November 14–16, 2012
Boston, Massachusetts, USA

Association for
Computing Machinery

Advancing Computing as a Science & Profession

IMC'12

Proceedings of the ACM
Internet Measurement Conference

Sponsored by:

ACM SIGCOMM, ACM SIGMETRICS, and USENIX

Supported by:

Akamai, Cisco, Microsoft Research, MLab, NSF, Narus, Telefonica, and ThousandEyes

Association for
Computing Machinery

Advancing Computing as a Science & Profession

The Association for Computing Machinery
2 Penn Plaza, Suite 701
New York, New York 10121-0701

Notice to Past Authors of ACM-Published Articles
ACM intends to create a complete electronic archive of all articles and/or other material previously published by ACM. If you have written a work that has been previously published by ACM in any journal or conference proceedings prior to 1978, or any SIG Newsletter at any time, and you do NOT want this work to appear in the ACM Digital Library, please inform permissions@acm.org, stating the title of the work, the author(s), and where and when published.

ISBN: 978-1-4503-1705-4 (Digital)

ISBN: 978-1-4503-1933-1 (Print)

Additional copies may be ordered prepaid from:

ACM Order Department
PO Box 30777
New York, NY 10087-0777, USA

Phone: 1-800-342-6626 (USA and Canada)
+1-212-626-0500 (Global)
Fax: +1-212-944-1318
E-mail: acmhelp@acm.org
Hours of Operation: 8:30 am – 4:30 pm ET

Printed in the USA

Message from the General Chairs

Welcome to the 2012 *ACM Internet Measurement Conference* in Boston. For the many of you returning to Boston, we hope you have the opportunity to reconnect with colleagues and friends in the area while you are here. For those visiting for the first time, we hope you have the opportunity to explore the charms of our historic small city, and the academic and technology hub that encompasses Boston, aka "The Hub" [Oliver Wendell Holmes, 1858 (who was really only referring to the state house)].

This year's conference continues the tradition of a strong technical program at IMC. It was our pleasure working with our colleagues Ratul Mahajan and Alex Snoeren who co-chaired the technical program committee and selected the program. Without the hard work of the the PC chairs and PC committee members, this fine conference would literally not have been possible, The diverse and exciting program spans 35 long and 10 short papers in addition to a panel on how Internet measurement data can facilitate interdisciplinary research, and a new Community Feedback Session.

We thank John Heidemann and Walter Willinger for their organization of the First IMC Workshop on Internet Visualization (WIV 2012) as a co-located workshop prior to this year's main event. Co-located workshops add to the vitality of our field's top conferences, so we hope to see other new experimental workshops at future meetings of IMC.

We are grateful to the many supporters of IMC 2012 for their generosity, many of whom have made repeated contributions to the conference over the years. Our corporate sponsors are: Akamai Technologies, Cisco Systems, Measurement Lab, and Microsoft (gold sponsors); and Narus, Telefonica, and ThousandEyes (silver sponsors).

We are also grateful to the National Science Foundation (gold sponsor), who provided funding for travel and registration costs enabling graduate student participation at the conference for students who would otherwise be unable to attend. Between NSF and our corporate sponsors, we were able to fund 10 domestic applicants and 9 international applicants. We would like to thank Chen-Nee Chuah from the IMC Steering Committee for overseeing the student travel grant selection process.

In the past, IMC conferences have been organized by the IMC Steering Committee together with the Technical Program chairs. This marks the first year that IMC has moved to having General Co-chairs organize the annual conference. Nonetheless the IMC Steering Committee continues to provide invaluable advice, oversight, "history" and vision for the conference. Our thanks to the current IMC Steering Committee and the many steering committee members before them who have made IMC the premier conference in its field.

John Byers
Boston University

Jim Kurose
UMass Amherst

Program Chairs' Welcome

It is our pleasure to welcome you to the *2012 Internet Measurement Conference – IMC 2012.* Even though the roots of IMC are in Internet measurements, it has now become the premier venue for measurement-based research into all kinds of networks that comprise the Internet ecosystem at large, including data centers, social networks, cellular networks, and the applications that run on these networks. This year's program reflects that diversity of the IMC community.

IMC 2012 received 183 papers that complied with the submission guidelines, of which 45 were accepted for publication. As usual, we solicited both long papers with deep treatment of topics and short papers that convey exciting work in progress, offer high-level visions, or present more succinct viewpoints. We received 101 long papers and 82 short papers, and we accepted 35 long papers and 10 short papers (which implies that short papers experienced a lower acceptance rate).

All submitted papers underwent a rigorous review process by a highly skilled and diverse program committee (PC) of 32 members (including us). Reviewing was done over two rounds. In the first round, each paper was reviewed by three PC members. 119 papers were picked for the second round, and each paper was reviewed by at least two more PC members. The final decisions were based on all the reviews, extensive online discussions, and a day-long meeting which was attended in-person by all but four PC members.

Along with the papers, we are publishing a review summary document for each accepted paper. The document contains almost-verbatim reviews, without the numerical scores, and a response by authors as to how they considered review feedback in preparing the final versions of the paper. This "experiment" was started in IMC 2011 to provide transparency into the review process, and we decided to continue it based on feedback from conference attendees. We made two small changes to it: participation was mandatory for the authors, and the document is being published separately to enable tracking of how frequently it was downloaded and viewed by the community.

We made a major change to IMC paper awards this year. In previous years, IMC has offered one best paper award, but only papers that made their data publicly available were eligible. While this encouraged data sharing, great work by authors who had legitimate reasons for not being able to share their data was left unrecognized. We decided to decouple the concerns by offering two awards: one best paper award for which all accepted papers are eligible, and one community award for which only papers that share their data with the community are eligible.

In addition to technical presentations, this year's program contains a panel and a community feedback session. The motivation for the panel is summed up well by its title: "Facilitating rigorous interdisciplinary research using network measurement data." Composed of panelists from both inside and outside of the network measurement community, we hope it will promote a timely conversation because the datasets produced by our community are being increasingly used by other communities (e.g., economics and public policy). The community feedback session, a continuation from last year, provides a forum for short talks on topics that are relevant to the IMC audience such as announcing a new tool or dataset and sharing experience with collecting or analyzing data.

We want to thank many people who helped make this year's program possible. First and foremost, we are grateful to the authors who submitted their thoughtful work. Our PC members were remarkable. They provided detailed and thoughtful feedback on the papers in a timely manner, and each of them stepped up to the plate when we made a special request. Mark Crovella, Nina Taft, and Ben Zhao handled out-of-band papers with which we were conflicted, kc claffy will moderate the panel, and Krishna Gummadi, Dina Papagiannaki, and Zhi-Li Zhang served on the awards committee. Finally, we appreciate the continuous support and feedback that we received from the IMC steering committee members.

We hope that you find the IMC 2012 program exciting and thought-provoking and that the conference facilitates stimulating discussions with other researchers and practitioners from around the world.

Ratul Mahajan
IMC'12 Program Co-Chair
Microsoft Research

Alex C. Snoeren
IMC'12 Program Co-Chair
UC San Diego

Table of Contents

Session 4: OSN Evolution

Session Chair: Krishna Gummadi *(MPI-SWS)*

Session 5: Video on Demand

Session Chair: Nina Taft *(Technicolor)*

Session 6: Network Characterization

Session Chair: Sharon Goldberg *(Boston University)*

Session 7: Mobile Performance

Session Chair: Alex C. Snoeren *(University of California, San Diego)*

Session 12: New Protocols & Policy

Session Chair: Ratul Mahajan *(Microsoft Research)*

2012 Internet Measurement Conference Organization

General Co-Chairs

John Byers, Boston University
Jim Kurose, University of Massachusetts Amherst

Technical Program Co-Chairs

Ratul Mahajan, Microsoft Research
Alex C. Snoeren, UC San Diego

Technical Program Committee

Aditya Akella, UW-Madison
Aruna Balasubramanian, Washington
Meeyoung Cha, KAIST
Kameswari Chebrolu, IIT Bombay
Kenjiro Cho, IIJ
Chen-Nee Chuah, UC Davis
kc claffy, CAIDA / UC San Diego
Mark Crovella, Boston University
Xenofontas Dimitropoulos, ETH Zurich
Nandita Dukkipati, Google
Nick Feamster, Georgia Tech
Sharon Goldberg, Boston University
Matthias Grossglauser, EPFL
Krishna Gummadi, MPI-SWS
Ramana Kompella, Purdue
Christian Kreibich, ICSI
Harsha Madhyastha, UC Riverside
Ratul Mahajan (Chair), Microsoft Research
Alan Mislove, Northeastern University
Vivek Pai, Princeton University
Dina Papagiannaki, Telefonica
Vern Paxson, UC Berkeley
Costin Raiciu, U. Politehnica of Bucharest
Vyas Sekar, Intel
Alex C. Snoeren (Chair), UC San Diego
Peter Steenkiste, CMU
Nina Taft, Technicolor
Xiaowei Yang, Duke
Jennifer Yates, AT&T Research
Ming Zhang, MSR
Zhi-Li Zhang, Minnesota University
Ben Zhao, UC Santa Barbara

IMC Steering Committee

Mark Allman, ICSI
Paul Barford, University of Wisconsin
Chen-Nee Chuah, UC Davis
Renata Teixeira, CNRS and UPMC Sorbonne Universités

2012 Internet Measurement Conference Sponsors

The Steering Committee, Organizing Committee, attendees, and friends of the 2012 ACM Internet Measurement Conference are grateful to the sponsors and supporters of this conference. These supporters' generosity and investment in the network measurement research community has helped make this conference possible.

2012 IMC Sponsors

acm sigcomm

ACM SIGMETRICS

In cooperation with

USENIX

2012 IMC Gold Supporters

Akamai

Cisco

Microsoft Research

MLAB

NSF

2012 IMC Silver Supporters

NARUS

Telefónica

ThousandEyes

Analysis of a "/0" Stealth Scan from a Botnet

Alberto Dainotti, Alistair King, kc Claffy
CAIDA, University of California, San Diego
La Jolla, CA, USA
{alberto,alistair,kc}@caida.org

Ferdinando Papale, Antonio Pescapé
University of Napoli Federico II
Naples, Italy
ferdinando.papale@gmail.com
pescape@unina.it

ABSTRACT

Botnets are the most common vehicle of cyber-criminal activity. They are used for spamming, phishing, denial of service attacks, brute-force cracking, stealing private information, and cyber warfare. Botnets carry out network scans for several reasons, including searching for vulnerable machines to infect and recruit into the botnet, probing networks for enumeration or penetration, etc. We present the measurement and analysis of a horizontal scan of the entire IPv4 address space conducted by the Sality botnet in February of last year. This 12-day scan originated from approximately 3 million distinct IP addresses, and used a heavily coordinated and unusually covert scanning strategy to try to discover and compromise VoIP-related (SIP server) infrastructure. We observed this event through the UCSD Network Telescope, a /8 darknet continuously receiving large amounts of unsolicited traffic, and we correlate this traffic data with other public sources of data to validate our inferences. Sality is one of the largest botnets ever identified by researchers, its behavior represents ominous advances in the evolution of modern malware: the use of more sophisticated stealth scanning strategies by millions of coordinated bots, targeting critical voice communications infrastructure. This work offers a detailed dissection of the botnet's scanning behavior, including general methods to correlate, visualize, and extrapolate botnet behavior across the global Internet.

Categories and Subject Descriptors

C.2.3 [**Network Operations**]: Network Monitoring;
C.2.5 [**Local and Wide-Area Networks**]: Internet;

General Terms

Measurement, Security

Keywords

Darknet, Network Telescope, Internet Background Radiation, Botnet, SIP, Scan, Probing, Stealth, Covert, Coordination, Sality, Bot, VoIP

1. INTRODUCTION

Botnets are collections of Internet hosts ("*bots*") that through malware infection have fallen under the control of a single entity ("*botmaster*"). Botnets of up to few million hosts have been observed [4, 23, 54]. Innocent users carry on with their legitimate activities, unaware that their infected PCs are executing various types of malicious activity in the background, including spamming, phishing, denial-of-service (DOS) attacks, brute-force password cracking, stealing of credentials, espionage and cyber warfare. The news media and scientific literature have documented many criminal activities carried out by botnets over the last few years [15, 20, 35, 59], including on mobile phones [42].

Botnets perform network scanning for different reasons: propagation, enumeration, penetration. One common type of scanning, called "horizontal scanning", systematically probes the same protocol port across a given range of IP addresses, sometimes selecting random IP addresses as targets. To infect new hosts in order to recruit them as bots, some botnets, e.g., Conficker [27, 46], perform a horizontal scan continuously using self-propagating worm code that exploits a known system vulnerability. In this work we focus on a different type of botnet scan – one performed under the explicit command and control of the botmaster, occurring over a well-delimited interval.

Several botnets have been analyzed in the literature, including characterizing botnet scanning techniques either based on packet captures from darknets and honeynets [38, 39], or by examining botnet source code [11]. Documented scans by botnets have been of relatively small size (e.g. around 3000 bots) [39] and lightly coordinated, e.g., many bots randomly (typically uniformly randomly [39]) probing the same target address range.

In February 2011, the UCSD /8 Network Telescope instrumentation [7] captured traffic reflecting a previously undocumented large-scale stealth scanning behavior (across the entire IPv4 space, we believe) from a botnet using about 3 million unique source IP addresses. We identified the malware responsible for this massive and sophisticated scanning activity as a binary module of the Sality botnet [23] known to target SIP (Session Initiation Protocol [49]) servers [22]. We hence refer to this interesting scanning event as *"sipscan"* throughout the rest of this paper.

Our contributions in this study include techniques to characterize a large-scale intentionally surreptitious scan of the entire IPv4 space (that is, a *"/0"* scan), including use of additional data to confirm that the scan was not using spoofed source IP addresses, but rather was being sourced by a large botnet. We correlated darknet traffic over this period with two other publicly available sources of Internet traffic data that strongly suggest the scan was not just of this /8 but over the entire IPv4 Internet address space. Finally, we created animations and visualization to help us understand the strictly ordered progression of the entire /0 scan, and correlate its address space and geographic coverage with its traffic volume. These tools also enabled us to delineate different phases of its scanning activity and its adaptation to changing network conditions. These methods and tools have already yielded substantial insight into the first observed /0 scan by a botnet, but we anticipate a wide range of applicability to other analyses of unidirectional or even bidirectional traffic.

Section 2 summarizes related work. Sections 3 describes the anatomy of the scan, including high-level characteristics and validation that it was indeed carried out by a botnet targeting the entire IPv4 space. Section 4 analyzes more detailed properties of the scan, including the impressively covert scanning strategy, bot turnover rate, coverage and overlap in target addresses, and highly orchestrated adaptivity and coordination of the bots. Section 6 summarizes our findings and contributions.

2. BACKGROUND AND RELATED WORK

Botnets have been an active area of research for almost a decade, starting with early generation botnets that used IRC channels to implement centralized Command & Control (C&C) infrastructures [9, 17]. In 2007 the Storm botnet signaled a new generation of botnet capabilities, including the use of peer-to-peer protocols to support distributed C&C channels [33, 51, 58]. These botnets are harder to detect and dismantle because there is no single point of failure, and they often use sophisticated techniques such as encrypted communication [58] and *Fast flux* DNS resolution [14]. Researchers have also studied methods for automated discovery of botnets [31, 40, 56], formal models of botnet communication [16, 18], and their use for orchestrated spam campaigns [36, 45].

Botnets commonly scan large segments of Internet address space, either seeking hosts to infect or compromise, or for the purpose of network mapping and service discovery. Analyzing and detecting these events can improve our understanding of evolving botnet characteristics and spreading techniques, our ability to distinguish them from benign traffic sources, and our ability to mitigate attacks. But analysis of network probing activities of botnets has received little attention in the literature.

In 2005, Yegneswaran, Barford, and Paxson analyzed six months of network traffic captured by honeynets [62]. Based on statistical properties of traffic, they characterized and classified 22 large-scale events into three categories: worm outbreaks, misconfigurations, and botnet probings. These first-generation botnets were less evolved in several ways than those we see today: in size (a maximum of 26,000 bots), scope (largest target scope was a /8 network), and communication capabilities (centralized IRC-based command and control). Li, Goyal, and Chen [38] analyzed traffic data they collected from 10 contiguous /24 networks operating as honeynets throughout 2006. Through analysis of the probing traffic they were able to infer properties of the botnet, e.g., geographical location of, and operating system running on infected machines. We use a similar approach to infer characteristics of the botnet scan we study in this paper. These three authors collaborated with Paxson on a more comprehensive analysis of data from both 2006 and 2007, which was corroborated both by data from the DShield project [34] and by the inspection of botnet source code [39]. Analyzing the traffic from 10 contiguous /24 darknets/honeynets they identified 203 botnet scans with different characteristics, all scanning at most a /8 network, and all with inferred bot populations significantly smaller (200-3700) than the February 2011 scan captured at our darknet (3 million IP addresses), They found that these first-generation botnets employed simple scanning strategies, either sequential or uniform random scanning, and elementary orchestration capabilities: many bots scanning the same address range independently, with high redundancy and large overlap in target addresses. Other studies have found similar results via examination of botnet source code to understand the scanning strategies [10, 11]. Barford and Yegneswaran [11] inspected four widely-used IRC botnet code bases, finding only primitive scanning capabilities with *"no means for efficient distribution of a target address space among a collection of bots"*. However these studies did not analyze any new-generation botnets.

The scan that we observe and analyze in this study differs from previous work in several ways: (i) it is recent (2011) and related to a new-generation, widely-deployed, peer-to-peer botnet (Sality [23]); (ii) it is observed from a larger darknet (a /8 network); (iii) the population of bots participating in the scan is several orders of magnitude larger; (iv) the target scope is the entire IPv4 address space; (v) it adopts a well-orchestrated stealth scan strategy with little redundancy and overlap.

This last point is the most surprising finding in terms of novelty and impact. The remarkably stealth scanning employed by new-generation botnets gives us reason to suspect that many large-scale scans may have occurred in recent years but gone unnoticed by any modern instrumentation for studying it. Despite the lack of any literature documenting the observation of highly coordinated large-scale network scans from botnets, the concept has been discussed, both in a worst-case theoretical analysis of attack potential [57], and for the more benign application of Internet-wide service discovery [37]. For service discovery, these authors considered a scan strategy based on reverse-byte sequential increments of target IP addresses, which they named "Reverse IP Sequential (RIS)". Although they dismissed this option for being difficult to extrapolate metrics from partial scans, we discovered that this was exactly the technique used by the Internet-wide scan ("sipscan") we study in this paper (Section 4.1). Heidemann's *et al.* reachability census was Internet-wide but ran independently from two hosts, not coordinated in the way botnets are [32].

Another relatively novel aspect of the scan we analyze is that it targets SIP infrastructure, which is not typically in published lists of services probed by botnets [39]. Only in the past 2 years have SIP servers been reported as the object of large-scale attacks [47,52,64]. As more of the world's voice communications move to an IP substrate, fraudulent activity targeting SIP-based VoIP services offers an attractive source of revenue to cybercrime [24]. In April 2010, Sheldon reported a series of brute-force password-guessing attacks on SIP servers worldwide, sourced from the Amazon EC2 cloud [52, 64]. Later in 2010, several sources reported on a new malware named "*sundayaddr*", which behaved like a few-hundred node botnet comprised of unix-like machines (e.g., Linux, FreeBSD) trying to brute-force accounts on SIP servers [30, 47]. The layout of the SIP headers in the attacking packets was almost identical to that of SIPVicious, a tool suite written in Python designed to perform security auditing of SIP services [26]. It seems therefore likely that the attack code was a slightly modified version of SIPVicious [47].

In November 2010, the author of SIPVicious reported another large-scale attack against several SIP servers worldwide, using a more significantly different SIP header than used by SIPVicious [25, 53]. Both of these events were reported by several parties and were largely discussed on public SIP operational mailing lists [6,8]. In contrast, to the best of our knowledge the scan that we document in this study was not publicly reported with respect to either observed network traffic or server activity (e.g. logs). Symantec identified and analyzed the binary responsible for what we call the "sipscan", which they discovered while monitoring Sality, a large peer-to-peer based botnet [22, 23]. A host infected by Sality downloads the scanning binary via a component of the main bot executable, which is responsible for downloading and executing additional malware whose URLs are communicated by other botnet peers [23]. During our analysis we had access to the same binary code and verified that it matches the SIP headers we observed in the sipscan. Symantec did not publish any information about the stealth scanning strategy or in particular on the reverse byte order adopted by the sipscan (Section 4.1). Our study, based instead on network traffic measurement and analysis, is complementary to what has been found by reverse-engineering the code running on the bots, showing novel insights into the botnet population and the orchestration and coordination of the scan. Since Sality is one of the largest known botnets but relatively undocumented in research literature, another contribution of our study is to shed light on the scanning behavior of this new-generation botnet.

3. ANALYSIS PART I: ANATOMY OF THE SIPSCAN

3.1 Overview

The sipscan probes each target IP address with two packets: (i) a UDP packet to port 5060 carrying a SIP header and (ii) a TCP SYN packet attempting to open a connection on port 80. We observe the sipscan at a darknet – i.e., there are no devices on it responding to incoming traffic – so we do not observe any further packets for the same flows except for TCP SYN retransmits.

Figure 1 depicts the SIP header of the packets sent by the sipscan. This SIP header is a request to register a random user account on a SIP server, but random account registrations are usually not accepted by SIP servers. Thus, if the targeted host is a SIP server, the registration will likely fail but will result in a "404 Not Found" response code, which is enough to reveal to the bot that the target is indeed a SIP server. We presume that the goal is to identify SIP servers for later use, e.g., to perform brute-force attempts to register user accounts.

The sipscan SIP header is similar to the header built by the SIPVicious security auditing tool suite to generate probe packets [26]. In November 2010, the author of this tool reported a large distributed attack against SIP servers with headers similar to those his tool used; this attack was observed by several parties and was likely carried out by a botnet [25, 53]. In the case of both the November 2010 scan and the February 2011 scan we observed, the botnet developers probably used the Python code of SIPVicious as a reference to write their attack code. The most notable difference between such attacks and SIPVicious headers is in the "User-Agent" header, where the attack code replaced the string "friendly-scanner" with the less suspicious "Asterisk PBX"[1].

The observed sipscan header has two distinctive characteristics compared to the attack of November 2010 (and in general compared to the miscellaneous SIP malware packets observed at the UCSD telescope): the user name, which is always composed of ten digits, and the "To:"/"From:" fields, which contains a SIP URI instead of simply the number [49]. Based on the properties of its SIP header, we defined a payload signature to identify all the sipscan packets seen by the UCSD Network Telescope. Each source host sends the TCP packet together with the UDP packets, allowing us to easily infer which TCP SYN packets on port 80, among all those received by the telescope, were associated with the sipscan).

Figure 2 shows the packet rate of the sipscan UDP packets (left axis) and the number of unique IPs per hour (right axis) sending

[1]Asterisk is a widely deployed open-source PBX software supporting both PSTN and VoIP.

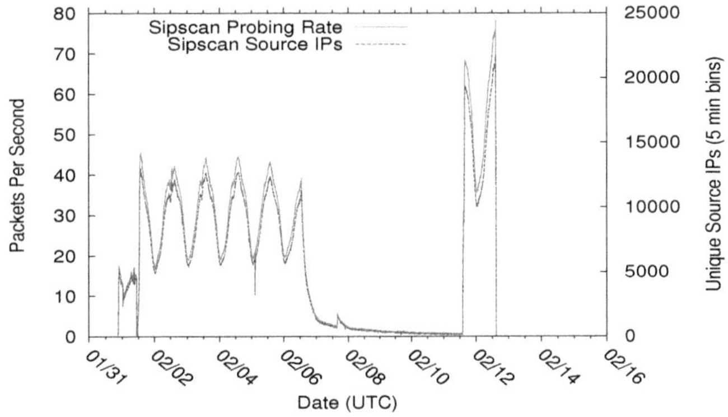

Figure 2: Overview of the scan. The continuous line shows the packets per second, in 5 minute bins, of UDP probing packets from the sipscan observed by the UCSD Network Telescope. The dashed line represents the corresponding number of distinct source IP addresses per bin.

such packets to addresses in the UCSD Network Telescope. The scan goes through different phases over approximately 12 days: it starts with a packet received on Monday 31 January 2011 at 21:07 UTC, and ends with a sharp drop of packets on Saturday 12 February around 15:00 UTC. Approximately 100 residual packets were observed in the following two days. During the scan, peaks of 21,000 hosts with distinct IPs probed the telescope's /8 address space in a single 5-minute interval.

# of probes (1 probe = 1 UDP + multiple TCP pkts)	20,255,721
#of source IP addresses	2,954,108
# of destination IP addresses	14,534,793
% of telescope IP space covered	86,6%
# of unique couples (source IP - destination IP)	20,241,109
max probes per second	78.3
max # of distinct source IPs in 1 hour	160,264
max # of distinct source IPs in 5 minutes	21,829
average # of probes received by a /24	309
max # of probes received by a /24	442
average # of sources targeting a destination	1.39
max # of sources targeting a destination	14
average # of destinations a source targets	6.85
max # of destination a source targets	17613

Table 1: Summary of the scanning event characteristics. The scan originated from almost 3 million distinct IP addresses and hit about 14.5 million addresses of the address space observed by the UCSD Network Telescope.

Table 1 lists the main characteristics of the scan. The portion of the scan observed by the UCSD Network Telescope involved around 3 million distinct source addresses, generating 20 million probes – we define a probe as a UDP scanning packet with the payload signature from Figure 1, plus TCP SYN packets to the same destination. These probes covered more than 14.5 million target IP addresses, that is, 86.6% of the darknet address space.

3.2 Verification of unspoofed source addresses

Because darknet addresses do not respond to received packets, we cannot generally assume that packets are not using spoofed (fake) source IP addresses. Effective scanning requires the use of real source addresses to receive responses, so there is reason to assume that these IP addresses are not spoofed. Conversely, evidence that the addresses are not spoofed would increase our confidence in the hypothesis that this behavior is in fact a large-scale scan. We found the following evidence that the observed packets were not actually spoofed.

```
1  2011-02-02 12:15:18.913184 IP (tos 0x0, ttl 36, id 20335, offset 0, flags [none], proto UDP (17), length
       412) XX.10.100.90.1878 > XX.164.30.56.5060: [udp sum ok] SIP, length: 384
2          REGISTER sip:3982516068@XX.164.30.56 SIP/2.0
3          Via: SIP/2.0/UDP XX.164.30.56:5060;branch=1F8b5C6T44G2CJt;rport
4          Content-Length: 0
5          From: <sip:3982516068@XX.164.30.56>; tag=147181381840286342321834266 8
6          Accept: application/sdp
7          User-Agent: Asterisk PBX
8          To: <sip:3982516068@XX.164.30.56>
9          Contact: sip:3982516068@XX.164.30.56
10         CSeq: 1 REGISTER
11         Call-ID: 4731021211
12         Max-Forwards: 70
```

Figure 1: Example of the payload of a UDP packet generated by the sipscan (line 1 is tcpdump output [5] with timestamp and information from IP and UDP headers). The payload contains a SIP request to register a user on the contacted host. A variant of the signature (which we also matched) has the string ":5060" appended to the "Contact: " header field (line 9). In the figure we replaced the value of the most significant byte of the destination address with "XX".

- In [19] we studied the country-wide outage that occurred in Egypt between the 27th of January and the 2nd of February 2011. During the last two days of the outage - which overlap with the period of activity of the sipscan - most of the country was completely isolated from the rest of the Internet. We verified that no sipscan packets with source IP addresses that geolocated to Egypt were observed by the telescope during the outage. Figure 3 shows the re-announcement of all the BGP prefixes geolocated to Egypt that were withdrawn during the outage (continuous line, left y axis), and the packet rate of UDP packets from the sipscan geolocated to the same country (dashed line, second y axis). The graph shows Egyptian hosts contributing to the scanning activity only after the country is reconnected to the Internet. We used the same methodology described in [19] to analyze BGP data from the RIPE RIS [3] and Routeviews [60] repositories, and geolocation data from MaxMind [41] and Afrinic [1].
- Random IP spoofing would use also source IPs from our /8 darknet set of addresses, which we never see in this set of packets. We also mapped the source addresses of the scan to originating ASes (autonomous systems, or independent networks in the global routing system) using BGP data, and verified that they matched only assigned ranges of IP addresses.
- In Section 3.4 we analyze source port numbers in transport-layer headers from selected scanning bots. The consistency of these parameters over time suggests that the source addresses are not spoofed: IP spoofing requires the use of raw sockets and usually involves random selection of spoofed addresses, whereas the progression of source ports followed by these bots is typical of packets sent through standard sockets that use ephemeral ports assigned by the operating system based on a single, global counter.

3.3 Botnet activity

This convincing evidence that the source IP addresses are authentic supports our hypothesis that a botnet is generating the packets, rather than one or a few hosts, or a worm spreading. Over the course of twelve days, we observed about 3 million source addresses, which mapped to countries and networks all over the world (Section 4.4). Figure 2 displays a clearly delimited beginning and end of the behavior, with strong diurnal periodicity and variations of intensity. Spreading worms tend to exhibit closer to exponential growth in IP addresses infected and trying to spread further [65].

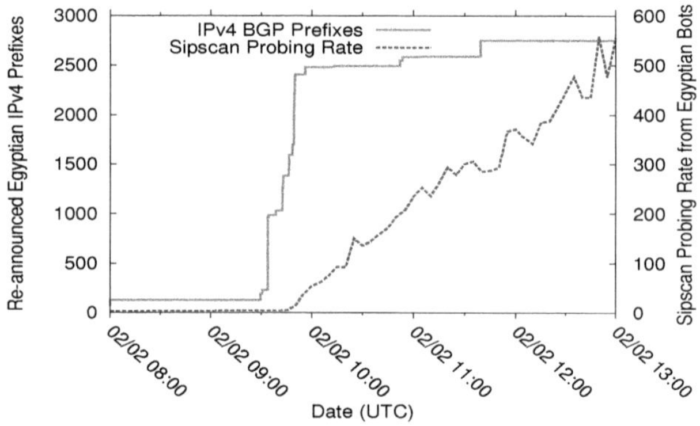

Figure 3: The case of the Internet black-out in Egypt helps to verify that source addresses from the sipscan are not spoofed. The continuous line shows the reannouncement of routes to Egyptian IPv4 prefixes when the country reappears on the Internet on 2 February 2011. The sipscan starts approximately on the 1 February, but we start seeing probes from source IPs geolocated to Egypt only when the Egyptian networks get reannounced through BGP updates.

We discovered an even more compelling piece of evidence that this traffic was generated by a botnet when we examined traffic data during last year's nation-wide censorship episode in Egypt. In [19] we showed that, during the Egyptian outage, some Conficker-infected hosts were still able to randomly send infecting packets to the Internet, even if they were in networks not visible via BGP. Outbound connectivity (from Egyptian hosts "upstream" to the rest of the Internet) was still possible from some networks in Egypt through the use of default routes. But while we saw Conficker traffic originating from IPs geolocated in Egypt, we saw no sipscan traffic from Egypt, consistent with the sipscan hosts not acting independently, but rather receiving instructions from a command & control 'botmaster' host (i.e., requiring bidirectional connectivity) outside of Egypt.

To simultaneously represent both the temporal and spatial dynamics of the event, we created a "World Map" animation available at [13]. Figure 4 is a single frame of the animation (capturing a window of 5 minutes and 20 seconds of data) from Wed 2 Feburary 09:34:00 2011. The circles are centered at the geographical coordinates of source IP addresses. For each time bin, the size of the circle is proportional to the number of hosts geolocated to those coordi-

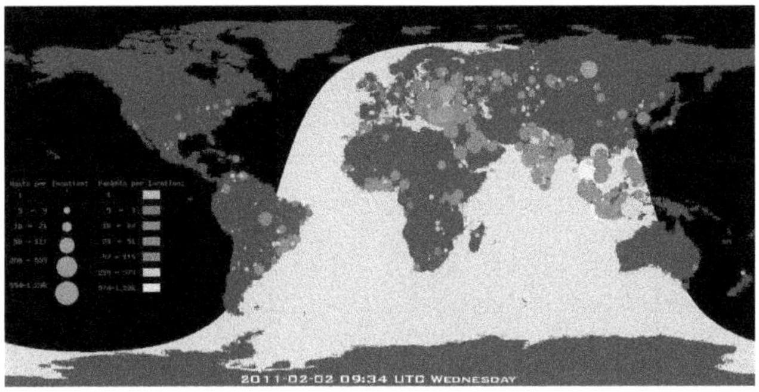

Figure 4: Snapshot of our "World Map" animation of the sipscan available at [13] (Wed Feb 2 09:34:00 2011). The animation shows, in 5:20-minutes of data represented per frame, circles at the geographical coordinates of source hosts (bots) with size proportional to the number of hosts geolocated to those coordinates, and color to the number of packets sent. The animation depicts the spatial and temporal dynamics of the scan.

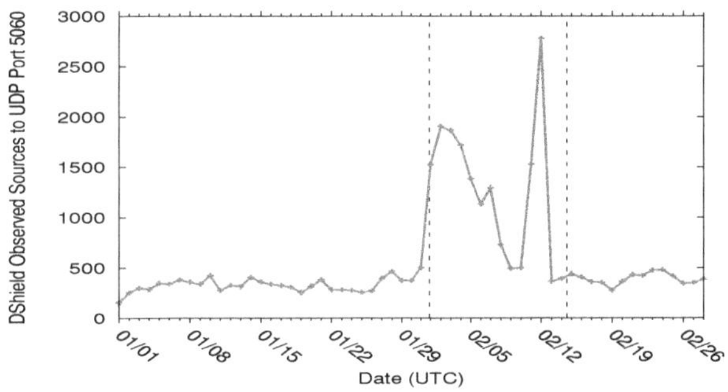

Figure 5: Daily count of unique source IP addresses in packets to port 5060 extracted from DShield sensor data [34]. The unique source IP count, for the months of January and February 2011, shows an increase of almost one order of magnitude between the 1st and the 12th of February. Its profile matches the sipscan shown in Figure 2, suggesting that sensors (darknets and honeynets) in other /8 networks received the same kind of traffic. The start and end times of the sipscan are denoted in this graph by the two dashed vertical lines.

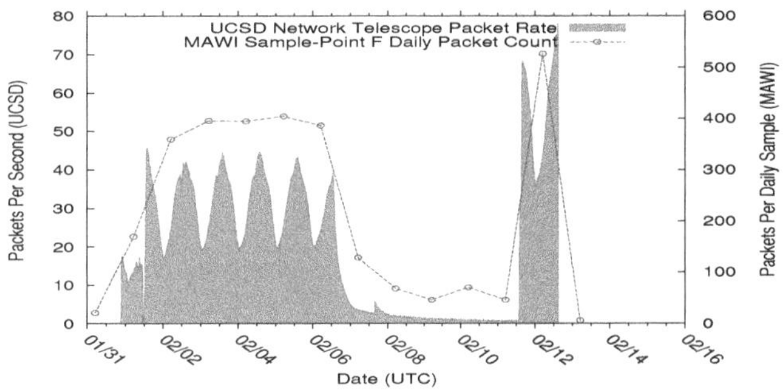

Figure 6: Sipscan UDP packets observed by (i) the UCSD Network Telescope (y axis, packets per second) and (ii) MAWI WIDE Samplepoint-F (y2 axis, packets per daily sample of xx minutes). The samples found on the small link monitored by the MAWI working group perfectly follow the profile of the sipscan observed by the UCSD Network Telescope, strongly suggesting that the sipscan targeted also other /8 networks.

nates, whereas the color reflects the number of packets sent (these two values are not proportional because, as we show in Section 4, there are both hosts sending a single probe and hosts sending multiple probes at different rates). The animation illustrates the traffic volume and geographic scope of the scan over time. Geolocation of IP addresses was done using the MaxMind GeoLite database released on March 1st, 2011, temporally proximate to the event [41]. The software used to create the animation is an improved version of the code originally developed at CAIDA by Huffaker *et al.* and available at [2]. The animation visually represents, for the first time, an Internet-wide scan conducted by a large botnet.

3.4 A "/0" scan

Observation from the UCSD Network Telescope is limited to packets destined to the corresponding /8 network. However, we also discovered evidence that the scan targeted the entire IPv4 address space (a /0 scan): similar traffic patterns observable on other network segments, and a continuity in source port usage in the packets we observed.

3.4.1 Targeting the UCSD Network Telescope

Even if approximately 15% of addresses of our darknet were not hit by the scan, the sipscan uniformly targeted the entire address range of the /8 network. In Section 4.3 we show that the missing (15%) targets may be due to a specific configuration parameter that would trade completeness of IPv4 address space coverage for redundancy in the utilization of the bots.

3.4.2 DShield repository

We have found circumstantial evidence of sipscan traffic in the DShield repository [34]. DShield is a constantly updated repository of scanning and attack reports. In particular it reports aggregated data of traffic observed on several "sensors" (i.e., small honeynets and darknets) operated by different participating organizations. Figure 5 shows the number of distinct source IP addresses per day observed by the DShield sensors on port 5060 from the 1 January to 28 February 2011. The large spikes in the traffic profile of the source IP addresses match the sipscan profile shown in Figure 2, indicating that the same phenomenon was probably targeting other networks besides the /8 monitored by the UCSD Network Telescope.

3.4.3 MAWI WIDE Samplepoint-F

We also examined traffic traces from a 150Mbps link on a trans-Pacific line that are made available by the MAWI WIDE project [29] (link "samplepoint-F"). The trace set is made of daily traces in pcap format, of 15 minutes each, where the IP addresses are anonymized and the transport-layer payload is removed [28]. This anonymization scheme prevented us for searching the trace specifically for the sipscan packets, since we can see neither the UDP payload signature nor the source IP addresses of the packets. Instead, from the analysis of the sipscan SIP headers (Figure 1), we built a flow-level signature with the following conditions for each UDP flow: (i) destination port 5060; (ii) made of a single packet; (iii) flow-size (in this case matching the packet size) between 382 and 451 bytes. We obtained the packet size range by examining all SIP header fields that were not fixed size, and how they varied (e.g. IP addresses in ascii format take between 7 and 15 bytes). We further sanitized the remaining flows considering some isolated cases of spikes in the MAWI traces which were using source ports outside of the most common ranges observed on the telescope (see Figure 7). The final result, depicted in Figure 6, is that there are almost no packets matching the flow-level signature in the days outside of the sipscan, whereas their profile during that period roughly follows the profile of the sipscan (The lack of tight precision between the two data sets in Figure 6 is due to the MAWI samples being coarser-

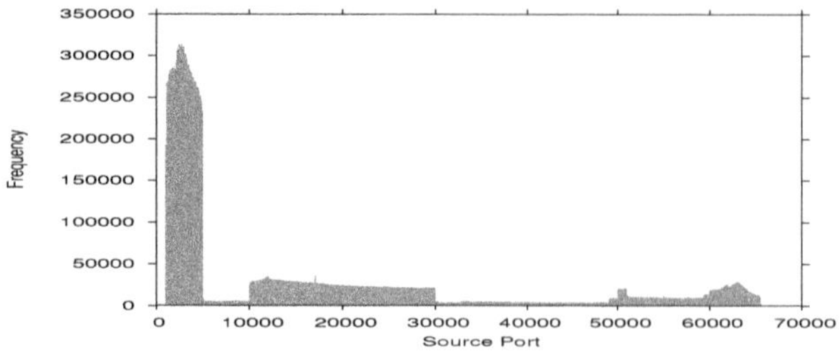

Figure 7: Distribution of the source port numbers (bin size = 100) The most common range is 1025-5000, used by several versions of OSs from the Microsoft Windows family.

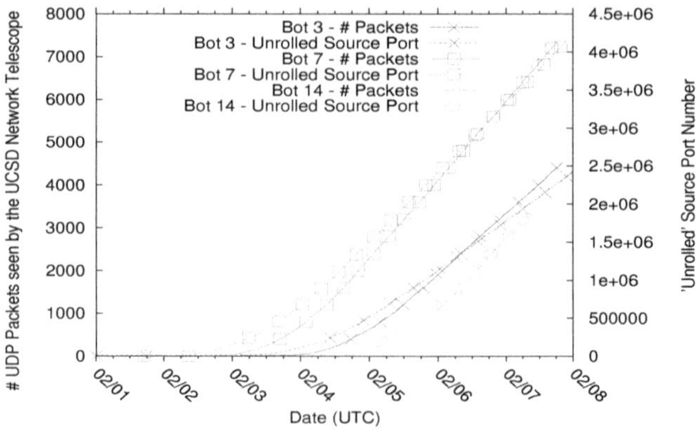

Figure 8: Estimating the global scan scope by exploiting source port continuity in scanning bots: continuous lines represent the count of probes (a UDP packet plus at a least one TCP SYN packet) observed by the UCSD Network Telescope (y axis), whereas the dashed lines represent the number of connections/sessions opened by each bot as inferred by unwrapping its source port numbers (second y axis). Each bot probes the darknet on average (approximately) every 285 global probes, suggesting that during its absence reaches the remaining 255 /8 networks in the IPv4 address space.

grained, 15 minutes each once per day, and from a relatively small link).

This finding is important because the anonymization technique used for MAWI traces preserves matching prefixes and IP classes between IP addresses [28]. The analysis of this data therefore revealed that, on average, 8 different /8 classes were targeted every day by the packets traveling on this link.

3.4.4 *Exploiting source-port continuity*

The positive correlations of our data source with the DShield and MAWI data sources convinced us that the sipscan hit other /8 networks as well as our own. We also found the following evidence that the sipscan most likely targeted all the /8 networks in the IPv4 address space.

We identified a few bots scanning at a roughly constant pace over several days. Analyzing the sequence of source ports in their scanning packets revealed that some of these bots used incremental source ports within a specific range assigned by the operating system. For example, Windows XP and other Microsoft operating systems assign a new ephemeral source port in the range 1025-5000 by incrementing a global counter for each opened TCP or UDP socket [44]. We inferred how many other connections/sessions a bot opened between each probe sent to the darknet by following the sequence of source ports the bot used and "unwrapping" them, taking into account their range. In [39], Li *et al.* used the same methodology to estimate the global scope of botnet scans. We could only apply this technique to the few persistent bots (see Section 4.2) running on an operating system configured to assign source ports in this manner.

Figure 8 depicts the behavior of three of these bots (the bot number indicates its rank based on the number of probes they sent). The continuous lines represent the count of probes (a UDP packet plus at least one TCP SYN packet) observed by the UCSD Network Telescope (y axis), whereas the dashed lines represent the number of connections/sessions opened by each bot as inferred by unwrapping its source port numbers (second y axis). For each bot the two curves follow approximately the same trend, suggesting that the view from the telescope is representative of the global behavior of the bot. The UCSD Network Telescope covers 1/256th of the entire IPv4 address space, so a uniformly random scanning bot will probe this /8 darknet approximately every 256 probes, or every 512 new connections opened (every probe includes a UDP and TCP connection attempt). We find these subclass of bots actually hitting our darknet every 570 packets (on average), which would be consistent with their hosting computer opening other connections/sessions unrelated to the scan, such as legitimate user activity or communication with the botmaster. In the next section we will show how the bots select their target IP addresses by first incrementing the most significant byte. Therefore we can assume that the external 255 probes from the bot reach all the other /8 networks in the IPv4 address space. In Section 4 we will also explore another feature of the data in Figure 8: the bots proceed at different rates and are active over different time intervals. We will refer to this finding later in the paper.

4. ANALYSIS PART II: PROPERTIES OF THE SIPSCAN AND OF THE BOTNET

4.1 Reverse IP Sequential order

A first manual observation of the sipscan destination addresses revealed that the bots were coordinated, presumably by a botmaster, to choose targets in a pre-defined sequence while scanning the entire IPv4 address space. Such coordination has not yet been documented in botnet-related research literature (see Section 2). Even more interesting, the target IP addresses incremented in reverse-byte order – likely to make the scan covert. Reverse-byte order scanning was considered in the context of supporting network-friendly Internet-wide service discovery [37], but was discarded for being difficult to extrapolate metrics from partial scans. A pseudo-random approach in selecting target addresses was also used as a technique for non-aggressive Internet-wide measurement surveys [32]. But to the best of our knowledge, this reverse-byte order scanning has been neither empirically observed in malicious scans nor discovered in botnet source code.

Manual examination of a sequence of 20 million addresses is practically infeasible; even its visual representation is a challenge. We used a visual map based on the space-filling Hilbert Curve [43,50] to verify that the target IP addresses incremented in reverse-byte order for the three bytes that we could observe (the most significant byte is fixed in our data to the /8 of the darknet observation point).

The Hilbert curve is a continuous fractal curve that can be used to map one-dimensional data into two dimensions filling a square, such as shown in Figure 9. Other researchers have effectively used the Hilbert space layout to visualize results of Internet-wide scanning or other Internet-wide data [21, 32]. The original order of the data is preserved along the Hilbert curve in two dimensions,

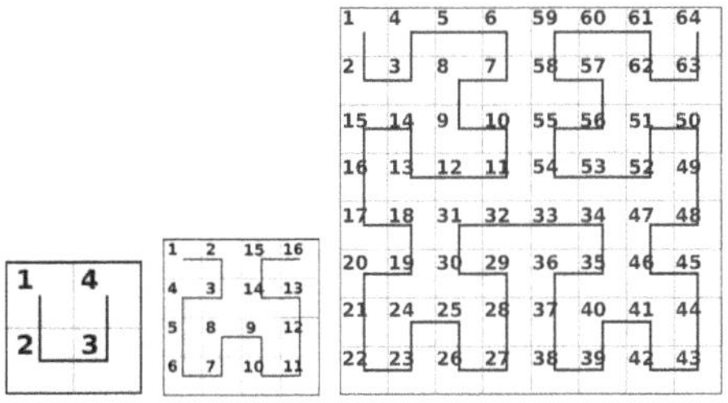

Figure 9: Examples of Hilbert's space-filling curves: orders 1, 2 and 3.

and conveniently displays data that is structured in powers of two. Hilbert curves of order 4, 8, and 12 have 2^8, 2^{16}, 2^{24} points, respectively, which in turn correspond to the masks for Class C (/24), Class B (/16), and Class A (/8) address blocks in the IPv4 numbering space. When mapping IP addresses to these two-dimensional Hilbert curves, adjacent address blocks appear as adjacent squares, even CIDR blocks (in between Class A, B, and C block sizes) are always represented as squares or rectangles.

We visualized the progression of the IP addresses targeted by the sipscan through an animation. Each frame represents the IPv4 address space of our darknet using a Hilbert curve of order 12, in which each cell corresponds to one IP address of the darknet, thus varying the 3 least significant bytes through all the possible combinations. The curve is displayed as a bitmap of size 4096x4096, with each pixel being assigned an IP address. For each frame, the pixels corresponding to the IP addresses that have been probed prior to that point in time are highlighted. We also added a brightness decay effect to better highlight the addresses probed in the last few frames while displaying the animation.

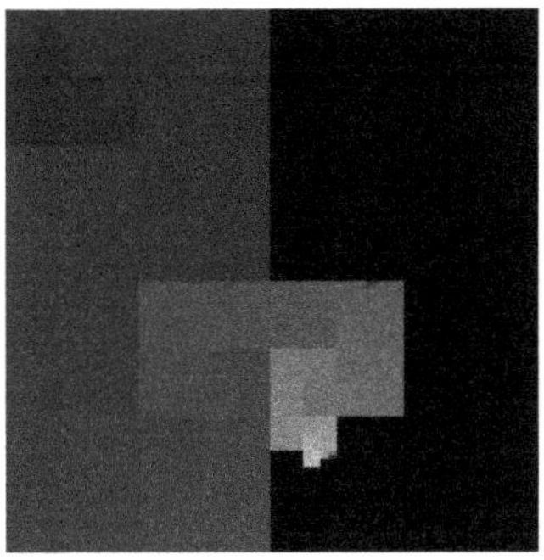

Figure 10: Snapshot of our animation representing the progression over time of the IP addresses targeted by the sipscan [13]. The darknet address space is represented as a Hilbert curve of order 12 in which the order of the three least significant bytes of each address is reversed before mapping it into the curve. Highlighted pixels correspond to IP addresses that have been probed up to that time (5 Feb 2011 11:47 GMT, in this frame). The animation proves the reverse-byte order progression is rigorously followed by the bots during the entire 12 days, independent of the varying rate of the sipscan. [The above snapshot is a modified version of the original frame from the reverse byte order animation at [13]; we over-emphasized the fading effect to better illustrate, in a single picture, the path the scan took through the address space.]

Drawing the Hilbert curve using IP addresses sequenced in their natural byte order does not reveal a particular pattern in the target progression, showing the square uniformly filling across the 12 days of the scan. This animation of target progression is available at [13]. In contrast, reversing the order of the three varying (i.e., least significant) bytes yields a representation that clearly illustrates the reverse sequential IP order rigorously followed by the sipscan: throughout the 12 days all the bots "march" together toward filling the entire address space. Figure 10 shows the frame for 5 February 2011 11:47 GMT from the full reverse-byte order animation available at [13]. This animation proves the strong coordination of bot activity: the progression is strictly observed by all the bots for the entire execution of the scan, independent of (i) variations in global scanning speed, (ii) the rates at which different bots proceed (see Section 3.4), (iii) the large number of hosts involved at the same time and thus the possible distributed architecture of the botnet (e.g., multiple C&C channels).

We also created a composite animation which combines both the natural and reverse byte order heatmaps with the world map animation into a single synchronized view of both the sources and the targets of the sipscan. This composite animation is available at [13].

The reverse IP sequential order used in this scan has significant implications. Observing this scan from a generic /24 network, would result in a very low number of packets per day: the average speed, during the largest phase of the scan – from the 2nd to the 6th of February – increments the least significant byte 34 times per day, unlikely to be detected by automated systems. This stealth technique is even more effective when combined with the constant turnover of bots that we illustrate in the next section.

4.2 Bot Turnover

The scanning statistics in Table 1, in particular the number of unique source IPs (about 3 million), total number of probes (about 20 million), and the average number of destinations a source targets (6.85), suggest that there is a large turnover in the use of the bots. Figure 11 shows the constant use of new bots throughout the entire scan, except for the interval from approximately 7 February 00:00 GMT to 11 February 12:00 GMT, which exhibits significantly reduced botnet activity. The continuous line with square

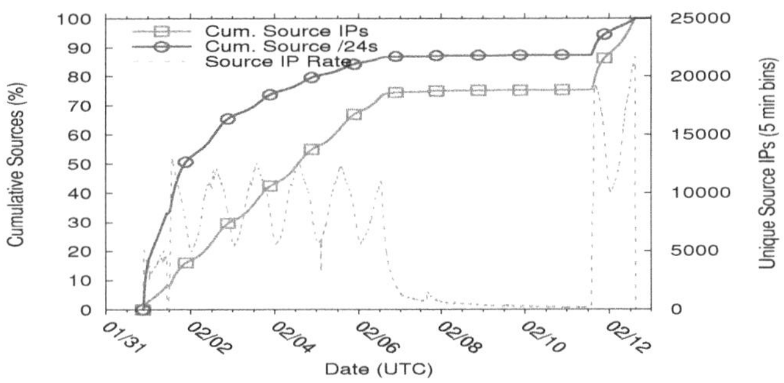

Figure 11: Arrival of new bots. The continuous line with squares shows the cumulative percentage of bots that probed our darknet throughout the 12-day scan. The continuous line with circles is the cumulative percentage of source /24 networks. The slope of these curves indicates a constant arrival (during the botnet's active periods) of new bots participating in the scan. The dashed line represents the number of unique source IPs scanning per 5-minute interval, representing the evolution of the scan over time.

symbols shows the cumulative percentage of bots that probed our darknet over the 12-day scan. Its linear slope indicates a constant arrival of new bots participating in the scan. To partially take into account the effect of dynamic IP address assignment, we also plot the cumulative sum of unique /24 networks containing the source IP addresses (continuous line with circles). The slope of this curve proves that new bots take part in the scan for its entire duration.

Figure 12 shows the distribution of the number of packets sent by each bot. The diagram on the left uses a log-log scale to show all the data, whereas the diagram on the right uses a linear scale to zoom in to the left side of the distribution up to 10 packets. More than 1 million bots (more than 1/3 of the total) sent a single probe and never participated further in the scan. The number of bots that sent more than 100 packets during the scan is two orders of magnitude smaller. This difference suggests rapid turnover of bots during the scan. We hypothesize that this behavior is related to how the C&C channels managed and assigned tasks to bots. For example, a C&C channel may assign a list of target IP ranges to a queue of bots, in which case it is unlikely that a single bot could reach the head of the queue twice. In such a situation, bots that reappear in the scan would have likely been assigned to a C&C channel with a smaller pool of bots.

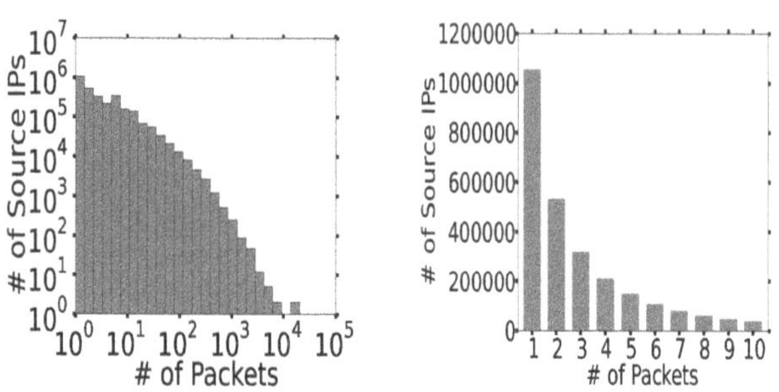

Figure 12: (left) Full histogram of packets sent per bot (log-log scale); (right) zoomed histogram of packets sent per bot for bots that sent up to 10 packets (linear axis) Most bots sent few packets, e.g., over a third of the bots sent a single packet during the entire scan.

In combination with the reverse-byte order property of the scan, the high bot turnover rate makes the scan impressively covert. Not only would an automated intrusion detection system on a /24 network see only 34 packets to the same port, but they would most likely arrive from 34 distinct IP addresses, making detection highly unlikely.

4.3 Coordination and Adaptation

4.3.1 Coverage and Overlap

The scan fails to cover the entire darknet's /8 address space, probing only 86.6% of it (Table 1). On the other hand, there is a non-negligible overlap in terms of bots hitting the same target: about 5.7 million IP addresses were probed by more than one bot, and on average a targeted IP is probed by 1.39 distinct bots. Whether probed zero, one, or multiple times, the probed IP addresses are scattered all over the address space without clusters or holes, in both the standard and reverse representation of the address bytes. These properties – coverage and overlap of target addresses – are independent of the number of bots active at any given time, the overall rate of the scan, or specific subnets being scanned. But we did discover a correlation between coverage and overlap in targets, which we believe is likely a function of a parameter of the scan configured by the botmaster to support trading off completeness and redundancy of scanning.

The representation with the Hilbert curve of the probed IP addresses in reverse byte order reveals three regions with different densities. These regions are labeled A, B, C, in a detail of the Hilbert-curve map in Figure 13(a) and correspond to three different phases of the scan as indicated in Figure 13(c). Brighter areas indicate a greater coverage of the corresponding address space: the scan starts with a very high percentage of targets probed ("A"), after few hours a parameter is changed and the coverage significantly drops ("B"), finally the parameter is adjusted again and an intermediate level of target coverage remains for the rest of the scan

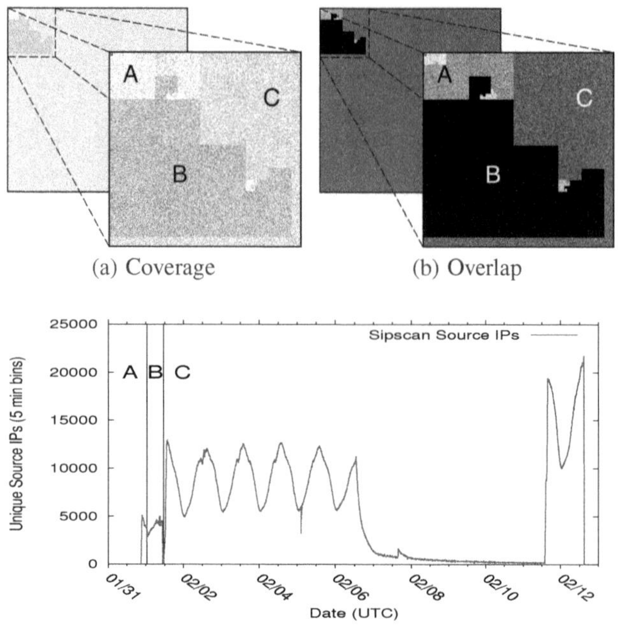

(a) Coverage (b) Overlap

(c) Phases over time

Figure 13: Different phases (A, B, C) of the scan characterized by different but correlated rates of coverage and overlap of the target IP space, (a) Slice of the Hilbert-curve map (with reversed-byte order IP addresses) highlighting areas of different density indicating different coverage of the target space. (b) shows the same phenomenon in terms of overlap: the lit pixels in the map represent target addresses probed by more than one bot. The three regions perfectly match between the two maps. (c) Scanning source IPs throughout scan, showing the transitions from Phase A to B and from Phase B to C.

Start time	Jan 31 21:00	Feb 1 00:45	Feb 1 11:20
# of probes	179,143	486,394	19,590,184
% of IP space covered	93.81%	76.27%	86.98%
Average bots per target	1.66	1.01	1.40

Table 2: Characteristics of the three phases of the scan, with different coverage and overlap of the target address space, show a trade-off between the two properties.

("C"). The same regions are visible in Figure 13(b), where we use the Hilbert-curve map to highlight the overlap in targets: IP addresses (in reverse-byte order) that were probed more than once are depicted in white.

Table 2 shows statistics calculated separately for the three phases of the scan. The correlation between coverage and overlap of the scan is evident, and is consistent with a probabilistic mechanism in the choice of the targets that can be configured by the botmaster to trade off completeness and redundancy of scanning. The finding illustrated in Figure 14 further substantiates the hypothesis that the three phases correspond to different configurations of the scan. The figure shows, for each phase, the distribution of the number of packets sent in each "reverse /16 subnet" (we define a reverse /16 subnet as the set of all possible IP addresses obtainable when the least two significant bytes are fixed). The three curves refer to populations of different size, which explains the different smoothness of their shapes (e.g., phase C is considerably longer thus covering a larger number of reverse /16 subnets). However, all of them are highly centered around a different value (average values are 395.6

(A), 196.3 (B), 312.6 (C)) and mostly non-overlapping, reflecting a consistent and distinctive behavior in each phase.

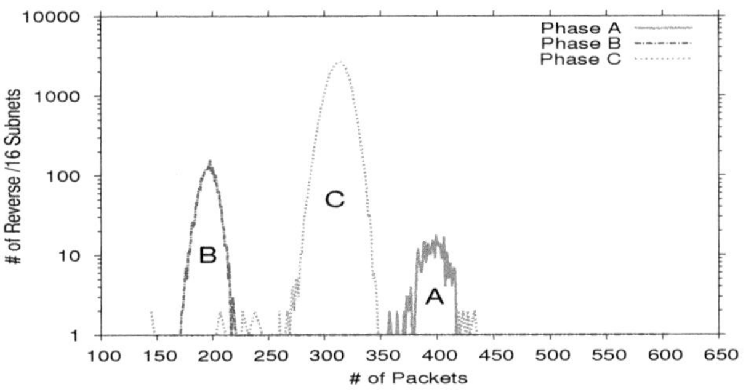

Figure 14: Consistent and distinctive behavior of the different phases of the scan. The curves represent, for each phase A, B, C, the distributions of packets observed at the UCSD Network Telescope in each "reverse /16 subnet". The distributions are all centered around different values and mostly non overlapping.

Finally, in both Figures 13(a) and 13(b), we also observe better coverage and larger overlap in the transition from one region to the other, suggesting that the botmaster re-issued a command to scan those IP ranges to the bots after changing the configuration parameter (possibly because the scan was stopped without collecting the results of the previous command). The higher coverage in these transition areas provides further evidence of a probabilistic approach in the choice of the target IPs (probably happening at the level of the single bots): re-issuing the commands for that range of target IPs results in a partially different set of probed targets.

Even given non-negligible redundancy, an average of 1.39 bots hitting the same target is small compared to the large number of bots involved. Such low redundancy is novel, or at least undocumented in the literature, which has mostly reported on bots that independently scan the same address range in a random uniform fashion [12,39]. The small overlap and thus high efficiency in terms of completeness vs. redundancy achieved by this botnet is an impressive consequence of strongly orchestrated behavior.

4.3.2 Adaptivity

The strong coordination of bot activity is also visible in terms of adaptation capabilities. Starting around 7 February 00:00 GMT through around 11 February 12:00 GMT, the scan proceeds very slowly, with only a few active bots (Figure 2). A possible hypothesis is that most of the C&C channels are down during this period. However, we observe that the target IP ranges that would have normally been assigned to these C&C channels were automatically redirected to those channels that were still up.

Figure 15 illustrates this behavior. Dashed lines in the graph represent the probing rate per hour of the three bots discussed in Section 3.4. During this period the bots do not change their speed, suggesting that the C&C channel they refer to has not changed its characteristics in terms of numbers of bots managed, etc. (i.e., the number of bots competing for a certain C&C channel does not change, therefore the rate at which each bot gets assigned a new "reverse" /24 stays the same). However, over this same time interval we observe a significant change in the sequences of IP ranges assigned to these bots. The continuous lines in Figure 15 show, for each of the three bots, the distance between subsequent target IPs, calculated by subtracting the target IPs after reversing their byte order and converting them into 32-bit numbers. The graph shows a drop of about one order of magnitude in the distance, meaning that the

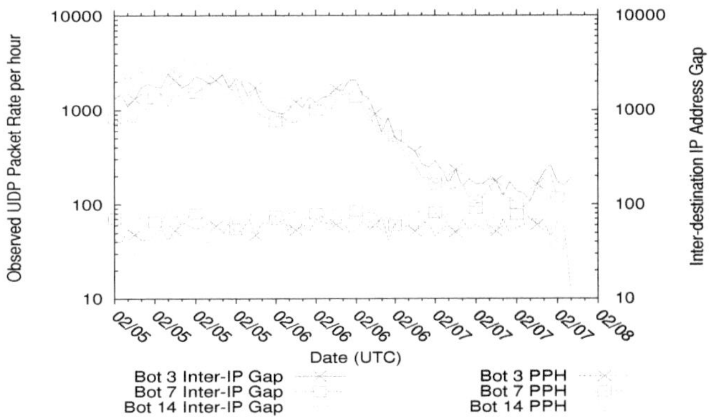

Figure 15: Adaptive assignment of target IP ranges to different C&C channels. Dashed lines represent probes per hour (PPH) carried out by 3 different bots. Their speed did not change significantly on 7 February but the global speed of the scan decreased considerably, probably because some C&C channels went off-line. However, the target IP ranges assigned to these bots became denser during this period, to compensate for the absence of other C&C channels: continuous lines represent the distance between subsequent target IPs of each respective bot, showing an order of magnitude decrease in that time interval.

corresponding C&C channel(s) receive a "denser" list of targets to compensate for the disappearance of the other C&C channels.

4.4 Botnet characteristics

Observing a horizontal scan of this magnitude from such a large darknet allows unique insight into the characteristics of the botnet that performed it. The size of the darknet, combined with the reverse IP sequential ordering of the targets, allowed the telescope to capture probes across the entire life of the scan, providing an unprecedented view of the population of the Sality botnet.

A white paper from Symantec [23] estimated the size of the Sality botnet at approximately a million bots, by measuring the number of hosts that a 'rogue' server under their control communicated with. We identified a total of 2,954,108 unique source IPs for bots that participated in the sipscan. As the authors of [59] demonstrate, it is difficult to accurately determine the size of the botnet population when using source IP addresses collected from traffic sent by infected hosts. This difficulty arises due to the effects of dynamic IP address assignment (DHCP), which can result in several IP addresses being used by a single bot (especially over a 12-day interval), and NAT, which can cause multiple bots to appear as a single IP. However, Figure 11 shows continuous growth in the number of unique /24 networks hosting bots over the entire duration of the scan. This diversity of /24 networks can be used as an approximation for the number of new bots that arrive over the course of the scan.

We leverage the large population of source addresses observed to further understand how hosts compromised by botnets are distributed globally. To this end, we determine the Autonomous System Number (ASN) for each bot using a Routeviews BGP routing snapshot [60] taken on Monday 14 February 2011 at 12:00 UTC, proximate to the scanning episode. Using this table, we perform longest-prefix matching to resolve each source IP to its origin AS.

The ASes enumerated in Table 3 are the 10 most common across the bots used by the sipscan botmaster. We also list the AS name and home country extracted from whois data. Similar to the Conficker [55] and Mega-D [4] botnets, we see a dominant AS at the top of the list (TTNet), which alone accounts for over 10% all participating bots, followed by a long tail of small ASes. However,

Rank	%	ASN	AS Name	Country
1	10.81	9121	TTNet	Turkey
2	4.57	8452	TE	Egypt
3	4.40	9829	BSNL-NIB	India
4	4.22	17974	TELKOMNET	Indonesia
5	4.20	45899	VNPT	Vietnam
6	3.01	7738	TELEMAR	Brazil
7	2.65	8708	RDSNET	Romania
8	2.51	24560	AIRTELBROADBAND	India
9	2.07	9050	RTD	Romania
10	1.94	9737	TOTNET	Thailand

Table 3: Top 10 origin ASes of bots used in the sipscan. As noted in other work [55], we see a dominant AS at the top of the list (Turkey, with 10% of the overall bot population), followed by a long tail. The country and AS name data have been extracted from whois data for each AS.

	Conficker [55]		Mega-D [55]		Sipscan	
Rank	ASN	Country	ASN	Country	ASN	Country
1	4134	China	3352	Spain	9121	Turkey
2	4837	China	3269	Italy	8452	Egypt
3	7738	Brazil	6739	Spain	9829	India
4	3462	Taiwan	9121	Turkey	17974	Indonesia
5	45899	Vietnam	6147	Peru	45899	Vietnam
6	27699	Brazil	19262	USA	7738	Brazil
7	9829	India	4134	China	8708	Romania
8	8167	Brazil	7738	Brazil	24560	India
9	3269	Italy	7418	Chile	9050	Romania
10	9121	Turkey	22927	Argentina	9737	Thailand

Table 4: Comparison of the top 10 ASes observed in three different botnets: the Conficker botnet as surveyed by [55], the Mega-D botnet as reported by [4,55], and the Sality (sipscan) botnet. We observe a trend toward Eastern European countries which have not featured as prominently in previous botnets.

although the scale of the leading ASes may resemble other botnets, the networks featured in the top 10 are quite different (Table 4). Only four of the ASes in the top 10 of the sipscan appear in the top 10 of either Conficker [55] or Mega-D [55]. Notably, TTNet in Turkey, which [55] lists in 10th place, represents the largest AS by more than a factor of two in the sipscan botnet.

Both the Conficker and Mega-D AS distributions indicate a move toward larger representation of bots in Asian and South American countries, corroborating the results of [55]. However, we see a considerable rise in bots in Eastern European countries, which becomes even more apparent on a per-country level (Table 5).

Simply aggregating bots by their ASN can be misleading because many large organizations/providers have multiple ASNs. To complement our AS findings, we geolocate the bot's IP address using a MaxMind GeoLite database [41] snapshot from March 1 2011 (again, proximate to the scan episode). Table 5 presents the top 10 countries for bots in both the sipscan and the Mega-D botnets [4]. Once we aggregate bots to a country granularity, the distribution of locations changes appreciably, with the Russian Federation making an appearance in the top 10 lists of both Mega-D and sipscan[2].

	Mega-D [4]		Sipscan	
Rank	%	Country	%	Country
1	14.82	USA	12.55	Turkey
2	11.74	Russian Federation	12.54	India
3	6.33	Turkey	8.64	Brazil
4	6.32	Poland	7.23	Egypt
5	5.32	Thailand	5.77	Indonesia
6	4.11	Brazil	5.59	Romania
7	3.89	Germany	5.58	Russian Federation
8	3.23	United Kingdom	5.36	Vietnam
9	2.53	India	5.10	Thailand
10	2.25	Spain	3.01	Ukraine

Table 5: Top 10 Countries of bots used in the sipscan compared to the Mega-D botnet. Geolocation data for sipscan sources was obtained using the MaxMind GeoLite database [41]. Aggregating bots by country rather than AS helps identify regions that are heavily compromised by bots but have many small ASes, such as the Russian Federation, which is not in the list of top 10 ASes.

Contrary to similarly large botnets [4,48,55,61], the sipscan bots do not have a dominant presence in China. China has been recorded in the top ten lists of these other botnets, but in the sipscan, China is in 27th place (0.57%) - close to U.S.'s 29th place position (0.44%). Heatmaps of overall Sality bot locations [23] also indicate a corresponding lack of Sality bot presence in China. We believe this under-representation of China, when compared to previous botnets, may be considered a limitation of the Sality botnet rather than a specific design choice by the botmaster. Although the data presented in [23] is largely in aggregated graphical form, it does appear to corroborate our findings in terms of geographical distribution. As noted earlier however, we are able to identify a much larger bot population.

In addition to analyzing the networks that host the bots, we also investigated the bots themselves. Output of the p0f passive OS fingerprinting tool [63] reported that more than 97% of bots were running operating systems of the Microsoft Windows family. The distribution of UDP source port values shown in Figure 7 also shows that the majority of packets fall into the 1025-5000 range of ports, which was used by Microsoft Windows until Vista and Server 2003. There are, however, a non-negligible number of bots that p0f identified as running the Linux operating system. We believe these machines are likely not bots but rather NAT gateways proxying packets from infected hosts.

5. BINARY ANALYSIS

We had the opportunity to analyze the binary code responsible for this scanning. The binary is a separate executable that Sality-infected computers download via a URL as directed by the peer-to-peer botnet infrastructure [22, 23]. Although our work focuses on the Internet measurement aspect of the event, we partially reverse engineered this code to validate some of our inferences. This section summarizes the most relevant findings.

We found that each bot contacts a hard-coded IP address (the C&C channel) in order to receive a probing command from the botmaster. The command followed by the bots we observed is one of three different command types that the binary supports. Through this command, the botmaster sends the target IP to the bot in the form of an ASCII string (dotted quad decimal format). By analyzing the code, we verified that this address is the actual address probed by the bot. In particular, the bot properly manages the endianness of the target IP addresses, e.g., when converting the ASCII string into binary and then when contacting the target.

Each bot reports through the C&C channel the results of both the TCP and UDP probes immediately after receiving a response from the victim. It then selects and probes a new target by incrementing the most significant byte of the target address received by the botmaster. This increment is repeated 15 times, for a total of 16 targets probed, each one from a different /8 network. The bot then sleeps for a fixed amount of time before contacting the botmaster again to receive a new target IP.

These findings, along with the progression of the target IP addresses observed through the UCSD Network Telescope, indicate

[2] [55] only provides Conficker results at an AS level.

that both the botmaster and each bot incremented the target IPs in reverse-byte order, and that the sequence followed by the scan reflected the original orders of the botmaster (who was sending addresses as quad decimal dot-separated ASCII strings). In other words, the reverse byte order probing was most likely not due to a bug or error in managing the endianness of the target IP addresses.

Inspecting the binary also revealed that several interesting properties of the scan would have not been visible by relying solely on the reverse-engineering the bot binary. For example, the code running on a single bot shows only the selection of 16 target addresses (whose increments to the most significant byte could have been attributed to a coding mistake, without the knowledge of the overall pattern). But analysis of traffic from the UCSD Network Telescope revealed a heavily coordinated behavior of many bots around the world, allowing inference of the mechanisms adopted by the botmaster in orchestrating the scan.

6. DISCUSSION

Botnets commonly scan large segments of the Internet's address space for various purposes, such as infecting or compromising hosts, recruiting hosts into a botnet, or collating a list of future targets. Awareness of evolving botnet characteristics and spreading techniques can improve our ability to navigate and mitigate their impacts. As mentioned in Section 2, although many aspects of botnet behavior have been documented, we are not aware of any published investigation of a million node botnet covertly scanning the entire IPv4 space. Most of the available literature are studies of older generation (pre-2007) botnets, which are substantially smaller in size, scope, and capability from newer-generation botnets. Studies of newer generation bots have focused on aspects other than the scanning behavior, such as the command and control, peer-to-peer infrastructure, or the domain of abuse, e.g., spam campaigns inflicted by the botnet. We present a new angle on the study of new-generation botnets: their scanning activity as observable in large darknets, most aspects of which cannot be inferred by reverse-engineering the bot malware.

This work offers contributions in two areas: documenting and visualizing behavioral aspects of a current generation botnet, and thoroughly analyzing the multiple synergistic characteristics of its extraordinarily well-coordinated scanning.

The scan that we analyzed in this study was new, or at least not previously documented, in four ways. It was sourced by a current-generation (2011), widely-deployed, peer-to-peer botnet (Sality [23]). Although earlier-generation version of Sality were first reported in June 2003, it was not until February 2011 that Sality operators deployed a new module designed to locate and compromise SIP servers in a distributed, heavily coordinated manner. The population of bots participating in the scan is several orders of magnitude larger than any previously documented botmaster-orchestrated scanning. Previous Internet-wide scanning behavior perpetrated by botnets was due to worm-spreading modules inside the bot, e.g, in Conficker, rather than botmaster-coordinated scanning. Not only was this sipscan coordinated, but it was impressively well-engineered to maximize coverage, minimize redundancy and overlap among target IP addresses by scanning bots, and evade detection by even state-of-the-art intrusion detection capabilities.

We used the detailed packet traces captured by the darknet to richly analyze many properties of the botnet, including several interacting properties of the botnet's heavily coordinated scanning. The size of the botnet, the fact that it was a /0 scan, i.e., of the entire IPv4 address space, and the reverse-byte ordering sequence of IP addresses targets were unprecedented and impressive enough characteristics, the last of which we only discovered using animated visualization techniques. This animation also revealed that the scan operated in distinct phases, with observable phase transitions. We presume the botmaster triggered these phase changes using configuration parameters in the malware, in order to trade off address coverage vs. redundancy in scanning. Time-series analysis of the active IP addresses operating as bots revealed an unusually rapid turnover rate and associated low re-use rate of the bot population, all heavily coordinated by the botmaster to scan in a extremely regular, stealth pattern.

We did have the opportunity to dissect the binary, which we used to validate our inferences. But most of these aspects of the scanning behavior would not be revealed by reverse-engineering of the bot binary; they require inference by measurement and analysis of actual bot-generated traffic (e.g, the mechanism that selects the IP addresses to be scanned is not entirely encoded in the bot binary, rather the intelligence lies in the botmaster and C&C).

We also developed several animation and visualization techniques to facilitate our own exploration of the phenomena. For example, using the Hilbert-curve map clearly revealed the strictly ordered reverse-byte incrementing behavior of the progression of the entire scan; without this visualization technique it is not clear that we would have verified this sequence (for all the three observable changing bytes) at all. Animations of the scan over time [13] also exposed the three different phases of the scanning, and juxtaposing the Hilbert maps with a geographic map of bot activity as well as a traffic time-series allowed us to visualize multiple dimensions of the scanning simultaneously. We anticipate this technique will be useful by us and others for analysis of other large-scale Internet probing behavior.

As the world's voice communications completes its transition to an all-IP network, the vulnerability of VoIP infrastructure, and the emerging capabilities of botnets to illegitimately commandeer its resources, present a daunting challenge for Internet architects, engineers, and policymakers. Analysis of this scan provides an illustrative if ominous indicator of the more sophisticated capabilities to surreptitiously survey and exploit critical infrastructure vulnerabilities on a planetary scale. Our darknet packet capture allowed a detailed analysis of a botnet's comprehensive and covert scanning behavior, and in the process we developed generalizable methods to correlate, visualize, and extrapolate botnet behavior across the global Internet.

A dataset with detailed information (e.g., timestamp and source IP geolocation) for each sipscan UDP probing packet we captured is available at [13].

Acknowledgements

We would like to thank: Joe Stewart of SecureWorks for helping us to identify the sipscan binary; Ken Chiang at Sandia National Labs for helping reverse engineering the binary; Saverio Niccolini at NEC for brainstorming on the SIP header of the sipscan; and Marco Stendardo for helping with the scripts used in the analysis. We are also grateful to all the CAIDA folks for their support, and in particular to Dan Andersen for enabling the storage, transport, and processing of massive data volumes on systems available 24/7. Antonio Pescapé has been partially supported by the PLATINO project financed by the MIUR and by the LINCE project of the FARO programme, jointly financed by Compagnia di San Paolo and Polo delle Scienze e delle Tecnologie of University of Napoli Federico II. Support for CAIDA's effort on this project, as well as support for the UCSD network telescope operations and data collection, curation, analysis, and sharing is provided by DHS S&T NBCHC070133 and NSF CNS-1059439.

7. REFERENCES

[1] AfriNIC: The Registry of Internet Number Resources for Africa. http://www.afrinic.net.

[2] Cuttlefish. http://www.caida.org/tools/visualization/cuttlefish/.

[3] RIPE NCC: Routing Information Service (RIS). http://www.ripe.net/data-tools/stats/ris/routing-information-service.

[4] Secureworks. ozdok/mega-d trojan analysis. http://www.secureworks.com/research/threats/ozdok/.

[5] tcpdump. http://www.tcpdump.org.

[6] The asterisk-users mailing-list archives. http://lists.digium.com/pipermail/asterisk-users/2010-November/thread.html, November 2010.

[7] UCSD Network Telescope, 2010. http://www.caida.org/data/passive/network_telescope.xml.

[8] The voipsec mailing-list archives. http://voipsa.org/pipermail/voipsec_voipsa.org/2010-November/thread.html, November 2010.

[9] M. Abu Rajab, J. Zarfoss, F. Monrose, and A. Terzis. A multifaceted approach to understanding the botnet phenomenon. In *Proceedings of the 6th ACM SIGCOMM conference on Internet measurement*, IMC '06, pages 41–52, New York, NY, USA, 2006. ACM.

[10] P. Bacher, T. Holz, M. Kotter, and G. Wicherski. Know your enemy: Tracking botnets. http://www.honeynet.org/papers/bots, 2008.

[11] P. Barford and V. Yegneswaran. An Inside Look at Botnets. In M. Christodorescu, S. Jha, D. Maughan, D. Song, and C. Wang, editors, *Malware Detection*, volume 27 of *Advanced in Information Security*. Springer, 2006.

[12] P. Barford and V. Yegneswaran. An Inside Look at Botnets. *Advances in Information Security, Malware Detection*, vol. 27, 2007, Springer.

[13] CAIDA. Supplemental data: Analysis of a "/0" Stealth Scan from a Botnet. http://www.caida.org/publications/papers/2012/analysis_slash_zero/supplemental/, 2012.

[14] C. Castelluccia, M. A. Kaafar, P. Manils, and D. Perito. Geolocalization of proxied services and its application to fast-flux hidden servers. In *Proceedings of the 9th ACM SIGCOMM conference on Internet measurement conference*, IMC '09, pages 184–189, New York, NY, USA, 2009. ACM.

[15] J. Cheng. Symantec: Flashback botnet could generate up to $10k per day in ad clicks. http://arstechnica.com/apple/2012/05/symantec-flashback-botnet-could-generate-up-to-10k-per-day-in-ad-clicks/, May 1 2012.

[16] C. Y. Cho, D. Babi ć, E. C. R. Shin, and D. Song. Inference and analysis of formal models of botnet command and control protocols. In *Proceedings of the 17th ACM conference on Computer and communications security*, CCS '10, pages 426–439, New York, NY, USA, 2010. ACM.

[17] E. Cooke, F. Jahanian, and D. McPherson. The zombie roundup: understanding, detecting, and disrupting botnets. In *Proceedings of the Steps to Reducing Unwanted Traffic on the Internet*, SRUTI'05, pages 6–6, Berkeley, CA, USA, 2005. USENIX Association.

[18] D. Dagon, G. Gu, C. Lee, and W. Lee. A taxonomy of botnet structures. In *Computer Security Applications Conference, 2007. ACSAC 2007. Twenty-Third Annual*, pages 325 –339, dec. 2007.

[19] A. Dainotti, C. Squarcella, E. Aben, K. C. Claffy, M. Chiesa, M. Russo, and A. Pescapé. Analysis of country-wide internet outages caused by censorship. In *Proceedings of the 2011 ACM SIGCOMM conference on Internet measurement conference*, IMC '11, pages 1–18, New York, NY, USA, 2011. ACM.

[20] J. Davis. Hackers take down the most wired country in europe. http://www.wired.com/politics/security/magazine/15-09/ff_estonia, July 1 2011.

[21] Duane Wessels. Mapping the IPv4 address space, 2009. http://maps.measurement-factory.com/.

[22] N. Falliere. A distributed cracker for voip. http://www.symantec.com/connect/blogs/distributed-cracker-voip, February 15 2011.

[23] N. Falliere. Sality: Story of a peer-to-peer viral network. http://www.symantec.com/content/en/us/enterprise/media/security_response/whitepapers/sality_peer_to_peer_viral_network.pdf, July 2011.

[24] S. Gauci. 11 million Euro loss in VoIP fraud.. and my VoIP logs, December 2010. http://blog.sipvicious.org/2010/12/11-million-euro-loss-in-voip-fraud-and.html.

[25] S. Gauci. Distributed sip scanning during halloween weekend. http://blog.sipvicious.org/2010/11/distributed-sip-scanning-during.html, Nov 4 2010.

[26] S. Gauci. Sipvicious. tools for auditing sip based voip systems. http://code.google.com/p/sipvicious/, Apr 2012.

[27] C. W. Group. Conficker working group lessons learned. http://www.confickerworkinggroup.org/wiki/uploads/Conficker_Working_Group_Lessons_Learned_17_June_2010_final.pdf, June 2010.

[28] M. W. group. Guidelines for protecting user privacy in wide traffic traces. http://mawi.wide.ad.jp/mawi/guideline.txt, Oct 1999.

[29] M. W. group. Mawi working group traffic archive. http://mawi.wide.ad.jp, Apr 2012.

[30] M. Gruber, F. Fankhauser, S. Taber, C. Schanes, and T. Grechenig. Security status of voip based on the observation of real-world attacks on a honeynet. In *Privacy, security, risk and trust (passat), IEEE third international conference on social computing (socialcom)*, pages 1041 –1047, oct. 2011.

[31] G. Gu, J. Zhang, and W. Lee. BotSniffer: Detecting botnet command and control channels in network traffic. In *Proceedings of the 15th Annual Network and Distributed System Security Symposium (NDSS'08)*, February 2008.

[32] J. Heidemann, Y. Pradkin, R. Govindan, C. Papadopoulos, G. Bartlett, and J. Bannister. Census and survey of the visible internet. In *Proceedings of the 8th ACM SIGCOMM conference on Internet measurement*, IMC '08, pages 169–182, New York, NY, USA, 2008. ACM.

[33] T. Holz, M. Steiner, F. Dahl, E. Biersack, and F. Freiling. Measurements and mitigation of peer-to-peer-based botnets: a case study on storm worm. In *Proceedings of the 1st Usenix Workshop on Large-Scale Exploits and Emergent Threats*, LEET'08, pages 9:1–9:9, Berkeley, CA, USA, 2008.

[34] S. Institute. Dshield.org: Distributed intrusion detection system. http://www.dshield.org, Apr 2012.

[35] C. Kanich, N. Weavery, D. McCoy, T. Halvorson, C. Kreibichy, K. Levchenko, V. Paxson, G. M. Voelker, and S. Savage. Show me the money: characterizing

spam-advertised revenue. In *Proceedings of the 20th USENIX conference on Security*, SEC'11, pages 15–15, Berkeley, CA, USA, 2011. USENIX Association.

[36] C. Kreibich, C. Kanich, K. Levchenko, B. Enright, G. M. Voelker, V. Paxson, and S. Savage. Spamcraft: an inside look at spam campaign orchestration. In *Proceedings of the 2nd USENIX conference on Large-scale exploits and emergent threats: botnets, spyware, worms, and more*, LEET'09, pages 4–4, Berkeley, CA, USA, 2009. USENIX Association.

[37] D. Leonard and D. Loguinov. Demystifying service discovery: implementing an internet-wide scanner. In *Proceedings of the 10th annual conference on Internet measurement*, IMC '10, pages 109–122, New York, NY, USA, 2010. ACM.

[38] Z. Li, A. Goyal, and Y. Chen. Honeynet-based botnet scan traffic analysis. In W. Lee, C. Wang, and D. Dagon, editors, *Botnet Detection*, volume 36 of *Advances in Information Security*, pages 25–44. Springer, 2008.

[39] Z. Li, A. Goyal, Y. Chen, and V. Paxson. Towards situational awareness of large-scale botnet probing events. *Information Forensics and Security, IEEE Transactions on*, 6(1):175 –188, march 2011.

[40] W. Lu, M. Tavallaee, and A. A. Ghorbani. Automatic discovery of botnet communities on large-scale communication networks. ASIACCS '09, pages 1–10, New York, NY, USA, 2009. ACM.

[41] MaxMind. MaxMind GeoLite Country: Open Source IP Address to Country Database. `http://www.maxmind.com/app/geolitecountry`.

[42] C. Mullaney. Android.bmaster: A million-dollar mobile botnet. `http://www.symantec.com/connect/blogs/androidbmaster-million-dollar-mobile-botnet`, February 9 2012.

[43] R. Munroe. xkcd: Map of the Internet. `http://xkcd.com/195/`, 2006.

[44] M. D. Network. bind function. `http://msdn.microsoft.com/en-us/library/ms737550%28VS.85%29.aspx`, 2012.

[45] A. Pathak, F. Qian, Y. C. Hu, Z. M. Mao, and S. Ranjan. Botnet spam campaigns can be long lasting: evidence, implications, and analysis. SIGMETRICS '09, pages 13–24, New York, NY, USA, 2009. ACM.

[46] P. Porras, H. Saidi, and V. Yegneswaran. Conficker. Technical report, SRI International, Mar 2009.

[47] A. H. Project. Sip brute force attack originating from amazon ec2 hosts. `http://honeynet.org.au/?q=sunday_scanner`, October 25 2010.

[48] A. Ramachandran and N. Feamster. Understanding the network-level behavior of spammers. SIGCOMM '06, pages 291–302, New York, NY, USA, 2006. ACM.

[49] J. Rosenberg, H. Schulzrinne, G. Camarillo, A. Johnston, J. Peterson, R. Sparks, M. Handley, and E. Schooler. SIP: Session Initiation Protocol. RFC 3261 (Proposed Standard), June 2002.

[50] H. Sagan. *Space-filling curves.* Universitext. New York: Springer-Verlag. xv, 193 p. DM 54.00; öS 421.20; sFr. 54.00 , 1994.

[51] S. Sarat and A. Terzis. Measuring the storm worm network, October 2007.

[52] S. Sheldon. Sip brute force attack originating from amazon ec2 hosts. `http://www.stuartsheldon.org/blog/2010/04/sip-brute-force-attack-originating-from-amazon-ec2-hosts/`, April 11 2010.

[53] S. Sheldon. Sip brute force attacks escalate over halloween weekend. `http://www.stuartsheldon.org/blog/2010/11/sip-brute-force-attacks-escalate-over-halloween-weekend/`, Nov 1 2010.

[54] S. Shin and G. Gu. Conficker and beyond: a large-scale empirical study. In *Proceedings of the 26th Annual Computer Security Applications Conference*, ACSAC '10, pages 151–160, New York, NY, USA, 2010. ACM.

[55] S. Shin, G. Gu, N. Reddy, and C. Lee. A large-scale empirical study of conficker. *Information Forensics and Security, IEEE Transactions on*, 7(2):676 –690, april 2012.

[56] S. Shin, Z. Xu, and G. Gu. EFFORT: Efficient and Effective Bot Malware Detection. In *Proceedings of the 31th Annual IEEE Conference on Computer Communications (INFOCOM'12) Mini-Conference*, March 2012.

[57] S. Staniford, V. Paxson, and N. Weaver. How to own the internet in your spare time. In *Proceedings of the 11th USENIX Security Symposium*, pages 149–167, Berkeley, CA, USA, 2002. USENIX Association.

[58] J. Stewart. Protocols and encryption of the storm botnet. `http://www.blackhat.com/presentations/bh-usa-08/Stewart/BH_US_08_Stewart_Protocols_of_the_Storm.pdf.`, 2008.

[59] B. Stone-Gross, M. Cova, L. Cavallaro, B. Gilbert, M. Szydlowski, R. Kemmerer, C. Kruegel, and G. Vigna. Your botnet is my botnet: analysis of a botnet takeover. In *Proceedings of the 16th ACM conference on Computer and communications security*, CCS '09, pages 635–647, New York, NY, USA, 2009. ACM.

[60] University of Oregon. University of Oregon Route Views project. `http://www.routeviews.org`.

[61] Y. Xie, F. Yu, K. Achan, R. Panigrahy, G. Hulten, and I. Osipkov. Spamming botnets: signatures and characteristics. In *Proceedings of the ACM SIGCOMM 2008 conference on Data communication*, SIGCOMM '08, pages 171–182, New York, NY, USA, 2008. ACM.

[62] V. Yegneswaran, P. Barford, and V. Paxson. Using honeynets for internet situational awareness. In *Fourth Workshop on Hot Topics in Networks (HotNets IV)*, 2005.

[63] M. Zalewski. p0f v3. `http://lcamtuf.coredump.cx/p0f3/`, 2012.

[64] L. Zeltser. Targeting VoIP: Increase in SIP Connections on UDP port 5060. `http://isc.sans.edu/diary.html?storyid=9193`, July 2010.

[65] C. C. Zou, L. Gao, W. Gong, and D. Towsley. Monitoring and early warning for internet worms. In *Proceedings of the 10th ACM conference on Computer and communications security*, CCS '03, pages 190–199, New York, NY, USA, 2003. ACM.

Detecting Prefix Hijackings in the Internet with Argus

Xingang Shi[†§] shixg@cernet.edu.cn
Yang Xiang[‡§] sharangxy@gmail.com
Zhiliang Wang[†§] wzl@cernet.edu.cn
Xia Yin[‡§] yxia@tsinghua.edu.cn
Jianping Wu[†‡§] jianping@cernet.edu.cn

[†]Institute for Network Sciences and Cyberspace, Tsinghua University
[‡]Department of Computer Science & Technology, Tsinghua University
[§]Tsinghua National Laboratory for Information Science and Technology (TNList)

ABSTRACT

Border Gateway Protocol (BGP) plays a critical role in the Internet inter-domain routing reliability. Invalid routes generated by mis-configurations or forged by malicious attacks may hijack the traffic and devastate the Internet routing system, but it is unlikely that a secure BGP can be deployed in the near future to completely prevent them. Although many hijacking detection systems have been developed, they more or less have weaknesses such as long detection delay, high false alarm rate and deployment difficulty, and no systematic detection results have been studied. This paper proposes *Argus*, an agile system that can accurately detect prefix hijackings and deduce the underlying cause of route anomalies in a very fast way. *Argus* is based on correlating the control and data plane information closely and pervasively, and has been continuously monitoring the Internet for more than one year. During this period, around 40K routing anomalies were detected, from which 220 stable prefix hijackings were identified. Our analysis on these events shows that, hijackings that have only been theoretically studied before do exist in the Internet. Although the frequency of new hijackings is nearly stable, more specific prefixes are hijacked more frequently. Around 20% of the hijackings last less than ten minutes, and some can pollute 90% of the Internet in less than two minutes. These characteristics make *Argus* especially useful in practice. We further analyze some representative cases in detail to help increase the understanding of prefix hijackings in the Internet.

Categories and Subject Descriptors

C.2.0 [**Computer-Communication Networks**]: [General Security and Protection]; C.2.3 [**Network Operations**]: [Network Monitoring]

Keywords

BGP, Security, Prefix Hijacking, Hijacking Detection

1. INTRODUCTION

The Internet is composed of tens of thousands of Autonomous Systems (ASes) which operate individual parts of the infrastructure. As Border Gateway Protocol (BGP) [27] controls the packet forwarding path between ASes, it plays a critical role in the efficiency and reliability of the Internet. However, because of the lack of security considerations, several BGP security problems have not been well resolved yet [25]. For example, the route information received from neighbors can not be validated, so invalid routes may cause packets being forwarded along wrong paths. This is known as the prefix hijacking problem.

Prefix hijacking is often generated by accidental misconfigurations, and may cause serious routing problems and economic losses [24]. For instance, in 2008, Pakistan Telecom hijacked YouTube for two hours [29], while in 2010, one AS of China Telecom hijacked more than 50,000 prefixes (15% of the Internet) of 170 different countries [28]. Malicious users also use prefix hijacking to intercept or drop certain traffic, or to launch spam or DDoS attacks.

To improve the security of BGP, several methods have been proposed, which broadly fall into three categories: cryptographic based prevention, anomaly mitigation, and anomaly detection. Cryptographic approaches [17, 21] usually use the Public Key Infrastructure (PKI) to ensure the authentication of routing announcements and prevent hijacking. They often consume significant router resources due to their computation and storage complexity, and are unlikely to be widely deployed very soon [10]. Anomaly mitigation approaches [30, 18] propose to ignore or demote suspicious routes once they are detected. These approaches are hard to deploy, and their misjudgments may disturb the routing system. At last, anomaly detection approaches [36, 16, 34, 12] aim to discover anomalous information or behavior in BGP announcements and raise alarm. As a viable secure scheme in the current stage, they offer valuable information for the understanding and diagnosis of the routing system, and help to push ISPs to deploy cryptographic solutions.

This paper focuses on the third category, anomaly detection. Although many workable detection systems have been developed, more or less, they have weaknesses such as long detection delay, high false alarm rate and great deployment difficulty. Our solution, *Argus*, exploits a key observation about IP prefix hijacking: polluted routers (i.e., routers whose traffic is hijacked) usually can not communicate with the hosts in the victim prefix, while normal routers can. This observation makes hijacking distinguishable from other anomalous route events, and let *Argus* achieve four superior capabilities over existing solutions: (1) Low false positive rate: *Argus* closely correlates the control-plane anomaly and the data-plane reachability information of a large number of vantage points, so that prefix hijacking can be accurately distinguished from other BGP events. (2) Low false negative rate: *Argus* monitors a much wider range of routing anomalies, including origin AS and AS-path anomalies, and considers the sub-prefix problem, so the chance of missing a hijacking event is much lower. (3) Realtime detection: *Argus* usually detects a hijacking within a few seconds, while existing methods often need orders of magnitudes longer. (4) Agile: *Argus* is very easy to deploy, and does not need to upgrade any existing network infrastructure or device.

Based on our earlier prototype [32] of *Argus*, [1] this paper makes four new contributions as follows:

- System improvement and service. We carefully evaluate the performance of *Argus*, and continuously improve it from several aspects. In particular, we tune the system parameters based on our monitoring practice, and add a scheme to collect and choose live IP addresses, resulting in better detection accuracy. We contribute it to the community by providing several public online services, and by raising alerts in realtime via different channels. We also discuss the limitations of *Argus* to facilitate further studies in this field.

- Hijacking monitoring and analysis. Since being deployed one year ago, *Argus* has already identified 220 stable prefix hijackings (i.e., hijackings that last longer than 10 seconds) from 40K anomalous BGP events. We systematically analyze these events, and get many interesting results. In particular, hijackings that have only been theoretically studied before do exist in the Internet. Although the frequency of new hijackings is nearly stable, more specific prefixes are hijacked more frequently. Around 20% of the hijackings last less than ten minutes, and some can pollute 90% of the Internet in less than two minutes. These characteristics make *Argus* especially useful in practice, and to the best of our knowledge, we are the first to present these statistics and trend of prefix hijackings in the Internet.

- Hijacking confirmation and diagnosis. Starting from March 2012, we directly contact the corresponding network operators if a stable prefix hijacking is detected. We provide detailed information collected by *Argus* to help their diagnosis work. More than 30% of those hijackings have been confirmed, and we did not received any objection to our judgments.

- Cause analysis of anomalous route events. We extend *Argus* to not only detect prefix hijackings, but also deduce the possible cause of anomalous route events and classify them into different categories. We further analyze several representative cases in detail, in order to help increase the understanding of hijackings in the Internet.

[1]In particular, most of Section 4.1 and Section 4.2, and part of Section 4.4 are replications of those in [32], with moderate revisions.

This paper is organized as follows. Section 2 introduces the necessary background of prefix hijacking and some related work. Section 3 illustrates our key observation for hijacking detection, and Section 4 describes the design details of *Argus*. Section 5 presents our Internet monitoring practice in the past year, while Section 6 further studies some representative hijacking cases and other anomalous route events. The pros and cons of our system are discussed in Section 7, and finally, Section 8 concludes.

2. BACKGROUND AND RELATED WORK

2.1 Prefix Hijacking

Each AS in the Internet manages a number of networks, which can be expressed as IP prefixes. BGP propagates routes (AS-paths) between neighboring ASes to determine how these networks can be reached, i.e., through which AS-path. An AS-path $p = \langle a_n, \cdots, a_0 \rangle$ is a sequence of ASes, where the last one, a_0, is called the origin AS of p. When the network connectivities change, BGP UPDATEs will be generated, and new AS-paths will be announced throughout the Internet.

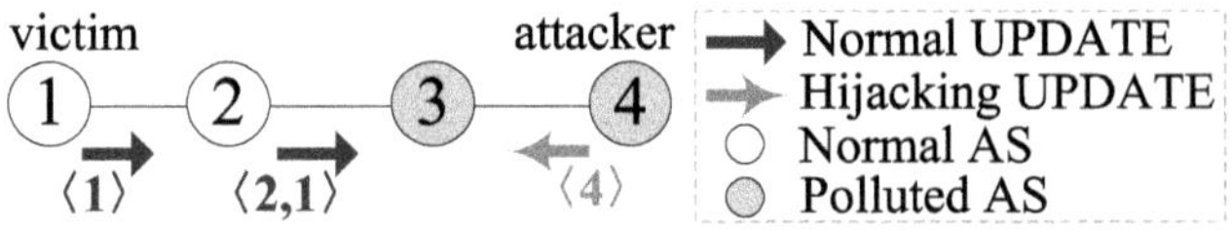

Figure 1: An example of BGP prefix hijacking.

As shown in Figure 1, AS1 announces a route for its prefix f with an AS-path $\langle 1 \rangle$, and AS2 and AS3 will get a route to f (i.e., $\langle 1 \rangle$ and $\langle 2, 1 \rangle$ respectively). However, AS4 can also announce a route for f with a forged but shorter AS-path $\langle 4 \rangle$. As AS3 considers the shorter path to be better [2] than the valid path it has previously received (i.e., $\langle 2, 1 \rangle$), it will forward the traffic destined to f to AS4. In this way, AS4 effectively hijacks the traffic by forging a route. We call AS3 *polluted* by the route announced by AS4, and indicate that by a gray circle in the figure.

A manipulator hijacks the traffic destined to a victim prefix either accidentally or intentionally. Based on how the hijacked traffic is finally dealt with, hijackings can be classified into the following two categories:

- Blackholing: the traffic is dropped, although the manipulator can eavesdrop on it at first.

- Imposture or Interception: the traffic is handled either by mimicking the victim's action, or by forwarding to the victim.

This paper only focuses on detecting blackholing due to the following reasons. First, mis-configurations will typically cause blackholing. Second, Although a malicious attacker may perform any of these actions, it is very difficult for him to mimic all behaviors of the victim, or to successfully forward the traffic to the victim, if not impossible. Third, detecting interception is very hard [9] since any AS can be viewed as a man-in-the-middle. Last, an end-to-end mechanism can be much more effective in protecting traffic from either imposture or interception.

[2]This is a simplified example, as the length of an AS-path is only one factor in BGP's route decision process.

Table 1: Pros and Cons of Hijacking Detection Methods

Methods	Detection delay	Attacker Information	Accuracy	Sub-prefix hijacking	Scalability	Deployment
Control-plane [8, 22, 12, 4]	Realtime	Yes	Low	Yes	Good	Easy
Data-plane [36, 34]	Minutes	No	Medium	No	Poor	Easy
Combination [16]	Minutes	Yes	High	Yes	Good	Hard
Correlation (*Argus*)	Realtime	Yes	High	Yes	Good	Easy

2.2 Related Work

Existing hijacking detection proposals can be classified into three categories based on the type of information they use, as compared in Table 1.

The control-plane approaches [8, 22, 12, 4] passively monitor the BGP routing information to collect anomalous events. They are easy to deploy, react in realtime, and can deduce information like who the attacker is or when the attack starts. However, they are fairly inaccurate and usually raise many unnecessary alarms, since they can not tell normal route events from hijackings very well [35].

The data-plane approaches [34, 36] continuously probe the Internet to detect whether any data path changes. The probing often involves a large number of networks, and the paths are collected by tools such as *traceroute*, hence these methods suffer from poor scalability and large latency. Due to a lack of control-plane information, they can not detect sub-prefix hijacking, and can provide little diagnosis such as who the attacker is.

Control and data plane information can be combined to complement each other. In [16], data-plane probing is launched only after an anomalous UPDATE is received, so the scalability is much better than a pure data-plane method. However, this system relies on some complicated probing methods like traceroute, nmap and IP/TCP timestamp, and also bears large latencies up to several minutes. More importantly, since customized software have to be installed on its vantage points, this solution is hard to deploy. Typically, a limited number of Planetlab nodes are used, which suffer from many side effects. In particular, the Planetlab nodes are unaware of BGP, so the benefits of combining control and data plane are limited. For example, the method can not distinguish prefix hijacking from BGP anycast, since both will result in different probing results. The nodes are mostly located in stub academic networks, so the data paths that can be probed are not diversified enough, and the capability of detecting hijackings is reduced.

We think the deep-rooted reason of their inefficiency is a lack of *close and pervasive correlation* between the control and the data plane. *Argus* makes a step forward, through correlating the control-plane route and data-plane reachability on a number of distributedly located diagnosis nodes in realtime.

There are also many measurement studies on BGP related problems, for example, analyzing route changes and their root causes [11, 14], measuring how the Internet end-to-end performance is impacted by BGP policy, timer or updates [31, 13], quantifying path exploration and slow convergence [26], and studying global black-holes in the Internet [20]. We monitor and identify anomalous route events and prefix hijackings, and systematically study the statistics and trend of these events that occurred over the past year, to help better understand the characteristics of Internet hijackings.

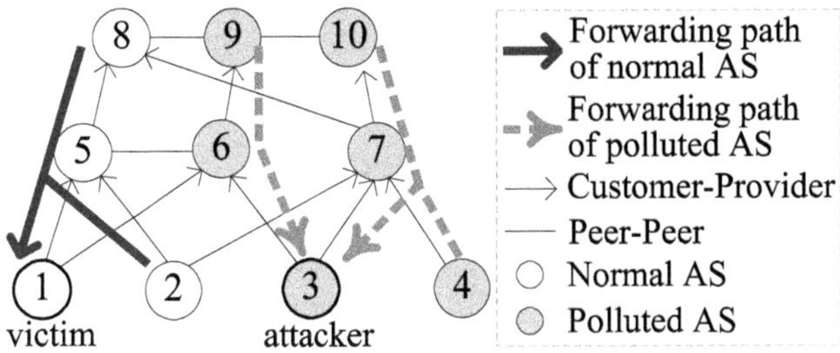

Figure 2: Different forwarding paths from normal ASes and polluted ASes during a hijacking.

3. KEY OBSERVATION

Prefix hijacking can be caused by changing either the origin AS, or some AS-path segments in a route announcement. Typically, only a portion of the ASes in the Internet can be polluted by a hijacking, due to the complexity and diversity of the Internet. As shown in Fig. 2, the attacker AS3 announces itself as the origin AS of the prefixes owned by the victim AS1,[3] and successfully pollutes AS4, AS6, AS7, AS9 and AS10. [4] These ASes will change their routes and forward the traffic which is originally destined to AS1 along the dashed line, while the other unpolluted ASes will forward such traffic along the solid line as usual. Unless the attacker forwards the hijacked traffic to AS1, a host in a polluted AS will not be able to communicate with a host in the victim, AS1, since the traffic goes to a black-hole.

Generally speaking, when the prefix hijacker acts as a black-hole, it is likely that a data-plane probe sent from an unpolluted AS to the victim prefix can successfully arrive at the destination and get a reply, while a probe from a polluted AS will most probably get no reply. This simple observation is the key basis of *Argus*, our prefix hijacking detection system. Next, we analyze this data-plane reachability problem in more detail.

As shown in Fig. 3, after an anomalous AS-path affects a portion of ASes in the Internet, the reachability to the affected prefix reflects different scenarios: [5]

1. When multi-origin (e.g., due to AS multi-homing, BGP anycast or static route) or traffic engineering is deployed, a new origin AS or new AS-path segments are introduced, and traffic may reach the destination prefix via different paths. In this case, both the normal ASes and the affected ASes can reach the destination prefix. (Fig. 3(a))

[3]Other cases, such as announcing false AS-path segments, will be discussed in Section 4.

[4]We assume AS6 prefers AS3 to AS1.

[5]By reachability, we mean one host can communicate with the other one in both directions, i.e., probe and reply.

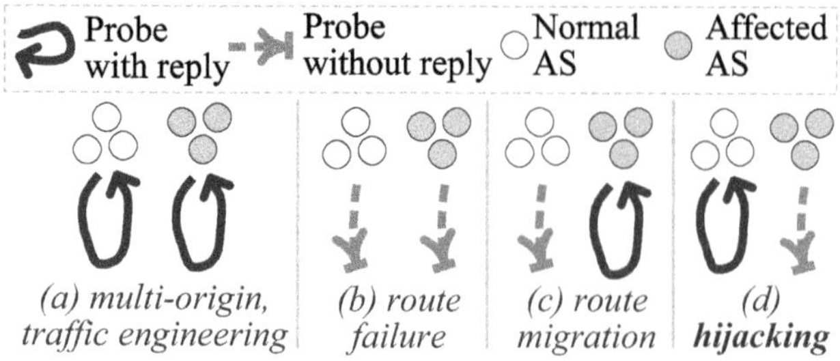

Figure 3: Data-plane reachabilities in different route events.

2. When node or link failure happens, there may not exist a valid route to the destination prefix, then no AS can reach it. Firewalls or inactive hosts may also lead to this result. (Fig. 3(b))

3. When route migrates (e.g., due to network merge or prefix acquisition, the ownership of a prefix changes, or new AS-path segments are used, either temporarily or permanently), ASes that have learned the new route are able to reach the destination prefix, while ASes have not learned the new route are not. (Fig. 3(c))

4. Under a hijacking as explained above, normal ASes can reach the destination prefix while polluted ASes can not. (Fig. 3(d))

The relation between the routes (control-plane) and the reachabilities (data-plane) in different ASes can be regarded as a fingerprint of a route event, and by this fingerprint, we can figure out whether a route change is actually caused by a hijacking. In *Argus*, we use *show ip bgp* to get the BGP routes, and use *ping* to test the reachability. These two commands are very simple, and are commonly enabled in a vast number of public route-servers and looking-glasses. These diagnosis nodes lie in different ASes nearly all over the Internet, and using them can greatly enhance our detection capabilities.

However, the real situation in the Internet is more complicated than the four scenarios above. Since there exists a convergence process after a route event happens, different ASes often experience route change at different time, and the control-plane does not always coincide with the data-plane. For example, as shown in Fig. 4, AS6 has already recovered from the pollution but its route UPDATE has not yet reached AS9. At this moment, probe from AS9 can get a response, even though AS9 is using a polluted AS-path.

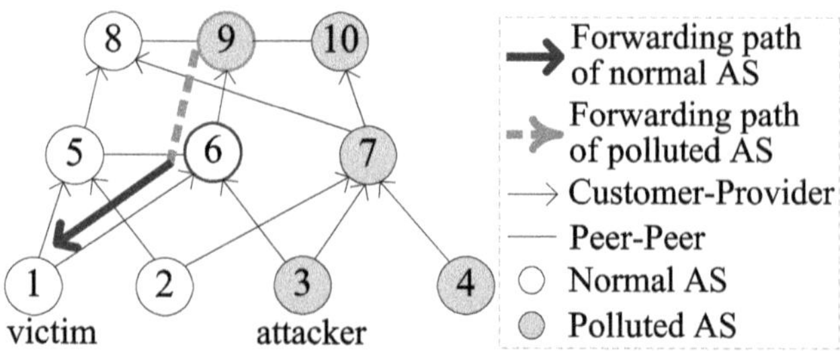

Figure 4: A polluted AS can reach the victim prefix during route convergence.

On the other hand, a normal AS not affected by a route change may also lose connectivity to certain destinations due to reasons not related to BGP [20]. Therefore, directly matching the control-plane status and data-plane probing results at each diagnosis node is error-prone. Instead, *Argus* correlates the control-plane and data-plane information of a large number of diagnosis nodes in a statistical manner. The details of this correlation process will be described in Section 4, and evaluated in Section 5.

4. PREFIX DETECTION SYSTEM - ARGUS

4.1 Overview

Argus is composed of three main modules: the Anomaly Monitoring Module (*AMM*), the Live-IP Retrieving Module (*LRM*), and the Hijacking Identification Module (*HIM*). The whole system is depicted in Figure 5.

The Anomaly Monitoring Module receives live BGP UPDATEs from BGPmon [3], a real-time BGP feed in the Route Views project [33] that collects UPDATEs from routers all over the world. When the *AMM* receives an UPDATE, it will check whether the embedded AS-path has an anomalous origin AS or an anomalous AS-path segment according to its local routing information database, as described in Section 4.2.

The Live-IP Retrieving Module maintains a pool of live IPs by periodically collecting from various sources. For an anomalous prefix f, it will carefully select an live IP as the probing target of the identification module. Details of the *LRM* will be discussed in Section 4.3.

The Hijacking Identification Module is responsible for collecting information from a number of vantage points, computing the fingerprint for the anomalous route event, and making final decisions about whether the suspicious prefix is really hijacked. It is the core of *Argus*, and Section 4.4 will present it in detail.

4.2 Monitor Anomalies

In *Argus*, we consider three types of route anomalies: origin anomalies (*OA*), adjacency anomalies (*AA*), and policy anomalies (*PA*), as illustrated in Fig. 6.

An origin anomaly (*OA*) happens when the origin AS in the AS-path of a prefix changes to a different AS, or a new prefix appears. This is the simplest case of prefix hijacking, and is the focus of all existing hijacking detection solutions. For example, in Figure 6(a), AS3 is not the origin AS of the prefix f, thus any AS-path for f ending with $\langle 3 \rangle$ is anomalous. *Argus* maintains a database which keeps track of the normal origin AS of each prefix to help detect origin anomalies.

Hijacking can also be caused by changing some AS-path segments, e.g., by using a command like *as-path prepend* incautiously, or by intentionally removing some ASes to shorten the path length. Such hijackings are key security issues considered by the IETF [5], but have not got enough attentions in measurement studies. To detect such anomalies, it is impractical to maintain all the AS-paths due to their enormous quantity. Instead, *Argus* only focuses on the neighboring ASes pairs and triples that occur in an AS-path.

In an AS-path of a prefix, if any pair of neighboring ASes has not appeared in any UPDATE before, *Argus* will report an adjacency anomaly (*AA*), since such a pair indicates that the adjacency between two ASes changes. Figure 6(b) illus-

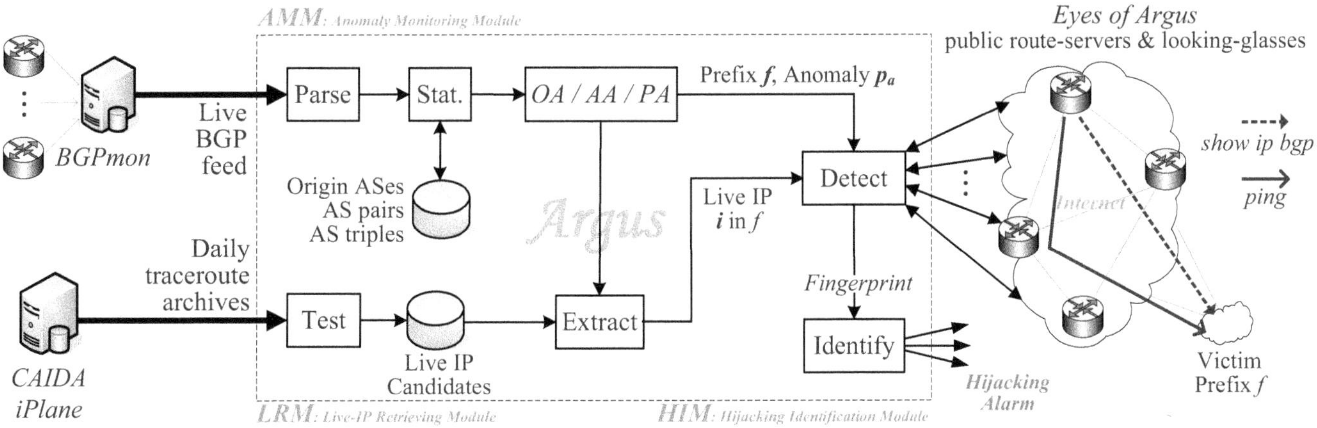

Figure 5: The architecture of *Argus*.

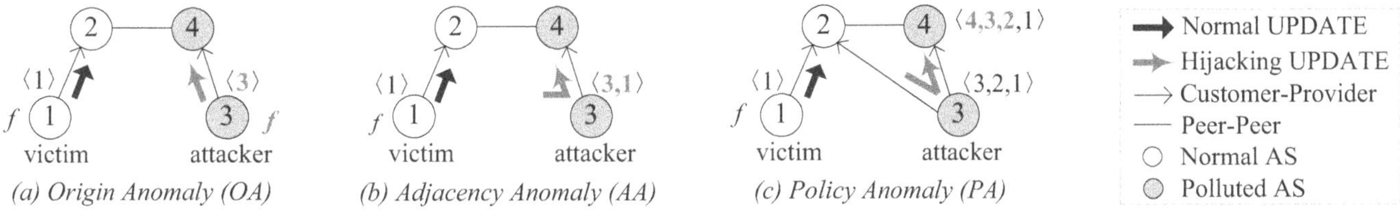

Figure 6: The three kinds of anomalies considered in *Argus*.

trates such an example, where AS3 does not directly connect to AS1, but erroneously announces an AS pair $\langle 3, 1\rangle$ in the AS-path.

On the other hand, since BGP is policy based, it often cares about whether routes learned from one neighbor should be propagated to another neighbor. Such a relationship between one AS with its two neighbors usually constitutes a BGP policy. For example, in Figure 6(c), although AS3 directly connects to AS2 and AS4, it should not announce routes learned from its provider AS2 to another provider AS4, so the triple $\langle 4, 3, 2\rangle$ should not appear in any route. In case that a new triple of neighboring ASes appears, e.g., an AS-path containing $\langle 4, 3, 2\rangle$ is received in this example, *Argus* will report a policy anomaly (*PA*).

In most cases, an AS uses the same policy for all the prefixes learned from the same neighbor, and does not care about the other non-adjacent ASes, so we think monitoring adjacency and policy anomalies can be an effective replacement for monitoring the whole AS-path. The latter needs to maintain all normal AS-paths while the former only needs to maintain all normal neighboring AS pairs and triples, as is done in *Argus*.

By considering the above three kinds of anomalies, *Argus* can detect a much wider range of hijackings, as will be demonstrated in Section 5.

Once the *AMM* detects an anomaly, it will notify the *HIM* to identify whether a hijacking truly happens. If not, it will add the new origin AS or the AS pair/triple into the local database since they are normal. The database will also be refreshed periodically by removing those origin ASs or AS pairs/triples inactive for a long period (i.e., more than two months).

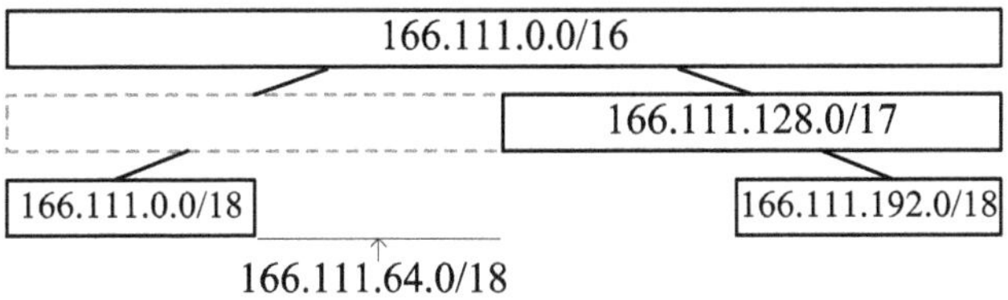

Figure 7: Finding an address block covered by 166.111.0.0/16 but not by any of its sub-prefixes.

4.3 Retrieve Live IPs

When anomaly is detected for a prefix f, the Live-IP Retrieving Module (*LRM*) tries to find a live IP address i in f. The reachability to this address is a key factor for determining whether f is hijacked. Due to the longest prefix matching mechanism, i should be covered by f, but not by any sub-prefix of f. Fig. 7 shows such an example, where the anomalous prefix 166.111.0.0/16 has three sub-prefixes announced, and our algorithm will try to find a live IP in the range of 166.111.64.0/18.

The *LRM* accomplishes this task by maintaining a local database of candidate live IP addresses in all announced prefixes in the Internet. These IPs are collected from CAIDA's Ark [2] and iPlane [23] daily traceroute results [6], and from many DNS records [6].

When a live IP address is asked for, the *LRM* will first retrieve all live IP addresses in the database according to the given prefix, and then launch parallel probings to select one that is currently reachable. This process is very quick, and

[6]These two projects perform traceroute from various vantage points to construct a router level atlas of the Internet.

usually completes within one second. When no reachable IP can be found, for example, when the server hosting the *LRM* is also polluted, the most active IP in the probing history will be selected. Inevitably, using an IP reachable in history may introduce false negatives if it is not alive at the moment, but our experiments show that this probability tends to be relatively low.

4.4 Identify Hijackings

The Hijacking Identification Module (*HIM*) employs a number of public route-servers and looking-glasses, called as the *eyes of Argus*, to finally determine whether an anomaly detected by the *AMM* is actually a prefix hijacking or not. At each *eye*, *Argus* activates two processes, one for gathering the control-plane route status of the victim prefix f, and the other for obtaining the data-plane reachability to the selected live IP i.

Specifically, *Argus* uses *show ip bgp* to extract the best BGP route $p_{t,j}(f)$ that its j-th *eye* chooses for the anomalous prefix f, in the t-th second. Then it checks whether $p_{t,j}(f)$ is affected by the anomalous origin AS (or AS pair/triple) reported by the *AMM*. Meanwhile, *Argus* uses *ping* to test whether the live IP i is reachable from each *eye*. Both of the two commands are very fast, so realtime results can be collected once every second.

After an anomaly is reported, we continuously do that for W seconds on N *eyes*. At the t-th second ($1 \leq t \leq W$), we compose the control-plane results of all *eyes* into a binary vector $C_t = \{C_{t,j} | 1 \leq j \leq N\}$, where

$$C_{t,j} = \begin{cases} 0, & \text{if } p_{t,j}(f) \text{ is affected by the anomaly} \\ 1, & \text{if } p_{t,j}(f) \text{ is not affected by the anomaly} \end{cases}$$

and compose the data-plane reachability results into a binary vector $D_t = \{D_{t,j} | 1 \leq j \leq N\}$, where

$$D_{t,j} = \begin{cases} 0, & \text{if the } j\text{-th } eye \text{ gets no reply from the IP } i \\ 1, & \text{if the } j\text{-th } eye \text{ gets a reply from the IP } i \end{cases}$$

Our key observation in Section 3 tells that, the relationship between C_t and D_t can expose the underlying cause of a route event, e.g., users in an unpolluted AS should be able to get a reply ($C_{t,j} = D_{t,j} = 1$) while users in a polluted AS should not ($C_{t,j} = D_{t,j} = 0$). Due to the possible inconsistency between the control and data plane at a node, we do not directly compare $C_{t,j}$ and $D_{t,j}$ of the same j-th *eye* one by one. Instead, we utilize the *correlation coefficient* of the two vectors C_t and D_t to measure this relationship, mathematically defined as

$$F_t = \frac{\sum_{j=1}^{N} \left[(C_{t,j} - \overline{C_t})(D_{t,j} - \overline{D_t}) \right]}{\sqrt{\sum_{j=1}^{N} (C_{t,j} - \overline{C_t})^2 \times \sum_{j=1}^{N} (D_{t,j} - \overline{D_t})^2}} \quad (1)$$

where $\overline{C_t}$ and $\overline{D_t}$ are the average of $C_{t,j}$'s and $D_{t,j}$'s ($1 \leq j \leq N$) on all *eyes*, respectively. We also call F_t and $\overline{D_t}$ the *fingerprint* and *reachability* of the route event at time t, respectively.

Fig. 8 schematically illustrates the fingerprint and reachability distribution of different route events. When F_t is close to 1, D_t and C_t have a strong positive correlation (i.e., most polluted *eyes* cannot get reply from the victim prefix, while most normal *eyes* can), then very probably a prefix hijacking is going on. Since routing may be inconsistent and instable, we raise a hijacking alarm only when F_t is greater than a threshold μ for at least a period of T seconds. The choice of μ and T will affect the detection accuracy, as will be discussed in Section 5. We compute F_t in each second for a total of 120 seconds.

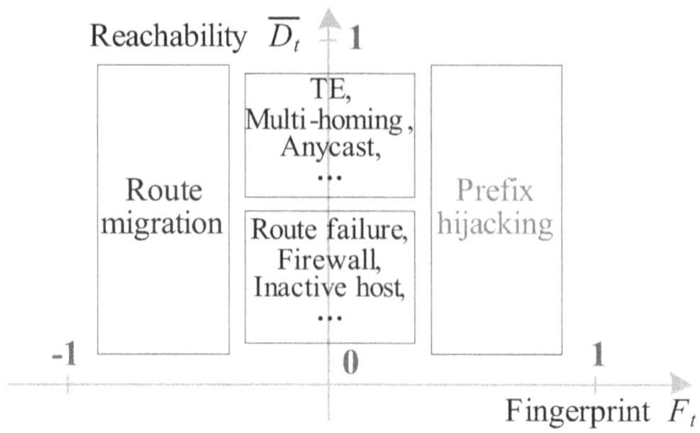

Figure 8: Fingerprint and reachability of different route events.

When F_t is close to -1, a strong negative correlation exists between C_t and D_t (i.e., most polluted *eyes* can get reply while most normal *eyes* cannot), then the anomaly is very possibly just a route migration.

When D_t and C_t are not strongly correlated (i.e., F_t is close to 0), there are two possible situations: (1) if the average data-plane reachability $\overline{D_t}$ approaches 1, which means most *eyes* can communicate with hosts in the target prefix, then the anomalous route is often a normal backup route, used for multi-homing, BGP anycast, backup path, or traffic engineering; (2) if $\overline{D_t}$ approaches 0, which means most *eyes* can not reach the target prefix, then a route failure or a firewall may exist in the middle, or because the probing target we choose is not alive.

We can see that *Argus* has very little dependency on external nodes. It only receives live BGP feed, collects active IP addresses, and logins to route-servers or looking-glasses to execute two simple commands. All of these resources are publicly and widely available, thus it is very easy to deploy, and can monitor the Internet closely and pervasively.

We note that, when the denominator of equation (1) is zero, we set F_t to be zero. This happens when either C_t or D_t is a vector of all zero's or all one's. In particular, when C_t is a vector of all one's, all our *eyes* are polluted, and we will not raise hijacking alarms any more. However this rarely happens, as will be shown in the next section.

Based on *Argus*, we have built several online services. We raise realtime hijacking alarms via a public mailing list and twitter, which network operators can subscribe freely. We post the information of all anomalous routes and hijackings, together with their statistics, on our website, to facilitate further processing and analysis. We also provide web service APIs that can access our monitoring system in realtime so that other systems can integrate the hijacking detection capability. We make the services robust by deploying them in different ASes, so even when some of them are polluted under an attack, the victim AS can still be informed as soon as possible. All the detail of these services can be found at `argus.csnet1.cs.tsinghua.edu.cn`.

5. INTERNET MONITORING PRACTICE

Argus has been continuously monitoring the Internet for one year, starting from May 2, 2011. During this period, 40K anomalous route events were reported [7], and 220 stable hijackings were identified. Due to a lack of the ground truth, we use several methods to verify our identification results. First, we query all valid Route Origin Authorizations (ROAs) [17], which are digitally signed and can be used to verify whether a prefix is announced by its authorized owner AS. Those anomalies with ROA records can be used as a validation set to test our algorithm: if any such anomaly is identified as a hijacking, then it must be a false positive. However the ROA records are still rather incomplete, and only 266 anomaly alarms can be used for validation, so we also query the Internet Routing Registry (IRR)[7] to get more prefix-origin pairs, where matching records are found for 3988 anomalies. [8] Although the IRR information is not guaranteed to be correct, we use it for a rough evaluation. Second, we announce all the identified hijackings via several public channels like twitter and mailinglist, [9] and have recently started to directly contact the corresponding network operators. Till now, we have not got any objection to our identification results, and 10 out of 31 network operators being contacted have confirmed our results. Last, we also query the IRR to get other auxiliary information, such as import/export policies, and query other databases such as *whois* and Cyclops [12] to validate our results. Since that needs a lot of labor work, the analysis is still on going.

5.1 System Parameters and Performance

The higher the correlation between the control and the data plane, the more likely a hijacking is going on. When an anomaly is reported by the Anomaly Monitoring Module (*AMM*), the Hijacking Identification Module (*HIM*) starts to compute the fingerprint F_t for this anomaly, in every second of a continuous period of W seconds. Since the Internet often converges in less than two minutes except for some unusual cases, and prefix hijacking is one kind of T_{short} event, which moves from a longer or less preferred to a shorter or more preferred path, with convergence time typically less than 40 seconds [26], we set $W = 120$ seconds. During this period, if F_t is larger than a hijacking fingerprint threshold μ, we say the event is in a *suspicious hijacking state*, and if the duration of the suspicious state, denoted by d, is no smaller than a hijacking duration threshold of T seconds, we classify this anomaly as a stable hijacking. Using a large hijacking fingerprint threshold μ or duration threshold T may miss some real hijacking events, while using a small μ or T may cause unnecessary alarms.

To model the high correlation coefficient a hijacking should have, μ can not be too small. Fig. 9 shows how the false positive rate (FPR) changes with μ, where μ varies from 0.4 to 1.0. When we use the 266 route anomalies that have corresponding ROAs as the validation set [10], and the threshold

[7] We have aggregated the raw BGP UPDATEs from different routers into anomalous events, using algorithms like in [26].

[8] The IRR currently contains about 36% of all the Internet prefixes, while the ratio that an origin anomaly can be matched in it is 20%.

[9] Full details about these channels can be found at http://argus.csnet1.cs.tsinghua.edu.cn/about/.

[10] These anomalies are all caused by normal route events, so FPR is the percentage of hijackings identified in this set.

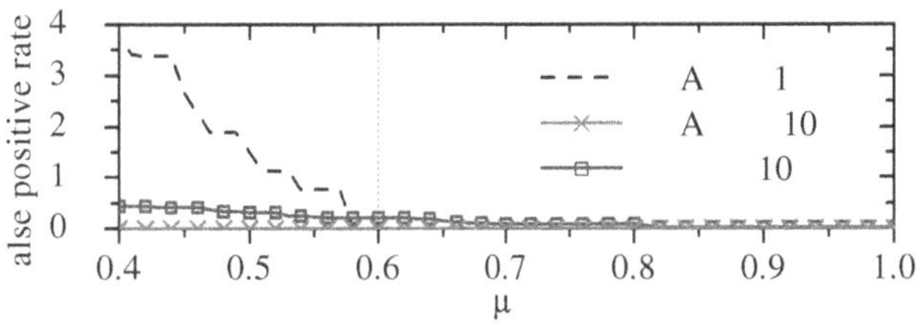

Figure 9: False Positive Detection Rate v.s. μ.

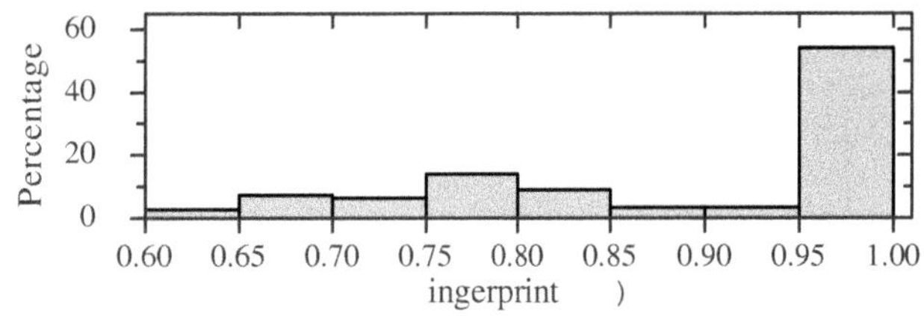

Figure 10: Fingerprint distribution of all identified stable hijackings ($\mu = 0.6$).

T is set as 10 seconds, no anomaly is ever falsely identified as a hijacking. If the 3988 alarms with IRR *route origin* records are used as the validation set, only 0.3% alarms are falsely identified as hijackings when $\mu = 0.5$, and the error decreases to 0.2% when $\mu = 0.6$, as represented by the line with squares. Since IRR records are often outdated and not guaranteed to be correct, the real error should be even smaller. For comparison, the dash line represents the results using ROAs but without filtering the alarms by their duration (i.e., when $T = 1$). If $\mu = 0.5$, there are four cases misclassified as hijackings, and when $\mu = 0.6$, there is no false identification.

Fig. 10 plots the fingerprint distribution of all identified stable hijackings when we use the default threshold $\mu = 0.6$ and $T = 10$. It is clear that most stable hijackings have a fingerprint much larger than 0.6, as indicated by the peak near 1.0. This confirms our conjecture that the control-plane route status C_t and the data-plane reachability D_t has a very high positive correlation when hijacking happens.

Fig. 11 shows the cumulative distribution function (CDF) of the duration of all suspicious hijacking alarms (i.e., when the fingerprint $F_t > \mu$). Many alarms are transient with a short lifetime, and the distributions do not change much when μ varies from 0.6 to 0.9. In practice, we use $T =$ 10 seconds to filter those non-stable route events that may cause μ temporarily high. Even If they are real hijackings,

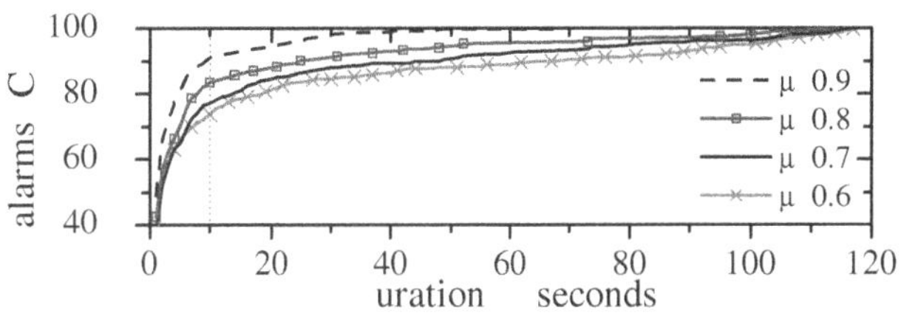

Figure 11: Duration of suspicious alarms (CDF).

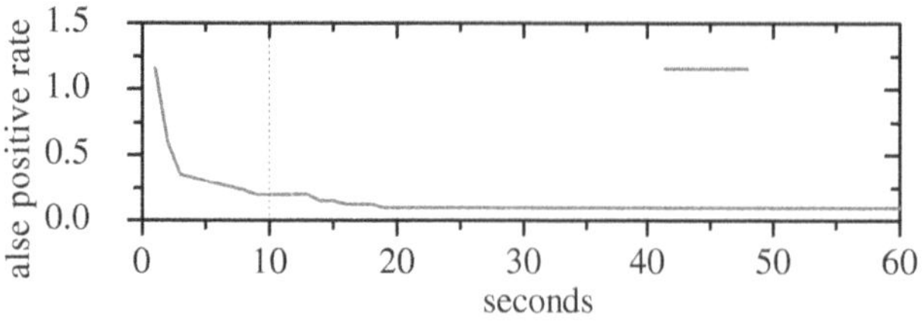

Figure 12: False Positive Detection Rate v.s. T.

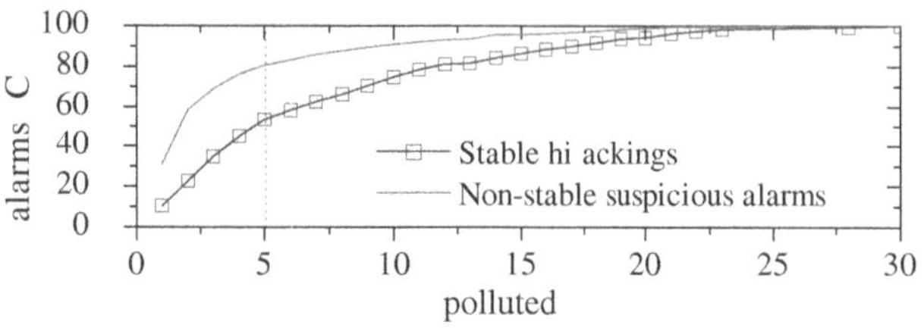

Figure 13: The numbers of polluted *eyes* in stable hijackings and non-stable suspicious alarms.

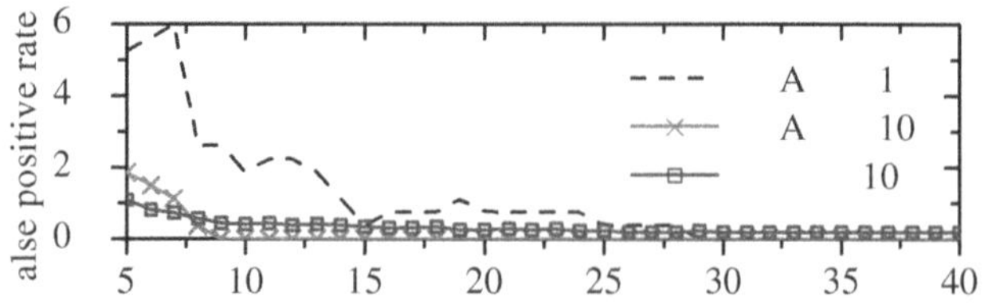

Figure 14: False positive detection rate v.s. #*eyes*.

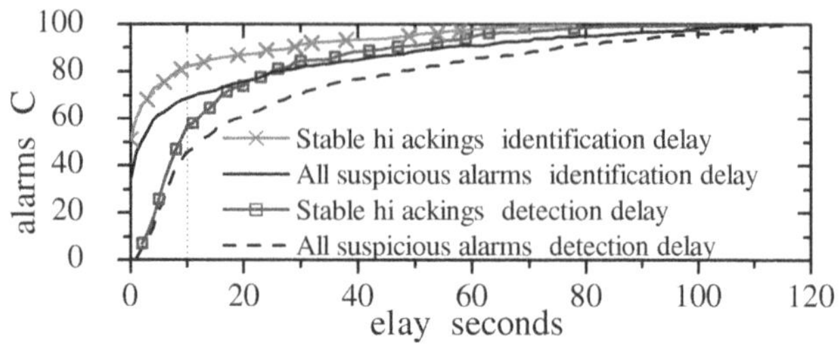

Figure 15: Hijacking detection delay (CDF).

they can do little harm to the Internet since the routes can hardly converge in such a short time.

Fig. 12 shows how the FPR decreases with T, under a default $\mu = 0.6$. Since there is no false identification when the ROA records are used, this curve is plotted using the IRR records as the validation set. When $T > 10$, the false rate is less than 0.2%, while if we do not use such a duration threshold, the false rate will increase to 1.1%.

To illustrate the effectiveness of T, we compare the numbers of *eyes* that are polluted by the 220 stable hijackings and the 570 non-stable suspicious alarms in Fig. 13. The distributions show that, non-stable hijackings usually affect a much fewer number of *eyes* than stable hijackings. For example, in 81% cases, less than five *eyes* are affected if the alarm duration $d < T$, while in more than 50% cases, more than five *eyes* are affected if $d > T$. We note that, it rarely happens that more than 40 *eyes* are affected, even for stable hijackings, and we will elaborate on this point later.

Fig. 14 presents how the false positive rate decreases when more *eyes* are used, where the 266 anomalies with ROAs and the 3988 anomalies with IRR records are used as the validation set, respectively. It is clear that using more than 40 *eyes* achieves a fair accurate result, while less than ten *eyes* may bring a few errors.

Fig. 15 reports the cumulative distribution of the detection delay (i.e., from when the first anomalous BGP UPDATE is received to when the first time that F_t exceeds μ), for the 790 suspicious hijacking alarms and 220 stable hijackings, respectively. About 50% suspicious alarms, and 60% stable hijacking have a detection delay of no more than 10 seconds. This is considered as much faster than existing data-plane based hijacking detection methods, which cost at least a few minutes.

We note that, the speed of *Argus* can be further improved, since this delay includes the time used for logging in to the *eyes* and the delay of route propagation, which are in average 6.4 and 4.6 seconds. They can be effectively reduced by putting *Argus* in a network of better quality, and by using more *eyes*. If these latencies are deducted from the detection delay, the real identification delay costs less than 10 seconds in 70% suspicious alarms and 80% stable hijackings, and costs less than one second in 35% suspicious alarms and 50% stable hijackings. In this manner, we claim that *Argus* achieves *realtime* detection.

5.2 Do we miss many real hijackings?

It is very hard to judge whether *Argus* can detect all or at least a large fraction of blackholing prefix hijackings in the Internet, since no one knows the ground truth. We make several efforts to improve its detection capability.

The BGP UPDATEs from BGPmon [3] is considered to cover a large portion of the Internet [33]. For example, the number of peers from which BGPmon collected live data ranged from 110 to 130 in the last year, and these peers were distributed in more than 70 ASes. To handle the relative large data volume [11], we used a server with a six-core Intel Xeon CPU and 16G memory, and experienced no data loss in the whole year. [12] In these UPDATEs, the anomaly monitoring module monitors three types of anomalies, including *OA*, *AA* and *PA*. To the best of our knowledge, we are the first to monitor hijackings which utilize forged adjacency or policy, although they have been theoretically studied before [15]. The successful detection of such hijackings demonstrates the superior capabilities of *Argus*.

Our identification method depends on the reachability to a live host in the target prefix. If no such a host can be found, we just guess one and probe it from our *eyes*. However, if no *eye* can reach it, a possible hijacking may be missed, and we say this is a blindfolded case. We improve the live-IP retrieving module by collecting live IPs from multiple sources, and the number of blindfolded cases decreases from 58% to 19% [13]. We also consider the sub-prefix problem

[11] The peak volume exceeded 10MB/s.

[12] On average, we handled around 10GB BGP data each day, and the peak volume exceeded 20Mbps.

[13] This is just an upper bound for missing hijackings, since

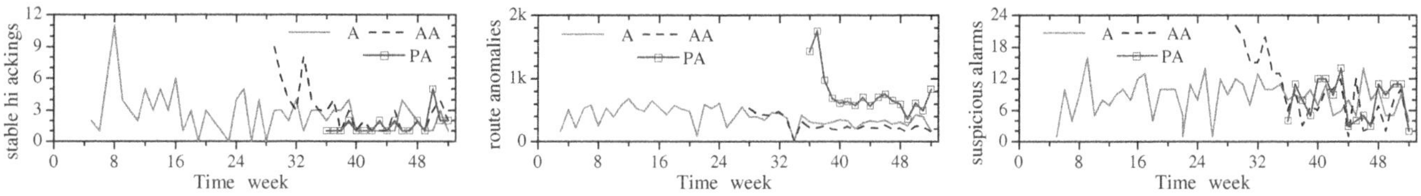

(a) Stable hijackings (b) Route anomalies (c) Suspicious hijacking alarms

Figure 16: The weekly numbers of stable hijackings, route anomalies and suspicious alarms.

as explained in Section 4.3 and illustrated in Fig. 7. In our results, around 10% stable hijackings will not be identified if sub-prefix is ignored, i.e., the live IP belongs to a sub-prefix of the prefix we are interested in.

In the identification module, we now keep a pool of 389 route-servers and looking glasses widely distributed in 41 transit ASes, [14] to sense both the control and the data plane status of the Internet in a pervasive manner. Transit ASes, including default-free ASes, can sense the diverse paths to different prefixes in the Internet. In contrast, other distributed monitoring platforms, such as the Planetlab, often concentrate in stub ASes, such as academic networks, and often use a default route for their traffic. To avoid overloading the eyes, for each anomalous event, we randomly choose $40 \sim 80$ eyes from our server pool, and use them to compute the corresponding fingerprint and reachability. Using more than one eye in the same transit AS can improve accuracy and provide better redundancy, since different eyes may experience different paths to the same prefix [15] and different inconsistencies between their control and data plane.

When computing the fingerprint F_t, a hijacking may be missed due to the division-by-zero problem. However, in our data, the chance that $\overline{C_t}$ equals 1 (i.e., no eye is polluted) is only 3%, and the chance that $\overline{D_t}$ equals 0 (i.e., all eyes are blindfolded) is less than 20%. [16] The case that $\overline{C_t} = 0$ (i.e., all eyes are polluted) or $\overline{D_t} = 1$ (i.e., all eyes can reach the live IP) never occurs. So the probability that a hijacking is missed due to the failure point of F_t is very likely to be small.

It is worth to note that, the number of ASes in which eyes are employed is very important. In the early stage of our system deployment, our eyes covered less than 20 transit ASes in the Internet, and almost half of the anomalous events could not be seen by any of our eyes. This is definitely a major contributor to the false negatives of our system at that time. However, we kept adding more usable eyes, especially in more ASes, and now less than 2% anomalous events may be missed by all the eyes used in identification.

Last, we do not use very large μ and T, so hijackings with unstable fingerprints can also be identified. As has been demonstrated, they do not affect the false positive rate very much.

In conclusion, although there is no direct proof for the false negative possibility of *Argus*, we believe it can detect a large fraction of blackholing hijackings in the Internet, and can liberate network operators from a vast number of alarms. In the rest of this paper, we will make a systematic analysis on our monitoring results.

5.3 Monitoring Results

The 40K anomalous route events reported by the *AMM* consist of 20K origin anomalies, 6.7K adjacency anomalies and 13.3K policy anomalies. From these events, the *HIM* identified 220 stable hijackings, in which 122 hijackings introduced origin anomalies, while 71 and 27 hijackings introduced adjacency and policy anomalies, respectively. However, since the monitoring of the three kinds of anomalies started at different time, these numbers are not directly comparable. Instead, in Fig. 16(a) and 16(b), we plot the weekly numbers of stable hijackings and route anomalies of each type, starting from May 2011. Notice there is no data for *AA* and *PA* anomalies until November 2011. For comparison, we also plot the weekly numbers of the 790 suspicious hijacking alarms in Fig. 16(c).

As shown in Fig 16(a), the frequencies of different types of stable hijackings are somewhat steady and comparable in the whole year, with an average of three new hijackings per week. The higher values in the starting points may just be caused by accumulation. One notable point is that, adjacency and policy based hijackings do exist in the Internet, and to the best of our knowledge, we are the first to detect and study them.

The trend of anomalies and suspicious hijackings is almost similar to that of stable hijackings. The only difference is that, the number of policy anomalies is far larger than the other types of anomalies, but the number of policy based hijackings is not that large. It is reasonable because the number of neighboring AS triples (i.e., policies) is much larger than the number of origins or neighboring AS pairs [17], while most anomalies are not hijackings.

Fig. 17 plots the CDF of the hijacking duration for all stable hijackings. The duration is computed off-line by examining when the corresponding route anomalies disappear from the routing UPDATEs, representing how long a hijacking will affect the Internet. It covers a very large range, from less than 10 minutes to longer than one week, both of which have a non-negligible fraction and are worth further studies. For example, more than 20% hijackings last less than 10 minutes, and these short (but not transient) hijackings ask for a realtime detector such as *Argus*. On the other hand, those long hijackings indicate that, this security problem is either ignored by or is still unknown to some ISPs, or it is

many such cases are indeed not hijackings, but are caused by route failure, firewall, no active hosts, etc..

[14] A complete list of the eyes we employ can be found at http://argus.csnet1.cs.tsinghua.edu.cn/static/eyes.txt.

[15] The chance that two eyes in the same AS experience different paths is 39% in our experiments.

[16] When our eyes cover more than 20 transit ASes and the improved live IP selection algorithm is used.

[17] In the past year, 925K neighboring AS triples, 606K prefix-origin pairs and 108K AS edges were monitored by *Argus*.

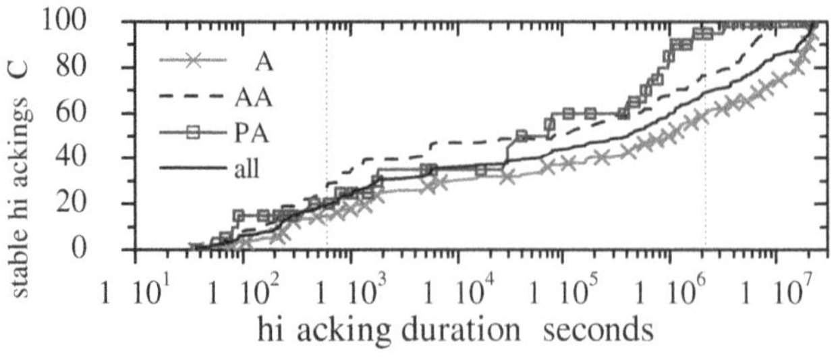

Figure 17: Duration of stable hijackings (CDF).

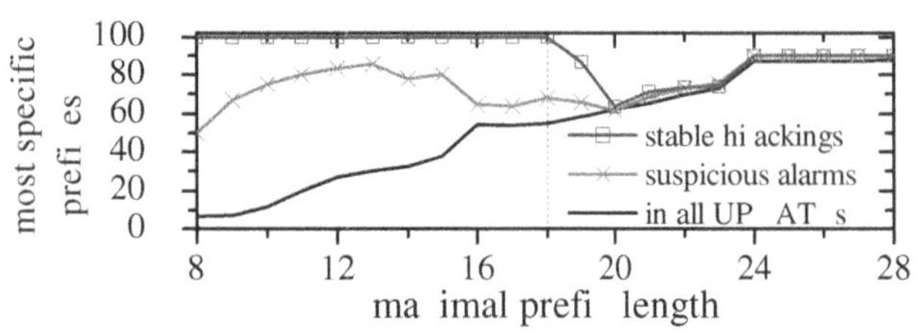

Figure 18: Ratio of most specific prefixes at different prefix length.

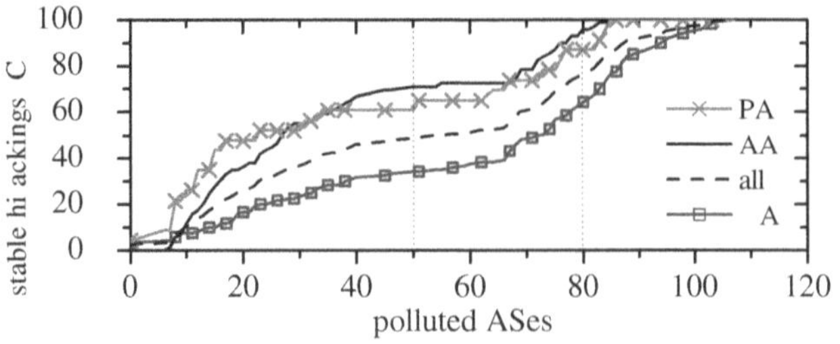

Figure 19: The number of polluted ASes (CDF).

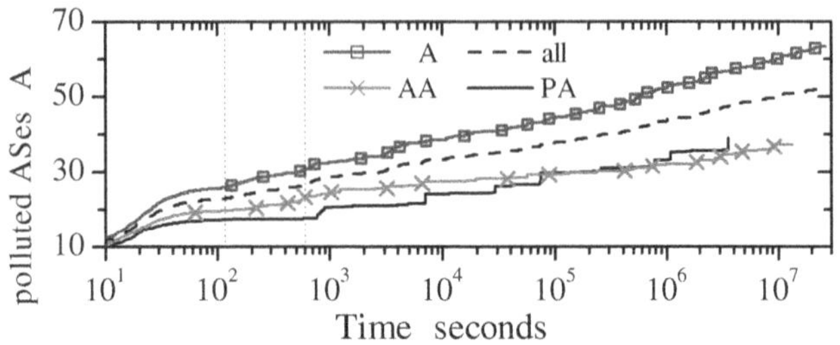

Figure 20: Hijacking pollution speed.

very hard to defend against. It should also be noted that, in order to reduce the workload of the eyes, we only use BGP UPDATEs to determine when a hijacking event ends, so it is possible that some long lasting hijackings are just route migrations which happen to exhibit hijacking characteristics in their early stage.

In total, we detected around 40K anomalous prefixes, of which 1132 appeared in suspicious alarms, while 263 appeared in stable hijackings. We call a prefix *most specific* if it has no sub-prefix announced to the Internet. Since routers prefer most specific prefixes, it is reasonable that hijackings also prefer them so that they can pollute the Internet more effectively, as in the Youtube event [29]. Fig. 18 shows the ratio of such most specific prefixes, in all announced prefixes, hijacked prefixes and suspicious prefixes, respectively, where hijackings show a clear favor for most specific ones. In stable hijackings, about 91% prefixes are most specific, while the ratio in all announced prefixes is 87%. This favor is especially evident for shorter prefixes whose impact is greater. In all the prefixes with a length less than 18, the average percentage of most specific prefixes is only 50%, while the ratio becomes 100% in stable hijackings (the ratio is 70% in all suspicious alarms). On the other hand, sub-prefix hijackings (using a *more specific* prefix than a normal one) contribute around 10% in stable hijackings.

To illustrate how these hijackings affect the Internet, Fig. 19 depicts how many ASes in the Internet a hijacking can successfully pollute (hijack), and Fig. 20 depicts how fast hijackings can pollute them. Since most ASes in the Internet are stub/customer ASes which use default routes to their providers for many prefixes, they cannot be seen in any of the UPDATEs for those prefixes. The numbers in these two figures only cover the transit ASes seen in the UPDATEs for the corresponding (hijacked) prefixes, while the actually affected area should also include their customers. In Fig. 19, more than 20% stable hijackings can pollute at least 80 ASes, while in Fig. 20, on average, more than 20 ASes are polluted within only two minutes. For each hijacking that affects more than 80 transit ASes, we also compute the ratio of the number of polluted ASes (in a certain period) to the number of ASes that can be seen in all UPDATEs for the corresponding prefix. This metric can be regarded as a rough estimator of *what percentage of the Internet is polluted*, and in some cases, more than 50% of the Internet are polluted within 20 seconds, and more than 90% of the Internet are polluted in less than two minutes.

On the other hand, in Fig. 19, origin based hijackings usually can pollute more ASes than adjacency or policy based hijackings. For example, about 70% in the former case can pollute at least 50 transit ASes, while only around 30% of the latter two cases have this capability. Similarly, origin based hijackings often pollute the Internet in a faster way, as shown in Fig. 20. For example, on average, an origin based hijacking can pollute about 26 transit ASes in two minutes, and can pollute more than 30 in ten minutes. Part of the reasons may be that, when forging prefix-origin pairs, most specific prefixes are often used, with short AS-paths.

It is also interesting that a hijacking can hardly pollute all ASes. Due to this reason, the chance that all our *eyes* are polluted is also low, which helps them to get a more accurate detection result.

6. CASE STUDIES

In this section, we analyze the characteristics and root causes of some interesting hijackings, as well as some non-hijacking anomalies, in order to help increase the understanding of prefix hijackings in the Internet.

Table 2 summarizes the hijacking cases discussed in this section, including five cases with origin anomalies, three with adjacency anomalies and two with policy anomalies. Most of these hijackings have been confirmed by the corresponding network operators, while for other cases, we will present enough evidence.

Table 2: **Case study: ten prefix hijackings detected in the past year.**

	Time	Prefix	Normal Origin	Anomalous Origin	Delay
OA_1	2011-12-27	166.111.32.0/24, ...	AS4538	AS23910	10
OA_2	2012-03-20	193.105.17.0/24	AS50407	AS15763	5
OA_3	2012-04-04	91.217.242.0/24	AS197279	AS48559	9
OA_4	2011-06-23	76.72.238.0/24, ...	AS701	AS27005	6
OA_5	2012-03-22	12.231.155.0/24	AS7018 (12.128.0.0/9)	AS13490	7
	Time	Prefix	AS-path	Anomalous AS Pair	Delay
AA_1	2012-04-23	210.1.38.0/24	3043 174 38082 38794 24465	38794 24465	12
AA_2	2012-03-31	184.164.255.0/24	4739 6939 2381 47065 19782 47065	47065 19782	4
AA_3	2011-12-19	205.153.112.0/22	3303 174 17368 26263	17368 26263	3
	Time	Prefix	AS-path	Anomalous AS Triple	Delay
PA_1	2012-04-19	77.223.240.0/22	4739 24709 25388 21021 12741 47728	21021 12741 47728	9
PA_2	2012-04-16	195.10.205.0/24	3043 174 20764 31484 3267 3216 35813	20764 31484 3267	5

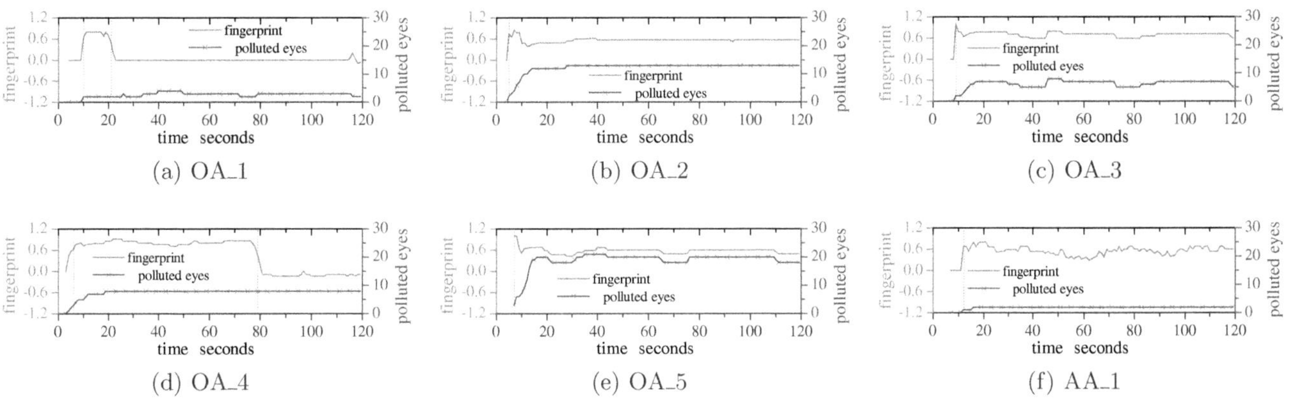

Figure 21: Case studies of hijackings: fingerprint and the number of polluted eyes.

In Fig. 21, for each hijacking with origin anomaly, we plot the corresponding fingerprint and the numbers of polluted *eyes* in each second, to demonstrate the timely and accurate reaction of *Argus*. We also indicate the time delay when *Argus* begins or stops to report hijacking alarms by a dotted line, if it exists. For other cases, since the curves are very similar, we just present one of them, and omit the others due to space limitations.

6.1 Hijackings with Origin Anomalies

Missing route filters: OA_1 was caused by a route filter failure. In this case, AS23910 learned two routes to 166.111.32.0/24 and 166.111.111.0/24, which were owned by AS4538. The Network operators confirmed that, since AS23910 accidentally removed its corresponding filters for a short period, these two routes were incorrectly redistributed into BGP, and then announced to the Internet, with AS23910 as the origin. This corresponds to the period when $F_t > 0.6$ in Fig. 21(a).

Network maintenance misplay: in OA_2, AS50407 was a customer of the victim AS15763. The network operators of AS50407 said they made a mistake when they were carrying out network maintenance, and hijacked the prefix 193.105.17.0/24 for 12 minutes. In Fig. 21(b), after the hijacking was detected, the fingerprint kept above 0.6 for the remaining window.

Premature migration attempt: OA_3 was caused by a premature route migration that was not well planned. In this case, AS197279 was to migrate 91.217.242.0/24 to another AS AS48559 "in the coming week or so", as said in their reply to our alarm. However, before the planned time, AS48559 announced itself as the owner of this prefix, which AS197279 was still keeping announcing at that time. Since live hosts have not moved into AS48559, polluted *eyes* could not reach them, and F_t increased above 0.6. The hijacking lasted about 17 minutes and *Argus* detected it within 9 seconds, as shown in Fig. 21(c). OA_4 is a similar case, where AS27005 announced the same prefix as AS701 did. There is a little difference from OA_3: live hosts in AS27005 became reachable after 70 seconds (still in the detection window), while live hosts in AS701 also kept reachable until several hours later, so F_t later decreased to 0 in Fig. 21(d).

Sub-prefix hijacking: OA_5 was confirmed by AS7018, which was the owner of a prefix 12.128.0.0/9. One of its sub-prefixes, 12.231.155.0/24, was incorrectly announced by AS13490 at March 22, 2012, and the hijacking lasted about 16 minutes. As shown in Fig. 21(e), this sub-prefix hijacking polluted around 20 *eyes* in 20 seconds, which is faster than the other cases. Interestingly, we also noticed that this sub-prefix was officially assigned to and announced by AS54357 nine days later, and *Argus* successfully detected that event and classified it as a route migration (i.e., the fingerprint was close to -1.0).

6.2 Hijackings with Adjacency Anomalies

Mis-configuration in traffic engineering: in the case

import: from AS12741 action pref=150; accept AS12741
export: to AS12741 announce AS21021

(a) PA_1: Routing policy of AS21021.

remarks: --- Uplinks ---
import: from AS3267 action pref=85; accept ANY
export: to AS3267 announce AS31484 AND AS196931
import: from AS20764 action pref=85; accept ANY
export: to AS20764 announce AS31484 AND AS196931

(b) PA_2: Routing policy of AS31484.

Figure 23: IRR records of PA_1 and PA_2.

of AA_1, AS24465 was connecting to two providers, and was using AS-Path prepending (ASPP) to achieve inbound Traffic Engineering. It normally announced its prefix 210.1.38.0/24 to one provider AS4750, but prepended itself for 4 times in the AS-path announced to the other provider AS7693. The hijacking happened when AS24465 connected to a new provider AS38794 and announced the prefix to it. However traffic could not go through the new one, and *Argus* immediately notified the operators of AS38794. When they replied 50 minutes later, we found the problem was fixed, and ASPP was also used in the new route.

AS-path poisoning experiment: AA_2 was caused by a rerouting experiment launched by Georgia Tech and University of Washington [19], using AS47065. They announced a looped path $\langle 47065, x, 47065\rangle$ for prefix 184.164.255.0/24, so that AS x would not accept this route later, and the corresponding traffic would not go through x. They repeated the experiments periodically for many times, and *Argus* continuously reported adjacency anomalies. If things went well, we should have identified no hijackings, since the destination should be reachable even when the path changed. [18] However, in an experiment when x was set to 19782, the target prefix became unreachable on our *eyes* that were using the new path, but was still reachable on the *eyes* that were using the normal path without loop, and *Argus* reported hijackings accordingly.

Short-lived neighbor: AA_3 was caused by AS17368 pretending to be a neighbor of AS26263, which was the owner of the victim prefix 205.153.112.0/22. The hijacking polluted 4 *eyes*, and lasted 14 minutes. Later, this adjacency disappeared and was never announced again.

6.3 Hijackings with Policy Anomalies

Import policy violation: PA_1 was caused by an import filter failure of AS21021. As described by the IRR records of AS21021 (Fig. 23(a)), it will import a route from AS12741 if and only if the corresponding AS-path is originated by AS12741. However, in this case, it accepted a route originated by AS47728, and the anomalous triple $\langle 21021, 12741, 47728\rangle$ was detected by *Argus*. When the traffic was hijacked by this route, *Argus* reported this case.

Export policy violation: PA_2 was caused by an export filter failure of AS31484. According to the IRR records of AS31484, it has two providers, AS20764 and AS3267. The route filter in the IRR, as shown in Fig. 23(b), means AS31484 will accept ANY route announced by the two providers, but will only announce routes originated from AS31484 or AS196931 (its customer) to them. In this case, AS31484 incorrectly announced routes learned from its provider AS3267 to the other provider AS20764, so *Argus* detected the anomalous triple $\langle 20764, 31484, 3267\rangle$. Later, it successfully identified the hijacking.

[18] Actually *Argus* reported route migrations, as expected.

6.4 Non-hijacking Anomalies

As we have mentioned before, *Argus* can also classify non-hijacking anomalies into different types, including route migration, traffic engineering, etc., as shown in Fig. 8. We analyze three cases to demonstrate this capability. Fig. 22 explains how they are different from hijackings, where for each case, we plot the corresponding fingerprint F_t, the reachability $\overline{D_t}$ to the anomalous prefix, and the number of polluted eyes.

TE using BGP anycast: Root DNS servers usually use BGP anycast to balance and optimize DNS requests. In this case, the anomalous prefix 193.0.16.0/24 was used by the root DNS server k, and was operated by RIPE NCC. *Argus* detected that this prefix was suddenly announced by a new origin AS197000. Since all its *eyes*, either polluted or not, could reach the target prefix (i.e., $D_t = 1$), while the fingerprint F_t was close to 0, it was identified as traffic engineering. Fig. 22(a) shows the corresponding F_t and D_t.

TE with backup links: In this case, AS12476 announced an AS-path with ASPP to AS6453, which was its provider but had never appeared as the its neighbor before. The new path exposed this backup link accidentally. Similarly to the first case, F_t was always 0 while D_t was always 1, as shown in Fig. 22(b).

Route migration: AS12653 and AS7700 were operated by the same ISP (KB Impuls Hellas, Greece). During the route migration, AS12653 stopped announcing routes, while AS7700 started to take the place. In the route convergence process, almost all *eyes* that had learned the new routes could reach the target prefix, while *eyes* using the old routes could not. This led to a negative F_t (i.e., less than -0.6), as is in Fig. 22(c).

7. DISCUSSION

To show the advantages of *Argus*, we compare it with some representative hijacking detection systems proposed earlier. A control plane based system such as Cyclops [12] will report the 20K *OA* anomalies, while *Argus* can identify 122 stable hijackings out of them. This can lower the burden to handle hijackings by two orders of magnitude. Data plane methods [34, 36] have to continuously measure the Internet for each prefix they care, while *Argus* only probe the Internet for two minutes when an anomaly appears. The measurement overhead in one year can be roughly computed as (40K anomalies) × (2 minutes) × (80 eyes) for *Argus*, and as (400K prefixes) × (1 year) × (1 eye) for the system in [36], resulting in a difference of four orders of magnitude. The overhead of iSPY [34] is less since it only monitors the prefixes owned by the organization who deploys the system, but if the entire Internet is to be protected, the overhead will be comparable to that in [36]. Moreover, these data plane methods cannot detect sub-prefix hijackings (around 10% in our data), unless every possible sub-prefix is monitored. They also cannot distinguish BGP anycast and route migration from hijackings since they are based on data path changes. The method utilizing both data and control plane information [16] relies on host-specific fingerprints, such as

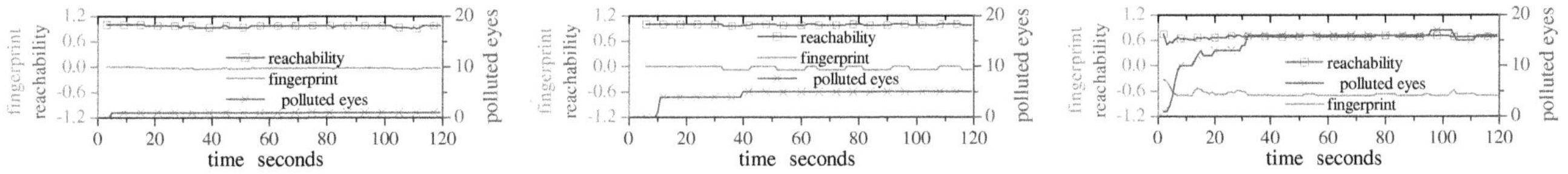

(a) BGP anycast (b) Backup link (c) Route migration

Figure 22: Case studies of non-hijacking anomalies: fingerprint, reachability and the number of polluted eyes.

OS property, IP ID, timestamp, etc., thus may also fail when BGP anycast or route migration happens. Besides, its detection delay is at least a few minutes while *Argus* needs only a few seconds.

Argus also has some limitations. It relies on ping to detect blackholing behavior, so malicious attackers can evade the system by actively responding to ping. However, we believe our earlier measurement results are still reasonable, and we will integrate other fingerprinting methods into *Argus*. A carefully crafted AS-path based on existing path segments may also evade our detection although building such a path is very difficult, and advanced detection and protection methods are still needed. Another weakness may lie in our metric F_t, which can be specifically attacked by carefully choosing the time/prefix to hijack, and how to devise more robust hijacking fingerprints is worth further study. Many components of *Argus* can be continuously improved, e.g., by adding eyes in different ASes, and refreshing live hosts [1]. Finally, much more can be done on the classification of route anomalies, and the characterization of realworld hijackings.

8. CONCLUSIONS

In this paper, we present *Argus*, a system for detecting IP prefix hijackings. Compared with existing methods, *Argus* has many advantages, and our one year practice in monitoring the Internet shows it can accurately distinguish prefix hijackings from a vast number of anomalies in a very short time, and can further deduce the possible root causes. It is very easy to deploy, and we are now providing it as a public service, which has already successfully helped many network operators to diagnose their network operations. In the future, we plan to incorporate more diagnosis information and make it more intelligent.

9. ACKNOWLEDGEMENT

We are grateful to the anonymous IMC reviewers and our shepherd Mark Crovella for their insightful comments. We also want to express our gratitude towards the network operators we have contacted for their generous cooperation and feedback. This work is supported by the National Key Technology R&D Program of China (Grant No. 2008BAH37B03), and the National Basic Research Program of China (973 Program, Grant No. 2009CB320502).

10. REFERENCES

[1] Ant censuses of the internet address space. `http://www.isi.edu/ant/traces/index.html`.

[2] Archipelago Measurement Infrastructure. `http://www.caida.org/projects/ark/`.

[3] The BGPmon project. `http://bgpmon.netsec.colostate.edu`.

[4] BGPmon.net. `http://bgpmon.net/`.

[5] Charter of the IETF Secure Inter-Domain Routing Working Group. `http://tools.ietf.org/wg/sidr/charters`.

[6] DNS records collected by Hurricane Electric. `http://bgp.he.net/net/166.111.0.0/16#_dns`.

[7] Irr - internet routing registry. `http://www.irr.net/`.

[8] Ripe myasn system. `http://www.ris.ripe.net/myasn.html`.

[9] H. Ballani, P. Francis, and X. Zhang. A study of prefix hijacking and interception in the internet. In *SIGCOMM*, 2007.

[10] S. M. Bellovin, R. Bush, and D. Ward. Security requirements for bgp path validation. `http://tools.ietf.org/html/draft-ymbk-bgpsec-reqs-02`, 2011.

[11] M. Caesar, L. Subramanian, and R. H. Katz. Towards root cause analysis of internet routing dynamics. In *Berkeley EECS Annual Research Symposium*, 2004.

[12] Y.-J. Chi, R. Oliveira, and L. Zhang. Cyclops: The AS-level connectivity observatory. *ACM SIGCOMM Computer Communication Review*, pages 7–16, 2008.

[13] N. Feamster, D. G. Andersen, H. Balakrishnan, and M. F. Kaashoek. Measuring the effects of internet path faults on reactive routing. In *SIGMETRICS*, 2003.

[14] A. Feldmann, O. Maennel, Z. M. Mao, A. W. Berger, and B. M. Maggs. Locating internet routing instabilities. In *SIGCOMM*, 2004.

[15] S. Goldberg, M. Schapira, P. Hummon, and J. Rexford. How secure are secure interdomain routing protocols? In *SIGCOMM*, 2010.

[16] X. Hu and Z. M. Mao. Accurate real-time identification of ip prefix hijacking. In *IEEE Symposium on Security and Privacy*, pages 3–17, 2007.

[17] G. Huston and G. Michaelson. RFC 6483: Validation of Route Origination Using the Resource Certificate Public Key Infrastructure (PKI) and Route Origin Authorizations (ROAs). `http://tools.ietf.org/html/rfc6483`, 2012.

[18] J. Karlin, S. Forrest, and J. Rexford. Pretty good BGP: Improving BGP by cautiously adopting routes. In *ICNP*, pages 290–299, 2006.

[19] E. Katz-Bassett. Announcement of university of washington routing study. `http://mailman.nanog.org/pipermail/nanog/2011-August/039337.html`.

[20] E. Katz-Bassett, H. V. Madhyastha, J. P. John, A. Krishnamurthy, D. Wetherall, and T. E. Anderson. Studying black holes in the internet with hubble. In *NSDI*, 2008.

[21] S. Kent, C. Lynn, J. Mikkelson, and K. Seo. Secure border gateway protocol (S-BGP). *IEEE Journal on Selected Areas in Communications*, 18:103–116, 2000.

[22] M. Lad, D. Massey, D. Pei, Y. Wu, B. Zhang, and L. Zhang. PHAS: A prefix hijack alert system. In *USENIX*, 2006.

[23] H. Madhyastha, T. Isdal, M. Piatek, C. Dixon, T. Anderson, and A. Krishnamurthy. iPlane: An information plane for distributed services. In *OSDI*, pages 367–380, 2006.

[24] R. Mahajan, D. Wetherall, and T. Anderson. Understanding bgp misconfiguration. In *SIGCOMM*, pages 3–16, 2002.

[25] S. Murphy. Rfc 4272: Bgp security vulnerabilities analysis. `http://tools.ietf.org/html/rfc4272`, 2006.

[26] R. Oliveira, B. Zhang, D. Pei, R. Izhak-Ratzin, and L. Zhang. Quantifying path exploration in the Internet. In *Proc. of the 6th ACM SIGCOMM Internet Measurement Conference (IMC)*, Rio de Janeriro, Brazil, 2006.

[27] Y. Rekhter, T. Li, and S. Hares. RFC 4271: Border gateway protocol 4. `http://tools.ietf.org/html/rfc4271`, 2006.

[28] Renesys. China's 18-minute mystery. `http://www.renesys.com/blog/2010/11/chinas-18-minute-mystery.shtml`, 2010.

[29] RIPE. Youtube hijacking: A ripe ncc ris case study. `http://www.ripe.net/news/study-youtube-hijacking.html`, 2008.

[30] L. Subramanian, V. Roth, I. Stoica, S. Shenker, and R. H. Katz. Listen and whisper: Security mechanisms for BGP. In *NSDI*, pages 127–140, 2004.

[31] F. Wang, Z. M. Mao, J. Wang, L. Gao, and R. Bush. A measurement study on the impact of routing events on end-to-end internet path performance. In *SIGCOMM*, 2006.

[32] Y. Xiang, Z. Wang, X. Yin, and J. Wu. Argus: An accurate and agile system to detecting ip prefix hijacking. In *Workshop on Trust and Security in the Future Internet*, 2011.

[33] B. Zhang, R. Liu, D. Massey, and L. Zhang. Collecting the internet as-level topology. *SIGCOMM Comput. Commun. Rev.*, 35(1):53–61, 2005.

[34] Z. Zhang, Y. Zhang, Y. C. Hu, Z. M. Mao, and R. Bush. iSPY: Detecting ip prefix hijacking on my own. In *SIGCOMM*, pages 327–338, 2008.

[35] X. Zhao, D. Pei, L. Wang, D. Massey, A. Mankin, S. F. Wu, and L. Zhang. An analysis of BGP multiple origin as (MOAS) conflicts. In *1st ACM SIGCOMM Workshop on Internet Measurement*, 2001.

[36] C. Zheng, L. Ji, D. Pei, J. Wang, and P. Francis. A light-weight distributed scheme for detecting ip prefix hijacks in real-time. In *SIGCOMM*, pages 324–334, 2007.

Concurrent Prefix Hijacks: Occurrence and Impacts*

Varun Khare
vkhare@cs.arizona.edu
The University of Arizona

Qing Ju
qingju@cs.arizona.edu
The University of Arizona

Beichuan Zhang
bzhang@cs.arizona.edu
The University of Arizona

ABSTRACT

A *concurrent prefix hijack* happens when an unauthorized network originates IP prefixes of *multiple* other networks. Its extreme case is leaking the entire routing table, *i.e.*, hijacking all the prefixes in the table. This is a well-known problem and there exists a preventive measure in practice to safeguard against it. However, we investigated and uncovered many concurrent prefix hijacks that didn't involve a full-table leak. We report these events and their impact on Internet routing. By correlating suspicious routing announcements and comparing it with a network's past routing announcements, we develop a method to detect a network's abnormal behavior of offending multiple other networks simultaneously. Applying the detection algorithm to BGP routing updates from 2003 through 2010, we identify five to twenty concurrent prefix hijacks every year, most of which are previously unknown to the research and operation communities at large. They typically hijack prefixes owned by a few tens of networks, last from a few minutes to a few hours, and pollute routes at most vantage points.

Categories and Subject Descriptors

Computer Systems Organization [**Computer-Communication Networks**]: Network Operations—*Network Monitoring*

General Terms

Algorithms, Measurement, Verification

Keywords

BGP Security, Prefix Hijacking

*The material in this article is based upon the work partially supported by DHS grant N66001-08-C-2028 and by Open Project of Shenzhen Key Lab of Cloud Computing Technology & Applications (SPCCTA). Any opinions, findings, and conclusions or recommendations expressed in this material are those of the author(s) and do not necessarily reflect the views of the sponsors.

1. INTRODUCTION

The Internet is an interconnection of tens of thousands of independently administered Autonomous Systems (ASes), which originate their allocated IP prefixes to the Internet via the Border Gateway Protocol (BGP). Due to the lack of authentication of BGP messages, an unauthorized network can originate prefixes owned by other networks [24, 18], *i.e.*, hijacking other prefixes, to divert traffic for those prefixes towards unauthorized network. Malicious attackers have been known to use prefix hijacking to hide their network identity in sending spam [28], inflict denial-of-service attacks by dropping traffic, or even manipulate content of the traffic before forwarding it to destination [14]. Configuration errors in BGP routers have also caused prefix hijacking, leading to service outages for other networks.

A concurrent prefix hijack is an event where an unauthorized network announces prefixes of *multiple* other networks. Its extreme case is leaking the entire routing table, *i.e.*, hijacking all the prefixes in its BGP table. The first well-known case of such prefix hijacking is the full table leak from AS 7007 [1] on April 25, 1997, which lasted for hours and disrupted services for many networks. A more recent event was in September 2008 when AS 8997 falsely announced 117K prefixes [3].

A commonly held belief is that full-table or near full-table leaks is becoming rare. The wide awareness of the problem helps reduce configuration errors and a new BGP configuration option called "max-prefix limit" helps stop such leaks. Once configured for a BGP session, the max-prefix limit specifies the maximum number of prefixes that can be received from a peer, and if that limit is exceeded, the BGP session by default is reset to stop the potential table leak. However without actual data on prefix hijacks it is unclear if such a belief is close to reality. Furthermore it is unclear whether concurrent prefix hijacks of medium or small scales happen on the Internet or not. If they do occur then what are their characteristics, *e.g.*, when did they occur, who instigated them, how many victim prefixes were hijacked, how often did they happen and how long did they last, etc.

Detecting prefix hijacks is a hard problem. Existing techniques fall into two categories. In schemes such as [16, 23, 10, 32, 34], authoritative prefix ownership is known a priori and is used to compare against observed routing messages or forwarding paths. The knowledge of prefix ownership allows accurate detection of prefix hijacks, but in many scenarios complete and up-to-date ownership information is not available. Detection schemes such as [6, 4, 29, 27] do not require such authoritative information. They collect prefix origin information from routing updates or Internet registrars and apply various filters to identify suspicious events. However, since prefix hijacks and some legitimate operational practices have similar behaviors [33], pinpointing real hijacks without prefix ownership information has been a notoriously hard problem. These schemes usually generate a large number of alarms, many of which may be false positives.

While individual hijacks are difficult to identify, concurrent hijacks are relatively easier even without prefix ownership information. When a network originates prefixes of another network, it can be a hijack or due to an operational arrangement not known to the public. But when a network simultaneously originates prefixes of *many* other networks, it is highly likely to be a real hijack since operational arrangements with many different networks are unlikely to take effect at the same time. Based on this observation, we develop a scheme that detects concurrent prefix hijacks by correlating suspicious origin announcements and identifying networks that are offending many other networks simultaneously. In order to facilitate real-time detection and reaction, we tune the scheme's parameters to minimize false positives.

Applying this scheme to RouteViews Oregon BGP data from 2003 through 2010, we detect 5 to 20 concurrent prefix hijacks each year. They typically hijack prefixes of a few tens of other networks, last from a few minutes to a few hours, and pollute routes at most vantage points, meaning that the damage to data traffic could be widespread. We verify detected events in 2008, 2009, and 2010 via email communication with network operators. We sent 582 emails and received 63 valid replies, from which 53 confirmed prefix ownership, and 51 of those confirmed an individual prefix hijack. All the 21 detected events were confirmed as real hijacks as each event had at least one confirmed individual prefix hijack. This means that our scheme detected concurrent prefix hijacks with zero false positive in these three years . Interestingly most events are not mentioned in operator mailing lists such as NANOG [9] or identified in research literature, implying that the network community in general is not aware of these hijacks. Furthermore, most operators of victim prefixes told us that they were unaware of their prefixes being hijacked. To our best knowledge, this is the first time these under-radar prefix hijacks are discovered, verified, and documented.

The rest of the paper is organized as follows. Section 2 describes the detection scheme. Section 3 reports detected incidents and analyzes the results. We discuss related work in Section 4 and conclude the paper in Section 5.

2. THE DETECTION ALGORITHM

While our current focus is to identify and analyze concurrent prefix hijacks from archived data, we also have a long-term goal of being able to automatically detect and resolve these hijacks based on real-time BGP updates. Therefore we have the following two requirements on the detection algorithm: (1) requiring no authoritative prefix ownership information, and (2) minimizing false positives. The first one allows anyone who has access to BGP updates to be able to detect prefix hijacks. For example, if YouTube prefixes are hijacked, any ISP or monitoring service (*e.g.*, Cyclops [16]) that has received the false routing announcements would be able to detect it. The second requirement allows fast response to hijacks. If there are significant false positives, operators have to be involved to judge whether a detected event is a real hijack or not, which takes time. For instance, when a YouTube prefix was hijacked in 2008, it took 80 minutes for YouTube to launch the first countermeasure [13]. Minimizing false positives helps automate and speed up response to detected hijacks. Inevitably our detection algorithm will have more false negatives. These are easily covered by existing detection schemes which report a large number of suspicious events and can be examined by operators later.

The current detection algorithm processes archived BGP tables and updates in five steps to detect routing events where one network hijacks prefixes of multiple other networks at the same time.

Step A: single view of origin changes.

We collect prefix origin changes observed from a single BGP monitor. Every BGP update contains a prefix and an AS path, and we treat the last AS in AS path as origin of the prefix. As we process data yearly, the algorithm reads all BGP tables and updates from a single monitor in one year and records which AS originates which prefix during which time period. This time series of (prefix, origin AS) set forms a single monitor's view of origin changes.

Step B: global view of origin changes.

Since BGP is a path vector protocol, different monitors see different things depending upon where they are relatively to the routing events. When a network hijacks prefixes of multiple other networks, some monitors may not see it at all, and some monitors may only see part of it. Therefore in the second step we combine the single views of individual monitors into a global view of origin changes. The result is a time series of (prefix, origin AS) set over the entire year. It is origin AS *set* because a prefix can be announced by multiple ASes for legitimate reasons [33].

Step C: filter out potentially legitimate changes.

Since many origin changes are legitimate, in this step we try to filter them out to reduce noise in later steps. Accurately identifying all legitimate origin changes is almost impossible, otherwise we would be able to identify all prefix hijacks accurately. What we do here is to run a few best-effort heuristics to discard origin changes that are likely to be legitimate. As long as the heuristics are reasonable, their accuracy is not critical to final results. If some legitimate origin changes are kept, they will become noise and be filtered out in a later step. If some illicit origin changes are discarded in this step, the worst case is some more false negatives in the final results, and as we explained earlier, false negatives can be captured by existing schemes and our scheme focuses on minimizing false positives.

Every prefix is associated with a stable set and a related set containing ASes that probably can legitimately announce the prefix.

Stable Set captures ASes that are likely owners of a prefix. Usually the owner AS of a prefix is expected to announce the prefix persistently for a long duration. Figure 1 shows the CDF of cumulative announcement duration of every (prefix, origin AS) pair in 2009. While about 55% of prefix-origin AS pairs are live throughout the entire year, 25% are live for somewhere between one day and one year, and 20% are extremely short-lived, lasting less than one day. Further analysis shows that the middle section of the curve

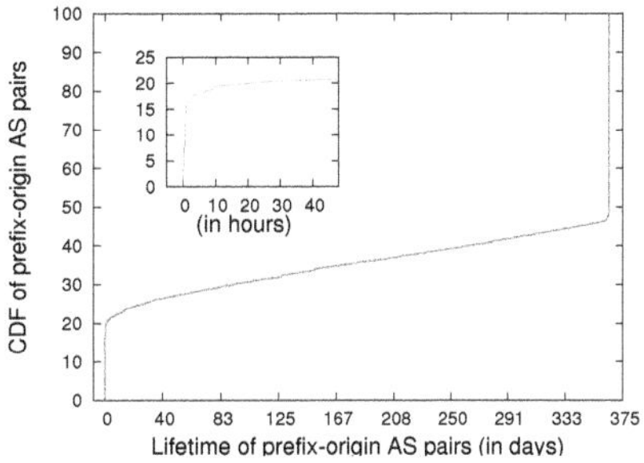

Figure 1: Lifetime of Prefix-Origin pairs in 2009

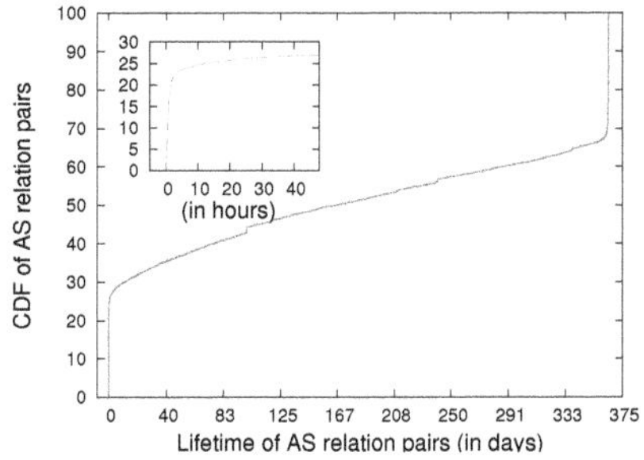

Figure 2: Lifetime of AS relation pairs in 2009

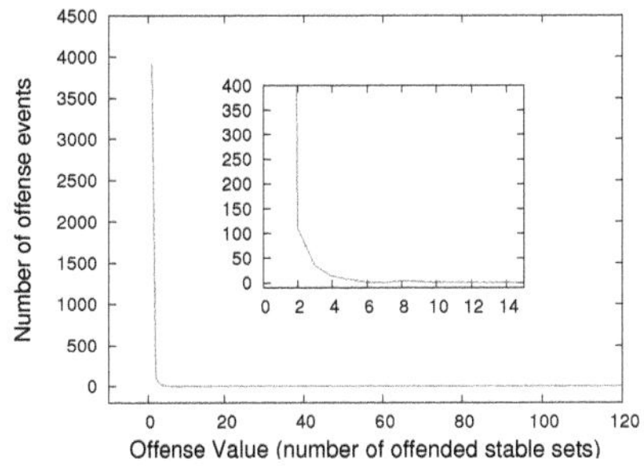

Figure 3: Offense Value of Events in 2009

are due to new prefixes that start to be announced during the year or prefixes that ceased to be announced sometime in the middle of the year. This leaves about 20% short-lived announcements that are deemed to be suspicious. Therefore any AS announcing a prefix cumulatively for one day or more within a year is included in the prefix's stable set. We choose one day as a threshold because (1) it is near the knee point of the curve, and (2) we assume operators are watching their networks and hijacks are dealt with within 24 hours mostly.

Related Set captures ASes that are not the owner of the prefix but can legitimately announce it in operation. It is impossible to enumerate all operational practices that lead to such legitimate announcements. We have found the following four cases useful for our detection algorithm.

First, an AS in a prefix's stable set also belongs to related set of all its sub-prefixes. This captures the case where ISPs de-aggregate prefixes and announce the sub-prefixes. Sometimes operators implementing TE de-aggregate prefixes to steer traffic within particular IP address range through specific paths [25].

Second, for all ASes in a prefix's stable set, their direct provider ASes also belong to this prefix's related set. This captures the case where a provider network may announce its customer's prefixes, *e.g.*., during failures.

For this purpose we use a simple heuristic to identify stable provider-customer inter-AS links. We start with a list of well-known tier-1 ASes, and given an AS path, the link from a tier-1 AS to a non-tier1 AS is provider-customer, and any link after that is also provider-customer due to the commonly deployed No-Valley policy. This can be considered as a subroutine in most of the existing AS relationship inference algorithms (*e.g.*, [19]), and thus the accuracy in inferring provider-customer relationship should be similar, although we do not need to infer peer-peer or sibling-sibling relationship, which is the challenging part of general AS relationship inference.

Since we are processing continuous routing updates, there is an issue that existing relationship inference algorithms do not deal with: the lifetime of links and relationships. Figure 2 presents CDF of the announcement duration of every AS relation pair in 2009. About 33% of AS relation pairs are live for the entire year, about 41% are live for somewhere between a day and a year, and nearly 26% are extremely short-lived, lasting less than a day. The short-lived links are more likely to be caused by configuration errors or route leaks. Thus we consider a provider-customer relationship stable if the link has been announced for one day or more cumulatively in a year. One day is chosen as the threshold since it is near the knee point of the curve. Only when the relationship is stable will the provider AS be added into the related set of customer's prefixes.

Third, ASes participating in an Internet Exchange Point (IXP) (as listed on IRL [7]) can legitimately announce the IXP's prefixes, and similarly the IXP AS can also legitimately announce the prefixes of its participating ASes.

Fourth, ASes belonging to the same organization are related and can legitimately announce each others prefixes. We simply infer such relation from the domain name of the contact emails listed in the WHOIS [12] database.

Step D: offense value.

Any AS not belonging to a prefix's stable set or related set but originating the prefix is deemed to be an *offending AS*, attempting to potentially hijack the prefix. In such case, we also say that the AS is offending the prefix's stable set, which represents the owner of the prefix. For an offending AS, we define its **offense value** as the number of unique stable sets that this AS is offending at any given moment. The offense value captures how many other networks are being potentially hijacked simultaneously. Based on the filtered global view of origin changes, we compute offense value for every AS for the entire year.

Step E: concurrent prefix hijacks.

Figure 3 presents the distribution of offense values of all possible concurrent hijack events in 2009. Most events pose small offense values of less than three and some of them are found to be legitimate cases after detailed analysis. We choose 10 as a threshold for identifying real concurrent prefix hijacks: if the offense value is no less than 10, then the event is reported as a concurrent hijack. This value is chosen because (1) it is close to the knee point in Figure 3, (2) it is conservative than the actual knee point so as to minimize false positive, and (3) it is not too conservative to capture non-trivial hijacks, that is, hijacks other than full-table or near-full-table leaks.

Summary.

Algorithm 1 summarizes the above steps. It uses one year of archived BGP tables and updates, available at Route Views Oregon monitors [11], to construct stable and re-

Date mm/dd/yy	Offender ASN	Type of Network	Offense Value	Victim ASes	Victim Prefixes	Victim IP Addresses	Duration	Monitor Pollution
04/08/10	23724	Small ISP	2365	2289	12115	113,924,096	21 mins	94.4%
04/22/10	11269	Small ISP	19	19	83	731,904	2.32 mins	94.6%
05/19/10	10834	Small ISP	15	14	85	141,824	42.90 mins	94.6%
08/12/10	5	Stub	15	15	32	98,816	5.28 mins	10.8%
09/10/10	27986	Small ISP	18	18	356	628,480	9.07 mins	94.6%
10/04/10	33770	Small ISP	20	20	188	393,216	20.67 mins	91.9%
02/14/09	8895	Small ISP	27	31	243	289,280	1.96 hours	95.35%
04/07/09	36873	Stub	13	15	45	27,392	9.98 mins	95.12%
05/05/09	10834	Small ISP	99	91	1108	1,713,664	3.06 hours	95.23%
07/12/09	29568	Small ISP	15	17	56	20,480	23.45 mins	50.00%
07/22/09	8997	Small ISP	170	173	351	101,500,416	1 min	4.76%
08/12/09	4800	Small ISP	13	13	39	18,176	0.53 mins	95.23%
08/13/09	4800	Small ISP	75	68	492	685,568	7.82 hours	95.23%
12/04/09	31501	Small ISP	18	19	77	1,574,400	1.02 mins	21.43%
12/15/09	39386	Large ISP	23	24	67	664,064	1 min	88.10%
04/28/08	44237	Small ISP	13	13	21	82,688	7.91 mins	86.4%
06/17/08	8953	Small ISP	105	113	218	113,920	2.12 mins	90.9%
08/26/08	24739	Small ISP	16	16	42	107,008	17.98 mins	95.3%
09/22/08	8897	Small ISP	17686	15270	116,753	1,511,397,056	21.95 hours	40.5%
12/31/08	1967	Stub	17	17	49	469,504	5.72 mins	26.2%
12/31/08	6849	Large ISP	37	38	52	25,856	2.21 hours	85.7%

Table 1: Concurrent Prefix Hijacking Events in 2008, 2009 and 2010 (all confirmed)

Algorithm 1 Concurrent Prefix Hijacks Detection

```
for all BGP routing message
  if AS X announces prefix p at time t
    if AS X ∉ StableSet(p) or RelatedSet(p)
      Update AS X offense value by StableSet(p)
  elsif AS X withdraws prefix p at time t
    if AS X ∉ StableSet(p) or RelatedSet(p)
      Reduce AS X offense value by StableSet(p)
Report hijack: if AS offense value >= 10
```

lated sets. Thereafter every BGP routing announcement is checked whether it is suspicious or legitimate by checking origin AS against stable and related set of prefix. Anytime the offense value of an AS exceeds the threshold of 10, it is reported to be a concurrent hijack.

3. CONCURRENT PREFIX HIJACKING RESULTS

In this section, we report detected concurrent prefix hijacks and the verification, followed by some major characteristics and a case study.

3.1 Concurrent Prefix Hijacks in 2008–2010

Table 1 lists concurrent prefix hijacks detected in 2010, 2009 and 2008 using BGP data collected by RouteViews Oregon collector. For each event, we classify offending AS as a large ISP if it has more than 50 customers, or a small ISP if it has less than 50 customers, or a stub network if it has no customers. Most of these events are caused by small ISPs with 50 or less customers.

To verify the detection results, we contacted operators of victim networks via emails. The email addresses were extracted from WHOIS [12] records of victim prefixes. Given that prefix ownership, ISP peering relationship and operation practices change over time, older results may not be reliably verified. Thus we did not attempt to verify results older than 2008. We are in the process of verifying results of 2011 and 2012, and plan to publish them online [8] once available.

In the emails we asked about two things: (1) whether the victim prefix is owned by AS(es) in its stable set or not, and (2) whether the hijack routing announcement on the given date and time is legitimate or not. The first question is intended to evaluate the accuracy of stable set inference (i.e., prefix ownership), and the second question is to evaluate the accuracy of detecting individual hijack announcement. A hijack *event* is confirmed if at least one prefix origination by the offending AS is illicit. For each email reply received, we first check the response to the first question. Only after the operator has confirmed prefix ownership will we consider the response to the second question.

We sent out 582 emails in total and received 63 valid replies, among which 53 networks confirmed that they own the prefixes but 10 networks said that they did not own the prefixes. The latter was caused by outdated or inaccurate WHOIS [12] records. For example, some operators said that the prefix was an old allocation that had been returned to their providers. Among the 53 responses that confirmed prefix ownership, 51 networks reported that all ASes in the prefix's stable set are legitimate, while 2 networks reported that some ASes in the stable set are not legitimate. This shows that in most cases the stable set captures prefix ownership correctly, but there exist cases (2 out of 53) where ASes in the stable set do not own the prefix, *i.e.*, their prefix origination are not legitimate, which may cause small false negatives in the final detection result.

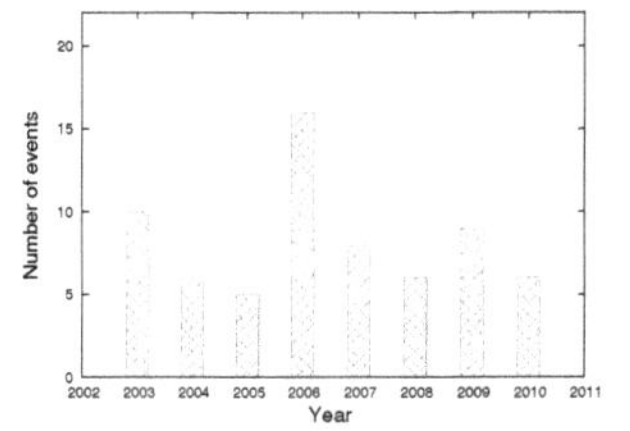

Figure 4: Hijacks per year

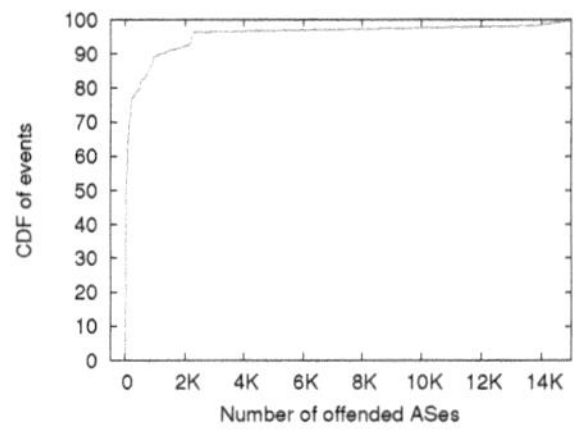

Figure 5: Offended ASes

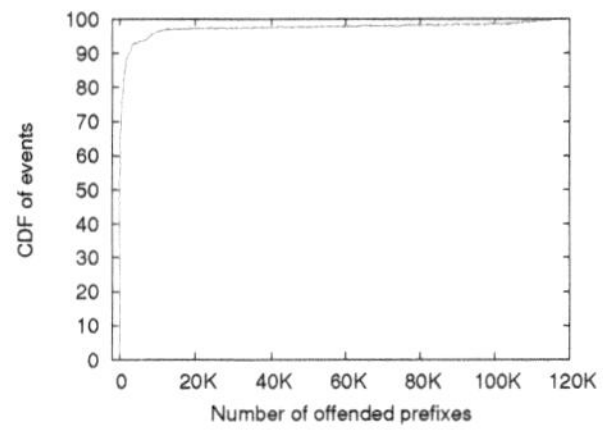

Figure 6: Victim Prefixes

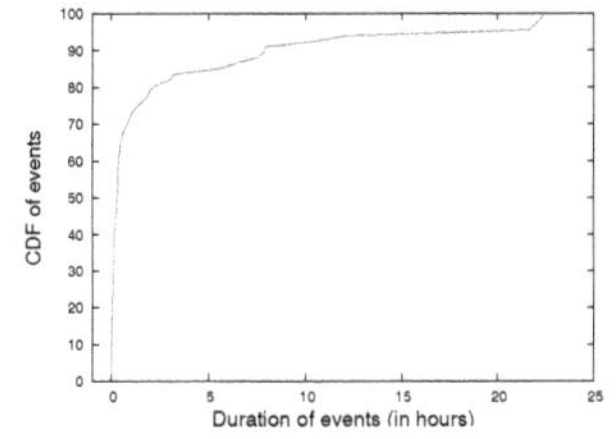

Figure 7: Event Duration

In the 53 emails that confirmed prefix ownership, 51 of them confirmed that the suspicious routing announcement was indeed false, *i.e.*, individual prefix hijacks. The other 2 emails explained that the suspicious routing announcements were legitimate. In one case the prefix owner peered with the offending AS, and in the other case the prefix owner and the offending AS belonged to the same company. However, these 2 cases did not cause any false positive in the final result. All the 21 events listed in Table 1 were confirmed as real hijack events since each event had at least one confirmed individual prefix hijack. Therefore by correlating suspicious routing announcements along the time dimension, our algorithm was able to identify a significant number of concurrent prefix hijacks with zero false positive.

Among the 51 confirmed individual prefix hijacks, 49 operators stated that they were unaware of the hijacks; only 2 operators had knowledge of the hijacks and had resolved it by contacting the provider of attacker AS. To some extent this is expected since when a prefix is being hijacked, the prefix owner network does not see the false routing announcement due to BGP's path vector routing. We made attempts to verify whether the network community knew about these events. NANOG is a forum where network operators regularly discuss and attempt to resolve network problems. We scanned the NANOG mailing list on the dates when these prefix hijacks occurred in 2008, 2009 and 2010 and only found discussions about a couple of very large leaks by AS 8997 in 2008 [3] and by AS23724 in 2010 [2]. Furthermore research literature does not report more events than NANOG. The fact that many hijacks happened but went unnoticed highlights the need for fast and accurate detection schemes.

3.2 Concurrent Prefix Hijacks in 2003–2010

Applying our algorithm to BGP data collected by RouteViews Oregon collector, we detect totally 60 concurrent prefix hijacks from 2003 through 2010, with about 5 to 20 events each year (Figure 4). The details of all the events are provided online [8]. Here we present some major characteristics of the events.

3.2.1 General Impacts

We measure the impacts of these hijack events by the number of ASes, the number of prefixes, and the number of monitor they affected and also the duration of the events. Figure 5 shows the CDF of the number of ASes whose prefixes were hijacked during these events. The top 20% of hijacks affected thousands of ASes, while the next 20% affected between 30 to 100 ASes and finally the remaining 60% affected 30 or less ASes. During these events multiple victim prefixes were hijacked.

Figure 6 shows the CDF of the number of victim prefixes per event. The top 20% of concurrent hijacks involve thousands of prefixes and sometimes as much as half the size of global routing table. The next 20% involve 100 or more prefixes and the remaining 60% involve less than 100 prefixes.

Figure 7 presents the CDF of the duration of each event. Most concurrent prefix hijacks are short-lived, lasting from a few minutes to a couple of hours, but still 20% of them lasted for more than 3 hours. The very short-lived events might be caused by typos in router configurations and were quickly caught and fixed. Adopting tools like router configuration checker [17] may help prevent these from happening. However, the existence of hijacks that lasted for a few hours or more raises the concern of serious damage to the prefix owner's network service.

Figure 8 shows the CDF of the percentage of monitors that were polluted in each hijack event. We say a monitor is *polluted* if it accepts at least one of the hijack routing announcements. In other words, if the monitor is a real router, it would forward traffic towards the hijacker. Since the RouteViews Oregon collector peers with BGP monitors in many different ISPs, the percentage of polluted monitors reflects the scope of the hijack's impacts. The figure shows that the top 70% of hijacks pollute 85% or more monitors, which means most hijack announcements propagate to most of the Internet.

3.2.2 Locality of Victim Prefixes

Concurrent prefix hijacking is caused by an AS falsely originating multiple victim prefixes at the same time. But what are the geographical locations of these victim prefixes? For instance, are these prefixes close to the attacker AS or distributed across the globe? We capture the locality of victim prefixes by the percentage of victim prefixes that are originated within the same country as the attacker AS. The geographic locations of victim prefixes were found by using Geo-Lite City [5], and the geographic location of attacker AS was found by looking up its WHOIS [12] record.

Majority of concurrent hijacks involved victim prefixes in the same country as offending AS. Figure 9 presents locality of victim prefixes for hijack events in years 2008 to 2010. For 55% of events more than 80% of victim prefixes are within the same country as attacker AS. Furthermore for about 35% of events every victim prefix is within the same country as attacker AS. This suggests that the false routing announcements do not involve random prefixes but are most likely meant to affect traffic for networks within a local region. Note that though victim prefixes are often in the same country as the attacker AS, the false routing updates are propagated to most of the Internet, causing wide-spread reachability problem to victim prefixes.

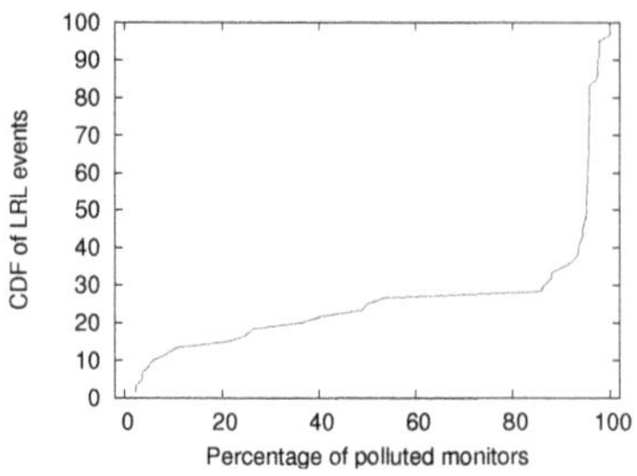

Figure 8: Monitor pollution

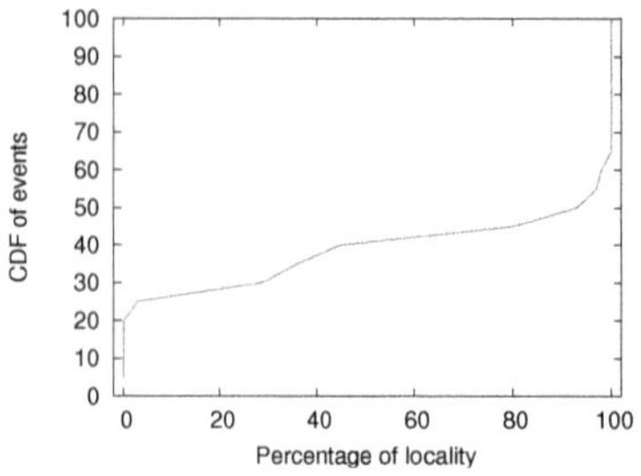

Figure 9: Locality of victim prefixes

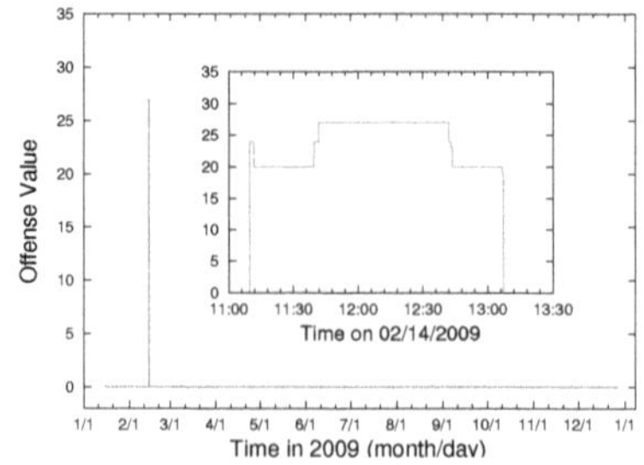

Figure 10: Prefix Hijacks by AS 8895 in 2009

3.2.3 A Case Study

Based on received operator emails, we now present an in-depth study of a verified concurrent prefix hijack that occurred in 2009. This event was caused by AS 8895 on February 14th, 2009 when it falsely originated 243 prefixes, which could potentially impact 289K IP addresses belonging to 34 ASes in Saudi Arabia. The event lasted for nearly 2 hours during which network services of all the involved Saudi ASes were interrupted. The scope of event was global as 41 out of 43 RouteViews Oregon monitors reported the false announcements. Most individual suspicious announcements were confirmed by offended ASes as illegitimate thereby verifying the event.

The network operators of victim prefixes and the offending AS confirmed that the stated hijacks were due to router misconfiguration. The network operator of AS 8895, *i.e.*, ISU/KACST stated that they used to be the major Internet gateway in the Saudi Arabia region and therefore an upstream provider for many local Saudi ISPs. In the past two years other Internet gateways have been launched within the region, one of them being AS 39386, *i.e.*, Saudi Telecom. In that period ISU/KACST shifted focus on educational sectors, universities, libraries and etc. Both these things resulted in many local ISPs switching providers to Saudi Telecom. But due to router misconfiguration AS 8895 kept announcing prefixes of many of its ex-customers which had switched providers to AS 39386.

Figure 10 illustrates how the offense value of AS 8895 reveals this event. Recall that *offense value* is the number of stable sets whose prefixes are hijacked by the offending AS. The offense value of AS 8895 was zero for the entire year except February 14th, 2009 when the leak occurred. The false announcement started at 11:10AM when AS 8895 announced prefixes of an increasing number of its ex-customers. The offense value fluctuated a couple of times but remained near constant at 34 for more than an hour. Finally offense value started to drop and got back to zero at 1:10 PM when the misconfiguration was fixed and false routing announcements stopped.

4. RELATED WORK

False BGP routing announcements are a well-known problem [15]. It includes hijacking allocated address space, as well as unallocated or private address space [18]. A number of solutions have been proposed to eradicate the problem of false routing announcements. They can be categorized into two categories: prevention [22, 26, 30, 21, 31], and detection [32, 23, 27, 16, 6].

The prevention techniques attempt to restrict ASes from making false routing announcements. Many prevention proposals [22, 26, 30] require extensive cryptographic key distribution infrastructure, and/or a trusted central database, and hence are difficult to deploy. PGBGP [21] and QBGP [31] attempts to prevent propagation of suspicious announcements. Each router monitors the origin AS for each prefix, any new prefix origination is considered anomalous, and router avoids using anomalous routes if old route is available.

The detection techniques focus on identifying prefix hijack events through monitoring of control plane or data plane and therefore can be categorized as (a) traceroute based solution and (b) control-plane based solution. These detection solutions do not require changes to BGP protocol and thus are more easily deployable. Traceroute based solutions, such as iSPY [32] and Lightweight Probing [34], periodically probe data paths to a specific prefix. Thus they are best to be used by prefix owners to protect their allocated prefix block.

Control-plane-based solutions, such as [27], can monitor the entire routing table passively, but they usually suffer from too many false positives as well as false negatives due to limited vantage points and the lack of ground truth of operational practices [20]. Certain control-plane-based solutions, such as PHAS [23] and MyASN [10], use information provided by prefix owners to filter out false positives, thus they are most effective when prefix owners register their prefixes and keep the registration up to date.

5. CONCLUSIONS

By identifying networks that announce prefixes of multiple other networks, we are able to discover 5 to 20 concurrent prefix hijacks every year from 2003 through 2010. For most of these events it is the first time they are discovered, verified, and documented. They typically last from a few minutes to a few hours and affect most monitors, implying these events may inflict significant damage to data traffic. Email communication with network operators verifies that the results of 2010, 2009, and 2008 have no false positives. Encouraged by the success of this method, we are implementing an online detection system that will process real-time BGP updates to generate up-to-date results.

6. ACKNOWLEDGEMENT

We are grateful to our shepherd, Sharon Goldberg, for her guidance and help in revising the paper. We would also like to thank anonymous reviewers for their valuable comments.

7. REFERENCES

[1] AS 7007 incident. http://en.wikipedia.org/wiki/AS_7007_incident.

[2] ASN 23724. www.merit.edu/mail.archives/nanog/msg07826.html.

[3] ASN 8997. www.merit.edu/mail.archives/nanog/2008/msg00704.html.

[4] BGPmon. http://www.bgpmon.net.

[5] GeoLite City. http://www.maxmind.com/app/geolitecity.

[6] Internet Alert Registry. http://iar.cs.unm.edu/.

[7] Internet Topology Collection. http://irl.cs.ucla.edu/topology.

[8] LRL. dyadis.cs.arizona.edu/projects/lsrl-events.

[9] North American Network Operators' Group. http://www.nanog.org.

[10] RIPE myASn System. http://www.ris.ripe.net/myasn.

[11] Route Views Project. http://www.routeview.org.

[12] Whois Database. http://www.whois.net/.

[13] YouTube Hijacking: A RIPE NCC RIS case study. http://www.ripe.net/news/study-youtube-hijacking.html.

[14] Ballani, H., Francis, P., and Zhang, X. A Study of Prefix Hijacking and Interception in the Internet. In *ACM SIGCOMM* (2007).

[15] Butler, K., Farley, T., McDaniel, P., and Rexford, J. A survey of bgp security issues and solutions. *Proceedings of the IEEE 2010*, 1 (Jan. 2010), 100–122.

[16] Chi, Y.-J., Oliveira, R., and Zhang, L. Cyclops: AS-level Connectivity Observatory. *SIGCOMM CCR 38*, 5 (2008), 5–16.

[17] Feamster, N., and Balakrishnan, H. Detecting BGP Configuration Faults with Static Analysis. In *Proc. NSDI* (2005).

[18] Feamster, N., Jung, J., and Balakrishnan, H. An empirical study of "bogon" route advertisements. *SIGCOMM Comput. Commun. Rev. 35*, 1 (Jan. 2005), 63–70.

[19] Gao, L. On Inferring Autonomous System Relationships in the Internet. In *IEEE ACM Transactions on Networking* (2000), vol. 9, pp. 733–745.

[20] Hu, X., and Mao, Z. M. Accurate Real-time Identification of IP Prefix Hijacking. In *IEEE Symposium on Security and Privacy* (2007).

[21] Karlin, J., Forrest, S., and Rexford, J. Pretty Good BGP: Improving BGP by Cautiously Adopting Routes. In *ICNP* (2006).

[22] Kent, S., Lynn, C., Mikkelson, J., and Seo, K. Secure Border Gateway Protocol (S-BGP). *IEEE JSAC 18* (2000), 103–116.

[23] Lad, M., Massey, D., Pei, D., Wu, Y., Zhang, B., and Zhang, L. PHAS: A Prefix Hijack Alert System. In *USENIX Security* (2006).

[24] Mahajan, R., Wetherall, D., and Anderson, T. Understanding bgp misconfiguration. In *SIGCOMM '02* (2002).

[25] Meyer, D., Zhang, L., and Fall, K. Report from the IAB Workshop on Routing and Addressing. draft-iab-raws-report-01.txt, 2007.

[26] Ng, J. BGP Extensions for Secure Origin BGP, April 2004. ftp://ftp-eng.cisco.com/sobgp/drafts/draft-ng-sobgp-bgp-extensions-02.txt.

[27] Qiu, J., Gao, L., Ranjan, S., and Nucci, A. Detecting Bogus BGP Route Information: Beyond Prefix Hijacking. In *SecureComm* (2007).

[28] Ramachandran, A., and Feamster, N. Understanding the Network Level Behavior of Spammers. In *ACM SIGCOMM* (2006).

[29] Siganos, G., and Faloutsos, M. Neighborhood Watch for Internet Routing. In *IEEE INFOCOM* (2007).

[30] Subramanian, L., Roth, V., Stoica, I., Shenker, S., and Katz, R. Listen and Whisper: Security Mechanisms for BGP. In *NSDI* (2004).

[31] Zhang, M., Liu, B., and Zhang, B. Safeguarding Data Delivery by Decoupling Path Propagation and Adoption. In *INFOCOM* (2010).

[32] Zhang, Z., Zhang, Y., Hu, Y. C., Mao, Z. M., and Bush, R. iSPY: Detecting IP Prefix Hijacking on My Own. In *SIGCOMM* (2008).

[33] Zhao, X., Pei, D., Wang, L., Massey, D., Mankin, A., Wu, S., and Zhang, L. BGP Multiple Origin AS Conflicts. In *IMW* (2001).

[34] Zheng, C., Ji, L., Pei, D., Wang, J., and Francis, P. A Light-Weight Distributed Scheme for Detecting IP Prefix Hijacks in Real-Time. In *ACM SIGCOMM* (2007).

Classifying Internet One-way Traffic

Eduard Glatz
ETH Zurich
Zurich, Switzerland
eglatz@tik.ee.ethz.ch

Xenofontas Dimitropoulos
ETH Zurich
Zurich, Switzerland
fontas@tik.ee.ethz.ch

ABSTRACT

Internet background radiation (IBR) is a very interesting piece of Internet traffic as it is the result of attacks and misconfigurations. Previous work primarily analyzed IBR traffic to large unused IP address blocks called network telescopes. In this work, we build new techniques for monitoring one-way traffic in live networks with the main goals of 1) expanding our understanding of this interesting type of traffic towards live networks as well as of 2) making it useful for detecting and analyzing the impact of outages. Our first contribution is a classification scheme for dissecting one-way traffic into useful classes, including one-way traffic due to unreachable services, scanning, peer-to-peer applications, and backscatter. Our classification scheme is helpful for monitoring IBR traffic in live networks solely based on flow-level data. After thoroughly validating our classifier, we use it to analyze a massive data-set that covers 7.41 petabytes of traffic from a large backbone network to shed light into the composition of one-way traffic. We find that the main sources of one-way traffic are malicious scanning, peer-to-peer applications, and outages. In addition, we report a number of interesting observations including that one-way traffic makes a very large fraction, i.e., between 34% and 67%, of the total number of flows to the monitored network, although it only accounts for 3.4% of the number of packets on average, which suggests a new conceptual model for Internet traffic in which IBR traffic is dominant in terms of flows. Finally, we demonstrate the utility of one-way traffic of the particularly interesting class of unreachable services for monitoring network and service outages by analyzing the impact of interesting events we detected in the network of our university.

Categories and Subject Descriptors

C.2.3 [COMPUTER-COMMUNICATION NETWORKS]: Network Operations—*Network monitoring*

General Terms

Measurement, Security

Keywords

Measurement methods, Traffic Analysis (anomaly detection, classification)

1. INTRODUCTION

Studying the background radiation of the Internet has been instrumental for understanding Internet threats, like the prevalence of Denial of Service (DoS) attacks [29] and the propagation of Slammer [27] and Blaster [4] worms. IBR traffic has been primarily studied with the help of network telescopes [28], which are large unpopulated IP address blocks (e.g. /8) that seamlessly filter out all benign traffic. In live networks, i.e., popuated networks IBR traffic can be extracted by dissecting two-way from one-way traffic, i.e., traffic connections that do not receive a network reply. In this work, we build techniques for monitoring one-way traffic in live networks.

We make three main contributions. First, we *design and validate a comprehensive classification scheme for dissecting one-way traffic* that relies solely on flow-level data, e.g., NetFlow. Our scheme uses 13 carefully-designed rules, which encode novel heuristics as well as leverage and combine existing techniques that have been proven effective for certain types of traffic. We associate each one-way flow with up to 17 different *signs*, which help dig into the causes of one-way flows. The key features of our scheme are that: 1) it relies on flow data; 2) it is very easy to configure; 3) it provides transparency into the classification process; and 4) it is easily extensible.

Our second contribution is that *we use our classification scheme to shed light into IBR traffic towards a large live network by analyzing a massive data set of unsampled flow records summarizing 7.41 petabytes of traffic* recorded over eight years (from 2004 to 2011). We find that in the studied years one-way traffic makes between 34% and 67% of the total number of flows, but it only accounts on average for 3.4% of the packets. This suggests a new conceptual model of Internet traffic in which IBR traffic is a needle in a haystack in terms of packets (and bytes), but it is very dominant in terms of flows. Besides, we find that scanning is the largest component of one-way traffic corresponding to 83.5% and 62.6% of the one-way flows and packets, respectively. The second major contributor is traffic caused by peer-to-peer (P2P) applications. Finally, we find that in 2011 the volume of IBR traffic in terms of flows is almost equal to 2004 with small fluctuations in the years between. The fraction of IBR traffic in the total number of flows has been consistently decreasing from 67% in 2004 to 34% in 2011.

Third, *we show how one-way flows assigned to the class of unreachable services provide new possibilities for service availability monitoring enabling in particular to passively assess the impact of outages*, which is not possible with traditional approaches based on active probing. To demonstrate the utility of our scheme, we describe and measure the impact of interesting outages and misconfiguration we discovered in the network of our university.

In the next section we provide preliminary insights into the one-way traffic classification problem. Next, in Section 3 we describe our data sets and their sanitization steps. Our classification scheme is introduced in Section 4 and validated in Section 5. In Section 6 we use our scheme to characterize the composition of IBR traffic in a live network, while in Section 7 we outline how our work is useful for service availability monitoring. Finally, we present related work and conclude our paper in Section 8 and 9.

2. PRELIMINARIES

Network communication inherently reflects dialogs taking place between applications running on distributed systems including any accompanied control and error messages. Regular communication involves two-way traffic consisting of packets in opposite direction. In contrast, one-way traffic results from communication errors or other unusual situations that result in packets in one direction. In this work, we look at one-way communication at the network level. We define a *two-way flow* (or equivalently a *bi-flow*) as the aggregate of two standard 5-tuple flows that have reverse values in the source and destination IP address and port number fields. A 5-tuple traffic flow is a flow of packets that have common values in the IP address, port number, and layer-4 protocol fields. We define an *one-way flow* as a flow that does not have a matching reverse flow. A two-way flow may still be the result of a failed communication at the transport or application level, e.g., a TCP reset packet produces a two-way flow, therefore *one-way flows provide a conservative view of failed communication attempts* in the Internet.

One-way traffic is important as it is associated with interesting events, such as unreachable services, scanning, and misconfigurations. To draw useful information from one-way traffic we need to infer what is causing it. The goal of one-way traffic classification is to classify one-way traffic into classes of malicious and benign causes. We identify three main causes of one-way traffic:

- **Failures & Policies:** this group comprises *attempts to access a service that do not succeed* due to failures or policies. Possible reasons are firewall blocking, temporary or permanent outages of network elements, stopped service processes on end-hosts, and routing misconfigurations. For example, the use of laptops outside of enterprise networks they are configured for produces one-way traffic. Similarly, one-way traffic is the result of attempts to use services that are blocked by security policies, like when testing connectivity with the ping tool to non-responding destinations. Furthermore, one-way traffic can in special cases result from network congestion.

- **Attacks:** *vulnerability scanning* is a very common attack vector. However, unsolicited probes typically do no receive a reply resulting in many one-way flows. Another attack case is *backscatter traffic* from DoS attacks using spoofed source IP addresses, which also results in one-way flows towards the spoofed IP addresses. Third, *prefix hijacking* results in one-way traffic towards a "black hole".

- **Special application behavior:** *P2P applications* try to reconnect to systems they have been in contact before as such systems are often preferred peers by application design. However, the dynamic nature of P2P networks and in particular nodes unexpectedly leaving a network result in one-way reconnection attempts. A second, but rare scenario is *applications using sessions that run the two communication directions over different connections*. For example, an interesting case we have identified is the application layer protocol of LANsource [15] that runs over UDP and uses different destination ports for each communication direction.

Properly identifying Internet one-way traffic from measurement data imposes specific requirements on monitoring. In particular, traffic sampling and poor spatial network coverage, i.e., missing one direction of a communication that may take a different path due to asymmetric routing, may result in artificial one-way flows. In principle, dealing with asymmetric routing requires to either know how flows are routed or to monitor every link along a network cut between a monitored network and the Internet. For these reasons, it is practically easier to measure one-way traffic near the edge, e.g., in enterprise, university, or small ISP networks, where it is possible to monitor the entire border traffic activity without sampling. Edge networks comprise the vast majority of Internet domains.

3. DATASETS AND SANITIZATION

We use data from a regional academic backbone network that serves 46 single-homed universities and research institutes. The monitored address range contains 2.2 million IP addresses, which correspond to a continuous block slightly larger than a /11. We have been archiving unsampled flow records since 2003 from hardware-based NetFlow meters on the border routers of the monitored network. The meters capture all the traffic that crosses the border destined to or coming from the Internet. In a single peering link, we observe in 2011 on average 108.1 million flows per hour, which corresponds to 3,064 million packets. The stored flow records are not anonymized. From each record we extract for our classification scheme the following fields: IP addresses, port numbers, protocol number, byte/packet counts, and timestamps. We do not use TCP flags because they are not supported by the fast hardware-based NetFlow, although they can be easily integrated in our classification. Over time we have accumulated a massive archive with more than 100 TBytes of compressed NetFlow records.

A challenge in analyzing our data is computational overhead especially for tasks that cannot be parallelized. For example, using a optimized C++ program to parse one day of data and compute the average number of one-way flows per host takes 10 hours and 10-20 Gbytes of main memory. The computational overhead includes time for disk I/O, decompression (*bzip2*), sorting flows by their start time, preprocessing (as discussed in the following paragraphs), and updating a hash table, which keeps per host state. Memory consumption is dominated by the hash table. The computation time can be drastically reduced by using flow meters that support on-the-fly bidirectional flow monitoring, like YAF [16]. To make the computational overhead more tractable, we use two 400-hour samples per year, which correspond to approximately one month per year. In particular, we analyze the first 400 hours of each February and August between 2004 and 2011. The studied traffic data correspond to 457 gigaflows and 7.41 petabytes and cover approximately 9% of the total number of flows observed during the eight year period. This is one of the largest traffic traces that has been analyzed in the literature.

For each 400-hour sample, in the top rows of Table 1 we report the time the monitoring and collection infrastructure was functioning properly and the traffic volume it corresponds to. Overall the availability of the infrastructure was higher than 99.5% with only short interruptions due to router restarts and corrupted data. To eliminate the impact of interruptions in our analysis, we use daily averages and discard the days in which the short interruptions occurred.

3.1 Data Sanitization

In this section we describe how we addressed a number of data sanitization challenges for extracting one-way flows. In particular, we outline our methodology for eliminating double-counting, defragmentating flows, and pairing bi-flows. To speed up searching for matching flows, we split time into intervals and limit our search within an interval. In Section 3.1.4 we analyze the impact of the interval size. In the future, the standardization of bidirectional flow monitoring [34] will likely make one-way flow extraction much easier.

3.1.1 Double-Counting Elimination

Although we collect flows from border routers only, if a flow is routed through multiple border routers, it will be reported multiple times in our NetFlow data. To address this problem we use a map provided to us by network operators of SWITCH (ISP serving Swiss Universities) that specifies which ports of the border routers are connected to the internal backbone and which to the Internet. Our NetFlow data carry information about the input and output port of a flow. We use this information to filter out flows. We only keep flows that are routed between the Internet and the intranet. Double-counting elimination has a significant impact on our data reducing the total traffic volume by 32.3%.

3.1.2 Defragmentation

We call the standard 5-tuple NetFlow records *raw flows*. NetFlow may fragment a traffic flow when the active timeout expires or when the flow cache is filled up and flushed. In addition, the optional NetFlow *fast aging* feature, with which our meters are configured, leads to additional fragmentation. Fast flow aging reduces the utilization of the flow table by exporting a flow if no more than a few packets are observed within the first few seconds of the creation of a flow table entry. It realizes an efficient process to age out entries for short flows. To address flow fragmentation due to fast aging, we split time into intervals and for each raw flow we search within its time interval for other raw flows with the same 5-tuple. We merge matching flows updating their byte/packet counts and start/end timestamps. We call the merged flows *defragmented flows*. Note that if a flow spans multiple intervals it will yield one defragmented flow for each interval. In the bi-flow pairing process we account for these cases. In the third and fourth row of Table 1 we show the numbers of raw and defragmented flows. We observe that defragmentation has a significant impact reducing the number of flows by a fraction ranging between 20.6% and 39.6% for different years.

3.1.3 Bi-flow Pairing

For TCP and UDP a two-way flow is the aggregate of two defragmented flows that have the same 5-tuple with reverse values in the source and destination IP address and port fields. For each defragmented flow in an observation interval, we search for flows in the same or in the adjacent intervals and group matched flows into a bi-flow. A one-way flow is a flow that does not have a matching reverse flow in the same or in an adjacent interval.

A special situation exists for other protocols, like ICMP, Encapsulated IPv6, and Encapsulated Secure Payloads (ESP). The port fields in our NetFlow data do not carry interesting semantics for protocols other than TCP and UDP. For these protocols we define a flow and match bi-flows based on a 3-tuple consisting of the IP addresses and protocol fields. This definition may underestimate the number of one-way flows involving protocols other than TCP and UDP.

Interestingly, it is not officially documented how NetFlow defines a flow for these protocols. According to certain sources NetFlow aggregates packets with common values in the source/destination IP address, protocol, and ICMP type/code fields into an ICMP flow [37]. For protocols other than TCP, UDP, and ICMP, NetFlow sets port fields to zero [37]. We find that this behavior is not met by our NetFlow data. Only 5% of all ICMP flows carry the ICMP type and code information, while all remaining ICMP flows have this information set to zero.

3.1.4 Impact of the Interval Size

We next analyze the impact of the interval size by computing flow metrics for a full day of data using different interval sizes. We select a 10-minute reference interval within which we can search efficiently for flow fragments and pairs. In Figure 1 we show the impact of the interval size with respect to the 10-minute (600 secs) interval. We observe, as expected, that longer intervals lead to slightly lower flow counts as fewer flows cross interval boundaries. This decrease is less for two-way flows due to their longer duration. We observe that doubling the interval size slightly decreases absolute count metrics by 3-5%. On the other hand, the decrease of the relative volume of one-way flows is only 1.2% and does not decrease further with an increasing interval size. Therefore, we conclude that with a 10-minute interval absolute count metrics slightly overestimate the number of flows, while relative count metrics, which is the type of metrics we primarily report, are very accurate.

4. ONE-WAY TRAFFIC CLASSIFICATION

Our classification scheme has the following key features:

- **Flow-based Classification:** We leverage solely flow monitoring data, i.e., NetFlow. Compared to packet-

	2004	2005	2006	2007	2008	2009	2010	2011
Hours	799.0	800.0	792.0	780.0	799.0	799.0	800.0	800.0
Total terabytes	270.8	304.5	424.4	641.5	842.6	1035.2	1763.2	2132.7
Raw flows (1e9)	30.96	29.35	30.32	49.03	63.16	77.05	90.91	86.49
Defragmented flows (1e9)	24.31	22.47	22.53	29.62	44.03	58.55	72.21	66.91
Two-way flows (1e9)	6.117	6.712	8.046	10.84	17.61	22.97	28.71	26.55
Two-way packets (1e9)	381.1	418.6	558.0	834.0	1080.8	1286.8	2092.3	2372.7
One-way flows (1e9)	12.19	9.102	6.502	8.040	8.967	12.78	15.01	14.06
One-way packets (1e9)	34.09	20.89	24.04	31.09	27.59	49.65	39.56	79.03

Table 1: Size of data sets per year in total hours, bytes, flows and packets. The different flow counts represent the processing steps from raw data to defragmented flows and finally to flows separated into two- and one-way flows.

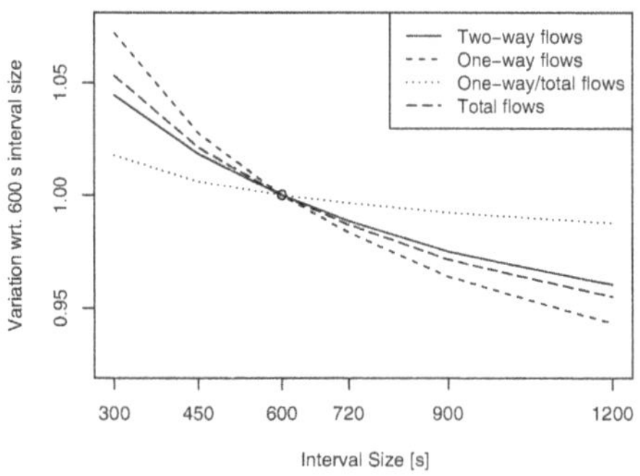

Figure 1: Impact of time interval size on flow metrics aggregated for a full day. The decrease of the fraction of one-way to total flows is not more than 1.2% for a doubled interval size.

level data and DPI that have been used in the past to monitor IBR traffic, flow monitoring provides fewer details, but is less expensive, scales better to monitoring large IP address blocks, and is more generally available.

- **Easy Configuration:** Our classifier does not require training, which is a drawback of many traffic classification techniques. It can be applied with minimal configuration, without extensive overhead.
- **Comprehensibility:** We use legible rules instead of complex classification structures, like self-organizing maps, to make our classifier comprehensible to non-machine-learning experts. Our scheme is based on the rules summarized in Table 3 that can be easily reviewed and verified both by researchers and network operators. Traffic classification schemes should be easily understandable to be engaged and deployed by network operators.
- **Extensibility:** Our classifier can be easily extended with additional traffic features and classification rules. For example, if a flow monitor is configured to collect additional data, like TCP flags, then these can be easily integrated into new or existing classification rules.

We classify one-way flows using a two step process that resembles the way medical diagnosis identifies the cause of a health problem. We first define a set of *signs*, which are informative attributes for digging into the cause of one-way flows. We then check each flow against all signs and find the ones it matches. Finally, we classify a flow based on the collection of signs that are present or absent. Our classification scheme is based on a set of rules that take as input the signs of a flow and determine the appropriate class, including the unknown class.

4.1 Signs

Flow signs are derived from *sign tests*. A sign test determines if a flow exhibits a specific sign and may be as simple as checking a flow feature value or as complex as performing a behavioral assessment of an involved end-host. We introduce in total 17 signs exploiting in 4 cases techniques from the literature that have been shown effective for detecting scan and peer-to-peer traffic. We classify our signs in four categories based on the entity they characterize: 1) a pair of communicating hosts, 2) a remote host as a source of a one-way flow, 3) a local host as a target of a one-way flow, or 4) a flow. In Table 2 we summarize our signs and show in which category they belong.

4.1.1 Host-Pair Signs

Host-pair signs characterize a pair of end-hosts with a one-way flow. They reflect the mix of one- and two-way flows of a host pair. In Figure 2 the graphs a to d illustrate communication patterns that correspond to the four possible combinations of a biflow and an outflow between a host pair with an inflow. Hosts are represented by nodes, where the local host is the node in the left and directed links represent the presence of one or more flows. We use the sign *end-hosts-communicating* to mark one-way flows between hosts that are involved in a productive communication, i.e., they have one or more biflows between them, with occasional failed connections, i.e., one-way flows. We assign this sign to one-way flows with the communication pattern shown in the graphs b and d in Figure 2.

Furthermore, we introduce a sign called "InOut" to capture the pattern of graph c in Figure 2. In particular, the "InOut" sign identifies host pair communication situations in which a one-way ICMP flow is a reply to another outgoing one-way flow exchanged between the same host pair. We assign ICMP one-way flows with the sign "InOut" to a special class that includes suspected benign one-way flows.

4.1.2 Remote Host Signs

We use four signs to characterize remote hosts that generate one-way flows towards the monitored network. If we observe one-way flows from a well-known source port of a remote host to a local ephemeral port and at the same time we do not observe any two-way flows nor opposite direction

Sign Type	Sign Name	Detection Criterion/Algorithm	Sign Short Name for Rules
Host pair behavior	End-hosts-communicating	One-way flow between productive host pair	PotOK
	Limited dialog	One-way flows between unproductive host pair	InOut
Remote host behavior	Service sole reply	no biflow on srcIP $\wedge$ dstPort$\geq$1024 $\wedge$ srcPort $<$ 1024	Backsc
	Remote scanner 1	TRW algorithm (suspected scanner)	TRWscan
	Remote scanner 2	Host classification (suspected scanner)	HCscan
	Remote non-scanner	TRW algorithm (suspected regular host)	TRWnom
Local host behavior	Unused local address	Unpopulated local IP address	GreyIP
	Service unreachable	Unanswered request to local service	Unreach
	Peer-to-peer	Flow towards local P2P host	P2P
Flow feature	Artifact	UDP/TCP flow with both port numbers=0	Artef
	Single packet	Flow contains one packet only	Onepkt
	Large flow	Flow carries $\geq$ 10 packets or $\geq$ 10240 bytes	Large
	Bogon	Source IP belongs to bogon space	Bogon
	Protocol	IP protocol type of flow	TCP, UDP, ICMP, OTHER

Table 2: Overview of defined signs based on the behavior of one or both involved hosts or based on the numeric values of one or more flow attributes.

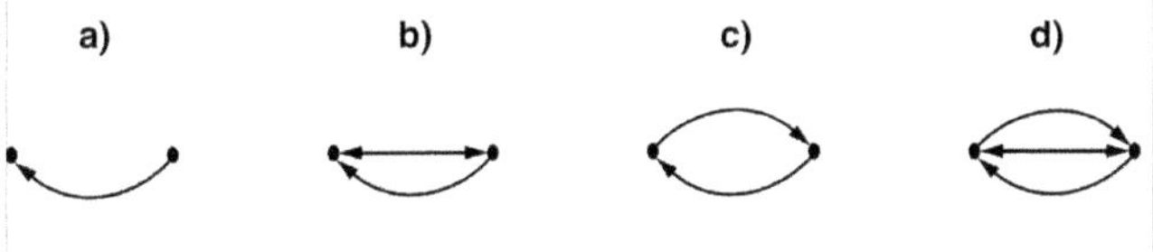

Figure 2: Mixture of incoming one- and two-way flows exchanged between a host pair shown as a graph. Hosts are represented by nodes and the presence of inflow/outflow/biflows by arrows.

one-way flows between the two hosts, then we assign the *service sole reply* sign. We use this sign to detect backscatter from attack traffic towards a service of the remote host. We check for the absence of biflows within a 30-minute time interval to limit computational overhead.

Besides, we leverage two state-of-the-art algorithms to detect remote scanners. We introduce three signs that describe either a positive or a negative test result. The first two signs are based on the well-known Threshold Random Walk (TRW) [19] algorithm, which uses sequential hypothesis testing to qualify a remote host as scanner or benign (or undecidable). We denote these signs with "TRWscan" and "TRWnom". The second algorithm [3] is a variant of TRW that inspects the behavior of a remote host in a relaxed way and classifies it as a scanner if a test condition is met. A negative test result is not supported, i.e., it does not qualify a host as benign. The test assesses the *service fanout* of a remote host, i.e., the count of 2-tuples {dstIP,dstPort} the host attempted to access, and its overall success in connection establishment. Each connection attempt is qualified either as "good" if it results in a two-way flow or as "bad" if it results in a one-way flow. This way, a remote host is classified as a scanner if it has a bad service fanout larger than two times the good service fanout (and at least 4). The host classification is done in a first pass. During a second pass any flow sourced by a classified scanner is labeled with the sign "HCscan". Both algorithms restrict their tests to 30 minute time windows to keep memory demands in bounds.

4.1.3 Local Host Signs

We use three signs to characterize local hosts within the monitored network. We mark with the sign *unused local address* ("GreyIP") local IP addresses that never sourced any flow over a full observation period of 400 hours and, therefore, are unpopulated.

We introduce the sign *service unreachable* to trace outages of well-known services. We define a service as an endpoint described by the 3-tuple {localIP, protocol, localPort} with the constraint that the port number is well-known, i.e., below 1024. We consider only TCP and UDP flows. We consider a local service valid if it serves at least 20 clients during any 30-minute interval over a full observation period. We label one-way flows that target valid services with the sign *service unreachable* ("Unreach").

The sign *peer-to-peer* marks one-way flows caused by stale host caches of P2P applications. Behavioral P2P application identification has been studied extensively [20, 31, 18]. We make use of three rules from the literature (H1,2,3 from [18]) that identify a local host as a member of a P2P network based on the observation of typical P2P behavioral patterns. We require that at least 2 out of 3 P2P rules are matched or a match occurs for at least 5 time windows of 30 minute duration. First, we prepare a list with detected local P2P hosts by analyzing two-way flows of a full observation period. Then, we mark any TCP/UDP one-way flow targeted at a high port towards such hosts with the *peer-to-peer* sign.

4.1.4 Flow Signs

The remaining signs are either direct flow attributes or are derived from them by the rules shown in Table 2. The sign *artifact* is used for TCP and UDP flows with both port numbers set to zero. Such flows are the result of packet fragments for which the correct port numbers are not available due to the missing layer-4 header. If a flow contains a source address that belongs to bogon space using the data of [9] then we mark it with the sign *bogon*.

4.2 Classifier

A class is associated with one or more rules. We define the following classes:

- **Service Unreachable:** access attempt to temporary unavailable services.
- **Malicious Scanning:** probing for the exploitation of vulnerabilities in end systems.
- **Benign P2P:** P2P applications trying to access peers listed in their local host cache that are not anymore available.

Class Name	Rule #	Flow Membership Rules
Malicious Scanning	1	$\{TRWscan, \overline{PotOk}\} \Rightarrow Scanner$
	2	$\{HCscan, \overline{PotOk}\} \Rightarrow Scanner$
	3	$\{GreyIP, \overline{Backsc}, \overline{ICMP}, \overline{bogon}\} \Rightarrow Scanner$
	4	$\{Onepkt, \overline{GreyIP}, \overline{ICMP}, \overline{TRWnom}, \overline{bogon}, \overline{P2P}, \overline{Unreach}, \overline{PotOk}, \overline{Backsc}, \overline{Large}\} \Rightarrow Scanner$
	5	$\{ICMP, \overline{TRWnom}, \overline{InOut}, \overline{bogon}, \overline{PotOk}\} \Rightarrow Scanner$
Backscatter	6	$\{Backsc, \overline{TRWscan}, \overline{HCscan}, \overline{P2P}, \overline{InOut}, \overline{PotOk}\} \Rightarrow Backscatter$
Service Unreachable	7	$\{Unreach, \overline{TRWscan}, \overline{HCscan}, \overline{bogon}, \overline{P2P}\} \Rightarrow Unreachable$
Benign P2P Scanning	8	$\{P2P, \overline{TRWscan}, \overline{HCscan}, \overline{bogon}\} \Rightarrow P2P$
Suspected Benign	9	$\{PotOk, \overline{Unreach}, \overline{P2P}, \overline{bogon}\} \Rightarrow Benign$
	10	$\{Large, \overline{GreyIP}, \overline{TRWscan}, \overline{HCscan}, \overline{P2P}, \overline{Unreach}, \overline{ICMP}, \overline{Backsc}, \overline{bogon}\} \Rightarrow Benign$
	11	$\{TRWnom, \overline{GreyIP}, \overline{HCscan}, \overline{P2P}, \overline{Unreach}, \overline{bogon}, \overline{Backsc}\} \Rightarrow Benign$
	12	$\{ICMP, InOut, \overline{TRWscan}, \overline{HCscan}, \overline{bogon}\} \Rightarrow Benign$
Bogon	13	$\{bogon, \overline{TRWscan}, \overline{HCscan}, \overline{Backsc}\} \Rightarrow Bogon$

Table 3: Rules used to classify one-way flows. Each rule specifies which signs have to be present or absent (sign names with overbars). An overview of defined signs can be found in Table 2.

- **Backscatter:** replies to DoS attack traffic that uses randomly chosen source IP addresses to hide the real identity of an attacker.
- **Suspected Benign:** one-way flows may exist as part of benign applications using data and control connections in parallel and employing one of them for acknowledgment only. Another cause may be temporary failures within an otherwise productive communication.
- **Bogon:** one-way flows originating from bogon IP space.
- **Other:** one-way flows that do not match any of the above classes.

We derive our classification rules with a systematic process shown in Figure 3. We start with an initial set of rules and in each iteration we classify flows, compute a conflict report of the resulting classification and update the rules. The conflict report describes flows classified in multiple classes. Specifically, it reports: 1) the classes that intersect; 2) the size of the intersections; 3) an ordered (by their popularity) list of sign combinations in the intersections; and 4) the number of remaining unclassified flows. Based on the conflict report and in particular the sign combinations, we then manually update the rules to resolve conflicts and to reduce the number of unclassified flows. Each flow is checked against 17 different signs, which in theory yields a maximum of 131,072 possible sign combinations. However, most combinations do not occur in practice. In our data, we observe a total of 1,035 different sign combinations. Moreover, one could ignore sign combinations that are only observed in a small number of flows resulting in a sharp reduction on the number of interesting combinations. We iteratively repeat this procedure until we resolve all conflicts and cannot further significantly reduce the number of unclassified flows. Based on the described procedure we derived a first version of our classification rules after eight iterations. Then, we further refine our rules based on our validation. The final classifier includes 13 classification rules shown in Table 3.

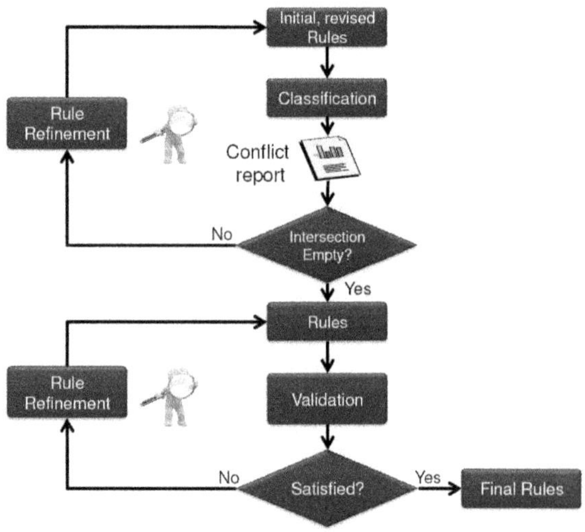

Figure 3: Rule refinement stages

For the initial rule set we defined rules that contained only signs that must be present based on expert knowledge. This resulted in many flows that were classified in multiple classes, summing up on average to 21.9% of the flows with a peak of 40.6%. Through carefully studying conflicting sign sets provided by the conflict report we revised the rules by adding extra predicates describing signs that must be absent to resolve all class conflicts. Finally, we investigated all sign sets of significant size that were not yet catched by any rule to minimize the count of unclassified flows (assigned to class "Other"). This way we could classify on average 98.0% of all one-way flows with a low of 95.6% in August 2008.

Our classifier processes input flows in three passes. In a first pass it initializes local services, local P2P hosts and inactive local IP addresses. In a second pass matching signs are assigned to flows and in a final pass rules are applied to account each flow to a unique class. We have implemented our classifier in C++ and run it on a dedicated Linux cluster with a fast RAID disk subsystem. We collect logs of the overhead of the three passes combined for all 16 runs. In general, the overhead scales with the size of the dataset, but also depends on dataset characteristics. On average a run processed 28.6 gigaflows in 23.1 hours (with a maximum of 37.4 hours) and required 3.4 GB of memory (with a peak of 6.1 GB). Considering the monitoring period length of 400 hours these figures are well within real-time bounds set by the speed of the flow data collection process. Note that we exclude the overhead for preprocessing (time binning, flow defragmentation, biflow-pairing) as it largely depends on the available input data (e.g. NetFlow export or YAF-created flow records). On our NetFlow records the preprocessing required the most resources while still safely remaining within real-time bounds.

Our classification scheme has one parameter that needs configuration: the time window size used for P2P and services identification and for scanner detection. We set it by default to 30 minutes, but on a smaller network the window size should be increased (see also Section 5).

5. VALIDATION

In this section we evaluate the accuracy of our classifier and optimize its rule set. Validating a one-way traffic classification scheme is very challenging. A major challenge is the scarcity of information available from one-way traffic consisting of very short flows carrying few packets and frequently no payload. We address this challenge, first, by building more accurate host profiles based on flow data over long time windows, second, by carefully examining one-way packets for violation of relevant protocol state machines, and third, by exploiting DPI and application identification techniques.

We first use a traffic summarization technique [5] based on frequent item-set mining (FIM) to summarize flows of different classes into frequent item-sets, which can be then easily inspected by an analyst. We apply this approach in each class and measurement period between 2004 and 2011. In summary, we find that for different classes and periods up to 75% of the flows were correctly classified. However, with this approach we cannot assess the remaining flows and the number of false negatives. In addition, a validation of one-way traffic classification solely based on flow data often provides insufficient evidence, as we miss information like TCP flag and ICMP types/codes. For this reason, we built a dedicated validation setup in a smaller network to obtain more detailed data.

5.1 Validation Setup

We built a monitoring setup and collected packet traces at the Internet gateway of the Swiss university Hochschule für Technik Rapperswil (HSR) occupying a /16 IP address range. The campus network is sparsely populated with a total of 3,949 active IP addresses seen during our experiment. We use a dedicated host that is tapping traffic between the border router and the firewall. On the border router no filtering is activated, enabling us to see all traffic routed to this IP range. To reliably collect packet data, we use an Endace DAG card that provides exact packet timestamps. Mandated by the IT security policy, we anonymize all IP addresses using a prefix-preserving scheme. Note that anonymization does not allow us to use active probing for our validation as proved to be useful in [30].

We collected packet traces for 19 consecutive days and extracted flows using the YAF flow meter [16] configured for bidirectional flow export. We then split flows into 10-minute intervals and defragmented flows within each interval resulting in a total of 322.7 million (mio) flows, which include 219.6 mio (68.1%) incoming one-way flows, 8.06 mio outgoing one-way flows (2.5%) and 95.1 mio two-way flows (29.5%). The small fraction of two-way flows can be explained by the scarce population of the monitored network. We retain packet data for a sub-period of three randomly chosen days.

To obtain application labels we configured YAF with its optional DPI application identification feature that assigns application labels to flows it recognizes. However, the coverage achieved by YAF is limited. Thus, we used an additional DPI application identifier to add a second set of application labels for almost all flows. This additional DPI application identifier originally was developed to evaluate the BLINC classifier [21] and in an improved version to evaluate several competing approaches to application identification [24].

To learn more on the occurrence of one-way flows using bogus source IP addresses, we periodically downloaded the full bogon list provided by [9] throughout the data collection process. This list not only contains the official IANA-reserved address ranges, but includes all IP ranges assigned to regional registrars that have not yet been handed out to costumers.

5.2 Validation Criterias

To determine class memberships we built a DPI classifier that uses an extensive set of 33 rules that make heavy use of details available only from packet-level data. Due to space limitations, we describe our DPI-based classification in the companion technical report [12]. In the following paragraphs, we summarize the key additional information we extracted from the packet-level data and how we exploited it.

Extended Host Profiles: For each host we maintain a host profile over the full observation period of 457 hours (19 days) that tracks its connection success and subsequently is used to feed the TRW algorithm. This is feasible in our /16 network, i.e., it required 12 GBytes of memory for 10.2 mio extended host profiles, but does not reasonably scale for larger networks carrying more traffic. Besides, extended host profiles in combination with application identification are useful for identifying P2P hosts and local services.

ICMP types and codes: For ICMP flows we analyze if type and code information and the communication situation of the involved host pair fit a class. For example, we deem a flow as backscatter if it is an echo reply and the receiver never sent a request to the sender. In addition, we check if the source of an ICMP flow is not already identified as a scanner, which interestingly is true for more than 92.1% of all incoming one-way ICMP flows.

Protocol State Machine: As an additional way to identify malicious scan traffic, we analyze how well individual flows follow the transport layer protocol state machine. Malformed packets are frequently used to exploit weaknesses of protocol stacks or to penetrate non-stateful firewalls. For

TCP flows we test if the flags of consecutive packets fit into acceptable state changes in the TCP protocol machine and run sanity checks on the sequence numbers of segments.

Application Identification: We apply application identification techniques [16, 21, 24] on two-way flows to discover local services and to detect hosts running P2P applications.

Precise Timestamps: We rely on packets timestamps to identify the initiator of a connection, which is not possible using NetFlow timestamps. Initiator detection is useful in combination with DPI and extended host profiles for mapping local services.

5.3 Validation Results

We run both the flow-based classifier and our DPI classifier over the evaluation dataset. Then, we compare the results of both classification runs and fill-in a *confusion matrix* showing predicted (flow-based) versus actual (DPI-based) class memberships. Based on the confusion matrix, we calculate the *recall* (also called sensitivity), *specificity* and *precision* metrics for all defined classes. Recall measures the portion of actual positives which are correctly identified as such; specificity measures the proportion of actual negatives which are correctly identified; and precision measures the portion of the classified positives which are correctly identified.

For the flow-based classification we use the same settings as we apply to the full dataset with the exception of the time window parameter for remote host profiling, which we increase by a factor of 32 to 16 hours instead of 30 mins. This compensates for the smaller probability to observe randomly targeted scan flows in the evaluation dataset caused by the smaller IP address range. Similarly to the full-dataset analysis, we classify incoming one-way flows. Our validation uses the full evaluation dataset to build host profiles and a subset of 34.8 mio incoming one-way flows for DPI. For this subset we could validate 99.4% of all one-way flows.

The test results are summarized in Table 4. We obtain very good results for the classes "Malicious Scanning", "Service Unreachable" and "Benign P2P Scanning" with recalls above 95.3%, specificitiy values greater than 91.3% and precision exceeding 95.4%. The class "Suspected Benign" has a recall of 85.1% and a precision of 75% caused by flows in the borderline between the classes "Suspected Benign" and "Malicious Scanning" that are hard to separate. On the other hand, its specificity is excellent at 99.9%. For the class "Backscatter" we observe a recall of 62.4%. We miss primarily ICMP replies and error messages as ICMP type and code information is not available in our flow data. However, the recall can be easily improved by using ICMP type/code fields when available to find ICMP replies. Besides, a specificity of 100% and a precision of 88.4% shows this class is still very useful. Finally, we observe a low recall for the class "Bogon" of 40.4% and at the same time a perfect specificity and precision of 100.0%. This is because the bogon list used by the flow-based classifier is a subset of the bogon list used by our DPI classifier. We intentionally exclude the full-bogon information from flow-based classification because historical full-bogon data is not available. Again, it is trivial to extend the flow-based classifier to use full-bogon lists for analyzing present or future data.

Class Name	Recall [%]	Specificity [%]	Precision [%]
Malicious Scanning	99.9 (99.6)	91.2 (88.8)	99.8 (99.6)
Backscatter	62.4 (62.4)	100.0 (100.0)	88.4 (87.2)
Service Unreachable	99.6 (99.5)	100.0 (100.0)	96.1 (92.5)
Benign P2P Scanning	95.3 (91.8)	99.9 (99.8)	95.5 (85.0)
Suspected Benign	85.1 (70.5)	99.9 (99.9)	75.0 (70.5)
Bogon	40.4 (40.2)	100.0 (100.0)	100.0 (100.0)

Table 4: Results of validation. The values in parentheses provide a lower bound by counting non-validated flows as classification mismatches.

5.4 Impact on Flow Classifier

For flow-based scan detection we use two sets of rules. The first set is based on scan detection algorithms providing strong evidence. The second set defines rules that point towards scanning, but provide weaker evidence. In particular, it includes flows 1) towards unpopulated IP addresses or 2) that consist only of a single packet and do not match any other rule. The validation shows that the second rule set is in fact useful for scan detection, which led us to add this rule set to the class "Malicious Scanning" eliminating an initially defined class "Suspicious Other". In particular, 65.1% of the flows matching these rules are actually detected as scanners when observing host behavior for an extended time period.

Another change introduced during validation concerns the assignment of ICMP flows. We observe that 92.1% of all ICMP flows seen are sourced by identified scanners. Without ICMP type/code information, it is difficult to satisfactorily distinguish backscatter ICMP flows from scanning. Consequently, we moved a rule initially assigned to the class "Backscatter", assuming ICMP replies from DoS attacks, to the class "Malicious Scanning". Furthermore, we added the sign "InOut" that helps to identify host pair communication situations in which an ICMP flow is a reply to a one-way flow exchanged between the same host pair. We use this sign in the class "Suspected Benign".

6. ONE-WAY TRAFFIC COMPOSITION

In this section we apply our classification scheme on a massive dataset of flows records collected between 2004 and 2011 to shed light into the composition and characteristics of one-way traffic.

Aggregate Statistics: We first find that in terms of flows one-way traffic is a very large component of Internet traffic. During the studied period one-way flows correspond to between 34% and 67% of the total number of flows towards the monitored network. This is important for systems that need to keep per flow state, like stateful firewalls and flow meters. On the other hand, due to their short-lived nature, one-way traffic corresponds on average only to 3.4% and 0.79% of the total number of packets and bytes, respectively. This indicates that IBR traffic is not a significant in terms of additional bandwidth consumption and packet processing overhead.

Table 5 provides for each measurement period and class the fraction of one-way traffic in terms of flows and packets. On average the class "Malicious Scanning" accounts for 83.5% of all one-way flows. It is followed by the classes "Benign P2P" (6.7%), "Service Unreachable" (4.8%), "Suspected Benign" (2.6%), "Other" (2.2%), "Backscatter" (0.3%) and "Bogon" (0.1%), where in parentheses we show the average fraction of one-way flows per class over the eight year period. The packet perspective provides a different view. "Mali-

Period	Malicious Scanning	Backscatter	Unreachable	Benign P2P	Suspected Benign	Bogon	Other
2004-02	87.2%/57.9%	0.1%/0.2%	4.8%/9.2%	5.5%/10.3%	1.1%/3.7%	0.1%/0.1%	1.1%/18.7%
2004-08	93.9%/82.0%	0.0%/0.1%	0.6%/1.3%	3.4%/9.8%	1.0%/4.1%	0.0%/0.0%	1.0%/2.7%
2005-02	87.2%/65.6%	0.0%/0.1%	5.8%/12.1%	4.1%/9.1%	1.8%/10.5%	0.0%/0.0%	1.0%/2.7%
2005-08	95.4%/74.7%	0.0%/0.1%	0.4%/0.7%	1.8%/4.3%	1.5%/5.3%	0.3%/0.1%	0.7%/14.9%
2006-02	89.3%/71.8%	0.1%/0.2%	0.6%/4.4%	4.2%/9.9%	3.3%/10.2%	0.2%/0.1%	2.3%/3.5%
2006-08	87.8%/47.3%	0.1%/0.0%	0.4%/0.3%	5.3%/4.1%	3.2%/46.9%	0.0%/0.0%	3.1%/1.4%
2007-02	86.9%/83.6%	0.1%/0.1%	1.7%/1.2%	6.5%/7.1%	2.8%/6.2%	0.0%/0.0%	2.0%/1.8%
2007-08	80.7%/63.5%	0.2%/0.2%	2.2%/2.9%	9.5%/17.6%	3.5%/10.3%	0.2%/0.1%	3.7%/5.5%
2008-02	68.3%/34.4%	0.2%/0.2%	1.1%/1.9%	23.9%/49.4%	3.0%/10.4%	0.0%/0.0%	3.5%/3.7%
2008-08	70.5%/47.8%	0.3%/0.4%	15.2%/26.3%	6.5%/11.4%	3.2%/8.5%	0.0%/0.0%	4.4%/5.5%
2009-02	74.2%/55.7%	0.1%/0.0%	15.3%/25.3%	5.9%/11.1%	2.7%/5.6%	0.0%/0.0%	1.8%/2.3%
2009-08	86.2%/75.2%	0.1%/0.1%	3.7%/6.0%	5.7%/10.2%	2.3%/5.2%	0.0%/0.0%	2.0%/3.3%
2010-02	88.2%/77.5%	0.3%/0.2%	2.6%/5.1%	4.0%/7.7%	2.9%/5.9%	0.1%/0.0%	2.0%/3.5%
2010-08	85.8%/74.3%	0.2%/0.2%	3.1%/4.7%	6.3%/12.5%	2.6%/5.5%	0.0%/0.0%	1.9%/2.7%
2011-02	81.4%/61.5%	0.6%/1.2%	6.2%/12.9%	7.3%/18.7%	2.6%/3.5%	0.0%/0.0%	1.9%/2.3%
2011-08	72.8%/28.3%	2.2%/4.3%	12.3%/46.7%	6.9%/15.1%	3.7%/4.3%	0.0%/0.0%	2.0%/1.4%

Table 5: Fraction of flows/packets falling into the defined one-way flow classes. The class *Other* represents the remainder of flows not captured by the other classes. Note, that we do not list rules that achieve a low coverage eliminating the flow artifacts class that results from fragmented packets without layer-4 header.

cious Scanning" accounts for 62.6% of all one-way packets, "Benign P2P" for 13.0%, "Service Unreachable" for 10.1%, "Suspected Benign" for 9.1%, "Other" for 4.7%, "Backscatter" for 0.5%, and "Bogon" for 0.03%.

We observe that one-way traffic is clearly dominated by scanning. In terms of packets, scanning accounts for a smaller fraction of 62.6% of the total number of one-way packets. This is because one-way flows classified as scanning consist on average of 1.6 packets per flow. In contrast, one-way flows of the classes "Service Unreachable" and "Benign P2P" consist of 4.1 and 12.1 packets per flow, respectively. This difference is because TCP one-way flows to unreachable services are much more persistent in SYN packet retransmission attempts than TCP scanning. In addition, we find that one-way flows in the class "Benign P2P" are often multi-packet UDP flows that sharply increase the average number of packets per flow.

Changes Over Time: Besides, we observe a number of notable changes over time. In Figure 4 we compare how the mean daily number of one- and two-way flows evolved between 2004 and 2011. The volume of one-way flows has exhibited small fluctuations between 2004 and 2011 and, interestingly, in 2011 it is almost equal to 2004. On the other hand, the number of two-way flows has grown significantly by 343%. A study by Akamai estimated the global Internet penetration increase in 2010 as 17% [2]. If we extrapolate this figure over eight years, it yields a growth by 351%, which is very close to our observations.

Besides, we observe that the fraction of one-way flows has dropped significantly over time as shown in Figure 5. In 2004 one-way flows accounted for 67% of the total number of flows. Their share gradually dropped and since Aug. 2007 one-way flows account consistently for one out of three incoming flows. Between 2004 and 2007, a very large fraction of one-way flows targeted a small number of destination port numbers, which were used by loud worms, like Sasser. For this reason, we connect the decline of share of one-way flows to that presently aggresive scanning is not as common malware propagation vector as in the period between 2004 and 2007.

Figure 6 shows how one-way traffic breaks down into different classes in terms of flows. The fraction of "Malicious Scanning" flows varies, started at a high of 87.2% in 2004 and stayed at this or a higher level until 2006. Then, in 2007 we note a decline that leads to a low of 68.3% in Aug. 2008.

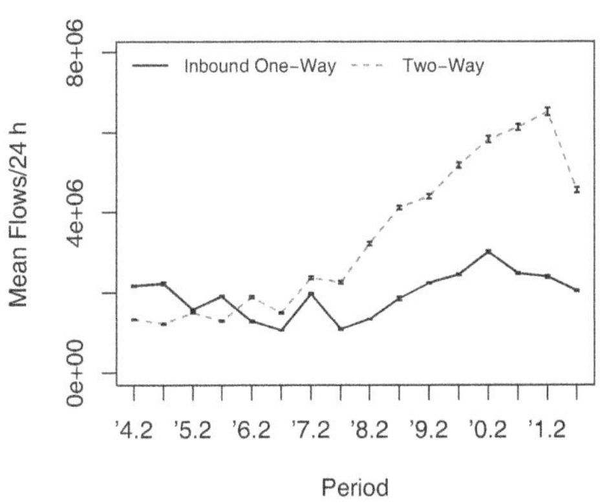

Figure 4: Evolution of one and two-way mean daily flow counts over time. The vertical bars mark 95% confidence intervals.

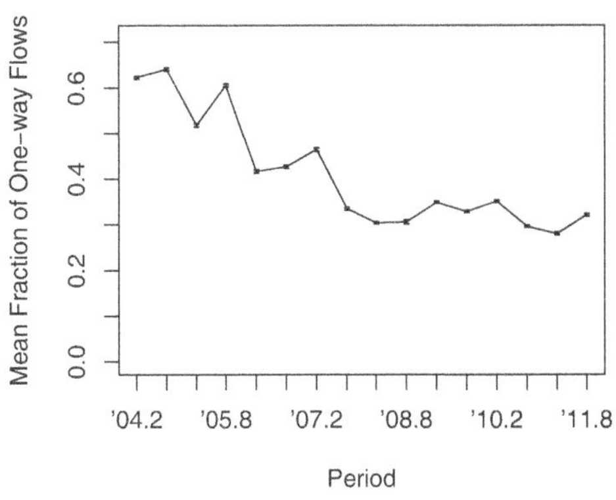

Figure 5: One-way flows as a (mean) fraction of the total number of flows, i.e., both one- and two-way flows, between 2004 and 2011. The share of one-way flows has declined between 2004 and 2007 and remains almost constant since then.

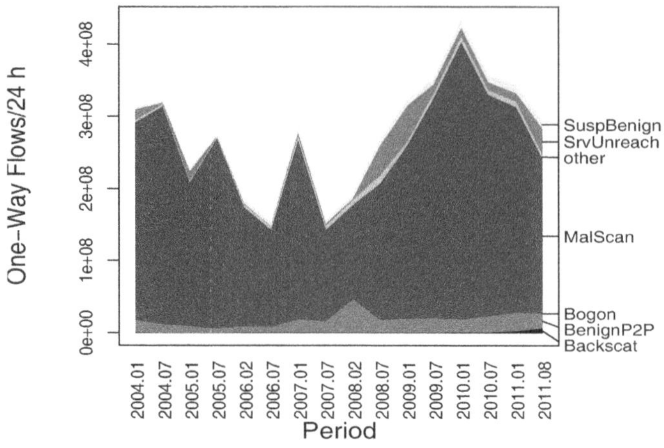

Figure 6: Composition of one-way traffic in flow counts per class.

This decline correlates with an increase of the class P2P one-way traffic that falls early into the same period and also an increase of class "Unreachable" later on. The high counts in class "Service Unreachable" between Aug. 2008 and Feb. 2009 are caused by unanswered NTP requests towards an NTP server. Investigating further this incident, we found that the increased number of requests pushed the operator to introduce access restrictions to this server. As we analyze more in the next section, this class of one-way flows is very useful to administrators to monitor the reachability of services. The peak in benign P2P one-way traffic between Aug. 2007 and Feb. 2008 can be attributed to two IP addresses that are reported to be fake servers by the eMule Bulletin Board. Fake eMule servers are commonly used to collect eMule user data for research or legal prosecution. Minor contributors to this class are XBSlink traffic sourced by Xbox 360 and PS2/3 game equipment, and the MMORPG (massively multiplayer online role-playing game) Heroes of Might and Magic.

7. SERVICE AVAILABILITY MONITORING

In this section, we show how one-way flows of the class "Service Unreachable" are very helpful for monitoring the availability of local networked services. Most existing schemes for monitoring the availability of services within an enterprise, a data center, or a university network are based on active probing and/or server logs. In contrast, flow data provide a new passive approach to monitor local services. The key intuition is that outages result in both 1) a drop (or halt) in the number of two-way flows and 2) a correlated rise in the number of one-way flows towards a destination. These changes can be easily detected by monitoring the number of one- and two-way flows towards local services. Compared to previous approaches, flow-based outage detection enables to leverage the regular traffic of a network as probe traffic. This approach offers the following key advantages: 1) *It exploits passive measurements* in contrast to injecting network overhead for active probing; 2) *It provides a tangible assessment of the impact of outages* by enabling to count the actual number of remote client IP addresses that fail to reach a service; 3) *It automatically discovers running local services* circumventing the need to manually configure (new) services; and 4) *It enables to concurrently monitor many services* by taking advantage of data from the strategical network location of gateways.

In the next paragraphs, we first outline our analysis methodology and secondly we show how our approach enables to assess the impact of outages using as a case study illustrating interesting misconfigurations and outages we detected in the campus network of ETH Zurich by applying our scheme on one week of data.

7.1 Methodology

Using one-way flows classified with our scheme in the class "Service Unreachable" as well as bidirectional flows as input, we compute the following three metrics to evaluate the reachability of local services within the network of ETH Zurich. We focus on services running on well-known port numbers.

We define the *availability* of a service as the number of time intervals a service is alive, i.e., it has bidirectional flows, over the number of intervals it is either alive or unresponsive, i.e., it only has incoming one-way flows. We ignore intervals in which a service does not have any incoming flows. The availability metric helps group services into permanently and temporarily offered ones.

Available services are not necessarily reachable to *all* clients due to access policies, misconfigurations, or other reachability problems. We define the *reachability* of a service as the fraction of the number of distinct client IP addresses with bidirectional flows to the service over the total number of distinct client IP addresses to the service during a time interval. The reachability metric is useful for identifying misconfigurations and outages.

Finally, the *outage impact* of a service is the number of unique client IP addresses that are involved in one-way flows of the class "Service Unreachable" during a time interval. As several clients can be behind a remote NAT, this metric provides a lower bound on the actual number of clients that are affected by an outage and is very useful for assessing the impact of failures.

7.2 Outages and Misconfigurations

In this section we demonstrate the utility of one-way flows detected with our classification scheme for monitoring the availability of networked services.

We applied our scheme on a randomly-selected week of NetFlow data from our archive and initially focused on services discovered within the address range of the Department of Information Technology and Electrical Engineering of ETH Zurich. We discovered services as 2-tuples $\{localIP, localPort\}$ with a well-known port number that had more than 20 unique clients during any time interval. As with bi-flow pairing, we used a 10-minute time interval. We discovered in total 43 remotely accessible departmental services for which we computed our three metrics. To validate our observations, we met and discussed with the network administrators of our department providing them details about the availability, reachability, and outages of the services. The administrators confirmed the validity of the discovered services and provided feedback on a number of interesting outages we summarize in the next paragraphs.

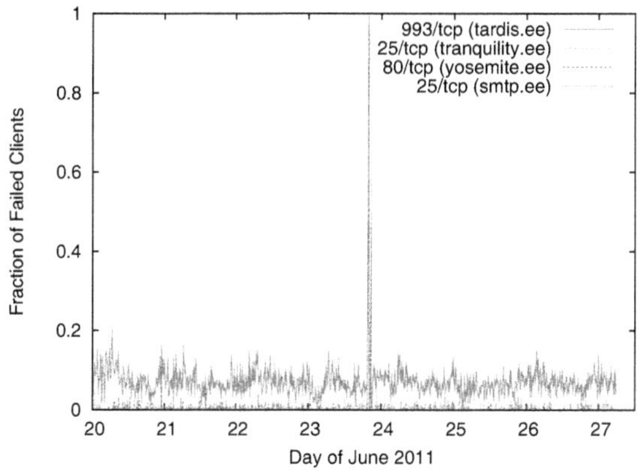

Figure 7: Coinciding outage observed on the 23rd of June 2011 19:40 UTC on most university services resulting in failed accesses from 287,583 unique clients.

We identified a group of 32 services available at least 99% of the time and 11 services that either fail very often or are not operated all the time.

For all frequently used services we found a coinciding global outage on the 23rd of June 2011 starting at approximately 19:40 UTC and lasting approximately 15 minutes as shown in Figure 7. This was a general problem in the reachability of the department network from the outside. To learn more about this outage, we analyzed three key services of the entire university: the main web, webmail, and software distribution services of ETH Zurich. Surprisingly, we found that at the same point in time the services were not accessible indicating a campus-wide reachability problem. During the identified 15-minute interval the outage impact metric revealed that 287,583 unique clients failed to access target services! Our investigation showed that the outage occurred during a planned router software upgrade. Although, temporal disruptions due to the upgrade were expected, the scale of the disruption revealed was suprisingly larger than expected. Present server availability monitoring techniques based on active probing and server logs miss this important information about the impact of an outage. Understanding the impact of outages in terms of the number of affected clients is very useful since this information helps to better provision network repairs and upgrades so that the number of affected clients is minimized. In addition, the number of failed client connections relates to the quality of an offered service and to lost revenues. In the examined case, although the detected outage resulted from a planned router software upgrade scheduled to take place during late evening hours, the number of affected clients, which our analysis revealed, turned out to be much higher than expected, which is important for better planning of such events. In addition, we visually inspected the time series of the volume of one-way flows for the top departmental services and found that the outage resulted in a sharp increase in requests targeting mail services due to the automated retry behavior of mail clients. On the other hand, for web services the volume of one-way flows during the outage did not substantially differ from the volume of two-way flows during regular operation, indicating a more network-friendly retry behavior.

Our inspection of the reachability metric for the discovered services revealed two actionable cases. First, we found an NTP server that was consistently not reachable on average by 12.9% of its clients. The outage impact metric showed that in this case too, a suprisingly large number of clients failed to receive a reply: during the studied week in total 2.2 million unique clients were involved in one-way flows to the NTP server. Investigating this further unveiled that standard NTP "hello world" configuration examples use the `swisstime.ee.ethz.ch` server in our department, making it likely one of the most popular NTP servers in the Internet. In addition, `swisstime.ee.ethz.ch` is often preconfigured in embedded devices. The failure rate, i.e., fraction of one-way flows, varies for different countries of origin. In the top client countries we observe Belgium with failure rate 65.7%, India with 20.2%, and Germany with 16.8%. Our investigation found two main causes of low reachability: 1) an IP filter was configured to prevent access from a /8 address block, which was frequently the source of attacks; and 2) certain devices appear to compute invalid CRC checksums resulting in dropped requests. From these findings we learned both that the traffic flow volume to the studied network was heavily affected from the popular NTP server and that a misconfigured application computes invalid CRC checksums.

Second, we noticed that the SMB service (Microsoft remote file server access) offered on 445/tcp was targeted by far more one-way flows (112% more) than two-way flows. An in-depth analysis revealed that almost all one-way flows were sourced by a likely misconfigured client that persistently tried to connect to this service. All remaining services achieved a reachability of 97.1% or more with most of them ranking at the 99.9% figure.

8. RELATED WORK

The related work falls into the following three categories.

8.1 IBR Traffic in Network Telescopes

Studying IBR traffic has been very useful for understanding Internet threats. In 2001, Moore *et al.* [29] were the first to use network telescopes to monitor background radiation and answer questions such as "how prevalent are denial-of-service attacks in the Internet today?". Yegneswaran *et al.* [39] employed scan logs collected by Dshield [11] during four months in 2001 and 2002 to analyze quantitative characteristics of intrusion activity in the global Internet. They made a number of interesting observations including that a very small collection of correlated sources are responsible for a significant fraction of intrusion attempts. In 2004, Pang *et al.* [30] used traces, lasting 80-hours to one week, from three sites to conduct a detailed characterization of traffic towards four large unused address blocks. Among other observations, they highlighted the dynamism of background radiation, which unlike normal traffic, can exhibit significant changes on a nearly daily basis. In 2010, Wustrow *et al.* [38] examined background radiation between 2006 and 2010 to four /8 unused blocks. They observed among other findings that background radiation continues to be very dynamic and identified interesting artifacts that lead to address space pollution. In addition to characterizing traces from network telescopes, in this work we consider the need to dissect one-way traffic to live networks, introduce and validate a one-way traffic classifier to facilitate this goal and characterize a massive data set of IBR traffic towards a live network.

8.2 IBR Traffic in Live Networks

A number of more recent studies have focused on one-way traffic. In 2012, Brownlee [6] described a tool called *iatmon* for classifying one-way traffic based on packet interarrival times and remote scanner patterns of the schema of Treurinet [35]. In addition, the author described observations about the different types of scanning in six months of data from the UCSD Network Telescope [7]. Our work is complementary to the *iatmon* tool, as we focus on flow instead of packet-based classification. Besides, the work by Lee and Brownlee [26] used three one-day packet traces captured in 2000, 2003, and 2006 in the University of Auckland to analyze the lifetime and size distribution of one and two-way flows. In our work, we provide new insights into one-way flows based on a substantially larger trace and introduce novel methods to classify their causes. Allman *et al.* [3] used TCP connection logs from the Lawrence Berkeley National Laboratory collected between 1994 and 2006 to characterize how scanning changed over time. In addition, they correlated observed patterns to well-known malware activity. Our study follows on until 2011 and focuses primarily on how to classify one-way traffic. Jin *et al.* [17] used flow data towards grey IP space of a campus network and developed a heuristic to identify external scanners. We follow along this direction and highlight the need to classify one-way traffic and identify a number of different causes in addition to scanning. Guha *et al.* [13] characterized the fraction of useful flows generated by mobile hosts in an enterprise network and found that 34% of the flows fail mainly due to hosts mobility. Compared to this work, we focus on understanding the nature of incoming (instead of out-going) one-way traffic.

8.3 Network Outages

Many previous studies have developed techniques for detecting network outages caused by events like prefix hijacking using control plane data (e.g., BGP updates) [36, 8, 25], active probing with tools like traceroute and ping [40, 41], or both [14, 22, 23, 33].

Recently, two studies have provided first insights on using passive network traffic measurements, like NetFlow or packet traces, to detect and characterize network outages. In particular, Schatzmann *et al.* [32] described a flow-based approach to identify reachability problems in remote networks caused by events like prefix hijacking. Dainotti *et al.* [10] used IBR traffic to a /8 network telescope to characterize large-scale remote outages caused by earthquakes and country-wide censorship. Compared to these studies, we use IBR traffic towards a live network to detect and characterize fine-grained outages affecting local networked services.

9. CONCLUSIONS

One-way traffic towards live networks is an exotic piece of Internet traffic. In the past it has been primarily studied with the help of a small number of large network telescopes. Although network telescopes have been very useful for understanding Internet attacks and misconfigurations, only a very small number of telescopes have been available to researchers, while the exhaustion of the IPv4 address space is likely to further drain their availability.

To shed light into IBR traffic towards live networks, in this work we introduce a classification scheme for one-way traffic. Classifying one-way traffic based solely on flow-level data is very challenging as one-way flows contain very few packets often without any payload. To address these challenges, we design, carefully optimize, and validate 13 classification rules that leverage communication patterns of involved end hosts to classify one-way traffic. Our techniques are useful for monitoring IBR traffic in any edge network and therefore significantly broaden the availability of network telescopes. They are also useful to network operators for passively monitoring the reachability of local networked services and in particular for analyzing the impact of outages, which is not possible with existing service monitoring techniques based on active probing or server logs.

We use our classifier to analyze the composition of a massive dataset of traffic flow records from a regional backbone network and make the following key observations:

- One-way traffic makes between 34% and 67% of the total number of flows, although it only accounts for only 3.4% and 0.79% of the total number of packets and bytes, respectively.
- The main sources of one-way traffic are: 1) scanning, which accounts for 83.5% of the one-way flows and 62.6% of the one-way packets; 2) peer-to-peer applications, which account for 6.7% of the one-way flows and 13.0% of the one-way packets; and 3) unreachable services, which account for 4.8% of the one-way flows and 10.1% of the one-way packets.
- The fraction of one-way flows to the total number of flows has declined from 67% in 2004 to 34% in 2011.
- The number of two-way flows has grown significantly by 343% between 2004 and 2011. In contrast, the absolute volume of one-way flows in 2011 is almost equal to 2004.

Finally, we focus on the particularly interesting class of one-way traffic caused by unreachable services and show, using the network of ETH Zurich as a case study, how this class is very useful for detecting important network outages and for assessing their impact.

With this paper we make the code of our classification scheme publicly available [1]. In addition, to shed further light into the composition of one-way traffic and to facilitate correlating data from multiple IBR traffic monitors, we release non-sensitive details about the evolution of one-way and two-way traffic between 2004 and 2011 based on the studied datasets. In particular, for each 10-minute time interval, we make available statistics about the synthesis of one-way traffic, the popularity of different signs, the targeted services, and the geographical distribution of sources.

Acknowledgements

We are grateful to SWITCH for providing us precious data for studying one-way traffic. In addition, we are thankful to Dominik Schatzmann for helping with double-counting elimination and to Simon Leinen for providing us valuable feedback on service reachability monitoring. Lastly, we wish to acknowledge anonymous reviewers for their helpful comments and suggestions.

10. REFERENCES

[1] One-way Traffic Classification Website. `http://www.ow-class.ethz.ch/`.

[2] Akamai Technologies. The state of the internet report (3rd quarter, 2009). Technical report, 2009.

[3] M. Allman, V. Paxson, and J. Terrell. A brief history of scanning. In *Proceedings of the 7th ACM SIGCOMM conference on Internet measurement*, page 82. ACM, 2007.

[4] M. Bailey, E. Cooke, F. Jahanian, D. Watson, and J. Nazario. The blaster worm: Then and now. *IEEE Security and Privacy*, 3:26–31, July 2005.

[5] D. Brauckhoff, X. Dimitropoulos, A. Wagner, and K. Salamatian. Anomaly extraction in backbone networks using association rules. In *Proceedings of the 9th ACM SIGCOMM conference on Internet measurement conference*, IMC '09, pages 28–34, New York, NY, USA, 2009. ACM.

[6] N. Brownlee. One-way traffic monitoring with iatmon. In *Passive and Active Measurement Conference*, 2012.

[7] CAIDA. UCSD Network Telescope. `http://www.caida.org/data/realtime/telescope/`.

[8] Y.-J. Chi, R. Oliveira, and L. Zhang. Cyclops: the as-level connectivity observatory. *SIGCOMM Comput. Commun. Rev.*, 38(5), Sept. 2008.

[9] T. Cymru. The Bogon Reference. `http://www.team-cymru.org/Services/Bogons/`, 2012.

[10] A. Dainotti, R. Amman, E. Aben, and K. C. Claffy. Extracting benefit from harm: using malware pollution to analyze the impact of political and geophysical events on the internet. *SIGCOMM Comput. Commun. Rev.*, 42(1):31–39, 2012.

[11] Cooperative Network Security Community - Internet Security. `www.dshield.org`.

[12] E. Glatz and X. Dimitropoulos. Classifying internet one-way traffic. TIK-Report 336, ETH Zurich, May 2012.

[13] S. Guha, J. Chandrashekar, N. Taft, and K. Papagiannaki. How healthy are today's enterprise networks? In *Proceedings of the 8th ACM SIGCOMM conference on Internet measurement*, pages 145–150. ACM, 2008.

[14] X. Hu and Z. M. Mao. Accurate real-time identification of ip prefix hijacking. In *Proceedings of the 2007 IEEE Symposium on Security and Privacy*, SP '07, 2007.

[15] IANA - Internet Assigned Numbers Authority. PORT NUMBERS. `http://www.iana.org/assignments/port-numbers`, 2011.

[16] C. Inacio and B. Trammell. Yaf: yet another flowmeter. In *Proceedings of the 24th international conference on Large installation system administration*, pages 1–16. USENIX Association, 2010.

[17] Y. Jin, Z. Zhang, K. Xu, F. Cao, and S. Sahu. Identifying and tracking suspicious activities through IP gray space analysis. In *Proceedings of the 3rd annual ACM workshop on Mining network data*, page 12. ACM, 2007.

[18] W. John and S. Tafvelin. Heuristics to classify internet backbone traffic based on connection patterns. *International Conference on Information Networking (ICOIN)*, pages 1–5, 2008.

[19] J. Jung, V. Paxson, A. Berger, and H. Balakrishnan. Fast portscan detection using sequential hypothesis testing. In *Proceedings of the IEEE Symposium on Security and Privacy*, pages 211–225, 2004.

[20] T. Karagiannis, A. Broido, and M. Faloutsos. Transport layer identification of p2p traffic. *Proceedings of the 4th ACM SIGCOMM conference on Internet measurement*, pages 121–134, 2004.

[21] T. Karagiannis, K. Papagiannaki, and M. Faloutsos. Blinc: multilevel traffic classification in the dark. In *Proceedings of the 2005 conference on Applications, technologies, architectures, and protocols for computer communications*, SIGCOMM '05, 2005.

[22] E. Katz-Bassett, H. V. Madhyastha, J. P. John, A. Krishnamurthy, D. Wetherall, and T. Anderson. Studying black holes in the internet with hubble. In *Proceedings of the 5th USENIX Symposium on Networked Systems Design and Implementation*, NSDI'08, 2008.

[23] E. Katz-Bassett, C. Scott, D. R. Choffnes, I. Cunha, V. Valancius, N. Feamster, H. V. Madhyastha, T. Anderson, and A. Krishnamurthy. Lifeguard: practical repair of persistent route failures. In *Proceedings of the ACM SIGCOMM 2012*, 2012.

[24] H. Kim, K. Claffy, M. Fomenkov, D. Barman, M. Faloutsos, and K. Lee. Internet traffic classification demystified: myths, caveats, and the best practices. In *Proceedings of the 2008 ACM CoNEXT conference*, page 11. ACM, 2008.

[25] M. Lad, D. Massey, D. Pei, Y. Wu, B. Zhang, and L. Zhang. PHAS: A prefix hijack alert system. In *In Proc. USENIX Security Symposium*, 2006.

[26] D. Lee and N. Brownlee. Passive measurement of one-way and two-way flow lifetimes. *SIGCOMM Comput. Commun. Rev.*, 37(3):17–28, 2007.

[27] D. Moore, V. Paxson, S. Savage, C. Shannon, S. Staniford, and N. Weaver. Inside the slammer worm. *IEEE Security and Privacy*, 1:33–39, July 2003.

[28] D. Moore, C. Shannon, G. Voelker, and S. Savage. Network telescopes: Technical report. Technical report, CAIDA, 2004.

[29] D. Moore, G. M. Voelker, and S. Savage. Inferring internet denial-of-service activity. In *SSYM'01: Proceedings of the 10th conference on USENIX Security Symposium*, Berkeley, USA, 2001.

[30] R. Pang, V. Yegneswaran, P. Barford, V. Paxson, and L. Peterson. Characteristics of Internet background radiation. In *Proceedings of the 4th ACM SIGCOMM conference on Internet measurement*, pages 27–40. ACM New York, NY, USA, 2004.

[31] M. Perényi, T. D. Dang, A. Gefferth, and S. Molnr. Identification and analysis of peer-to-peer traffic. *JOURNAL OF COMMUNICATIONS*, 1(7), 2006.

[32] D. Schatzmann, S. Leinen, J. Kogel, and W. Muhlbauer. Fact: Flow-based approach for connectivity tracking. In *Passive and Active Measurement conference*, Mar. 2011.

[33] X. Shi, Y. Xiang, Z. Wang, X. Yin, and J. Wu.

Detecting prefix hijackings in the internet with argus. In *Proceedings of the 12th ACM SIGCOMM conference on Internet measurement*. ACM, 2012.

[34] B. Trammell and E. Boschi. Bidirectional flow export using IPFIX. RFC 5103, January 2008.

[35] J. Treurniet. A network activity classification schema and its application to scan detection. *IEEE/ACM Trans. Netw.*, 19(5):1396–1404, Oct. 2011.

[36] US Homeland Security. BGPmon. `http://bgpmon.net/`.

[37] Wikipedia. Netflow. `http://en.wikipedia.org/wiki/Netflow`.

[38] E. Wustrow, M. Karir, M. Bailey, F. Jahanian, and G. Huston. Internet background radiation revisited. In *Proceedings of the 10th annual conference on Internet measurement*, IMC '10, pages 62–74, New York, NY, USA, 2010. ACM.

[39] V. Yegneswaran, P. Barford, and J. Ullrich. Internet intrusions: global characteristics and prevalence. *SIGMETRICS Perform. Eval. Rev.*, 31(1):138–147, 2003.

[40] Z. Zhang, Y. Zhang, Y. C. Hu, Z. M. Mao, and R. Bush. ispy: detecting ip prefix hijacking on my own. *IEEE/ACM Trans. Netw.*, 18(6), Dec. 2010.

[41] C. Zheng, L. Ji, D. Pei, J. Wang, and P. Francis. A light-weight distributed scheme for detecting ip prefix hijacks in real-time. In *Proceedings of the 2007 conference on Applications, technologies, architectures, and protocols for computer communications*, SIGCOMM '07, 2007.

RasterZip: Compressing Network Monitoring Data with Support for Partial Decompression

Francesco Fusco
ETH Zurich
Switzerland
fusco@tik.ee.ethz.ch

Michail Vlachos
IBM Research - Zurich
Switzerland
mvl@zurich.ibm.com

Xenofontas Dimitropoulos
ETH Zurich
Switzerland
fontas@tik.ee.ethz.ch

ABSTRACT

Network traffic archival solutions are fundamental for a number of emerging applications that require: a) efficient storage of high-speed streams of traffic records and b) support for interactive exploration of massive datasets. Compression is a fundamental building block for any traffic archival solution. However, present solutions are tied to general-purpose compressors, which do not exploit patterns of network traffic data and require to decompress a lot of redundant data for high selectivity queries. In this work we introduce RasterZIP, a novel domain-specific compressor designed for network traffic monitoring data. RasterZIP uses an optimized lossless encoding that exploits patterns of traffic data, like the fact that IP addresses tend to share a common prefix. RasterZIP also introduces a novel decompression scheme that accelerates highly selective queries targeting a small portion of the dataset. With our solution we can achieve high-speed on-the-fly compression of more than half a million traffic records per second. We compare RasterZIP with the fastest Lempel-Ziv-based compressor and show that our solution improves the state-of-the-art both in terms of compression ratios and query response times without introducing penalty in any other performance metric.

Categories and Subject Descriptors

D.4.1 [**Data**]: Coding and Information Theory— *Data compaction and compression*

General Terms

Algorithms

Keywords

Network monitoring, network traffic archives, data compression, NetFlow

IMC'12, November 14–16, 2012, Boston, Massachusetts, USA.

1. INTRODUCTION

In many network monitoring tasks, it would be extremely useful to "travel back in time" and trace the causal nexus of events that led to important outcomes, like failures or security breaches. For this reason, an increasing number of applications need to efficiently search massive network traffic archives. For example, when a breach of credit card numbers is detected, analysts strive to find past traffic connections that are linked to the adversarial action to determine which systems and data were affected. Large-scale traffic repositories are also vital for network operators in validating claims against Service Level Agreements (SLAs), for scientists in studying Internet traffic, and for law enforcement agencies in lawful interception. All these applications need to support very efficient drill-down queries to find "needles in a haystack".

In the context of long term traffic archiving, compression is an essential enabling technology. It substantially reduces the size of an archive, while it directly relates with the efficiency of drill-down queries. Domain-optimized compression technologies have been researched, developed and sometimes standardized in several information technology fields, including, but not limited to bioinformatics [6, 21], biochemistry, and web information retrieval [26]. Previous experience shows that substantial gains can be obtained by designing compressors tailored to the data and requirements posed by specific domains.

In contrast, the de-facto approach to reduce the volume of network traffic repositories consists of applying general-purpose compression utilities, such as *gzip*, *bzip2*, and *lzop* [12, 17]. However, general-purpose compressors present limitations when used in the context of large-scale traffic repositories. The main shortcoming is that network traffic data archives exhibit distinct data patterns and pose specific requirements, which are not taken into account and exploited by general-purpose compressors.

In particular, the values stored in a traffic archive often share a common prefix (e.g., first few bits of IP addresses and timestamps), typically lie within a particular range (e.g., port numbers and protocols), and exhibit a large number of repetitions within a relatively short time window. A compressor optimized for network traffic data should exploit these patterns to *substantially reduce data volumes.*

Second, traffic data have to be compressed without introducing severe performance penalties when performing drill-down operations. Therefore, supporting efficient data retrieval from large-scale compressed repositories is necessary. Traffic archival solutions should provide mechanisms enabling *selective, fine-grained and high-speed* data decompression operations that minimize the amount of redundant data to be decompressed, especially in the case of drill-down operations targeting a small subset of the collected data. In contrast, general purpose compressors are optimized for compressing data in large blocks, which need to be retrieved, and fully decompressed, even for queries targeting a small part of the datasets.

Third, traffic archival solutions need to handle high rates of input streams, which are only expected to increase in the future. For example, present commercial flow collectors are designed to process up to hundreds of thousands flow records per second [1]. However, even higher rates can be observed caused by denial of service attacks, oversubscription of streams from many probes to a single collector or very high traffic rates on gateway routers of large institutions. Therefore, a compression algorithm designed for network traffic archival solutions has to provide *high-speed compression* of data streams.

Our work introduces 'RasterZip', a compressor optimized for the requirements and data patterns of network traffic archives. RasterZip compresses blocks of homogeneous network attribute types. It intelligently combines and adapts a number of compression techniques to exploit the *shared prefixes*, *bounded ranges*, and *frequent value repetitions* commonly observed in network traffic attributes. RasterZip first homogenizes each block based on a transposition that exploits the prefix structure and bounded range of traffic attributes and finally compresses it using an efficient online run-length encoding (RLE). Our encoding can sustain high-speed (de)compression exploiting features of modern CPUs instruction sets. More importantly, RasterZip introduces a novel decompression scheme based on **partial and adaptive decompression** to accelerate highly selective queries. With partial decompression, attribute values stored at specified positions can be retrieved from a RasterZip-compressed data block without requiring the entire block to be decompressed. Our adaptive decompression scheme dynamically selects at runtime between full or partial decompression based on a very light-weight decision classifier that predicts which strategy is expected to be the fastest.

We conduct an extensive evaluation of RasterZip using traffic traces from two different networks. The results show that: first, RasterZip can reach stream compression rates of more than half a million traffic flows per second, which is in par with the fastest general-purpose compressor (*lzop*). Second, decompression speed is better than *lzop*, which is one of the fastest decompressors. Third, RasterZip produces significantly more compact archives than *lzop*. Our experiments suggests an expected data reduction of approximately 22-24%. This directly suggests that compared to the state-of-the-art high-speed compressor, RasterZip reduces storage expenses for network traffic archives by an analogous amount.

In summary, our work makes the following contributions:

- **Domain-Specific Compressor.** RasterZip leverages network data patterns; enables interactive queries over archived data; supports online high-speed stream compression; and exploits features of modern hardware.
- **Novel Decompression.** RasterZip introduces a novel decompression scheme that provides fine-grained decompression granularity at the attribute level in order to accelerate queries for "needles in a haystack".
- **Outperform General-Purpose Compression.** Compared to the widely-used state-of-the-art *lzop* compressor, RasterZip accelerates queries, reduces expenses for storage by 22-24% due to more compact compression, and does not incur any penalty.

Although our design is focused on network traffic data, there are several monitoring domains and applications that demonstrate similar traits (shared prefixes, bounded data-ranges, and frequent data repetitions), and, therefore, can also benefit from our compressor. For example, data centers and cloud computing environments typically produce voluminous monitoring data to capture environmental (e.g. temperature) and performance metrics [12]. Such resource monitoring streams inherently contain numerous repetitions and shared prefixes and therefore can also benefit from RasterZip.

The remainder of the paper is structured as follows. In Section 2, we describe common strategies, recent trends and unsolved challeges in archiving network traffic flow records. Section 3 describes the internals of RasterZip. We evaluate our compressor in Section 5 and we discuss the cost of storage for large-scale traffic archives in Section 7. Finally, Section 8 concludes our paper.

2. BACKGROUND ON FLOW RECORD ARCHIVING AND SCOPE OF WORK

Modern network infrastructures come with built-in traffic monitoring functionalities. Switches and routers are equipped with embedded meters, referred to as *flow meters*, that analyze the network traffic to produce network flow records, which are then sent towards a centralized flow collector using an export protocol, such as Cisco's NetFlow [7]. A network flow is typically defined as the set of packets that have five header fields in common: source and destination IP addresses, source and destination port numbers, and the layer-4 protocol. Flow records carry detailed statistics describing each observed network flow, such as transferred bytes, number of packets, TCP flags, and timestamps.

Flow record analysis has many applications, including billing [10], traffic engineering [11], and anomaly detection [20]. Large-scale historical network flow record repositories are also used for forensics operations, for intrusion detection, and for conducting long-term network traffic studies. Such applications require flow storage infrastructures capable of storing high-speed data streams in a compressed format, while enabling highly efficient drill-down operations.

Existing Relational Database Management Systems (RDBMSs) present severe performance degradations when dealing with multi-gigabyte datasets [18] and offer limited support for data compression. A more commonly used strategy for collecting flow records consists of storing flow records or even *raw* NetFlow packets on disk as multiple files. This approach provides significantly higher insertion rates than RDBMSs, and allows users to compress their repositories using off-the-shelf general-purpose compression utilities. In this way, however, accessing the data involves time consuming decompression operations. NfDump [17], a widely-used flow processing tool, trades compression ratios for decompression speed by compressing data with the general-purpose compression utility *lzop* (based on the LZO algorithm), which is up to five times faster in decompression than *gzip*, but provides lower compression ratios [25].

Recent research has shown that advances in database technologies, stream compression and stream indexing, enable the development of more advanced flow record storage infrastructures that are more effective in compressing data and that are more suitable for drill-down operations.

- *Columnar databases* have been identified as a significantly better alternative to relational databases in the context of flow record collection [9, 14, 16]. By storing distinct attributes of flow records as separate physical columns, columnar databases offer better opportunities for compression [2] and are suited for queries that are highly selective at the attribute level (e.g., for queries that require just a few fields of a flow record to be accessed). These queries are common for after-the-fact analysis, where network operators are rarely interested in accessing the entire set of flow record attributes.

- *Compressed bitmap indexes* have been shown to be effective for indexing network traffic attributes [9, 13, 3]. They are a companion technology of columnar databases. Given a columnar database with k rows, a bitmap index is a binary array of length k that indicates the row positions, where an attribute assumes a specific value, e.g., `srcPort=443`. Bitmap indexes are intelligently compressed to allow for performing boolean operations in the compressed space between multiple compressed bitmap indexes. This enables to efficiently support multi-attribute queries, e.g., `srcPort=`X `AND srcIP=`Y, by combining the compressed bitmap indexes corresponding to columns of distinct attributes. Given a single- or multi-attribute query, compressed bitmap indexing enables to find very fast the n ($n \leq k$) row positions j_1 .. j_n that match the query. Compared to tree-based indexes (e.g., B-Trees), compressed bitmap indexes: i) are more compact, ii) provide high-speed indexing and iii) are optimized for read-only data. If data columns are compressed in small data blocks, the matching row positions can be exploited to selectively decompress the data blocks that store the requested data. This capability is very desirable for accelerating drill-down queries targeting a small portion of the dataset.

- *Stream-based reordering techniques* have been proposed in the context of network flow record collection to introduce better opportunities for compression [14]. The techniques profit from the fact that it is not necessary to strictly order flow records by time. Therefore, the order of incoming flow records can be altered to improve their compression.

In our previous work [14], we introduced a flow-record reordering technique, called online Locality Sensitive Hashing (**oLSH**), which is optimized for columnar databases. oLSH treats each multi-attribute flow-record as a multi-dimensional numerical vector and uses Locality Sensitive Hash functions [8] to bring flow records that are close to each other according to their euclidean distance to nearby stream positions.

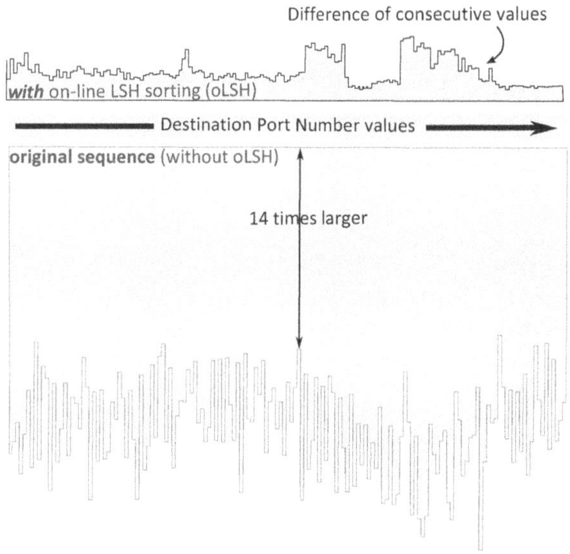

Figure 1: Effect of record reordering on column data homogenity. Storing the streaming records without reordering (bottom) results in a difference of consecutive values that is up to 14 times larger than when the online-LSH approach is used (top).

Figure 1 illustrates an example of the benefits of oLSH, which is described in detail in [14]. For one hour of network traffic we create a columnar archive for a multi-attribute flow record stream with and without the oLSH reordering enabled. For the destination port attribute, we compute the sum of differences between consecutive values for fixed-size blocks. The unordered stream shown on the bottom depicts significantly lower homogeneity: the cumulative difference between consecutive values is up to 14 times larger compared to the reordered stream using oLSH on top. It is evident that the reordering process is very effective in clustering values that belong to *adjacent ranges* and, thus, that share *common prefixes*.

In our previous work [14], we have also shown that by applying this transformation to a flow-record stream, the performance of the speed-optimized compressor LZO used to compress individual attributes separately in a columnar manner is substantially improved and in fact, LZO can match *gzip* in terms of compression ratio, while providing substantially higher decompression speed.

The main goal and outcome of our research (illustrated in Figure 2) is to move beyond general-purpose compressors by designing a domain-optimized compression algorithm that offers better compression ratios than *gzip* and *bzip2* while at least matching LZO, which was used in our previous work [14], both in terms of compression and decompression speed in the context of flow record archival.

Compared to general-purpose compressors, our compressor can fully profit from recent advances in flow record collection research including columnar databases, compressed bitmap indexes and stream-based flow record sorting techniques:

1. It is designed to exploit specific data patterns commonly present in network traffic attributes.

2. It is optimized for compressing data columns of colum-

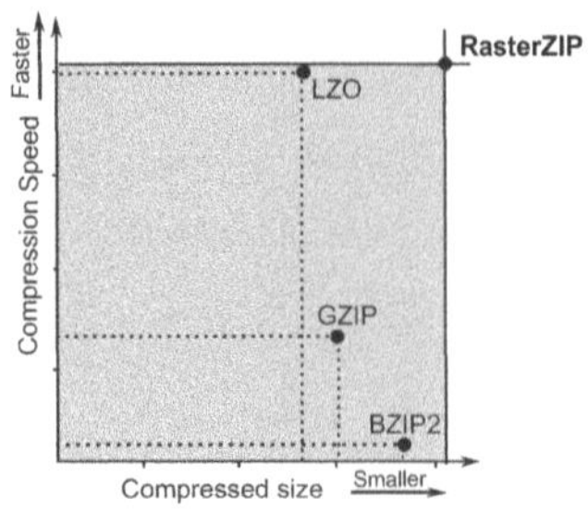

Figure 2: RasterZip versus general-purpose compressors.

nar databases in small data blocks allowing fine-grained decompression operations.

3. It can exploit bitmap indexes to retrieve attribute values stored at specific positions from a compressed block without performing a full decompression.

3. RASTERZIP COMPRESSION

RasterZip is a block-based compressor optimized for small data blocks intended to be used in columnar-databases. This means that the compression routine operates on blocks of *homogeneous* attribute values (e.g., timestamps). Our compressor has been designed to leverage the common prefix structure that is present in many network attributes (e.g., timestamps) and also produced by the oLSH transformation. RasterZip takes as input a column, e.g., of IP addresses, and *scans its bytes column-wise* (as shown in Figure 3) to take advantage of the observation that in this manner adjacent bytes are often identical. The column-wise order forms the input to our compressor, which is based on *run-length encoding* (RLE) principles. We call the new compression algorithm *RasterZip*, because we scan data in a raster-like fashion. In this section, we describe our compression techniques in detail.

3.1 Overview

The compression routine receives as input data blocks of homogeneous attribute values. Each block consists of m values of size n bytes. In our setting n corresponds, for example, to two bytes for port numbers, or four bytes for IPv4 addresses. Each data block of every attribute is treated as an $m \times n$ matrix of bytes, stored in row-major order.

Traditional data archiving approaches process the data row by row for reasons of efficiency and simplicity. Because of the data reordering, consecutive row-records share similar/adjacent values and hence have common prefixes. RasterZip compresses data efficiently by processing them column by column, where each cell represents one byte of the currently processed data attribute. This conceptual and practical distinction of our approach is shown in Figure 3. Note, that since rows share common prefixes, we expect very high compression for the first byte-columns. For the last byte-columns where higher variability is generally observed, lower compression ratios are to be expected.

Based on the above discussion, compression consists of two logical steps. First, the matrix is logically transposed and then the resulting matrix is traversed row-by-row to compress long sequences of repeated symbols. We provide

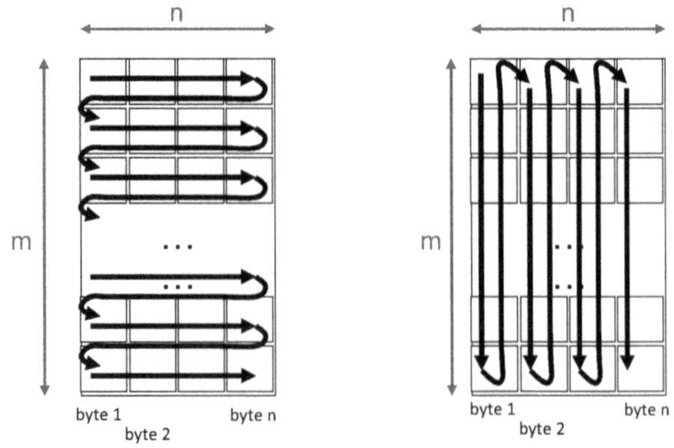

Figure 3: Left: Traditional compression approaches process data bytes in a row-wise fashion. Right: RasterZip scans the data bytes of an attribute in a columnar manner, in order to exploit the prefix structure of the input data.

an in-depth description of the two steps and the resulting encoding.

1. **Transposition.** The $m \times n$ matrix is transposed, i.e., the ith row becomes the ith column for all $i \in \{1, \ldots, m\}$. Given that the first bytes of subsequent data items (i.e., subsequent entries in each of the first few columns in the original matrix) are often the same, transposing the matrix creates rows with many identical bytes in a row. As a small example, given an input of three IPv4 addresses (3×4 byte matrix), stored in memory as

   `10.4.20.22|10.4.20.23|10.4.21.24`

   the transposition yields the following representation:

   `10.10.10.4.4.4.20.20.21.22.23.24`

   This transformation results in long sequences of identical bytes not only for IP addresses, but also for other fields such as timestamps, flow duration, and so on.

   We emphasize, that the above *transposition* is merely logical. One does not need to carry out the matrix transposition, but only traverse the data in a different order.

2. **Repeated symbol compression**: RasterZip efficiently compresses long sequences of repeated symbols (runs) using a technique based on run-length encoding (RLE) principles. RLE encodes the input stream as a list of pairs (r, l) where r is the symbol and l is the length. For example, RLE encodes the sequence 9,9,9,4,4,4,3 as (9,3),(4,3),(3,1).

   RasterZip encodes runs in a more structured and efficient way that provides higher decompression performance compared to the standard RLE encoding, *particularly when highly compressible and incompressible content are interleaved in the input stream.* In addition, our encoding has been designed to enable random access on the compressed data. This is particularly useful for supporting partial data decompression.

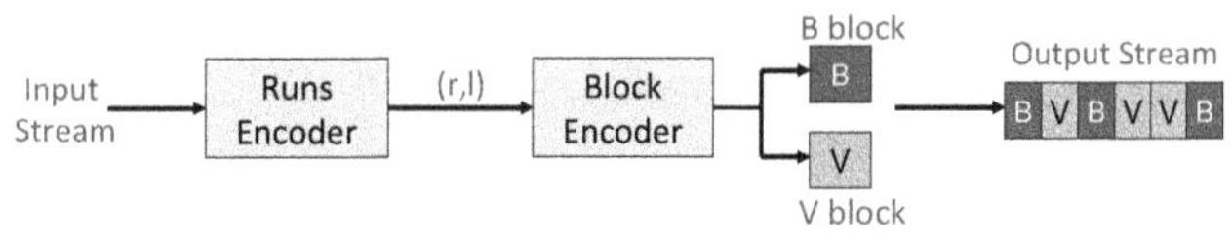

Figure 4: Flowgraph of RasterZip compression. Sequences of repeated symbols in the input stream are detected by the Runs Encoder and encoded as Bitmap (`B`) or Verbatim (`V`) blocks by the Block Encoder.

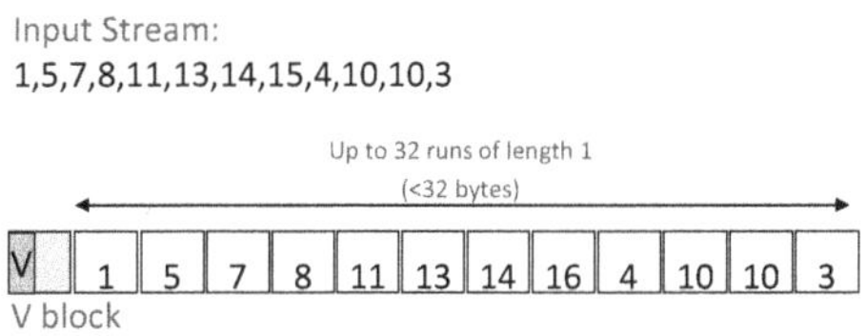

Figure 5: V-blocks are used to store content that is incompressible with RLE. V blocks store value repetitions of length 1. Runs of length 2 are split in two runs of length 1.

Figure 4 depicts a flowgraph of the compressor. The input stream for the compressor is the matrix given in column-major order. This is the currently processed data window, representing the output of the online-LSH component. The *Runs Encoder* scans the input stream and outputs to the *Block Encoder* pairs of the form (r, l) representing sequences of repeated symbols. The *Block Encoder* groups together runs in multiples of 32 and encodes each group by dynamically selecting between two different subblock types: a `Verbatim (V) block` and a `Bitmap (B) block`, which are described in the next section.

3.2 The Encoding

The encoding includes two different block types: `Verbatim (V) blocks` store RLE-incompressible content whereas `Bitmap (B) blocks` store RLE-compressible content.[1] Specifically:

1. **V-blocks** store a group of up to 32 runs whose length is exactly one. Runs of length 2 are stored as two runs of length 1 (i.e., the block encoder never receives runs of length 2 from the runs encoder). Therefore, such a block stores data that is hard to compress using RLE. A one-byte header is prepended. The header specifies the block type using 1 bit (i.e. that it is a `V-block`) and the number of runs which are stored in the block using five bits ($2^5 = 32$ runs). Because this block-type only stores runs of length 1, lengths need not be explicitly stored. Figure 5 depicts how an incompressible input stream is encoded with a `V-block`.

2. **B-blocks** encode up to 32 runs where at least one run has length greater than 1. `B-blocks` consist of:

   - A *header* (1 byte) specifying the block type and the number of runs (similarly to `V-blocks`).

[1]A block of attribute values is encoded into multiple subblocks of type `V` or `B`. The terms `V-block` and `B-block` refer to subblocks. The proper interpretation of the term block should be clear from the context.

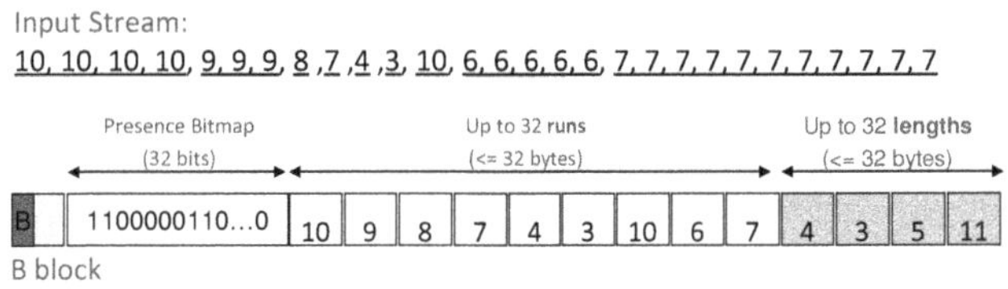

Figure 6: B-blocks store RLE-compressible content. B blocks encode up to 32 consecutive runs where at least one run has a length greater than 1. Only lengths greater than 1 are explicitly stored.

   - A *presence bitmap* (32 bits) indicating which runs have length greater than 1.
   - A *Runs part* storing up to 32 runs.
   - A *Lengths part* storing up to 32 lengths.

   Therefore, unlike plain RLE, RasterZip does not store runs and lengths as pairs. Instead, runs are stored sequentially, followed by the sequence of the corresponding lengths. The reason for this becomes apparent in the following, where we describe how the `V-` and `B-blocks` are created in an online fashion.

   Note that a `B-block` stores mixed content of compressible and incompressible content. In fact, the presence bitmap (32 bits) exactly indicates which of the runs have length greater than 1. Recall that runs of length 2 are always treated as 2 consecutive runs of length 1. So, length is only explicitly stored for runs with length greater than 2. This is indicated by setting the corresponding bit in the presence bitmap to one.

   An example of a `B-block` is given in Figure 6. For the initial sequences of 10's and 9's the lengths are explicitly stored (4 and 3, respectively), whereas for the singular values that follow, no explicit length is recorded. This is captured in the presence bitmap, by setting the appropriate bits to 1 or 0.

   We also emphasize that, having allocated one byte for each length, we could have represented sequences of up to $2^8 = 256$ consecutive identical symbols. However, by not storing explicitly lengths 1 and 2, we can increase the maximum sequence length that can be represented to 258. In fact, since runs of length 1 are just marked in the bitmap and runs of length 2 are always treated as two runs of length 1, each length-byte in the `B-block` can store lengths in the range $[3, 258]$. This allows us to pack long sequences of the same symbol even more effectively.

Online Blocks Creation Now we describe how the two types of blocks can be created by the Block Encoder in a streaming fashion. First, note that a `V-block` can be treated as a special case of a `B-block`, as it is a `B-block` whose presence bitmap does not have any bits set to 1. Therefore, the block creation always commences by assuming that the current block is a `B-block`. Whenever a run of length greater than 2 is observed, the presence bitmap is updated and the corresponding length is appended as well. After 32 runs are processed, we check whether the completed block contains at least one run of length greater than 2 by examining if at least one bit is set in the presence bitmap. In that case, the block is finalized and a new `B-block` is created. Otherwise, the presence bitmap is dropped and the block is changed into a `V-block` by simply flipping the first bit in the header byte. Pseudocode of this process is given in Algorithm 1.

Algorithm 1 Compress(input)

```
Input: Uncompressed input stream
Output: Compressed output stream
{split runs of length two}
while (r, l) := getNextRun(input) do
  {Update the bitmap}
  if l > 1 then
    set_bit(bitmap, curr_run)
    lengths[curr_len++] := l
  end if
  {Add the current run}
  runs[curr_run++] := r
  if curr_run = 32 then
    {Output a V or a B block}
    if bitmap = 0 then
      h := create_header(V, curr_run)
      output.appendHeader(h)
      output.appendBytes(runs, curr_run)
    else
      h := create_header(B, curr_run)
      output.appendHeader(h)
      output.appendBitmap(bitmap)
      output.appendBytes(runs, curr_run)
      output.appendBytes(lengths, curr_len)
    end if
    curr_run := 0
    curr_len := 0
    bitmap := 0
  end if
end while
```

3.3 Encoding properties and advantages

The proposed encoding presents several desirable properties with an emphasis on exploiting features of modern CPU architectures for enhanced performance. In particular RasterZip provides:

▪ **Low memory footprint during compression**: Through the whole compression process, the algorithm is only required to allocate memory for a single RasterZip sub-block. A sub-block is very small: at most 69 bytes (header + bitmap + runs + lengths = 1 + 4 + 32 + 32). We also note that the average sub-block size is even smaller in practice. We observed an average of 40 bytes in our experiments. The cache-line size on modern processors is 64 bytes; therefore, at most 2 cache-lines are used during the compression. This leads to a low number of cache-misses and enhanced performance of the proposed compression algorithm. In contrast, popular compression algorithms, such as the Lempel-Ziv based compression schemes, use hash tables or dictionaries to store previously seen data [23], and as such, result in many cache misses in practice.

▪ **Efficient handling of incompressible content**: RasterZip encodes data that is hard to compress using RLE (i.e., the length of each run is less than 3) with a `V-block`. This block-type enables fast decompression of incompressible data, because decompressing a `V-block` merely requires copying up to 32 bytes to the output, which can be implemented using the *memcpy()* function. On the contrary, decompressing hard to compress data encoded with the original RLE encoding requires a *conditional branch* (if statement) for every symbol, even if the length is as short as 1 or 2.

The next two points show how RasterZip exploits features offered by modern CPU architectures. These characteristics are useful primarily during the decompression process, as they allow the efficient traversal of RLE subblocks and the computation of the *span* of each subblock.

▪ **Fast traversing of compressed data**: The simple structure of `V` and `B` blocks allows compressed data to be traversed quickly. A `V-block` storing n runs always consists of $1+n$ bytes, and n can be read from the first byte after masking the three most significant bits to 0. Similarly, the size of a `B-block` is $1+4+n+b$ bytes, where b corresponds to the number of bits set to one in the bitmap. The value of b can be efficiently computed using specialized *bit counting* instructions offered on modern processors. For example, Intel introduced POPCNT to the SSE4.2 instruction sets, which offers a dedicated assembly instruction to perform the bit counting operation.[2]

▪ **Efficient computation of the block span**: given a block, its *span* is the number of bytes of uncompressed data stored in it. For both block types, the span can be efficiently computed: the span of a `V-block` is the number of runs that it stores. Computing the span of a `B-block` requires summing up the lengths greater than 2 and adding the number of runs with length 1. More formally:

$$Span_B = (n-b) + \sum_{i=1}^{b} l[i]$$

where n is the number of runs, b denotes the number of bits set to 1 in the bitmap, and $l[i]$ is the length of the ith run whose length exceeds 2. Since b is at most 32, and therefore the array of lengths cannot be longer than 32, it is possible to *unroll the loop* for this computation using a switch statement with 32 entries. This optimization enables the fast computation of the block span, which is an essential component of the decompression process.

Additional properties of the encoding scheme: The described encoding represents runs in batches of 32. However, the number of runs encoded in `V-` or `B-blocks` is in principle a tunable parameter[3]. In practice, there are trade-offs to be considered: i) a smaller number of runs corresponds to finer-grained decompression granularity and lower performance when copying individual `V-blocks` to the output, and, ii) a larger number of runs favors `B-` over `V-blocks`, making the compressor less capable of mixing RLE-compressible and incompressible content efficiently. We fix the number of runs to 32, which resulted to be a good compromise between compression ratio and decompression performance.

[2]Modern compilers, such as GCC, offer the intrinsic function *__builtin_bitcount(unsigned int)* for using POPCNT in C. The *-msse4* compilation flag instructs the GNU GCC compiler to use the POPCNT instruction.

[3]The 1-byte header of both `V-` and `B-blocks` can be accommodated for up to 128 runs by using 7 instead of 5 bits to store the number of runs belonging to the block ($2^7 = 128$ runs). In the case of `B-blocks` the maximum number of runs has to be the same as the length, expressed in bits, of the presence bitmap.

4. DECOMPRESSION

Recall that for a certain attribute, a columnar archive contains multiple RasterZip-compressed blocks, which in turn are made of multiple RLE-subblocks (`V` or `B`). At runtime, user queries are evaluated using an index (e.g., a compressed bitmap index), which returns the row positions that match within the data column. Therefore, the query processor receives as input a list of row positions from which it determines the blocks that need to be decompressed.

The row positions list also specifies the positions of the attribute values stored by a specific RasterZip-compressed block that belongs to the result set. Compared to general-purpose compressors, our approach can exploit this information to provide partial data decompression: it decompresses only the RLE subblocks that are part of the result set.

We first start by examining two block decompression strategies: a *full decompression* and a *partial decompression*. The latter approach decompresses only the RLE-subblocks that contain parts of the result set. Intuitively the first approach is better when a block contains many results; the second approach when only few results need to be retrieved. Finally, we show how to adaptively select between full and partial decompression at runtime. We introduce an adaptive decompression component that intelligently shifts between full- or partial decompression, according to which approach is expected to result in lower decompression time.

4.1 Full-Decompression (FD)

Assume that a compressed block is marked for decompression because it contains results for a given query. The block contains m data items each with size of n bytes and the index shows the row positions $r_1, \ldots, r_k$ $(k \leq m)$ within the block. The Full-Decompression strategy is shown in Figure 7. It decompresses the entire block (i.e., all RLE-subblocks) which is then stored in column-major order. Block transposition back to row-major order does not need to be performed, because the required data rows can be retrieved directly, as we explain below.

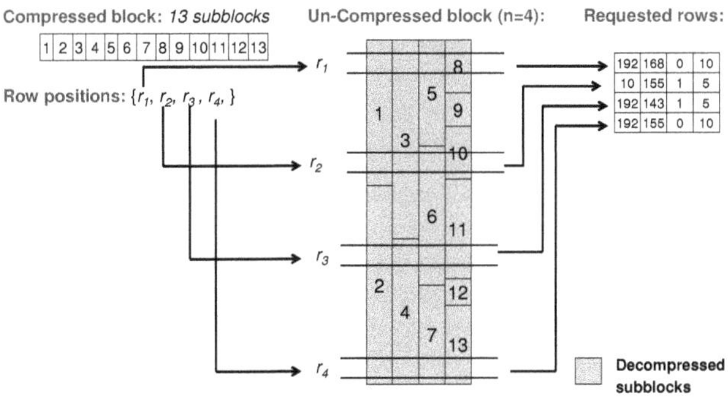

Figure 7: Full-Decompression (FD) decompresses the entire set of RLE subblocks and then uses the row positions to compute the indices of the bytes that need to be retrieved in the uncompressed matrix stored in column-major order.

Consider each decompressed archive block as an $m \times n$ matrix. Each required row position r can be retrieved by accessing the bytes at the offsets $r, r+m, .., r+(n-1)m$, since the offset between the bytes that belong to a certain row is exactly m.

An example of the retrieval procedure is given in Figure 8, which on the left illustrates a block with three IPv4 addresses and 4 bytes per row. Because the decompressed matrix is in column-major order, as shown in the right of Figure 8, to access a row r at position x, the decompressor traverses the data every 4 bytes at offsets: $x, x+4, x+8, x+12$.

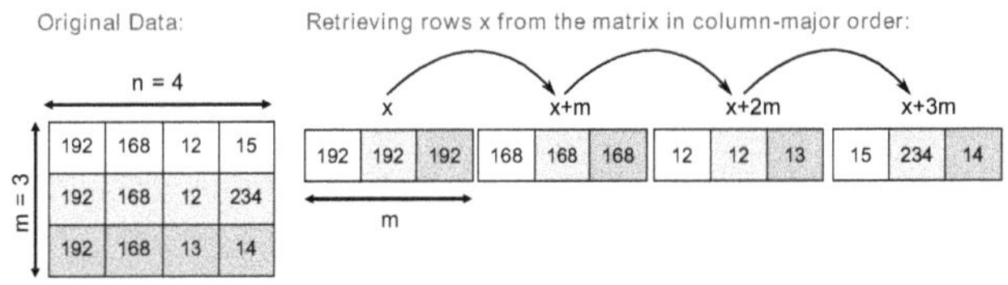

Figure 8: The row at position x from a 3×4 matrix stored in column-major order is retrieved by accessing the four bytes at the offsets $x, x+m, x+2m, x+3m$.

4.2 Partial-Decompression (PD)

The Full-Decompression decompresses all RLE-subblocks, even if they contain no results. Partial-Decompression decompresses only subblocks that contain query results. An illustration of this approach is given in Figure 9.

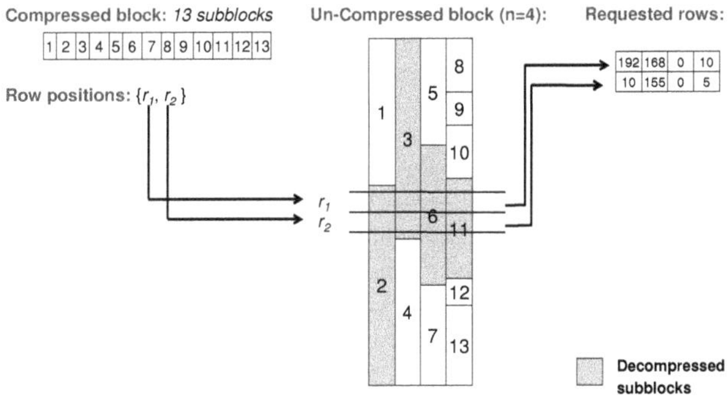

Figure 9: Partial Decompression (PD) decompress only RLE subblocks containing at least a byte that is required for retrieving the requested rows.

The partial decompression algorithm first calculates the set of offsets O in the matrix (stored in column-major order) that should be accessed to retrieve the requested rows. The offsets O are used to determine whether an RLE-subblock (`V-` or `B-block`) must be decompressed: a subblock b that compresses the matrix byte offset i to j needs to be decompressed if there is an offset $k \in O$, where $i \leq k \leq j$. The decompressor can efficiently find which subblocks need to be decompressed using the procedure we outline below. After decompressing the required subblocks, the requested rows are extracted using the same byte-traversal technique described for the Full-Decompression. The process described above is summarized in Algorithm 2.

Implementing Partial-Decompression: A naive approach to determine which RLE-subblock needs to be decompressed is to test, for each subblock, whether it contains at least one byte of the rows in the query (line 6 of Algorithm 2). For this purpose, we need to compute the *subblock range*, which is the range of byte offsets stored in an RLE subblock. If the span of a subblock is σ and the sum of the

Algorithm 2 PartialDecompress($Rows$, B, n)

Input: A list of row positions $Rows$
A compressed block B
The size n of each attribute value

Output: The attribute values stored in the requested row positions

$O := \emptyset$ ◁ start with an empty set of offsets

foreach $r \in Rows$ ◁ build the set of offsets
  $O := O \cup$ getOffsets(r, n)

foreach $b \in SubBlocks(B)$ ◁ linear subblock scan
  $(i, j) :=$ subBlockRange(b)
  if $\exists\, k \in O : k \leq j \wedge k \geq i$ **then**
    decompressSubBlock(b, i, $output$)
  end if
    {Byte-traversal technique as in Figure 8}
return retrieveRowsFromColunMajor($Rows$,$output$,n)

spans of the preceding subblocks is S, then the range of a subblock is $[S{+}1, S{+}\sigma]$. Recall that the RasterZip encoding allows to efficiently compute the span of a subblock. In order to test whether a sublock range contains a byte of a queried row, the naive approach would require to map the offsets of the queried row bytes into the transposed matrix and then to test each subblock. If at least one of the new offsets lies in the range between $S+1$ and $S+\sigma$, then the corresponding subblock should be decompressed. This naive strategy is very simple, but requires many comparisons. In practice, it leads to very slow performance. Even if only a small fraction of rows have to be extracted, the decompression speed is considerably worse than performing a full-decompression.

We next describe a practical and efficient implementation of Algorithm 2 that uses a fixed amount of memory to store the set of offsets and substantially reduces the number of needed comparisons. The main idea of the implementation is to represent the set of offsets as a bitmap instead of a list of integers. Each bitmap entry corresponds to a certain range of bytes. A bitmap entry is set to 1 if and only if at least one byte in the corresponding range belongs to one of the queried rows. In the next paragraph, we describe the technique in more detail.

The transposed $m \times n$ matrix (in column-major order) is partitioned into s fixed size cells, where s is a small constant. Intuitively, a grid of s slots is logically superimposed on the matrix. A bitmap of length s, called *grid bitmap*, is used to mark each cell that contains at least one byte that is part of the query result (see Figure 10 where $s = 16$). Given the set of rows to be retrieved, the bits that need to be set to 1 can be determined very efficiently. First, the offsets of the desired row bytes are mapped into the transposed matrix. The mapped offsets are (still) in the range $[1, m \cdot n]$. Then, by linearly rescaling the offsets in the range $[1, s]$ we find the positions of the grid bitmap that need to be set.

Given the grid bitmap, it can be determined efficiently whether a subblock needs to be decompressed: its subblock range simply needs to be linearly rescaled as well by a factor of $s/(mr)$. If any bit is set in the grid bitmap in this rescaled range, the block needs to be decompressed. This process can exploit the bit counting assembly instruction and does not need any comparisons. The number s of cells is a tunable parameter that allows to trade off precision for performance. More detailed grids (i.e. with larger values of s) are more

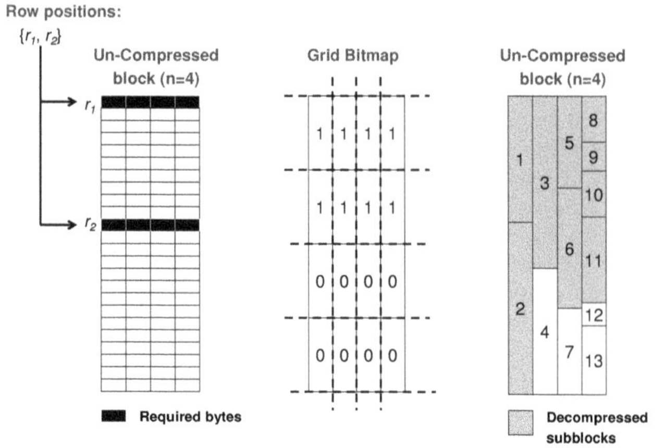

Figure 10: A Grid Bitmap is used to partition the uncompressed $m \times n$ matrix into 16 distinct cells ($s = 4 \times 4$). Given a query, the bit corresponding to each cell is set to 1 if there is at least a byte in the cell that has to be retrieved from the compressed data. A subblock has to be decompressed if and only if it overlaps with a cell that has been marked with a 1 in the corresponding Grid Bitmap.

precise in estimating the subblocks to be decompressed, but require more space to be stored, and consequently, are slower to query in average due to cache misses.

4.3 Adaptive Block Decompression

We have so far described two algorithms for block decompression. In this section we examine how to *adaptively* choose between the two algorithms at runtime. Partial decompression is preferred when a small fraction of RLE-subblocks need to be decompressed. Otherwise, the cost for computing the span of multiple RLE-subblocks makes full decompression a better strategy.

We introduce an adaptive decompression component that uses two runtime parameters, namely the *selectivity* of a query (within a block) and the *compression ratio* of a block, to predict which decompression strategy will result in faster decompression. Below, we describe how the two parameters relate to the decompression strategy:

- **Selectivity**: If the selectivity within a block is low (i.e., a large fraction of rows have to be retrieved), then many RLE subblocks need to be decompressed. In this case, full-decompression is preferable. In contrast, for high selectivity queries, a small fraction of subblocks is decompressed. In this case partial-decompression is faster.

- **Compression ratio**: The compression ratio is defined as the ratio between the size of the compressed data and the size of data before compression [23]. When the compression is better (lower compression ratio), then a block is compressed into fewer RLE-subblocks, and a larger fraction of the subblocks needs to be decompressed. Therefore, better compressed blocks benefit more from full decompression. Conversely, when RasterZip achieves worse compression ratios, a small fraction of RLE-subblocks have to be decompressed.

The selectivity of a query and the compression ratio of a block largely determine the fraction of RLE-subblocks that need to be decompressed and therefore can be used to predict which of the two strategies will perform better. In addition, the selectivity (s) and compression ratio (c) can be *efficiently computed at runtime before accessing the compressed subblocks.* We exploit these two parameters to build an *adaptive decompression component* shown in Figure 11. The adaptive decompression component accepts as input a compressed block b and a set R of row positions and, then, it uses a model to decide if partial or full decompression will provide a lower response time.

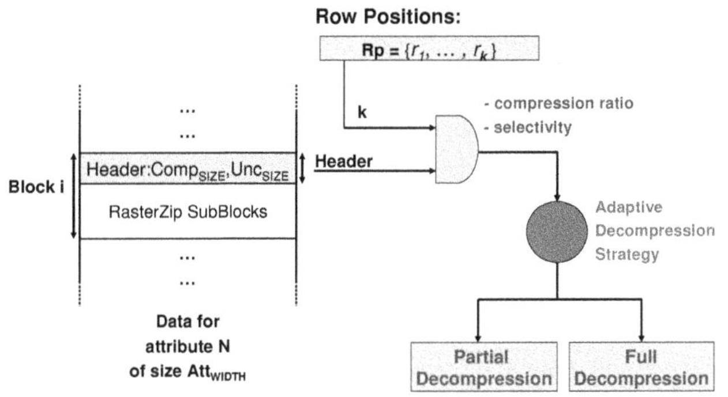

Figure 11: The adaptive decompression component decides at runtime the more efficient decompression strategy (partial or full) to be used for answering a query where k rows of the data block have to be accessed. It accepts as input the row selectivity s and the block compression ratio c.

Given a block b, the compression ratio can be efficiently computed from the block header, which stores the size of the block before and after compression (Unc_{SIZE} and $Comp_{SIZE}$ in Figure 11). The selectivity is computed by dividing the number of rows to be decompressed by the total number of attribute values packed in b. The adaptive decompression component, chooses between the two strategies using a simple and yet effective model built from profiling RasterZip. The model is a $l \times l$ matrix, where the two dimensions are selectivity and compression ratio. The value in a cell indicates the decompression strategy that is expected to provide faster decompression for the corresponding range of selectivity and compression ratio values.

A profiled model is data- and attribute-agnostic: once built using real or synthetic data, it can be applied for different datasets and queries. To profile RasterZip we executed queries of different selectivity on compressed traffic flow records and measured the time required to decompress the queried rows using both the partial and full decompression strategies. For each cell of the model matrix, we computed the average response time for the two decompression strategies. We finally selected the decompression strategy with the lowest average decompression time.

An actual example of the model is shown in Figure 12. Note that partial-decompression is preferable for blocks that exhibit poor compression and/or high selectivity. For the remaining cases, full-decompression should be chosen. In summary, the adaptive decompression component allows our methodology to combine the power of both full- and partial-decompression strategies.

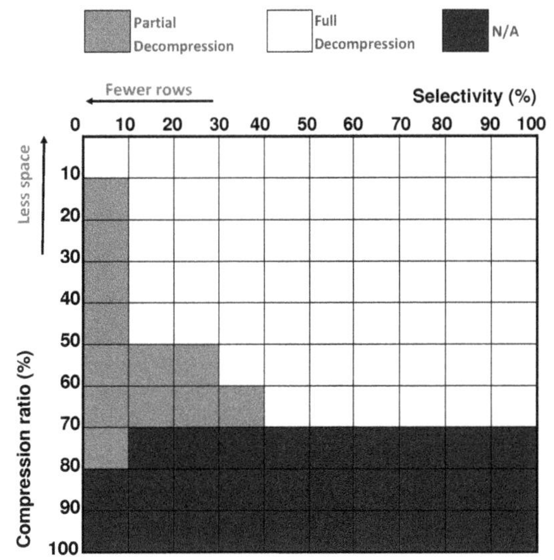

Figure 12: A 10×10 grid model built using a profiling dataset for deciding when to decompress using Partial-Decompression (PD) or Full-Decompression (FD). We indicate with *N/A*, cells that were not filled using the profiling dataset. Partial-Decompression is preferable for blocks that exhibit low compression ratios and/or high block selectivities.

4.4 Error detection

Contrary to block-based compression utilities, such as *bzip2*, RasterZip does not define a framing format and does not come with built-in support for error detection. In fact, RasterZip delegates this task to the upper layers where error detection mechanisms can be implemented using well-known approaches.

For example, RasterZip-encoded data blocks can be interleaved with a fixed size bit pattern, the block delimiter, that allows data block boundaries to be recognized and a checksum can be prepended to each RasterZip-encoded block. Data corruption can be detected by comparing the stored checksum with the checksum computed over the data decompressed using the full decompression algorithm. This approach is not applicable when the partial decompression strategy is used. However RasterZip could be modified to include an additional checksum at the end of `V-` and `B-blocks`. We leave this extension to future work.

5. EVALUATION

To evaluate the performance of RasterZip we built the archival solution shown in Figure 13 and use it to archive and query traffic flow records collected from real networks. The streaming flow records (13.A) are hashed into hash-buckets containing chains of 'similar' records (13.B). Data blocks are created from each hash chain and then indexed (13.C) and archived (13.D) in compressed data blocks using a columnar-approach. At query time, the index returns the row positions of interest in the archive. This information is used by the query processor to identify for each requested attribute the compressed data blocks within the corresponding data column that contain the result set.

For our comparison experiments, we compress attribute blocks in the component D of Figure 13 both with LZO and RasterZip. In this manner, both LZO and RasterZip benefit from the online record rearrangements provided by the component 13.B. The reordering is realized using oLSH, a flow record sorting methodology that we introduced in our previous work [14].

We choose a block size of 4000 records, which we found empirically to provide the best trade-off between compression ratio and response time. The indexing (13.C) is realized using the COMPAX compressed bitmap indexing encoding introduced in our previous work [14]. The only evaluation metric that depends on the selected index is the query response time. As shown in our previous work, the index lookup makes a negligible fraction of the query response time, which is dominated by the time for decompressing blocks even when a high-speed compressor such as LZO is used. In addition, the evaluated compressors are used with the same index to yield a fare comparison.

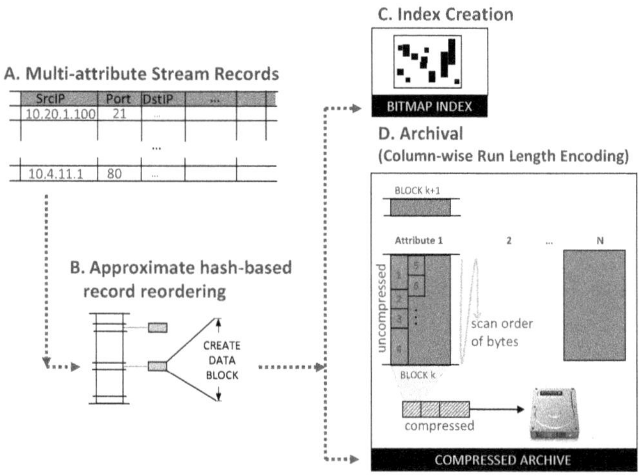

Figure 13: An overview of the compression methodology for streaming records.

Our experiments show that the column-major RLE-based compression significantly improves the compression ratio achieved with LZO. Additionally, because RasterZip provides *subblock decompression* it has better response times for high selectivity queries.

All experiments have been conducted on a commodity desktop machine equipped with 2 GB of DDR3 memory and an Intel Core 2 Quad processor (Q9400) running GNU/Linux (2.6.28 kernel) in 32-bit mode. The processor has four cores running at 2.66 GHz and 6 MB of L2 cache. We store the compressed archives on a 320 GB desktop hard drive[4].

As input to the system we provided uncompressed flow traces stored on a commodity solid state drive[5]. The drive provides a sustained reading speed of 170 MB/s, which corresponds to more than 5 Million flows/second (f/s). The system has been configured to fetch flows sequentially from the solid state drive and to store both indexes and compressed columns to the mechanical desktop hard drive. This simple setup allows us to reproduce flow rates that can only be observed in large ISP networks. We use two data sets in the evaluation:

- Six days of NetFlow traces of access traffic from a *large hosting environment* (HE).
- A two month NetFlow trace of internal and external traffic in an medium-sized enterprise *production network* (PN).

Each flow record includes the following attributes: source and destination IP addresses and L3 ports, the L3 protocol, TCP flags, source and destination Autonomous System (AS) number, number of packets, number of bytes, the time of the first packet and the duration of the flow. Information about the datasets are summarized in Table 1. The *gzip* and *bzip2* columns report the storage footprint when compressing the *raw* data with the *gzip* and *bzip2*, respectively.

Table 1: Utilized Datasets

Data	# flows	Length	Raw	*gzip*	*bzip2*
HE	231.9 M	6 days	6.9 GB	2.5 GB	2.2 GB
PN	1.2 B	62 days	37 GB	8.1 GB	6.9 GB

5.1 Compression Ratio

In Table 2, we report the size of the archives compressed with RasterZip and LZO. First, we note that the approximate flow reordering scheme allows LZO, which is optimized for compression speed rather than for achieving high compression ratios, to almost match the compression ratio of *gzip* (shown in Table 1). By properly exploiting the prefix structure of partially reordered traffic records, RasterZip can further reduce the disk consumption for both datasets. In fact, we observe that RasterZip uses 22% and 24% less space than LZO for the HE and PN datasets, respectively. It also uses less space than the simple approach of compressing raw data with *gzip* or *bzip2*. Compared to the values in Table 1, RasterZip offers 20% compression than *gzip* and even 9-10% better compression than the slow, but heavily space-optimized *bzip2*.

Table 2: Disk space requirements for different compression algorithms.

Dataset	LZO	RasterZip
HE	2.6 GB	2.0 GB
PN	8.2 GB	6.2 GB

5.2 Insertion Rate

Our system has been designed for compressing and indexing high-speed streams of flow records in real-time. RasterZip aims at reducing the disk usage of compressed archives and at supporting very high insertion rates. Having showed that RasterZip reduces the disk usage of two reference compressors, we evaluate the insertion rate it can support. For this purpose, we use the two datasets and compare the insertion rate our archive achieves when data columns are compressed on-the-fly using LZO and RasterZip.

[4]The hard drive is a 7200 rpm Hitachi HDP725032GLA380 equipped with 8 MB of cache. The system is capable of performing cached reading at 2400 MB/s and unbuffered disk reads at 80 MB/s (measured with `hdparm`).

[5]Intel X-25M G1, 80 GB model

Table 3: Record processing rates when using RasterZip or LZO for compressing data columns.

Dataset	LZO	RasterZip
HE	474K f/s	471K f/s
PN	513K f/s	512K f/s

As shown in Table 3, RasterZip realizes almost identical insertion rates with LZO, which is the fastest known compressor of the reference Lempel-Ziv family. The average insertion rate is close to 500 thousand flows/second (f/s) for both datasets regardless of the compression algorithm used. To put this number into perspective, medium-large networks exhibit peak rates of 50 thousand f/s. Therefore, we learn that RasterZip substantially reduces the disk consumption of LZO (and *gzip*) and supports very high insertion rates.

5.3 Adaptive Decompression Selection

Next, we evaluate the adaptive decompression component to see if it can properly select between the full and partial decompression strategies at run-time.

Profiling stage: We constructed the model for the adaptive decompression component by profiling the decompression speed of the two decompression strategies using real network data and queries of different selectivity. Specifically, we created a set P containing the distinct IP addresses present in one hour of traffic from the production network dataset (PN). Then, we performed a query for every element in P and for every data block that was decompressed to answer the query we computed the following four metrics: the compression ratio of the block (percentage), the selectivity of the query (percentage), and the time required to decompress the block using full and partial decompression. We used these metrics to profile a very compact grid model of size 8×8 bits as described in Section 4.3.

Evaluation stage: We evaluate the adaptive decompression component by comparing the block decompression time it provides with the decompression time offered by the full and partial decompression strategies. For this purpose, we issue the IP queries described above over a different time frame. In Figure 14 we illustrate the query response time using full, partial, and adaptive decompression. The figure on the bottom shows how the response time varies with selectivity for a fixed compression ratio (20%), while the one on the top shows how the response time varies with the compression ratio when the selectivity is fixed to 20%. The line corresponding to adaptive decompression is at the bottom for the vast majority of the queries. This illustrates that the adaptive decompression component effectively selects the decompression strategy that is faster. This is feasible simply by relying on a very compact model stored in a 8×8 bitmap. We use this model for the rest of our evaluation experiments.

5.4 Overall Performance

Finally, we measure the overall query response time of the archives compressed using RasterZip with the adaptive decompression component enabled. We compare the response time of this setup with the response times that the system offers when LZO is used for data compression. Note that the response time for answering queries, as we have shown in our previous work [14], is dominated by the time spend

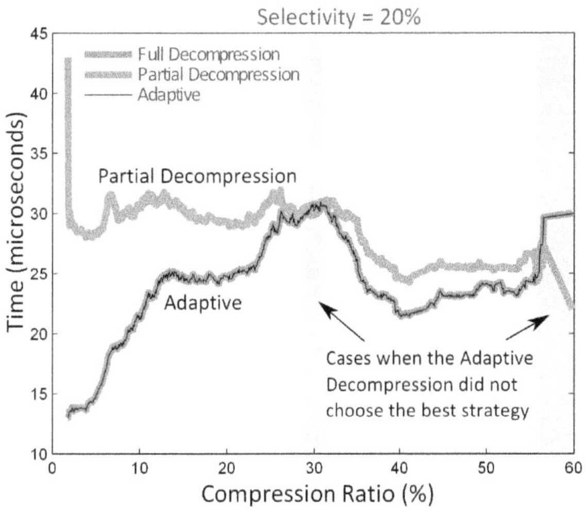

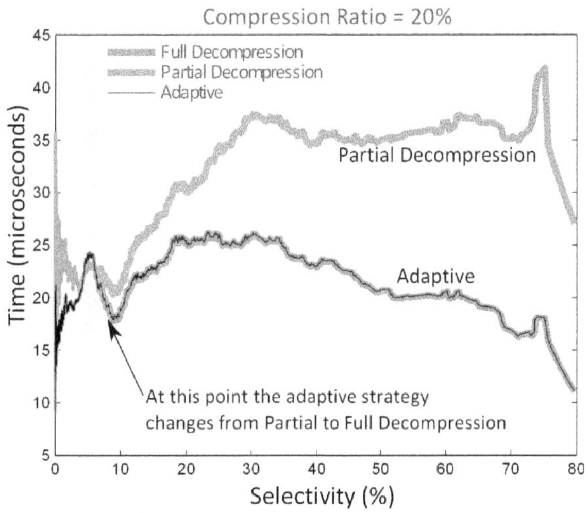

Figure 14: The Adaptive strategy chosen on-the-fly intelligently shifts between Full-Decompression and Partial-Decompression. Shown for a fixed compression ratio (bottom) and selectivity (top).

in decompressing data blocks rather than by the time spend in looking up the compressed bitmap indexes to find blocks that need to be decompressed.

To compare the two compressors, we query for flow records using ports corresponding to well-known applications.[6] For this purpose, we extracted the 311 ports listed in the file */etc/services* of the test machine and executed destination port queries over 7 days of each dataset (PN and HE). This corresponds to 2,177 different queries, each selecting all the existing flow records attributes (i.e.,`"SELECT * FROM flows WHERE dstPort=X"` in SQL parlance). Note that using single- or multi-attribute queries, e.g., `dstPort=`X `AND dstIP=`Y, does not play a role in the comparison between LZO and RasterZip because it would only affect the index lookup time of a query equally for both compressors. What is important is to compare the two compressors over a range of query selectivity values. Varying the selectivity can be done in multiple ways. In our experiments, we selected to do this by issuing single-attribute queries as this is a simple

[6]The Internet Assigned Numbers Authority (IANA) assigns port numbers to applications.

way to do it. We ordered queries by the number of rows retrieved (the selectivity) and, for each query, we plot in Figures 15 and 16 the ratio between the response time when the query is executed over a RasterZip compressed archive and the response time for the same query executed over an LZO compressed archive. Values lower than one correspond to queries where RasterZip offers better response times than LZO.

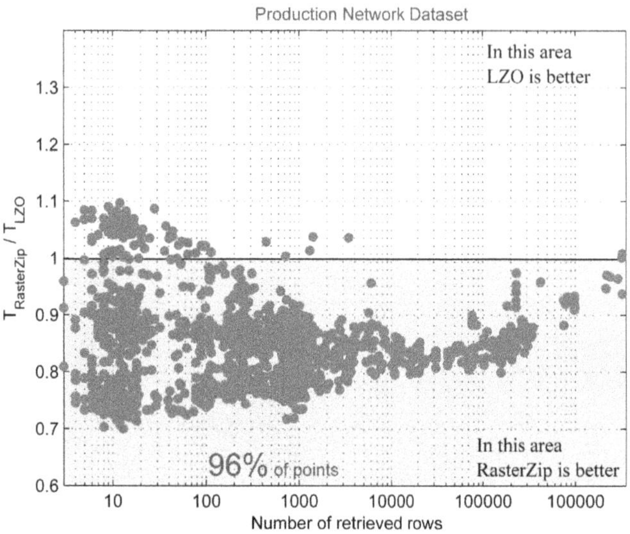

Figure 15: RasterZip over LZO query response time for the Production Network dataset (PN).

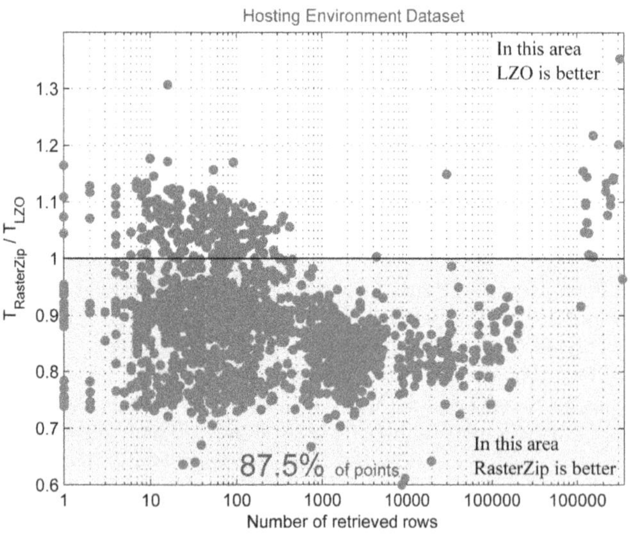

Figure 16: RasterZip over LZO query response times for the Hosting Environment dataset (HE).

RasterZip provides better query response time than LZO for more than 87% – 96% of the queries depending on the dataset (see Figure 15 and 16 for the PN and HE dataset, respectively). For high selectivity queries, the query response time is in the order of milliseconds. The few cases where RasterZip offers worse response time than LZO correspond to: a) a small fraction of the high selectivity queries (left top side of the two figures) and b) to extremely low selectivity queries. Examples of the second type of queries can be observed on the extreme right side of Figure 16, which is based on the data set from the hosting environment. These points correspond to queries on port 80 (HTTP protocol), which, in the hosting environment, match an extremely large fraction of the flows. Such queries of extremely low selectivity are not typically useful for network administrators, since they match too many flows. Our system is optimized for high selectivity queries, i.e., searching for "needles in a haystack", which are shown in the middle and left side of Figures 15 and 16.

6. RELATED WORK

General-purpose compression has been extensively studied in the previous decades, which led to a set of state-of-the-art algorithms and associated utilities that are presently extensively-used. The well-known Lempel-Ziv family of algorithms [28] includes *gzip* and LZO, which is the fastest member of the family [27]. Due to the high compression and decompression speed, LZO is a compressor widely used to accelerate I/O bound data-intensive workloads (e.g., in Hadoop clusters [19]).

Although the available compression gain margins have become extremely tight, in this work we show that by exploiting the patterns of network traffic data we can improve the compression ratio of LZO (and also of *gzip* and *bzip2*) by a significant fraction of 22-24%, while reducing query response times and without incuring any penalty. The RadixZip Transform [24] is similar to our approach in that it transposes bytes by the sort order of their prefixes to boost the compression of token based streams, such as urls and logs. RadixZIP offers up to 20% better compression ratios and up to 10% higher decompression speed than *bzip2*, the widely used block based compressor based on the Burrows-Wheeler Transform (BWT). In contrast with RadixZip and *bzip2*, which are optimized for achieving high compression ratios, RasterZip is optimized for speed and achieves much faster (de)compression speeds. Additionally, it has been designed to support fine-grained partial decompression operations, which are hard to accommodate in *bzip2* even with the help of an index. In fact, *bzip2*-compressed data is made of data blocks that can be independently decompressed. However, the block size is large (between 100Kb and 900Kb), and as a result, even highly selective queries can require the decompression of the entire archive.

Silk [15], nfdump [17], and flowtools [22] are commonly-used tools for storing streams of flows. They all store flow records as flat files, which are eventually compressed using general purpose compressors and compression algorithms, such as *gzip*, *bzip2*, and LZO.

Recently, compression algorithms have been used to boost the performance of columnar databases. A comparison of the performance of different general-puropose compression algorithms for columnar databases can be found in [2]. In our previous work [14], we built a columnar database that uses a novel indexing scheme optimized for network flow records and the LZO general-puropose compressor. In this, work we visit the subject of compression and introduce a domain-optimized compression scheme that provides fine-grained decompression granularity and high compression efficiency. Recently, Giura *et al* [16] optimized a columnar database called NetStore for storing flows. NetStore provides the capability to select, at runtime, among different standard compression tools. However, when deployed on a significantly less powerful machine (4 cores instead of 8, 2 Gb of RAM instead of 6 Gb), our solution provides insertion rates that are two orders of magnitude higher.

7. WHAT IS THE COST OF STORAGE?

The costs for storing and maintaining large repositories is commonly underestimated, mostly because the price of desktop hard drives dropped significantly in the last few years. Unfortunately, the *disk space is cheap* motto only holds at small scales. Historical network traffic repositories can be massive. For example, large traffic archives maintained by academic and research institutions, like the flow record repository of the Communication Systems Group at ETH and the UCSD Network Telescope data of CAIDA, are both close to 100 Terabytes [4]. Organizations, like medium and large ISPs, cloud providers, and law enforcement agencies, monitor much more traffic and need to handle even bigger traffic data. Large-scale repositories must be highly available and fault-tolerant to prevent data loss. Fault-tolerance can be achieved by replicating data in a distributed setting (e.g., the Google approach) or by using enterprise class storage products (e.g, disk arrays with RAID support). In both cases, the operational costs include additional expenses for energy consumption and for performing backups over tape drives. Based on current storage prices [5], the cost for storing 100 Terabytes is, for example, between \$40,000 and \$72,000 per year for different types of service. High storage costs prevent the wider availability of rich Internet measurement data, and are, in fact, the sole reason why even existing traffic repositories that have been very influencial in studying Internet threats are threatened with deletion [4]. A compression technology that can substantially reduce data volume has a direct and very tangible economical impact, which can be measured in several thousands of dollars per year for few dozens of Terabytes. RasterZip, by compressing more than 20% better than *gzip*, reduces costs accordingly.

8. CONCLUSION

In this work we introduce RasterZip, the first high-performance compressor specifically designed for network traffic archives that exploits the prefix structure of partially reordered data to provide fine-grained decompression granularity. RasterZip supports online high-speed stream compression, enables interactive queries over archived data, leverages network data patterns, and exploits features of modern hardware. In addition, we introduce a novel decompression scheme that provides fine-grained decompression granularity at the attribute level in order to accelerate queries for “needles in a haystack”. Our evaluation shows that RasterZip outperforms general-purpose compressors on traffic flow data from two different networks. Compared to the widely-used state-of-the-art *lzop* compressor, RasterZip accelerates queries, reduces expenses for storage by 22-24% due to more compact compression, and does not incur penalty in any other performance metric.

9. REFERENCES

[1] StealthWatch FlowCollector. http://www.lancope.com/products/stealthwatch-flowcollector/.

[2] D. Abadi, S. Madden, and M. Ferreira. Integrating Compression and Execution in Column-Oriented Database Systems. In *Proc. 32nd ACM SIGMOD Int. Conf. on Management of Data*, pages 671–682, 2006.

[3] E. W. Bethel, S. Campbell, E. Dart, K. Stockinger, and K. Wu. Accelerating Network Traffic Analysis Using Query-Driven Visualization. In *Proc. of IEEE Symposium on Visual Analytics Science and Technology*, pages 115–122, 2006.

[4] CAIDA. Targeted serendipity: the search for storage. `http://blog.caida.org/best_available_data/2012/04/04/`, 2012.

[5] S. D. S. Center. Sdsc project storage pricing options. `http://project.sdsc.edu/pricing.php`.

[6] X. Chen, M. Li, B. Ma, and J. Tromp. DNACompress: fast and effective DNA sequence compression. *Bioinformatics*, 18(12):1696–1698, 2002.

[7] B. Claise. RFC 3954: Cisco Systems NetFlow Services Export Version 9, 2004.

[8] M. Datar, N. Immorlica, P. Indyk, and V. S. Mirrokni. Locality-Sensitive Hashing Scheme Based on p-Stable Distributions. In *Proc. of the 20th Annual Symposium on Computational Geometry*, pages 253–262, 2004.

[9] L. Deri, V. Lorenzetti, and S. Mortimer. Collection and Exploration of Large Data Monitoring Sets Using Bitmap Databases. In *Proc. of the 2nd Int. Workshop on Traffic Monitoring and Analysis*, TMA'10, pages 73–86, 2010.

[10] N. Duffield, C. Lund, and M. Thorup. Charging from Sampled Network Usage. In *Proc. of the 1st ACM SIGCOMM Workshop on Internet Measurement (IMW)*, pages 245–256, 2001.

[11] A. Feldmann, A. Greenberg, C. Lund, N. Reingold, J. Rexford, and F. True. Deriving Traffic Demands for Operational IP Networks: Methodology and Experience. *IEEE/ACM Transactions on Networking (ToN)*, 9:265–280, 2001.

[12] A. Friedl and S. Ubik. Perfmon and Servmon: Monitoring Operational Status and Resources of Distributed Computing Systems. Technical Report 10, CESNET, Prague, Czech Republic, 2008.

[13] F. Fusco, X. Dimitropoulos, M. Vlachos, and L. Deri. pcapindex: an index for network packet traces with legacy compatibility. *SIGCOMM Comput. Commun. Rev.*, 42(1):47–53.

[14] F. Fusco, M. Vlachos, and M. P. Stoecklin. Real-time creation of bitmap indexes on streaming network data. *The VLDB Journal*, 21(3):287–307, June 2012.

[15] C. Gates, M. Collins, M. Duggan, A. Kompanek, and M. Thomas. More Netflow Tools for Performance and Security. In *Proc. of the Conf. on Large Installation Systems Administration*, pages 121–132, 2004.

[16] P. Giura and N. Memon. Netstore: an efficient storage infrastructure for network forensics and monitoring. In *Proc. of the 13th Int. Conf. on Recent advances in intrusion detection*, RAID'10, pages 277–296, 2010.

[17] P. Haag. NFDump. http://nfdump.sourceforge.net/.

[18] R. Hofstede, A. Sperotto, T. Fioreze, and A. Pras. The network data handling war: MySQL vs. NfDump. In *Proc. of the 16th EUNICE/IFIP Conf. on Networked services and applications: engineering, control and management*, EUNICE'10, pages 167–176, 2010.

[19] S. B. Joshi. Apache hadoop performance-tuning methodologies and best practices. In *Proc. of the 3rd joint WOSP/SIPEW Int. Conf. on Performance Engineering*, ICPE '12, pages 241–242, 2012.

[20] A. Lakhina, M. Crovella, and C. Diot. Mining Anomalies Using Traffic Feature Distributions. In *Proc. ACM SIGCOMM Conf. on Applications, Technologies, Architectures, and Protocols for Computer Communications*, pages 217–228, 2005.

[21] T. W. Lam, W.-K. Sung, S.-L. Tam, C.-K. Wong, and S.-M. Yiu. Compressed indexing and local alignment of DNA. *Bioinformatics*, 24(6):791–797, 2008.

[22] S. Romig, M. Fullmer, and R. Luman. The OSU Flow-tools Package and Cisco NetFlow Logs. In *Proc. Conference on Large Installation Systems Administration (LISA)*, pages 291–303, 2000.

[23] D. Salomon. *Data Compression: The Complete Reference.* Springer-Verlag, 2nd edition, 2000.

[24] B. D. Vo and G. S. Manku. RadixZip: Linear Time Compression of Token Streams. In *Proc. Int. Conf. on Very Large Data Bases*, pages 1162–1172, 2007.

[25] A. Wagner. *Entropy-Based Worm Detection for Fast IP Networks.* PhD thesis, ETH Zurich, 2008.

[26] H. Yan, S. Ding, and T. Suel. Compressing term positions in web indexes. In *Proc. of the 32nd ACM SIGIR Conf. on Research and development in information retrieval*, SIGIR '09, pages 147–154, 2009.

[27] L. Yang, R. P. Dick, H. Lekatsas, and S. Chakradhar. Online memory compression for embedded systems. *ACM Trans. Embed. Comput. Syst.*, 9:27:1–27:30, 2010.

[28] J. Ziv and A. Lempel. A Universal Algorithm for Sequential Data Compression. *IEEE Transactions on Information Theory*, 23(3):337–343, 1977.

Wire-Speed Statistical Classification of Network Traffic on Commodity Hardware

Pedro M. Santiago del Rio
UAM, Madrid, Spain
pedro.santiago@uam.es

Dario Rossi
Telecom ParisTech, France
dario.rossi@enst.fr

Francesco Gringoli
UNIBS, Brescia, Italy
francesco.gringoli@ing.unibs.it

Lorenzo Nava
UNIBS, Brescia, Italy
lorenzo.nava@ing.unibs.it

Luca Salgarelli
UNIBS, Brescia, Italy
luca.salgarelli@ing.unibs.it

Javier Aracil
UAM, Madrid, Spain
javier.aracil@uam.es

ABSTRACT

In this paper we present a software-based traffic classification engine running on commodity multi-core hardware, able to process in real-time aggregates of up to 14.2 Mpps over a single 10 Gbps interface – i.e., the maximum possible packet rate over a 10 Gbps Ethernet links given the minimum frame size of 64 Bytes.

This significant advance with respect to the current state of the art in terms of achieved classification rates are made possible by: (i) the use of an improved network driver, PacketShader, to efficiently move batches of packets from the NIC to the main CPU; (ii) the use of lightweight statistical classification techniques exploiting the size of the first few packets of every observed flow; (iii) a careful tuning of critical parameters of the hardware environment and the software application itself.

Categories and Subject Descriptors

C.2.3 [**Network Operations**]: Network Monitoring

Keywords

Statistical Identification, Commodity Hardware, Traffic Monitoring

1. INTRODUCTION AND MOTIVATION

The ability to identify which application is generating every single traffic session is recognized as a crucial building block of today IP networks and unavoidable requisite for their evolution [6]. Effective techniques could open new possibilities for actual deployment of QoS, for enforcing user traffic to comply with policies, for legal interception and intrusion detection [14].

Classic techniques based on Deep Packet Inspection (DPI) have been thoroughly analyzed during the years: though specialized hardware based on Network Processor [17] and FPGAs [18] have been considered, the emergence of multi-core commodity hardware has gained increasing attention and exhaustive performance analyses have been reported also for advanced systems using off-the-shelf Graphics Processing Units (GPUs) [28, 27]. Unfortunately, despite the powerfulness of the underlying hardware none of aforementioned approaches is able to actually sustain a 10 Gbps throughput.

The latest years have also seen a flurry of proposals exploiting different "features" (in machine learning terms) to perform the classification [20]. Statistical techniques based on the size and directions of the first few packets of a flow [1, 5] emerged as especially appealing due to their low complexity if compared to current state of the art DPI approaches. Furthermore, such techniques can be used when traffic is encrypted, while DPI approaches simply cannot. However, most of the previous work on statistical classification focused on assessing the *accuracy* of the different techniques (that we take for granted given results in [1, 5, 14, 16]) without measuring their *achievable classification rates*.

In this work, we argue that commodity multi-core hardware offers intrinsic scalability at low cost, while providing the unbeatable flexibility of software-only solutions. Hence, we take a different twist with respect to works employing specialized hardware based on Network Processor or FPGAs: furthermore, our software based solution is the first to achieve two important milestones. First, using both real Tier-1 traces and synthetic traffic, we demonstrate that multi-Gbps statistical traffic classification is feasible with open-source software on off-the-shelf hardware. Second, our solution is able to sustain higher classification rates than previous work [27, 17, 28, 16] with a sizeable gain in terms of the maximum amount of classification actions per second and manageable packet rates.

In more detail our software can easily handle a real Tier-1 traffic aggregate (i.e., a CAIDA OC192 trace [29]) replayed at 10 Gbps, corresponding to 1.6 million packets per second (Mpps) and 58 thousand flow classifications per second (Kfps). Using two interfaces, our system sustains classification rates of 20 Gbps, 3.2 Mpps, 116 Kfps. Yet, the upper bound of the system performance is much higher, as we manage to handle classification rates up to 14.2 Mpps and 2.8 Mfps without any losses (benchmark with synthetic

IMC'12, November 14–16, 2012, Boston, Massachusetts, USA.

worst-case traffic scenario with trains of 64B packets, 5 packets per flow, over a 10 Gbps link).

Such astonishing performance follows the use of a light-weight classification algorithm (which bases its decisions upon the size of the first 4 packets of every unidirectional flow [1, 5]), as well as of the most recent advances in terms of packet processing techniques [11]. Yet, as we will see in the following, engineering the system so that it sustains wire-speed classification in the worst-case traffic scenario required investigation of several delicate architectural trade-offs of the software, as well as the careful tuning of hardware parameters. We believe the removal of all software bottlenecks in the workflow to be another major contribution of this paper.

The paper sheds light on traffic monitoring and measurement, giving advices and guidelines for designing high performance traffic analysis tools which may be helpful for researchers and network program designers. In this light, we have released the code of our implementation to the community as open-software[1] which may enlighten researchers and designers about how to implement their own network monitoring tools (or modify the existing ones) to cope with current high speeds, i.e. 10Gbps and beyond.

Finally, we point out that to stress-test our system, we also had to develop highly efficient traffic injection engines able to either generate infinite synthetic traffic or replay huge traces thus saturating 10 Gbps links during very long experiments. As final contribution of this paper, we make these latter tools, whose scope of applicability goes beyond that of the Internet traffic classification, available as open-source software[2] as a research byproduct.

2. RELATED WORK

We present recent advances in (i) packet capturing engines, (ii) flow management and (iii) traffic classification techniques. We summarize performance for each category in Tab. 1, further providing a comparison of our results with respect to the current state of the art.

Packet capturing engines. Although modern Network Interface Cards (NICs) hardware can handle high packet rates, standard operating system network stacks are still affected by a few software bottlenecks (e.g., per-packet operations like buffer allocation and transfer to user-space). To overcome such issues, several approaches bypass standard stacks by (i) processing multiple packets in batch to limit IRQs and DMA transactions; (ii) exposing memory of packet buffers to the user-space for zero-copy access; (iii) tying every capture thread with its own ring buffer to a fixed CPU to increase cache memory hits (Non-Uniform Memory Access, NUMA) and (iv) using Receive Side Scaling (RSS) to split incoming flows among different input queues/capture threads. We report in Tab. 1 packet capture performance for a number of systems including: PF_RING with Threaded NAPI [10] and variants [4]; Netmap [24, 23]; PacketShader [11]; and PFQ [2]. As can be seen from the table, performance at 10 Gbps are impressive and this demonstrates that off-the-shelf hardware can now be used in place of costly Network Processors. Finally, since these systems achieve comparable performance, *the choice of a specific technique is not critical for our purposes, and falls on PacketShader [11]* (see Sec. 3).

Flow matching. Monitoring at the flow level requires to match each packet to the correct flow bin. In software based solutions such as Tstat [25] or YAF [12] this is usually accomplished using hash-based structures over the flow 5-tuple. To the best of our knowledge, however, performance of flow matching code in complex monitoring systems is rarely evaluated alone and extrapolating such data from overall measurements can be tough or even misleading. For instance, [12] describes a flow management module in detail, explaining how to optimize flow management using slab allocator [3] for fast recycling of expired flow records, but benchmarks of the system performance are not publicly available. Otherwise, the performance analysis for flow matching modules has been done either monitoring real ISP deployments [9] or over offline traces [25, 30]. However, as real 10 Gbps traffic is not by itself a stress-test scenario, this calls for synthetic benchmarks.

Explicit performance are reported instead in [8] where a dual Xeon box hosts a dedicate Endace DAG card which achieves matching of up to 6 Mpps. In [22] an Intel IXP2850 Network Processor is shown matching 10 million concurrent flows at 10 Gbps at full packet rate. Switching to off-the-shelf setup, an application note from Intel [15] reports flow matching of trains of 64 bytes packets at 17 Mpps out of 24 Mpps received over 16× 1 Gbps interfaces, where each NIC is tied to a different core of an Intel multi-core CPU system (unfortunately the study does not report the number of concurrent flows). A similar architecture [7] matches up to 11 Mpps for 1 million concurrent flows at 10 Gbps using "FastFlow" algorithms spawned over 6 cores. *For comparison, our system is able to handle aggregate flow rates up tp 2.8 Mfps using just two cores.*

Statistical traffic classification. Several techniques have been proposed for the classification of Internet traffic. Traditional ones are based either on the analysis of the transport layer port numbers as in CoralReef [19], or on Deep Packet Inspection of the packet payload as most commercial tools do. Statistical techniques, instead, observe basic properties like packet lengths and interarrival times to classify traffic and are celebrated for their accuracy and speed [20]. However, while the former has been experimentally demonstrated [14, 16] on real traces, the latter is far from being assessed. As a result, the classification rates and scalability of these new algorithms are either unknown or really far from those needed for real world deployment [6]: e.g., [1, 5] merely discuss the complexity of the classification technique, while the most recent performance analysis in [16] reports as few as $30 \cdot 10^3$ classification per seconds with Naïve Bayes. *On a off-the-shelf setup similar to that used in [16], we achieve* $2.8 \cdot 10^6$ *classification per seconds running custom implementation of Naïve Bayes, thus boosting performance of a factor of 100.*

Furthermore we can compare our results to that achieved by non-commercial Deep Packet Inspection (DPI) systems [17, 28, 27], that run pattern matching algorithms on multicore GPUs. It is worth noting that while the amount of GPUs power is already enough to process up to 40 Gbps traffic, bottlenecks in the communication subsystem crushes the actual performance down to a mere 5.2 Gbps corresponding to 1 Mpps and 5 Kfps [28]. Similarly, [17] and [27] achieve 3.5 Gbps and 6 Gbps of aggregated traffic rate, corresponding to less than 2 Mpps. *Our technique not only sustains*

[1]`http://www.eps.uam.es/~psantiago/hptrac.html`
[2]`http://www.eps.uam.es/~psantiago/hpcap.html`

Table 1: Maximum processing rate in the state of the art, and advances offered by this work.

Category	*Ref.*	*Rates* MFlow/s	MPkts/s	Gb/s	*Comments*
Packet capture	[10, 4]	-	14.8	10	60B frames
	[24, 23]	-	14.2	10	64B frames
	[11]	-	14.2	10	64B frames
	[2]	-	12	10	Sender limitation
	this work[11]	-	*14.2*	*10*	*64B frames*
Flow handling	[8]	-	6	10	Using Endace DAG cards
	[15]	-	17	-	Using 16 cores (16x1Gbps interfaces)
	[7]	1	10	10	Using 6 cores
	this work	*2.8*	*14.2*	*10*	*Using 2 cores*
Traffic classification	[27]	-	1.8	6.7	Using a GPU, synthetic traffic
	[17]	-	-	3.5	Using real traffic
	[28]	0.005	1	5.2	Using a GPU, real traffic
	[16]	0.03	-	-	Offline experiments on real traffic (Weka)
	this work	*0.116*	*3.2*	*20*	*Real Tier-1 OC192 traffic over 2×10Gbps NIC*
		2.8	*14.2*	*10*	*Synthetic traffic (64B frames, 5pkts/flow)*

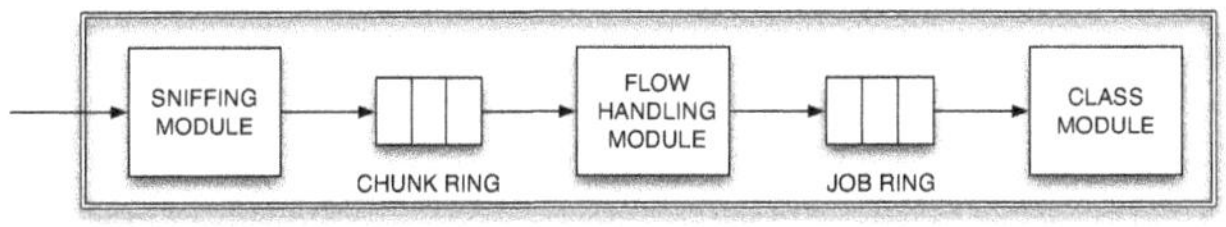

Figure 1: System modules.

10 Gbps of aggregated traffic, but potentially much more as we handle $2.8 \cdot 10^6$ *classifications per second.*

3. SYSTEM MODULES

We report in Fig. 1 the three main blocks that compose our classification system, the two data ring structures for packet/flow queuing and the logical connections that push information from left to right.

Sniffing module. We capture incoming packets making use of PacketShader [11], a customized version of the Intel ixgbe driver that can fetch chunks of multiple frames from the NIC using one single DMA data transfer, greatly reducing the I/O overhead and the per-packet buffer allocation cost. Thanks to a native feature of the Intel 82599EB 10 Gbps Ethernet controller[13], incoming frames are partitioned in RSS queues according to a hash function: one sniffing module (a thread running in user space that has direct access to the kernel-space buffers) can then be set up to fetch frames only from a given RSS queue. Following Intel paradigm, we also tie every capture thread to a specific CPU core (thread affinity) so as to keep the data locally in that CPU cache (hence limiting cache thrashing between processor sockets). This same feature extends parallelism from the NIC to the user layer, as RSS queues feed different cores with multiple chunks at the same time, pushing them through multiple lanes of the PCIe bus and hence increasing the overall throughput with respect to a single core solution. Packets are then organized in a circular ring and made available to the user space with zero-copy technology. Here a thread running on the same CPU copies the chunks from the kernel ring and enqueues resulting data to a *Chunk Ring* of Fig. 1: if the ring is full, a chunk might be lost. We set the chunk size to 128 packets.

Flow Handling module. A thread then dequeues packets from the Chunk Ring and perform lookup into a *Flow Table*. A hash over the packet 5-tuple is used as a primary key to access a hash table, while collisions are handled by chaining (a data structure based on linked list of flow buckets). Once the bucket is found (or a new one is appended if the flow was not already known), a new feature is added to the flow structure, namely the length of the corresponding packet (read from the IP header). Each flow is considered active within a timeout (default 15 sec) after the reception of the last packet. When the timeout expires, its position in the linked list can be reused by a new flow (no deallocation overhead). Once a configurable number of packets for a given flow has been seen (4 in this work), a new classification Job is fired to the *Job Ring* of Fig. 1 if a position is available (otherwise, the Job will likely be inserted the next time a packet from that flow will be analyzed). We set the flow hash table size[3] to 50 millions.

Classification Module. Classification threads run a custom implementation of Naïve Bayes with Gaussian density estimation. Given the first four packets of a flow have been received, the algorithm associates the flow to the protocol whose model scores the maximum likelihood for the generation of the flow. For each protocol model the algorithm uses the size of the packets as indexes into the four lookup tables that have been associated to that protocol during the training phase: the values extracted are then summed together, we optimize, in fact, the algorithm by storing the logarithms of the table values to avoid products as reported in [26]. By comparing the values obtained for each of the protocols for which a model is available, the algorithm chooses the application and the classification of the flow terminates: for more details please refer to [5]. Although classification accuracy, in terms of packets *correctly* classified, is a key issue, it is not the goal of this paper because it has been already

[3]For reason of space, we are unable to report a detailed sensitivity analysis of the hash table size; here, we merely stress that we set a hash size large enough to significantly mitigate the occurrence of chaining.

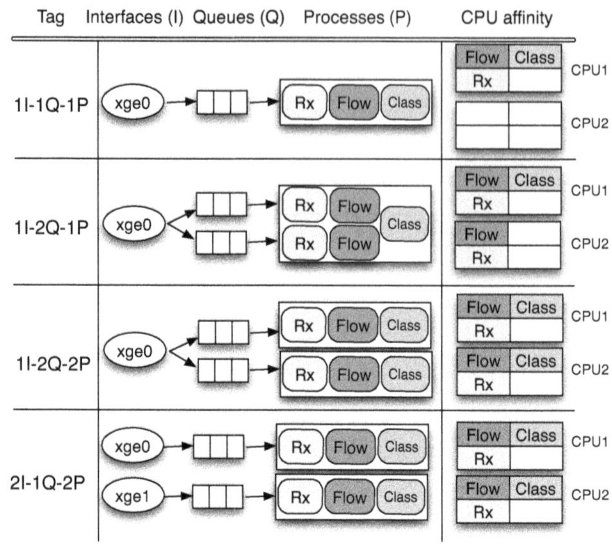

Figure 2: Different architectural configurations of our system.

analyzed. Thus, we have chosen a representative classification technique, such as Naïve-Bayes, whose accuracy has been previously showed as enough for traffic classification purposes [20]. Once chosen the classification technique, we evaluated its performance in terms of computational cost and the feasibility of its implementation on a real system (based on commodity hardware and open software). Note that the computational complexity, given a model, is not a function of accuracy.

To increase the speed at which Jobs are extracted from the Job Ring, multiple threads can be spawned according also to the complexity of the algorithm. Each thread extracts one Job from the ring, processes the data, and writes the classification verdict in the flow bucket inside the Flow Table. New packet for that flow will be marked with this verdict in their Type Of Service (TOS) field of the IPv4 header[4]. By default, we set only one thread to classify: as we will see in the next section, this is sufficient to classify all Jobs generated by flow handling module.

4. SYSTEM CONFIGURATION

Contrary to traditional network applications, new capture engines extend the capture data rates by several orders of magnitude. This implies that probably current networking software is not able to work adequately at this speed. In addition to this, multi-core hardware opens a new opportunity to develop applications that take advantage of the parallelism that such engines allow, whereas current applications were developed in the pre-multicore area. Thus, careful engineering of the system (e.g., CPU and memory affinity, threads/process choice) is needed to achieve the highest classification rates of Tab. 1 under worst-case traffic. Configurations explored in this paper are sketched in Fig. 2.

1I-1Q-1P. This is the simplest configuration: traffic received at the same RSS queue of a single interface is captured by a thread which in turn pushes packets to one chunk ring in the user space. All packets are matched in the flow table sequentially: one classification thread works on the single Job ring. *In this case, though, some CPU cores are not utilized.* Note that using a single RSS queue may be preferable to multi-queue in some cases —whenever the performance is enough to cope with line-rate. For instance: to get smaller CPU usage (and therefore less power consumption), not to re-implement monitoring tools which have not been designed for parallel processing, or to avoid packet reordering issues due to multi-queue[31].

1I-2Q-1P. This configuration holds the single process model of the previous one but two RSS queues are used: this means two threads for fetching packets chunks and two separate flow matching modules. Each capturing flow is executed on a different CPU, but only one hash table is used. Since a single Job ring is used, data coming from two different CPUs is merged again in a single data flow. *In this case, locking is used to enable concurrent accesses to the flow table, and this might decrease the overall performance.*

1I-2Q-2P. Though similar to the previous configuration (two RSS queues, two threads for capturing, bound to different CPUs), the two threads for flow-handling *reside in different processes*, each on the same CPU of the corresponding sniffer. This means that two separated flow tables are maintained and no locking is required thanks to the hash function used at the NIC for dividing packets into the two queues: each single flow lives on a single queue only (no mixing). Moreover, the classification code (threads) and data structures (Job rings) are duplicated and fairly spread among the two CPUs with no data flow merge. *In this case, locking is solved at the price of doubling the amount of memory.*

2I-1Q-2P. The last configuration is exactly as the first one, but two NICs are used: for each NIC a complete capture and classification chain is instantiated, each complete chain lives on a separated CPU. *Given the number of cores in our system, we cannot explore other configurations when 2 interfaces are in use.*

5. PERFORMANCE EVALUATION

First, we describe our experimental testbed, covering hardware, software and traffic details. Then, we benchmark system performance in two scenarios: (i) we locate and solve system bottlenecks using synthetic traffic in a worst-case scenario (64B packets at maximum rate); (ii) we assess our system in a real scenario, replaying traces from a Tier-1 link over one or two 10 Gbps interfaces.

5.1 Experimental testbed

Hardware setup. Our setup consists of two general-purpose servers: one acts as traffic generator, the other receives and classifies the traffic. Both are equipped with 24 GB of DDR3 memory and feature two Intel Xeon E5620 processors, counting four cores each (with hyper-threading capabilities disabled to obtain actual parallelism among cores) working at 2.40 GHz. Concerning connectivity, each server is equipped with one dual port 10Gbps Intel X520-SR2 NIC, and servers are directly connected with a fiber link. This NIC model is based on 82599 chipset, that enables multi-queue techniques, up to 16 RSS queues per interface and direction.

[4]For reason of space, we do not assess packet forwarding after classification in this paper.

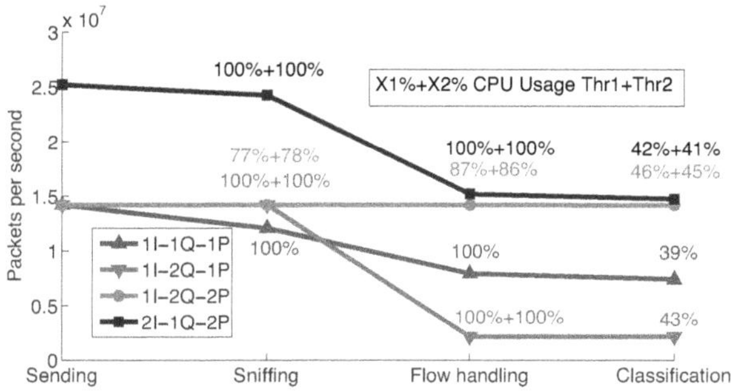

Figure 3: System Performance. Worst-case scenario: synthetic traffic 64B packets, 5 packet/flow.

Software. Ubuntu 10.04 server 64-bit is installed on both servers with a 2.6.35 Linux kernel. In order to inject traffic, we have developed a tool on top of PacketShader API to send traffic at maximum rate: generic tools such as tcpreplay[5] can not, in fact, saturate 10Gbps links. Our tool[6] instead is able either to inject infinite synthetic traffic or to replay very long packet-level traces at maximum speed.
Traffic. We utilized both synthetic traffic and real traces. *Synthetic traffic* consists of TCP segments encapsulated into 64B-size Ethernet frames, forged with incremental IP addresses and TCP ports. We stress once more that, though all packets have 64B-size, the packet length features are extracted from the IPv4 header: hence, our benchmark methodology does not affect the relevance of the classification results. For each flow (5-tuple combination), we send 5 packets, since the 5-th packet will be the first to have the chance to be classified (on the basis of the packet-length features of the previous 4 packets). At a maximum rate of 14.2 Mpps for 64B frames, this translate into 2.8 Mfps. *Real traffic* consists of a packet-level trace sniffed in 2009 at an OC192 (9953 Mbps) backbone link of a Tier-1 ISP located between San Jose and Los Angeles, available from CAIDA [29]. All the packets in the trace are anonymized and captured without payload, the average of the original packet size in the trace is 744 bytes and the average number of packets per flow is 49.

5.2 Stress test: finding the bottlenecks

We first stress test the system in a worst-case scenario, i.e., using synthetically generated 5-packets long flows, sending 64B frames at maximum rate, i.e., 14.2 Mpps or 2.8 Mfps per interface. We measure the amount of packets processed by each module during 60-second experiments (but we also tested the system on 24-hr long experiments on the best configuration without observing losses). Note that using two interfaces we were only able to send at ≈25 Mpps (instead of the theoretic maximum 28.4 Mpps) due to limitations in the sender.

Fig. 3 shows the performance of each module (sniffing, flow handling and classification) for the different configurations. In the parallel coordinates plot, a negative slope in the curves reflects a bottleneck: i.e., a module is not able to process all packets generated by the previous one. Curves in Fig. 3 are annotated with the CPU usage of each module: if a module runs two threads, CPU usage is expressed summing the two corresponding values.CPU usage is computed using `sysstat` utilities[7]. We obtained the CPU load per thread every 5 seconds and then we averaged. Background CPU usage (when there is no classification systems running) and experimental variance are negligible.
The simplest configuration. The simplest configuration 1I-1Q-1P sniffs traffic from one interface, uses one RSS queue and one process. In this case, it can be observed that not all packets can be sniffed using a single RSS queue (a single core). Particularly, only 12.1 Mpps are sniffed out of the 14.2 Mpps sent: notice that the CPU usage of the sniffing module is 100% which pinpoints a processing bottleneck. Similarly, flow module is only able to process 7.9 Mpps out of 12.1 Mpps sniffed packets. As CPU utilization of the flow handling module is also 100%, we have strong indication of a second processing bottleneck. Finally, a slight negative slope can be observed in the classification module. This is not due to a CPU bottleneck (39%), but rather to the fact that only flows with 5 packets can be classified and there have been packet losses in previous modules. The classification rates sustained by 1I-1Q-1P configuration are thus 7.9 Mpps and 1.5 Mfps.
Using 2 RSS queues. In order to remove bottlenecks observed in the first configuration, we increment the number of RSS queues and the number of cores dedicated to packet sniffing and flow management. Thus, we test two configurations, namely 1I-2Q-1P and 1I-2Q-2P. As shown in Fig. 2 and explained in Sec. 4, the former configuration uses one process with two threads for sniffing, one per queue, and two threads for flow handling, having a unique hash table and a unique classification thread. Conversely, 1I-2Q-2P configuration uses two processes, one per queue, which do not share neither data structures nor processing cores. We can observe that the bottleneck in the sniffing module is removed in both cases: i.e., at 14.2 Mpps, two RSS queues are enough to receive and process the traffic. Besides, the 1I-2Q-2P configuration with two processes consumes less CPU power.
Locking issue. The behavior of the flow handling module is different for 1I-2Q-1P and 1I-2Q-2P. Indeed, 1I-2Q-1P is not able to process all packets received by the sniffing module, and performance are even worse than in the case with only one RSS queue. The bottleneck in this configuration is tied to the contention in the access to shared data structures, such as the hash table and the Job ring. To arbitrate concurrent access to shared memory, synchronization and locking mechanisms are necessary but they are detrimental to overall performance. As in the first configuration, all flows generated by the flow handling module can be classified. With 1I-2Q-1P configuration, the performance of the whole system fall to 2.1 Mpps and 0.4 Mfps.
Wire-speed classification. Using two RSS queues and two independent processes, we remove both sniffing bottleneck and flow management locking issues. With 1I-2Q-2P, the system sniffs, processes and classifies all packets sent at wire-speed without losses. Notice further that not even a single CPU core is saturated (sniffing 77%+78%, flow management 87%+86%, classification 45%+46%), so that the remaining processing power could be useful to perform other

[5]`http://tcpreplay.synfin.net/`
[6]`http://www.eps.uam.es/~psantiago/hpcap.html`
[7]`http://sebastien.godard.pagesperso-orange.fr/documentation.html`

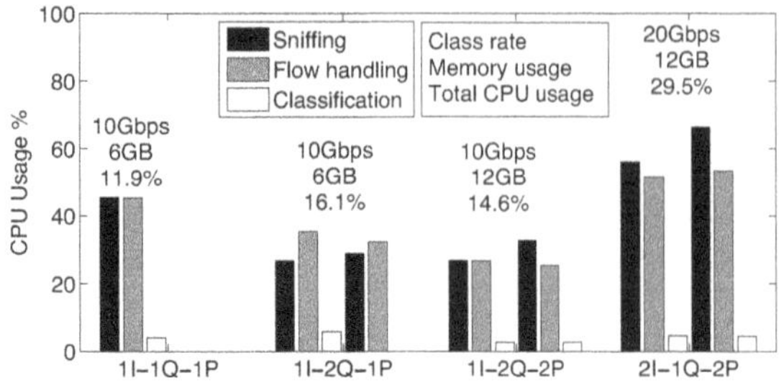

Figure 4: Real scenario: CAIDA trace with original packet length.

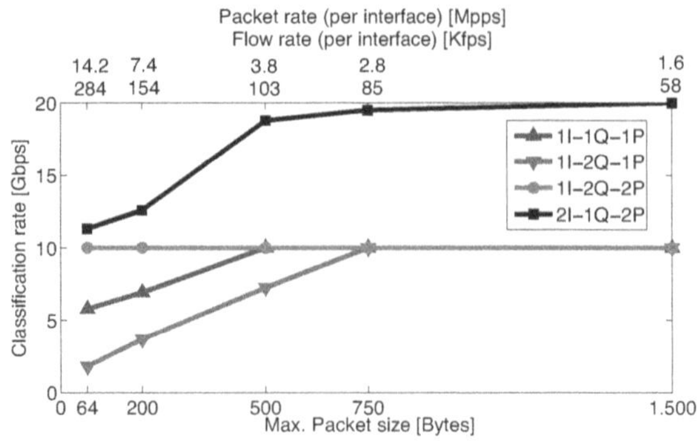

Figure 5: CAIDA trace with capped packet length.

tasks (such as packet forwarding or statistics collection). This also means that the processing capabilities of 1I-2Q-2P configuration exceed the maximum data rate at 10 Gbps., i.e., 14.2 Mpps and 2.8 Mfps.

Using 2 interfaces. The latest configuration, 2I-1Q-2P uses two interfaces to receive traffic, but a single RSS queue per interface due to the limit in the number of cores. As expected, behavior is similar to 1I-1Q-1P, with bottlenecks in both sniffing (24.2 Mpps received out of 25.2 Mpps sent) and flow handling (15.2 Mpps processed out of 24.2 Mpps received).

5.3 Real scenario: classifying at 20 Gbps

Original packet size. We now test performance on real Tier-1 traffic. We replay traces by sending packets back-to-back at 10 Gbps by filling payload with zeros. Using full packet size in Fig. 4, all system configurations sustain maximum rate: i.e., 1.6 Mpps and 58 Kfps on a single 10Gbps interface, or 3.2 Mpps and 116 Kfps on two interfaces. CPU usage and memory occupancy report that cores are far from being saturated: this proves that our system could classify more than 20 Gbps traffic in a realistic scenario. Notice that the simplest configuration (only 3 threads) is enough to classify all traffic with the smallest CPU load (hence the lowest carbon footprint).

Capped packet size. Finally, in Fig. 5 for each frame of size S_i we control the maximum amount of bytes sent on the wire as $\max(S_i, L)$ with L the maximum frame size, that we vary in the range $[64, 1500]$B to tune the flow and packets arrival rates for a fixed datarate of 10 Gbps – hence finding the packet and flow processing rate bottleneck of each configuration. From the figure, we gather that the simplest configuration 1I-1Q-1P can sustain up to 3.8 Mpps and 103 Kfps using only 3 cores.

6. CONCLUSIONS

We propose an all software solution for statistical traffic classification on commodity hardware. Our system achieves a significant advance with respect to the state of the art in several ways. First, it demonstrates the feasibility of online statistical traffic classification, that was so far confined on offline analysis published in the literature. Second, it significantly outperforms state of the art classification techniques. Indeed, while the raw classification throughput on real traffic aggregates is about 3× higher than [27] and 4× higher than [28], however our system is able to sustain flow classification rates 93× higher than [16] and 560× higher than [28]. Additionally, this paper sheds light on traffic monitoring and measurement, giving advices and guidelines for designing high performance traffic analysis tools which may be helpful for researchers and designers. In this light, we released the code of our implementation to the community as open-software which may be useful for researchers and designers in order to implement their own network monitoring tools (or modify the existing ones) to cope with current high speeds (10Gbps and beyond).

Notice that the above performance gap between our work and the previous ones, is hard to remove. Indeed, on the one hand, while GPUs in [28] could in principle process 40 Gbps equivalent of traffic, this is forbidden by a bottleneck in the path from the NIC to the GPU. That is, current approaches force to pass through main memory, and waste processing time, to transfer data between the NIC and the GPU creating a bottleneck — although there are preliminary results which may avoid such limitation, they can be only used with Infiniband technology yet[21]. On the other hand, the statistical technique is anyway much more lightweight than DPI (only process packet headers), so that it would benefit more from a GPU. This gap is intrinsic to the nature of the statistical classification process, that avoid to transfer packet payload from the NIC to GPUs unlike DPI. Thus, statistical approaches are unachievable for DPI, even making use of different hardware, such as GPUs.

While this work constitutes a significant advance, we believe that further optimization are possible, which are part of our current ongoing work. First, we aim at wire-speed performance on two interfaces, which should be achieved with a 2I-2Q-4P configuration on a 12 core server. Second, we plan to implement C4.5 trees, due (i) their known discriminative power, and (ii) the fact that they can be efficiently implemented as if-then-else branches. Finally, we want to optimize flow management, avoiding to compute hash in software, by exporting the hash computed by the NIC to map packets to RSS queues, which should requires only simple modification to the NIC driver.

Acknowledgements

This work has been carried out when Pedro was at LINCS[8], with the support of the Spanish FPU scholarship, and has been partly supported by the FP7 IP mPlane project. This work was supported in part by a grant from the Italian MIUR, under the PRIN project IMPRESA.

[8]`http://www.lincs.fr`

7. REFERENCES

[1] L. Bernaille, R. Teixeira, and K. Salamatian. Early application identification. In *ACM CoNEXT 2006.*

[2] N. Bonelli, A. Di Pietro, S. Giordano, and G. Procissi. On multi-gigabit packet capturing with multi-core commodity hardware. In *Passive and Active Measurement (PAM) 2012.*

[3] J. Bonwick. The slab allocator: An object-caching kernel memory allocator. In *USENIX Summer Technical Conference 1994.*

[4] A. Cardigliano, J. Gasparakis, and F. Fusco. vPF_RING: Towards wire-speed network monitoring using virtual machines. In *ACM IMC 2011.*

[5] M. Crotti, M. Dusi, F. Gringoli, and L. Salgarelli. Traffic classification through simple statistical fingerprinting. *ACM SIGCOMM Comput. Commun. Rev.*, 37(1):5–16, 2007.

[6] A. Dainotti, A. Pescape, and K. Claffy. Issues and future directions in traffic classification. *Network, IEEE*, 26(1):35 –40, 2012.

[7] M. Danelutto, L. Deri, and D. De Sensi. Network monitoring on multicores with algorithmic skeletons. In *International Conference on Parallel Computing (PARCO) 2011.*

[8] L. Deri. IP traffic monitoring at 10 Gbit and above. `http://www.terena.org/activities/ngn-ws/ws2/deri-10g.pdf`.

[9] A. Finamore, M. Mellia, M. Meo, M. Munafo, and D. Rossi. Experiences of Internet traffic monitoring with Tstat. *Network, IEEE*, 25(3):8–14, 2011.

[10] F. Fusco and L. Deri. High speed network traffic analysis with commodity multi-core systems. In *ACM IMC 2010.*

[11] S. Han, K. Jang, K. Park, and S. Moon. PacketShader: a GPU-accelerated software router. In *ACM SIGCOMM Comput. Commun. Rev.*, volume 40, pages 195–206, 2010.

[12] C. Inacio and B. Trammell. YAF: yet another flowmeter. In *International conference on Large installation system administration (LISA) 2010.*

[13] Intel. Intel Í 82599 10 GbE Controller Datasheet. *October*, (December), 2010.

[14] H. Kim, K. Claffy, M. Fomenkov, D. Barman, M. Faloutsos, and K. Lee. Internet traffic classification demystified: myths, caveats, and the best practices. In *ACM CoNEXT 2008.*

[15] A. Lim and R. Kinsella. Data plane packet processing on embedded intel architecture platforms. `http://download.intel.com/design/intarch/papers/322516.pdf`.

[16] Y. Lim, H. Kim, J. Jeong, C. Kim, T. Kwon, and Y. Choi. Internet traffic classification demystified: on the sources of the discriminative power. In *ACM CoNEXT 2010.*

[17] Y. Liu, D. Xu, L. Sun, and D. Liu. Accurate traffic classification with multi-threaded processors. In *IEEE International Symposium on Knowledge Acquisition and Modeling Workshop (KAM) 2008.*

[18] A. Mitra, W. Najjar, and L. Bhuyan. Compiling PCRE to FPGA for accelerating SNORT IDS. In *ACM/IEEE Symposium on Architecture for networking and communications systems (ANCS) 2007.*

[19] D. Moore, K. Keys, R. Koga, E. Lagache, and K. C. Claffy. The CoralReef software suite as a tool for system and network administrators. In *USENIX conference on System administration 2001.*

[20] T. Nguyen and G. Armitage. A survey of techniques for Internet traffic classification using machine learning. *Communications Surveys & Tutorials, IEEE*, 10(4):56–76, 2008.

[21] NVIDIA Corporation. NVIDIA GPUDirect Technology. `http://developer.download.nvidia.com/devzone//devcenter/cuda/docs/GPUDirect_Technology_Overview.pdf`.

[22] Y. Qi, B. Xu, F. He, B. Yang, J. Yu, and J. Li. Towards high-performance flow-level packet processing on multi-core network processors. In *ACM/IEEE Symposium on Architecture for networking and communications systems (ANCS) 2007.*

[23] L. Rizzo. netmap: a novel framework for fast packet I/O. In *USENIX Annual Technical Conference 2012.*

[24] L. Rizzo, M. Carbone, and G. Catalli. Transparent acceleration of software packet forwarding using netmap. In *IEEE INFOCOM 2012.*

[25] D. Rossi and M. Mellia. Real-time TCP/IP analysis with common hardware. In *IEEE ICC 2006.*

[26] D. Rossi, S. Valenti, P. Veglia, D. Bonfiglio, M. Mellia, and M. Meo. Pictures from the Skype. *ACM Performance Evaluation Review (PER)*, 36(2):83–86, 2008.

[27] G. Szabó, I. Gódor, A. Veres, S. Malomsoky, and S. Molnár. Traffic classification over Gbit speed with commodity hardware. *IEEE J. Communications Software and Systems*, 5, 2010.

[28] G. Vasiliadis, M. Polychronakis, and S. Ioannidis. MIDeA: a multi-parallel intrusion detection architecture. In *ACM conference on Computer and communications security (CSS) 2011.*

[29] C. Walsworth, E. Aben, k. claffy, and D. Andersen. The CAIDA anonymized 2009 Internet traces. `http://www.caida.org/data/passive/passive_2009_dataset.xml`.

[30] D. Wang, Y. Xue, and Y. D. Memory-efficient hypercube flow table for packet processing on multi-cores. In *IEEE GLOBECOM 2011.*

[31] W. Wu, P. DeMar, and M. Crawford. Why can some advanced Ethernet NICs cause packet reordering? *IEEE Communications Letters*, 15(2):253–255, 2011.

Fathom: A Browser-based Network Measurement Platform

Mohan Dhawan*
Rutgers University
mdhawan@cs.rutgers.edu

Justin Samuel
UC Berkeley
jsamuel@cs.berkeley.edu

Renata Teixeira✿
CNRS & UPMC
renata.teixeira@lip6.fr

Christian Kreibich
ICSI & UC San Diego
christian@icir.org

Mark Allman
ICSI
mallman@icir.org

Nicholas Weaver
ICSI & UC San Diego
nweaver@icsi.berkeley.edu

Vern Paxson
ICSI & UC Berkeley
vern@cs.berkeley.edu

ABSTRACT

For analyzing network performance issues, there can be great utility in having the capability to measure directly from the perspective of end systems. Because end systems do not provide any external programming interface to measurement functionality, obtaining this capability today generally requires installing a custom executable on the system, which can prove prohibitively expensive. In this work we leverage the ubiquity of web browsers to demonstrate the possibilities of browsers themselves offering such a programmable environment. We present *Fathom*, a Firefox extension that implements a number of measurement primitives that enable websites or other parties to program network measurements using JavaScript. Fathom is lightweight, imposing $< 3.2\%$ overhead in page load times for popular web pages, and often provides 1 ms timestamp accuracy. We demonstrate Fathom's utility with three case studies: providing a JavaScript version of the *Netalyzr* network characterization tool, debugging web access failures, and enabling web sites to diagnose performance problems of their clients.

Categories and Subject Descriptors

C.2.0 [**Computer-Communication Networks**]: General; C.4 [**Performance of Systems**]: Measurement techniques; D.2.8 [**Software Engineering**]: Metrics—*performance measures*

General Terms

Design, Measurement, Performance, Security

Keywords

Network troubleshooting, network performance, end-host network measurement, web browser, browser extension

*This work was done while the author was visiting ICSI.

✿This work was done while the author was visiting UC Berkeley & ICSI.

IMC'12, November 14–16, 2012, Boston, Massachusetts, USA.

1 Introduction

Network measurements from the perspective of end systems often play a vital role both for researchers who want to develop general insight into how the Internet functions, and for practitioners aiming to diagnose individual performance issues. To gain insight into network operation, researchers traditionally either (i) beg acquaintances to install a custom measurement tool, or (ii) use or instantiate infrastructure to conduct the measurements (e.g., PlanetLab). Neither of these options scales to supporting broad measurement of the network's edge, limiting the scope of the insight we can obtain. Practitioners, on the other hand, have less interest in developing general knowledge about networked systems and more interest in understanding the performance of their own systems, including understanding *why* their users experience suboptimal performance. While systems developed by the research community for general measurement may aid practitioners in small ways, these systems do not run on regular users' end systems and hence do not offer help with *specific* measurement or debugging of user problems.

While researchers and practitioners come to the need for measurement of user end systems from opposite ends of the spectrum—i.e., one looking for broad, general results, and the other seeking specific information—both find obtaining such measurements problematic due to the lack of general support in end systems. While getting users to install programs can suffice for particular, limited situations, the approach does not scale up: one cannot rely upon users repeatedly conducting such installations as a building block for facilitating measurement. One difficulty in this regard concerns users not wanting to continually undergo the hassle of the process. Another difficulty is the challenge that implementors face in developing portable executables that run correctly across a wide range of system configurations. A third issue is one of safety: such installations, whether for standalone binaries or native code that extends an existing system, generally require privileged access and trust in the behavior of the introduced program.

In this work we aim to overcome these difficulties by minimizing the impediments to writing and installing measurement programs across a large number of end systems. Our vehicle for doing so is *Fathom,* a browser-based extensible measurement platform. Fathom provides a measurement-oriented API that standard JavaScript loaded from any web page can tap into to facilitate empirical observation.

We argue that building a measurement platform into the web browser hits a sweet spot for both deployability and flexibility, thus providing Fathom with the potential to flourish where other measurement systems have floundered. The ubiquity of web browsers, and the central role they play for a vast array of disparate network activities, provide an unparalleled scaling potential that holds great promise for benefiting common measurement and troubleshooting scenarios (§ 2). Like other measurement platforms, Fathom requires users to install a piece of software, a step that generally presents a significant hurdle to widespread adoption. However, the user only has to do so *once* to enable a vast range of measurements. By bundling useful Fathom applications with the platform itself (most notably, a connectivity debugger that works even in complete absence of connectivity), we provide users an immediate incentive for installation.

We begin by framing desiderata for a browser-based measurement platform (§ 3), which guide both Fathom's design and its implementation. Our design (§ 4) includes a set of APIs covering a wide range of measurement and troubleshooting applications, significantly expanding the capabilities of in-page JavaScript code. To ensure safety, we equip Fathom with a security model that balances user approval, permission management, and code-signing (§ 4.2 and § 4.3). Consideration of possible implementation strategies motivates our decision to implement Fathom as a JavaScript-only extension for the Firefox browser, paying close attention to the constraints imposed by modern-day browser environments (§ 5). We demonstrate that careful design of a JavaScript-driven measurement platform enables experimenters to conduct measurements with modest overhead for the user (§ 6.1) and high accuracy (§ 6.2). We report on additional experiences gained using Fathom in three different use cases (§ 7). We discuss portability and adoption incentives (§ 8), and close with a survey of related browser extension work and measurement platforms (§ 9).

Contributions: Fathom explores the feasibility of building a generic network measurement and troubleshooting platform into modern browsers. We view our contribution as developing a realization of broad capability that the community has been working towards for a number of years. Fathom builds on the lessons of previous efforts and reflects a promising, practical approach that (*i*) fosters innovation via open-endedness, as opposed to implementing a particular tool; (*ii*) provides unparalleled access to the edge via the ubiquity of browsers; (*iii*) enables novel analyses supported via passive collection of context and active experimentation; (*iv*) combines existing security primitives in a novel way to safely expand in-page JavaScript capabilities.

Fathom is open source and we invite interested readers to visit `http://fathom.icsi.berkeley.edu` to download the platform and provide feedback.

2 Motivating Scenarios

We begin by sketching examples of measurement efforts that benefit from both an end system vantage point and a large footprint. The list here is far from exhaustive; our design is general, and hence adaptable to a range of other tasks, too.

Web performance debugging: With a browser-based vantage point website operators can significantly improve their ability to diagnose slow load times. Along those lines, Google's analytics code recently started collecting basic page rendering times [24]. This captures facts, but cannot provide troubleshooting assistance, for which page authors currently lack critical information. The web pages' isolation from the host system here works against the developer, preventing access to helpful indicators such as system load and I/O characteristics. For example, the Google Maps forum [19] shows discussions whereby Google engineers explicitly ask users to quantify the "slowness" of page loads, including ancillary system-level information such as CPU and network activity. By allowing Google engineers access to a measurement platform in the user's browser they could directly extract the required information. Researchers can also leverage this capability to better understand web performance and complexity (e.g., [7, 10]) both at scale and across sites.

Web access failures: Similar to the performance debugging case, a browser-based platform can also directly assist users in diagnosing website failures. In this scenario, the browser could provide a "diagnose" button that launches measurements to identify common causes of access failures (e.g., loss of connectivity or DNS issues). While web failures have been studied in a passive fashion [1, 42], giving users a way to conduct real-time assessment offers the potential to both (*i*) better diagnose the problem with contemporaneous active measurements and (*ii*) inform users what might be done to fix the problem (or at least who to ask to fix the problem).

Local network debugging: Poor performance can also stem from issues in the local network and hence combining external- and local-network measurements can help pinpoint the location of the problem [10]. Further, when multiple local systems use the measurement platform we can discover this—e.g., using multicast DNS or UPnP—and coordinate the vantage points for a richer analysis of the failure.

ISP performance: A wide range of tools perform active measurements from end systems to a controlled server, including speed tests [4], general performance diagnostics [20, 28, 31], traffic tampering [46], and traffic shaping detectors [12, 25]. While each of these tools performs custom tests, they share the basic need to conduct active probing from end systems.

Large-scale topology mapping: Many efforts within the research community over the years have tried to understand the Internet's topology by conducting traceroute(-like) measurements from multiple vantage points [8, 44, 47]. A browser-based platform would facilitate such studies from a breadth of vantage points currently not practical.

3 Platform Design Goals

We identify the broad design goals for an end-system based measurement platform as follows:

Rich measurement capabilities: The examples in § 2 show that we require support for both *passive* and *active* observations. Passive measurements provide precise and continuous understanding of the activity in the browser, ranging from system-level information such as CPU load, memory availability, and traffic load, to browser-level activity such as HTTP session tracking and fine-grained page-level activity (e.g., DOM[1] updates and event loop activity). Note that this enables far broader analyses than available to in-browser JavaScript debuggers (e.g., Firebug). While network problems may often manifest in passive measurements, their root cause frequently reveals itself only using active probing. We therefore require a wide range of network I/O primitives, reaching as far down in the networking stack as feasible.

Extensibility: As sketched in § 2, we strive for a general measurement facility rather than providing a simple interface to ready-made measurements. Therefore, instead of providing APIs for specific measurements, the platform should provide APIs that support the *implementation* of as wide an array of measurements as possible.

Security and privacy: While Fathom strives to maximize utility to practitioners and experimenters, the platform must not compromise the privacy of the user (e.g., expose browsing history). Addition-

[1]Document Object Model, a browser-independent tree abstraction representing a web page.

```
var fathom = window.fathom;
var DATA = "Hello world";
var ADDR = "226.0.0.2", PORT = 23456;

fathom.socket.multicast.open(socketCB);

function socketCB(sock) {
  if (sock && !sock['error']) {
    fathom.socket.multicast.send(sendCB,
        sock, DATA, ADDR, PORT);
  }
}

function sendCB(result) { ... }
```

Figure 1: Asynchronous multicast network output in Fathom.

ally, the platform must not allow for the abuse of host or network resources.

Measurement accuracy: We require the measurement platform to accurately track time and the outcome of network I/O events. Precise timing supports the ability to both understand when an event happened and to schedule future events.

Low system overhead: We desire the platform's runtime overhead to be as low as possible for two reasons: (*i*) high overhead can alter test results for intensive experiments (e.g., bandwidth measurements) and (*ii*) the platform resides in a user's application and hence we do not want to unduly impact the user's browsing activity.

Portability: Measurement code should work portably on any implementation of the platform. This implies that measurement code should execute without requiring compilation to different execution environments.

Fathom's design (§ 4) addresses the first three goals and its implementation (§ 5) the remaining goals.

4 Fathom

We design Fathom to provide a rich set of APIs for measurements. Since Fathom significantly expands the capabilities of in-page JavaScript code, it requires a carefully thought-out security and privacy model.

4.1 API design

Fathom's APIs remain conceptually independent of the underlying platform implementation and cover a broad range of network I/O capabilities as well as means to obtain system information and historical performance baselines. Our case studies (§ 7) and development experience drove the design.

To make its services available to in-page JavaScript code, Fathom creates a new JavaScript object, registers its APIs as methods on this object as requested by the measurement code (see § 4.3), and adds it to the page's `window` object as `window.fathom`. Web application code can invoke these APIs to perform both passive and active measurements on the end system. To do so, the caller provides a callback function which Fathom will invoke when the result of the call becomes available. This approach provides natural asynchronicity in the presence of potentially blocking network I/O. Fathom passes a single object to the callbacks. A set of properties on the object conveys error codes and return values. Figure 1 shows an example of sending data over a multicast socket. Fathom currently provides four main API families (listed in Table 1):

`fathom.socket` provides socket management. These functions export low-level socket functionality and serve as the basis for active measurements, including opening TCP and UDP sockets, setting socket options, and performing both blocking and non-blocking I/O operations.

`fathom.proto` supplies clients and servers for common application-layer protocols including DNS, multicast DNS, HTTP, and UPnP.

`fathom.system` realizes controlled access to system-provided tools and information to invoke select services on the host that can provide information otherwise unavailable or inconvenient to re-implement. Fathom sanitizes the call arguments, handles onerous output parsing, and returns results to the caller while abstracting platform specifics. Examples in this family include the host's *ping* and *traceroute* implementations. In contrast to other runtime plugins such as Java (see § 5.1), Fathom's API *never* allows invocation of arbitrary system commands.

Lastly, `fathom.utils` collects additional helpful APIs, particularly access to aggregate statistics for passively collected data (`metrics.*`) and configuration settings for the browser (`browser.*`), such as proxy configuration.

`fathom.utils.metrics.*` performs low-level system sampling and monitors the browser's HTTP activity. Fathom currently conducts passive data collection in three domains: each web page, the browser itself, and the host's system and network resource usage. For web pages, collection includes socket connection times, DNS resolution times, HTTP response times and goodput, as well as the trigger times for `DOMContentLoaded` and `Load` page events.[2] From the browser, it collects its overall memory use as well as network transmission statistics. Finally, from the host system it collects CPU load, memory use and availability, per-process load, and network interface statistics including packet/byte counters, transmission errors, and—for wireless links—signal strength and noise levels. Per-page CPU load proves tricky to measure. Fathom can expose any browser specific performance measurement API [37] to web pages to measure JavaScript overhead, but authors would still need to instrument their code for reliable profiling. Furthermore, the CPU load induced by active embedded objects such as Flash manifests outside of the browser.

Fathom keeps a history of these metrics to provide *baseline* performance metrics for the pages. JavaScript code using Fathom can then obtain aggregate statistics of these data points in order to diagnose detected anomalies in the document loading process. Fathom stores browser and system metrics in client-side persistent storage, while the web page metrics end up in the site's HTML5 `localStorage` facility. This separation of storage for the baseline metrics enables websites to selectively retain or discard collected datasets for individual browsing sessions, reduces Fathom's persistent storage requirements, and minimizes information leakage across different origins.

Since Fathom monitors the browser's entire HTTP activity, web pages not requiring Fathom's capabilities will also incur an overhead in page load times. To exclude any added overhead, we propose that sites that require Fathom's diagnostic capabilities could explicitly request them. To signal to the server that the client supports Fathom, Fathom adds an *X-Fathom* header in the HTTP request for each page. Web sites that wish to enable diagnostic measurements for the page and its additional resources echo this header in their response. Via local browser configuration the user can request passive data collection for sites as needed.

Comparison: Flash and Java constitute the main competitors to Fathom, so it behooves us to compare their capabilities directly. Fathom's network I/O capabilities subsume Flash's, with the exception of the latter's built-in multimedia streaming capabilities.

[2]When downloading a page's DOM has finished, the browser triggers a `DOMContentLoaded` event. When the page's additional components (such as images) have finished downloading as well, the browser triggers a `Load` event.

API	Availability in JavaScript	Flash	Java Applet[1]	Default policy (§ 4.3)
`fathom.socket.tcp.*`	◐	◐[2]	●	U[3] / SM→U
`fathom.socket.udp.*`	○	○	●	U[3] / SM→U
`fathom.socket.broadcast.*`	○	○	●	U
`fathom.socket.multicast.*`	○	◐	●	U
`fathom.proto.dns.*`	○	○	●[4]	–
`fathom.proto.http.*`	◐	●	●	SM→U
`fathom.proto.mdns.*`	○	○	●[4]	U
`fathom.proto.upnp.*`	○	○	●[4]	U
`fathom.system.getActiveInterfaces()`	○	○	●	U
`fathom.system.getResolvers()`	○	○	●	U
`fathom.system.getRoutingTable()`	○	○	◐[5]	U
`fathom.system.doTraceroute()`	○	○	◐[5]	–
`fathom.system.doPing()`	○	○	◐[5]	–
`fathom.utils.browser.*`	◐[6]	◐[6]	◐[6]	U
`fathom.utils.timer.*`	●	●	●	–
`fathom.utils.metrics.*`	○	○	○	U
JavaScript & DOM access	●	◐[7]	◐[8]	–

[1] Given signed code and trust confirmed by the user, i.e., unconstrained host access with user-level privileges.

[2] No support for listening sockets.

[3] For listening sockets.

[4] If implemented by the experimenter.

[5] By directly calling system binaries in OS-specific locations.

[6] Implicitly or partially; for example, XML-HttpRequest connections transparently inherit browser proxy settings. In Flash, socket connections do not inherit, others do.

[7] By abusing the `getURL` function; no access to return values.

[8] JavaScript–Java interaction via LiveConnect; details depend on platform and implementation.

Table 1: Primary Fathom namespaces and APIs. Due to lack of space, we show select individual functions only for the `system` family of calls, given its diversity. The final column indicates input mechanisms required by the default client policy (see § 4.3): "U" symbolizes that a capability requires user input, "SM→U" means that server manifests suffice to permit the capability while their absence necessitates user input, and "–" indicates permission without additional confirmation. Fathom by design provides full access to JavaScript functions and the DOM without the need of an additional API; we include the ability here to compare to other platforms.

In particular, Fathom supports listening sockets, UDP, protocol-specific APIs, as well as controlled access to host commands and historical performance baselines. With Java, the situation depends on the execution context: without host-specific customization, untrusted applets only allow a limited set of network I/O APIs and require communication with the applet's origin server. As pointed out in § 5.1, signed and trusted applets (as well as Java applications) provide an over-privileged environment that supports all of Fathom's capabilities, without abstracting from platform specifics and without reliable DOM interaction. Table 1 summarizes the respective capabilities.

4.2 Privacy

Our first goal is to ensure Fathom does not allow measurements to exfiltrate sensitive information from a user's browser or host. To do so, Fathom's design mandates that its network I/O stack operates independently of the browser's stack. Hence, any state the browser would normally associate with a connection is unavailable to Fathom. For example, when Fathom script code running in a web page from site `a.com` issues HTTP connections to site `b.com`, such connections do not transmit current session cookies for `b.com` even though the user might currently be logged in to that site in a separate tab. This mechanism effectively defeats classic attacks leveraging same-origin violations, such as cross-site scripting (XSS) or cross-site request forgery (CSRF). Like any JavaScript code, Fathom scripts can only access host-local state (including cookies) for the site the script originated from (`a.com`, in this case).

By providing websites with the ability to collect additional client-side data in the form of both active and passive measurements, Fathom increases the ability for websites to fingerprint visitors [15]. In addition, clients using anonymizing proxies expose themselves to additional de-anonymization risks due to web pages having access to TCP and UDP sockets that can bypass the browser's proxy settings, as well as communicating with local network services (such as the local DNS resolver) that may expose identifying information. Current tools for obtaining anonymity or resisting fingerprinting try to automate disabling or changing sensitive browser functionality [45], but require vigilance on the user's part. Thus, it seems reasonable to expect developers of such technologies (or users employing it) to consider disabling Fathom as needed. Additionally, when the browser has a proxy setup, Fathom's default policy (see below) could disallow active measurement except through the proxy or by explicit agreement of the user. Doing so would also reduce the chances of fingerprinting through arbitrary active communication.

The storage of local data about a user's browsing history is another important privacy concern. Most popular browsers have adopted private browsing modes that, when enabled, aim to eliminate the local storage of information that could later reveal a user's browsing history [2]. Additionally, users expect that "clearing their history" removes all data the browser keeps that one could use to infer their history—behavior that Fathom conforms with.

4.3 Security

We next discuss Fathom's model for controlling scripts such that the platform has adequate protection against facilitating active attacks. We note that in the limit any communication we allow can become part of a distributed attack, but the same applies to browsers without Fathom [29, 50]. We strive to provide enough control that Fathom does not exacerbate the situation significantly. In our present design, Fathom sets its security posture for a given script based on the following inputs:

I.1: **Client Policy.** Once users have installed Fathom, they may tune the client policy by customizing a general local security policy that comes with Fathom. This policy specifies the conditions under which Fathom makes API calls available to scripts. For groups of APIs, the policy defines which destinations they may access, whether they require permission to execute, and the form of that permission. Permission forms include user confirmation,

Resource Schema	Description
`http://*.google.com:*`	`fathom.http.*` APIs may contact any *.google.com name on arbitrary ports
`*://{upnp}:*`	any API can contact hosts found via `fathom.upnp.*` calls
`udp://10.1/16:53,5353`	`fathom.udp.*` APIs may contact hosts within 10.1/16 on the DNS and mDNS ports

Table 2: Example resource schemas in Fathom script manifests.

script manifests, and code signing, with multiple forms possible in order to indicate priorities. Users can adjust this policy at any time. Table 1 shows the default policies for the various API groups.

***I.2*: User Confirmation.** Fathom can directly ask users whether it should allow some activity at script run time. We do not consider this a particularly appealing mechanism because (*i*) framing questions in a way users will understand is challenging, and (*ii*) a system that overly interferes with a user's workflow may lead users to disable Fathom, or train them to grant permission requests blindly [16]. (Note that Fathom's status icon in the browser's toolbar always indicates to the user when a web page employs Fathom APIs.)

***I.3*: Script Manifests.** Each Fathom script includes a *script manifest* that succinctly declares desired resources. Fathom ensures that in-page JavaScript code can only access resources declared in the manifest, subject to the effective client policy. Currently, these resources include Fathom APIs and active measurement targets. APIs and their permissible targets get expressed in tandem in *resource schemas* of the following form:

$$[API\_subset] : //[destinations] : [ports]$$

A resource schema requests access to certain destinations and ports for a subset of the Fathom API. Similar to import statements in other languages, Fathom supports API aggregation, allowing authors to request access to specific functions (e.g., to `fathom.proto.dns.query()`) or to all routines in a family (e.g., `fathom.proto.dns.*`). Destinations come in three forms: (*i*) domains with wildcarding (such as `*.a.com`), (*ii*) IP address ranges (e.g., 192.168/16), and (*iii*) *derived* IP addresses (e.g., `{upnp}`), covering cases where one Fathom API returns an address that the author wants to subsequently pass to another API, but which the script author cannot specify in advance.[3] Table 2 shows examples of Fathom resource schemas.

Fathom enforces resource schemas by initially only making a single API function available: `fathom.init()`. This function receives the script manifest (in JSON form), and subsequently hooks only the requested APIs into the `window.fathom` object. Scripts thus have no way to access APIs they did not request.

***I.4*: Server Manifests.** In addition to script manifests, we allow targets to explicitly control permissible incoming traffic via *server manifests*. These manifests reside at a well-known location on web servers, currently `/fathom.json`. Server manifests can whitelist connectivity for scripts originating from specific domains or IP addresses. Users can configure their client policy to allow APIs to proceed without prompting whenever server manifests permit interaction with the given destination. This scenario forms the default for most APIs initiating connections.

***I.5*: Code Signing.** Finally, experimenters can sign Fathom scripts cryptographically to express authorship. Such signatures provide two key benefits. First, signatures establish an identity behind Fathom code, which allows users to reason about scripts in terms of their trust in the author, instead of (or in addition to) making judgments based on the resources the script intends to use (API calls and targets). This trust in authorship likely proves easier for non-technical users to understand. Second, signed code allows users to configure permissions at the granularity of author identities instead of script origin. Furthermore, Fathom can identify scripts abstractly, across origins, and even when users save Fathom-bearing pages to disk.

Examples: With the above inputs Fathom can derive effective policies for each arriving script at run time. For instance, Fathom can let an arriving script proceed without user prompting if (*i*) the client policy (*I.1*) permits execution without prompting for the API resources the script requests (via its script manifest, *I.3*) and (*ii*) the desired destination agrees via a server manifest (*I.4*), given (*iii*) this server manifest actually exists and indeed agrees. In a more simple scenario, if a script bears the signature (*I.5*) of an author whom the user added to their local whitelist indicating full trust in the code, then the script will execute without any prompting.

By design, policy inputs can come into conflict. The client policy resolves such cases. Consider a script that declares (via *I.3*) its need to use `fathom.socket.tcp.*` to open a connection to a given target that has agreed to such communication (via *I.4*). If the user's client policy (*I.1*) requests prompting for permission to use `fathom.socket.tcp.*` then Fathom will prompt the user (via *I.2*) before running the code regardless of the server's consent and any possible signing.

Our hope is that with more extensive experience, a subset of inputs will emerge that proves sufficient, since fewer mechanisms would simplify explication and maintenance of the security framework. Moreover, expanded user experience will allow us to better understand how Fathom's input mechanisms can accommodate the users' potentially limited awareness of the implications of the different permission levels.

Comparison: Fathom's security model borrows from the Java and Flash platforms, with careful consideration of current browsers' same-origin policies. Like Java, we employ code signing and provide user consent as a means to enable functionality, but in contrast to Java's *carte blanche* permissions after user consent to signed code (§ 5.1), Fathom retains precise API-level control and allows neither execution of arbitrary binaries nor file system access. Like Flash, we employ server manifests to establish an explicit consent signal for the Fathom core that permits cross-site connections [33]. Script manifests exist in several technologies, including Java, Flash, and Android apps, as well as Firefox and Chrome extensions. However, our notion of resource schemas renders resource control more explicit than any of these technologies.

5 Implementation

Web browsers are complex systems, hence the design of a browser-based measurement platform requires careful thought. We first discuss the implementation choices within the browser, and then we describe our prototype of Fathom, which we implement as a Firefox extension.

5.1 Implementation space

To maximize ease of adoption, we would like Fathom to depend on the browser's architecture as little as possible while still imple-

[3]For example, UPnP's discovery phase produces IP addresses to which the script may want to connect via HTTP in order to retrieve a device's service profile. Resource schemas allow precise expression of such dependencies, in contrast to broad notions such as "local network." Fathom tracks hostnames and IP addresses returned by its APIs.

Technology	Rich APIs	Accuracy	Portability Browser	Portability OS
Standard JS	✗	Low	✓	✓
Extension (JS)	✓	Good	✗	✓
Plugin (runtime)	✓	High	✗	✗
Plugin (custom)	✓	High	✗	✗
Browser	✓	High	N/A	✗

Table 3: Design space for a browser-based platform. Note: the accuracy of JavaScript-based extensions depends upon the underlying extension API.

menting the design discussed above. In the following, we discuss several points along this design space. Table 3 summarizes the capabilities of each approach.

Standard JavaScript: While it is possible to implement some types of measurements in JavaScript (see discussion in § 7.1), the lack of low-level socket interfaces and access to host properties, leaves this approach suboptimal. Additionally, measurement accuracy would require careful implementation as timer accuracy depends heavily on browser architecture and load.

Browser extensions: Extensions enhance the functionality of the web browser and allow implementation of measurement tasks in portable JavaScript, platform-dependent C/C++, or both. The API richness available to JavaScript extensions varies considerably across browsers. Those extensions execute with browser privileges and have access to most system resources, including the network and file systems, and remain portable across different operating systems for a particular browser. Since most modern browsers compile JavaScript to native code using JIT compilers, extensions do not impose any significant performance overhead. JavaScript extensions present good candidate vehicles for realizing a measurement platform, assuming sufficient API richness and accuracy. C/C++ extensions increase measurement capability at the expense of portability.

Runtime plugins: In this category, Java, Flash, and Silverlight technologies allow developers to implement experiments and easily distribute them to users who have the required runtime plugin installed. Indeed, Java is a popular choice for measurement experiments due to its rich APIs and performance, but it comes with crucial shortcomings that largely also apply to the Flash platform. First, Java's sandboxing keeps execution effectively fully separate from the containing web page. By contrast, measurement code that executes within a web page can directly interact with current web applications. Second, the runtimes' security policies tend to prohibit activities that could aid network measurements (such as `traceroute` or `ping` invocations). Java's code-signing feature provides a way to work around this limitation: after the user accepts an initial dialog presenting the code author's identity, even self-signed applets may access arbitrary runtime APIs and thus behave like host-native applications *with full user privileges*, including permission to create and delete files or contact arbitrary network locations. While no doubt useful in principle, this *carte blanche* ability far exceeds the permissions required to implement measurement and troubleshooting code. Third, the availability of the runtime presents a limiting factor, as virtually no modern web sites use Java applets.[4] Fourth, even when installed, code portability remains uncertain. For example, JavaScript interaction from plugin code remains highly platform-dependent, and the Android operating system supports only an API-limited dialect of Java.

[4]OSX and Windows no longer include a Java runtime by default, while several recent critical security incidents relating to Java [17, 26, 35] further erode users' willingness to install the platform.

Custom plugins: We could develop our own native measurement plugin in C/C++. While enabling great performance and host access, portable interaction with the browser remains uncertain. For example, Microsoft recently dropped support for the cross-browser NPAPI [53] in its browsers. Sandboxing technologies like NaCl [55] and Xax [13] allow the execution of native applications within the browser without compromising on performance, but their sandboxed environment respects the browser's security policies and disables application code from performing TCP/IP or UDP networking, or even local file I/O.

Browser changes: One could build the entire platform into an open-source browser, which would provide ideal feature support. This approach would present a substantial development effort and would likely find little immediate support from browser vendors. While not immediately feasible, if a general purpose measurement platform proves useful—especially to web site operators—the functionality could be moved into browsers in the future.

After considering the major browsers and the design space sketched above, we chose to implement our prototype of Fathom as a JavaScript-only extension for the Firefox browser. Several aspects informed this choice: (*i*) Firefox enjoys great popularity and exists on a wide range of different platforms; (*ii*) its XPCOM interface provides a rich API to extensions; (*iii*) as we describe further below, this API allows us to perform low-level socket I/O directly from JavaScript. The latter currently sets Firefox apart from other browsers, for which we would need to implement at least parts of Fathom in native code. The extension realizes the design details outlined in § 4 and currently consists of 3,200 lines of JavaScript.

5.2 Firefox's architecture

Before describing Fathom's architecture in detail, we briefly explain the major components of the Firefox browser relevant to Fathom's design. Firefox's DOM subsystem creates an abstract representation of the visited web pages, which the rendering engine uses for layout and page imaging. A single, shared JavaScript engine parses and interprets both web page and extension code, the browser's *UI thread*. While the browser restricts web page code to stringent security policies, the extension code runs with browser-level privileges. The network engine implements application-layer network protocols such as HTTP and FTP. To do this, it employs the Netscape Portable Runtime (NSPR), Mozilla's platform-neutral API for low-level network I/O and *libc*-like functions. The XPCOM subsystem implements a number of core architecture facilities such as threads and memory management. It also exposes these features to the JavaScript runtime. Furthermore, it includes *js-ctypes* [40], a JavaScript wrapper to the *ctypes* library, allowing extensions implemented in JavaScript to call functions in shared C libraries.

5.3 Architectural challenges

Firefox's architecture poses a number of challenges for extension development, particularly given the design goals for a network monitoring platform as we outlined in § 3.

First, without the *js-ctypes* wrapper, we could not perform socket-level I/O from JavaScript and would need to resort to native code. Even given *js-ctypes*, implementation of some socket APIs requires handling platform dependent data types (such as `union`-based network address structures) which creates a challenge for achieving a truly OS-neutral Fathom. We overcame this problem by providing sufficient padding in the relevant JavaScript datatypes to accommodate varying `union` sizes on different platforms.

Second, despite low-level socket access, ICMP responses and raw sockets remain unavailable. Thus, Fathom cannot provide access to packet-level traces, which would be useful for detailed diag-

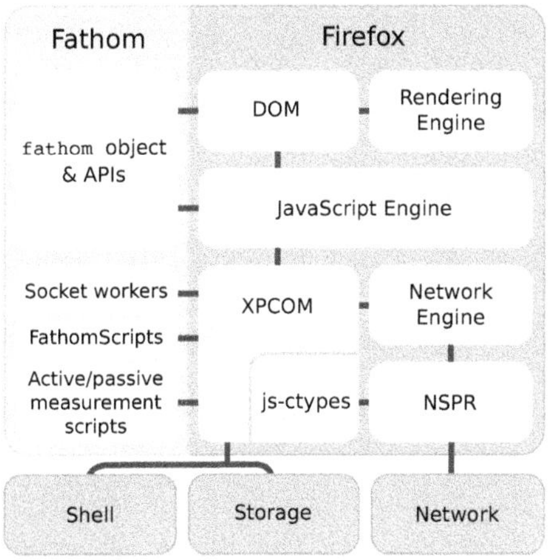

Figure 2: Fathom's architecture in Firefox. Fathom augments the browser's XPCOM subsystem with measurement capabilities and extends each web page's DOM with a `fathom` object and associated measurement APIs. Worker threads enable asynchronous API implementation.

nosis. Fathom overcomes the problem by leveraging access to the browser's command execution API to directly invoke select services on the host, like *ping* or *traceroute* and sidestep this architectural challenge.

Third, JavaScript executing as part of a web page or browser extensions accesses the objects on the web page from the browser's UI thread. Call blocking or long-running functions while executing in this thread would render the entire browser's UI unresponsive.

Fourth, while Firefox extensions can use a threading mechanism called Chrome Workers[5] [39], these threads do not follow the standard OS model of a shared address space with synchronization primitives. Instead, a message-passing system similar to Web Workers exclusively manages communication with worker threads, imposing additional latency.[6]

Fifth, to conserve system resources, recent Firefox versions clamp callback timer accuracy for in-page JavaScript to low precision when the user is viewing a page in a different tab. This clamping can add further function call latency.

5.4 Fathom's architecture

Figure 2 shows the schematic architecture of Fathom running in Firefox. Once installed, the extension creates a component in the XPCOM subsystem that performs two main tasks. First, it installs measurement scripts that handle data collection for passive in-browser measurement. Second, it provides measurement and network I/O APIs to in-page JavaScript. We next discuss the main implementation decisions of Fathom's prototype.

Asynchronous API callflow: As mentioned in § 5.3, in-page and extension JavaScript code as well as the application's UI thread share a single thread of execution. Since Fathom likewise consists of JavaScript code, its focus on network I/O requires careful API design on our part to avoid the possibility of rendering the entire application unresponsive. In order to invoke potentially blocking I/O calls without delaying the rest of the browser and without suffering delays due to browser load, Fathom performs *all* such calls in independently executing Chrome Worker threads and uses asynchronously invoked user-provided callbacks when I/O operations complete. Fathom allocates these worker threads on per-socket granularity as *socket workers*. Firefox's event management on such threads thus ensures that I/O operations queue up and get processed as I/O progresses. Figure 3 illustrates the callflow.

[5]"Chrome" here refers to a privilege level within the Firefox browser, not to the Google Chrome web browser.

[6]While XPCOM exports an interface to manage OS-level threads, we opted for Chrome Workers as they provide a natural, Web Worker-like asynchronous interface and also give thread safety guarantees.

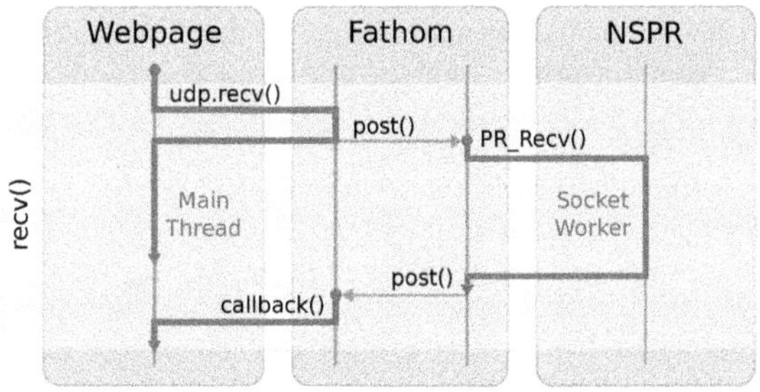

Figure 3: Asynchronous callflow in Fathom between the main thread and a socket worker, for a `recv()` invocation on a UDP socket.

Timer throttling: The throttling of frequently executing timer callbacks in background tabs, as mentioned in § 5.3, could affect measurements implemented in inactive in-page JavaScript code. For example, a measurement in a background tab that invokes the `fathom.socket.udp.receive()` API call in a callback invoked periodically via JavaScript's `setInterval()` mechanism, Firefox would clamp the timeout at 1000ms, perhaps significantly slowing down and affecting the measurement. As a workaround, Fathom users can package an entire measurement into a single function (with nested state and functions) and provide the *source* of that function—a *FathomScript*—to Fathom (JavaScript's `toSource()` feature makes this easy). Fathom then launches a low-privileged Web Worker, prepares it such that it offers the Fathom API, and proceeds to execute the function in the Worker. This guarantees independence from in-page timer clamping. Script authors need only be aware of this feature in special cases requiring the use of low-latency I/O inside Fathom (see § 7.1).

Maintaining baseline measurements: For passive measurements, the current implementation of Fathom samples browser and system information every 5 seconds and makes the last 2,000 samples available to all web pages. Each sample takes approximately 450 bytes. While the Fathom implementation stores a sliding window with the last 20 user sessions per domain for baseline metric measurements, all the parameters of the baseline metrics are configurable. We plan to evaluate different techniques for keeping baseline measurements in our future work.

Security model: Our present implementation supports all of the approaches outlined in § 4.3 other than code-signing, which we anticipate adding in the near future. While Firefox already supports signing JavaScript code [38], we have opted not to employ the mechanism directly in Fathom, due to technical shortcomings.[7] We do, however, follow Firefox's approach of signing the JavaScript code of an entire web page, including scripts it pulls in additionally, which provides protection against runtime page modifications.

Controlling resource consumption: Our design incorporates

[7]Firefox requires bundling the required files into a JAR file, requires a `jar:` protocol handler for the download, insists on specific `Content-Type` header MIME values, and uses a rather simplistic dialog to convey signer identity to the user.

tracking Fathom's resource usage—e.g., number of open connections or amount of data transmitted and received in the last time unit. Currently we do not restrict resource usage, which is consistent with other runtime plugins such as Flash and Java. As we accrue experience with Fathom we may decide exposing resource usage policy to users and/or developers as it becomes necessary. In the current implementation, if a user judges that a given experiment is overloading her system, she can simply close the web page. Given how simple it is for users to stop measurement pages, experimenters have a strong incentive to use system's resources conscientiously.

6 Performance Evaluation

We evaluate Fathom's performance using two metrics—overhead on web browsing and timing accuracy. We conduct all experiments with Firefox v7.0.1 on a 2.20GHz Intel Core2 Duo machine with 2GB RAM, running Ubuntu 10.04, and connected to a 100 Mbps local network.

6.1 Overhead

We evaluate Fathom's page load overhead for eight popular web sites (CNN, Craigslist, ESPN, Google Maps, New York Times, Slashdot, Yahoo! and YouTube) with diverse JavaScript complexity and number of HTTP requests. For each site, we compare the time interval between initiating a page load and the firing of the `Load` event in a Fathom-enhanced browser against a normal browser. The `Load` event fires at the end of the page loading process when all page components have rendered. To obtain the ground truth, we enhance the browser with a lightweight extension that captures only the page load times. We also compare Fathom's overhead with that of Firebug [36], a popular browser extension to debug web page performance. Firebug performs extensive diagnostic measurements, which increase the page load time. We use Firebug as a reference and not as a direct comparison.

We perform 50 page loads for each benchmark and record the timestamp values for the `Load` event and the clock-time spent within Fathom's code for collecting the metrics. To measure the worst case performance overhead Fathom imposes, we conduct all experiments on a browser with a warm cache. Table 4 shows the average absolute load times and Fathom's relative overhead for the benchmarks. The count of HTTP requests, scripts, and images indicates the range between the minimum and the maximum number of requests of each type until the page finishes loading. Requests that start after the page has loaded are not included in these numbers, as Fathom's activity for such requests will not affect the load time.

Overall, Fathom imposes 1–3% overhead for all the benchmarks. We note that as the number of HTTP requests increase, the average execution time within Fathom also increases. We expect this behavior, because Fathom observes all HTTP activity to collect passive measurements. We also observe that with the increase of HTTP requests, Fathom does not always incur a corresponding increase in the absolute overhead. This is because Fathom's overhead is not additive. Since we implement Fathom in JavaScript, its execution will only block the single-threaded JavaScript interpreter, while the rest of the browser can continue loading the page. Thus, Fathom's overhead gets masked in part by network latency and the browser's parallelism during the document loading process.

6.2 Accuracy

Network measurement platforms require accurate timestamps and timers. Fathom leverages the browser's JavaScript API to record timestamps and the XPCOM API to implement a timer. As with all

	No browsing		Passive browsing		Active browsing	
	Avg.	Stdev.	Avg.	Stdev.	Avg.	Stdev.
Send (ms)	0.52	0.29	0.54	0.28	0.52	0.39
Recv (ms)	0.41	0.33	0.50	0.75	0.54	0.89

Table 5: Difference in timestamps from Fathom and `tcpdump` for sent and received packets under different browsing conditions.

measurement, competing activity (browser, host and network) can affect accuracy of timestamps and firing of timers.

Timestamp accuracy: We measure the accuracy of Fathom's timestamps by sending probe packets between two machines on the same local network and recording timestamps for those packets in Fathom and via packet capture with `tcpdump` on the same machine. Since the timestamps from Fathom and `tcpdump` stem from the same clock, the difference between the timestamps for each packet are due to the time required to traverse the network stack between the interface and the browser.

We test timestamp accuracy under different browsing conditions with a train of 106 probe packets with a payload of 200 bytes each. In the "no browsing" scenario, there is no other browsing activity in progress. For the "passive browsing" scenario, we load four web sites (CNN, Google Maps, NYTimes and YouTube) in separate browser tabs and send the probe train after the sites finish loading. For the "active browsing" scenario, we send the probe train while simultaneously loading the same four sites in other tabs.

Table 5 shows the results of the experiment. The "send" row indicates the difference in timestamps from the time Fathom dispatches the probe to the resulting timestamp from `tcpdump`. Similarly, the "recv" row indicates the delay from the timestamp given by `tcpdump` to its arrival in Fathom. In all the browsing scenarios we find the accuracy of the timestamps in Fathom—which inherit the XPCOM granularity of 1 ms—to be within 1 ms of the `tcpdump` reported event time. Further, the standard deviation for all experiments is also below 1 ms. In the passive and active browsing scenarios, Fathom's receive timestamp accuracy remains lower than in the "no browsing" case, but the accuracy is still less than 1 ms.

We next explore Fathom's timestamp accuracy under heavy cross-traffic on the host. We repeat the experiment for 10 probe trains of 10 packets while performing an *iperf* [21] transfer with 4 TCP connections between two hosts on the same local network. In this experiment, the average difference in the "send" timestamps increases to 729 ms. This test represents a worst-case scenario when users fully utilize their network; the heavy concurrent network traffic from *iperf* completely fills the egress queue, which prevents timely transmission of Fathom-generated probes.

Timer: We measure the accuracy of Fathom's timer by testing how precisely it can dispatch 200-byte probes at 200 ms intervals. We use the timer to send 51 probe trains of 100 probes each and measure the average (μ) and standard deviation (σ) for the observed intervals between consecutive probes. Since the accuracy for XPCOM timers is 1 ms, a σ of more than 1 ms would mean that the timer loses precision. We study timer accuracy in four scenarios: (i) no browsing, (ii) passive browsing, as described above (and for which asynchronous activity due to both ads and scripts can lead to concurrent activity), (iii) active browsing, as described above, and (iv) CPU stress case, where we emulate a competing process in the host that overloads the CPU.

For the no-browsing and stress tests, we find the mean timer interval to be within 1 ms of the expected value of 200 ms. Further, for both cases the 5th percentile was 199 ms and the 95th per-

Benchmark	# HTTP	# Scripts	# Images	Avg. load time (ms)	Avg. Fathom load time (ms)	Avg. Firebug load time (ms)	Avg. execution time within Fathom (ms)	Avg. Fathom overhead(%)	Avg. Firebug overhead (%)
Craigslist	4	2	0	512	517	532	9	1.1	4
YouTube	28–34	2–3	17–23	869	896	957	37	3.1	10
Google Maps	39–40	7–8	26–28	1233	1268	1585	60	2.9	29
Yahoo	49–58	4–5	31–43	1168	1180	1747	42	1.0	50
Slashdot	35–60	2–12	22–30	2381	2414	4083	51	1.4	71
ESPN	85–89	7–8	61–63	1761	1805	2325	96	2.5	32
CNN	89–104	6–9	22–59	1458	1504	2263	174	3.1	55
NY Times	115–125	23–26	77–80	1144	1159	1798	91	1.3	57

Table 4: Average page load overhead of Fathom for popular web pages over 50 runs.

centile was 201 ms. For the passive and active scenarios, we use 10 probe trains of size 10, with probes sent at 200 ms intervals. In the passive-browsing scenario, the average lies within 2 ms of the expected, the 5th percentile was 1 ms, and the 95th percentile was 267 ms. For the active browsing scenario, the average lies within 33 ms of the expected, the 5th percentile was 12 ms, and the 95th percentile was 669 ms. This large drop in accuracy compared to the no-browsing and stress experiments occurs because multiple tabs in the same browser window share the same browser runtime.

To sum up, Fathom often achieves 1 ms timestamp accuracy, but the accuracy of timestamping sent packets degrades under both heavy network traffic and concurrent tabs within the browser. The degradation in timing accuracy due to competing activity is a well-known difficulty when measurements are running in shared environments like end-systems. For example, it is well-known that measurements running in PlanetLab will suffer due to concurrent activity [48]. Measurement scripts that use Fathom should be aware of these issues and perform extra tests to verify the accuracy of their experiments. For example, scripts can invoke Fathom APIs to request CPU load and network cross-traffic on the host to test existing operating conditions.

7 Case Studies

In this section, we demonstrate Fathom's utility by implementing three example usage cases that together exercise different aspects of its API: providing a JavaScript version of ICSI's Netalyzr testsuite, debugging web access failures, and enabling Google Maps to diagnose poor web page performance. Our goal is to illustrate how Fathom can support disparate measurement needs.

7.1 Netalyzr

We test Fathom's suitability as a platform for conducting a wide range of active measurements by reproducing many of the tests present in our Netalyzr testsuite [28]. Netalyzr relies on a Java applet for its client-side tests, so supporting this range of measurements can serve as a litmus test for Fathom's flexibility. We developed a Fathom-powered JavaScript version of the suite,[8] focusing in particular on tests not feasible in standard JavaScript.

API requirements: In the following, we consider Netalyzr's full set of test categories and discuss Fathom's significance in the tests.

Address-based tests: This category primarily investigates whether the client resides behind a NAT, and if so, how the NAT renumbers the client-side address and port numbers. It requires the equivalent of `getsockname()`, i.e., access to the local address and port of a socket. Standard JavaScript does not provide these, but Fathom's TCP APIs do.

UDP and TCP port reachability: Tests in this category measures the extent to which the client can communicate freely on approximately 30 ports used by standard protocols. For TCP, standard JavaScript APIs can approximate these tests somewhat clumsily, while for UDP no mechanisms exist. Fathom provides raw TCP and UDP access, making these tests easy.

Access link properties: Netalyzr leverages Java's raw UDP access to implement basic latency testing, upstream/downstream bandwidth measurement, and in-path buffer size measurements. Standard JavaScript APIs provide no equivalent functionality, but Fathom's UDP access allowed us to realize the tests.

HTTP functionality & correctness: These tests determine the presence of HTTP proxies and, if found, the use of caching and caching correctness. The JavaScript XMLHttpRequest API is insufficient to implement Netalyzr's proxy tests as it provides inadequate control over raw message headers and browser caching. Fathom's TCP APIs allow us to realize these tests.

DNS functionality & correctness: This category broadly covers DNS feature support tests, lookup performance measurements, lookup result correctness, and tests for known security problems. While standard JavaScript APIs can use the success status of HTTP requests as an implicit signal of success for the underlying DNS lookup, one cannot obtain the actual IP address resulting from the request, which virtually all tests in this category require. Fathom's DNS API allows us to conduct these tests.

IPv6 support: This category includes reachability tests to IPv6-only servers as well as performance comparisons to servers reachable over IPv6 as well as IPv4. As the address family effectively remains abstracted, standard JavaScript can handle these tests via URL requests from the servers in question.

API usability: The Java-to-JavaScript porting effort also allow us to compare programming paradigms. JavaScript's basic single-threaded execution model with callback-driven asynchronicity differs substantially from Java's lightweight threading model. Accordingly, restructuring the client's overall execution flow required significant reworking of the basic design, while porting the tests themselves felt quite straightforward. Netalyzr's tests execute in individual threads using I/O that may block, with a main thread monitoring test durations. In writing our JavaScript version, we restructured each test into a larger set of individual functions chained together via callbacks invoked by Fathom upon I/O progress. The main test sequence likewise leverages test completion callbacks. We implemented the Fathom-driven Netalyzr subset in two weeks, the majority of which went into replicating the overall test execution, reporting harness, and GUI. Each test took on the order of an hour to port.

Fathom bandwidth tests: Netalyzr's testsuite includes measurements of the available send and receive bandwidths. We implement two versions of the bandwidth test:

- **In-Fathom.** To estimate the maximum possible send/receive rate that Fathom can achieve, we invoke NSPR's UDP `send`/`recv` APIs within a tight loop to saturate the available network bandwidth. Since executing a tight loop increases CPU load, we repeat the experiment and invoke the NSPR `send`

[8] `http://netalyzr.fathom.icsi.berkeley.edu`

Send / Receive	Payload (bytes)	Iperf (Mbps)	In-Fathom (Mbps) Loop	In-Fathom (Mbps) Callback	Web page (Mbps) Loop	Web page (Mbps) Callback
Send	**0**	13.60	6.64	2.42	1.66	0.75
	1024	93.90	92.35	81.41	49.48	24.51
Recv	**0**	4.89	4.55	0.79	0.84	0.02
	1024	93.70	73.36	52.85	22.63	1.69

Table 6: Fathom's send/receive data rates for different payloads.

API within a `setTimeout` with delay 0, which enables other events in the event queue to get processed.

- **Web page.** To get an estimate of the send/receive traffic that JavaScript on a web page can achieve, we perform the same tests but invoking Fathom's socket `send`/`recv` APIs, both within a loop and using a timer.

We perform all tests between a laptop and a desktop connected over a 100 Mbps Ethernet and compare them with the speed achieved by *iperf*. We determine the maximum available send bandwidth using a Fathom client and an *iperf* server. We determine the maximum available receive bandwidth using a Fathom-based server and an *iperf* client. Table 6 shows the results. We observe that under the In-Fathom category, using the NSPR APIs we get much higher traffic rates than the web pages using Fathom's APIs. We expect this, since NSPR APIs are synchronous, while due to the asynchronous nature of Fathom APIs every additional callback in the call sequence affects the bandwidth rates.

We also observe that send rates increase as the payloads increase and match *iperf* send rates at high payload size. But the maximum achievable receive rate did not exceed 73.4 Mbps. Although we could not experimentally verify the cause of the imbalance in the send and receive rates, the discrepancy could arise due to the js-ctypes library used for Fathom's socket APIs. We suspect js-ctypes, which does not benefit from JavaScript's JIT optimizations [18, 6], may pose a significant performance bottleneck.

A natural way to improve the send/receive bandwidths is to parallelize the tests. We tried using HTML5 Web Workers, which spawn OS-level threads to concurrently perform the bandwidth tests. We observed that the reported bandwidth did not increase when running the test in a tight loop. We attribute this to a limitation of the Workers, which cannot access the page's JavaScript namespace, including the `window` object. Workers, thus, cannot access Fathom APIs defined on the `window.fathom` object. All accesses to Fathom APIs must require another level of indirection using the asynchronous message passing `postMessage` API between the Worker thread and the main UI thread (which has access to the `window.fathom` object). This indirection limits the achieved bandwidth.

To enable better bandwidth tests from a web page, script authors should therefore implement bandwidth tests via FathomScripts (recall § 5.4), as they obviate the message passing overhead.

Summary: Our implementation of key Netalyzr tests that prove difficult or infeasible to realize in standard JavaScript (local network configuration, UPnP probing, DNS features, and particularly UDP-based latency and bandwidth tests) confirm Fathom's versatility. For tests leveraging low-level APIs, particularly `fathom.socket.*`, the coding effort compares to that required in Java, while tests that could leverage Fathom's APIs (e.g. `fathom.proto.upnp.*`) instead of needing full protocol implementations required a fraction of the code.

7.2 Web access failure debugging

While troubleshooting suites such as Netalyzr work well when the user has access to sufficient connectivity to download and run the testsuite, such an approach fails in the presence of more fundamental connectivity problems. Indeed, a frequent request we receive from Netalyzr users is to expand the connectivity tests in that direction, particularly in Netalyzr's command-line interface. For such scenarios, we developed a "Debug my connection" measurement application. We include this script as a built-in part of the Fathom distribution (which provides an immediate incentive for users to install Fathom), but emphasize that we implement it solely in JavaScript using the existing Fathom API. The script is currently 400 LOC.

Implementation: We structure the connectivity debugger by starting at the host's link-level network interface configuration and progressing upward through the protocol stack, identifying and reporting problems at each layer. The test begins by obtaining basic system usage statistics from Fathom's usage baseline, including memory usage and process load. Using `fathom.system.getActiveIntefaces()`, we detect whether the system actually connects to any network. If so, we report recent link quality and throughput counters for the active interfaces, as reported by `fathom.system.getNetworkUsage()`, and, again using the baseline counters, report on cross traffic originating from outside of the browser. We then move up to the network layer and test the availability of a default route in the system's routing table, as well as IP-level connectivity (via `fathom.system.doPing()`) to the gateway and DNS resolver(s) (via `fathom.system.getResolvers()`), and relevant browser-level configuration settings such as proxies (via `fathom.utils.browser.getProxyConfig()`). Moving up to the transport level, we attempt retrieval of an image from `www.google.com`, and the test completes.

At each stage, we report on the outcome of the tests involved. In the current version, users click on a "Debug my connectivity" button provided in the browser toolbar in order to initiate diagnosis, but we envision hooking the connectivity debugger into relevant parts of the browser in order to automatically provide contextual information to the user. For example, upon failing DNS lookups, we can automatically test the DNS configuration, and for unavailable servers we can test whether the user experiences a full outage or one just affecting the destination site.

Collaborative debugging: We can further troubleshoot possible connectivity problems in the local network by leveraging Fathom's rendezvous and server-side abilities. In particular, we can leverage Fathom's UPnP and zeroconf capabilities (via `fathom.proto.{mdns,upnp}.*`) as follows. First, using UPnP we can try to locate UPnP-enabled gateway devices. If available, such devices can report uplink type, upstream/downstream throughput counters, and other information [51]. Second, using UPnP and Zeroconf we can locate *other* Fathom-enabled devices. Since Fathom supports listening sockets, we can then engage in both local and remote latency and throughput tests. Correlating the resulting numbers allows us to pinpoint packet loss problems.

To test this approach, we have implemented a Fathom-powered web application in 320 lines of code that lets two Fathom instances detect each other using UPnP and initiate probes to measure unidirectional loss and latency between each pair of Fathom-enabled nodes. The script then compares these values with historic values of loss rates and delays for the local networks, obtained from Fathom's passive data collection. Values greater than expected cause the application to report poor local network performance. Crucially, in order to conduct this testing the user neither needs to

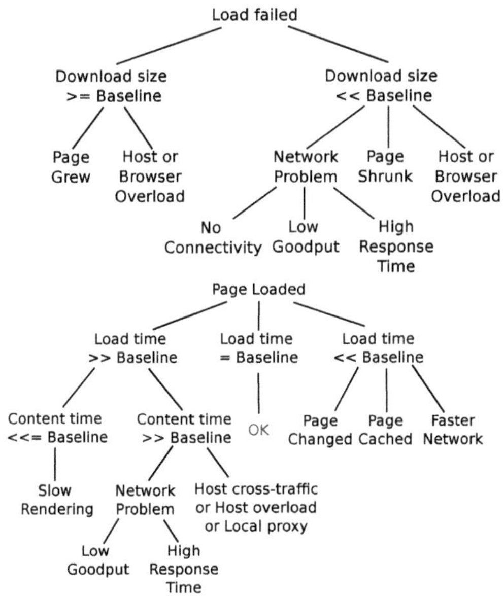

Figure 4: Diagnosis logic when the page load failed (top) vs. when it succeeded (bottom).

understand command-line tools that might serve similar purposes, nor orchestrate the testing procedure manually. Currently, the web application consists of stand-alone web pages. Integrating its functionality into the debug button forms part of our future work.

7.3 Web services debugging: Google Maps

Fathom substantially expands the ability of web site developers to understand the context and impediments that affect the way their pages render in the client's browser. Fathom's API enables a range of potential measurements of interest in this context, such as pinpointing of loss in the home or backbone [11], system and I/O load on the client's device, and network connectivity configurations that hamper performance (e.g., via slow HTTP proxies). In the following, we demonstrate Fathom's utility in troubleshooting client-side issues for web services by playing the role of the developer for Google Maps. We make two modifications to the Google Maps web page code. First, we embed a diagnostic script that uses Fathom APIs to obtain results for passive and active measurements. Second, we provide a debug button on the Google Maps page, which enables a user to initiate execution of the debug script. In the special case when the button itself does not render (because page loading failed), users can employ Fathom's connectivity debugger as explained in the previous section.

Implementation: The debug script first verifies if the `Load` event for the Google Maps web page fired, confirming full page load. Figure 4 illustrates the decision logic Fathom follows for failures (top) and successes (bottom) of page load attempts. If the *load time*—i.e., the time elapsed between the first HTTP request and when the `Load` event fires—resembles[9] the corresponding baseline value, then the algorithm reports a normal load and terminates.

If the load time turns out far smaller than the baseline value, the baseline metric does not apply to the current scenario. Possible causes include changing content size, page caching, and improving network conditions (such as when the user moved to a faster network). Fathom tracks all HTTP-level metrics for the last 20 user sessions. Using DOM `localStorage`, it makes the results available to all scripts of the same origin. We then average these values to generate baseline values for Google Maps. As a result, the debug script can identify the problem by checking if the amount of downloaded content for the web page reduced substantially, if the data rate for individual resources in the web page improved, and also if the browser fetched a web page resource entirely from the cache.

If the load time far exceeds the baseline, it could indicate a network impediment or a host problem. To distinguish between the two cases, the debug script examines the *content time*, i.e., the time elapsed to download the content of the web page. A content time less than or equal to the baseline indicates that a problem with the host machine or the browser slowed down the rendering. Such a condition could also arise if the user explicitly stops the loading of the web page and then invokes the debug script. Our debug script uses `fathom.system.*` APIs to determine resource utilization. If content time proves larger than the baseline, the problem most likely resides in the network. We debug slow networks as discussed in the previous section.

Emulating Google Maps: Since we did not have access to Google Maps servers, we modified the site's JavaScript code at runtime. When visiting the Google Maps page, we inject the debug script and the Fathom debug button using Greasemonkey [30]. Our debug script uses Fathom APIs to implement all diagnostic cases shown in Figure 4.

We implemented Fathom's Google Maps debug script in 640 lines. It imposes no observable runtime overheads. The bulk of the script implements parsing routines to interpret responses from `fathom.system.*` as well as statistical utilities to compute average and standard deviation for metric values. Fathom's system, network, and browser-level APIs directly provide all values except for cross-traffic, which we measure using a combination of APIs: cross-traffic at the host is the fraction of HTTP traffic observed by the browser over the TCP-level traffic approximated from the link-level network measurements. In order to estimate cross-traffic given only transport level information from the browser, Fathom must also account for the effect of framing. To do so, Fathom assumes all link-level traffic to be TCP and subtracts the per-packet overhead from the traffic counters (in bytes) to get approximate transport level TCP traffic. It then compares this value against the TCP traffic values available from the browser.

We used our debug script and performed 10 trials of loading the Google Maps home page with packet loss of 10, 20, 30 and 50 percent and packet delays of 0.5, 1.0, 1.5 and 2.0 seconds. We emulate packet loss and delays with *netem*. In each case, before starting the experiments, we loaded the Google Maps home page repeatedly to allow Fathom to calculate the starting baseline metrics using 20 normal sessions.

While the page load time increased in the presence of packet loss rates up to 20%, the content download time remained within two standard deviations. Higher packet loss rates severely affected the goodput and the page took much longer to load. We observed that for all packet delays (starting from 0.5 seconds), the debug script indicated load times larger than two standard deviations and the content download time also increased. In all cases, the debug script identified a change in the network operating conditions. As the number of completed connection trials increased, more samples fell into the range of two standard deviations and so Fathom could include the HTTP metric values from the newer sessions. The debug script thus adjusted the baseline correspondingly, with the result that some of the later trials reported normal operating conditions.

[9] We say that a value is similar to the corresponding baseline value if it lies within $\pm 2\ \sigma$ of the baseline value.

8 Discussion

Portability: While Fathom currently works only in Firefox, we envision broadening support to other browsers and environments. The Android version of Firefox shares the desktop version's architecture and thus required only minor Fathom compatibility work.[10] In Chrome [3], the implementation would require a combination of content scripts for hooking the API into `window`, an extension core for mediation between web page and OS,[11] and a native binary for all remaining functionality, including invocation of commands on the host. Fathom's callback-driven API would map well to Chrome's architecture. Internet Explorer and Safari prove tricky; the former will require the development of a browser helper object, while the latter's limited extension JavaScript API requires falling back to a plugin component.

Incentives for adoption: Fathom provides strong incentives for end-users, researchers and website operators. For end-users, Fathom's built-in troubleshooting capabilities provide an immediate incentive to install the platform, as a means to help debug connectivity problems that users would otherwise need to solve manually. Our experience with Netalyzr shows that there is in fact a desire for such debugging tools among a set of users who will return to the Netalyzr site to run its set of diagnostics, and who see fit to leave feedback [27]. As Fathom can support troubleshooting tasks both in the presence of fundamental connectivity problems (which preclude the use of website-driven services such Netalyzr) as well as with the ease of visiting a webpage when connectivity permits, we believe this incentive holds at least as strongly for Fathom as it does for Netalyzr. For researchers, Fathom's appeal lies in the fact that it does not require manual installation of code specific to their experiments; once the user has installed Fathom, *any* Fathom-driven experiment will work with the convenience of visiting a web page, lowering barrier-to-entry for both users and experimenters. For site operators, similar incentives apply: once users have installed Fathom, both they and the site operators benefit from increased understanding of performance impediments.

Support for long-running measurements: Quite often experimenters may need to execute long running measurement tasks, such as when studying the evolution of network topology [8, 47] or the dynamics of network performance [5]. Fathom's browser-based nature prompts the question of how long users normally view a particular page before moving on, closing its tab, or closing the browser's window altogether. One dataset collected by the Mozilla TestPilot project and recording browsing behavior of 2,000 Firefox users [41] provides limited insight into this aspect: in general web surfing, 20% of browser windows remain open for at least an hour, 7% for more than a day.[12] With the aid of gentle reminders to users of experiments still actively running in a tab or window, Fathom should thus be able to provide a reasonable level of longer-term data collection. Fathom's current implementation does support execution of such long running tasks if the measurement script is invoked within a *FathomScript* (recall in § 5.4). This mechanism would allow independence from user interaction with the web page (and thus immunize the experiment from potentially reduced scheduling priorities or other service degradations imposed by the browser when a tab does not have focus), but it would still require the end-user to keep the measurement tab open. This is because Fathom controls resource consumption by deallocating all requested resources when the corresponding browser tab/window is closed. Also, Fathom currently does not save any measurement state in the event of browser or system shutdown. We anticipate introducing a special API for experimenters to launch experiments that can run in the background to avoid tying the longevity of a measurement task to a browser tab. This approach will provide independence from accidental tab closures but requires more careful thought regarding the resource management of long-running measurement tasks. For example, we must consider (i) what experiment state and resources must be preserved across browser or system reboots, and (ii) the security implications of running a background task and providing it with access to host and web resources.

[10]Fathom for the Android platform is available on `http://fathom.icsi.berkeley.edu`.

[11]This could leverage Chrome's upcoming support for TCP and UDP sockets in extensions, see `http://developer.chrome.com/trunk/apps/app_network.html`.

[12]The dataset's collection was limited to one week and thus forms a lower bound for longer-running window instances.

9 Related Work

We divide related work in three main areas: browser-based approaches to profile page performance, server-based measurement platforms, and efforts that piggyback measurements with applications already running on end systems.

Browser-based page performance profiling. A number of browser-based approaches help page developers benchmark and debug web page performance. The Firebug [36] extension and the dynaTrace [14] application break down the time to load pages, but these measurements are only accessible from the browser, not the web page itself. As a result, web page developers cannot remotely execute tests from real users' browsers. The Boomerang JavaScript library [54] overcomes this obstacle and, like Fathom, gives web pages a vantage point directly from the end-system. Janc et al. combined JavaScript and Flash to measure throughput and jitter in HTTP downloads [22, 23]. Neither effort strives to provide a generic API. While the forthcoming NavigationTiming API [52] standardizes latency measurements by providing timestamps for fixed events during a page's loading cycle, it does so only for the page itself, not embedded components. Fathom furthermore adds the ability to contrast passive timing collection with active measurements. Rivet [34], another recent effort, leverages reflection and dynamic characteristics of JavaScript to implement a remote debugger for web applications. As a regular JavaScript library, Rivet does not fundamentally add functionality to JavaScript in web pages. Unlike Fathom, Rivet therefore cannot enable additional passive or active measurement tasks.

Measurement platforms. Researchers often use PlanetLab [9] as a measurement platform. More recently, Google launched M-Lab [32] as another measurement platform. Both PlanetLab and M-Lab are based on well-connected servers, and not on end systems as is Fathom. Scriptroute [49] added the capability for any Internet user to run measurements using scripts in a sandboxed, resource-limited environment in PlanetLab. We share Scriptroute's goal of building a community platform for network measurements. However, our focus on taking measurements directly from end systems brings new challenges in particular: portability across operating systems and small performance overhead.

Piggybacking measurements with applications. Dasu [5] is a Vuze plugin that analyzes BitTorrent traffic to characterize ISP performance. Because Dasu piggybacks on BitTorrent, it has a large user base. BitTorrent's frequent use for sharing pirated content, however, can make its use problematic from a policy perspective. We instead opt for deploying measurements on the web browser, which is even more ubiquitous than BitTorrent. The Measurement Manager Protocol (MGRP) [43] is an in-kernel service that runs on end systems to reduce overhead for active measurement tools. MGRP allows measurement tools to send probe trains where application packets piggyback on measurement probes. Neither MGPR nor Dasu provide a programmable measurement platform.

10 Conclusion

In this paper, we describe *Fathom*, a browser extension that uses web browser APIs to build a measurement platform. Fathom provides a programmable interface for writing and launching measurements from the convenience of the web browser. We have implemented a Fathom prototype for the Firefox web browser. Our evaluation shows that it can achieve timestamp accuracies of 1 ms, and generally has runtime overheads of $< 3.2\%$ for popular websites. We also demonstrate its utility in three case studies: providing a JavaScript version of the *Netalyzr* network characterization tool, debugging of web access failures, and enabling web sites to diagnose performance problems of their clients.

Acknowledgements: We thank the anonymous reviewers and our shepherd, KC Claffy, for their comments and feedback on the paper. This work was supported in part by the National Science Foundation under grants CNS-0831535 and CNS-1111672. Any opinions, findings, conclusions or recommendations expressed in this material are those of the authors and do not necessarily reflect the views of the National Science Foundation. We also thank Comcast and Google for their support.

11 References

[1] S. Agarwal, P. Mohan, N. Liogkas, and V. Padmanabhan. Webprofiler: cooperative diagnosis of web failures. In *Proc. COMSNETS*, 2010.

[2] G. Aggrawal, E. Bursztein, C. Jackson, and D. Boneh. An analysis of private browsing modes in modern browsers. In *Proc. USENIX Security*, 2010.

[3] A. Barth, A. Felt, P. Saxena, and A. Boodman. Protecting browsers from extension vulnerabilities. In *Proc. NDSS*, 2010.

[4] S. Bauer, D. Clark, and W. Lehr. Understanding broadband speed measurements. *MITAS project white paper*, 2010.

[5] Z. S. Bischof, J. S. Otto, M. A. Sánchez, J. P. Rula, D. R. Choffnes, and F. E. Bustamante. Crowdsourcing ISP characterization to the network edge. In *Proc. ACM SIGCOMM Workshop on Measurements Up the Stack*, 2011.

[6] Bugzilla. `https://bugzilla.mozilla.org/show_bug.cgi?id=687306`.

[7] M. Butkiewicz, H. V. Madhyastha, and V. Sekar. Understanding website complexity: Measurements, metrics, and implications. In *Proc. IMC*, 2011.

[8] K. Chen, D. R. Choffnes, R. Potharaju, Y. Chen, F. E. Bustamante, D. Pei, and Y. Zhao. Where the sidewalk ends: Extending the Internet AS graph using traceroutes from P2P users. In *Proc. CoNEXT*, 2009.

[9] B. Chun, D. Culler, T. Roscoe, A. Bavier, L. Peterson, M. Wawrzoniak, and M. Bowman. PlanetLab: An overlay testbed for broad-coverage services. *ACM SIGCOMM Computer Communication Review*, 33(3), July 2003.

[10] H. Cui and E. Biersack. Trouble shooting interactive web sessions in a home environment. In *Proc. ACM SIGCOMM Workshop on Home Networks*, 2011.

[11] L. DiCioccio, R. Teixeira, M. May, and C. Kreibich. Probe and Pray: Using UPnP for Home Network Measurements. In *Passive and Active Measurement Conference (PAM)*, Vienna, Austria, March 2012.

[12] M. Dischinger, M. Marcon, S. Guha, K. P. Gummadi, R. Mahajan, and S. Saroiu. Glasnost: Enabling end users to detect traffic differentiation. In *Proc. USENIX NSDI*, 2010.

[13] J. R. Douceur, J. Elson, J. Howell, and J. R. Lorch. Leveraging legacy code to deploy desktop applications on the web. In *Proc. USENIX OSDI*, 2008.

[14] dynaTrace Software. Diagnose and prevent AJAX performance issues. `http://ajax.dynatrace.com/`.

[15] P. Eckersley. How unique is your web browser? In *Proc. Privacy Enhancing Technologies Symposium (PETS)*, 2010.

[16] A. P. Felt, S. Egelman, M. Finifter, D. Akhawe, and D. Wagner. How to Ask For Permission. In *Proc. USENIX Workshop on Hot Topics in Security*, 2012.

[17] FireEye. Zero-day season is not over yet. `http://blog.fireeye.com/research/2012/08/zero-day-season-is-not-over-yet.html`.

[18] A. Giammarchi. An introduction to js-ctypes. `http://webreflection.blogspot.com/2011/09/introduction-to-js-ctypes.html`.

[19] Google. Google Maps help forum. `http://www.google.com/support/forum/p/maps/thread?tid=24f446d4cc24d07a`.

[20] Internet2. Network Diagnostic Tool (NDT). `http://www.internet2.edu/performance/ndt/`.

[21] Iperf. `http://iperf.sourceforge.net/`.

[22] A. Janc. Nettest. `http://code.google.com/p/nettest/`.

[23] A. Janc, C. Wills, and M. Claypool. Network performance evaluation in a web browser. In *Proc. IASTED PDCS*, 2009.

[24] S. Kambala. Speed metrics in Google Analytics. `http://googlecode.blogspot.com/2011/12/speed-metrics-in-google-analytics.html`.

[25] P. Kanuparthy and C. Dovrolis. ShaperProbe: End-to-end detection of ISP traffic shaping using active methods. In *Proc. IMC*, 2011.

[26] A. Kingsley-Hughes. Flashback Malware Worth Up To $10,000 A Day To Criminals. `http://www.forbes.com/sites/adriankingsleyhughes/2012/05/01/flashback-malware-worth-up-to-10000-a-day-to-criminals/`, May 2012.

[27] C. Kreibich, N. Weaver, G. Maier, B. Nechaev, and V. Paxson. Experiences from Netalyzr with engaging users in end-system measurement. In *Proc. ACM SIGCOMM Workshop on Measurements Up the Stack*, 2011.

[28] C. Kreibich, N. Weaver, B. Nechaev, and V. Paxson. Netalyzr: Illuminating the edge network. In *Proc. IMC*, 2010.

[29] V. Lam, S. Antonatos, P. Akritidis, and K. Anagnostakis. Puppetnets: misusing web browsers as a distributed attack infrastructure. In *Proc. ACM CCS*, 2006.

[30] A. Lieuallen, A. Boodman, and J. Sundström. Greasemonkey. `http://www.greasespot.net/`.

[31] M. Mathis, J. Heffner, P. O'Neil, and P. Siemsen. Pathdiag: Automated TCP diagnosis. In *Proc. PAM*, 2008.

[32] Measurement Lab. `http://www.measurementlab.net/`.

[33] D. Meketa. Policy file changes in Flash Player 9 and Flash Player 10. `http://www.adobe.com/devnet/flashplayer/articles/fplayer9_security.html`.

[34] J. Mickens. Rivet: Browser-agnostic Remote Debugging for Web Applications. In *Proc. USENIX ATC*, pages 30–38, 2012.

[35] Mitre.org. Cve-2012-4681. http://cve.mitre.org/cgi-bin/cvename.cgi?name=2012-4681.

[36] Mozilla. Firebug. http://getfirebug.com/.

[37] Mozilla. Perfmeasurement.jsm. https://developer.mozilla.org/en/JavaScript_code_modules/PerfMeasurement.jsm.

[38] Mozilla. Signed Scripts in Mozilla. http://www.mozilla.org/projects/security/components/signed-scripts.html.

[39] Mozilla Developer Network. ChromeWorker. https://developer.mozilla.org/en/DOM/ChromeWorker.

[40] Mozilla Developer Network. js-ctypes. https://developer.mozilla.org/en/js-ctypes.

[41] Mozilla TestPilot. Tab Switch Study. https://testpilot.mozillalabs.com/testcases/tab-switch-study.

[42] V. N. Padmanabhan, S. Ramabhadran, S. Agarwal, and J. Padhye. A study of end-to-end web access failures. In *Proc. CoNEXT*, 2006.

[43] P. Papageorge, J. McCann, and M. Hicks. Passive aggressive measurement with MGRP. In *Proc. ACM SIGCOMM*, 2009.

[44] V. Paxson. End-to-end routing behavior in the Internet. *Proc. ACM SIGCOMM*, 1996.

[45] M. Perry. Torbutton design documentation. https://www.torproject.org/torbutton/en/design/.

[46] C. Reis, S. Gribble, T. Kohno, and N. Weaver. Detecting in-flight page changes with web tripwires. In *Proc. USENIX NSDI*, pages 31–44, 2008.

[47] Y. Shavitt and E. Shir. DIMES: Let the Internet measure itself. *ACM SIGCOMM Computer Communication Review*, 35(5), 2005.

[48] J. Sommers and P. Barford. An active measurement system for shared environments. In *Proc. IMC*, 2007.

[49] N. Spring, D. Wetherall, and T. Anderson. Scriptroute: A public Internet measurement facility. In *Proc. USENIX Symposium on Internet Technologies and Systems*, 2003.

[50] J. Ullrich. Javascript DDoS Tool Analysis. http://isc.sans.org/diary/Javascript+DDoS+Tool+Analysis/12442.

[51] UPnP Forum. Internet Gateway Device (IGD) V 2.0. http://upnp.org/specs/gw/igd2.

[52] W3C. Navigation timing, editor's draft november 14th, 2011. https://dvcs.w3.org/hg/webperf/raw-file/tip/specs/NavigationTiming/Overview.html.

[53] Wikimedia Foundation, Inc. Netscape Plugin Application Programming Interface. http://en.wikipedia.org/wiki/NPAPI.

[54] Yahoo! Exceptional Performance Team. This, is boomerang. http://yahoo.github.com/boomerang/doc/.

[55] B. Yee, D. Sehr, G. Dardyk, J. B. Chen, R. Muth, T. Orm, S. Okasaka, N. Narula, N. Fullagar, and G. Inc. Native Client: A sandbox for portable, untrusted x86 native code. In *Proc. IEEE S&P*, 2009.

Mitigating Sampling Error when Measuring Internet Client IPv6 Capabilities

Sebastian Zander
CAIA, Swinburne University of Technology
Melbourne, Australia
szander@swin.edu.au

Lachlan L. H. Andrew
CAIA, Swinburne University of Technology
Melbourne, Australia
landrew@swin.edu.au

Grenville Armitage
CAIA, Swinburne University of Technology
Melbourne, Australia
garmitage@swin.edu.au

Geoff Huston
Asia Pacific Network Information Centre (APNIC)
Brisbane, Australia
gih@apnic.net

George Michaelson
Asia Pacific Network Information Centre (APNIC)
Brisbane, Australia
ggm@apnic.net

ABSTRACT

Despite the predicted exhaustion of unallocated IPv4 addresses between 2012 and 2014, it remains unclear how many current clients can use its successor, IPv6, to access the Internet. We propose a refinement of previous measurement studies that mitigates intrinsic measurement biases, and demonstrate a novel web-based technique using Google ads to perform IPv6 capability testing on a wider range of clients. After applying our sampling error reduction, we find that 6% of world-wide connections are from IPv6-capable clients, but only 1–2% of connections preferred IPv6 in dual-stack (dual-stack failure rates less than 1%). Except for an uptick around IPv6-day 2011 these proportions were relatively constant, while the percentage of connections with IPv6-capable DNS resolvers has increased to nearly 60%. The percentage of connections from clients with native IPv6 using happy eyeballs has risen to over 20%.

Categories and Subject Descriptors

C.2.3 [**Computer-Communication Networks**]: Network Operations—*Network Monitoring*; C.4 [**Performance of Systems**]: Measurement Techniques

Keywords

IPv6 deployment, banner-ad-based measurement

1. INTRODUCTION

In response to the foreseen exhaustion of IPv4 address space, the IETF standardised the IPv6 protocol as a long-term replacement for IPv4 in 1998 (for an introduction to IPv6 see [1,2]). As of May 2012 most of the IPv4 address space is now allocated and according to predictions, the Regional Internet Registrars (RIRs) will run out of IPv4 addresses between 2012 and 2014 [3]. The question is: how many clients can access Internet resources with IPv6?

IMC'12, November 14–16, 2012, Boston, Massachusetts, USA.

Over the last decade several researchers studied the progress of IPv6 deployment [4]. Many of these studies were based on active probing of servers and network topology, or passive measurements based on server or traffic logs, routing data, or DNS root server data [5–11]. These provide valuable information about the IPv6 capabilities of servers or networks, and the proportion of clients that already use IPv6. However, these studies do not provide information about the IPv6 capabilities of clients. While most hosts run IPv6-capable operating systems, they are often not configured to use IPv6 (because there are virtually no IPv6-only services) or their access networks are not IPv6-capable.

More recently, a few researchers used active web-based measurements (based on a technique developed by S. Steffann [12]) to investigate the IPv6 capabilities of clients [13–15]. On certain participating web sites the clients' web browsers download not only the "normal" web pages and images, but also a few very small invisible images from a test server. One image can only be retrieved with IPv4, a second only with IPv6 and a third with either IPv4 or IPv6. Based on the images successfully retrieved one can determine the clients' IPv6 capabilities.

With this method the client sample has a bias based on the participating web sites. In previous studies only one or two web sites were used, or the analysis was limited to a region (e.g. EU countries). Also, the original method did not provide any means to verify whether a client actually attempted all image downloads or aborted some, for example because the user moved to a different web page quickly. Furthermore, previous studies focussed only on certain aspects (e.g. how many clients preferred IPv6 [13]).

We propose an improved version of the web-based measurement method, commonly implemented with JavaScript (JS-test). Our method not only measures the fraction of clients that prefer IPv6 over IPv4, but also the fraction of clients that are IPv6-capable (*including* latent Teredo [16] capabilities), or use an IPv6-capable DNS server for query resolution. We also analyse the capabilities based on the clients' operating system (OS) and country, and we estimate IPv6-related dual-stack failures and the use of "happy eyeballs" (fast fail-over from IPv6 to IPv4 [17]).

To increase the number of participating sites our test provides information not only to us, but also to the site operators themselves via Google Analytics. Since some web service providers are interested in the IPv6 capabilities of visiting clients, this has lead to an increase in participating sites. We also propose a novel method of selecting the clients to be tested. We embedded the test script in a

Flash ad banner (FA-test), which is served to clients via Google's AdSense. The test is carried out as soon as the ad is *displayed* by a browser. The ad's distribution is controlled by Google, but ads can potentially reach a very broad set of clients, through popular AdSense-enabled web sites (e.g. YouTube).

We compare the coverage of JS-test and FA-test and show that Google distributes the ads well. Normalised on the total number of tests, the FA-test reaches far more IP addresses located in more /24 networks compared to the JS-test. However, due the ad's running costs the number of FA-tests was limited, and the ad presentation was somewhat biased towards Asian web sites. Also, the FA-test could not test iPhones or iPads due to the absence of Flash.

We then identify sources of potential sampling error and propose techniques to mitigate it. We interpret our results as statistics of connections to avoid potential bias, for example due to multiple clients behind proxies or Network Address Translators (NATs). To mitigate the sampling error we re-weight the data based on the clients' countries and the proportion of Internet traffic of different countries. We compare the proportions of OSs and browsers measured with reference statistics and show that our raw statistics appear biased, but the re-weighted statistics are similar to the reference. We then estimate the IPv6 capabilities based on the re-weighted statistics.

The paper is organised as follows. Section 2 describes our measurement method. Section 3 describes the dataset and compares the client samples of JS-test and FA-test. Section 4 analyses sources of bias and presents our approach to mitigate the sampling error. Section 5 presents the IPv6 capability statistics measured. Section 6 discusses related work and compares it with our findings. Section 7 concludes and outlines future work.

2. MEASUREMENT METHOD

We describe the improved web-based measurement method, discuss the different ways tested clients are selected, and outline our experimental setup. Finally, we argue that our tests do not significantly affect the experience of users.

2.1 Web-based measurements

When users visit web sites their web browsers normally download several web pages, scripts, images etc. At certain participating web sites this includes a small test script that fetches a few invisible one-pixel images via HTTP from URLs pointing to our test web server (similar to a page hit counter). We refer to the script as *test* and a single image download as *sub-test*. For URLs containing host names the client's resolver has to first perform DNS look-ups against our authoritative test DNS server prior to sending HTTP requests. The following sub-tests allow us to test IPv4, IPv6, dual-stack, and (latent) Teredo [16] capabilities of clients, as well as whether the client's resolving DNS server is IPv6-capable:

1. The image can only be retrieved with IPv4 because the DNS server only returns an A record (IPv4-only).
2. The image can only be retrieved with IPv6 because the DNS server only returns an AAAA record (IPv6-only).
3. The image can be retrieved with IPv4 or IPv6 because the DNS server returns A and AAAA records (dual-stack).
4. The image URL is an IPv6 *address literal*. Windows Vista and Windows 7 hosts without native IPv6 will not query for DNS AAAA records, but with an IPv6 address literal they can use Teredo [18].
5. The image URL puts our authoritative DNS server behind an IPv6-only name server record. The DNS server can only be accessed if the client's resolving DNS server can perform DNS queries over IPv6.

A sub-test is deemed successful if the image could be retrieved, otherwise it is deemed a failure. After all sub-tests have been successfully completed or a timeout of ten seconds (whichever occurs first), the test script sends another HTTP request to the test web server that acts as a *test summary*. The test summary allows us to determine whether a browser has waited a sufficient amount of time for all sub-tests to complete. Without the summary it is impossible to know whether a sub-test was not successful because a client lacked the capability or because the test was interrupted.

The test script starts sub-tests in quick succession, but to which degree the images are fetched in parallel depends on the web browser's connection management. We assume that browsers try to fetch objects as quickly as possible without unnecessary delay. The URLs for each sub-test and summary resolve to different IPv4 and/or IPv6 addresses, which means browsers cannot multiplex different sub-tests over one TCP connection.

2.2 Client sample

Clients interact with our measurement system in two different ways. Several participating web sites link our JavaScript test script (JS-test) and visiting hosts are tested. To encourage participation in our JS-test, the script also logs the IPv6 capabilities of clients with Google Analytics and the site administrators can inspect the statistics (test script is available at [19]). The client sample is biased towards the participating web sites, but since the test is implemented in JavaScript the vast majority of visiting clients can be tested. We assume there are not many clients with disabled JavaScript [20].

We also implemented a Flash ActionScript test and embedded it in a Flash ad banner (FA-test). The ad is served to hosts via Google's AdSense. The test is carried out as soon as the ad is *displayed* by the web browser, the user does not have to click on it. We selected the ad's keywords and languages to achieve broad placement across different countries and sites. The FA-test reaches a more diverse client population, but cannot be carried out by clients without Flash, such as iPhones/iPads during our measurements.

2.3 Experimental setup

Figure 1 shows a logical diagram of our experimental setup. The DNS server handles the incoming DNS queries and the web server serves the test images. All servers are time-synchronised with NTP. Local Teredo and 6to4 relays are located close to the web server to reduce IPv6 tunnelling delay (Teredo server and client-side 6to4 relay are out of our control). We collect HTTP log data, DNS log data, and capture the traffic with tcpdump.

Several data fields are used to convey information from a tested client to our test servers, and to prevent caching of DNS records or test images at the client or intermediate caches (see Figure 1). The following data is prepended to the host name *as well as* appended as URL parameters: test time, test ID, test version, and sub-test name. Test time is the time a test started taken from the client's clock (Unix time plus milliseconds). Test ID is a "unique" random 32-bit integer number determined by the test script.[1] Test version is the test script's version number and sub-test name is a unique identifier for the sub-test, e.g. "IPv4-only".

[1]FA-tests use a hash value computed from Google's clickTAG, as Google prohibits the use of the ActionScript random() function.

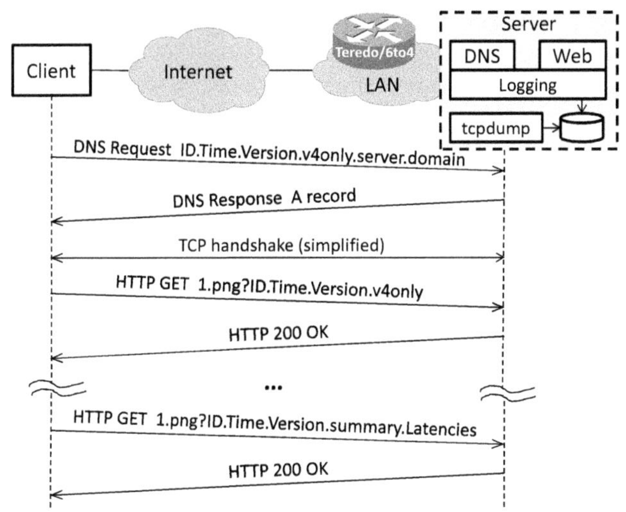

Figure 1: Experimental setup

The JS-test uses cookies to ensure clients are only tested once every 24 hours (per web site). The main reason for this is to reduce the load on our test servers. However, some clients may ignore the JS-test cookies and perform the test multiple times within 24 hours. The FA-test cannot use cookies due to Google's restrictions, so clients may be tested multiple times. For both tests there can be web proxies or NATs in front of multiple clients that look like repeating clients. Nevertheless, the number of IPs repeating the test within 24 hours is low (see Section 3.1)

2.4 User impact

The JS-test is only executed after the web page has loaded completely. Hence it does not delay the loading of the page. The JS-test script is 12 kB large (including the Google Analytics code). The loading of the FA-test is controlled by Google. Our ad is only 16 kB large, not larger than many other ads and well below Google's size limit of 50 kB. The test images are only 157 bytes large and invisible (loaded but not displayed). The total size of the test data transferred is well under 20 kB, less than 6% of the average web page size of 320 kB (as determined in [21]).

Our test opens six different TCP connections to download the test images (five for the sub-tests plus one for the summary). The download is done in the background by the browsers. The maximum number of concurrent open connections is at least 30 for most browsers [22]. Whether the test connections will cause existing connections to be closed depends on how many connections are already open. But in any case the test does *not* affect the loading of the current page and the next page will not load slower than when loaded for the first time.

We argue that overall our test does not have a significant impact on the user's browsing experience. We conducted a few simple tests in which test users did not experience any noticeable impact. Also, our test does not trick users into revealing any sensitive information. Instead, we utilise information that web clients normally send to *every* visited web server.

3. DATASET

We use the data collected between 16th of May 2011 and 19th of February 2012. We discarded 1% of tests as "invalid", such as tests with malformed or truncated URLs in the server logs. We also discarded tests of clients referred by three large web sites that only participated for one or two days. We analyse the data in blocks of days (24 hours). However, we will present most of the statistics averaged over weekly periods to reduce the error of the estimates. We now describe the properties of our dataset.

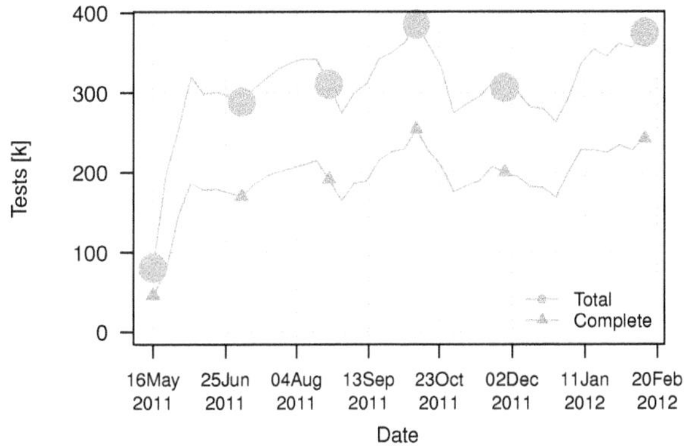

Figure 2: Total number of tests and number of completed tests per day

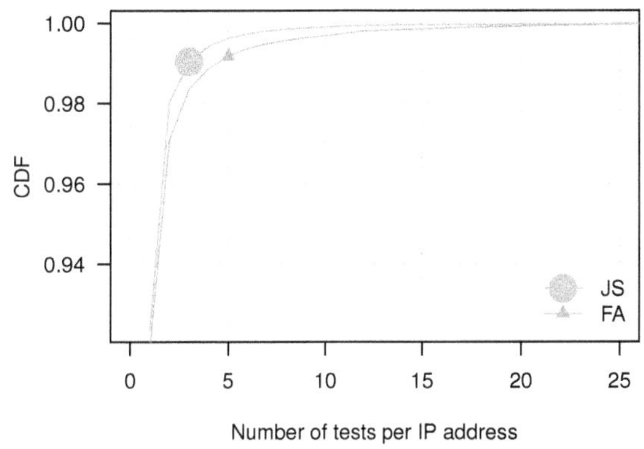

Figure 3: Number of tests per day per IP address for JS-test and FA-test

3.1 Number of tests

Figure 2 shows the weekly averages of the number of total and completed (with test summary) tests per day. Apart from the initial period the total number of tests per day was 250 000–300 000 and the number of completed tests was 180 000–200 000 per day (of which 30 000–35 000 were FA-tests and the rest were JS-tests).

The statistics we present in Section 5 are proportions. If the samples are independent, then the standard error for proportion estimates is $SE = \sqrt{\frac{\hat{p}(1-\hat{p})}{n}}$, where $\hat{p}$ is the estimated proportion and n is the number of samples. Generally, for our statistics the relative error is below 1% and hence we do not plot error bars. However, due to the way we sample the clients there is an additional sampling error, which we discuss in Section 4.

Figure 3 shows the CDFs of the number of tests per day for each IPv4 address. FA-tests have a higher repeat rate (FA-tests cannot use cookies), but it is only slightly higher since Google distributed the ads well. Less than 8% of IPs performed the test more than once per day and less than 0.1% (JS-test) or 0.3% (FA-test) of IPs performed the test more than 10 times per day. This suggests that single IPs do not dominate our statistics.

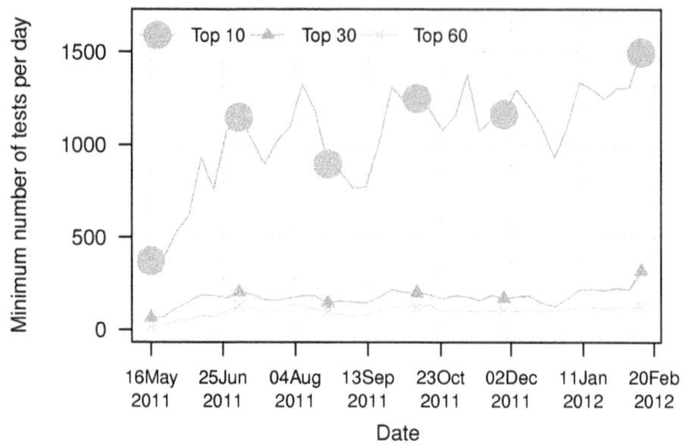

Figure 4: Minimum number of tests per day for the top-10, top-30 and top-60 traffic generating countries [24,25]

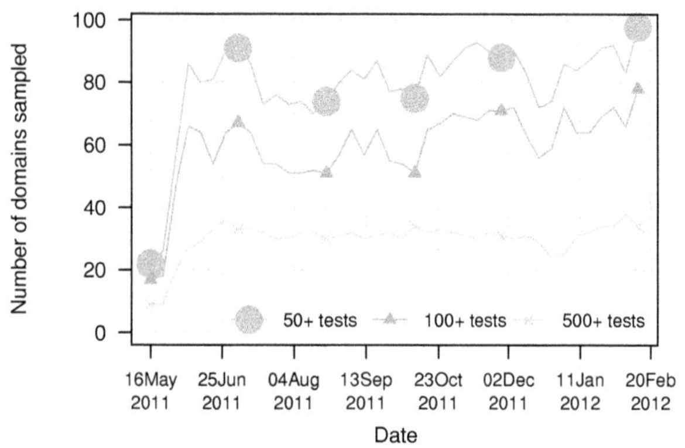

Figure 5: Number of domains with at least 50, 100 and 500 tests per day

3.2 Country and domain coverage

According to MaxMind's GeoIP [23] our dataset includes clients from 95% of all country codes including all 196 sovereign countries (the missing 5% are dependent territories). For about one third of the sovereign countries we observed at least 100 tests per day (with a few outliers), and these countries accounted for almost 100% of the Internet's traffic according to [24,25]. Figure 4 shows the *minimum* number of samples per day per country for the top-10, top-30 and top-60 countries, which generate 76%, 90%, 98% of the Internet's traffic according to Cisco and Wikipedia statistics [24,25] (we use the 5% quantile as minimum to exclude a few outliers). Apart from the initial period the minimum number of samples per day was higher than 750 for any of the top-10 countries, higher than 200 for any of the top-30 countries and at least 100–150 for any of the top-60 countries.

Figure 5 shows the number of domains sampled that generated at least 50, 100 or 500 tests per day (based on HTTP referrer information for JS-tests and Google ad placement information for FA-tests). Apart from the initial period, there always were 30–35 domains that each generated at least 500 tests a day and 55–75 domains that each generated at least 100 tests per day.

3.3 Client and subnet coverage

Figure 6 shows the number of unique versus total tested IPv4 addresses (left) and unique versus total tested /24 networks (right) for the measurement period (a /24 is obtained by setting an IPv4 address' last octet to zero). The dashed lines show the maxima (unique equals total). Since the IPv6 capability of clients depends on the clients themselves *and* on the clients' ISPs, a good spread over different /24 is also desirable.

The FA-test reaches a much larger proportion of unique IP addresses. The chance of the same IP address being tested multiple times is much lower than for the JS-test. It appears that Google tries to distribute the ads to a wide audience (at least in our case where the ad is not clicked often). For /24 networks the FA-test initially also tested unique /24 networks at a higher rate, but over time has slowed to a rate only slightly higher than that of the JS-test. The FA/JS-test sampled 0.40%/0.48% of the routed IP addresses and 22.2%/21.7% of the routed /24 networks (the total number of routed addresses divided by 256). Overall both tests sampled 0.75% of the routed IP addresses and 28.7% of the routed /24 networks. The percentages are based on Routeviews data [26] (2.52 billion routed addresses in February 2012).

Figure 7 plots the percentages of /24 networks from each /8 prefix where at least one IP was sampled for JS-test and FA-test versus each other. We classified the /8 prefixes based on which RIR mainly assigned them, and use the category "Several" for prefixes assigned by multiple RIRs. The figure shows that the JS-test covers significantly more /24s in many prefixes assigned by ARIN, and slightly more /24s in some prefixes assigned by RIPE or several RIRs (the latter mainly in the old class B space). On the other hand, the FA-test covers significantly more /24s in prefixes assigned by APNIC and a few more /24s in some prefixes assigned by LACNIC.

4. SAMPLING ERROR MITIGATION

Now we discuss sources of potential bias and present methods to mitigate the error. Our main method is based on re-weighting the data. We compare our OS and browser statistics from the raw and re-weighted data with reference statistics and show that the re-weighted statistics are a much better match than the raw statistics.

4.1 Error analysis and data re-weighting

Our data collection can be modelled as probability sampling, since random clients are tested. However, our client sample is not uniform. Different sites hosting the JS-test have different audiences. Hence, the JS-test error has two parts: a sampling error due to the random choice of sites and the bias of results conditional on a given site. We view the total error as sampling error since, averaged over all possible random choices of sites, the average per-site bias would be zero. The FA-test has an actual bias towards low-revenue sites showing our Google ad, and we abuse terminology by referring to this also as sampling error.

Bias may be caused by clients that do not respond to the test. The JS-test uses JavaScript, but all major browsers are JavaScript-capable and JavaScript is usually enabled as many web pages rely on it. According to [20] only 1–2% of clients have JavaScript disabled. Also, disabled JavaScript may be uncorrelated with IPv6 capability. We do not expect significant error to be introduced by this non-response.

The FA-test requires Flash, which may not be present on all clients. Most notably during the time of our experiments iOS (iPhone, iPad) did not support Flash, and on some Unix OS Flash also does not always work out-of-the-box. Since IPv6 capability depends on the OS, it is likely that the lack of Flash in non-Windows OS introduces bias. Furthermore, bias could be introduced by clients that use ad-blockers, which prevent the execution of ads. However, it is unclear what percentage of clients use ad-blockers and whether their use is correlated with IPv6 capability.

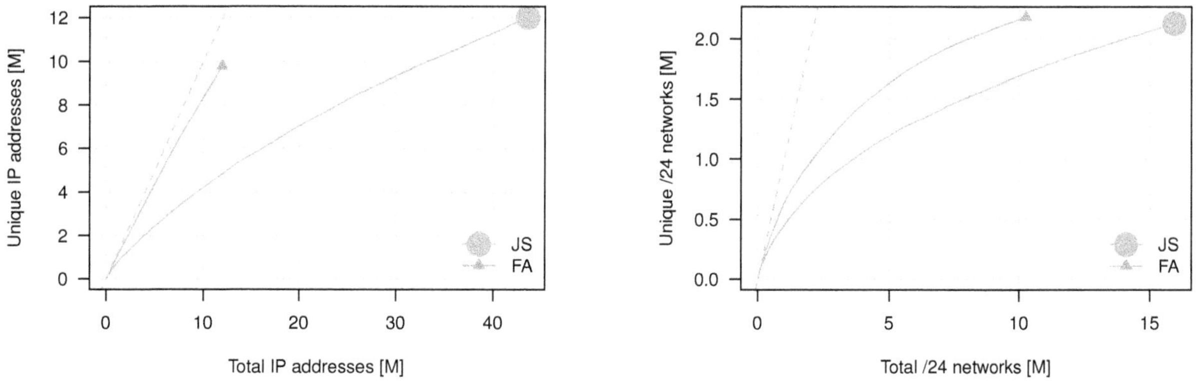

Figure 6: Unique vs. total tested IPv4 addresses (left) and unique vs. total tested /24 networks (right). The dashed lines show the maxima (all observed IPs or /24s are unique).

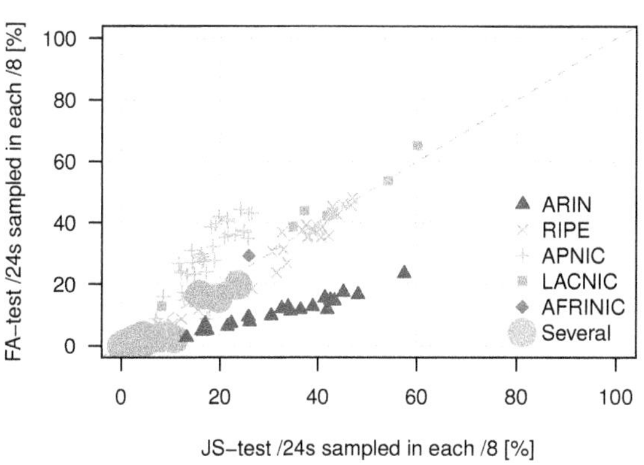

Figure 7: Percentage of /24 networks from each /8 prefix where at least one IP was sampled for JS-test (x-axis) and FA-test (y-axis)

Another source of potential bias are clients that do not perform some sub-tests, not because they lack the capabilities, but because of other reasons. For example, if a user moves to another web page quickly, this effectively aborts a test. To eliminate this bias we analyse only *completed* tests (with test summary). For these we can be sure that the clients attempted all sub-tests.

Our sample of tested clients is biased towards the web sites activating the JS-tests and FA-tests. For example, Indonesian JS-test connections are well over-represented due to a large participating Indonesian web site. Furthermore, the participating web sites change over time. To mitigate this bias we weight each test based on the tested client's country.[2] Let P_c be the weight of country c ($\sum P_i = 1$), T be the total number of tests, and T_c be the number of tests of country c . Then the weight for a test W_t is:

$$W_t = P_c \frac{T}{T_c} \,. \tag{1}$$

Our weights P_c are based on traffic statistics estimated by Cisco [24] for 16 countries that generate 79% of the Internet's traffic and Wikipedia country traffic statistics [25]. The traffic proportion ranks of the 16 countries in both datasets are broadly consistent. Spearman's rank correlation is 0.54 (1.0 indicates perfect positive correlation) and a hypothesis test indicates correlation (at 99% significance level). However, the Wikipedia data appears biased towards non-Asian countries. Hence, we use the Cisco estimates for the 16 countries covered and the Wikipedia statistics for the remaining countries.

We use MaxMind's GeoLite country database [23] to map IPv4 client addresses to countries, which has a claimed accuracy of 99.5%. Note that the ISO 3166-1 country codes represent not only sovereign countries, but also dependent territories and special areas of geographical interest.

Similar re-weighting approaches were used to mitigate bias before. For example, to deal with non-response the US Current Population Survey divided all sampled households into 254 adjustment cells and for each cell the sampling weight of non-respondents was redistributed to the other households in the cell [27].

We interpret the measurement results as *statistics of connections*[3] and not of clients. Interpreting the measurements as statistics of clients would result in an "observation bias". Also, IP addresses are not very good identifiers for clients (even when combined with browser ID strings). Using statistics of connections we avoid potential bias caused by multiple clients behind web proxies or NATs, or clients that change their IP addresses more often (home users, mobile users, frequently offline clients). Furthermore, we avoid potential bias because we are more likely to observe clients that are more likely to use the Internet, which potentially have more up-to-date systems and are more up to date with IPv6.

4.2 Effectiveness of re-weighting

To determine the possible bias in the raw data and the effectiveness of our re-weighting we compare the clients' OS, web browser, and Windows version distributions from our data with reference "population statistics". Since nobody has true population statistics we use the data of multiple statistics providers as reference.

We used the two-sample t-test (statistical hypothesis test) to compare the JS-test and FA-test combined raw and re-weighted data with the reference. The test determines whether the difference of the means of two samples is significant or due to random chance. The null hypothesis is that the difference between the two means is zero. If the null hypothesis is rejected, then there is a statistically significant difference.

[2]For <1% of JS-tests, where the IPs were proxies located in different countries than the clients (e.g. BlackBerry connections), we assume a client's country was the referring web sites' country (our data shows that many sites had relatively high locality).

[3]Here "connections" refers to instances of end-host connectivity and not to transport-layer connections.

Table 1: OS percentage of connections for raw (R) and re-weighted (W) data (mean±standard deviation)

	Reference [%]	JS R [%]	JS W [%]	FA R [%]	FA W [%]	Total R [%]	Total W [%]
Windows	81.5±4.5	89.1±1.8	83.5±1.6	96.6±1.0	93.1±0.8	90.3±1.8	86.2±0.9
MacOS X	8.8±3.1	3.3±0.5	8.0±0.4	2.9±0.9	6.1±0.8	3.2±0.4	7.5±0.3
iOS	4.4±1.4	1.7±0.2	3.3±0.5	0.0	0.0	1.4±0.2	2.5±0.4
Linux	1.2±0.4	2.1±0.5	4.3±1.3	0.5±0.1	0.8±0.2	1.8±0.3	3.1±0.6

Table 2: Windows 7, XP, Vista percentage of all Windows connections for raw (R) and re-weighted (W) data (mean±std. deviation)

	Reference [%]	JS R [%]	JS W [%]	FA R [%]	FA W [%]	Total R [%]	Total W [%]
Windows 7	44.3±4.3	41.5±2.9	48.6±3.5	38.0±6.8	42.7±4.2	40.9±3.3	45.6±3.1
Windows XP	40.3±5.2	51.8±1.5	41.3±2.6	52.7±7.7	42.8±3.2	51.9±2.2	42.8±2.4
Windows Vista	13.2±3.0	6.4±1.8	9.3±1.1	9.2±2.0	14.4±1.2	6.9±1.4	11.0±0.8

Table 3: Browser percentage of connections for raw (R) and re-weighted (W) data (mean±standard deviation)

	Reference	JS R [%]	JS W [%]	FA R [%]	FA W [%]	Total R [%]	Total W [%]
MS IE	39.9±8.4	18.4±4.1	35.8±2.3	49.9±10.3	52.4±2.2	23.5±4.6	42.3±1.6
Firefox	24.5±2.3	47.7±1.5	27.5±1.9	20.8±3.9	20.8±1.6	43.2±2.9	24.7±2.3
Chrome	21.9±4.9	22.9±2.5	22.6±2.3	24.4±5.8	21.0±2.1	23.3±3.1	21.3±1.8
Safari	7.0±1.6	6.0±1.3	9.6±1.4	2.2±0.5	4.2±0.5	5.3±1.1	8.1±0.7
Opera	2.3±1.0	3.8±1.1	2.9±0.2	2.7±1.0	1.4±0.2	3.7±1.0	2.4±0.2

Table 1 compares the percentages of OSs for JS-test, FA-test, and both tests combined for both the raw and re-weighted data with the reference data (unweighted average of AT Internet, Clicky, Net Market Share, StatCounter, StatOwl, W3Counter, WebmasterPro, Wikimedia from [28]). The FA test is biased towards Windows, as iOS could not run Flash and possibly Flash on Linux also did not work for some distributions/browsers. For both tests the MacOS X percentage is surprisingly low compared to the reference, but it may be that our observed web sites are less frequently used by MacOS X clients. The re-weighted statistics are much closer to the reference data, except that the JS-test appears to have a bias towards Linux (possibly due to the participating sites attracting a higher than average Linux user fraction).

According to the t-tests, for the combined raw data the null hypothesis must be rejected for all OSs (at 99% confidence level). In contrast for the re-weighted data we cannot reject the null hypothesis for Windows, MacOS X and iOS, but must reject it for Linux (at 99% confidence level). The re-weighted means are similar, except for Linux, which is over-represented.

Table 2 shows the percentages of Windows XP, Vista and 7 as percentages of all Windows connections for our data and the reference (as above from [28]). The raw data is biased towards more Windows XP and fewer Windows Vista and Windows 7 connections (e.g. for the JS-test a large Indonesian blog site had a high Windows XP fraction). But the re-weighted data is close to the reference data.

According to the t-test for the combined raw data the null hypothesis is rejected for Windows XP and Windows Vista, but not for Windows 7 (at 99% significance level). However, for the combined re-weighted data the null hypothesis cannot be rejected for any of the three Windows versions.

Table 3 shows the browser percentages of all connections and the reference data (based on unweighted averages of June 2011, December 2011 and March 2012 data from StatCounter, Net Applications, W3Counter, Wikimedia, Clicky from [29]). The raw JS-tests have a much higher percentage of Firefox and a much lower percentage of MS IE than the reference data. But the re-weighted numbers are much closer to the reference. As said above, the FA-test is biased towards Windows hence MS IE has a larger share and the other browsers have a smaller share (in particular Safari, which is not popular on Windows). Most of the re-weighted data is closer to the reference data, except the percentage of MS IE.

According to the t-tests for the combined raw data the null hypothesis is rejected for all browsers except Chrome (at 99% significance level). In contrast for the re-weighted data the null hypothesis cannot be rejected for any browser (at 99% significance level).

In conclusion, most of the OS and browser statistics from the raw data appear to have bias, while all statistics based on the re-weighted data are relatively similar to the reference, with the exception of Linux being over-represented. The results indicate that the re-weighting is very effective. Nevertheless, we cannot determine whether it is similarly effective for the IPv6 capability statistics.

4.3 Discussion and limitations

The per-country re-weighting mitigates the bias introduced because the proportions of tests observed from different countries differ significantly from the countries' traffic proportions. However, there is still a bias towards the clients visiting the particular set of web sites observed. Nevertheless, our set of web sites is relatively large and diverse, consisting of 55–75 different domains (universities, ISPs, gaming sites, blog sites) that refer at least 100 tested clients per day. Furthermore, we will show that a number of the statistics (but not all) from re-weighted JS-tests and FA-tests match well despite the totally different set of web sites.

Using per connection statistics instead of per client/IP statistics means we avoid additional observation bias. We showed in Figure 3 that in general our statistics are not dominated by some IPs that generated a huge number of connections. However, we encountered two daily statistics with overall low numbers (e.g. clients that preferred IPv6) that were largely dominated by a single IP address. We corrected these outliers manually (by ignoring the IPs).

5. IPV6 CAPABILITY ANALYSIS

First we analyse the overall and OS IPv6 capabilities. Then we compare statistics for JS-test and FA-test. Finally, we analyse per-

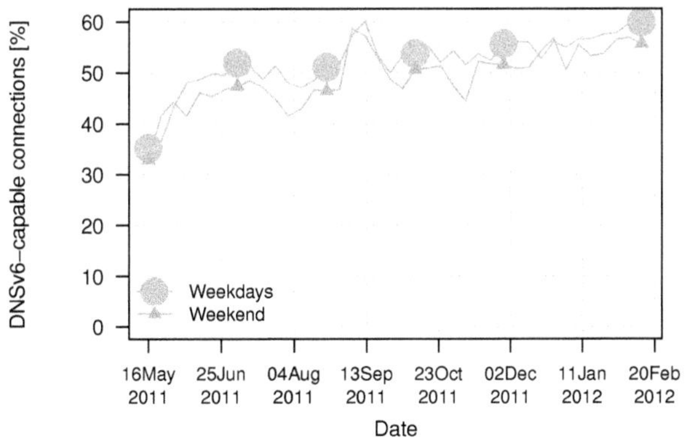

Figure 8: Percentage of all connections with IPv6-capable resolving DNS server

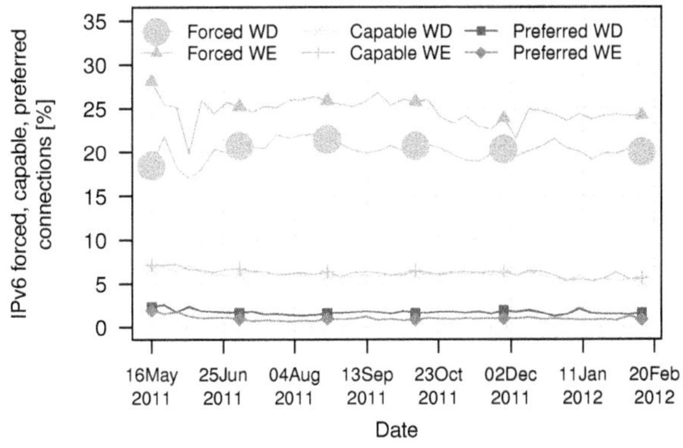

Figure 9: Percentage of all connections from hosts that were IPv6-capable, preferred IPv6 in dual-stack, or could be forced to use IPv6 with a literal URL

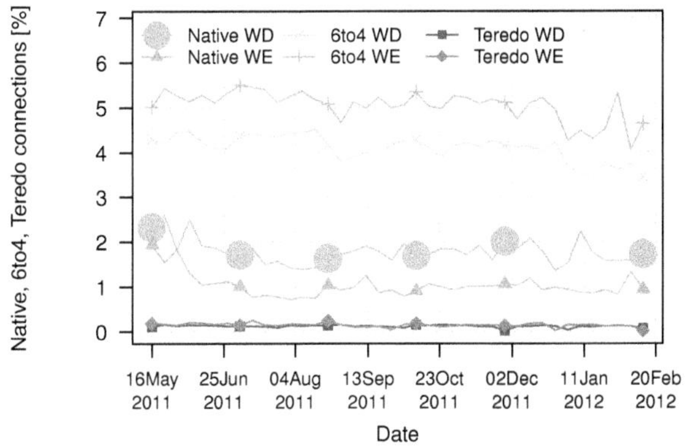

Figure 10: Percentage of all connections from IPv6-capable hosts by IPv6 type (native, 6to4, Teredo)

country IPv6 capabilities, dual stack failures and happy eyeballs usage.

5.1 Overall IPv6 capabilities

First we analyse the proportions of the connections where the client's resolving DNS server was IPv6-capable (DNSv6-capable), the client was IPv6-capable (IPv6-capable), the client preferred IPv6 over IPv4 in dual-stack (IPv6-preferred), or could be forced to use IPv6 with a literal URL (IPv6-forced). We plot the proportions for weekdays/workdays (WD) and weekends (WE).

Figure 8 shows the percentage of DNSv6-capable connections. The graph shows a clear uptrend from 40% to nearly 60% during our measurement period, meaning the percentage of connections from clients with resolving dual-stack DNS servers has increased. A slightly smaller weekend percentage suggests that fewer home user connections are DNSv6-capable.

Figure 9 shows the percentages of IPv6-capable, IPv6-preferred, and IPv6-forced. The percentage of IPv6-capable decreased slightly from 6–7% around World IPv6 day 2011 (Wednesday 8th of June), during which major Internet network and service providers enabled IPv6 as a test, to 6% with not much difference between weekdays and weekends. The percentage of IPv6-preferred connections decreased from its peak of 2.5% around IPv6 day to 1–2% in July 2011 and has remained relatively constant since then. The percentage of IPv6-preferred is higher during weekdays suggesting that home users were less likely to prefer IPv6 (probably because they were less likely to use native IPv6).

The percentage of IPv6-forced is basically the percentage of IPv6-capable plus 15–20% of connections originating from Windows Vista and Windows 7 hosts that support IPv6 via Teredo, but by default do not query for DNS AAAA records (see Section 2.1). The percentage of Teredo is almost 5% higher on weekends suggesting that Teredo is more likely used by home users. We think this is because Teredo is less likely to work in company networks due to being disabled or filtered by firewalls.

Only 6% of connections were from IPv6-capable clients, but for 11–12% of connections we observed DNS AAAA requests. We think the difference is mainly due to hosts that request AAAA records even if they have no IPv6 interfaces. For example, some older Firefox browsers cause this and it is a common default on Linux [30]. However, IPv6 failures may also contribute to the difference. A detailed analysis is future work.

Figure 10 shows a breakdown of the IPv6-capable connections into those using "native" IPv6 (including point-to-point tunnels and 6rd [31]), 6to4, or Teredo based on the IPv6 address prefixes.[4] Over 70% of the connections from IPv6-capable hosts used 6to4 tunnelling (4–5% of all connections), 20–30% of IPv6-capable connections came from hosts with native addresses (1–2% of all connections), and only 2–3% of IPv6-capable connections used Teredo – manually fully-enabled Windows Teredo or Teredo on other OS (0.1–0.2% of all connections).

Native IPv6 peaked in the week of IPv6-day, then decreased slightly and has remained relatively steady since (with a possibly very small uptrend). The percentage of 6to4 has decreased slightly over time. On weekends there are significantly fewer connections from hosts using native IPv6, but more connections from hosts using 6to4. During the week this reverses. This suggests a higher native IPv6 usage at work places.

Figure 11 shows that 90–100% of connections from hosts with native IPv6 prefer IPv6 in dual-stack. However, the percentage has decreased over time. We suspect this happened because of an increased use of happy eyeballs, which fails over very quickly from IPv6 to IPv4 (see Section 5.6). Only 0.5–1% of IPv6-capable 6to4 connections preferred IPv6 in dual-stack, and well under 0.1% of Teredo connections preferred IPv6 in dual-stack (Teredo omitted in Figure 11).

[4] The 6to4 protocol uses the prefix 2002::/16 and the Teredo protocol uses the prefix 2001:0::/32 [1, 2]. We ignore older IPv6-over-IPv4 tunnelling technologies since they are not common [5, 13].

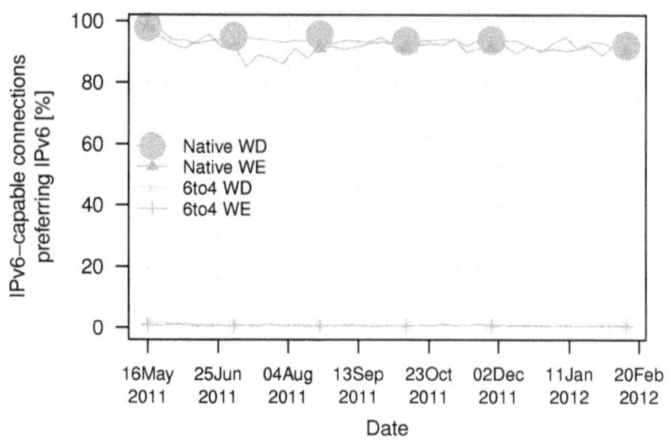

Figure 11: Percentage of IPv6-capable connections that preferred IPv6 in dual-stack (native IPv6, 6to4). Capable clients with Teredo never preferred IPv6.

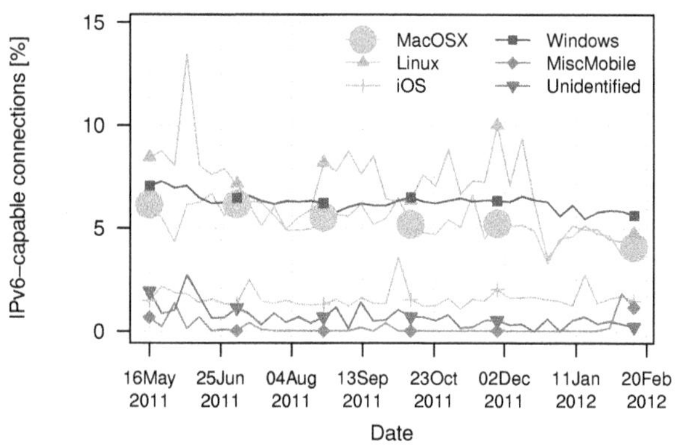

Figure 12: Percentage of all connections from IPv6-capable hosts by operating system

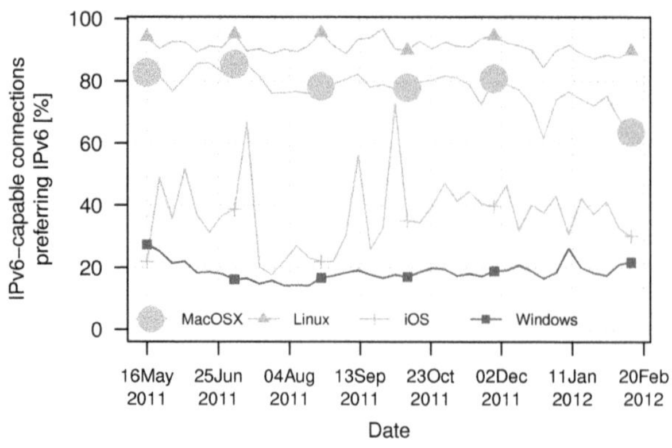

Figure 13: Percentage of IPv6-capable connections where the host preferred IPv6 by operating system

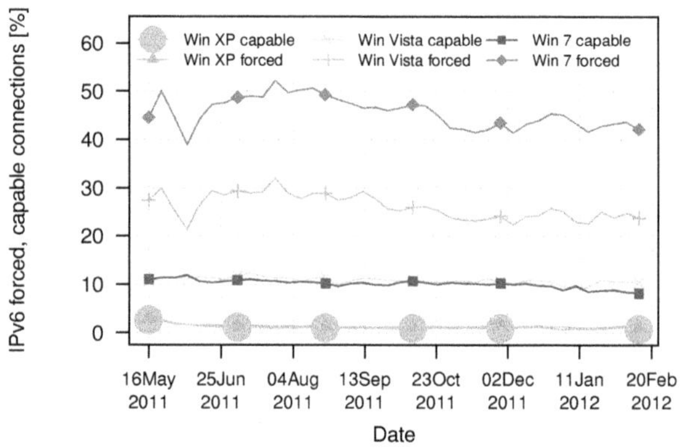

Figure 14: Percentage of IPv6-capable and IPv6-forced for Windows XP, Vista, and 7 connections

5.2 Operating system IPv6 capabilities

Figure 12 shows the percentages of IPv6-capable connections and Figure 13 shows the percentage of connections from IPv6-capable clients that preferred IPv6 for different OSs.[5] Over 6% of connections were from IPv6-capable Windows clients, but only for 20% of these (with native IPv6) the clients actually preferred to use IPv6 in dual-stack. In contrast MacOS X and Linux clients have a similar 6–7% of IPv6-capable connections, but most of them were native IPv6 and preferred to use IPv6 in dual-stack. Only 1–2% of connections came from IPv6-capable iOS clients, but about 30–40% (with native IPv6) preferred IPv6 in dual-stack.[6]

Figure 12 shows a significantly increased IPv6-capability for Linux around IPv6-day 2011. Many of the connections came from Ubuntu clients that enabled IPv6 via point-to-point tunnels on that day and even for a few weeks afterwards. In the raw data the spike is even higher (up to 30%), since multiple of our participating web sites were monitored by a company that uses Ubuntu-based probes located in different countries. We filtered out these probes as they are not "genuine" clients.

[5]We distinguish between MacOS X, Linux, BSD variants, Solaris, iOS, Windows, mobile OS (Symbian, BlackBerry, and Android), and unidentified OS. OSs with too few occurrences are not shown.

[6]Note that due to the low number of observed IPv6-capable iOS connections the standard error here is 5–10%.

Figure 14 shows the percentages of IPv6-capable and IPv6-forced connections for all connections of each Windows version (Windows XP, Vista, and 7 only, as 99% of the tested Windows clients ran these versions). Only 1% of connections from Windows XP hosts were IPv6-capable and the percentage of IPv6-forced was equally low (6to4 and Teredo are not enabled by default on Windows XP). Windows Vista and Windows 7 had a similar 10% of IPv6-capable connections, but the percentage of IPv6-forced was 20% larger for Windows 7 (6to4 and Teredo are enabled by default on Windows Vista and 7, but the lower IPv6-forced percentage suggests that Teredo was either disabled or failed to establish a tunnel more often on Vista [32]).

The percentages of connections from IPv6-capable Windows XP, Vista and 7 clients that preferred IPv6 in dual stack were 20–30%, 10%, and 20% respectively (since there were no significant trends we omitted the figure). Windows XP has the highest IPv6-preferred (native IP) percentage, which is not very surprising since in contrast to Windows Vista or 7 6to4 is not enabled by default. The IPv6-preferred percentage is significantly higher for Windows 7 than for Windows Vista, maybe because more IPv6-savy Windows users avoid Vista.

5.3 Client sample dependencies

Figure 15 compares the IPv6-forced, IPv6-capable and IPv6-preferred proportions for JS-tests and FA-tests. IPv6-forced was higher for FA-tests since the proportion of Windows was higher.

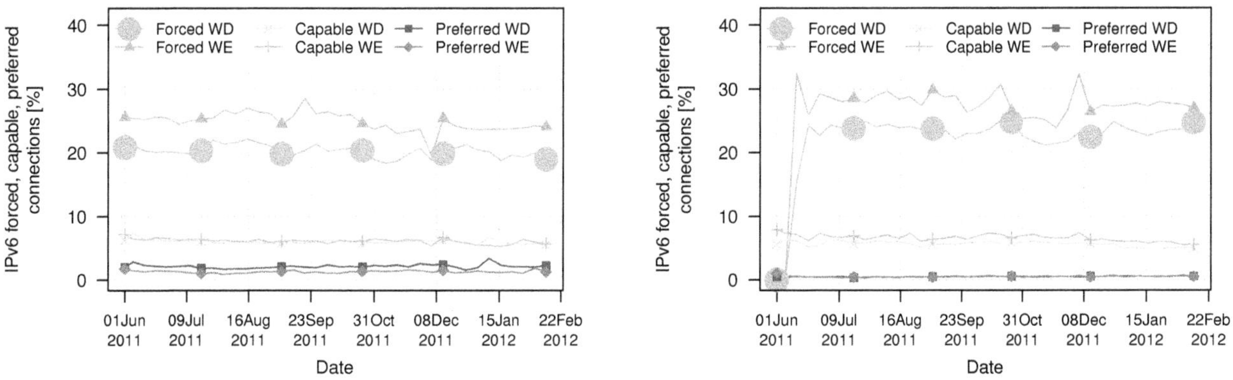

Figure 15: Percentage of IPv6-forced, IPv6-capable and IPv6-preferred for JS test (left) and FA test (right)

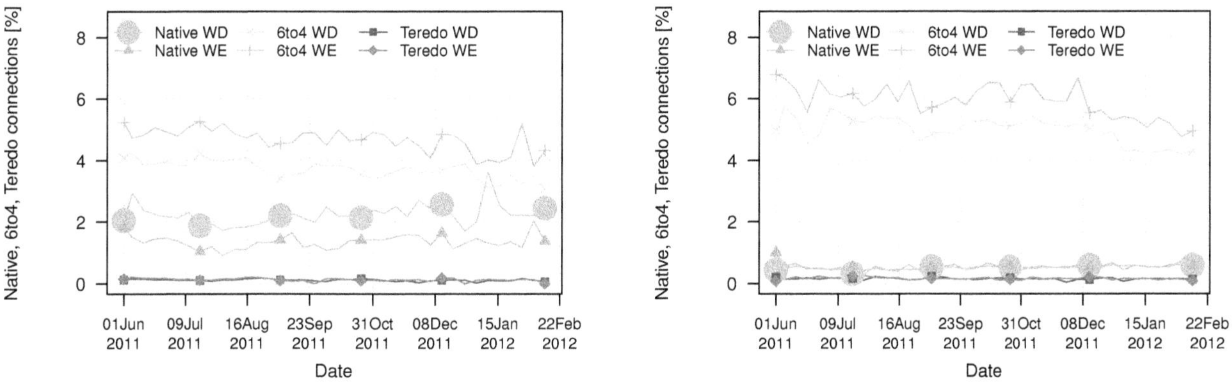

Figure 16: Percentage of all connection from IPv6-capable hosts by IPv6 type for JS test (left) and FA test (right)

IPv6-capable was similar for both tests (for FA-tests it was slightly lower and the difference between weekday and weekend was larger). IPv6-preferred was lower for FA-tests. FA-tests covered fewer MacOS X and Linux connections, the two OSs that strongly preferred IPv6, but also the IPv6-capable proportion for these two OSs was lower for FA-tests.

Figure 16 shows the breakdown of the IPv6-capable connections for JS-tests and FA-tests. The percentage of 6to4 was higher for FA-tests, whereas the percentage of native IPv6 was higher for JS-tests. However, for both tests the 6to4 percentage decreased slightly over time and the native IPv6 percentage peaked around IPv6 day, then decreased to a low in July 2011 and since then has increased very slightly. The weekday/weekend difference for 6to4 was consistent across both tests, but the weekday/weekend difference for native IPv6 was different. For JS-tests the percentage was significantly higher on weekdays, but for FA-tests there was no difference between weekdays and weekends. We suspect some JS-test web sites attracted IPv6-capable hosts during the week (e.g. APNIC web site), whereas the FA-test was more biased towards home users.

For both JS-tests and FA-tests 90–95% of connections from clients with native IPv6 addresses preferred IPv6 in dual-stack, but only 0.5–1% of 6to4 connections and under 0.1% of Teredo connections preferred IPv6 in dual-stack.

5.4 Country IPv6 capabilities

We now analyse the proportions of IPv6-capable and IPv6-preferred connections for the top-12 countries in each category over the whole measurement period. The number of Teredo connections does not vary much for different top-12 countries, hence we omit an analysis for brevity. We analysed JS-tests and FA-tests separately, but here focus on the results for FA-tests, since we think the JS-test is more biased because of the participating web sites.

Figure 17 shows the percentages of IPv6-capable connections for the FA-test for Brazil (BR), France (FR), Indonesia (IN), Italy (IT), Japan (JP), Korea (KR), Poland (PL), Romania (RO), Russia (RU), Taiwan (TW), Ukraine (UA), and the USA (US). For the JS-test the percentages and order of the countries differ, but 9 of the 12 countries (75%) in the top-12 are identical.

Figure 18 shows the percentage of IPv6-preferred connections for the FA-test for China (CN), France (FR), Germany (DE), Great Britain (GB), Japan (JP), Malaysia (MY), Poland (PL), Russia (RU), Taiwan (TW), Thailand (TH), Ukraine (UA), and the USA (US). Again, for the JS-test the percentages and order of the countries differ, but 8 of the 12 countries (66% of countries) in the top-12 are identical. Colitti *et al.* [13] analysed the world's top-10 countries of clients that preferred IPv6 previously. While their ranking differs from ours we note that 6 (JS-test) or 7 (FA-test) of their top-10 countries are also in our top-12.

5.5 Dual-stack failures

It would be interesting to know the proportion of connections that failed the dual-stack sub-test, because the clients tried to retrieve the test image unsuccessfully over IPv6. However, we cannot differentiate reliably between IPv6-related dual-stack failures

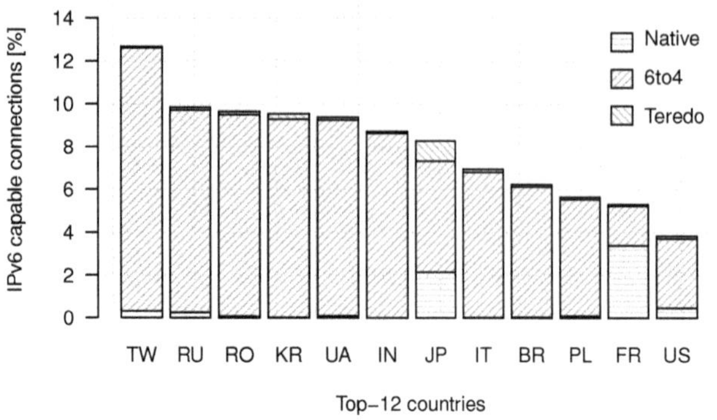

Figure 17: Percentage of IPv6-capable connections of top-12 countries for FA-test

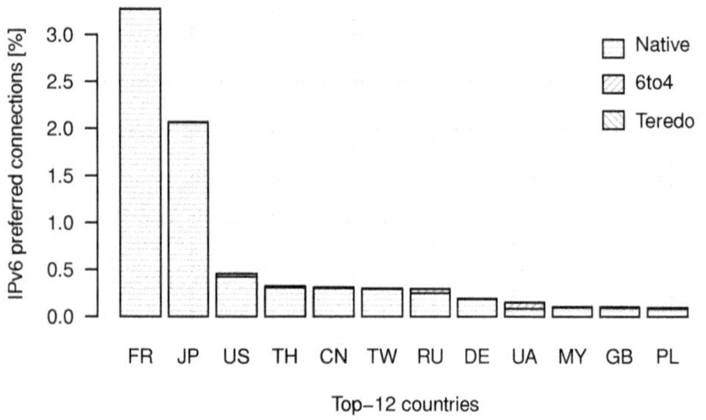

Figure 18: Percentage of IPv6-preferred connections of top-12 countries for FA test

or other connectivity failures. Nevertheless, we can estimate an upper bound.

Let e^{A}_{dual} be the dual-stack sub-test failure rate for connections where only a DNS A request was observed, e^{A+AAAA}_{dual} be the dual-stack sub-test failure rate for connections where both A and AAAA requests were observed, and $e^{A+AAAA}_{v4only+dual}$ be the proportion of connections with failed IPv4-only *and* dual-stack sub-tests for clients that asked for A+AAAA records. We assume that non-IPv6 related failures do not depend on whether clients asked for A+AAAA records or A record only. We estimate the proportion of dual-stack failures because of failed IPv6 to:

$$\varepsilon = e^{A+AAAA}_{dual} - e^{A}_{dual} - e^{A+AAAA}_{v4only+dual} \,. \qquad (2)$$

Still some of these failures may have other causes than failed IPv6, hence our estimated proportion is an upper bound. Figure 19 shows the estimated dual-stack error rate because of failed IPv6 (we only logged DNS requests since mid July 2011). Overall, well under 1% of connections with AAAA requests failed the dual-stack sub-test because of IPv6, but the error rate increased during our measurement.

5.6 Happy eyeballs

When a dual-stack client resolves a host name to IPv6 and IPv4 addresses, it will often try to reach the destination host using IPv6 first. If the client cannot reach the destination with IPv6, it will fail back to use IPv4. With older browsers/OSs this fail-over could take a long time (sometimes up to a minute). "Happy eyeballs" [17] en-

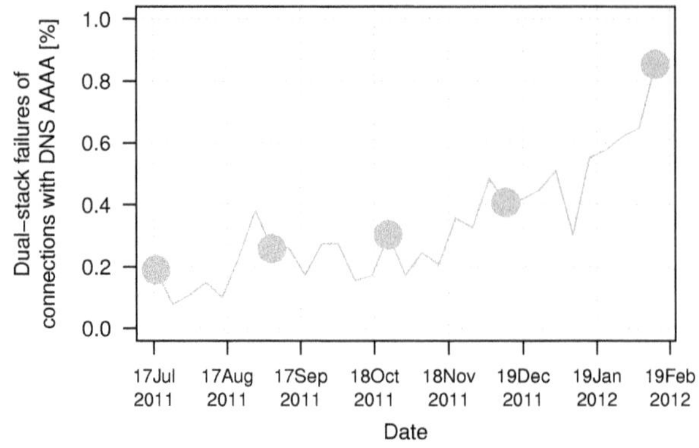

Figure 19: Percentage of connections with DNS AAAA requests with dual-stack failure due to IPv6 problems (upper bound)

ables browsers/OSs to reduce connection-setup times by minimising fail-over delays. They fail over to IPv4 very quickly if IPv6 connections cannot be established.

We estimated the percentage of clients with native IPv6 that use happy eyeballs. If for a dual-stack sub-test a host tried to open IPv4 and IPv6 TCP connections simultaneously (within a one second time window) and one connection succeeded while the other was abandoned, we count this as happy eyeballs attempt. Figure 20 shows that we observed happy eyeballs for 10–20% of hosts with native IPv6 and the percentage increased. For 75% of these connections clients preferred IPv6 over IPv4, but for 25% of them clients failed over to IPv4.

Figure 21 shows the web browsers that used happy eyeballs (according to the browser ID strings). Most of the happy eyeballs came from hosts using Chrome, which has had working happy eyeballs support since May 2011 [33]. A smaller number of happy eyeballs came from Firefox and Safari. Since July 2011 MacOS X Lion had happy eyeballs support and the combination of Safari and MacOS X Lion works [34]. According to our data there were happy eyeballs from Safari running on MacOS X and on iOS.

Firefox had a happy eyeballs implementation since version 7, but prior to version 10 it was disabled by default [34]. Also, the initial Firefox implementation had problems; it was effectively removed in September 2011 and replaced by an improved version in November 2011 [35]. This explains the period without happy eyeballs from Firefox. Happy eyeballs was turned on by default in Firefox 10 (released end of January 2012), which is clearly visible in the graph.[7]

We also computed the average latency between the IPv6 and IPv4 connection requests. For Chrome it was on the order of 200–250 ms, close to the nominal 300 ms fail-over time [34]. For Firefox since version 10 the delay was also on the order of 200–250 ms, whereas for Safari the delay was 150–200 ms.

6. RELATED WORK

A number of researchers studied the progress of IPv6 deployment. The survey paper [4] provides an excellent overview and also identifies areas that need further study.

Some studies examined routing or DNS data, or used active measurements to identify the IPv6 capabilities of domains and

[7]Firefox automatically updates on a daily basis, assuming a user restarts it on request or reboots. Hence, an update can relatively quickly change the abilities of the Firefox population.

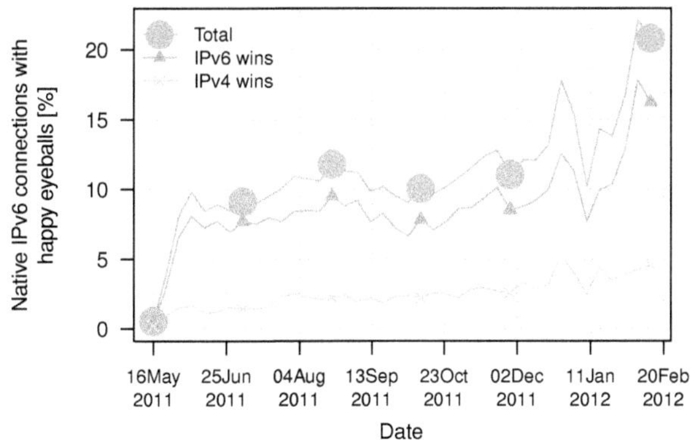

Figure 20: Percentage of connections from clients with native IPv6 that used happy eyeballs – overall and by winning protocol (IPv4 or IPv6)

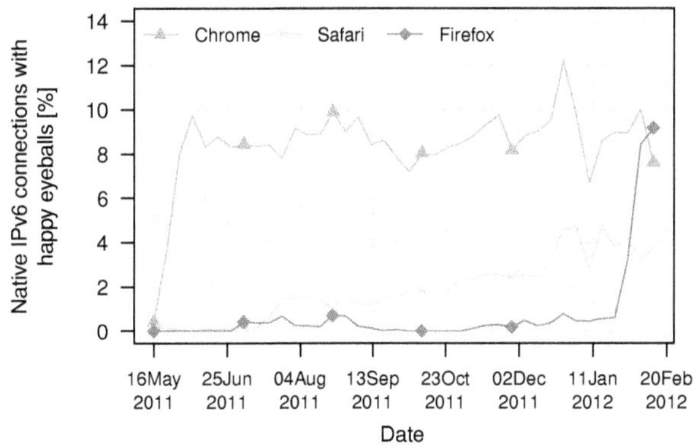

Figure 21: Percentage of connections from clients with native IPv6 that used happy eyeballs by web browser

servers. They do not provide any insights into the IPv6-capabilities of clients and we only briefly mention them. Leber [6] tracked the percentage of Autonomous Systems (ASs) that advertised IPv6 prefixes, and the percentage of top level domains and top-1000 web servers (based on Alexa) that were IPv6-capable (had DNS AAAA records). Prior [7] monitored the IPv6 capability of web, email, DNS, and NTP servers of certain domains. Kuehne [8] surveyed the IPv6 deployment by querying web and email servers of the top domains from Alexa for DNS AAAA records. Nikkah *et al.* [36] compared the performance of IPv4 and IPv6 based on accessing a larger number of IPv6-capable web servers. CAIDA [37] visualised the IPv6 Internet topology based on routing information and active probing.

Other studies analysed server logs and traffic traces. They only reveal the fraction of clients that preferred IPv6 over IPv4, but they cannot reveal the IPv6 capabilities of all clients. Also, some of these studies did not analyse the former, but focussed on other aspects, such as the IPv6 technologies used. Karpilovsky *et al.* [9] analysed the proportion of different IPv6 technologies used based on NetFlow data, but they did not analyse the overall proportion of IPv6 traffic. Shen *et al.* [10] studied the IPv6 deployment and the applications using IPv6 in China based on NetFlow records. They focused on the IPv6 techniques and addressing schemes used, but did not estimate the proportion of IPv6 traffic. Malone [5] analysed the proportion of IPv6 addresses from three server logs (Web, FTP, DNS) in 2007 and found that 0.3–0.4% of the connections used IPv6. Labovitz [11] measured an IPv6 traffic proportion of 0.03–0.04% in 2010 based on flow measurements from 100 Internet Service Providers (ISPs). Defeche and Wyncke [38] studied the use of IPv6 in the BitTorrent file sharing community and found that the fraction of IPv6-capable peers was 1%. The IPv6 proportions observed in [5, 11, 38] span almost two magnitudes, probably because each study observed a very specific set of clients.

Recently, a few studies used a web-based measurement method to study the IPv6 capabilities of clients based on Steffann's [12] approach. Colitti *et al.* [13] measured the proportion of hosts that preferred IPv6 and the IPv6 technologies used for different countries based on a fraction of Google users in 2008–2009. They found that only 0.25% of hosts used IPv6. Kreibich *et al.* [30] analysed Netalyzr logs and reported that 4.8% of sessions used IPv6. However, they note that this is an upper bound due to possible caching effects and "geek bias" (Netalyzr only tests hosts of users who choose to be tested). Smets *et al.* [14] estimated the IPv6 deployment for EU states based on over 30 participating web sites in 2010. They found that the proportion of IPv6-capable hosts varied from under 1% (Cyprus) to over 12% (Sweden) with an average of 6%. Aben [15] measured the IPv6 deployment based on DNS AAAA records for popular servers, advertised IPv6 routing prefixes, and active web-based measurements embedded in the RIPE web site. Aben found that in 2011/2012 around 6–7% of clients were IPv6 capable and 2–3% of clients preferred IPv6. Anderson [39] measured a client dual-stack failure rate of 0.015% at two web sites in Norway in May 2011.

We measured 6% of IPv6-capable connections, which is consistent with the 6% observed in [14] (for EU countries) and the 6–7% measured in [15]. We measured 1–2% of connections that preferred IPv6 over IPv4. This is much higher than the 0.25% measured in [13], but lower than the 2–3% reported in [15] and the 4.8% upper bound reported in [30]. Our dual-stack failure rate is much higher than the rate reported in [39], because our proportion is based on the connections with DNS AAAA requests and not on all connections. As proportion of all connections our estimate is 0.02–0.09%.

Compared to most previous studies we sampled a wider range of clients and domains, including clients sampled by our novel Google-ad based measurement approach. Also, we provide a more comprehensive analysis, e.g. we distinguish between IPv6-preferred and IPv6-capable (including latent Windows Teredo) clients, and analyse the IPv6 capabilities of the clients' resolving DNS servers. Furthermore, only our study analyses the client sample properties, discusses the sampling error and proposes methods to mitigate the error.

7. CONCLUSIONS AND FUTURE WORK

Despite the predicted exhaustion of unallocated IPv4 addresses in the next two years, it remains unclear how many clients can use its successor IPv6. We proposed a refined web-based measurement approach that mitigates intrinsic measurement biases, and demonstrated a novel web-based technique using Google ads to perform IPv6 capability testing on a wider range of clients. To mitigate the sampling error we re-weighted the raw data. We compared raw and re-weighted OS and browser statistics with reference statistics and showed that our raw statistics appear biased, but the re-weighted statistics are similar to the reference. We then used the re-weighted statistics to estimate the IPv6 capabilities of clients.

We observed slightly over 6% of connections from IPv6-capable clients, but over 70% of these were from Windows clients that used 6to4 tunnelling and did not prefer IPv6 in dual-stack. Only 1–2% of connections were from clients with native IPv6, but over 90% of them preferred IPv6 in dual-stack. The dual-stack failure rate (as percentage of connections with DNS AAAA requests) was under 1%, but we observed an increasing trend. The use of happy eyeballs (fast fail-over from IPv6 to IPv4) rose to over 20% of connections from clients with native IPv6.

The percentage of connections with IPv6-capable resolving DNS servers increased significantly from 40% to nearly 60%. On the other hand, the percentage of connections from IPv6-capable clients and the percentage of clients that preferred IPv6 peaked around IPv6 day 2011, decreased slightly and then remained relatively constant. The IPv6-capable percentage actually decreased slightly. However, this decrease was caused by a decline in 6to4 connections, while the percentage of native IPv6 connections increased very slightly. Overall, the trends suggest that the adoption of IPv6 by clients is still very slow, at least in the client sample we observed. However, the increasing percentage of connections with IPv6-capable DNS servers is encouraging, as it could indicate an increased number of dual-stack DNS servers and possibly an increased IPv6-capability of ISPs.

We noticed a clear difference between weekdays and weekends, most likely driven by the different capabilities of work and home clients. The proportion of native IPv6 connections was higher during the week, whereas the proportion of 6to4 and Teredo was higher on weekends. The proportion of IPv6-capable connections was roughly similar for Windows, MacOS X and Linux. However, while 80% of the Windows connections relied on 6to4, most MacOS X and Linux connections used native IPv6.

An additional 15–20% of all connections from Windows 7 and Windows Vista clients could use IPv6 with Teredo. However, by default the Windows resolver does not ask for DNS AAAA records if the only IPv6 network interface is a Teredo interface, so these clients are not truly IPv6-capable. Without Teredo only 10% of connections from Windows Vista or Windows 7 clients were IPv6-capable, but with Teredo the percentage increased to 20–30% for Windows Vista and 40–50% for Windows 7.

Our Google ad based measurement technique could be used for other types of client-based measurements, if they can be performed with the functionality of ActionScript available in Google Flash ad banners. Our current test script already measures the delays for fetching the test images [32], and this information could possibly be used to analyse clients' network access technologies. Another possibility is to estimate the bottleneck capacities of clients with a tailored packet-pair measurement approach. Our proposed reweighting method could be applied to other problems where a geographically biased sample of Internet clients is observed.

In the future we plan to increase the sample size, estimate the size of the sampling error, and improve the sampling error reduction. We also plan to extend our measurement methodology, so that we can determine IPv6 failures more accurately and identify their causes.

Acknowledgements

We thank our shepherd Kenjiro Cho and the anonymous reviewers for their helpful comments. This research was supported under Australian Research Council's Linkage Projects funding scheme (project LP110100240) in conjunction with APNIC Pty Ltd and by Australian Research Council grant FT0991594.

8. REFERENCES

[1] I. van Beijnum. *Running IPv6* . Apress, Nov. 2005.

[2] S. Frankel, R. Graveman, J. Pearce, M. Rooks. Guidelines for the Secure Deployment of IPv6. NIST SP 800-119, Dec. 2010.

[3] G. Huston. IPv4 Address Report. http://www.potaroo.net/tools/ipv4/index.html.

[4] kc claffy. Tracking IPv6 Evolution: Data We Have and Data We Need. *ACM SIGCOMM Computer Communication Review (CCR)*, (3):43–48, Jul 2011.

[5] D. Malone. Observations of IPv6 Addresses. In *Passive and Active Measurement Conference (PAM)*, pages 21–30, 2008.

[6] M. Leber. Global ipv6 deployment. http://bgp.he.net/ipv6-progress-report.cgi.

[7] M. Prior. IPv6 Status Survey. http://www.mrp.net/IPv6_Survey.html.

[8] T. Kuehne. Examining Actual State of IPv6 Deployment, 2008. http://www.circleid.com/posts/81166_actual_state_ipv6_deployment.

[9] E. Karpilovsky, A. Gerber, D. Pei, J. Rexford, A. Shaikh. Quantifying the Extent of IPv6 Deployment. In *Passive and Active Measurement Conference (PAM)*, pages 13–22, 2009.

[10] W. Shen, Y. Chen, Q. Zhang, Y. Chen, B. Deng, X. Li, G. Lv. Observations of IPv6 Traffic. In *ISECS Computing, Communication, Control, and Management (CCCM)*, pages 278–282, August 2009.

[11] C. Labovitz. IPv6 Momentum? http://ddos.arbornetworks.com/2010/10/ipv6-momentum/.

[12] S. Steffann. IPv6 test, 2008. http://ipv6test.max.nl/.

[13] L. Colitti, S. Gunderson, E. Kline, T. Refice. Evaluating IPv6 Adoption in the Internet. In *Passive and Active Measurement Conference*, pages 141–150. April 2010.

[14] R. Smets. IPv6 Deployment Monitoring, December 2010. http://ipv6-ghent.fi-week.eu/files/2010/12/1335-Rob-Smets-v2.pdf.

[15] E. Aben. Measuring World IPv6 Day - Long-Term Effects, 2011. https://labs.ripe.net/Members/emileaben/measuring-world-ipv6-day-long-term-effects.

[16] C. Huitema. Teredo: Tunneling IPv6 over UDP through Network Address Translations (NATs). RFC 4380 (Proposed Standard), February 2006.

[17] D. Wing, A. Yourtchenko. Happy Eyeballs: Success with Dual-Stack Hosts. RFC 6555 (Proposed Standard), April 2012.

[18] Microsoft Technet. DNS Client Behavior in Windows Vista. http://technet.microsoft.com/en-us/library/bb727035.aspx.

[19] G. Huston, G. Michaelson. IPv6 Capability Tracker, 2012. http://labs.apnic.net/tracker.shtml.

[20] N. C. Zakas. How many users have JavaScript disabled?, Oct. 2010. http://developer.yahoo.com/blogs/ydn/posts/2010/10/how-many-users-have-javascript-disabled/.

[21] S. Ramachandran. Web metrics: Size and number of resources, 2010. https://developers.google.com/speed/articles/web-metrics.

[22] Browserscope. Community-driven project for profiling web browsers. http://www.browserscope.org/?category=network.

[23] MaxMind's GeoIP Country Database. http://www.maxmind.com/app/geoip_country.

[24] Cisco Systems. Visual Network Index. http://www.cisco.com/en/US/netsol/ns827/networking_solutions_sub_solution.html.

[25] Wikimedia Traffic Analysis, March 2012. http://stats.wikimedia.org/wikimedia/squids/SquidReportPageViewsPerCountryOverview.htm.

[26] Advanced Network Technology Center, University of Oregon. University of Oregon Route Views Project, 2012. http://www.routeviews.org/.

[27] A. Korinek, J. A. Mistiaen, M. Ravallion. An Econometric Method of Correcting for Unit Nonresponse Bias in Surveys. *Journal of Econometrics*, 136(1):213–235, 2007.

[28] Wikipedia. Usage share of operating systems, May 2012. http://en.wikipedia.org/w/index.php?title=Usage_share_of_operating_systems&oldid=490169177.

[29] Wikipedia. Usage share of web browsers, May 2012. http://en.wikipedia.org/w/index.php?title=Usage_share_of_web_browsers&oldid=490374342.

[30] C. Kreibich, N. Weaver, B. Nechaev, V. Paxson. Netalyzr: Illuminating the Edge Network. In *ACM SIGCOMM Conference on Internet Measurement*, pages 246–259, 2010.

[31] R. Despres. IPv6 Rapid Deployment on IPv4 Infrastructures (6rd). RFC 5569 (Informational), January 2010.

[32] S. Zander, L. L. H. Andrew, G. Armitage, G. Huston, G. Michaelson. Investigating the IPv6 Teredo Tunnelling Capability and Performance of Internet Clients. *SIGCOMM CCR*. (accepted for publication, to appear).

[33] Chrome Repository. Chrome Happy Eyeballs. http://src.chromium.org/viewvc/chrome?view=rev\&revision=85934.

[34] E. Aben. Hampered Eyeballs. https://labs.ripe.net/Members/emileaben/hampered-eyeballs.

[35] Mozilla Bugzilla. Firefox happy Eyeballs. https://bugzilla.mozilla.org/show_bug.cgi?id=621558.

[36] M. Nikkhah, R. Guérin, Y. Lee, R. Woundy. Assessing IPv6 through web access a measurement study and its findings. In *Conference on Emerging Networking EXperiments and Technologies (CoNEXT)*, pages 26:1–26:12, 2011.

[37] CAIDA. IPv4 and IPv6 AS Core: Visualizing IPv4 and IPv6 Internet Topology at a Macroscopic Scale in 2010. http://www.caida.org/research/topology/as_core_network/.

[38] M. Defeche, E. Vyncke. Measuring IPv6 Traffic in BitTorrent Networks. IETF draft-vyncke-ipv6-traffic-in-p2p-networks-01.txt, March 2012.

[39] T. Anderson. IPv6 Dual-stack Client Loss in Norway. http://fud.no/ipv6/.

MAPLE: A Scalable Architecture for Maintaining Packet Latency Measurements

Myungjin Lee†, Nick Duffield‡, Ramana Rao Kompella†
†Purdue University, ‡AT&T Labs–Research

ABSTRACT

Latency has become an important metric for network monitoring since the emergence of new latency-sensitive applications (*e.g.*, algorithmic trading and high-performance computing). To satisfy the need, researchers have proposed new architectures such as LDA and RLI that can provide fine-grained latency measurements. However, these architectures are *fundamentally ossified* in their design as they are designed to provide only a specific pre-configured aggregate measurement—either average latency across all packets (LDA) or per-flow latency measurements (RLI). Network operators, however, need latency measurements at both *finer* (*e.g.*, packet) as well as *flexible* (*e.g.*, flow subsets) levels of granularity. To bridge this gap, we propose an architecture called MAPLE that essentially stores packet-level latencies in routers and allows network operators to query the latency of arbitrary traffic sub-populations. MAPLE is built using scalable data structures with small storage needs (uses only 12.8 bits/packet), and uses a novel mechanism to reduce the query bandwidth significantly (by a factor of 17 compared to the naive method of sending packet queries individually).

Categories and Subject Descriptors

C.2.3 [**Computer Communication Networks**]: Network management

General Terms

Measurement, algorithms

Keywords

Latency, bloom filter, approximation

1. INTRODUCTION

For the longest time, networking engineers and researchers have focused mainly on obtaining high end-to-end throughput in IP networks. In recent years, however, *latency* has evolved into a metric that is as important as throughput in IP networks. While low latency is a desirable property for any network-based application, this obsession towards low end-to-end latency stems from the stringent requirements of many new kinds of datacenter, cloud, and wide-area applications that have become popular in the recent times. For instance, several cloud applications (*e.g.*, Salesforce, Google App Engine, modern Web services) involve complex back-end processing, such as accessing storage, SQL database transactions, etc. After removing time for computation and wide-area RTTs, the budget for datacenter network accesses is significantly reduced. Similar requirement exists for partition/aggregate type workloads found in search and social collaboration applications, where jobs that do not finish within a certain time are typically cancelled thus affecting the overall result, and in some cases, lost revenue [7]. Even more stringent latency requirements, in the order of 10s of microseconds, exist for high-performance computing (HPC) applications [1] and financial trading applications [31].

Network operators managing such latency-sensitive applications need sophisticated tools for high-fidelity latency measurements at various places in the network that will help them identify root causes of SLA violations, determine offending applications that may hurt the performance of others, perform traffic engineering, and so on. In light of the importance of these measurements, there has been some recent research on developing measurement mechanisms such as the lossy difference aggregator (LDA) [26] and reference latency interpolation (RLI) [27]. A *key limitation* of these techniques is that they only obtain latency measurements at the granularity of a fixed pre-configured aggregate (across all packets in LDA, and per-flow latencies in RLI). By making the granularity of the aggregates for latency measurements part of the architecture, these prior architectures are quite *ossified*, lacking flexibility to obtain arbitrary latency measurements than what they are already pre-programmed to achieve. What network operators need instead is a holistic architecture that provides the ability to obtain arbitrary latency measurements from switches. Such an architecture would help operators with powerful tools to help debug and manage low-latency applications in their networks. Designing such an architecture is the main objective of this paper.

In our quest to obtain arbitrary latency measurements from switches, we ask, "What is the finest granularity of latency measurements a network operator may be interested in ?" LDA and RLI implicitly assumed that aggregate or flow-level granularity of measurements is what operators may care about. In this paper, we argue instead that there are many compelling scenarios where finer-granularity measurements may be important.

For example, for diagnosing client delays in online services, it may be critical to know whether a DNS query (that is typically a single packet) got delayed, or whether a backend transaction got delayed in the network, or whether there were processing delays. As another canonical example, in a real-time bidding (RTB) ecosystem for online ads, bidders (*e.g.*, agency trading desks) must respond to bid requests within a tight deadline (say, less than 120 ms) by typically shipping their response message with bidding price in a single packet [4]. Failing to meet the deadline makes the bidders miss an opportunity of exposing commercials of their customers (*i.e.*, advertisers) to the public. As a result, the customers can experience bad practice of marketing, potentially causing significant revenue loss to the customers. Similarly, for financial trading applications, one may care about the delay of a single stock trade (that may be carried in one packet). For HPC applications built on message passing libraries (*e.g.*, MPI), latency of even a single message may be quite important. In addition, one may wish to focus on latencies for a *subset* of packets that belong to a flow, perhaps to hone in on the ones that exhibited abnormal latency, or to track the latency time-series of the flow. Thus, clearly, in order to satisfy these requirements, we need a more flexible architecture than the one-size-fits-all approach of existing solutions such as LDA (aggregate) or RLI (per-flow).

Since the finest granularity of latency measurements is on a *per-packet basis*, we start with an architecture that achieves these measurements in a scalable fashion. Then, any other forms of aggregation (per-flow, per-prefix), that may be of importance to network operators, are easily composable from these packet-level measurements. Such an architecture essentially decouples the collection of measurements (at the granularity of a packet), and aggregation (across arbitrary subpopulations) during query time. This key intuition forms the basis for our proposed architecture MAPLE.

MAPLE essentially consists of two main components—a scalable packet latency store (PLS) and a query engine—at each router. PLS stores the latencies of all packets that appear at the router. In high speed networks, storing all the packets and their associated latencies is going to be expensive; hence we store latencies only for a small amount of time (*e.g.*, 1s) in high-speed SRAM, and rely on flushing them periodically to a higher capacity data store. Since storing the entire packet and delay requires high storage (in terms of bits/packet), we propose a novel approach that first clusters packets and associates a delay value for each cluster, and then, uses a novel hardware data structure called shared-vector Bloom filter (SVBF) to significantly reduce the memory requirement. SVBF makes the architecture technologically feasible in high-speed switches where SRAM is a very scarce and precious resource. We show how the entire PLS can enable an efficient streaming implementation in hardware that can keep up with line rates.

The second component of MAPLE, the query engine, essentially allows end-hosts or a centralized entity to initiate a query for the packet. These queries need to be within a particular timeframe of the original packet; otherwise, the store in the router may not have any history of the packet. By constructing queries across arbitrary packets, end-hosts can easily obtain per-packet latencies for all (or a sample) of packets within a given subpopulation, using which they can compose the aggregate latency measurements for that flow. We also consider mechanisms to reduce query bandwidth by providing the ability to perform range queries.

Thus, the main contributions in this paper are as follows:

1) We propose MAPLE for maintaining per-packet latency measurements in a scalable fashion (§2). Our architecture allows network operators to obtain any aggregate of measurements thus subsuming the functionality of existing architectures, while providing newer and more powerful capabilities.

2) We propose novel mechanisms that use streaming algorithms for clustering packet delays, and storing them compactly using a novel data structure called SVBF that is much more storage-efficient (requires only 12.8 bits/packet) than a variant of regular hash tables (that may require 147 bits/packet) and also minimizes memory accesses for inserts and lookups (§3). We also propose a range query mechanism to reduce the amount of query bandwidth required (§4).

3) We built a software prototype of our architecture. In our evaluations (§5), we found that SVBF achieves almost 6× lower per-packet latency estimate error compared to prior data structures for comparable storage. We also found that the range query achieves significant reduction in query bandwidth (almost 17×) compared to naive packet query.

2. MAPLE ARCHITECTURE

In this section, we outline a flexible architecture for obtaining high-fidelity latency measurements in the network. Before we describe the architecture, we first state our measurement goals followed by a brief discussion on why previous solutions cannot satisfy these goals.

2.1 Measurement goals

Our goal is to enable a high-fidelity latency measurement architecture that satisfies the following requirements:

- *R1) Per-packet latency measurements.* The architecture should allow network operators to obtain latency information about a single packet at various routers in the network.

- *R2) Measurements across arbitrary aggregates.* It should enable operators to easily compute measurements across arbitrary aggregates (*e.g.*, per-prefix, flows, sub-flows).

- *R3) Measurements across arbitrary locations.* We need support for latency measurements both within and across routers by allowing network operators complete freedom to selectively turn on interfaces between which they need measurements.

Such an architecture will provide detailed latency information that will help network operators to debug their networks and satisfy the demands of modern latency-sensitive network applications.

2.2 Limitations of previous solutions

We consider mainly passive measurement solutions since, as pointed out by prior work [26, 27], it is difficult to estimate packet-level latencies by injecting active probes. As

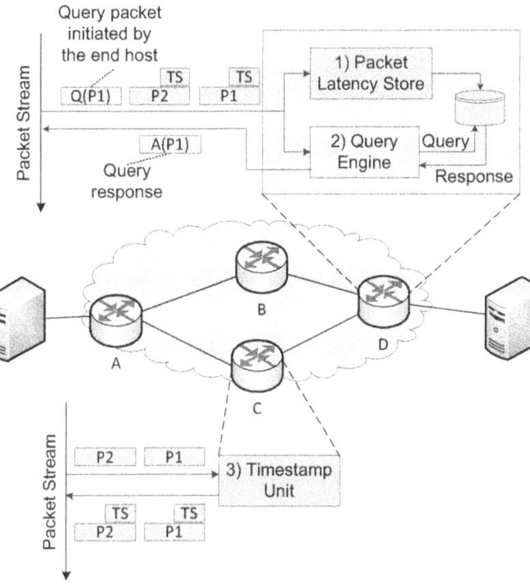

Figure 1: MAPLE architecture.

mentioned before, there have been mainly two solutions, LDA [26] and RLI [27], that have been proposed for fine-grained latency measurements in the recent past. (Another solution for per-flow latency measurements is Consistent NetFlow [28], but it is quite similar in spirit to RLI, and arguments applicable to RLI are applicable there too.)

LDA provides only aggregate measurements and cannot be modified simply to satisfy all the requirements listed before. For instance, it cannot satisfy $R1$. $R2$ could potentially be satisfied by configuring different LDAs on a per-aggregate basis, but this approach will not scale well, as all potential aggregates need to be pre-configured, and there can be many such aggregates. RLI provides per-flow measurements, and hence, it can satisfy $R2$ partially for aggregates that can be obtained from individual per-flow measurements. For example, one can aggregate all the flows per-prefix from per-flow measurements but *cannot* obtain finer granularity measurements than flow, such as a packet (or flow subsets). In addition, LDA and RLI cannot easily satisfy requirement $R3$, because of the FIFO ordering assumption in LDA and temporal delay correlation assumption in RLI, both of which may not hold true across arbitrary measurement points.

2.3 Architecture

Given existing solutions fall short of satisfying the requirements we outlined earlier, we propose Measurement Architecture for Packet LatEncies (MAPLE). Our architecture (shown in Figure 1) is based on three key ideas: First, in order to satisfy requirement $R1$, we need MAPLE to store per-packet latency measurements in some scalable way; any form of aggregation within routers cannot be used to satisfy $R1$. Thus, at its heart, MAPLE contains a scalable packet latency store (called PLS) designed to simply store latencies of *all* packets in a scalable and efficient fashion. Since storing all packets will mean significant storage requirement that will be prohibitively expensive if not technologically infeasible, it stores packet latencies only for a small amount of time, τ, say 1-100s, in high speed memory. Every τ seconds, the store will be (optionally) flushed to an off-chip secondary storage (*e.g.*, DRAM, SSD), where it can be held for a longer time. We discuss PLS in §3.

Second, to satisfy requirement $R2$, it essentially contains a generic query engine that allows clients to query switches about the latency of a packet (using its hash, for instance) that has traversed that particular switch. These queries need to be within the storage timeframe (either high-speed or off-chip storage), otherwise the switch may lose the packet latency record. We expect that queries are mostly going to be only for specific applications or customers which are experiencing trouble. Instead of a per-packet query, we also provide a range query mechanism to reduce query bandwidth. By querying latencies of specific packets that form an aggregate, the client can obtain latency measurements across arbitrary sub-populations. More details are discussed in §4.

Finally, it is simpler to satisfy requirement $R3$, if we enable packet headers to carry timestamps (Figure 1). While we understand that it may be complicated in the short-term to make header changes (as prior work [27, 26] pointed out), we believe this is a cleaner longer-term option that switch vendors are already considering. In our discussions with prominent switch vendors, they mention that implementing a timestamp within the switch is not a problem, and, in some cases, such as Fulcrum [3], they already have an internal timestamp within the switch. Thus, the assumptions in LDA (FIFO ordering) and RLI (temporal delay correlation) are no longer required in our architecture thus enabling a more flexible architecture. However, if timestamping is not feasible, for restricted settings, such as packets within a router, or when there is a series of routers in a FIFO order, we can still use temporal delay correlation assumption made in prior work [27] and obtain approximate delays on a per-packet basis. In that sense, our architecture builds on *any* scheme to obtain one-way delay for each packet.

Note that in all cases, we assume high precision time synchronization (similar to LDA and RLI) between the two measurement points, which has become feasible in modern times due to the increasing adoption of IEEE 1588 [2].

3. PACKET LATENCY STORE (PLS)

Simply put, the goal of PLS is to store a packet and its associated latency value in a scalable fashion. In normal settings, this goal would be relatively straightforward to accomplish using a simple linear-probing or linked-list-based hashtable implementation [15]. Unfortunately, hashtables are not efficient in their storage since they typically require storing a packet hash (32 bits) and associated timestamp (20 bits). For a million packets, we need about 50 Mbits which is already quite expensive; for an OC-192 link, even this storage will last only 0.2s unfortunately (assuming 5M packets per second). Even if we use a slightly coarser timestamp (say 10 bits), it will reduce the memory need only slightly. Besides, collision resolution techniques are not easy to implement in a hardware in a pipelined fashion, and may incur unpredictable insert/lookup times (*e.g.*, depending on the number of accesses required to find an empty slot).

If we need to store *precise* latency values for each and every packet, relying on hashtables is probably the best recourse unfortunately. Luckily, for the kind of applications we envision, such as performance diagnosis or detecting SLA violations, we can exploit the fact that *the latency values for each and every packet need not be precise, and can be approximate instead.* If we assume some amount of inaccuracy is tolerable, then we can significantly reduce the memory usage—this is the key intuition behind our approach.

Our approach In our approach, we exploit two key ideas. First, within a given measurement interval, there are typically only a few dominant latency values (depending on the utilization) where most of the packet latencies are clustered. In the worst case, the latency values can be all over the entire permissible range, but in general, this is typically rare. Thus, instead of storing packets and their associated latencies, we can first cluster packets into *equivalence classes* based on the delay values, and associated a single delay value, called *cluster center*, for all packets within the cluster. Second, for each cluster, we can leverage approximate membership query data structures such as Bloom filters [10], that have gained significant prominence in networking applications recently, for better efficiency in storage (in terms of bits/packet) as well as implementation in hardware (just a bit vector and few hash functions). We discuss these in more detail next.

3.1 Selecting representative delays

Depending on whether the clusters are chosen statically or dynamically, there are two broad choices for selecting the cluster centers. For the static case, we consider logarithmic center selection, while we explore online clustering algorithms (k-means and k-medians) for determining centers dynamically.

Logarithmic delay selection. In this method, we first select a range of latency values that packets can experience, and then divide this range into logarithmic sub-ranges. For instance, if the delay range is 0.1-10,000 μs, we have 5 sub-ranges; 0.1-1 μs, 1-10 μs, and so on. If we have γ sub-ranges, we assign k/γ representative delays linearly for each sub-range. If $k = 50$, and $\gamma = 5$, each sub-range assigns 10 representative delays linearly. While this method does not take the pattern of delays into account, the complexity of choosing representative delays is minimal. Because the distance between two center delays in a sub-range is equal, the relative and absolute error of a packet latency estimate remains bounded and stable regardless of packet delay distributions. However, accuracy may not be close to the optimal accuracy as we can obtain with given k delay centers.

k-means and k-medians clustering. If we know distribution of packet delays in an interval *a priori*, selecting representative delays can be formulated as a clustering problem. In literature, there are two broad classes of algorithms—k-means and k-medians—that can help determine good cluster centers [23]. Typically, both types of algorithms minimize the average absolute error of packet latencies, because they choose centers that minimize total sum of distances between each member with its closest center.

Formally, for observations $x_1, x_2, \ldots, x_n$, the k-means algorithm aims to partition them into k sets, $S_1, \ldots, S_k$, $k \leq n$, so as to minimize the sum of squares of distances within cluster from the center (mean), i.e.,

$$\arg\min_{\{\mu_i\}} \sum_{i=1}^{k} \sum_{x_j \in S_i} ||x_j - \mu_i||^2$$

where μ_i is the mean of the cluster S_i. k-medians clustering algorithm minimizes the distance to the median of a cluster as opposed to the least-squares distance that k-means obtains. The advantage of k-medians is that it is more resilient to outliers which have too large or small values.

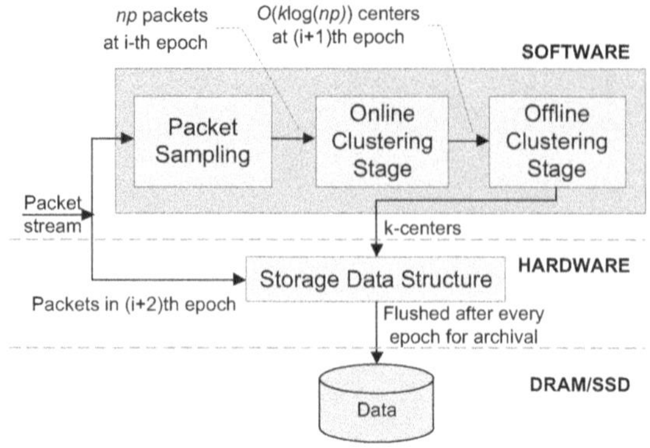

Figure 2: Architecture for streaming representative delay selection and storage provisioning.

There are two key concerns with using these algorithms directly in our setting though. First, the basic algorithms cannot be directly implemented in a streaming fashion due to their high run-time complexity, $O(n^{k+1} \log n)$. There exist heuristics such as the classic Lloyd's algorithm [30], but still it can be quite computationally intensive. Second, the centers are determined *after* running the algorithm on all the packets in a given measurement interval, but we need the centers to be determined *before* the packets start streaming in. We discuss how to address these issues next.

3.2 Streaming clustering

In order to address the first problem concerning the high run-time complexity, we use a streaming version of k-medians clustering algorithm in our architecture. For the second problem of lagged availability of centers, we use a pipelined architecture, where computed centers from a previous epoch are used to cluster packets for this epoch.

Online version of clustering algorithm. There exist a few time-efficient k-medians clustering algorithms [12, 22, 21] in literature. In our architecture, we leverage an online clustering algorithm proposed in [12] because the algorithm makes no assumption about the characteristics of the streaming data and is space-efficient. We need to make several modifications to make the algorithm more efficient than the version in [12]. We describe briefly how the algorithm works and our modifications to speed up the algorithm next.

Given a stream of n data points and k centers we wish to find, this algorithm consists of two stages—online and offline clustering. At a high level, the online stage works in many (not necessarily equal) phases over the entire epoch to find $O(k \log n)$ candidate medians that the offline clustering stage subsequently reduces to k centers. In each phase, it uses Meyerson's online facility location algorithm [32], and chooses to open a new center with probability δ/f, where δ is the distance of the current point x to the closest already-open center, and f is the cost. In this algorithm, cost f is $L/(k(1 + \log n))$, where L is the lower bound cost of the optimal. Note that L is refined at the beginning of every phase by multiplying the previous value of L by a fixed constant β. (Refer to the PolyLogarithmic Space algorithm in page 4 of [12] for the exact description.) The current phase terminates if either the number of opened centers or the associated cost function exceeds some threshold (details in [12]). The algorithm terminates when all the packets are consumed, and leaves behind a set of $O(k \log n)$ candidate medians.

We make a few modifications to the original algorithm to contain the run-time complexity. First, since speed is critical, we use only one thread instead of $2 \log n$ parallel threads in the original algorithm in [12] (see PARA-CLUSTER in page 4 of the paper). Second, the online algorithm requires searching for the closest existing center out of $O(k \log n)$ centers in each phase, which is hard even for small k to do in 1 cycle. We therefore run the online algorithm only on *sampled* packets; a 10% sampling rate trivially gives 10 cycles to do these lookups. For $k = 50$ and $n = 400,000$, we observe about 1000 centers which can be looked up with a balanced binary tree using 10 memory accesses. We observe in our evaluations that 1-10% sampling rate has virtually no effect on the quality of the centers produced by the algorithm.

Handling lagged availability of centers. The problem here is that we cannot compute the centers and cluster on the same packet stream in one pass. Besides, the streaming algorithm itself operates in two stages, online and offline. To address this problem, we design a three-stage pipeline consisting of the following stages to handle this issue: The first stage consists of the online clustering algorithm that computes the $O(k \log n)$ centers that operates on packets in epoch i. The second stage consists of the offline clustering which will result in k centers by consuming these $O(k \log n)$ centers. Finally, we cluster the packets in epoch $i+2$ depending on the closest center that matches the packet's latency in the final stage. Since these stages operate in a pipelined fashion, the centers computed will be based on the dynamics of packets computed *two epochs back*. Assuming some amount of stationarity across measurement intervals (our evaluation shows holds true in practice), this pipelined approach should work well. However, to cover for the worst case where these centers may be significantly dissimilar to each other, we propose a hybrid clustering approach that combines static allocation with dynamic allocation, which we explain next.

Hybrid clustering. The basic idea of hybrid clustering is to choose $k/2$ centers with logarithmic clustering and remaining $k/2$ centers are computed by streaming k-medians algorithm. To enable hybrid clustering algorithm, we make two more modifications in the online version of clustering algorithm explained earlier. First, at the online clustering stage, the centers chosen by the logarithmic clustering are always selected as a new center in each phase and the number of data points added to the centers is incremented by one. Second, when $O(k \log(np))$ candidate centers (where p is sampling rate) need to be processed at the offline clustering stage, we exclude the $k/2$ centers picked by the logarithmic clustering from $O(k \log(np))$ centers, the rest candidate centers are fed into the offline algorithm, and finally $k/2$ centers are obtained. While we choose to split the total number of centers equally between static and dynamic allocation schemes, this equal split is somewhat arbitrary and other variants (*e.g.*, 2/3-1/3 split) could also work equally well (although we have not explored this thoroughly yet).

3.3 Storage provisioning

So far, we have reduced the problem of storing $< s, l >$ tuple to $< s, c_i >$ where l is the actual latency of packet s and c_i is the ith center ($0 \leq i < k$). Once the k representative delays are selected by the clustering algorithm, we need to determine how much storage is required to store packet latencies. Depending on the data structure that one uses, the actual required memory size can be different. Note that the goal of the data structures is essentially to store and look up the center id corresponding to a packet; the actual latency value corresponding to the center will need to be looked up in a separate table. During the lookup phase, instead of returning the static latency value corresponding to the center, we can dynamically return the *actual mean* of all the packets that map to a given center. Implementing this would require essentially two additional counters per center (latency sum and packet counts). We call these *refined latency estimates.*

3.3.1 Naive approach: PBF

Given these k cluster centers, we can now simply match each incoming packet latency value to determine the right center, and for each center maintain a separate Bloom filter (BF) in which we record the packet's presence. This naive and intuitive data structure called Partitioned Bloom Filter (PBF) as shown in Figure 3(a).

Insert To store a packet and its latency, it finds the right BF corresponding to the latency value by performing a closest center match in parallel (shown in Figure 3(a)). Since the number of centers k is quite small, doing this in parallel in hardware should be relatively easy to do. It then accesses the BF corresponding to this center, and inserts it into the BF just like a regular BF insert, i.e., by hashing using multiple hash functions and setting the bits indexed by the hash values to 1. Since BF inserts are $O(1)$, PBF insert time is $O(1)$, ignoring the small hardware cost for parallel match of the packet latency with the various centers.

Lookup To look up the latency of a packet, PBF checks whether the packet is present in any of the BFs; the delay represented by the BF that returns a match is the estimated latency of the queried packet. Clearly, the complexity of the lookup operation is $O(k)$ since k BFs need to be consulted.

Limitations A big problem with PBF is that, PBF needs to allocate storage for each of the k groups differently since the frequency counts for each group could be different. Of course, PBF could use the estimated frequency counts, but since our centers are calculated based on packets two epochs back, these estimates may not be accurate. Thus, the only options are to allocate higher amounts of storage per BF than necessary, or once the capacity of a BF is reached, it stops adding packets, leading to false negatives.

3.3.2 Prior approach: COMB

The second option we explore is using a recent generic data structure called combinatorial Bloom filters (COMB) designed for supporting multiset membership testing [20]. While PBF strictly partitions all BFs, COMB uses a single BF, but represents different groups using different subsets of hash functions. COMB contains three parameters, an f-bit vector in which θ bits are set to 1 to indicate the code for a group, and h different hash functions for each bit-position (in total $h \cdot f$ hash functions).

Insert For given center c_i, it first looks up the code $C(c_i)$ corresponding to the group; for each bit position that is set (θ bits will be set in each code), it picks the corresponding set of hash functions to index into the BF, and sets the

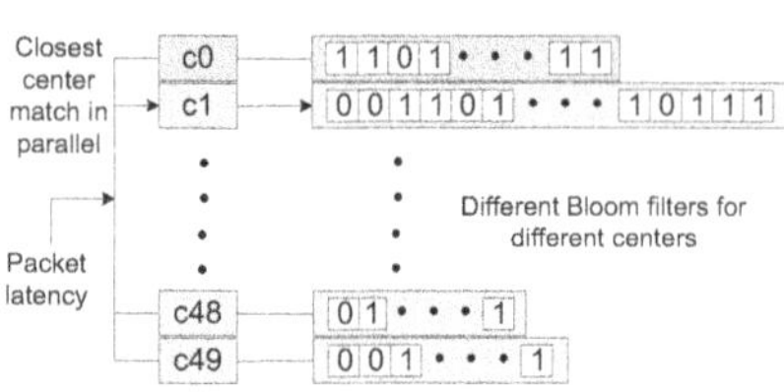

(a) PBF, $O(1)$ insert, $O(k)$ lookup

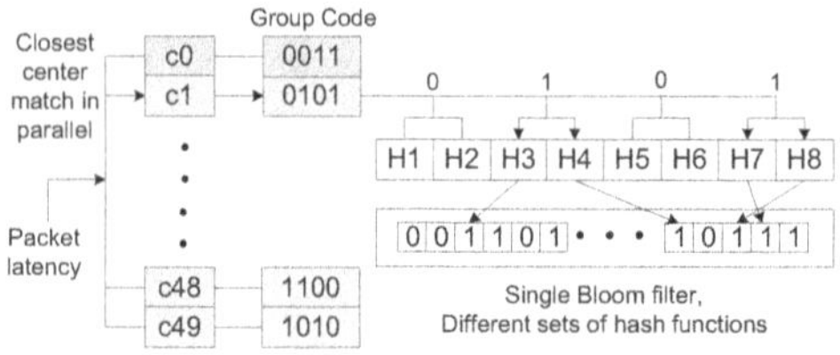

(b) COMB, $O(1)$ insert, $O(f)$ lookup

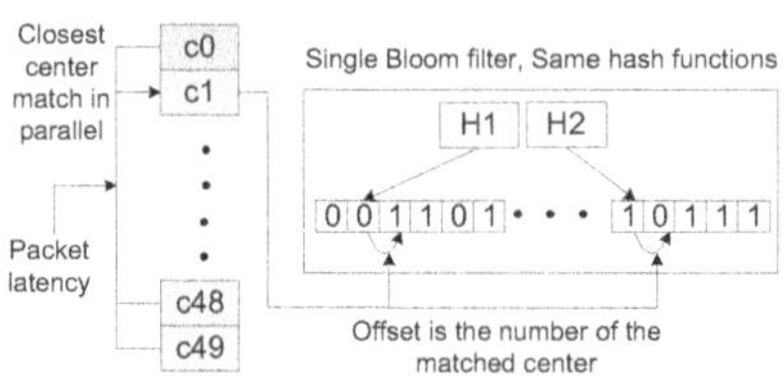

(c) SVBF, $O(1)$ insert, $O(1)$ lookup

Figure 3: Different variants of Bloom filters with different insert and lookup and $O(f)$ lookup where f is the size of bit vector. SVBF has $O(1)$ insert and $O(1)$ lookup assuming reading the k vector takes 1 memory access.

appropriate bits to 1 (just like a regular BF insert). Thus, for each packet, it requires setting up to $h \cdot \theta$ bits in the BF.

Lookup For each packet, it tests the positions indexed by hashing the packet with $h \cdot f$ hash functions. The f-bit code is formed by setting a bit position to 1, only if *all* bits indexed by the hash functions associated with the bit position indicate a 1 in the BF. The code then indicates the center.

Limitations The biggest advantage of COMB is that, unlike PBF, it does not need to know the number of packets in each group. However, storage requirement increases as θ increases, which decreases storage efficiency (as we shall compare shortly). Another limitation is that lookup complexity is high since all the $h \cdot f$ hash functions need to be queried, and all these bits are randomly located.

3.3.3 Our new data structure: SVBF

In the philosophy of maintaining one BF for all the groups, we could consider another, perhaps simpler alternative. Here, instead of storing packet s directly, we can store its concatenation with the group id, c_i, i.e., $s' = s \oplus c_i$, where $\oplus$ is a concatenation operator. Inserts are fast, but lookups (that involve querying a packet with all concatenations of group ids, *i.e.* k queries) are quite slow. Further, these cannot be parallelized since all the bits are scattered all across the BF.

To address this problem, we propose a new data structure called SVBF that essentially preserves the simplicity of a single BF, but reduces the lookup complexity significantly. Specifically, we store the bits corresponding to different delay values for the same packet close-by so that during queries we can read all the bits in a burst instead of reading them sequentially from various bit positions.

Insert The insert operation is quite similar to a regular BF, except for a small modification. In regular BF, each packet is hashed using multiple hash functions, and bits at those indices are set to 1. In SVBF, we use the center's index of the packet as an offset into a vector of delay values. Thus, we set the bit corresponding to $(h_j(s)+i) \mod m$, where j is the hash function index, $i \in [0, k-1]$ is the center index of the packet, and m is the size of SVBF. We do this for all hash functions. This is shown in Figure 3(c) where a packet that matches the second center $c1$ (center index 1) is added into the BF using hash functions H1 and H2. The offset at which the bit is set is 1 for this second center.

Lookup Given packet s, we first hash the packet to obtain various hash indices $h_j(s) \mod m$. From each of these bases, we read the next set of k bits, i.e., $h_j(s) \mod m$ to $(h_j(s)+k-1) \mod m$, to obtain bitmap B_j. We compute the bit-wise AND across all these bitmaps, $B = B_1 \& B_2 \& \ldots$. In the final bitmap (B), the offset where a bit is set to 1 is the center index.

Data structure	#Hash	Capacity (m/n)	Insert	Lookup
hashtable	1	147 bits/pkt	1	1
PBF	9	12.8 bits/pkt	9	450
COMB(50, 1)	9	12.8 bits/pkt	9	450
COMB(11, 2)	7	18.5 bits/pkt	14	77
COMB(8, 3)	6	24.2 bits/pkt	18	48
SVBF	9	12.8 bits/pkt	9	27

Table 1: Example of complexity of storage data structures for single port memory. 32 bit word is assumed for lookup in SVBF. Classification failure rate $p_{cf} = 0.1$ and $k = 50$. hashtable is tuned for $p_{fc} = 0.02$. The unit for insertion and lookup is the number of memory accesses.

While SVBF looks like a simple BF, there are two major differences. First, a BF only supports a membership check of a single sort, but SVBF supports multiset membership check. Second, the biggest advantage of this scheme is that, it relies on 'burst reads' which are simpler than random reads that COMB and BF suffer from. Thus, instead of k memory accesses, we need at most $\lceil k/w \rceil + 1$ memory accesses for each hash index as shown in Table 2. For example, for $k = 50$, we can obtain the bit maps in a total of $3 \times h$ memory accesses assuming a 32-bit machine word, and h is the number of hash functions. In Table 1, we show an example that outlines the storage complexity, lookup and insert times of SVBF compared to other data structures.

3.3.4 Classification failures

BFs are known to suffer from *false positives* occasionally, in which case a given element is not in the BF, but the BF returns with a positive answer. In PBF, this translates to a *classification failure* problem, since two (or more) BFs, one legitimate and one (or more) false positive may both (all) indicate a hit—the question is which one to trust. Similarly, COMB too may suffer from classification failures where more than θ bits in the bit vector are set to one. Even SVBF may suffer from classification failure, since the bitmap B described above may have more than one position set to 1 occasionally. We formally analyze this in §3.4.

Tie-breaking heuristic One option when classification fails due to the false positives, is to just not return an answer; this may be an acceptable choice given the system inherently trades off some amount of accuracy in order to scale

Data structure	#Hash functions	Capacity (m/n)	Insert	Lookup	Note
PBF	$h_{\text{PBF}} = -\log_2(1-(1-p_{\text{CF}})^{1/(k-1)})$	$\geq h_{\text{PBF}}/\log 2$	h_{PBF}	$k \times h_{\text{PBF}}$	lookup can be parallelized
COMB	$h_{\text{COMB}} = -\log_2(1-(1-p_{\text{CF}})^{1/(f-\theta)})$	$\theta \times h_{\text{COMB}}/\log 2$	$\theta \times h_{\text{COMB}}$	$f \times h_{\text{COMB}}$	random access for lookup
SVBF	$h_{\text{SVBF}} = -\log_2(1-(1-p_{\text{CF}})^{1/(k-1)})$	$h_{\text{SVBF}}/\log 2$	h_{SVBF}	$(\lceil k/w \rceil + 1) \times h_{\text{SVBF}}$	serial burst read in the unit of word

Table 2: Complexity of storage data structures for single port memory. w is the size of memory word. log **is natural log.**

better. We can also choose to resolve such conflicts using the following *tie-breaking heuristic*. When a packet can potentially match many groups, we report the latency value of the group with the largest number of packets among all conflicting groups. For identifying this, we assume we can store *running* packet counts for each group in an extra counter. This approach now can introduce *false classification* because the decisions can be wrong. But, we observed that this heuristic works well when the distribution of the cardinalities of BFs is skewed (*e.g.*, long tailed, heavy tailed), and can improve accuracy in many cases. However, as we mention in §4, the result of a query will be explicitly tagged so that the application which uses this data can be informed about the 'guess'ing nature of the answer.

3.4 Analysis of PLS

Now we discuss why simple hash table cannot scale in terms of space requirement while achieving $O(1)$ insert and lookup, and analyze the dependence of collision performance of the proposed data structures on storage dimensioning.

3.4.1 Hash table

While hash tables are typically simple, at a minimum they require the packet hash (32 bits) and group id (6 bits for 50 centers), thus requiring at least 38 bits per packet. Collision avoidance schemes present a further challenge for scaling. Thus, in order to perform a comparison with a BF, we consider a simpler hash table with no collision avoidance scheme, in which the packet digest is used to address a memory location in which the group id is stored (collisions will override the group id). For our analysis we consider n packets whose digest values are distributed independently and uniformly across m locations. Following §3.3.4, the false classification probability p_{FC} is proportion of packets allocated to already occupied locations: $p_{\text{FC}} = 1-\frac{m}{n}(1-(1-1/m)^n)$; see e.g. Section 3.3.2 of [25]. Although the required capacity m is not given as an explicit function of a target p_{FC}, we have the approximation $p_{\text{FC}} \approx n/(2m)$ when $n \ll m$. For example, when $p_{\text{FC}} = 0.02$ (a median false classification rate that SVBF achieves in §5.3) then $m = 24.6n$. Considering $k = 50$, each bucket is 6 bits. Then, $m/n = 147$ bits/packet, even higher than the regular hash tables. Thus, this simple variant does not scale.

3.4.2 Collision analysis & storage dimensions

We now analyze the frequencies of classification failures due to storage collisions for queries on the PBF, COMB and SVBF data structures. First, it is convenient to identify a generic collision analysis that applies to each storage method. Following the terminology of §3.3, the *false positive* probability p_{FP} denotes a probability that a given set of storage locations pertaining to a single delay group are occupied. Then, *classification failure* for a packet in delay group i occurs if it has a false positive in any other delay group j: $p_{\text{CF}}^{(i)} = 1 - \prod_{j \neq i}(1 - p_{\text{FP}}^{(j)})$.

Consider now specifically a BF with m locations and h hash functions. We assume an independent hash digest distribution over all packets. For simplicity, we assume that the query packet is mapped by the hash functions to h distinct locations[1]. As is well known, the false positive probability that a set of h bits are all set after the insertion of n background objects is $p_{\text{FP}} = p(m,n,h) = (1-(1-1/m)^{nh})^h$.

Collisions in PBF Each delay group i has capacity m_i ($\sum_i m_i = m$) and n_i background packets allocated to it ($\sum_i n_i = n$). Given a classification failure probability for a packet in a delay group i, by averaging over all n packets in their respective delay groups, we have

$$p_{\text{CF}} = 1 - \sum_j \frac{n_j}{n} \prod_{i \neq j}(1 - p(m_i, n_i, h)) \qquad (1)$$

Since the operational allocations m_i and n_i are not known in advance, for design purposes one would assume uniformity, in which case (1) reduces to (3) below.

Collisions in COMB All delay group locations for the query flow may be set by any of the background flows. Since COMB uses θ bits to denote a group id in a code, it is equivalent to virtually put $\theta{\cdot}n$ items into m locations. Hence

$$p_{\text{CF}} = 1 - (1 - p(m, \theta \cdot n, h))^{f-\theta} \qquad (2)$$

Collisions in SVBF All delay group locations for the query flow may be set by any of the background flows. Hence

$$p_{\text{CF}} = 1 - (1 - p(m,n,h))^{k-1} \qquad (3)$$

When all BF sizes m_i are equal, a standard convexity argument shows that $p_{\text{CF}}(\text{SVBF}) \leq p_{\text{CF}}(\text{PBF})$ for any $\{n_i\}$.

Storage Dimensioning We use the foregoing analysis to show how to dimension SVBF for given target classification failure rate p_{CF}. For large, n, $p(m,n,h) \approx q(n/m, h)$ where $q(\alpha, h) = (1-e^{-\alpha h})^h$. As is well known, $\alpha \mapsto q(\alpha, h)$ is minimized at when $h = \alpha^{-1}\log(2)$, in which case, $p_{\text{CF}}(\text{SVBF}) = 1-(1-2^{-h})^{k-1}$. Thus, given a target p_{CF} of $\varepsilon > 0$, we must choose h and $\alpha^{-1}\log 2$ to be bounded below by $-\log_2(1-(1-\varepsilon)^{1/(k-1)})$. The lower bound for h and upper bound for α compatible with two possible target classification failure rates $\varepsilon = 10^{-1}$ and 10^{-5} are displayed as a function of the number k of delay groups in Figure 4. Observe that, due to the logarithmic dependence, after an initial phase, the curves are relatively flat as a function of k. They do not depend very strongly on the target rate: decreasing ε by 4 orders of magnitude changes the bounds by only about half an order of magnitude. Table 2 provides

[1] This happens with probability $m^{-h}m!/(m-h)! \geq 1 - h^2/(2m)$

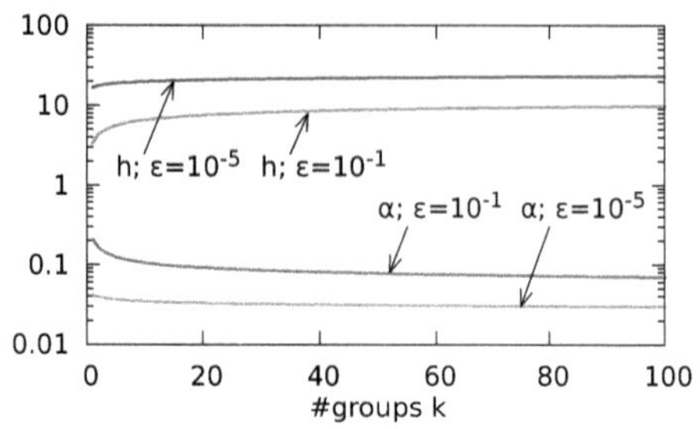

Figure 4: Dimensioning SVBF: lower bound on #hash functions h, and upper bound on load $\alpha = n/m$, as function of #delay groups k, for two target p_{cf} classification failure rates $\varepsilon = 10^{-1}$ and 10^{-5}.

overview of insert and lookup complexities and storage requirements of the three data structures. Given $\varepsilon = 10^{-1}$, parameter tuning examples are shown in Table 1.

4. LATENCY QUERY INTERFACE

In this section, we describe the packet latency query interface that allows a 'querying client' (henceforth, just client) to query routers for specific packet latency measurements.

Query using packet hash. In the very basic query, a client can request a particular router for latency of a given packet identified by the packet hash. This implicitly assumes that the packets are first hashed using the invariant fields in a packet header (*e.g.*, IP addresses, IP id, port numbers) and the packet payload (a few bytes is often sufficient [17]) before inserting into the SVBF. We also assume that the client knows that the path taken by the packet; otherwise, the client needs to ask all the routers in the network which may increase the number of bogus queries. We assume that it will be possible to determine this based on the forwarding tables. In cases where multiple parallel paths are exploited (*e.g.*, flow-based VLB in VL2 [19] or ECMP), a selected path for a flow at random in VL2 needs to be stored or hash functions for ECMP computation needs to be published. When centralized controllers (*e.g.*, Hedera [6]) are involved in forwarding, such forwarding information can be saved for offline-queries. We leave this issue as part of our future work.

The switch then performs a lookup operation of the packet in the SVBF to return the latency estimate to the client. Because of classification failure possibility in SVBF, we return latency estimates with a 2-bit type that identifies one of three types: (1) `Match` that indicates that the packet was uniquely identified in the SVBF. (2) `Multi-Match` indicating that multiple matches were reported, but the latency estimate corresponds to the answer using the tie-breaking heuristic we discussed in §3.3.4. (3) `No-Match` that indicates the packet's latency estimate could not be located.

If the host wishes to obtain flow-level (or any other aggregate) latency statistics, it needs to send all packet digests of a particular flow of interest to the particular switch/router it believes the packets may have traversed along the path from the source to the destination. Sending one packet for querying each packet to the switch may lead to too many packets. Luckily, packet digests could be easily batched in one query message (about 375 32-bit labels can be embedded within one 1500 byte query packet). Since packet hashes are random d-byte strings, this is the only way to form the aggregate unfortunately. We can reduce the query bandwidth by potentially querying only a sample corresponding to the aggregate as opposed to all the packets, that may represent a trade-off between query bandwidth and accuracy. While exploring this trade-off is outside the scope of this paper, we briefly describe an idea next that has the potential to reduce the query bandwidth significantly.

Query using flow key and IP identifier. We can reduce query bandwidth overhead with the help of a range search capability. Since packet hashes do not lend themselves to this range search easily, we consider an alternate scheme. Instead of storing the packet hash, we store the concatenation of the packet's flow key and the IP identifier (IPID) field. Since IPID field is typically implemented to increment IPIDs of packets linearly in most operating systems, the use of IPID field allows us to support flow-level (or sub-flow level) queries quite easily. We believe that in data center environments orchestrated by a single organization, enforcing such *de facto* implementation can be possible. Note that we evaluate this scheme against intact packet traces with *no* modification on IPID field collected from a tier-1 ISP link and two links in data centers in §5.4.

The client in this case can query packets using the tuple $(f_k, [IPid_i, IPid_j])$. Note that this does not stipulate that all packets that belong to a flow will need to have contiguous IDs. But since TCP transmits packets in bursts usually, we can break down a flow in to several tuples

$$f_k = (f_k, [IPid_{i1}, IPid_{i2}]), (f_k, [IPid_{i3}, IPid_{i4}]), \ldots,$$

and chain them together in one message. This reduces the query bandwidth significantly, almost by a factor of 17× in our evaluation (§5.4). The receiving router will sequentially query all packets $(f_k, IPid_{i1})$, $(f_k, IPid_{i1+1})$, ..., $(f_i, IPid_{i2})$. Further, we can make the query interface specify whether it wants the individual latency values or the aggregate values, so that the router can send either individual packet latency values or aggregate them in its response. This will also reduce the response overhead significantly.

Query timing. For both types of queries, we need the client to mention a rough time of the packet as part of the query, so that the router can look up the appropriate SVBF data structure corresponding to the time when the packet may have gone through the router. Given the fact that PLS resets the SVBF's every epoch, it is important to make sure that the previous epoch and the next epoch are also queried for the packet in order to make sure there are no fringe effects, i.e., the timing is close to the start/end of an epoch and it may lie before or after the epoch.

Querying clients. MAPLE is largely oblivious to who originates the query. In some environments, we could envision end hosts could be the clients. For example, an end host that is running a low-latency trading application or a high-performance computing application, whenever it detects packet delays exceed some level, may originate a query packet to determine which router is responsible for the higher delay. Similarly, we can consider private datacenter owners such as Google, Microsoft, etc., that may want to debug their systems may provide this ability for individual hosts to query routers periodically for obtaining latency statistics.

We can also consider public cloud environments such as Amazon EC2 where customers may demand certain SLAs on network performance. We could imagine the cloud provider installing a debugging stub-module within the host hypervisor (similar to other recent works [36]) that essentially, at the signal of a management host controlled by the network operator, can start storing each packet's hash that matches a given hurting application, or a hurting customer. It can then query these packets along the route to its destination to determine its latency. In this case, it makes sense to put this stub module within the hypervisor since it is the one that knows which packets are going out of its system; the management host cannot possibly know how to query for the packets since it does not know either the packet hash or the IP id sequence.

In the first usage scenario, we essentially trust the end host to not overwhelm the switch by injecting too many queries. This is possible in a tightly controlled datacenter or cluster environment, but may not be, for example, possible in a public cloud environment such as Amazon EC2 (the second scenario). In such cases, we need some other protection mechanisms (*e.g.*, charging models, rate limiting) to ensure the number of queries to switches does not exceed some limit.

5. EVALUATION

In this section, we evaluate the practicality of our MAPLE architecture. Specifically, our experiments are designed to answer the following questions. (1) How do the different clustering algorithms perform ? (2) How do the various data structures we discussed in §3.3 compare in terms of their accuracy for a given storage budget ? (3) How efficient is the query interface in terms of latency estimates of arbitrary aggregates, bandwidth reduction and inaccuracies in query timing ? (4) How does it compare with previous approaches such as RLI ? We first describe our experimental setup before answering these questions.

5.1 Experimental setup

While we envision the eventual deployment to be in the form of a hardware prototype, for the purposes of evaluation, we prototyped various pieces, notably the streaming clustering algorithm and the storage data structure, of MAPLE in software. We implemented the online portion of the k-medians algorithm from scratch (about 300 lines of C++ code), while we used the C clustering library [5] for the offline part. However, the library had to be modified to support clustering data with weight (*i.e.*, count of entries clustered to a candidate center at the online stage). For most of the experiments, we use 50 centers ($k = 50$) that, as we shall show, represent a good balance between accuracy and complexity.

In our setup, we feed several packet traces (real router as well as using synthetic queueing models) into the software prototype to study its efficacy. We can however easily replace the packet traces with live traffic in our environment. For the most part, we kept our evaluation setup very similar to prior work [27]. We also used the same traces—a tier-1 trace (*ISP*) collected at an OC-192 link and a real router trace (*RR*)—as the authors of [27] to facilitate a fair comparison with prior work. Benson *et al.* [9] have recently published data center traces (*UNIV1* and *UNIV2*) that belong to a university data center edge router. However, the data center traces are not sufficient workloads (data rates of 2-60Mbps) for testing the scalability of our architecture. Nevertheless, since the traces reflect real flow size distribution in data centers, we use them in §5.4 to evaluate query bandwidth saving that can be achieved by the range query mechanism discussed in §4.

The *RR* trace was collected at a pair of ingress and egress interfaces in a real router. Therefore, it contains two timestamps of every packet that passes the router; and this immediately allows us to compute real delays of packets. On the other hand, the *ISP* trace was collected at a single interface, which means that it only has one timestamp of every packet arriving at the interface. Thus, to facilitate our experiments with this trace, we simulate the delays of packets; we subject packets to a simple, synthetic queueing model with open-loop RED queue management strategy with parameters configured similar to the setup in [27]. We configure the packet processing time in terms of byte/second and queue length in the model. Real packet lengths and inter-arrival distribution govern dynamics of packet delay values and losses.

The *ISP* trace we used in our setup has about 22.4M packets in a period of 60s. We divide the 60s period into 60 measurement epochs each with 1s duration. Recall that our architecture operates in epochs and freezes the storage for lookup after every epoch. The number of packets in an epoch ranges from 358K to 404K. We find about 40K hosts and 4.2M flows (considering same flow key across two epochs as two different flows) on average in each epoch. We also conducted experiments using an *RR* trace set that contains two different traces; one has 2.6 million packets for 5 minutes achieving 53% utilization of an OC-3 link, and the other has 4.0 million packets during the same period (88% link utilization). The traffic source is artificial in that, it is generated by Harpoon traffic generator, but all packets were subject to latency factors in a real router. Qualitatively, we found consistent results across both *ISP* and *RR* traces and hence we do not discuss the results on *RR* traces any further.

5.2 Performance of clustering algorithms

We first compare static (logarithmic), dynamic (pipelined k-medians) and the hybrid strategy that combines the two. For reference we also include a *hypothetical* non-pipelined k-medians (called *oracle*) approach, that essentially runs the k-medians on the data directly, determines the centers, and then clusters the packets into these centers. In all algorithms, we assume a perfect data structure for storing the approximate delays, i.e., no Bloom filters to introduce any interference. This gives us a baseline for comparison. As mentioned before, we compare these schemes assuming $k = 50$ centers. While we conduct experiments with three traces of different link utilization scenarios to comprehensively understand the tradeoffs, we omit showing all the curves due to space limitations. We show the absolute error CDF for only the high (85 %) utilization case in Figure 5(a).

In our experiments, we observe that oracle achieves the smallest absolute error at higher quartiles among all methods across all link utilization scenarios as it minimizes the summation of absolute distance between entries and their closest centers, which is exactly the absolute error. Since its objective is to decrease the absolute error, it may allocate centers that may increase the relative error for some packets, particularly the low-latency packets. We observe a similar trend in the k-medians clustering method as well. Logarithmic clustering generally achieves higher accuracy

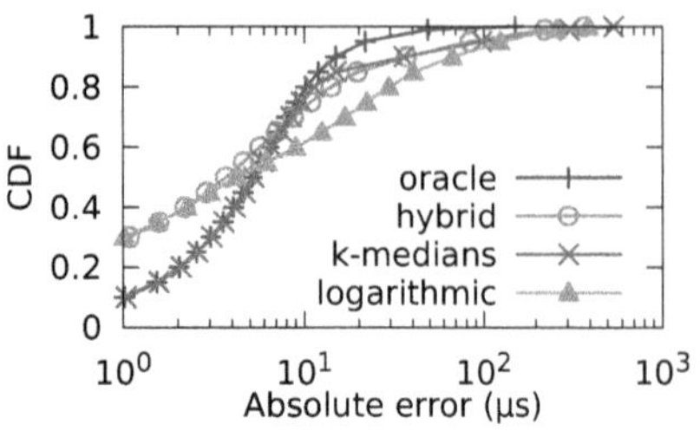

(a) Clustering schemes

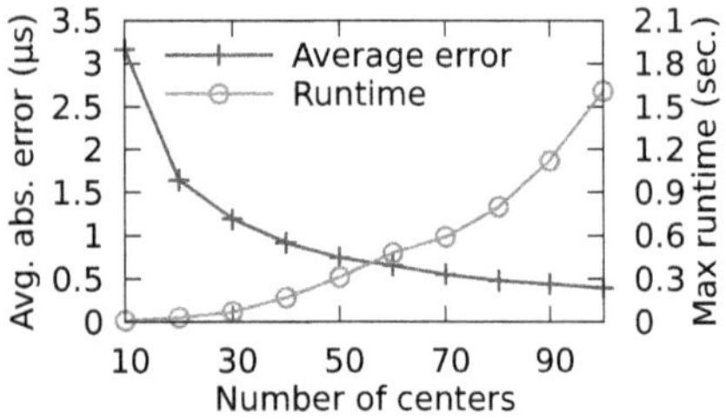

(b) Tradeoff in deciding centers

Figure 5: Comparing different clustering schemes and exploring trade-off between average error and maximum running time for offline stage.

than other methods in terms of relative error because its centers are placed at equal distances within each sub-range (*e.g.*, 1-10μs and 10-100μs). On the contrary, analyses on absolute error suggest that the logarithmic clustering suffers from inaccurate estimates at higher percentiles. For instance, k-medians clustering is almost twice more accurate than logarithmic clustering at 90 %ile (35μs absolute error in k-medians and 67μs in logarithmic) in Figure 5(a). This basically stems from the logarithmic clustering's failing to adjust its centers as packet delays vary. This may further worsen its accuracy as configurations such as link capacity may change in future. Comparatively, the other schemes adapt to this trend quickly and place more centers close to where the actual delays are, leading to better accuracy.

The k-medians clustering method has the similar performance that the oracle has in terms of both absolute and relative errors under low and moderate utilization cases, and even till the 3rd quartile of high utilization case. At top 25 %ile of high utilization scenario (Figure 5(a)), accuracy of the k-medians is worse than that of oracle because of the inherent variations across epochs; this is in essence the price we pay for an online clustering algorithm. Finally, we observe that the hybrid clustering approach balances both absolute and relative errors by inheriting the good properties of static and dynamic center determination approaches. For instance, in Figure 5(a), we see how the hybrid scheme inherits the better accuracy of logarithmic approach up to 50 %ile and better accuracy of k-medians at top 50 %ile. Henceforth, unless otherwise mentioned, we use the hybrid scheme in the rest of the paper.

Impact of packet sampling. In §3.2, we discussed that we employ packet sampling in the clustering phase to reduce the processing overhead. We now study the impact of varying the sampling rate on the accuracy of the per-packet latency estimates. In our experiments, we found virtually no difference between the different absolute error CDFs (and hence, refrain from showing the actual plots) between the sampled and unsampled variants. One could imagine this happens because most packet delays are clustered to statically chosen centers instead of those close to the k-medians. However, this is not the case, as only 53% and 1.5% packets are clustered to those static centers at high and low levels of link utilization respectively. The actual reason is that the k centers output by the algorithm are similar even when we sample packets. We observe that the cosine similarity (defined as $\cos\varphi = \frac{A \cdot B}{|A||B|}$) between two vectors A and B of k centers output by sampled and unsampled k-medians algorithm is over 0.98 for sampling rates as low as 1%.

Number of centers vs. running time. The running time of the offline algorithm depends on the final number of centers required, i.e., k, and the number of candidate centers output by the online clustering stage. As k increases, the running time of the algorithm increases, but the resulting error also decreases. This is the main trade-off involved in choosing an appropriate value of k. Figure 5(b) explores this trade-off under moderate (58%) link utilization scenario as k is increased from 10 to 100. (We only plot the curve corresponding to the sampling rate 0.1 here, but other sampling rates also exhibited similar trends.) From the plot, we can clearly observe the sweet spot that represents a reasonable trade-off between running time and average absolute error is $k = 50$. We can possibly choose up to 70 or 80 centers as well as the running time is less than the epoch interval (1s). Of course, depending on the target platform and computational resources we can expect on the processor, the number of centers may vary. But this trade-off implies we can easily determine the value of k appropriate for the target platform.

5.3 Comparison of data structures for PLS

Next, we compare the performance of various data structures for PLS—SVBF, PBF and COMB. For fair comparisons, we configure all of these with the same 5Mbit memory in total. It is not easy to fix the amount of memory in PBF since the total memory needs to be explicitly partitioned across all the BFs. We split the total memory across each BF proportional to the number of packets that are mapped to a given BF (according to the frequency counts two epochs back). For the others, we derive the optimal parameter configurations, such as number of hash functions, for different data structures using the formulae in §3.4. For this memory, the theoretical analysis suggests using 9 hash functions for SVBF and PBF. For COMB, there are two other parameters, θ (number of bits that need to be set in the group code) and f (length of the code). Out of feasible combinations to support $k = 50$ groups, we choose the configuration with f=8 and θ=3 that has the smallest lookup time (that is proportional to f). By fixing these parameters, the number of hash functions per bit, h needs to be set to 3 according to the analysis in §3.4. Thus, all in all, we ensured that the comparisons are as fair as possible between the various schemes.

In our comparisons, we mainly study the classification failure rate, false classification rate, and finally the impact of these on the accuracy of latency estimates. We search latencies of all packets for 58 epochs (the first 2 epochs are used for clustering only). For false classification rate, we use the tie-breaking heuristic described in §3.3.4 and compute the rate at which the heuristic leads to an incorrect answer.

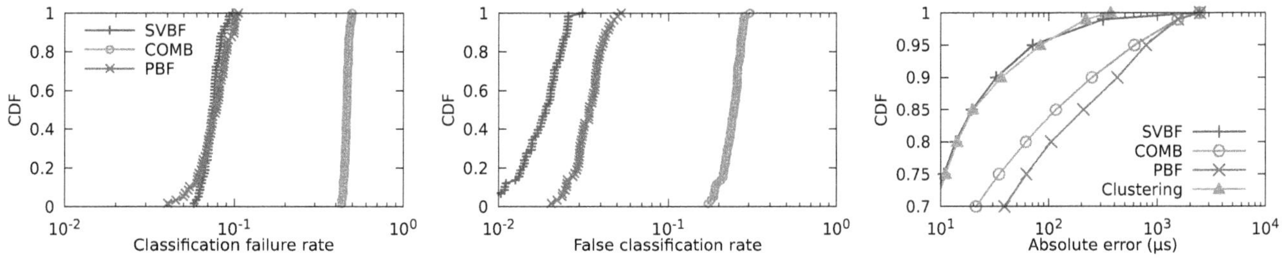

(a) Classification failure (b) False classification (c) Estimation accuracy

Figure 6: Analysis of classification failure, false classification, and estimation accuracy.

Classification failure and false classification rates. We show the classification failure rate of each data structure in Figure 6(a). SVBF and PBF (as expected) achieve least classification failure rate of about 10% at most across all epochs, while COMB obtains 50% at most—almost 5× higher than SVBF. Note that for PBF due to the fact that for a given BF, the number of packets may exceed the capacity, we observed almost 24% of packets could not be admitted altogether (false negatives). Applying the tie-breaking heuristic results in a false classification rate that is lower than the classification failure rate, but not by much. Still, as shown in the Figure 6(b), the median false classification rate of COMB is almost 12× higher than SVBF. This shows the efficacy of our SVBF compared to existing data structures such as COMB. As shown in Table 1, COMB requires almost twice the number of bits per packet to achieve the classification failure rates as SVBF. We next study how this decrease in classification failure effects the actual delay estimation.

Accuracy of per-packet latency estimation. Figure 6(c) shows absolute errors of per-packet latency estimates for three data structures. In addition to them, there is an additional curve titled 'Clustering' that essentially assumes a perfect data structure, but does not use the refined latency estimates (described in §3.3) using the observed mean of the data packets. (We can always plot that too, and that would strictly be better than the rest, but we chose this as a nice reference point to see the effects of the refinement.)

We show mainly the upper quartile in this graph where the difference is the most pronounced. Clearly, at lower than 75 %ile, either SVBF or COMB would return the same (correct) group id if the packet is not misclassified; it is only for the misclassified packets that the accuracy is likely to be worse since the tie-breaking heuristic may pick the wrong latency estimate for the packet. (If we choose not to report them, then they will be counted as false negatives.) We can notice that COMB and PBF suffer from much higher discrepancies as early as the 70 %ile onwards, while in contrast we can see that the Clustering and SVBF have an absolute error that is significantly lower in comparison. For example the 85 %ile absolute error for COMB is close to $116\mu s$ while SVBF has an error of $19\mu s$ at the same percentile. From the figure, we can see that not until almost the 98 %ile onward do we see any difference between Clustering and SVBF.

Insert and lookup time complexity. We study the complexity of insert and lookup time of each data structure. We tested 0.4 million packets for insert and lookup using a Linux machine with 2.66GHz Intel CPU. Figure 7 shows the complexity in microsecond precision. From the figure, we observe that SVBF works faster than COMB in both insert (45% gain on average) and lookup (28%) operations. These experimental gains of SVBF are close to the theoretical ones which are 50% ((18-9)/18) for insert and 44% ((48-27)/48) for lookup based on the number of memory accesses in Table 1. While PBF achieves the same performance of SVBF for insert operation, PBF is four times slower than SVBF for lookup operation on average. Note that SVBF is implemented as software and can be optimized further in hardware platform.

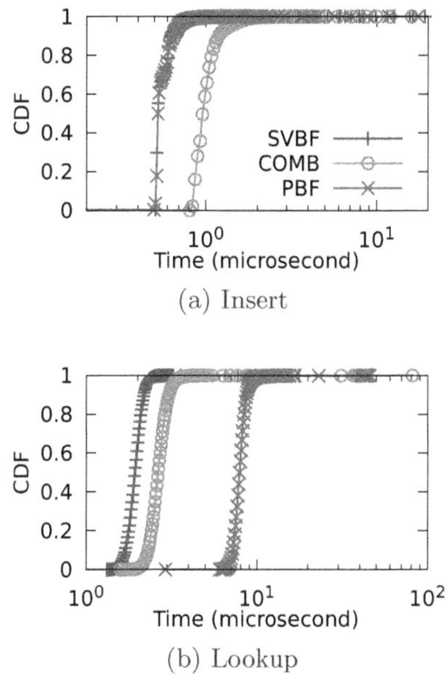

Figure 7: Comparison of insert and lookup times.

5.4 Query interface

Since our architecture can support querying any packet, it can allow the querying host to compute aggregate statistics across arbitrary traffic sub-populations.

Accuracy of aggregate statistics. We first verify the accuracy of obtained aggregate statistics (by querying packets that belong to that aggregate) at different levels–sub-flow, flow, host, and prefix/16. By performing flow-level aggregation, i.e., by grouping packets with the same flow key, our

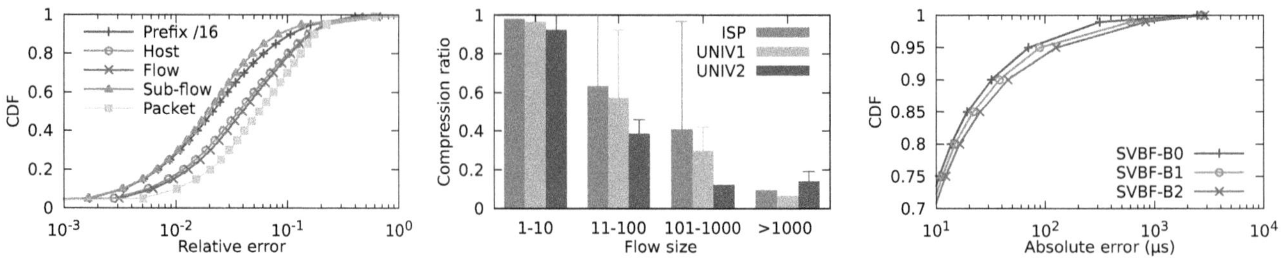

(a) Accuracy of aggregates (b) Query bandwidth compression (c) Impact of query timing

Figure 8: Average latency statistics at different aggregation levels, query message compression ratio depending on flow size, and impact of query timing using high utilization scenario.

architecture achieves similar functionality as previous work RLI [27]. However, perhaps more unique to our architecture, due to the fact that it stores measurements on a per-packet basis, we can choose to aggregate at sub-flow level, while RLI cannot easily achieve this. We compute the average delay of 10 consecutive packets within the same flow key (among large flows whose size is more than 10 packets) as the sub-flow average delay. Such a feature could be useful, for instance, to understand which set of packets within a large flow are exhibiting abnormal latencies.

Figure 8(a) shows the aggregate statistics in terms of relative error for the high link utilization scenario. We also draw a curve for packet latencies as a reference curve. From the figure, we observe that as aggregation level becomes higher, relative error reduces. Latency estimates at sub-flow level, however, have the least relative errors. This is not inconsistent, since many flow/host/prefix-level statistics, although aggregated with packets within a given epoch, are computed with only a single packet (46% flows, 41% hosts, and 13% prefix/16), while sub-flow statistics are computed for flows that at least have 10 packets. Thus, sub-flow latency estimates get more influence on canceling individual errors out by aggregation. Specifically, median relative error is 5.5% at packet level, 3.9% at flow level, 3.6% at host level, 2.1% at prefix/16 level and 1.9% at sub-flow level. Similar trends are found under low and moderate utilization scenarios.

In terms of absolute errors, we observe that prefix/16 average latency is more accurate than other aggregation levels, at low link utilization. As link utilization increases, however, we find little difference in absolute error among all four aggregation levels. We omit graphs for brevity, but we observe a 95 %ile absolute error of less than $0.05\mu s$, $2\mu s$ and $55\mu s$ across all four aggregation levels.

Compression of query bandwidth with IP ids. We study the query bandwidth saving using the IPID idea outlined in §4. For each flow within an epoch, we compare the bandwidth of range query messages with individual packet queries. Figure 8(b) shows the bar graph of compression ratio depending on flow size for 60 epochs with *ISP*, *UNIV1* and *UNIV2* traces. The bar denotes average compression ratio and the whisker bar means 75 %ile value from the figure. We observe that as flow size increases, higher query bandwidth saving is achieved (for flows with more than 1000 packets in *UNIV1*, average compression ratio is 6%—17× less bandwidth than the naive packet query method). We also observe that more compression at larger flow sizes is achieved with data center traces compared to *ISP* trace.

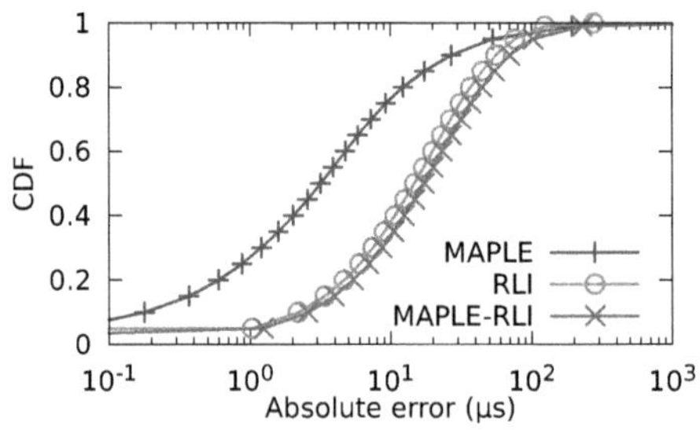

Figure 9: Comparison of flow estimates with RLI.

Impact of inaccurate query timing. We evaluate the impact of inaccurate query timing when clients issue per-packet latencies. In the experiments, all packet queries in an epoch i are asked to a SVBF of that epoch (true SVBF) and additional b number of SVBFs of previous epochs $i-b$ (bogus SVBFs). Multiple matches are resolved using the same tie-breaking heuristic. In Figure 8(c), we show the results for 2 bogus SVBFs. Clearly, as the number of epochs considered increases, the accuracy decreases slightly. For instance, 95 %ile absolute error shifts from 70 to 89 to $125\mu s$ as bogus SVBFs are added, but the 75 %ile errors are not that impacted, increasing the error from 10.7 to $12.2\mu s$.

5.5 Comparison with prior architecture

We now compare our MAPLE architecture with RLI [27], that also averages approximate latencies of packets (obtained via latency interpolation) that belong to a flow. MAPLE uses accurate packet latencies (using timestamps) but stores them approximately in the SVBF data structure. MAPLE can also use RLI-approximated latency for each packet, but this leads to two sets of approximations (we denote this as MAPLE-RLI). We study these various effects in Figure 9. (For brevity, we only show the high utilization curve; the trends for the other two utilizations were similar.)

We make two observations in Figure 9. First, there is little difference in absolute error between MAPLE-RLI and RLI, while RLI has slightly higher accuracy than MAPLE-RLI, which is expected. Specifically, under high utilization scenario, RLI has $76\mu s$ absolute error at 95 percentile, but MAPLE-RLI has $102\mu s$ at the same percentile. Median error by RLI is $15\mu s$ and the error of MAPLE-RLI is $17\mu s$. The second observation is that MAPLE (with true latencies) achieves much higher (half to one order of magnitude higher) accuracy than RLI. For instance, about 90% flows have less than $1\mu s$ absolute error with MAPLE, but RLI only has 50% flows with such absolute error under moderate utilization scenario (not shown for brevity). Put differently, in Figure 9, MAPLE achieves 5× less median error than RLI. This shows that MAPLE, if implemented, may provide more accurate latency estimates than RLI, even with the approximations in the storage data structure. Of course, if actual packet latencies are available to RLI, there is no need for interpolation in RLI, and per-flow latencies are trivially obtained with 100% accuracy. So, we do not discuss the obvious case.

6. IMPLEMENTATION

We envision that the streaming k-medians algorithm will be implemented in software. We assume there is an additional processor (or core) devoted to implementing this architecture. We assume that this core will perform the streaming k-medians on the sampled data. There have been some prior efforts [29] on implementing k-medians directly in hardware that we can also leverage. In environments where there is not enough processing capacity, we can rely on the static clustering approach we discussed in §3. This will however yield worse accuracy than the hybrid clustering.

The actual storage data structure (SVBF) outlined in Figure 2, will need to be implemented in hardware in high-speed SRAM. Bloom filters in general require simple hashing operations and updating bit maps and thus are amenable to high-speed implementations (see [38] for example). For implementing the hash functions, we can use the H3 [34] hash functions or the BOB [24] ones that are amenable to easy hardware implementations. We need to also maintain two extra counters per center, one for tracking number, and the other for sum of delays of all packets that map to a given center. These counters will enable the refined latency estimate heuristic (in §3.3) and the tie-breaking heuristic (in §3.3.4). The SVBF data structure needs to be flushed every epoch to an off-chip storage, which can be either DRAM or SSDs. Along with each SVBF, the associated k centers for that particular epoch need to be stored. For smaller k, this is only a small amount of extra storage. Depending on the technological constraints such as the amount of available high-speed memory and link speeds, the epoch size could be determined.

Assuming an OC-192 interface, we have roughly 5 million packets per second, for which we will require about 60 Mbits of memory per second (assuming 12 bits/packet). Of course, this is assuming the interface is running at full capacity, which is often not the case. Rather, latency spikes are often generated by microburst typically occurring under low average utilization [9]. Thus, if we assume 20% utilization, we only require 12 Mbits of memory per second to capture such latency spikes. 16 GB of DRAM (which is commodity today) could be used to store packet latencies for almost 3 hours. Flash memory densities are even higher; today 256 GB SSDs are possible which will enable storing packet latency state for 47 hours, which is enough time for network operators to debug and process the information. Even for 100% utilization, the DRAM and SSD can sustain for 36 minutes and 9.5 hours respectively.

Queries will need to be handled in software. For each query, depending on the approximate time of the packet in the query, the appropriate SVBF (and the two neighbors just in case) will be queried by the processor (or core) (perhaps shared with the k-medians implementation). Only the words corresponding to the hash indexes will need to be fetched from the secondary memory (SSD or DRAM), which are then looked up according to the algorithm outlined in §3.3.3.

7. RELATED WORK

There exists a lot of research in measuring per-hop latencies, although in the wide-area context, where ISPs typically rely on injecting active probes and obtaining link or hop latency statistics using tomographic approaches [14, 16, 39]. These approaches do not satisfy any of our high-fidelity measurement requirements in §2.1 and thus we need high-fidelity passive measurement mechanisms. In this regard, we already discussed three prior approaches relevant to ours—LDA [26], RLI [27] and Consistent NetFlow [28].

The idea of storing packet-level information has been pursued in other prior contexts; trajectory sampling for identifying packet trajectories in [17] and SPIE for IP traceback in [37]. Neither provides latency estimates unfortunately, although trajectory sampling could be augmented with a timestamp, but only a small number of packets are sampled at each router (see [26, 27] for comparison of these approaches with trajectory sampling). SPIE on the other hand stores only packets and not their associated timestamps; thus, a simple Bloom filter was sufficient there, while we needed the clustering and SVBF in our setting.

The idea of 'in-band' diagnosis was proposed in NetReplay [8] and Orchid [33]. NetReplay proposes the idea of replaying packets to collect feedback from the network. Orchid [33] also proposes the idea of in-band network troubleshooting, where packets collect feedback from routers along the path. Our approach, however is more focused on estimating, storing and retrieving packet-level latency measurements, and is complementary to these approaches.

Song *et al.* propose fast hash table [38] to provide constant lookup time by exploiting counting bloom filter. Fast hash table does not address large space requirement because of an extra counting bloom filter and the need to store both packet digest and its delay. Supporting membership check across multiple groups is non-trivial for Bloom filter. Several data structures [11, 13, 20] have been proposed to address this problem. COMB [20] is a multi-group membership check data structure that is highly relevant to our work and hence, we discussed this in §3.3.

Our SVBF data structure shares some similarity with the bit slicing idea proposed in the database community [35, 18]. Specifically, the concept of colocating bits corresponding to different centers to which a packet may potentially match is similar to laying out bits corresponding to records in a document on the disk, one of which a given keyword may match to. The bit slicing idea may be applied to PBF to make the lookup time complexity close to SVBF's, but it needs BF sizes to be uniform. One may think of normalizing the sizes of all BFs, but that means each BF needs to be the size of the largest BF, which is all packets in the worst case. This is clearly a considerable wastage.

8. CONCLUSION

This paper proposed a scalable and flexible measurement architecture called MAPLE. The core of the architecture consists of two novel mechanisms; a streaming clustering algorithm to cluster packet latencies into small number of latency clusters in a streaming fashion, and a data structure called SVBF to store packet latencies efficiently in a router. In addition, it provides a flexible query interface for network operators to query the latency of individual packets. Together, the architecture provides both fine-grained as well as flexible latency measurements to help network operators manage low-latency applications efficiently. Our evaluations using a software prototype indicate that our architecture can scale efficiently both in terms of storage needs as well as in terms of query bandwidth.

Acknowledgments

The authors are indebted to Aditya Akella, our shepherd, and the anonymous reviewers for comments on previous versions of this manuscript. This work was supported in part by NSF Award CNS 0831647 and 1054788.

9. REFERENCES

[1] Cut-through and store-and-forward ethernet switching for low-latency environments. `http://www.cisco.com/en/US/prod/collateral/switches/ps9441/ps9670/white_paper_c11-465436.html`.

[2] Data Center Fabric with Nanosecond Accuracy - Use IEEE1588 PTP on Nexus 3000 Switches. `http://www.cisco.com/en/US/prod/collateral\/switches/ps9441/ps11541/white_paper_c11-690975.html`.

[3] FocalPoint TDM Support. `http://www.fulcrummicro.com/product_library/applications/TDM_App_Note.pdf`.

[4] OpenRTB API Specification Version 2.0. `http://www.iab.net/media/file/OpenRTB_API_Specification_Version2.0_FINAL.PDF`.

[5] The C Clustering Library. `http://bonsai.hgc.jp/~mdehoon/software/cluster/software.htm`.

[6] M. Al-Fares, S. Radhakrishnan, B. Raghavan, N. Huang, and A. Vahdat. Hedera: Dynamic flow scheduling for data center networks. In *USENIX/ACM NSDI*, 2010.

[7] M. Alizadeh, A. Greenberg, D. A. Maltz, J. Padhye, P. Patel, B. Prabhakar, S. Sengupta, and M. Sridharan. Data center TCP (DCTCP). In *ACM SIGCOMM*, 2010.

[8] A. Anand and A. Akella. NetReplay: a new network primitive. *ACM SIGMETRICS Performance Evaluation Review*, 37, 2010.

[9] T. Benson, A. Akella, and D. A. Maltz. Network traffic characteristics of data centers in the wild. In *ACM/USENIX IMC*, 2010.

[10] B. H. Bloom. Space/time trade-offs in hash coding with allowable errors. *Communications of the ACM*, 1970.

[11] F. Chang, F. Chang, and W. chang Feng. Approximate Caches for Packet Classification. In *IEEE INFOCOM*, 2004.

[12] M. Charikar, L. O'Callaghan, and R. Panigrahy. Better Streaming Algorithms for Clustering Problems. In *ACM STOC*, 2003.

[13] B. Chazelle, J. Kilian, R. Rubinfeld, and A. Tal. The bloomier filter: an efficient data structure for static support lookup tables. In *ACM SODA*, 2004.

[14] Y. Chen, D. Bindel, H. Song, and R. H. Katz. An Algebraic Approach to Practical and Scalable Overlay Network Monitoring. In *ACM SIGCOMM*, 2004.

[15] T. H. Cormen, C. E. Leiserson, R. L. Rivest, and C. Stein. *Introduction to Algorithms*. The MIT Press, 2nd edition, 2001.

[16] N. Duffield. Simple network performance tomography. In *ACM/USENIX IMC*, 2003.

[17] N. G. Duffield and M. Grossglauser. Trajectory sampling for direct traffic observation. In *IEEE/ACM Transactions on Networking*, 2000.

[18] C. Faloutsos and S. Christodoulakis. Signature Files: an Access Method for Documents and Its Analytical Performance Evaluation. *ACM Transactions on Information Systems*, 2(4):267–288, Oct. 1984.

[19] A. Greenberg, J. R. Hamilton, N. Jain, S. Kandula, C. Kim, P. Lahiri, D. A. Maltz, P. Patel, and S. Sengupta. VL2: a scalable and flexible data center network. In *ACM SIGCOMM*, 2009.

[20] F. Hao, M. Kodialam, T. Lakshman, and H. Song. Fast multiset membership testing using combinatorial bloom filters. In *IEEE Infocom*, 2009.

[21] P. Indyk. A Sublinear Time Approximation Scheme for Clustering in Metric Spaces. In *IEEE FOCS*, 1999.

[22] P. Indyk. Sublinear Time Algorithms for Metric Space Problems. In *ACM STOC*, 1999.

[23] A. K. Jain and R. C. Dubes. Algorithms for clustering data: Prentice-Hall, 1981.

[24] B. Jenkins. Algorithm alley. Dr. Dobb's Journal, September 1997.

[25] D. E. Knuth. *The Art of Computer Programming, Volume II: Seminumerical Algorithms, 2nd Edition.* Addison-Wesley, 1981.

[26] R. R. Kompella, K. Levchenko, A. C. Snoeren, and G. Varghese. Every MicroSecond Counts: Tracking Fine-grain Latencies Using Lossy Difference Aggregator. In *ACM SIGCOMM*, 2009.

[27] M. Lee, N. Duffield, and R. R. Kompella. Not All Microseconds are Equal: Fine-Grained Per-Flow Measurements with Reference Latency Interpolation. In *ACM SIGCOMM*, 2010.

[28] M. Lee, N. Duffield, and R. R. Kompella. Two Samples are Enough: Opportunistic Flow-level latency estimation using Netflow. In *IEEE Infocom*, 2010.

[29] M. Leeser, J. Theiler, M. Estlick, and J. Szymanski. Design tradeoffs in a hardware implementation of the k-means clustering algorithm. In *Sensor Array and Multichannel Signal Processing Workshop*, 2000.

[30] S. Lloyd. Least squares quantization in PCM. *Information Theory, IEEE Transactions on*, 28(2):129–137, Mar. 1982.

[31] R. Martin. Wall street's quest to process data at the speed of light. `http://www.informationweek.com/news/infrastructure/showArticle.jhtml?articleID=199200297`.

[32] A. Meyerson. Online Facility Location. In *IEEE FOCS*, 2001.

[33] M. Motiwala, A. Bavier, and N. Feamster. Network troubleshooting: An in-band approach. In *USENIX NSDI*, 2007.

[34] M. Ramakrishna, E. Fu, and E. Bahcekapili. Efficient hardware hashing functions for high performance computers. *IEEE Transactions on Computers*, 46(12), Dec. 1997.

[35] C. S. Roberts. Partial-Match Retrieval via the Method of Superimposed Codes. *Proceedings of the IEEE*, 67(12):1624–1642, Dec. 1979.

[36] A. Shieh, S. Kandula, A. Greenberg, and C. Kim. Seawall: performance isolation for cloud datacenter networks. In *USENIX HotCloud*, 2010.

[37] A. C. Snoeren, C. Partridge, L. A. Sanchez, C. E. Jones, F. Tchakountio, B. Schwartz, S. T. Kent, and W. T. Strayer. Single-packet IP traceback. *IEEE/ACM Transactions on Networking (ToN)*, 10, 2002.

[38] H. Song, S. Dharmapurikar, J. Turner, and J. Lockwood. Fast Hash Table Lookup Using Extended Bloom Filter: An Aid to Network Processing. In *ACM SIGCOMM*, 2005.

[39] Y. Zhao, Y. Chen, and D. Bindel. Towards unbiased end-to-end network diagnosis. In *ACM SIGCOMM*, 2006.

Can you GET Me Now? Estimating the Time-to-First-Byte of HTTP Transactions with Passive Measurements

Emir Halepovic, Jeffrey Pang, Oliver Spatscheck
AT&T Labs - Research
180 Park Avenue
Florham Park, NJ, United States
{emir,jeffpang,spatsch}@research.att.com

ABSTRACT

Cellular network operators have a compelling interest to monitor HTTP transaction latency because it is an important component of the user experience. Existing techniques to monitor latency require active probing or use passive analysis to estimate round-trip time (RTT). Unfortunately, it is impractical to use active probing to monitor entire cellular networks, and RTT is only one component of HTTP latency in cellular networks. This paper presents a new passive technique to estimate HTTP transaction latency that overcomes the scaling and completeness limitations of prior approaches. We validate our technique in an operational cellular network and present results for traffic in the wild.

Categories and Subject Descriptors

C.2.3 [**Computer-Communication Networks**]: Network Operations

Keywords

Time To First Byte, Round-Trip Time, Network measurement, Cellular, Wireless, Mobile

1. INTRODUCTION

Quick application response time has always been a crucial component of a satisfactory user experience [10], and recent studies suggest that differences of only 250 milliseconds will cause a user to visit a Web site less often [2]. As more and more applications migrate to the Web and interact with the cloud, the latency of network protocol transactions is an increasingly important component of overall user response time. In particular, this trend implies a growing importance of HTTP transaction latency, as HTTP is the dominant protocol for the mobile Web, RESTful APIs, and video streaming [3].

Cellular network operators have a compelling interest to monitor the latency of HTTP transactions because changes in their networks can directly influence these latencies. A standard measure of HTTP transaction latency is the total time-to-first-byte (TTFB). The total TTFB is informally defined as the time elapsed from a user's request for an object to the reception of the first byte of that object. This time represents the lower bound on the delay the user will experience before an application can start rendering the requested content. Of particular interest to network operators is the TTFB of a single HTTP transaction, i.e., time between the start of the TCP handshake and the arrival of the HTTP response at the user device. This elapsed time, which we refer to as TTFB hereafter for brevity, captures all the latency components that a cellular network can directly influence.[1] Unfortunately, conventional methods to measure TTFB rely on using active probing tools,[2] which in practice limits the scale and representativeness of measurements to a small number of vantage points. This limitation is particularly problematic for wireless network operators because it is impractical to run probes at all physical locations that their users will visit and physical context plays a large role in the wireless network latency users experience.

As a consequence, passive estimation techniques are generally preferred to measure latency at scale. For example, well-known passive techniques estimate round-trip time (RTT) by measuring the arrival times of packets at the probe location [7, 8, 9, 16]. However, these prior approaches have drawbacks that limit their usefulness as a proxy for TTFB. First, prior approaches do not capture additional delays that may occur prior to the first packet being sent over the network. These delays are common and significant in cellular networks due to layer 2 connection setup signaling [13]. Second, approaches that only measure TCP handshake time don't account for the transmission delay of the HTTP request and response, which can be significantly larger than TCP handshake packets. Finally, the same approaches don't account for server delay in processing the HTTP request. As a result, prior passive latency estimation techniques provide only limited visibility into changes that can impact HTTP response time in cellular networks.

In this paper, we design and evaluate a new passive measurement technique to estimate TTFB, taking into account the signaling and large packet transmission delays specific to cellular networks. Our approach works at a large scale and only requires information available within the network

[1]The TTFB of a single HTTP transaction excludes potential delays due to DNS and HTTP redirects included in the total TTFB, but we find that a large fraction of HTTP transactions are not preceded by these delays (Section 3.3).

[2]E.g.: *keynote.com, webpagetest.org, loadimpact.com*

IMC'12, November 14–16, 2012, Boston, Massachusetts, USA.

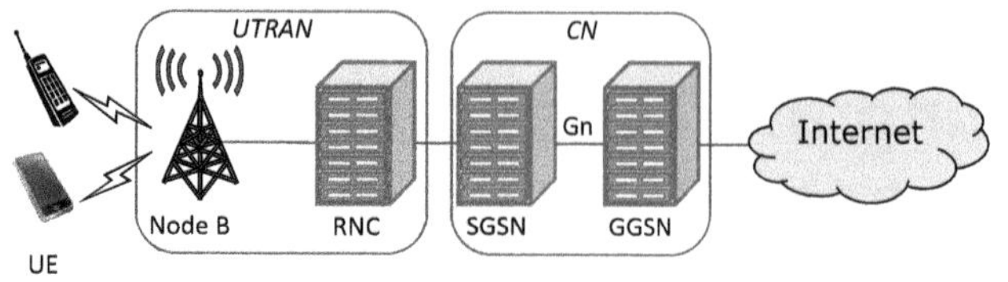

Figure 1: UMTS network architecture.

core, which meets two key challenges faced by a network operator. The main insight in our TTFB estimation approach is to utilize TCP timestamps (user domain) as well as the arrival times of packets at the probe location (network domain). Our approach addresses the limitations of previous techniques and challenges caused by peculiarities of traffic in the wild. This allows the operator to fully quantify the influence on TTFB of RTT, cellular network latency, connection setup delay, transmission time of HTTP messages, and server processing delay.

Finally, we present measurement results of TTFB in a deployment on a large U.S. cellular network. We find that TTFB can better reflect user response time than RTT, as connection setup signaling, which RTT ignores, comprises up to 68% of total TTFB. Comparison of TTFB values reveals up to 72.5% difference across domains, and up to 36% across applications, whereas RTT shows no appreciable difference. We believe our work demonstrates a practical method for operators to monitor a critical component of the mobile user experience.

2. BACKGROUND AND RELATED WORK

The most significant component of TTFB is the network latency. In cellular data networks, the network latency of delivering a packet comprises of three components: radio connection setup time, radio access network (RAN) scheduling and transmission, and core network transmission. To illustrate, consider a UMTS network (Figure 1). When a User Equipment (UE) such as a smartphone wants to send a packet, the UMTS Terrestrial Radio Access Network (UTRAN) must first allocate a radio resource control (RRC) connection for the UE if it has not already done so. Second, the UTRAN must schedule and then deliver the packet from the UE to the Core Network (CN). Finally, the packet is sent through the core network and the Internet to the destination. RAN scheduling and core network transmission typically incur RTTs of 100s of milliseconds on 3G networks [15] and 50-60 milliseconds in 4G Long Term Evolution (LTE) networks [5]. A new HTTP connection will typically incur two RTTs in a TTFB, one for the TCP 3-Way Hand Shake (3WHS) and one for the HTTP request and response. While these latencies are significant, radio connection setup time often adds an order of magnitude higher delay.

Radio connection setup delay is the time it takes for the UTRAN to allocate a radio connection to the UE. To understand why the connection setup delay is significant, we must understand the RRC state machine [11]. To efficiently utilize the radio resources, both UTRAN and UE maintain the state machine, which is synchronized via signaling on the control channel. There are typically three RRC states in a UMTS network: IDLE, CELL-FACH, CELL-DCH.[3] The state machine transitions to a higher resource state (state promotion), i.e., IDLE to CELL-DCH, when the UE has more data to send/receive and to a lower resource state (state demotion), i.e., CELL-DCH to CELL-FACH, when the UE has less data to send/receive. The reason for a significant connection setup delay is a state promotion, which involves signaling latency between the UE and the UTRAN. This latency is variable because signaling messages can be lost due to contention. Since RRC state is demoted after only a few seconds [12], a connection setup delay will typically occur for each user-initiated request.

The state promotion time is 1.5 to 2 seconds in UMTS [12], 260 milliseconds in LTE [5], and 80 ms in Wi-Fi [5]. These delays are an order of magnitude larger than the corresponding RAN scheduling and core network transmission delays, and they grow even larger when there is contention for radio resources. In addition, operators will evolve existing cellular networks by introducing new RRC states and by tuning RRC timers, which will change the magnitude and frequency of the connection setup delay [11]. Hence, to effectively monitor TTFB in cellular data networks, it is imperative that any estimation technique has the capability to measure all three components of network latency.

2.1 Limitations of Existing Techniques

Previous passive techniques attempt to estimate the RTT of TCP connections that pass through a passive packet monitor along the connections' end-to-end path. In a UMTS cellular data network, the monitor is typically located on the Gn link (Figure 1), where all cellular data traffic passes, because they are usually located in a small number of physical locations [4, 14].[4]

There are several approaches to estimate RTT. SYN-ACK estimation uses the interval between the SYN and acknowledgment (ACK) packets of the TCP 3WHS, and Slow-Start estimation measures intervals between bursts of data packets within a minimum of 5 consecutive data packets [8]. Jaiswal, et al. [7] estimate RTT by replicating the sender's state machine to infer congestion window size. Veal, et al. [16] estimate RTT as inter-arrival time between data and ACK packets matched by TCP timestamps.

All these techniques estimate network latency by recording the arrival time of IP packets at the monitor. Thus, a crucial limitation of these approaches is that they can not capture the connection setup delay that occurs before the first IP packet of a transaction leaves the UE for the UTRAN. Moreover, they don't measure the transmission time incurred for the HTTP request and response. In this paper, we design a new approach that overcomes this limitation by passively inferring the timing of packets at the UE.

3. DESIGN

In order to capture all potential components of cellular network latency, we focus on measuring the TTFB of HTTP transactions that begin with new TCP connections.[5] Figure 2 depicts the typical packet exchange at the beginning

[3]The same state machine mechanism applies when additional states are used, such as URA-PCH, and in LTE and Wi-Fi with PSM [5].

[4]In LTE, the equivalents to the Gn link are the S1u and S11 links.

[5]These transactions are most likely to be user initiated because typical web servers tear down persistent HTTP connections after only a few seconds [1].

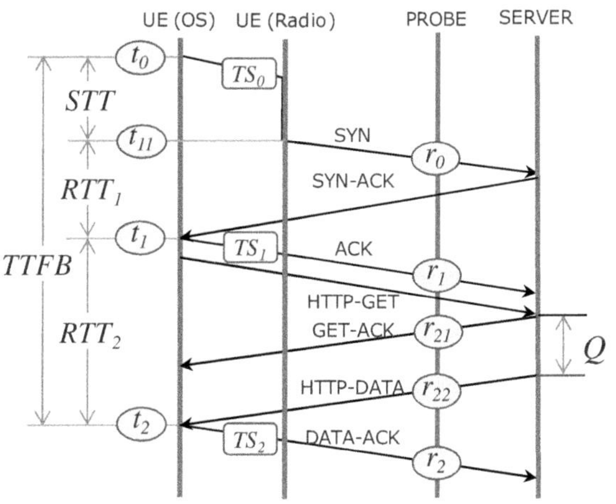

Figure 2: Typical HTTP data transfer.

Table 1: TTFB and its components.

Metric	Actual	Estimate
$TTFB$	$t_2 - t_0$	$G(TS_2 - TS_0)$
STT	$t_{11} - t_0$	$G(TS_1 - TS_0) - (r_1 - r_0)$
RTT_1	$t_1 - t_{11}$	$(r_1 - r_0)$
RTT_2	$t_2 - t_1$	$(r_2 - r_1)$
Q	unknown	$(r_{22} - r_{21})$
G	unknown	$\frac{r_2 - r_1}{TS_2 - TS_1}$

of such HTTP transaction. The vertical lines represent elapsed time at the UE operating system (OS), radio interface, probe, and server. Bubbles labeled t_i and r_i represent arrival times of packets, and TS_i are TCP timestamps in packets, which we describe in Section 3.1. The SYN, SYN-ACK, and ACK packets comprise the TCP 3WHS, while the HTTP-GET and HTTP-DATA packets correspond to the HTTP request and the first packet of the response. As RRC state transition is the largest part of the radio connection setup, we refer to this delay as State Transition Time (STT) hereafter. Q is the server processing delay.

We define the actual TTFB as the time elapsed between the SYN packet departure and the arrival of the first HTTP-DATA packet at the UE, i.e. $t_2 - t_0$. We stress that our definition of TTFB differs from the conventional one by not including DNS latency, as explained later. However, it includes the complete TCP 3WHS, STT when it occurs, as well as the HTTP request and the first packet of the response. Previous estimation techniques only used arrival times r_i to estimate latency (e.g., RTT $= r_1 - r_0$ [14, 8]), thereby missing the crucial STT that occurs between t_0 and r_0. Unfortunately, t_0 and t_2 are only directly measurable at the UE and available only for active probing techniques. In this section, we describe how we can estimate $t_2 - t_0$ and break down its constituent latency components using only information measured at the probe. Our approach is summarized in Table 1.

3.1 Challenges

The naïve approach to estimating TTFB at the probe would be as the inter-arrival time between the SYN and DATA-ACK, i.e., $r_2 - r_0$. This estimate would be correct if the latency between the UE and the probe is always the same. However, as we already explained, the delay $r_0 - t_0$ is often much larger than the delays $r_1 - t_1$ and $r_2 - t_2$ due to STT. To overcome this limitation of the naïve approach, we need to estimate t_0 and t_2 directly.

To do this estimation, we leverage the observation that many TCP connections include the TCP timestamp option (75% of the top 500 servers in previous work [16] and 85% of TCP connections in our dataset). This option adds two fields to the TCP header: Timestamp Value (TSval) and Timestamp Echo Reply (TSecr) [6]. The sender sets TSval to the time at which the segment was sent, and the receiver echoes the TSval of the most recently received segment in TSecr. Therefore, each t_i is represented by the corresponding TS_i in each TCP packet (Figure 2).

Under the assumption that the clock the sender uses to compute TS_0 and TS_2 has a known frequency $\frac{1}{G'}$ ticks/sec, we would have the simple equivalence $t_2 - t_0 = G'(TS_2 - TS_0)$. Unfortunately, $\frac{1}{G'}$ is not known and it depends on the device generating the timestamp. Moreover, we will not be able to measure TTFBs with any finer time resolution than G' because the timestamps are quantized to integral values. Thus, two challenges are to reliably estimate G' using only information at the probe and to evaluate whether G' is sufficiently granular in real traffic to effectively measure TTFB. We also want to ensure that TTFB estimation is robust against changes in the rapidly evolving mobile technology.

Finally, typical probes at the Gn interface will encounter traffic rates of tens of Gbps, if not larger. Thus, in order to capture as many real-time samples as possible, the TTFB estimation approach should be light-weight in terms of processing cost and memory footprint. While sampling can be employed, a large number of samples is required to monitor the real-time health of the individual elements in the entire spatial extent of a cellular network, e.g., NodeBs (Figure 1) can number in the hundreds of thousands.

3.2 TTFB Estimation

Recall that the actual TTFB $= t_2 - t_0$. We would like to estimate TTFB directly as $TS_2 - TS_0$. However, as we explained in the previous section, the units of TS_i, i.e., the *timestamp granularity*, are unknown and UE-specific, so we have to convert them into comparable time units. For this purpose, we define the granularity factor, G, as an estimate of timestamp granularity:

$$G = \frac{r_2 - r_1}{TS_2 - TS_1} \,. \tag{1}$$

The granularity factor G is effective in estimating the timestamp granularity because we expect that the time elapsed between the HTTP-GET and DATA-ACK at the UE ($t_2 - t_1$) is the same as at the probe ($r_2 - r_1$), and we record r_2 and r_1 in known time units. Since we use sender's TCP timestamps only, there is no need for any kind of clock synchronization between the sender and receiver.

Our TTFB estimate, thus, is defined as follows:

$$TTFB \;=\; G(TS_2 - TS_0) \,. \tag{2}$$

We can also estimate the TTFB's constituent components using the formulas in Table 1.

With the above formulation, we need only collect the following values for each TCP connection: r_0, r_1, r_2, TS_0, TS_1, and TS_2. Since r_i times will almost never differ by more than several seconds, we can use a 16 bit clock to generate the r_i timestamps with millisecond granularity and compute the differences modulo 2^{16}. The TCP timestamps themselves are 4 bytes each, so the total state tracked per TCP connection can be only 18 bytes. We identify packets belonging to distinct TCP connections using the standard IP 4-tuple (12 bytes for IPv4). The tuple can be hashed to 8 bytes if memory is more constrained than processing resources.

Alternative Formulation. We also consider an alternative formulation which requires tracking less state. This formulation uses twice the conventional estimate of RTT and the state transition delay STT in connection setup, i.e.

$$TTFB' = 2(r_1 - r_0) + STT \; . \qquad (3)$$

STT is the difference between $G(TS_1 - TS_0)$, which includes STT, and $(r_1 - r_0)$, the conventional RTT estimate without STT. This option assumes that $RTT_1 \approx RTT_2$. This option does not need to track the HTTP request/response packets if we can obtain the timestamp granularity G without the HTTP request/response.

One way to obtain G without looking at the HTTP request/response is to maintain a database of timestamp granularities for each model of UE, since G is typically determined by the operating system and the device. We can then map each flow to the device model that generated it to obtain the correct G.[6] This requires a post-processing step after the measurement, but enables us to avoid tracking HTTP-GET and DATA-ACK packets.

The state required for the alternative option is only: r_0, r_1, TS_0, TS_1 (12 bytes), and there would be no need to track the HTTP-GET and DATA-ACK, allowing the probe to release memory resources sooner for each connection. Unfortunately, we found that $RTT_2 = 2.2RTT_1$ on average, which violates the underlying assumption of this approach and significantly alters the TTFB estimate (by up to 60% without STT).

Distinguishing State Transitions. Not all TTFB measurements will include STT, but we need to know which ones do to effectively understand if the change in STT impacted the observed TTFB. To estimate if a packet incurred a state transition, we use a Finite State Machine (FSM) to emulate a simplified RRC state machine for each UE IP address. We use the FSM model from [13], but only estimate transitions from IDLE to CELL-DCH, the most common transition for new user-initiated transactions. We validate the accuracy of this approach in the next section.

3.3 Limitations

Our approach assumes that TTFB transactions will look like Figure 2. While there are exceptions, which we describe here, the next section shows that enough follow this pattern to accurately estimate TTFB. First, our estimate assumes that the DATA-ACK immediately follows HTTP-DATA packet. The UE could use a delayed ACK after the first HTTP-DATA packet, but the error introduced would likely be small (e.g., 3.7% for a 40 ms delayed-ACK timer, in our data described in the next section). Second, we assume that the SYN packet is not lost before reaching the probe, so that the timestamp will represent initial user activity. Loss rather than delay of the SYN at the IP layer is unlikely, as the cellular link layer employs hybrid ARQ to retransmit lost packets. The delay of the uplink ACK that completes the 3WHS on the radio link may reduce the observed interval $r_2 - r_1$ and, in turn, introduce error into G, because G assumes this interval is proportional to $TS_2 - TS_1$. In the next section, we show error in G introduced by typical delay variance does not result in appreciable error in TTFB estimates.

Since TTFB estimation is performed per TCP connection, distinguishing between HTTP responses that carry content vs. redirect instructions is not a part of the estimation technique. This does not diminish the value of the estimates, which may be filtered or aggregated in the post-processing stage to produce the estimates for different case studies, such as video stream start-ups, aggregated redirects and initial content, discarding advertising and analytics, etc. (e.g., see Section 5).

Finally, our TTFB definition does not include the DNS request and response latency that precede many HTTP transactions (30-39% in our data). While our estimate will be affected by all network latency components that can also affect the DNS exchange, it may miss state transitions that are initiated by the DNS request. We note that our definition already captures state transitions for 7-14% of HTTP transactions in our data. We are currently exploring ways to estimate state transition delays caused by the DNS exchange, e.g., by leveraging the fact that DNS clients retry requests after just 1 second, which is shorter than STT in today's UMTS networks. DNS packets do not include any data comparable to TCP timestamps, hence the technique to estimate TTFB is not applicable to DNS delay.

4. VALIDATION

To validate the estimation of TTFB on real traffic, we collect two packet traces at Gn links of a major U.S. cellular carrier (Figure 1), which we refer to as "network traces" hereafter. The traces include the first 128 bytes of each data packet, capturing extended TCP/IP headers. The traces do not include any personally identifiable information. Each TCP connection is identified by the standard IP 4-tuple. The arrival timestamp, TCP flags and timestamps are extracted from packet headers for TTFB estimation. All other data is discarded. The first trace captures 2 minutes of traffic on September 2, 2011 (754,082 TCP connections and 61,362 unique UE IPs), while the second captures 9 hours and 5 minutes of traffic March 2, 2012 (5,626,320 TCP connections and 73,058 unique UE IPs). The two Gn links where traces were obtained serve large regions of the western U.S. with significantly different traffic load.

During the capture of network traces, we also capture `tcpdump` traces from active experiments on four popular UE devices. These traces, referred to as "UE traces" hereafter, record packets as they enter the UE's operating system. During the time of the second network trace, we simultaneously capture radio event logs from the RNC that our UE was connected to, which will be used to validate state transitions.

4.1 Validation of TTFB estimates

Timestamp Granularity Validation. The key ingredient of our estimation technique is the TCP timestamp granularity, estimated according to Equation 1. Since the timestamp granularity determines the time resolution at which we

[6]In a UMTS or LTE network, the device type can be obtained from GTP-C messages [4].

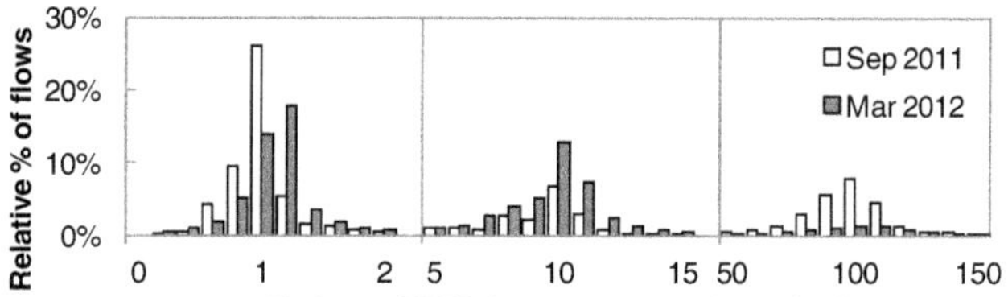

Figure 3: Distribution of G estimates.

can resolve TTFB estimates, we want to determine whether most TCP connections have a fine enough granularity. Resolutions from 1 to 10 ms are sufficient to differentiate changes in TTFB latencies since they are several multiples of this resolution. By examining packet traces of several popular UE devices, we find that common timestamp granularities are 1, 5, 10, and 100 ms. Next, we estimate G for TCP connections from the network traces and plot the distribution in Figure 3. Our estimates of G using Equation 1 correspond to the expected granularities, though the 5 ms granularity does not appear in a significant number of connections. For both network traces, we are able to see clusters around expected values of G from 96% of connections. In our validation below, we evaluate whether quantizing these estimated G values to 1, 5, 10, and 100 ms would result in higher accuracy, since other values are most likely due to estimation errors. Threfore, G is indeed accurate in the face of actual variance in scheduling and transmission delays.

We see a shift toward finer timestamp granularity over 6 months between trace collections, which corresponds to newer devices. If this trend continues, estimation accuracy will improve.

TTFB Validation. In order to determine the accuracy of our approach, we compare the TTFB estimates derived from the network traces against the actual TTFB as seen in the UE traces. Latencies from UE traces closely reflect the approach used in most popular active probing tools that execute within the Web browser or a standalone application, with the exception of the DNS exchange that we exclude. We use a UE with a 1 ms timestamp granularity in three scenarios: a) manual browsing, b) scripted browsing (without state transitions), and c) scripted browsing with state transitions. We find similar scripted browsing results for a UE with a 100 ms granularity (omitted for brevity). Scenario (a) consists of 731 connections to arbitrary Web sites, and (b) and (c) have 5,149 and 278 connections (respectively) to 26 popular Web sites (20% are mobile versions). Manual browsing connections may or may not include STT as the delay between page loads is arbitrary. Scripted browsing does not include STT as the delay is 1 second between loads. Scripted browsing with state transitions does include STT induced by a 20-second delay between loads.

The CDFs of the actual and estimated TTFB are shown in Figure 4 for all three scenarios. For competitive reasons, latency values in all plots are consistently normalized by the same constant. All scenarios show that our estimate (Equation 2) produces a distribution of estimates fairly close to the actual TTFB. A question posed earlier is how much the estimates would improve if we quantized estimated G values, since we know the actual timestamp granularity is usually 1 or 10 ms. To answer this question, we apply the following heuristic: when the G estimate falls in the range

Table 2: MSE for TTFB estimations.

Estimate	Quantized	Proposed	Alternative
Manual	3.95	4.86	7.05
Scripted	0.03	0.03	0.17
Scripted with STT	1.65	2.09	2.26

Table 3: Composition of TTFB (normalized).

State	STT	RTT_1	$RTT_2 - Q$	Q
No ST	0 (0%)	0.15 (32%)	0.31 (50%)	0.08 (18%)
With ST	0.79 (68%)	0.08 (7%)	0.29 (12%)	0.15 (13%)

(0.5, 1.5) ms, quantize G to 1 ms. This range is determined empirically from Figure 3. Figure 4 shows that using this approach (labeled Quantized) provides a slightly better estimate of TTFB. However, since the improvement is small and quantizing would result in incorrect results for fractional timestamp granularities, which are allowed, we do not use quantizing in our implementation.

The mean-squared-error (MSE) of estimates is shown in Table 2. The quantized estimate has the same error as the proposed one (Equation 2) in the scripted scenario, and a moderate advantage for other scenarios is indicated by lower MSE, as expected. For completeness, we also evaluate the alternative formulation (Equation 3) and it has higher error, especially for the scripted scenario. The error in scenarios that include STT is moderated by the relative magnitude of STT that dominates total TTFB. Due to its high error, we did not implement the alternative formulation.

State Transition Validation. Finally, to validate that our FSM can approximately distinguish TTFBs with and without state transitions, we compare our FSM's estimated transitions, which are based on the network trace, to the RNC radio event logs, which record when the UE really has a state transition.[7] We find that over 76% of our estimated transitions are correct. 10% of incorrect estimates are edge cases, such as starting and ending a measurement session, while the remaining 14% are cases when signaling traffic that is not observable at the Gn keeps the UE in active state. Since the FSM classifies a large majority correctly, it is sufficient to determine whether changes in TTFB values are due to changes in the STT.

5. DEPLOYMENT AND RESULTS

We have implemented our TTFB estimation technique in a probe platform on the production network of a major U.S. cellular carrier. In addition to performance estimation, the platform categorizes TCP flows by application, domain, and device type using HTTP signatures and GTP-C information [18]. In this section, we describe some early results from this deployment.

TTFB Latency Breakdown. The difference in TTFB for connections with and without a state transition is shown using CDFs in Figure 5. The averages of key constituent latencies in the TTFB, estimated using formulae in Table 1, are listed in Table 3. Both results demonstrate the large contribution of STT to total response time. STT comprises 68% of TTFB, on average, when a state transition occurs

[7]Due to load, resource, and vendor limitations, it is not practical to collect and process RNC logs continuously [17], which is why an estimation approach is needed.

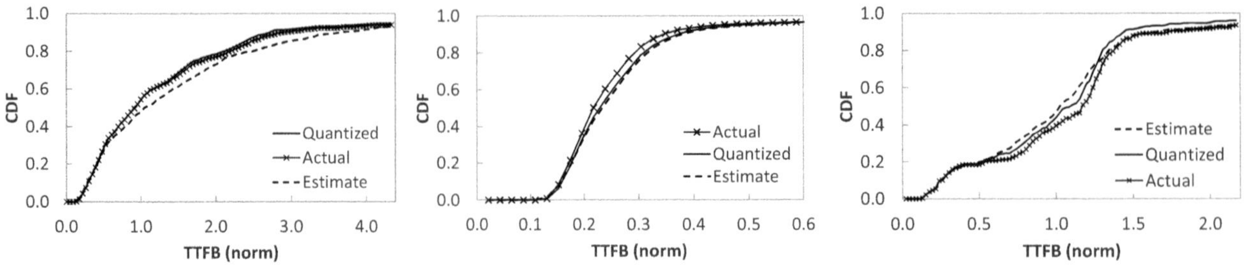

(a) Manual browsing (b) Scripted browsing (c) Scripted browsing with STT

Figure 4: Validation of TTFB estimates.

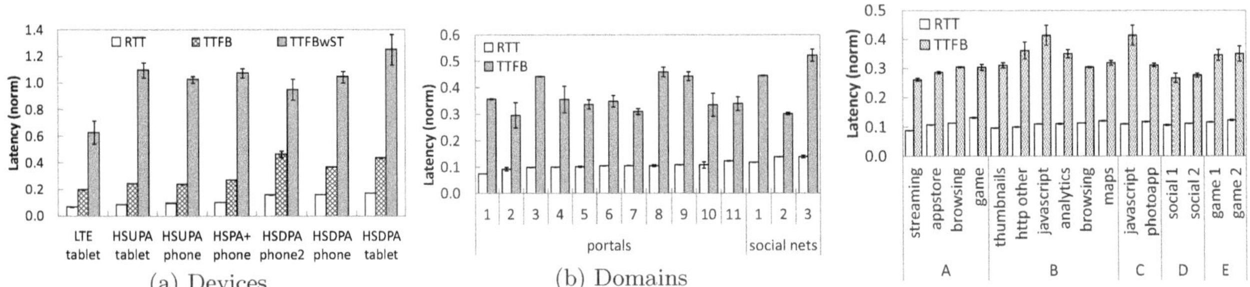

(a) Devices (b) Domains (c) Applications

Figure 6: Comparison of mean RTT vs. mean TTFB. Error bars indicate 95% confidence intervals.

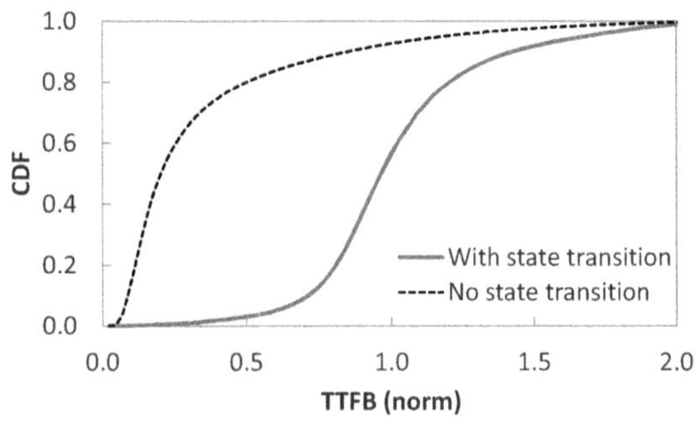

Figure 5: TTFB with and without STT.

(Table 3). In addition, we observe that the average server delay Q is non-negligible.

TTFB by Device, Domain, and Application. Next, we present three examples where TTFB offers a more complete picture of user experienced delay than RTT, using $5\frac{1}{2}$ hours of network data collected from 4:50PM ET on May 2, 2011. Figure 6 shows estimated RTT (as per [8]) and TTFB by device, domain, and application. Mobile devices with newer radio technology are expected to offer a better user experience, but we observe that the improvements can be subtle. Figure 6a shows that devices with HSUPA/HSPA+ have lower RTT and TTFB over those without (HSDPA), while there is no significant difference for TTFB with state transitions. However, the LTE device shows better performance across all metrics. This is due to the fact that LTE technology has both higher data rates and shorter state transition delays, while both HSDPA and HSUPA/HSPA+ devices have the same state transition delay.

Figure 6b compares the RTT and TTFB for different Web portals and social network domains. We observe up to 72.5% difference in TTFB between domains that have nearly identical measured RTT (social networks 2 and 3). This can be mostly attributed to varying processing delays and HTTP packet transmission delays, which RTT estimates do not capture. As cellular technologies with lower transmission delay are deployed, such as LTE, server processing delay will make up a larger faction of the TTFB (Table 3).

Figure 6c shows the RTT and TTFB of different applications, grouped by domain (all apps under the same letter are transactions to the same domain). We again see examples where TTFB differentiates user-perceived performance but RTT does not. For example, we have cases where there is no correlation between RTT and TTFB (domains B and C). The three application classes that stand out are analytics, http-other and javascript, which are served up to 36% slower than browsing and photoapp in domains B and C, respectively. The higher TTFB is likely the consequence of such transactions occurring in parallel with others.

6. CONCLUSION AND FUTURE WORK

This paper presented an accurate and light-weight technique to estimate TTFB of HTTP connections. Our early results from a deployment in a large cellular carrier demonstrate that TTFB, a large component of user response time, can vary substantially along many dimensions, even when measured RTT does not. Hence, measuring TTFB provides a more complete picture of the user experienced delay. In addition, our technique allows each component of TTFB to be studied separately, such as state transitions and server delay. While presented technique is applicable not only to cellular networks, there may be simpler methods available, depending on the transmission technologies in each particular case. In the future, we plan to improve the accuracy of our state estimation FSM by including more states. We are also evaluating ways to include the DNS exchange into our definition of TTFB.

7. REFERENCES

[1] Apache 2.2 keepalivetimeout directive. http://httpd.apache.org/docs/2.2/mod/core.html#keepalivetimeout.

[2] For impatient web users, an eye blink is just too long to wait. http://www.nytimes.com/2012/03/01/technology/impatient-web-users-flee-slow-loading-sites.html, 2012.

[3] J. Erman, A. Gerber, K. K. Ramadrishnan, S. Sen, and O. Spatscheck. Over the top video: The gorilla in cellular networks. In *ACM Internet Measurement Conference*, pages 127–136. ACM, 2011.

[4] A. Gerber, J. Pang, O. Spatscheck, and S. Venkataraman. Speed testing without speed tests: Estimating achievable download speed from passive measurements. In *ACM Internet Measurement Conference*, pages 424–430. ACM, 2010.

[5] J. Huang, F. Qian, A. Gerber, Z. M. Mao, S. Sen, and O. Spatscheck. A close examination of performance and power characteristics of 4G LTE networks. In *ACM International Conference on Mobile Systems, Applications, and Services (MobiSys)*, 2012.

[6] IETF. RFC 1323: TCP extensions for high performance, supersedes RFC 1072, RFC 1185, 1992.

[7] S. Jaiswal, G. Iannaccone, C. Diot, J. Kurose, and D. Towsley. Inferring TCP connection characteristics through passive measurements. In *IEEE INFOCOM*, volume 3, pages 1582–1592 vol.3, 2004.

[8] H. Jiang and C. Dovrolis. Passive estimation of TCP round-trip times. *SIGCOMM Comput. Commun. Rev.*, 32(3):75–88, 2002.

[9] S. Khirman and P. Henriksen. Relationship between quality-of-service and quality-of-experience for public Internet service. In *Passive and Active Measurement Workshop*, 2002.

[10] R. B. Miller. Response time in man-computer conversational transactions. In *Proceedings of the December 9-11, 1968, fall joint computer conference, part I*, AFIPS '68 (Fall, part I), pages 267–277, 1968.

[11] J. Perez-Romero, O. Sallent, R. Agusti, and M. A. Diaz-Guerra. *Radio Resource Management Strategies in UMTS*. Wiley, 1 edition, 2005.

[12] F. Qian, A. Gerber, Z. M. Mao, S. Sen, O. Spatscheck, and W. Willinger. TCP revisited: A fresh look at TCP in the wild. In *ACM Internet Measurement Conference*, pages 76–89. ACM, 2009.

[13] F. Qian, Z. Wang, A. Gerber, Z. M. Mao, S. Sen, and O. Spatscheck. Characterizing radio resource allocation for 3G networks. In *ACM Internet Measurement Conference*, 2010.

[14] P. Romirer-Maierhofer, A. Coluccia, and T. Witek. On the use of TCP passive measurements for anomaly detection: A case study from an operational 3G network. In *2nd COST TMA Workshop*, Zurich, Switzerland, 2010.

[15] P. Romirer-Maierhofer, F. Ricciato, A. D'Alconzo, R. Franzan, and W. Karner. Network-wide measurements of TCP RTT in 3G. In *International Workshop on Traffic Monitoring and Analysis (TMA)*, pages 17–25, Berlin, Heidelberg, 2009. Springer-Verlag.

[16] B. Veal, K. Li, and D. Lowenthal. New methods for passive estimation of TCP round-trip times. In *Passive and Active Measurement Workshop*, 2005.

[17] Q. Xu, A. Gerber, Z. M. Mao, and J. Pang. AccuLoc: Practical localization of performance measurement in 3G networks. In *ACM MobiSys*, 2011.

[18] Q. Xu, A. Gerber, Z. M. Mao, J. Pang, and S. Venkataraman. Identifying diverse usage behaviors of smartphone apps. In *ACM IMC*, 2011.

Towards Geolocation of Millions of IP Addresses*

Zi Hu John Heidemann Yuri Pradkin
USC/Information Sciences Institute {zihu, johnh, yuri}@isi.edu

ABSTRACT

Previous measurement-based IP geolocation algorithms have focused on accuracy, studying a few targets with increasingly sophisticated algorithms taking measurements from tens of vantage points (VPs). In this paper, we study how to scale up existing measurement-based geolocation algorithms like Shortest Ping and CBG to cover the whole Internet. We show that with many vantage points, VP proximity to the target is the most important factor affecting accuracy. This observation suggests our new algorithm that selects the *best few* VPs for each target from many candidates. This approach addresses the main bottleneck to geolocation scalability: minimizing traffic into each target (and also out of each VP) while maintaining accuracy. Using this approach we have currently geolocated about 35% of the allocated, unicast, IPv4 address-space (about 85% of the addresses in the Internet that can be directly geolocated). We visualize our geolocation results on a web-based address-space browser.

Categories and Subject Descriptors

C.2.1 [**Computer-Communication Networks**]: Network Architecture and Design—*Network topology*; C.2.5 [**Computer-Communication Networks**]: Local and Wide-Area Networks—*Internet*; C.2.6 [**Computer-Communication Networks**]: Internetworking

General Terms: Experimentation, Measurement

Keywords: IP geolocation, IPv4

1. INTRODUCTION

IP geolocation is the process of finding geographic locations of Internet Protocol addresses. IP geolocation is widely used today. For example, companies use IP geolocation to limit the content to certain countries (for example, television and movies that are often licensed differently by the viewer's country) and to customize advertising based on location. Internet researchers use IP geolocation to relate network phenomena to countries, such as studying the cultural impacts on social networking, or rates of computer crime by country and policy. Moreover, IP geolocation is essential in law enforcement to identify the appropriate jurisdiction to handle enforcement of computer crime statues.

*This work partially supported by the United States Department of Homeland Security contract number D08PC75599 All conclusions of this work are those of the authors and do not necessarily reflect the views of DHS.

IMC '12, November 14–16, 2012, Boston, Massachusetts, USA.

Several research and commercial geolocation systems exist, exploring many different approaches. They form three rough categories (Section 3): systems driven by databases ([11, 15]), measurement based geolocation (such as Geoping [15], CBG [4], and others), and target-assisted geolocation (such as Skyhook [17]). We focus on measurement-based systems here, since they provide better coverage and accuracy than database approaches and are independent of the target. Measurement-based algorithms all depend on *vantage points* (VPs) to actively probe the geolocation *targets*. We study both Geoping- and CBG-like algorithms.

Our goal is not to invent a new geolocation algorithm, but to understand how existing algorithms can *scale up* to many millions of targets and the entire IPv4 address space. We encounter several problems in scaling-up existing algorithms to the whole Internet. First, all existing work uses a relatively small set of VPs, typically tens of VPs [4, 9]. Second, existing work is tested on a relatively small set of targets, typically hundreds of targets. Typical targets are selected with known ground truth to evaluate algorithm accuracy. With dozens of VPs and hundreds of targets, current algorithms each have all VPs send many probes to each target. While this product is reasonable when both are small, with hundreds of VPs and a billion targets, the product is large. The result is a huge amount of traffic out of each VP, burdensome traffic into each target, where hundreds of probes arrive to *each* IP address in a target block, and a heavy load to bring this data together.

To scale geolocation to the entire Internet, our first contribution is *to study what factors affect geolocation scalability and accuracy* for the measurement-based geolocation protocols. We show that *traffic*, both outbound from VPs and inbound to targets, is a significant limitation to full-Internet geolocation, and show that fewer VPs can make inbound traffic manageable. We then show that most VPs provide little benefit to geolocation, suggesting that one can select only a few VPs to geolocate each IP address, getting reasonable accuracy while greatly reducing traffic. We develop three conjectures on factors that affect accuracy and show that good accuracy with a few VPs is possible (Section 4.1).

Our second contribution is to define *new algorithms to choose the right few VPs* (Section 4.2). Our idea is to select the closest VPs to the target, since closer VPs provide

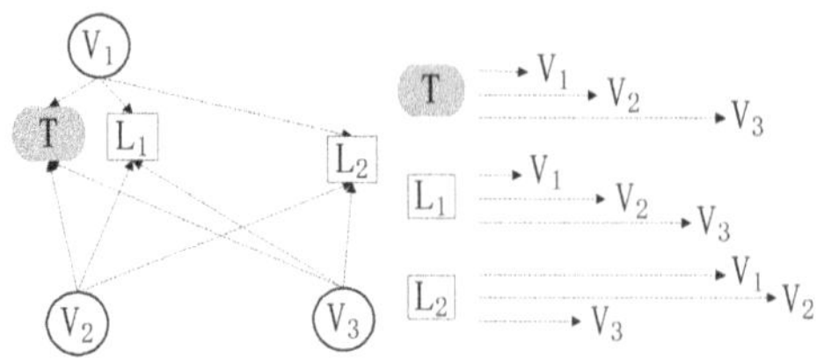

Figure 1: Vantage points (VP), targets and landmarks in Geoping (left), with RTT vectors for Geoping (right).

stronger constraints on location. We show that VP selection using trial measurements to each /24 address block works well (Section 4.2). Our experimental results show that representatives can identify close VPs and provide accuracy almost as good as many VPs. For Shortest Ping, the median error is the same with 10 close VPs compared to all 400 VPs, and for CBG median error is only 11% worse.

With the approaches outlined in this paper we are in the process of geolocating all responsive, public IPv4 addresses. This data is available at no cost to researchers [7].

2. PROBLEM STATEMENT

Our goal is to geolocate every allocated, unicast IPv4 address, with similar accuracy to basic Shortest Ping and CBG. While geolocation algorithms are well known, the main constraint in scaling them up to cover the entire Internet is probing traffic. We next review geolocation elements and these constraints.

2.1 Geolocation terminology

Measurement-based geolocation systems send probes from *vantage points* to geolocate *targets* in the Internet. Some systems also probe *landmarks* at known reference location. Figure 1 shows those entities: V_1, V_2 and V_3 are VPs, T is the target, L_1, L_2 are landmarks.

Targets are public IPv4 addresses that we wish to geolocate. In this paper we assume targets have fixed physical locations, at least over the duration of measurement. Some addresses represent objects that move, such as mobile phones or those using Mobile IP; their identification is future work.

Vantage points (VPs) are hosts in the Internet, always with known locations. They send messages (probes) to targets to determine the targets locations.

Landmarks are IP addresses with known locations used by some geolocation algorithms such as Geoping. Unlike VPs, landmarks do not actively send messages. Since VPs locations are usually known, they often also serve as landmarks.

Address blocks, (or *blocks*), are groups of consecutive addresses, with size determined by the number of leading address bits in common. IP address allocation policies result in blocks that often have common administration [1], often including physical location [15]. We exploit but do not require this assumption.

2.2 Problem Constraints

Unfortunately, it is intractable to probe billions of addresses from hundreds of VPs. Assume we have 500 VPs and each VP probes every IP address 10 times to get the minimum round-trip time (RTT). There are about 3.7 billion allocated, unicast IPv4 addresses. This simple probing from each VP would generate 1.8×10^{13} records (more than 400 TB at 24 B/record), a challenge to process centrally. Other challenges are the amount of traffic to targets and as traffic and processing at the VPs. When combined with the need to probe relatively quickly so that observations can be combined, these challenges motivate our optimizations.

The primary challenge is *incoming traffic to the targets*, both because of its volume and because it can be misinterpreted. While geolocation traffic is not huge, it can be noticed. Ten probes from 500 VPs is only 320 kB of traffic, equal to about a 10 seconds of a Skype video call (at 250 kb/s). While not a huge amount of traffic by itself, the network administrator of a /24 network (or her users) can easily be alarmed at this traffic rate as it covers all 256 addresses over much of an hour. Even a few percent of very vigilant network operators can result in abuse complaints due to concerns of denial-of-service attacks; we must minimize complaints in our use of a shared measurement infrastructure. To avoid complaints, we instead want to pace traffic; we discuss target rates in Section 4.4.

A secondary challenge is sustained, high-rate *traffic at the VPs*. Geolocation requires sustained, symmetric (inbound and out) traffic. At 1 Gb/s, one could cover the geolocatable space in 5 hours, but geolocation requires *geographically* distributed VPs. Current public measurement infrastructure, such as PlanetLab, caps sustained outgoing traffic to less than 10 Mb/s, thus pushing measurement time to more than 500 hours, and longer when the nodes are shared. A simple solution to traffic problems is to spread probes out in time.

Probe pacing must be limited so that measurements are *coherent*, consistent in the face of path or target changes, so arbitrarily slow measurements would be unusable. Probes cannot easily be combined if they cross changes in routing or target movement. According to Paxson, most paths have routes that are stable for days [16]. In our experiment, we assume that most paths are stable for more than two days, so we select a probing rate that allows measurements of each address to complete in at most that time. Detecting and adapting to changes is possible future work.

2.3 Our Approach

To make our goal tractable, we must reduce the workload by using fewer targets or fewer VPs. Prior work such as GeoCluster selects a single target to represent an entire cluster of IP addresses [15], significantly reducing the number of targets. However, our goal is to understand blocks that are geographically homogeneous, and to find blocks that are not.

We therefore instead focus on reducing the number of VPs. TBG shows that geolocation rarely works better than the distance to the nearest landmark [9]. Our approach is based on one similar observation: although one needs *many potential observation points* for accurate IP geolocation, *only a few add information*[1].

In Section 4.1 we formalize this observation as three conjectures and develop a geolocation system around it.

3. RELATED WORK

Three general approaches to geolocation have been proposed. The earliest is *database-driven*, using WHOIS [11, 14], DNS [15], or information from millions of users [10] to infer location, although with generally poor accuracy. Re-

[1] We thank Bill Woodcock of Packet Clearing House for suggesting this observation.

cent work has explored *target-assisted* geolocation, such as with GPS and WiFi-based method such as Skyhoook [17]. These approaches require geolocation code to run on the target, an approach incompatible with covering the entire Internet.

The focus of this paper is on *measurement-based* geolocation: systems that measure network delay from VPs to target to estimate location.

Geoping [15] is based on the assumption that hosts exhibiting similar network delays to other fixed hosts tend to be co-located. In Geoping, all VPs probe many landmarks at known locations, building a set of latency fingerprints (Figure 1). To geolocate an address, all VPs actively probe the target and compare the resulting fingerprint against known landmark fingerprints using Euclidean distance, placing the target at the best matching landmark. Shortest Ping is a simplification of Geoping where targets are mapped to the closest VP (effectively making VPs the only landmarks) [9]. We use Shortest Ping to approximate Geoping because of its efficiency, and its similar accuracy [9].

Constraint-based Geolocation (CBG) instead uses multilateration, where each VP draws a circle with its location as center and the distance (estimated from measured network delay by "bestline" [4]) to the target as radius. CBG locates the target in the overlap of all circles. Topology-based Geolocation (TBG) improves CBG accuracy by considering network topology and using a better latency-to-distance estimate [9]. Octant extends CBG by using both positive constraints (which the target might satisfies) and negative constraints (which the target doesn't satisfy) to reduce the estimated region for the target [18]. We explore basic CBG as representing a second class of algorithms.

Yong et al. propose a three-tiered geolocation algorithm which takes advantage of a massive landmark database and the fact that relative distances are preserved in delay measurements at small scales [20]. In the first tier, the algorithm utilizes the same idea of CBG to geolocate a target IP into a region. In the second tier, the algorithm employs the landmarks in the region of Tier 1 to narrow down the possible region, with the distance constraint-based method. Finally, the target is mapped to the closest landmark found in the region of Tier 2. We do not examine this algorithm because of the difficulty of generating a large landmark database with sufficient detail.

Although we focus on Shortest Ping and CBG as representatives of the two main classes of measurement-based geolocation, we expect that other approaches that also use VPs can also benefit from our evaluation.

4. METHODOLOGY

To address the problem of scaling current geolocation approaches (Section 2), we next describe how selecting a few, good VPs can reduce inbound traffic on each target while preserving accuracy. We first identify three conjectures that must be satisfied for our approach to work, then present specific VP selection algorithms, and finally we describe our overall system to geolocate the world.

4.1 Three Conjectures

To minimize traffic on each target, we probe each target only from a few VPs. In this section we explore three conjectures required to minimize traffic while maintaining accuracy:

1. A few VPs *can be as accurate* as many VPs
2. *Certain small subsets* have good accuracy
3. The *closest* VPs generally maximize accuracy

4.1.1 A Few VPs Can Be Accurate

We begin with our first conjecture: a few VPs *can be as accurate* as many VPs. If all VPs are important to accuracy, then there is no way to reduce traffic.

To evaluate this conjecture we begin with 400 vantage points and randomly select different subsets of 5 to 100 VPs. We do not consider more VPs, because our results are asymptotic with 100 VPs. For each trial we geolocate 25 targets with known locations, using both Shortest Ping and CBG. We repeat each trial 100 times with a different, random subsets of VPs. Our VPs are 400 PlanetLab nodes, while the targets are 25 universities around the world.

Our results depend on the numbers and locations of VPs and targets in several ways. Our premise is that global geolocation should use thousands of VPs and select the best few, so we must study VPs and targets that are both close to each other and distant. To understand the effects of a wide range of topologies, we consider random subsets of VPs (Figures 2c and 3c) and present distributions of accuracy (Figures 2b and 3b). To verify that we do not have degenerate cases (all VPs and targets co-located or distant), we verify that 12 of our 25 targets do not host PlanetLab nodes. Our results represent geolocating the current Internet to the extent that VPs and targets and their topology is representative. Although random samples of VPs present a wide range of topologies, we do not claim to fully represent all Internet topologies. With our targets and many PlanetLab-based VPs at universities, their connectivity is likely better than general Internet connectivity, so our accuracy is likely optimistic for the general Internet (today), with the prediction diverging less as Internet connectivity improves in the future. Ideally, future work would use a more diverse set of targets or VPs, but unfortunately public sources of targets with ground truth are limited today, and growing use of remote hosting makes developing new ground truth a very labor-intensive undertaking.

Figure 2a reports median and standard deviations of Shortest Ping accuracy. With more than 60 VPs, median error is small and stable. With fewer than 60 VPs, median error rises and standard deviation is high—some random subsets do well, but some do poorly. This experiment shows that many VPs add no information to geolocation, and that we can reduce the number of VPs, however which VPs are chosen affects accuracy.

Figure 3a shows this experiment repeated with CBG. These results are qualitatively similar to Shortest Ping: moderate numbers of VPs are stable, and use of only a few VPs shows very large variance in accuracy.

4.1.2 Certain Small Subsets Have Good Accuracy

We have shown that subsets can generally have good accuracy, but variance increases greatly as the number of VPs gets very small: some instances do well, but many cases result in large error. We next explore, for a given number of VPs, how different instances perform.

We use the same 400 possible VPs, 25 targets as Section 4.1.1. However, here we look at the distribution of accuracies for several specific sizes of VP subsets. Ideally, for

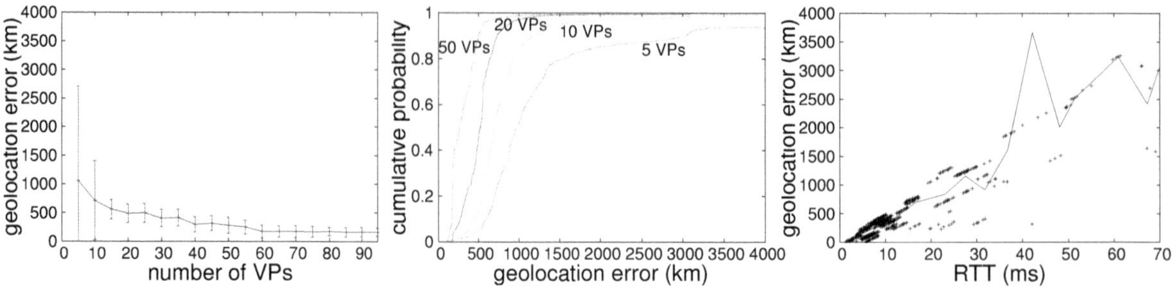

(a) Number of VPs vs. accuracy (b) Accuracy vs. subset sizes (c) VP distance vs. accuracy (to NYU)

Figure 2: Evaluation of three conjectures for Shortest Ping.

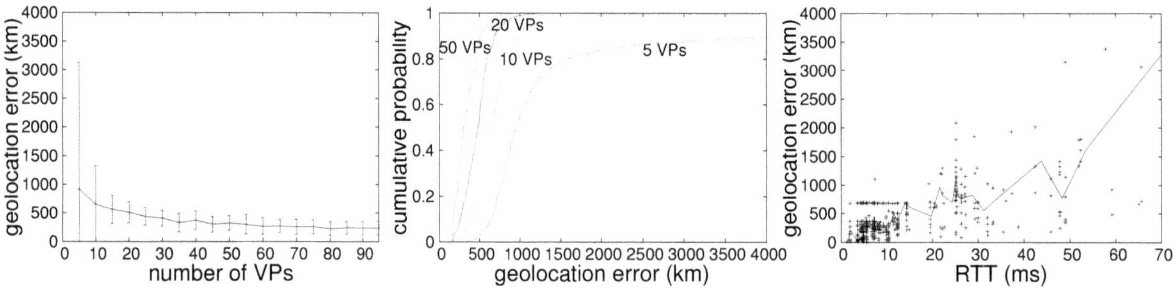

(a) Number of VPs vs. accuracy (b) Accuracy vs. subset sizes (c) VP distance vs. accuracy (to NYU)

Figure 3: Evaluation of three conjectures for CBG.

each size we would study all possible combinations, but that is computationally infeasible. (There are about 83×10^{12} possible combinations of 5 VPs selected from 400.) Instead, we evaluate Shortest Ping and CBG on each of 10,000 randomly chosen subsets.

Figures 2b (Shortest Ping) and 3b (CBG) show the cumulative distribution of median location error across all 25 targets for all 10,000 trials for the two algorithms. The result supports our second conjecture: different instances of same-size VP sets get different accuracy.

With fewer VPs, a small number of cases have very large error (about 5% of cases with 10 to 50 VPs, and 20% of cases with 5 VPs). However, many of the *best instances* have similar accuracy. For example, in Figure 2b, with 5 VPs, the worst instance has errors larger than 4000 km, while the error for the best is less than 42 km, close to the best instance with 50 VPs (error 30 km). (Error with *all* 400 VPs is smaller, at about 12 km, so 80× greater traffic does provide some improvement.) This experiment indicates that if we can select the *right* VP subset, we can achieve fairly good accuracy with just a few VPs.

4.1.3 The Closest VPs Generally Maximize Accuracy

Since we know some combinations of a few VPs provide good results, our final step is to predict which few those are. Our assumption is that *close* VPs provide stricter constraints than far away VPs. To quantify this intuition, we next explicitly compare VP distance and geolocation error. We fix the number of VPs to 10, drawn from the same 400, and geolocate our 25 targets. We carry out 800 trials, each with a different, randomly selected subset of 10 VPs. In each case, we plot the minimum RTT across all VPs with the geolocation error.

Figures 2c and 3c show our study for a single target (a computer at New York University in New York City, USA). This example is representative of all 25 targets. Each point in the figure represents one set of randomly chosen VPs. The line shows the mean geolocation error for all observations in each 5 ms bin of minimum RTTs.

This experiment shows that geolocation error for Shortest Ping has an almost linear relationship with minimum RTT (correlation coefficient 0.88). For CBG, the linear relation between geolocation and minimum RTT holds when the minimum RTT is small (less than 25ms); for larger values of minimum RTT the relationship is much noisier. CBG's correlation coefficient is 0.71 over the entire range. Both graphs show that that small geolocation errors usually have small minimum RTTs, supporting our claim that we can select a good set of VPs by estimating the closest VPs.

4.2 VP Selection and Geolocation

From these conjectures we next propose our VP selection algorithm. We work on /24 blocks, typically consider groups of 6 /8s, processing 150k–217k /24 blocks a time to spread load on the targets (Section 4.4). Although we select VPs based on a few representatives for the block, we geolocate every IP address in the block with those selected VPs to understand how often and which /24 blocks cover multiple locations.

Our algorithm has four steps:

1. Using Internet census histories, select several *representatives* for the block.
2. Probe those representatives from all VPs to *select nearby VPs* for the block.
3. Probe all addresses in the block from nearby VPs to generate *raw geolocation input*.
4. Centralize this input and process it with Shortest Ping (or CBG) to identify *IP geolocation*.

Finding Representatives: We begin by finding representatives for each block. Prior work studied IP hitlists and approaches to select representatives, IP addresses most likely to respond [3]. For geolocation, we *require* at least one representative that responds; we use three to provide some redundancy. If all three representatives do not respond, we just ignore the block. As with hitlist discovery, we use the results of prior IPv4 censuses and the hitlist prediction algorithm to select representatives. Because census histories are public, this step requires no network traffic. We distribute a list of representatives to all VPs for the next step.

Selecting Nearby VPs: To select close VPs, we probe representatives for each block from all VPs. We considered selecting VPs using information about AS paths from BGP to avoid probing from all VPs, but we found it impossible to get BGP data co-located with our 500 VPs. With only a few representatives per block, we probe fairly slowly (200 probes/s) in parallel across all VPs. We probe each representative 10 times, typically taking about 16 hours.

We use our own high-rate probing software, first developed for IPv4 census collection [6]. It probes each address on a target list in a pseudorandom order, spreading probes in time and space to minimize impact on the target networks.

After the representatives are probed, we retrieve all data in parallel to a central site. We estimate VP-representative RTT using the second-to-minimum measurement (discarding the lowest to avoid outliers). Finally, we select the closest VPs for each target block.

Given representatives for each block, we centrally compute target lists unique to each VP and distribute them.

Probing Blocks: VPs then probe targets using the same software. We use a higher probing limit of 500 probes/s, since with 85× (256/3, 3 representatives for each /24) more targets, traffic to each block is still limited. After probing, we copy the raw geolocation data to a central site.

Retrieving Data and Geolocating: Finally, with the raw data centralized, we first extract second-to-minimum RTT for each target, then run standard Shortest Ping and CBG.

4.3 VP Selection and Accuracy

We next examine how our VP selection affects geolocation accuracy. We know geolocation will have some error; our question is: does VP selection increase that error? We randomly select 18 /24 blocks from the ground truth dataset from CAIDA [13], each block with about 100 responsive IP addresses. We then compare the distribution of accuracy of 10 VPs selected by our algorithm against use of all 400 VPs, using both Shortest Ping and CBG.

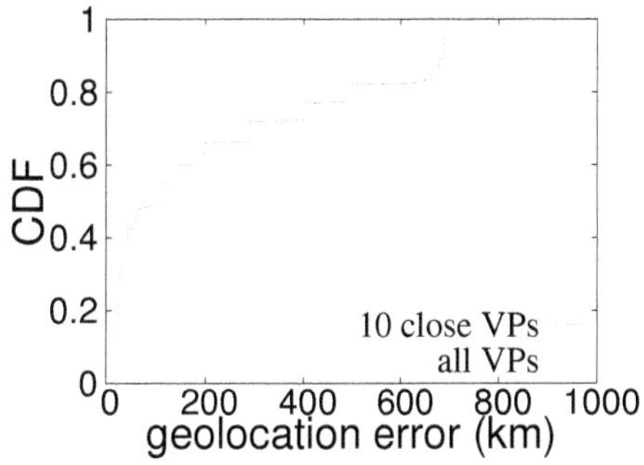

Figure 4: Geolocation error with 10 close vs. all VPs for Shortest Ping

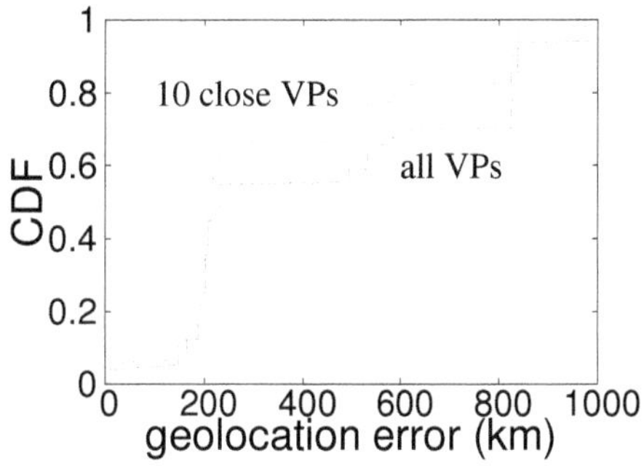

Figure 5: Geolocation error with 10 close vs. all VPs for CBG

Figures 4 and 5 shows accuracy for both Shortest Ping and CBG. For Shortest Ping, the accuracy of our 10 VPs is basically indistinguishable from use of all VPs. Median error is 105 km for both 10 close VPs and all VPs. For CBG, accuracy of using our selected 10 VPS is slightly worse than using all VPs: median error is 231 km instead of 208 km (11% worse). While one would expect this result for Shortest Ping, where accuracy only depends on the closest VP by definition, but we also get similar results for CBG and Geoping. So we conclude that our approach is successful, adding no or only slight error while using only about 2% the number of VPs.

4.4 Managing Probing Rates

Our approach must manage probing rate, going as fast as we can (to maximize coherence) but not so fast as to generate traffic that harms or worries the targets. Our main constraint is the amount of traffic arriving at each target. We evaluate incoming traffic per /24 block, with a goal of being no more than the Internet background radiation [19], that is 0.5 to 0.9 packets/s per /24 block. The traffic rate we generate is:

$$addr\_rate = \frac{probes\_per\_VP \times VPs \times tx\_rate\_per\_VP}{target\_blocks \times targets\_per\_block}$$

$$block\_rate = targets\_per\_block \times addr\_rate$$

Since probes-per-VP and number of VPs are fixed, we control our block-rate by capping the transmit rate and increasing the number of blocks. Our probing software sends probes for a given run in a pseudorandom order, so with a fixed transmit rate, adding targets spreads probes out over more time, decreasing the traffic to each target per unit time.

In our current practice we study 393k /24 blocks per run (6 /8s). For VP selection, we probe only 3 targets per block, so we cap each VPs transmit rate at 200 probes/s. With fewer VPs and more targets per block for geolocation we are able to probe at a greater rate of 500 probes/s, so we estimate that each /24 receives at most 0.64 probes/s.

Experimental verification: The above analysis assumes steady state and smooth flow; we expect traffic will be burstier in practice. To verify our analysis we recorded all incoming probes to one target over 16 hours for VP selection and about 12 hours for geolocation.

Because VPs are not synchronized and probe rates vary due to response, we see that traffic is moderately bursty. If we normalize time to one probe per interval, most periods see no traffic and a few see two or three probes. If we project to block probe rates, the mean observed probe rate is 0.13 probes/s (standard deviation: 0.20) during VP selection, and 0.48 probes/s (standard deviation: 0.79) during geolocation.

Our early use of PlanetLab generated traffic at about double our current rate and drew three complaints from targets. However, after limiting probing as described above, the complaints have stopped.

4.5 Visualization of Geolocation Data

Picturing the results of geolocating the entire IPv4 address space requires new visualization methods. We cannot simply project blocks onto the globe.

Several prior efforts have plotted the IPv4 address space on a Hilbert curve [12, 5, 1, 2]. A Hilbert curve keeps numerically close addresses physically close in two dimensions, and as a fractal it is easy to zoom in or out to control detail. We use it here to show the geographic location of IP addresses, rendering longitude and latitude as color.

As of August 2012, we have geolocated 78 /8s, about 35% of the allocated, unicast, IPv4 address-space. We can only geolocate addresses that respond to probes. From IPv4 censuses we know that those addresses are unevenly distributed; our best estimate is that our progress so far corresponds to about 85% of the addresses in the Internet that can be directly geolocated. Figure 6 shows the map of our geolocation results, and a web-based browser supports pan and zooming down to the individual IP level [8]. Each of the large squares corresponds to a /8 address block (for example, the reddish block near the top left is 2/8). The light green hatched regions are private or multicast address space, the blue hatched regions have not yet been geolocated. Areas that have been geolocated are colored by their location; colors are keyed to latitude and longitude, with hue corresponding to longitude and lightness to latitude, as shown in the country color map at the right bottom of Figure 6. While this color scheme makes some locations similar, we believe a continuous spectrum is important. Code for our color conversion function is freely available at our website.

Because of limited resolution, in this figure each pixel is colored to show the mean latitude and longitude of all addresses in a /18 block. We are evaluating different aggregation methods. While using the mean is our current method, we are considering the use of the modal location, the most common value, although that is sensitive to jitter.

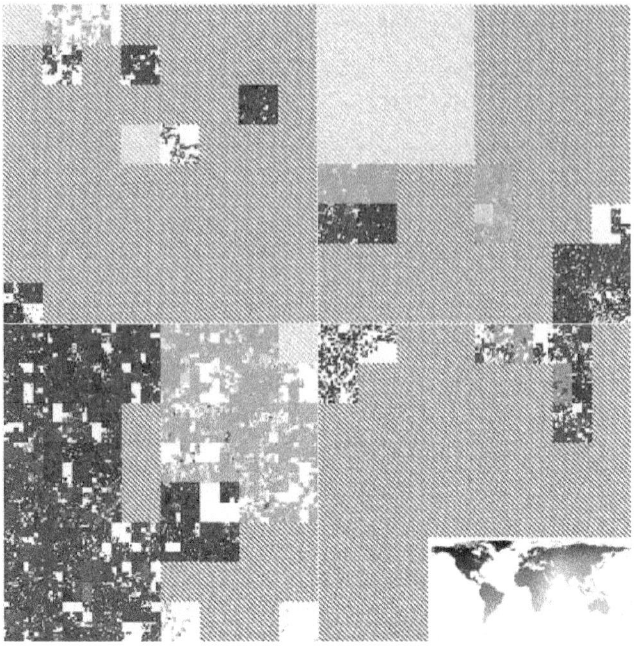

Figure 6: The IPv4 address space placed on a Hilbert curve, with colors corresponding to geolocation (hue follows longitude; lightness, latitude).

5. CONCLUSIONS

This paper studies how to adapt existing measurement-based geolocation algorithms to scale to cover each address in the entire IPv4 address space using many vantage points (VPs). We identify what factors affect geolocation scalability and accuracy, finding that the *right* subset of few VPs can preserve accuracy while greatly reducing traffic. Then we propose a VP selection algorithm to choose these right few VPs for targets, using the closest VPs since they provide the most information. Our experimental results show that the few closest VPs selected by our algorithm are almost as accurate as many VPs, within the limits of our university-centric set of VPs and targets. For Shortest Ping, median error is the same with 10 close VPs compared to all 400 VPs, and for CBG the median error is only 11% worse.

Currently we are geolocating the whole Internet with our proposed techniques. As of August 2012, we have geolocated 78 /8s, about 35% of the allocated, unicast, IPv4 address-space. Visualizations showing geolocation results on a Hilbert curve can be found at our website [8], and our data to-date is available to other researchers [7].

Acknowledgments: We thank Bill Woodcock (PCH) for discussions that prompted this work, Erik Klein (UCLA and USC/ISI) for comments about this work, Kim Claffy and Young Hyun (CAIDA) for discussion of probe rates, the anonymous referees and our shepherd, Vern Paxson, for questions that helped clarify our description. This work was determined to be non-human-subjects research by USC IRB (request IRR00001013, June 2011).

6. REFERENCES

[1] Xue Cai and John Heidemann. Understanding block-level address usage in the visible Internet. In *Proceedings of the ACM SIGCOMM Conference*, pages 99–110, New Delhi, India, August 2010. ACM.

[2] Brian Cort. IPSpace: An interactive visualization of the Internet. unpublished manuscript, October 2006.

[3] Xun Fan and John Heidemann. Selecting representative IP addresses for Internet topology studies. In *Proceedings of the ACM Internet Measurement Conference*, pages 411–423, Melbourne, Australia, November 2010. ACM.

[4] Bamba Gueye, Artur Ziviani, Mark Crovella, and Serge Fdida. Constraint-based geolocation of Internet hosts. *ACM/IEEE Transactions on Networking*, 14(6):1219–1232, December 2006.

[5] John Heidemann and Yuri Pradkin. Mapping the Internet address space. Poster, September 2007. described on the "Mapping the Internet address space" web page `http://www.isi.edu/ant/address/`.

[6] John Heidemann, Yuri Pradkin, Ramesh Govindan, Christos Papadopoulos, Genevieve Bartlett, and Joseph Bannister. Census and survey of the visible Internet. In *Proceedings of the ACM Internet Measurement Conference*, pages 169–182, Vouliagmeni, Greece, October 2008. ACM.

[7] Zi Hu, John Heidemann, and Yuri Pradkin. LANDER geolocation datasets. `http://www.isi.edu/ant/traces/geolocation`, August 2012. Also available through PREDICT (`www.predict.org`).

[8] Zi Hu, Yuri Pradkin, and John Heidemann. Ip geolocation in our browsable IPv4 map. Blog post `http://www.isi.edu/ant/blog/2012/07/02/ip-geolocation-in-our-browsable-ipv4-map/` and Web site `http://www.isi.edu/ant/address/browse/`, July 2012.

[9] Ethan Katz-Bassett, John P. John, Arvind Krishnamurthy, David Wetherall, Thomas Anderson, and Yatin Chawathe. Towards IP geolocation using delay and topology measurements. In *Proceedings of the ACM Internet Measurement Conference*, pages 71–84, Rio de Janeiro, Brazil, October 2006. ACM.

[10] Maxmind. web page `http://www.maxmind.com/app/ip-locate`.

[11] David Moore, Ram Periakaruppan, and Jim Donohoe. Where in the world is netgeo.caida.org?, July 2000.

[12] Randall Munroe. Map of the Internet. web page `http://xkcd.com/c195.html`, December 2006.

[13] Freebox ADSL networks. IP geolocation ground truth. web page `http://francois04.free.fr/liste_dslam.php`.

[14] University of Illinois. IP to latitude/longitude server. web page `http://cello.cs.uiuc.edu/cgi-bin/slamm/ip2ll`.

[15] Venkata N. Padmanabhan and Lakshminarayanan Subramanian. An investigation of geographic mapping techniques for Internet hosts. In *Proceedings of the ACM SIGCOMM Conference*, pages 173–185, San Diego, California, USA, August 2001. ACM.

[16] Vern Paxson. End-to-end routing behavior in the Internet. *ACM/IEEE Transactions on Networking*, 5(5):601–615, October 1997.

[17] Skyhook. web page `http://www.skyhookwireless.com/`.

[18] Bernard Wong, Ivan Stoyanov, and Emin Gün. Octant: A comprehensive framework for the geolocalization of Internet hosts. In *Proceedings of the 4th USENIX Symposium on Networked Systems Design and Implementation*, pages 313–326, 2007.

[19] Eric Wustrow, Manish Karir, Michael Bailey, Farnam Jahanian, and Geoff Houston. Internet background radiation revisited. In *Proceedings of the 10th ACM Internet Measurement Conference*, pages 62–73, Melbourne, Australia, November 2010. ACM.

[20] Wang Yong, Burgener Daniel, Flores Marcel, Kuzmanovic Aleksandar, and Huang Cheng. Towards street-level client-independent IP geolocation. In *Proceedings of the 8th USENIX conference on Networked systems design and implementation*, Berkeley, CA, USA, 2011. USENIX Association.

Evolution of Social-Attribute Networks: Measurements, Modeling, and Implications using Google+

Neil Zhenqiang Gong
EECS, UC Berkeley
neilz.gong@berkeley.edu

Wenchang Xu
CS, Tsinghua University
wencxu@gmail.com

Ling Huang
Intel Labs
ling.huang@intel.com

Prateek Mittal
EECS, UC Berkeley
pmittal@eecs.berkeley.edu

Emil Stefanov
EECS, UC Berkeley
emil@berkeley.edu

Vyas Sekar
CS, Stony Brook University
vyas@cs.stonybrook.edu

Dawn Song
EECS, UC Berkeley
dawnsong@cs.berkeley.edu

ABSTRACT

Understanding social network structure and evolution has important implications for many aspects of network and system design including provisioning, bootstrapping trust and reputation systems via social networks, and defenses against Sybil attacks. Several recent results suggest that augmenting the social network structure with user attributes (e.g., location, employer, communities of interest) can provide a more fine-grained understanding of social networks. However, there have been few studies to provide a systematic understanding of these effects at scale.

We bridge this gap using a unique dataset collected as the Google+ social network grew over time since its release in late June 2011. We observe novel phenomena with respect to both standard social network metrics and new attribute-related metrics (that we define). We also observe interesting evolutionary patterns as Google+ went from a bootstrap phase to a steady invitation-only stage before a public release.

Based on our empirical observations, we develop a new generative model to jointly reproduce the social structure and the node attributes. Using theoretical analysis and empirical evaluations, we show that our model can accurately reproduce the social and attribute structure of real social networks. We also demonstrate that our model provides more accurate predictions for practical application contexts.

Categories and Subject Descriptors

J.4 [**Computer Applications**]: Social and behavioral sciences

Keywords

Social network measurement, Node attributes, Social network evolution, Heterogeneous network measurement and modeling, Google+

IMC'12, November 14–16, 2012, Boston, Massachusetts, USA.

1. INTRODUCTION

Online social networks (e.g., Facebook, Google+, Twitter) have become increasingly important platforms for interacting with people, processing information and diffusing social influence. Thus understanding social-network structure and evolution has important implications for many aspects of network and system design including bootstrapping reputation via social networks (e.g., [39]), defenses against Sybil attacks (e.g., [14]), leveraging social networks for search [1], and recommender systems with social regularization [35].

Traditional social network studies have largely focused on understanding the topological structure of the social network, where each user can be viewed as a node and a specific relationship (e.g., friendship, co-authorship) is represented by a link between two nodes. More recently, there has been growing interest in augmenting this social network with *user attributes*, which we call as *Social-Attribute Network* (SAN). User attributes could be *static* (e.g., school, major, employer and city derived from user profiles), or *dynamic* (e.g., online interest and community groups). Recent studies have demonstrated the promise of social-attribute networks in applications such as link prediction [58, 17], attribute inference [17, 58], and community detection [62].

Despite the growing importance of such social-attribute networks in social network analysis applications, there have been few efforts at systematically measuring and modeling the evolution of social-attribute networks. Most prior work in the measurement and modeling space focuses primarily on the social structure [3, 4, 13, 26, 28, 33, 38]. Measuring social-attribute networks can simultaneously inform us the properties of social network structure, attribute structure, and how such attributes impact social network structure.

In this paper, we present a detailed study of the evolution of social-attribute networks using a unique large-scale dataset collected by crawling the Google+ social network struture and its user profiles. This dataset offers a unique opportunity for us as we were fortunate to observe the complete evolution of the social network and its growth to around 30 million users within a span of three months.

We observe novel patterns in the growth of the Google+ social-attribute network. First, we observe that the social reciprocity of Google+ is lower than many traditional social networks and is closer to that of Twitter. Second, in contrast to many prior networks, the social degree distributions in Google+ are best modeled by a lognormal distribution. Third, we observe that assortativity of

Google+ social network is neutral while many other social networks own positive assortativities. Fourth, we also see that the distinct phases (initial launch, invite only, public release) in the timeline of Google+ naturally manifest themselves in the social and attribute structures. Fifth, for the generalized attribute metrics (that we define), while some attribute metrics mirror their social counterparts (e.g., diameter), several show distributions and trends that are significantly different (e.g., clustering coefficient, attribute degree). Finally, via the social-attribute network framework, we study the impact of user attributes on the social structure and observe that nodes sharing common attributes are likely to have higher social reciprocity and that some attributes have much stronger influence than others (e.g., Employer vs. City).

Based on our observations, we develop a new generative model for SANs. Our model includes two new components, i.e., *attribute-augmented preferential attachment* and *attribute-augmented triangle-closing*, which extend the classical preferential attachment [5, 27] and triangle-closing [29, 43, 53, 2], respectively. Using both theoretical analysis and empirical evaluation, we show that our model can reproduce SANs that accurately reflect the true ones with respect to various network metrics and real-world applications. Such a generative model has a lot of applications [30] such as network extrapolation and sampling, network visualization and compression, and network anonymization [44].

To summarize, the key contributions of this work are:

- We perform the first study of the evolution of social-attribute networks using Google+. We observe novel phenomena in standard social structure metrics and new attribute-related metrics (that we define) and how attributes impact the social structure.
- We develop a measurement-driven generative model for the social-attribute network that models the impact of user attributes into the network evolution.
- Using both theoretical analysis and empirical evaluation, we validate that our model can accurately reproduce real social-attribute networks.

2. PRELIMINARIES AND DATASET

In this section, we begin with some background on augmenting social network structure with attributes. Then, we describe how we collected the Google+ data and how we augment the Google+ social network with user attribute information. We also present some basic measurements describing the evolution of the Google+.

2.1 Social-Attribute Network (SAN)

In this section, we review the definition of *Social-Attribute Network* (SAN) [17] and introduce the basic notations used in the rest of this paper.

Given a directed social network G, in which nodes are users and edges represent friend relationships between users, and M distinct binary attributes, which could be static (e.g., name of employer, name of school, major, etc.) or dynamic (e.g., interest groups), a SAN is an augmented network with M additional nodes where each such node corresponds to a specific binary attribute. For each node u in G with attribute a, we create an undirected link between u and a in the SAN.

Nodes in a SAN corresponding to nodes in G are called *social nodes* and denoted as the set V_s, while nodes representing attributes are called *attribute nodes* and denoted as the set V_a. Figure 1 shows an example SAN. Links between social nodes are called *social links* and denoted as the set E_s, while links between social nodes and attribute nodes are called *attribute links* and denoted as the set E_a. Thus a Social-Attribute Network is denoted as $SAN = (V_s, V_a, E_s, E_a)$.

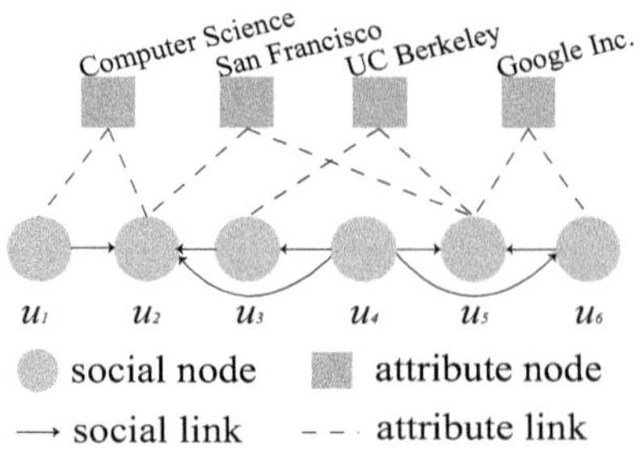

Figure 1: *Illustration of a SAN with six social nodes and four attribute nodes. Note that the social links between users are directed whereas the attribute-user links are undirected.*

For a given social or attribute node u in a SAN, we denote its *attribute neighbors* as $\Gamma_a(u) = \{v|v \in V_a, (u,v) \in E_a\}$, *social neighbors* as $\Gamma_s(u) = \{v|v \in V_s, (v,u) \in E_s \cup E_a$ *or* $(u,v) \in E_s \cup E_a\}$, *social in neighbors* as $\Gamma_{s,in}(u) = \{v|(v,u) \in E_s\}$ and *social out neighbors* as $\Gamma_{s,out}(u) = \{v|(u,v) \in E_s\}$. Note that an attribute node can only have social neighbors.

2.2 Google+ Data

Google+ was launched with an invitation-only test phase on June 28, 2011, and opened to everyone 18 years of age or older on September 20, 2011. We believed this was a tremendous opportunity to observe the real-world evolution of a *large-scale* social-attribute network. Thus, we began to crawl daily snapshots of public Google+ social network structure and user profiles; our crawls lasted from July 6 to October 11, 2011. The first snapshot was crawled by breadth-first search (without early stopping). On subsequent days, we expanded the social structure from the previous snapshot. For most snapshots, our crawl finished within one day as Google did not limit the crawl rate during that time.

We believe our crawl collected a large Weakly Connected Component (WCC) of Google+. This may be surprising as many past attempts on Flickr, Facebook, YouTube etc., were unable to do so [38]. The key difference is that these were only able to access outgoing links. In contrast, each user in Google+ has both an outgoing list (i.e., "in your circles") and an incoming list (i.e., "have you in circles"). This allows us to access both outgoing and incoming links making it feasible to crawl the entire WCC.

We have two points of reference that suggest our coverage is high ($\geq 70\%$): 1) TechCrunch estimated the number of Google+ users on July 12, 2011 is around 10 million [52]; our crawled snapshot on the same day has 7 million users. (2) Google announced 40 million users had joined Google+ in middle October [19]; our crawled snapshot on October 11 has around 30 million users.

We take each user u in Google+ as a social node in SAN, and connect it to her outgoing friends via outgoing links and incoming friends via incoming links. We use four attribute types *School*, *Major*, *Employer* and *City* that were available and easy to extract. Specifically, we find all distinct schools, majors, employers and cities that appear in at least one user profile and use them as attribute nodes. Recall that a social node u is connected to attribute node a via an undirected link if u has attribute a. In this way, we construct a SAN from each crawled snapshot, resulting in 79 SANs during the period from July 6 to October 11, 2011.

Figures 2 and 3 show the temporal evolution of the number of nodes and links in the Google+ SAN. From the results we clearly see three distinct phases in the evolution of Google+: Phase I from

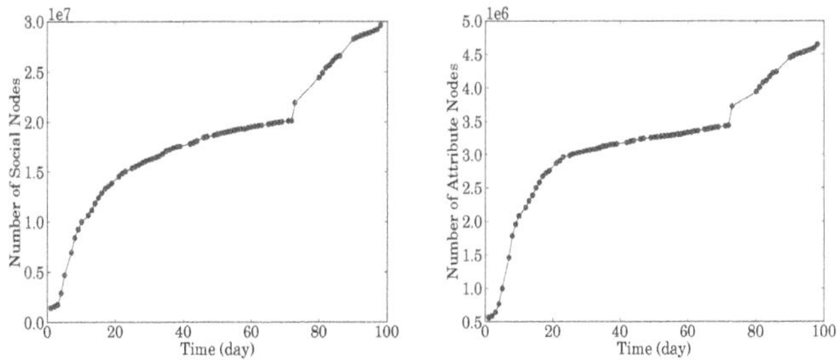

(a) Social nodes (b) Attribute nodes

Figure 2: *Growth in the number of social and attribute nodes in the Google+ dataset.*

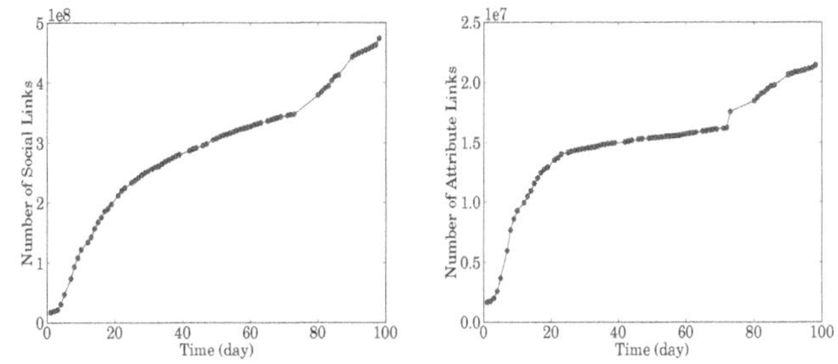

(a) Social links (b) Attribute links

Figure 3: *Growth in the number of social and attribute links in the Google+ dataset*

day one to day 20, which corresponds to the early days of Google+ whose size increased dramatically; Phase II from day 21 to day 75, during which Google+ went into a stabilized increase phase; and Phase III from day 76 to day 98, when Google+ opened to public (i.e., without requiring an invitation), resulting in a dramatic growth again. We point this out because we observe a similar three-phase evolution pattern for almost all network metrics that we analyze in the subsequent sections.

In the following sections, we use the last or largest snapshot, unless we are interested in the time-varying behavior.

Potential biases: We would like to acknowledge two possible biases. First, users may keep some of their friends or circles private. In this case, we can only see the publicly visible list. Thus we may not crawl the entire WCC and underestimate the node degrees. However, as discussed earlier, we obtain a very large connected component that covers more than 70% of known users which is sufficiently representative. Second, users may choose not to declare their attributes, in which case we may underestimate the impact of attributes on the social structure. However, we find that roughly 22% of users declare at least one attribute which represents a statistically large sample from which to draw conclusions. Furthermore, by validating the attribute-related results via further subsampling the attributes we have, we show that our attributes are representative of the entire attributes.

3. SOCIAL STRUCTURE OF THE GOOGLE+ SAN

In this section, we begin by presenting several canonical network metrics commonly used for characterizing social networks such as the reciprocity, density, clustering coefficient, and degree distribution [38, 25, 28, 41]. These metrics are useful to expose the inherent structure of a social network in terms of the friend relationships and whether there are "community" structures beyond a one-hop friend relationship. It is particularly useful to revisit these metrics in the context of Google+ both because of its scale and because it enables a somewhat hybrid relationship model compared to other networks such as Facebook, Twitter, Flickr, and email networks. Furthermore, since we have a unique opportunity to observe the network as it grew, we also analyze how these properties changed as the Google+ SAN evolved.

3.1 Reciprocity

The reciprocity metric for directed social networks represents the fraction of social links that are mutual; i.e., if there is a $A \rightarrow B$ edge what is the likelihood of the reverse $B \rightarrow A$ edge. Previous work studied the global reciprocities for *specific snapshots* of social networks and measured it to be 0.62 on Flickr, 0.79 on YouTube [38], and 0.22 on Twitter [28]. We focus on the *evolution* of global reciprocity for Google+ in Figure 4a. The result shows an interesting behavior where the reciprocity fluctuates in Phase I, decreases in Phase II and decreases even faster in Phase III. We speculate that this arises because of the hybrid nature of Google+. Initially many people treat the network like a traditional social network (e.g., Facebook) where the relationships are mutual. However, as time progresses and people appear to become familiar with the Twitter-like publisher-subscriber model also offered by Google+, the reciprocity decreases.

3.2 Density

The ratio of links-to-nodes, $\frac{|E_s|}{|V_s|}$, captures the *density* [1] of a social network. To put this in context, previous studies show that the social density increases over time on citation and affiliation networks [33], on Facebook [4], and fluctuates in an increase-decrease-increase fashion on Flickr [26], and is relatively constant on email communication networks [25].

Figure 4b shows the evolution of this social density metric in Google+. We observe that social density in Google+ network has a sharp decrease followed by an increase in Phase I, a continued increase in Phase II, and a sudden drop in Phase III (when Google+ opened to the public) followed by a steady increase again. This three-phase pattern can be explained in conjunction with the trends in Figures 2a and 3a. In the early part of Phase I, even though the rate of users joining Google+ is high, the rate of adding links is low, possibly because many of a user's existing friends have not yet joined. This causes social density to decrease. As users acquire friends with a rate higher than the rate of new users in later part of Phase I and the same trend continuing in Phase II, the social density increases. In Phase III, the number of users in Google+ had a sudden jump due to the public release but the number friendship links increases less dramatically, which once again causes the social density to drop significantly around t=70, but then starts slowly increasing again. Our findings have implications for network modeling. Specifically, many network models either assume constant density [5, 24] or power-law densification [33], which is not consistent with Google+.

3.3 Diameter

In directed social networks, the distance between two user nodes u and v, $dist(u, v)$ is defined as the length of the shortest directed path whose head is v and tail is u. Note that only social links E_s are used in this definition. We find that the distribution of the distance between nodes has a dominant mode at a distance of six, with most nodes (90%) having a distance of 5, 6, or 7 (not shown).

[1] In graph theory, density is defined as the fraction of existing links with respect to all possible links. We follow the terminology in [26] in order to compare with previous results.

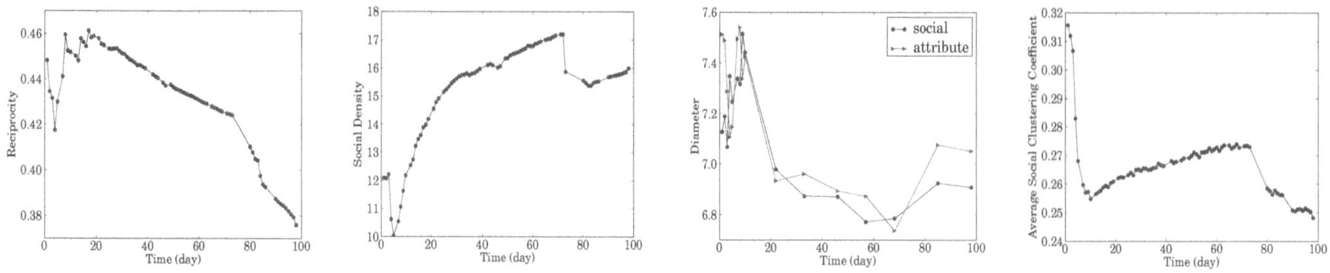

(a) Reciprocity (b) Social density (c) Diameter (d) Social clustering coefficient

Figure 4: *Evolution of four key metrics: reciprocity, density, diameter and clustering coefficient on the Google+ SAN. In each case, we observe distinct behaviors in the three phases corresponding to early initialization, time to public release, and time after public release.*

Based on the distance distribution, we can also define the *effective diameter* as the 90-th percentile distance (possibly with some interpolation) between every pair of connected nodes [33]. Unfortunately, computing the effective diameter is infeasible for large networks, so we use the HyperANF approximation algorithm [8], which has been shown to be able to approximate diameter with high accuracy.

Previous work observed effective diameter shrinks in citation networks, autonomous networks and affiliation network [33], in Flickr and Yahoo! 360 [26], and in Cyworld [3]. However, we observe that the effective diameter follows a three-phase evolution as seen in Figure 4c, which again can be explained in conjunction with the trends in Figures 2a and 3a. In Phase I, user joining rate outpaces link creation rate, causing the diameter to increase; in Phase II, user joining rate is lower than link acquisition rate, resulting in decreasing diameter; and in Phase III user joining rate is much higher, resulting in a diameter increasing phase again. Again, our observations have implications for network modeling. Existing network models either assume logarithmically growing diameter [55, 5] or shrinking diameter [30, 33].

3.4 Clustering Coefficient

Given a network G and node u, u's clustering coefficient is defined as

$$c(u) = \frac{L(u)}{|\Gamma_s(u)|(|\Gamma_s(u)| - 1)},$$

where $L(u)$ is the number of links among u's social neighbors $\Gamma_s(u)$ and the average *social clustering coefficient* is defined as $C_s = \frac{1}{|V_s|}\sum_{u \in V_s} c(u)$ [55]. Intuitively, this captures the community structure among a user's friends.

Again, computing the average clustering coefficient is expensive. Thus, we extend the constant-time approximate algorithm proposed by Schank et al. for undirected networks [45], and develop an algorithm to approximate the clustering coefficients for a directed network. With $\lceil \frac{\ln 2\nu}{2\epsilon^2} \rceil$ random samples, our constant time algorithms can bound the error of average clustering coefficient within ϵ with probability at least $1 - \frac{1}{\nu}$. In practice, we set the error to be $\epsilon = 0.002$ and $\nu = 100$. Algorithm details and theoretical analysis can be found in Appendix A.

Kossinets et al. [25] observed constant average social clustering coefficient over time in an email communication network. However, we find that the evolution of average social clustering coefficient of Google+, which is shown in Figure 4d, again follows a three-phase evolution pattern where the clustering coefficient dramatically decreases in Phase I, increases slowly in Phase II and decreases again in Phase III. Our findings indicate that the community structure among users' friends is highly dynamic, which inspires us to do dynamic community detection.

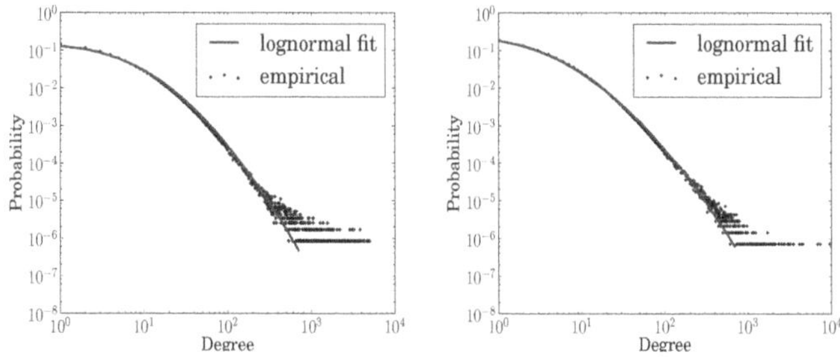

(a) Outdegree (b) Indegree

Figure 5: *Indegree and outdegree distributions for the social nodes in the Google+ SAN along with their best-fit curves. We observe that both are best modeled by a discrete lognormal distribution unlike many networks that suggest power-law distributions.*

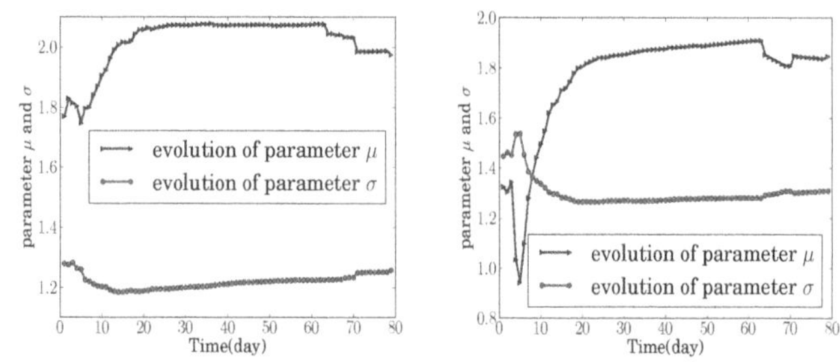

(a) Outdegree (b) Indegree

Figure 6: *Evolution of the lognormal parameters for the indegree and outdegree distributions.*

3.5 Degree Distributions

Next, we focus on the social *indegree* and *outdegree* of users in Google+. In each case, we are also interested in identifying an empirical best-fit distribution using the tool [54, 10], which compares fits of several widely used distributions (e.g., power-law, lognormal, power-law with cutoff using) with respect to *goodness-of-fit*. We find that unlike many studies on social networks, in which social degrees usually follow a power-law distribution [13, 38], social degrees are best captured by a discrete lognormal distribution in Google+. Recall that a random variable $x \in \mathbb{Z}^+$ follows a power-law distribution if $p(x = k) \propto k^{-\alpha}$, where α is the exponent of the power-law distribution. On the other hand, a random variable $x \in \mathbb{Z}^+$ follows a discrete lognormal distribution if $p(x = k) \propto \frac{1}{k}\exp(-\frac{(\ln k - \mu)^2}{2\sigma^2})$ [7], where μ and σ are the mean and standard deviation respectively of the lognormal distribution.

Figure 5 shows these degree distributions and their discrete lognormal fits, and Figure 6 shows the evolutions of the parameters for the fitted discrete lognormal distributions. We see the evolution of the outdegree and indegree distributions follows a similar trend but with the fluctuation differing in magnitude (Figures 6a, 6b).

Lognormally distributed degree distributions imply that there are probabilistically more low degree social nodes in Google+ than those in power-law distributed networks.

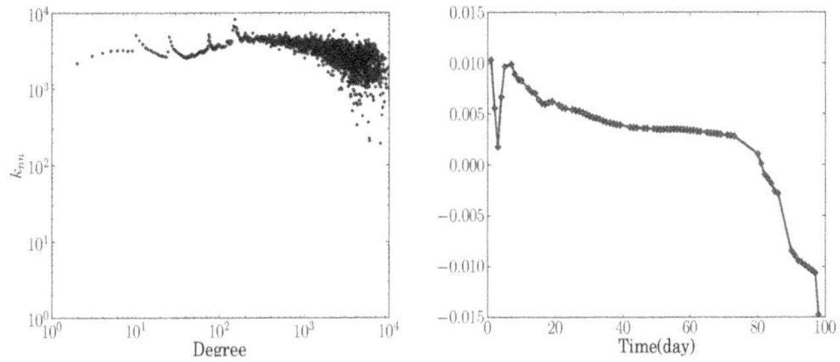

(a) k_{nn} metric (b) Assortativity

Figure 7: *Two metrics for capturing the joint-degree distribution: (a) k_{nn} shows a log-log plot of the outdegree versus the average indegree of friends and (b) shows the evolution of the assortativity coefficient.*

3.6 Joint Degree Distribution

Last, we examine the joint degree distribution (JDD) of the Google+ social structure. JDD is useful for understanding the preference of a node to attach itself to nodes that are similar to itself. One way to approximate the JDD is using the degree correlation function k_{nn}, which maps outdegree to the average indegree of all nodes connected to nodes of that outdegree [42, 38]. An increasing k_{nn} trend indicates high-degree nodes tend to connect to other high-degree nodes; a decreasing k_{nn} represents the opposite trend. Figure 7a shows the k_{nn} function for Google+ social structure.

The JDD can further be quantified using the *assortativity coefficient* r that can range from -1 to 1 [41]. r is positive if k_{nn} is positively correlated to node degree k. Figure 7b illustrates the evolution of the assortativity coefficient. We observe that r keeps decreasing in all three phases but at different rates. Furthermore, unlike many traditional social networks where the assortativity coefficient is typically positive—0.202 for Flickr, 0.179 for LiveJournal and 0.072 for Orkut [38, 41]—Google+ has almost neutral assortativity close to 0. The neutral assortativity can possibly be explained by the hypothesis that Google+ is a hybrid of two ingredients, i.e., a traditional social network and a publisher-subscriber network (e.g., Twitter). Traditional social networks usually have positive assortativity; publisher-subscriber networks often have negative assortativity because high-degree publisher nodes tend to be connected to low-degree subscriber nodes. Thus a hybrid of them results in a network with neutral assortativity. The evolution pattern of Google+' assortativity coefficient (i.e., positive in Phase I, around 0 in Phase II, and negative in Phase III) manifests the competing process of the two ingredients of Google+. More specifically, the traditional network ingredient slightly wins in Phase I, resulting in a slightly positive assortativity coefficient. A draw between them in Phase II results in the neutral assortativity. In Phase III, the publisher-subscriber ingredient wins, resulting in a slightly negative assortativity coefficient. This implies that Google+ is more and more like a publisher-subscriber network.

3.7 Summary of Key Observations and Implications

Analyzing the social structure of Google+ and its evolution over time, we find that:

- In contrast to many traditional networks, we find that Google+ has low reciprocity, the social degree distribution is best modeled by a lognormal distribution rather than a power-law distribution, and the assortativity is neutral rather than positive.
- Google+ is somewhere between a traditional social network (e.g., Flickr) and a publisher-subscriber network (e.g., Twitter), reflecting the hybrid interaction model that it offers. Moreover, it's more and more closer to a publisher-subscriber network.
- The evolutionary patterns of various network metrics in Google+ are different from those in many traditional networks or assumptions of various network models. These findings imply that existing models cannot explain the underlying growing mechanism of Google+, and we need to design new models for reproducing social networks similar to Google+.

4. ATTRIBUTE STRUCTURE OF THE GOOGLE+ SAN

In the previous section we looked at well-known social network metrics. In this section, we focus on analyzing the attribute structure of the Google+ SAN. To this end, we extend the metrics from the previous section to the attributes as well. Finally, we show the importance of using attributes in understanding the social structure by studying their impact on metrics we analyzed earlier (e.g., reciprocity, clustering coefficient, and degree distribution). These attribute-related studies will characterize the attribute structure, give us insights about the underlying growing mechanism of Google+, and eventually guide us design a new generative model for Google+ SAN.

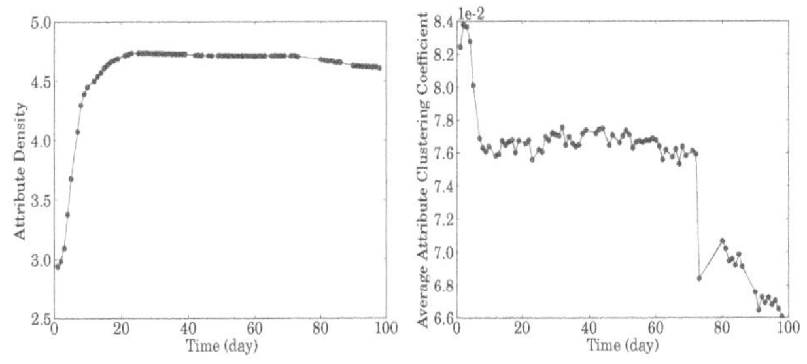

(a) Attribute density (b) Clustering coefficient

Figure 8: *Evolution of the attribute density and average attribute clustering coefficient in the Google+ SAN.*

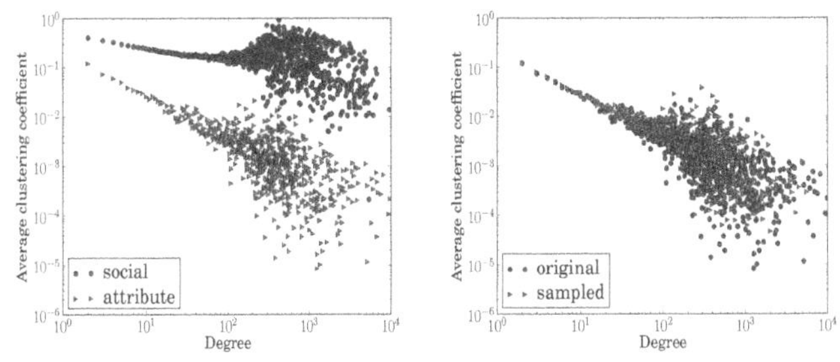

(a) Distributions in the original SAN (b) Comparison with a subsampled SAN

Figure 9: *Distributions of clustering coefficient with respect to node degrees. (a) Comparison of social and attribute clustering coefficient distributions in the original SAN. (b)Comparison of distributions of attribute clustering coefficients in the original SAN and the subsampled SAN.*

4.1 Attribute Metrics

Density: We consider a natural extension of the social density metric from §3.2 and define *attribute density* as $\frac{|E_a|}{|V_a|}$. Different from our observations with social density in Figure 4b, in Figure 8a, We observe the attribute density increases rapidly in Phase I, stays relatively flat in Phase II, and slightly decreases in Phase III. The reason for the decrease in Phase III is the large volume of new (i.e., non-invitation) users joining Google+ with many new attribute nodes whose social degrees are small.

Diameter: We extend the distance metric from §3.3 to define the *attribute distance* between two attribute nodes a and b as $dist(a, b) = \min\{dist(u, v)|u \in \Gamma_s(a), v \in \Gamma_s(b)\} + 1$.[2] Intuitively, attribute distance is the minimum number of social nodes that a attribute node has to traverse before reaching to the other one; i.e., attribute distance is the distance between two attribute communities. Similarly, we can consider the effective diameter using this attribute distance. Figure 4c also shows the evolution of the attribute diameter and shows that it very closely mirrors the social diameter.

Clustering coefficient: Similarly, we generalize the social clustering coefficient from §3.4 to define the *attribute clustering coefficient* $c(u)$ for the attribute node u, and the average attribute clustering coefficient as $C_a = \frac{1}{|V_a|}\sum_{u \in V_a} c(u)$. This attribute clustering coefficient $c(u)$ characterizes the power of attribute u to form communities among users who have the attribute u. Compared to Figure 4d, we find in Figure 8b that the average attribute clustering coefficient evolves in a different pattern since it's relatively stable in Phase II.

We also show the distribution of average social and attribute clustering coefficients as a function of node degree in Figure 9a. We observe that both social and attribute clustering coefficients follow a power-law distribution with respect to node degrees, but attribute clustering coefficient distribution has a larger exponent. Moreover, we see that in general attribute clustering coefficients are lower because many shared attributes (e.g., city or major) will not naturally translate into a social relationship.

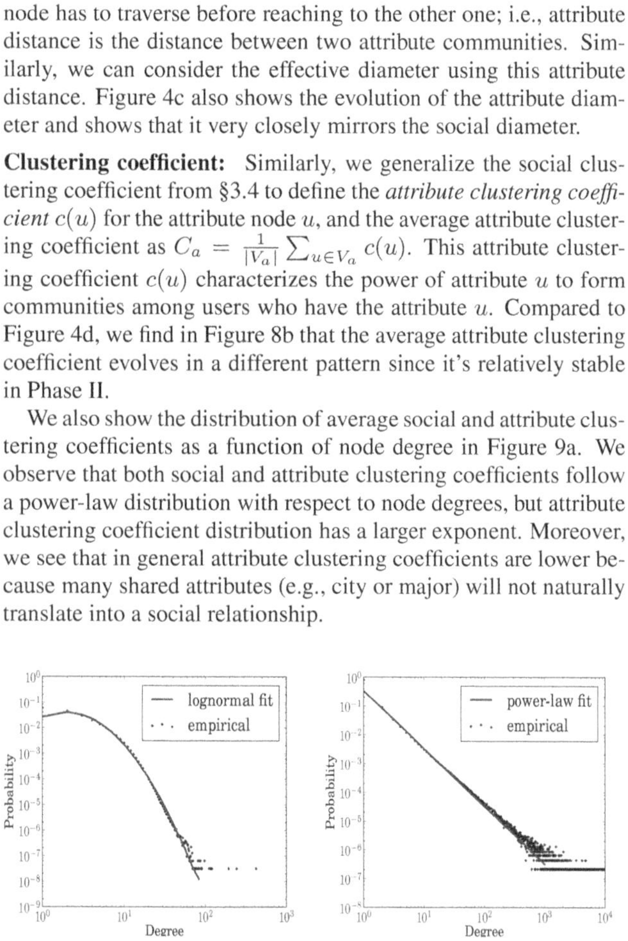

(a) Attribute degree of social nodes (b) Social degree of attribute nodes

Figure 10: *Distributions of attribute-induced degrees in the Google+ SAN along with their best fits. The attribute degree of social nodes is best modeled by a lognormal whereas the social degree of attribute nodes is best modeled by a power-law distribution.*

Degree distributions: As discussed earlier, SANs introduce edges between social and attribute nodes. Thus, we consider two new notions of node degrees: (1) *social degree* of attribute nodes (i.e., the number of users that have this attribute) and (2) *attribute degree* of social nodes (i.e., the number of attributes each user has). We find that the attribute degree of social nodes is best modeled by a lognormal distribution whereas the social degree of attribute nodes is best modeled by a power-law distribution. Figure 10 and Figure 11 show the degree distributions and evolution of their fitted parameters.

[2]Other definitions are possible, e.g, using average instead of min. We choose min because of its computational efficiency.

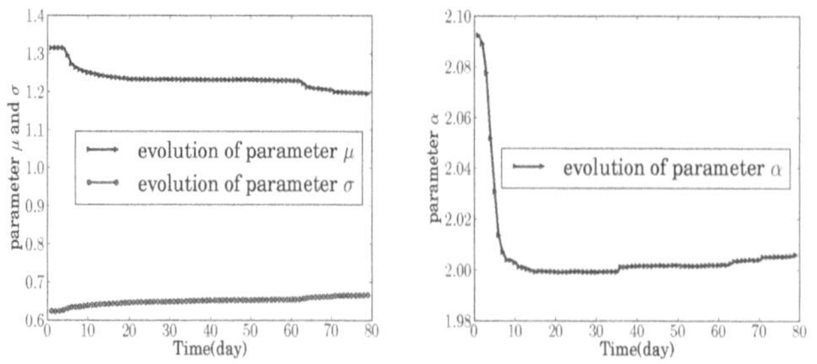

(a) Attribute degree of social nodes (b) Social degree of attribute nodes

Figure 11: *Evolution in lognormal and power-law parameters for the attribute and social degree distributions*

In terms of the evolution, we find the attribute degree evolution seen in Figure 11 is significantly different from the previous observation in Figure 6: its mean decreases in Phase I, remains roughly constant in Phase II, and decreases again in Phase III. However, its standard deviation increases slightly in all phases. Finally, for the social degree which follows a power-law distribution, the exponent decreases fast in Phase I, and increases slightly in Phase II and Phase III.

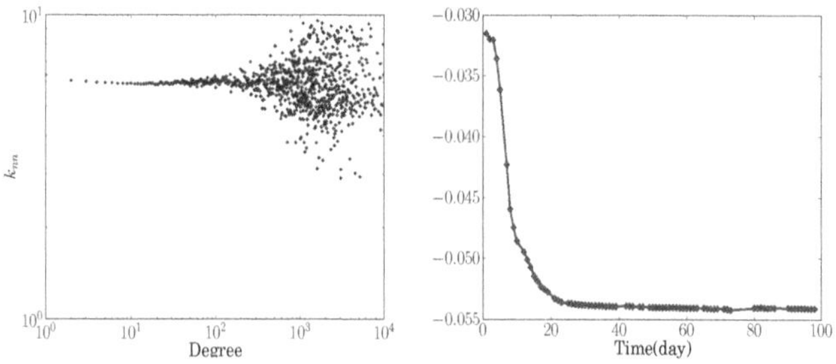

(a) Attribute k_{nn} (b) Evolution of assortativity

Figure 12: *(a) Joint degree of attribute nodes: Log-log plot of the social degree versus the average attribute degree of social neighbors of attribute nodes. (b) The evolution of the attribute assortativity coefficient.*

Joint degree distribution: Next, we extend the joint degree distribution (JDD) analysis to attribute nodes. For each social degree k, we compute k_{nn} as the average attribute degree of social neighbors of attribute nodes that have social degree k. Intuitively, it captures the tendency of attribute nodes with high social degree to connect to social nodes with high attribute degree; i.e., if many nodes share a particular attribute, then are these nodes likely have many attributes? Figure 12 shows the k_{nn} function for attribute JDD and the evolution of the attribute assortativity. Intuitively, we expect this relationship to be neutral and the result confirms this intuition; e.g., there are many Google+ users in New York but that does not imply the people in New York have many attributes. One interesting observation is that attribute assortativity coefficient evolves slightly differently compared to social assortativity coefficient (Figure 7b); it is stable in Phase III whereas social assortativity decreases significantly.

4.2 Influence on Social Network Structure

Next, we look at how attributes influence the social structure of the Google+ SAN w.r.t the metrics discussed in §3.

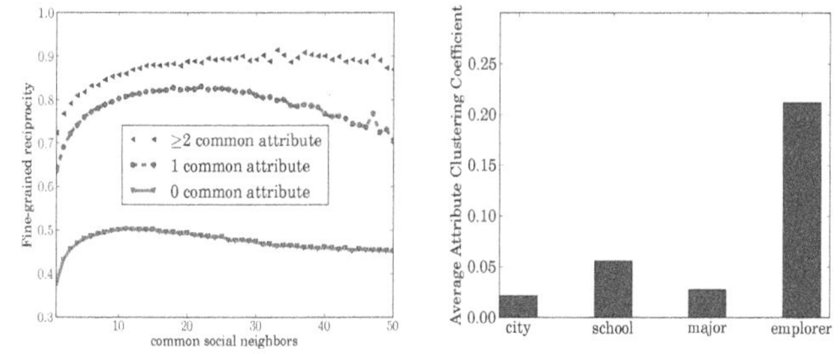

(a) Reciprocity (b) Clustering coefficients

Figure 13: *Influence of attribute on reciprocity and clustering coefficients.*

Reciprocity: We study how the number of common attribute neighbors influences reciprocity in conjunction with the number of common social neighbors. Let a and s denote the number of attribute and social neighbors of a given node, respectively. For each pair (s, a), we compute $r_{s,a}$ as the percentage of links that are reciprocal among all the links whose endpoints have s social neighbors and a attribute neighbors.

To compute this, we look at all *one directional* links at the snapshot collected halfway and then compute the number of such links that become *bidirectional* at the last snapshot. We split these by the number of common social and attribute neighbors between these nodes at the halfway stage and show the $r_{s,a}$ values in Figure 13. We see that the reciprocity is almost twice as high for nodes that share common attribute neighbors compared to nodes without common attributes, regardless of the number of common social neighbors. While sharing common social neighbors improves link reciprocity, there is a natural diminishing returns property beyond 10 common social neighbors, and even decreasing for much larger values. We speculate that nodes sharing too many social neighbors are likely users with many "weak" ties. For recent reciprocity prediction problem [9, 21], our findings imply that any reciprocity predictor should incorporate node attributes instead of pure social structure metrics.

Clustering coefficient: Next, we compute the average attribute clustering coefficient for the 4 attribute types: Employer, School, Major and City. For example, we compute the attribute clustering coefficients for all attribute nodes belonging to the attribute type Employer, and then average them to obtain the average attribute clustering coefficient for Employer. Figure 13b shows that attribute types vary in their influence on forming communities and that users with the same Employer attributes are much more likely to form communities than users sharing other attribute types. This has interesting implications for link prediction and attribute inference.

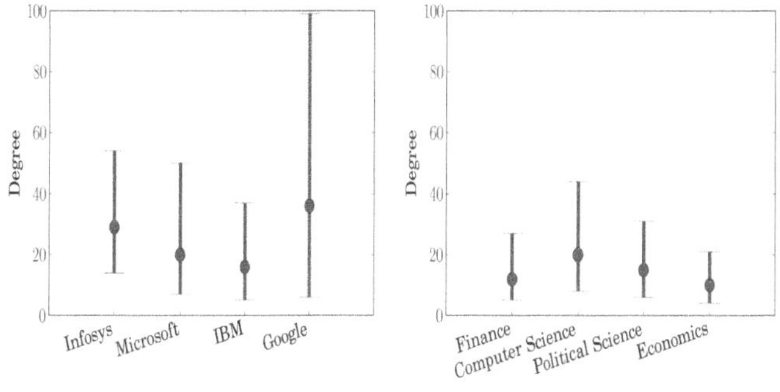

(a) Employer (b) Major

Figure 14: *Influence of attribute on social degree*

Degree distribution: For brevity, we only focus on the Employer and Major attributes and show the result for the top attribute values observed within each category. We plot the median, 25th, and 75th percentile of the social outdegree of nodes that have these attribute values in Figure 14. We see that the users with Employer=Google and Major=Computer Science are likely to have higher degrees. We also computed the full degree distributions for these attribute values and saw that they follow different lognormal distributions (not shown). We speculate this could be a specific artifact of the Google+ network as many of the early adopters likely consist of Google employees and users in the IT/CS industry.

4.3 Validation via Subsampling

One natural question is whether the attributes of 22% of users we collected is a good representative of the entire attributes. To this end, we use subsampling method to validate our attribute-related results. We use attribute clustering coefficient distribution with respect to node degrees as an example, and observe similar results for other metrics. For each user with attributes, we remove her attributes with probability 0.5, from which we obtain a subsampled SAN. Then we calculate the attribute clustering coefficient distributions for the original and this subsampled SANs. Figure 9b shows that the results of the original and subsampled SANs are almost identical. Given the assumption that whether a user fills in her attributes is a random and independent event, our results demonstrate that the attributes of 22% of users is a representative sample of the attributes of all the users.

4.4 Summary of Key Observations and Implications

In this section, we studied the attribute structure of the Google+ SAN and how such attribute structure impacts the social structure. Our key observations are:

- While some attribute metrics mirror their social counterparts (e.g., diameter), several show distributions and trends that are significantly different (e.g., clustering coefficient, attribute degree). These observations will guide us to design models for SAN.
- We confirm that attributes have interesting impact on the social structure. e.g., nodes are likely to have higher reciprocity if they share common attributes. These findings have various implications. For instance, reciprocity predictor should incorporate node attributes.
- We also observe that some attribute types naturally have stronger influence than others. For example, users sharing the same employer have higher probability to be linked compared to users sharing the same city. Data mining tasks such as link prediction and attribute inference should potentially benefit from these findings.

5. A GENERATIVE MODEL FOR SAN

From the previous sections, we have seen novel phenomena in the social and attribute structure of the Google+ SAN and that the attribute structure impacts the social structure significantly. A natural question is whether we can create an accurate generative network model that can reproduce both the social and attribute structures we observe. Such a generative model can help us understand the growing mechanism of SAN, and allow other applications such as network extrapolation and sampling, network visualization and compression, and network anonymization [30].

Prior work on generative models focus primarily on the social structure [5, 24, 2, 33, 29]. Consequently, these approaches can-

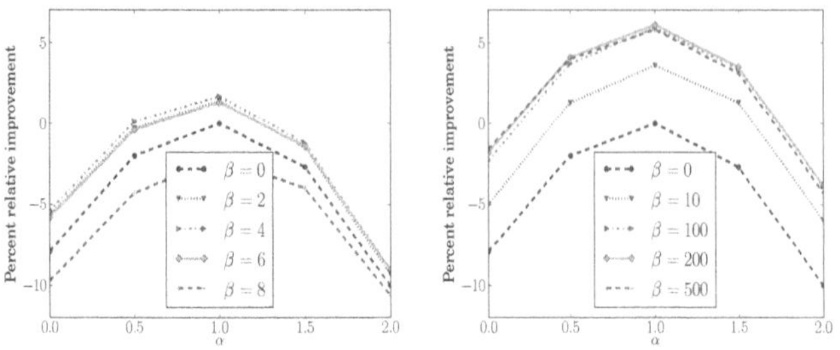

(a) PAPA model (b) LAPA model

Figure 15: *Comparison between Power Attribute Preferential Attachment (PAPA) and Linear Attribute Preferential Attachment (LAPA) models. All result numbers are percentage of relative improvements over the loglikelihood of the PA model, i.e., with α =1 and β = 0.*

not model the attribute structure or their impact on social structure. To address this gap, we provide a new generative model taking into account the attribute structure from first principles rather than overlaying it after-the-fact. To this end, we extend a prior generative model [29], using attribute-augmented models for link generation and addition , which are key building blocks for such generative models. As we will show, this provides more realistic synthetic SAN that closely matches the Google+ SAN.

5.1 Building Block 1: Attribute-Augmented Preferential Attachment

Leskovec et al. showed that the Preferential Attachment (PA) [5] is a suitable choice for creating edges [29]. The key idea in PA is that a new node u is likely to connect to an existing node v with a probability proportional to v's degree. As we saw earlier, users who share attributes are also more likely to be connected. Thus, we consider two ways to augment the PA model:

- *Power Attribute Preferential Attachment (PAPA):* $f(u, v) \propto d_i(v)^\alpha(1 + a(u, v)^\beta)$
- *Linear Attribute Preferential Attachment (LAPA):* $f(u, v) \propto d_i(v)^\alpha(1 + \beta \cdot a(u, v))$

Here, $f(u, v)$ is the probability with which social node u adds a link to social node v, $d_i(v)$ is the indegree of v and $a(u, v)$ is the number of common attributes that social nodes u and v share.[3] Notice that when $\alpha = \beta = 0$, both reduce to a uniform distribution (i.e., v is sampled uniformly at random) and when α=1,β=0 both reduce to the PA model.

The relative improvement of a model with parameter α, β over the PA model is defined as $\frac{l_{PA} - l(\alpha,\beta)}{l_{PA}}$, where l denote the log-likelihood of the model with respect to the empirically observed Google+ SAN. Figure 15 shows the relative improvements of these models over the PA model for varying values of α, β. First, LAPA models perform better than PAPA models, which indicates that attribute likely influence friend requests in a linear way. Second, the PA model (α =1, β = 0) is 7.9% better than a uniform random model (α =0, β = 0). A LAPA model with α =1 and β = 200 achieves a further 6.1% improvement over the PA model. Third, $\alpha = 1$ achieves the best loglikelihood for any given β, which indicates that social degree has a linear effect on friend requests. In

[3]In a more general setting, we can also weight attribute types differently; e.g., Employer is stronger than City.

Algorithm 1: Social-Attribute Network Model

T, simulated time steps
Initialization.
for $1 \le t \le T$ **do**
  Social node arrival. Sample a set of new social nodes $V_{t,new}$.
  for $v_{new} \in V_{t,new}$ **do**
    Attribute degree sampling. Sample the number of attributes $n_a(v_{new})$ for v_{new} from a lognormal distribution.
    for $1 \le i \le n_a(v_{new})$ **do**
      Attribute linking.
    end
    First outgoing linking.
    lifetime sampling.
    sleep time sampling.
  end
  Collect woken social nodes $V_{t,woken}$.
  for $v_{woken} \in V_{t,woken}$ **do**
    Outgoing linking.
    sleep time sampling.
  end
end

summary, we conclude that there is a combined linear effect of both social degree and attributes.

5.2 Building Block 2: Attribute-Augmented Triangle-Closings

Triangle closing, where a node u selects a node v from its 2-hop neighbors and adds an edge, is an essential part of many generative network models [29, 61, 33, 2, 43, 53]. We explore if node attributes can improve triangle closing.

In the context of SAN, we can consider two types of triangle-closing: one is closing a triangle with no attribute node involved (e.g., $u_4 \rightarrow u_2$ in Figure 1), and the other is closing a triangle which includes an attribute node (e.g., $u_1 \rightarrow u_2$ in Figure 1). Following prior work, we refer them as *triadic* and *focal* closure respectively [25]. In the friend requests we observe in Google+, 84% percent are triadic (common friend), 18% percent are focal (common attribute), and 15% percent are cases where the nodes share both common friends and common attributes (e.g., $u_6 \rightarrow u_5$ in Figure 1).

This suggests the importance of incorporating attributes in the triangle closure. To this end, we consider three models:

- *Baseline*: Select a social neighbor v within a 2-hop radius uniformly at random.
- *Random-Random (RR)*: Select a social neighbor $w \in \Gamma_s(u)$ uniformly at random, and then select a social neighbor $v \in \Gamma_s(w)$ uniformly at random which is shown to have very good performance in previous work [29].
- *Random-Random-SAN (RR-SAN)*: select a neighbor $w \in \Gamma_s(u) \cup \Gamma_a(u)$ uniformly at random, and then select a social neighbor $v \in \Gamma_s(w)$ uniformly at random.[4]

We compare these models using friend requests that are triadic closures, focal closures, or both. Our experimental results confirm that RR model performs 14% better than the Baseline model [29], and our RR-SAN model performs 36% better than RR model. This confirms that attributes play a significant role in the triangle-closing phenomenon as well and has natural implications for applications such as link prediction and friend recommendation.

5.3 Our Generative Model for SAN

[4]We also tried a weighted model where we select neighbors proportional to link weights. For brevity, we do not show this because it performs similarly.

Our stochastic process models several key aspects of SAN evolution: node joining, how nodes issue outgoing links and receive incoming links, and how they link to attribute nodes. The key differences from prior work [29] are the two building blocks we described earlier: Linear Attribute Preferential Attachment (LAPA) and Random-Random-SAN (RR-SAN) triangle-closing.

Here, nodes arrive at some pre-determined rate. On arrival, each node picks an initial set of attributes and social neighbors (using the LAPA model). After joining the network, each node subsequently "sleeps" for some time, wakes up, and adds new links based on the RR-SAN model. We describe the model formally in Algorithm 1 and discuss each step next. From the analysis below, we find that the key step for generating lognormal social *outdegree* distribution is to make the lifetime of nodes follow a *truncated normal distribution*.

Initialization: The SAN is initialized with a few social and attribute nodes and links. We observed that the starting point has no detectable influence when the number of initialization nodes is small compared to the overall network. We currently use a complete social-attribute network with 5 social nodes and 5 attribute nodes.

Social node arrival: Social nodes arrive as predicted by a node arrival function $N(t)$, which could be estimated from real social networks. In our simulations, we simply let $N(t) = 1$ modeling each node arrival as a discrete time step.

Attribute degree: Each node picks some number of attributes sampled from a lognormal distribution with mean μ_a and variance σ_a^2.

Attribute linking: Each new social node v_{new} with $n_a(v_{new})$ attributes, we connect it to $n_a(v_{new})$ attribute nodes with the stochastic process defined as follows: for each attribute, with probability p, a new attribute node a is generated; otherwise an existing attribute node a is chosen with probability proportional to its social degree.

First outgoing links: Each new node issues an outgoing link to a social node according to the LAPA model.

Lifetime sampling: The lifetime l of v_{new} is sampled from a truncated normal distribution, i.e., $p(l) \propto \exp(-\frac{(l-\mu_l)^2}{2\sigma_l^2})$ for $l \geq 0$. (Prior models use an exponentially distributed lifetime value [29, 61].)

Sleep time sampling: Sleep time s of any node v with outdegree d_o can be sampled from any distribution with mean m_s/d_o. Our model only depends on mean sleep time. The intuition of making mean sleep time reversely proportional to outdegree is that a node with larger outdegree has higher tendency to issue outgoing links. (Prior models assume a power-law with cutoff distributed lifetime value [29, 61].)

Outgoing linking. Each woken social node v_{woken} issues a new outgoing link according to our RR-SAN triangle-closing model.

5.4 Theoretical Analysis

By design, the attribute degree distribution of social nodes follows a lognormal distribution. Next, we show via analysis that the outdegree of social nodes and the social degree of attribute nodes follow a lognormal and power-law distribution respectively. For brevity, we provide a high-level sketch of the proofs.

Let $\phi(x)$ and $\Phi(x)$ denote the probability density function and cumulative density function of standard normal distribution. Let $\gamma_l = -\frac{\mu_l}{\sigma_l}$, $g(\gamma) = \frac{\phi(\gamma)}{1-\Phi(\gamma)}$ and $\delta(\gamma) = g(\gamma)(g(\gamma) - \gamma)$.

THEOREM 1. *If the sleep time is sampled from some distribution with mean m_s/d_o, then the social out degrees of SANs generated by our model follow a lognormal distribution with mean $(\mu_l + \sigma_l g(\gamma_l))/m_s$ and variance $\sigma_l^2(1 - \delta(\gamma_l))/m_s^2$.*

PROOF. For any social node v, assume its final outdegree is D_o, then we have

$$\sum_{d_o=1}^{D} s(d_o) \leq l,$$

where $s(d_o)$ is the random sleep time whose mean is m_s/d_o. Thus, with mean-field approximation, we obtain

$$m_s \sum_{d_o=1}^{D} \frac{1}{d_o} \leq l.$$

Moreover, according to Euler's asymptotic analysis on harmonic series, we have

$$\sum_{d_o=1}^{D} \frac{1}{d_o} \approx \ln D_o.$$

That is, $\ln D_o \approx l/m_s$. Lifetime l is also a normal distribution truncated for $l \geq 0$, thus having mean $\mu_l + \sigma_l g(\gamma_l)$ and variance $\sigma_l^2(1 - \delta(\gamma_l))$. Thus, $\ln D_o$ follows a truncated normal distribution with mean $\mu_o = (\mu_l + \sigma_l g(\gamma_l))/m_s$ and variance $\sigma_o^2 = \sigma_l^2(1 - \delta(\gamma_l))/m_s^2$. So D_o follows a lognormal distribution with mean μ_o and variance σ_o^2. □

Next, we derive the distribution of social degree of attribute nodes using mean-field rate equations [6].

THEOREM 2. *The social degrees of attribute nodes in the SANs generated by our model follow a power-law distribution with exponent $\frac{2-p}{1-p}$.*

PROOF. Without loss of generality, we assume one attribute link joins the SAN at each discrete time step. Let D_i denote the social degree of the attribute node i that joins the network at time t_i. According to the stochastic process in our algorithm, we have

$$\frac{dD_i}{dt} = \frac{(1-p)D_i}{\sum_i D_i} = \frac{(1-p)D_i}{t + m_0}$$

,where m_0 is the initial number of attribute links. Solving this ordinary differential equation with initial condition $D_i = 1$ at $t = t_i$ gives us

$$D_i = (\frac{t + m_0}{t_i + m_0})^{(1-p)}.$$

So the probability of $D_i < D$ is

$$Pr(D_i < D) = 1 - Pr(t_i + m_0 \leq (t + m_0)D^{-\frac{1}{1-p}}).$$

According to our model, $Pr(t_i)$ has a uniform distribution over the set $\{1, 2, \cdots, t\}$. Thus we obtain

$$Pr(D_i < D) = 1 - \frac{(t + m_0)D^{-\frac{1}{1-p}} - m_0}{t}.$$

Then the distribution of D_i can be calculated as

$$Pr(D) = \frac{dPr(D_i \leq D)}{dD} = \frac{t + m_0}{t(1-p)} D^{-\frac{2-p}{1-p}}.$$

As $t \to \infty$, we obtain $Pr(D) \propto D^{-\frac{2-p}{1-p}}$. So the social degrees of attribute nodes follow a power-law distribution with exponent $\frac{2-p}{1-p}$. □

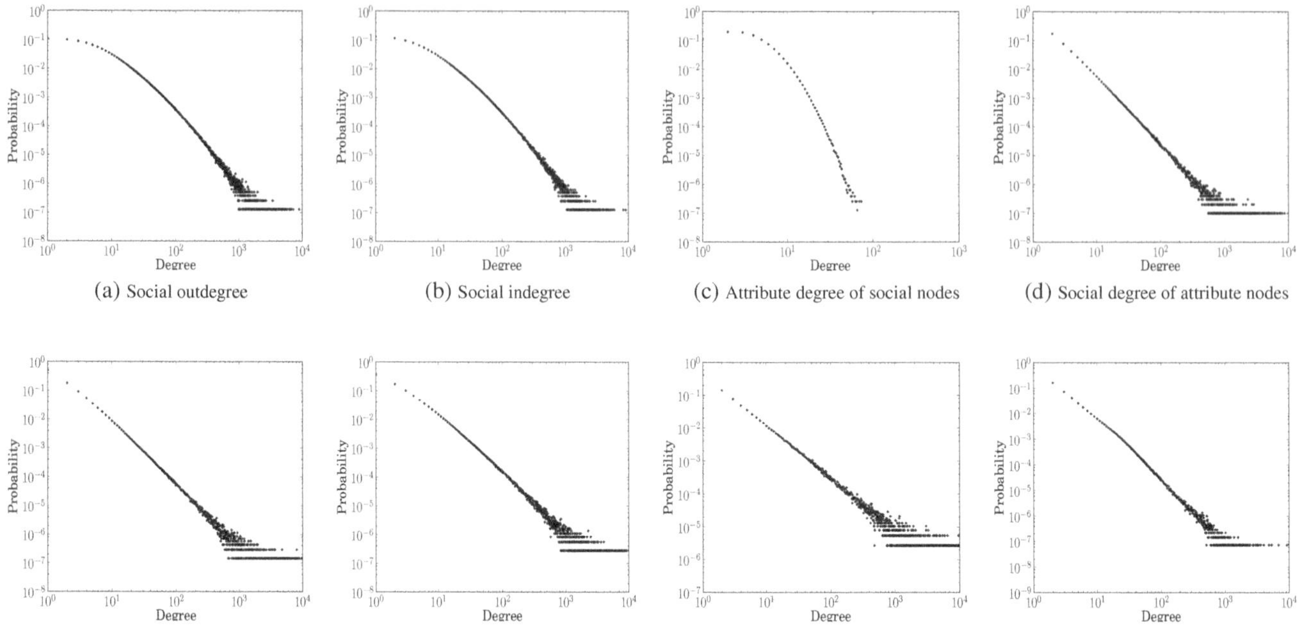

(a) Social outdegree (b) Social indegree (c) Attribute degree of social nodes (d) Social degree of attribute nodes

(e) Social outdegree (f) Social indegree (g) Attribute degree of social nodes (h) Social degree of attribute nodes

Figure 16: *Degree distributions of synthetically generated SAN using our model in (a)-(d) vs.* Zhel *shown in (e)-(h).*

Mitzenmacher [40] did a comprehensive study on generative models (e.g., PA, multiplicative models, random monkey) for power-law and lognormal distributions. In this work, we have proposed two new generative models.

6. EVALUATION

In this section, we validate our SAN generative model. Because the SAN area is still very nascent there are few standard models of comparison. We pick the closest generative model by Zheleva et al [61]. Note that their model is actually orthogonal to ours since it's modeling dynamic node attributes while ours is modeling static node attributes. Furthermore, their original model generates undirected social networks. In order to compare with our model and directed Google+ SANs, we extend their model to generate directed social networks[5]. We refer to the extended model as the *Zhel* model throughout this section. We start with network metrics, including single-node degree distribution, joint degree distribution and clustering coefficient. Then, following the spirit of [43], we also evaluate our model using real application contexts.

For comparison, we use the Google+ snapshot crawled on July 15, 2011, which has roughly 10 million nodes and we believe it is representative of Google+ SAN. Using this Google+ snapshot, we run a guided greedy search to estimate appropriate parameters for our model and *Zhel* to generate synthetic SAN that best match the Google+.

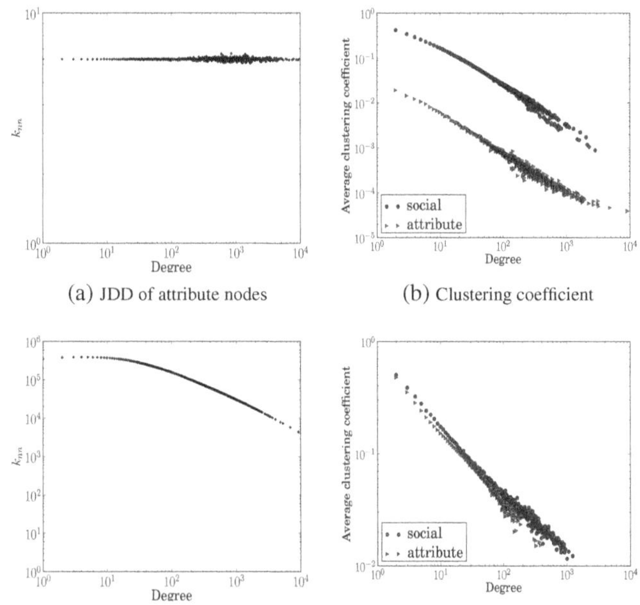

(a) JDD of attribute nodes (b) Clustering coefficient

(c) JDD of attribute nodes (d) Clustering coefficient

Figure 17: *Joint degree and clustering coefficient distributions of our model (a)–(b) vs.* Zhel *in (c)–(d).*

6.1 Network Metrics

In this section, we qualitatively compare our model to the *Zhel* model, and demonstrate that our model can generate synthetic SAN that better reproduces various network metrics closer to Google+ SAN.

Degree distributions: We first examine the degree distributions of the synthetic SAN generated by our model and the *Zhel* model in Figure 16. The most visually evident result looking at Figure 16a and Figure 16b is that our model can generate synthetic networks with social indegree and outdegree following lognormal distributions similar to the Google+ SAN that we saw in Figure 5. In contrast, Figure 16f and Figure 16e confirm that the *Zhel* model generates indegree and outdegree following power-law distributions. Similarly, comparing Figure 16c and 16g to Figure 10a, the attribute degree of social nodes in our model follows the lognormal distribution that matches that of the Google+ SAN, whereas the *Zhel* model generates attribute degrees that follow a power-law distribution. Finally, Figure 16d and 16h confirm that both our

[5]Extending their model is straightfoward. For instance, when the original model issues an undirected link, we change it to be a directed outgoing link.

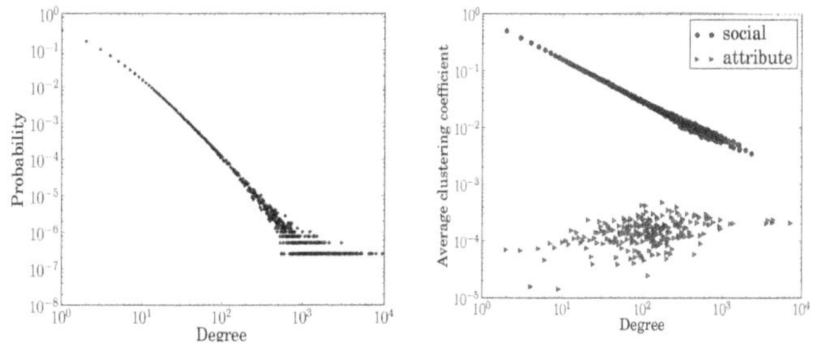

(a) Social indegree w/o LAPA (b) Clustering coefficient w/o focal closure

Figure 18: *The effect of LAPA and focal closure.*

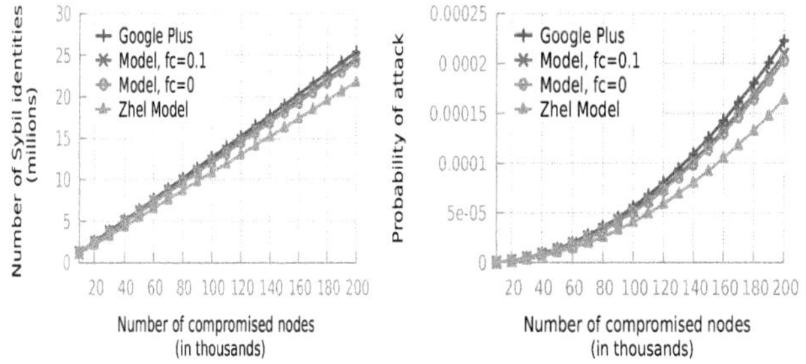

(a) Sybil defense (b) Anonymous communication

Figure 19: *Application fidelity of our model. (a) Sybil defense: SybilLimit false negatives as a function of number of compromised nodes. (b) Social network based anonymity: Probability of end-to-end timing analysis as a function of number of compromised nodes.*

model and *Zhel* generate social degrees of attribute nodes that follow power-law distribution, which is again consistent with Google+ SAN from Figure 10b.

Joint degree distributions: The ability to mirror more fine-grained properties beyond the degree distributions has been shown to be a key metric for evaluating generative models [37]. Thus, we look at the joint degree distribution approximated by degree correlation function k_{nn} in Figure 17a and 17c for our model and *Zhel*. Compared to Figure 12, we see that the JDD of attribute nodes in our model generated SAN matches Google+ SAN much better than *Zhel*. We observe similar pattern for JDD of social nodes.

Clustering coefficient: Fig. 17b and Fig. 17d shows the clustering coefficient distributions of synthetic SANs generated by our model and *Zhel*, respectively. When comparing them to Fig. 9a we see that our model generates synthetic SAN with both social and attribute clustering coefficient distributions matching well to those of Google+ SAN, which is not the case for *Zhel*.

Significance of building blocks: Recall that our model has two key building blocks that extend preferential attachment via LAPA and also extending triangle closing via focal closure. A natural question is what each of these components contribute toward the overall generative model.

First, we investigate how LAPA impacts the structure of the generated SAN in our model. To this end, we consider an intermediate model with the classical PA (but with the RR-SAN enabled) and compute the previous metrics for SANs generated by this intermediate model. We find that all metrics except the distribution of social *indegree* are qualitatively the same. Figure 18a shows that the distribution of social indegree of the synthetic SAN generated by our intermediate model is very close to a power-law distribution, different from the lognormal distribution generated by our full model shown in Figure 16b and derived from the real Google+ SAN shown in Figure 5. This suggests that the LAPA component is necessary for modeling a key aspect of the Google+ SAN.

Second, we investigate the impact of RR-SAN. The key metric impacted by the focal closure component of RR-SAN is the attribute clustering coefficient. Figure 18b shows the social and attribute clustering coefficients of synthetic SANs generated by our model without RR-SAN (with classical RR enabled). Looking at Figure 17b and Figure 18b together, we see that RR-SAN has a significant impact on the attribute clustering coefficient.

These results confirm both attribute-augmented building blocks, LAPA and RR-SAN, play important but complementary roles in our model in generating synthetic SAN that closely mirrors the real Google+ SAN.

6.2 Application Fidelity

Next, we use two real-world application contexts to evaluate the fidelity of our generative model and the *Zhel* model with respect to a real Google+ snapshot. In each case, we use the metric of interest relevant to each application. Note that all these applications only rely on the social structure.

Sybil defense: In a Sybil attack [14], a single entity emulates the behavior of a large number of identities to compromise the security and privacy properties of a system. Sybil attacks are of particular concern in decentralized systems, which lack mechanisms to vet identities and perform admission control. Several recent works have proposed the use of social trust relationships to mitigate Sybil attacks [14, 59]. Next, we show the fidelity of our model using a representative social network based Sybil defense mechanism called SybilLimit [59].

In order to prevent an adversary from obtaining a large number of attack edges (edges between compromised and honest users), SybilLimit bounds the effective node degree in the social network topology. Following their guidelines, we also imposed a node degree bound of 100 in evaluating their proposal on the different SANs. Figure 19a depicts the number of Sybil identities that an adversary can insert, as a function of number of compromised nodes in the network. We compromised the nodes uniformly at random, and set the SybilLimit parameter $w = 10$. The parameter fc governs the attribute link weight in our RR-SAN component; $fc = 0$ means no focal closure.

We can see that (a) SybilLimit results using the synthetic topology generated by our model are a close match to the real Google+ data, and (b) our model outperforms the baseline approach (*Zhel* model). For example, when the number of compromised nodes is 200,000 the average number of Sybil identities in the Google+ topology is about 25.3 million, while our model predicts 24.5 million (error of 3.1% using $fc = 0.1$). In contrast, the baseline approach has almost 4× worse error with a prediction error of 12.5%. This shows the importance of using attribute information to influence the structure of the social structure (the *Zhel* model only uses the social structure to influence the attribute structure.)

Anonymous communication: Anonymous communication aims to hide user identity (IP address) from the recipient (destination) or from third parties on the Internet such as autonomous systems. The Tor network [12] is a deployed system for anonymous communication that serves hundreds of thousands of users a day. It is widely used by political dissidents, journalists, whistle-blowers, and even law enforcement/military. Recent work [22, 11] has proposed leveraging social links in building anonymous paths for improving resistance to attackers. For example, the Drac [11] system selects proxies (onion routers) by performing a random walk on the social network. For low-latency communications, if the first and the last hops of the forwarding path (onion routing circuit) are compromised, then the adversary can perform end-to-end timing analysis and break user anonymity. Figure 19b depicts the probability of end-to-end timing analysis when random walks on social networks are performed for anonymous communication, using the Google+ social network and our synthetic network. Similar to our Sybil-Limit experiments, we compromise nodes uniformly at random in the network, and impose an upper bound of 100 on the node degree. Again, we can see the accuracy of our model, as well as the improvement over prior work.

6.3 Summary

Via evaluating our model with respect to network metrics and real-world applications, we find that:

- Our model can reproduce SANs that well match Google+ SAN with respect to various network metrics (e.g., degree distributions, joint degree distributions and clustering coefficients.), but the *Zhel* model cannot match several metrics (e.g., social degree distributions, joint degree distributions and clustering coefficient.).
- Our model also performs better than the *Zhel* model for real-world applications such as Sybil defense and anonymous communication.
- The two attribute-augmented building blocks, i.e., LAPA and RR-SAN, play important but complementary roles in our model.

7. DISCUSSION

Using attributes to strengthen defenses: Our evaluation largely focuses on how our model better matches the real-world SAN. We hypothesize that several attack defenses (e.g., Sybil proofing) can also be enhanced by taking into account the attribute structure. For example, we could check if the attribute structure of the nodes matches normal nodes, or even if an attacker manages to obtain a "compromised" edge to one node we can limit the influence of this compromised edge by checking the attribute structure.

LAPA Computation: The LAPA model as described requires a costly linear time (in number of nodes) step when a new node arrives. This is because we have to consider the number of common attributes between the new node and each current node, unlike PA which only needs the global degree distribution. Fortunately, we can approximate LAPA using a practical heuristic. The high-level idea is to pick one of the new node's attributes at random and use PA within the nodes having this attribute. This approximates LAPA as nodes sharing more attributes are more likely to get selected.

Dynamic attributes: Our model currently focuses on static attributes that nodes pick when they join the SAN. In our future work, we plan to incorporate dynamic attributes, and investigate whether the static attribute structure also influences the selection of dynamic attributes. Note that static attributes influence the social structure in our model while the dynamic attributes are influenced by the social structure in the model from Zheleva et al [61].

Parameter inference: We currently use a guided greedy search to empirically estimate model parameters. While this works quite well, we plan to develop a more rigorous parameter inference algorithm based on maximum-likelihood principle [31, 57].

Parsimoniousness of our model: In § 6, we have shown that each component of our model is necessary. However, it's an interesting future work to design a more parsimonious model.

Implications for social network designs: Our results that users sharing common employer attributes are more likely to be linked than users sharing other attributes can help design a better friend recommendation system, which is a very fundamental component of online social networks.

Relationship to heterogeneous networks: Our SAN can be viewed as a heterogeneous network since it consists of multiple types of nodes and links. Heterogeneous networks are shown recently to work better than traditional homogeneous networks for various data mining tasks such as link prediction [17, 58, 48, 49], attribute inference [17, 58] and community detection [51, 50, 62]. It is an interesting future work to generalize our new attribute-related metrics and generative model to other heterogeneous networks.

8. RELATED WORK

Given the growing role of social networks in users' lives and the potential for using such insights for building better systems and applications, there is a rich literature on measuring and modeling social networks. Next, we discuss our work in the context of this related work. At a high-level, our specific new contributions are: (1) we characterize the evolution of a new large-scale network (Google+), and (2) we provide measurement-driven insights and models on the impact of attributes on social network evolution.

Measuring social networks: Many prior efforts characterize social networks using the network metrics we also describe in §3 [26, 28, 29, 38, 25]. Most of these focus on static snapshots; a few notable work also focus on evolutionary aspects similar to our work [3, 56, 4]. With multiple Google+ snapshots crawled around its public release, Schioberg et al. [46] studied a few network metrics, geographic distribution of the users and links, and correlation of users' public information of Google+.

Concurrently, Gonzalez et al. [18] characterize several key features of Google+ during its first 10 months, and compare them to those of Facebook and Twitter. Using a static Google+ snapshot crawled after its public release, Magno et al. [36] identify the key differences between Google+ and Facebook and Twitter, study the adoption patterns of Google+ in different countries, and characterize the variation of privacy concerns across different cultures. Zhao et al. [60] study the early evolution of the Renren social network, and analyze its network dynamics at different granularities to determine their influence on individual users. While we follow the spirit of these works, our work is unique in terms of the specific dataset (i.e., three phases of Google+), the scale of the network, and the fact that we had a singular opportunity to study the evolution across different phases.

There has been recent realization of the importance of user attributes in characterizing social networks [38, 61]. These focus on the influence of social structure on dynamic node attributes (e.g., interest groups). Our work focuses on the orthogonal dimension of analyzing and modeling the influence of static node attributes on social structure formation using Google+.

Modeling social networks: There are two broad classes of models for generating social networks: *static* and *dynamic*. Static models try to reproduce a single static network snapshot [15, 55, 37, 47]. Dynamic models can provide insights on how nodes arrive and create links; these include models such as preferential attachment [5], copying [24], nearest neighbor [2], forest fire [33]. Sala et al. [43] evaluated such models using both network metrics and application benchmarks and showed that the nearest neighbor model outperforms others. The dynamic/generative model by Leskovec et al. mimics the nearest neighbor model in a dynamic setting [29], and thus we use it as our starting point in §5, However, these models are known to generate networks with power-law degree distributions. Many social networks including Google+, however, exhibit lognormal degree distributions [16, 32, 34]. Our dynamic model extends these prior work to provably generate a lognormal distribution for social outdegree. Our model also provides a more general framework by capturing both social and attribute structure.

Modeling social-attribute networks: There has been relatively little work on generating SANs, though a few recent work jointly generating both social structure and node attributes can be viewed as SAN models; the most relevant work is from Zheleva et al. [61] and Kim and Leskovec [23]. Zheleva et al. [61] focus on dynamic attributes; their model generates undirected networks with power-law distribution for social degree and non-lognormal distribution for attribute degree (see Figure 16). Kim and Leskovec model the social and attribute structure simultaneously [23]. Here, both the social degree of attribute nodes and attribute degrees of social nodes follow binomial distribution, which differs from empirically observed SANs. Our model can generate SANs that we confirm through both analysis and simulations to be consistent with real SANs.

9. CONCLUSION

Using a unique dataset collected by crawling Google+ since its launch in June 2011, we provide a first-principled understanding of the attribute structure and its impact on the social structure and their evolutions with the SAN model. We observe several interesting phenomena in the structure and evolution of Google+. For example, the social degree distributions are lognormal, the assortativity is neural while many other social networks have positive assortativities, and the distinct phases in the evolution manifest themselves in the network structure. We also provide new metrics for characterizing the attribute structure and demonstrate that attributes can significantly impact the social structure. Building on these empirical insights, we provide a new generative model for SANs and validate that it is close to the real Google+ SAN using both network metrics and real application contexts. We believe that our work is one of the first steps in this regard and that there are several interesting directions for future work to harness the power of using the attribute structure for designing better social network based systems and applications.

10. ACKNOWLEDGMENTS

We would like to thank Mario Frank, our shepherd Ben Zhao and the anonymous reviewers for their insightful feedback. This work is supported by the NSF TRUST under Grant No. CCF-0424422, NSF Detection under Grant no. 0842695, by the AFOSR under MURI Award No. FA9550-09-1-0539, by the Office of Naval Research under MURI Grant No. N000140911081, the NSF Graduate Research Fellowship under Grant No. DGE-0946797, the DoD National Defense Science and Engineering Graduate Fellowship, by Intel through the ISTC for Secure Computing, and by a grant from the Amazon Web Services in Education program. Any opinions, findings, and conclusions or recommendations expressed in this material are those of the author(s) and do not necessarily reflect the views of the funding agencies.

11. REFERENCES

[1] Microsoft Bing Social vs. Google Search Plus Your World: Showdown. http://www.pcworld.com/article/255476/microsoft_bing_social_vs_google_search_plus_your_world_showdown.html.

[2] A. VAZQUEZ. Growing network with local rules: Preferential attachment, clustering hierarchy, and degree correlations. *Physical Review E* (2003).

[3] AHN, Y.-Y., HAN, S., KWAK, H., MOON, S., AND JEONG, H. Analysis of topological characteristics of huge online social networking services. In *WWW* (2007).

[4] BACKSTROM, L., BOLDI, P., ROSA, M., UGANDER, J., AND VIGNA, S. Four degrees of separation. In *WebSci* (2012).

[5] BARABÁSI, A.-L., AND ALBERT, R. Emergence of scaling in random networks. *Science 286* (1999), 509–512.

[6] BARABÁSI, A.-L., ALBERT, R., AND JEONG, H. Mean-field theory for scale-free random networks. *Physica A 272* (1999).

[7] BI, Z., FALOUTSOS, C., AND KORN., F. The dgx distribution for mining massive, skewed data. In *KDD* (2001).

[8] BOLDI, P., ROSA, M., AND VIGNA, S. Hyperanf: Approximating the neighbourhood function of very large graphs on a budget. In *WWW* (2011).

[9] CHENG, J., ROMERO, D., MEEDER, B., AND KLEINBERG, J. Predicting reciprocity in social networks. In *IEEE Conference on Social Computing* (2011).

[10] CLAUSET, A., SHALIZI, C. R., AND NEWMAN, M. E. J. Power-law distributions in empirical data. *SIAM Review*, 51 (2009).

[11] DANEZIS, G., DIAZ, C., TRONCOSO, C., AND LAURIE, B. Drac: an architecture for anonymous low-volume communications. In *PETS* (2010).

[12] DINGLEDINE, R., MATHEWSON, N., AND SYVERSON, P. Tor: The second-generation onion router. In *USENIX Security* (2004).

[13] DONG, Z.-B., SONG, G.-J., XIE, K.-Q., AND WANG, J.-Y. An experimental study of large-scale mobile social network. In *WWW* (2009).

[14] DOUCEUR, J. R. The sybil attack. In *Proc. IPTPS* (2002).

[15] ERDŐS, P., AND RÉNYI., A. On random graphs i. *Publ. Math. Debrecen 6* (1959), 290–297.

[16] GÓMEZ, V., KALTENBRUNNER, A., AND LÓPEZ, V. Statistical analysis of the social network and discussion threads in slashdot. In *WWW* (2008).

[17] GONG, N. Z., TALWALKAR, A., MACKEY, L., HUANG, L., SHIN, E. C. R., STEFANOV, E., SHI, E., AND SONG, D. Jointly predicting links and inferring attributes using a social-attribute network (san). In *SNA-KDD* (2012).

[18] GONZALEZ, R., CUEVAS, R., REJAIE, R., AND CUEVAS, A. Google+ or google-?: Examining the popularity of the new OSN. In *arXiv:1205.5662v2* (2012).

[19] GOOGLE EVIDENCE OF THE HIGH COVERAGE OF OUR CRAWLED DATASET. https://plus.google.com/106189723444098348646/posts/EanXz8fLwDh.

[20] HOEFFDING, W. Probability inequalities for sums of bounded random variables. *Journal of the American Statistical Association 58*, 301 (1963), 713–721.

[21] HOPCROFT, J., LOU, T., AND TANG, J. Who will follow you back? reciprocal relationship prediction. In *CIKM* (2011).

[22] JOHNSON, A., SYVERSON, P. F., DINGLEDINE, R., AND MATHEWSON, N. Trust-based anonymous communication: adversary models and routing algorithms. In *ACM CCS* (2011).

[23] KIM, M., AND LESKOVEC, J. Multiplicative attribute graph model of real-world networks. *Internet Mathematics 8*, 1-2 (2012), 113–160.

[24] KLEINBERG, J. M., KUMAR, S. R., RAGHAVAN, P., RAJAGOPALAN, S., AND TOMKINS, A. The web as a graph: Measurements, models and methods. In *Proceedings of the International Conference on Combinatorics and Computing* (1999).

[25] KOSSINETS, G., AND WATTS, D. Empirical analysis of an evolving social network. *Science* (2006).

[26] KUMAR, R., NOVAK, J., AND TOMKINS, A. Structure and evolution of online social networks. In *KDD* (2006).

[27] KUMAR, R., RAGHAVAN, P., RAJAGOPALAN, S., SIVAKUMAR, D., TOMKINS, A., AND UPFAL, E. Stochastic models for the web graph. In *FOCS* (2000).

[28] KWAK, H., LEE, C., PARK, H., AND MOON, S. What is twitter, a social network or a news media? In *WWW* (2010).

[29] LESKOVEC, J., BACKSTROM, L., KUMAR, R., , AND TOMKINS, A. Microscopic evolution of social networks. In *KDD* (2008), pp. 462–470.

[30] LESKOVEC, J., CHAKRABARTI, D., KLEINBERG, J., FALOUTSOS, C., AND GHAHRAMANI, Z. Kronecker graphs: An approach to modeling networks. *Journal of Machine Learning Research (JMLR)* (2010).

[31] LESKOVEC, J., AND FALOUTSOS, C. Scalable modeling of real graphs using kronecker multiplication. In *Proceedings of ICML* (2007), pp. 497–504.

[32] LESKOVEC, J., AND HORVITZ, E. Planetary-scale views on a large instant-messaging network. In *WWW* (2008).

[33] LESKOVEC, J., KLEINBERG, J. M., AND FALOUTSOS, C. Graphs over time: densification laws, shrinking diameters and possible explanations. In *KDD* (2005), pp. 177–187.

[34] LIBEN-NOWELL, D., NOVAK, J., KUMAR, R., RAGHAVAN, P., AND TOMKINS, A. Geographic routing in social networks. *PNAS 102*, 33 (2005).

[35] MA, H., ZHOU, D., LIU, C., LYU, M. R., AND KING, I. Recommender systems with social regularization. In *WSDM* (2011).

[36] MAGNO, G., COMARELA, G., SAEZ-TRUMPER, D., CHA, M., AND ALMEIDA, V. New kid on the block: Exploring the google+ social graph. In *IMC* (2012).

[37] MAHADEVAN, P., KRIOUKOV, D., FALL, K., AND VAHDAT, A. Systematic topology analysis and generation using degree correlations. In *SIGCOMM* (2006).

[38] MISLOVE, A., MARCON, M., GUMMADI, K. P., DRUSCHEL, P., AND BHATTACHARJEE, B. Measurement and analysis of online social networks. In *Proc. of ACM SIGCOMM Internet Measurement Conference* (2007).

[39] MISLOVE, A., POST, A., GUMMADI, K. P., AND DRUSCHEL, P. Ostra: Leveraging trust to thwart unwanted communication. In *Proc. NSDI* (2008).

[40] MITZENMACHER, M. A brief history of generative models for power law and lognormal distributions. *Internet Mathematics 1*, 2 (2003), 226–252.

[41] NEWMAN, M. E. J., AND PARK, J. Why social networks are different from other types of networks. *Phys. Rev. E 68*, 3 (2003).

[42] PASTOR-SATORRAS, R., VAZQUEZ, A., AND VESPIGNANI, A. Dynamical and correlation properties of the Internet. *Phys. Rev. Lett. 87* (2001).

[43] SALA, A., CAO, L., WILSON, C., ZABLIT, R., ZHENG, H., AND ZHAO, B. Y. Measurement-calibrated graph models for social network experiments. In *WWW* (2010).

[44] SALA, A., ZHAO, X., WILSON, C., ZHENG, H., AND ZHAO, B. Y. Sharing graphs using differentially private graph models. In *IMC* (2011).

[45] SCHANK, T., AND WAGNER, D. Approximating clustering coefficient and transitivity. *Journal of Graph Algorithms and Applications 9*, 2 (2005), 265–275.

[46] SCHIOBERG, D., SCHNEIDER, F., SCHIOBERG, H., SCHMID, S., UHLIG, S., AND FELDMANN, A. Tracing the birth of an osn: Social graph and profile analysis in google+. In *WebSci* (2012).

[47] STANTON, I., AND PINAR, A. Constructing and sampling graphs with a prescribed joint degree distribution. *CoRR abs/1103.4875* (2012).

[48] SUN, Y., BARBER, R., GUPTA, M., AGGARWAL, C. C., AND HAN, J. Co-author relationship prediction in heterogeneous bibliographic networks. In *ASONAM* (2011).

[49] SUN, Y., HAN, J., AGGARWAL, C. C., AND CHAWLA, N. V. When will it happen?: relationship prediction in heterogeneous information networks. In *WSDM* (2012).

[50] SUN, Y., NORICK, B., HAN, J., YAN, X., YU, P. S., AND YU, X. Integrating meta-path selection with user-guided object clustering in heterogeneous information networks. In *KDD* (2012).

[51] SUN, Y., YU, Y., AND HAN, J. Ranking-based clustering of heterogeneous information networks with star network schema. In *2009*.

[52] TECHCRUNCH EVIDENCE OF THE HIGH COVERAGE OF OUR CRAWLED DATASET. http://techcrunch.com/2011/07/12/google-users-10-million-chart/.

[53] TOIVONEN, R., KOVANEN, L., KIVELÄ, M., ONNELA, J.-P., A, J. S., AND KASKI, K. A comparative study of social network models: Network evolution models and nodal attribute models. *Social Networks 31* (2009), 240–254.

[54] TOOLS FOR FITTING DEGREE DISTRIBUTIONS. http://tuvalu.santafe.edu/$\sim$aaronc/powerlaws/.

[55] WATTS, D. J., AND STROGATZ, S. H. Collective dynamics of 'small-world' networks. *Nature 393* (JUNE 1998).

[56] WILSON, C., BOE, B., SALA, A., PUTTASWAMY, K. P., AND ZHAO, B. Y. User interactions in social networks and their implications. In *Proc. of the 4th ACM European conference on Computer systems* (2009).

[57] WIUF, C., BRAMEIER, M., HAGBERG, O., AND STUMPF, M. P. A likelihood approach to analysis of network data. *PNAS 103*, 20 (2006).

[58] YANG, S., LONG, B., SMOLA, A., SADAGOPAN, N., ZHENG, Z., AND ZHA, H. Like like alike - joint friendship and interest propagation in social networks. In *WWW* (2011).

[59] YU, H., GIBBONS, P. B., KAMINSKY, M., AND XIAO, F. Sybillimit: A near-optimal social network defense against sybil attacks. In *Proc. IEEE Symposium on Security and Privacy* (2008).

[60] ZHAO, X., SALA, A., WILSON, C., WANG, X., GAITO, S., ZHENG, H., AND ZHAO, B. Y. Multi-scale dynamics in a massive online social network. In *Proc. of ACM SIGCOMM Internet Measurement Conference (2012)*.

[61] ZHELEVA, E., SHARARA, H., AND GETOOR, L. Co-evolution of social and affiliation networks. In *KDD* (2009).

[62] ZHOU, Y., CHENG, H., AND YU, J. X. Graph clustering based on structural/attribute similarities. In *VLDB* (2009).

APPENDIX

A. A CONSTANT TIME ALGORITHM FOR APPROXIMATING CLUSTERING COEFFICIENTS

Before going to details of the algorithm and analysis, we introduce a few notations. In both directed or undirected SANs, a triple t consists of three nodes (v, u, w) satisfying $v, w \in \Gamma_s(u)$, where u is called the center and v, w are called the endpoints of t. Moreover, α_t and β_t denote respectively the center node and the two endpoints of t.

Algorithm 2: Constant Time Approximate Algorithm for Computing the Average Clustering Coefficient

Input: (SAN, Ω, K), where $SAN = (V_s, V_a, E_s, E_a)$, Ω is the set of nodes whose average clustering coefficient C_Ω is approximated and K is the number of samples needed.

Output: Approximate average clustering coefficient $\tilde{C}_\Omega$.

begin
- $L \longleftarrow 0$
- $k \longleftarrow 0$
- **while** $k < K$ **do**
  - $k \longleftarrow k + 1$
  - Sample a node u uniformly at random from Ω
  - Sample a pair of nodes v and w uniformly at random from $u's$ social neighbors $\Gamma_s(u)$
  - $L \longleftarrow L + F(v, u, w)$
- **end**
- $\tilde{C}_\Omega \longleftarrow L/(2^I K)$

end

For a directed SAN and a set of triples T, we define a mapping $F : T \longrightarrow \{0, 1, 2\}$, where $F(t = (v, u, w)) = 0$ if v and w are not connected, $F(t = (v, u, w)) = 1$ if they are connected by one directed link and $F(t = (v, u, w)) = 2$ if they are reciprocally linked. For an undirected SAN, the mapping is defined as $F : T \longrightarrow \{0, 1\}$, where $F(t = (v, u, w)) = 0$ if v and w are not connected, otherwise $F(t = (v, u, w)) = 1$. Let I be an indicator variable of the directedness of a SAN, where $I = 0$ when the SAN is undirected, otherwise $I = 1$. With the indicator variable I, we have $0 \leq F(t) \leq 2^I$, which is useful for deriving the approximation bounds in the follows.

For any set of nodes Ω, their average clustering coefficient can be represented as $C_\Omega = \frac{1}{|\Omega|}\sum_{u\in\Omega} c(u) = 2^{-I}\sum_{t\in T_\Omega}\frac{1}{|\Omega|\tau(\alpha_t)}F(t)$, where $T_\Omega = \{t|\alpha_t \in \Omega\}$ and $\tau(\alpha_t) = \frac{1}{2}|\Gamma_s(\alpha_t)|(|\Gamma_s(\alpha_t)| - 1)$ is the number of triples whose center node is α_t. If t is a uniformly distributed random variable over Ω, then we have $C_\Omega = 2^{-I}E[F(t)]$. This observation informs us the design of our approximate algorithm, which is shown in Algorithm 2. Our algorithm computes the average social clustering coefficient when setting $\Omega = V_s$, and the average attribute clustering coefficient when setting $\Omega = V_a$. Note that our algorithm can also be used to compute average clustering coefficient distribution with respect to node degrees. The following theorem bounds the error of our algorithm.

THEOREM 3. *With the number of samples $K = \lceil\frac{\ln 2\nu}{2\epsilon^2}\rceil$, the approximated average clustering coefficient $\tilde{C}_\Omega$ output by our algorithm satisfies $|\tilde{C}_\Omega - C_\Omega| \leq \epsilon$ with probability at least $1 - \frac{1}{\nu}$.*

PROOF. Assume $t_1, t_2, \cdots, t_K$ are K independently and uniformly distributed random variables over the triple set T_Ω. Then we have $C_\Omega = E[\frac{1}{2^I K}\sum_{i=1}^{K} F(t_i)]$. According to Hoeffding's bound [20], we obtain

$$Pr(|\frac{1}{K}\sum_{i=1}^{K} F(t_i) - E[\frac{1}{K}\sum_{i=1}^{K} F(t_i)]| \geq 2^I\epsilon) \leq 2e^{-2K\epsilon^2}.$$

Thus,

$$Pr(|\tilde{C}_\Omega - C_\Omega| \leq \epsilon) \geq 1 - 2e^{-2K\epsilon^2}.$$

So we get $K = \lceil\frac{\ln 2\nu}{2\epsilon^2}\rceil$ by setting $\nu = 2e^{-2k\epsilon^2}$. □

Evolution of a Location-based Online Social Network: Analysis and Models

Miltiadis Allamanis
Computer Laboratory
University of Cambridge
ma536@cam.ac.uk

Salvatore Scellato
Computer Laboratory
University of Cambridge
ss824@cam.ac.uk

Cecilia Mascolo
Computer Laboratory
University of Cambridge
cm542@cam.ac.uk

ABSTRACT

Connections established by users of online social networks are influenced by mechanisms such as preferential attachment and triadic closure. Yet, recent research has found that geographic factors also constrain users: spatial proximity fosters the creation of online social ties. While the effect of space might need to be incorporated to these social mechanisms, it is not clear to which extent this is true and in which way this is best achieved.

To address these questions, we present a measurement study of the temporal evolution of an online location-based social network. We have collected longitudinal traces over 4 months, including information about when social links are created and which places are visited by users, as revealed by their mobile *check-ins*. Thanks to this fine-grained temporal information, we test and compare whether different probabilistic models can explain the observed data adopting an approach based on likelihood estimation, quantitatively comparing their statistical power to reproduce real events. We demonstrate that geographic distance plays an important role in the creation of new social connections: node degree and spatial distance can be combined in a *gravitational attachment* process that reproduces real traces. Instead, we find that links arising because of *triadic closure*, where users form new ties with friends of existing friends, and because of *common focus*, where connections arise among users visiting the same place, appear to be mainly driven by social factors.

We exploit our findings to describe a new model of network growth that combines spatial and social factors. We extensively evaluate our model and its variations, demonstrating that it is able to reproduce the social and spatial properties observed in our traces. Our results offer useful insights for systems that take advantage of the spatial properties of online social services.

Categories and Subject Descriptors

H.4 [**Information Systems Applications**]: Miscellaneous; H.2.8 [**Database Management**]: Database applications—*data mining*

Keywords

social network, graph evolution, gravity models

1. INTRODUCTION

Measurement studies of popular online social services have greatly improved the understanding of how users create social connections online [22]. Research efforts have taken advantage of the availability of large-scale datasets to study the temporal evolution of online social ties [15]. Models of network growth have been proposed to reproduce the global properties observed in real online social networks, such as power-law degree distributions and high clustering coefficient [17].

The fundamental importance of such models is due to the fact that they explain properties observed in measured traces in terms of the actions of individual users: for instance, mechanisms such as preferential attachment [2] and triadic closure [14] are inspired by the actions of individuals creating their social connections. Thus, by offering insights about how users behave, measurements and models of network evolution provide practical applications to link prediction systems [19, 21], but also suggest solutions to large-scale engineering problems faced by online service providers [24]. However, researchers have often neglected factors that are not inherently connected to the structure of the social network itself. In this work we aim to fill this gap, studying the influence of *spatial factors* on connections created by users of a location-based social service.

Spatial properties of social services. Recently, online social networks have integrated location-based features: services such as Foursquare and Gowalla have pioneered the idea of sharing one's geographic location with friends, attracting millions of users over a short period of time. These services offer an additional source of information about user behavior: the geographic mobility of individuals.

Recent works have taken advantage of this opportunity to shed some light on the relationship between spatial factors and online social interactions. For instance, the probability of seeing a social connection between users of online social services decreases with spatial distance [20, 1]. Similar but quantitatively different spatial constraints have been also found in mobile phone communication networks [16, 23].

Online social ties can also be inferred by mining geographic coincidences [7], suggesting that spatial encounters have an effect on the creation of new online connections. The places that online users visit offer even more accurate predictive power about future social connections [8, 27].

The importance of space. The importance of space for online social network goes beyond the definition of more accurate models. In fact, a better understanding of the spatial aspects of the evolution of social networks would greatly benefit engineering approaches based on the spatial constraints of online social ties.

For instance, online interactions tend to be spatially clustered: this geographic locality of interest has been exploited in Facebook interactions, to improve service responsiveness with distributed proxies [31], and in a company's email network, to partition email traffic across storage locations [13]. Spatial differences in content requests arising from online social sharing have been used to reduce latency and bandwidth costs associated to content delivery [29]. The spatial patterns observed in Facebook social connections have been exploited to predict the geographic location of users given their friends' locations [1]. Such engineering efforts confirm that understanding the effect that space has on online social services remains of crucial importance for modern large-scale online platforms.

However, the effect of space on the mechanisms that drive how online users create their links is still largely unknown. In more detail, there has been no investigation of the spatial aspects of the temporal evolution of an online social network: a better understanding of these mechanisms would pave the way to predictive models including geographic factors.

Our work. In this work we study the temporal evolution of a location-based social network: over a period of 16 weeks we have collected daily snapshots of a location-based social network with hundred of thousands of users, Gowalla, including the places visited by users and their social connections (Section 2). Thanks to this fine-grained temporal information about network evolution and users' mobility, we test and compare different edge attachment models that can explain the observed data, adopting an approach based on *likelihood estimation* [32]. This allows us to quantitatively compare these models according to their statistical ability to reproduce the real traces.

In more detail, we analyze these core facets of temporal network evolution:

- **how edges are created**: we test different edge attachment models based on the social and spatial properties of nodes: we show that node degree and spatial distance are simultaneously influencing edge creation, demonstrating that *a gravitational attachment model captures real network evolution better than purely social or spatial models* (Section 3);

- **how social triangles are created**: since social networks tend to have a dominant fraction of new edges closing triangles, we test several different models of triadic closure, some of them involving also spatial distance: we find that *social factors are more important than spatial constraints when an edge closes a triangle* (Section 4);

- **how users' mobility affects new edges**: because social connections might arise among users visiting the same place, we study models of edge creation that exploit the properties of shared places to connect users; we discover that both *the popularity of a place and the popularity of users visiting that place* help to predict which social connections are established (Section 5);

In addition, we study the temporal patterns of user behavior. We focus on the lifetime of a node, that is, the amount of time a user is actively creating new edges, and the inter-edge waiting time, which governs the amount of time elapsed before a node will create a new edge (Section 6).

Based on our findings, *we describe a new family of models of network growth which are able to reproduce both the social and spatial properties observed in the real data* (Section 7). Such models combine a *global gravitational attachment* process with a *local triadic closure* mechanism based on shared friends and shared places; the result is an evolutionary random process that grows a spatial network edge-by-edge. We demonstrate that the resulting synthetic networks exhibit social and spatial properties similar to the real network, while a similar model that considers preferential rather than gravitational attachment, effectively ignoring the effect of geographic distance, fails to reproduce real properties.

This work sheds light on the effect of geographic constraints on the evolution of online social networks. Our results offer useful insights for researchers and practitioners, with promising implications for the wide range of applications that already take advantage of the spatial properties of online social services.

2. MEASUREMENT METHODOLOGY

In this section we illustrate the measurement methodology used in our work to acquire data on a large-scale location-based service, Gowalla. We describe this service, our data collection procedure and we present the basic properties of the resulting dataset. We also introduce the likelihood estimation technique we adopt to quantify how edge attachment models explain the real traces.

2.1 Gowalla

Gowalla is a location-based social networking service created in 2009 that allows users to add friends and share their location with them. It allows users to "check-in" at places through a dedicated mobile application, publicly disclosing their location on the service. These check-ins can then be pushed to friends. As a consequence, friends can see where a user is or has been. Users can create mutual friendship relationships, requiring each user to accept friendship requests. Gowalla was discontinued at the end of 2011 as the company was acquired by Facebook.

2.2 Data collection

Using the public API provided by Gowalla to allow other applications and services to access their content, we have downloaded daily snapshots of Gowalla data between May, 4th and August, 19th 2010.

We built a multi-threaded self-limiting crawler to access their API without incurring into rate limitation. Since users were identified by consecutive numeric IDs, each day we were able to exhaustively gather profiles of all the registered user accounts on the service. Each user profile included information about the number of social connections of that user and the timestamp and the place of his/her last check-in. This

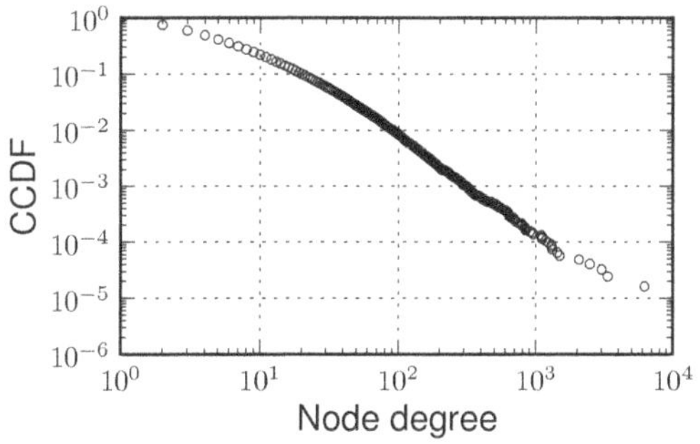

(a) Node degree

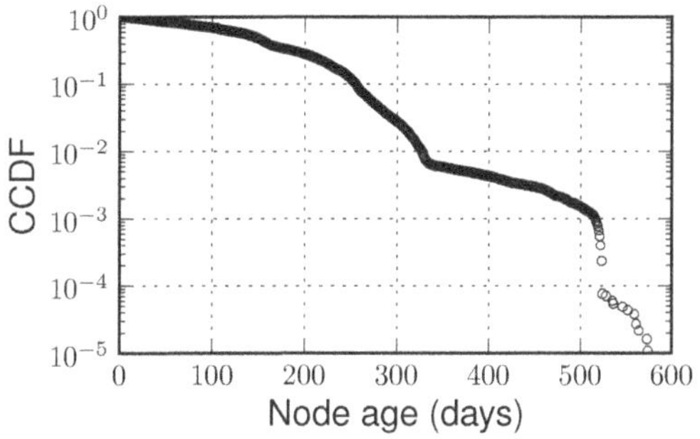

(b) Node age

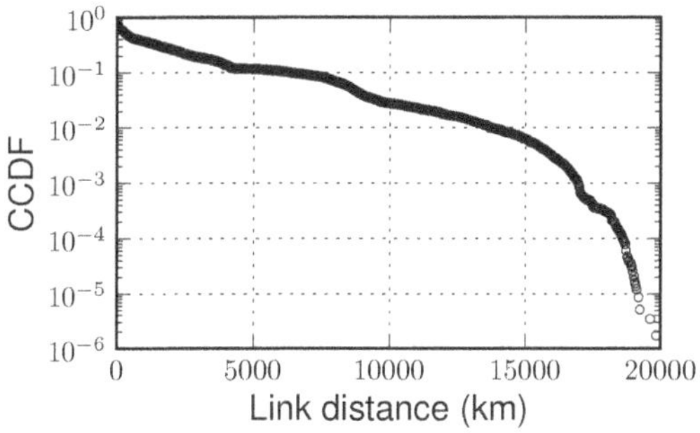

(c) Link length

Figure 1: Complementary Cumulative Distribution Function (CCDF) of node degree (a), node age (b) and link geographic length (c) at the end of the measurement period.

allowed us to additionally download the friend list or the timestamped list of check-ins for all those users which either had new friends or new check-ins with respect to the previous day; we did the same for all the new users that were not registered before. As a result, we have a sequence of daily snapshots, each one including social connections and check-ins for each registered user. We also acquired the geographic coordinates of each place where users had checked in.

This dataset represents a sequence of *complete* snapshots of a large-scale location-based service, offering a chance to study how a social network grows over time and also over space. In particular, we have temporal information about all the social links created during our measurement process. This will allow us to study which social and spatial factors influence how links are created at the microscopic level. Finally, even though we have no temporal information about social connections created before our measurement started,

N	122,030
K	577,014
$\langle k \rangle$	9.28
$\langle C \rangle$	0.254
N_{GC}	116,910 (95.8%)
D_{EFF}	5.43
$\langle l \rangle$	1,792 km
$\langle D \rangle$	5,479 km

Table 1: Properties of the spatial social network at the end of the measurement period: number of nodes N, number of edges K, average node degree $\langle k \rangle$, average clustering coefficient $\langle C \rangle$, number of nodes in the giant component N_{GC}, 90-percentile effective network diameter D_{EFF} average geographic distance between nodes $\langle D \rangle$, average link length $\langle l \rangle$.

we have a reasonable estimation of the first time each user joined the network by observing the list of previous check-ins.

At the end of our measurement period we find about 400,000 registered users, with a total of more than 10 million check-ins across about 1,400,000 distinct places. More precisely, there are only 183,709 users with at least one check-in and only 162,239 with at least one friend. We focus our analysis on 122,030 users that have both friends and check-ins.

2.3 Notation

Formally, we represent the social network of Gowalla users as an undirected graph. We denote by N and K the total number of nodes and edges, while $G_t = (N_t, K_t)$ is the graph composed of the earliest t edges $(e_1, \ldots, e_t)$, with G_T being the final network at the end of the measurement process. The time when edge e was created is $t(e)$ and $t(u)$ is the time when node u joined the network. The degree of node u at time t is $k_u(t)$, while the number of nodes with degree k at time t is denoted as $n_k(t)$.

Every node of this network is embedded in a metric space: in our case, the metric space is the 2-dimensional surface of the planet and we adopt the great-circle distance over the Earth as distance metric. Rank-distance has been suggested as an alternative density-aware distance measure [20]: however, in our study the growing social graph would cause the measure to change as new nodes are added. Thus, we choose to adopt the simpler great-circle distance. We define the location of each user as the geographic location of the place where he/she has more check-ins overall at the end of the measurement period. We denote by D_{ij} the distance between nodes i and j. We assign a length l_{ij} to each social link so that $l_{ij} = D_{ij}$: since node positions do not change over time, link lengths and distances between nodes do not change either.

2.4 Basic properties

The number of nodes and the number of links grows approximately linearly over time, with the number of links growing at a faster pace. on average, the network gains about 375 new nodes and about 1,900 new edges per day. As a result, the average degree of the social network slowly increases: we find that a relationship $K_t \propto N_t^{\rho}$ holds with an exponent $\rho \approx 1.11$, which denotes superlinear growth of the edges with respect to the number of nodes, a sign of densification of the network as time passes by [18]. The main properties of the spatial social network at the end of the measurement period are reported in Table 1. At the end of the measurement period the social network under analysis contains 122,030 nodes and 577,014 edges, with an average degree of 9.28 and an average clustering coefficient of 0.254. The giant component includes 96% of all observed nodes: the 90-th percentile of nodes network distances is 5.43 hops. There is evidence of the small-world effect, as found in other offline and online systems [22, 17]: while the shortest path lengths tend to be only a few hops, the average clustering coefficient is high, suggesting that strong local structures tend to be connected by occasional shortcuts.

The degree distribution exhibits a heavy tail, as depicted in Figure 1(a), with some nodes accumulating thousands of friends. In contrast, both the distribution of node age and link geographic distance, in Figures 1(b)-1(c), do not exhibit heavy tails but instead an almost exponential decay (notice the linear x-axis). We should note that whenever distance is calculated, we have used logarithmic binning with a minimum distance of 1 km. This allows a more robust analysis of the distribution of distances but preserves the distance characteristics of the dataset. There is a large fraction of short-range geographic connections: about 50% of social links span less than 100 km, with only a small fraction being longer than 4,000 km. The distribution of node age shows how users have joined the service with irregular temporal bursts; overall the trend can be approximately described as exponential, particularly for lower values of node age.

2.5 Limitations

Although our dataset represents a complete snapshot of Gowalla, this service was relatively small compared to other massive online social services. Furthermore, we underline a potential demographic bias: typical users of location-based services may have different mobility patterns and social habits than other Web users. In addition, some properties observed in our traces could be attributed to user engagement and Gowalla marketing and would not reflect user behavior in other online geosocial networks. Notwithstanding these limitations potentially present in our dataset, our analysis sheds new light on the spatial and social properties of Gowalla users and our findings can pave the way for further investigation on other services.

2.6 Model likelihood estimation

We take advantage of the fine-grained temporal information of our traces and we adopt a quantitative approach to compare how different attachment models describe the empirical data. We compute the likelihood that a model has to generate the observed events in our sequence of traces. The Maximum Likelihood Principle can then be applied: this principle is used to compare a family of models numerically and, as a result, pick the "best" model (and parameters) to explain the data.

Studying networks with likelihood methods requires a probabilistic model describing the evolution of the graph itself. In other words, the network is considered the result of an evolutionary stochastic process which drives its growth, both in terms of new nodes and new edges [32]. Given real data about the evolution of a network, one can test the extent to which the assumptions of a model are supported by the data.

In our case, estimating the likelihood of a model M involves considering each individual edge $e_t = (i, j)$ created during our measurement period and computing the likelihood $P_M(e_t)$ that the source i selects the actual destination j according to the model M. Thus, the likelihood $P_M(G)$ that model M reproduces graph G is given by the product of the individual likelihoods according to model M:

$$P_M(G) = \prod_t P_M(e_t) \tag{1}$$

We use log-likelihood for better numerical accuracy, obtaining

$$\log(P_M(G)) = \log(\prod_t P_M(e_t)) = \sum_t \log(P_M(e_t)) \tag{2}$$

Equation (2) suggests a simple algorithm to compute the log-likelihood of a given model M: for each new edge created during the graph evolution, we compute the probability that it would be created according to model M, we take the logarithm of this probability and we sum all the values obtained for each edge. When this procedure is repeated for several models, we can choose the model with the highest likelihood to explain the data.

Since every edge is undirected and we do not have information about which user initiated the social contact, we consider every new edge $e_t = (i, j)$ in both directions in the rest of our analysis, to avoid any bias. This methodology can be extended easily to handle directed graphs.

3. EDGE CREATION

In this section we study how the creation of individual edges is influenced by social and spatial properties of the nodes, exploring the effect of node degree, node age and spatial distance on the the edge attachment process.

3.1 Edge attachment by node degree

The preferential attachment model [2] posits that the probability of creating a new connection with a node is proportional to the number of its existing connections. This cumulative advantage held by high-degree nodes results in a degree distribution with heavy tail, as some nodes accumulate a large number of connections. We test if a similar mechanism is governing our data by computing the probability $P_{deg}(k)$ that a new link will be created with a node with degree k:

$$P_{deg}(k) = \frac{|\{e_t : e_t = (i, j) \wedge k_j(t-1) = k\}|}{\sum_t n_k(t-1)} \tag{3}$$

where the normalization factor considers all nodes with degree k just before the edge creation. If preferential attachment is not governing the growth $P_{deg}(k)$ should not depend on k: instead, we see in Figure 2(a) that $P_{deg}(k) \propto k^{0.74}$, denoting how nodes with higher degrees are more likely to attract new edges than nodes with fewer connections. Although the trend is not exactly linear as in the original preferential attachment model, node degree is related to the creation of new edges.

3.2 Edge attachment by node age

The amount of time a node has been part of the network could also be a factor which drives the creation of edges.

Older nodes might have more visibility on the service; at the same time, when new users join the network they might experience intense activity as they create their first connections. We compute $E(a)$, the number of edges created by nodes of age a normalized by the number of nodes that ever achieved age a [17]:

$$E(a) = \frac{|\{e_t : e_t = (i,j) \wedge t(e) - t(i) = a\}|}{\sum_t |\{n : T - t(n) \geq a\}|} \quad (4)$$

where T is the time when the last node joined the network during the measurement period. As reported in Figure 2(b), there is a spike at age 0: this represents nodes that join the network, create some links and then never come back. The number of created edges then quickly goes down with age a but grows again for higher values of a. This denotes that older nodes might benefit from receiving incoming links. The overall effect suggests that there is an abnormal spike of links created when a node joins the network followed by lower levels of edge creation: older nodes tend then to establish further links.

3.3 Edge attachment by node distance

The probability of having a social connection between two individuals decreases with their distance, although the exact functional form of this relationship is still under debate and appears slightly different in different systems [20, 1, 26]. We compute the probability $P_{geo}(d)$ that a new edge spans geographic distance d, normalized by the number of nodes at distance d from the source:

$$P_{geo}(d) = \frac{|\{e_t : e_t = (i,j) \wedge D_{ij} = d\}|}{\sum_t |\{n : D_{in} = d\}|} \quad (5)$$

Our data show how $P_{geo}(d)$ decreases with distance d, as reported in Figure 2(c), even though the trend appears noisy: in particular, the data roughly follow a trend $P_{geo}(d) \approx d^{-\alpha}$ with $\alpha = 0.6$ (depicted). While a similar functional form has been found in other spatial social networks, but with different exponents α, this is the first time it is measured at microscopic level on individual edge creation events. The main difference is that in this case there is a lower value of α, while other systems exhibit values closer to 1 [26]. Nonetheless, geographic distance affects the edge creation process in a straightforward way: longer links have a lower probability of appearance than short-range ones.

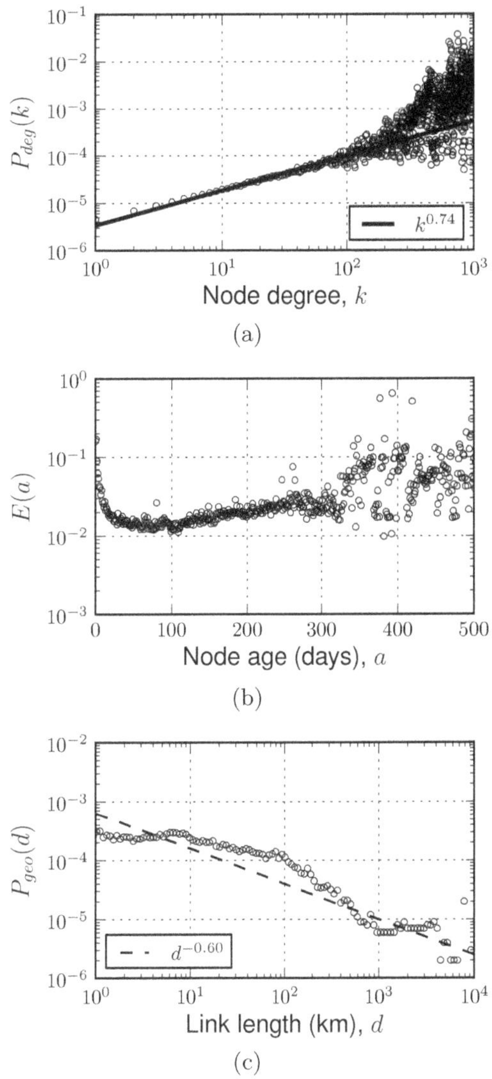

Figure 2: Probability of creating a new social link as a function of node degree (a), age of the node (b) and geographic distance of the node (c).

3.4 Evidence of gravitational attachment

The effect of node degree on network evolution is well captured by the preferential attachment model, where the probability of connection between nodes i and j, P_{ij}, is proportional to the degree of node j, $P_{ij} \propto k_j$. This model generates networks with degree distribution exhibiting a heavy tail, as there are a few nodes, the so called "hubs", that accumulate an extremely high number of connections. Real-world examples such as transportation and communication networks can be described by a preferential attachment model, but geographic distance is an important parameter as well. In fact, long-range connections tend to exist mainly between well-connected hubs [5].

The effect of geographic distance can be included in the attachment probability, $P_{ij} \propto k_i k_j f(D_{ij})$, where f is a decreasing *deterrence function* of the geographic distance D_{ij} between the nodes. Thus, long distances tend to be covered only to connect to important hubs, while nodes with less connections become attractive when they can be reached over a short distance. When the deterrence function has a simple functional form such as $f(d) \sim d^{-\alpha}$, then the probability of a connection between two nodes becomes similar to the gravitational attraction between celestial bodies, $P_{ij} \propto \frac{k_i k_j}{D_{ij}^{\alpha}}$. Hence, this family of attachment models has been known as *gravity models* [6]. We want now to understand whether there is any evidence that similar factors are shaping the evolution of our real spatial social network.

A consequence of the gravity model is that nodes with higher degrees tend to attract longer links: thus, we define $\lambda_i(k)$ as the geographic length of the k-th edge created by user i and we study $\lambda(k)$ for different values of k. The influence of degree k on the geographic properties of social links appears strong: as described in Figure 3, both the average and the median value of the geographic length $\langle\lambda(k)\rangle$ of the k-th edge increase with k: while the average length of the first edge is about 1,100 km, the 100th edge is about 2,400

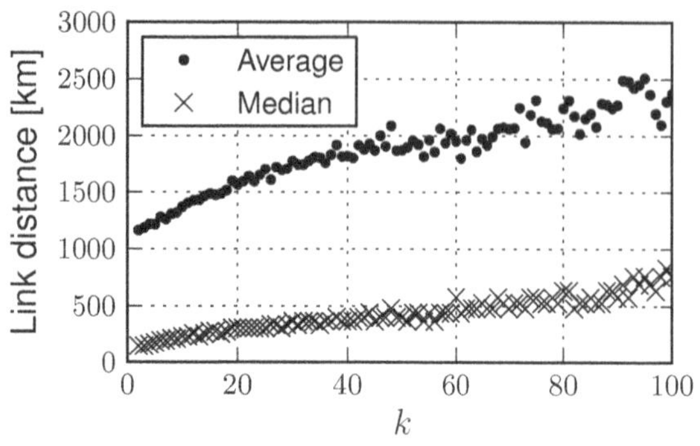

Figure 3: Average and median geographic span gap of the k-th edge created by a node as a function of k.

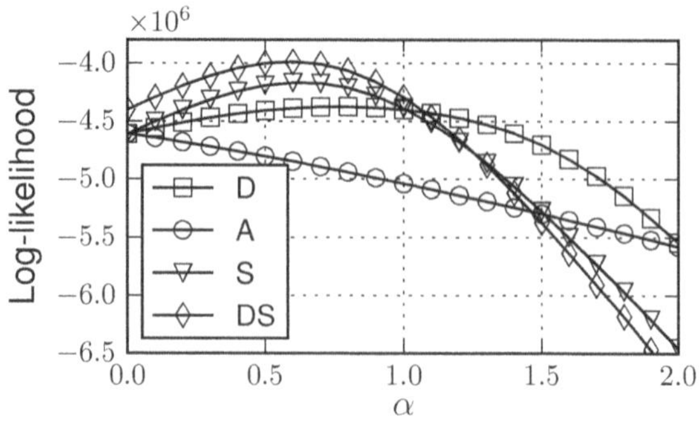

Figure 4: Log-likelihood of each edge attachment model as a function of their parameter α. The gravity model DS outperforms all the others.

km. The median value shifts in accordance with k, increasing from 150 km to more than 900 km for higher degrees. These findings are compatible with a gravity model where node degree and geographic distance simultaneously influence social connections created over space, as we will see in the next section.

3.5 Evaluation of attachment models

With our analysis we have discovered that individual node properties and geographic distance affect how edges are created. Our aim is now to understand what type of edge attachment mechanisms better explain the temporal evolution of the network.

We deliberately choose simple models, since our goal is not to accurately reproduce the temporal evolution of the network but rather to understand which factors mainly drive its growth. We consider 4 different edge attachment models, each one with a single parameter α:

- D: the probability of creating an edge with node n is proportional to a power α of its degree: $k_n(t)^\alpha$
- A: the probability of creating an edge with node n is proportional to a power α of its age: $a_t(n)^\alpha$
- S: the probability of creating an edge with node n is inversely proportional to a power α of its spatial distance from source i: $D_{in}^{-\alpha}$
- DS: the probability of creating an edge with node n is proportional to its degree and inversely proportional to a power α of its spatial distance from i: $k_n(t)D_{in}^{-\alpha}$

Figure 4 displays the log-likelihood values obtained by each model as a function of the parameter α. First, we note that the models S and DS, which incorporate geographic distance, have higher log-likelihood than the other two models D and A, with the maximum log-likelihood achieved by DS. The maximum log-likelihood for DS is achieved for $\alpha \approx 0.6$, which is in agreement with the results obtained measuring $P_{geo}(d)$. Node age does not seem a key factor for edge attachment, as the model A shows decreasing values of log-likelihood for values of α between 0 and 2, with its maximum log-likelihood of -4.4×10^6 reached instead only for $\alpha = -0.8$, failing to outperform S and DS. Indeed, we have tested models which also combine node age with geographic distance and node degree, but they do not exhibit significant improvements with respect to the models without node age. Hence, it seems that *the main driving factors, of those examined, in edge attachment are node degree and geographic distance* and that a gravity model which combines them is the most suitable option.

4. SOCIAL TRIADIC CLOSURE

The edge attachment mechanisms previously investigated only take into account the influence of global network properties on new edge creation. However, local network properties can be equally or more important: for instance, new links tend to connect users that already share friends, creating social triangles that are extremely common on social networks [19]. This mechanism, where a node just copies a connection from a node it is already connected to, has turned out to be essential to reproduce the structure observed in many networks [25]. Hence, in this section our aim is to study the extent to which new links generate social triangles and whether different models based on local network properties can reproduce the patterns observed in the data.

4.1 Measuring triangle creation

Social connections tend to link together individuals that are already at close social distance: the vast majority of new links tend to be between nodes that already share at least a connection, thus only 2 hops away from each other, with larger social distances exponentially less likely [17]. We notice a similar pattern in our data: Figure 5(a) shows that the number of edges E_h that connect nodes h hops away exponentially decays with h. Furthermore, many edges also connect nodes that were not in the same connected component, as when a new node joins the network and creates its first link.

A better understanding of this process can be achieved by considering not only how many new links connect nodes h hops away, but also considering the number of nodes at that social distance. In fact, since E_h exponentially decreases with h and the number of available nodes increases with h, the probability P_h that a new link spans h hops must be decreasing much faster than exponentially. More precisely, we compute P_h as

$$P_h = \frac{|\{e_t : e_t = (i,j) \wedge d_{t-1}(i,j) = h\}|}{\sum_t |\{n : d_{t-1}(i,n) = h\}|} \qquad (6)$$

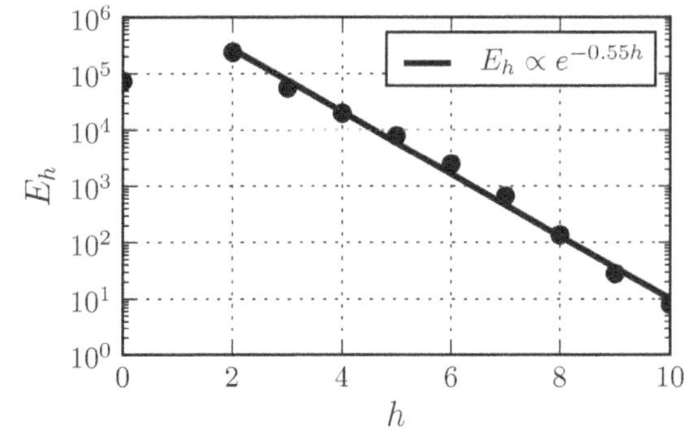

(a)

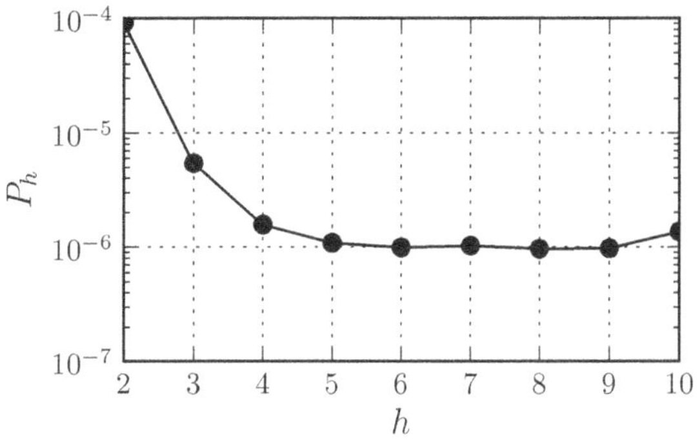

(b)

Figure 5: Number of new links E_h created between nodes h hops away (a) and probability P_h that a new link connects nodes h hops away. The single E_h value at $h = 0$ denotes the number of edges connecting nodes previously in separate disconnected components.

where $d_t(i, j)$ is the number of hops between nodes i and j at time t. Figure 5(b) plots P_h as a function of h: the probability quickly decays and finally reaches a constant value. Triadic closure seems to be the predominant factor shaping network growth over time: new edges are most likely to connect people who already share at least one friend.

In summary, our analysis of triadic closure provides evidence that two users sharing at least one friend are much more likely to create direct connections than two users without friends in common.

4.2 Triangle-closing models

Since a vast majority of new edges close social triangles, our aim is now to understand what factors influence which node to choose when an edge is closing a triangle. Again, we make use of the maximum likelihood principle to test and compare whether different triangle-closing models would be able to generate the triangles created during the real network evolution.

We consider the case when a source node s has to choose another target node t 2 hops away to create a new link. A simple model would be for node s to choose t uniformly at random from all the nodes at a distance of 2 hops, which will be our baseline model. We then take into account more complex models where a source node s first chooses according to a given strategy an intermediate node i among its neighbors

	random	shared	degree	distance	gravity
random	**12.34**	9.48	-3.47	-28.17	-35.26
shared	**14.54**	11.47	-0.95	-24.74	-34.46
degree	7.33	5.16	-6.79	-25.17	-41.98
distance	-0.92	-3.70	-16.94	-39.32	-41.53
gravity	2.71	0.25	-12.11	-33.01	-43.18

Table 2: Performance of different triangle closing models: on each row there is the model to pick the intermediate node and on each column the model to then pick the target node. The value in each cell gives the percentage improvement over the baseline, which is the log-likelihood of choosing a random node two hops away from the source.

and then picks a target t among i's neighbors with, potentially, a different strategy. The edge (s, t) is then created, closing the triangle (s, i, t). Since every strategy involves only choosing a node among the neighbors of a given node, we consider 5 different strategies to choose a neighbor v of a given node u:

- random: uniformly at random;
- shared: proportional to the number of shared friends between u and v;
- degree: proportional to the degree of the neighbor v;
- distance: inversely proportional to the geographic distance between u and v;
- gravity: proportional to the degree of v and inversely proportional to the geographic distance between u and v.

Since there are 5 different triangle-closing models, there are 25 combinations: we compute the log-likelihood of each combination and we measure the percentage improvement over the log-likelihood of the baseline model. The results are presented in Table 2: the general trend is that random and shared offer the largest improvements over the baseline, with a maximum improvement of 14.54% in the combination shared-random and 12.34% for random-random. Instead, models based on degree or on distance have performance much lower than the baseline, with degradation up to 40% when the gravity model is adopted. In particular, the random-random model works surprisingly well, as it favors connections between nodes that have multiple 2-hop paths between them and that have higher degrees, while being extremely simple and computationally fast.

These results show that *triadic closure is mainly driven by social processes*. Nonetheless, it only reproduces some aspects of network evolution, as edges that do not close triangles are also arising in the network. As we will see, we can exploit users' mobility information to understand how other online social connections are created, adopting closure models based on the *places* visited by online users.

5. MOBILITY-DRIVEN CLOSURE

The edge attachment mechanisms discussed so far do not include any information on users' mobility. However, the places where users check in could help explain how new social ties are created. According to the *common focus* theory [10],

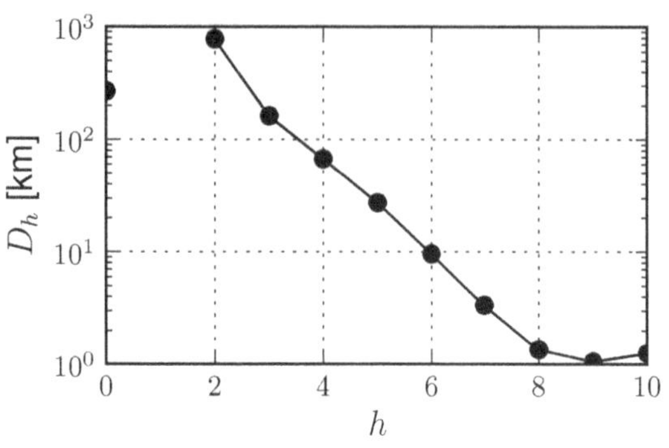

Figure 6: Average geographic distance D_h of new links created between nodes h hops away. The single value at $h = 0$ denotes the average geographic distance of links connecting nodes previously in separate disconnected components.

individuals who visit the same places tend to establish new social connections. In this section we measure the impact that users' mobility has on network evolution. In agreement with the common focus theory, we study edge attachment mechanisms that connect users that visit the same places.

5.1 Measuring mobility-based attachment

In our Gowalla traces, 32.28% of all new edges are established between users that share at least one common place. In particular, about 10% of new links are created between users that do share common places, but no common friends. This means that adopting only social triadic closure mechanisms would fail to reproduce that users create new social connections beyond their 2-hop neighborhood.

The importance of social ties that connect users without friends in common is confirmed when we examine the average geographic distance D_h of all new edges that connect nodes previously h hops away, shown in Figure 6. There is an evident trend: *social connections at shorter social distance tend to have higher geographic distances, while links spanning more hops have lower spatial distance.* A potential explanation is that both social and spatial factors tend to affect the edge creation process: a new link is created either between users sharing friends, even if they are far from each other, or between spatially close users, even if they have no friends in common. In particular, *geographic proximity becomes complementary to social closeness*: both factors are shaping the network, but in different ways. The challenge is to go beyond geographic distance when modeling the evolution of the network: mobility-based attachment provides the additional source of information, based on the places visited by users. Such information may be important to model network evolution, since it provides more accurate geographic information than users' home locations.

5.2 Mobility-driven closure models

We consider mobility-driven closure models to be two-step processes. A source node s first selects a place $p \in P_s$, where P_s is the set of all places where node s has checked in; then, given place p a target note $t \in Q_p$ is selected, where Q_p is the set of all nodes that have checked in at place p. We consider different strategies that a node u adopts to select a place p from the set P_u:

- random: uniformly at random;
- friends: proportional to the number of user u's friends that have visited p;
- user-checkins: proportional to the number of check-ins made by user u at p;
- tot-checkins: proportional to the total number of check-ins made at p by all users;
- tot-users: proportional to the total number of users who have checked in at p;
- place-distance: inversely proportional to the distance between user u's home location and p;
- place-gravity: proportional to the total number of check-ins made by all users at place p and inversely proportional to the distance between user u's home location and p.

Given a selected place p, we then consider another set of strategies to select a target user t from Q_p:

- random: uniformly at random;
- degree: proportional to user t's degree;
- deg-diffusion: proportional to user t's degree and inversely proportional the logarithm of user t's total number of visited places;
- user-checkins: proportional to user t's number of check-ins at p;
- tot-checkins: proportional to user t's total number of check-ins;
- inv-tot-checkins: inversely proportional to user t's total number of check-ins;
- distance: inversely proportional to the distance between user t's home location and p;
- gravity: proportional to user t's degree and inversely proportional to the distance between user t's home location and p.

To test and evaluate mobility-driven models we use again the maximum likelihood principle; we only evaluate the likelihood that a model has to reproduce real edge attachments where the source and target nodes share at least one place. We adopt a baseline model that selects at random target users from the set of all users that share places with the source. Table 3 presents the results for all the possible combinations.

In general, in the first step the best improvement is given by selecting a popular place that has already been visited by many users, friends or not. For the second step, node degree plays an important role, akin to a local preferential attachment. The greatest improvement over the baseline is provided by first selecting a place that has been visited many times (tot-checkins) and then choosing a node proportionally to its degree "diffused" over the number of visited places (deg-diffusion). This mobility measure corrects for the fact that popular users that visit only a few places might be more related to that place, thus enticing other visitors to

	random	degree	deg-diffusion	user-checkins	tot-checkins	inv-tot-checkins	distance	gravity
random	0.28	6.88	9.24	0.16	-17.02	-4.51	-19.36	-7.04
friends	4.70	**11.60**	**13.63**	4.74	-10.63	-1.56	-14.88	-1.71
user-checkins	0.05	6.59	8.94	-0.03	-17.27	-4.80	-19.69	-7.41
tot-checkins	6.09	**13.13**	**15.18**	6.14	-9.29	0.04	-13.15	-0.02
tot-users	5.10	**12.33**	**14.33**	5.16	-9.96	-1.08	-14.19	-0.84
place-distance	-23.41	-15.57	-13.21	-23.56	-40.82	-28.27	-43.67	-30.17
place-gravity	0.37	7.22	9.46	0.32	-16.26	-5.29	-19.60	-6.81

Table 3: Performance of mobility-driven closure models: on each row there is a model to pick the intermediate place and on each column a model to then pick the target node. The value in each cell gives the percentage improvement over the baseline, which is the log-likelihood of choosing a node at random among all the nodes that share at least one place with the source.

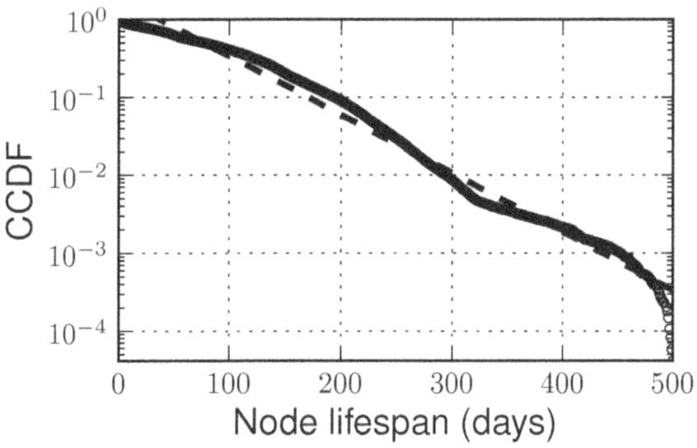

Figure 7: Complementary Cumulative Distribution Function (CCDF) of node lifespan and exponential fit.

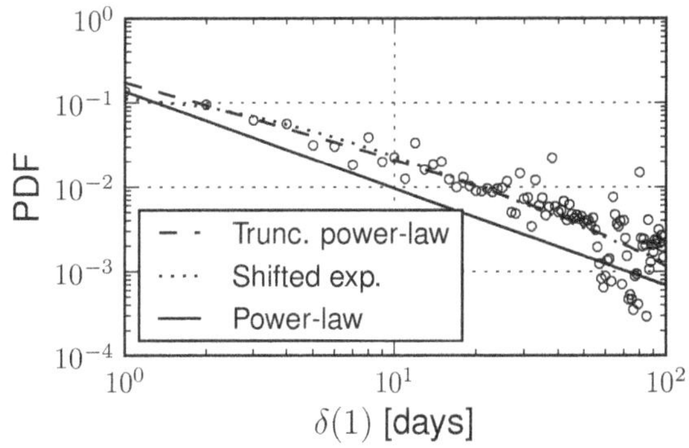

Figure 8: Probability Distribution Function (PDF) of $\delta(1)$, the temporal gap elapsing between the time when the first and the second edge are created by a user. The fits show a power law, an exponentially truncated power law and a shifted exponential.

connect. The tot-checkins-degree model has a similar but slightly inferior performance, yet it is simpler and computationally faster.

In addition to the models presented in Table 3, we experimented with variations of tot-users and tot-checkins where we use a probability of attachment *inversely* proportional to the total number of users or check-ins. All these models provided inferior performance compared to the baseline.

6. TEMPORAL EVOLUTION

In this section we study how users create new connections as they spend more time on the network. We study the amount of time users remain active for, their lifespan; then, we investigate the inter-edge temporal gap between the creation of consecutive edges. In this section we consider only users that joined the service after our measurement process started, in order to observe their behavior from the very first moment.

6.1 Node lifespan

We define the *lifespan* of a node as the difference between the time the node created the last and the first edge. Figure 7 plots the distribution of lifespan for all users: the distribution shows an approximately exponential behavior, with a deviation only at longer lifespans for few users who were early adopters and started using the service from the very first days. The fit is reasonably accurate for a wide range of lifespan values.

6.2 Inter-edge temporal gap

Different users can show significant differences in the pace they add new edges: users with higher degree create new ties at a faster rate. Thus, we study $\delta_i(k)$, the temporal gap between the k-th and $k+1$-th edges of user i, for different values of k.

Figure 8 displays the probability distribution of $\delta(1)$, the amount of time between the first and the second edges created by a user. Even though many users add their second edge after a few days, some wait for several weeks. The distribution can be reproduced by different functional forms: an exponentially truncated power law $\delta(1)^{-\alpha_1} exp(-\delta(1)/\beta_1)$ yields a slightly higher log-likelihood than a pure power-law, a shifted exponential and an exponential; the average log-likelihood improvement over the exponential fit is about 5%. This result also holds for different values of k.

Then, we study the effect of current degree k: in particular, we are interested in how the probability distribution of $\delta(k)$ changes with k. A first indication is given in Figure 9(a), which plots the average temporal gap $\langle\delta(k)\rangle$ between the k-th and $k+1$-th edges for different values of k: users with higher degrees tend to wait, on average, for a shorter amount of time. In fact, users wait on average 20 days before adding their second edge but only 7 days when they have about 100 friends. While α_k tends to be unrelated to k, the exponential cut-off β_k becomes smaller as k grows larger, as seen in Figure 9(b). The final effect is that nodes with higher degrees are more likely to wait for

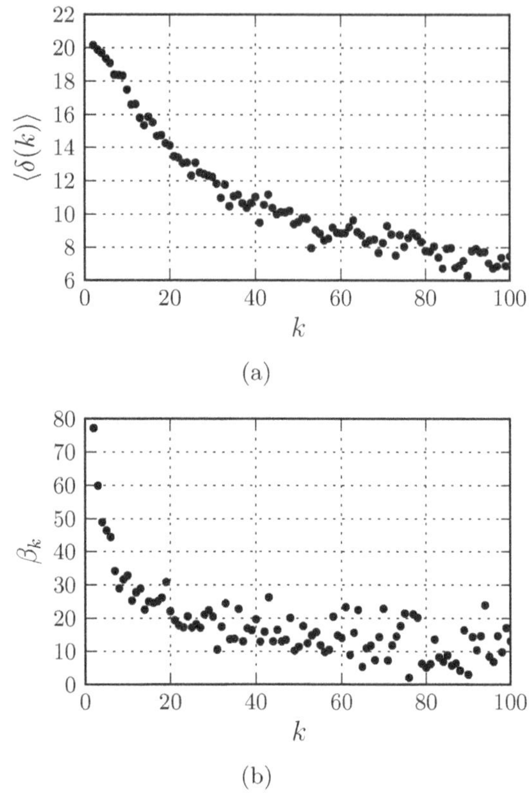

Figure 9: Average temporal gap $\langle\delta(k)\rangle$ between the k-th and $k+1$-th edge (a) and exponential cut-off β_k (b) in the truncated power law $p(\delta(k)) \propto \delta(k)^{-\alpha_k} exp(-\delta(k)/\beta_k)$, as a function of node degree k.

a shorter time span, as the truncated tail of the power law $P(\delta(k))$ increasingly constrains larger gap values.

It is not surprising that nodes with higher degree add links at a higher pace: given a fixed temporal period, as in our measurement, higher degree nodes add more links than lower degree ones, so their activity has to be faster in the same temporal period. Nonetheless, this heterogeneous temporal behavior is crucial to foster the heterogeneity observed in the degree distribution of social systems [17].

7. PUTTING IT ALL TOGETHER: NEW MODELS

We have seen that a gravity-based attachment, combining spatial distance and node degree, influences how new edges are created (in Section 3). At the same time, we have discussed that triadic and mobility-based closure are mainly shaped by social factors rather than geographic ones (in Section 4 and 5). These two mechanisms seem to be complementary: while the gravity attachment is responsible for edges connecting together different parts of the network, the closure mechanisms seem involved in the creation of local edges between nodes that already share either a friend or a place. Finally, we have analyzed how nodes tend to become faster and faster in creating new edges as they get more connections (in Section 6). Building on all these results, our aim is now to define network growth models which are able to reproduce the spatial and social properties observed in the real network. We stress that the goal of our models is not to accurately reproduce the network or predict edge creation events, but to describe the fundamental mechanisms affecting user behavior.

7.1 Model definition

Following the methodology presented in [17], we describe our model as a simple algorithm to grow a network one node, and one edge, at a time. Our model combines global attachment mechanisms and local closure mechanisms:

1. A new node u joins the network according to a certain arrival discipline and positions itself over the space;
2. A new node u samples its lifetime from an exponential distribution;
3. Node u adds its first edge to node v according to a global connection model (preferential or gravity-based attachment);
4. A node with degree k samples a time gap δ from a distribution $p(\delta(k)) \propto \delta(k)^{-\alpha_k} exp(-\delta(k)/\beta_k)$ and then goes to sleep for δ time steps;
5. When a node wakes up, if its lifetime has not expired yet it creates a new edge: with probability p the node uses the random – random social triangle-closing model, otherwise it uses the tot-checkins – degree mobility-based closure.
6. The node repeats step 4.

The probability p allows us to assess the impact that the local closure models have on overall accuracy. In particular, we adopt two variations: we use $p = 1$ so that the model only includes social triadic closure, and we adopt $p = 0.66$ to introduce also mobility-driven closure (this value is motivated by the observed frequency of edge attachments in the real data). This yields a total of 4 different combinations: gravity-based (G), gravity-based with mobility-driven closure (GM), preferential attachment (P) and preferential attachment with mobility-driven closure (PM).

Finally, we note that local closure models only account for about two-thirds of all new social links. The remaining fraction includes ties between users that do not share common friends and that do not visit the same places. Thus, we introduce a variation into our models whose aim is to adopt global attachment models also during a node's lifetime, and not only in step 3. In more detail, when a node wakes up in step 5, with probability $q = 0.33$ it creates an edge according to the global attachment mechanisms; otherwise, the model proceeds as defined. This yields 4 additional model combinations, for a total of 8 combinations. We will present our results separately for combinations that do and do not trigger global attachment mechanisms during a node's lifetime.

7.2 Evaluation

To test our model we take the real network at the beginning of our measurement, G_t, and simulate its growth by adding the missing nodes and check-ins, with their real geographic locations, and the check-ins according to when and where they happen in the real network. However, once they

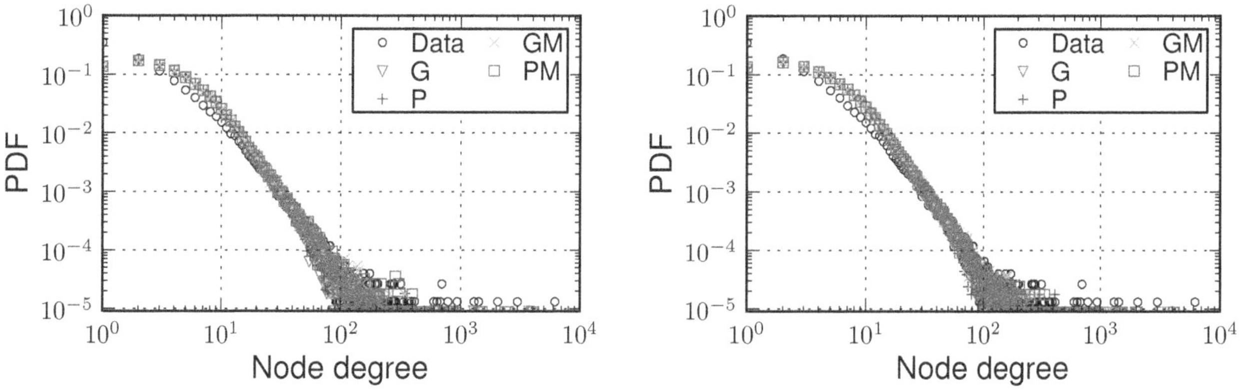

(a) Without global attachment (b) With global attachment

Figure 10: Probability distribution function (PDF) of node degree for real data and different models: gravity-based (G), gravity-based with mobility-driven closure (GM), preferential attachment (P), preferential attachment with mobility-driven closure (PM).

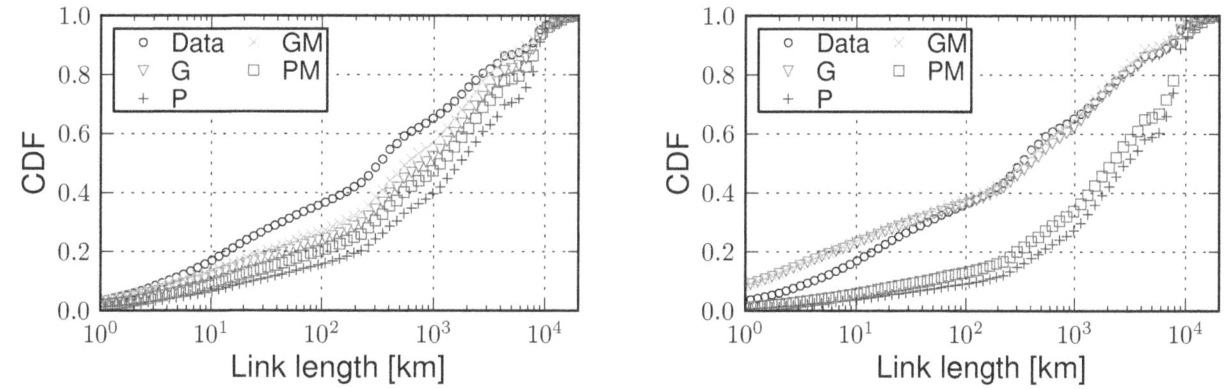

(a) Without global attachment (b) With global attachment

Figure 11: Cumulative distribution function (CDF) of link geographic length for real data and different models: gravity-based (G), gravity-based with mobility-driven closure (GM), preferential attachment (P), preferential attachment with mobility-driven closure (PM).

join the network they add new edges according to our algorithmic model. We stop the evolution when the simulated network has the same number of nodes as the real one, G_T.

All 8 model combinations are run 10 times with different random seeds and then their properties are averaged over all these realizations. When computing the properties shown in Figures 10, 11, 12 and 13 we only consider edges added after the start of our measurement period, both in the real network and in the simulated models, to avoid that the properties of the initial graph G_t dominate the final result.

The degree distribution observed in the real network and the two models are depicted in Figure 10: all models are able to reproduce the distribution, capturing the social properties of the real network. There is no noticeable difference between models with and without global attachment. However, as shown in Figure 11, the probability distribution of link geographic length is closer to the real one for gravity-based model, while models P and PM have links with longer geographic length. We note that models with global attachment have more similar characteristics than those without: the effect is that models G and GM reproduce better the real distribution, while social links created by models P and PM tend to span longer geographic distance. This suggests a positive effect of a gravity-based global attachment mechanism on the accuracy of the model.

Another important difference between the gravity-based and the preferential attachment models is highlighted by considering the geometric average distance of the links of a user as a function of the node degree. As seen in Figure 12, models G and GM show an increasing trend as the original data, while, on the contrary, models P and PM have weaker correlation between node degree and geographic length of the links. Again, global attachment emphasizes the difference between gravity-based and preferential attachment models, with the first ones reproducing more accurately the real trend. A similar behavior is observed in Figure 13 the preferential attachment models create triangles on a much wider geographic scale than models G and GM, which are closer to the real data.

We note that when mobility-based closure is used results always marginally improve with respect to models with only social triadic closure. This performance increase can be

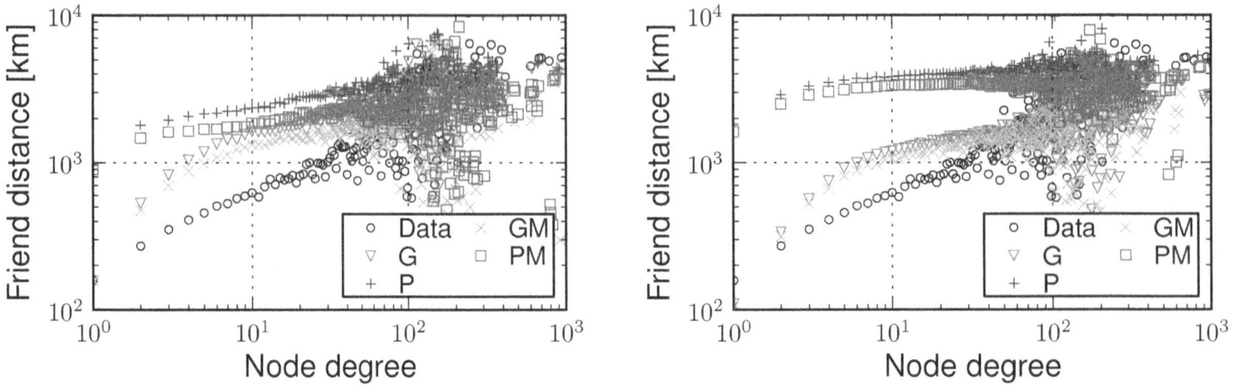

(a) Without global attachment

(b) With global attachment

Figure 12: Average geographic friend distance as a function of node degree for real data and different models: gravity-based (G), gravity-based with mobility-driven closure (GM), preferential attachment (P), preferential attachment with mobility-driven closure (PM).

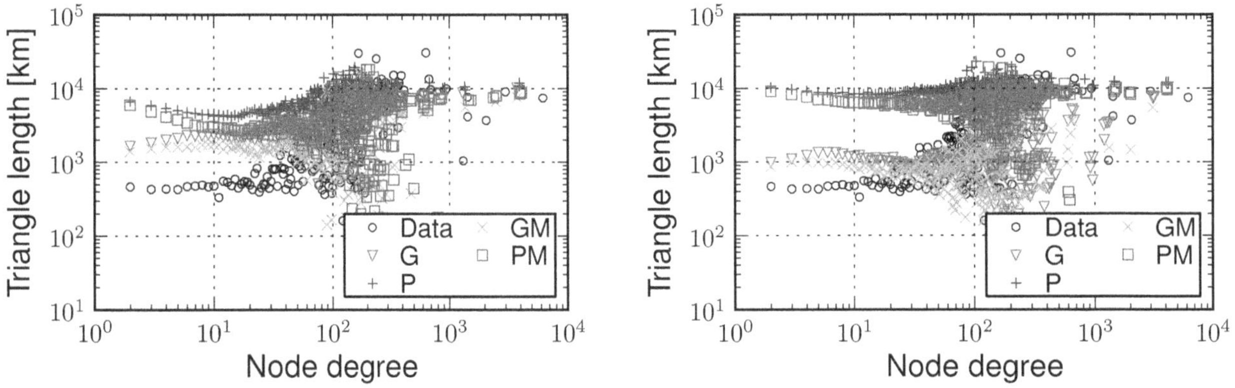

(a) Without global attachment

(b) With global attachment

Figure 13: Average geographic triangle length as a function of node degree for real data and different models: gravity-based (G), gravity-based with mobility-driven closure (GM), preferential attachment (P), preferential attachment with mobility-driven closure (PM).

attributed to the latent geographic information embedded in user check-ins. The effect of global attachment is even stronger, as it enhances the accuracy of gravity-based models, while also reducing the validity of preferential attachment models. These results confirm that the effect of geographic distance can not be neglected when social networks are studied and modeled: preferential attachment mechanisms need to be modified into gravity-based mechanisms, which are able to correctly balance the effects of node attractiveness and the connection costs imposed by spatial distance. Furthermore, mobility-based closure improves model accuracy, offering additional information about the geographic whereabouts of online users.

7.3 Implications

The importance of our findings goes beyond the definition of accurate models of network evolution. Our results show that the effect of geographic distance cannot be neglected when online social networks are studied and modeled. In reality, preferential attachment and triadic closure together are already able to reproduce the global social properties observed in real social networks, namely the degree distribution and the level of clustering. However, neglecting spatial information about where users are located fails to account for the effect of distance. In real systems users preferentially connect over short distances, resulting in a considerable fraction of short-range ties; instead, ignoring spatial constraints would predict an unlikely majority of long-range connections. This goes against empirical evidence, both in offline and online social systems.

Our findings support the idea that distance has a simple effect on the creation of social ties: the probability of connection between two individuals decreases as a negative power of the spatial distance between them. Yet, this effect must be combined with a process based on "popularity" or "visibility" that introduces heterogeneity across users, such as attachment to the best connected nodes, in order to fully recreate the self-reinforcing mechanisms that lead to the scale-free degree distributions observed in social graphs.

Gravity mechanisms provide an elegant and insightful way

of combining the effect of distance and the influence of social factors. Surprisingly, the influence of distance on the formation of social triads appears negligible, as other factors become more important at this level. The main implication of the gravity mechanism is that one user may be interested in another because the other user is hugely popular, regardless of their spatial distance, or because the other user is spatially close, *regardless of popularity and importance.* These mechanisms can be adopted in scenarios where the future evolution of an online social graph has to be estimated: some examples include security mechanisms for online services [1], the design of distributed storage solutions for massive social graphs [24] and the delivery of user-generated content [29].

The overall picture is that proximity both over physical and social dimensions fosters the creation of new social links; the result is that the likelihood of a new connection increases when two individuals share many other connections or when two individuals are close to each other. We also point out that no friend recommendation mechanism was in place on the online service under analysis during the measurement period.

This dual role of proximity has promising applications in a wide range of systems. In particular, despite the abundance of friend recommendation services, only few of them have included spatial closeness in their systems [8, 27]. Our work provides new insights for further research in this direction.

8. RELATED WORK

The temporal patterns of network evolution have been the focus of many studies and several models have been put forward to describe the basic mechanisms that drive network growth. A set of works studied the evolution of online social networks, discussing the densification and diameter reduction observed during the growth of the graph [11, 15]. Even though online social graphs tend to be have an heterogeneous degree distribution in agreement with the preferential attachment principle, these findings highlighted that, in social networks, different mechanisms seems to be in place. More in detail, Leskovec et al. [18] propose a "forest-fire" copying process: when a new node joins the network and connects to a first neighbor, it starts recursively creating new links among the neighbors of the first neighbor, effectively copying the connection already in place. This process mixes preferential attachment, as more connected nodes are more likely to be selected, and transitivity, which fosters new connections between nodes in social proximity. This confirms the importance that triadic closure holds for the evolution of social graphs, as we have seen in our results.

Other works have also been focusing on triadic closure: Simmel noted that people sharing many friends might be more likely to become connected [28]. This effect was then measured in online social networks [19, 14] and included in growth models. With respect to these results, our work explores, for the first time, the effect of spatial distance on network evolution: specifically, we study how distance influences preferential attachment and triadic closure.

Other works have been focusing on general models for spatial networks. One of the earliest examples is the Waxman model, where nodes are distributed at random over space and then connected with probability exponentially decreasing with distance [30]. The Waxman model has also been modified as a growth model, where new nodes join the network and connect with a similar rule [12]. Barthélemy proposed to combine preferential attachment with spatial distance, studying how the resulting graphs move away from being scale-free as the effect of spatial distance is increased [4], albeit this case only considered an exponential decay with distance as in the original Waxman model. Barrat et al. [3] also considered a similar model for weighted networks where preferential attachment is driven by the weight of the existing connections and hampered by spatial distance. While these works contain the initial ideas about including spatial influence in models of network growth, they were based on systems such as transportation networks that lacked social properties. Hence, they tend to focus on an exponential decay of the probability of connection as a function of distance, differently to what observed in social graphs, and they ignore properties arising from triadic closure. Our contribution builds on these findings and bridges together several different insights in order to obtain a suitable model for spatial social graphs.

Another set of works have investigated the spatial properties of social networks: the influence of geographic distance on social connections was firstly discussed in the LiveJournal community [20]. This influence appears so important that it can be exploited to predict where people live given their friends' locations [1]. Other studies on mobile phone communication networks have found that social triangles tend to extend over large geographic distances [16] and that community detection approaches should take spatial distance into account to achieve better results [9]. The fostering effect of geographic proximity on social ties has been demonstrated considering both purely spatial coincidences [7] and repeated visits to venues [27]. Our work extends these results by analyzing the effect of spatial distance not on the static structure of social networks but on their temporal evolution.

Finally, we adopt the maximum likelihood methodology from and we base our growth model on results presented in [17], where the evolution of four different online social networks was discussed. Again, our work differs as it addresses the effect of geographic distance on the temporal mechanisms that govern network evolution, providing a more complete understanding of the factors driving social behavior. Furthermore, we describe a model of network growth which successfully reproduces both social and spatial properties observed in online social graphs.

9. CONCLUSIONS

In this work we studied the evolution of the social graph of a location-based service. We collected data about social links created and places visited by users over a period of 4 months and we studied the effect of spatial factors on the growth of the network.

We tested different models of edge attachment and we found that on a *global scale* node degree and spatial distance simultaneously affect how individuals create social connections. On the other hand, on a *local scale* we studied triadic closure models based on shared friends and on shared places: in these cases social factors are more important than spatial ones. Finally, we explored the temporal properties of network evolution, studying how much time users remain active on the service and how the time elapsed between the creation of consecutive social connections becomes shorter as users have more friends.

Based on our findings, we defined and tested network growth models combining a global gravity-based attachment with local closure models based on shared friends and places. Our models are able to reproduce the structural and spatial properties observed in the traces. Our results highlight basic factors driving social network growth that could impact a range of research efforts and practical applications. Overall, this work builds up on previous results and provides further evidence that spatial factors should not be neglected when studying and modeling online social services.

Acknowledgments

This research was partly funded by a Google Research Award.

10. REFERENCES

[1] L. Backstrom, E. Sun, and C. Marlow. Find me if you can: improving geographical prediction with social and spatial proximity. In *Proceedings of WWW'10*, 2010.

[2] A.-L. Barabási and R. Albert. Emergence of Scaling in Random Networks. *Science*, 286(5439), 1999.

[3] A. Barrat, M. Barthélemy, and A. Vespignani. The effects of spatial constraints on the evolution of weighted complex networks. *Journal of Statistical Mechanics*, (05), 2005.

[4] M. Barthélemy. Crossover from scale-free to spatial networks. *Europhysics Letters*, 63, 2003.

[5] M. Barthélemy. Spatial Networks. *Physics Reports*, 499, 2011.

[6] V. Carrothers. A Historical Review of the Gravity and Potential Concepts of Human Interaction. *Journal of the American Institute of Planners*, 22, 1956.

[7] D. J. Crandall, L. Backstrom, D. Cosley, S. Suri, D. Huttenlocher, and J. M. Kleinberg. Inferring social ties from geographic coincidences. *PNAS*, 107(52):22436–22441, 2010.

[8] J. Cranshaw, E. Toch, J. Hong, A. Kittur, and N. Sadeh. Bridging the gap between physical location and online social networks. In *Proceedings of UbiComp'10*, Copenhagen, Denmark, 2010.

[9] P. Expert, T. S. Evans, V. D. Blondel, and R. Lambiotte. Uncovering space-independent communities in spatial networks. *PNAS*, 108(19):7663–7668, May 2011.

[10] S. L. Feld. The Focused Organization of Social Ties. *American Journal of Sociology*, 86(5):1015–1035, 1981.

[11] D. Fetterly, M. Manasse, M. Najork, and J. Wiener. A large-scale study of the evolution of web pages. In *Proceedings of WWW'03*, 2003.

[12] M. Kaiser and C. C. Hilgetag. Spatial growth of real-world networks. *PRE*, 69:036103, Mar 2004.

[13] T. Karagiannis, C. Gkantsidis, D. Narayanan, and A. Rowstron. Hermes: clustering users in large-scale e-mail services. In *Proceedings of SoCC'10*, 2010.

[14] D. Krackhardt and M. S. Handcock. Heider vs Simmel: emergent features in dynamic structures. In *Proceedings of ICML'06*, 2006.

[15] R. Kumar, J. Novak, and A. Tomkins. Structure and Evolution of Online Social Networks. In *Proceedings of KDD'06*, 2006.

[16] R. Lambiotte, V. Blondel, C. Dekerchove, E. Huens, C. Prieur, Z. Smoreda, and P. Vandooren. Geographical dispersal of mobile communication networks. *Physica A*, 387(21), 2008.

[17] J. Leskovec, L. Backstrom, R. Kumar, and A. Tomkins. Microscopic evolution of social networks. In *Proceedings of KDD'08*, 2008.

[18] J. Leskovec, J. Kleinberg, and C. Faloutsos. Graphs over time: densification laws, shrinking diameters and possible explanations. In *Proceedings of KDD'05*, 2005.

[19] D. Liben-Nowell and J. Kleinberg. The link prediction problem for social networks. In *Proceedings of CIKM'03*, 2003.

[20] D. Liben-Nowell, J. Novak, R. Kumar, P. Raghavan, and A. Tomkins. Geographic routing in social networks. *PNAS*, 102(33):11623–11628, 2005.

[21] R. N. Lichtenwalter, J. T. Lussier, and N. V. Chawla. New perspectives and methods in link prediction. In *Proceedings of KDD'10*, 2010.

[22] A. Mislove, M. Marcon, K. P. Gummadi, P. Druschel, and B. Bhattacharjee. Measurement and Analysis of Online Social Networks. In *Proceedings of IMC '07*, 2007.

[23] J.-P. Onnela, S. Arbesman, M. C. González, A.-L. Barabási, and N. A. Christakis. Geographic constraints on social network groups. *PLoS ONE*, 6(4):e16939, 2011.

[24] J. M. Pujol, V. Erramilli, G. Siganos, X. Yang, N. Laoutaris, P. Chhabra, and P. Rodriguez. The little engine(s) that could: scaling online social networks. In *Proceedings of SIGCOMM'10*, 2010.

[25] D. M. Romero and J. Kleinberg. The Directed Closure Process in Hybrid Social-Information Networks, with an Analysis of Link Formation on Twitter. In *Proceedings of ICWSM'11*, 2011.

[26] S. Scellato, A. Noulas, R. Lambiotte, and C. Mascolo. Socio-spatial Properties of Online Location-based Social Networks. In *Proceedings of ICWSM'11*, 2011.

[27] S. Scellato, A. Noulas, and C. Mascolo. Exploiting place features in link prediction on location-based social networks. In *Proceedings of KDD'11*, 2011.

[28] G. Simmel. *The Sociology of Georg Simmel*. The Free Press, 1908.

[29] S. Traverso, K. Huguenin, V. Trestian, I. Erramilli, N. Laoutaris, and K. Papagiannaki. TailGate: Handling Long-Tail Content with a Little Help from Friends. In *Proceedings of WWW'12*, 2012.

[30] B. M. Waxman. Routing of multipoint connections. *Selected Areas in Communications*, 6(9):1617–1622, 1988.

[31] M. P. Wittie, V. Pejovic, L. Deek, K. C. Almeroth, and B. Y. Zhao. Exploiting locality of interest in online social networks. In *Proceedings of CONEXT'10*, 2010.

[32] C. Wiuf, M. Brameier, O. Hagberg, and M. P. H. Stumpf. A likelihood approach to analysis of network data. *PNAS*, 103(20):7566–7570, 2006.

New Kid on the Block: Exploring the Google+ Social Graph

Gabriel Magno
UFMG
Belo Horizonte, Brazil
magno@dcc.ufmg.br

Giovanni Comarela
UFMG
Belo Horizonte, Brazil
giovannicomarela@dcc.ufmg.br

Diego Saez-Trumper
Universitat Pompeu Fabra
Barcelona, Spain
diego.saez@upf.edu

Meeyoung Cha
KAIST
Republic of Korea
meeyoungcha@kaist.edu

Virgilio Almeida
UFMG
Belo Horizonte, Brazil
virgilio@dcc.ufmg.br

ABSTRACT

This paper presents a detailed analysis of the Google+ social network. We identify the key differences and similarities with other popular networks like Facebook and Twitter, in order to determine whether Google+ is a new paradigm or yet another social network. This work is based on large-scale crawls of over 27 million user profiles that represented nearly 50% of the entire network in 2011. We observe that the average path length between users is slightly higher than other networks, possibly because Google+ is a new system where relationships are still rapidly growing. Google+ shows a higher level of reciprocity than Twitter, which also has directed social links. The newly available "places lived" field could be used to study how users are distributed around the world and how aggressively the service has been adopted in different countries. We find that Google+ is popular in countries with relatively low Internet penetration rate. Based on the amount and types of information publicly shared in user profiles, we also find that the notion of privacy varies significantly across different cultures.

Categories and Subject Descriptors

J.4 [**Computer Applications**]: Social and behavioral sciencesMiscellaneous; H.3.5 [**Online Information Services**]: Web-based services

General Terms

Human Factors, Measurement

Keywords

Google+, Online Social Network, Geo-location

1. INTRODUCTION

Social networks are a global information infrastructure, where individuals bring their social relations online and share information, photos, songs, videos, as well as ideas. Social networking sites like Facebook now reach 82% of the world's Internet-using population or about 1.2 billion people in total according to comScore [11]. In fact social networking became the most popular online activity worldwide. Accordingly, a number of researchers have tried to understand user behaviors and characteristics of various online social networks, where Twitter and Facebook have been the two most popularly examined platforms [26, 7, 39, 3].

To compete in this field, Google has launched in June 2011 its own social networking service called Google+ (https://plus.google.com/). The platform was announced as a new generation of social network and included several new features, such as *circles* that allow users to share different content with different people and *hangouts* that let users to create video chatting session and invite up to nine people from their circles of friends to share the environment [22].

Since its launch, the Google+ social network has been adding new users at a rapid pace. In fact, it is known as the fastest growing network ever, reaching 20 million visitors in only 21 days [10]. The service has later reached 62 million registered users as of December 2011 [24] and a total of 250 million registered users of whom 150 million are active as of June 2012 [15].

Once Google+ has become a popular social media network, it is important to understand how it compares to other social network models. Typical questions follow. How are people connected on Google+? Who are the most popular users? How are users distributed worldwide? What is the impact of geography on the social relationships?

Furthermore, the rapid adoption rate of the service raises interesting questions about online privacy. One crucial question is on what the default privacy settings should be. Along these lines, it is worth examining how "closed" social networking sites are, compared to the "open" Internet. Google has positioned itself as promoter of the Internet openness against other social networking services that are often described "walled garden" [5] due to limited access to their internal web pages. Then, is Google+ different? How open is it and how does it impact user interactions?

To answer these questions we have crawled more than 27,556,390 user profiles and 575,141,097 relationship links among users, as well as any publicly available data about the users such as gender, geo-location, and relationship status. A relatively large number of users leave personal information publicly available for anyone to see. This kind of information allows us to analyze user behavior patterns and compare them to previous research results obtained for other social networks, e.g., Facebook and Twitter.

IMC'12, November 14–16, 2012, Boston, Massachusetts, USA.

Based on the gathered data, we characterize the novel social network model provided by Google+ in depth, its user base, its geographical distribution, and compare its main characteristics with other social network services. Among various findings, some of the main results are summarized as follows:

1. Our analysis on the top users based on the circles list indicate that the majority of the top users (7 out of 20) are well-known individuals from information technology industry;

2. By looking into users who share their work or home contact information publicly (1% of all suers), we observe that a large fraction of the users who share telephone numbers are male and single;

3. We find that users share strikingly different amounts of information to public in their profiles depending the country they live in;

4. By examining the social links between the users in relation to their countries, we observe that physical distance is crucial in the likelihood of forming a social link between two users;

5. The fraction of global and national links also vary according the countries, indicating the different patterns of usages of the Google+ service across different cultures.

As another contribution of this paper, we make the collected data available to the wider research community at `http://gplus.camps.dcc.ufmg.br`. Our Google+ data set could facilitate new projects in social computing and computer network research that need actual data for their experiments.

The rest of this paper is organized as follows. We begin with a detailed description of the Google+ platform and the data collection methodology in Section 2. In Section 3, we study the social graph of the Google+ users and describe in detail the public attributes available in Google+. Next, we analyze the impact of geographical distance and relationships in Google+ in Section 4. We examine the economic indicators of a country and their relationship to the adoption rate of Google+ within that country. We discuss related work and implications in Section 5 and Section 6. Finally, we summarize our findings and conclude in Section 7.

2. METHODOLOGY

We briefly describe key features of the Google+ service and the way we gathered data.

2.1 Platform Description

The Google+ service was released in June of 2011 [22]. In the first 90 days, the service has been on field trial and only those users who received an invitation could create an account. During this time, the network grew *virally* through social contacts. In September 20th, 2011, the service became publicly open and no invitation was required for a sign up [21]. These two different mechanisms of spreading would have attracted different kinds of users to Google+. For instance, users who joined through invitations are likely tech-savvy users who typically adopt new services early, compared to the users who join through open sign-up.

In Google+, users can manage their contact list through *circles*. Circles are labeled groups of friends, which allows a user to share or receive information with and from a specified subset of his contacts. For example, a user may manage "family", "colleagues", and "alumni" circles. When a user adds someone in one of his circles, he starts to receive updates from that person. This manual grouping of contacts alleviates some of the privacy problems that existed in other "flat" social networks, where default privacy settings are set to maximize the visibility of users profile and only a small number of members change it [20]. There are two types of circles, namely in- and out-circles. While the latter represents the list of users that a given user has added to her circles, the former represents the list of other users who added that user to their circles.

Circle names and their user lists are private information that only the circle creator can see. A user can identify all the others who included the user in their circles (i.e., followers), because the user receives a notification when someone adds him to a circle. Similar to Twitter, people can add other users to their circles without confirmation. This is different from networks like Facebook, where all social links are reciprocal and both sides of the users should agree to own a social link. In the user profile page two lists are shown by default: The "Have user in circles" list, like a followers list, and "In user's circles", similar to the followees list in Twitter. The user has the option to set these lists as private.

Figure 1: Google+ home page of Larry Page.

Google+ users can publish ideas (status), images, videos and any kind of URL. Whenever a user post something, she has the option to set the visibility of that content, choosing which of her circles can see it. On the other side, a user can choose from which circles she will receive content. Therefore, circles are the way to manage information flow in Google+. The continued information flow through circles is referred to as "stream" in the system.

There are several features that allow users to interact with others. User interactions are centered around content; users can comment, share (like retweet in Twitter), and click on the "+1" button (similar to Like button in Facebook) on a given content. When a user clicks on the "+1" button, she is publicly recommending that particular content to others and it will be saved in her "+1's tab" similar to bookmark. There are other features such as photo albums (that allow users to upload, share and organize photos), hangout (a kind of collaborative video chat with friends), and games.

2.2 Data Collection

In order to collect user profiles in Google+, we implemented a breadth-first search (BFS) crawler in Python, considering both the public in-circles and out-circles lists (i.e. bidirectional BFS). We began our crawl with Mark Zuckerberg, the co-creator and chief executive of Facebook, because he was known to be one of the most popular users in Google+ at the time of data collection. Given that users are connected in social networks, our crawler although started from a single seed node soon reached other popular users in Google+. We could not repeat the crawl with randomly chosen seed nodes, because numeric user IDs were not supported at the time of data collection. Although the BFS technique is simple and efficient, it exhibits several well-known limitations such as the bias towards sampling high degree nodes, which may affect the degree distribution [18, 35].

The data collection process started on November 11th, 2011, and ended on December 27th, 2011. We used a total of 11 machines with different IP addresses to efficiently gather large amount of data. The profile information was retrieved by making HTTP requests to publicly available user profile pages. In total we crawled **27,556,390** profile pages, collecting public user information and its circles lists. With the social links of the users we have constructed a directed graph that has **35,114,957** nodes and **575,141,097** edges. As of the data collection date, we estimated that our data set represented 56% of all registered Google+ users[2].

There is a limit on the maximum number of users that could appear in any public circle, which is 10,000 users. Since the Google+ social graph was gathered in both directions (in-circles and out-circles), we were able to recover almost all "lost edges." In order to estimate the fraction of missed links, we compared the number of users shown in their profile page with the actual number of edges we collected. In our dataset there are 915 users with more than 10,000 in-circles users, which should have 37,185,272 incoming edges according to their profile pages, while we found 27,600,503 links for those users in our graph. By dividing the difference of these numbers by the total number of edges, we estimate that 1.6% of the edges are lost because of the 10,000 limit on the circle list.

3. GRAPH ANALYSIS

In order to characterize social relationships of Google+ users, we define a social graph. The vertices of the social graph are Google+ users present in our dataset. A user v added by user u to her circles results in a directed edge from u to v. Therefore the social relations among Google+ users make a directed graph $G(V, E)$, where V represents the set of users and E is the set of directed edges (u, v), $u,\ v \in V$. Given the social graph construction, we analyze two types of properties: first on the node characteristics and then on the graph structure. The former capture the characteristics of Google+ users, as defined by the fields of the user profile, while the latter represents relationships between users.

Table 1: Top 20 users ranked by in-degree

Rank	Name	About
1	Larry Page	IT (Google)
2	Mark Zuckerberg	IT (Facebook)
3	Britney Spears	Musician
4	Snoop Dogg	Musician
5	Sergey Brin	IT (Google)
6	Tyra Banks	Model
7	Vic Gundotra	IT (Google)
8	Paris Hilton	Socialite
9	Richard Branson	Businessman (Virgin Group)
10	Dane Cook	Comedian
11	Jessi June	Model
12	Trey Ratcliff	Blogger
13	will.i.am	Musician
14	Felicia Day	Actor
15	Thomas Hawk	Blogger
16	Tom Anderson	IT (Myspace)
17	Pete Cashmore	IT (Mashable)
18	Guy Kawasaki	IT (Apple) & Writer
19	Wil Wheaton	Actor & Writer
20	Ron Garan	Astronaut (NASA)

3.1 Node Characteristics

To get a sense for what users expect from the Google+ service, we first examine who the most popular users are. Table 1 shows the top 20 users based on their in-degrees (i.e., how many circles these users are added to by others). The top list of Google+ is a mix of singers, bloggers, actors, and IT professionals. When we compare the list to that of Twitter in [26], only one user appears in both lists; singer Britney Spears ranked second as of mid 2009. The top list is particularly different from that of Twitter in that (1) we do not see any news media outlet like the New York Times and CNN, while (2) we see founders of large Internet-based companies like Google and Facebook. In fact 7 out of the 20 users are IT related, which is uncommon in other social networks.

Next focusing more on the average user, we examine what kinds of interactions they perform on the network. In general, users of social networking sites reveal different types of personal information in their profile, such as basic descriptors (e.g., gender, relationship status, cities lived), contact information (e.g., e-mail, phone number, address, Web site), personal interests (e.g., favorite TV shows, movies, books, quotes, music), education information (e.g. field of study, degree), work information (e.g., employer, position), etc.

Google+ users also publish information about themselves in their profiles. Some pieces of information are in "restricted fields", where users have to choose among some options, while in "open fields" users can write anything they want. Only the fields "relationship", "looking for", and gender are restricted fields. The rest of the fields are open fields. In the field called, places lived, a user can write the name of any place she lived and the Google+ system automatically tries to mark the place on the map.

For all the fields, except for the name that is public by default, a user can control the privacy setting and set visibility of that field. There are five options: (1) *public*, which means open to anyone in the Internet, (2) *extend circles*, which means open to people that are in circles and people that are in the circles of those, (3) *your circles*, which means open to people in one's circles, (4) *only you*, and (5) *custom*, which means a user can choose exactly which circles may view that field.

We have collected information about all the fields of users that were publicly accessible. In Table 2, we show the number and fraction of users that have made each type of information available.

Table 2: Public attributes available in Google+

Attribute	Available	%
Name	27,556,390	100.00
Gender	26,914,758	97.67
Education	7,471,191	27.11
Places lived	7,371,461	26.75
Employment	5,917,609	21.47
Phrase	4,075,132	14.79
Other profiles	3,713,546	13.48
Occupation	3,656,447	13.27
Contributor to	3,622,627	13.15
Introduction	2,149,191	7.80
Other names	1,210,760	4.39
Relationship	1,186,903	4.31
Braggin rights	1,074,964	3.90
Recommended links	1,001,349	3.63
Looking for	753,704	2.74
Work (contact)	60,434	0.22
Home (contact)	58,876	0.21

3.2 Privacy concerns

Studies on human behavior [38] show that individuals with profiles on social networking sites may have greater risk taking attitudes than those who do not. And sharing contact information, such telephone numbers, may increases risks. As far as contact details are concerned, the work in [38] shows how many Facebook users disclose identity information in the form of contact details. The majority of the users in the sample used by the study publicly showed their e-mail address (64.1%). Only a few Facebook members published their mobile phone number (10.7%). Similarly, only a minority (10.7%) of the participants revealed their home address on Facebook.

Google+ allows their users to publish contact information in their profiles. Some users publicly share their work or home contact information. In our data set, a total of 72,736 users share telephone number in Google+, which represent 0.26% of the population. We call these users *tel-users* and because they represent a class of risk taking users we look into the details of the profile of these users.

In order to examine how much information *tel-users* share publicly compared to all users, we show the CCDF (Complementary Cumulative Distribution Function) of the number of fields in the profile shared for each user in Figure 2, removing the fields of Home and Work information from the contabilization. (The list of the fields available are given in Table 2.) As we can see, *tel-users* generally share more information in their profiles than other Google+ users, which confirm their risk taking attitude. For example, 10% of all Google+ users share more than six fields, while 66% of the *tel-users* do the same.

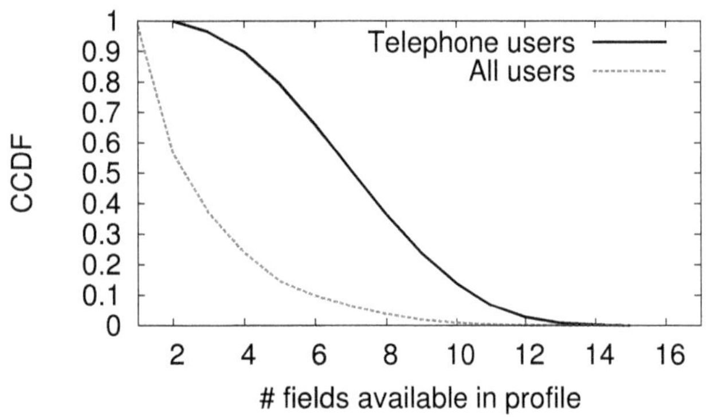

Figure 2: Number of fields shared by users in the profile

Concerning the information sharing behavior of Google+ users, table 3 displays the percentage of users who give information about gender, relationship, and location for all users and *tel-users*, considering only those users that had the field public. Among all users of the dataset, 68% are male and 31% are female. However, the difference is much higher when we consider *tel-users*; 86% are male and 11% female, indicating that female Google+ users are less likely to share phone numbers than male Google+ users. Similar to the observations confirmed in [16], more risk taking behaviors can be found for men and greater concern from women with regard to information provided on the Web.

What is particular about Google+ is that it asks users to provide a very detailed level of information about their relationship status as opposed to other social networks. The nine default options from which users can choose from are listed in the table. Conducting the same comparison of all users and *tel-users* over the relationship status, we find that user behaviors are similar between the two groups.

Table 3: Information shared by all users and *tel-users*

	All users	Tel-users
Total	27,556,390	72,736
Gender (N)	26,914,758	71,267
Male	67.65%	85.99%
Female	31.46%	11.26%
Other	0.89%	2.75%
Relationship (N)	1,186,903	29,068
Single	42.82%	57.24%
Married	26.59%	21.03%
In a relationship	19.80%	10.23%
It's complicated	3.16%	3.98%
Engaged	4.39%	2.98%
In an open relationship	1.26%	2.77%
Widowed	0.50%	0.58%
In a domestic partnership	1.08%	0.77%
In a civil union	0.39%	0.41%
Location (N)	6,621,644	45,676
United States	31.38%	8.92%
India	16.71%	31.90%
Brazil	5.76%	4.72%
United Kingdom	3.35%	2.19%
Canada	2.30%	1.52%
Other	40.50%	50.77%

However, those users who set their relationship status as "single", "it's complicated", "in an open relationship", "widowed", and "in a civil union" were more likely to share their phone numbers publicly than others. In particular, we saw a high percentage of single users (57.24%) compared to all the users (42.82%). In contrast, only half of the users "in a relationship" shared their phone numbers.

The fraction of *tel-users* does not follow the rank of the top 10 countries in Figure 6. While the US take up 31.38% of all users, it counts for only 8.92% of those users who have made their phone numbers available in Google+. In contrast, India now becomes the most populated country based on the fraction of *tel-users* count (31.90%). The fraction of Indian users in the *tel-users* group is twice as big as in all other country users group.

While the different level at which users of a given country reveal their phone numbers is interesting, this may come as no surprise when we account for the fact that people's perception of what is "private" is different. According to a report in [9], 65% of people in Germany find mobile phone number as personal, whereas only 28% of people in Romania think the same.

3.3 Structural characteristics

We next present characteristics of the Google+ social graph. For each network metric, we also show the results for the Twitter graph from other research [7] for comparison.

3.3.1 Degree Distribution

One of the most common structural measures analyzed in complex networks such as the Google+ social graph is the distribution of the number of the incoming and outgoing node connections or what is so called "degree." Figure 3 shows the CCDF for the variables out-degree and in-degree of the Google+ social graph. We can see that these curves have approximately the shape of a Power Law distribution. The CCDF of a Power Law distribution is given by $Cx^{-\alpha}$, $x, \alpha, C > 0$. If we compare the curves with Twitter, we observe similar patterns, altough Google+ shows slightly lower degrees.

By using a simple statistical linear regression (in the log-log scale) we estimated the exponent α that best models the data. We obtained $\alpha = 1.3$ (with $R^2 = 0.99$) for in-degree and $\alpha = 1.2$ (with $R^2 = 0.99$) for out-degree. Although both curves are similar, the out-degree curve drops sharply around 5000. We conjecture this is because Google maintains a policy that allows only some special users to outpass a specified threshold (unknown) and add more than 5000 friends to their circles.

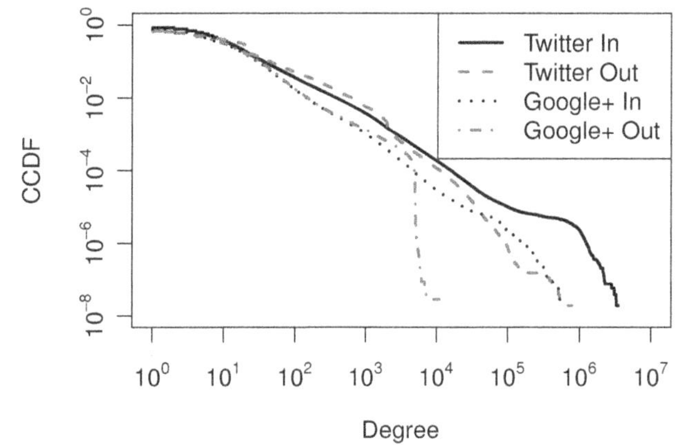

Figure 3: Degree Distributions

The overall power-law trend shown in the degree distribution is characteristics of the human social networks. This means that a small fraction of the individuals have disproportionately large number of neighbors, while most users have a small number of neighbors. Examples of such hubs are listed in Table 1. For instance, Larry Page is listed in 3.7 million circles as of August 2012, while the majority are listed in no more than 10 circles. As studied in many other research, hubs play a central role in information propagation in social networks.

3.3.2 Reciprocity

In order to evaluate discrepancies between in- and out-degrees for a given node we use a simple metric called Relation Reciprocity (RR) of a node $u \in V$ as:

$$RR(u) = \frac{|OS(u) \cap IS(u)|}{|OS(u)|} \quad (1)$$

where $OS(u)$ is the set of nodes (i.e, users) that have an incoming edge from u and $IS(u)$ is the set of nodes with outgoing edges pointing to u.

Figure 4(a) shows the distribution of the Relation Reciprocity. This metric is able to effectively differentiate very popular users, such as celebrities and companies, with very low reciprocity from ordinary users, that have moderate to high RR.

The analysis of the relation reciprocity in circles links suggests a strong signature of the Google+ users. More than 60% of the users have RR higher than 0.6, which shows some sort of structural balance between the users of this new social networking service. This concept is related to the fraction of reciprocal relationships in a social graph. Based on our datasets, we calculate the percentage of global reciprocal relations and find 32% in Google+, compared to 22.1% reported for Twitter [26].

The high reciprocity rate in Google+ may be related to the scarcity of large media outlet profiles, since by the time of our collection the "pages" feature was new and not very popular. Media outlet attract very large numbers of followers, but do not exhibit followees. Different kinds of online sharing services exhibit higher reciprocal relations, such as 68% for Flickr [8] and 84% for Yahoo! 360 [25].

3.3.3 Clustering Coefficient

Another common characteristic of social networks is a high average clustering coefficient (CC). The CC of a node u, denoted by $C(u)$, is defined as the probability of any two of its neighbors (outgoing) being neighbors themselves [41]. This metric is associated to the number of triangles that contain a node u. For a directed graph, the maximum number of triangles connecting the $|OS(u)|$ outgoing neighbors of u is $|OS(u)|(|OS(u)| - 1)$. Thus, the CC measures the ratio between actual triangles and their maximal value. During clustering coefficient analysis we only consider the nodes with $|OS(u)| > 1$, since this is a necessary condition for this computation.

Figure 4(b) shows the distribution for the CC of nodes in the social graph. We randomly sampled one million nodes and computed CC for each one of them. We can see that 40% of all users have a CC greater than 0.2. An approximate calculation, based on the results presented for Facebook in [39], allows us to estimate the clustering coefficient for part of Facebook population. In [39], we have that only users with degree smaller than 50 have an average CC greater than this value. However, these users represent less than 1% of the entire network [39], suggesting that Google+ has a higher average cluster coefficient than Facebook, which represent a more tightly connected network. Comparing with Twitter (as shown in Figure 4(b)), we can also see higher values of CC in Google+.

3.3.4 Strongly Connected Component

The study of the connected components of a social graph is a key factor to understand its structural properties. For example, if we know the WCCs (Weakly Connected Components) of a graph then we have information about the number of isolated nodes in the network as well if it has a giant component. Due to the data collection procedure used to crawl Google+ in this work, which is a bidirectional snow ball, the social graph G consists of only one WCC. As a consequence, we do not have information about the isolated nodes, but we know that we have collected a giant component of the graph (see Table 4).

In order to investigate the connectivity of G we decided to measure the number and size of all its Strongly Connected Components (SCC). A strongly connected component of a social graph (directed) is a subgraph, such that a node can be reached from any other node following edges between them. SCCs have an important role in directed social networks (like Google+) because they are central to information dissemination to the users that are part of the them. Graphs with large SCCs are amenable to quick information dissemination processes.

We identified 9,771,696 SCCs in G. To reach this number we used a procedure involving two Depth First Searches [12]. Figure 4(c) presents the CCDF of the size of all SCCs found in G. In this figure we can see that almost all of them are small. In fact, there is only one with more than 100 nodes, which is the SCC with 25,240,000, that means that G has a giant component and the graph we collected is highly connected.

3.3.5 Degrees of Separation

The degree of separation essentially describes the shortest possible routes between two nodes of our graph. Although the degree of separation has been commonly thought of in the social context, the concept has many applications in social networking such as infor-

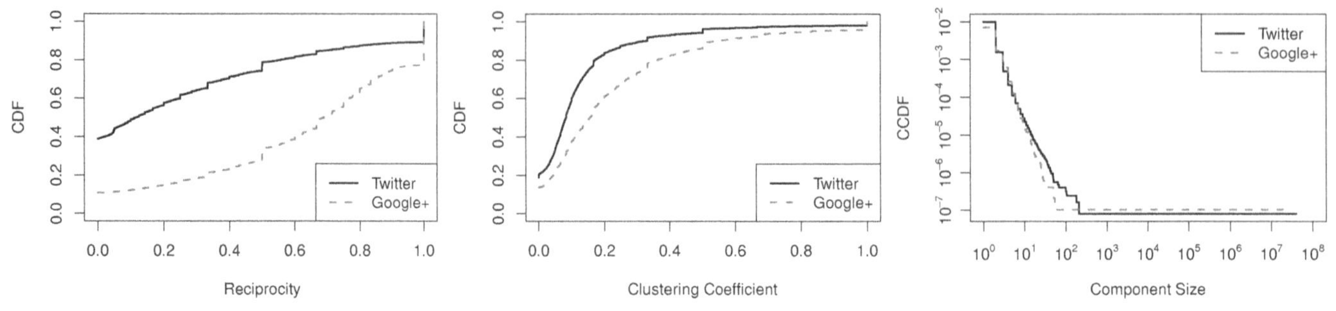

(a) Reciprocal links (b) Clustering coefficients of nodes (c) Size of the strongly connected components

Figure 4: Distributions of various network properties in Google+

Table 4: Comparison of topological characteristics of Google+ and other online social networks

Network	Nodes	Edges	% Crawled	Path length	Reciprocity	Diameter	In-degree	Out-degree
Google+	35M	575M	56%	5.9	32%	19	16.4	16.4
Facebook	721M	62G	100%	4.7	100%	41	190.2	190.2
Twitter	41.7M	106M	100%	4.1	22%	18	28.19	29.34
Orkut	3M	223M	11%	4.3	100%	9	-	-

mation dissemination and friend recommendation [13]. We present an analysis of how many hops there are between two users in the Google+ social graph. In order to have the exact distribution we would need to compute the shortest path from all nodes to all nodes of the network. Due to the computational cost of this task we decided to use a random sampling procedure [1]. We sampled k different users and for each one of them we computed the shortest path to all others users in the network. We started with $k = 2000$ and increased its until 10000, stopping in this value once there were no more changes in the distribution.

Figure 5 presents the final estimate of the path length distribution for two cases: the directed graph G and its undirected version. In the first case we can see that the most common value is 6 with an average of 5.9. In the second we have 5 as the most common and an average of 4.7. The graph G has a diameter of 19 and for its undirected version 13. This means that most users are only a few hops away from a random user, which has the important implication that information can spread quickly and widely throughout the network.

Although we have found the same mode of the well-known study of Milgram [31], it is important to remark that we are analyzing the public graph of Google+. So, adding back the edges omitted by users due to privacy constraints may reduce the average path length further. Comparing with other networks, we refer to Twitter with a mode of 4 and average of 4.12 [26], Facebook with an average of 4.74 hops [3] and a median of 6 for the MSN messenger network [27].

Table 4 summarizes the key structural features of Google+ and three others important OSNs in order to conclude this section. Statistics on other social networks are borrowed from [26, 3, 39, 32]. We can see some important differences, for example the Google+ social graph has a higher average path length and reciprocity. Its diameter is comparable to Twitter, but smaller than Facebook. Moreover, we can see that the number of friends (both in- and out-degrees) are much smaller when compared to Facebook.

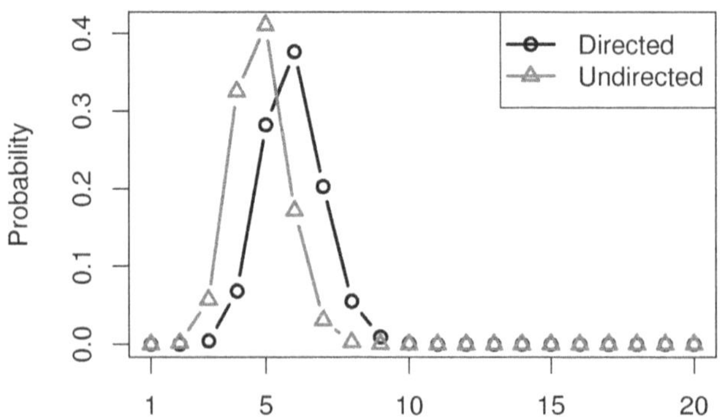

Figure 5: Estimated path length distribution

4. PATTERNS ACROSS GEO-LOCATIONS

Google+ users can list all the places they have lived at a field in their profile called "Places lived," which is incorporated to the Google Map for visualization. Nearly 27% of the users in our dataset provide geo-location information. This feature is unique in Google+, for other social networks like Facebook only allows users to list their current location and, at most, their hometown information.

Using the places lived field, we analyzed how Google+ users are distributed around the world. For this, we first extracted the coordinates of the last location from the places lived field for each user and translated the coordinates into a valid country identifier. In this fashion, we were able to identify the country of 6,621,644 users.

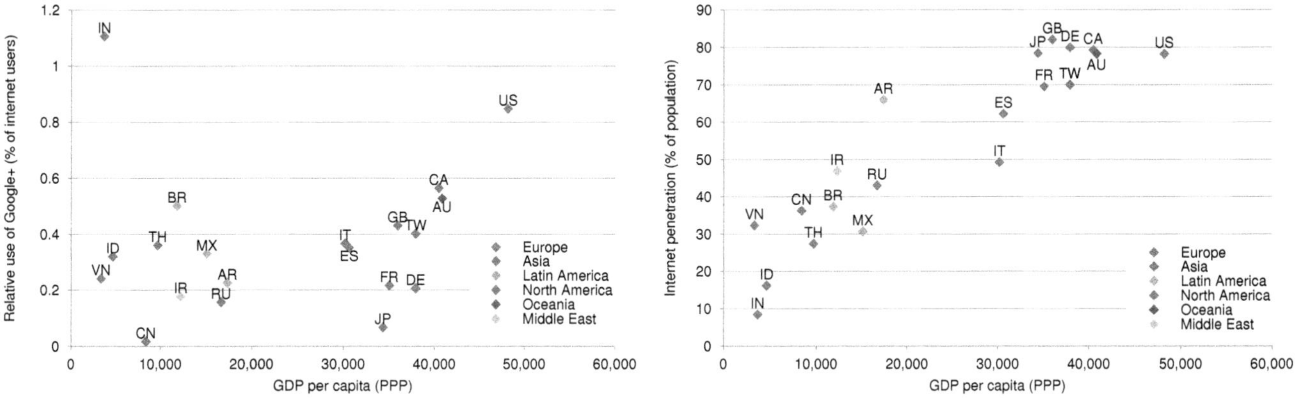

(a) GDP Per Capita and Use of Google+

(b) GDP Per Capita and Internet Penetration

Figure 7: Usage of Internet and Google+ among countries

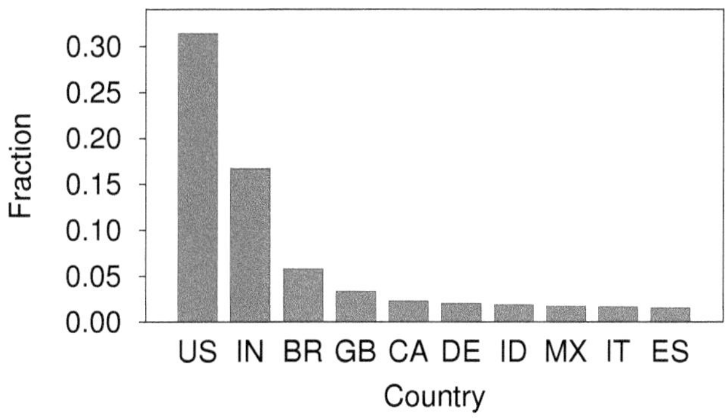

Figure 6: Top 10 countries with Google+ users

Figure 6 shows the top 10 countries in our dataset with their respective percentages of the registered users.[1] More than 30% of the users who share their location information are identified as living in the US. We observe Google+ is relatively popular in India and Brazil, which are also two of the countries with high presence of Google's other social network, Orkut [19]. United Kingdom, Canada, and Germany also appear in the list, which are countries known to have high Internet Penetration Rate (IPR) or the percentage of Internet users out of the population of that country.[2] Interestingly, countries like Indonesia and Mexico appear in our top list, which are not part of the top countries based on the Internet penetration rate.

4.1 Economics

Intrigued by the unique mix of countries based on Internet penetration rate, we further investigate which countries have high percentage of their Internet population on Google+. To do that we define *Google+ Penetration Rate*, that can be computed for each country C as follows:

$$GPR = \frac{\text{number of users in our dataset living in } C}{\text{Internet population of } C}. \quad (2)$$

[1]County codes represent the following. US: United States; IN: India; BR: Brazil; GB: United Kingdom; CA: Canada; DE: Germany; ID: Indonesia; MX: Mexico; IT: Italy; ES: Spain.

[2]Statistics about the Internet penetration rate and population were obtained from http://www.internetworldstats.com

Note that our measure is meaningful only for the relative ranking of different countries, because our data is a sample taken from Google+ and in the sample only 27% of the users provide geolocation information.

Figure 7(a) shows the Google+ penetration rate for the top 20 countries. The top country in Google+ adoption now becomes India. We also see that countries like Taiwan and Thailand appear in the top ten list. For comparison, we show the Internet penetration rate of the same top 20 countries in Figure 7(b). The top five countries of Internet penetration are United Kingdom, Germany, Canada, Japan, and Australia. Both of the figures have Gross Domestic Product (GDP) per capita in the X-axis.

We make several observations. First, while there is a linear relationship between the GDP per capita of a country and its Internet penetration rate (identified as the data points clustered near a straight line in Figure 7(b)), we do not see the same trend in Google+ penetration rate. Countries with lower GDP per capita like Brazil, Mexico, and Thailand have equal footing in the penetration rate as with much wealthier countries such as United Kingdom, Australia, and Canada.

Second, certain countries showed a large gap between the Internet and Google+ penetration rate such as Japan, Russia, and China. In both of these countries, domestic social networks like Mixi in Japan, Odnoklassniki in Russia, and QQ in China are widely used. International social networking services like Facebook and Twitter are known to have little presence in these countries. Also in case of China, international social networking sites have been blocked [17].

Third, countries with lower Internet penetration like India and Brazil had a very high Google+ penetration rate. As we mentioned before, these two countries are known to favor Google's other social network, Orkut. It is possible that users in India and Brazil are familiar with the Google product, hence are more likely to adopt the service quickly than other countries.

4.2 User Occupation

Among various statistics we examined, the occupation-job title of the top users clearly distinguished Google+ from other well-known social networks, as we examined in Table 2. Interestingly, the top occupations also varied slightly across different countries. Table 5 shows the occupation-job title of the 10 most connected users in each of the top 10 countries, based on their in-degree (i.e., how many circles these users are added to by others). At a glance, the top list of Google+ is a mix of singers, bloggers, actors, and IT (i.e.,

Table 5: Occupation-Job Title of the top users

Country	Profession codes of the top-10 users*									Jaccard
United States	Co	Mu	IT	Mu	IT	Mu	Bu	IT	Mo	Ac	1.00
India	Mu	So	IT	Mu	Mo	Mo	IT	Bu	IT	Mu	0.57
Brazil	Co	TV	Jo	Wr	Ar	Bl	Bl	Co	Mu	Co	0.18
United Kingdom	Bu	Mu	IT	IT	Mu	Mu	IT	Mo	So	IT	0.57
Canada	IT	IT	Mu	Co	Bu	Ac	IT	Mu	Co	Ac	0.83
Germany	Bl	IT	IT	Jo	Bl	IT	Jo	Ec	Mu	Bl	0.22
Indonesia	Mu	IT	So	Mo	Mo	IT	Mu	Ec	Ph	Jo	0.30
Mexico	Mu	Mu	Mu	IT	Mu	Bl	Bl	Mu	Ac	Jo	0.33
Italy	Jo	Jo	IT	IT	Jo	IT	Jo	Mu	Mu	IT	0.29
Spain	Jo	Po	Po	IT	Mu	Mu	IT	Mu	Po	IT	0.25

* Co: Comedian; Mu: Musician; IT: Information Technology Person; Bu: Businessman; Mo: Model; Ac: Actor; So: Socialite; TV: Television Host; Jo: Journalist; Bl: Blogger; Ec: Economist; Ar: Artist; Po: Politician; Ph: Photographer; Wr: Writer

Information Technology) professionals. When we compare the list to that of Twitter [26], the top list is particularly different in that we do not see any news media outlet like the New York Times and CNN, while we see founders of large Internet-based companies like Google and Facebook. In fact, seven out of the top 20 global users were IT related in Google+, which is uncommon in other social networks.

In the table, we also show the Jaccard index, used to compare the similarity and diversity of occupations in these country when compared to occupation-job titles in US. The top users in Canada have a very similar profile to that of the United States. Furthermore, the US, Canada, UK, and India share several top professions, which we may be due to the common British colonization. In contrast, Brazil, Italy, and Spain show a different set of celebrities and professions, and is worth noting that these three countries are Latin cultures, different from anglo-saxon cultures (US, CA, GB).

The top countries have very different kinds of popular users. IT professionals are popular in Google+. In Brazil, there are no famous IT related public figures, hence the list is dominated by comedians and bloggers. In Mexico, half of the top users are related to music. Italy is the country with more journalists among top users, 4 in total. Spain is the only country having Politicians in the top 10 user list. These lists suggest that each country has a different pattern of utilization of the information network provided by Google+, because the occupations of the top individuals represent what a typical user expect from Google+.

4.3 Openness

We next examine how these 10 countries differ in the notion of privacy, by looking at the number of different types of information publicly shared by users in their profiles (e.g., name, gender, education, occupation). As mentioned earlier, the name field is mandatory. Also, because of our methodology to utilize geo-location, all of the sample users studied in this section have shared "places lived" field. Therefore, the minimum number of shared fields is 2.

Figure 8 shows the CCDF of the number of fields users of the top 10 countries shares in their profiles. We present the X-axis in the range 2-14 for better visualization. We observe that, although the difference between the countries is not very pronounced, the ranking is slightly different.

Indonesia and Mexico share more information than other more popular countries like United States and United Kingdom. Germany is the most conservative when it comes to sharing personal information; it was the only country having less than 10% of the users sharing more than 12 fields and also the only country having less than 30% of the users sharing more than 10 fields.

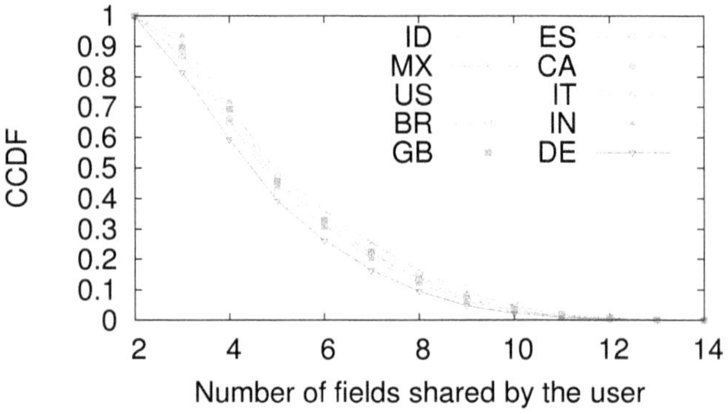

Figure 8: Number of fields in profiles in each country

4.4 Average Path Miles

We now investigate the relationship between social network structure and geographical properties. We start by answering the following question: *is the geographical location of users an important factor in the formation of social links?* To understand if the distance has some influence on the formation of social links as described in circles, we estimated the physical distance of pairs of users in three cases: (1) every pair of socially connected users (approximately 60 million pairs), (2) pairs of reciprocally connected users (approximately 13 million pairs) and (3) randomly chosen pairs of users (20 million, not linked by a social relation). We then computed the physical distance between them. It is important to remark that we conducted this analysis only for users that share geo-location information, which represents 26.75% of the crawled Google+ network.

Figure 9(a) shows the cumulative distribution on the expected physical distance—which we call the *path mile*, similar to the notion of the path length—between pairs of circle friends and random user pairs in Google+. The friendship links in Google+ have higher geographical proximity than a random pairs of users. Nearly 58% of the users (friends) were separated by less than a thousand miles and 15% of them were separated by in fact 10 miles. This observation reinforces the high chance that the Google+ network largely capture the offline social relationships among users. As expected, users with symmetric links (reciprocal) live closer than those with asymmetrical links, indicating the influence of physical distance on the intensity of the relationship.

One natural question that arises from this result is whether it depends, or not, on the country size. For example, do geographically large countries like US have a higher average path mile than small

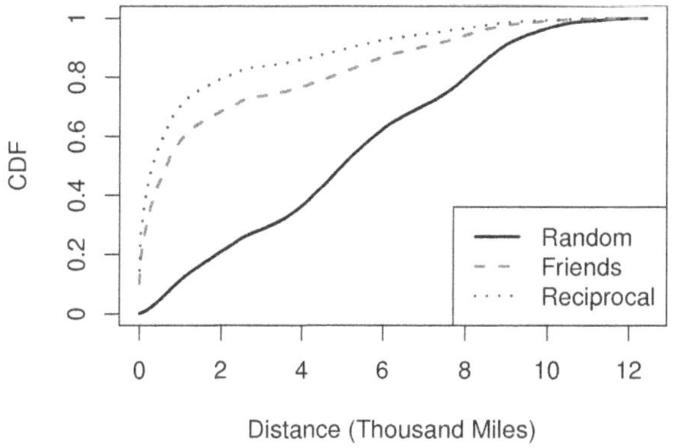

(a) Path Mile distribution of Google+ users

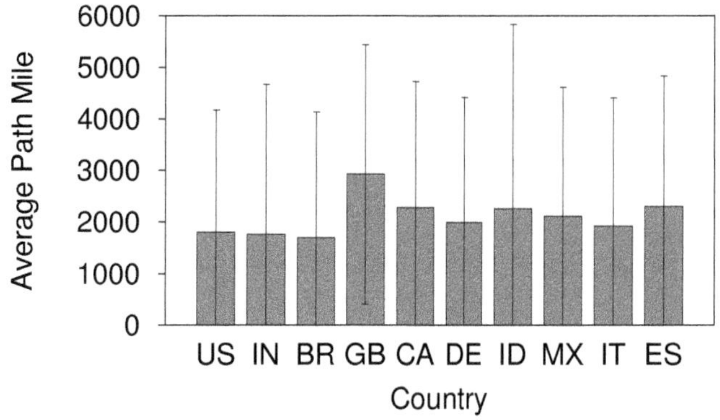

(b) Average path mile with standard deviation

Figure 9: Path Mile distributions

countries like Italy? If this is the case, large countries should have better investment in content distribution in order to minimize jitter and delay especially for the delivery of user generated videos. Figure 9(b) shows the average path miles along with the standard deviation error bar for the top 10 countries. Contrary to our expectation, there is no specific pattern relating the size of the country and its average path mile. One possible explanation could be that small countries have a considerable fraction of edges going outside the country. In fact, this result is discussed in next section.

4.5 Social links across geography

The final question we ask is about the impact of country on friendship link formation. In particular, we ask: are users in the same country more likely to be friends in Google+ than users in different countries? To answer this question, we constructed a graph of countries, where each node is represented by one of the top 10 countries and the weight of each directed edge is given by the proportion of outgoing links from one country to another. Self-loop edges hence would represent the fraction of friendship links that bind two users in the same country.

Figure 10 shows the visualization of the links across the top 10 countries of Google+. The size of each node is normalized to represent the proportion of Google+ users in the associated country and the thickness of each edge is proportional to its weight. Edges with weight smaller than 0.01 were omitted to improve visibility. With this result we find that US has an important role in the overall landscape of Google+, as seen from the dominant influx of edges from most countries to the US. Moreover, the US is a node with low reciprocity, which means that there are a significant number of people of other places adding people in the US to their circles while those in the US, in general, prefer to form friendships among themselves.

Highly populated countries like Brazil, India, and Indonesia (and the US as already mentioned) tend to have a high weight in the self-loop edges. For the remaining six countries, the proportion of self-loops is much smaller. In particular, only 30% of the links are self-loops in United Kingdom and 33% in Canada. These two countries, as a result, have a large number of out-going edges to the US, which might be explained by geographical proximity and cultural similarity (e.g., sharing the same spoken language).

It is also worth noticing that in Figure 10, the countries that exhibit self-loop edges grater than 0.50 are those that do not have English as their first languages, which are Indonesia, India, Brazil, Italy. Perhaps because of its economical and technological leadership, the US also exhibits a high degree of self-loop edges. This indicates the language barrier in the set up of cross-national social relationships. Furthermore, this also means that the nature of language and geography will introduce interesting opportunity for growth strategies (e.g., launch of Google+ in a new non-English speaking country will likely show a similar organic growth pattern with many national links).

The average path mile discussed earlier could mean that content distribution in Google+ faces similar challenges for both small and large countries. In fact, smaller countries like United Kingdom may require more sophisticated measures to reduce delay in content delivery, as seen from its high average path mile. Furthermore, we see varying patterns of link formation across different countries. When it comes to building recommender systems, it may make sense to recommend domestic users and their content for those countries that have high degree of self-loop such as Brazil and India. However, it may be of more interest to the users to recommend foreign users and content to those in Germany and United Kingdom due to their low fraction of self-loops.

5. RELATED WORK

Characterization of social networks and user behavior is fundamental to the understanding and engineering of these services on the Internet. Many studies focus on the characterization of the most popular social network models, such as Facebook, Twitter, Orkut, Cyworld and others. Some of the important findings of these studies include establishing power law distributions for in- and out-degree, short average distance between pairs of users, a very large connected component, and a small number of extremely popular users. Thus, in the remainder of this section, we restrict our coverage of related work to studies that concentrate on characterization of other social network models.

Mislove et al. [32] studied graph theoretic properties of social networks, based on the friend network of Orkut, Flickr, LiveJournal, and YouTube. They confirmed the power-law, small-world, and scale-free properties of these social network services. Ahn et

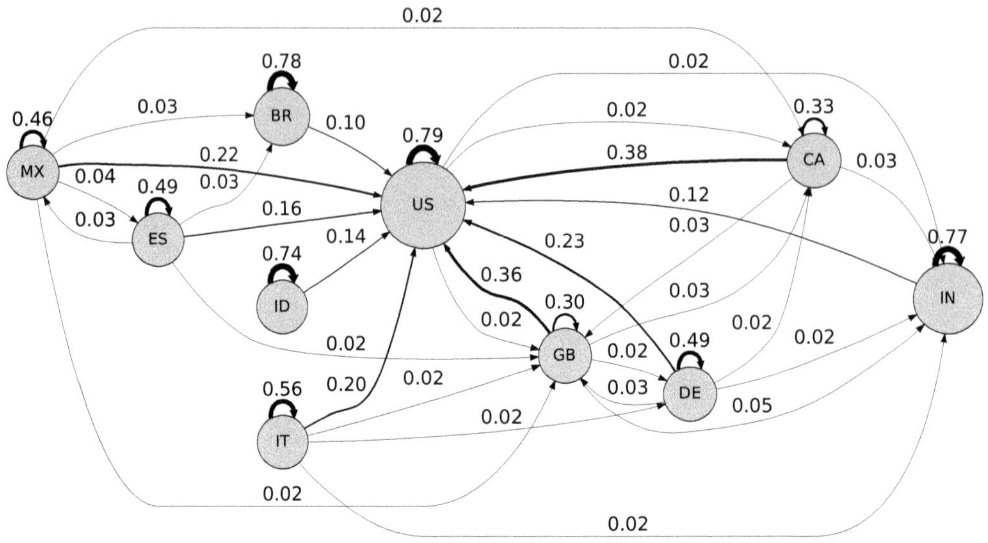

Figure 10: Link distribution across the top countries

al. [1] studied the network properties of Cyworld, a popular social networking service in South Korea. They compared the explicit friend relationship network with the implicit network created by messages exchanged on Cyworld's guestbook. They found similarities in both networks: the in-degree and out-degree were close to each other and social interaction through the guestbook was highly reciprocal.

Recently, Ugander et al. [39, 3] used the complete Facebook dataset to study the social graph of Facebook. They show - among other things - that the degree of separation in that platform is 4.7, while we find that in Google+ it is 5.9. This difference may be explained by the fact that Google+ is a new platform at it should get denser in the future, as studied by [28] for different networks. Two recent references [26, 7] focus on the study of the Twitter graph. Other studies comparing different social network models were done by [32, 4]. In general, Google+ presents a combination of the characteristics of other networks, such as Facebook and Twitter.

When it comes to research on geo-location of users in online social networks, Liben-Nowell et al. [29] analyzed the geographical location of LiveJournal users and found a strong correlation between friendship and geographic proximity. This work confirms that most social links in the blog network are correlated with physical distance and only 33% of the friendships are independent of geography. We find a similar pattern in the friendship structure of Google+ in this paper. Recently, Scellato et al. [37] showed that there is a strong relationship between geographical distance and the probability of being friends in social networks. They discuss the implications of geo-location for social networking sites. Rodrigues et al. [36] investigate the word-of-mouth based content discovery by analyzing URLs in Twitter. They showed that propagation and physical proximity have correlation. Finally, Poblete et al. [34] studied a large amount of data gathered from Twitter and showed the various usages of the system depending across different countries.

Most existing work focus on several extremely popular social networks. Although it started much later in time, Google+ has grown rapidly as one of the top 10 popular social networks in the world. While there exist a large number of newspaper articles [24, 23, 40, 14] and blog articles [33, 6] on Google+, no research paper has looked into its structure or user behavior in a research oriented way. This work provides a first look into the social graph and the geo-location patterns of Google+ users.

6. IMPLICATIONS

So far, we have made a series of observations about the service, network topology, and users of the Google+ social network based on large-scale data. In this section, we discuss the implications of these findings.

First, given that Google+ is a new social network, our first interest is to compare the topological structure of Google+ against other social networks. Compared to other social networks, Google+ cherishes openness in content sharing and is not a "walled garden" service like Facebook, where only the members can access content [30]. On the other hand, Google+ enforces a strong notion of friendship links by allowing users to manage different circles of friends. Our data analyses in Section 3 and Section 4 indicate that Google+ is in fact truly a social network, where the social links are correlated in geography reflecting offline friendship (i.e., friends are more likely to be located close), is far more reciprocal (i.e., bidirectional links), and have higher clustering coefficient (i.e., have triangle structures) compared to Twitter. The average path length is shown slightly longer than the other networks. As shown earlier, it is 5.9 in Google+ compared to 4.1–4.7 in other networks. A possible reason stem from the Google+ network is new and is still in the growing phase.

Second, observing the patterns of Google+ penetration worldwide can give insight into other new social networking service providers who would like to enter the market. While most new social network services typically starts their operation as a third party application or an adds-on service to the existing OSN services, Google+ is leading a full-fledged competition in the field. Therefore the pattern of how this new service is being adopted is important. While popular social networks like Facebook are known to have extremely high penetration rate of 50% or above [42], there is still room for a new social network service to become a hit in some countries. In particular, Google+ have been successfully adopted by countries with lower GDP per capita and this trend is important because the Internet penetration rate of these countries are growing fast–meaning the user base could potentially grow more rapidly for Google+.

Third, our findings about the privacy concern of users indicate that users exhibit different privacy notions and expectations in Google+, based on geography. Such differences could be taken into account when trying to build a recommender system or run an advertisement campaign on top of Google+, for instance, the system could feature newly emerging musicians to users in Mexico, while recommend journalists to newly joining users in Italy. Also, running a political campaign on Google+ may not turn out successful for many countries, except for in Spain. Another example would be that marketers could build appealing profiles for companies by following the right level of privacy concerns in each country.

Third, based on the information about the circle list and the geography of users, we have examined how the social links are distributed across different countries. The resulting map in Figure 10 shows an interpreting landscape of user interactions. We find very different user behaviors in this case. Certain countries like Brazil, India, and Indonesia appear far more inward looking when forming social links, than those outward looking countries like United Kingdom and Canada. This means that based on the geographical location of where a user lives, her expectation towards finding a stronger local community in the network is different. We believe this kind of social network analysis allows us to study the collective and deviant behavior of particular demographics, which are increasingly considered important and useful both in research and practice.

7. CONCLUDING REMARKS

In this paper we study characteristics of the Google+ social graph. We present a comprehensive description of the platform, highlighting the main differences from other popular social network models. Our study is based on a large amount of data gathered encompassing 27 million user profiles and their connections to other users. With this dataset we analyze unique features of the Google+ demographics, especially on the gender, occupation, relationship status, and geo-location of users. We construct a graph representing the social relations of Google+ and analyze its structural properties, such as reciprocity, clustering coefficient, and node degree distribution. The Google+ social graph has a giant connected component that included 70% of the crawled users, which means that information can flow freely among all such users.

We also compute the average physical distance between two connected users. Exploiting the geo-location of users, we could see how aggressively Google+ has been adopted in different countries. We investigate relationships between economic indexes of countries and the adoption rate of Google+. We find that Google+ is popular in countries with relatively low Internet penetration rate. By examining the top users based on the circle link information, seven out of the top 20 users turned out to be in the information technology industry, a trend that is rather uncommon in other online social networks, where popular figures are media outlets, celebrities, and public figures. By looking into users who share their contact information publicly, we observe that a large fraction of the users are male and single.

There are several interesting directions for future research. First, we are interested in measuring the speed at which a new social network service grows and whether we can predict the phase transitions in the growth sparks (e.g., tipping point when a network suddenly shows a rapid growth or the point where the growth stabilizes and turns into a dormant phase). By collecting multiple snapshots of the Google+ topology, we hope to gain insight in the dynamic changes in the internal structure of the social network over various adoption phases. Second, having seen the key differences of Google+ from other online social networks, we would like to understand how different privacy settings and openness impact the types of conversations and the patterns of content sharing in Google+. By gathering status updates of the most prolific users, we hope to understand what people expect to read and share from Google+ as opposed to other walled-garden or media-like social networks.

Acknowledgements

We thank our shepherd Zhi-Li Zhang and the anonymous reviewers for their valuable comments. This research was partially funded by the Brazilian National Institute of Science and Technology for the Web (MCT/CNPq/INCT grant number 573871/2008-6). Gabriel Magno, Giovanni Comarela and Virgilio Almeida were partially supported by grants from CNPq, CAPES and FAPEMIG. Diego Saez-Trumper was supported by the HIPERGRAPH project (TIN2009-14560-C03-01) from the Spanish Economy and Competitiveness Ministry. Meeyoung Cha was supported by Basic Science Research Program through the National Research Foundation, Korea (2011-0012988).

8. REFERENCES

[1] Y.-Y. Ahn, S. Han, H. Kwak, S. Moon, and H. Jeong. Analysis of topological characteristics of huge online social networking services. In *Proc. of ACM International World Wide Web Conference*, pages 835–844, 2007.

[2] P. Allen. Google+ growth accelerating. passes 62 million users. adding 625,000 new users per day. prediction: 400 million users by end of 2012., December 2011. `http://bit.ly/gp_nusers`.

[3] L. Backstrom, P. Boldi, M. Rosa, J. Ugander, and S. Vigna. Four degrees of separation. *CoRR*, abs/1111.4570, 2011.

[4] F. Benevenuto, T. Rodrigues, M. Cha, and V. Almeida. Characterizing user behavior in online social networks. In *Proc. of ACM SIGCOMM Internet Measurement Conference*, pages 49–62, 2009.

[5] S. Brin. Web freedom faces greatest threat ever, warns google's sergey brin., April 2012. `http://www.guardian.co.uk/technology/2012/apr/15/web-freedom-threat-google-brin`.

[6] H. Carpenter. I already use facebook and twitter. why do i need google+?, July 2011. `http://tinyurl.com/7pwauo2`.

[7] M. Cha, H. Haddadi, F. Benevenuto, and K. P. Gummadi. Measuring User Influence in Twitter: The Million Follower Fallacy. In *Proc. of AAAI International Conference on Weblogs and Social Media*, 2010.

[8] M. Cha, A. Mislove, and K. P. Gummadi. A measurement-driven analysis of information propagation in the flickr social network. In *Proc. of ACM International World Wide Web Conference*, pages 721–730, 2009.

[9] E. Comission. Attitudes on data protection and electronic identity in the european union, June 2011. `http://bit.ly/wkZhGR`.

[10] comScore. Google+ Reaches 20 Million Visitors in 21 Days, July 2011. `http://tinyurl.com/3ox3lp9`.

[11] comScore. It's a Social World: Top 10 Need-to-Knows About Social Networking and Where It's Headed, December 2011. `http://tinyurl.com/cfhqxke`.

[12] T. H. Cormen, C. Stein, R. L. Rivest, and C. E. Leiserson. *Introduction to Algorithms*. McGraw-Hill Higher Education, 2nd edition, 2001.

[13] D. Easley and J. Kleinberg. *Networks, Crowds, and Markets: Reasoning About a Highly Connected World*. Cambridge University Press, 2010.

[14] E. Eldon. Larry page is super excited to announce that google+ has 90m users, January 2012. `http://tinyurl.com/82mkntq`.

[15] engadget. Google+ has 250 million users, more mobile than desktop, June 2012. `http://tinyurl.com/d3ausse`.

[16] J. Fogel and E. Nehmad. Internet social network communities: Risk taking, trust, and privacy concerns. *Computers in Human Behavior*, 25(1):153–160, 2009.

[17] Freshtrax. Top 10 most popular websites in china, March 2010. `http://bit.ly/xgRIAq`.

[18] M. Gjoka, M. Kurant, C. T. Butts, and A. Markopoulou. A walk in facebook: Uniform sampling of users in online social networks. *CoRR*, abs/0906.0060, 2009.

[19] Google. Orkut demographic data, January 2012. `http://www.orkut.com/MembersAll`.

[20] R. Gross and A. Acquisti. Information revelation and privacy in online social networks. In *Proc. of ACM CCS Workshop on Privacy in the Electronic Society*, pages 71–80, 2005.

[21] V. Gundotra. Google+: 92, 93, 94, 95, 96, 97, 98, 99... 100., September 2011. `http://bit.ly/gp_noinvite`.

[22] V. Gundotra. Introducing the google+ project: Real-life sharing, rethought for the web, June 2011. `http://bit.ly/gp_released`.

[23] J. Halliday. Google+ saw 67m visits in november, with 2.7m from uk, says comscore, January 2012. `http://tinyurl.com/7ydcnck`.

[24] Q. Hardy. Google+ gains traction, researcher says, December 2011. `http://nyti.ms/wrEsOx`.

[25] R. Kumar, J. Novak, and A. Tomkins. Structure and evolution of online social networks. In *Proc. of ACM SIGKDD International Conference on Knowledge Discovery and Data Mining*, pages 611–617, 2006.

[26] H. Kwak, C. Lee, H. Park, and S. Moon. What is twitter, a social network or a news media? In *Proc. of ACM International World Wide Web Conference*, pages 591–600, 2010.

[27] J. Leskovec and E. Horvitz. Planetary-scale views on a large instant-messaging network. In *Proc. of ACM International World Wide Web Conference*, pages 915–924, 2008.

[28] J. Leskovec, J. Kleinberg, and C. Faloutsos. Graphs over time: densification laws, shrinking diameters and possible explanations. In *Proc. of ACM SIGKDD International Conference on Knowledge Discovery and Data Mining*, pages 177–187, 2005.

[29] D. Liben-Nowell, J. Novak, R. Kumar, P. Raghavan, and A. Tomkins. Geographic routing in social networks. *Proceedings of the National Academy of Sciences of the United States of America*, 102(33):11623–11628, 2005.

[30] R. MacManus. Tim berners-lee calls facebook a walled garden - is that fair?, November 2010. `http://www.readwriteweb.com/archives/tim_berners-lee_says_facebook_is_a_walled_garden.php`.

[31] S. Milgram. The small world problem. *Psychology Today*, 2:60–67, 1967.

[32] A. Mislove, M. Marcon, K. P. Gummadi, P. Druschel, and B. Bhattacharjee. Measurement and Analysis of Online Social Networks. In *Proc. of ACM SIGCOMM Internet Measurement Conference*, 2007.

[33] J. Mitchell. Google+ is going to mess up the internet, January 2012. `http://tinyurl.com/84x7o3a`.

[34] B. Poblete, R. Garcia, M. Mendoza, and A. Jaimes. Do All Birds Tweet the Same? Characterizing Twitter Around the World. In *Proc. of ACM Conference on Information and Knowledge Management*, Glasgow,UK, 2011.

[35] B. F. Ribeiro and D. F. Towsley. Estimating and sampling graphs with multidimensional random walks. *CoRR*, abs/1002.1751, 2010.

[36] T. Rodrigues, F. Benevenuto, M. Cha, K. P. Gummadi, and V. Almeida. On Word-of-Mouth Web Based Discovery of the Web. In *Proc. of ACM SIGCOMM Internet Measurement Conference*, 2011.

[37] S. Scellato, C. Mascolo, M. Musolesi, and V. Latora. Distance matters: geo-social metrics for online social networks. In *Proc. of ACM SIGCOMM Workshop on Social Networks*, Berkeley, CA, USA, 2010. USENIX Association.

[38] T. Taraszow, E. Aristodemou, G. Shitta, Y. Laouris, and A. Arsoy. Disclosure of personal and contact information by young people in social networking sites: An analysis using Facebook profiles as an example. *International Journal of Media and Cultural Politics*, pages 81–101, 2010.

[39] J. Ugander, B. Karrer, L. Backstrom, and C. Marlow. The anatomy of the facebook social graph. *CoRR*, abs/1111.4503, 2011.

[40] T. Wasserman. Google+ most popular with male users, students, February 2012. `http://tinyurl.com/7kz2k3m`.

[41] D. J. Watts and S. H. Strogatz. Collective dynamics of 'small-world' networks. *Nature*, 393(6684):440–442, June 1998.

[42] ZDNet. Top 10 countries in Facebook adoption, January 2012. `http://zd.net/xmA4rt`.

Multi-scale Dynamics in a Massive Online Social Network

Xiaohan Zhao[†], Alessandra Sala[*], Christo Wilson[†], Xiao Wang[‡], Sabrina Gaito[§], Haitao Zheng[†], Ben Y. Zhao[†]
[†]Department of Computer Science, UC Santa Barbara
[*]Bell Labs, Ireland, [‡]Peking University, [§]Università degli Studi di Milano
{xiaohanzhao, bowlin, htzheng, ravenben}@cs.ucsb.edu, alessandra.sala@alcatel-lucent.com, wangxiao@net.pku.edu.cn, gaito@dsi.unimi.it

ABSTRACT

Data confidentiality policies at major social network providers have severely limited researchers' access to large-scale datasets. The biggest impact has been on the study of network dynamics, where researchers have studied citation graphs and content-sharing networks, but few have analyzed detailed dynamics in the massive social networks that dominate the web today. In this paper, we present results of analyzing detailed dynamics in a large Chinese social network, covering a period of 2 years when the network grew from its first user to 19 million users and 199 million edges. Rather than validate a single model of network dynamics, we analyze dynamics at different granularities (per-user, per-community, and network-wide) to determine how much, if any, users are influenced by dynamics processes at different scales. We observe independent predictable processes at each level, and find that the growth of communities has moderate and sustained impact on users. In contrast, we find that significant events such as network merge events have a strong but short-lived impact on users, and they are quickly eclipsed by the continuous arrival of new users.

Categories and Subject Descriptors

J.4 [**Computer Applications**]: Social and Behavioral Sciences; H.3.5 [**Information Storage and Retrieval**]: Online Information Services

General Terms

Algorithms, Measurement

Keywords

Dynamic Graphs, Online Social Networks

1. INTRODUCTION

A number of interrelated processes drive dynamics in social networks. A deeper understanding of these processes can allow us to better model and predict structure and dynamics in social networks. In turn, improved models and predictors have numerous practical implications on the design of infrastructure, applications, and security mechanisms for social networks.

Details of these dynamic processes are best studied in the context of today's massive Online Social Networks (OSNs), *e.g.* Facebook [38], LinkedIn [24], and Renren [13]. Unfortunately, the providers of large social networks generally consider their dynamic network data to be trade secrets, and have few incentives to make such data available for research. Instead, studies have analyzed citation networks [22], content sharing networks [18], and high level statistics of social networks [1]. Others [21, 26, 10] sought to validate generative models such as preferential attachment (PA) [5].

Our goal is to better understand in detail the evolutionary dynamics in a social network. This includes not only the initial growth process during a social network's formation, but also the ongoing dynamics afterwards, as the network matures. Much of the prior work in this area, including generative graph models and efforts to validate them [5, 21, 26, 10], has focused on capturing network dynamics as a single process. In contrast, we are interested in the question "how are individual user dynamics influenced by processes at different scales?" How much are the dynamics of users influenced by external forces and events, such as the activities of friends in communities they belong to, or by large-scale events that occur at the network level?

In this work, we explore these questions empirically through a detailed analysis of social network dynamics at multiple scales: at the individual user level, at the level of user communities, and at the global network level. We study a dynamic graph, *i.e.* a sequence of detailed timestamped events that capture the ongoing growth of a large Chinese online social network. With over 220 million users, it is the largest social network in China, and provides functionality similar to Facebook. We focus our analysis on first two years of its growth, from its first user in November 2005, to December 2007 when it had over 19 million members. This captures the network's initial burst of growth, as well as a period of more sustained growth and evolution. Our anonymized data includes timestamps of all events, including the creation of 19 million user accounts and 199 million edges. This dataset is notable because of three features: its scale, the absolute time associated with each event, and a rare network *merge* event, when the network merged with its largest competitor in December 2006, effectively doubling its size from 600K users to 1.3 million users in a single day.

IMC'12, November 14–16, 2012, Boston, Massachusetts, USA.

Our analysis of network dynamics in this dataset focuses on three different levels of granularity: nodes, communities, and networks. At each level, we search for evidence of impact on user behavior. Along the way, we also make a number of intriguing observations about dynamic processes in network communities and network-wide events.

Individual Nodes. The creation of links between individual users has been studied in a number of contexts, and is long believed to be driven by generative models based on the principle of preferential attachment, *i.e.* users prefer to connect to nodes with higher degree [5]. Our goal is to extend the analysis of this model with respect to two new dimensions. First, preferential attachment defines how a sequence of edges are created in logical order, but how do node dynamics correlate with absolute time? Second, does the strength of the preferential attachment model strengthen or weaken as the network grows in scale and matures?

Communities. Intuitively, the behavior of a user is likely to be significantly impacted by the actions of her friends in the network. This has been previously observed in offline social networks [39]. Our goal is to empirically determine if user activity at the level of communities has a real impact on individual users. To do so, we first implement a way to define and track the evolution of user communities over time. We use the Louvain algorithm [6] to detect communities, track the emergence and dissolution of communities over time, and quantify the correlation of user behavior to the lifetime, size, and activity level of the communities they belong to.

Networks. Finally, we wish to quantify the impact, if any, of network-level events on individual user behavior. By network-level events, we refer to unusual events that affect the entire network, such as the merging of two distinct social networks recorded in our dataset. We analyze user data before and after the merge of our social network and its competitor, and quantify the impact of different factors on user behavior, including duplicate accounts, and user's edge creation preferences over time.

Key Findings. Our analysis produces several significant findings. First, we find that nodes (users) are most active in building links (friendships) shortly after joining the network. As the network matures, however, we find that new edge creation is increasingly dominated by existing nodes in the system, even though new node arrivals is keeping pace with network growth. Second, we find that influence of the preferential attachment model weakens over time, perhaps reflecting the reduced visibility of each node over time. As the network grows in size, users are less likely to be aware of high degree nodes in the network, and more likely to obey the preferential model with users within a limited neighborhood. Third, at the level of user communities, we find using the Louvain algorithm that users in large communities are more active in creating friends and stay active for a longer time. In addition, we found that a combination of community structural features can predict the short-term "death" of a community with more than 75% accuracy.

Finally, in our analysis of the network merge event, we use user activity to identify duplicate accounts across the networks. Aside from duplicate accounts, we find that the network merge event has a distinct short-term impact on user activity patterns. Users generate a high burst in edge creation, but the cross-network activity fades and quickly becomes dominated by edge creation generated by new users. Overall, this quickly reduces average distance between the two networks and melds them into a single monolithic network.

2. NETWORK LEVEL ANALYSIS

We begin our study by first describing the dataset, and performing some basic analysis to understand the impact of network dynamics on first order graph metrics. Our data is an anonymized stream of timestamped events shared with us by a large Chinese social network, whose functionality is similar to those of Facebook, Google+ and Orkut. Our basic measurements in this section set the context for the analysis of more detailed metrics in later sections.

Dataset of Dynamics in a Massive Social Network. The first edge in our large social network was created on November 21, 2005. The social network was originally built as a communication tool for college students, but expanded beyond schools in November 2007.

Our anonymized dataset encompasses the timestamped creation events of all users and edges in the social network. The dataset covers more than 2 years, starting on November 21, 2005 and ending December 31, 2007. In all, the dataset includes the creation times of 19,413,375 nodes and 199,563,976 edges. To perform detailed analysis on the social graph, we produce 771 graphs representing daily static snapshots from the timestamped event stream. Note that in this paper, we will use the term *node* to mean an OSN *user* and *edge* to mean a friendship link.

An unusual event happened on December 12, 2006, when our network merged with a second, competing online social network that was created in April 2006. On the merge date, our social network had 624K users with 8.2 million social links, and the second online social network had 670K users with 3 million social links. Wherever possible, we treat the merge as an external event to minimize its impact on our analysis of network growth. We also present detailed analysis of the network merge event in Section 5.

On our network, default user policy limits each user to 1,000 friends. Users may pay a fee in order to increase their friend cap to 2,000. However, prior work by the network has shown that very few users take advantage of such features. We make the same observation about our dataset: the number of users with >1,000 friends is negligibly small.

Network Growth. Figure 1(a) depicts the growth of the large Chinese social network in terms of the number of nodes and edges added each day. Day 0 is November 21, 2005. Overall, the network grows exponentially, which is expected for a social network. However, there are a number of real world events that temporarily slow the growth, and manifest as visible artifacts in Figure 1(a). The two week period starting at day 56 represents the Lunar New Year holiday; a two-month period starting on day 222 accounts for summer vacation; the merge with the competing social network causes a jump in nodes and edges on day 386; additional dips for the lunar new year and summer break are visible starting at days 432 and 587, respectively. In Figure 1(b), we plot daily growth as a normalized ratio of network size from the previous day. It shows that relative growth fluctuates wildly when the network is small, but stabilizes as rapid growth begins to keep rough pace with network size.

Graph Metrics Over Time. We now look at how four key graph metrics change over the lifetime of our data

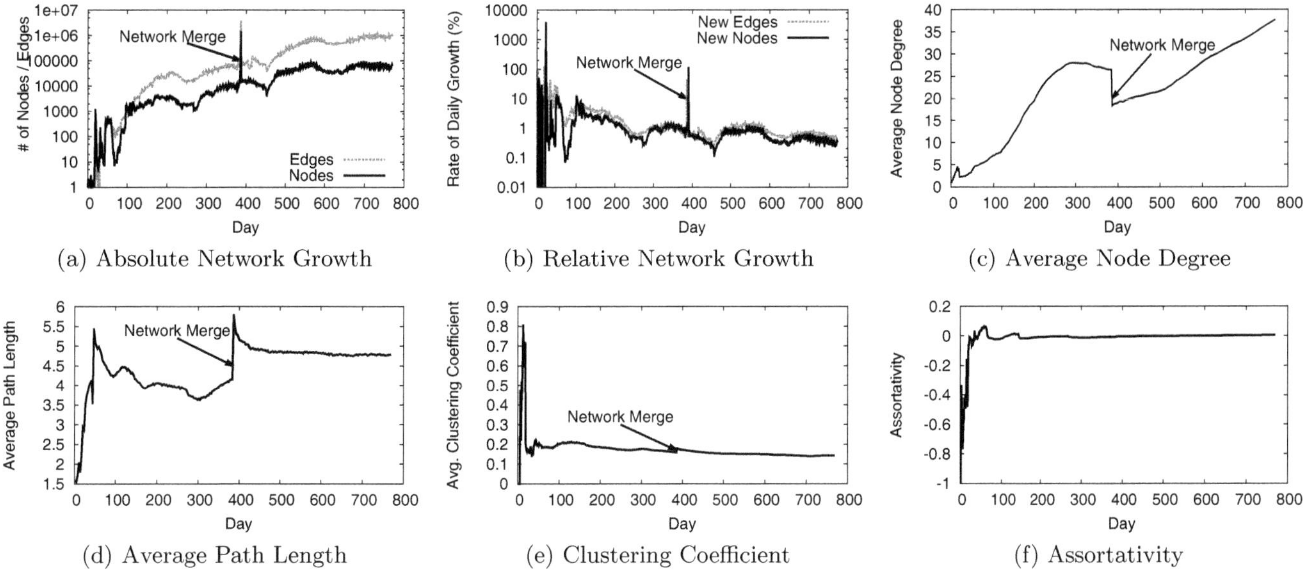

(a) Absolute Network Growth (b) Relative Network Growth (c) Average Node Degree

(d) Average Path Length (e) Clustering Coefficient (f) Assortativity

Figure 1: Network growth over time, and its impact on four important graph metrics.

stream, and use them to identify structural changes in the large Chinese social network. We monitor average degree, average path length, average clustering coefficient, and assortativity. As before, the analysis of each metric starts from November 21, 2005.

Average Degree. As shown in Figure 1(c), average node degree grows for much of our observed time period, because the creation of edges between nodes out paces the introduction of new users to the network. When we take a closer look, we see that around days 120, 275, 475 and 650, the average degree grows faster. This means that more edges are created around this time period, which happens to match up nicely with the beginning of new academic semesters over multiple years. On day 305, however, a period of rapid growth in users starts to reduce average degree in the network. This comes from a sudden influx of new users due to several successful publicity campaigns by the social network. Next, on day 386 (December 2006), average degree drops suddenly when 670K loosely connected nodes from a competing social network merges with our social network. Average degree resumes steady growth following the event, again showing edge growth out pacing node growth and increasing network densification [22].

Average Path Length. We follow the standard practice of sampling nodes to make path length computation tractable on our large social graphs. We compute the average path length over a sample of 1000 nodes from the SCC for each snapshot, and limit ourselves to computing the metric once every three days. As seen in Figure 1(d), the results are intuitive: path length drops as densification increases (*i.e.* node degree increases). There is a significant jump when nodes from the second online social network join the large social network on day 386, but the slow drop resumes as densification continues after the merge.

Average Clustering Coefficient. Clustering coefficient is a measure of local density, computed as the ratio of the existing edges between the immediate neighbors of a node over the maximum number of edges possible between them. We plot average clustering coefficient in Figure 1(e). In early stages of network growth (before day 60), the network was very small and contained a large number of small groups with loose connections between them. Groups often formed local cliques or near-cliques, resulting in high clustering coefficients across the network. Once the network grows in size, average clustering coefficient transitions to a smooth curve and decreases slowly. The network merge produces a small jump, since the competing social network had many small clusters of 3 or 4 nodes that boosted average clustering coefficient.

Assortativity. Finally, we plot assortativity in Figure 1(f). Assortativity is the probability of a node to connect to other nodes with similar degree, computed as the Pearson correlation coefficient of degrees of all node pairs. In the early stages of the network, the graph is sparse and dominated by a small number of supernodes connecting to many leaf nodes. This produces a strong negative assortativity that fluctuates and then evens out as the network stabilizes in structure. Assortativity evens out at around 0, meaning nodes in our network have no discernible inclination to be friends with nodes of similar or different degree.

Summary. We observe that the high-level structure of our network solidifies very quickly. Several key properties stabilize after the first 2 months, with others establishing a consistent trend after 100 days. While the notable network merge with a second, competing social network introduces significant changes to network properties, the effects quickly fade with time and continued influx of new users to the merged network.

3. EDGE EVOLUTION

In this section, we study the behavior of individual nodes in terms of how they build edges over time. Many studies have shown that nodes build edges following the preferential attachment (PA) model [5, 21, 26, 10]. Specifically, when a new node joins the network and creates edges, it chooses the

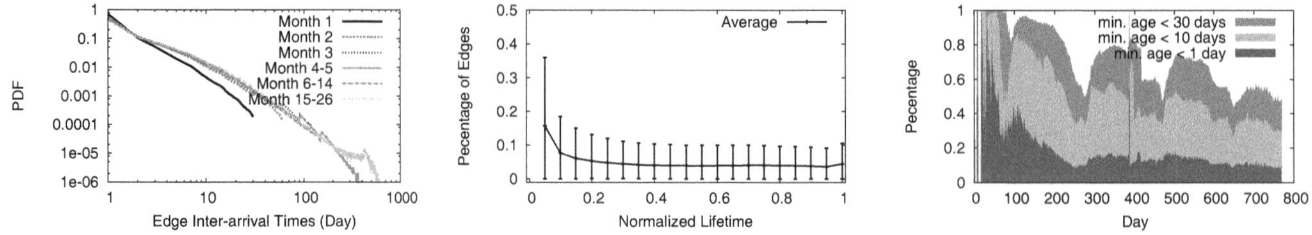

(a) Distribution of Edge Inter-arrival Times

(b) Edge Creation vs. Normalized Lifetime

(c) Node Age and Edge Creation

Figure 2: Time dynamics of edge creation. (a) The probability distribution of the edge inter-arrival times follows a power-law distribution. (b) The normalized activity level over each user's lifetime. Users create most of her friendships early on. (c) The portion of edges created by new nodes each day. When the network is young, new edges are mostly triggered by newly joined nodes. However, as the network matures, the majority of new edges connect older users.

destination of each edge proportionally to the destination's degree. In other words, nodes with higher degrees are more likely to be selected as the destination of new edges, leading to a "rich get richer" phenomenon.

Using our dynamic network data, we extend the analysis of this model in two new dimensions. First, while PA defines how a sequence of edges is created in logical order, we seek to understand how node activities correlate with absolute time. Second, we are interested in whether, as the network evolves, the PA model's predictive ability grows or weakens over time.

3.1 Time Dynamics of Edge Creation

Edge Inter-arrival. We begin by analyzing the edge creation process in absolute time, focusing on the speed that nodes add edges. First, we look at the inter-arrival time between edge creation events. For each node, we collect the inter-arrival times between all its edges, then place them into buckets based on the age of the node when the edge was created. We then aggregate all users' data together for each bucket, *e.g.* the "Month 1" bucket contains all edge inter-arrival times where one or both of the nodes was less than 1 month old.

We plot the results in Figure 2(a). We observe that the time gap between a node's edge creation events follows a power-law distribution. The scaling exponent is between 1.8 and 2.5, shown in Figure 2(a). The exponent values can be used in an edge creation gap model. However, it is difficult to evaluate its significance without a direct comparison to data from other networks. Overall, this power-law distribution provides a realistic model of a user's idle time between edge creations at different stages of her lifetime.

Edge Creation Over Lifetime. The above result motivates us to examine the normalized activity level within each user's lifetime. We plot in Figure 2(b) the distribution of new edges based on the normalized age of the users involved. To avoid statistical outliers, we consider only nodes with at least 30 days of history in our dataset and degree of at least 20. As expected, users create most of their friendships early on in their lifetimes. Edge creation converges to a constant rate once most offline friends have been found and linked.

Node Age and Edge Creation. We observe above that nodes tend to generate a significant portion of their edges soon after joining the network. Since most generative graph models use new nodes to drive edge creation, we ask the question "What portion of the new edges created in the network are driven by the arrival of new nodes?" For each day in our dataset, we take each edge created on that day and determine its minimal age, *i.e.* the minimum age of its two endpoints. The distribution of this value shows what portion of new edges are created by new nodes.

We compute and plot this distribution in Figure 2(c). We show the relative contribution by nodes of different ages by plotting three stacked percentages, showing the portion of daily new edges with minimal age $\leq$ 1 day, $\leq$ 10 days, and $\leq$ 30 days. We see that when the network is young ($\leq$ 60 days), the vast majority of new edges connect brand new nodes (*i.e.* 1 day old). As the network stabilizes and matures, that portion quickly drops, and continues to decrease over time. Edges with minimal age of 10-30 days dominate new edges for much of our trace, but their contribution steadily drops over time from 95% around day 100 to 48% by day 770. Note that this drop occurs even after the daily relative network growth has reached a constant level (see Figure 1(b)). It is reasonable to assume that in today's network (4.5 years past the end of our data), the vast majority of new edges connect mature users who have been in the network for significant amounts of time.

This result in Figure 2(c) is important, because it shows a dramatic change in the driving force behind edge creation as the network matures. Most generative graph models assume edge creation is driven by new nodes. However, our data indicates that existing models will only accurately capture the early stages of network creation. Capturing the continuous evolution of a mature network requires a model that not only recognizes the contribution of mature nodes in edge creation, but also its continuous change over time.

3.2 Strength of Preferential Attachment

Next, we take a look at the preferential attachment model and how well it predicts changes over time and network growth. We follow the method in [21] to measure the strength (or degree) of preferential attachment using edge probability $p_e(d)$. This function defines the probability that an edge chooses its destination with degree d, normalized by the total number of nodes of degree d before this time step:

$$p_e(d) = \frac{\Sigma_t\{e_t(u,v) \wedge d_{t-1}(v) = d\}}{\Sigma_t|v : d_{t-1}(v) = d|} \quad (1)$$

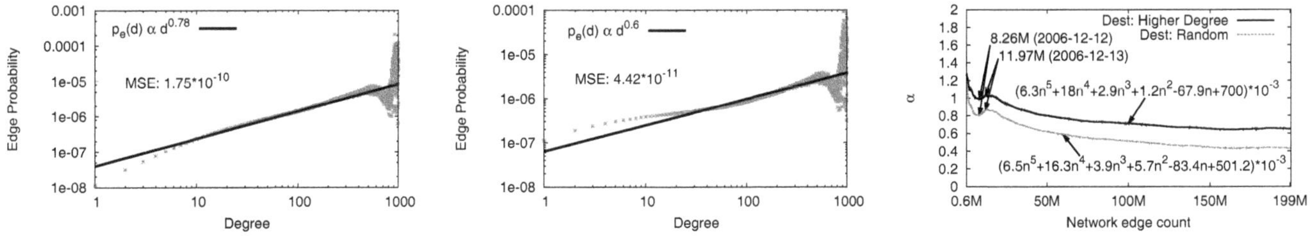

(a) $p_e(d)$, higher-degree node as destination (b) $p_e(d)$, random destination selection (c) Evolution of $\alpha(t)$

Figure 3: (a)-(b) Fitting the measured edge probability $p_e(d)$ with d^α, when our large Chinese social network reaches 57M edges. In (a), $p_e(d)$ is calculated by selecting the higher-degree node as each edge's destination. In (b) the destination is selected randomly. The mean square error (MSE) is very low, confirming the goodness of the fit. (c) As the network grows, α drops from 1.25 to 0.65. It can be approximated by a polynomial function of the network edge count n.

where $\{e_t(u,v) \wedge d_{t-1}(v) = d\} = 1$ if the destination v of the edge $e_t(u,v)$ is of degree d, and 0 otherwise.

Intuitively, if a network grows following the PA model, its edge probability $p_e(d)$ should have a linear relationship with d: $p_e(d) \propto d$. The authors of [21] verified this conclusion using synthetic graphs, and also tested the PA model on four real social networks: Flickr, Delicious, Answers, and LinkedIn. The first three networks follow the PA model $p_e(d) \propto d^\alpha$ with $\alpha \approx 1$, while for LinkedIn, $\alpha = 0.6$. From these observations, we can define a criterion for detecting preferential attachment: when $\alpha \to 1$, the network grows with a strong preferential attachment, and when $\alpha \to 0$, the edge creation process becomes increasingly random.

Using this criterion, we validate the PA model over time on our large Chinese social network by fitting $p_e(d)$ measured at time t to $d^{\alpha(t)}$ and examining $\alpha(t)$ over time. Our study seeks to answer an important question: "Does our network display the same level of preferential attachment consistently over time?" In other words, does $\alpha(t)$ stay constant over time? And if not, is the preferential attachment stronger (or weaker) at a particular stage of network growth?

We make some small adjustments to the computation of $p_e(d)$ on our dataset. First, because our data does not state who initiated each friendship link (edge directionality), we perform our test with two scenarios. The first is biased in favor of preferential attachment, because it always selects the higher degree end-point as the destination. The second scenario chooses the destination node randomly from the two end-points. Second, to make the computation tractable on our large number of graph snapshots, we compute $p_e(d)$ once after every 5000 new edges. Finally, to ensure statistical significance, we start our analysis when the network reaches a reasonable size, *e.g.* 600K edges.

Results. We start by examining whether $p_e(d) \propto d^{\alpha(t)}$ is a good fit. For this we use the Mean Square Error (MSE) between the measured $p_e(d)$ and the fitted curve. We observe that the MSE decreases with the edge count, ranging from 1.8e-5 to 3.5e-13. This confirms that the fit is tight for the measured edge probability. To illustrate the results, Figures 3(a)-(b) show the edge probability $p_e(d)$ when the network reaches 57M edges, using the two destination selection methods. The corresponding MSEs of the fit are 1.7e-10 and 4.4e-11, respectively.

Next, we examine $\alpha(t)$ over time in Figure 3(c). We make two key observations. *First*, $\alpha(t)$ when using the higher-degree method is always larger than when using random selection. This is as expected since the former is biased in favor of preferential attachment. More importantly, the difference between the two results is always 0.2. This means that despite the lack of edge destination information, we can still accurately estimate $p_e(d)$ from these upper and lower bounds.

Second, $\alpha(t)$ decays gradually over time, dropping from 1.25 (when the network first launched) to 0.65 (two years later at 199M edges). Since the number of nodes with node degree 1000 in the last snapshot is very small (0.0001% of the total nodes in the network), we believe the decrease in $\alpha(t)$ is not caused by the hard limit on node degree. This results shows that when the network is young, it grows with a strong preferential attachment. However, as the network becomes larger, its edge creation is no longer driven solely by popularity. Perhaps this observation can be explained by the following intuition. When a social network first launches, connecting with "supernodes" is a key factor driving friendship requests. But as the network grows, it becomes harder to locate supernodes inside the massive network and their significance diminishes. Alternatively, we could explain this phenomenon in another way. When the network is young, a new user is likely to find few of her offline friends to connect to, and "supernodes" easily draw users' attention because of their popularity. As the network grows, users find more and more of their offline friends on the online social network. As a result, users pay more attention to people who they may know instead of popular users.

Finally, we observe a small ripple at the early stage of the network growth, when $\alpha(t)$ experiences a surge on December 12, 2006 (8.26M edges). This is due to the network merge event, which generated a burst of new edges that produce a bump in $\alpha(t)$ for that single day.

3.3 Summary of Observations

Our analysis produces three conclusions:

- *In a node's lifetime, edge creation rate is highest shortly after joining the network and decreases over time.*
- *Edge creation in early stages of network growth is*

- *driven by new node arrivals, but this trend decreases significantly as the network matures.*
- *While edge creation follows preferential attachment, the strength degrades gradually as the network expands and matures.*

These results set the stage for the following hypothesis. An accurate model to capture the growth and evolution of today's social networks should combine a preferential attachment component with a randomized attachment component. The latter would provide a degree of freedom to capture the gradual deviation from preferential attachment.

4. COMMUNITY EVOLUTION

In online social networks, communities can be defined as groups of densely connected nodes based on network structure. More specifically, they are groups of nodes where more edges connect nodes in the same community than edges between different communities [29]. Note that these are implicit groups based on structure, and not explicit groups that a user might join or leave. Communities effectively capture "neighborhoods" in the social network. As a result, we believe they represent the best abstraction with which to measure the influence of social neighborhoods on user dynamics. We ask the question, "how do today's social network communities influence their individual members in terms of edge creation dynamics?"

To answer our question, we must first develop a method to scalably identify and track communities as they form, evolve, and dissolve in a dynamic network. There is ample prior work on community detection in static graphs [29, 7, 37, 6]. More recent work has developed several algorithms for tracking dynamic communities across consecutive graph snapshots [17, 32, 23, 35, 34]. Some of these techniques are limited in scale by computational cost, others require external information to locate communities across snapshots of the network.

In the remainder of this section, we describe our technique for scalably identifying and tracking communities over time based on network structure. We then present our findings on community dynamics in our social network, including community formation, dissolution, merging, and splitting. Finally, we analyze community-level dynamics, and use our detected communities to quantify the correlation between node and community-level dynamics. To make computation tractable across our large dataset, we choose a modified Louvain algorithm to produce the large majority of our results. To ensure that our choice of community detection algorithm does not significantly bias our results, we validate a portion of our findings using a second community detection algorithm that does not rely on modularity.

4.1 Tracking Communities over Time

Tracking communities in the presence of network dynamics is a critical step in our analysis of network dynamics at different scales. Prior work proved that dynamic community tracking is an NP-hard problem [35]. Current dynamic community tracking algorithms [17, 32, 23, 35, 34, 11] are approximation algorithms that "track" a community over multiple snapshots based on overlap with an incarnation in a previous snapshot. For scalability and efficiency, we use the similarity-based community tracking mechanism [11] for our analysis. In this section, we first introduce background on community detection algorithms and related definitions. Then, we briefly describe our mechanism, which is a modified version of [11] that provides tighter community tracking across snapshots using the incremental version of the Louvain algorithm [6]. At a high level, we use incremental Louvain to detect and track communities over snapshots, and use community similarity to determine when and how communities have evolved.

Background. Communities can be defined based on network structure as groups of well-connected nodes. There are dense connections inside communities but sparse connections between communities [29]. Modularity [27] is a widely used metric to quantify how well a network can be clustered into communities. It is defined as the difference between the fraction of edges falling in communities and the expected fraction when edges are randomly connected. It is formally defined in Equation 2, where A is the adjacency matrix ($A_{ij} = 1$ if node i and j are connected, and $A_{ij} = 0$ otherwise), k_i is the degree of node i, m is the total number of edges and $\delta(c_i, c_j) = 1$ if node i and j are in the same community and $\delta(c_i, c_j) = 0$ otherwise. The value of modularity should be between -1 and 1, and a large modularity means the network can be well clustered into communities.

$$Q = \frac{1}{2m} \sum_{ij} (A_{ij} - \frac{k_i k_j}{2m}) \delta(c_i, c_j) \tag{2}$$

Several algorithms are designed to optimize modularity. [29] proposes a simple method to optimize modularity, reducing complexity to $O(n^3)$. [28] improves the algorithm further using hierarchical clustering method and its complexity is $O(n^2)$. [7] further reduces the complexity to $O(m \cdot d \cdot log(n))$ using balanced binary trees and max heaps. [37] improves the computation efficiency by avoiding unbalanced partitions.

Similarity-based Community Tracking. Louvain [6] is a scalable community detection algorithm that significantly improves both modularity and efficiency using greedy local modularity optimization. It uses a bottom up approach that iteratively groups nodes and communities together, and migrates nodes between communities until the improvement to modularity falls below a threshold δ. To the best of our knowledge, Louvain is the only community detection algorithm that scale to graphs with tens of millions of nodes[1].

Our approach leverages the fact that Louvain can be run in incremental mode, where communities from the current snapshot are used to bootstrap the initial assignments in the next snapshot. Given how sensitive community detection is to even small changes in modularity, this approach enables more accurate tracking of communities by providing a strong explicit tie between snapshots. Finally, we follow the lead of [11], and track communities over time by computing the similarity between communities. Similarity is quantified as community overlap and is computed using set intersection via the Jaccard coefficient.

Community Evolution Events. Using similarity to track communities allows us to detect major community events, including their birth, death, merges, and splits. We define a community A *splits* at snapshot i when A is the highest correlated community to at least two communities

[1]https://sites.google.com/site/findcommunities/

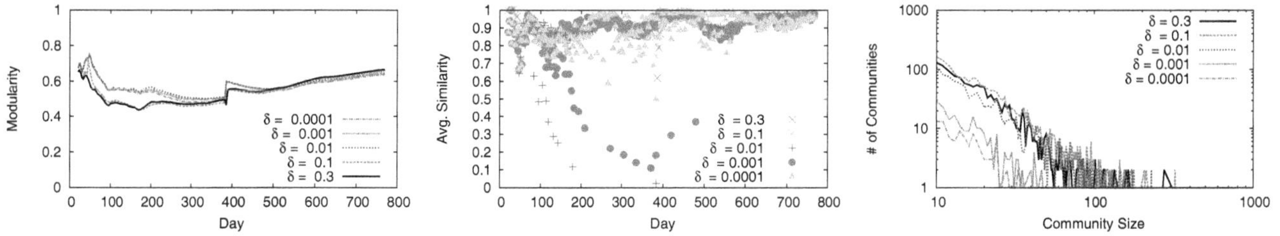

(a) Modularity (b) Average Community Similarity (c) Community Size Distribution on Day 602

Figure 4: Tracking communities over time and the impact of δ. (a) The value of modularity always stays above 0.4, indicating a strong community structure. The choice of δ has minimum impact, and $\delta = 0.01$ is sensitive enough to detect communities. (b) The value of average similarity over time at different δ values. Small δ values like 0.0001 and 0.001 produce less robust results. (c) The distribution of community size observed on Day 602. The algorithm is insensitive to the choice of δ once $\delta \geq 0.01$. The same conclusion applies to other snapshots.

B and C at snapshot $i+1$. When at least two communities A and B at snapshot i contribute most of their nodes to community C at snapshot $i+1$, A and B have merged.

When a community A splits into multiple communities $X_1, X_2 ... X_n$, we designate X_j as the updated A in the new snapshot, where X_j is the new community who shares the highest similarity with A. We say that all other communities in the set were "born" in the new snapshot. Similarly, if multiple communities merge into a single community A, we consider A to have evolved from the community that it shared the highest similarity with. All other communities are considered to have "died" in the snapshot.

Choosing δ. The δ threshold in Louvain is an important parameter that controls the trade off between quality of community detection and sensitivity to dynamics. If δ is too small, the algorithm is too sensitive, and over-optimizes to any changes in the network, needlessly disrupting the tracking of communities. If δ is too large, the process terminates before it optimizes modularity, and it produces inaccurate communities.

Choosing the best value for δ means optimizing for the dual metrics of high modularity and robustness (insensitivity) to slight network dynamics. First, we use network-wide modularity as a measure of modularity optimization for a given δ value. Second, to capture robustness to network dynamics, we use community similarity [11]: the ratio of common nodes in two communities to the total number of different nodes in both communities. More specifically, for two consecutive snapshots, we compute the average similarity between communities that exist in both snapshots. We run the Louvain algorithm on our snapshots using several different δ threshold values, and select the best δ that generates both good modularity and strong similarity. We repeat this procedure on shrinking ranges of δ until modularity and similarity can no longer be improved.

Sensitivity Analysis. We run the Louvain algorithm on our dynamic graph snapshots generated every 3 days. We start from Day 20, when the network is large enough (64 nodes) to support communities, and only consider communities larger than 10 nodes to avoid small cliques.

We scale δ between 0.0001 and 0.3, and plot the resulting modularity and average similarity in Figure 4. As shown in Figure 4(a), in all snapshots the modularity for all thresholds is more than 0.4. According to prior work [20], modularity ≥ 0.3 indicates that our social network has significant community structure. As expected, a threshold around 0.01 is sensitive enough for Louvain to produce communities with good modularity. Note that the big jump in modularity on Day 386 is due to the network merge event.

Figure 4(b) shows that thresholds 0.0001 and 0.001 produce lower values of average similarity (*i.e.* they are less robust and more sensitive) compared to higher thresholds between 0.1 and 0.3. Thus, Louvain with $\delta > 0.01$ generates relatively good stability of communities between snapshots.

Lastly, we examine whether detected communities are highly sensitive to the choice of δ. As an example, Figure 4(c) plots the distribution of community sizes observed on Day 602. The conclusion from this figure is that once the threshold exceeds 0.01, the impact of δ on community size is reduced to a minimum. The same conclusion applies to other snapshots as well.

Based on the results in Figure 4, we repeat the Louvain algorithm within a finer threshold range of 0.01 to 0.1. We find that a threshold value of 0.04 provides the best balance between high modularity and similarity. We use $\delta = 0.04$ to track and measure dynamic communities in the rest of our analysis on the dataset.

4.2 Community Statistics Over Time

We now leverage the Louvain-based community tracking technique to analyze the dynamic properties of our social network communities. We begin in this section by looking at the community size distribution, how it changes over time, and the distribution of lifetimes for all communities. In Section 4.3, we take a closer look at the dynamic processes of community merges and splits. We explore the possibility of predicting community death from observed dynamics. Finally, in Section 4.4, we analyze the impact of community membership on individual user dynamics, and gauge how and to what extent community dynamics are observed to have influenced individual user dynamics.

Community Size. The size distribution of communities is an important property that reflects the level of clustering in the network structure. Since the network is constantly evolving, we can compute a community size distribution for each snapshot in time. We already observed in Figure 4(c) that the distribution of community sizes follows a power-law.

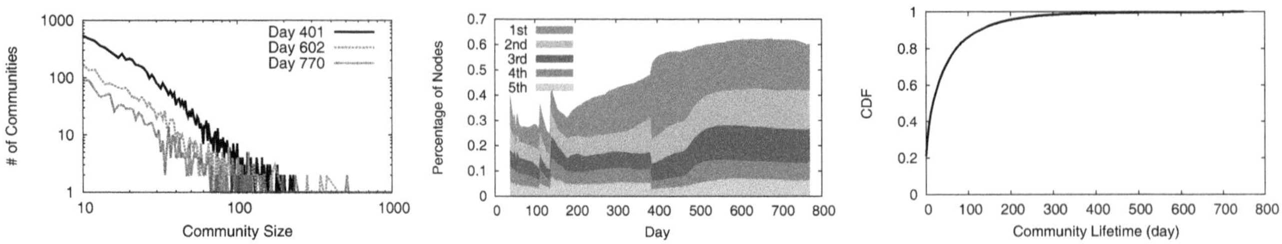

(a) Community Size Distribution (b) % of Nodes Covered by Top 5 Communities (c) CDF of Community Lifetime

Figure 5: Analysis on the evolution of communities. (a) Community size distribution on Days 401, 602, and 770. All three lines follow a power-law distribution, and show a gradual trend towards larger communities. (b) The portion of nodes covered by the top 5 communities grows considerably as the network matures. (c) Distribution of community lifetimes shows most communities only stay in the network for a very short time, and are quickly merged into other communities. This indicates a high level of dynamics between communities.

Our goal is to understand not only the instantaneous community size distribution, but also how the distribution changes over time as the network evolves. Thus, we compute the distributions for days 401, 602, and 770; 3 specific snapshots roughly evenly spaced out in our dataset following the network merge event. We plot the resulting community size distributions in Figure 5(a). The figure shows that the three snapshots consist of a large number of small communities and a long tail of large communities, consistent with the power-law distribution. This is consistent with other daily snapshots as well. More importantly, these snapshots show a gradual trend towards larger communities. Over the year of time between snapshots 401 and 770, the number of small communities shrunk by an order of magnitude. In turn, the sizes of the largest communities increase significantly.

To take a closer at how communities grow over time, we focus on the portion of the network that is covered by a small number of the largest communities. We take the top five communities sorted by size, and plot the percentage of the overall network they contain in Figure 5(b). We see that their coverage of the network shows a clear and sustained growth over time. They grow from less than 30% around day 100 to more than 60% of the entire network by the end of our dataset. Over time, this trend seems to indicate that as the network matures, connectivity becomes uniformly strong throughout the main connected component, while distinctions between communities fade.

Community Lifetime. In a dynamic network, how long a community remains in the network is another important statistical property. By using our community identification method between snapshots, we measure the distribution of community lifetime. Figure 5(c) shows that most of the communities only stay in the network for a very short period of time. Specifically, 20% of communities have lifetimes of less than a day, meaning that they disappear in the next snapshot after they are first detected. 60% of the communities have lifetimes less than 30 days, at which point they are merged into other communities. This shows an extremely high level of dynamics at the community level.

4.3 Community Merging and Splitting

Community merging and splitting are the main reasons underlying community death and birth. Therefore, understanding these processes in detail is critical to understanding dynamics at the community level as a whole. We study these processes in detail, with three questions in mind: What factors influence the split and merge processes for communities? What features, if any, are good indicators for whether a community will merge soon? Finally, can we predict which communities will merge together?

First, we study whether community size impacts splitting or merging. For splitting events, we only consider the largest two communities resulting from the split. Similarly for merge events, we focus on the two largest communities merging to become one community. We use as a metric the ratio of the size of the second largest community to the size of the largest community. The smaller the ratio is, the larger the size difference is between the two communities. In Figure 6(a), we plot the ratio of community splitting with a red line and community merging with a black line. We observe that for 78% of merged community pairs, this ratio is less than 0.005. This reflects that for most merge events, there is a large size discrepancy between the smaller community and a larger community. This is consistent with our observation that small communities tend to disappear over time, while the biggest communities continue to grow in size.

The community splitting process acts in a totally different manner. The red line in Figure 6(a) shows that the ratio for 68% split communities pairs are more than 0.5. Thus, when a community splits into smaller communities, the community tends to split into two comparable size communities. One possible explanation for this observation is that users only have a finite amount of time or energy to devote to online friendships, *e.g.* an online version of Dunbar's Number [9]. Once a community grows beyond this number, existing users cannot continue to add more friends. This leads to non-uniform distribution of new edges as users arrive, which creates pockets of stronger connectivity in the community and fragments it. The limit in social relationships has been observed in prior measurement studies [38].

Predicting Merging. Since community merge is the only reason causing the death of the communities, we are curious whether there are any structural features specific to the merge process, and whether we can accurately predict if a community is going to merge with another in the next snapshot. We identify three structural metrics, including *community size*, *in-degree ratio*, the ratio of the edges inside a community over the sum of the degrees of nodes in the

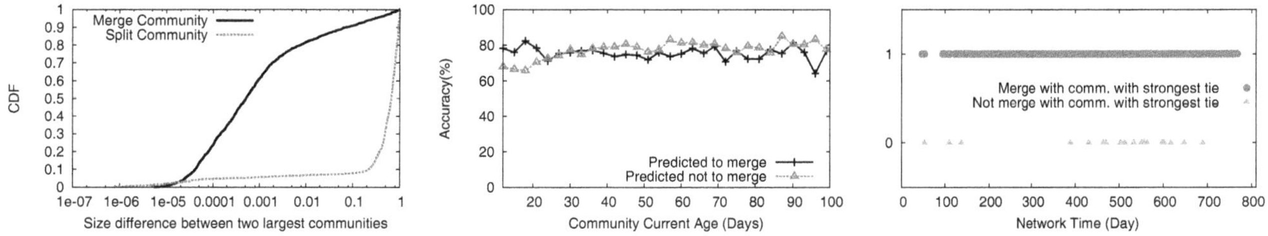

(a) Community Size Difference (b) Accuracy on Merge Prediction (c) Patterns of Merged Communities

Figure 6: Analysis of community merge and split events. (a) The distribution of the normalized size difference between the largest two components when they split or merge. Small communities always merge into large communities, and a community tends to split into two communities of comparable sizes. (b) The accuracy of our prediction on whether a community will merge with another in the next snapshot. We achieve a reasonably good accuracy of 75%. (c) With very high probability (99%), a community merges with the community that has the most edge connections (or the strongest tie) to itself.

community, and the *similarity* of a community to itself in the previous snapshot (defined in Section 4.1).

Since these metrics evolve over time, we also consider short-term changes in these features as additional factors. For example, consider the community size feature. We can identify its *first order change indicator* as a feature: if a community is smaller than its incarnation in the previous snapshot, we use -1 to indicate the decrease. Similarly, we use 1 to mark an increase and 0 to mark no change. For each metric, we can also consider its *second order change indicator*. If the change in community size from snapshot $i-1$ to i is larger than the size change from snapshot $i-2$ to $i-1$, we use 1 to indicate acceleration in this metric. Similarly, we use -1 to mark a deceleration in this metric. In total, we start with the three basic metrics and add on their standard deviation, their first order change indicator, and their second order change indicator.

Leveraging these feature metrics, we can now predict whether a community will merge with another in the next snapshot. Specifically, we apply a support vector machine over these features, together with the age of each community. For consistency, we do not consider communities created on the day of the network merge with the competing network because those changes are driven by external events. To examine the accuracy of our prediction, we compute two metrics: 1) the ratio of the number of communities predicted to merge in the next snapshot to the number of communities who actually merge, and 2) the ratio of the number of communities predicted to not merge in the next snapshot to the number of communities who do not merge.

Figure 6(b) plots our two accuracy metrics as a function of the community age. They show that our method achieves reasonable prediction accuracy. It achieves an average accuracy of 75% in predicting community merges and 77% in predicting no merges. This means that we can reliably track communities' short-term evolution.

We are also interested in predicting which destination community a given community will merge into. After examining each merged community pair, we make an interesting observation. With a very high probability (99%), a community i will merge with another community j that has the largest number of edges to i, or the strongest tie with i. Figure 6(c) illustrates this trend by plotting red dots for all merge events where a community merges with the peer with the strongest tie, and a green triangle otherwise. The results show that the trend is consistent over time. Thus, we conclude that the inter-community edge count is a reliable metric for predicting the destination of community merges.

4.4 Impact of Community on Users

To understand how communities impact users' activity, we compare edge creation behaviors of users inside communities to those outside of any community. Overall, our results show that community users score higher on all dimensions of activity measures, confirming the positive influence of community on users.

Edge Inter-arrival Time. Figure 7(a) plots the CDF of edge inter-arrival times for community and non-community users. We observe that users within different communities display similar edge inter-arrival statistics, and merge their results into a single CDF curve for clarity. The considerable distance between the two curves confirms that community users are more enthusiastic in expanding their social connections than non-community users.

User Lifetime. Next, we examine how long users stay active after joining the network, and whether engagement in a community drives up a user's activity span. We define a user i's lifetime as the gap between the time i builds her last edge and the time i joins the network.

Figure 7(b) plots the CDF of user lifetime for users in different size communities as well as non-community users. $[x, y]$ represents communities of size between x and y. We find that the lifetime distribution depends heavily on the size of the community. The larger the community is, the longer its constituent user's lifetimes are. Compared to non-community users, users engaging in a community tend to stay active for a longer period of time. This confirms the positive impact of community on users.

In-Degree Ratio. Although we know that communities have more edges inside than outside statistically, we want to quantify how each user within each community connect to each other. We compute each user's in-degree ratio, *i.e.* the ratio of her edge count within her community to her degree. Figure 7(c) shows the CDF of the in-degree ratio for users in communities of different sizes. We observe that users in larger communities have a larger in-degree ratio, indicating that they form a greater percentage of edges within

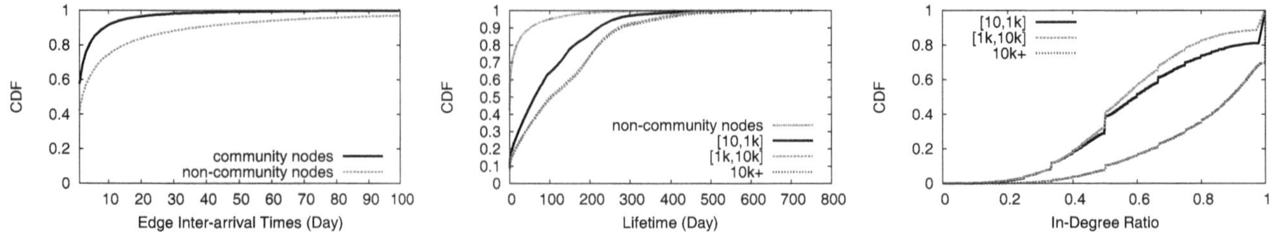

(a) Edge Inter-arrival Time (b) Node Lifetime (c) Edge In-Degree Ratio

Figure 7: Comparing activity of users inside and outside communities. Community users score higher on all dimensions of activity measures, confirming the positive influence of community on users. (a) Edge inter-arrival time. Community nodes create edges more frequently than non-community nodes. (b) Node lifetime. Community users are grouped by their community sizes. $[x, y]$ represents communities of size between x and y. Community nodes stay active longer than non-community nodes. (c) Community user's in-degree ratio. Nodes in larger communities are more active within their own communities.

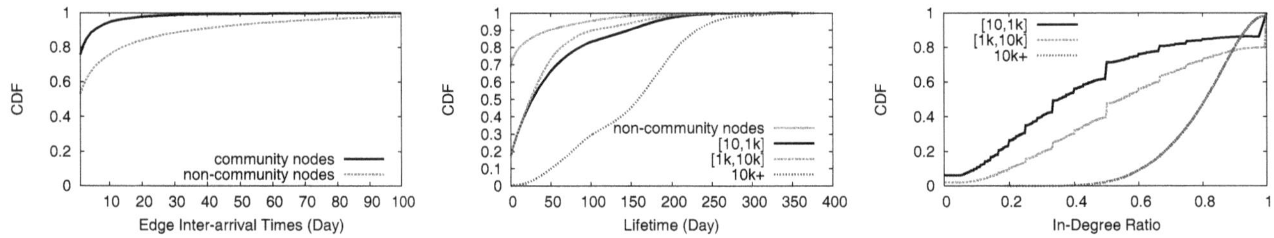

(a) Edge Inter-arrival Time (b) Node Lifetime (c) Edge In-Degree Ratio

Figure 8: Verification of results on the impact of communities on users' activities, using the Absolute Potts Model (APM) community detection algorithm. The results from communities detected by APM are consistent with our results using communities detected by our incremental Louvain approach.

their own community. In particular, 11-30% of nodes only interact with peers in their own communities. These results show that like offline communities, online social communities also encourage users to interact "locally" with peers sharing mutual interests.

4.5 Verification by Alternative Community Detection Algorithm

One concern with our work is whether our results are strongly biased by our choice of community detection algorithm. Since our incremental Louvain approach is the only algorithm able to process our large dataset, we choose to validate a small subset of our results using an alternative algorithm for community detection.

We select the Absolute Potts Model (APM) community detection algorithm [31]. This algorithm detects communities by minimizing a metric from Potts model, which describes the network energy under such network partition. The formal definition of this metric for unweighted graphs is shown in Equation 3, where A_{ij} is the element of adjacency matrix, $J_{ij} = (1 - A_{ij})$ is the missing edge in this network and σ_i is the community which node i belongs to. If node i and node j are in the same community, *i.e.* $\sigma_i = \sigma_j$, $\delta(\sigma_i, \sigma_j)$ is 1; otherwise, it is 0. γ is used to weight the strength of the missing edges, which is 0.0001 in our experiment.

$$H = -\frac{1}{2}\sum_{i \neq j}(A_{ij} - \gamma J_{ij})\delta(\sigma_i, \sigma_j) \tag{3}$$

Because of the significant computational costs, we run the APM community detection algorithm on our first-year network data, *i.e.* from snapshot 20 to snapshot 383. Then we run the measurement in Figure 7 on communities detected by APM, and present all of the results in Figure 8. Figure 8(a) shows the CDF of edge inter-arrival time of users in communities and users out of communities. We find that users in communities are more active in creating new connections compared to those outside of communities. Figure 8(b) shows the node lifetime distribution in communities of different sizes. We observe that users in larger communities have longer lifetimes. The edge in-degree ratio distribution in Figure 8(c) shows that users in larger communities are more likely to connect users inside the same community than users outside the community. All these results are qualitatively consistent with the observations in Figure 7. This confirms our results on community membership's impact on user activity. But more broadly, it provides evidence that our choice of that community detection algorithms does not significantly skew our analytical results.

4.6 Summary of Results

Our efforts on tracking and analyzing the evolution of communities lead to the following key findings:

- *Our social network displays a strong community structure, and the size of the communities follows the power-law distribution.*
- *The majority of communities are short-lived, and within a few days they quickly merge into other larger*

communities. These merge events can be reliably predicted using structural features and dynamic metrics.

- *The membership to a community has significant influence on users' activity. Compared to stand-alone users, community users create edges more frequently, exhibit a longer lifetime, and tend to interact more with peers in the same community.*

5. MERGING OF TWO OSNS

On December 12, 2006, our large Chinese OSN merged with a second competing online social network in China. This combined entity became the largest Chinese online social network that exists today. Our access to the graph topological and temporal data that characterizes this merge gives us a unique opportunity to study how this network-level event impacts users' activity. For clarity, we refer to our original social network as network X and the competitor it merged with as network Y.

In this section, we analyze the forces at work during the merge. First, we look at the edge creation activity of users over time in order to isolate users that have become inactive. This enables us to estimate how many duplicate accounts there were between network X and network Y. Second, we examine edge creation patterns within and between the two OSNs, and show that user preferences vary by OSN and over time. We observe that the merge is the primary driver of new edge creation for only a short time; edges to new users that joined the combined network after the merge rapidly take over as the driving force. Finally, we calculate the distance between users in each group to quantify when the two distinct OSNs become a single whole. We calculate that the average path length from one OSN to the other drops rapidly in the days following the merge, even when edges to new users are ignored. This demonstrates that the two OSNs quickly become a single, indistinguishable whole.

5.1 Background

Our original Chinese social network opened for business in November 2005 to university students. Before the two networks merged, network X counted 624K active users and 8.2M edges. Network Y was a competing OSN created in April 2006 that also targeted university students. Before the merge, network Y included 670K active users and 3M edges.

On December 12, 2006, the two OSNs officially merged into a single OSN. During the actual merge event, both OSNs were "locked" to prevent modification by users, and all information from network Y was imported and merged into network X's databases. Starting the next day, users could log-in to the combined system and send friend requests normally, *e.g.* users with profiles in network X could friend users in network Y and vice versa. New users just joining the system would not notice any difference between profiles of users from the two networks.

Since both networks targeted university students, it was inevitable that some users would have duplicate profiles after the merge. Network X used users' registration emails to identify whether a user has a duplicate profile in network Y. If a user uses one email to register both networks, the new merged social network allowed the user to choose which profile they wanted to keep during their first log-in to the site after the merge.

Definitions. In this section, we investigate the details of the merge between the two networks. To facilitate this analysis, we classify the edges created after the merge into three different groups. *External edges* connecting users from network X to users in network Y, whereas *internal edges* connect users within the same OSN. *New edges* connect a user in either OSN with a new user who joined the combined network after the merge. Time based measurements are presented in "days after the merge," *e.g.* one day after the merge is day 387 in absolute terms, since the merge occurs during day 386 of our dataset.

5.2 Measuring the Merge

User Activity Over Time. We start our analysis by examining the number of active users in both OSNs over time. We define a user as "active" if it has created an edge within the last t days. In our data, 99% of users create at least one edge every 94 days (on average), hence we use that as our activity threshold t.

Figure 9(a) shows the number of active users over time for network X, while Figure 9(b) focuses on network Y users. Each "all edges" line highlights the number of users actively creating edges in each group. Although we have 384 days of data after the merge, the x-axis of Figures 9(a) and 9(b) only extends 290 days. Since our minimum activity threshold is 94 days, we cannot determine whether users have become inactive during the tail of our dataset.

We now address the question: *how many duplicate accounts were there on both OSNs?* Users with accounts on both services were prompted to choose one account or the other on their first log-in to the combined OSN after the merge. However, the discarded accounts were not deleted from the graph. Thus, it is likely that any accounts that are inactive on the first day after the merge are discarded, duplicate accounts.

Figures 9(a) and 9(b) reveal that 11% of network X accounts and 28% of network Y accounts are immediately inactive. Thus, it is likely that at least 39% of users had duplicate accounts between the two networks before the merge. Interestingly, users demonstrate a strong preference for keeping network X accounts over network Y accounts.

As time goes on, the number of active accounts in each group continues to drop. Presumably, these users lose interest in the merged network and stop generating new friend relationships. After 284 days, the number of inactive network X accounts doubles to 23%, while 52% of network Y accounts are inactive. The relative decrease in active accounts over time (12% on network X versus 24% on network Y demonstrates that network X users are more committed to maintaining their OSN presence. This observation corresponds to our earlier finding that users with duplicate accounts tended to keep their network X accounts. Network X users form a self-select population of more active OSN users when compared to network Y users.

The "new users," "internal," and "external" lines give the first glimpse of the types of connections favored by users in both OSNs. For each line, a user is considered active only if they have created an edge of the corresponding type in the last 94 days. Users in both graphs show similar preferences: edges to new users are most popular, followed by internal and then external edges. The large activity gap between internal and external edges highlights the strong homophily among each group of users. Internal and external edge creation activity declines more rapidly than edges to new users. This makes sense intuitively: the number of

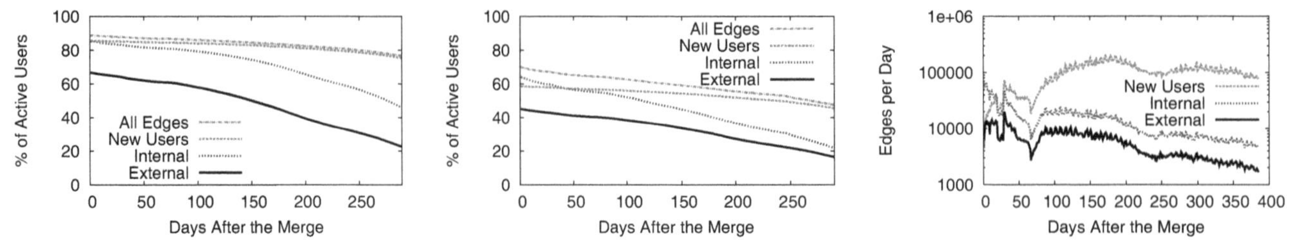

(a) Active users over time for network X (b) Active users over time for network Y (c) Edge creation per day

Figure 9: (a)-(b) The number of active users over time. Accounts that are inactive on day 0 after the merge are likely to by discarded, duplicate accounts. Overall user activity declines over time. (c) Number of edges of different types created per day after the merge. Edges to new users quickly become the most popular edge type, although there is a small peak for external edges as well.

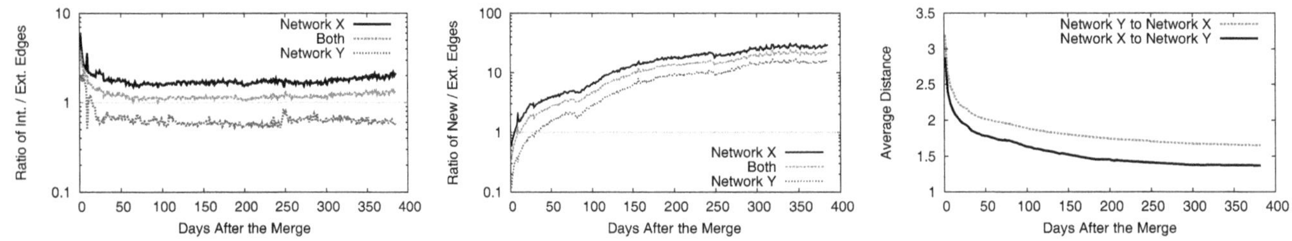

(a) Ratio of internal to external edges (b) Ratio of new to external edges (c) Distance between 2 OSNs over time

Figure 10: (a) Ratio of internal to external edges over time. Network X users create more edges overall, and are biased towards internal edges, weighting the average upward. (b) Ratio of new to external edges per day. Both networks overwhelmingly prefer edges to new users, although they reach this point at different rates. (c) The average distance in hops between the two OSNs drops over time as more internal and external edges are created. By day 50, the two networks are essentially one large, well connected whole.

users in the two networks is static, and hence the pool of possible friends slowly drops over time as edges are created.

Edge Creation Over Time. Next, we switch focus to look at the characteristics of edges, rather than individual users. By looking at the relative amounts of internal, external, and edges to new users that are created each day, we can identify what types of connections are driving the dynamic growth of the network after the merge.

Figure 9(c) shows the number of internal, external, and new edges created per day. Initially, internal and external edges are more numerous than edges to new users. However, 3 days after the merge new edges begin to outnumber external edges, and by day 19 new edges out pace internal edges as well. This result demonstrates that new users quickly become the primary driver of edge creation, as opposed to new edges between older, established users. This is not surprising: since the merged network is growing exponentially, the number of new users eventually dwarfs the sizes of network X and network Y, which remain static.

Note that this result does not conflict with the results presented in Section 3. Section 3 examines the edge creation patterns over the lifetime of *all* users in our data. In this section, we are comparing the edge creation patterns of users who existed before the merge to *everyone* who joined after. Thus, the age "buckets" in this section are very course.

We now ask the question: *are there differences between the types of edges created by network X and network Y users?* Although Figure 9(c) demonstrates that internal edges always outnumber external edges, the reality of the situation is more complicated when the edges are separated by OSN.

Figure 10(a) plots the ratio of internal to external edges over time for network X and network Y. Initially, users on both OSNs favor creating internal edges (*i.e.* the ratio is >1). However, by day 16, the ratio for network Y users starts to permanently favor external edges. The reason for this strange result is that network X users create more than twice as many edges than network Y users. In our dataset, network X users create 3.9 million internal edges, while network Y users only create 1.5 million. However, unlike internal edges, external edges affect the statistics for *both* groups. Thus, the number of external edges (2.2 million total in our dataset) is driven by the more active user base. Even though network X users create less external edges than internal edges, the number is still proportionally greater than the number of internal edges created between network Y users. The "both" line in Figure 10(a) is always >1 because network X users create more edges overall, which pushes the average upwards.

Figure 10(b) plots the ratio of edges to new users versus external edges over time for both networks. This plot reveals that the inflection point where users switch from preferring external edges to new edges is different for the two OSNs. The ratio becomes $\geq$1 for network X 5 days after the merge, whereas network Y takes 32 days. Despite these differences, both OSNs demonstrate the same overall trend for the ratio to eventually tip heavily in favor of edges to new users.

Distance Between the two networks. Finally, we examine the practical consequences of edge creation between the two networks. Our goal is to answer the question: *at what point do the two networks become so interconnected that they can no longer be considered separate graphs?*

To answer this question, we calculate the distance, in hops, between users in each group. Intuitively, the distance between the groups should decrease over time as 1) more external edges are created, and 2) more internal edges increase the connectivity of users with external edges. In our experiments, we select 1,000 random users from each OSN on each day after the merge and calculate the shortest path from each of them to *any* user in the opposite OSN. Thus, the lowest value possible in this experiment is 1, *e.g.* the randomly selected user has an external edge directly to a user in the opposite OSN. New users and edges to new users are not considered in these tests.

Figure 10(c) shows that the average path length between the two OSNs rapidly declines over time. Although average path lengths for both OSNs initially start above 3 hops, within 47 days average path lengths are <2. Path lengths from network X to network Y are uniformly shorter, and by the end of the experiment the average path length is <1.5.

The distance between networks X and Y rapidly approaches an asymptotic lower bound in Figure 10(c). Once this bound is reached, it is apparent that the graphs can become no closer. We conclude that by day 50, when both lines begin to approach the lower bound, the two networks can no longer be considered separate OSNs. These results demonstrate how quickly the two disjoint OSNs can merge into a single whole, even when edge creation is biased in favor of internal edges (see Figure 10(a)).

5.3 Summary of Results

Our analysis produces several high-level conclusions:

- *There were a large number of duplicate accounts between the two networks that become inactive immediately after the merge.*
- *Edges to new nodes quickly become the driving force behind edge creation.*
- *Despite user's preference against external edges, the two networks very quickly merge into a single, well-connected graph.*

We also observe that the merge alters user's edge creation patterns for a short time (until equilibrium is restored):

- *The total number of edges created per day increases, driven by the sudden appearance of so many new users.*
- *Users' preferences for internal/external edges changes drastically in the days following the merge.*
- *Network X users are more active than network Y users. Thus, the external edges created between network X and network Y force network Y users to become more active than they normally would be.*

6. RELATED WORK

Dynamic OSN Measurement. Several studies have measured basic dynamic properties of graphs. [22] analyzed four citation and patent graphs, and proposed the forest fire model to explain the observed graph densification and shrinking diameter. [21] studied details of dynamics in four OSNs to confirm preferential attachment and triangle closure features. Similar conclusions were reached by studies on Flickr [26] and a social network aggregator [10]. [16] measured network temporal radius and found out that there is a gelling point to distribution. In addition, [2] measured weighted dynamic graphs, [1] analyzed the growth of a Korean OSN, and [36] considered temporal user interactions as graph edges instead of static friendship. Finally, [12, 18] analyzed blogspace dynamics.

Some studies focused on analyzing social network dynamics through explicitly defined groups [4, 40, 14] or disconnected components [19, 25, 15]. [18] tried to identify blog communities and detect bursts in different temporal snapshots. [30] utilized the clique percolation method [8] to identify overlapping community dynamics in mobile and citation graphs. Unlike these studies, our work focuses on the evolution of implicit communities in a densely connected, large-scale social graph.

Dynamic Community Detection and Tracking Algorithms. There are two approaches to detecting and tracking dynamic communities. One approach is to minimize the self-defined temporal cost of communities between snapshots. [35] proved that this problem is NP-hard and then several works [35, 34, 23] proposed approximation algorithms. However, these algorithms only scale to graphs with thousands of nodes. [32] and [17] propose dynamic community detection algorithms that scale to graphs with hundreds of thousands of nodes. The drawback of [32] is that it cannot track individual community evolution.

The other approach is to match communities detected by static community detection algorithms across temporal snapshots. [11] maps communities between snapshots if their similarity is higher than a threshold. [3, 33] tracks communities between snapshots based on critical community events. These algorithms do not consider any temporal correlation when detecting communities between snapshots.

7. CONCLUSION

This work presents a detailed analysis of user dynamics in a large Chinese online social network, using a dataset that covers the creation of 19 million users and 199 million edges over a 25-month period. More specifically, we focus on analyzing edge dynamics at different levels of scale, including dynamics at the level of individual users, dynamics involving the merge and split of communities, and dynamics involving the merging of two independent online social networks.

Our analysis produced a number of interesting findings of dynamics at different scales. First, at the individual node level, we found that the preferential attachment model gradually weakens in impact as the network grows and matures. In fact, edge creation in general becomes increasingly driven by connections between existing nodes as the network matures, even as node growth keeps pace with the growth in overall network size. Second, at the community level, we use an incremental version of the popular Louvain community detection algorithm to track communities across snapshots. We empirically analyze the birth, growth, and death of communities across merge and split events, and show that community merges can be predicted with reasonable accuracy using structural features and dynamic metrics such as acceleration in community size. Finally, we analyze detailed dynamics following a unique event merging two comparably-sized social networks, and observe that its impact, while significant in the short term, quickly fades with the constant arrival of new nodes to the system.

While our results from this network may not generalize to all social networks, our analysis provides a template for understanding the dynamic processes that are active at different scales in many complex networks. A significant takeaway from our work is that the actions of individual users are not only driven by dynamic processes at the node-level, but are also significantly influenced by events at the community and network levels. A comprehensive understanding or model of an evolving network must account for changes at the network and community levels and their impact on individual users.

Acknowledgments

We would like to thank our shepherd Alan Mislove and the anonymous reviewers for their feedback. This work is supported in part by NSF grant CNS-1224100 and by DARPA GRAPHS. Any opinions, findings, and conclusions or recommendations expressed in this material are those of the authors and do not necessarily reflect the views of the funding agencies.

8. REFERENCES

[1] AHN, Y., HAN, S., KWAK, H., MOON, S., AND JEONG, H. Analysis of topological characteristics of huge online social networking services. In *Proc of WWW* (2007).

[2] AKOGLU, L., MCGLOHON, M., AND FALOUTSOS, C. RTM: Laws and a recursive generator for weighted time-evolving graphs. In *Proc. of ICDM* (2008).

[3] ASUR, S., PARTHASARATHY, S., AND UCAR, D. An event-based framework for characterizing the evolutionary behavior of interaction graphs. *ACM TKDD 3*, 4 (2009), 16.

[4] BACKSTROM, L., HUTTENLOCHER, D., KLEINBERG, J., AND LAN, X. Group formation in large social networks: membership, growth, and evolution. In *Proc. of KDD* (2006).

[5] BARABÁSI, A., AND ALBERT, R. Emergence of scaling in random networks. *Science 286*, 5439 (1999), 509.

[6] BLONDEL, V., GUILLAUME, J., LAMBIOTTE, R., AND LEFEBVRE, E. Fast unfolding of communities in large networks. *J. Stat. Mech* (2008).

[7] CLAUSET, A., NEWMAN, M., AND MOORE, C. Finding community structure in very large networks. *Physical review E 70*, 6 (2004).

[8] DERÉNYI, I., PALLA, G., AND VICSEK, T. Clique percolation in random networks. *Physical review letters 94* (2005).

[9] DUNBAR, R. Neocortex size as a constraint on group size in primates. *Journal of Human Evolution 22*, 6 (1992).

[10] GARG, S., GUPTA, T., CARLSSON, N., AND MAHANTI, A. Evolution of an online social aggregation network: an empirical study. In *Proc. of IMC* (2009).

[11] GREENE, D., DOYLE, D., AND CUNNINGHAM, P. Tracking the evolution of communities in dynamic social networks. In *Proc. of ASONAM* (2010).

[12] GUO, L., TAN, E., CHEN, S., ZHANG, X., AND ZHAO, Y. Analyzing patterns of user content generation in online social networks. In *Proc. of KDD* (2009).

[13] JIANG, J., WILSON, C., WANG, X., HUANG, P., SHA, W., DAI, Y., AND ZHAO, B. Y. Understanding latent interactions in online social networks. In *Proc. of IMC* (2010).

[14] KAIRAM, S., WANG, D., AND LESKOVEC, J. The life and death of online groups: predicting group growth and longevity. In *Proc. of WSDM* (2012).

[15] KANG, U., MCGLOHON, M., AKOGLU, L., AND FALOUTSOS, C. Patterns on the connected components of terabyte-scale graphs. In *Proc. of ICDM* (2010).

[16] KANG, U., TSOURAKAKIS, C., AND FALOUTSOS, C. Radius plots for mining tera-byte scale graphs: Algorithms, patterns, and observations. In *Proc. of SDM* (2010).

[17] KIM, M., AND HAN, J. A particle-and-density based evolutionary clustering method for dynamic networks. *Proceedings of the VLDB Endowment 2*, 1 (2009), 622–633.

[18] KUMAR, R., NOVAK, J., RAGHAVAN, P., AND TOMKINS, A. On the bursty evolution of blogspace. *World Wide Web 8*, 2 (2005), 159–178.

[19] KUMAR, R., NOVAK, J., AND TOMKINS, A. Structure and evolution of online social networks. In *Proc. of KDD* (2006).

[20] KWAK, H., CHOI, Y., EOM, Y., JEONG, H., AND MOON, S. Mining communities in networks: a solution for consistency and its evaluation. In *Proc. of IMC* (2009).

[21] LESKOVEC, J., BACKSTROM, L., KUMAR, R., AND TOMKINS, A. Microscopic evolution of social networks. In *Proc. of KDD* (2008).

[22] LESKOVEC, J., KLEINBERG, J., AND FALOUTSOS, C. Graphs over time: densification laws, shrinking diameters and possible explanations. In *Proc. of KDD* (2005).

[23] LIN, Y., CHI, Y., ZHU, S., SUNDARAM, H., AND TSENG, B. Facetnet: a framework for analyzing communities and their evolutions in dynamic networks. In *Proc of WWW* (2008).

[24] LINKEDIN INFRASTRUCTURE TEAM. Data infrastructure at linkedin. In *Proc. of ICDE* (2012).

[25] MCGLOHON, M., AKOGLU, L., AND FALOUTSOS, C. Weighted graphs and disconnected components: patterns and a generator. In *Proc. of KDD* (2008).

[26] MISLOVE, A., KOPPULA, H., GUMMADI, K., DRUSCHEL, P., AND BHATTACHARJEE, B. Growth of the flickr social network. In *Proc. of WOSN* (2008).

[27] NEWMAN, M. Analysis of weighted networks. *Physical Review E 70*, 5 (2004), 056131.

[28] NEWMAN, M. Fast algorithm for detecting community structure in networks. *Physical Review E 69* (2004).

[29] NEWMAN, M., AND GIRVAN, M. Finding and evaluating community structure in networks. *Phys.Rev. E 69*, 2 (2004).

[30] PALLA, G., BARABASI, A., AND VICSEK, T. Quantifying social group evolution. *Nature 446*, 7136 (2007), 664–667.

[31] RONHOVDE, P., AND NUSSINOV, Z. Local resolution-limit-free potts model for community detection. *Physical Review E 81*, 4 (2010), 046114.

[32] SUN, J., FALOUTSOS, C., PAPADIMITRIOU, S., AND YU, P. Graphscope: parameter-free mining of large time-evolving graphs. In *Proc. of KDD* (2007).

[33] TAKAFFOLI, M., SANGI, F., FAGNAN, J., AND ZAIANE, O. A framework for analyzing dynamic social networks. *Applications of Social network Analysis (ASNA)* (2010).

[34] TANTIPATHANANANDH, C., AND BERGER-WOLF, T. Constant-factor approximation algorithms for identifying dynamic communities. In *Proc. of KDD* (2009).

[35] TANTIPATHANANANDH, C., BERGER-WOLF, T., AND KEMPE, D. A framework for community identification in dynamic social networks. In *Proc. of KDD* (2007).

[36] VISWANATH, B., ET AL. On the evolution of user interaction in facebook. In *Proc. of WOSN* (2009).

[37] WAKITA, K., AND TSURUMI, T. Finding community structure in mega-scale social networks. *CoRR abs/cs/0702048* (2007).

[38] WILSON, C., BOE, B., SALA, A., PUTTASWAMY, K. P. N., AND ZHAO, B. Y. User interactions in social networks and their implications. In *Proc. of EuroSys* (April 2009).

[39] ZACHARY, W. An information flow model for conflict and fission in small groups. *Journal of anthropological research* (1977), 452–473.

[40] ZHELEVA, E., SHARARA, H., AND GETOOR, L. Co-evolution of social and affiliation networks. In *Proc. of KDD* (2009).

Watching Videos from Everywhere: A Study of the PPTV Mobile VoD System

Zhenyu Li[†], Jiali Lin[†], Marc-Ismael Akodjenou[†],
Gaogang Xie[†], Mohamed Ali Kaafar[*] [‡], Yun Jin[♯], Gang Peng[♯]
[†]ICT, CAS, China,
[‡]INRIA France, [*]National ICT Australia,
[♯]PPlive, China
{zyli, linjiali, akodjenou, xie}@ict.ac.cn, kaafar@inrialpes.fr,
{yunjin, gangpeng}@pptv.com

ABSTRACT

In this paper, we examine mobile users' behavior and their corresponding video viewing patterns from logs extracted from the servers of a large scale VoD system. We focus on the analysis of the main discrepancies that might exist when users access the VoD system catalog from WiFi or 3G connections. We also study factors that might impact mobile users' interests and video popularity. The users' behavior exhibits strong daily and weekly patterns, with mobile users' interests being surprisingly spread across almost all categories and video lengths, independently of the connection type. However, by examining the activity of users individually, we observed a concentration of interests and peculiar access patterns, which allows to classify the users and thus better predict their behavior. We also find a skewed video popularity distribution and then demonstrate that the popularity of a video can be predicted using its very early popularity level. We further analyzed the sources of video viewing and found that even if search engines are the dominant sources for a majority of videos, they represent less than 10% (resp. 20%) of the sources for the highly popular videos in 3G (resp. WiFi) network. We report that both the type of connections and mobile devices in use have an impact on the viewing time and the source of viewing. Based on our findings, we provide insights and recommendations that can be used to design intelligent mobile VoD systems and help improving personalized services on these platforms.

Categories and Subject Descriptors

C.2.4 [**Computer Applications**]: Distributed applications; C.4 [**Performance of Systems**]: Measurement techniques

General Terms

Measurement, Performance, Human Factors

Keywords

Mobile VoD, user behavior, video popularity, view source

1. INTRODUCTION

The advanced wireless technologies (*e.g.* WiFi, 3G and 4G) and smart mobile devices (*e.g.* iPad, iPhone, Android systems) enable users to watch Internet videos from almost everywhere. Today video content providers often, if not always, offer client applications that can be installed on mobile users' tablets and smart phones, making the video viewing ubiquitous and contributing to the growing popularity of mobile video services.

A recent report [1] indicated an increase of 50% of the global mobile video traffic in 2011 compared to the previous year, and expected that the volume of video traffic will reach 25 times its current volume by 2016. Video providers naturally strive to meet such a huge demand through the design of better system architectures. Understanding the current system's artifacts, *e.g.* users' behavior, viewing patterns and trends of video popularity is of tremendous importance to design and optimize the efficiency of the systems, from the consumption of network resources to the economic models. User- and video-related trends are two key factors combining to influence the day-to-day performance of the VoD distribution network. Analyzing and predicting these factors is highly valuable to build scalable and robust distribution networks and caching systems.

There have been several measurement studies on landline based video systems, *e.g.* [15][14][5] for VoD systems, [10] for P2P VoD systems, [9] for P2P live streaming, [3] and [7] for IPTV systems. However, the observations reported so far may not be applicable to mobile video systems because of mobility-related constraints, limited bandwidth and small screen size of mobile devices. For example, Li *et al.* [12] found that viewing patterns in mobile TV systems are different from those observed in landline-based TV broadcast and VoD systems.

In this paper, we analyze the viewing behavior of mobile users and study the patterns of video consumptions using a unique dataset extracted from the log servers of PPTV, a leading video provider in China offering both live streaming and VoD services. The dataset spans over 14 days in December 2011 and consists in a collection of approximately 86 million videos requests generated by more than 3.5 million users. This unique dataset enables us to dig into both mobile users' behavior and video consumption patterns. From a user behavior perspective, we focus on temporal patterns, viewing time, user interests and individual users' activity, while for video-related patterns, we analyze the level of video popularity and sources of video viewing. We are particularly interested in identifying the impact of types of connection and mobile device on these metrics. Our main findings and observations are summarized as follows:

- We observe that the behavior of users shows strong daily and weekly patterns, with a relatively short viewing time. Longer viewing times are associated with the use of WiFi rather than 3G and with the use of tablets (*e.g.* iPad) compared to smart phones (*e.g* iPhone). We also found a surprisingly high number of requests of long videos from 3G users. The completion rate (*i.e.* the viewing time normalized by the video length) for short videos is on average around 0.5, with lower rates observed for long videos. This is however varying with the time of the day, as we observed that completion rates are much higher in early morning.
- We analyze the activity of individual users by aggregating the number of views and find that it follows a stretched exponential distribution model. The stretched factor is correlated with the connection type. Interestingly, the users viewing videos through a mix of both WiFi and 3G connections watch a higher number of videos than those using exclusively one type of connection.
- We study the interests of users according to video category and found that such interests vary over the course of the day. The interests are also correlated with geolocations. In general, individual users request and view videos from only a few categories, pointing to a high concentration of interests.
- We measure that 10% of the requested set of top popular videos attracted more than 80% of the views, in accordance with the Pareto principle ("a minor proportion of causes generate a major proportion of effects"). Although the observation period of 14 days is relatively short to assess general behavior of video popularity distributions, we find a high correlation between the amount of early viewing of videos and their near-future popularity, especially for animation videos and variety shows.
- We finally observe that even though the view source is dependent on the type of access to the network, overall the category page is the primary source of views and is often used to request highly popular videos. Another source is the PPTV video search engine which is the main source of views for more than half of the total video catalog, especially for low-popularity videos. The video search engine thus contributes to the diversity of video views.

In the light of these results, it is desirable that the research community investigates the inclusion of several features into the design of intelligent mobile VoD systems. Firstly, the Pareto principle of video popularity indicates that it might be necessary for content delivery networks (CDNs) to cache only the 10% top popular videos, since they contribute to more than 80% of the views. The high correlation coefficient between early view records of videos and their popularity can be used to decide whether a video should be cached just a few hours after its release. Secondly, it is important to notice that the effectiveness of the cache can be optimized by allocating most of the capacity to store the first chunks of videos, since the normalized viewing time of the vast majority of views is low. Thirdly, despite the variety of users' behaviors, users' interests reside in a few categories only, which could be leveraged to design efficient recommendation systems and targeted advertisement. Finally, the types of connection and mobile device should be considered as important factors. The CDN can better predict the peculiar behavior of its mobile users by taking these factors into account and thus optimize further the placement of servers and the routing strategies.

The remaining of this paper is organized as follows: Section 2 describes the dataset. In Section 3, we perform an in-depth analysis of users' behavior. Section 4 examines video popularity patterns, followed by an analysis of viewing source in Section 5. In section 6, we evaluate the design of a caching system that uses the observations we made. We discuss the related work in Section 7. Section 8 concludes our work.

2. DATASET

2.1 Dataset Description

Our dataset was collected from the log servers of PPTV[1], a leading video content provider offering live streaming and VoD services in China. PPTV provides free access to 22 categories of videos, including movies, TV series, animation or variety shows. Users can view videos either through a Web browser or through a free client application available for various types of mobile devices (*e.g.* iPad, iPhone, Android pads and Android phones).

Table 1: Main fields of logs

Field	Example
Timestamp	13:10:01 Dec. 4 2011
Geo-location	BJ, SH, overseas, etc.
Connection type	WiFi, 3G or unknown
User ID	33ab8c95437fd
File name	Tom and Jerry_episode1.mp4
Video category	Movie, TV series, animation
Device	iPhone, iPad, Android phone, etc.
Viewing time	55 seconds
Viewing source	video search, category page, etc.
Streaming type	VoD, live

Since most of the views of mobile accesses are generated by mobile devices-based software (as opposed to web browsers), we only consider the views records from the software. After a view is terminated, a record is pushed to the log servers. Table 1 lists an example of the main fields contained in the logs.

The timestamp field is formatted as GMT+8 (Beijing's time zone). The geo-location field can refer to one of the provinces in mainland China, HongKong-Macao-Taiwan or

[1]http://www.pptv.com/

an overseas location. Connection type has three possible values: WiFi, 3G and unknown. A unique user ID is generated when a client application is installed on a mobile device. Note that it is possible for some users to share a device (*e.g.* members of the same household) and as such a user in this paper relates to a client application which may correspond to different users sharing the same device. The video name field contains a unique identifier of the video. The viewing time field contains the duration of a view in seconds, not including the possible pauses in viewing. Finally, the viewing source field identifies how users discover videos, *i.e.* category page, video search, recent views, recommendation, favorite, top popular videos, cover and next episode.

We uniformly sampled the logs of VoD and live streaming requests that came from the client application on mobile devices for a period spanning two weeks from Dec. 1st, 2011 to Dec. 14th, 2011. Overall we collected 111,702,242 view logs, out of which 108,851,161 views are VoD requests. By filtering out the logs with unknown connection type, the data finally contained 86,521,403 logs, with a proportion of 92.58% access with a WiFi connection and 7.42% via a 3G connection. These views were generated by 3,759,129 users watching 427,316 unique videos. Hereafter, we will refer to this final filtered dataset as the `mobile dataset` and use it as the base of our analysis.

Table 2: Dataset statistics

Access method	% of views from		
	Tablets (iPad+aPad)	Smart phones (iPhone+aPhone)	others
3G	5.37	94.63	~0
WiFi	44.89	55.10	0.01
WiFi+3G	42.08	57.91	0.01

Table 2 shows the distribution of views generated by different types of mobile devices. Almost all the views are from four types of mobile devices, *i.e.* iPad, iPhone, Android pad and Android phone (the latter two are abbreviated aPad and aPhone in this paper). The number of views from smart phones and tablets is similar when a WiFi connection is used while for 3G accesses most of the views come from smart phones.

2.2 Limitations

The dataset contains 14 days of viewing logs. This relatively short period of time does not allow us to fully observe users' behavior and videos' consumption patterns, as the series of viewing rates and video popularity trends usually span larger time scales. Besides, the dataset is a uniform sample and not a total collection of logs. We will thus focus on normalized values and avoid metrics that might be affected by a sampling bias.

Another limitation is that the dataset does not contain detailed video attributes, such as video length, video uploading time, video tags, bit rate or others. Among these attributes, video length is certainly one of the most important for the analysis of viewing time. In order to obtain this information, we used another large sample of viewing logs from the Web portal of PPTV (with 91 million entries, mostly from PCs). In this Web sample the video length is included, along with an identifier for the video file with the same format as in our `mobile dataset`. We were then able to obtain the corresponding length of 268,867 videos that were contained in both samples. Although these videos only cover 62.9% of the unique videos in `mobile dataset`, they still account for 95.8% of the views.

Finally, even though the viewing behavior during user's mobility would be of interest in this work, the dataset does not contain any relevant location information.

3. USERS' BEHAVIOR AND INTERESTS

We analyze in this section both aggregated viewing behavior and individual behavior of the users, and discuss the implications of our key observations.

3.1 Daily and Weekly Patterns

System designers need insights on the workload of the systems to perform adequate capacity design. In this article, we define workload as the number of video requests to the system. Figure 1 plots the variation of this workload over time, for both WiFi and 3G connection types. Each of the two curves is produced in the following way: we aggregate the number of views with a bin for each hour and counted the number of views of the same hour of week. Finally the number of views per hour is normalized by the total number of views through WiFi and 3G, respectively. Note that since the total number of views through WiFi is different from the number of views through 3G, one cannot quantitatively compare the two curves.

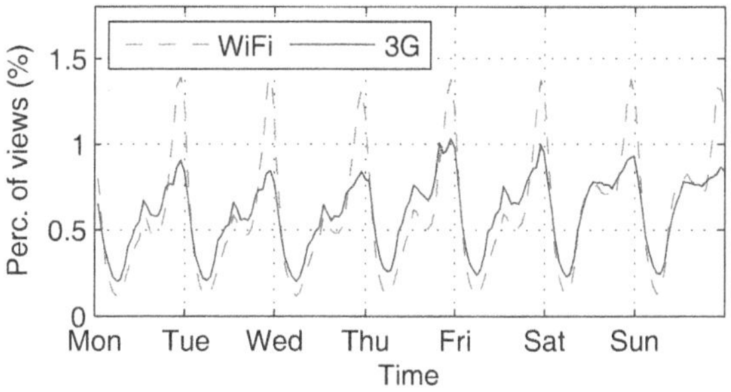

Figure 1: Weekly patterns of access using WiFi and 3G

Both WiFi and 3G workloads exhibit strong daily and weekly patterns. The lowest level of workload happens between 5AM and 7AM every day. The number of views reaches its first minor peak at 1PM in weekdays and at 2PM in weekends. The peak of day is observed around 11PM during both weekdays and weekends. We also observe that the number of views in the afternoon of the weekends is much higher than weekdays for both WiFi and 3G workloads.

Comparing 3G and WiFi workload patterns is also enlightening. The gap between the first minor peak (around 1PM) and the peak of the day (around 11PM) in WiFi network is much larger than that in 3G network, especially in weekends. The most probable reason is that the peak of the day happens during nights when users are most likely at home, thus favoring WiFi to obtain a better quality of video streaming and to save cost.

The daily pattern is similar to the one observed in landline-based VoD systems [10]. However the weekly pattern we observed is different from mobile TV systems [12], where for the 3G connections the viewing pattern of the weekend was almost the same as the pattern of the weekdays.

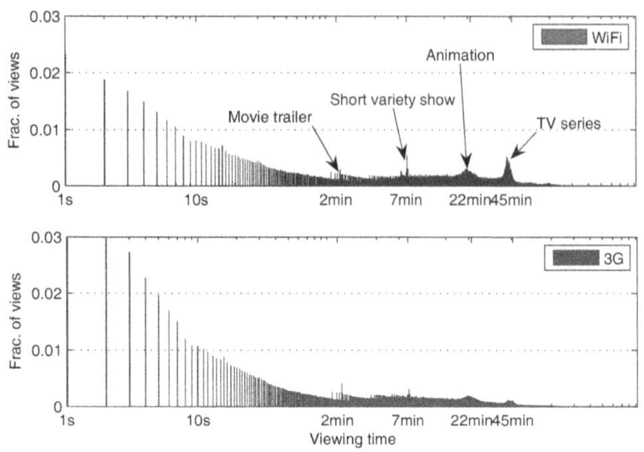

Figure 2: Distribution of viewing time via WiFi and 3G connections

3.2 Video Viewing Time

Viewing time is another indicator of workload, which can be also used for cache policy design. In particular, if most of the views last only a few minutes, it would be efficient to cache the first chunks of videos in content delivery networks (CDNs) so as to maximize the effectiveness of system storage.

Figure 2 shows the histogram distribution of viewing time for WiFi and 3G connection types. The y-axis is the normalized number of views. For both connection types, a considerable fraction of views last less than 10 seconds and generally, the number of views decreases with the growth of viewing time. There are noticeable peaks around 2 minutes, 7 minutes, 21 minutes and 45 minutes in both distributions. They correspond to typical video length for the following types of videos: movie trailer, short variety shows, animation and TV series. The peaks correspond to users watching entirely these types of videos. The variations in 3G viewing time distribution are not as marked as in the WiFi viewing time, indicating that there are fewer users watching full videos in 3G. A possible reason is that the 3G network has a relatively lower speed and obviously higher cost. Another possible reason is the limited power capacity of smart phones, which make up the most of the views via 3G connections as shown in Table 2.

Table 3: Cumulative distribution of viewing time

	0 s	10s	1 min	10 min	20 min
WiFi	23.9%	32.3%	48.7%	74.4%	83.8%
3G	42.7%	54.5%	67.5%	88.5%	94.1%

Table 3 summarizes the cumulative distribution of viewing time. The number of views with 0 seconds is considerably large, especially for views via 3G. 32.3% of the views via WiFi connections and 54.5% via 3G connections last less than 10 seconds. This can be due to the low access speed or to the poor rendering quality of mobile devices, with which users would quickly abandon the viewing of the video. Examining the views with longer durations, we find that only 26% of views via either WiFi or 3G last more than 10 minutes.

We further evaluate the impact of mobile devices on viewing time in Table 4. We only consider views via WiFi since views are more evenly distributed on tablets and smart phones as shown in Table 2. Views from tablets tend to last longer than those from smart phones. This may be explained by the smaller screen size and lower power capacity of smart phones. We also observe a small proportion of views with very long viewing time, often caused by the viewing of movies and TV series. Additionally, we find that views from Android phones last longer than the views from iPhones. While Android phones have various types of hardware with various screen sizes and battery capacities, all iPhones have the same type of hardware. Some Android phones with larger screens or longer battery life may offer better video streaming quality than iPhone, which in turn contributes to making the viewing time longer. We conclude that the type of connections and mobile devices impact the viewing time, with the larger screen size and longer battery life being possible factors lengthening the viewing time.

Table 4: Impact of devices on viewing time (WiFi)

Device	50th prctile (s)	95th prctile (min)
iPad	121	45.1
iPhone	44	34.7
aPad	80	45.8
aPhone	58	42.8

3.3 Normalized Viewing Time

The viewing time is also affected by video length, which varies from several seconds to more than 2 hours. In order to have a better grasp of how complete are the viewings, we define a rate of completion of a video as the *normalized viewing time (NVT)*, which is the ratio of the viewing time to the total length of the video. By definition, NVT can also be considered as a good indicator of the user's interest in a video.

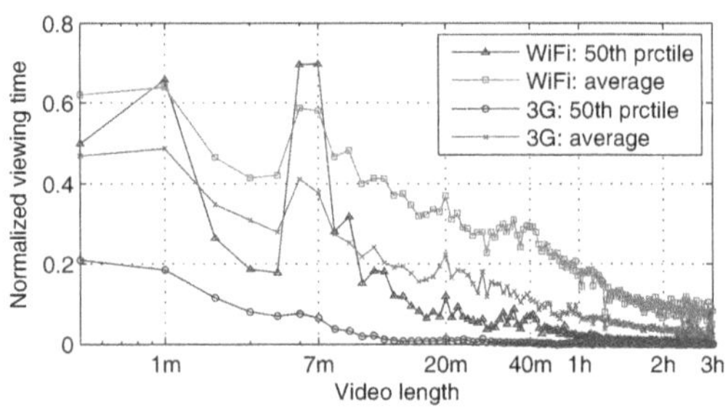

Figure 3: Normalized viewing time against video length

We bin the views by video length in minutes and compute the average and median NVT for each bin. Figure 3 shows the NVT against video length for WiFi and 3G connection types. As expected, the NVT for WiFi is larger than for 3G. It is however interesting to notice that the NVT for WiFi and 3G share similar patterns. In general, the NVT for shorter videos is higher than longer videos. For example with WiFi connections, while the NVT is around 0.4 for videos with length smaller than 12 minutes, it is only around 0.1 for those longer than 1.5 hours. We also observe several abrupt variations as the video length increases. The most noticeable is around the 7-minute length (the typical length for short variety shows). The median NVT value with length around 7 minutes even reaches 0.7 for WiFi connections.

Table 5: Average NVT against popularity of videos

Top	0.5%	1%	5%	10%	50%	100%
WiFi	0.205	0.222	0.275	0.284	0.304	0.336
3G	0.074	0.083	0.109	0.124	0.173	0.229

Yu *et al.* [15] found that in landline-based VoD systems, the viewing time is inversely proportional to the popularity of videos. We observe similar behavior in the PPTV mobile VoD systems as shown in Table 5. Regardless of the connection type, on average, the NVT grows with the decrease of video popularity. With WiFi connections the NVT grows from 0.205 for the top 0.5% of videos to 0.336 for all videos; with 3G connections the NVT grows from 0.074 for top 0.5% videos to 0.229 for all videos.

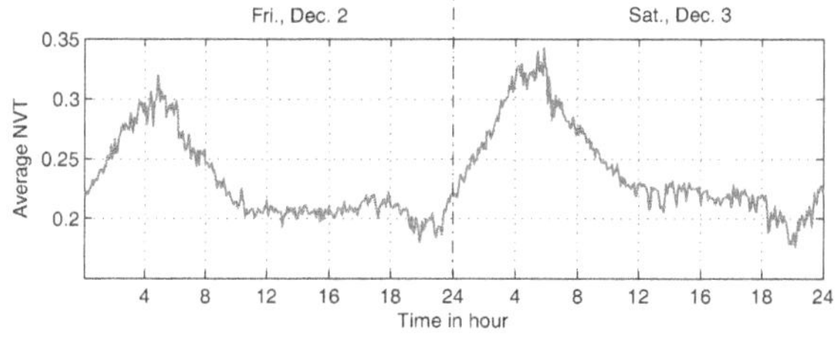

Figure 4: Normalized viewing time evolution over time of day

We further examine the evolution of NVT over time of days for WiFi connections in Figure 4. Note that the evolution of NVT for 3G networks exhibits the same trend as for the WiFi connections. Views are binned by 5-minute time frames and then the average of each bin is computed. Figure 4 shows the results for two days. We observe that the average NVT in early morning is higher than in other time of days, which is consistent with what was observed in mobile TV systems [12]. The NVT remains stable during day time and reaches its minimum in the evening.

3.4 User Interest

Internet video providers often store popular videos according to users' interest on CDN servers close to users. The storage locations of a video should be chosen by taking into account several factors, including the variation of users' interests over time and users' geo-locations. Here we measure user interest using the categories of the videos that the users watched.

3.4.1 User interests over time

Figure 5 depicts the popularity (measured by the proportion of views) of different categories over 2 days. Other days exhibit similar trends as shown in the figure. We bin the views by 5-minute time frames and compute the popularity for each category. For both WiFi and 3G connections, the top 4 categories, *i.e.* movies, TV series, animation and variety shows, make up about 94% of views. While TV series is the top category in terms of views for both connection types, we observe a rather unexpected fact that 3G users watch more movies than WiFi users. By further examining the movie views for 3G connections, we found that 58% of views were abandoned before playback. Several factors may contribute to explain this observation, including low speed of 3G connections, high connection costs, etc. We are unfortunately unable to investigate further these factors using the limited information contained in our dataset.

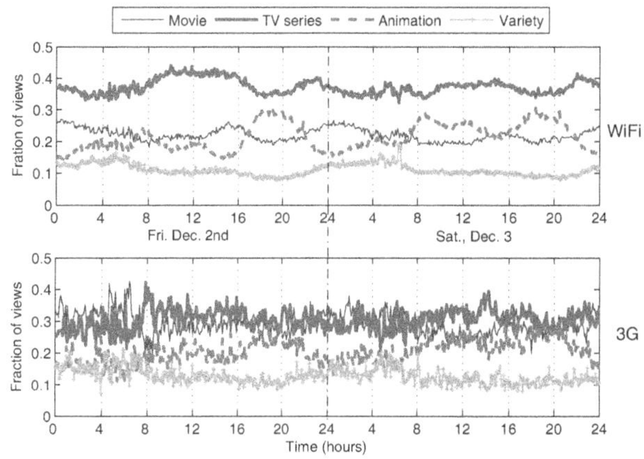

Figure 5: # of views from different categories over time

Looking at the evolution in time of the number of views, the curves for 3G connections are slightly less stable than those for WiFi connections. That may be however due to the fact that there are fewer samples in each time bin for the 3G connections, making the curves less smooth.

The popularity of movies and TV series share similar evolution trends: decreasing at early morning, remaining at a high level from 8AM to 4PM, decreasing again after 4PM, and climbing up from 8PM. The popularity trend of animation vidoes, as opposed to movies and TV series, exhibits a different shape. The popularity reaches its first peak around 8AM and grows fast from 4PM to reach a daily peak around 7PM. We believe the main reason behind these differences is that the majority of animation audiences are young students, who watch videos after study time.

The popularity of variety shows is less variable, but exhibits peaks around 6AM. A closer inspection of the data for this type of video revealed that at this time of day, the fraction of views from overseas reaches its peak. As shown later in this section, overseas users prefer to watch variety shows. By comparing the trends on Friday and Saturday, we observe a higher fraction of animation views in Saturday than in Friday. This might also be explained by the viewing of videos by young students.

3.4.2 User interest across locations

We first bin views by locations (*i.e.* provinces) and examine the popularity of categories for each location. We find that users from the provinces of mainland China share similar interests. However, the views from overseas and HongKong-Macao-Taiwan (HMT) show high discrepancies with mainland China on video categories. We thus further group the provinces of mainland China as one cluster and compared users' interests between mainland China, overseas and HMT in Figure 6. In the figure, "M-WiFi" is short for "Mainland China-WiFi", "O-WiFi" is short for "Overseas-WiFi".

Overall, about 7% (resp. 6%) of the views are from overseas (resp. HMT). We see different patterns of users'

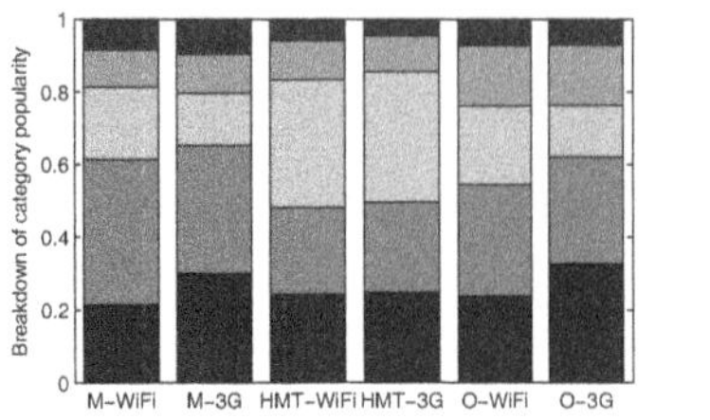

Figure 6: Popularity of categories across locations

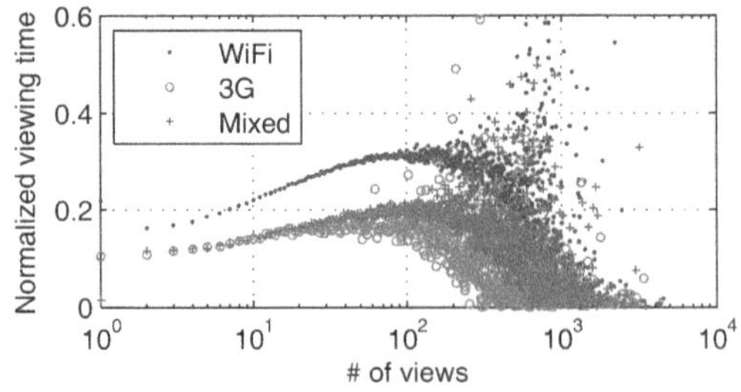

Figure 7: Average NVT against number of views

interests in different locations. The users located in HMT are mainly interested in animation videos which represent 35.3% of the views, about twice as many as the percentage for other locations. Figure 6 also shows that overseas users tend to prefer videos of variety shows a little more than users from other locations. The users from mainland China on the other hand favor TV series.

While the impact of the connection type on HMT measurements seems very limited, it is clear that 3G users in mainland China and overseas favor viewing movies more than users with WiFi connections. This observation is consistent with the insight offered by Figure 5.

3.5 Activity of Individual Users

Understanding individual user behavior is important for the design of recommendation systems and targeted advertisement. In our dataset, users are identified by a unique user ID in the log entries. We divide users into 3 categories according to their connection types, *i.e.* WiFi, 3G and mixed-access users. WiFi and 3G users are defined as those viewing videos exclusively through either connection type during the observation period, while a mixed-access user is defined as one who accessed via each connection type at least once.

Table 6: Statistics for individual user activity

	% of users	# of views (percentile)	
		50th	95th
WiFi	83.57	6	89
3G	8.49	3	39
Mixed	7.94	27	186

Table 6 gives the number of users for the 3 categories and shows statistics for individual user activity. The number of views is aggregated for individual users from the dataset. We observe that the number of WiFi users is one order of magnitude greater than that of 3G and mixed-access users. WiFi users view twice as many videos as 3G users. For mixed-access users, the median number is about one order of magnitude larger than that for 3G users.

3.5.1 *Per user NVT analysis*

We now focus on the possible correlation between the number of views and the normalized viewing time for individual users. We bin users by their number of views and compute the average NVT for each bin. In Figure 7, the relationship between the number of views and the NVT shows an interesting feature. The measured NVT grows with the number of views but the growth seems to stop when the number of views reached a level of 100 views. Above this level the average NVT is more dispersed, but the relation is globally reversed as the average NVT decreases with the number of views.

3.5.2 *Distribution of user activity*

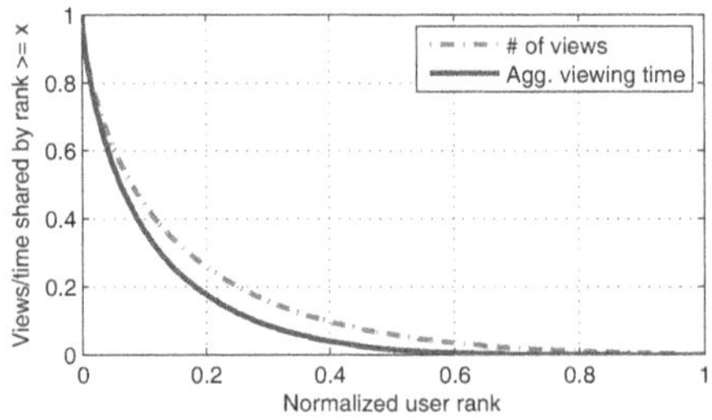

Figure 8: Rank distribution for users' activities

User activity can be quantified in our dataset through the per-user viewing time and the number of views. We examine the rank distribution of users for both viewing time and aggregated number of views and plot the results in Figure 8. The figure gives the important insight that the top 20% of the users generated 75% of the views and 80% of the viewing time. Since viewing time can be directly mapped to system workload, it means 80% of the workload is generated by 20% of users, following the Pareto principle.

We next examine the activity distribution per category of users. For each category, we sort the users according to the number of views in a descending order. We then plot the rank distribution of individual users' activity in Figure 9, *i.e.* rank index i versus the number of views made by the i-th ranked user. Note that the x-axis and the right y-axis are in logarithmic scale.

The well-known power law rank distribution would be observed as a straight line in log-log scale. It can be seen on Figure 9 that the rank distribution for the three connection types WiFi, 3G and mixed-access significantly deviate from such a straight line. We can clearly see a flat head and a thin tail, showing that the distributions do not follow a power law model.

Laherrere *et al.* [11] suggest a stretched exponential (SE) distribution, also known as the complementary Weibull distribution, to model such a deviation from the straight line in a log-log plot. The complementary cumulative distribution function (CCDF) of the SE distribution is given as $P(X \ge x) = e^{-(\frac{x}{x_0})^c}$, where c is the stretched factor and x_0 is a constant parameter. In the rank-ordering technique, N objects are ranked in a descending order of their reference

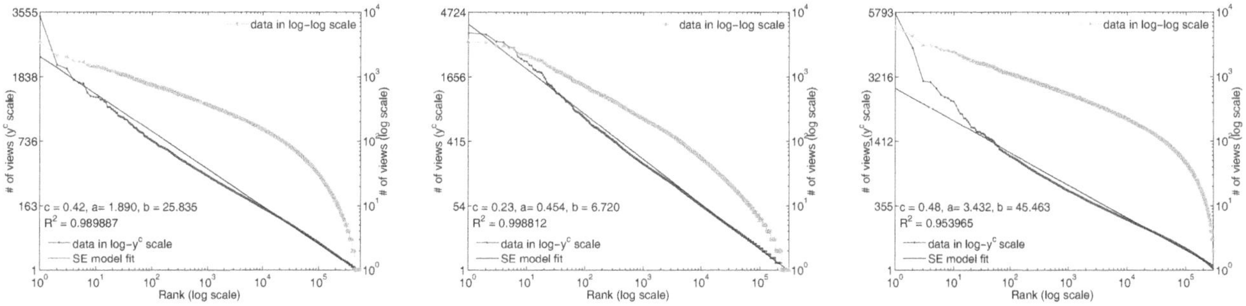

(a) WiFi (b) 3G (c) Mixed

Figure 9: Rank distribution of aggregated number of views for individual users

numbers. Then $P(X \geq x_i) = i/N$, where i $(1 \leq i \leq N)$ is the number of objects with reference numbers larger or equal to x_i. That is $\log(i/N) = -(\frac{x}{x_0})^c$. By substituting x_i for y_i, we have ${y_i}^c = -a \log i + b$, where $a = {x_0}^c$ and $b = {y_1}^c$. The log-y^c plot of ranked data following a SE distribution should be a straight line.

We leverage the SE fit method provided by Guo *et al.* [8], where the parameters for the distribution are obtained by maximum likelihood estimation. The goodness of fit is measured by the coefficient of determination, R^2. In Figure 9, the left y-axis is in y^c scale. As it can be seen the fit is very good for all 3 types of connections although exhibiting different stretched factors. The first several points in Figure 9c are significantly higher than the SE model predictions, which is known as the "King effect" [11].

Taking a closer look at the estimates of the distributions, the distribution for 3G connections has the smallest stretched factor, implying that it is more skewed towards (a few) core users. We further divide users in each category into subcategories by the type of mobile devices (*e.g.* iPad, iPhone, etc.). Although not shown here, we also observed SE distributions for each subcategory with a stretched factor equal to the factor measured for the category. For example, all the 3G subcategories are with the same stretched factor 0.23. We believe that different stretched factors for different types of users reflect the intrinsic characteristics of users' specific activities.

3.5.3 *Interests of individual users*

Internet video systems often rely on individual users' interests in videos for personalized recommendation. We investigate whether a user tends to watch videos from a small number of categories only. To this end we compute category entropy, which is introduced in [4] and defined for a user i as:

$$e_i = \frac{-\sum_{k=1}^{K} p_{ik} \times ln p_{ik}}{lnK} \quad (1)$$

where K is the number of categories, $p_{ik} = \frac{u_{ik}}{u_i}$, u_{ik} is the number of videos viewed by user i and belonging to category k, u_i is the total number of videos viewed by user i. The category entropy is a number between 0 and 1, with "0" corresponding to a user viewing videos of a single category only and "1" when the user watches videos uniformly chosen from all possible categories. PPTV offers $K = 22$ categories of videos for VoD streaming. We divide users into 2 groups, those viewing more than 1 video and those viewing more than 50 videos within 14 days. Figure 10 shows the distribution of the category entropy.

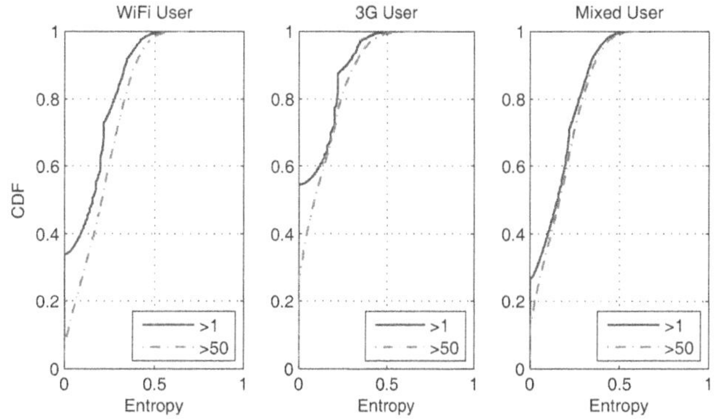

Figure 10: CDF of category entropy

Almost all users have a category entropy less than 0.5, independent of the number of viewed videos. Focusing on the users who view more than 50 videos, we observe as many as 29% of the users with 3G connections viewing videos of only 1 single category, which is larger than the WiFi (9%) and mixed users (15%). We conclude that individual users tend to view videos from a limited set of categories.

3.6 Summary and Implications

Our findings on user behavior are summarized as follows.

- Users' behavior through both WiFi and 3G connections shows strongly daily and weekly patterns. As opposed to previous work, we observed at large scale significantly different 3G and WiFi weekly patterns.
- In general, the viewing time is very short. Only about 25% of the views via either WiFi or 3G last longer than 10 minutes, and we note that a considerable fraction of views are abandoned before playback. The views via WiFi connections last longer than those via 3G. Mobile devices also have an impact on the viewing time, with larger screen sizes and longer battery life being possible factors explaining this longer viewing time.
- Longer videos have shorter normalized viewing time (NVT). The NVT is inversely proportional to the popularity of the videos and varies during the course of the day. The views taking place in the early morning have longer average NVTs.

- Movies and TV series account for 60% of views, independently from the connection type. There are surprisingly more views via 3G to request movies than via WiFi, although more than half of them are abandoned before playback. Users' interests also change over time and we observed different video "tastes" according to users' geo-location.
- Individual users' activity follows the Pareto principle: a minor proportion of causes generate a major proportion of effects. About 20% of users generate 80% of views and users requesting videos via both 3G and WiFi connections view a higher number of videos. The aggregated number of views per user follows a stretched exponential model with a stretched factor depending on the connection type. Besides, individual users and especially those using 3G connections tend to focus on videos from a limited set of categories.

These observations might prove useful for caching policy of CDNs, buffering policy in client software, system design, recommendation and advertisement systems:

- The system maintenance and upgrade operations should be scheduled between 5AM and 7AM to minimize the impact on users. Since the system's capacity is designed according to the peak workload, a major part of the system resources would be not used in the early morning.
- Short viewing time implies that the effectiveness of cache could be optimized by allocating most of the capacity to store the first chunks of videos on the CDN servers. The fact that the viewing time is also impacted by the connection type points to the need for different caching policies for different types of network access.
- A flexible buffering policy in the client application could consider the length, popularity of videos and the time of day to perform effective buffering, which is key for user engagement [5]. Firstly, client software should not aggressively buffer several chunks of videos, but rather adopt a more efficient adaptive caching policy. Secondly, video providers' customized client applications would benefit from the pre-fetching of more chunks of videos for buffering in the early morning, since views exhibit a high completion rate during this period. Finally, as noticed previously, buffering policies should take into account the type of connection and the type of mobile device used.
- Recommendation systems and content providers could exploit the patterns we observed to better fit users' variable interests across time and locations. A time-aware recommendation system could weight the candidate items based on the time of day, and for example propose to its users animation videos with a higher probability after school time. Advertisers could consider the fact that users with 3G connections are more likely to watch movies than those with WiFi connections.

4. VIDEO POPULARITY

In this section, we focus on the video popularity in the PPTV mobile VoD system. The video popularity characteristics not only help us to understand the underlying human collective behaviors, but also provide insights into optimization of the cache policy and deployment of CDNs.

Individual videos are identified by the unique file names of videos in the PPTV video system. Video popularity can be measured by either the number of views or the aggregated viewing time. We examine the correlation between these two popularity metrics with the Spearman rank correlation coefficient ρ. The coefficient ρ is defined as

$$\rho = 1 - \frac{6\sum(x_i - y_i)^2}{n(n^2-1)} \quad (2)$$

where x_i and y_i are the ranks of the i-th video according to two different metrics, n is the total number of videos under consideration. It is a non-parametric measure of correlation, which quantifies how well an arbitrary monotonic function could describe the relationship between two variables. The coefficient lies in [-1,1], a value of "1" indicating perfect positive correlation and "-1" indicating perfect negative correlation.

The value of the correlation coefficient of the two popularity metrics is $\rho = 0.884$, indicating a high correlation. Thus, in the following we will use the number of views as the measure of video popularity. Unless otherwise specified, we consider the aggregated number of views to be the popularity of a video for the time period covered by our dataset.

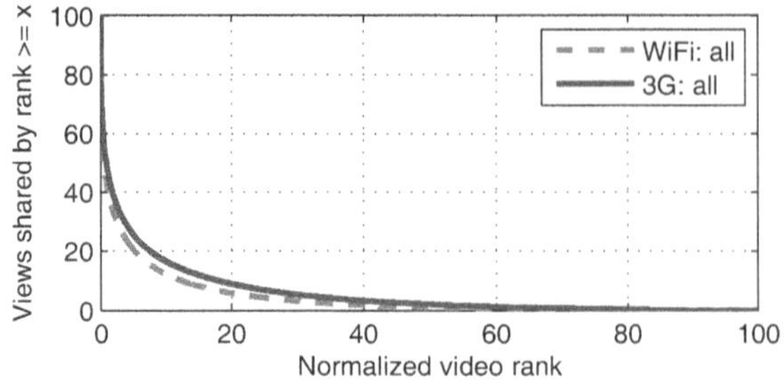

Figure 11: Pareto principle for video popularity

4.1 Video Popularity Distribution

We examine the video popularity distribution by ranking videos by popularity. We normalize video ranks between 0 and 100 and compute the normalized aggregated views of the least x-th popular videos. Figure 11 shows a highly skewed distribution for both WiFi and 3G connections. The top 10% of the popular videos attract more than 80% of views. The distribution for 3G connections seems to be slightly less skewed than the WiFi's. The differences of viewing source between the two types of connections could be a contributing factor. As will be shown next, users with 3G connections are more likely to use search portals to discover videos than users with WiFi connections, which makes the video viewing of a more diverse origin. The skewed distribution indicates that the video popularity follows the Pareto principle, in this case that a very small number of top popular videos attract the majority of views.

Although not shown here, we found that the overlap rate of top ranked videos via WiFi and 3G connections is moderately high. For example, the overlap rate of the top 1,000 popular videos is 0.75.

These observations imply that by caching only the top 10% of popular videos on CDNs, more than 80% of requests can be satisfied. However, the popularity of videos changes overtime and is the object of the following subsection.

4.2 Video Rank Stability

We bin views of WiFi and 3G connections by 30-minute time frames. The rank stability coefficient for the top k popular videos in the i-th ($i > 1$) bin is defined as

$$R_k(i) = \frac{|S_k(i) \cap S_k(i-1)|}{k} \quad (3)$$

where S_i is the set of top k popular videos during the i-th time frame. The coefficient has values within [0, 1], where a value of "1" indicates no change and a value of "0" that all the videos in the top list change.

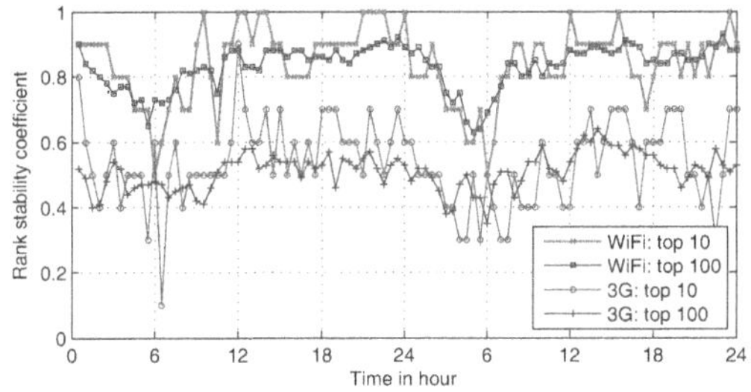

Figure 12: Video rank stability coefficient over time

Figure 12 shows the change of the coefficient of the top 10 and top 100 popular videos over 2 days. Our first observation is that the top videos for WiFi connections have between 20% and 30% more stability than for 3G. This can be explained by the fact that there are fewer views in each bin for 3G and the difference in the number of views among popular videos is smaller. Thus a small variation of views would change the rank ordering of videos, which in turn results in a lower rank stability. We note that the top videos are less stable in the early morning and more stable after noon, which is the highest workload period of the day. This observation is consistent with the results in landline-based VoD systems [15] and mobile IPTV systems [12]. We also observed that the top 100 videos have similar stability as the top 10 videos, independently of the connection type, while in landline-based VoD systems [15], the top 100 videos are less stable than the top 10 videos.

The cache should adaptively change the top popular videos it stores to maximize efficiency. An important question at this point and that we examine in the following is whether it is possible to predict the near-future popularity of videos.

4.3 Video Popularity Evolution and Prediction

Focusing on the evolution of video popularity, we examine videos by ranking them in a descending order according to their popularity for WiFi and 3G connections. We select the 1st-ranked video (*i.e.* the most popular video), the 10th-ranked video and the 50th-ranked video for both types of connections and plot their popularity evolution trends over time in Figure 13. We note that popular videos watched via WiFi attract more views than via 3G, probably because of the higher number of views in WiFi network.

Figure 13 shows that both 3G and WiFi exhibit similar patterns in terms of video popularity evolution, including a strong daily pattern similar to the pattern of the total aggregated views of Figure 1. The figure shows that the number of views of popular videos has a clear decreasing

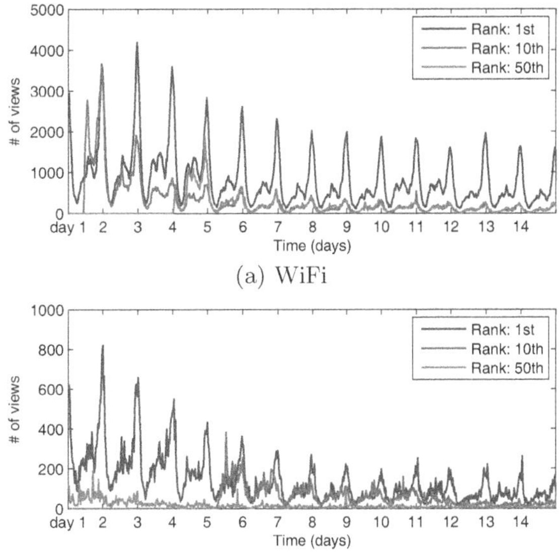

Figure 13: Popularity over time for top videos

trend after the peak day and thus that a given video rarely belongs to the top list for a long time.

Another interesting finding is that the 10th-ranked videos for both WiFi and 3G connections experience a sharp increase in popularity immediately after their uploading, independently of when they were uploaded in the course of the day.

The above observation motivates us to examine whether it is possible to predict the near-future popularity of videos using their early views records. We unfortunately couldn't extract the exact upload time of videos from our data. We form an estimate of the upload time in the following way: we consider a video as being a fresh upload if it was not viewed in the three preceding days (*i.e.* from Dec. 1 to Dec. 3, 2011) and mark its upload time to be the first time it was viewed in our dataset. A drawback of this method is that it would consider the least popular videos uploaded before Dec. 1, 2011 to be freshly uploaded videos. In order to avoid this effect and since we are only interested in top popular videos, we further filter out the videos with less than 10 views.

Table 7: Pearson correlation coefficient between early views records and the popularity of videos

Network	k hours after uploading				
type	1h	2h	4h	8h	16h
WiFi (19,312)	0.542	0.836	0.841	0.813	0.888
3G (9,403)	0.049	0.777	0.926	0.944	0.961

With this method, we can estimate the upload time of videos uploaded after Dec. 3, 2011. We first focus on popularity prediction of videos uploaded on Dec. 4, 2011. Table 7 shows the Pearson correlation coefficient between the number of views a video attracted within k hours after its estimated upload time and the number of views of that video in the dataset. The Pearson correlation coefficient is a measure of the correlation (linear dependence) between two variables X and Y defined as

$$\rho_{X,Y} = \frac{E[(X - \mu_X)(Y - \mu_Y)]}{\sigma_X \sigma_Y} \quad (4)$$

where E is the expected value operator, μ_X is the expected value of X and σ_X is its standard deviation.

We also present the number of videos under consideration in Table 7. For both WiFi and 3G connections, the first 4-hour viewing volume yields an accurate estimation with higher correlations. The early records of a longer duration only increase the correlations marginally, especially for WiFi connections.

Table 8: Pearson correlation coefficient between the first 4-hour viewing volume and the popularity on different days

	Dec. 4	Dec. 5	Dec. 6	Dec. 7
WiFi	0.841	0.630	0.880	0.913
3G	0.926	0.575	0.712	0.861

We also evaluate the Pearson correlation coefficient between the first 4-hour viewing volume and the near-future popularity for other days, including Dec. 5, Dec. 6 and Dec 7. The results are shown in Table 8. The coefficients are moderately high for all days: ranging from 0.63 to 0.913 for WiFi connections and from 0.575 to 0.926 for 3G. These results indicate that video popularity can be accurately predicted only with early views records.

We conjecture that such a high correlation is due to the fact that users are expecting the regular upload of new episodes of TV series, animation series and variety shows. To confirm our conjecture, we divide the videos by categories and compute the correlation coefficients between the first 4-hour viewing volume and the video popularity. The results are shown in Table 9.

Table 9: Correlation coefficient between the first 4-hour viewing volume and the popularity for different categories on Dec. 4

Category	WiFi (19,312)	3G (9,403)
Movie	0.304(2.9%)	-0.026(7.6%)
TV series	0.802(40.3%)	0.292(46.9%)
Animation	0.982(14.1%)	0.996(25.3%)
Variety	0.993(9.9%)	0.984(7.9%)
Others	0.884(32.8%)	0.822(12.3%)

We see a very high correlation for animation and variety videos for both types of connection, ranging from 0.982 to 0.996. While the correlation for TV series for WiFi connections is moderately high (0.802), it is very low for 3G. This difference suggests that users using 3G connections tend to not watch TV episodes just after their release date. The very low correlation for movies indicates that it is challenging to accurately predict the popularity of such content using only the very early viewing volume.

4.4 Summary and Implications

The key observations on video popularity are summarized below.

- Video popularity follows the Pareto principle. The top 10% of the popular videos attract more than 80% of views for both WiFi and 3G connection types. The overlap rate of the top ranked videos is moderately high for both connection types.
- The videos' popularity constantly changes overtime. The video rank stability for WiFi connections is between 20% and 30% higher than in 3G.
- Top popular videos exhibit a sharp increase of views several hours after their release. The early viewing volume of videos and their popularity are highly correlated, especially for animation videos and variety shows.

These observations have the following implications:

- Independently of the connection type, the quality of more than 80% of the views can be improved if the caching policy considers only the top 10% of popular videos.
- The popularity prediction can greatly benefit from the early viewing volume of the videos and can be used by designers to improve system performance.
- The flash crowd just after the release of popular videos, especially for TV episodes, animation videos, variety shows via WiFi connections, suggests an opportunity to leverage P2P techniques to reduce server loads.

5. VIEW SOURCE

The PPTV mobile VoD system provides 8 sources for users to discover videos: category page (*i.e.* the front page of each category), video search in PPTV, recent views (of the client), recommendation, favorites, top popular videos, cover (*i.e.* the first page of the client software) and next episode (of TV series or variety shows). An in-depth understanding of how users discover videos in WiFi and 3G networks and its correlation with video popularity is useful for both software developers and advertisers.

5.1 Sources of Views

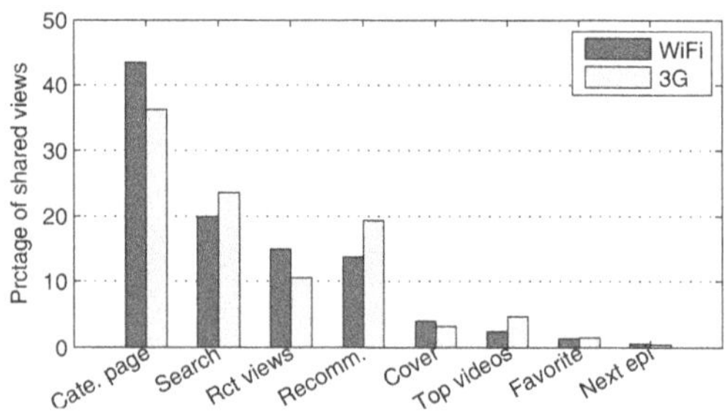

Figure 14: Percentage of views from different sources in WiFi and 3G networks

Figure 14 depicts the distribution of views from each source for WiFi and 3G connections. Category page and video search are the two main sources of views for both types of connections. They account for more than 60% of the views. We see that users with WiFi connections are more likely to use the category pages than those with 3G, while the latter use the search engine more often. These observations also show that users with 3G connections tend to find the videos of their interests directly rather than browse video pages.

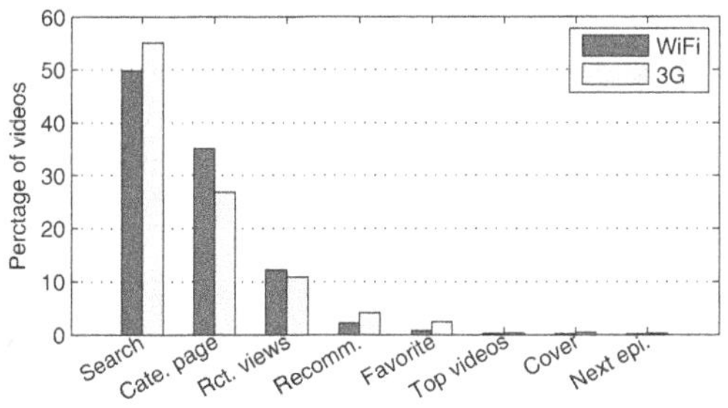

Figure 15: Percentage of videos dominated by different view sources

5.2 Dominant Sources for Individual Videos

We now look at the dominant sources for individual videos. We define the source which accounts for the largest proportion of views as a video's *dominant source* [16]. We extract the dominant source for each video and plot the result in Figure 15. We observe that the category page and the video search are the dominant view sources for 85% of the videos. However, in contrast to Figure 14, video search is the top source of views for individual videos. There are more individual videos dominated by search with 3G connections than with WiFi connections, which is consistent with our previous observation.

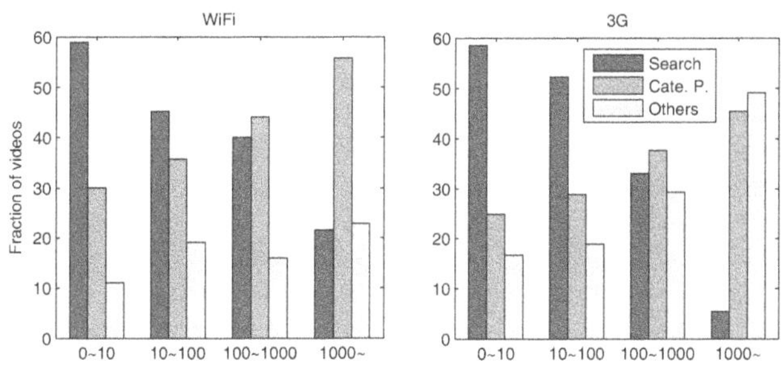

Figure 16: Percentage of videos for dominant sources with different views

Focusing on the view source of popular videos, we bin videos by their popularity and examine the dominant sources. Figure 16 shows the distribution of dominant sources for each bin for WiFi and 3G connections. All the other sources, except search and category page, are grouped as "Others".

With both types of connections, while video search is the dominant source for low-popularity videos, category pages are favored to access highly popular videos. Video searches represent less than 10% (resp. 20%) of the sources for the highly popular videos with 3G (resp. WiFi) connections. This observation suggests that videos are more likely to become popular if they are pushed to the category pages. It is also interesting to note that with 3G connections, half of the highly popular videos are not dominated by category pages as with WiFi connections but rather by a collection of other sources. Users with 3G connections would seem to carefully choose videos, before viewing from various sources.

5.3 The Impact of Search

We have found that video searches are the dominant source of viewing for individual videos, especially for low-popularity videos. Intuitively, one might consider that video search enables users to quickly find various videos matching their interests, which would result in an increase of the diversity of views. In order to verify this intuition, we use the Gini coefficient to measure statistical dispersion and examine the distributional inequality [16].

Sorting the videos in an ascending order according to their popularity, the Gini coefficient is defined as:

$$G = 1 - \sum_{k=1}^{n}(X_k - X_{k-1})(Y_k + Y_{k-1}) \qquad (5)$$

where n is the number of videos, X_k is the fraction of the first k videos, and Y_k is the fraction of the views attracted by the first k videos. A Gini coefficient of "0" indicates a perfect equality where views are uniformly shared by all videos, while "1" indicates a maximum inequality, *e.g.* one video alone attracts the entire views.

Table 10: Gini Coefficient with/without video search

Network type	w/ search	w/o search
Wifi	0.918	0.941
3G	0.884	0.930

In order to evaluate the impact of video search, we compute the Gini coefficient under two scenarios: when video search is present (*i.e.* the actual dataset) and when video search is removed. In order to evaluate the second scenario, we updated the popularity of each video by excluding the views from video search. The Gini coefficients with and without video search with WiFi and 3G connections are listed in Table 10.

The coefficients are above 0.88 for both types of connections, implying a dispersed distribution of video views. The 3G connections have a lower coefficient than the WiFi connections, indicating a lower dispersion. By removing the views from video search the coefficient increases by 0.023 for WiFi and 0.046 for 3G. This indicates that video search increases the diversity of viewing and that the video search plays a more important role with 3G than with WiFi connections.

5.4 Summary and Implications

Our two main findings of view source analysis can be summarized as follows.

- While category page is the primary source of views overall, video search is the dominant source of viewing for most of individual videos, especially for low-popularity videos. Users with 3G connections tend to use video search to discover videos more often than those with WiFi connections.
- Videos that are present on category pages are more likely to become popular, while video search increases the diversity of views.

Our findings offer insights on how video content is discovered in a large video repository. They emphasize the importance of different content discovery and give indications to content providers and advertisers on video promotions. The differences between WiFi and 3G connections should also be taken into account.

6. APPLICATION: DESIGN OF AN EFFICIENT CACHING SYSTEM

An efficient caching system typically stores replicas of videos as close as possible to end users, in order to improve user experience and alleviate server load. In the preceding sections we observed that caching the top 10% popular videos and the first few chunks of the videos could be part of a caching strategy to optimize the overall performance. In this section, we aim to evaluate such a performance gain using trace-driven simulations and comparing different caching strategies. We first assume a global virtual cache, where requests are first sent to the cache. Since we are primarily interested in the performance improvement potentially obtained by leveraging our findings, we do not assume any particular distribution for the locations of content cache servers. We assume that a video can be cached at chunks level and that it is divided in a set of 1-minute chunks. We consider the following 3 caching strategies:

1. Full caching: Each day the cache is refreshed with the top 10% popular videos as observed the day before. All the chunks of the selected videos are stored in the cache.

2. Partial caching: Each day the cache is refreshed with the top 10% popular videos as observed the day before. However as suggested by our findings, we only cache the first few chunks of each video. The fraction of cached chunks of each video is computed as a function of the normalized viewing time (NVT), as depicted on Figure 3. Specifically, considering the video lengths (in minutes), we estimate the expected video's viewing time with the average NVT. The number of chunks for each video to be cached corresponds then to the fraction of chunks covering the expected viewing time.

3. Full caching with limited size: In this strategy we further take into account the constraint of limited cache size. The daily cache size is set to the size used in the partial caching strategy of the same day. But all chunks of the selected videos are stored in the cache, which is populated with the top popular videos until it has reached it maximal capacity. Due to the limited cache size, less than 10% of the top popular videos will be stored.

For a viewing request i, let h_i denote the number of chunks' hits and let r_i denote the number of requested chunks, then the cache hit rate of the view i is defined as $C_i = \frac{h_i}{r_i}$. We perform the simulations by replaying the requests of 13 days, from Dec. 2 to Dec. 14. Table 11 shows the average cache hit ratio over all viewing requests. Note that the cache size is defined as the number of stored chunks in the cache. The table also shows the average value of each day's cache size.

Table 11: Cache performance

Cache scheme	avg. cache size	avg. hit rate
Full	658,630	75.3%
Partial	133,019	63.3%
Full+limited	133,019	52.6%

We observe a high average hit rate for the full caching strategy, showing the effectiveness of only caching the top 10% previously observed popular videos. Compared to the full caching strategy, the partial caching offers a reduction of 80% in cache size, at the expense of a reduction of only 12% of the hit rate. Our results also suggest that the variant of the full caching with limited size yields a lower hit rate when compared to the partial caching. This preliminary analysis indicates that the partial caching strategy provides a better tradeoff between cache size and hit rate.

7. RELATED WORK

User behavior and video consumption patterns in Internet video systems have been examined in the context of VoD [15][14] [5], IPTV [7][3], P2P VoD [10] and live streaming [9], including YouTube[2]. By measuring a VoD system, Yu *et al.* [15] made several observations on user arrival rate, video popularity and the impact of recommendation. Yin *et al.* [14] analyzed a live VoD system from the 2008 Olympics, focusing on how the dynamic nature of the system impacted user behavior. Dobrian *et al.* [5] examined the impact of video quality on user engagement and found that the buffering ratio is the most important factor. Guo *et al.* [8] modelized the video access patterns of several Internet video systems with stretched exponential distributions.

Another major type of video services is IPTV. Cha *et al.* [3] measured an IPTV system and analyzed the characteristics of viewing sessions and the patterns of channel popularity. Gopalakrishnan *et al.* [7] and Qiu *et al.* [13] modeled interactive usage and user activity in IPTV systems.

Measurement studies [10][9] on P2P-based VoD and live streaming systems emphasized the aspects of peer stability, chunk availability and scheduling mechanisms. We have discussed the possibility of using P2P techniques on mobile VoD systems in this paper. As a UGC (user-generated content) video system, YouTube constitutes a huge repository of short videos in the context of VoD streaming. Cha *et al.* [2] characterized the video popularity in YouTube. They identified several popularity distributions and gave suggestions on the design of caching and P2P content distribution.

Watching videos with mobile devices becomes more and more popular. Li *et al.* [12] analyzed traffic patterns and user behavior for a mobile TV system. They showed that the wireless connectivity allowed smooth video viewing with mobile devices and modeled the sojourn time in channels with two piecewise distributions. Finamore *et al.* [6] compared YouTube traffic generated by mobile devices with traffic generated by PCs. Their key observation is that aggressive buffering policies cause a considerable waste of bandwidth for mobile devices. In this paper, we observed the short viewing times and suggested adaptive caching policies which could be also leveraged in YouTube.

As opposed to previous research, to the best of our knowledge, our paper is among first to systematically analyze the user viewing behavior and the corresponding video consumption patterns for mobile VoD systems. We examined the impact of the connection type and the type of mobile device on viewing behavior, video popularity and viewing sources. We also compared our findings with landline-based VoD systems and mobile TV systems where applicable.

8. CONCLUSION

Understanding user behavior patterns in mobile video systems is of prime importance for content providers, system designers and researchers. In this paper, using a unique data from a mobile VoD system, we systematically analyzed users' behavior and the corresponding video popularity patterns, emphasizing the impact of the connection type (3G or WiFi) and the type of mobile device used (tablet or smart phone). We have made several key observations and discussed their implications on caching and buffering policies and the design of systems, software and on-line advertising. We observed short viewing times (especially via 3G), a stretched exponential distribution for user activity, a concentration of individual users' interests and that the video popularity conformed to the Pareto principle. We also highlighted several surprising findings: 3G users request more movies than other categories of videos; users requesting videos via both 3G and WiFi view a significantly higher number of videos; the early viewing volume of a video is a good predictor of popularity for animation and variety shows. These observations constitute useful insights for system designers, CDNs and developers alike.

Substantial study remains to address issues such as the impact of the type of client application (*e.g.* wired clients, web browsers and mobile clients) on video consumption patterns; the reasons underlying the differences in user behavior depending on whether they connect using WiFi or 3G; how to design better content delivery (*e.g.* P2P delivery) in mobile VoD systems as well as designing effective caching strategies in content delivery networks. Identifying the main discrepancies that might exist between the wired and wireless-based accesses to VoD content would also be worth investigating. In future work, we will study these potentially fundamental differences, exploiting both mobile and Internet-based VoD datasets.

Acknowledgement

The authors would like to thank PPLive for providing the dataset and Yi Sun from ICT-CAS for the useful discussions. We are also grateful to our shepherd Ming Zhang and anonymous reviewers for their feedback. This work was supported in part by National Basic Research Program of China with Grant 2012CB315801, by National Natural Science Foundation of China (NSFC) with Grants 61133015 and 60903207, by Strategic Priority Research Program of the Chinese Academy of Sciences with Grant XDA06010303. The work was also supported by the NSFC-ANR (France) pFlower project and EC EINS project.

9. REFERENCES

[1] Cisco visual networking index: Global mobile data traffic forecast update, 2011-2016. Technical report, Cisco, 2012.

[2] M. Cha, H. Kwak, P. Rodriguez, Y.-Y. Ahn, and S. Moon. I tube, you tube, everybody tubes: analyzing the world's largest user generated content video system. In *Proceedings of IMC '07*, 2007.

[3] M. Cha, P. Rodriguez, J. Crowcroft, S. Moon, and X. Amatriain. Watching television over an ip network. In *Proceedings of IMC '08*, 2008.

[4] Y. Ding, Y. Du, Y. Hu, Z. Liu, L. Wang, K. Ross, and A. Ghose. Broadcast yourself: understanding youtube uploaders. In *IMC '11*, 2011.

[5] F. Dobrian, V. Sekar, A. Awan, I. Stoica, D. Joseph, A. Ganjam, J. Zhan, and H. Zhang. Understanding the impact of video quality on user engagement. In *Proceedings of the ACM SIGCOMM*, 2011.

[6] A. Finamore, M. Mellia, M. M. Munafò, R. Torres, and S. G. Rao. Youtube everywhere: impact of device and infrastructure synergies on user experience. In *Proceedings of IMC'11*, 2011.

[7] V. Gopalakrishnan, R. Jana, K. K. Ramakrishnan, D. F. Swayne, and V. A. Vaishampayan. Understanding couch potatoes: measurement and modeling of interactive usage of iptv at large scale. In *Proceedings of IMC '11*, 2011.

[8] L. Guo, E. Tan, S. Chen, Z. Xiao, and X. Zhang. The stretched exponential distribution of internet media access patterns. In *Proceedings of PODC '08*, 2008.

[9] X. Hei, C. Liang, J. Liang, Y. Liu, and K. Ross. A measurement study of a large-scale p2p iptv system. *IEEE Transactions on Multimedia*, 9(8):1672 –1687, dec. 2007.

[10] Y. Huang, T. Z. Fu, D.-M. Chiu, J. C. Lui, and C. Huang. Challenges, design and analysis of a large-scale p2p-vod system. In *Proceedings of SIGCOMM '08*, 2008.

[11] J. Laherrere and D. Sornette. Stretched exponential distributions in nature and economy: "fat tails" with characteristic scales. *The European Physical Journal B*, 2:525–539, January 1998.

[12] Y. Li, Y. Zhang, and R. Yuan. Measurement and analysis of a large scale commercial mobile internet tv system. In *Proceedings of IMC '11*, 2011.

[13] T. Qiu, Z. Ge, S. Lee, J. Wang, J. Xu, and Q. Zhao. Modeling user activities in a large iptv system. In *Proceedings of IMC'09*, 2009.

[14] H. Yin, X. Liu, F. Qiu, N. Xia, C. Lin, H. Zhang, V. Sekar, and G. Min. Inside the bird's nest: measurements of large-scale live vod from the 2008 olympics. In *Proceedings of the ACM IMC '09*, 2009.

[15] H. Yu, D. Zheng, B. Y. Zhao, and W. Zheng. Understanding user behavior in large-scale video-on-demand systems. In *Proceedings of EuroSys '06*, 2006.

[16] R. Zhou, S. Khemmarat, and L. Gao. The impact of youtube recommendation system on video views. In *Proceedings of IMC '10*, 2010.

Program Popularity and Viewer Behaviour in a Large TV-on-Demand System

Henrik Abrahamsson
Swedish Institute of Computer Science
Box 1263, Kista, Sweden
henrik@sics.se

Mattias Nordmark
TeliaSonera AB
Stockholm, Sweden
mattias.nordmark@teliasonera.com

ABSTRACT

Today increasingly large volumes of TV and video are distributed over IP-networks and over the Internet. It is therefore essential for traffic and cache management to understand TV program popularity and access patterns in real networks.

In this paper we study access patterns in a large TV-on-Demand system over four months. We study user behaviour and program popularity and its impact on caching.

The demand varies a lot in daily and weekly cycles. There are large peaks in demand, especially on Friday and Saturday evenings, that need to be handled.

We see that the cacheability, the share of requests that are not first-time requests, is very high. Furthermore, there is a small set of programs that account for a large fraction of the requests. We also find that the share of requests for the top most popular programs grows during prime time, and the change rate among them decreases. This is important for caching. The cache hit ratio increases during prime time when the demand is the highest, and caching makes the biggest difference when it matters most.

We also study the popularity (in terms of number of requests and rank) of individual programs and how that changes over time. Also, we see that the type of programs offered determines what the access pattern will look like.

Categories and Subject Descriptors

C.4 [**Computer Systems Organization**]: Performance of Systems; C.2.3 [**Computer Systems Organization**]: Computer-Communication Networks—*Network Operations*

General Terms

Measurement, Performance

Keywords

IPTV, TV-on-Demand, Program Popularity

IMC'12, November 14–16, 2012, Boston, Massachusetts, USA.

1. INTRODUCTION

Today increasingly large volumes of TV and video are distributed over IP-networks and over the Internet. Many telecom and broadband companies have become TV operators and distribute TV channels using IP multicast in their networks. The TV services also evolve, and are more and more changing towards TV-on-Demand and time-shifted viewing where the users can choose to watch the programs after its scheduled time. Distributing individual TV streams to each viewer requires a lot of bandwidth and server capacity. How to best use caching of popular content closer to the viewers is therefore an important issue to reduce network load.

In this paper we study access patterns in a large TV-on-Demand system over four months. We study user behaviour and program popularity and its impact on caching.

There are several studies of viewing behaviour in IPTV systems where traditional scheduled TV is distributed over IP networks [8], [17], [18]. This include studies of TV channel popularity and channel switching. Our work is different in that we look at TV-on-Demand where the viewers choose programs to watch outside of the TV schedule. The programs are not distributed using multicast but transferred with unicast streams to the viewers.

In this sense our work is closer to studies of content access patterns in traditional Video-on-Demand systems (VoD) [26]. But TV-on-Demand is different from traditional VoD in several ways. The TV-on-Demand service is more diverse. It is a mix of TV program libraries, time-shifted viewing, and rental video. Time-shifted viewing here means that the viewer can choose to watch ongoing scheduled TV-programs from the beginning. The TV schedule gives a large inflow of new programs each day. The programs available also come from a wide range of TV channels. There is a large variation in program types (news, drama, children's programs, movies, etc.) which each can have different access patterns. Many programs, like news and weather forecasts, also have a very short lifespan and are typically only interesting for a few hours.

The two main contributions of this paper are: (1) an investigation of program popularity and access patterns for TV and video on demand in a real network, (2) a trace-based study of caching. We characterize access patterns for different program categories, we show how program popularity changes over time and how this differs between different program types. We then use the request sequence in our data set for trace-driven simulation and study cache hit ratios for different cache sizes, cache replacement policies and population sizes.

Table 1: The data set in figures

	Requests	Clients	Programs
Total (over 125 days)	10294948	307347	89889
Daily median	80174	30232	7523
Daily max	121053	42451	8751
Daily min	56720	22194	6316

Our main results are:

- The popularity (ranking) of rental movies, news, and TV shows changes over time in very different ways. News programs are often only requested for a few hours, movies are popular for months and increase in rank during weekends, TV shows increase in rank when the next episode is shown, children's programs are top ranked in the mornings and early evenings. This means that programs jumps in and out of the top 100 list. It also means that the *type* of content offered is essential for what the access pattern will look like.
- The program popularity conforms with the Pareto principle, or 80-20 rule. There is a small set of programs that account for a large fraction of the requests: the 2% most popular programs get 48% of the requests, and the 20% most popular programs get 84% of the requests.
- The share of requests for the top 100 most popular programs increases during prime time and the change among the top 100 decreases during prime time and during weekends when the demand is the highest.
- The cacheability is very high. The hit ratio with LRU is above 50% when caching 5% of the average daily demand, and the hit ratio increases during prime time when it is needed most.

The rest of the paper is structured as follows: In Section 2 we describe the TV-on-Demand service and introduce the data set. In Section 3 we study access patterns and the daily and hourly change in user interest. In Section 4 we look at the program popularity in more detail, how the access patterns differs between different program categories, and how the popularity of individual programs changes over time. In Section 5 we show what impact the access patterns has on cacheability and cache hit ratios. Related work is in Section 6, we discuss future work in Section 7 and conclude the paper in Section 8.

2. THE DATA SET

We study logs from the TeliaSonera TV-on-Demand service. The program selection is a mix from a wide range of TV channels (news, drama, children's programs, movies, etc.). It is a mix of TV program libraries, time-shifted viewing, and rental video.

The TeliaSonera TV service also includes multicast distribution of traditional scheduled TV. Here we only study logs of on-demand requests but the TV schedule with many ongoing channels gives a constant inflow of new programs that become available for on-demand requests. In our data set, on average 8% of the programs each day have not been requested before.

The data set is a mysql database with logs from RTSP sessions where we for each session have:
<Timestamp, Length, ServerID, ClientID, AssetID>.

The timestamp shows when the session ended and by subtracting the length of the session we get the time when the request arrived. The AssetID identifies what TV program is requested. For each asset, we also have additional out-of-band information about providers and program descriptions that help us categorize the programs into genres.

The data set is summarized in Table 1. It contains TV-on-Demand requests over 125 days between May 12th and September 13th 2011. During this period almost 90000 different programs were requested. The data set includes more than 300000 clients making more than ten million requests.

Figure 1 shows the number of requests, viewers, and programs per day. There are distinct weekly cycles where the

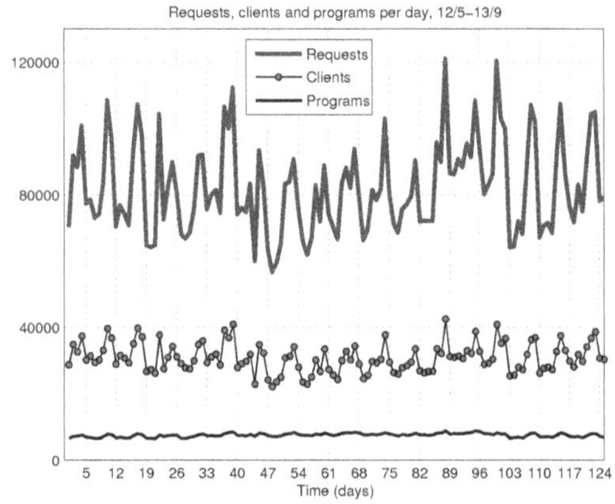

Figure 1: Number of requests, active clients, and distinct programs requested per day over 125 days. The grid shows weeks starting from Mondays.

number of active clients and the number of requests increase a lot during the weekends.

On average more than 30000 clients are active per day often increasing up to 40000 at the weekends. Some viewers are much more active than others and watch more TV programs. Viewers also subscribe to different TV packages and have access to different number of TV channels and program libraries. We can see that 5% of the viewers account for 41% of the requests and 20% of the viewers account for 75% of the requests. Figure 2 shows a log-log-plot of the number of requests per viewer. While many clients only watch a few on-demand programs per month, the most active viewer had more than 137 requests per day on average. Some of these sessions were 5-30 minutes long but many where short, jumping between different on-demand programs.

The clients in the data set are all in the same time zone and in the same geographical region. Later in Section 5, when looking at caching, we will also study smaller subsets of the population. We have one geographically close subset with 23304 clients in the same town. For the smaller populations in the study we randomly chose clients and include into sets of different size up to 10000. We will use the labels *region* (307347), *town* (23304), *rand10000*, *rand1000* etc. for the different populations.

On average 7523 different programs are requested per day. As expected, some programs are much more popular than

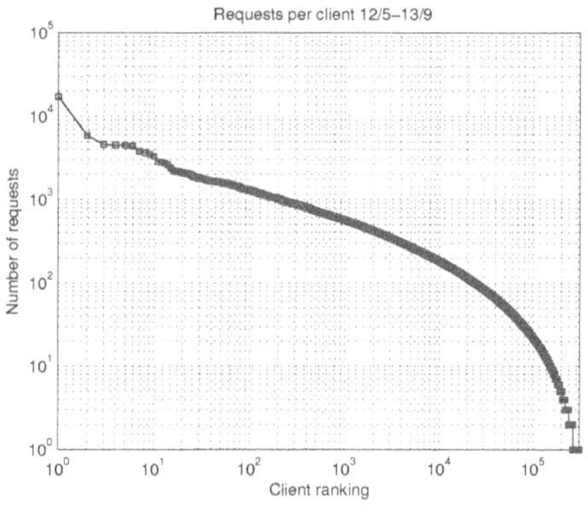

Figure 2: Log-log plot of requests per client over 125 days.

Table 2: The week 19-25/5 in figures

	Requests	Clients	Programs
Total (over 7 days)	585147	105698	14067
Daily median	76931	31542	6813
Hourly median	2626	1723	1190
Hourly max	16037	9019	2987
Hourly min	186	131	128

others. On average the top 10 programs each day get 11% of the requests, the top 100 get 35%, and the top 1000 account for 71% of the requests. We will look at the program popularity in more detail in Sections 3 and 4.

3. ACCESS PATTERNS

3.1 Access pattern over a week

Figure 3 shows the number of requests per hour during one week from Thursday to Wednesday.

We can see here in detail the typical daily and weekly variation in demand. There are large, predictable peaks in demand in the evenings. The number of requests are often four times higher or more during the peak hour compared to the average demand during daytime. As expected, the number of requests are the highest on Friday and Saturday evening. The demand during daytime also increases during weekends.

The number of distinct programs requested per hour follows a similar pattern to that of the demand but the peaks are not as pronounced. The number of different programs requested often doubles in the evenings compared to daytime. In this particular week the median number of programs requested per hour was 1190, the hourly maximum was 2987 programs (Saturday 21:00-22:00) and the minimum was 128 programs (Wednesday 04:00-05:00).

The bar plot in Figure 3 also shows the number of requests for the top 10 and top 100 most popular programs each hour. Figure 4 shows the share of requests per hour that the top 100 most popular programs account for. On an hourly basis the top 100 on average get 50% of the requests. The top 100 obviously have a large part of the traffic during night when not much more than 100 programs are requested. But more interestingly the top 100's share of requests also increase significantly during prime time. The number of different programs requested increases during the evenings

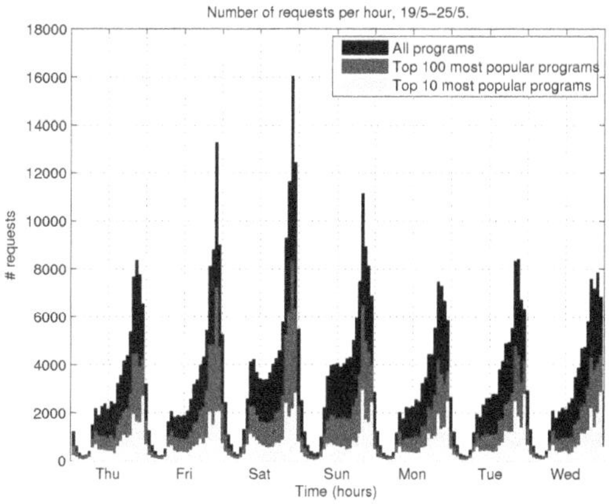

Figure 3: Number of requests per hour during a week. The grid points out the hours between 11:00-12:00 and 23:00-00:00 each day.

and so a hundred programs constitute a smaller share of the requested program volume. But even so the top 100's share of requests increase significantly.

3.2 Daily and hourly change in user interest

Which programs are most popular change over time. On average 6 of the top 10 programs are replaced each day. Figure 5a shows the daily change among the top 100 and top 1000 most requested programs. Here we also see the daily change among all requested programs. On average 73% of the requested programs are the same as yesterday. On average 56% of the top 100 and 42% of the top 1000 is different from the day before.

We notice in Figure 5a a weekly pattern with less change in top 100 during weekends (from Fridays to Saturdays and Saturdays to Sundays). This suggests that what the most

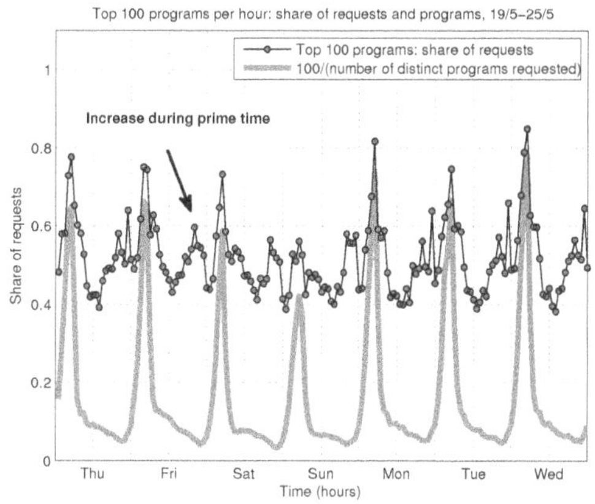

Figure 4: The figure shows the share of requests per hour that the top 100 most popular programs account for. It also shows the share of programs requested that a hundred programs comprises. The top 100's share of requests increases during night when few programs are requested but more interestingly it also increases during prime time when the demand is the highest. The grid points out the hours between 11:00-12:00 and 23:00-00:00 each day.

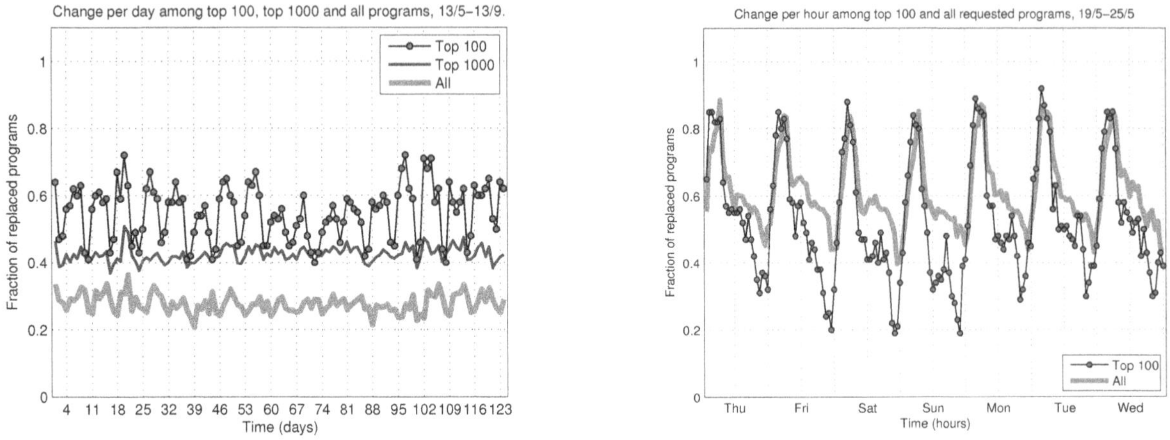

(a) (b)

Figure 5: (a) Daily change among the top 100 and top 1000 most requested programs. (b) Hourly change among the top 100 most requested programs. The figures also shows the fraction of all programs that was not requested the day and hour before.

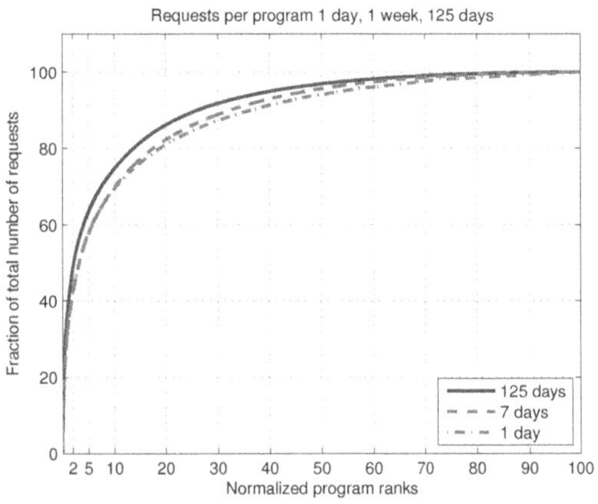

Figure 6: Cumulative distribution of requests to programs (1 day, 7 days and 125 days).

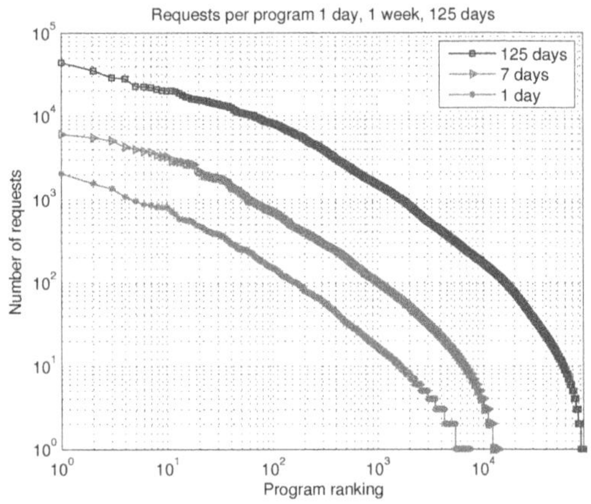

Figure 7: Log-log plot of requests per program (1 day, 7 days, 125 days).

popular items will be is more predictable during weekends when the demand also is the highest. This is even clearer on an hourly basis.

Figure 5b shows the hourly change among the top 100 most requested programs. On average 51 out of the 100 most requested programs are the same as the hour before. But the amount of change in the top 100 varies from hour to hour in a distinct daily cycle. During night up to 92% of the top 100 programs are changed from one hour to the next. While during prime time (19:00 to 23:00) the top 100-list becomes much more stable with down to 19% change among the top 100 programs.

4. PROGRAM POPULARITY

There is a small set of popular programs that account for a very large part of the requests. The Pareto principle, or the 80-20 rule, is often referred to when describing video popularity and the concentration of user interest towards a few popular programs [7], [26]. The users spread of requests across programs in the TV-on-Demand system conforms with this principle. The 20 % most popular programs account for more than 80% of the requests.

We calculated the number of requests for each program, sorted them in order of popularity, and plotted the cumulative distribution function shown in Figure 6. Here we can see the number of requests per program as a CDF-plot for 1 day, 1 week and for the entire 125-day period.

If we consider the entire 125-day period, then the 2% most popular programs account for 48% of the requests, the 10% most popular programs account for 74% of the requests, and the 20% most popular programs receive 84% of the requests. The figures are similar on daily and weekly basis as well.

This skewness in popularity for TV-on-Demand is somewhere in between what has been described in the literature for user-generated content and traditional Video-on-Demand systems. For Youtube traffic, investigated by Cha et al. [7], 10% of the videos accounted for 80% of the requests. In the chinese PowerInfo Video-on-Demand system described by Yu et al. [26], 10% of the videos accounted for 60% of the accesses. TV-on-Demand systems are more dy-

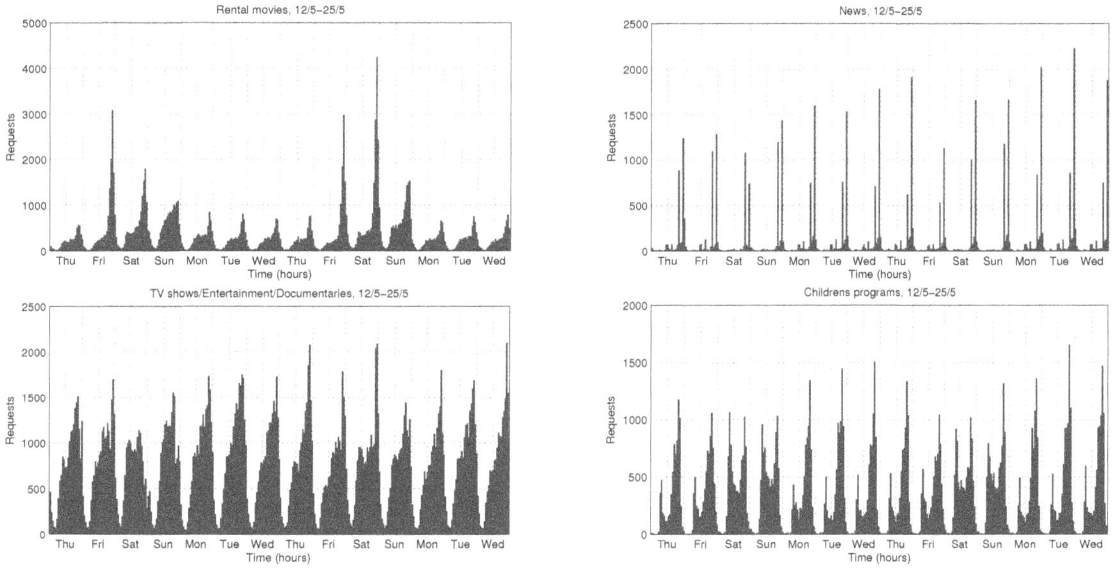

Figure 8: Access patterns per program category: rental movies, TV news, TV drama, and children's programs. Requests per hour over two weeks. The grid points out the hours between 11:00-12:00 and 23:00-00:00 each day.

namic than traditional VoD systems with a large daily inflow of new content. As we will see in Section 4.2, there are programs that are popular for several weeks and accumulate a lot of requests, but there are also many programs that have a very short life-span and are only requested for a few hours.

Figure 7 shows the number of requests per program as a log-log plot. It shows the number of times that a program has been accessed versus the ranking of the program in the data set.

There are a large number of research papers that deal with the popularity distribution of web pages and video. Much of the debate concerns whether the distribution of requests is Zipf-like or not [6, 7, 9, 13, 26]. Here we do not try to fit the curve to a specific probability distribution. However, we note that the curve does not follow a straight line on the log-log scale. This implies that the distribution of TV-on-Demand requests does not follow a Zipf-like distribution.

The 80-20 rule, and the concentration of requests to a small set of programs is important for caching. This is independent of what exact probability distribution best describes the access frequency. In Section 5 we perform trace-driven simulation, and directly use the sequence of requests to investigate the impact on caching.

4.1 Access patterns per program category

Different categories of programs have different access patterns. Figure 8 shows the number of requests per hour over two weeks for programs in four different categories: rental video, TV news, drama and children's programs. The figure demonstrates some clear and expected differences in access patterns.

The top left figure shows the access pattern for rental movies. These are movies that a viewer can pay to access for 24 hours. We can see that movie rentals are concentrated over weekends with large peaks in demand during Friday and Saturday evenings.

For TV news the traditional TV schedule determines to a large extent also when the program is requested on demand. The TV news is scheduled daily at 19:00 and 22:00. At the same time it becomes available for time-shifted viewing and we can see that most requests are close to these times.

For the other two categories we note that the TV reality and drama shows are watched during the daytime to a larger degree than other programs. We also see that the children's programs have peaks in demand in the mornings and early evenings. This is especially true for weekends.

4.2 Access patterns for individual programs: how program popularity changes over time

The popularity of a program changes with time and the demand pattern varies depending on the program type. Figure 9 shows the number of requests per day for 20 different programs over 125 days.

The top figures show the most requested rental movies and TV news programs in the data set. For each movie we can see a slow decline in popularity over time. The movies are requested many weeks after their premiere. There is also a clear weekly pattern with peaks in demand at the weekends. For TV news programs the access patterns are very different compared to movies. A news program is mostly requested the first evening and then quickly becomes outdated and loses its popularity when available on demand.

The figures at the bottom show the access pattern for five episodes of a daily TV reality show and five episodes of a weekly home improvement show. We can see that the request patterns for different episodes of the same show are surprisingly similar. For the reality show we can also see that after the initial peak in demand the program popularity quickly decline with time. The programs are requested daily also the following three months but there are often only a few requests per day.

4.2.1 The life of a rental movie

Figure 10a shows the number of requests per day and the rank for a comedy-drama rental movie. We can see the decline in popularity over 16 weeks from the premiere. The

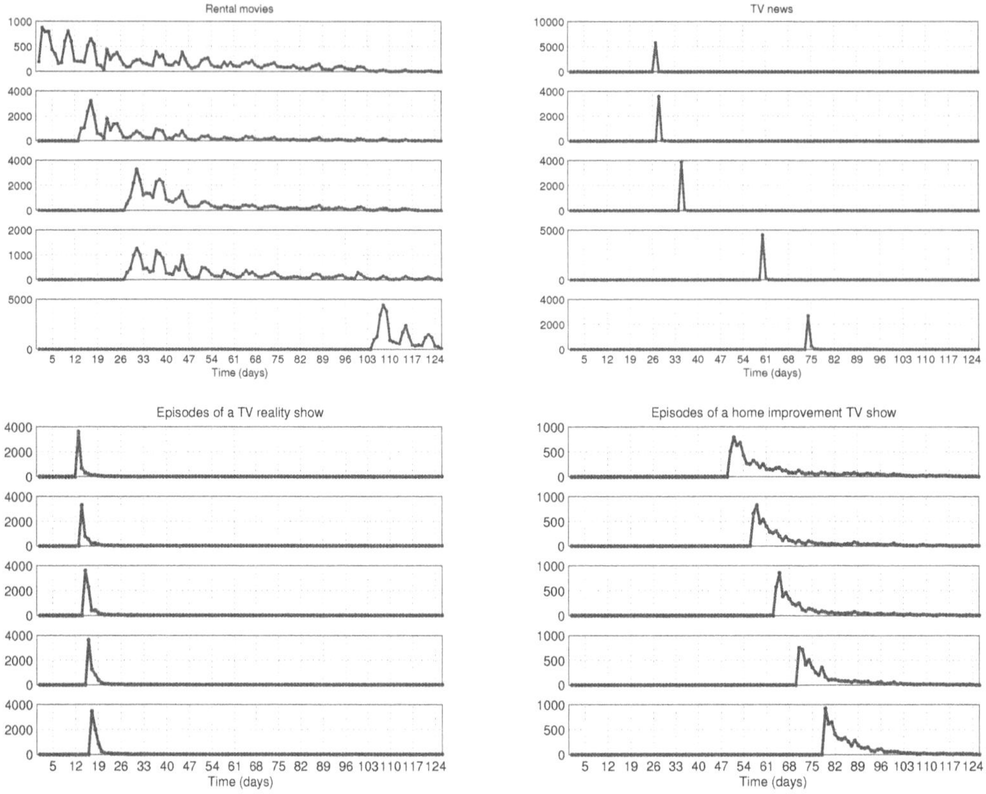

Figure 9: Requests per day for 5 movies, TV news programs and episodes of a reality show and a home improvement show.

figure also demonstrates the typical peaks in popularity for a rental movie during weekends where the number of requests increases and the program increase in rank.

Figure 10b shows the change in rank in more detail among the top 100 most popular programs each day. We can see that the movie jumps in and out of the top 10 and top 100 lists a number of times. This has implications for the choice of caching strategy. It is essential to have the right programs in the cache at Friday and Saturday evenings when the total demand is the highest. If the replacement policy acts on popularity over a short time window the program might be evicted when popularity temporarily goes down during weekdays and the program will not immediately be available in the cache when the demand increases again next weekend.

Figure 10b also compare the rank for our movie among all programs with the rank among only rental movies. The movie is the number one most popular movie for 14 days in a row and it stays in the top 10 for one month and in the top 20 for two months.

Figure 11 shows the rank and the number of requests per hour during the first week that the movie is available. The movie quickly climbs in rank and becomes one of the most popular programs. It is in the top ten during the evenings but the rank of the program sometimes drops during the daytime and during night. There are large, predictable daily variations in demand with peaks in the evenings. The number of requests increases significantly during Friday and Saturday.

4.2.2 *The life of a TV news program*

TV news programs have a very short lifespan compared to movies. Figure 12 shows the rank and number of requests per hour for a news program that was sent live at 19:00.

Most of the requests are the first hour when the program becomes available. The news program immediately becomes the most requested program that hour and number one on the ranking. The popularity then quickly declines. There are almost no requests at all for a news program after the first day. The access pattern is very different compared to what we see in Figure 11 for the simultaneously available movie.

4.2.3 *TV series and children's programs – periodic increase in popularity*

The interest in a TV program usually decreases with time. But more often than not the popularity of a program can also increase temporarily or periodically. We saw in the previous sections that the number of requests for a program varies during the day and the week. We also saw for rental movies that the ranking increased during weekends.

Many TV shows are part of a series of programs. When the next episode is sent there is often also renewed interest for old episodes available on-demand. Figure 13 shows an example with the rank and number of started sessions per day for an episode of a weekly home improvement TV show. We can see that the program increase in rank every Thursday when the series is shown on the traditional scheduled TV.

Figure 14 shows the number of requests per day and the

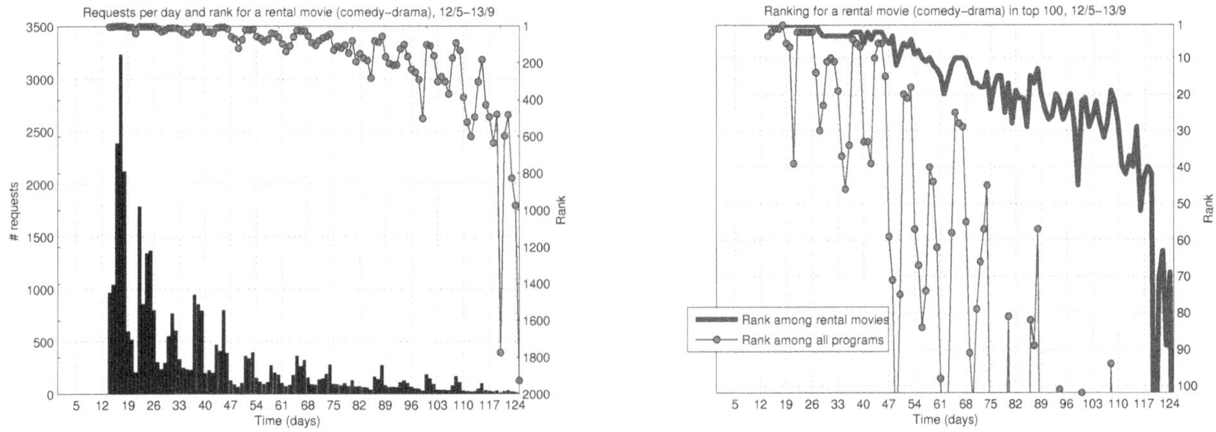

(a) (b)

Figure 10: (a) Requests per day and ranking for a rental movie (comedy-drama). The bar graph shows requests per day with the scale on the Y-axis shown to the left. The plotted line shows the ranking of the program among all other programs requested that day. The scale of the ranking is shown on the Y-axis to the right. The grid points out weeks starting on Mondays. (b) Detailed look at the rank among all programs (top 100) and among rental movies.

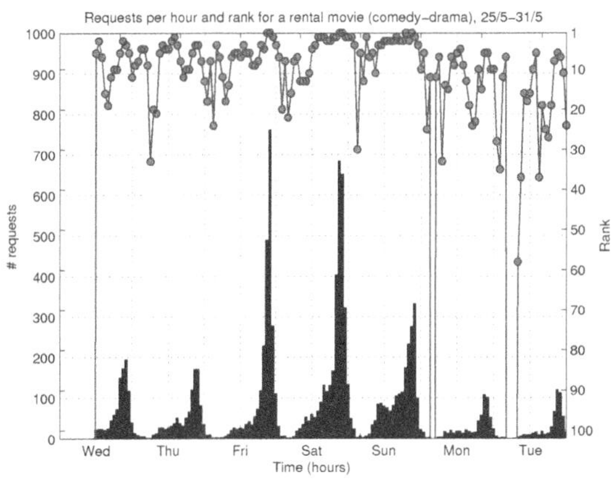

Figure 11: Requests per hour and ranking for a rental movie (comedy-drama). The grid points out the hours between 11:00-12:00 and 23:00-00:00.

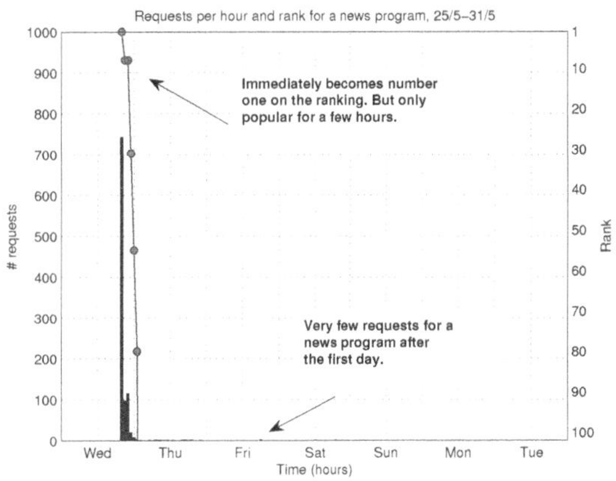

Figure 12: Requests per hour and ranking for a TV news program.

ranking for a cartoon. After the initial peak in interest the popularity decreases and remains at a steady level over the month when the program is available. This is different if we look at the ranking on an hourly basis. Figure 15 shows the ranking of the program per hour during the first week. The pattern is the same for the next three weeks as well. The program varies in popularity. It goes in and out of the top 100 list, often twice a day.

The number of requests for children's programs increases in the mornings and in the early evenings. This is a daily recurring pattern. Also, at these times of the day there is little demand for other TV-programs so few requests are needed to get into the top ranking.

5. IMPACT ON CACHING

In previous sections we have seen many aspects of the access patterns in a TV-on-Demand system. In this section we study the impact on caching. We examine the proportion of requests that are not first-time requests for a program and therefore potentially could be served from a cache. We look at this for different population sizes and time periods.

We then use trace-driven simulation to investigate the cache friendliness of the workload with a limited cache size and the classic LRU and LFU cache replacement policies. We run the sequence of requests in our data set through caches of different size and look at the resulting cache hit ratios.

5.1 Cacheability

For on-demand caching, the first request for a program needs to go to the central server. But if we imagine an unlimited cache size then all other requests could potentially be served from the local cache. It is therefore interesting to examine the proportion of requests that are not first-time requests. We here call that *cacheability*.

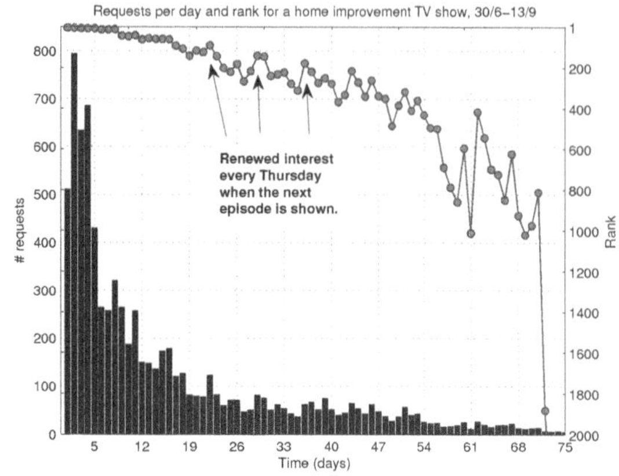

Figure 13: Requests per day and ranking for an episode of a weekly home improvement TV show. The grid points out weeks starting on Mondays.

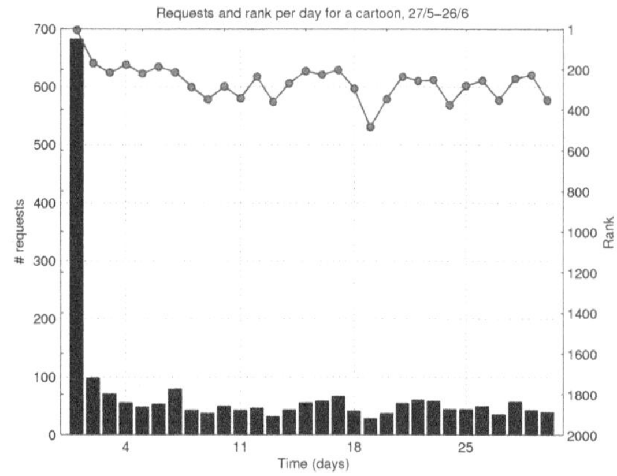

Figure 14: Requests per day and ranking for a cartoon.

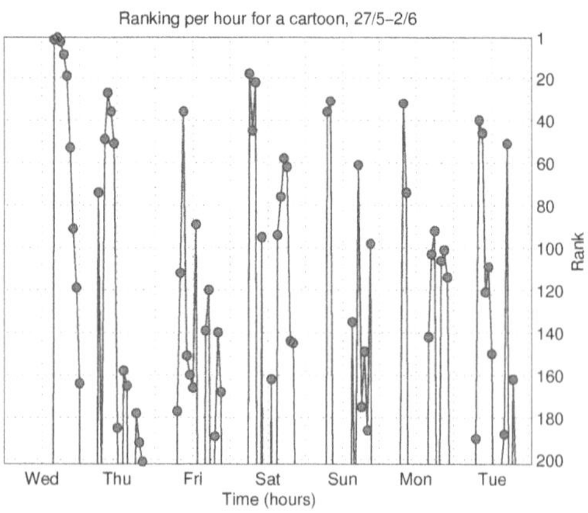

Figure 15: Ranking per hour for a cartoon. The grid points out the hours between 11:00-12:00 and 23:00-00:00 each day. The program jumps up and down in popularity. It always climbs to top 40 in the mornings and are often in top 100 in the early evenings.

We follow the definition of *cacheability* used by Ager et al. [2]. But our data set do not include information about program size so here we only consider requests. Cacheability is then the share of requests that are not first-time requests. If k_i is the total number of requests for a program k then the cacheability is $\sum_{i=1}^{n}(k_i - 1)/\sum_{i=1}^{n}(k_i)$, where n is the number of programs.

The share of first time requests is very low in the TV-on-Demand system if we consider all clients over a long period of time. The cacheability over 125 days is: 99.13%.

In Figure 16 we also look at the cacheability per day and per hour and for populations of different size. The calculation of cacheability starts from the beginning of each time interval. It is not considering what have been requested the hour or day before. For all clients in the region during the week in Figure 16, the median cacheability per hour is 59%. However, there are large daily variations. During night many programs are requested only once and the cacheability is low. During Friday and Saturday evenings the cacheability is above 80%.

Figure 17 shows examples of cacheability over 125 days for smaller populations. For very small populations the probability that a viewer will choose a program that nobody else in the group has requested before is high. So the share of first-time requests is high and the cacheability is low. But we see that already for groups of 1000 viewers the cacheability is above 60%. We calculated the cacheability for five different groups of 1000 viewers. The median was 63.9% and the group with lowest result had a cacheability of 61.7%.

5.2 Limited cache size

We saw in the previous section that the cacheabilty in the TV-on-Demand system is very high. But in practice there is a limited cache size. In order to investigate the cache friendliness of the TV-on-Demand workload we use trace-driven simulation. We run the sequence of requests in the data set through caches of different size and study the cache hit ratios for three classic caching policies:

Least Recently Used (LRU): with the LRU strategy we delete from the cache the program that has not been requested for the longest time.

Least Frequently Used (LFU): with LFU we discard the program that is requested least often. This is done by keeping track of the hit ratio for all programs currently in the cache (in cache LFU).

Clairvoyant: we also implement a clairvoyant strategy with the ability to look into the future and delete the program that will not be needed for the longest time. This is used for comparison to obtain an upper limit on the cache hit ratio. It is implemented by going through the traces twice. First, for each request of a program we look up and determine when the program will be requested next. This is then used in the simulation to determine what program should stay in the cache.

Figure 18 shows cache hit ratios for the LRU, LFU and Clairvoyant replacement policies for increasing cache sizes. The hit ratios are calculated over 3 days. The size of the programs are not taken into account. We calculate request (or program) hit rate and not the byte hit rate. The x-axis shows cache size in number of programs. The median number of distinct programs requested per day is 7523. To put the hit ratio and cache size in relation to the daily demand we therefore look specifically at cache sizes of 376

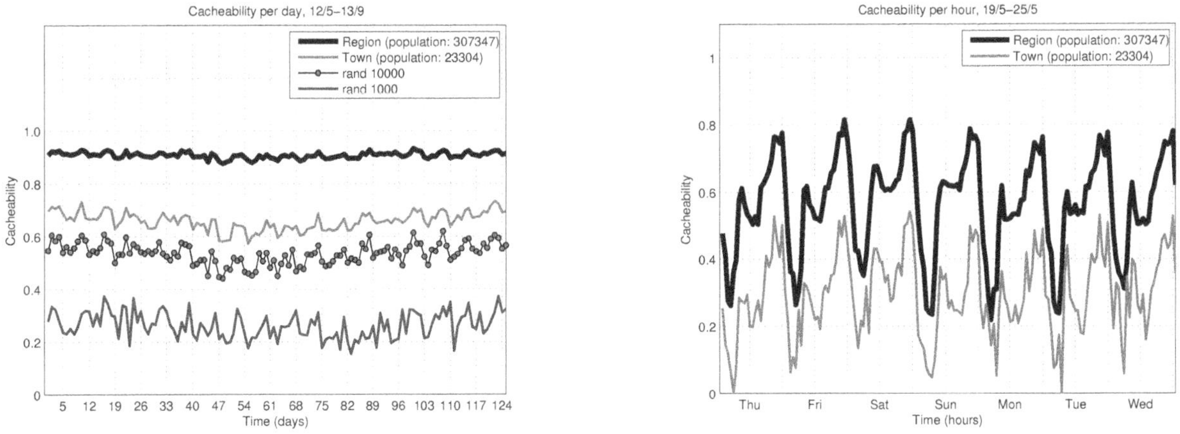

Figure 16: Cacheability per day and per hour. Comparison between different population sizes.

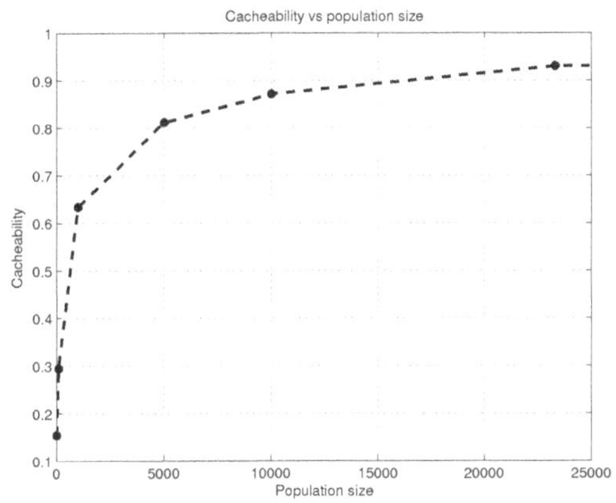

Figure 17: Example of cacheability versus population size.

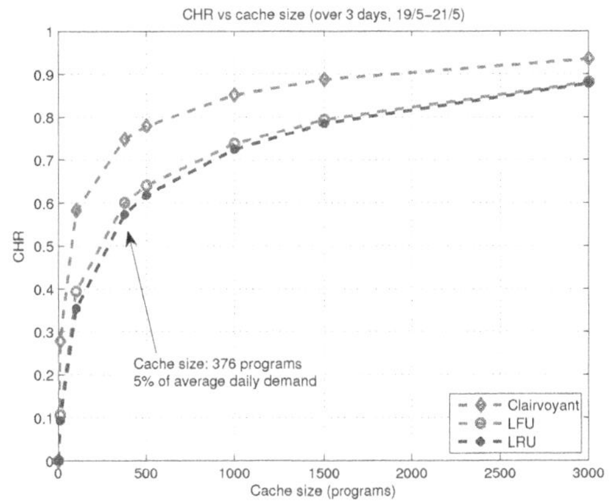

Figure 18: Cache hit ratio versus cache size, requests from all clients over 3 days. Comparison of the LRU, LFU and Clairvoyant replacement policies.

programs, which is 5% of average daily demand. We can see that caching 5% of the daily demand gives a hit ratio of 57% for LRU, 60% for LFU and 75% for the Clairvoyant replacement policy.

In Figure 18 we include the requests from all viewers. In Figure 19 we investigate the impact of population size. Here we use the LRU replacement policy and compare the cache hit ratios for populations of different size. For a cache size of 376 programs (5% of the daily demand) the town subset of 23304 clients get a hit ratio of 51%. This is close to the result for the full set of clients. For the small population with 1000 clients we get a hit ratio of 43%. The cacheability for this particular population of 1000 viewers was 0.64 over 125 days and we see the curve approaching that value at a cache size of 3000 programs.

The cache hit ratio also varies over time. Figure 20 shows hit ratio per hour for all viewers, the LRU replacement policy and a cache size of 376 programs. The hit ratio was calculated over 17 weeks and the figure shows the median (and max and min) value for each hour of the week. We can see that the cache hit ratio varies over the day and it increases when it is needed as most. During prime time, when there are the most requests, the hit ratio is over 60%.

From the results presented above we highlight three observations:

- The cacheability and the potential for caching is very high.
- The hit ratio with a simple LRU replacement policy is above 50% when caching 5% of the average daily demand.
- The hit ratio increases during prime time when it is needed most. This is consistent with the observations in Section 3 that the share of requests for the most popular programs increases during prime time.

We have here looked at the cache friendliness of the TV-on-demand workload in terms of cacheability and cache hit ratios for the basic LRU and LFU replacement policies. In Section 7 on future work we discuss how our observations about access patterns and program popularity can potentially be used to design a more informed caching strategy.

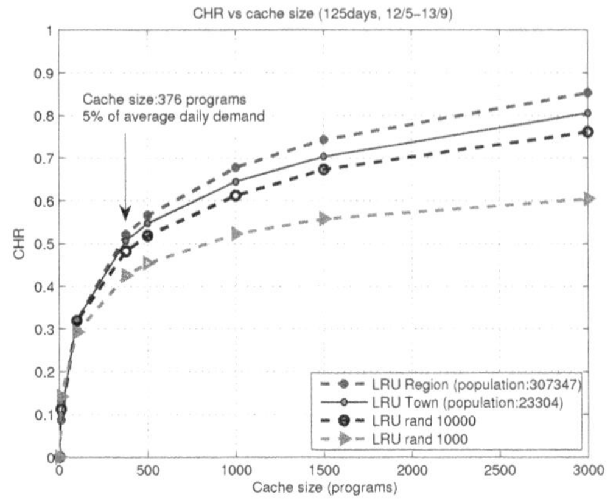

Figure 19: Cache hit ratio versus cache size. Comparison of cache hit ratios for populations of different size.

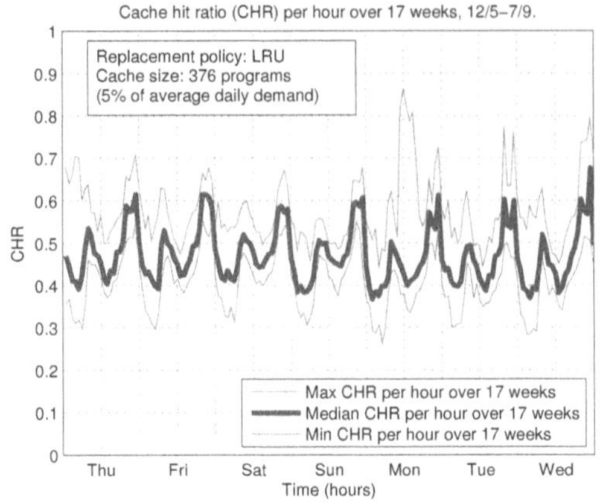

Figure 20: Cache hit ratio per hour over 17 weeks

6. RELATED WORK

There are several studies of viewing behaviour in IPTV systems where traditional scheduled TV is distributed over IP networks. Cha et al. [8] study viewing behaviour including channel popularity and channel switching in an operational IPTV network. Qiu et al. model TV channel popularity [18] and user activities [17] in a large IPTV system. Our work is different in that we look at TV-on-Demand where the viewers choose programs to watch outside of the TV schedule. In this sense our work is closer to studies of traditional VoD systems.

Yu et al. [26] present a large measurement study of the chinese PowerInfo Video-on-Demand system. This work is similar to ours in that they investigate many aspects of user behaviour and content access patterns. The PowerInfo system is a traditional VoD system. The videos in the library are old TV shows and movies and there are usually only a few new movies introduced to the system per day. This is different from the TV-on-Demand system that we study where there is a large inflow of new programs from the TV-schedule, time-shifted viewing, and programs with a very short life-span. Our work is also different in other aspects in that we investigate how the access pattern depend on genre, we study cacheability and use trace-based simulation to investigate what impact the access patterns have on caching.

There are many other interesting studies of VoD systems and video popularity. Griwodz et al. [12] model long-term popularity of videos on the time scale of days based on VHS rental statistics. Lou et al. [16] give examples of the popularity evolution of video files from a Chinese television station. Tang et al. [19] analyse and model many aspects of media server access. Avramova et al. [3] model the popularity evolution of TV-on-demand and video traces. Dan and Carlsson [9] measure and analyse BitTorrent content popularity. Guo et al. [13] study the probability distributions of Internet media workloads and analyse caching using a mathematical model. Yin et al. [25] study live VoD workloads from the 2008 Beijing Olympics. There are also many studies of Youtube and user generated videos [4, 7, 10, 14].

Gopalakrishnan et al. [11] study user behaviour in a large IPTV system. This is similar to our work but their focus is on modeling the interactive user behaviour in an IPTV environment, including how users fast-forward, pause and rewind to control their viewing.

In this paper we also investigate cacheability and we look at the potential for caching in a TV-on-Demand system. Caching has been widely studied for web content and video [6, 15, 22, 24]. More recently, Ager et al. [2] studied the cacheability for HTTP- and P2P-based applications. There are also several studies of caching strategies in IPTV on-demand systems [1, 5, 20, 21, 23], but these studies use analytical models and simulations whereas we present a trace-based study from a real TV-on-Demand system.

7. FUTURE WORK

In this paper we have studied many aspects of the access patterns in a TV-on-Demand system. We have looked at the cache friendliness of the workload in terms of cacheability and hit ratios for basic replacement policies. For future work we hope that our observations can be used as a basis for developing better caching strategies for TV-on-Demand systems.

When studying the cache friendliness of the request stream in Section 5 we used the basic LRU and LFU cache replacement policies. With these the last requested program is always cached and the choice of what to evict from the cache is between the least recently and the least frequently requested program. A more advanced system could use more knowledge about access patterns and program popularity to decide what program to put in the cache and what program to evict.

One such strategy could be to keep track of all programs in the system, also those that are not currently in the cache. One could monitor the popularity by counting requests, let the programs age over time and for each program keep a value that describes the probability that it will be requested. There are several observations in this paper that can be useful for such an informed caching strategy:

Give preference to new programs
With time-shifted TV ongoing scheduled programs immediately get a lot of requests. Some programs, like TV-news, also have a very short life-span. The value of a program should not have to be built up by requests over a long time.

Categorize programs by genre to predict change in popularity over time

We saw in Section 4 that the access pattern very much depends on the type of program. A news program that is top-ranked the first evening age quickly and have a very low probability for being requested the next evening. A rental movie however is popular for months and increase in rank during weekends. By categorizing programs by genre the probability for future requests can be predicted. The categorization of programs can also be more detailed. The request patterns for different episodes of the same show are often very similar as we saw in Figure 9, Section 4.2. For a new episode of a show it is a reasonable assumption that the popularity of the program will change over time in a way similar to that of the previous episodes.

Focus on prime time
The value of a program should reflect the probability that it will be requested during prime time. There are large peaks in demand in the evenings and at the weekends that need to be handled. If caching is used to limit the maximum link load then it is essential to have the right programs in the cache on Friday and Saturday evenings. There are program like cartoons that are top-ranked in the mornings and early evenings that probably should not be in the cache.

The observations and the predictions outlined above can be used to optimise the caching performance. However, the basic monitoring of request frequency is still needed as a basis, and to handle unexpected changes and sudden peaks in program demand for instance due to large news events.

8. CONCLUSIONS

We have analysed the access patterns in a large TV-on-Demand system and studied the potential for caching.

Our contribution in this paper is three-fold. As a first-order result, we provide reconfirmation of known observations with an independent dataset. We demonstrate that there is a small set of programs that account for a large part of the requests. The program popularity conforms with the Pareto principle, or 80-20 rule. The demand follows a diurnal and weekly pattern, and there are large peaks in demand on Friday and Saturday evenings that need to be handled.

Second, we provide systematic evidence of TV-on-Demand access pattern characteristics that are intuitive yet unconfirmed in the literature. We show that news programs have a very short lifespan and are often only requested for a few hours, children's programs are top ranked in the mornings and early evenings, and movie rentals are concentrated over weekends.

Finally, we also provide novel insights into access patterns that have not been reported previously to the best of our knowledge. We show how the popularity of TV-on-Demand programs changes over time. We see that the access pattern in a TV-on-Demand system very much depend on what type of content it offers. Furthermore, we find that the share of requests for the top most popular programs grows during prime time, and the change rate among them decreases. The cacheability is very high and the cache hit ratio increases during prime time when it is needed most.

We believe that these observations and findings can guide the design of future systems for TV-on-Demand infrastructures.

9. ACKNOWLEDGMENTS

This work has been performed within the SICS Center for Networked Systems funded by VINNOVA, KKS, SSF, ABB, Ericsson, Saab SDS, TeliaSonera, T2Data, Vendolocus and Peerialism.

10. REFERENCES

[1] H. Abrahamsson and M. Björkman. Simulation of IPTV caching strategies. In *Proceedings of SPECTS'10*, Ottawa, Canada, 2010.

[2] B. Ager, F. Schneider, J. Kim, and A. Feldmann. Revisiting Cacheability in Times of User Generated Content. In *Proceedings of 13th IEEE Global Internet Symposium*, San Diego, CA, USA, March 2010.

[3] Z. Avramova, S. Wittevrongel, H. Bruneel, and D. Vleeschauwer. Analysis and Modeling of Video Popularity Evolution in Various Online Video Content Systems: Power Law versus Exponential Decay. In *Proceedings of International Conference on Evolving Internet*, 2009.

[4] Y. Borghol, S. Mitra, S. Ardon, N. Carlsson, D. Eager, and A. Mahanti. Characterizing and Modeling Popularity of User-generated Videos. In *Proceedings of IFIP International Symposium on Computer Performance, Modeling, Measurements and Evaluation (PERFORMANCE)*, 2011.

[5] S. Borst, V. Gupta, and A. Walid. Distributed caching algorithms for content distribution networks. In *Proceedings of INFOCOM'10*, San Diego, USA, 2010.

[6] L. Breslau, P. Cao, L. Fan, G. Phillips, and S. Shenker. Web Caching and Zipf-like Distributions: Evidence and Implications. In *Proceedings of IEEE INFOCOM*, 1999.

[7] M. Cha, H. Kwak, P. Rodriguez, Y. Ahn, and S. Moon. Analyzing the Video Popularity Characteristics of Large-Scale User Generated Content Systems. *IEEE Transactions on Networking*, 17:1357–1370, October 2009.

[8] M. Cha, P. Rodriguez, J. Crowcroft, S. Moon, and X. Amatriain. Watching Television Over an IP Network. In *Proceedings of Internet Measurement Conference (IMC'08)*, Greece, 2008.

[9] G. Dan and N. Carlsson. Power-law Revisited: A Large Scale Measurement Study of P2P Content Popularity. In *Proceedings of IPTPS'10*, San Jose, USA, April 2010.

[10] P. Gill, M. Arlitt, Z. Li, and A. Mahanti. YouTube Traffic Characterization: A view From the Edge. In *Proceedings of ACM SIGCOMM Internet Measurement Conference*, San Diego, USA, October 2007.

[11] V. Gopalakrishnan, R. Jana, K. Ramakrishnan, D. Swayne, and V. Vaishampayan. Understanding Couch Potatoes: Measurement and Modeling of Interactive Usage of IPTV at large scale. In *Proceedings of Internet Measurement Conference (IMC'11)*, 2011.

[12] C. Griwodz, M. Bär, and L. Wolf. Long-term Movie Popularity Models in Video-on-Demand Systems or The Life of an on-Demand Movie. In *Proceedings of ACM Multimedia'97*, Seattle, USA, 1997.

[13] L. Guo, E. Tan, S. Chen, Z. Xiao, and X. Zhang. The stretched exponential distribution of internet media access patterns. In *Proceedings of the twenty-seventh*

ACM symposium on Principles of distributed computing (PODC'08), New York, USA, 2008.
[14] X. Kang, H. Zhang, G. Jiang, H. Chen, X. Meng, and K. Yoshihira. Measurement, Modeling, and Analysis of Internet Video Sharing Site Workload: A Case Study. In *Proceedings of ICWS'08*, 2008.
[15] J. Liu and J. Xu. Proxy Caching for Media Streaming Over the Internet. *IEEE Communications Magazine*, 42:88–94, 2004.
[16] J. Lou, Y. Tang, M. Zhang, and S. Yang. Characterizing User Behavior Model to Evaluate Hard Cache in Peer-to-Peer Based Video-on-demand Service. In *Proceedings of MMM'07*, pages 125–134, 2007.
[17] T. Qiu, Z. Ge, S. Lee, J. Wang, J. Xu, and Q. Zhao. Modeling User Activities in a Large IPTV System. In *Proceedings of Internet Measurement Conference (IMC'09)*, USA, 2009.
[18] T. Qiu, Z. Ge, S. Lee, J. Wang, Q. Zhao, and J. Xu. Modeling Channel Popularity Dynamics in a Large IPTV System. In *Proceedings of SIGMETRICS*, pages 275–286, Seattle, USA, June 2009.
[19] W. Tang, Y. Fu, L. Cherkasova, and A. Vahdat. Modeling and Generating Realistic Streaming Media Server Workloads. *Computer Networks*, 51:336–356, 2007.
[20] D. D. Vleeschauwer, Z. Avramova, S. Wittevrongel, and H. Brueel. Transport Capacity for a Catch-up Television Service. In *Proceedings of EuroITV'09*, pages 161–170, Leuven, Belgium, June 2009.
[21] D. D. Vleeschauwer and K. Laevens. Performance of caching algorithms for IPTV on-demand services. *IEEE Transactions on broadcasting*, 55:491 – 501, 2009.
[22] J. Wang. A Survey of Web Caching Schemes for the Internet. *ACM SIGCOMM Computer Communication Review*, 29:36–46, 1999.
[23] T. Wauters, W. V. de Meerssche, F. D. Turck, B. Dhoedt, P. Demeester, T. V. Caenegem, and E. Six. Co-operative Proxy Caching Algorithms for Time-Shifted IPTV Services. In *Proceedings of 32nd EUROMICRO Conference on Software Engineering and Advanced Applications (SEAA)*, pages 379–386, Dubrovnik, Croatia, September 2006.
[24] A. Wolman, G. M. Voelker, N. Sharma, N. Cardwell, A. Karlin, and H. M. Levy. On the scale and performance of cooperative Web proxy caching. In *Proceedings of the 17th ACM Symposium on Operating Systems Principles (SOSP '99)*, 1999.
[25] H. Yin, X. Liu, F. Qiu, N. Xia, C. Lin, H. Zhang, V. Sekar, and G. Min. Inside the Bird's Nest: Measurements of Large-Scale Live VoD from the 2008 Olympics. In *Proceedings of Internet Measurement Conference (IMC'09)*, USA, 2009.
[26] H. Yu, D. Zheng, B. Zhao, and W. Zheng. Understanding User Behavior in Large-Scale Video-on-Demand Systems. In *Proceedings of EuroSys2006*, pages 333–344, Leuven, Belgium, 2006.

Video Stream Quality Impacts Viewer Behavior: Inferring Causality Using Quasi-Experimental Designs

S. Shunmuga Krishnan
Akamai Technologies
sarumuga@akamai.com

Ramesh K. Sitaraman
University of Massachusetts, Amherst
& Akamai Technologies
ramesh@cs.umass.edu

ABSTRACT

The distribution of videos over the Internet is drastically transforming how media is consumed and monetized. Content providers, such as media outlets and video subscription services, would like to ensure that their videos do not fail, startup quickly, and play without interruptions. In return for their investment in video stream quality, content providers expect less viewer abandonment, more viewer engagement, and a greater fraction of repeat viewers, resulting in greater revenues. The key question for a content provider or a CDN is whether and to what extent changes in video quality can *cause* changes in viewer behavior. Our work is the first to establish a causal relationship between video quality and viewer behavior, taking a step beyond purely correlational studies. To establish causality, we use Quasi-Experimental Designs, a novel technique adapted from the medical and social sciences.

We study the impact of video stream quality on viewer behavior in a scientific data-driven manner by using extensive traces from Akamai's streaming network that include 23 million views from 6.7 million unique viewers. We show that viewers start to abandon a video if it takes more than 2 seconds to start up, with each incremental delay of 1 second resulting in a 5.8% increase in the abandonment rate. Further, we show that a moderate amount of interruptions can decrease the average play time of a viewer by a significant amount. A viewer who experiences a rebuffer delay equal to 1% of the video duration plays 5% less of the video in comparison to a similar viewer who experienced no rebuffering. Finally, we show that a viewer who experienced failure is 2.32% less likely to revisit the same site within a week than a similar viewer who did not experience a failure.

Categories and Subject Descriptors

C.4 [**Performance of Systems**]: Measurement techniques, Performance attributes; C.2.4 [**Computer-Communication Networks**]: Distributed Systems—*Client/server*

IMC'12, November 14–16, 2012, Boston, Massachusetts, USA.

Keywords

Video quality, Internet Content Delivery, User Behavior, Causal Inference, Quasi-Experimental Design, Streaming Video, Multimedia

1. INTRODUCTION

The Internet is radically transforming all aspects of human society by enabling a wide range of applications for business, commerce, entertainment, news and social networking. Perhaps no industry has been transformed more radically than the media and entertainment segment of the economy. As media such as television and movies migrate to the Internet, there are twin challenges that *content providers* face whose ranks include major media companies (e.g., NBC, CBS), news outlets (e.g., CNN), sports organizations (e.g., NFL, MLB), and video subscription services (e.g., Netflix, Hulu).

The first major challenge for content providers is providing a *high-quality streaming experience* for their viewers, where videos are available without failure, they startup quickly, and stream without interruptions [24]. A major technological innovation of the past decade that allows content providers to deliver higher-quality video streams to a global audience of viewers is the content delivery network (or, CDN for short) [8, 17]. CDNs are large distributed systems that consist of hundreds of thousands of servers placed in thousands of ISPs close to end users. CDNs employ several techniques for transporting [2, 12] media content from the content provider's origin to servers at the "edges" of the Internet where they are cached and served with higher quality to the end user. (See [17] for a more detailed description of a typical CDN architecture.)

The second major challenge of a content provider is to actually *monetize* their video content through ad-based or subscription-based models. Content providers track key metrics of viewer behavior that lead to better monetization. Primary among them relate to viewer *abandonment, engagement, and repeat viewership.* Content providers know that reducing the abandonment rate, increasing the play time of each video watched, and enhancing the rate at which viewers return to their site increase opportunities for advertising and upselling, leading to greater revenues. The key question is whether and by how much increased stream quality can *cause* changes in viewer behavior that are conducive to improved monetization. Relatively little is known from a scientific standpoint about the all-important *causal* link between video stream quality and viewer behavior for online media. *Exploring the causal impact of quality on behavior and developing tools for such an exploration are the primary foci of our work.*

While understanding the link between stream quality and viewer behavior is of paramount importance to the content provider, it also has profound implications for how a CDN must be architected. An architect is often faced with tradeoffs on *which* quality metrics need to be optimized by the CDN. A scientific study of which quality metrics have the most impact on viewer behavior can guide these choices. As an example of viewer behavior impacting CDN architecture, we performed small-scale controlled experiments on viewer behavior a decade ago that established the relative importance of the video to startup quickly and play without interruptions. These behavioral studies motivated an architectural feature called prebursting [12] that was deployed on Akamai's live streaming network that enabled the CDN to deliver streams to a media player at higher than the encoded rate for short periods of time to fill the media player's buffer with more data more quickly, resulting in the stream starting up faster and playing with fewer interruptions. It is notable that the folklore on the importance of startup time and rebuffering were confirmed in two recent important large-scale scientific studies [9, 15]. Our current work sheds further light on the important nexus between stream quality and viewer behavior and, importantly, provides the first evidence of a causal impact of quality on behavior.

1.1 Measuring quality and viewer behavior

The advent of customizable media players supporting major formats such as Adobe Flash, Microsoft Silverlight, and Apple HTTP streaming has revolutionized our ability to perform truly large-scale studies of stream quality and viewer behavior as we do in this work, in a way not possible even a few years ago. It has become possible to instrument media players with an analytics plug-in that accurately measures and reports both quality and behavioral metrics from every viewer on a truly planetary scale.

1.2 From correlation to causality

The ability to measure stream quality and viewer behavior on a global scale allows us to correlate the two in a statistically significant way. For each video watched by a viewer, we are able to measure its quality including whether the stream was available, how long the stream took to start up, and how much rebufferring occurred causing interruptions. We are also able to measure the viewer's behavior including whether he/she abandoned the video and how long he/she watched the video.

As a first step, we begin by simply correlating important quality metrics experienced by the viewers to the behavior that they exhibit. For instance, we discover a strong correlation between an increase in the delay for the video to start up and an increase in rate at which viewers abandon the video. Several of our results are the first quantitative demonstration that certain key streaming quality metrics are correlated with key behavioral metrics of the viewer. However, the deeper question is not just whether quality and behavior are *correlated* but whether quality can *causally* impact viewer behavior. While correlation is an important first step, correlation does not necessarily imply causality. The holy grail of a content provider or a CDN architect is to discover causal relationships rather than just correlational ones, since they would like to know with *some certainty* that the significant effort expended in improving stream quality will in fact result in favorable viewer behavior.

In fact, a purely correlational relationship could even lead one astray, if there is no convincing evidence of causality, leading to poor business decisions. For instance, both video quality (say, video bitrates) and viewer behavior (say, play time) have been steadily improving over the past decade and are hence correlated in a statistical sense. But, that fact alone is not sufficient to conclude that higher bitrates cause viewers to watch longer, unless one can account for other potential "confounding" factors such as the available video content itself becoming more captivating over time.

While inferring causality is generally difficult, a key tool widely used in the social and medical sciences to infer causality from observational data is a Quasi Experimental Design (QED) [23]. Intuitively, a QED is constructed to infer if a particular "treatment" (i.e., cause) results in a particular "outcome" (i.e., effect) by pairing each person in the observational data who has had treatment with a random untreated person who is "significantly identical" to the treated person in all other respects. Thus, the pairing eliminates the effect of the hidden confounding variables by ensuring that both members of a pair have sufficiently identical values for those variables. Thus, evaluating the differential outcomes between treated and untreated pairs can either strengthen or weaken a causal conclusion that the treatment causally impacts the outcome. While it is impossible to completely eliminate all hidden factors, our causal analysis using QEDs should be viewed as strengthening our correlational observations between treatments and outcomes by eliminating the common threats to a causal conclusion.

1.3 Our Contributions

Our study is one of the largest of its kind of video stream quality and viewer behavior that collects and analyzes a data set consisting of more than 23 million video playbacks from 6.7 million unique viewers who watched an aggregate of 216 million minutes of 102 thousand videos over 10 days.

To our knowledge, our work is the first to provide evidence that video stream quality *causally* impacts viewer behavior, a conclusion that is important to both content providers and CDNs. Further, our adaptation of Quasi-Experimental Designs (QEDs) is an unique contribution and is of independent interest. QEDs have been used extensively in medical research and the social sciences in the past decades. We expect that our adaptation of QEDs for measurement research in networked systems could be key in a variety of other domains that have so far been limited to correlational studies.

Our work is also the first to quantitatively explore viewer abandonment rates and repeat viewership in relation to stream quality, last-mile connectivity, and video duration. In addition, we also study viewer engagement (e.g., play time) in relation to stream quality (e.g., rebuffering) that has also been recently studied in [9] in a correlational setting, but we take a step beyond correlational analysis to establish a causal relationship between quality and engagement using QEDs. Our work makes the following specific contributions on the impact stream quality on viewer behavior.

- We show that an increase in the startup delay beyond 2 seconds causes viewers to abandon the video. Using regression, we show that an additional increase of the startup delay by 1 second increases the abandonment rate by 5.8%.

- Viewers are less tolerant to startup delay for a short video such as news clip than a long video such an hour-long TV episode. In a quasi experiment, the likelihood of a viewer of short video abandoning earlier than a similar viewer of a long video exceeded the likelihood that the opposite happens by 11.5%.
- Viewers watching video on a better connected computer or device have less patience for startup delay and abandon sooner. In particular, viewers on mobile devices have the most patience and abandon the least, while those on fiber-based broadband abandon the soonest. In a quasi experiment, the likelihood that a viewer on fiber abandoned earlier than a similar viewer on a mobile device exceeded the likelihood that the opposite happens by 38.25%.
- Viewers who experienced an increase in the normalized rebuffer delay, i.e., they experienced more interruptions in the video, played the video for lesser time. In a quasi experiment, a viewer who experienced a rebuffer delay that equals or exceeds 1% of the video duration played 5.02% less of the video in comparison to a similar viewer who experienced no rebuffering.
- A viewer who experienced a failed visit is less likely to return to the content provider's site to view more videos within a specified time period than a similar viewer who did not experience the failure. In a quasi experiment, the likelihood that a viewer who experienced failure returns to the content provider's site within a week is less than the likelihood of a similar viewer who did not experience failures by 2.32%.

We show that above results are statistically significant using the sign test. Further, these results show a significant level of causal impact of stream quality on viewer behavior. In this regard, it is important to recall that small changes in viewer behavior can lead to large changes in monetization, since the impact of a few percentage points over tens of millions of viewers can accrue to large impact over a period of time. Finally, our work on deriving a causal relationship by systematically accounting for the confounding variables must not be viewed as a definitive proof of causality, as indeed there can be no definitive proof of causality. But, rather, our work *significantly increases the confidence in a causal conclusion* by eliminating the effect of major confounding factors that could threaten such a conclusion.

2. BACKGROUND

We describe the process of a user watching a stream, defining terms along the way that we will use in this paper.

Viewer. A viewer is a user who watches one or more streams using a specific media player installed on the user's device. A viewer is uniquely identified and distinguished from other viewers by using a GUID (Globally Unique Identifier) value that is set as a cookie when the media player is accessed. To identify the viewer uniquely, the GUID value is generated to be distinct from other prior values in use.

Views. A view represents an attempt by a viewer to watch a specific video stream. A typical view would start with the viewer initiating the video playback, for instance, by clicking the play button of the media player[1] (see Figure 1). During a view, the media player begins in the startup state where it connects to the server and downloads a certain specified amount of data, before transitioning to the play state. In the play state, the player uses the data from its buffer and renders the video on the viewer's screen. Meanwhile, the player continues to download data from the server and stores it in the buffer. Poor network conditions between the server and the player could lead to a situation where the buffer is drained faster than it is being filled. This could lead to a condition where the buffer is empty causing the player to enter the rebuffer state where the viewer experiences an interruption or "freeze" in the video play back. While in the rebuffer state, the player continues to fill its buffer from the server. When the buffer has a specified amount of data, the player enters the play state and the video starts to play again (see Figure 1). A view can end in three ways: a *successful view* ends normally when the video completes; a *failed view* ends with a failure or error due to a problem with the server, network, or content; and, finally, *an abandoned view* ends with the viewer *voluntarily* abandoning the stream either before the video starts up or after watching some portion of it. Note that a viewer may abandon the view by closing the browser, stopping the stream, or clicking on a different stream. There are other secondary player-initiated events or viewer-initiated events that are part of the viewing process. For instance, a viewer could initiate actions such as pausing, fast-forwarding, or rewinding the video stream. Further, the player may switch the bitrate of the encoded media in response to network conditions, such as reduce the bandwidth if there is packet loss. We do not explicitly analyze behaviors associated with these secondary events in this paper, though these could be part of future work.

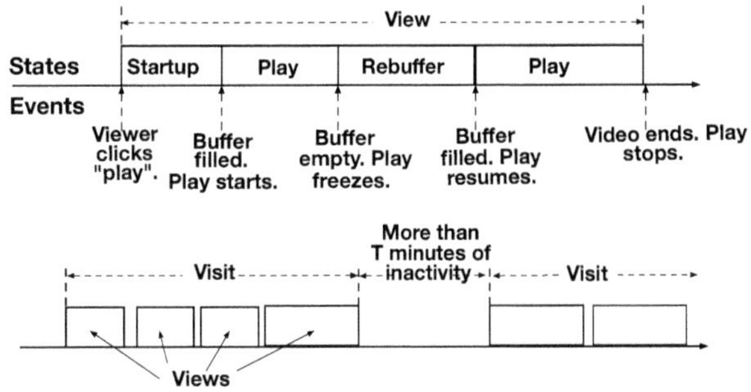

Figure 1: Views and Visits.

Visits. A visit is intended to capture a single session of a viewer visiting a content provider's site to view videos. A visit is a maximal set of contiguous views from a viewer at a specific content provider site such that each visit is separated from the next visit by at least T minutes of inactivity, where we choose $T = 30$ minutes[2](see Figure 1).

Stream Quality Metrics. At the level of a view, the key metrics that measure the quality perceived by the viewer are shown in Figure 2. Failures address the question of whether

[1]For some content providers, a "pre-roll" advertisement is shown before the actual content video is requested by the media player. In that case, our view starts at the point where the actual video is requested.

[2]Our definition is similar to the standard notion of a visit (also called a session) in web analytics where each visit is a set of page views separated by a period of idleness of at least 30 minutes (say) from the next visit.

Key Metrics	Definition
Failures	Number (or, percentage) of views that fail due to problems with the network, server, or content.
Startup Delay	Total time in startup state.
Average Bitrate	The average bitrate at which the video was watched.
Normalized Re-buffer Delay	Total time in rebuffer state divided by the total duration of the video.

Figure 2: View-level stream quality metrics.

the stream was available or if viewing of the video initiated by the viewer failed due to a problem with the network or the server or the content itself (such as a broken link). A failed view can be frustrating to the viewer as he/she is unable to watch the video. A second key metric is startup delay which is the amount of time the viewer waits for the video to start up. Once the video starts playing, the average bitrate at which the video was rendered on the viewer's screen is a measure of the richness of the presented content. This metric is somewhat complex since it is a function of how the video was encoded, the network connectivity between the server and the client, and the heuristics for bitrate-switching employed by the player. Finally, a fourth type of metric quantifies the extent to which the viewer experienced rebuffering. Rebuffering is also frustrating for the viewer because the video stops playing and "freezes". We can quantify the rebuffering by computing the rebuffer delay which is total time spent in a rebuffer state and normalizing it by dividing it by the duration of the video.

Many of the above view-level metrics can be easily extended to visit-level or viewer-level metrics. One key visit-level metric that we examine in this paper is a *failed visit* which is a visit that ends with a failed view. A failed visit could have had successful views prior to the failed view(s). However, a failed visit is important because the viewer tries to play a video one or more times but is unable to do so and leaves the site right after the failure, presumably with a level of frustration.

In our paper, we use many of the key metrics in Figure 2 in our evaluation of the impact of quality on viewer behavior, though these are by no means the only metrics of stream quality. It should be noted that many of the above metrics were incorporated into measurement tools within Akamai and have been in use for more than a decade [24, 1]. The lack of client-side measurements in the early years led to measurements based on automated "agents" deployed around the Internet that simulated synthetic viewers [1, 19] that were then supplemented with server-side logs. In recent years, there is a broad consensus among content providers, CDNs, and analytics providers that these metrics or variations of these metrics matter.

Metrics for Viewer Behavior. Our metrics are focused on the key aspects of viewer behavior that are often tracked closely by content providers which we place in three categories (see Figure 3). The first category is abandonment where a viewer voluntarily decides to stop watching the video. *Here we are primarily concerned with abandonment where the viewer abandons the video even before it starts playing.* A viewer can also abandon a stream after watching a portion of the video which results in a smaller play time,

Type	Metric	Definition
Abandonment	Abandonment Rate	% views abandoned during startup.
Engagement	Play time	Total time in play state (per view).
Repeat Viewers	Return Rate	Prob. of return to site within time period

Figure 3: Key metrics for viewer behavior.

which we account for in the next category of metrics. The second category is viewer engagement that can be measured by play time which is simply the amount of video that the viewer watches. The final category speaks to the behavior of viewers over longer periods of time. A key metric is the return rate of viewers measured as the probability that a viewer returns to the content provider's site over period of time, say, returning within a day or returning within a week.

3. DATA SETS

The data sets that we use for our analysis are collected from a large cross section of actual users around the world who play videos using media players that incorporate the widely-deployed Akamai's client-side media analytics plug in[3]. When content providers build their media player, they can choose to incorporate the plugin that provides an accurate means for measuring a variety of stream quality and viewer behavioral metrics. When the viewer uses the media player to play a video, the plugin is loaded at the client-side and it "listens" and records a variety of events that can then be used to stitch together an accurate picture of the playback. For instance, player transitions between the startup, rebuffering, seek, pause, and play states are recorded so that one may compute the relevant metrics. Properties of the playback, such as the current bitrate, bitrate switching, state of the player's data buffer are also recorded. Further, viewer-initiated action that lead to abandonment such as closing the browser or browser tab, clicking on a different link, etc can also be accurately captured. Once the metrics are captured by the plugin, the information is "beaconed" to an analytics backend that can process huge volumes of data. From every media player at the beginning and end of every view, the relevant measurements are sent to the analytics backend. Further, incremental updates are sent at a configurable periodicity even as the video is playing.

3.1 Data Characteristics

While the Akamai platform serves a significant amount of the world's enterprise streaming content accounting for several million *concurrent* views during the day, we choose a smaller but representative slice of the data from 12 content providers that include major enterprises in a variety of verticals including news, entertainment, and movies. We consider only on-demand videos in this study, leaving live videos for future work. We tracked the viewers and views for the chosen content providers for a period of 10 days (see Figure 4). Our data set is extensive and captures 23 million

[3]While all our data is from media players that are instrumented with Akamai's client-side plugin, the actual delivery of the streams could have used *any* platform and not necessarily just Akamai's CDN.

	Total	Avg Per Visit	Avg Per Viewer
Views	23 million	2.39	3.42
Minutes	216 million	22.48	32.2
Videos	102 thousand	1.96	2.59
Bytes	1431 TB	148 MB	213 MB

Figure 4: Summary of views, minutes watched, distinct videos, and bytes downloaded for our data set.

Viewer Geography	Percent Views
North America	78.85%
Asia	12.80%
Europe	7.75%
Other	0.60%

Figure 5: The geography of viewers in our trace at the continent-level.

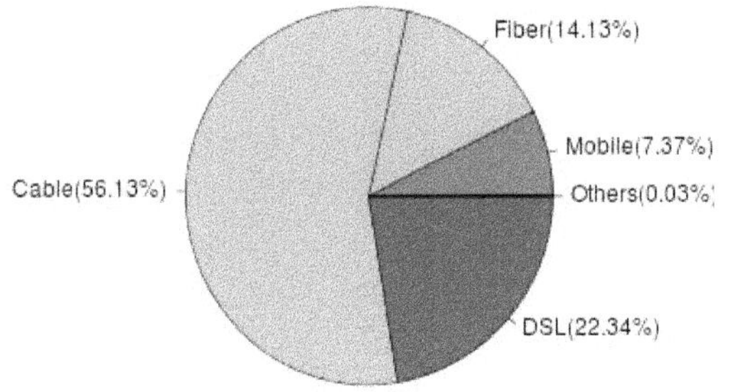

Figure 6: Connection type as percent of views.

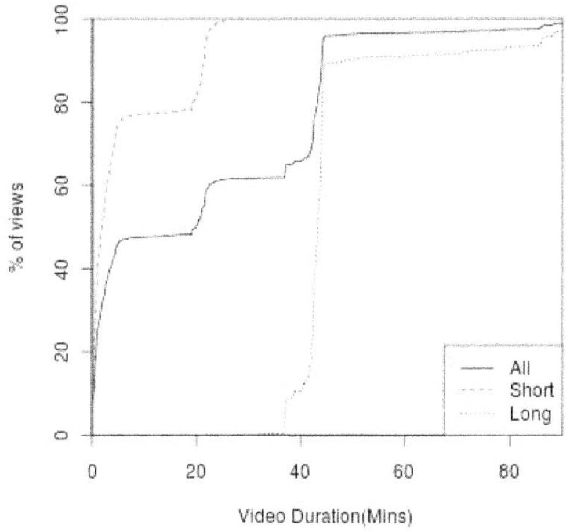

Figure 7: A CDF of the total video duration. The median duration is 19.92 minutes over all videos, 1.8 minutes for short, and 43.2 minutes for long videos.

views from 6.7 million unique viewers, where each viewer on average made 3.42 visits over the period and viewed a total of 32.2 minutes of video. In each visit, there were on average 2.39 views but only 1.96 unique videos viewed, indicating that sometimes the viewer saw the same video twice.

The geography of the viewer was mostly concentrated in North America, Europe and Asia with small contributions from other continents (see Figure 5). More than half the views used cable, though fiber, mobile, and DSL were significant. The fiber category consisted mostly of AT&T Uverse and Verizon FiOS that contributed in roughly in equal proportion. The other connection types such as dialup were negligible (see Figure 6). Video duration is the total length (in minutes) of the video (See Figure 7). We divide the videos into short that have a duration of less than 30 minutes and long that have a duration of more than 30 minutes. Examples of short video include news clips, highlight reels for sports, and short television episodes. The median duration was 1.8 minutes, though the mean duration was longer at 5.95 minutes. In contrast, long video consists of long television episodes and movies. The median duration for long videos was 43.2 minutes and the mean was 47.8 minutes.

4. ANALYSIS TECHNIQUES

A key goal is to establish a *causal* link between a stream quality metric X and viewer behavior metric Y. The first key step is to establish a *correlational* link between X and Y using the statistical tools for correlation and regression. Next, in accordance with the maxim that "correlation does not imply causation", we do a more careful analysis to establish causation. We adapt the innovative tool of Quasi Experimental Design (QED) used extensively in the social and medical sciences to problem domains such as ours.

4.1 Correlational Analysis

To study the impact of a stream quality metric X (say, startup delay) with a viewer behavioral metric Y (say abandonment rate), we start by visually plotting metric X versus metric Y in the observed data. The visual representations are a good initial step to estimating whether or not a correlation exist. As a next step, we also quantify the correlation between X and Y. There are many different ways to calculate the correlation. Primary among them are Pearson's correlation and Kendall's correlation that is a type of rank correlation. As observed in [9], Kendall's correlation is more suitable for a situation such as ours since it does not assume any particular distributional relationship between the two variables. Pearson's correlation is more appropriate when the correlated variables are approximately linearly related, unlike the relationships that we explore in our work. Kendall's correlation measures the whether the two variables X and Y are statistically dependent (i.e., correlated) without assuming any specific functional form of their relationship. Kendall's correlation coefficient τ takes values in the interval $[-1, 1]$ where $\tau = 1$ meaning that X and Y are perfectly concordant, i.e., larger values of X are always associated with larger values for Y, $\tau = -1$ meaning that X and Y are perfectly discordant, i.e., larger values of X are always associated with smaller values of Y, and τ near 0 implying that X and Y are independent.

4.2 Causal Analysis

A correlational analysis of stream quality metric X (say,

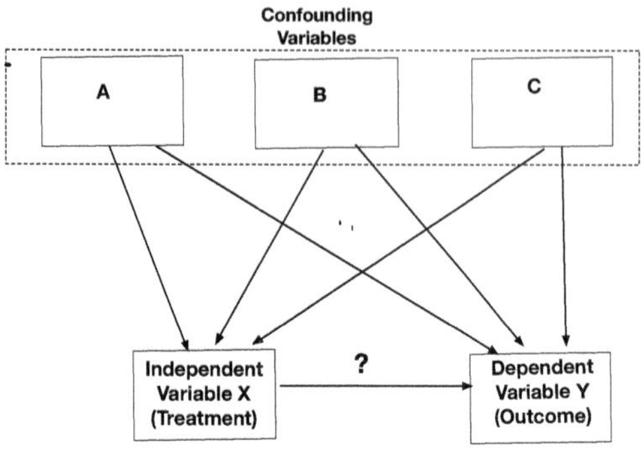

Figure 8: An example of a QED Model. The confounding variables are kept the same while the treatment variable is varied to observe impact on outcome.

startup delay) and a viewer behavior metric Y (say, abandonment rate) could show that X and Y are associated with each other. A primary threat to a causal conclusion that an *independent variable* X causes the *dependent variable* Y is the existence of *confounding variables* that can impact both X and Y (see Figure 8). To take a recent example from the medical literature, a study published in Nature [20] made the causal conclusion that children who sleep with the light on are more likely to develop myopia later in life. But, as it turns out, myopic parents tend to leave the light on more often, as well as pass their genetic predisposition to myopia to their children. Accounting for the confounding variable of parent's myopia, the causal results were subsequently invalidated or substantially weakened.

More relevant to our own work, lets consider a potential threat to a causal conclusion that a stream quality metric X (say, startup delay) results in a viewer behavior Y (say, abandonment). As a hypothetical example, suppose that mobile users tend to have less patience for videos to startup as they tend to be busy and are "on the go", resulting in greater abandonment. Further assume that mobile users tend to have larger startup delays due to poor wireless connectivity. In this situation, a correlation between startup delay and abandonment may not imply causality unless we can account for the confounding variable of how the viewer is connected to the Internet. In our causal analyses, we systematically identify and account for all or a subset of the following three categories of confounding variables as relevant (see Figure 8).

Content. The video[4] being watched could itself influence both quality and viewer behavior. For instance, some videos are more captivating than others leading viewers to watch more of it. Or, some videos may have higher perceived value than others, leading viewers to tolerate more startup delay. The manner in which the video is encoded and the player heuristic used by the media player could also impact stream quality. For instance, the player heuristics that could differ from one content provider to another specifies how much of the video needs to be buffered before the stream can startup or resume play after rebuffering.

Connection Type. The manner in which a viewer connects to the Internet, both the device used and typical connectivity characteristics can influence both stream quality and viewer behavior. We use the connection type of the viewer as a confounding variable, where the connection type can take discrete values such as mobile, DSL, cable, and fiber (such as AT&T's Uverse and Verizon's FiOS).

Geography. Geography of viewer captures several social, economic, religious, and cultural aspects that can influence viewer behavior. For instance, it has been observed by social scientists that the level of patience that consumers exhibit towards a delay in receiving a product varies based on geography of the consumer [5]. Such a phenomena might well be of significance in the extent to which the viewer's behavior is altered by stream quality. In our work, we analyze viewer's geography at the granularity of a country.

4.2.1 The Quasi Experimental Design (QED) Method

A primary technique for showing that an independent variable X (called the treatment variable) has a causal impact on a dependent variable Y (called the outcome variable) is to design a *controlled experiment*. To design a true experiment in our context, one would have to randomly assign viewers to differing levels of stream quality (i.e., values of X) and observe the resultant viewer behaviors (values of Y). The random assignment in such an experiment removes any systematic bias due to the confounding variables that are threats to a causal conclusion. However, the level of control needed to perform such an experiment at scale for our problem is either prohibitively hard, expensive, or even impossible. In fact, there are legal, ethical, and other issues with intentionally degrading the stream quality of a set of viewers to do a controlled experiment. However, there are other domains were a controlled experiment can and are performed, example, $A|B$ testing of web page layouts [11].

Given the inability to perform true experiments, we adapt a technique called QED to discover causal relationships from observational data that already exists. QEDs were developed by social and medical scientists as a similar inability to perform controlled experiments is very common in those domains [23]. In particular, we use a specific type of QED called the matched design [18] where a treated individual (in our case, a view or viewer) is randomly matched with an untreated individual, where both individuals have identical values for the confounding variables. Consequently, any difference in the outcome for this pair can be attributed to the treatment. Our population typically consists of views or viewers and treatment variable is typically is binary. For instance, in Section 7, viewers who experienced "bad" stream quality in the form a failed visit are deemed to be treated and viewers who had normal experience are untreated. We form comparison sets by randomly matching each treated viewer with an untreated viewer such that both viewers are as identical as possible on the confounding variables. Needless to say, the more identical the viewers are in each pair

[4]Note that our notion of video content is url-based and thus also incorporates the content provider. If the same movie is available from two content providers, they would constitute two different pieces of content for our analysis.

the more effective the matching is in neutralizing the confounding variables. Note that matching ensures that the distributions of the confounding variables in the treated and untreated set of viewers are identical, much as if viewers were randomly assigned to treated and untreated sets in a controlled experiment. Now, by studying the behavioral outcomes of matched pairs one can deduce whether or not the treatment variable X has a causal effect on variable Y, with the influence of the confounding variables neutralized. Note that treatment variable need not always be stream quality. Depending on the causal conclusion, we could choose the treatment variable to content length or connection type, if we would like to study their impact on viewer behavior.

Statistical Significance of the QED Analysis.

As with any statistical analysis, it is important to evaluate whether the results are *statistically significant* or if they could have occurred by random chance. As is customary in hypothesis testing [14], we state a null hypothesis H_o that contradicts the assertion that we want establish. That is, H_o contradicts the assertion that X impacts Y and states that the treatment variable X has no impact on the outcome variable Y. We then compute the "p-value" defined to be the probability that the null hypothesis H_o is consistent with the observed results. A "low" p-value lets us reject the null hypothesis, bolstering our conclusions from the QED analysis as being statistically significant. However, a "high" p-value would not allow us to reject the null hypothesis. That is, the QED results could have happened through random chance with a "sufficiently" high probability that we cannot reject H_o. In this case, we conclude that the results from the QED analysis are not statistically significant.

The definition of what constitutes a "low" p-value for a result to be considered statistically significant is somewhat arbitrary. It is customary in the medical sciences to conclude that a treatment is effective if the p-value is at most 0.05. The choice of 0.05 as the significance level is largely cultural and can be traced back to the classical work of R.A. Fisher about 90 years ago. Many have recently argued that the significance level must be much smaller. We concur and choose the much more stringent 0.001 as our significance level, a level achievable in our field given the large amount of experimental subjects (tens of thousands treated-untreated pairs) but is rarely achievable in medicine with human subjects (usually in the order of hundreds of treated-untreated pairs). However, our results are unambiguously significant and not very sensitive to the choice of significance level. All our results turned out to be highly significant with p-values of 4×10^{-5} or smaller, except for one conclusion with a larger p-value that we deemed statistically insignificant.

The primary technique that we employ for evaluating statistical significance is the sign test that is a non-parametric test that makes no distributional assumptions and is particularly well-suited for evaluating matched pairs in a QED setting [26]. We sketch the intuition of the technique here, while deferring the specifics to the technical sections. For each matched pair (u, v), where u received treatment and v did not receive treatment, we define the differential outcome denoted by $outcome(u, v)$ as the numerical difference in the outcome of u and the outcome of v. If H_o holds, then the outcomes of the treated and untreated individuals are identically distributed, since the treatment is assumed to have no impact on the outcome. Thus, the differential outcome is equally likely to be a positive number as a negative number. Thus, for n independently selected matched pairs, the number of positive values of the differential outcome (call it X) follows the binomial distribution with n trials and probability 1/2. In a measured sample consisting of a total of n non-zero values of the differential outcome, suppose that x have positive values. Given that H_o holds, the probability (i.e., p-value) of such an occurrence is at most $Prob(|X - n/2| \geq | x - n/2|)$, which is sum of both tails of the binomial distribution. Evaluating the above tail probability provides us the required bound on the p-value.

As an aside, note that a different but distribution-specific significance test called the paired T-test may be applicable in other QED situations. A paired T-test uses the Student's T distribution and requires that the differential outcome has a normal distribution. Since our differential outcome does not have a normal distribution, we rely on the distribution-free non-parametric sign test that is more generally applicable.

Some Caveats.

It is important to understand the limitations of our QED tools, or for that matter *any* experimental technique of inference. Care should be taken in designing the quasi-experiment to ensure that the major confounding variables are explicitly or implicitly captured in the analysis. If there exists confounding variables that are not easily measurable (example, the gender of the viewer) and/or are not identified and controlled, these unaccounted dimensions could pose a risk to a causal conclusion, if indeed they turn out to be significant. *Our work on deriving a causal relationship by systematically accounting for the confounding variables must not be viewed as a definitive proof of causality, as indeed there can be no definitive proof of causality. But, rather, our work increases the confidence in a causal conclusion by accounting for potential major sources of confounding.* This is of course a general caveat that holds for all domains across the sciences that attempt to infer causality from observational data.

5. VIEWER ABANDONMENT

We address the question of how long a viewer will wait for the stream to start up, a question of great importance that has not been studied systematically to our knowledge. However, the analogous problem of how long a user will wait for web content to download has received much attention. In 2006, Jupiter Research published a study based on interviewing 1,058 online shoppers and postulated what is known in the industry as the "4-second rule" that states that an average online shopper is likely to abandon a web site if a web page does not download in 4 seconds [21]. But, a recent study [16] implied that the users have become impatient over time and that even a 400 ms delay can make users search less. Our motivation is to derive analogous rules for streaming where startup delay for video is roughly analogous to download time for web pages.

ASSERTION 5.1. *An increase in startup delay causes more abandonment of viewers.*

To investigate if our assertion holds, we classify each view into 1-second buckets based on their startup delay. We then compute for each bucket the percentage of views assigned to that bucket that were abandoned. From Figure 9, we see that the percent of abandoned views and startup delay are positively correlated with a Kendall correlation of 0.72.

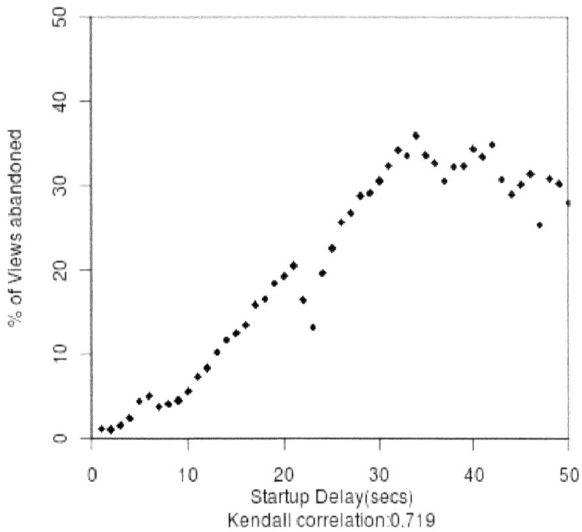

Figure 9: Percentage of abandoned views and startup delay are positively correlated.

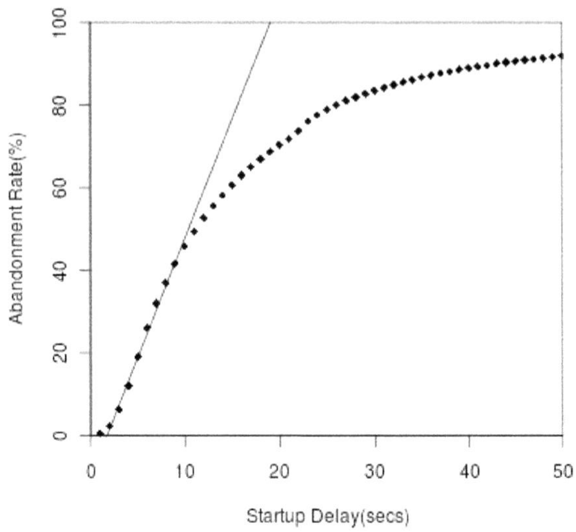

Figure 10: Viewers start to abandon the video if the startup delay exceeds about 2 seconds. Beyond that point, a 1-second increase in delay results in roughly a 5.8% increase in abandonment rate.

Suppose now that we build a media delivery service that provides a startup delay of exactly x seconds for every view. What percent of views delivered by this system will be abandoned? To *estimate* this metric, we define a function called AbandonmentRate(x) that equals

$$100 \times \text{Impatient(x)}/(\text{Impatient(x)} + \text{Patient(x)}),$$

where Impatient(x) is all views that were abandoned after experiencing less than x seconds of startup delay and Patient(x) are views where the viewer waited at least x time without abandoning. That is, Impatient(x) (resp., Patient(x)) corresponds to views where the viewer did not (resp., did) demonstrate the patience to hold on for x seconds without abandoning. Note that a view in Patient(x) could still have been abandoned at some time greater than x. Also, note that a view where the video started to play before x seconds does not provide any information on whether the viewer would have waited until x seconds or not, and so is considered neither patient or impatient. Figure 10 shows the abandonment rate computed from our data which is near zero for the first 2 seconds, but starts to rise rapidly as the startup delay increases. Fitting a simple regression to initial part of the curve shows that abandonment rate increases by 5.8% for each 1-second increase in startup delay.

Assertion 5.2. *Viewers are less tolerant of startup delay for short videos in comparison to longer videos.*

Researchers who study the psychology of queuing [13] have shown that people have more patience for waiting in longer queues if the perceived value of the service that they are waiting for is greater. Duration of the service often influences its perceived value with longer durations often perceived as having greater value. People often tolerate the 30 minute delay for the checkin process for a 4-hour plane ride but would find the same wait excessive for a 10-minute bus ride. On the same principle, is it true that viewers would be more patient for the video to startup if they expect to be watching the video for longer period of time?

To investigate our assertion, we first classify the views based on whether the content is short with duration smaller than 30 minutes (e.g., news clip), or long with duration longer than 30 minutes (e.g., movies). The Kendall correlation between the two variables, percent of abandoned videos and startup delay, were 0.68 and 0.90 for short and long videos respectively, indicating a strong correlation for each category. Further, Figure 11 shows abandonment rate for each type of content as a function of the startup delay. One can see that viewers typically abandon at a larger rate for short videos than for long videos.

Assertion 5.3. *Viewers watching videos on a better connected computer or device have less patience for startup delay and so abandon sooner.*

The above assertion is plausible because there is some evidence that users who expect faster service are more likely to be disappointed when that service is slow. In fact, this is often touted as a reason for why users are becoming less and less able to tolerate web pages that download slowly. To study whether or not this is true in a scientific manner, we segment our views into four categories based on their connection type that indicates how the corresponding viewer is connected to the Internet. The categories in roughly the increasing order of connectivity are mobile, DSL, cable modem, and fiber (such as Verizon FIOS or AT&T Uverse). In all four categories, we see a strong correlation between the two variables, percent of abandoned views and startup delay. The Kendall correlations for mobile, DSL, cable, and fiber are 0.68, 0.74, 0.71, and 0.75 respectively. Further, in Figure 12, we show the abandonment rate for each connection type. We can see that viewers abandon significantly less on mobile in comparison with the other categories, for

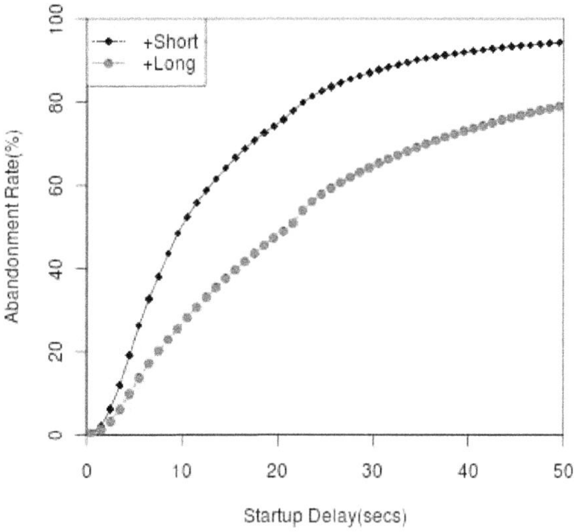

Figure 11: Viewers abandon at a higher rate for short videos than for long videos.

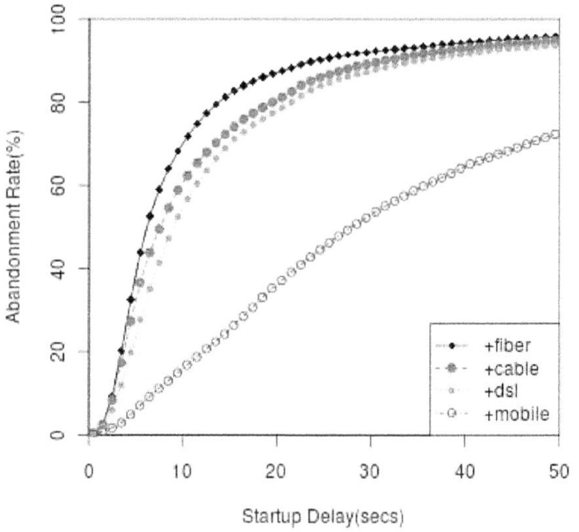

Figure 12: Viewers who are better connected abandon sooner.

a given startup delay. Some difference in abandonment is discernible between the other categories in the rough order of cable, DSL, and fiber though they are much smaller.

5.1 QED for Assertion 5.2

First, we devise a QED to study the impact of content length on abandonment (Assertion 5.2). Therefore, we make the content length (long or short) the treatment variable and the outcome measures patience of the viewer to startup delay. The viewer's patience to startup delay can be influenced by both the viewer's geography and connection type which we use as the confounding variables. Specifically, we form matched pairs (u, v) such that view u is a short video that was abandoned and view v is a long video that was abandoned and u and v are watched by viewers from the same geography, and the viewers have the same connection type. The matching algorithm is described as follows.

1. *Match step.* Let the treated set T be all abandoned views for short content and let untreated set C be all the abandoned views for long content. For each $u \in T$ we pick uniformly and randomly a $v \in C$ such that u and v belong to viewers in the same geography and have the same connection type. The matched set of pairs $M \subseteq T \times C$ have the same attributes for the confounding variables and differ only on the treatment.

2. *Score step.* For each pair $(u, v) \in M$, we compute an $outcome(u, v)$ to be $+1$ if u was abandoned with a smaller startup delay than v. If u was abandoned with a larger startup delay than v, then $outcome(u, v) = -1$. And, $outcome(u, v) = 0$, if the startup delays when u and v were abandoned are equal. Now,

$$Net\ Outcome = \left(\frac{\sum_{(u,v)\in M} outcome(u, v)}{|M|} \right) \times 100.$$

Note that a positive value for net outcome provides positive (supporting) evidence for Assertion 5.3, while a negative value provides negative evidence for the assertion. The results of the matching algorithm produced a net outcome of 11.5%. The net outcome shows that the matched pairs that support Assertion 5.2 exceed those that negate the assertion by 11.5%. The positive net outcome provides evidence of causality that was not provided by the prior correlational analysis alone by eliminating the threats posed by the identified confounding variables.

To derive statistical significance of the above QED result, we formulate a null hypothesis H_o that states that the treatment (long versus short video) has no impact on abandonment. If H_o holds, the $outcome(u, v)$ is equally likely to be positive (+1) as negative (-1). We now use the sign test that we described in Section 4.2 to derive a bound on the p-value. Since we matched $n = 78,840$ pairs, if H_o holds, the expected number pairs with a positive outcome is $n/2 = 78,840/2 = 39,420$. Our observational data however had $x = 43,954$ pairs with positive scores, i.e., $x - n/2 = 4534$ pairs in excess of the mean. We bound the p-value by showing that it is extremely unlikely to have had 4534 positive pairs in excess of the mean by computing the the two-sided tail of the binomial distribution with n trials and probability 1/2:

$$p\text{-}value \leq \text{Prob}\left(|X - \frac{n}{2}| \geq |\, x - \frac{n}{2}\right) \leq 3.3 \times 10^{-229} \quad (1)$$

The above bound for the p-value is much smaller than the required significance level of 0.001 and leads us to reject the null hypothesis H_o. Thus, we conclude that our QED analysis is statistically significant.

5.2 QED for Assertion 5.3

To investigate a causal conclusion for Assertion 5.3, we set up a QED where the treatment is the connection type of the user and the outcome measures the relative tolerance of the viewer to startup delay. For each pair of network types A and B, we run a matching algorithm where the treated set T is the set of all abandoned views with connection type A and untreated set is all abandoned views with connection type B. The matching algorithm used is identical to the one described earlier except that the match criterion in step 1 is changed to match for identical content and identical geography. That is, for every matched pair (u, v), view u has network type A and view v has network type B but both are views for the same video and belong to viewers in the same geography.

The results of the matching algorithm are shown in Figure 13. For instance, our results show that the likelihood that a mobile viewer exhibited more patience than a fiber viewer is greater than the likelihood that opposite holds by a margin of 38.25%. Much as in Section 5.1, we use the sign test to compute the p-value for each QED outcome in the table. All QED outcomes in Figure 13 turned out to be statistically significant with exceedingly small p-values, except the dsl-versus-cable comparison that was inconclusive. Specifically, our results show that a that a mobile viewer exhibits more patience than other (non-mobile) viewers, and the result holds with exceedingly small p-values ($< 10^{-17}$). Our results also provide strong evidence for DSL and cable users being more patient than fiber users, though the p-value for the dsl-versus-fiber was somewhat larger (4.6×10^{-5}) but still statistically significant. The dsl-versus-cable comparison was however inconclusive and not statistically significant as the p-value of the score was 0.06 that is larger than our required significance level of 0.001.

Treated \ Untreated	dsl	cable	fiber
mobile	33.81	35.40	38.25
dsl	-	-0.75	2.67
cable	-	-	3.65

Figure 13: Net QED outcomes support the causal impact of connection type on viewer patience for startup delay, though the impact is more pronounced between mobile and the rest. The p-value for all entrees are very small ($< 10^{-17}$), except dsl-versus-cable (0.06) and dsl-versus-fiber (4.6×10^{-5}).

6. VIEWER ENGAGEMENT

We study the extent to which a viewer is engaged with the video content of the content provider. A simple metric that measures engagement is play time. Here we study play time on a per view basis, though one could study play time aggregated over all views of a visit (called *visit play time*) or play time aggregated over all visits of a viewer (called *viewer play time*). Figure 14 shows the CDF of play time over our entire data set. A noticeable fact is that a significant number of views have very small play time with the median play time only 35.4 seconds. This is likely caused by "video surfing" where a viewer quickly views a sequence of videos to see what might of interest to him/her, before settling in on the videos that he/she wants to watch. The fact that a viewer watched on average of 22.48 minutes per visit (cf. Figure 4) is consistent with this observation. Play time is clearly impacted by both the interest level of the viewer in the video and the stream quality. Viewer interest could

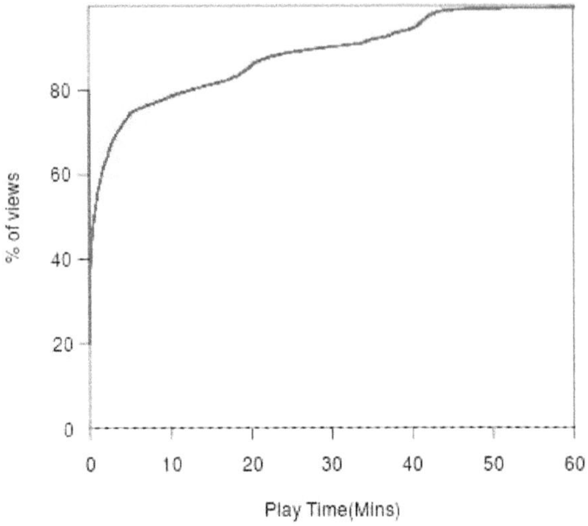

Figure 14: A significant fraction of the views have small duration.

itself be a function of complex factors, for instance, Italian viewers might be more interested in soccer world cup videos than American viewers, even more so if the video is of a game where Italy is playing. In understanding the impact of stream quality on viewer engagement, the challenge is to neutralize the bias from confounding variables *not* related to stream quality such as viewer interest, geography, and connection type. Since more rebuffer delay is expected of videos with a longer duration, we use normalized rebuffer delay[5] that equals 100 × (rebuffer delay/video duration).

ASSERTION 6.1. *An increase in (normalized) rebuffer delay can cause a decrease in play time.*

To evaluate the above assertion, we first classify views by bucketing their normalized rebuffer delay into 1% buckets. Then, we compute and plot the average play time for all views within each bucket (see Figure 15). The decreasing trend visualizes the negative correlation that exists between normalized rebuffer delay and play time. The Kendall correlation between the two metrics is -0.421, quantifying the negative correlation.

6.1 QED Analysis

To examine the causality of Assertion 6.1, we devise a QED where the treatment set T consists of all views that suffered normalized rebuffer delay more than a certain threshold γ%. Given a value of γ as input, the treated views are matched with untreated views that did not experience rebuffering as follows.

1. *Match step.* We form a set of matched pairs M as follows. Let T be the set of all views who have a normalized rebuffer delay of at least γ%. For each view u in T, suppose that u reaches the normalized rebuffer delay threshold γ% when viewing the tth second of the

[5]Note that normalized rebuffer delay can go beyond 100% if we rebuffer for longer than the total duration of the video.

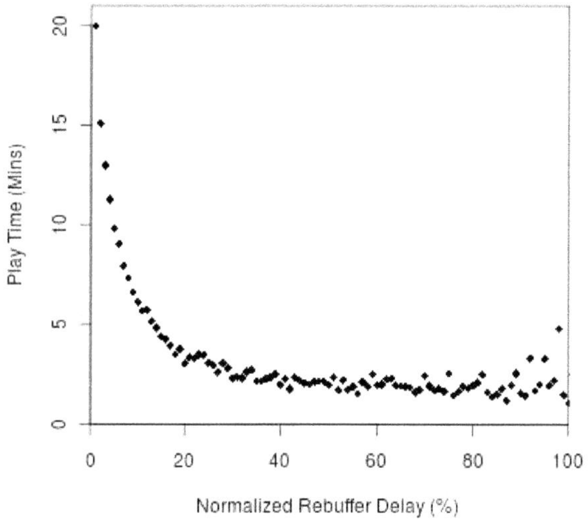

Figure 15: Correlation of normalized rebuffer delay with play time.

video, i.e., view u receives treatment after watching the first t seconds of the video, though more of the video could have been played after that point. We pick a view v uniformly and randomly from the set of all possible views such that

(a) the viewer of v has the same geography, connection type, and is watching the same video as the viewer of u.

(b) View v has played at least t seconds of the video without rebuffering till that point.

2. *Score step.* For each pair $(u, v) \in M$, we compute

$$outcome(u, v) = \frac{\text{play time of v} - \text{play time of u}}{\text{video duration}}.$$

$$Net\ Outcome = \left(\frac{\sum_{(u,v) \in M} outcome(u, v)}{|M|} \right) \times 100.$$

Note that closer we can make the matched views u and v in variables other than the treatment, the more accurate our QED results. Though as a practical matter, adding too many matching parameters can highly reduce the availability of matches, eventually impacting the statistical significance of the results. It is worth noting step 1(b) above where we ensure that v watches the video to at least the same point as when u first received treatment. Thus, at the time both u and v play the tth second of the video, they have viewed the same content and the only difference between them is one had rebuffering and the other did not. The net outcome of the matching algorithm can be viewed as the difference in the play time of u and v expressed as a percent of the video duration. Figure 16 shows that on average a view that experienced normalized rebuffer delay of 1% or more played 5.02% of less of the video. There is a general upward trend in the net outcome when the treatment gets harsher with increasing values of γ. Much as in Section 5.1, we use the sign test to compute the p-values for each QED outcome. All p-values were extremely small as shown in Figure 16, making the results statistically significant.

Normalized Rebuffer Delay γ (percent)	Net Outcome (percent)	P-Value
1	5.02	$< 10^{-143}$
2	5.54	$< 10^{-123}$
3	5.7	$< 10^{-87}$
4	6.66	$< 10^{-86}$
5	6.27	$< 10^{-57}$
6	7.38	$< 10^{-47}$
7	7.48	$< 10^{-36}$

Figure 16: A viewer who experienced more rebuffer delay on average watched less video than an identical viewer who had no rebuffer.

7. REPEAT VIEWERSHIP

We study the viewers who after watching videos on a content provider's site return after some period of time to watch more. Repeat viewers are valued highly-valued by media content providers as these viewers are more engaged and more loyal to the content provider's site. Even a small decrease (or, increase) in the return rate of viewers can have a large impact on the business metrics of the content provider. Clearly, a number of factors, including how captivating the video content is to the viewer, influence whether or not a viewer returns. However, we show that stream quality can also influence whether or not a viewer returns.

The most drastic form of quality degradation is failure when a viewer is unable to play a video successfully. Failures can be caused by a number of issues, including problems with the content (broken links, missing video files, etc), the client software (media player bugs, etc), or the infrastructure (network failure, server overload, etc). More frustrating than a failed view is a failed visit where a viewer tries to play videos from the content providers site but fails and leaves the site immediately after the failure, presumably with some level of frustration. (Note that the definition of a failed visit does not preclude successful views earlier in that visit before the last view(s) that failed.) We focus on the impact of a failed visit experienced by a viewer on his/her likelihood of returning to the content provider's site.

ASSERTION 7.1. *A viewer who experienced a failed visit is less likely to return to the content provider's site to view more videos within a specified time period than a similar viewer who did not experience a failed visit.*

To examine if the above assertion holds, we classify each of our views as either failed or normal (i.e., not failed). For each failed visit (resp., normal visit), we compute the *return time* which is defined to be the next time the viewer returns to the content provider's site. (Return time could be infinite if they do not return to the site within our trace window.) Figure 17 shows the CDF of the return time for both failed visits and normal visits. It can be seen that there is significant reduction in the probability of return following a failed visit as opposed to a normal one. For instance, the probability of returning within 1 day after a failed visit is 8.0%

versus 11% after a normal one. Likewise, the probability of returning within 1 week after a failed visit is 25% versus 27% after a normal one.

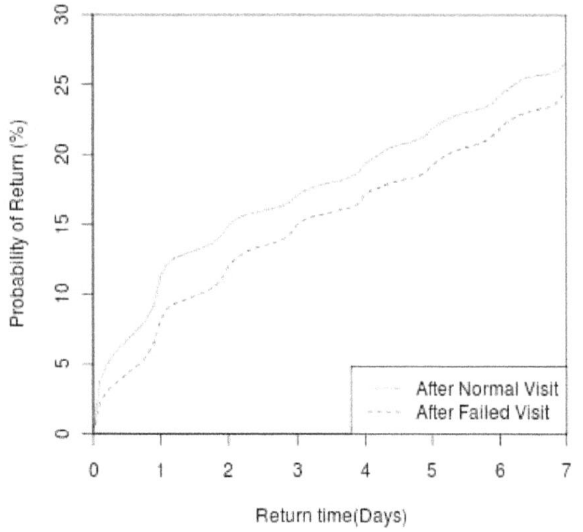

Figure 17: Probability of the return after a failed visit and after a normal visit. The probability of returning within a specified return time is distinctly smaller after a failed visit than after a normal one.

7.1 QED Analysis

We perform a QED analysis to strengthen Assertion 7.1 by considering viewers[6] with a failed visit to be the treated set T. For each $u \in T$ we find a matching viewer v that is similar to u in all the confounding variables. As before, we ensure that viewers u and v are from the same geography, have the same connection type, and are viewing content from the same content provider. However, there is a subtle characteristic that need to be matched. Specifically, we need also ensure that the propensity of u to watch videos *prior* to when u received treatment is equivalent to the corresponding propensity of v. This ensures that any differential behavior *after* the treatment can be attributed to the treatment itself.

To reinforce the last point, a viewer who watches more video at a site is more likely to have had a failed view. Therefore, the treated set T of viewers has a bias towards containing more frequent visitors to site who also watch more video. Figure 18 shows the CDF of the aggregate play time of a viewer across all visits. It can be seen that the treated set T has viewers who have watched for more time in aggregate. To neutralize this effect, we match on the number of prior visits and aggregate play time in step 1 (c) below and make them near identical, so that we are comparing two viewers who have exhibited similar propensity to visit the site *prior* to treatment. The use of a similarity metric of this kind for matching is common in QED analysis and is similar in spirit to propensity score matching of [22].

[6]Note that in this matching we are matching viewers and not views as we are evaluating the repeat viewership of a viewer over time.

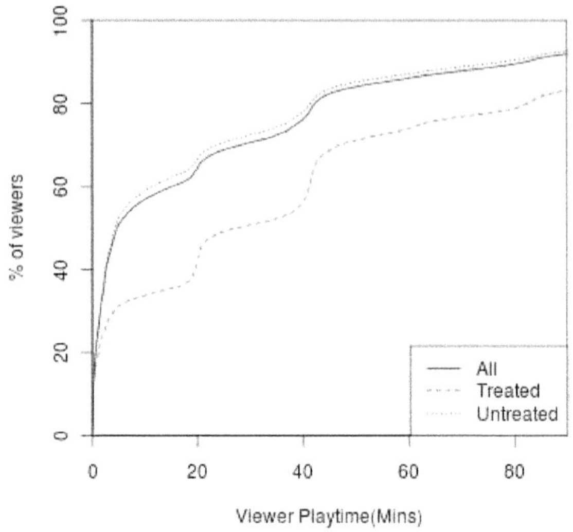

Figure 18: CDF of the viewer play time for all, treated, and untreated viewers.

The matching algorithm follows.

1. *Match step.* We produce a matched set of pairs M as follows. Let T be the set of all viewers who have had a failed visit. For each $u \in T$ we pick the first failed visit of viewer u. We then pair u with a viewer v picked uniformly and randomly from the set of all possible viewers such that
   (a) Viewer v has the same geography, same connection type as u, and is watching the content from the same content provider as u.
   (b) Viewer v had a normal visit at about the same time (within ± 3 hours) as the first failed visit of viewer u. We call the failed visit of u and the corresponding normal visit of v that occurred at a similar time as matched visits.
   (c) Viewer u and v have the same number of visits and about the same total viewing time (± 10 minutes) prior to their matched visits.
2. *Score step.* For each pair $(u, v) \in M$ and each return time δ. We assign $outcome(u, v, \delta)$ to -1 if u returns within the return time and v does not, $+1$ if v returns within the return time and u does not, and 0 otherwise.

$$Net\ Outcome(\delta) = \left(\frac{\sum_{(u,v) \in M} outcome(u, v, \delta)}{|M|} \right) \times 100.$$

Figure 19 shows the outcome of the matching algorithm for various values of the return time (δ). The positive values of the outcome provide strong evidence of the causality of Assertion 7.1 since it shows that viewers who experienced a normal visit returned more than their identical pair with a failed visit. To take a numerical example, for $\delta = 1$ day, 458,621 pairs were created. The pairs where the normal viewer returned but its identical failed pair did not exceed

Return Time δ (in days)	Outcome (percent)	P-Value
1	2.38	$<10^{-57}$
2	2.51	$<10^{-51}$
3	2.42	$<10^{-44}$
4	2.35	$<10^{-37}$
5	2.15	$<10^{-22}$
6	1.90	$<10^{-11}$
7	2.32	$<10^{-6}$

Figure 19: A viewer who experienced a failed visit is less likely to return within a time period than a viewer who experienced a normal visit.

the pairs where the opposite happened. The amount of pairs in excess was 10,909 pairs, which is 2.38% of the total pairs. Using the sign test, we show that the p-value is extremely small (2.2×10^{-58}), providing strong evidence of statistical significance for the outcome. Note that as δ increases, the outcome score remained in a similar range. However, one would expect that for very large δ values the effect of the failed event should wear off, but we did not analyze traces that were long enough to evaluate if such a phenomenon occurs. All p-values remain significantly smaller than our threshold of significance of 0.001, allowing us to conclude that the results are statistically significant.

8. RELATED WORK

The quality metrics considered here have more than a dozen years of history within industry where early measurement systems used synthetic "measurement agents" deployed around the world to measure metrics such as failures, startup delay, rebuffering, and bitrate, example, Akamai's Stream Analyzer measurement system [1, 24]. There have been early studies at Akamai on streaming quality metrics using these tools [19]. However, truly large-scale studies were made possible only with the recent advent of client-side measurement technology that could measure and report detailed quality and behavioral data from actual viewers. To our knowledge, the first important large-scale study and closest in spirit to our work is the study of viewer engagement published last year [9] that shows several correlational relationships between quality (such as rebuffering), content type (such as live, short/long VoD), and viewer engagement (such as play time). A recent sequel to the above work [15] studies the use of quality metrics to enhance video delivery. A key differentiation of our work from prior work is our focus on establishing *causal* relationships, going a step beyond just correlation. While our viewer engagement analysis was also correlationally established in [9], our work takes the next step in ascertaining the causal impact of rebuffering on play time. Besides our results on viewer engagement, we also establish key assertions pertaining to viewer abandonment and repeat viewership that are the first quantitative results of its kind. However, it must be noted that [9] studies a larger set of quality metrics, including join time, average bitrate, and rendering quality, and a larger class of videos including live streaming, albeit without establishing causality.

The work on quasi-experimental design in the social and medical sciences has a long and distinguished history stretching several decades that is well documented in [23]. Though its application to data mining is more recent. In [18], the authors use QEDs to answer questions about user behavior in social media such as Stack Overflow and Yahoo Answers.

There are a number of other studies on perceived quality though they tend to be small-scale studies or do not link the quality to user behavior [10, 7]. There has also been prior work for other types of systems. For instance, the relationship between page download times and user satisfaction [3] for the web and quantifying user satisfaction for Skype [6]. There has also been work on correlating QoS with QoE (quality of experience) for multimedia systems using human subjects [27]. These of course have a very different focus from our work and do not show causal impact. There has been significant amount of work in workload characterization of streaming media, P2P, and web workloads [25, 4]. Even though we do characterize the workload to a degree, our focus is quality and viewer behavior.

9. CONCLUSIONS

Our work is the first to demonstrate a *causal* nexus between stream quality and viewer behavior. The results presented in our work are important because they are the first quantitative demonstration that key quality metrics causally impact viewer behavioral metrics that are key to both content providers and CDN operators. As all forms of media migrate to the Internet, both video monetization and the design of CDNs will increasingly demand a true causal understanding of this nexus. Establishing a causal relationship by systematically eliminating the confounding variables is immensely important, as mere correlational studies have the potential costly risk of making incorrect conclusions.

Our work breaks new ground in understanding viewer abandonment and repeat viewership. Further, it sheds more light on the known correlational impact of quality on viewer engagement by establishing its causal impact. Our work on startup delay show that more delay causes more abandonment, for instance, a 1 second increase in delay increases the abandonment rate by 5.8%. We also showed the strong impact of rebuffering on the video play time. For instance, we showed that a viewer experiencing a rebuffer delay that equals or exceeds 1% of the video duration played 5.02% less of the video in comparison with a similar viewer who experienced no rebuffering. Finally, we examined the impact of failed visits and showed that a viewer who experienced failures is less likely to return to the content provider's site in comparison to a similar viewer who did not experience failures. In particular, we showed that a failed visit decreased the likelihood of a viewer returning within a week by 2.32%. While reviewing these results, it is important to remember that small changes in viewer behavior can lead to large changes in monetization, since the impact of a few percentage points over tens of millions of viewers can accrue to large impact over a period of time.

As more and more data become available, we expect that our QED tools will play an increasing larger role in establishing key causal relationships that are key drivers of both the content provider's monetization framework and the CDN's next-generation delivery architecture. The increasing scale of the measured data greatly enhances the statistical significance of the derived conclusions and the efficacy of our tools. Further, we expect that our work provides an important tool for establishing causal relationships in other areas of measurement research in networked systems that have so far been limited to correlational studies.

10. ACKNOWLEDGEMENTS

We thank Ethendra Bommaiah, Harish Kammanahalli, and David Jensen for insightful discussions about the work. Further, we thank our shepherd Meeyoung Cha and our anonymous referees for their detailed comments that resulted in significant improvements to the paper. Any opinions expressed in this work are solely those of the authors and not necessarily those of Akamai Technologies.

11. REFERENCES

[1] Akamai. *Stream Analyzer Service Description.* `http://www.akamai.com/dl/feature_sheets/Stream_Analyzer_Service_Description.pdf`.

[2] K. Andreev, B.M. Maggs, A. Meyerson, and R.K. Sitaraman. Designing overlay multicast networks for streaming. In *Proceedings of the fifteenth annual ACM symposium on Parallel algorithms and architectures*, pages 149–158. ACM, 2003.

[3] N. Bhatti, A. Bouch, and A. Kuchinsky. Integrating user-perceived quality into web server design. *Computer Networks*, 33(1):1–16, 2000.

[4] M. Cha, H. Kwak, P. Rodriguez, Y.Y. Ahn, and S. Moon. I tube, You Tube, Everybody Tubes: Analyzing the World's Largest User Generated Content Video System. In *Proceedings of the 7th ACM SIGCOMM conference on Internet measurement*, pages 1–14, 2007.

[5] H. Chen, S. Ng, and A.R. Rao. Cultural differences in consumer impatience. *Journal of Marketing Research*, pages 291–301, 2005.

[6] K.T. Chen, C.Y. Huang, P. Huang, and C.L. Lei. Quantifying skype user satisfaction. In *ACM SIGCOMM Computer Communication Review*, volume 36, pages 399–410. ACM, 2006.

[7] M. Claypool and J. Tanner. The effects of jitter on the peceptual quality of video. In *Proceedings of the seventh ACM international conference on Multimedia (Part 2)*, pages 115–118. ACM, 1999.

[8] John Dilley, Bruce M. Maggs, Jay Parikh, Harald Prokop, Ramesh K. Sitaraman, and William E. Weihl. Globally distributed content delivery. *IEEE Internet Computing*, 6(5):50–58, 2002.

[9] Florin Dobrian, Vyas Sekar, Asad Awan, Ion Stoica, Dilip Joseph, Aditya Ganjam, Jibin Zhan, and Hui Zhang. Understanding the impact of video quality on user engagement. In *Proceedings of the ACM SIGCOMM Conference on Applications, Technologies, Architectures, and Protocols for Computer Communication*, pages 362–373, New York, NY, USA, 2011. ACM.

[10] S.R. Gulliver and G. Ghinea. Defining user perception of distributed multimedia quality. *ACM Transactions on Multimedia Computing, Communications, and Applications (TOMCCAP)*, 2(4):241–257, 2006.

[11] R. Kohavi, R. Longbotham, D. Sommerfield, and R.M. Henne. Controlled experiments on the web: survey and practical guide. *Data Mining and Knowledge Discovery*, 18(1):140–181, 2009.

[12] L. Kontothanassis, R. Sitaraman, J. Wein, D. Hong, R. Kleinberg, B. Mancuso, D. Shaw, and D. Stodolsky. A transport layer for live streaming in a content delivery network. *Proceedings of the IEEE*, 92(9):1408–1419, 2004.

[13] R.C. Larson. Perspectives on queues: Social justice and the psychology of queueing. *Operations Research*, pages 895–905, 1987.

[14] E.L. Lehmann and J.P. Romano. *Testing statistical hypotheses.* Springer Verlag, 2005.

[15] X. Liu, F. Dobrian, H. Milner, J. Jiang, V. Sekar, I. Stoica, and H. Zhang. A case for a coordinated internet video control plane. In *Proceedings of the ACM SIGCOMM Conference on Applications, Technologies, Architectures, and Protocols for Computer Communication*, pages 359–370, 2012.

[16] Steve Lohr. For impatient web users, an eye blink is just too long to wait. *New York Times*, February 2012.

[17] E. Nygren, R.K. Sitaraman, and J. Sun. The Akamai Network: A platform for high-performance Internet applications. *ACM SIGOPS Operating Systems Review*, 44(3):2–19, 2010.

[18] H. Oktay, B.J. Taylor, and D.D. Jensen. Causal discovery in social media using quasi-experimental designs. In *Proceedings of the First Workshop on Social Media Analytics*, pages 1–9. ACM, 2010.

[19] Akamai White Paper. *Akamai Streaming: When Performance Matters*, 2004. `http://www.akamai.com/dl/whitepapers/Akamai_Streaming_Performance_Whitepaper.pdf`.

[20] G.E. Quinn, C.H. Shin, M.G. Maguire, R.A. Stone, et al. Myopia and ambient lighting at night. *Nature*, 399(6732):113–113, 1999.

[21] Jupiter Research. *Retail Web Site Performance*, June 2006. `http://www.akamai.com/html/about/press/releases/2006/press_110606.html`.

[22] P.R. Rosenbaum and D.B. Rubin. Constructing a control group using multivariate matched sampling methods that incorporate the propensity score. *American Statistician*, pages 33–38, 1985.

[23] W.R. Shadish, T.D. Cook, and D.T. Campbell. *Experimental and quasi-experimental designs for generalized causal inference.* Houghton, Mifflin and Company, 2002.

[24] R.K. Sitaraman and R.W. Barton. Method and apparatus for measuring stream availability, quality and performance, February 2003. US Patent 7,010,598.

[25] K. Sripanidkulchai, B. Maggs, and H. Zhang. An analysis of live streaming workloads on the internet. In *Proceedings of the 4th ACM SIGCOMM Conference on Internet Measurement*, pages 41–54, 2004.

[26] D.A. Wolfe and M. Hollander. Nonparametric statistical methods. *Nonparametric statistical methods*, 1973.

[27] W. Wu, A. Arefin, R. Rivas, K. Nahrstedt, R. Sheppard, and Z. Yang. Quality of experience in distributed interactive multimedia environments: toward a theoretical framework. In *Proceedings of the 17th ACM international conference on Multimedia*, pages 481–490, 2009.

Confused, Timid, and Unstable: Picking a Video Streaming Rate is Hard

Te-Yuan Huang Nikhil Handigol Brandon Heller Nick McKeown Ramesh Johari
Stanford University
{huangty,nikhilh,brandonh,nickm,ramesh.johari}@stanford.edu

ABSTRACT

Today's commercial video streaming services use dynamic rate selection to provide a high-quality user experience. Most services host content on standard HTTP servers in CDNs, so rate selection must occur at the client. We measure three popular video streaming services – Hulu, Netflix, and Vudu – and find that accurate client-side bandwidth estimation above the HTTP layer is hard. As a result, rate selection based on inaccurate estimates can trigger a feedback loop, leading to undesirably variable and low-quality video. We call this phenomenon the *downward spiral effect*, and we measure it on all three services, present insights into its root causes, and validate initial solutions to prevent it.

Categories and Subject Descriptors

C.2.0 [**Computer Systems Organization**]: Computer-Communication Networks—*General*; C.4 [**Performance of Systems**]: [Measurement techniques]

General Terms

Measurement

Keywords

HTTP-based Video Streaming, Video Rate Adaptation

1. INTRODUCTION

Video streaming is a huge and growing fraction of Internet traffic, with Netflix and Youtube alone accounting for over 50% of the peak download traffic in the US [18]. Several big video streaming services run over HTTP and TCP (*e.g.* Hulu, Netflix, Vudu, YouTube) and stream data to the client from one or more third-party commercial CDNs (*e.g.* Akamai, Level3 or Limelight). Streaming over HTTP has several benefits: It is standardized across CDNs (allowing a portable video streaming service), it is well-established (which means the CDNs have already made sure service can reach through NATs to end-hosts), and cheap (the service is simple, commoditized, and the CDNs compete on price). These benefits have made possible the huge growth in affordable, high-quality movie and TV streaming, for our viewing delight.

IMC'12, November 14–16, 2012, Boston, Massachusetts, USA.

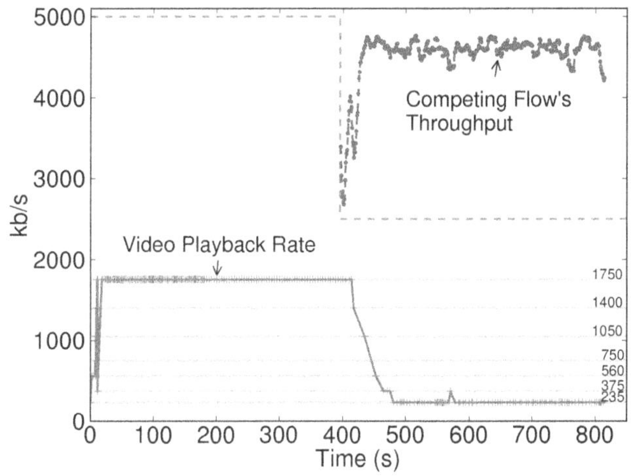

Figure 1: (Service A) A video starts streaming at 1.75Mb/s over a 5Mb/s network. After 395 seconds, a second flow starts (from the same server). The video could stream at 1.75Mb/s (given its fair share of 2.5Mb/s), but instead drops down to 235kb/s.

When video is streamed over HTTP, the video service provider relies on TCP to find the available bandwidth and choose a video rate accordingly. For example, if a client estimates that there is 1.5Mb/s available in the network, it might request the server to stream video compressed to 1.3Mb/s (or the highest video rate available at or below 1.5Mb/s). The video streaming service provider must walk a tightrope: If they pick a video rate that is *too high*, the viewer will experience annoying rebuffering events; if they pick a streaming rate that is *too low*, the viewer will experience poor video quality. In both cases, the experience degrades, and user may take their viewing elsewhere [9]. It is therefore important for a video streaming service to select the highest safe video rate.

This paper describes a measurement study of three popular HTTP-based video streaming services (Hulu, Netflix, and Vudu) to see how well they pick the video rate. According to the latest Consumer Reports [21], Netflix is the most popular video streaming provider in the United States, while

Vudu is one of the most satisfying streaming services. Hulu is also popular for its TV content. Our results show that when the home network is quiet, all three do a good job and pick a rate close to the maximum possible given the available network bandwidth. But all three services do a poor job when there is competing traffic (*e.g.* from another video stream, a backup, or a large download). Figure 1 shows a typical example in which the video is streamed at only 1/7th of its fair share of the available network bandwidth.

We attribute the problem to the difficulty of selecting the best video rate from "above" HTTP. We will present evidence that all three video streaming services underestimate available bandwidth because of interactions between the video playback buffer, HTTP and TCP's congestion control algorithm. In some cases the cause is on-off scheduling when the playback buffer fills, causing TCP to re-enter slow-start (Section 5.1). In all cases, it appears that when the bit rate is reduced, the client has less accurate data upon which to estimate the available bandwidth. When bandwidth estimates are scant or noisy, it is perhaps safer to stream at a lower rate and avoid wreaking havoc in home networks. On the other hand, given how well TCP shares bandwidth among long-lived flows, the video service provider could safely send at a higher rate and rely on TCP to be a good neighbor.

We explore the bandwidth estimation problem in each of the three video services. Throughout the paper we refer to the services by the names A, B and C. All of our results can be reproduced by observing the services externally, so the data is not confidential. However, we refer to the services as A, B, and C to stress that the paper is not a comparison of the services; rather, we wish to show that any HTTP-based streaming service must wrestle with the problem of picking a streaming rate based on observations above HTTP.

Our measurements lead us to recommendations, which we demonstrate by trace-driven emulations of the video services: ensure that TCP achieves its fair share by using sufficiently large HTTP requests, take advantage of a large playback buffer (a client typically holds several minutes of video), do not focus on keeping the playback buffer full (this will naturally fall foul of TCP dynamics), be less conservative in trying higher video rates, and rely on TCP to prevent the video stream from taking more than its fair share.

In what comes next we describe how the three video services work, then demonstrate in Section 4 how badly they perform in the presence of a competing flow. In Section 5 we explain why each service picks a much lower video rate than necessary and explain how this condition depends on the interaction between HTTP, TCP and conservatism. We describe ways to pick rates more accurately in Section 6 and validate rate selection changes. In Section 7 we describe related work, then conclude in Section 8.

2. HOW VIDEO STREAMING WORKS

To understand why the three video streaming services all suffer from the same problem, we first need to understand how they work. This information will later be useful for deploying a local proxy as well as for enabling our own emulator to download video segments from the CDNs directly.[1] We start out with the similarities before describing unique aspects to each. All three video streaming services share the following features:

[1]Even though we are able to download the video segments, only the legitimate player would be able to play the video.

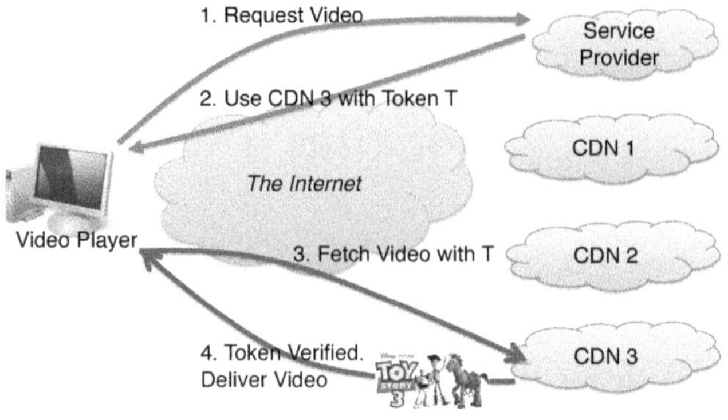

Figure 2: Common architecture of video streaming services over HTTP.

1. Video content is streamed over HTTP from third party CDN providers.

2. The video service runs on several different clients (*e.g.* web browser plugin, game console, TV).

3. Watching a video has two phases: authentication and streaming (see Figure 2).

4. Authentication (over HTTPS): When a client requests a video, the service provider authenticates the user account and directs the client to a CDN hosting the video. The video service provider tells the client which video streaming rates are available and issues a token for each rate.

5. Streaming: The client picks a video rate and requests a video by presenting a token (as a credential) to the designated CDN.

6. Picking a video rate: The client starts up with a preconfigured starting video rate. The client monitors the arriving traffic to pick the video rate. Because the service runs over "vanilla HTTP", the client makes the decision and the CDN server is not involved in picking the video rate.[2]

Although the three services are very similar, they differ from each other in some important ways.

Service A: Our measurements for Service A are based on a web-browser client. The Service A client sends HTTP byte range requests to the CDN, requesting 4-second segments of video over a persistent TCP connection. Unless it switches to a new rate, the client reads the whole video from the same server. The client always starts out requesting the lowest video rate, continuously estimates the available bandwidth, and only picks a higher rate if it believes it can sustain it.

Service B: Service B's desktop client runs over a proprietary protocol; thus, our measurements for Service B are based on its client on the Sony PlayStation 3 (PS3), which operates over HTTP. Service B's PS3 client also requests

[2]Services that control both the server and the client (*e.g.* YouTube) can involve the server and the client when picking a rate.

Provider	Platform	Download Strategy
Service A	Web Browser	Segment-by-segment download (Persistent connection)
Service B	Sony PlayStation 3	Segment-by-segment download (New connection)
Service C	Sony PlayStation 3	Progressive download (Open-ended download)

Table 1: Summary of the download strategies of the three services.

Provider	HTTP Request Format	Available Playback Rates (kb/s)
Service A	GET /*filename*/byte_range?token	235, 375, 560, 750, 1050, 1400, 1750(SD), 2350, 3600(HD)
Service B	GET /filename/clip_num?br=*bitrate*&token	650, 1000, 1500, 2000, 2500, 3200
Service C	GET /*filename*?token	SD: 1000, 1500, 2000
		HD: 3000, 4500, 6750, 9000

Table 2: Summary of the available playback rates for each of the three services.

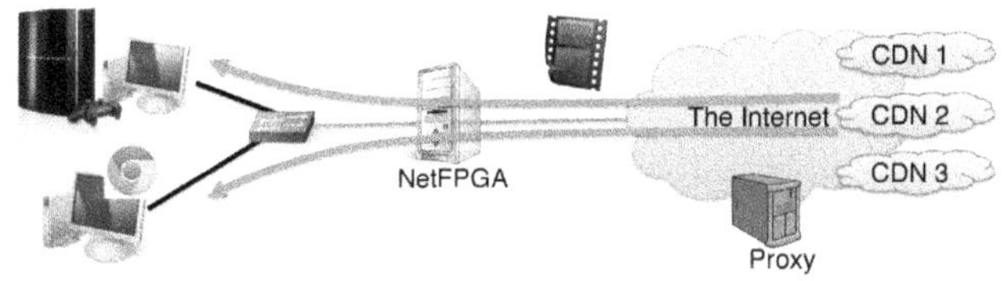

Figure 3: Our experimental setup includes a NetFPGA bandwidth limiter and a proxy.

one segment at a time, but each segment is stored as a separate file and each request for a new segment is sent over a new TCP connection. Each request is for about eight seconds of video. The video rate is specified in the HTTP GET request; the player starts at one of the two lowest playback rates, and steps up as it detects more bandwidth is available.

Service C: Our measurements for Service C are also based on its PS3 client, which has access to a broader range of video qualities compared to its desktop client. Service C's PS3 client sends an open-ended HTTP request; *i.e.*, it requests the whole file in one go. To change video rate, the client must reset the TCP connection and request a new filename. While Service A controls the occupancy of the playback buffer by varying the rate at which they request new segments, Service B and Service C rely on the TCP receive window: when the playback buffer is full, TCP reduces the receive window to slow down the server.

Table 1 and Table 2 summarize the three services.

3. MEASUREMENT SETUP

In this section we describe our experimental setup and measurement approach. In particular, we describe how to control bottleneck bandwidth (including the use of a local proxy to eliminate network path variation), how to measure the playback rate, and the competing traffic we employ.

3.1 Bandwidth Control and Proxy

Our experiments measure the behavior of video streams from Services A, B and C when they compete with other TCP flows. To create a controlled environment, where we can set the bottleneck link rate, all the video streams must pass through a rate limiter between the CDN and the client. Figure 3 shows how we place a NetFPGA machine [15] inline to limit bandwidth. In most cases, we limit the bandwidth to 5Mb/s, and the buffer size to 120kbit, sufficient to sustain 100% throughput with a 4–20 ms RTT. We use these configuration parameters throughout the paper, unless stated otherwise. The competing flow always passes through the NetFPGA too, and it shares the bottleneck link with the video stream.

In instances where we want a tightly controlled experiment, we download videos from a local proxy instead of the CDN, so as to eliminate any variance caused by the location of the CDN server or in Internet paths.

3.2 Measuring the Video Playback Rate

To understand the system dynamics, we need to know what video playback rate the client picks. Because this information is not externally visible, we have to deduce the mapping between the filenames requested by the client and the playback rate of the video inside the file. We developed a different technique for each service.

Service A: To figure out the mapping between filenames and the corresponding video rates, we first extract tokens from our traces and get the size of each file (via HTTP). We divide the file size by the duration of the video to get the rough video playback rate. The Service A client provides a debug window for users to monitor the current video playback rate, and we use these rates to validate our mapping.

Service B: Unfortunately, Service B doesn't provide a debug facility to validate the video playback rate. However, one of the parameters in the client's HTTP request seems to indicate the requesting video playback rate. But we needed to verify this. While the segment size requested with the parameter set to 3200 kb/s is about 3.1 times larger than the segments with 1000 kb/s, the same relationship does not hold between other video rates. Instead, we use an indirect method of verification. We set the link bandwidth to a value slightly higher than each of the parameter values and see if the client converges to requesting with that parameter value. Indeed, the value of the parameter closely follows the bandwidth setting. For example, when we set the available bandwidth to 3,350 kb/s, the HTTP parameter converges to 3200. Similarly, when we set the bandwidth to 1,650 kb/s, the HTTP parameter converges to 1500.

Service C: Like Service A, Service C also has a mapping between the requested filename and the video playback rate. Unfortunately, Service C does not directly tell us the current rate. However, because the TCP flow is limited by the receive window when the playback buffer is full, the average TCP throughput matches the video playback rate. We confirmed that the converged receiver-limited TCP throughput reflects the rate information embedded in the requested filename.

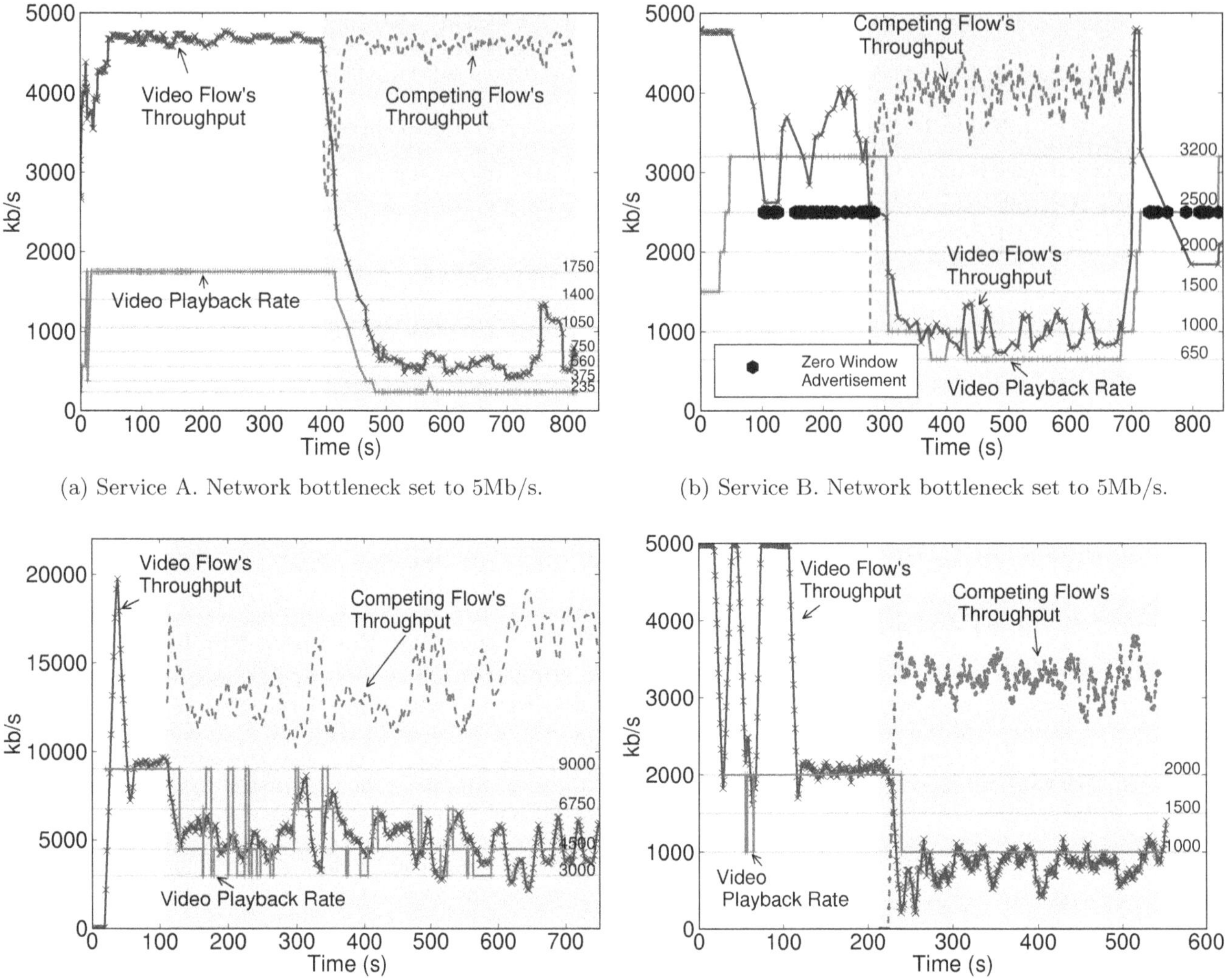

(a) Service A. Network bottleneck set to 5Mb/s.

(b) Service B. Network bottleneck set to 5Mb/s.

(c) Service C HD. Network bottleneck set to 22Mb/s.

(d) Service C SD. Network bottleneck set to 5Mb/s.

Figure 4: The downward spiral effect is visible in all three services.

The video rates available from each of the three services are summarized in Table 2; some playback rates may not be available for some videos.

3.3 The Competing Flows

The competing flow is a TCP flow doing a long file download. To eliminate any unfairness due to variations in network path properties, we ensure that the competing flow is served by the same CDN, and usually, by the same server. For Service A and Service C, the competing flow is generated by an open-ended byte range request to the file with the highest rate. Further, we use the DNS cache to make sure that the competing flow comes from same termination point (the server or the load-balancer) as the video flow. For Service B, since the files are stored as small segments, an open-ended request only creates short-lived flows. Instead, we generate the competing flow by requesting the Flash version of the same video stored in the same CDN, using rtmpdump [20] over TCP.

4. THE DOWNWARD SPIRAL EFFECT

All three services suffer from what we call the "downward spiral effect" – a dramatic anomalous drop in the video playback rate in the presence of a competing TCP flow. The problem is starkly visible in Figure 4. In all four graphs, the video stream starts out alone and then competes with another TCP flow. As soon as the competing flow starts up, the client mysteriously picks a video playback rate that is far below the available bandwidth. Our goal is to understand why this happens.

To gain a first inkling into what is going on, we calculate the upper bound of what the client might *believe* the instantaneous available bandwidth to be, by measuring the arrival rate of the last video segment. Specifically, we calculate the throughput upper bound as the size of a received video segment divided by the time it took to arrive (the time from when the first byte arrived until the last byte arrived), which excludes the initial server response time. In all of the graphs, the video playback rate chosen by the client is quite strongly correlated with the calculated throughput. As we will see, herein lies the problem: if the client is selecting the video rate based on some function of the throughput it perceived, and the throughput is so different from the actual available bandwidth, then it is not surprising the client does such a poor job. Let's now see what goes wrong for each service in turn. For ease of discussion, we will use *video throughput* to refer to the throughput a client perceived by downloading a video segment.

4.1 Service A

Figure 4(a) shows the playback rate of a Service A video session along with the client's video throughput over time. Starting out, the video stream is the only flow and the client requests the highest video rate (1750kb/s). The competing flow begins after 400 seconds; the video rate steadily drops until it reaches the lowest rate (235kb/s), and it stays there most of the time until the competing flow stops. In theory, both flows should be able to stream at 2.5Mb/s (their fair share of the link) and the client should continue to stream at 1750kb/s.

We repeated the experiment 76 times over four days. In 67 cases (91%) the downward spiral happens, and the client picks either the lowest rate, or bounces between the two or three lowest rates. In just seven cases (9%) was the client able to maintain a playback rate above 1400kb/s. To ensure accuracy and eliminate problems introduced by competing flows with different characteristics (*e.g.* TCP flows with different RTTs), we make the competing flow request the *same* video file (encoded at 1750kb/s) from the *same* CDN. Unlike the video flow, the competing flow is just a simple TCP file download and its download speed is only dictated by TCP congestion control algorithm and not capped by the video client.[3]

Why does throughput of the video flow drop so much below available fair-share bandwidth? Is it an inherent characteristic of streaming video over HTTP, or is the client simply picking the wrong video rate?

We first confirm that the available bandwidth really is available for streaming video. We do this using a feature provided by the Service A client that allows users to manually select a video rate and disable the client's automatic rate selection algorithm. We repeat the above experiment, but with a slight modification. As soon as the client picks a lower rate, we manually force the video to play at 1750kb/s. Figure 5 shows the results. Interestingly, the client maintains a playback rate of 1750kb/s without causing rebuffering events, and the throughput also increases. This suggests that the downward spiral effect is caused by underestimation of the available bandwidth in the client's rate selection algorithm. The bandwidth is available, but the client needs to go grab it.

4.2 Service B

Figure 4(b) shows the same downward spiral effect in Service B. As before, the bottleneck bandwidth is 5Mb/s and the RTT is around 20 ms. We start a video streaming session first, allow it to settle at its highest rate (3200kb/s) and then start a competing flow after 337 seconds, by reading the same video file from the same server.

[3]To eliminate variation caused by congestion at the server, we verified that the same problem occurs if we download the competing video file from a different server at the same CDN.

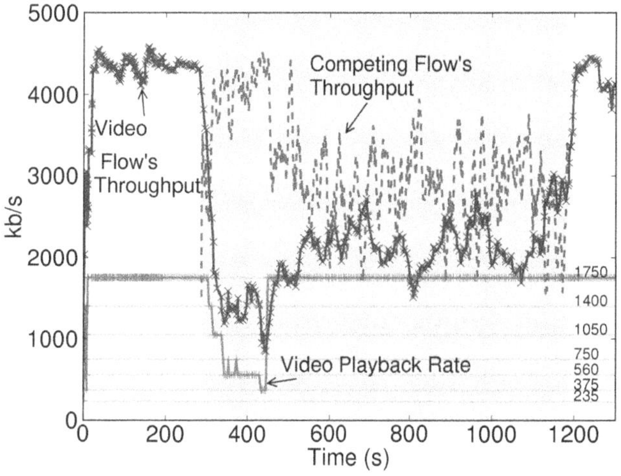

Figure 5: (Service A) The client manages to maintain the highest playback rate if we disable automatic rate selection.

The client should drop the video rate to 2500kb/s (its fair share of the available bandwidth). Instead, it steps all the way to the lowest rate offered by Service B, 650kb/s, and occasionally to 1000kb/s. The throughput plummets too.

4.3 Service C

We observe the downward spiral effect in Service C as well. Since Service C does not automatically switch between its HD and SD bitrates, we do two separate experiments.

In the HD experiment, as shown in Figure 4(c), we set the bottleneck bandwidth to 22Mb/s. To start with, the client picks the highest HD video rate (9Mb/s). When the client's playback buffer is full, the video flow is limited by the receive window, and the throughput converges to the same value as the playback rate. We start the competing flow at 100 seconds, and it downloads the same video file (9Mb/s video rate) from the same CDN.

Each flow has 11Mb/s available to it, plenty for the client to continue playing at 9Mb/s. But instead, the client resets the connection and switches to 4.5Mb/s and then 3Mb/s, before bouncing around several rates.

SD is similar. We set the bottleneck bandwidth to 5Mb/s, and the client correctly picks the highest rate (2000kb/s) to start with, as shown in Figure 4(d). When we start the competing flow, the video client drops down to 1000kb/s even though its share is 2.5Mb/s. Since Service C only offers three SD rates, we focus on its HD service in the rest of the paper.

5. WALKING THE DOWNWARD SPIRAL

To understand how the downward spiral happens, we examine each service in turn. Although each service enters the downward spiral for a slightly different reason, there is enough commonality for us to focus first on Service A (and Figure 4(a)) and then describe how the other two services differ.

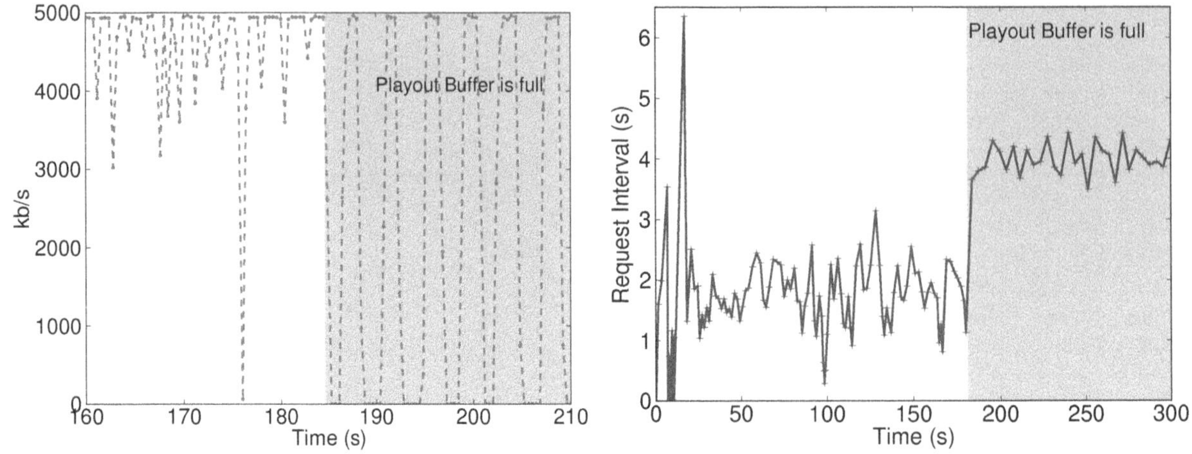

(a) TCP throughput before and after the buffer fills. (b) Request interval before and after the buffer fills.

Figure 6: (Service A) Before and after the playback buffer fills at 185 seconds.

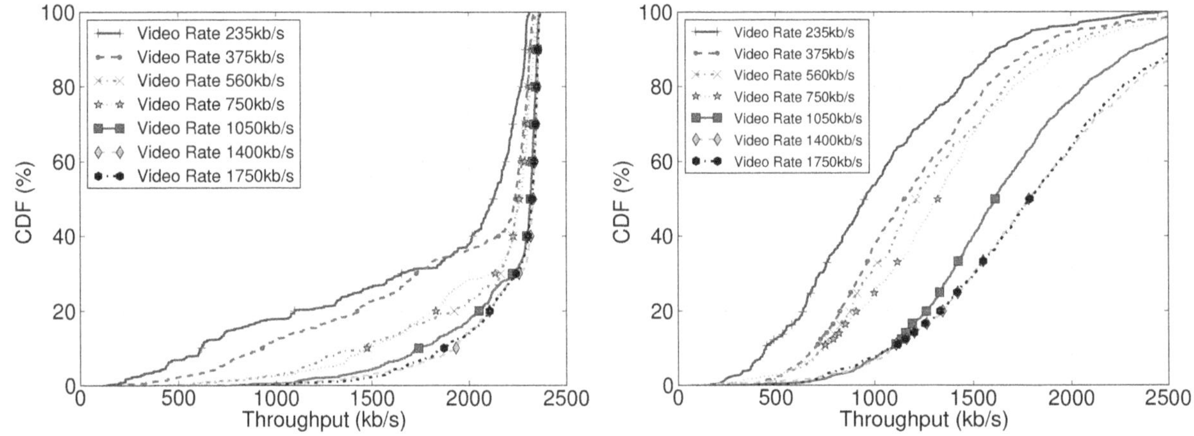

(a) Service A with no competing flow. (b) Service A with one competing flow.

Figure 7: (Service A) Throughput at HTTP layer with and without a competing flow.

5.1 Initial Condition: No Competing Flow

In the absence of a competing flow (first 400 seconds), the Service A client correctly chooses the highest playback rate. Because the available network bandwidth (5Mb/s) is much higher than the playback rate (1750kb/s), the client busily fills up its playback buffer and the bottleneck link is kept fully occupied. Eventually the playback buffer fills (after 185 seconds) and the client pauses to let it drain a little before issuing new requests. Figure 6(a) shows how the TCP throughput varies before and after the playback buffer fills up. After the buffer is full, the client enters a periodic ON-OFF sequence. As we will see shortly, the ON-OFF sequence is a part of the problem (but only one part). Before the buffer fills, the client requests a new 4-second segment of video every 1.5 seconds on average (because it is filling the buffer). Figure 6(b) confirms that after the buffer is full, the client requests a new 4-second segment every 4 seconds, on average. The problem is that during the 4-second OFF period, the TCP congestion window (*cwnd*) times out — due to inactivity longer than 200ms — and resets *cwnd* to its initial value of 10 packets [5, 6]. Even though the client is using an existing persistent TCP connection, the *cwnd* needs to ramp up from slow start for each new segment download.

It is natural to ask if the repeated dropping back to slow-start reduces the client's video throughput, causing it to switch to a lower rate. With no competing flow, it appears the answer is 'no'. We verify this by measuring the video throughput for many requests. We set the bottleneck link rate to 2.5Mb/s, use traces collected from actual sessions to replay the requests over a persistent connection to the same server, and pause the requests at the same interval as the pauses in the trace. Figure 7(a) shows the CDF of the client's video throughput for requests corresponding to various playback rates. The video throughput is pretty accurate. Except for some minor variation, the video throughput accurately reflects the available bandwidth, and explains why the client picks the correct rate.

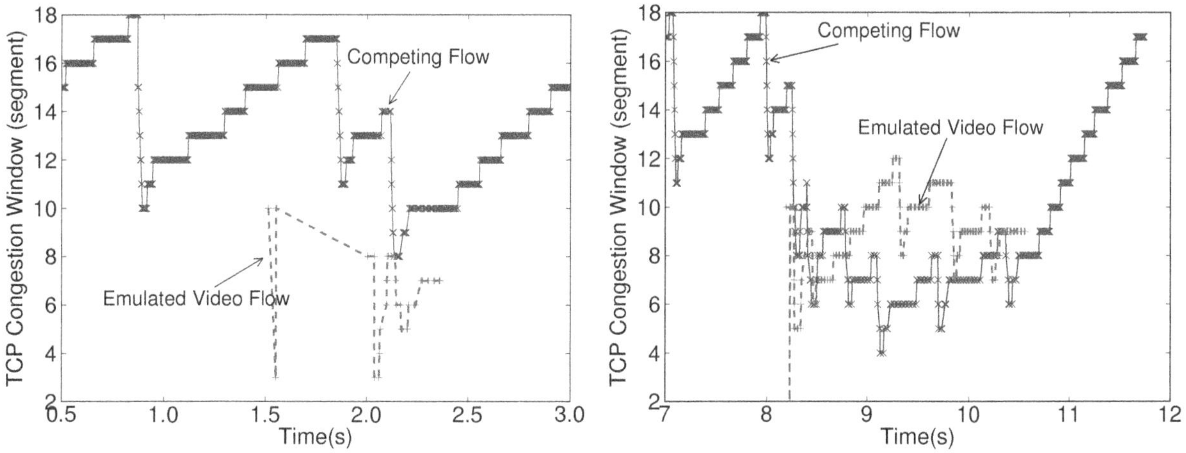

(a) A 235kbps Segment.

(b) Five contiguous 235kbps segments concatenated into one.

Figure 8: (Service A) The evolution of *cwnd* for different segment sizes.

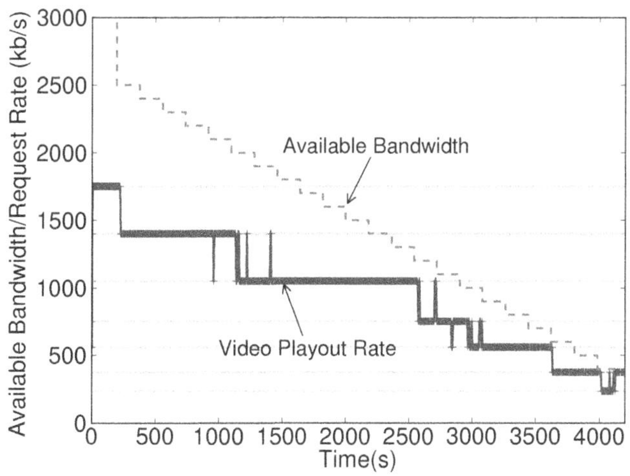

Figure 9: (Service A) The client picks a video rate depending on the available bandwidth. The horizontal gray lines are the available rates.

5.2 The Trigger: With a Competing Flow

Things go wrong when the competing flows starts (after 400 seconds). Figure 7(b) shows the client's video throughput are mostly too low when there is a competing flow.[4] If we look at the progression of *cwnd* for the video flow after it resumes from a pause, we can tell how the server opens up the window differently when there is a competing flow. Because we don't control the server (it belongs to the CDN) we instead use our local proxy to serve both the video traffic and the competing flow, and use the `tcp_probe` kernel module to log the *cwnd* values. The video traffic here is generated by requesting a 235kbps video segment. Figure 8(a) shows how *cwnd* evolves, starting from the initial value of 10 at 1.5 seconds, then *repeatedly being beaten down by the competing* `wget` *flow*. The competing `wget` flow has already filled the buffer during the OFF period, and so the video flow sees very high packet loss. Worse still, the segment is finished before *cwnd* climbs up again, and we re-enter the OFF period. The process will repeat for every ON-OFF period, and the throughput is held artificially low.

For comparison, and to understand the problem better, Figure 8(b) shows the result of the same experiment with a segment size five times larger. With a larger segment size, the *cwnd* has longer to climb up from the initial value; and has a much greater likelihood of reaching the correct steady state value.

Now that we know the video throughput tends to be low (because of TCP), we would like to better understand how the client *reacts* to the low throughputs. We can track the client's behavior as we steadily reduce the available bandwidth, as shown in Figure 9. We start with a bottleneck link rate of 5Mb/s (and no competing flow), drop it to 2.5Mb/s (to mimic a competing flow), and then keep dropping it by 100kb/s every 3 minutes. The dashed line shows the available bandwidth, while the solid line shows the video rate picked by the client. The client chooses the video rate conservatively; when available bandwidth drops from from 5Mb/s to 2.5Mb/s, the video rate goes down to 1400kb/s, and so on.

We can now put the two pieces together. Consider a client streaming at a playback rate of 1750kb/s, the median video throughput it perceives is 1787kb/s as shown in Figure 7(b). According to Figure 9, with a video throughput of 1787kb/s, the client reduces its playback rate to 1050kb/s. Thus, 50% of the time the playback rate will go down to 1050kb/s once the competing flow starts.

It is interesting to observe that the Service A client is behaving quite rationally given the throughput it perceives. The problem is that because Service A observes the throughput *above* TCP, it is not aware that TCP itself is having

[4]In Figure 7(b), the bottleneck bandwidth is set to 5Mb/s so that the available fair-share of bandwidth (2.5Mb/s) is the same as in Figure 7(a). Note that some segment downloads are able to get more than its fair share; in these cases, the competing flow experiences losses and has not ramped up to its fair share yet. This is the reason why some of the CDF curves does not end with 100% at 2.5Mb/s in Figure 7(b).

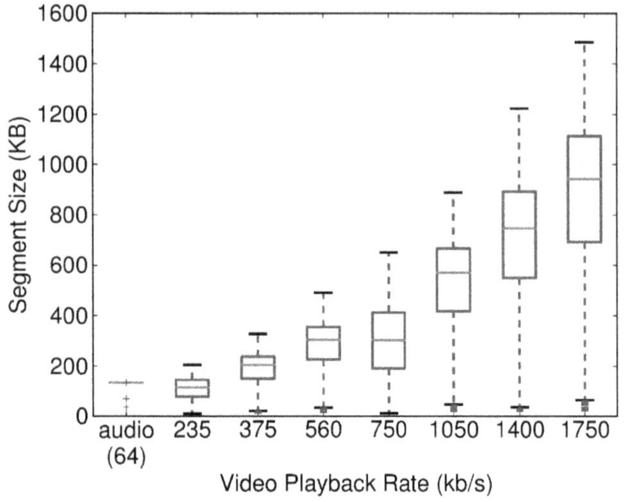

Figure 10: (Service A) The segment size for different video rates.

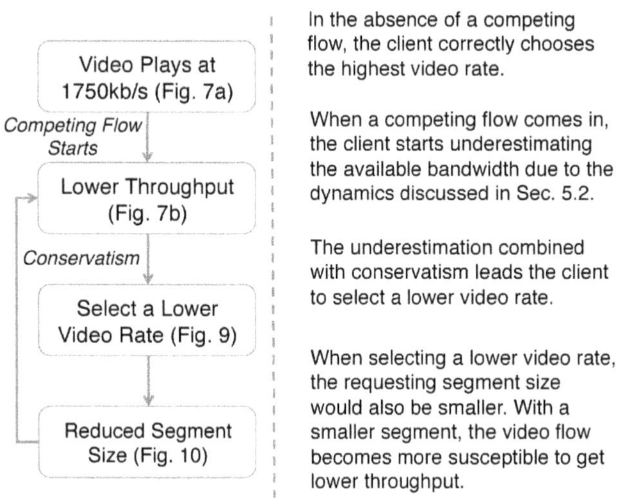

Figure 11: (Service A) The feedback loop.

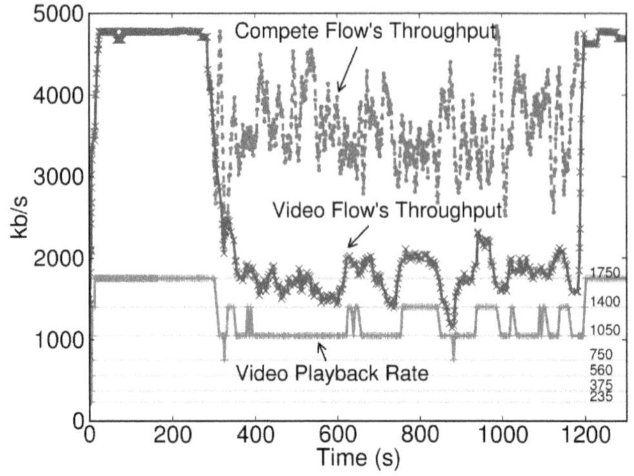

Figure 12: (Service A) When streaming from another CDN, the playback rate stabilizes at 1050kb/s.

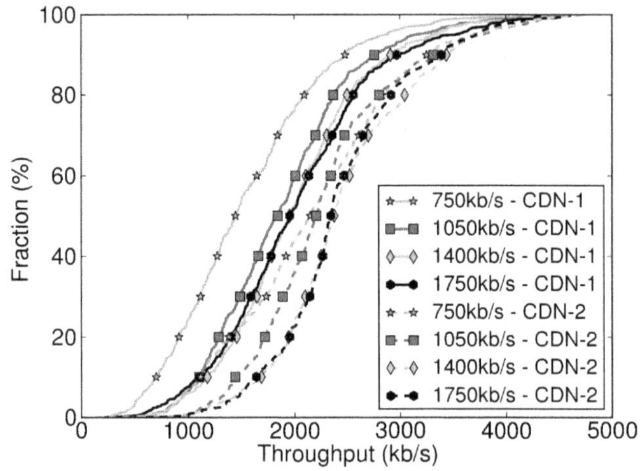

Figure 13: (Service A) Different network path properties (CDNs) lead to different video throughput.

trouble reaching its fair share of the bandwidth. Coupled with a (natural) tendency to pick rates conservatively, the rate drops down.

5.3 The Spiral: Low Playback Rate

Finally, there is one more phenomenon driving the video rate to its lowest rate. Recall that each HTTP request is for four seconds of video. When the video rate is lower, the four-second segment is smaller, as shown in Figure 10. With a smaller segment, the video flow becomes more susceptible to perceiving lower throughput, as shown in Figure 7(b). With a lower throughput, the client reduces the playback rate, creating the vicious cycle shown in Figure 11. The feedback loop will continue until it reaches a steady state where the perceived available bandwidth is large enough to keep the rate selection algorithm at the chosen rate. In the worst case, the feedback loop creates a "death spiral" and brings the playback rate all the way down to its lowest value.

To summarize, when the playout buffer is full, the client enters a periodic ON-OFF sequence. The OFF period makes the TCP connection idle for too long and reset its congestion window. Also during the OFF period, the competing TCP flow fills the router buffer, so the video flow sees high packet loss when it returns to the ON period. Worse still, the video could finish downloading its video segment before its *cwnd* climbs up to its fair share and thus re-enters the OFF period. This process repeats for every ON-OFF period; as a consequence, the video flow underestimates the available bandwidth and switches to a lower video rate. When switching to a lower rate, the client requests a smaller video segment, which makes the video flow further underestimate the available bandwidth, forming a vicious cycle.

5.4 With Different Network Conditions

Our experiments so far were all for the same CDN. Figure 12 shows different behavior for a different CDN. The path properties are different, and Figure 13 shows that the

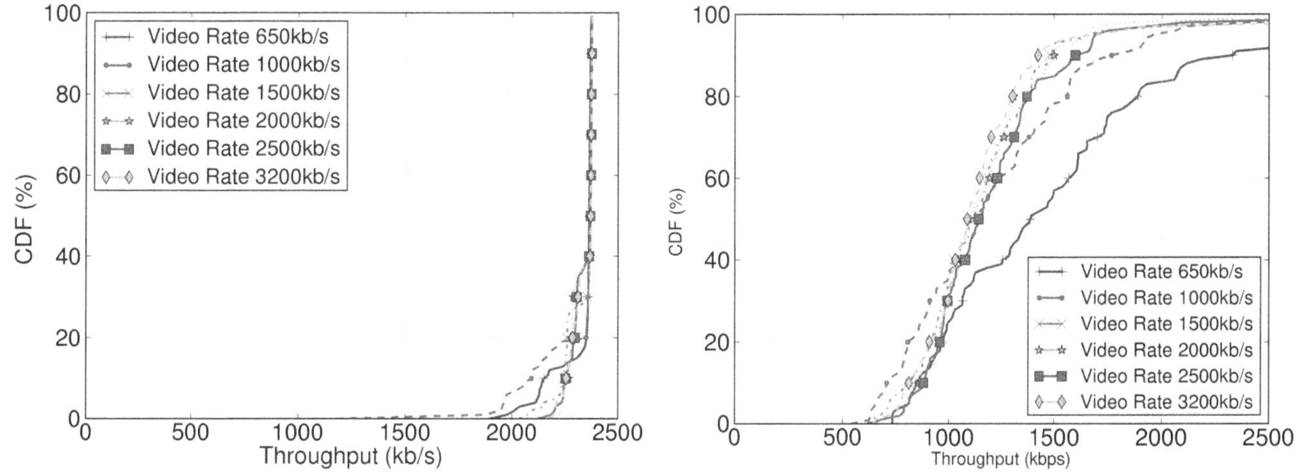

(a) Service B with no competing flow.

(b) Service B with one competing flow.

Figure 16: (Service B) The TCP throughput changes in the presence of a competing flow.

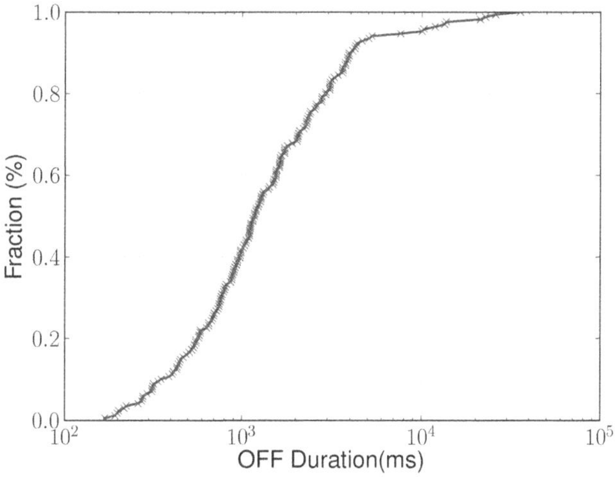

Figure 14: (Service B) Almost all the OFF periods in a single video session are greater than RTO (200ms).

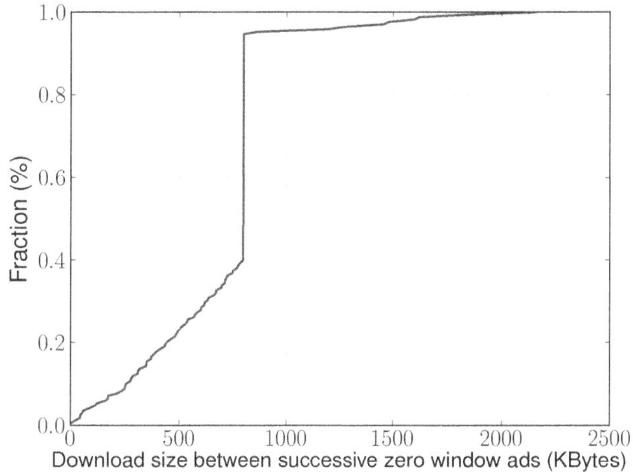

Figure 15: (Service B) When the video stream is receiver-limited, the client does not request many bytes during an ON period.

video throughput is higher — hence the Service A client picks a higher rate (1050kb/s).

For comparison, we asked 10 volunteers to rerun this experiment with Service A in their home network connected to different ISPs, such as AT&T DSL, Comcast, Verizon and university residences. Even though there was sufficient available bandwidth for the highest video rate in the presence of a competing flow, seven people reported a rate of only 235kb/s-560kb/s.

5.5 Service B

Service B also exhibits ON-OFF behavior, but at the TCP level and not the HTTP level, i.e., the pause could happen while downloading a video segment. When its video playback buffer is full, the client stops taking data from the TCP socket buffer. Eventually, the TCP socket buffer also fills and triggers TCP flow control to pause the server by sending a *zero window advertisement*. In Figure 4(b), each *zero window advertisement* is marked by a hexagon. The client starts issuing *zero window advertisements* at around 100s and continues to do so until a few seconds after the competing flow starts. Figure 14 shows the CDF of the duration of the OFF periods. Almost all the pauses are longer than 200ms, so *cwnd* is reset to its initial value. Thus, Service B effectively exhibits an ON-OFF behavior similar to that of Service A.

Worse still, during an ON period, Service B does not request many bytes; Figure 15 shows that over half of the time, it reads only 800kbytes, which is not enough for the *cwnd* to climb up to its steady state before the next OFF period. Figure 4(b) and Figure 16(b) show the result, that the TCP throughput is only around 1Mbps to 1.5Mbps, causing Service B to pick a video rate of 1000kb/s, or even 650kb/s. As we saw earlier, when competing with another flow, the smaller the request, the higher the likelihood of perceiving

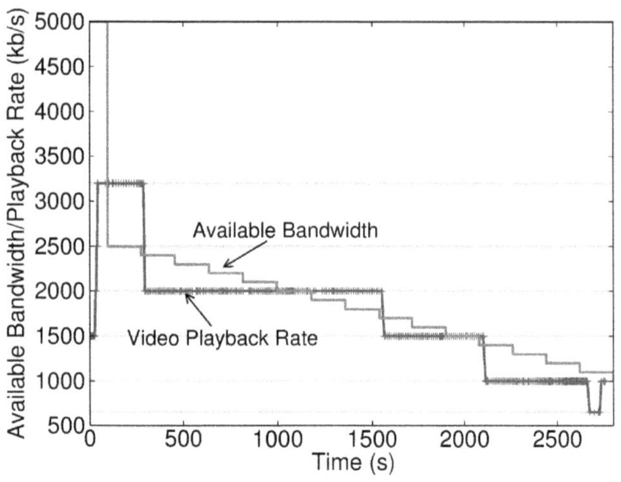

Figure 17: (Service B) While not too conservative, the client is limited by its TCP throughput.

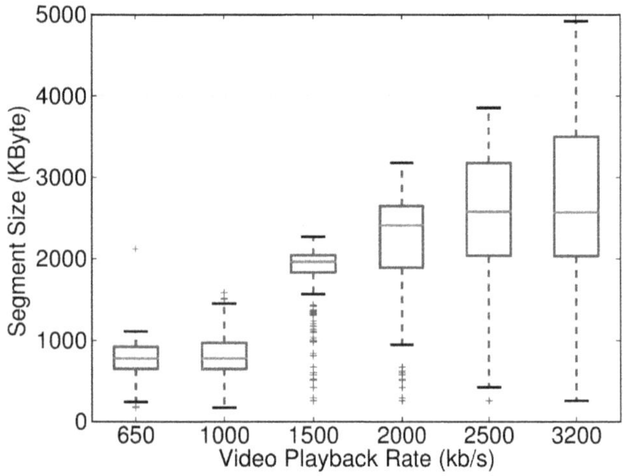

Figure 18: (Service B) Segment size varies with video playback rate.

a lower throughput. The problem would be even worse if it was coupled with a conservative rate selection algorithm. Fortunately, Service B is not nearly as conservative as the other two services, as shown in Figure 17.

Similar to Service A, the segment size gets smaller with decreasing playback rate – from 3MByte to 1MByte, as shown in Figure 18. However, segment size does not play a significant role in the downward spiral effect of Service B, since the ON-OFF behavior is at the TCP level and the number of bytes for each ON period is not determined by segment size.

5.6 Service C

Service C performs an open-ended download, instead of going segment-by-segment. Thus, it is not constrained by segment size and does not pause between HTTP requests. The download is only slowed down when the receive window fills, and the client reduces the number of bytes in flight. However, the OFF period for Service C is less than an RTO and therefore does not trigger TCP to reset its window size.

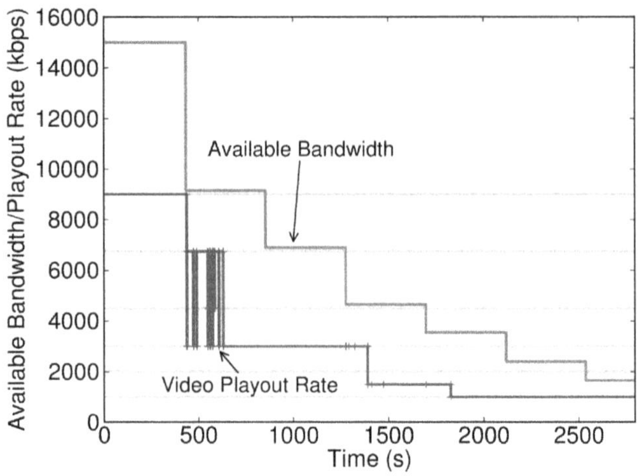

Figure 19: (Service C) The client is conservative in its rate selection.

The problem with Service C is mainly caused by its conservativeness and being sensitive to temporal behaviors in TCP. Figure 19 shows the conservativeness of Service C; it steps down to 3Mb/s even when the available bandwidth is more than 9Mb/s. As shown in Figure 4(c), Service C regulates itself at 9Mb/s after its playout buffer is full. Thus, the competing flow would take over the rest of the 13Mb/s available bandwidth when it starts and make Service C perceive less than 9Mb/s of available bandwidth. As a consequence, the video flow steps down to the video rate of 3Mb/s. Since Service C does an open-ended download, it has to reset the current TCP connection to stop downloading the current video file when switching to a different video rate. The client then starts a new connection for the file with the newly selected rate. This would make the video flow perceive less bandwidth during the transition, as TCP needs to go through the phase of connection establishment and slow start. As a result, whenever Service C switches to a higher video rate, this overhead of transition makes the client perceive less bandwidth and bounce back to a lower video rate.

6. ACTIVELY INTERVENING

We can verify our explanation in Section 5 by modifying the system. For example, a modified server might tell the client the highest rate achieved during a segment download, or an augmented HTTP interface might report the recent bandwidth history to the client. Unfortunately, this is not an option for our three services, because they use unmodified HTTP CDN services. The experiments we describe next therefore leave the ecosystem unchanged, and only require client changes. Our intent is not to propose a new client design, but rather to confirm our understanding of the root causes of the downward spiral by trying small changes to the algorithm.

6.1 The Custom Client

For brevity, we focus on Service A. Our approach is to replay a movie, using the same CDN and segments as Service A, but with our own client algorithm. The three services keep their algorithms secret, but our measurements provide

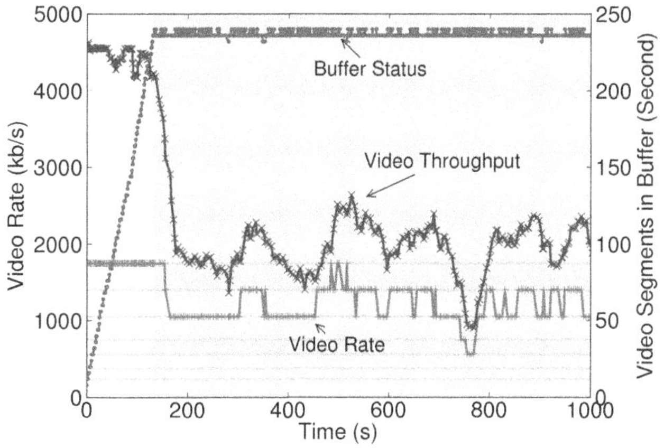

Figure 20: Custom client, similar to Service A – equally conservative, with a 10-sample moving average filter – displays the downward spiral.

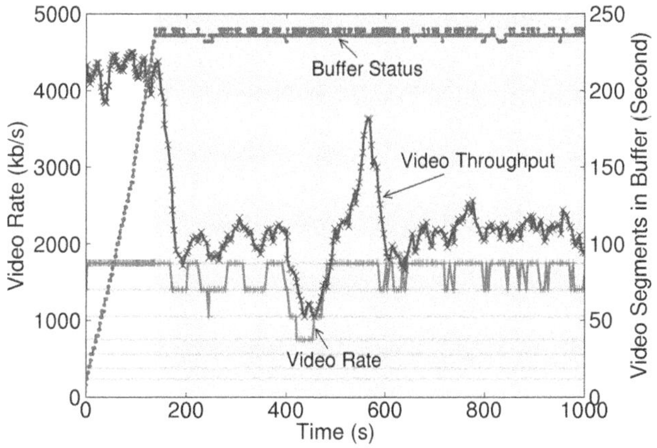

Figure 21: Custom client – with 10% conservatism, but with a 10-sample moving average filter.

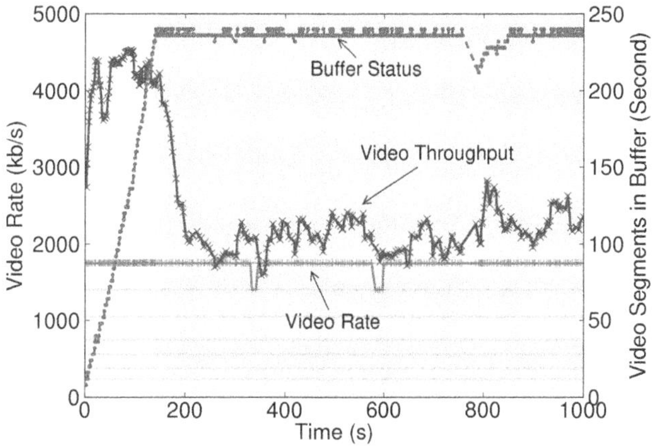

Figure 22: Custom client – with 10% conservatism, and with an 80th-percentile filter.

a reasonable baseline. For Service A, Figure 9 indicates the bandwidth below which the client picks a lower video rate. Assume that Service A estimates bandwidth by simply dividing the download size by the download time and passing it through a fixed-size moving-average filter. We can estimate the size of the filter by measuring how long it takes from when the bandwidth drops until the client picks a new rate. A number of traces from Service A suggest a filter with 10 samples, though the true algorithm is probably more nuanced.

To closely mimic the Service A client, our custom client requests the video segments with the same sizes from the same locations in the CDN: we capture the segment map given to the client after authentication, which locates the video segments for each supported playback rate. Hence, our custom client will experience the same segment-size variation over the course of the movie, and when it shifts playback rate, the segment size will change as well. Since our custom client uses tokens from an earlier playback, the CDN cannot tell the difference between our custom client and the real Service A client. To further match Service A, the playback buffer is set to 240 seconds, the client uses a single persistent connection to the server, and it pauses when the buffer is full. We first validate the client, then consider three changes: (1) being less conservative, (2) changing the filtering method, and (3) aggregating segments.

6.2 Validating our Custom Client

Figure 20 shows the custom client in action. After downloading each segment, the custom client selects the playback rate based on Service A's conservative rate selection algorithm, observed in Figure 9. Once the playback buffer is full, we introduce a competing flow. Like the real client, the playback rate drops suddenly when the competing flow starts, then fluctuates over the course of the movie. The downward spiral does not bottom out, which we suspect is due to some subtle differences between Service A's algorithm and ours.

6.3 Less Conservative

Bandwidth estimates based on download sizes and durations tend to under-report the available bandwidth, especially in the presence of a competing flow. If the algorithm is conservative, it exacerbates the problem. We try a less conservative algorithm, with a conservatism of 10% instead of 40%. Conservatism of 40% means the client requests for a video rate of at most 1.2Mb/s when it perceives 2.0Mb/s, while 10% means it requests at most 1.8Mb/s when perceiving 2.0Mb/s. According to Figure 9, Service A requests video rate with a conservatism of approximately 40%. Figure 21 shows that the video rate is higher, even though the playback buffer stays full. The result is higher quality video, high playback buffer occupancy (*i.e.* resilience against rebuffering) and four minutes of buffering to respond to changes in bandwidth. Note that even though the algorithm is less conservative, the underlying TCP ensures the algorithm stays a "good citizen" and only gets its fair share of available bandwidth.

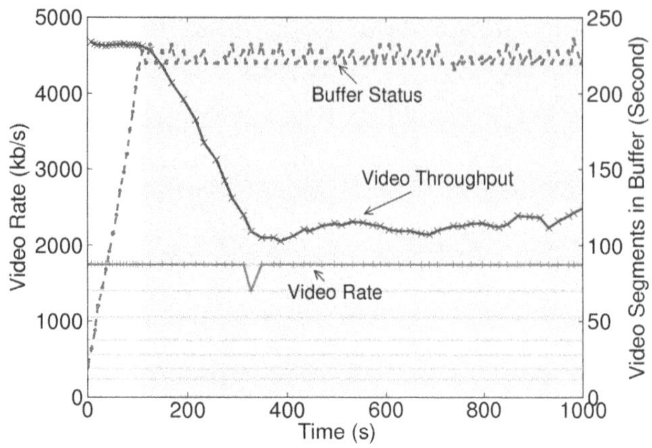

Figure 23: Custom client with increased segment size (5x).

6.4 Better Filtering

Averaging filters provide a more stable estimate of bandwidth, but a single outlier can confuse the algorithm. For example, a few seconds of low-information movie credits reduces the segment size and the algorithm might drop the rate. In place of averages, we consider medians and quantiles to reduce the vulnerability to outliers. Figure 22 shows what happens if we use the 80th-percentile of measured rate of the past ten segment download. Variation is greatly reduced, and the majority of the movie plays at the highest-available rate. The playback buffer has small fluctuations, but it is still far from a rebuffer event.

6.5 Bigger Segments

As noted earlier, bigger segments provide better estimates of the available bandwidth, allowing TCP to escape slow-start. Figure 23 shows what happens if our client aggregates five requests into one. With the larger segment size, the video throughput is more stable, and both the playback rate and buffer size are more stable.

In summary, larger segments let TCP reach its fair share and improve the video throughput. Picking higher rates less conservatively and filtering measurements more carefully can improve video quality. But we should note that these improvements are for one movie on one service. Given the prevalence of the downward spiral effect, these should not be interpreted as hard recommendations, merely as added detail to our understanding of the problem.

7. RELATED WORK

The related work largely considers three overlapping areas: systems for video streaming; measurements to understand their performance, and the design and analysis of rate selection algorithms.

Video Streaming Services. The first category covers video streaming approaches using HTTP, such as the commercial ones from Adobe, Apple, and Microsoft described in [22], which differ in their alignment of video switching rates, whether A/V streams are combined, and whether requests are issued as byte ranges or for pre-specified segments. A more recent technique is MPEG DASH (Dynamic Adaptive Streaming over HTTP) [7] which standardizes the formatting of video content and leaves open the specific client player algorithm. These techniques underpin the major commercial services like YouTube, Netflix, and Hulu.

Video Streaming Measurement. The second category measures the performance of individual video streaming clients experiencing local traffic conditions ("in the lab"), all the way to distributed measurement systems that compare the performance of thousands of clients ("in the wild").

The work most similar to ours is [3], where the authors also parse HTTP messages to determine playback rates and use a bandwidth limiter to test clients under varying network conditions. However, [3] focuses on the unfairness problem among two video players, while in this work we focus on the unfairness problem between a video player and a long-lived TCP flow. This paper considers a significantly different scenario: it focuses on a video client competing against *another video client*. In this context, they observe similar pathologies: poor bandwidth estimation, leading to instability. However, they explain their observations entirely in terms of the application-layer ON-OFF behavior of video clients; even if one video client perfectly obtained its fair share when ON, it can fail to correctly estimate available bandwidth (depending on the amount of overlap with the ON periods of the other client). By contrast, our paper demonstrates that this is only a symptom of a more general problem: inaccurate bandwidth estimation occurs *even* when the competing flow does not exhibit ON-OFF behavior. As we show in this paper, the problem arises because it is hard to estimate bandwidth above TCP. Others have identified the same problem but not explained its causes or validated potential fixes [4, 16].

Measuring the CDN servers rather than clients provides different insights. In [1], the authors examine the CDN selection strategy of Hulu, while in [2], the authors look at Netflix. Both papers find a predisposition for clients to stay with the original CDN, despite variation between CDNs and over time. In [9], the authors describe lessons learned from a distributed commercial measurement system to understand the effects of Quality-of-Experience (QoE) metrics on viewer engagement and retention. Rebuffer rates and average video quality are QoE metrics with measurable impacts on viewer engagement, which underscores the importance of getting rate measurement and selection right in the presence of competing flows. With the measurement-driven insights from the same system, [14] proposes a global video control plane to dynamically assign clients a choice of video rate and CDN that optimizes viewers' experience.

Other work looks at network characteristics of video streaming traffic, rather than focusing on the client or viewer experiences [11, 19, 24]. In particular, the authors in [19] show ON-OFF cycle behavior for YouTube and Netflix and use a model to study aggregates of video client and their effects on the network. Both CDN and network traffic papers do not consider local effects on measured bandwidth or their effects on rate stability.

Rate Selection Algorithms. The third category is work on rate selection algorithms. This work complements ours, as a control system always benefits from more accurate measurements. In [8], the authors propose an algorithm to maintain the playout buffer at a target level. In [17], the authors implement a different buffer-aware rate selection algorithm and experimentally measure user preferences for gradual and infrequent playback rate changes. In [23], the authors model the rate selection problem as a Markov Decision Process and use a dynamic programming technique to choose a streaming strategy that improves QoE. In [13], the authors use simulations to show how parallel HTTP sessions can improve playback quality. Server-side pacing is another approach to selecting rate used by YouTube, as described in [10, 12].

8. CONCLUSION

Despite some differences in specific service implementations, all three services we study display degraded performance in the presence of competing traffic, well below the video quality possible if the client used its fair share of bandwidth. At a high level, our measurement analysis and experiments suggest that the root cause of this failure is a lack of information. The HTTP layer is simply not privy to continuous high-fidelity feedback about the fair share at the bottleneck link.

There are two ways to interpret our observations. On one hand, we observe that determining the fair share of bandwidth available at the bottleneck is *precisely the role of TCP*. Thus, one path forward might be to suggest that we should design the client to improve information flow from TCP to the HTTP layer. In particular, we should ensure that TCP has a chance to reach its steady-state fair share; for example, increasing the segment size enables this effect.

However, we believe there may be a more radical solution: *do not attempt to estimate bandwidth at all!* The video streaming client has two competing goals: attain the highest bitrate possible while avoiding buffer underruns. Thus the objective is *not* to ensure the buffer stays full; the objective is to ensure the buffer does not go empty. Since the buffer holds several minutes of video, this shift in perspective suggests that if the buffer is full then the client has picked a rate that is *too low*. Rather, the client should *increase* the bitrate when the buffer is high and *decrease* it when the buffer falls low. Though this sounds aggressive, note that it is exactly the correct layer separation: it hands off to TCP the objective of obtaining the fair share of bandwidth, and tries to always ensure the client picks the highest rate possible. This suggests an intriguing path forward for future research: design video-streaming clients that deliver high performance by *eliminating* bandwidth estimation all together.

Acknowledgment

We are grateful to the anonymous reviewers and our shepherd Nina Taft for their valuable comments and feedback, which helped improve the final version. The authors would also like to thank Kok-Kiong Yap, Masayoshi Kobayashi, Vimalkumar Jeyakumar, Yiannis Yiakoumis and Netflix engineers for helpful discussions that shaped the paper. This work was supported by Mr. and Mrs. Chun Chiu Stanford Graduate Fellowship, Hewlett-Packard Fellowship, the Stanford Clean Slate Program, and the National Science Foundation under grants CNS-0904609, CNS-0644114, and CNS-0832820.

9. REFERENCES

[1] V. Adhikari, Y. Guo, F. Hao, V. Hilt, and Z.-L. Zhang. A Tale of Three CDNs: An Active Measurement Study of Hulu and its CDNs. In *Proceedings of IEEE Conference on Computer Communications Workshops (INFOCOM WKSHPS)*, pages 7–12, March 2012.

[2] V. K. Adhikari, Y. Guo, F. Hao, M. Varvello, V. Hilt, M. Steiner, and Z.-L. Zhang. Unreeling Netflix: Understanding and Improving Multi-CDN Movie Delivery. In *Proceedings of the IEEE INFOCOM 2012, Orlando, FL, USA*, pages 1620–1628, March 2012.

[3] S. Akhshabi, L. Anantakrishnan, C. Dovrolis, and A. Begen. What Happens When HTTP Adaptive Streaming Players Compete for Bandwidth? In *Proceedings of the ACM Workshop on Network and Operating Systems Support for Digital Audio and Video (NOSSDAV)*, June 2012.

[4] S. Akhshabi, C. Dovrolis, and A. Begen. An Experimental Evaluation of Rate Adaptation Algorithms in Adaptive Streaming over HTTP. In *Proceedings of the ACM Multimedia Systems Conference (MMSys)*, San Jose, CA, USA, Feburary 2011.

[5] M. Allman, V. Paxson, and E. Blanton. TCP Congestion Control. RFC 5681 (Draft Standard), Sept. 2009.

[6] M. Allman, V. Paxson, and W. Stevens. TCP Congestion Control. RFC 2581 (Proposed Standard), Apr. 1999. Obsoleted by RFC 5681, updated by RFC 3390.

[7] MPEG DASH specification (ISO/IEC DIS 23009-1.2), 2011.

[8] L. De Cicco, S. Mascolo, and V. Palmisano. Feedback Control for Adaptive Live Video Streaming. In *Proceedings of the ACM Multimedia Systems Conference (MMSys)*, Febrary 2011.

[9] F. Dobrian, A. Awan, D. Joseph, A. Ganjam, J. Zhan, V. Sekar, I. Stoica, and H. Zhang. Understanding the Impact of Video Quality on User Engagement. In *Proceedings of the ACM SIGCOMM*, Toronto, Canada, August 2011.

[10] M. Ghobadi, Y. Cheng, A. Jain, and M. Mathis. Trickle: Rate Limiting YouTube Video Streaming. In *Proceedings of the USENIX Annual Technical Conference (ATC)*, page 6, 2012.

[11] P. Gill, M. Arlitt, Z. Li, and A. Mahanti. Youtube Traffic Characterization: A View From the Edge. In *Proceedings of the ACM SIGCOMM conference on Internet Measurement (IMC)*, pages 15–28, 2007.

[12] L. Kontothanassis. Content Delivery Considerations for Different Types of Internet Video. In *Proceedings of the ACM Multimedia Systems Conference (MMSys) – Keynote*, Chapel Hill, NC, USA, Febrary 2012.

[13] C. Liu, I. Bouazizi, and M. Gabbouj. Parallel Adaptive HTTP Media Streaming. In *Proceedings of the IEEE International Conference on Computer Communications and Networks (ICCCN)*, pages 1–6, 2011.

[14] X. Liu, F. Dobrian, H. Milner, J. Jiang, V. Sekar, I. Stoica, and H. Zhang. A Case for a Coordinated Internet Video Control Plane. In *Proceedings of the ACM SIGCOMM*, Helsinki, Finland, August 2012.

[15] J. W. Lockwood, N. McKeown, G. Watson, G. Gibb, P. Hartke, J. Naous, R. Raghuraman, and J. Luo. NetFPGA–An Open Platform for Gigabit-Rate Network Switching and Routing. In *MSE '07:*

Proceedings of the 2007 IEEE International Conference on Microelectronic Systems Education, pages 160–161, 2007.

[16] K. Miller, E. Quacchio, G. Gennari, and A. Wolisz. Adaptation algorithm for adaptive streaming over HTTP. In *Proceedings of the IEEE International Packet Video Workshop (PV)*, pages 173–178, May 2012.

[17] R. Mok, X. Luo, E. Chan, and R. Chang. QDASH: a QoE-aware DASH system. In *Proceedings of the ACM Multimedia Systems Conference (MMSys)*, pages 11–22, Febrary 2012.

[18] Sandvine: Global Internet Phenomena Report. `http://www.sandvine.com/news/pr_detail.asp?ID=312`.

[19] A. Rao, A. Legout, Y. Lim, D. Towsley, C. Barakat, and W. Dabbous. Network characteristics of video streaming traffic. In *Proceedings of the ACM COnference on emerging Networking EXperiments and Technologies (CONEXT)*, page 25. ACM, 2011.

[20] RTMPDump. `http://rtmpdump.mplayerhq.hu/`.

[21] Consumer Report: Streaming Video Services Rating. `http://www.consumerreports.org/cro/magazine/2012/09/best-streaming-video-services/`.

[22] M. Watson. HTTP Adaptive Streaming in Practice. In *Proceedings of the ACM Multimedia Systems Conference (MMSys) – Keynote*, San Jose, CA, USA, Febrary 2011.

[23] S. Xiang, L. Cai, and J. Pan. Adaptive Scalable Video Streaming in Wireless Networks. In *Proceedings of the ACM Multimedia Systems Conference (MMSys)*, pages 167–172, Febrary 2012.

[24] M. Zink, K. Suh, Y. Gu, and J. Kurose. Characteristics of YouTube network traffic at a campus network - Measurements, models, and implications. In *Computer Networks, Volume 53, Issue 4*, pages 501–514. Elsevier, 2009.

Routing State Distance: A Path-based Metric for Network Analysis

Gonca Gürsun, Natali Ruchansky, Evimaria Terzi, and Mark Crovella
Department of Computer Science
Boston University

ABSTRACT

Characterizing the set of routes used between domains is an important and difficult problem. The size and complexity of the millions of BGP paths in use at any time can hide important phenomena and hinder attempts to understand the path selection behavior of ASes. In this paper we introduce a new approach to analysis of the interdomain routing system designed to shed light on collective routing policies. Our approach starts by defining a new metric for 'distance' between prefixes, which we call routing state distance (RSD). We show that RSD has a number of properties that make it attractive for use in visualizing and analyzing the state of the BGP system. Further, since RSD is a metric, it lends itself naturally to use in clustering prefixes or ASes. In fact, the properties of RSD allow us to define a natural clustering criterion, and we show that this criterion admits to a simple clustering algorithm with provable approximation guarantees. We then show that by clustering ASes using RSD, one can uncover macroscopic behavior in BGP that was previously hidden. For example, we show how to identify groups of ASes having similar routing policies with respect to certain destinations, which apparently reflects shared sensitivity to economic or performance considerations. These routing patterns represent a considerable generalization and extension of the notion of BGP atoms to the case where routing policies are only locally and approximately similar across a set of prefixes.

Categories and Subject Descriptors

C.2.3 [**Network Operations**]: Network monitoring; C.2.5 [**Local and Wide-Area Networks**]: Internet — BGP

Keywords

BGP, Interdomain Routing

1. INTRODUCTION

One of the principal challenges in working with measurements of Internet topology is to extract insight from massive, complex datasets. Many projects have collected extensive measurements of Internet topology at the router or autonomous-system (AS) level, but comparatively few tools have been developed to discover important patterns or structures in the resulting data. The lack of such tools makes it difficult to visualize the Internet topology, understand the routing behavior of ASes, and detect significant changes in Internet routing.

In this paper, we define a new metric for analyzing routing at the interdomain level, and we describe various kinds of useful data analysis that the metric enables. The metric is called *routing state distance (RSD)*; it measures 'closeness' between two prefixes in terms of *similarity of routing* to the prefixes.

The key idea behind *RSD* can be stated simply: the routing state distance between two prefixes is conceptually just *the number of ASes that disagree about the next hop* to the two prefixes. (Later we will make this notion precise and deal with the practical issues that arise in applying it to real BGP measurements.) The basic idea is illustrated in Figure 1. Figures 1(a), (b), and (c) each show the next hops from a set of ASes to different destinations. The routing state distance between the destinations in (a) and (b) is 3, because there are three ASes that choose different next hops between (a) and (b). Likewise, the routing state distance between the destinations in (b) and (c) is 5.

The key properties of *RSD* can be understood by contrasting it with typical measures of distance between ASes. The most common starting point is the AS graph – a graph in which nodes are ASes – and distance is traditionally thought of as some number of hops between ASes. In contrast, *RSD* is *not* defined in terms of a graph; rather, it is defined in terms of a set of *paths.* This has a number of advantages. First of all, it is well-known that measurements of the AS graph are highly incomplete (a recent review of this problem is [17]). By defining *RSD* in terms of AS paths rather than the AS graph, the problem of missing edges in the AS graph does not arise. This is a crucial advantage, given the large fraction of missing edges in AS graph measurements. Second, as we will show later, the set of paths to a prefix is a much richer characterization of the prefix's location than is its position in the AS graph. As a result, *RSD* can provide much more nuanced information about the relative location of two (or more) prefixes than can be provided by simply noting their position in a graph.

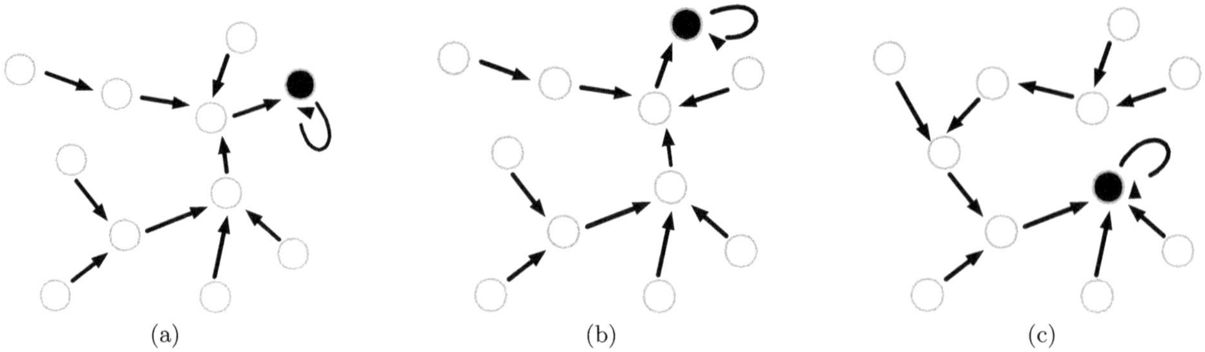

Figure 1: Example illustrating *RSD*. In each figure the filled node is the destination.

Having defined *RSD*, we next explore its utility. We show that it has a number of desirable properties. First, it is a metric (it obeys the triangle inequality), which makes it easy to reason about. Second, we show that it defines fine-grained neighborhoods — the number of prefixes that are within distance d of a given prefix declines smoothly with decreasing d. Third, we show that *RSD* generally exhibits *low effective dimension,* which means that 2-D visualizations can capture most of the information present in a set of *RSD* measurements. And fourth, we show that *RSD* has a natural clustering criterion, and that criterion has an associated clustering algorithm with provable approximation guarantees.

Most importantly, these four properties together allow us to develop an analytic toolkit that we use to uncover surprising patterns and behaviors that have not previously been documented in the interdomain routing system. Using the *RSD* toolkit we demonstrate the existence of collective routing behavior that we call *local atoms.* Roughly, a local atom is a set of prefixes that are routed similarly, but *only in some region* of the Internet. We show the existence of local atoms spanning a wide range of sizes, from macroscopic (Internet-wide) to microscopic. Although detecting these sorts of patterns in data is hard in general, we show that *RSD* and its associated clustering tools are natural and effective ways to uncover local atoms in BGP data.

Finally, we note that *RSD,* as a measure of distance between ASes, was first introduced by Gürsun et al. [10]. However, that paper used *RSD* for a specific purpose (as an input to a particular inference algorithm), and did not focus on the exploration of the theoretical and practical properties of *RSD* as a distance measure. In this paper, we fill this gap by studying the geometric properties of *RSD* and by defining notions of clustering appropriately tailored to this measure. Finally, we provide a thorough experimental study, which demonstrates the utility of *RSD* and the clusters identified by our clustering framework. Although our present study is motivated by the concept of *RSD* defined in [10], none of the results we present here were anticipated or discussed in that previous paper.

2. ROUTING STATE DISTANCE

In this section we define *RSD* starting from a general definition for arbitrary graphs. We then discuss how to customize *RSD* to address the practical issues that arise when applying it to BGP measurements.

2.1 Definition

To define RSD, we will assume a universe X of nodes, with $|X| = n$.[1] To fix a set of paths, we require that for each source-destination pair (x_1, x_2) there is a unique node x_3, which is the *next hop* on the path from x_1 to x_2. We denote this by $x_3 = \mathbf{N}(x_1, x_2)$. Note by following the nodes on $\mathbf{N}(\cdot, x_2)$ recursively, one will eventually reach x_2. We also assume that the next hop of every node x is the node itself; i.e., $\mathbf{N}(x, x) = x$. Thus, $\mathbf{N}$ encodes a set of paths that leads from each node to every other node, without any branches or loops.

We generally treat the function $\mathbf{N}$ as an $n \times n$ matrix. That is, we interpret $\mathbf{N}(x', x)$ as a matrix element that stores the next hop from node x' to node x. We also use $\mathbf{N}(x, :)$ (resp. $\mathbf{N}(:, x)$) to denote the x-th row (resp. column) of $\mathbf{N}$. We call $\mathbf{N}$ the *nexthop* matrix that encodes the paths over the set X.

Using the *nexthop* matrix, we can define the *Routing State Distance* (*RSD*) between two nodes x_1 and x_2 as follows:

$$RSD(x_1, x_2) = |\{x_i \mid \mathbf{N}(x_i, x_1) \neq \mathbf{N}(x_i, x_2)\}|. \quad (1)$$

That is, $RSD(x_1, x_2)$ is the number of positions where the columns $\mathbf{N}(:, x_1)$ and $\mathbf{N}(:, x_2)$ differ. Hence, by definition, *RSD* is an integer that takes values in $\{0, \ldots, n\}$. Referring back to Figure 1, each of the subfigures (a), (b), and (c) corresponds to a single column $\mathbf{N}(:, x)$ for different values of x. Intuitively, $\mathbf{N}(:, x)$ tells us what the 'direction' is to x from each node in X. Two nodes that appear to most other nodes to be in the same direction are considered close under *RSD*.

We now show that *RSD* satisfies the triangle inequality.

PROPOSITION 1. *For any nodes* x_1, x_2, *and* x_3, $\mathrm{RSD}(x_1, x_2) \leq \mathrm{RSD}(x_1, x_3) + \mathrm{RSD}(x_2, x_3)$.

PROOF. Assume the opposite, i.e., that $RSD(x_1, x_2) > RSD(x_1, x_3) + RSD(x_2, x_3)$. Then there must be a node x for which $\mathbf{N}(x, x_1) \neq \mathbf{N}(x, x_2)$, but for which $\mathbf{N}(x, x_1) = \mathbf{N}(x, x_3)$ and $\mathbf{N}(x, x_2) = \mathbf{N}(x, x_3)$, which is a contradiction. □

Oftentimes, we use *rsd* to refer to the normalized value of *RSD.* That is, for every x_1, x_2 we define the normalized *RSD* as follows:

$$rsd(x_1, x_2) = \frac{1}{n} RSD(x_1, x_2). \quad (2)$$

[1]Note that the definition given here is essentially equivalent to that in [10], but has been recast in somewhat different terms for simplicity of discussion.

By definition, $rsd(x_1, x_2) \in [0, 1]$ and – given that it is a rescaling of *RSD* – it also satisfies the triangle inequality. Intuitively, the the *rsd* value between two nodes x_1 and x_2 encodes the *fraction* of positions in which the columns $\mathbf{N}(:, x_1)$ and $\mathbf{N}(:, x_2)$ differ with each other.

2.2 Applying RSD to BGP Analysis

Having defined *RSD*, we next seek to apply it to a dataset of publicly available BGP paths so as to compute the *RSD* between prefix pairs in the dataset. However, computing *RSD* from BGP data raises some implementation considerations.

The first issue concerns the distinction between ASes (which choose next hops, but are not themselves destinations) and prefixes (which are destinations, but do not make next-hop choices). In fact, our framework can adapt to this situation easily. We slightly redefine the matrix $\mathbf{N}$: while the columns of $\mathbf{N}$ correspond to prefixes, the rows of $\mathbf{N}$ correspond to ASes. Thus, to analyze BGP, $\mathbf{N}(a, p)$ needs to be defined as the next hop from AS a on the path to prefix p.

The next issue concerns the fact that publicly available BGP data consists (essentially) of paths from a set of monitor ASes to a large collection of prefixes. For any given AS-prefix pair (a, p), these paths may not contain information about $\mathbf{N}(a, p)$. We address this by *approximating RSD.* We make the following observation: some ASes have a much larger impact on *RSD* than others. For example, a stub AS a has a highly uniform row $\mathbf{N}(a, :)$. If the stub AS a has a small set of providers, then for many prefixes $p_1, p_2, ...$, $\mathbf{N}(a, p_1) = \mathbf{N}(a, p_2) = ...$ In the limit of a stub AS that makes use of only a single provider, the row $\mathbf{N}(a, :)$ will be constant. Note that a constant row in $\mathbf{N}$ has no effect on the *RSD* value of any prefix pairs. Since the majority of ASes are stub ASes, *most ASes contribute little information to RSD.*

Thus, we observe that we can approximate *RSD* using just a subset of all ASes. In particular we should use the ASes with many neighbors since these ASes have many next hop choices and therefore can contribute the most information to *RSD*. We call these ASes the *basis set.* We select the basis set by identifying those ASes with the largest number of neighbors in our data.[2] Luckily, such ASes tend to appear on many paths in the publicly available data; hence we can often find $\mathbf{N}(a, p)$ when a is in the basis set.

To address the case when $\mathbf{N}(a, p)$ is not available (for AS a in the basis set), we performed extensive studies of the effect of missing *nexthop* information on *RSD*. We found that proportional approximation yields results that work well in practice. This approximation allows the matrix $\mathbf{N}$ to include 'don't know' elements. We then approximate *RSD* by the fraction of *known* positions in which $\mathbf{N}(:, p_1)$ and $\mathbf{N}(:, p_2)$ differ, times the number of ASes in the basis set. This ensures that the approximation to *RSD* always ranges between zero and the size of the basis set.

One consequence of using proportional approximation to *RSD* is that it can introduce minor violations of the triangle inequality. However we find that in practice, such violations are quite small and do not impair our ability to reason about *RSD* or use it as if it were a metric.

The last issue is that for some AS-prefix pairs there is more than one next hop. This happens when an AS uses detailed routing policies (such as hot-potato routing) that are not strictly per-neighbor. That is, traffic destined for the same prefix may take different next hops depending on where it enters the network. We address this problem the same way as in [14], i.e., by introducing the notion of 'quasi-routers.' Using the algorithm in [14] we divide each AS in the basis set into a minimal set of quasi-routers such that for each (quasi-router, prefix) pair there is a unique next hop AS. Thus, the rows of $\mathbf{N}$ correspond either to ASes or quasi-routers of ASes.

[2]Two nodes are neighbors if they appear consecutively on any path.

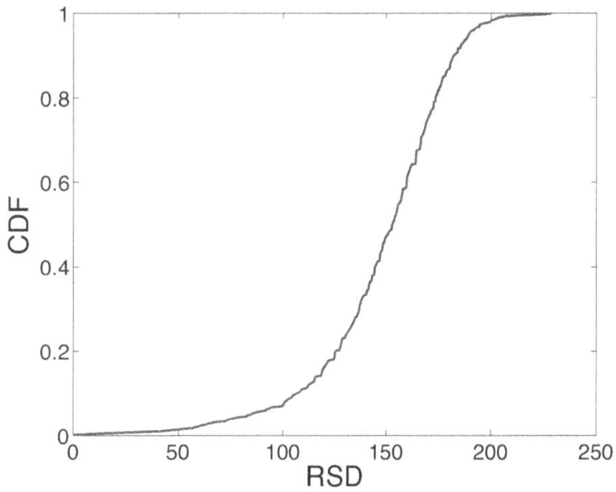

Figure 2: Distribution of $\mathbf{D}$ for 1000 prefix pairs.

Having addressed these issues, we can compute our version of *RSD* specialized for BGP, which we store in the $n \times n$ matrix $\mathbf{D}$. Clearly, the values of the cells of $\mathbf{D}$ depend on the number of rows in $\mathbf{N}$, i.e., the total number of ASes (or quasi-routers of ASes). For the rest of the discussion we will assume that we have m such ASes and therefore $\mathbf{N}$ is of size $m \times n$ and $\mathbf{D}(x, x') \in \{0, \ldots, m\}$. We also use $\widetilde{\mathbf{D}}$ to denote the normalized *rsd* for BGP.

3. DATASETS

To evaluate our methods, we use a collection of BGP tables collected on midnight UTC on December 6, 2011 from the Routeviews [18] and RIPE [16] repositories.

The full dataset is collected from 359 unique monitors; it consists of over 48 million AS paths, and contains 454,804 unique destination prefixes. However, the dataset does not contain paths from every monitors to every prefix. Rather, there is a subset of prefixes that appear in most tables, i.e., to which most monitors have paths. We chose a subset of 135,369 prefixes on this basis; these prefixes are typically present in most BGP tables in our dataset.

Next, we need to select a subset of monitors to serve as the basis set, as described in Section 2.2. We select the basis set by identifying 77 ASes with the largest number of neighbors in our data. Finally, we expand the basis set with quasi-routers to handle the cases where there is not a unique next hop to certain prefixes. This expands the size of the basis set from 77 to 243. Hence, our final $\mathbf{N}$ matrix is of size 243 $\times$ 135,369.

From $\mathbf{N}$ we can compute $\mathbf{D}$, our *RSD* metric based on BGP paths applied to prefixes. To illustrate the distribution

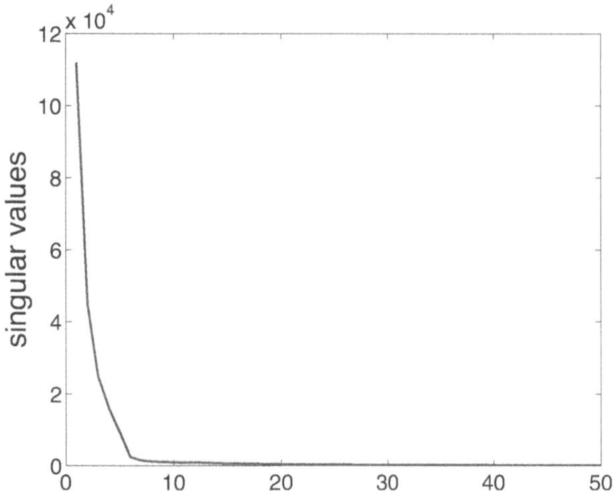

Figure 3: Singular values of **D**.

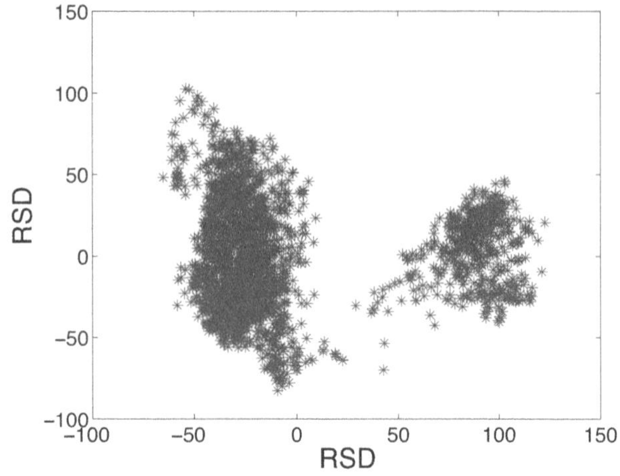

Figure 4: Visualization of *RSD* for 3000 randomly chosen prefixes. Axes are marked in units of *RSD* to give a sense of scale to the plots.

of **D** values, Figure 2 shows the CDF of **D** for a randomly chosen set of 1000 prefix pairs. The figure shows three important aspects of *RSD* applied to prefixes. First, it takes on values in the range 0 to 243, because there are 243 ASes and quasi-routers in the basis set. Second, it varies smoothly – there are no sudden jumps or steps in the distance function. This is in contrast to a metric like hop distance, in which going from hop distance 1 to hop distance 2 encompasses a huge increase in the number of prefix pairs. Finally, the gradual slope on the left of the figure shows that *RSD* can make fine distinctions between prefix pairs. The number of prefixes in a neighborhood grows very slowly for small to moderate values of *RSD*, which means that *RSD* can be used to identify fine-grained groups of prefixes. This capability will be important when we use *RSD* for clustering later in the paper.

4. VISUALIZATION WITH RSD

In this section, we motivate the use of *RSD* for visualization and we demonstrate that visualization using *RSD* can yield useful insights in the analysis of interdomain routing.

4.1 Why 2-D Visualization is Meaningful

As described in Section 2, the information provided by RSD can be organized into a distance matrix **D** in which $\mathbf{D}(i,j) = RSD(i,j)$. We seek a way to effectively visualize the information contained in **D**.

To do so, we start by observing that in practice, we find that **D** has *low effective rank.* That is, although **D** is a $n \times n$ matrix it can be well approximated by a matrix of rank r with $r \ll n$. A simple way to assess this is through a *scree plot,* which is a plot of the singular values of **D** in decreasing order. The sum of the first k squared singular values is equal to the fraction of total variance in **D** that can be captured in a rank-k approximation. Thus, the scree plot of **D** gives a direct assessment of the effective rank of **D**.

We start by choosing 3000 prefixes at random from the set of all 135,369 prefixes in our dataset. We then form the 3000×3000 matrix **D** consisting of the RSD values for all prefix pairs. The scree plot of **D** is shown in Figure 3.

The Figure shows that **D** has very low effective rank – almost all of the the variation in **D** is captured in five dimensions, and even a rank-2 approximation to **D** captures more than half of **D**'s total variance. (Results for other random samples look very similar).

The fact that **D** has low effective rank is important for a number of reasons. First, it suggests that (as we will demonstrate) *RSD* captures specific phenomena – were the matrix **D** purely random, it would have high effective rank. Second, from a visualization standpoint, it indicates that a large fraction of the total information captured by *RSD* can be represented in a 2-D or 3-D visualization.

Thus, Figure 3 suggests that even a 2-D visualization of **D** should give a reasonably accurate picture of its information content. The usual way to construct such a visualization is by using *multidimensional scaling* (MDS) [19]. Given a set of items I and a set of item-item distances $\{d_{ij}\}$, $i, j \in I$, MDS assigns each item a location x_i, $i \in I$ in some r-dimensional Euclidean space. The goal is that distances between items in Euclidean space should closely approximate the given set of input distances $\{d_{ij}\}$. That is, MDS seeks to minimize:

$$\min_{x_1,\ldots,x_{|I|}} \sum_{i<j} \left(||x_i - x_j|| - d_{ij}\right)^2 .$$

When $r = 2$, the result can be plotted; in such a plot, distances (i.e., *RSD* values) are approximately preserved.

4.2 The Emergence of Clusters

We use MDS to visualize the randomly chosen set of 3000 prefixes. The results are shown in Figure 4; distances between points in this figure approximate *RSD.* The figure shows remarkable high-level structure: there are two large clusters, with the smaller cluster comprising about 23% of all prefixes. We find this same clustering quite consistently for *any* random sampling of prefixes; it seems to be an Internet-wide phenomenon.

The fact that Internet prefixes cluster into two distinct groups under the *RSD* metric is surprising. In fact, understanding the reason behind the presence of the two clusters in Figure 4 is important and motivates our subsequent analyses. Hence, we will now explore the cause of these two clusters in depth.

First, we consider exactly what causes clustering under

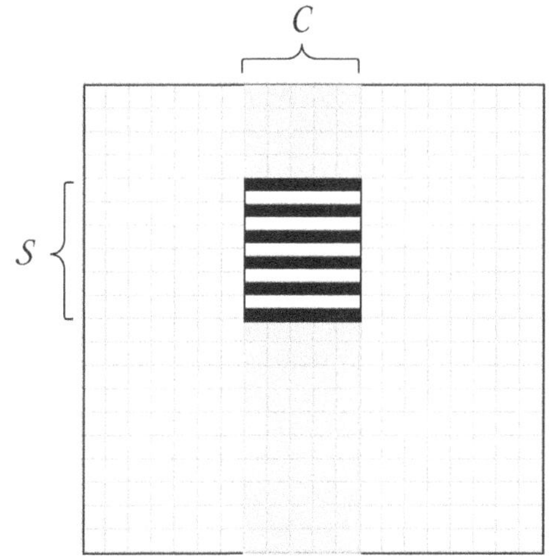

Figure 5: A cluster within the *nexthop* matrix **N**.

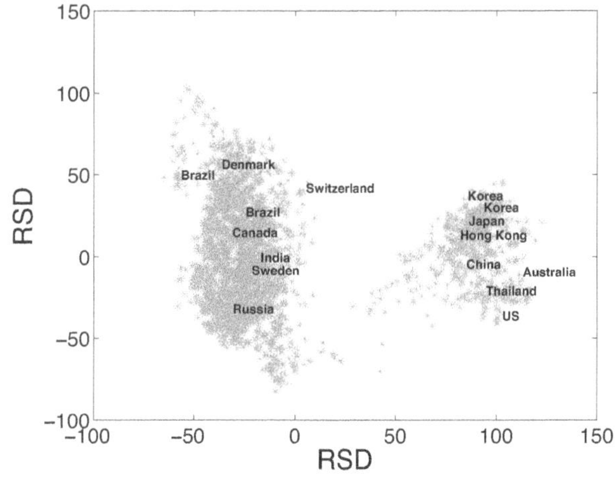

Figure 6: Locations of a random subset of prefixes.

RSD. Consider a cluster of prefixes C. This cluster corresponds to a set of columns of $\mathbf{N}$, i.e., $\mathbf{N}(:, C)$. Because the prefixes in C are close to each other in *RSD*, the columns of $\mathbf{N}(:, C)$ are similar to each other, at least in certain positions. This must be the case, by the definition of *RSD*.

This situation is shown in Figure 5. The figure shows the *nexthop* matrix $\mathbf{N}$, where cluster C is shown in gray. The fact that the columns are similar in certain positions S is signified by the horizontal bars. Note that for the columns to be similar, rows in S must be constant (or at least nearly constant).[3] The region where the rows are constant is the submatrix $\mathbf{N}(S, C)$. (We have assumed that the columns and rows of $\mathbf{N}$ have been reordered to bring out this structure.)

The key fact is that, in order for the prefixes in C to cluster together, there will typically be a subset of rows S with the following property: for any row within the submatrix $\mathbf{N}(S, C)$, the next hop AS in each cell must be (nearly) always the same AS. That is, the entries of $\mathbf{N}(S, C)$ are expected to be highly coherent.

Thus, we can identify a cluster with a coherent submatrix $\mathbf{N}(S, C)$. To understand what such coherent submatrices signify, we consider how they arise in the course of BGP routing. Expressed in terms of BGP, $\mathbf{N}(S, C)$ captures a set of source ASes (S) that *all make similar routing decisions* with respect to a set of destination ASes (C, i.e., the cluster). In Section 6, we use different measures to quantify and evaluate the coherence of the submatrix $\mathbf{N}(S, C)$.

We refer to the pair (S, C) as a *local atom.* A local atom is a generalization of the notion of BGP atoms [6]. Whereas a BGP atom is a set of prefixes that are routed the same way by all routers in the Internet, a local atom is a set of prefixes that are routed similarly *in some region* of the Internet (i.e., by the ASes in S). To be interesting, a local atom (S, C) should have a significant number of ASes in S and also prefixes in C.

To illustrate the concept of a local atom, we return to the example in Figure 4. The smaller cluster turns out to be the result of a local atom. We demonstrate this as follows. Sampling the prefixes in the smaller cluster, we find that they belong primarily to networks in the Far East, with a small portion belonging to networks in the US. For example, out of a random sample of 100 prefixes we find that 64% are Far East and Pacific Rim networks (including Korea, Japan, Taiwan, Thailand, Singapore, China, Hong Kong, Australia, and New Zealand) and 30% are from North America. However, there are also many Far Eastern (29%) and North American (20%) prefixes in the larger cluster (along with 33% European, which are almost completely absent in the smaller cluster).[4] Figure 6 shows examples of where a random selection of these prefixes occurs within the two clusters.

Given that Far Eastern and US prefixes occur in both clusters, why then should this specific set of Far Eastern and US prefixes group together in the smaller cluster?

The answer has to do with the next-hop decisions made by the source set S. There are 35 ASes in the S set; they are predominantly in Europe (52%) and North America (40%). These ASes prefer one particular provider for transit to the Far East and US. This provider is Hurricane Electric, ASN 6939 ('HE'). The overwhelming presence of AS 6939 as a next-hop results in the observed coherence of $\mathbf{N}(S, C)$. On the other hand, the set of ASes in S does not commonly agree on next hops to destinations in Europe. Therefore, these prefixes do not occur in the local atom. Instead, those prefixes appear in the larger cluster in Figure 4.

Figure 7 is a visualization of a portion of the *nexthop* matrix $\mathbf{N}$. In this plot, colors represent the five most popular next-hop ASes across both clusters. The prefixes (columns) consist of 50 samples chosen at random from each of the two clusters. The first 35 rows correspond to the ASes in set S and the remaining rows are other ASes shown for compar-

[3]Strictly speaking, it is possible to construct a cluster without a common set of similar rows; but such an arrangement is highly unlikely in practice as it requires a very specific structure. In all the cluster examples we study, we find that the prefixes cluster together because of a common set of similar rows.

[4]The assignment of a prefix to a geographic region was done by noting the AS that announced the prefix, and then combining information from the various routing registries along with inspection of network maps and peering relationships where available. In particular, for prefixes that were announced by internationally distributed ASes, care was taken to identify the region the prefix originated from.

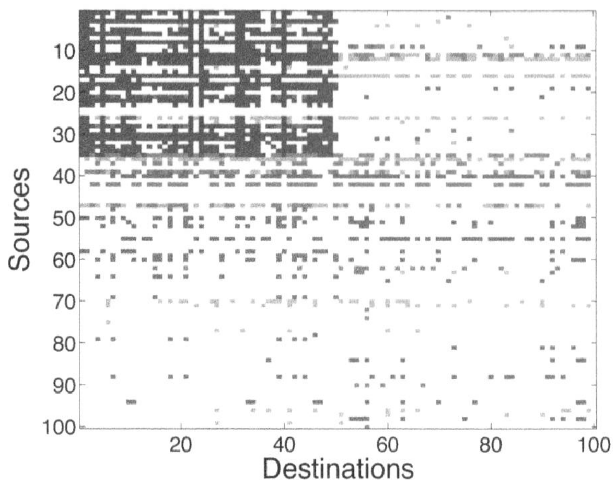

Figure 7: Coherence of the $\mathbf{N}(S, C)$ submatrix for the smaller cluster. The five most frequently-occurring ASes are shown in color: 6939 (Hurricane Electric, blue), 10026 (Pacnet, green), 3257 (TiNet, red), 3356 (Level3, turquoise), and 3549 (Global Crossing, magenta).

ison. The local atom (S, C) can be seen as the submatrix $\mathbf{N}(S, C)$ in the upper left part of the plot.

The figure shows the remarkable coherence of the $\mathbf{N}(S, C)$ submatrix. The similarity of the columns on the left side of the plot is the reason that those prefixes cluster together in Figure 4. It also shows that, while sources in S clearly distinguish between prefixes in the two clusters, other sources do not.

In fact, the prefixes that occur in the smaller cluster have the following property: if *any* path from a monitor to a prefix in our dataset passes through Hurricane Electric, then that prefix is in the smaller cluster. This remarkable fact is illustrated in Figure 8. The figure shows which prefixes can be reached from one or more monitors through three of the most commonly occurring ASes in our data: (a) Level 3, (b) Hurricane Electric, and (c) Sprint. The figure shows that what determines which prefixes go into the smaller cluster is whether the prefix can be reached through Hurricane Electric.

An example of routing to one such prefix is shown in Figure 9 (generated using BGPlay [4]). The prefix is one of those that falls into the smaller cluster. The figure shows how Hurricane Electric (ASN 6939) plays a special role with respect to this prefix for a large set of ASes. The presence of the smaller cluster is a result of routing patterns similar to Figure 9 for all the prefixes in the cluster.

To uncover the reasons behind this effect, we consulted with a number of the network operators whose BGP configurations contributed to the clustering (that is, operators of networks in the source set S). As a result, we can explain the reason for this unusual routing behavior with respect to Hurricane Electric: HE is a large ISP, but it has an open peering policy. That is, any ISP that has a presence in an exchange point in common with HE will be allowed to peer with HE at that exchange point [12]. HE is present in dozens of exchange points, mainly in the US and Europe (but with some in the Far East).

Note that most operators will prefer peer routes over provider routes in general. This implies that an ISP that peers with HE will typically use HE as the next-hop to reach any network that is a customer of HE (and not one of its own customers). Hence, we can identify S as largely consisting of networks that peer with HE, and D as the set of networks that are customers (or customers of customers, etc.) of HE.

Thus, the presence of two clusters among Internet prefixes is due to a large-scale phenomenon: for many ASes, Hurricane Electric is the preferred next hop for *any prefixes for which it provides transit.* Thus this local atom is a case of similar decision making by independent entities (ASes) when driven by common external factors; in this case, it seems that the particular, open peering policy used by HE is responsible for the observed similarity of routing behavior.

Hence, we conclude that clustering in *RSD* space has the potential to uncover local atoms, and local atoms are evidence of (generally unexpected) synchronization of routing decisions among certain ASes with respect to certain destinations. We then naturally ask the question: besides the macroscopic cluster shown in Figure 4, are there other local atoms, corresponding to other clusters, in our data? Presumably these clusters are at smaller scale and thus will be much harder to find. This motivates us to consider the problem of clustering in *RSD* space more analytically, and to look for efficient and effective methods of clustering for *RSD*.

5. CLUSTERING WITH RSD

Finding a natural clustering for prefixes using the *RSD* metric is challenging. Common clustering methods either operate over a continuous metric space (e.g., k-means) or others (e.g., k-median) require defining the notion of a 'representative' object for each cluster (i.e., the object that minimizes the sum of the distances to all other points in the cluster). Unfortunately, our data are not continuous; each data point is a column of the nexthop matrix and therefore its elements are categorical. Secondly, the notion of a representative in the *RSD* metric space is not clear. Further, most clustering algorithms require the number of clusters as input. Here we show that the *RSD* metric has a natural clustering formulation that does not have these drawbacks. Throughout this section, we will use the generic definition of *RSD* (or *rsd*) on a set of prefixes – which we refer to as nodes. In practice, we make the adaptations discussed in Section 2.2 and use $\mathbf{D}$ (resp. $\widetilde{\mathbf{D}}$) instead of *RSD* (resp. *rsd*).

5.1 The RS-CLUSTERING problem

Given a set X of n prefixes, our goal is to produce a *partition* $\mathcal{P}$ of X; every prefix $x \in X$ belongs only to one cluster of $\mathcal{P}$, denoted by $\mathcal{P}(x)$. (Note that we will often overload notation and use partition names like $\mathcal{P}$ as labeling functions that map prefixes to clusters.)

Intuitively, a good partition satisfies the property that the routing state distance between two prefixes x and x' in the same cluster ($\mathcal{P}(x) = \mathcal{P}(x')$) should be minimized, while the routing state distance between prefixes x and x' in different clusters ($\mathcal{P}(x) \neq \mathcal{P}(x')$) should be maximized. This intuition can be captured in the following formal definition of the RS-CLUSTERING problem.

PROBLEM 1 (RS-CLUSTERING). *Given a set of nodes* $X = \{x_1, \ldots, x_n\}$ *and the* $m \times n$ *nexthop matrix* $\mathbf{N}$*, find*

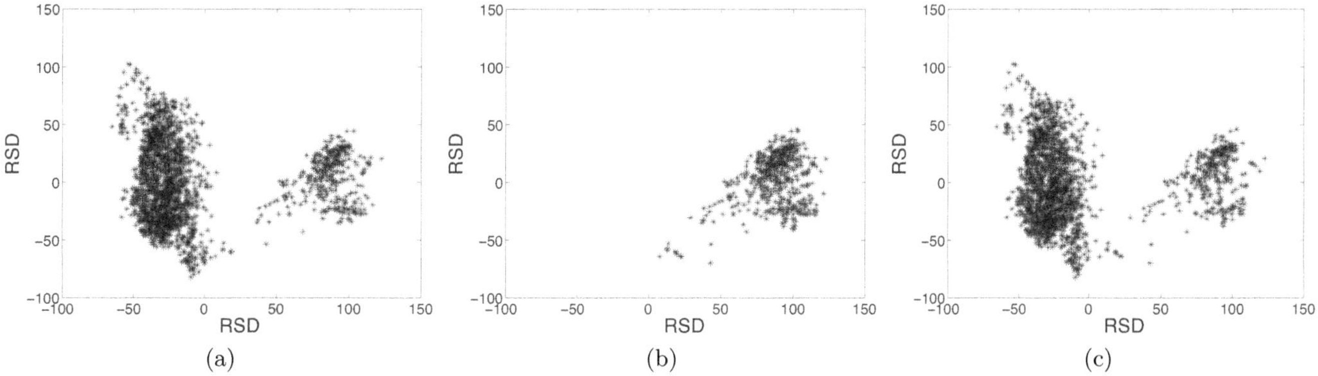

Figure 8: Prefixes that can be reached from one or more monitor ASes through (a) Level3, (b) Hurricane Electric, or (c) Sprint.

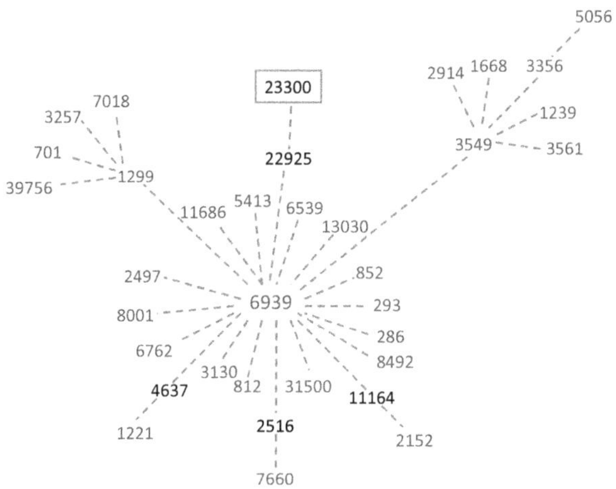

Figure 9: BGPlay snapshot of prefix 64.72.205.0/24 (origin AS: 23300) which occurs in the smaller cluster.

a partition $\mathcal{P}$ of the nodes in X such that

$$\text{P-Cost}(\mathcal{P}) = \sum_{\substack{x,x':\\ \mathcal{P}(x)=\mathcal{P}(x')}} \mathbf{D}(x,x') + \sum_{\substack{x,x':\\ \mathcal{P}(x)\neq\mathcal{P}(x')}} \left(m - \mathbf{D}(x,x')\right).$$

is minimized.

Observe that the definition of the RS-CLUSTERING problem does not require the number of clusters to be part of the input. That is, RS-CLUSTERING is *parameter-free.* This happens because the objective function of the clustering problem (i.e., the P-COST function) is not guaranteed to decrease as the number of clusters increases. This is in contrast with the objective functions of many classical clustering problems (e.g., k-means, k-median etc). Hence, there exists an optimal number of clusters that minimizes the P-COST function. A solution to RS-CLUSTERING provides both the clusters of the prefixes as well as the optimal number of clusters as part of its output.

Despite the fact that the RS-CLUSTERING problem is parameter free, its optimal solution cannot be computed in polynomial time. This is shown in the following proposition.

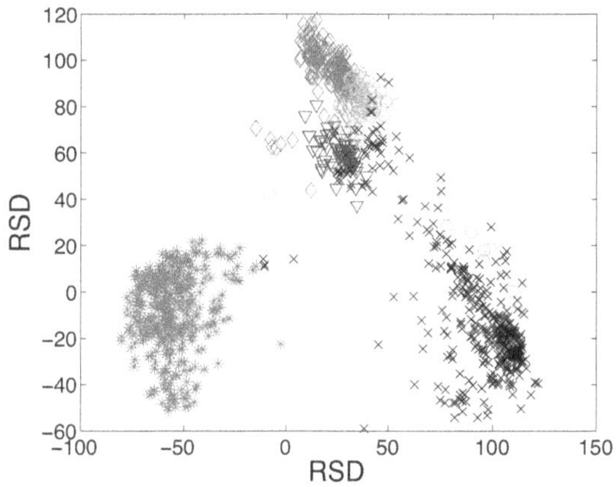

Figure 10: `Pivot` clustering of *RSD* with $\tau = 120$.

PROPOSITION 2. *The* RS-CLUSTERING *problem is NP-hard.*

The proof of the above proposition is by a reduction from the CLUSTERING AGGREGATION problem [2, 7, 8].

5.2 The `Pivot` algorithm

Based on the similarity between the RS-CLUSTERING problem with the CORRELATION CLUSTERING [3] and the CLUSTERING AGGREGATION [2, 8] problems, we propose solving the problem using the `Pivot` algorithm, which was first proposed for solving the CLUSTERING AGGREGATION problem.

The pseudocode of `Pivot` is shown in Algorithm 1. The algorithm takes as input the set of prefixes, their *RSD* values, and the value of a threshold parameter $\tau \in [0, m]$. The algorithm works as follows: starting from a random prefix x, it finds all prefixes that are within distance τ from x. All these prefixes are assigned in the same cluster – centered at prefix x. We call x the *pivot* of cluster C_x. The prefixes that are assigned in the cluster are removed from the set of prefixes X and the `Pivot` algorithm is reapplied to the remaining subset of prefixes that have not been assigned to any cluster.

Observe that `Pivot` requires the precomputation of all pairwise *RSD* distances. Given that these distances are known, the running time of `Pivot` is $O(n^2)$.

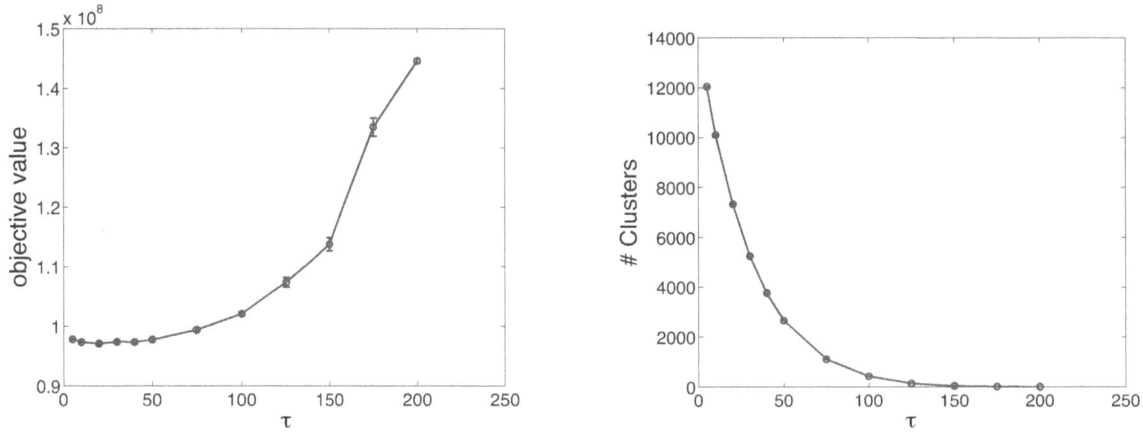

(a) (b)

Figure 11: (a) Value of P-COST and (b) number of clusters as clustering threshold τ varies.

Algorithm 1 The `Pivot` algorithm .

A set of prefixes $X = \{x_1, \ldots, x_n\}$ and a threshold $\tau \in [0, m]$.
A partition $\mathcal{P}$ of the prefixes

1: pick a random prefix $x \in X$
2: create a cluster $C_x = \{x' \mid \mathbf{D}(x, x') \leq \tau\}$
3: $X = X \setminus C_x$
4: `Pivot`(X, τ)

The quality of the solution output by `Pivot` can be measured using the P-COST function. An interesting observation is that a small rewriting of the P-COST function reveals that it is identical with the optimization function used for the CORRELATION CLUSTERING problem [2, 3]. Hence, using the results of Ailon et al. [2] we can state the following:

PROPOSITION 3. *For $\tau = m/2$, the* `Pivot` *algorithm is is an expected 3-approximation algorithm for the* RS-CLUSTERING *problem.*

Observe that `Pivot` is a randomized algorithm since at every recursive call it picks a random prefix to play the role of a pivot.

6. APPLICATIONS

In this section, we illustrate how the solutions of RS-CLUSTERING obtained using `Pivot`, automatically extract local atoms of $\mathbf{N}$.

We start by applying `Pivot` using the threshold $\tau = m/2$ as suggested by Proposition 3. This translates into $\tau = 120$ in our data.

Five large clusters identified by `Pivot` are shown in Figure 10. The sharpest separation is shown by the cluster in the lower left. Upon inspection, we find that the lower left cluster is in fact the Hurricane Electric cluster which was described in detail in Section 4. Note that whereas previously the Hurricane Electric cluster was identified manually, in this case it is extracted automatically through the use of `Pivot`. This provides good validation of the RS-CLUSTERING problem definition and our proposed solution obtained via `Pivot`.

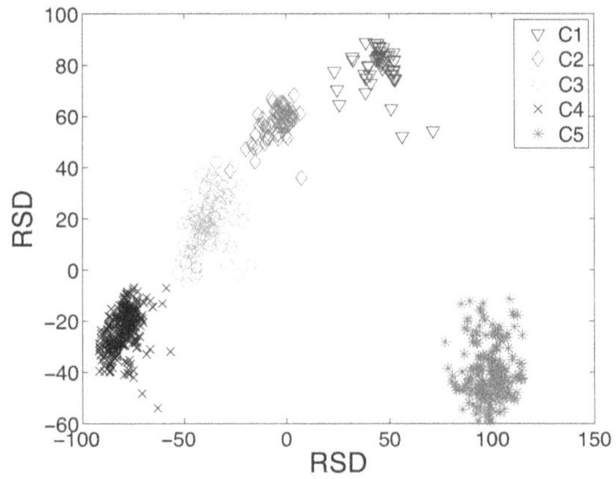

Figure 12: `Pivot` clustering of *RSD* with $\tau = 50$.

While Figure 10 shows that the Hurricane Electric cluster is clearly separated from the other prefixes, the other clusters are not so well separated. In fact, although `Pivot` with $\tau = m/2$ has a provable approximation bound, it is entirely possible that the algorithm may find a better solution with a different value of the threshold. We can assess the quality of a clustering simply by computing the value of the objective function P-COST. Figure 11(a) shows how the objective function varies by decreasing the threshold below $\tau = 120$. It shows that at a threshold τ of about 50, the quality of the clustering levels off, and below 25 or so it starts to climb again. Furthermore, Figure 11(b) shows the number of clusters found at each threshold, and shows that below a τ value of 50 the number of clusters becomes very large. In fact, below $\tau = 50$, many clusters are just singletons which are not interesting as local atoms. Hence we next apply `Pivot` using a threshold value of 50.

Five of the largest clusters found with a threshold of 50 are shown in Figure 12. (Note that these clusters are not the same as those shown in Figure 10; the two figures show outputs of different clustering runs.) Compared to those in Figure 10, these clusters show much sharper separation, and we find that each of these corresponds to a local atom. To

Table 1: Statistics for the clusters in Figure 12.

	C_1			C_2			C_3			C_4			C_5		
Size of cluster (C)	150			170			126			484			375		
Size of source set (S)	16			9			7			8			15		
Destinations	Ukraine 83%			Romania 33%			India 93%			Russia 73%			US 74%		
	Czech Rep. 10%			Poland 33%			US 2%			Czech Rep. 10%			Australia 16%		
Dominant Next Hops	9002	21011	3549	5588	3549	1299	9498	3257	174	12389	3257	1273	6939	174	16735
Next Hop Density	0.26	0.23	0.11	0.33	0.16	0.11	0.30	0.10	0.06	0.31	0.07	0.06	0.54	0.06	0.03
Coherence	0.70	0.82	0.74	0.88	0.67	0.58	0.69	0.43	0.39	0.67	0.28	0.29	0.80	0.25	0.90

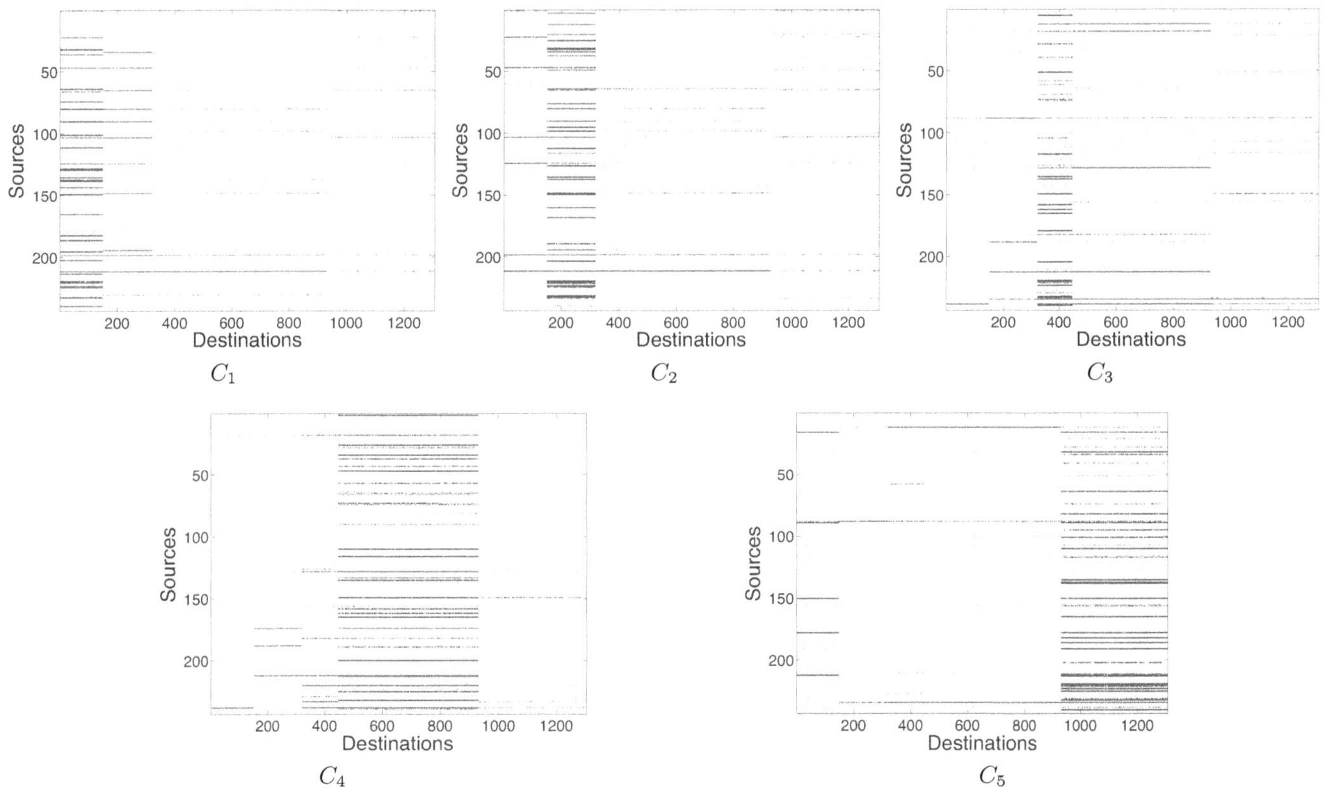

Figure 13: Visualization of the portion of **N** corresponding to the union of all five clusters. In each plot, we color the three most dominant next hops used in one cluster.

explore the nature of these local atoms, we start by characterizing them in Table 1.

The first two rows of the table give the size of the local atom. This is captured by the number of prefixes in the cluster (the size of C) and by the number of sources that show common routing behavior to those prefixes (the size of S). In each cluster, we find a significant number of ASes that show similar routing behavior to a large number of prefixes.

Next, we dive into the characteristics of each local atom. The next two rows characterize the geographic location of the prefixes (destinations). In each case, we have only listed the top-2 countries associated with the prefixes in the cluster, and we give the percent of prefixes that we find in each cluster from those countries. These rows show that in most cases, as much as 90% of the prefixes in a cluster are associated with only one or two countries. This shows that geography clearly influences the formation of local atoms.

The next three rows of Table 1 illustrate the nature of the 'common routing behavior' that the sources S exhibit with respect to the destinations C. The row labeled *Dominant Next Hops* lists the ASNs of the three most common next-hop ASes (in order of decreasing frequency) used by sources in S for destinations in C. The row *Next Hop Density* shows the fraction of entries in the cluster (across all 243 sources) that correspond to each of the three common next hops. And the row *Coherence* shows the fraction of entries *only in the submatrix* $\mathbf{N}(S, C)$ that correspond to each of the three common next hops. That is, the Coherence aims to quantify the cohesiveness of the nexthops appearing in the submatrix $\mathbf{N}(S, C)$.

The last two rows of Table 1 illustrate how common routing behavior is concentrated in the submatrix $\mathbf{N}(S, C)$. The much larger density of the dominant next hops used by sources in S as compared to among all sources shows that the sources in S are indeed making similar *nexthop* choices.

This is further illustrated graphically in Figure 13. In this figure, each plot is a view of the *nexthop* matrix $\mathbf{N}$. The same portion of $\mathbf{N}$ is shown in each plot, namely, the columns that correspond to prefixes forming the union of clusters C_1 through C_5. The difference between each plot is the choice of which next hop ASes are highlighted. In each plot, the three dominant next-hop ASes as given in Table 1 are colored in blue, green, and red, respectively. The figure shows how sharply the routing behavior of each local atom is defined. The common routing decisions made within each local atom appear as clearly isolated regions within the overall $\mathbf{N}$ matrix. This confirms our intuition of a local atom as equivalent to a coherent submatrix of $\mathbf{N}$.

7. OVERLAPPING CLUSTERING

The local atoms we have found so far have non-overlapping prefix sets. Consider the case of two coherent submatrices of $\mathbf{N}$ as shown in Figure 14. It is quite possible for BGP routing to result in this situation, but such local atoms can not be distinguished by the approach we have taken so far.

The `Pivot` algorithm outputs a *partition* of the prefixes. That is, every prefix x (column of $\mathbf{N}$) is only assigned to one cluster. However, as demonstrated by Figure 14, some columns should belong to both clusters, thus the expressiveness of partition-based clustering is limited. In this section, we propose a clustering that allows us to create clusters that can express such scenarios. Such clustering allows for *overlapping* clusters — the same node can be assigned to more

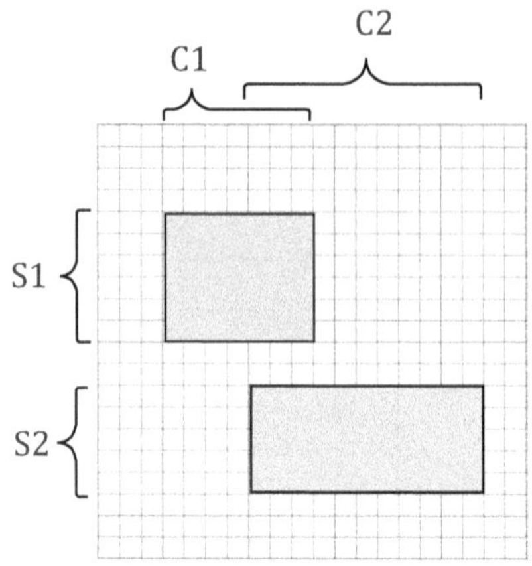

Figure 14: Overlapping clusters in $\mathbf{N}$.

than one cluster, and hence can capture the relationship shown in Figure 14.

Algorithm 2 The `Local` algorithm .

A set of prefixes $X = \{x_1, \ldots, x_n\}$, the matrix of their normalized *rsd* distances $\widetilde{\mathbf{D}}$ and integer p.
A labeling $\mathcal{L}$ that assigns at most p labels (clusters) for every $x \in X$.

$t = 0$
for every $x \in X$ **do**
  $\mathcal{L}_t(x) =$ `Initialize`(p)
end for
while true **do**
  $t = t + 1$
  $\mathcal{L}_t = \mathcal{L}_{t-1}$
  for every $x \in X$ **do**
    $\widetilde{\mathcal{L}}_t(x) =$ `NNLS`$(\widetilde{\mathbf{D}}, \mathcal{L}_t)$
    $\mathcal{L}_t(x) =$ `Boolean`$(\hat{\mathcal{L}}_t(x), p)$
  end for
  if $|\text{L-Cost}(\mathcal{L}_t) - \text{L-Cost}(\mathcal{L}_{t-1})| < \epsilon$ **then**
    return $\mathcal{L}_t$
  end if
end while

7.1 The Overlapping-Clustering problem

In this section, we define the Overlapping-Clustering problem. The output of this problem is a *labeling* $\mathcal{L}$, which assigns every node x to a *set* of clusters $\mathcal{L}(x)$. That is, every label corresponds to a cluster.

Since every node is assigned to a set (rather than to a single) cluster, we can compare a cluster-assignment for two nodes – e.g., x and x' – by comparing the corresponding labels. We do this by considering the *Jaccard distace* of the label sets $\mathcal{L}(x)$ and $\mathcal{L}(x')$, which is defined as follows:

$$J\left(x, x' \mid \mathcal{L}\right) = 1 - \frac{|\mathcal{L}(x) \cap \mathcal{L}(x')|}{|\mathcal{L}(x) \cup \mathcal{L}(x')|}.$$

That is, the Jaccard distance captures the extent to which two label sets overlap, as a fraction of the total number of labels in both sets.

To capture the kind of relationship shown in Figure 14,

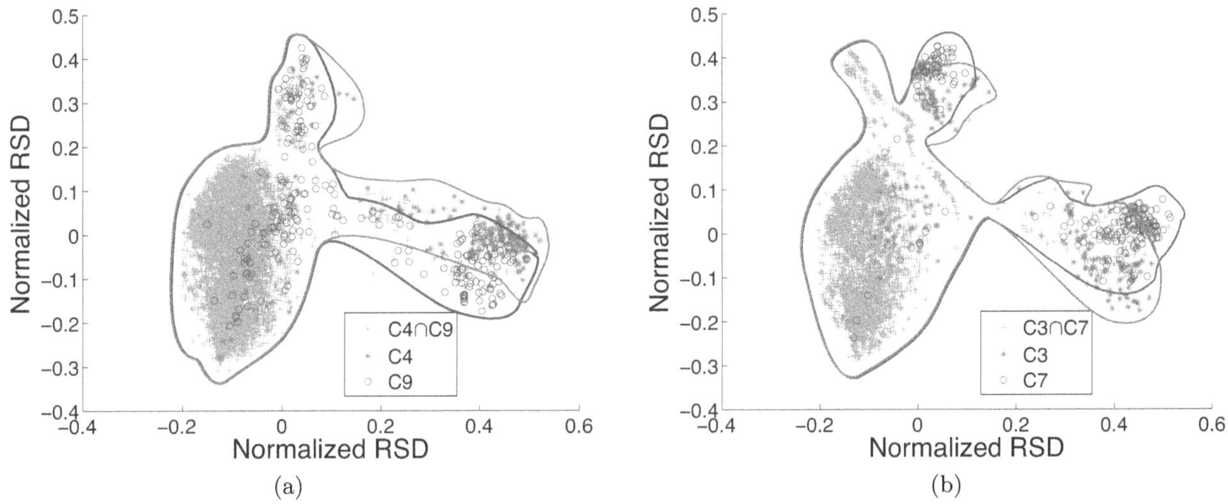

Figure 15: Cluster pairs (a) C_4/C_9 and (b) C_3/C_7. For each pair, the points in common are in green, while the points exclusive to each cluster are in red or blue. Cluster outlines are also overlaid for ease of interpretation.

the definition of the OVERLAPPING-CLUSTERING problem focuses on identifying a labeling of each prefix such that the Jaccard distance between the labels assigned to two prefixes approximates the *rsd* distance between the corresponding prefixes, to the maximum extent possible. Note that since the Jaccard distance is a real number in the interval $[0, 1]$ we seek to approximate the normalized version of *RSD*.

Our definition of OVERLAPPING-CLUSTERING builds on the recent work of Bonchi et al. [5]; its formal definition follows.

PROBLEM 2 (OVERLAPPING-CLUSTERING). *Given a set of nodes X, their $m \times n$* nexthop *matrix $\mathbf{N}$ and an integer p, identify a labeling of nodes $\mathcal{L}$ such that*

$$\text{L-COST}(\mathcal{L}) = \sum_{x,x' \in X \times X} \left| J\left(x, x' \mid \mathcal{L}\right) - \widetilde{\mathbf{D}}(x, x')\right|$$

is minimized and for every $x \in X$ it is guaranteed that $|\mathcal{L}(x)| \leq p$.

The definition of Problem 2 does not require the number of clusters in the output to be provided as part of the input. Rather, the problem requires as input the maximum number of clusters p in which a node can participate. Note that the L-COST function does not necessarily decrease as p increases. Thus, in theory there is an optimal value of p, which can be found by trying all possible values (i.e., $\{1, \ldots, n\}$) and report the clustering with the smallest L-COST value. In our experiments, we chose $p = 10$, because for $p > 10$ we observed no significant decreases in the objective function.

7.2 The `Local` algorithm

Bonchi et al. [5] showed that not only is Problem 2 NP-hard to solve, but it is also NP-hard to approximate. Therefore, we are content with efficient heuristics to minimize the L-COST objective function. In this section, we give a brief description of such a heuristic, which we call `Local`; this heuristic is an instantiation of the generic algorithm proposed in [5]. Although space does not permit a detailed description of our algorithm here, the code is available at: `CodeURL`.

The pseudocode of the `Local` algorithm is shown in Algorithm 2. On a high level it uses a local-search heuristic, which starts with a random assignment of prefixes to clusters and iteratively improves it to reduce the value of the L-COST function. More specifically, at the first step (`Initialize` routine), every prefix is assigned a random set of at most p labels. Subsequently, the labels of each prefix x are appropriately changed so that the cost of the objective function improves. This is done by the `NNLS` and the `Boolean` routines. First, `NNLS` finds a real-valued assignment of labels to a node by solving a non-negative least squares problem. The output of this step is weighted association of the prefix with every cluster– denoted by $\widetilde{\mathcal{L}}$ in Algorithm 2. Then, the routine `Boolean` transforms the real-valued assignment into one-zero assigment. Thus, the output of this step is a set of labels (i.e., clusters) that are associated with prefix x. The details of these steps are described by Bonchi et al. [5]. The two steps are repeated, till a local minimum – with respect to the objective function L-COST – is reached.

7.3 Overlapping Clustering Results

To demonstrate overlapping clustering using *RSD* we apply `Local` to our data with $p = 10$. This allows any prefix to be a member of as many as 10 clusters. To understand the results, it is easiest to look at pairs of clusters. All pairs of clusters have some overlapping subset, so pairs of clusters illustrate the general power of overlapping clustering for our data.

From our 10 clusters, we focus on two pairs which we denote C_4/C_9 and C_3/C_7. We show the two pairs visualized using MDS in Figure 15.

The figure shows that, as intended, clusters overlap. In each case, a large number of prefixes are in both clusters. What is perhaps less expected is that points that are close to each other in *RSD* space as visualized in 2-D are not necessarily contained in the same cluster. For example, note the regions on the right side of each plot in which points belonging to distinct clusters are shown to be near in *RSD*.

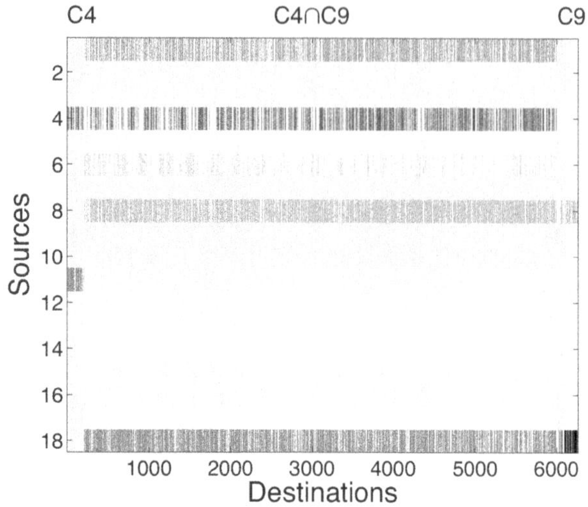

(a)

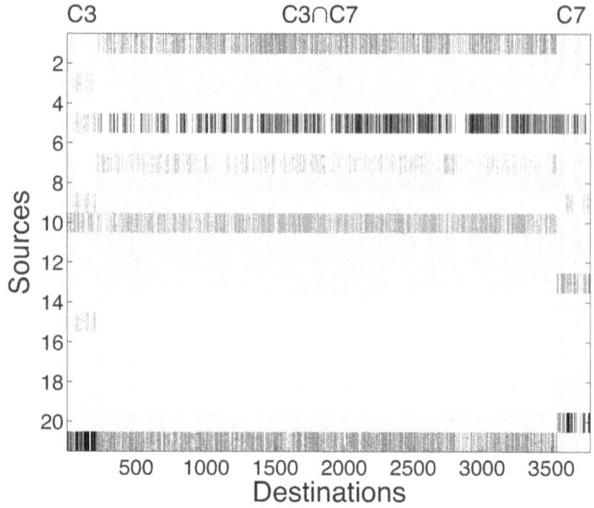

(b)

Figure 16: Submatrices of $\mathbf{N}$, with different nexthop ASes in different colors.

In fact, this effect is exactly what we had hoped overlapping clustering would capture. The reason for this effect is that point-pairs can be close to each other in *RSD* space *for different reasons.* Consider again Figure 14. There are two different sets of sources (S_1 and S_2) that have similar routing behavior and create coherent submatrices in $\mathbf{N}$. Each set of sources causes prefixes to cluster together, but independently so; the prefixes in C_1 are near each other in *RSD* space because of the similar routing decision of the ASes in S_1, while prefixes in C_2 are near each other in *RSD* space because of the similar routing decision of the ASes in S_2.

As a result, in contrast to the non-overlapping case, we do not find that clusters typically map to geographic sets or regions. Furthermore, clusters are not compact in *RSD* space as can be seen in Figure 15.

The overlapping clustering constructed by the `Local` algorithm allows us to discover the different sets of source ASes that have similar routing behavior. This is shown in Figure 16. The figure shows submatrices of $\mathbf{N}$ in which each next hop values has been given a color. These submatrices correspond to the cluster pairs C_4/C_9 and C_3/C_7. In each figure, we have ordered the columns so that the prefixes contained in each cluster are in the center, and the prefixes that are only in one cluster are on the sides. This allows us to visualize the sets of ASes that give rise to each cluster.

For example, in Figure 16(a), we can see that the AS in row 4 has the same next hop for all prefixes cluster C_4, but not for the prefixes that are only in C_9. Likewise, the AS in row 8 has the same next hop for prefixes in C_9, but not for those only in C_4. In the case of C_3/C_7, the cluster-defining rows are rows 5 and 10.

We conclude that these results give evidence that overlapping clustering (using an algorithm such as `Local`) can find clusters in which different sets of ASes each have cohesive routing behavior over overlapping sets of prefixes. This holds the promise of extracting a richer set of local atoms from BGP data.

8. DISCUSSION

Our sense is that *RSD*, owing to its simple definition, is a general tool that can be used in a variety of settings. These include further in-depth analysis of BGP, as well as its application to entirely different domains.

A promising direction for further application of *RSD* is to incorprate temporal analysis. Consider a set of nexthop matrices indexed in time, i.e., $\mathbf{N}_t, \mathbf{N}_{t+1}, \ldots$. In this setting, one can ask about the *RSD* of the same prefix at different points in time. For prefix x, this is simply the number of positions where $\mathbf{N}_t(:, x)$ and $\mathbf{N}_{t+1}(:, x)$ differ. Such a measure could have value over short timescales for detecting sudden, significant routing changes (such as a prefix hijacking) or over long timescales for characterizing the evolving routing structure of the Internet. Further, comparison of average *RSD* change across all or a selected set of prefixes from time t to time $t+1$ could give a sense of overall rate of change and stability in the interdomain routing system.

Another direction for further analysis of BGP follows from the observation that the *RSD* matrix $\mathbf{D}$ has low effective rank. Previous work on traffic matrices has shown that this property naturally leads to an effective method for anomaly detection [13]. Our initial investigations indicate that this method can very effectively identify prefixes that have unusual connectivity patterns in BGP (such as CDNs).

Another consequence of the low effective rank property of $\mathbf{D}$ is that $\mathbf{D}$ may be amenable to matrix completion. That is, it may be possible to accurately *estimate* the *RSD* between two pairs of prefixes if enough measurements of *RSD* between other pairs is available. This could be useful in situations where only partial path information is available.

Going beyond the analysis of BGP, *RSD* can be applied in any situation in which paths between nodes are an available data source. For example, it could be applied to collections of traceroute measurements, information dissemination in social media, or infection propagation in social and communication networks.

9. RELATED WORK

It's been widely reported that publicly available BGP tables provide an incomplete view of the AS graph [17]. In this regard, it is important to develop tools that can analyze the network using only the BGP path data instead of the AS graph. The way we define RSD based on paths eliminates the problem of missing edges in the AS graph so that ambiguities due to missing links do not arise.

In addition, our paper touches on the problem of visualization of prefixes (or ASes) based on BGP data. The authors in [11] visualize the set of core ASes using placement based on AS degree and geographic location. Small scale visualizations of selected BGP paths are available through `BGPlay` [4] and `bgpviz` [15]. However, to our knowledge, no macroscopic visualization method relies directly on BGP paths as we do, despite the fact that paths are the fundamental unit of measurement in BGP. In addition, relatively little work has been done on clustering of prefixes or ASes; the work that has been done relies on the inferred AS graph rather than BGP paths [9].

Finally, a number of studies explore aggregation of prefixes. In [6], the authors show that there are many cases in which a collection of prefixes is routed the same way. Such collections, so called *policy atoms*, consist of prefixes that share the same BGP paths. In [1], the authors study methods for calculating policy atoms and their characteristics in detail. The main goal of these works is using policy atoms to reduce the sizes of BGP tables. Our work differs from these works in the sense that we do not require that the prefixes in the same *local atom* routed the same way. Instead we cluster the prefixes that are routed similarly *in some regions* of the Internet. In fact, we generalize and extend the notion of *atoms* so that it can be used to analyze the routing behaviors at different granularities.

10. CONCLUSIONS

In this paper we have developed a new set of tools for extracting insight from BGP measurements. We defined a new metric for measuring distance between prefixes, called *RSD*. This metric captures the notion of 'closeness' of two prefixes with respect to the global routing state of the Internet. As such, it is a natural tool for visualizing the relationship between prefixes. But going beyond visualization, we show that *RSD* can uncover surprising patterns in routing data. In particular, we show that *RSD* exposes situations in which large numbers of ASes make similar routing decisions with respect to specific sets of prefixes. We call this situation a local atom, generalizing the notion of a BGP atom. We show that local atoms exist at the macroscopic scale (one involves 23% of all prefixes in the Internet) as well as at much smaller scales. To expose local atoms, we develop and demonstrate the power of two new clustering methods specifically tailored for use with *RSD*. We conclude that the combination of (1) computing *RSD*, (2) visualizing *RSD* using MDS, and (3) clustering *RSD* using `Pivot` and `Local` together constitute a powerful toolbox for discovering patterns in massive datasets of BGP paths.

Code for the `Pivot` and `Local` algorithms, as well as code for computing *RSD*, is available at `http://csr.bu.edu/rsd`. That site also provides a list of *RSD* values for the prefix pairs used in this study.

11. ACKNOWLEDGEMENTS

This work was supported by NSF grants CNS-1017529, CNS-0905565, CNS-1018266, CNS- 1012910, CNS-1117039, by a GAANN Fellowship, and by grants from Microsoft, Yahoo!, and Google. The authors thank the IMC referees and shepherd for their help in improving the paper. The authors also appreciate helpful discussions with various network operators.

12. REFERENCES

[1] Y. Afek, O. Ben-Shalom, and A. Bremler-Barr. On the structure and application of bgp policy atoms. In *ACM SIGCOMM Workshop on Internet measurment*, 2002.

[2] N. Ailon, M. Charikar, and A. Newman. Aggregating inconsistent information: Ranking and clustering. *J. ACM*, 55(5), 2008.

[3] N. Bansal, A. Blum, and S. Chawla. Correlation clustering. *Machine Learning*, 56:89–113, 2004.

[4] Bgplay. `http://bgplay.routeviews.org`.

[5] F. Bonchi, A. Gionis, and A. Ukkonen. Overlapping correlation clustering. In *ICDM*, pages 51–60, 2011.

[6] A. Broido and k. claffy. Analysis of RouteViews BGP data: policy atoms. In *NRDM*, 2001.

[7] V. Filkov and S. Skiena. Integrating microarray data by consensus clustering. *Intern. J. on Artificial Intelligence Tools*, 13:863–880, 2004.

[8] A. Gionis, H. Mannila, and P. Tsaparas. Clustering aggregation. *TKDD*, 1(1), 2007.

[9] C. Gkantsidis, M. Mihail, and E. W. Zegura. Spectral analysis of internet topologies. In *INFOCOM*, 2003.

[10] G. Gürsun, N. Ruchansky, E. Terzi, and M. Crovella. Inferring visibility: Who's (not) talking to whom? In *SIGCOMM*, 2012.

[11] B. Huffaker and k. claffy. CAIDA's IPv4 and IPv6 AS Core AS-level Internet Graph. `http://www.caida.org/research/topology/as_core_network/`, 2010.

[12] Hurricane Electric. Hurricane electric peering policy. `http://he.net/peering.html`.

[13] A. Lakhina, M. Crovella, and C. Diot. Diagnosing network-wide traffic anomalies. In *SIGCOMM*, 2004.

[14] W. Mühlbauer, S. Uhlig, B. Fu, M. Meulle, and O. Maennel. In search for an appropriate granularity to model routing policies. In *SIGCOMM*, 2007.

[15] RIPE. bgpviz. `http://www.ris.ripe.net/bgpviz`.

[16] Ripe's routing information service raw data project. `http://www.ripe.net/data-tools/stats/ris/ris-raw-data`.

[17] M. Roughan, W. Willinger, O. Maennel, D. Perouli, and R. Bush. 10 lessons from 10 years of measuring and modeling the internet's autonomous systems. *IEEE Journal on Selected Areas in Communications*, 2011.

[18] University of oregon route views project. `http://www.routeviews.org`.

[19] W. S. Torgerson. Multidimensional scaling: I. theory and method. *Psychometrika*, 17:401–419, 1952.

On the Incompleteness of the AS-level Graph: a Novel Methodology for BGP Route Collector Placement

Enrico Gregori
Institute of Informatics and Telematics, Italian National Research Council
Pisa, Italy
enrico.gregori@iit.cnr.it

Alessandro Improta
Information Engineering Department, University of Pisa and Institute of Informatics and Telematics, Italian National Research Council
Pisa, Italy
a.improta@iet.unipi.it

Luciano Lenzini
Information Engineering Department, University of Pisa
Pisa, Italy
l.lenzini@iet.unipi.it

Lorenzo Rossi
Institute of Informatics and Telematics, Italian National Research Council
Pisa, Italy
lorenzo.rossi@iit.cnr.it

Luca Sani
IMT - Institute for Advanced Studies
Lucca, Italy
luca.sani@imtlucca.it

ABSTRACT

In the last decade many studies have used the Internet AS-level topology to perform several analyses, from discovering its graph properties to assessing its impact on the effectiveness of worm-containment strategies. Yet, the BGP data typically used to reveal the topologies are far from being complete. Our contribution is three-fold. Firstly, we analyse BGP data currently gathered by RouteViews, RIS and PCH route collectors, and investigate the reasons for its incompleteness. We found that large areas of the Internet are not properly captured due to the geographic placement of the current route collector feeders and due to BGP filters, such as BGP export policies and BGP decision processes. Secondly, we propose a methodology to select the optimal number of ASes that should join a route collector project to obtain a view of the Internet AS level topology closer to reality. We applied this methodology to the global AS-level topology and to five regional AS-level topologies, highlighting that the particular characteristics of the Internet at a regional level cannot be ignored during this process. Thirdly, we provide a characterization of the ASes that we found to be part of at least one optimal solution set. By analysing these ASes we found that the current route collector infrastructure is rarely connected to them, highlighting that much more effort should be made in devising a route collector infrastructure that ideally would be able to capture a complete view of the Internet.

IMC'12, November 14–16, 2012, Boston, Massachusetts, USA.

Categories and Subject Descriptors

C.2.1 [**Computer-Communication Networks**]: Network Architecture and Design—*Network topology*; C.2.2 [**Computer-Communication Networks**]: Network Protocols—*Routing protocols*; C.2.3 [**Computer-Communication Networks**]: Network Operations—*Network monitoring*

Keywords

Autonomous Systems, BGP, incompleteness, Internet, measurement, topology

1. INTRODUCTION

During the last few years, the Internet has become more and more part of the everyday life of billions of people. Thanks to the Internet, it is now possible to do things that just a couple of decades ago would have been impossible, such as sending mail to the other side of the world in less than a second, checking one's bank account from home and retrieving any kind of information at any time with just a couple of clicks. Despite its increasing pervasiveness, very little is known about the real structure of the Internet and what happens to data once they have left the home router. This is a major issue, since it means that is impossible to detect any structural problem or Achilles' heels until an outage occurs.

To address this problem, several researchers started to analyse the Internet in a topological perspective in the hope of revealing any potential weaknesses at any level. The AS-level topology represents one of the most interesting perspectives. In this topology each node is represented by an AS that represents an organization (or part of it) that manages a certain amount of IP subnets, while the edges are represented by BGP connections between pairs of ASes. The most common approach is to exploit data gathered by BGP route collectors and/or Traceroute monitors and, then, to extract AS-level information about the Internet. Although several works have highlighted problems in using traceroute data to infer AS-level information – such as aliasing [1], biasing [2] and router-to-AS mapping [3, 4] – only a few have investigated the limitations of the BGP approach, and in doing so have mainly focused on the incompleteness of data gathered via BGP route collectors.

Our contribution is threefold. Firstly, we analyse the BGP data currently gathered by RouteViews, RIS and PCH route collectors, highlighting and explaining the causes of their incompleteness. We show that the current view of the Internet is extremely *narrow* – due to the extremely low number of ASes that are actively feeding the route collectors – and *biased* – due to the nature of the feeding ASes, which is mostly managed by worldwide ISPs. This top-down view does not allow the route collector infrastructure to discover a large set of p2p connections that may be established among ASes that are part of the lower part of the Internet hierarchy, as already highlighted in [5, 6, 7, 8]. In addition to this classic analysis we developed an innovative metric, named *p2c-distance*, which takes into account the presence of BGP decision processes and BGP export policies crossed by BGP UPDATE messages before reaching a route collector. This then provides a better understanding of the level of completeness of the data gathered. Unlike other approaches, we are thus able to analyse and quantify the level of incompleteness of BGP data by relying only on the route collector infrastructure and without exploiting any private data.

Secondly, in order to overcome the large amount of incompleteness highlighted, we select the minimum number of ASes that should provide full routing information to the route collector infrastructure. To do that we formulate a Minimum Set Cover (MSC) problem that exploits the inter-AS p2c-distance within a generic AS-level topology. Even though the MSC has been proved to be NP-complete [9], our methodology exploits the graph properties extracted the MSC solution. We first reduce the size of the graph in which the solution has to be searched by *a*) leveraging on the extreme low densities of the covering matrices, *b*) applying classic mathematical reduction techniques to these matrices and *c*) using a brute force approach on the remaining uncovered components of the original covering matrix.

Thirdly, we analyse and compare the solutions obtained by applying this methodology on the global topology and five regional AS-level topologies of the Internet, highlighting the impact that the geographical peculiarities of the Internet have on the selection of the optimal set of ASes. As already highlighted in [10], geography plays an important role in routing decisions inside worldwide ASes and, consequently, also on the establishment of local economic inter-AS relationships and on the related BGP export policies. Typically the routing decisions are carried out at a continental level. Thus, to have full coverage of a given world-wide AS and its neighbors, multiple BGP connections with the route collectors need to be set up, one for each continent where the ASes are located. Furthermore, we also carry out an analysis of the current status of the route collector regional infrastructure by identifying how many ASes in the optimal solution are currently connected to them, by working out how many new ASes should be connected in each region, and by providing their typical characteristics. We found that some parts of the world, such as Africa, completely hide their p2p connectivity from the current route collector infrastructure. To the best of our knowledge, this is the first work to provide a constructive and systematic approach to enhance the coverage of the current route collectors from a geographical perspective, by identifying the ASes that should feed them in every continent. We also provide a ranked list of ASes, which highlights those ASes that should be given more priority in joining a route collector project.

The paper is organized as follows. Section 2 describes briefly the state of the art about the studies on BGP data and its incompleteness. An analysis of the current view of the route collector infrastructure is given in Section 3. In Section 4 we describe the proposed monitor placement methodology and we define the p2c-distance. Section 5 analyses the results of the methodology on the global topology and on the five regional topologies. Section 6 concludes the paper.

2. RELATED WORK

Some issues about the extent of the incompleteness of BGP data were initially raised in [11], but only several years later was the first attempt to quantify such incompleteness performed. In [12], the authors compared the topology inferred from BGP data and the topology inferred from data contained in the Internet Routing Registries (IRRs), highlighting that about 40% of connections were missing in BGP-derived topologies. This topic was then to some extent neglected, but was recently re-evaluated in [13] and [5]. In [13] there is an analysis of the BGP data obtained from each AS participating in RouteViews and RIS, and their contribution was found to be heavily redundant. A completely different approach was applied in [5]. The AS-level topology inferred via BGP data was compared with a ground truth made up of proprietary router configurations of two major ISPs (a Tier-1 and a Tier-2 ISP), of two research networks (Abilene and GEANT) and several content providers. Their results were significant, but they are not reproducible and are heavily biased by the ground truth selected. Nevertheless, this work can still be considered a milestone in the analysis of the incompleteness of BGP data. Its most relevant result was that economic relationships established between ASes strongly affect the information that can be revealed by each monitor. The main rationale behind this lies in the economic-driven nature of the inter-domain routing introduced in [14], where the most common types of inter-AS economic relationships – provider-to-customer (p2c), customer-to-provider (c2p), peer-to-peer (p2p) and sibling-to-sibling (s2s) – are identified and where the related BGP export policy are described. In particular, an AS announces to its customers and siblings the routes obtained by its peers, customers, providers and siblings, while it announces to its providers and peers only the routes related to its customers (see Fig. 1). This means that p2p connections are hidden from any of the providers or peers of a given AS. Based on the above, in [5] was claimed that most of the connections that are missing are p2p connections, and that monitors should be placed in the periphery of the Internet to discover them. A similar conclusion about the invisibility of p2p connections was also drawn in [6], which proposed a tool based on traceroute probes that is able to discover missing p2p connections established on Internet Exchange Points (IXPs).

Despite this strong evidence of the incompleteness of BGP data gathered by route collectors, only a few works have addressed the issue of how new BGP monitors should be located to minimize this lack of information. In [15], the authors extended a model based on techniques developed in biological research for estimating the size of populations to work on the Internet AS graph. Their results showed that thousands of connections are missing, and the authors estimated that 700 route monitors would be able to see almost the totality of the connections. However, their heuristic only marginally took into account the existence of inter-AS economic relationships, thus the optimal number of route monitors found was seriously underestimated, as will be highlighted in Section 5.

3. THE DARK SIDE OF BGP-BASED MEASUREMENTS

Without any doubt, BGP data is the best data to infer the Internet AS-level topology, since the AS-level information is directly contained in the *AS Path* BGP attribute and no further heuristics have to be applied. BGP route collectors receive BGP routing information from cooperating ASes, hereafter *BGP feeders*, to which they establish a BGP session. Thanks to these routing data it is possible to re-create the dynamics of the inter-domain routing as seen from BGP feeders. In this section we analyse the incompleteness of BGP data from a different perspective. First, we outline the current route collector projects. Then, we focus on the analysis of data gathered by these projects and on the contribution of each of their BGP feeders. Finally, we investigate the impact of the geographical distribution of route collectors has on the ability to discover regional Internet properties.

3.1 BGP Route Collector Projects

There are three main projects that collect BGP data and make it publicly available on the web: RouteViews, RIS and PCH. RouteViews was conceived at the University of Oregon [16] as a tool for Internet operators to obtain real-time information on the global routing system from the perspectives of several different backbones and locations. Since its birth in 1997, this project has provided an invaluable amount of BGP data through its route collectors. RIS (Routing Information System) was developed by Réseaux IP Européens (RIPE), the European Internet Registry, which collects and stores Internet routing data from several locations around

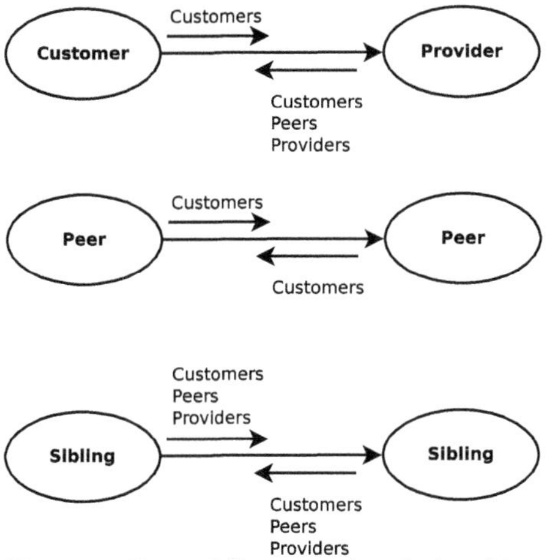

Figure 1: Inter-AS economic relationships

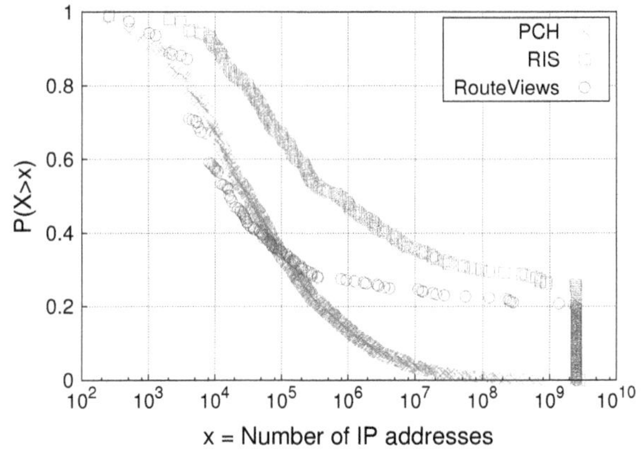

Figure 2: CCDF of the amount of IPv4 space obtained by each project

the globe deployed on the largest IXPs [17]. It offers also several tools that allow the Internet community to easily read and use BGP data. PCH (Packet Clearing House) [18] is a non-profit research institute that supports operations and analysis in the areas of Internet traffic exchange, routing economics and global network development. Since July 2010, PCH has been making BGP data available on its website, collected by several route collectors deployed on distinct IXPs. We gathered and analysed the BGP routing information provided by these three projects during February 2012. In this time interval, the number of active route collectors which provided BGP data in MRT format (RFC 6397) were 10 for RouteViews, 13 for RIS and 51 for PCH. Table 1 details the number of BGP feeders per route collector and their geographical location.

3.2 BGP feeder contribution analysis

Despite the well-known aims of these route collector projects, several of their BGP feeders do not provide any relevant contribution [8]. To better quantify the total contribution of BGP feeders, we subdivide them on the basis of the amount of IPv4 space[1] that each of them advertised to the route collectors (Table 1): *minor feeders* announce an IPv4 space smaller than that of a single /8 subnet, *full feeders* announce an IPv4 space closer to the full Internet IPv4 space currently advertised[2] (more than two billion IP addresses), while *partial feeders* include those ASes in between. Following this subdivision, the number of full feeders is 65 for RouteViews, 78 for RIS and 1 for PCH. Together they make up a set of 120 feeders, i.e. 5.99% of the total number of feeders. Figure 2 shows the amount of non overlapping IPv4 addresses announced from the BGP feeders of each project. In RouteViews and RIS projects, only about one in four/five feeders announce the full routing table (represented by the vertical tail of the CCDFs) to the route collectors, while in PCH the percentage is much lower.

A feature that can be used to gain a deeper insight into

[1]We compute the IPv4 space considering only *not overlapping* subnets, i.e. those subnets that are not included in any other subnet

[2]More information about the current IPv4 space advertised can be found at http://www.potaroo.net/tools/ipv4

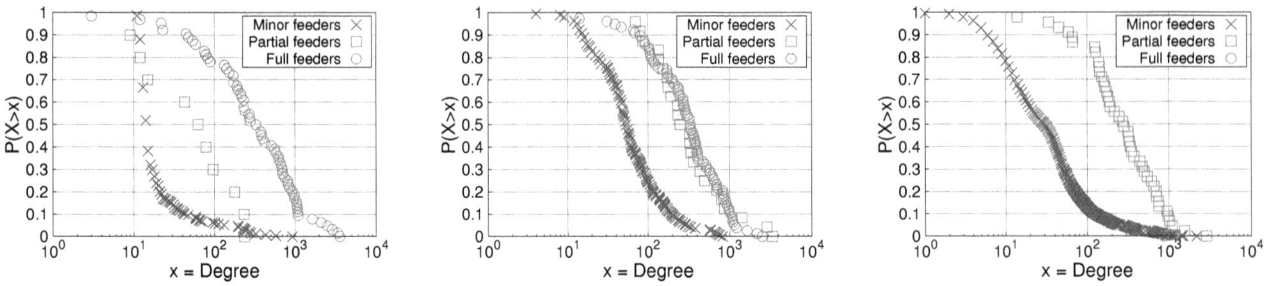

(a) RouteViews (b) RIS (c) PCH

Figure 3: CCDF of the node degree of ASes connected to route collectors

these different classes of BGP feeders is their node degree distribution (Fig. 3), which is computed on the union of the AS-level topologies inferred from RouteViews, RIS and PCH datasets. In each project the full feeder set is mainly composed of ASes that have developed a large number of BGP connections, which is a typical behavior of transit ISPs. To confirm this, we analysed the nature of these ASes by browsing their websites and parsing their entries in the IRRs. We found that 10 out of 13 Tier-1 ASes[3] are well-known national/international ISPs.

Since the vast majority of full feeders are large ISPs, the view of the Internet (at the AS-level) extracted from these projects is likely to represent more the Internet viewed by some of the most important ISPs in the world rather than the real Internet. A view of the Internet from the top of the AS hierarchy is not able to discover a large number of connections. In fact, due to BGP export policies, a route collector connected with ASes that are part of the top of the hierarchy is not able to reveal all the p2p connections that are established at the lower levels. On the other hand, the lower in the hierarchy the BGP feeder is located, the greater the chance to gathering information about an AS path involving a previously hidden p2p connection. Consider for example Fig. 4. In this case, if the route collector R is connected to AS E at the top of the hierarchy, it cannot reveal either the p2p connection between A and B, or the p2p connection between C and D. On the other hand, if R is connected to AS A, it can reveal the p2p connection between A and B, but not between C and D. It is fundamental that the route collector establishes a c2p relationship with its feeders. Otherwise, even if the route collector is connected to A, the connection (A, B) will not be revealed. A real example of the importance of obtaining the full routing table from BGP feeders located in the lowest part of the Internet hierarchy is represented by PCH. This data source is potentially extremely useful for discovering hidden AS connections, since its route collectors are deployed on 51 different IXPs and connected to 1,697 ASes, about three times the total number of BGP feeders of RIS and RouteViews. In addition, many of its BGP feeders have small node degree value (Fig. 3), which is a rough indication of their location at the bottom of the Internet hierarchy.

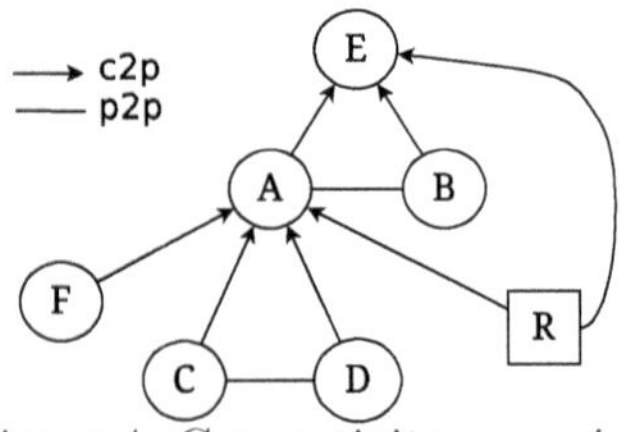

Figure 4: Connectivity scenario I

Nevertheless, as shown in Table 2, the number of AS connections detected by BGP data gathered by PCH and not discovered by RouteViews and RIS is extremely low, since 84,037 connection out of the total 85,674 discovered connections are already revealed by RouteViews and/or RIS. This happens because PCH mainly establishes p2p connections with its BGP feeders, i.e. its route collectors obtain only the routes announced by the customers of its BGP feeders. Consequently, it is likely that almost every connection found by PCH represents a p2c (c2p) economic agreement. Thus the issue of p2p connection discovery has not been solved even though it currently represents the largest set of hidden connections [6, 7, 19], greatly limiting the topology discovery potentiality of its route collectors.

A deeper insight into the amount of information provided by each BGP feeder can be found by analysing the difference between the direct node degree and the inner node degree

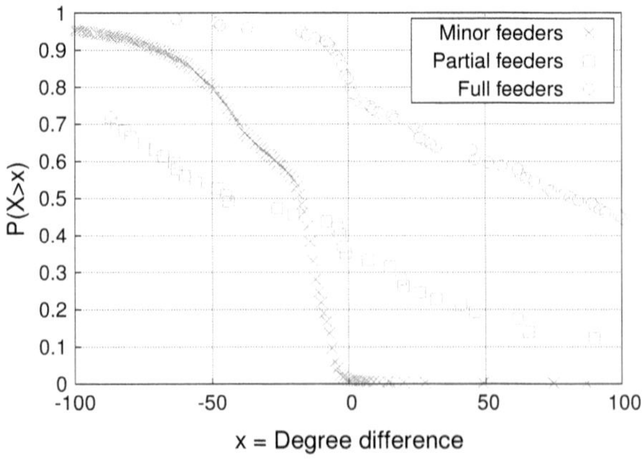

Figure 5: CCDF of the degree difference of BGP feeders

[3]A full list of ASes part of the Tier-1 set can be found at http://en.wikipedia.org/wiki/Tier_1_network

Route collector (Country)	*total feeders*	*# of feeders*		
		full	partial	minor
RouteViews				
route-views2 (US)	33	30	3	0
route-views4 (US)	15	13	2	0
route-views6 (US)	12	0	0	12
route-views.eqix (US)	14	10	0	4
route-views.isc (US)	13	10	0	3
route-views.kixp (KE)	1	0	0	1
route-views.linx (UK)	23	18	1	4
route-views.saopaulo (BR)	231	4	2	225
route-views.sydney (AU)	8	4	4	0
route-views.wide (JP)	4	2	0	2
RIS				
rrc00 (NL)	19	17	1	1
rrc01 (UK)	70	10	11	49
rrc03 (NL)	71	5	5	61
rrc04 (CH)	12	5	1	6
rrc05 (AT)	40	8	2	30
rrc07 (SE)	14	2	3	9
rrc10 (IT)	17	3	5	9
rrc11 (US)	26	8	3	15
rrc12 (DE)	45	11	4	30
rrc13 (RU)	19	9	1	9
rrc14 (US)	16	5	3	8
rrc15 (BR)	12	6	3	3
rrc16 (US)	6	1	1	4
PCH				
akl.pch.net (NZ)	7	0	0	7
ams.pch.net (NL)	390	0	17	373
atl.pch.net (US)	50	0	4	46
ber.pch.net (DE)	27	0	1	26
bos.pch.net (US)	2	0	0	2
bru.pch.net (BE)	5	0	0	5
bur.pch.net (US)	43	0	9	34
cai.pch.net (EG)	2	0	0	2
cdg.pch.net (FR)	120	0	1	119
chix.pch.net (US)	2	0	1	1
cpt.pch.net (ZA)	8	0	0	8
dac.pch.net (BD)	10	0	0	10
dub.pch.net (IE)	36	0	0	36
equinix-paris.pch.net (FR)	103	0	1	102
eze.pch.net (AR)	1	0	0	1
fra.pch.net (DE)	355	0	14	341
hkg.pch.net (HK)	34	0	4	30
iad.pch.net (US)	104	0	15	89
icn.pch.net (KR)	2	0	1	1
jpix.pch.net (JP)	33	0	2	31
ktm.pch.net (NP)	16	0	0	16
lax.pch.net (US)	24	0	6	18
lga.pch.net (US)	44	0	7	37
lhr.pch.net (UK)	330	0	16	314
lonap.pch.net (UK)	80	0	1	79
mia.pch.net (US)	44	0	6	38
mnl.pch.net (PH)	4	0	0	4
mpm.pch.net (MZ)	6	0	0	6
muc.pch.net (DE)	12	0	2	10
nbo.pch.net (KE)	2	0	0	2
nl-ix.pch.net (NL)	72	0	3	69
nrt.pch.net (JP)	9	0	2	7
nyiix.pch.net (US)	82	0	9	73
ord.pch.net (US)	45	0	6	39
paix-sea.pch.net (US)	12	0	4	8
pao.pch.net (US)	69	1	14	54
per.pch.net (AU)	7	0	0	7
sea.pch.net (US)	77	0	6	71
sfinx.pch.net (FR)	29	0	2	27
sgw.pch.net (SG)	64	0	7	57
sin.pch.net (SG)	16	0	0	16
sna.pch.net (US)	131	0	8	123
syd.pch.net (AU)	44	0	0	44
tie-ny.pch.net (US)	26	0	2	24
trn.pch.net (IT)	44	0	1	43
vie.pch.net (AT)	87	0	2	85
waw.pch.net (PL)	192	0	1	191
wlg.pch.net (NZ)	5	0	0	5
yow.pch.net (CA)	1	0	0	1
yyz.pch.net (CA)	33	0	2	31
zrh.pch.net (CH)	105	0	1	104

Table 1: February 2012 route collector status

(Fig. 5). The *direct* node degree of a BGP feeder X is defined as the cardinality of the set of its neighbors that are discovered using only BGP data directly announced by X to a route collector, and the *inner* node degree of X is defined as the cardinality of the set of its neighbors that are discovered using BGP data announced by every BGP feeder but X. A similar approach was proposed in [20], but with a different purpose.

It is thus possible to differentiate between two different classes of behavior of BGP feeders: *a*) ASes that announce just a partial view of the Internet (degree difference < 0), like those ASes that consider the route collectors as peers and not as customers, and *b*) ASes that contribute with connections not contained in any AS path announced by other BGP feeders (degree difference > 0), such as p2p and p2c connections that are hidden from the other BGP feeders due to the effect of BGP export policies crossed during the propagation of the routing information.

The first class is typical of minor feeders, whose connectivity is mostly discovered via other feeders (Fig. 5). On the other hand, the second class is typical of full feeders, that typically introduce previously undiscovered AS connections involving them.

However, some full feeders partially hide some of their interconnectivity despite advertising their full routing table to a route collector project. This phenomenon has been recorded in about 20% of the full feeders (see negative values of degree difference in Fig. 5) and is caused by the BGP decision process on the feeder side. Depending on the policies established among ASes and on technical decisions, some direct connections may not be announced to the route collector. However, for the same economic and technical reasons it is possible that the same direct connections hidden from the route collector are announced to other neighbors, propagated on the Internet, and finally detected by the route collector from another feeder as a side effect. Some other slight exceptions are related to minor and partial feeders with a positive degree difference (less than 5%). These feeders are likely to be located in the bottom part of the Internet hierarchy and some of their p2c connections may result as hidden to the route collector infrastructure because of the cross effect of their multi-homed nature and of multiple BGP decision process crossed by UPDATE messages before reaching the route collector infrastructure.

This last phenomenon highlights that the presence of multiple BGP decision processes along the AS path may limit the completeness of AS-level topology collected, since each BGP AS border router selects and announces only the best route per-destination (RFC 4271) to their neighbors. In summary, the information that a BGP feeder announces to the route collector is the result of its BGP decision process which, in turn, is fed only with routes that are the result of the BGP decision processes of its neighboring ASes, and so on. Each BGP decision process, from an AS-level measurement perspective, is a route filter, which can potentially reduce the AS-level connectivity information received from each route collector. As a consequence, the higher the dis-

	RouteViews	*RIS*	*PCH*
# of nodes	41,062	41,085	40,855
# of edges	112,854	134,903	85,674
# of common edges	84,037		

Table 2: Topology characteristics

Region	*# BGP feeders*	*# full feeders*
Africa	10	0
Asia-Pacific	159	15
Europe	1,279	68
Latin America	13	6
North America	444	42
World	2,004	120

Table 3: Geolocation of BGP feeders

tance of an AS from the BGP route collectors, the higher the number of BGP decision processes crossed and, thus, the higher the probability that one or more of them will filter out some AS connections.

3.3 Geographical coverage

The incompleteness of BGP data is even stronger if analysed from a geographical perspective. Table 3 details the total number of BGP feeders as well as the number of them that supply the full routing table to any of route collector projects. To perform this analysis we geolocated the IP address of each BGP feeder using the Maxmind GeoIPLite database [21] and considering the world being subdivided into five macro-regions: Africa, Asia-Pacific (i.e. Asia and Oceania), Europe, Latin America (the Caribbean, Central America, Mexico and South America) and North America. Table 3 highlights that most full feeders are located either in Europe or in North America. Interestingly, in Africa no full feeder is found even though Africa hosts one route collector of RouteViews and four of PCH. This means that every inference about the African part of the Internet is mostly obtained through views located in different regions. Thus, some relevant characteristics of the African part of Internet may be hidden from the current route collectors. This is not only a problem regarding Africa, in fact the number of feeders in other regions is low as well.

4. A NOVEL METHODOLOGY TO DEAL WITH BGP DATA INCOMPLETENESS

Given the large amount of incompleteness highlighted in Section 3, the first step to infer the real Internet AS-level topology and its properties is to introduce a larger number of new BGP feeders that announce their full routing tables. To quote Sir Arthur Conan Doyle, *"It is a capital mistake to theorize before you have all the evidence. It biases the judgment"*. One of the biggest obstacles is the vast number of ASes that make up the Internet. Obtaining routing information from each of them would require the participation of thousands administrators in a project that may not be appealing for many of them.

Given this situation, we focus on those ASes that play a major role in Internet connectivity, i.e. those ASes that offer IP transit to other ASes. Although there are far fewer of them than the total number of ASes, these ASes contribute substantially to provide Internet connectivity. In fact, both world-wide ISPs and small/medium ISPs are part of this set of ASes. This latter class of ASes is known to be the cause of the largest number of p2p connections [22] that are currently hidden from the route collector infrastructure.

In this section, we propose a methodology to identify the minimal set of BGP feeders that would be needed to gather as much BGP data as possible *about* the ASes whose connectivity plays a major role in their economic market, thus minimizing the number of hidden connections present in the core of the Internet and, at the same time, minimizing the impact of BGP filters, such as BGP export policies and BGP decision processes.

4.1 A new metric: p2c distance

As already highlighted, a major role in filtering is due to inter-AS economic relationships because of their influence on the amount of routing information that each AS announces to each other. Given the BGP export policies related to each economic relationship [14], a necessary (but not sufficient) condition for a route collector to reveal the full connectivity of a given AS is that there exists at least one AS path that is made up exclusively of p2c connections from that AS to the route collector. This is because only customers in a p2c connection are able to obtain routes towards all Internet destinations. In order to limit the filtering effects of BGP decision processes, it is preferable that routing information arrives at a route collector having crossed the lowest number of p2c connections as possible.

On the basis of the two conditions hypothesized above, we define a new metric that is able to capture the level of completeness of data gathered by the current set of route collectors. The *p2c-distance* of one AS X from another AS Y is defined as the minimum number of consecutive p2c connections that connect X to Y in the considered economic topology or, likewise, the minimum number of consecutive c2p connections that connect Y to X. This metric easily quantifies the distance and the amount of transit connections crossed by any BGP UPDATE message to reach a route collector, and can be exploited to reveal which part of the Internet is well-monitored and which part is still a dark zone. Note that this metric still relies on an inference made on the current Internet AS-level topology, but the p2c and c2p connections have been proved to be extremely accurate [5, 6, 7, 8].

To better understand how this metric works, consider the connectivity scenario depicted in Fig. 4. In this example, the route collector R has a p2c-distance of 1 from AS A and E, while the p2c-distance from B, C, D and F is not defined. This means that R has the possibility to reveal every p2p connection established by A, B and E. On the other hand, it also means that R is not able to reveal the p2p connectivity of C, D and F in any way, thus R will not reveal the connection (C, D) in any AS path. Nevertheless, R can discover the p2c (c2p) connectivity of each AS of the scenario.

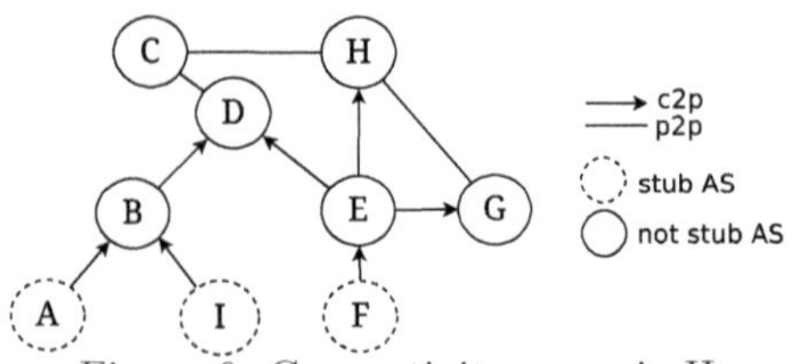

Figure 6: Connectivity scenario II

4.2 BGP feeder selection

Given the definition of p2c-distance, a complete view of the Internet can only be obtained by connecting a route collector to each stub AS, as already concluded in [5]. Stub ASes are ASes typically managed by local access providers (which provide connectivity to end users but not to other

ASes) and organizations that do not have the Internet transit as part of their core business (e.g. banks and car manufacturers), and appear in BGP data as the originating element, i.e. the right-most element, in every AS path that involves them. Due to the nature of their related organizations, these ASes tend to be customers in the economic relationships established with other ASes, representing a perfect starting point to minimize the p2c-distance of all ASes that make up the Internet. However, since p2c connections are already discovered by route collectors connected to the top of the hierarchy [5], most BGP data collected from a hypothetical route collector infrastructure connected to each of them would be redundant. Moreover, since it is not possible to infer a priori which stub AS is actually interested in establishing p2p connections, it is impossible to reduce the number of route collectors required to obtain full Internet AS-level connectivity. This means that, based on February 2012 BGP data, we need to have a connection to 33,845 ASes out of 41,127. This makes this approach practically unfeasible. We believe that a good trade-off between the possibility to discover hidden p2p connections and the feasibility of obtaining such data is represented by ASes that are actually interested in deploying p2p connections to improve the quality of their services, i.e. *non-stub ASes* [22]. The lack of interest of stub ASes in establishing p2p connections is highlighted by the fact that only 7% of them participate in at least one IXP[4], where ASes typically interconnect with settlement-free p2p connections to reduce the amount of their traffic directed to their providers (see [6, 19] and [24] for more details on IXPs).

Specifically, we aim to select new BGP feeders such that each non-stub AS has a finite and bounded p2c distance from the route collector infrastructure to minimize the effects of BGP filters and, consequently, increasing the possibility to reveal the hidden p2p connectivity of the actual core of the Internet. As will be shown later on, stub ASes will play a key role in the solution of the problem, even though we are not actually focusing on their connectivity.

4.2.1 Problem description

We model the problem of finding the optimal number of BGP feeders as an MSC problem which can be formulated as follows:

$$\text{Minimize} \quad \left(\sum_{AS_i \in \mathcal{U}} x_{AS_i} \right) \tag{1}$$

subject to

$$\sum_{AS_i : n \in S^{(d)}_{AS_i}} x_{AS_i} \geq 1 \qquad \forall n \in \mathcal{N} \tag{2}$$

$$x_{AS_i} \in \{0,1\}, \qquad \forall AS_i \in \mathcal{U} \tag{3}$$

where $\mathcal{U} = \{AS_1, AS_2, \ldots, AS_n\}$ is the set of ASes, $\mathcal{N} \subset \mathcal{U}$ is the set of non-stub ASes and $S^{(d)}_{AS_i}$ represents the *covering set* of AS_i, i.e. the set of ASes in $\mathcal{N}$ that have a p2c-distance value of at most d from AS_i, and x_{AS_i} is 1 if $S^{(d)}_{AS_i}$ is part of the final solution, 0 otherwise. Note that AS_i belongs to $S^{(d)}_{AS_i}$ for any $d \geq 0$. The parameter d defines the maximum number of BGP decision processes[5] that the update messages by each non-stub AS will traverse before reaching a BGP feeder and, thus, indicates the number of filters encountered that can cause loss of information. Note that imposing $d = 0$ implies that the solution is composed of the entire set of non-stub ASes. The larger the value of d, the heavier the filtering effect introduced by BGP decision processes but the smaller the number of required BGP feeders and, thus, the number of required BGP connections. This thus, makes the solution more feasible. To better understand the problem consider the scenario depicted in Fig. 6. In this example, $\mathcal{U} = \{A, B, C, D, E, F, G, H, I\}$ and $\mathcal{N} = \{B, C, D, E, G, H\}$. Thus we compute $S^{(1)}_A = S^{(1)}_I = \{B\}$, $S^{(1)}_B = \{B, D\}$, $S^{(1)}_C = \{C\}$, $S^{(1)}_D = \{D\}$, $S^{(1)}_E = \{E, D, G, H\}$, $S^{(1)}_F = \{E\}$, $S^{(1)}_G = \{G\}$, $S^{(1)}_H = \{H\}$.

The goal of this MSC problem is to obtain the minimum number of elements of $\mathcal{S}^{(d)}$ such that their union is $\mathcal{N}$ or, in other words, to select the minimum number of BGP feeders from $\mathcal{U}$ such that the p2c-distance of any non-stub AS from at least one of them is at most d. Returning to the example depicted in Fig. 6, one of the optimal solutions to cover every non-stub AS is $\{S^{(1)}_B, S^{(1)}_C, S^{(1)}_E\}$, i.e. we should select ASes B, C and E as BGP feeders.

4.2.2 Positioning algorithm

To carry out the MSC problem we introduce a directed graph $G^{(d)}(\mathcal{V}, \mathcal{E})$ where $\mathcal{V} = \{i \mid AS_i \in \mathcal{U}\}$ is the set of nodes and $\mathcal{E} = \{(i, j) \mid i, j \in \mathcal{V} \wedge AS_j \in \mathcal{N} \wedge AS_j \in S^{(d)}_{AS_i}\}$ is the set of edges. In other words, the set of nodes is represented by the full set of ASes, while an edge directed from node i to node j represents that the non-stub AS_j is contained in $S^{(d)}_{AS_i}$. The adjacency matrix related to the graph $G^{(d)}$ is a $|\mathcal{V}| \times |\mathcal{E}|$ matrix $A^{(d)}$ such that $A^{(d)}_{ij} \in \{0, 1\}$, and $A^{(d)}_{ij} = 1$ if $(i, j) \in \mathcal{E}$ and is made up of one row per AS and one column per non-stub AS. The problem can thus be translated into selecting the minimum number of rows such that $\sum_i A^{(d)}_{ij} \geq 1$ for every j.

Given the potentially high number of elements in the problem, a direct brute-force approach to solve it would not be effective. Nevertheless, we can still manage to obtain its exact solutions by reducing the size of the problem through applying matrix reduction techniques that are well known in the mathematical optimization literature, such as the possibility to delete dominated rows in the adjacency matrix without changing the solvability of the problem [25, 26].

In detail, we propose an algorithm that firstly consists in an iterative reduction process, consisting of four phases (Fig. 7): *phase a*) Selection of those ASes that are the only elements covering one or more non-stub ASes, *phase b*) Deletion of of dominated covering sets, *phase c*) Verification of whether if the dominated elements deleted during phase b) can be interchanged with the elements inserted so far in the solution, *Phase d*) Decomposition plus further inspection, in which the optimal solution is exhaustively searched on the reduced adjacency matrix and the algorithm checks whether

[4]We collected the set of ASes that participate to at least one IXP by downloading and parsing the participant list web page of 190 active IXPs. Data is available at [23].

[5]The number of BGP decision processes encountered before reaching a route collector is $d + 1$, since BGP feeders introduce an additional BGP decision process before providing BGP data to the route collectors.

```
1  Input: distance d, S^{(d)}_{AS_i} ∀AS_i ∈ \mathcal{U}
2
3  Pool = \mathcal{U}
4  \mathcal{P} = ∅
5  \mathcal{A} = ∅
6  \mathcal{R} = ∅
7  \mathcal{D} = ∅
8  Old_Pool = ∅
9
10 while Pool ≠ Old_Pool
11    Pool = Old_Pool
12    foreach AS_i ∈ \mathcal{N}
13       if |{AS_k | AS_k ∈ Pool ∧ AS_i ∈ S^{(d)}_{AS_k}}| == 1
14          remove AS_k from Pool
15          insert AS_k into \mathcal{P}
16          foreach AS_j ∈ Pool
17             S^{(d)}_{AS_j} = S^{(d)}_{AS_j} − S^{(d)}_{AS_k}
18             if |S^{(d)}_{AS_j}| == 0
19                remove AS_j from Pool
20
21    foreach AS_i ∈ Pool
22       foreach AS_j ≠ AS_i ∧ AS_j ∈ \mathcal{P}
23          if S^{(d)}_{AS_i} = S^{(d)}_{AS_j}
24             remove AS_j from Pool
25             insert (AS_i, AS_j) in \mathcal{A}
26          else if S^{(d)}_{AS_i} ⊂ S^{(d)}_{AS_j}
27             remove AS_i from Pool
28             insert ((AS_j, AS_i)) in \mathcal{D}
29          else if S^{(d)}_{AS_j} ⊂ S^{(d)}_{AS_i}
30             remove AS_j from Pool
31             insert ((AS_i, AS_j)) in \mathcal{D}
32
33
34 foreach AS_i in \mathcal{P}
35    foreach AS_j in \mathcal{D}(AS_i, AS_j)
36       if S^{(d)}_{\mathcal{P}} = S^{(d)}_{\mathcal{P}−AS_i+AS_j}
37          insert (AS_i, AS_j) in \mathcal{I}
38    foreach AS_j in \mathcal{A}(AS_i, AS_j)
39       insert (AS_i, AS_j) in \mathcal{I}
40
41 {Subpool} = decompose(Pool)
42
43 foreach Subpool_k in {Subpool}
44    {\mathcal{P}_k} = brute_force(Subpool_k)
45    foreach \mathcal{P}_{k_l} in {\mathcal{P}_k}
46       foreach AS_i in \mathcal{P}_{k_l}
47          foreach AS_j in \mathcal{D}(AS_i, AS_j)
48             if S^{(d)}_{\mathcal{P}_{k_l}} = S^{(d)}_{\mathcal{P}_{k_l}−AS_i+AS_j}
49                insert \mathcal{P}_{k_l} − AS_i + AS_j in {\mathcal{P}_k}
50          foreach AS_j in \mathcal{A}(AS_i, AS_j)
51             insert (AS_i, AS_j) in \mathcal{I}
52    \mathcal{P} = \mathcal{P} ⋃ \mathcal{P}_{k_0}
53    \mathcal{R}_k = {\mathcal{P}_{k_l}}_{l>0}
54
55 Output: solution set \mathcal{P}, alternative solution sets \mathcal{R}, interchangeable AS set \mathcal{I}
```

Figure 7: MSC resolver algorithm

any of the dominated elements deleted during phase b) may still be part of at least one optimal solution. Fig. 7 details the above phases.

Initially in phase a) (lines 12–19) the algorithm verifies the presence of any AS_k which is the only AS to cover a certain non-stub AS_i. More formally, the algorithm verifies if there

	# ASes					
	AF	*AP*	*EU*	*LA*	*NA*	*W*
ASes	770	6,576	17,657	2,490	16,032	41,127
Edges	1,980	19,829	77,465	8,175	43,331	144,475
Non-stub ASes	229	1,589	3,697	659	2,531	7,282
p2c	1,380	14,868	39,812	4,844	33,701	93,898
p2p	533	4,737	37,225	3,231	9,430	49,251
s2s	31	158	359	54	323	1,256

Table 4: Main characteristics of AS-level topologies

is a set of ASes that covers a non-stub AS_i with cardinality equal to one (line 13). In this case AS_k is removed from *Pool* and is inserted into the solution set $\mathcal{P}$ (lines 14–15) and, as a consequence, every non-stub AS in $S^{(d)}_{AS_k}$ is considered to be covered. Thus, each element in the set $S^{(d)}_{AS_k}$ is removed from every remaining covering set $S^{(d)}_{AS_j}$ (lines 16–17). Eventually, whenever one of the covering is emptied, the related AS is removed from the *Pool* (lines 18–19).

The same concepts are exploited in phase b) (lines 21–31), in order to check whether any covering set is already included in another set and, thus, can be put aside during the remaining computation. More formally, for each pair (AS_i, AS_j) the algorithm verifies if the related covering sets overlap each other exactly (line 23) or if one of the two dominates the other (lines 26 and 29). In the first case the pair (AS_i, AS_j) is put into the *alias set* $\mathcal{A}$, while in the second case the pair that comprises the dominating and the dominated ASes is put into the *dominated set* $\mathcal{D}$. In both cases, the computation continues by removing one AS of the pair from *Pool*. In the first case AS_j is arbitrarily removed (line 24), while in second case the dominated AS is removed (lines 27 and 30). The arbitrary removal of AS_j in the first case does not affect the results of the computation, since both ASes are completely interchangeable, i.e. their covering set is exactly the same. By reducing the number of elements in *Pool*, this phase may mean that additional non-stub ASes are covered by a single AS in *Pool*, so that new elements that have to be part of the final solution can be identified. Consequently, phases a) and b) are repeated until *Pool* cannot be reduced any further (line 12).

In phase c) (lines 34–39) the dominated elements that have been recorded are analysed to check if any of them could be part of one of the solutions, by verifying if they can be substituted with the related dominating elements and maintaining, at the same time, full coverage of $\mathcal{N}$. More formally, to verify if the dominated element AS_j can be substituted with its dominating element AS_i, the set of covered non-stub ASes $S^{(d)}_{\mathcal{P}}$ is compared with the set $S^{(d)}_{\mathcal{P}-AS_i+AS_j}$, which is obtained by switching AS_j with AS_i in $\mathcal{P}$. If the sets are equal (line 36), then AS_j is recorded being interchangeable with AS_i in the set of interchangeable ASes $\mathcal{I}$ (line 37).

Since the problem cannot be reduced any further, an exhaustive approach to obtain an exact solution is required. Phase d) (lines 41–53) firstly aims to solve the problem by further reducing the problem by applying the usual mathematical techniques to reduce the adjacency matrix $A^{(d)}$ (line 41) into independent sub-matrices. These sub-matrices can still be seen as small and independent MSC sub-problems, but due to their limited size they can be practically solved by applying a brute-force algorithm (line 44) or a branch-and-bound algorithm. To obtain all the possible solution sets $\{\mathcal{P}_k\}$ for the considered sub component k, we still have

p2c-distance	*# not stub ASes*					
	AF	*AP*	*EU*	*LA*	*NA*	*W*
1	0	15	67	6	39	120
2	0	78	165	21	126	310
3	0	124	252	47	165	489
> 3	229	1,372	3,213	585	2,202	6,363

Table 5: Regional distribution of p2c-distances

to test each of the dominating-dominated pairs in a similar way as is done in phase c). However, unlike phase c), the tests are performed on each solution $\mathcal{P}_{k_l}$ found, and whenever AS_j can substitute AS_i, a new solution is inserted into $\{\mathcal{P}_k\}$ (line 51).

As result of this procedure, the algorithm provides: *i)* a set $\mathcal{P}$ of ASes composed of the set of ASes that were inserted into the solution during phase a) and of one of the solution sets for each component found (in the algorithm indicated as $\mathcal{P}_{k_0}$); *ii)* a set $\mathcal{R}$ of ASes related to each component k found during phase d) consisting of the possible solutions not taken into account in $\mathcal{P}$; and *iii)* a set $\mathcal{I}$ containing all the ASes that can be interchanged.

Thus, $\mathcal{P} \cup \mathcal{I} \cup \mathcal{R}$ is the set of all the ASes that are part of at least one optimal solution, i.e. the set of ASes that are candidates for BGP feeders, while $\mathcal{P}$ is the solution found by the algorithm. The cardinality of $\mathcal{P}$ is the exact number of BGP feeders that should be selected from the set of candidates $\mathcal{P} \cup \mathcal{I} \cup \mathcal{R}$ in order to solve the MSC problem.

5. TOWARDS AN IDEAL ROUTE COLLECTOR INFRASTRUCTURE

Finding a list of ASes that should become BGP feeders exploiting the methodology illustrated in Section 4.2.2 entails computing the p2c-distances between ASes on a suitable economic-tagged AS-level Internet topology. A good starting point would seem to be the classic global AS-level topology of the Internet tagged according to one of the economic tagging algorithms proposed in the literature. However, as shown in our recent work [10], this could lead to misleading and incomplete results. An AS connection present in the global topology may hide multiple connections between the same two ASes but located in different geographic regions, each potentially regulated by different economic relationships. Applying our methodology to this coarse-level representation of the Internet may thus lead to an underestimation of the correct number of BGP feeders required to obtain a complete view of the Internet core. To illustrate this we show both the results obtained by applying our methodology to the global topology of the Internet, referred to as *World (W)*, and to five regional topologies: *Africa (AF), Asia-Pacific (AP), Europe (EU), Latin America (LA), North America (NA)*.

We first show the impact of the geography in BGP feeder selection, highlighting that the analysis of the Internet from a global point of view underestimates the number of BGP feeders required. Then, we analyse the candidate feeders selected by our methodology, identifying their particular characteristics. Finally, we compare the coverage of the current BGP feeders with the ideal set drawn by our methodology.

Region	$\lvert\mathcal{P}\rvert$ ($\lvert\mathcal{P} \cup \mathcal{I} \cup \mathcal{R}\rvert$)		
	$d = 1$	$d = 2$	$d = 3$
AF	117 (214)	97 (182)	95 (197)
AP	931 (1,688)	848 (1,666)	834 (1,625)
EU	2,271 (4,641)	2,089 (4,545)	2,063 (4,438)
LA	393 (707)	363 (669)	360 (660)
NA	1,535 (3,233)	1,428 (3,133)	1,409 (3,027)
W	4,311 (9,232)	3,937 (9,116)	3,859 (8,875)

Table 6: Positioning algorithm results

5.1 Global vs regional analysis

The global and the regional topologies have been inferred using the same BGP data analysed in Section 3 and exploiting enhanced versions of the algorithms[6] described in [27] and [10], which can be found in an internal report [23]. The main characteristics of these topologies are reported in Table 4.

Firstly, we compute the p2c-distances for each of the available topologies, as required by the positioning algorithm. Note that these values can also be used to highlight which zones of the Internet are poorly captured by the route collector infrastructure, thus providing further proof of the incompleteness of the current collected topologies. To confirm this, we analysed the p2c-distances of each non-stub AS from the route collector infrastructure by considering only routing information obtained via full feeders (see Table 5). Note that we consider to be ∞ the p2c-distance of ASes that cannot reach any route collector using only p2c connections. Most ASes are currently either too far from the route collector infrastructure or cannot be reached by any route collector via c2p connections alone, thus potentially representing hideouts for AS connectivity which need further investigation.

Once the p2c-distances had been calculated, we applied the positioning algorithm to each of the economic topologies available. The results are summarized in Table 6, where are shown the cardinality of the solution set $\mathcal{P}$ and, in round brackets, the cardinality of the candidate set $\mathcal{P} \cup \mathcal{I} \cup \mathcal{R}$ for each topology. In each geographic scenario the number of BGP feeders required is significantly smaller than the number of non-stub ASes (Tables 4 and 6). More importantly, the sum of BGP feeders required by regional scenarios is higher than the number of those required by the *World* scenario. This result was expected since the complete capture of the connectivity of an AS with a large geographic range may entail deploying multiple BGP feeders around the world. The inter-regional ASes typically follow a regional principle to route their traffic, in order to maximize their performance and minimize latency. To do this, they tend to subdivide their ASes into different routing areas by exploiting the features of Interior Gateway Protocols (IGPs) such as OSPF and IS-IS and they set up connections that can only be exploited in regional traffic routing. A total of 965 of 7,282 non-stub ASes are present in more than one single geographical topology and thus may fit this description.

[6]The results shown in this paper are obtained using the most conservative economic topology obtained by applying the algorithms described in [27] and [10] with the time parameter $N_{MAG} = 1$. Results for the remaining topologies can be found at [23]

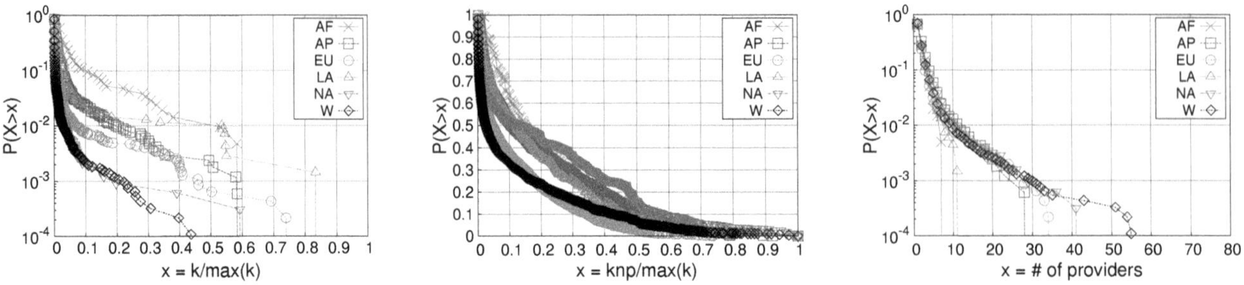

(a) Normalized node degree (b) Normalized average provider degree (c) Number of providers

Figure 8: CCDF of node properties of candidate BGP feeders

d	# candidate BGP feeders					
	AF	*AP*	*EU*	*LA*	*NA*	*W*
Full feeders	0 (−− %)	7 (46.67 %)	22 (32.35 %)	4 (66.67 %)	16 (38.10 %)	40 (33.33 %)
Partial feeders	1 (100 %)	3 (23.08 %)	10 (30.30 %)	2 (66.67 %)	5 (21.74 %)	15 (26.32 %)
Minor feeders	3 (33.33 %)	47 (34.81 %)	407 (33.78 %)	75 (33.63 %)	117 (30.47 %)	621 (33.99 %)

Table 8: Characteristics of feeders of the current route collector infrastructure

5.2 Candidate feeder analysis

We now focus on the characteristics of the elements of the set of candidate BGP feeders found by applying the monitor placement algorithm with parameter $d = 1$, which represents the best trade-off between AS-level connectivity discovery and the number of BGP feeders required. With $d = 1$, the positioning algorithm finds the set of BGP feeders required to obtain BGP routing information filtered by at most two BGP decision processes from each non-stub AS: the source AS and the BGP feeder itself. The results obtained with other values of d are available at [23].

Table 7 and Figure 8 show the most relevant characteristics of these elements. Figure 8 depicts a) the degree distribution, b) the *average provider degree* (k_{np}) distribution, where k_{np} is computed for each AS as the average degree of its providers, and c) the number of providers of the candidate feeders. Note that graphics a) and b) have been normalized with the maximum value of the node degree (k) found in the related region, in order to allow full-scope analysis and to trace the characteristics of a typical candidate BGP feeder. The most frequent classes of ASes found to be candidate are: a) stub ASes (see Table 7), b) ASes that have set up a small number of BGP connections (see Fig. 8a), and c) ASes that have chosen a rather small number (see Fig. 8c) of small-medium ISPs (see low-medium values of the normalized k_{np} in Fig. 8b) to be their providers.

Only a small percentage of these ASes are present on at least one IXP (see Table 7), and this implies that their typical interconnectivity behavior is to not establish public peering with other ASes. Thus, we can conclude that the typical AS that should become a BGP feeder of the current route collector infrastructure is a small multi-homed AS, that has set up multiple connections with different regional providers to guarantee route diversity and increase the reliability of its reachability. This is not surprising since these ASes are likely to be located at the bottom of the hierarchy and, thanks to multi-homing can cover several non-stub ASes at once.

5.3 Current status of the route collector infrastructure

We now analyse how many of the current BGP feeders are present in the ideal set of candidates found via the methodology proposed in Section 4. Their distribution for each region is shown in Table 8, as well as the percentage of the total number of feeders in the region that fall into that category. The main result is that only a small percentage of the current full feeders are actually part of an optimal solution in any of the topologies analysed. This is a direct consequence of their position in the Internet hierarchy, as already shown in Section 3. These ASes are not likely to have a large number of providers, thus their contribution is limited. Nevertheless, there are few other classes of current BGP feeders in the set of candidates, thus highlighting that, in terms of p2c-distance, only a few of them are placed in an optimal position. It is also interesting to understand how many BGP feeders should be added to the current route collector infrastructure in order to improve the quality of data. To determine these values, we used the methodology illustrated in Section 4.2.2 considering the current set of full feeders $\mathcal{F}$ as part of the initial set of solution $\mathcal{P}$, and considering the number of additional BGP feeders as $n = |\mathcal{P}| - |\mathcal{F}|$. Results per each geographic region are reported in Table 9.

Region	$\|\mathcal{P} \cup \mathcal{I} \cup \mathcal{R}\|$	
	On IXPs	*Stubs*
AF	27 (12.79 %)	114 (54.03 %)
AP	472 (28.04 %)	942 (55.97 %)
EU	1,931 (41.60 %)	2,250 (48.48 %)
LA	204 (29.14 %)	394 (56.29 %)
NA	406 (12.55 %)	1,509 (46.67 %)
W	2,944 (31.88 %)	4,221 (45.72 %)

Table 7: Characteristics of candidate BGP feeders

Region	$n = \|\mathcal{P}\| - \|\mathcal{F}\|$		
	$d = 1$	$d = 2$	$d = 3$
AF	117	97	95
AP	922	843	831
EU	2,249	2,072	2,050
LA	389	359	357
NA	1,519	1,423	1,405
W	4,266	3,785	3,714

Table 9: Additional feeders required in each region

A comparison of the number of additional ASes required and the number of non-stub ASes (see Table 4) reveals that the methodology covered every non-stub AS with a number of new BGP feeders which is about 50-60% of the number of non-stub ASes in each region. In addition, a priority for each AS found to be part of $\mathcal{P}$ can be identified by recording the amount of non-stub ASes that are found to be uniquely covered by an element in $\mathcal{P}$ during phase a) of the methodology[7]. The higher this value is, the larger the coverage of the element considered. The distribution of these values can be found in Fig. 9, while the complete AS ranking is available at [23].

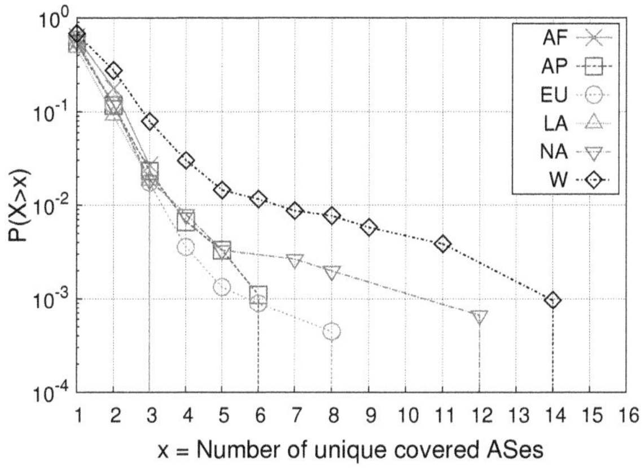

Figure 9: CCDF of the number of ASes uniquely covered

The number of elements covered uniquely by a single AS is never too large, since typically a customer demands its Internet reachability to a set of well-known ISPs. The distribution of this priority index also allows us to make a priority selection, adding first those ASes with the highest number of unique covered AS values (see Fig. 9). Exploiting this priority selection, by just adding a number of ASes comparable to the current number of feeders, the route collectors can now see about one in three non-stubs in each region (see Table 10). This means that the capture of a more complete AS-level view of the Internet is a feasible task in terms of numbers of elements to be connected and, consequently, of costs. Thus our methodology would seem to be a very useful tool to drive the growth of the route collector infrastructure.

It must be stressed that our methodology extracts the optimal solution for the input data provided, thus, if a new BGP feeder is introduced, the solution may no longer be optimal. In any case, it still represents an upper bound to the number of additional full feeders needed. In fact, the introduction of new data may add previously hidden connections and may lead the tagging algorithm exploited to infer a higher number of p2c connections. These new connections may change the p2c-distance of several ASes that might be reached by exploiting a lower number of feeders. However, it would still be possible to apply the methodology once again on the new data to obtain a new optimal value.

[7]The same ranking value is also inherited by every element in $\mathcal{I}$ that is related to an element in $\mathcal{P}$ due to their interchangeability. However, only one of them is required to be connected.

Region	*# Not stub ASes covered*	
	Current status	*Top priority introduction*
AF	0 (0.00%)	71 (31.00%)
AP	88 (5.54%)	452 (28.45%)
EU	209 (5.65%)	958 (25.92%)
LA	26 (3.95%)	148 (22.49%)
NA	148 (5.85%)	728 (28.77%)
W	384 (5.27%)	2,137 (29.35%)

Table 10: Coverage improvements by doubling the number of BGP feeders

6. CONCLUSIONS

The BGP route collector projects that have been developed to date are extremely valuable for researchers, as they are the most reliable source of information for gathering data on the infrastructure of the Internet. However, BGP data are currently only collected from a small amount of ASes, thus limiting the quality of the inferences that can be drawn from analysing such data. Studies on Internet topology structure must be fully aware of the high level of incompleteness of BGP data, since a topological analysis of the Internet as viewed from these monitors is like analysing a roadmap of a given country where the highways are known, but most of the secondary roads are not shown!

In this paper, we have quantitatively evaluated the currently available BGP route collector infrastructure, showing that it is only able to reveal complete AS-level connectivity information about a very small number of ASes. The current BGP feeders that are contributing with their full routing tables are typically large ASes such as provider-free and worldwide ISPs. This implies that the current vision of the BGP route collector projects cannot capture any of the p2p connections that small or medium-sized ASes may establish. The only solution to deal with this incompleteness is to dramatically increase the number of BGP feeders of these projects. In this perspective, we have outlined a systematic methodology to infer the minimum number of ASes that the route collector projects should introduce as BGP feeders in order to maximize the amount of information that can be collected. We found that multi-homed ASes with a small-medium size are the most useful contributors in a topology discovery perspective.

Our methodology provides a useful tool to select those ASes that are the most useful in enhancing the quality of topology information data. We are aware that this kind of data is extremely hard to obtain, but we also believe that the greatest problem in data gathering is that ASes are not stimulated enough to join any of the current projects, since no direct service is offered by the projects in change of the voluntary participation of ASes. Thus, it makes sense to imagine that currently the route collector projects are used by several large ISPs to promote their reachability. In particular, it might be a good idea to create services based on the real-time analysis of the inter-domain routing from different points of view in return of full routing tables, following the *do ut des* principle. Such services would be valuable for many ASes, ranging from local ISPs to CDNs, and thus encourage them to participate. Otherwise, it might be useful to exploit alternative tools to improve the amount of data available. Specifically, some of the traceroute-based projects [28, 29, 30, 31] are able to bypass the reluctance in disclosing the routing information of AS owners by placing agents directly on user applications and, thus, obtaining data that would not be collected otherwise.

7. ACKNOWLEDGMENTS

We would like to thank Massimo Pappalardo (University of Pisa) and Paolo Nobili (University of Salento) for their very useful advice provided during the formulation and solution of our MSC problem.

8. REFERENCES

[1] K. Keys, "Internet-Scale IP Alias Resolution Techniques," *ACM SIGCOMM CCR*, vol. 40, no. 1, pp. 50–55, 2010.

[2] D. Achlioptas, A. Clauset, D. Kempe, and C. Moore, "On the Bias of Traceroute Sampling: or, Power-law Degree Distributions in Regular Graphs," in *ACM STOC '05*, pp. 694–703, 2005.

[3] B. Huffaker, A. Dhamdhere, M. Fomenkov, and K. Claffy, "Toward Topology Dualism: Improving the Accuracy of AS Annotations for Routers," in *PAM '10*, pp. 101–110, 2010.

[4] Y. Zhang, R. Oliveira, H. Zhang, and L. Zhang, "Quantifying the Pitfalls of Traceroute in AS Connectivity Inference," in *PAM '10*, pp. 91–100, 2010.

[5] R. Oliveira, D. Pei, W. Willinger, B. Zhang, and L. Zhang, "The (In)Completeness of the Observed Internet AS-level Structure," *IEEE/ACM TON*, vol. 18, no. 1, pp. 109–122, 2010.

[6] Y. He, G. Siganos, M. Faloutsos, and S. Krishnamurthy, "Lord of the Links: A Framework for Discovering Missing Links in the Internet Topology," *IEEE/ACM TON*, vol. 17, no. 2, pp. 391–404, 2009.

[7] R. Cohen and D. Raz, "The Internet Dark Matter - on the Missing Links in the AS Connectivity Map," in *IEEE INFOCOM '06*, pp. 1–12, 2006.

[8] k. claffy, "Border Gateway Protocol (BGP) and Traceroute Data Workshop Report," *ACM SIGCOMM Computer Communication Review (CCR)*, vol. 42, pp. 28–31, Jul 2012.

[9] M. R. Garey and D. S. Johnson, *Computers and Intractability; A Guide to the Theory of NP-Completeness*. New York, NY, USA: W. H. Freeman & Co., 1990.

[10] E. Gregori, A. Improta, L. Lenzini, L. Rossi, and L. Sani, "Inferring Geography from BGP Raw Data," in *IEEE NetSciCom '12*, pp. 208–213, 2012.

[11] R. Govindan and A. Reddy, "An Analysis of Internet Inter-Domain Topology and Route Stability," in *IEEE INFOCOM '97*, pp. 850–857, 1997.

[12] H. Chang, R. Govindan, S. Jamin, S. Shenker, and W. Willinger, "Towards Capturing Representative AS-level Internet Topologies," *Computer Networks*, vol. 44, no. 6, pp. 737–755, 2004.

[13] K. Chen, C. Hu, W. Zhang, Y. Chen, and B. Liu, "On the Eyeshots of BGP Vantage Points," in *IEEE GLOBECOM '09*, pp. 3558–3563, 2009.

[14] L. Gao, "On Inferring Autonomous System Relationships in the Internet," *IEEE/ACM TON*, vol. 9, no. 6, p. 733, 2001.

[15] M. Roughan, S. J. Tuke, and O. Maennel, "Bigfoot, Sasquatch, the Yeti and Other Missing Links: What We Don't Know About the AS Graph," in *IMC '08*, pp. 325–330, 2008.

[16] "University of Oregon Route Views Project." http://www.routeviews.org.

[17] "RIPE NCC Routing Information Service." http://www.ripe.net/data-tools/stats/ris/routing-information-service.

[18] "Packet Clearing House." http://www.pch.net.

[19] B. Augustin, B. Krishnamurthy, and W. Willinger, "IXPs: mapped?," in *IMC '09*, pp. 336–349, 2009.

[20] A. Dhamdhere, H. Cherukuru, C. Dovrolis, and K. Claffy, "Measuring The Evolution of Internet Peering Agreements," in *Proceedings of the 11th international IFIP TC 6 conference on Networking - Volume Part II*, IFIP'12, (Berlin, Heidelberg), pp. 136–148, 2012.

[21] "Maxmind GeoIPLite database." http://www.maxmind.com/app/geoip_country.

[22] X. Dimitropoulos, D. Krioukov, M. Fomenkov, B. Huffaker, Y. Hyun, k. claffy, and G. Riley, "AS Relationships: Inference and Validation," *ACM SIGCOMM Computer Communication Review (CCR)*, vol. 37, pp. 29–40, Jan 2007.

[23] "Isolario project." http://www.isolario.it.

[24] E. Gregori, A. Improta, L. Lenzini, and C. Orsini, "The Impact of IXPs on the AS-level Topology Structure of the Internet," *Computer Communications*, vol. 34, pp. 68–82, 2010.

[25] S. Mecke and D. Wagner, "Solving Geometric Covering Problems by Data Reduction," in *ESA '04*, vol. 3221 of LNCS, pp. 760–771, 2004.

[26] G. L. Nemhauser and L. A. Wolsey, *Integer and combinatorial optimization*. New York, NY, USA: Wiley-Interscience, 1988.

[27] E. Gregori, A. Improta, L. Lenzini, L. Rossi, and L. Sani, "BGP and Inter-AS Economic Relationships," in *IFIP TC-6 Networking '11*, vol. 2, pp. 54–67, 2011.

[28] A. Faggiani, E. Gregori, L. Lenzini, S. Mainardi, and A. Vecchio, "On the Feasibility of Measuring the Internet Through Smartphone-based Crowdsourcing," in *WINMEE '12*, pp. 1–6, 2012.

[29] "Distributed Internet MEasurement System." http://www.netdimes.org/new/.

[30] K. Chen, D. R. Choffnes, R. Potharaju, Y. Chen, F. E. Bustamante, D. Pei, and Y. Zhao, "Where the Sidewalk Ends: Extending the Internet AS Graph Using Traceroutes from P2P Users," in *ACM CoNEXT '09*, pp. 217–228, 2009.

[31] P. Marchetta, P. Mérindol, B. Donnet, A. Pescapé, and J.-J. Pansiot, "Topology discovery at the router level: a new hybrid tool targeting ISP networks," *IEEE JSAC, Special Issue on Measurement of Internet Topologies*, vol. 29, October 2011.

Quantifying Violations of Destination-based Forwarding on the Internet

Tobias Flach
University of Southern California
Los Angeles, CA 90089, USA
flach@usc.edu

Ethan Katz-Bassett
University of Southern California
Los Angeles, CA 90089, USA
ethan.kb@usc.edu

Ramesh Govindan
University of Southern California
Los Angeles, CA 90089, USA
ramesh@usc.edu

ABSTRACT

Initially, packet forwarding in the Internet was destination-based – that is, a router would forward all packets with the same destination address to the same next hop. In this paper, we use active probing methods to quantify and characterize deviations from destination-based forwarding in today's Internet. From over a quarter million probes, we analyze the forwarding behavior of almost 40,000 intermediate routers. We find that, for 29% of the targeted routers, the router forwards traffic going to a single destination via different next hops, and 1.3% of the routers even select next hops in different ASes. Load balancers are unlikely to explain these AS-level variations, and in fact we uncover causes including routers inside MPLS tunnels that otherwise employ default routes. We also find that these violations can significantly affect the results of measurement tools that rely on destination-based forwarding, and we discuss some ideas for making these tools more robust against these violations.

Categories and Subject Descriptors

C.2.3 [**Computer-Communication Networks**]: Network Operations—*Network management*; C.2.6 [**Computer-Communication Networks**]: Internetworking—*Routers*

Keywords

Routing, Measurements, Forwarding, Ping, Traceroute

1. INTRODUCTION

Historically, most IP routers determined the next hop of a packet based solely on the destination of that packet [8]. As the routing fabric has evolved, networks have deployed several mechanisms that violate destination-based forwarding. Many Internet routers employ load balancing, with the majority of load balancers splitting traffic based on the flow identifier [3]. Tunneling using encapsulation (e.g., MPLS label switching or IP-in-IP encapsulation) can produce different routes than destination-based forwarding, as routers in the tunnel forward packets based on a label or the IP address of the tunnel endpoint. Finally, policy-based forwarding mechanisms may determine next hops using policies specified on arbitrary header fields to realize, for example, differentiated service.

Despite the existence of such mechanisms, a number of measurement systems still assume destination-based forwarding [6, 10, 15]. These systems are agnostic to whether routers forward based on destination or based on, say, labels. However, their correctness depends on the resulting routes being observably destination-based, in that all packets from a router to a destination follow the same path.

For example, reverse traceroute assumes forwarding is destination-based in order to stitch together a path out of segments of multiple paths to a common destination [10]. This stitching could yield false paths if routers forward based on factors other than just the destination address.

As another example, Doubletree attempts to minimize the number of probes required for topology discovery [6]. It uses hop-by-hop probing, like traceroute, to find (partial) paths between source-destination pairs, but stops probing for a pair if it observes an interface which was encountered earlier while probing on a different path to the same destination. In that case, Doubletree assumes that the remainder of the path is the same for both pairs. This may not hold if forwarding is not strictly destination-based.

Figure 1 illustrates how violations of destination-based forwarding can significantly distort path measurements. This figure shows the result of two probes sent to a PlanetLab node at the University of Auckland, New Zealand. We sent the first probe from a PlanetLab host at the University of Texas in Arlington, and we injected the second probe at one of the intermediate nodes observed on the first probe's path. The two probes take completely different AS-level paths because we injected the second probe at a router inside an MPLS tunnel. Because the injected packet lacked an MPLS label, the router forwarded it via a default route [14].

In this paper, we make two contributions. First, we devise a general methodology to detect destination-based forwarding violations; prior work (e.g., [4]) has described methodologies tailored towards specific kinds of violations like load balancing. Combining and adapting two existing probing techniques [7, 10], our technique uses source-spoofed IP *record-route* pings to quantify violations of destination-based forwarding. By injecting packets in routers in the middle of a source-destination path, we are able to detect violations caused by MPLS tunnels. In addition, these injected packets have different contents, so they can exercise load balancers or certain violations due to policy-based forwarding.

Our second contribution is an analysis of three research questions: How often is destination-based forwarding violated (Section 3)? What are the causes of these violations (Section 3 & 4)? What effect do these violations have on the accuracy of mea-

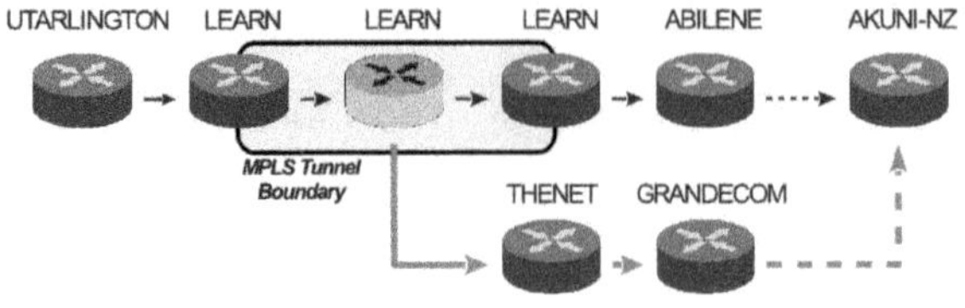

Figure 1: Observed partial paths for two probes to the same New Zealand destination. The first probe (thin/blue arrows) traverses the LEARN network via an MPLS tunnel. We inject the second probe (thick/red arrows) at the colored router inside the tunnel. The router forwards it based on the IP table entry for the destination. Each node is labeled with its AS. Dashed arrows indicate elided paths.

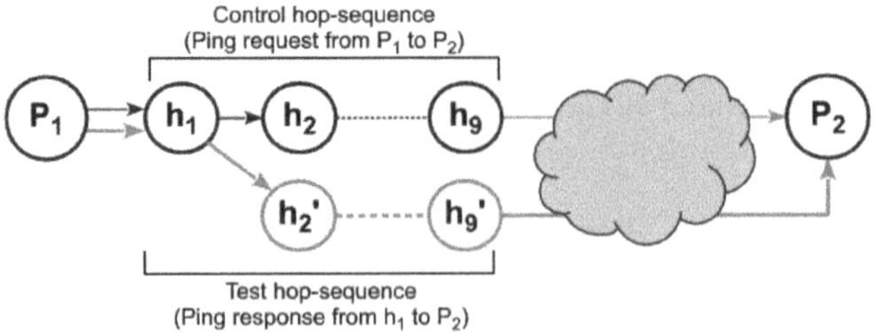

Figure 2: Example for two comparable paths to the same destination P_2. The thin/blue path (top) is traversed by an RR ping request sent directly to P_2. The thick/red path (bottom) is traversed by a spoofed RR ping request sent to h_1 and the response forwarded to P_2. Note that only the first nine hops can be recorded in either case, thus the remainder of the path to the destination is unknown.

surement systems that assume the prevalence of destination-based forwarding (Section 5)? To answer these questions, we employ our probing methods on PlanetLab and conduct large-scale experiments, measuring paths between PlanetLab hosts and from PlanetLab to the broader Internet. We measure over 250,000 paths spanning over 3,700 ASes and find that a *non-negligible fraction (4.4%) of probed ASes exhibit violations that cause AS-level differences in paths*. Moreover, we find that violations of destination-based forwarding can significantly skew the results obtained by tools like reverse traceroute and Doubletree. We also find that a tool like reverse traceroute can easily be made more robust to such violations, but it is less obvious how to make Doubletree more robust.

2. MEASUREMENT METHODOLOGY

In this paper, we use active probing to find routes that observably violate destination-based forwarding. We first measure a path $h_1, h_2, \ldots h_n$ from a PlanetLab source to a destination D. Then, for each router h_i on that path, we want h_i to send a packet to D, to test whether it forwards to the same next hop h_{i+1} observed in our original path. By forcing h_i to send the packet – that is, by changing the point where the packet is injected into the network[1] – we guarantee that it does not route based on encapsulation originated by another router, thus giving us visibility inside tunnels. Since we do not have direct access to h_i, we have to induce it into sending a packet to D, which we can do by sending it an ICMP Echo Request and measuring the path that h_i's response uses.

While traceroute cannot measure this path, an IP Record Route ping (henceforth *RR ping*) can [10]. An RR ping is an ICMP Echo Request with the Record Route (RR) IP option enabled. The IP standard requires that, if a packet has the RR option set, routers record the IP address of one of their interfaces into the packet header. However, the RR field only has space for nine entries, and some routers do not honor the standard. Thus, only the first nine routers that implement the RR option will record one of their interfaces, and later routers will not overwrite these entries. A router that receives an RR ping will copy the RR field into the ICMP Echo Response, and hops on the reverse path will fill the remaining slots. Many routers support the RR option [17], and the global distribution of PlanetLab allows probes to reach many IP addresses within the nine-hop limit [9]. Nevertheless we acknowledge that the limitations of RR might introduce some bias to our data.

Baseline Experiments: Our experiments use PlanetLab nodes to send RR pings and receive the responses. To describe our methodology, we discuss our baseline experiments conducted between source-destination pairs $\langle P_1, P_2 \rangle$ both on PlanetLab, resulting in a data set we label *Set PL/PL* (PlanetLab-to-PlanetLab). Later, we discuss extensions to this methodology.

For each such pair, P_1 first sends an RR ping request to another PlanetLab host P_2. Depending on the hop distance between the pair, the RR field in the response that P_1 receives will include all or part of the forward path to P_2 and may include all or part of the reverse path back to P_1. The hops on the *forward* path of this probe constitute what we call a *control hop-sequence*.

To detect violations to destination-based forwarding, we compare this hop sequence with sequences generated by sending *test* probes as follows (Figure 2). P_1 sends an RR ping to each forward path hop h_i, but *spoofs the source address as* P_2. Spoofing ensures that the response traverses the path between h_i and P_2. The response records hops in this path, when header space permits, and we use these hops to form what we call a *test hop-sequence*. This technique is strongly influenced by the methodology of reverse traceroute [10] and a prior technique used to estimate ICMP generation delays [7].

Thus, while the control probe is routed *through* the forward hops, we inject the i-th test probe *at* h_i. If forwarding were strictly destination-based, the control probe and the response to the test probe would follow the same path from h_i to P_2 because they are both destined to P_2, even though they have different source addresses (the response has h_i as the source address). On the other hand, if the next hop h'_{i+1} in the test hop-sequence is different from the next hop in the control hop-sequence, the hop h_i violates destination-based forwarding. In this case, we say that a *path fork* occurred at router h_i and that h_i satisfies the *fork condition*. However, the converse is not true: h_i may violate destination-based forwarding, but this violation may not always be visible in the way packets are forwarded at h_i.

Since a fork condition may be caused by a routing change between the control and the test probes, we repeat the pair of probes to ensure that the fork condition is reproducible. If a hop h_i reliably satisfies the fork condition, it is said to be a *violator*. Note that a violator need not violate destination-based forwarding for all traffic through it; our definition classifies the router as a violator if it exhibits the fork condition for at least one source-destination pair.

Extended Experiment Sets: As seen in the *Set PL/PL* part of Figure 3, only the first eight routers on a path between two PlanetLab nodes can be classified, and the source node must support spoofing. To target routers that are not observed on paths between

[1] In this study, we only modified the point of injection (and therefore the source address of the packet), to keep the methodology concise. Thus, we do not detect violations caused by differing port numbers, protocol types, etc.

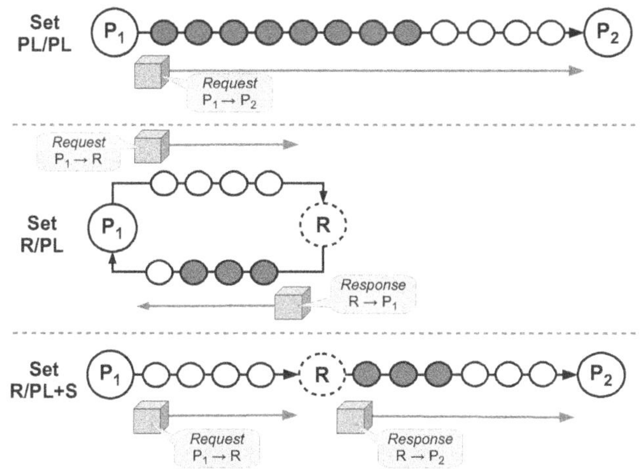

Figure 3: Overview of the coverage of nodes by each of the experiment sets and the ping packets associated with it. Violations can only be detected in filled nodes due to the RR hop limit.

PlanetLab nodes, we designed two additional sets of experiments. In *Set R/PL* (Router-to-PlanetLab) we send an RR ping from a PlanetLab node P_1 to a node R and use the hops visited by the response along the *reverse* path back to P_1 as the control hop-sequence. Then, P_1 sends an RR ping to each such hop as the test probe, again selecting the hops visited by the response as the test hop-sequence. Since we designed this approach to analyze paths back to the source of the ping, it has the advantage of not requiring spoofing. However, it has the drawback that R can be at most seven hops away from the source to leave space for at least two reverse hops in the RR field. We inject the test probe at the first reverse hop and use the second reverse hop to test the fork condition. The *Set R/PL* part of Figure 3 illustrates which hops this methodology can test. To determine which nodes are suitable choices for R for each PlanetLab node, we had the node send an RR ping to the .1 address in each routable /24 prefix and retained those that were responsive and within range.

Our third set, *Set R/PL+S* (Router-to-PlanetLab with spoofing), uses source spoofing to expand the coverage of the second set, as seen in Figure 3. Each PlanetLab node P_1 probes each nearby router R that it probed in R/PL, but P_1 sends multiple RR pings to R, spoofing as each of the other PlanetLab nodes in turn. This technique measures the (partial) path from R to a PlanetLab node P_2 even if P_2 is not near R. We use the hops $h_1, ..., h_m$ traversed by the response from R to P_2 as the control hop-sequence. We produce the test hop-sequences by sending probes from P_1 to $h_1, ..., h_m$ directly and extracting the hops visited by the response.

Establishing Fork Causality: In addition to determining violators, we also want to establish causality for forks. We explore two causes, load balancing and MPLS tunnels. Attributing violations to other causes is left for future work.

To characterize a violation as induced by load balancing, we employ two techniques. First, we measure the paths between our source-destination pairs with Paris traceroute, a traceroute variant that measures all load balancing paths to the destination [4]. Since traceroute and RR may record different IP addresses for a given router [17], we align the Paris traceroutes with our RR pings using IP alias data [12]. If a violating node is an alias for a load balancer seen by Paris traceroute on the same route, we classify the violation as being caused by load balancing. Since the alias data is likely incomplete, we use a second technique to attribute additional load balancing. Many routers act as packet-based load balancers for packets with IP options, including RR pings [17]. We can pinpoint these nodes by recording the control hop-sequence for a source-destination pair multiple times; we do this by issuing RR pings repeatedly. To find all possible paths with high probability we send 100 probes for each pair, and then compute the confidence interval for observing all next hops [4]. To avoid misclassifications in our analysis, we only used measurements with at least 99% confidence. Our results indicate that the 100 probes we sent per pair were sufficient to reach this confidence threshold in almost all cases. We mark a node as a load balancer if we observed at least two different next hops after that node on measurements to a single destination.

If a router inside an MPLS tunnel forwards the control probe based on a tunnel label, rather than based on the destination, it may choose a different route when it generates and sends the test probe towards the destination. To detect violations correlated with MPLS tunneling, that is cases where the violating node is observed in an MPLS tunnel, we use two detection mechanisms.

First, we rely on traceroute measurements which exhibit MPLS labels for nodes in *explicit MPLS tunnels* [5]. However, up to 50% of the tunnels have configurations which prevent this means of detection. That is, either the nodes do not appear in traceroute measurements at all (opaque or invisible tunnels) or their MPLS labels are obfuscated (implicit tunnels) [5, 18]. As such violations caused by them remain unclassified.

Second, we enhance our measurements to find possible instances of *default routing* regardless of tunnel visibility. Some routers in the middle of tunnels do not carry full routing tables and rely on tunnels to forward packets routed through them [14]. A router configured in this manner will use a default route to forward any packet it sources, and so all packets sent from the router will have the same next hop, regardless of the destination. To detect evidence suggesting such behavior, we sent a number of RR pings to a router, each using a different PlanetLab node as the spoofed source, thus causing the router to send responses to each of those PlanetLab destinations. If all these responses have the same first hop, regardless of the destination, and this hop differs from the next hop we observe on a route *through* the router, we assume the route through the router was traversing a tunnel.

Violation causes such as policy-based forwarding are harder to establish, and we have left these to future work.

3. RESULTS

Analysis methodology: We recorded all experimental datasets between December 16, 2011 and March 12, 2012. Before we conducted each experiment, we compiled a list of suitable PlanetLab nodes by selecting at most one active node per AS. For sets PL/PL and R/PL+S we also removed nodes from the sender set which employ spoofing filters since these experiments use spoofed source addresses in some probes. Since set PL/PL only investigates direct routes between PlanetLab nodes, we encountered fewer than 2,000 unique IPs on the paths between these nodes; sets R/PL and R/PL+S encountered about 25,000 IPs each when targeting arbitrary destinations within seven hops distance. Overall, we recorded more than 260,000 traces using 179 PlanetLab sites, 65 of which do not filter source-spoofed packets.

After we recorded the measurements, we compared each test hop-sequence with its corresponding control hop-sequence. We analyzed the data at two levels of granularity: IP addresses and AS numbers. To map an IP address stored in the RR field to its cor-

Traces recorded	262,034
Involved PlanetLab nodes	179
IP addresses targeted	39,699
IP addresses violating (IP forks)	11,487 (28.9%)
IP addresses violating (AS forks)	505 (1.3%)
ASes targeted	3,777
ASes w/ viol. IP addr. (IP forks)	669 (17.7%)
ASes w/ viol. IP addr. (AS forks)	165 (4.4%)

Table 1: Overview of combined results from all experiment sets (PL/PL, R/PL, R/PL+S)

Type	Freq. (IP)	Freq. (AS)
Non-violating	74.8%	97.8%
Load balancing	16.1%	0.0%
Explicit MPLS tunnel	0.4%	0.0%
Default routing	0.3%	0.3%
Unclassified	6.9%	1.7%
Invalid	1.5%	0.0%

Table 2: Node type frequencies in Set PL/PL for IP and AS forks

Type	Freq. (IP)	Freq. (AS)
Without violation	72.6%	89.9%
Load balancing	22.3%	0.0%
Explicit MPLS tunnel	0.2%	0.0%
Default routing	0.2%	0.2%
Unclassified	11.8%	10.0%

Table 3: Percentages of paths between source-destination pairs where a violation of particular type (or no violation at all) was observed in the PL/PL set (only considering first nine hops)

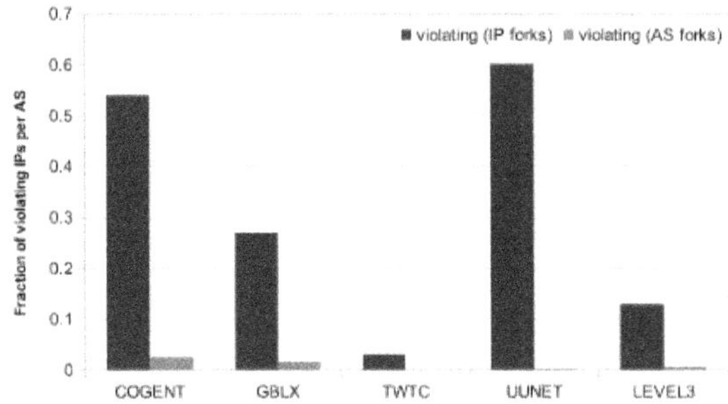

Figure 4: Fraction of violating IP addresses in an AS, that are violators for the most frequently targeted ASes (all experimental sets)

responding AS number, we used prefix-to-AS mappings provided by an iPlane dataset [15].

On the IP level, we classified a targeted node as a violating router if, for at least one pair of paths to a common destination, the next hop differed. In this case we observed an *IP fork*. If the next AS, different from the AS of the targeted node, differed between the control and test hop-sequences, we labeled it an *AS fork*.

Frequency of violations: Table 1 summarizes the experimental results. *Out of nearly 40,000 targeted IP addresses, 28.9% caused IP forks and 1.3% of the nodes caused an AS fork.* The existence of a non-trivial fraction of AS forks is interesting, and to our knowledge, has not been documented elsewhere. Our results also indicate that most of these forks occur at edge routers. It is not surprising that the fraction of nodes causing AS forks is significantly smaller than the number of nodes responsible for IP forks for the following reason. We expect the majority of IP forks to be the result of load balancing, and prior studies have shown that most load balancers only distribute traffic across multiple paths inside their own AS boundaries [3]. Thus, forks caused by load balancing usually converge before leaving the current AS and rarely translate to AS forks.

Causes of Violations: As discussed earlier, violations can have different causes, e.g., load balancing, MPLS tunneling, or other routing policies. In this section we classify forks by cause.

Table 2 provides a classification of the targeted nodes in set PL/PL (classifying violations in sets R/PL and R/PL+S is difficult since this requires traceroutes from the *R* router, which we could not obtain for these sets). The middle column shows statistics for all forks, whereas the right column only considers forks which also result in differing AS traversals. Table 3 shows statistics for the violation types observed on paths between source-destination pairs.

We determined *load balancing*, *Explicit MPLS tunnel*[2], and *default routing* violations as described in Section 2. We classified a node as *invalid* if we suspected routing instabilities or if the confidence of having observed all interfaces was below 99%. Any violation that did not fit in any of these categories is labeled as *unclassified*.

The distribution suggests that we can attribute the majority of IP forks to load balancing. However, for more than 6% of the cases we were unable to determine a violation cause. For many of these cases, we did not observe the violator on any recorded traceroute, e.g., due to ICMP error message filtering by some routers or missing IP address alias mappings. Thus, a fraction of these violations could still be the result of load balancing. However, *we did not observe any load balancers causing AS-level divergences.* All cases of *default routing caused AS forks*, as did a significant portion of the unclassified violations. Additional causes such as routing policies incorporating source addresses may be responsible for some path forks. In Section 4 we discuss some specific instances of the unclassified violations in more detail.

These frequencies may be a lower bound on the likelihood of observing violations on paths, because RR's nine hop limit restricts the coverage of our methodology. For example, as we discuss below, traceroutes from PlanetLab nodes to randomly selected destinations revealed that over 70% of the paths include at least one load-balancing node. However, many of these load balancers were in core networks that were located more than nine hops from our sources.

AS Characteristics: Next, we analyzed which ASes exhibited violations and with what frequency. Table 1 shows that we observed IP-level forks in 17.7% of the visited ASes and *AS forks in 4.4% of the ASes assessed.* However, the distribution of violating IP addresses across ASes is not uniform, with the number of IP addresses in an AS observed to cause a fork varying from 1% to over 70%. In Figure 4, we show the violation frequencies for the ASes in which we probed the most targets. While 55% of the targeted COGENT nodes are violating routers, less than 5% of the targeted TWTC addresses are responsible for a path fork. A likely explanation for these differences across ASes is the variability in AS engineering practices. For example, Sommers et al. found that COGENT is one of the top-10 ASes in terms of total MPLS tunnels

[2]Our traceroute data as well as results from an earlier study [18] indicate that about 25% of the paths contain an MPLS tunnel, but in our experiments most of them do not trigger a violation.

AS Name	Type	obs. IPs	viol. IPs
COGENT	Large ISP	3303	86
AR-TAST-LACNIC	Large ISP	62	18
SWISSCOM	Large ISP	600	13
GNAXNET-AS	Stub	35	12
GBLX	Tier-1	1119	12

Table 4: Statistics for ASes with the largest number of violating IP addresses (viol. IPs) causing AS forks (all experimental sets; obs. IPs describes the number of observed IPs in that AS in our measurements)

Diamond type	μ	σ	Median
Single AS	2.5	2.0	2
Multiple ASes	4.9	2.5	5

Table 5: Diamond length statistics from traces with violations from Set PL/PL

per AS, which likely contributes to the high number of violations in that AS [18].

We obtained similar results when considering only nodes responsible for AS forks. Table 4 shows the statistics for the ASes with the largest number of violating IP addresses and gives the UCLA Internet Topology Project's AS-type classification for the ASes [19]. As the table shows, AS forks can be found even in large ISPs and a Tier-1 provider, possibly due to the usage of MPLS and policy-based routing for traffic engineering.

Diamond lengths: In this section we analyze how much two paths deviate from each other once they traverse a violating router, before reconverging on their path to the common destination. The deviating path portion is termed a *diamond* [4]. To do so, we count the number of hops between the violating router and the first interface common to the two paths after the violating router. We refer to the common interface as the *merging router*, and we refer to the number of hops between the violating router and the merging router as the *diamond length*.[3] Note that due to the nine hop limit of the RR field, we may not observe the merging router. In obtaining these results, we omitted R/PL and R/PL+S datasets since we typically only observe a small number of hops past R, making it rarer to observe complete diamonds. In PL/PL cases when we do not observe the merge, we assume that the next (unrecorded) hop would be the merging router. While this likely results in an underestimation of the diamond lengths, the small number of such cases has a negligible effect on the overall outcome.

As shown in Table 5, diamonds where the forking and merging routers belong to the same AS have an average length of 2.5 nodes. This result roughly coincides with the average diamond length of load-balanced paths studied by Augustin et al. [3]. In contrast, *diamonds induced by AS forks are roughly twice as long on average*. When a path diverges at the AS level, it will usually traverse multiple nodes inside this AS before exiting to another AS where it could reconverge with the path traversed by the control probe.

4. CASE STUDIES

In Section 1 we briefly discussed a routing violation we found with our measurements (see Figure 1). In the example, the targeted IP is not globally routable. Normally, it only carries MPLS-encapsulated packets and local network management traffic. Because it normally only forwards traffic based on MPLS labels, it does not carry a full IP routing table. Instead, it has a default route pointing to the University of Texas System (THENet) that suffices to carry management traffic back to the network operators. In our case, a record route probe from a PlanetLab node at the University of Texas, Arlington (UTA), uncovered the router. Even though the IP was not globally routable, routes to it exist from the University of Texas system, and so our test probe from UTA reached the IP. However, the UTA node spoofed the test probe to claim it came from a different PlanetLab site. The target, lacking a non-default route to this other site, responded to the test probe via its default route. Despite the fact that the control and test probes visit completely different ASes, they do travel via similar locations. More concretely, in this example all probes follow routes via Arlington, Dallas, Houston and Los Angeles before leaving the RR scope.

There are other cases in our dataset showing similar behavior and we omit presenting them separately here.

However, many violations are hard to classify if no load balancing or MPLS labels are observed. This is especially true in cases where we have no corresponding traceroute data available for the measured path, i.e. when we analyze reverse paths. For example, below we describe a violation observed in the R/PL set. The control probes always observed the following hops:

```
1 dinet-gw.spb.citytelecom.ru
2 te4-1-20-adelaida.spb.cloud-ix.net
3 runnet-gw.msk.citytelecom.ru
4 msk-1-gw.runnet.ru
5 CORE-VL42.radio-msu.net
```

In contrast, the test probe response traversed a different path:

```
1 dinet-gw.spb.citytelecom.ru
2 * (vsevnet.ru)
3 border.vsevnet.ru
4 CORE-VL42.radio-msu.net
```

The paths fork in an AS in St. Petersburg, Russia and merge in a different AS in Moscow, but observe different intermediate ASes. Based on the measurements, we can only rule out load balancing as a possible cause for the violation. However, we cannot determine whether the point of injection or the different source address of the test probe traversing the reverse path is causing the forking router to forward the probes to different next hops.

5. IMPACT OF VIOLATIONS

In this section we discuss the possible impact of routing violations on two existing systems: Doubletree and reverse traceroute.

Impact on Doubletree: Doubletree reduces probing overhead in large-scale distributed traceroute measurements by stopping probing a path once it reaches a hop already observed on the path from another monitor to the destination [6]. Consequently, forking paths are not explored and remain invisible to the system (Figure 5).

To quantify the impact, we issued Paris traceroutes from over 170 PlanetLab nodes to 200 randomly chosen destinations.[4] In total, we acquired 30,911 traceroutes.

We found that 22,582 of these (73.1%) include at least one load balancing node. This differs from results by Augustin et al. who found that only 39% of their recorded traces contain a load balancer [3]. Since their study was published in 2007, we suspect that,

[3]If the two forks have different lengths we use the smaller value.

[4]We executed multiple trials with different destination sets to ensure that the results are not biased by the number of destinations selected. We synchronized the probing mechanism, such that traceroutes for the same destination were issued within a time frame of five minutes on all PlanetLab nodes, thus minimizing the probability of route changes.

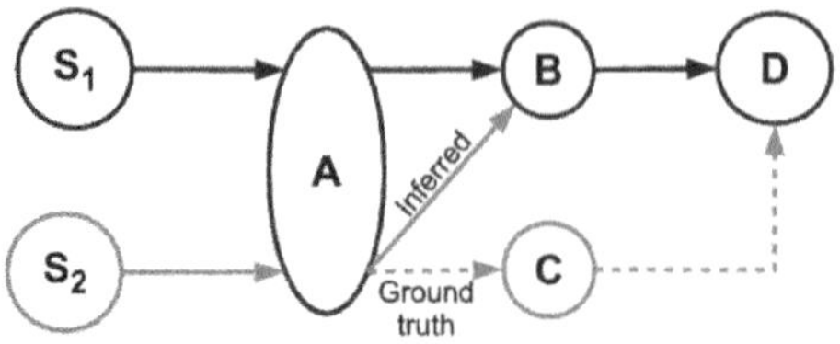

Figure 5: Scenario where Doubletree output deviates from the ground truth. Both paths from S_1 (blue edges) and S_2 (red edges) visit the common hop A. If Doubletree already observed the path $A \rightarrow B \rightarrow D$ it would not find the edge from A to C since the probing algorithm stops at the common node.

as part of the evolution of the Internet, more ASes have started to incorporate load balancing mechanisms into their topologies. This number is also larger than the results shown in Table 3. This discrepancy likely stems from the fact that traceroute provides data about all hops on a path, whereas RR has a 9 hop limit (see discussion of Table 3 in Section 3).

Of our recorded traces, 2997 (9.7%) visit a node with a violation unexplained by load balancing. Furthermore, 1260 traces (4.1%) encounter a node where traces towards the same destination forked into *different* ASes. These numbers are qualitatively consistent with Table 3. In that table, a little over 11% of the traces contained violations not explained by load balancing, with default routing and unknown causes usually resulting in AS forks.

We then determined the number of links that Doubletree would miss. Out of 49,272 observed links in the data, Doubletree would miss 11,222 links (22.8%) as a result of load balancers splitting traffic across multiple next hops. Furthermore, 601 links (1.2%) would remain unobserved due to other violations, with 150 unobserved links (0.3%) related to AS forks. Doubletree was shown to be unable to observe about 18% of links in an experiments [6]; our results are consistent with that number, but give some insight into the causes of unobserved links.

Impact on reverse traceroute: Reverse traceroute assumes forwarding is destination-based in order to incrementally piece together a path [10]. All the violations quantified in Section 3 would impact the accuracy of that technique; in particular, the statistics on diamond lengths give us a feel for the degree to which reverse traceroute can be affected.

Possible solutions: Both systems could employ Paris traceroute-like techniques to identify and incorporate load-balanced paths. However, Doubletree aims to reduce the number of probes required to establish a topology. Since Paris traceroute probes a node many times to ensure that all load balancing paths are explored, incorporating this technique to Doubletree would result in a significantly larger number of probes required to find the currently missing links. Thus, it is less clear how Doubletree should balance the tension between completeness and overhead reduction.

Additionally, systems could use the techniques in this paper to generate blacklists of violation candidates along a path, at the expense of additional probing overhead. Upon encountering these hops, systems could issue additional measurements to improve confidence in a result or flag it as suspect. For example, reverse traceroute could send additional spoofed RR pings, as described above, to find hops employing default routing that would otherwise distort results. Upon encountering these hops, reverse traceroute can easily adapt its IP timestamp-based technique to verify that hops discovered by its RR probes actually appear along the end-to-end path and not just on a default route. Similarly, in cases where an RR ping yields multiple reverse hops, reverse traceroute can then target each of those hops to check for consistent routes, as we did in this paper. Using a week of data from a reverse traceroute deployment monitoring routing failures [11], we analyzed probes sent for over 33,000 router-destination pairs. We found that 75% of them included multiple reverse hops, thus enabling the consistency check described above.

6. RELATED WORK

Systems such as reverse traceroute [10], Doubletree [6], and iPlane [15] assume destination-based forwarding. Other studies also make this assumption [2, 13, 16], but we omitted a detailed discussion of these due to space considerations.

Prior studies analyzed the prevalence of load balancing and MPLS deployments in the Internet. Augustin et al. describe measurements from fifteen RON nodes to over 68,000 destinations using Paris traceroute [3]. Their 2007 study found that about 39% of the paths between source-destination pairs contain at least one flow-based load balancer. In contrast, we have designed a generic mechanism to detect violations to destination based forwarding and demonstrate the existence of a non-trivial proportion of AS forks.

Using data from the CAIDA Archipelago project [1], Sommers et al. were able to detect MPLS tunnels based on traceroute data [18]. Besides extracting MPLS stacks from traceroute data, they inferred probable tunnels by comparing latency differences between consecutive hops. Their results indicate that about 25% of all paths in 2011 contained at least one tunnel. While their MPLS detection techniques are more advanced than ours, we did not incorporate their methodology due to the high number of false positives. Furthermore, our focus was on detecting violations to destination-based forwarding, and we use a different probing methodology because, as we have discussed above, not all MPLS tunnels trigger these violations.

Recently Donnet et al. demonstrated additional mechanisms to detect MPLS tunnels [5]. In their study they propose inference techniques for non-explicit tunnels based on using TTL signatures from traceroute and ping measurements. Incorporating their methods into our analysis would likely help to attribute some of the unclassified violations to non-explicit MPLS tunnels, and we leave this to future work.

7. CONCLUSION

We designed a probing methodology to uncover violations of destination-based forwarding. Our measurements reveal that an unexpectedly significant fraction of these violations cause forked paths to traverse different ASes as compared to the original path: 4.4% of targeted ASes and about 10.2% of paths exhibit such behavior. In general, these violations impact the accuracy of systems like Doubletree and reverse traceroute; the former can miss 22% of the links as a result of these violations. Finally, while it is conceptually easy to mitigate the impact of these violations in reverse traceroute by incorporating some of our mechanisms, it is less clear how to do so in Doubletree in a manner that also achieves one of that system's objectives, reducing probing overhead.

Acknowledgments

We would like to thank our shepherd, Peter Steenkiste, and the anonymous referees for their helpful comments on earlier versions of the paper. In addition we thank Byron Hicks from the Lonestar Education and Research Network (LEARN) for his insight on the causes of violations observed in his network. This work was funded in part by Google, Cisco, and the NSF (CNS-0121778 and CNS-0905568).

8. REFERENCES

[1] Archipelago IPv4 Routed /24 AS Links Dataset. http://www.caida.org/data/active/ipv4_routed_topology_aslinks_dataset.xml.

[2] B. Armbruster, J. C. Smith, and K. Park. A Packet Filter Placement Problem with Application to Defense Against Spoofed Denial of Service Attacks. *European Journal of Operational Research*, 176(2):1283–1292, 2007.

[3] B. Augustin, T. Friedman, and R. Teixeira. Measuring Load-balanced Paths in the Internet. In *IMC*, 2007.

[4] B. Augustin, T. Friedman, and R. Teixeira. Multipath tracing with Paris traceroute. In *E2EMON*, 2007.

[5] B. Donnet, M. Luckie, P. Mérindol, and J.-J. Pansiot. Revealing MPLS tunnels obscured from traceroute. *SIGCOMM Computer Communication Review*, 42(2):87–93, 2012.

[6] B. Donnet, P. Raoult, T. Friedman, and M. Crovella. Deployment of an Algorithm for Large-Scale Topology Discovery. *IEEE Journal on Selected Areas in Communications*, 24(12):2210–2220, 2006.

[7] R. Govindan and V. Paxson. Estimating router ICMP generation delays. In *PAM*, 2002.

[8] Internet Engineering Task Force. *RFC 1812: Requirements for IP Version 4 Routers*, June 1995.

[9] E. Katz-Bassett. *Systems for Improving Internet Availability and Performance*. PhD thesis, University of Washington, 2012.

[10] E. Katz-Bassett, H. V. Madhyastha, V. K. Adhikari, C. Scott, J. Sherry, P. van Wesep, T. E. Anderson, and A. Krishnamurthy. Reverse Traceroute. In *NSDI*, 2010.

[11] E. Katz-Bassett, C. Scott, D. R. Choffnes, I. Cunha, V. Valancius, N. Feamster, H. V. Madhyastha, T. E. Anderson, and A. Krishnamurthy. LIFEGUARD: Practical repair of persistent route failures. In *SIGCOMM*, 2012.

[12] K. Keys, Y. Hyun, M. Luckie, and K. Claffy. Internet-Scale IPv4 Alias Resolution with MIDAR: System Architecture - Technical Report. Technical report, Cooperative Association for Internet Data Analysis (CAIDA), May 2011.

[13] A. Kvalbein, A. F. Hansen, T. Čičic, S. Gjessing, and O. Lysne. Multiple routing configurations for fast IP network recovery. *IEEE/ACM Transactions on Networking*, 17(2):473–486, April 2009.

[14] Lonestar Education and Research Network (Austin, Texas): Private communication.

[15] H. V. Madhyastha, T. Isdal, M. Piatek, C. Dixon, T. E. Anderson, A. Krishnamurthy, and A. Venkataramani. iPlane: An Information Plane for Distributed Services. In *OSDI*, 2006.

[16] A. Riedl and D. A. Schupke. Routing Optimization in IP networks Utilizing Additive and Concave Link Metrics. *IEEE/ACM Transactions on Networking*, 15(5):1136–1148, October 2007.

[17] R. Sherwood, A. Bender, and N. Spring. Discarte: A Disjunctive Internet Cartographer. In *SIGCOMM*, 2008.

[18] J. Sommers, P. Barford, and B. Eriksson. On the Prevalence and Characteristics of MPLS Deployments in the Open Internet. In *IMC*, 2011.

[19] UCLA Internet Topology Collection. http://irl.cs.ucla.edu/topology/.

Revisiting Broadband Performance

Igor Canadi
University of Wisconsin-Madison
canadi@cs.wisc.edu

Paul Barford
University of Wisconsin-Madison
pb@cs.wisc.edu

Joel Sommers
Colgate University
jsommers@colgate.edu

ABSTRACT

Understanding the empirical characteristics of broadband performance is of intrinsic importance to users and providers, and has been a significant focus of recent efforts by the Federal Communications Commission (FCC) [9]. A series of recent studies have reported results of empirical studies of broadband performance (*e.g.,* [11, 15, 22]). In this paper, we reappraise previous empirical findings on broadband performance. Our study is based on a unique corpus of crowd-sourced data consisting of over 54 million individual tests collected from 59 metropolitan markets over a 6 month period by Speedtest.net. Following analytic approaches from prior studies, our results confirm many of the raw performance results (upload/download/latency) for ISPs in specific US markets. However, the size and scope of our data enable us to examine the details of characteristics that were not identified in prior studies, thereby providing a more comprehensive view of broadband performance. Furthermore, we also report results of broadband performance characteristics in 35 metropolitan markets outside of the US. This not only provides an important baseline for future study in those markets, but also enables relative comparison of broadband performance between markets world wide.

Categories and Subject Descriptors

C.2.3 [**Network Operations**]: Network management; C.4 [**Performance of Systems**]: Performance attributes; C.4 [**Performance of Systems**]: Measurement techniques

General Terms

Experimentation, Measurement, Performance

Keywords

Access networks, Broadband access

1. INTRODUCTION

High speed broadband connectivity to the home is the foundation for rich media applications and services. Over the past several years, the impact of streaming media enabled by broadband to the home has been dramatic. For example, the growing phenomenon of "cord cutting" — doing away with cable television subscriptions in lieu of streaming — has important implications for service providers, television, advertising and other industries [20].

The increasing reliance by consumers on high speed broadband connectivity has made its performance and reliability a matter of public interest. To that end, the US Federal Communications Commission (FCC) has initiated efforts to develop a national broadband strategy that promotes competition among providers and uses data-driven standards to ensure that service providers do not abuse their market power [8]. The "data driven" mandate led to the FCC's consumer broadband test site, which enables users to evaluate their broadband performance with several different tools [9].

While broadband performance test sites have been available for some time (*e.g.*, [3, 13]) measuring, characterizing, and understanding broadband performance in the large presents several significant challenges. The first is perspective: with nearly two billion Internet users world wide, the task of gathering "representative" data and extracting meaningful information even with a metropolitan area focus is daunting. Second, taking measurements of last mile performance necessitates instrumentation at an end host. While many tools (*e.g.,* [7, 15]) and systems (*e.g.,* [4]) for end host-based performance measurement exist, deploying them broadly and then using them to conduct systematic study intrinsically relies on user participation, which is obviously challenging. Third, different test methods and the diversity of infrastructure in the last mile complicate the interpretation and comparison of measurements. For example, users who run tests from their laptops may be limited by wireless interference instead of their broadband connection. We argue that the collective perspective offered by multiple tests methods is the best way to gain an understanding of broadband performance.

In this paper we present results of a study of broadband performance that seeks to reconfirm results from prior studies and to expand the knowledge base in this critical area. Our study is based on a unique data set provided by `speedtest.net` [3]. Speedtest is a popular end host-based performance measurement application that directs participating users to local servers in over 700 metropolitan markets world wide. We evaluate a data corpus of over 54 million performance tests collected over a 6 month period in 59 metro markets (24 US, 35 non-US).

While the goals of our work are aligned with prior broadband performance studies (*e.g.,* [11, 15, 17, 22]), our approach expands on prior studies in several important ways. Most importantly, we provide a crowd-sourced perspective on broadband performance. While Speedtest data are limited in several ways (see Section 2), the size, diversity and rich details of these data enable us to reconsider results from prior studies. Moreover, we identify new

IMC'12, November 14–16, 2012, Boston, Massachusetts, USA.

characteristics of broadband performance that to the best of our knowledge have not been previously reported. The scope of the Speedtest data also enables us to examine broadband performance from a world-wide perspective. Prior studies have typically focused on broadband performance in the US or Europe. We report results that compare and contrast broadband performance for major geographic areas all over the world.

The first component of our analysis considers broadband performance in 25 metropolitan areas in the United States. The metro areas represent a broad cross section of the population in terms of market size and geographic location. Our analyses focus on download, upload and latency measurements and consider recent results reported by Sundaresan *et al.* [22] as a point of comparison. We begin by reporting results of a small case study that compares Speedtest measurements to SamKnows measurements [4], which were the basis for many of the results in [22]. Next, we consider the question of whether or not users experience consistent performance from their providers, in many cases our findings support observations of prior work (*e.g.*, in terms of lower latencies for cable vs. DSL), but in others they are not (*e.g.*, in terms of provider quality ranking). We make no argument that in cases where our findings differ, that ours are "more valid". Rather, we believe that our findings show that performance comparisons are complex and dynamic, and benefit from on-going study.

The second component of our analysis takes advantage of the crowd-sourced nature of our data to dig into the details of local connectivity. We focus on two characteristics that emerge in our data that were not evident or highlighted in prior studies. The first characteristic is a tight clustering of measurements that show lower performance. While we can not absolutely validate the causes, this could be explained by older service plans that have not been upgraded, older equipment, or rate limiting. The second characteristic considers the question of latency versus distance from a test server. While this may seem obvious, prior studies identify buffers as a potential dominant factor in latency [17]. Our geographic analysis confirms that there is a strong correlation between latency and distance.

The final component of our analysis considers broadband performance in 35 metropolitan areas outside of the US. Our analysis methodology is consistent with studies of US and European broadband performance. Perhaps as expected, we find that broadband performance in Hong Kong is superior to the US on average. We find that performance in Europe is on par with the US on average. We find that performance in South American and African sites is below the US, while performance is relatively lower in India and Indonesia. These results highlight the relative penetration of high speed broadband world wide and have implications for economic development and competitiveness.

The remainder of this paper is organized as follows. In Section 2, we describe the details of the Speedtest measurement methodology, our data set and its limitations. In Section 3, we describe the details of the evaluations that we conduct on our data. The results of our analyses are reported in Section 4. We discuss prior studies that inform our work in Section 5. We summarize, conclude and discuss future work in Section 6.

2. DATA

In this section we describe the Speedtest data set used in our study. We provide an overview of the measurement algorithm used by Speedtest, the deployment of Speedtest servers around the world, and the specific types of data that are collected in their infrastructure. We list the 59 metro areas in which the data were collected. We also discuss limitations with the Speedtest data and how they may affect our comparisons with prior broadband performance studies.

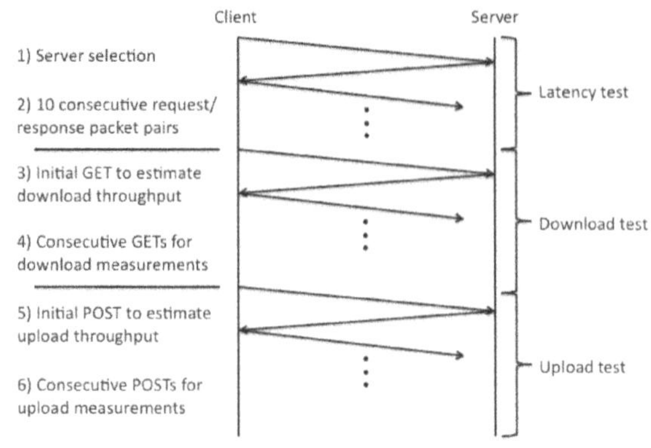

Figure 1: The Speedtest performance measurement protocol, which is activated when clients start a test.

2.1 Speedtest Measurements

`Speedtest.net` [3] is an openly available, Flash-based bandwidth/performance measurement application that is managed and maintained by Ookla, Inc. [2]. Over 3 billion performance tests have been run since 2006 when Speedtest came on line, and there are hundreds of thousands of tests performed per day, globally.

The testing protocol that is initiated by clients running the web-based Speedtest application is shown in Figure 1. When a client initiates a test, a request is automatically sent to the Speedtest server that is identified as being geographically nearest to the client. Alternatively, clients can specify a server for performing a test. There are Speedtest servers deployed in over 700 locations world wide.

The Speedtest wiki [1] explains the details of each test. Measurements of latency, download, and upload performance are conducted via HTTP (TCP port 80). Latency tests use a minimum of 10 RTT ping-style measurements and report the mean result. The first step in a download test is the transfer of a fixed-size file from server to client. This transfer is used to determine the size of a target file that will be used in the actual performance tests. The target file is fixed at a smaller size when the initial transfer indicates a lower bandwidth path. Larger size target files are used when the initial transfer indicates higher bandwidth. The second step in a test consists of repeated transfers of the target file using up to 8 parallel HTTP connections. Care is taken to avoid client caching. Throughput is sampled at up to 30 times per second; the top 10% and bottom 30% are discarded and the mean of the remaining samples is used as the overall throughput estimate. This approach is motivated by an attempt to obviate burst effects due to OS overhead and other host-system effects, and produce a maximum throughput estimate that corresponds to the expected case for the user. Test runs are designed to be relatively short in order to enhance user experience. The use of HTTP (and by extension, TCP) in the Speedtest protocol is prompted by a desire to gather performance measures similar to what many applications would experience.

Upload tests come after download tests. They are designed to follow a protocol that is similar to the download tests.

Each test results in a log entry stored at the local Ookla server that includes a unique test identifier, timestamp, upload and download throughput estimates (in Kb/s), latency estimate (in milliseconds), anonymized client IP address, browser user agent string, client geographic coordinates (longitude / latitude), server name and coordinates, geographic distance between client and server, and ISP name. While Speedtest can be run from either wireline or mobile clients, log entries are easily distinguished by device type and access type.

2.2 Data Sets Considered

The data we use in this study were collected from Speedtest servers located in 59 metro areas over a period of six months from June 1, 2011 through November 30, 2011. The goal in selecting metro areas was to provide a broad perspective on broadband performance. The criteria that were used for selection included geographic location of servers, metro market sizes and socio-economic information. The result were 24 metro areas in the US and 35 outside of the US.

For US, we selected 24 geographically diverse metro areas that can be grouped by population size: small (*e.g.,* Lawrence, KS; Sumter, SC; Grand Forks, ND), medium (*e.g.,* Portland, ME; Grand Rapids, MI; San Francisco, CA) and large (*e.g.,* New York, NY; Los Angeles, CA; Chicago, IL).

For areas outside of the US, we selected ten metro areas in Europe, and five in Asia, Pacific, Middle East, South America and Africa respectively for a total of 35. Similar to the US, these selections were based on a geographic diversity and market size with an attempt to select areas for each category that had roughly the same population. In order to gain a measure of consistency in our evaluations, we only include tests (directed to that server) that are conducted within a 200 miles radius. The full set of metro areas, along with summary statistics of the associated Speedtest results can be found in Table 2.

Our data indicates that roughly 300,000 users per day initiated tests to the 59 servers considered in this study. As noted above, we also have the browser user agent string. Figure 2 shows a breakdown of client operating system and browser types in our data. Further, each test entry includes the client's geographic coordinates. These coordinates are determined from GPS, if available, or by using the MaxMind GeoIP geolocation database [19], which is generally accurate at the city level. Locations of test clients in our data set are shown in Figure 3 (we only show test locations that are within a 200 mile radius of the Speedtest servers included in our study).

Figure 2: Profile of Speedtest users's Web browsers and Operating systems

2.3 Discussion

We believe that the data provided by Speedtest offer a unique and valuable perspective that enhances the general understanding of broadband performance. The broad use of Speedtest around the world enables detailed profiles of broadband performance to be established for diverse markets. The fact that Speedtest has been using substantially the same measurement methodology for years enables longitudinal study of broadband performance and comparisons across markets. The web-based delivery of tests precludes the need for deployment and management of dedicated systems or software at client sites and encourages broad use of the tool.

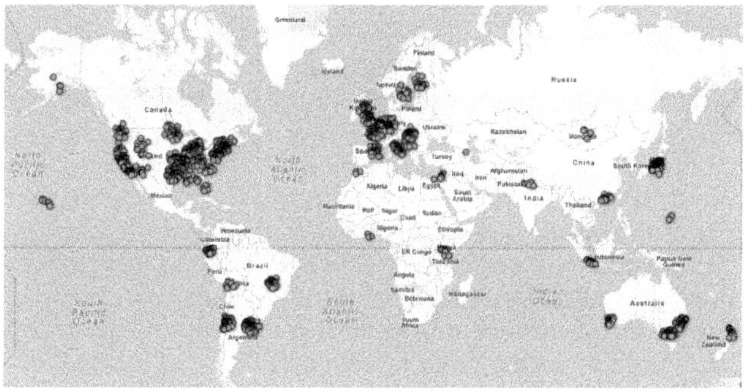

Figure 3: Locations of measurements

While the crowd-sourced nature of the data set is compelling, there are limitations that are important to recognize since they could have an influence on the findings in our study. Speedtest data are assembled based on diverse users running the test application. While some information about client hosts is available (*e.g.,* host operating system via the browser user agent string), this information cannot be verified. Furthermore, host systems are likely to vary widely in terms of hardware and software configurations. There also is no way to dictate when or how tests are run. Indeed, Speedtest may well be invoked when users believe their network performance is poor or otherwise problematic. This may bias results of performance tests toward below average operating conditions. We have no way of establishing baselines for performance or assessing testing bias in each metro area that we consider other than appealing to statistical characterizations and the relatively large numbers of tests conducted over the six month period from which our data is collected. Nevertheless, many of our conclusions described below are consistent with prior work, suggesting that any biases are fairly limited in nature or that prior work suffered from similar or the same biases.

An additional limitation that is specific to our objective of reproducing prior results is the fact that we cannot identify specific users in the Speedtest data. While this does not preclude all analyses, it does mean that can cannot evaluate the performance observed by specific users, which was the focus of certain aspects of prior broadband studies.

3. EVALUATION METHODOLOGY

Analyzing and drawing conclusions from a large, multidimensional data set presents a number of challenges. Toward the goal of reconfirming prior results, many of our evaluation techniques are taken directly from past studies which enables us to draw meaningful comparisons.

To assess the high level characteristics of throughput and latency, we provide summary statistics (average and standard deviation) for each metro area. We also use simple summary statistics for country-level aggregates and present the results using bubble plots, similar to prior work [15]. The location of each bubble is the average throughput performance and the area of bubbles is proportional to the number of measurements. When comparing different US operators, we also use bubble plots to present their average performance and popularity amongst users.

We consider characteristics of specific service providers using scatter plots of download and upload speed for each measurement.

Similar graphical analyses have been used in prior work, such as [22]. When plotting, we make every point a semi-transparent circle, which makes it easy to assess the areas of high and low density: high density areas appear darker, while low density areas appear lighter. We can also more easily distinguish different data points. Due to the large number of measurements for every ISP, in some cases we had to randomly sample the data used in the plots to create manageable figures. Every plot contains roughly 30,000 points that were (uniform) randomly selected from the full dataset. Finally, while scatter plots are a natural way to capture data from a single source, it is difficult to compare two scatter plots. Thus, to compare operators and show correlation between parameters, we use various types of line plots and bar charts.

The Speedtest measurement method estimates upload/download performance from a user to the closest server. If a user is geographically distant from the server, the measurement may reflect wide area effects such as congestion. For this reason, we only consider measurements within a radius of 200 miles of a given server. Latency measurements are potentially the most sensitive to distance (although we recognize that geographic distance may not correlate perfectly with network latency). In our latency analyses, unless otherwise noted, we discard measurements that are more than 50 miles away from the server.

Finally, we note that our data analysis was facilitated through development of a MySQL database on which we ran queries using a series of Python scripts. Statistical analysis and plotting were done using R.

4. BROADBAND PERFORMANCE RESULTS

In this section we report the results of our analysis. Our primary comparisons are with the dataset and findings of the recent study of Sundaresan *et al.* [22], but we also compare our results and data to the prior work of Kreibich *et al.* [15]. We expand on these prior works by examining new geographic regions, and discuss other findings specific to our dataset.

4.1 Alternative Broadband Testing Protocols

The study by Kreibich *et al.* uses data from their Netalyzr system [15], and the recent study by Sundaresan *et al.* [22] reported findings from empirical broadband performance data based on *SamKnows* deployments and from their own BISMark system. Below, we discuss these measurement methods and specifically compare the SamKnows testing method with Speedtest.

4.1.1 SamKnows

SamKnows operates a FCC-sponsored broadband access network study, and has developed a test methodology focused on measuring different aspects of a broadband Internet connection from the gateway's point of view [4]. The tests are executed from a device called a "whitebox", which is a device situated between the access network modem and home router. These devices are deployed in the homes of volunteers, and they contain software that attempts to run a connection test every two hours. The whitebox has the ability to monitor both wired and WiFi network traffic and does not perform tests when it senses any user activity, in order to obtain an accurate measure of access network capabilities.

To measure download and upload speeds, whiteboxes open three concurrent connections with a SamKnows server. First, a warm-up sequence is initiated in which each connection repeatedly downloads small chunks of the target payload. The warm-up period is used to avoid effects of TCP slow start, and network congestion. When three consecutive chunks are downloaded at the same speed, the real testing begins. The test is run for a fixed period of time, or a fixed-size payload. After the test ends, each connection reports reports the throughput it obtained, and the speeds from each connection are summed.

4.1.2 Comparison with SamKnows

Although there are some differences between SamKnows and Speedtest methodologies in the number of parallel connections, and methods of aggregating the raw results, we believe that the biggest difference in reported values is due to where and when the test is executed. SamKnows deploys their whiteboxes between a router and a modem, and the monitoring capabilities designed into the devices help to avoid cross-traffic effects from home networks. Speedtest, on the other hand, can be run from clients connected to home networks over wireless connections. It can also be run when there is activity on the line created by other clients.

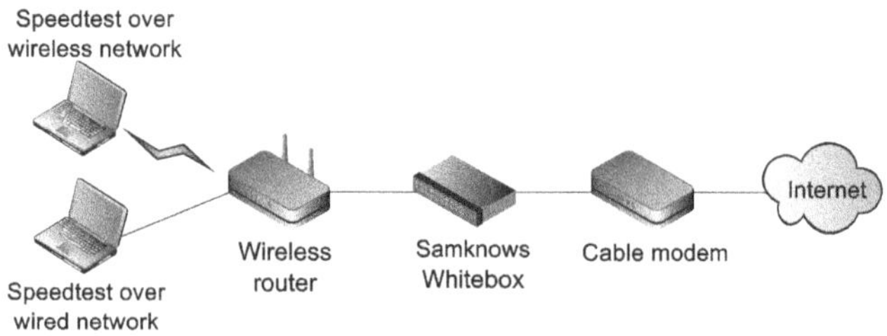

Figure 4: Setup of the network we used to compare Speedtest and Samknows test methodology.

To better understand and evaluate the mentioned differences, we ran both Speedtest and Samknows tests from a network connected to Charter's cable Internet service in Madison, WI. The operator's promised speed was 15 Mb/s download and 3 Mb/s upload with Powerboost [6]. Figure 4 shows the network setup that was used. End hosts were connected to a router through both wired and wireless connections. The router was connected to a SamKnows whitebox, which was in turn connected to the cable modem. We ran a total of 12 tests over the course of two weeks, six in the day time (9am – 4pm) and six in the night time (8pm – 2am). Every test consisted of three runs of each of the following: (1) executing Samknows download and upload test binaries on the whitebox; (2) running a Speedtest from a Macbook Pro connected to the router over 100 Mb/s wired Ethernet; and (3) running a Speedtest from a Macbook Air connected to the router over wireless 802.11g Ethernet.

Figures 5 and 6 show averages of the three runs for each measurement. SamKnows almost always reported higher download speeds than Speedtest over the wired network. However, the difference between the two was very small. Executing Speedtest experiments over the wireless network, on the other hand, shows much slower download performance in all tests except one. The wireless network we were testing on supports download speeds up to 54 Mb/s, so it should not be a bottleneck. The one test where we achieved the full potential of the Internet connection is intriguing; the cause for this surprisingly good performance is presently unclear. SamKnows tests also show higher upload speeds and more consistent results than Speedtest in almost every case. A clear limitation with our Speedtest data is that we have no way of separating the measurements conducted over a wireless network from the ones over a wired network.

To examine the behavior of the Speedtest application in the presence of cross traffic in the home network, we started a download of a large file over the wireless network and simultaneously ran Speedtest from another machine over the wired network. After executing the Speedtest measurement, we executed a SamKnows performance test from the whitebox. Note that while the whitebox usually does not start a test if the line is not idle, it is possible to disable that check, which we did for this experiment. Our results show that a single large file download affects Speedtest, which reports an average of 11 Mb/s, while the SamKnows whitebox reports the correct speed of 15 Mb/s. When we started multiple large file downloads and ran the Speedtest application and whitebox measurement, the results were poor for both Speedtest and SamKnows. The whitebox reported approximately 7.5 Mb/s, and the Speedtest application gave an even lower estimate.

Figures 7 and 8 show the standard deviation of the three runs, presenting the consistency of the results over short time spans. The standard deviation of SamKnows was the lowest for both upload and download throughput tests. In the data point where Speedtest over the wireless network matched the performance of the wired network, the standard deviation of the wireless tests was low and exhibited similar variability as the wired Speedtest and SamKnows measurements. In these experiments, we did not find any significant differences between tests performed during the night and during the day.

4.1.3 Netalyzr

Netalyzr is a Java-based tool that executes various types of probing in order to diagnose access network behavior and performance. Of relevance to our study is the fact that it uses UDP probes to estimate both latency and throughput. It uses a train of small UDP probes sent 100 millisecond intervals to measure latency, then employs a slow-start-like algorithm to detect maximum upload and download throughput. Due to a limitation of the Java environment, there are limits to the maximum throughput detected by Netalyzr (about 20 Mb/s). The client-side tool connects to a back-end server running on Amazon EC2.

A notable similarity between the Speedtest method and Netalyzr is that the measurements are initiated from a computer *behind* the access network gateway/router. This computer may be connected to the local network via WiFi or wired Ethernet, and test traffic is subject to interference with other traffic on the local network. While these end-host based measurements are subject to errors induced by interference (*e.g.*, cross-traffic interference, WiFi contention, etc.), it is arguable that these types of endhost-based measurements give a more accurate perspective of performance that *users* experience. Moreover, end-host based measurements are significantly easier to collect since no special measurement hardware is required. As a result, platforms like Netalyzr and Speedtest add a rich and complementary perspective on broadband performance.

4.2 Revisiting previous findings from US markets

One of the goals of our work is to reassess empirical findings from previous studies [11, 15, 22] in light of the dataset obtained from Speedtest.

Sundaresan *et al.* [22] analyzed SamKnows data from 8 of the biggest ISPs in the US market: Comcast, AT&T (SBC Internet Services), TimeWarner (Road Runner), Verizon, Cox, Qwest, Charter and Cablevision (Optimum Online). The advantages of their data were two fold. First, they have speed measurements from one user taken periodically every hour over the course of few months. Due to privacy reasons, we were not able to connect measurements with specific clients. This limitation prevented us from repeating some of their findings. Second, their tests were conducted from the gateway, thus avoiding bottlenecks and losses in home network. A study by Bauer *et al.* found that the SamKnows method was the most accurate broadband testing method [5], but we note that they found that the Speedtest method also gives a reasonably accurate characterization of access network performance. Furthermore, the Speedtest measurements capture real user experience, and measure the throughput speeds that users actually obtain, as opposed to what they might obtain in perfect conditions.

Figure 9 shows average speeds obtained by users of different ISPs. The center of each circle represents the average download and upload performance obtained by users of a specific ISP. The area of the circle is proportional to the number of measurements that were performed by users of a given ISP on Speedtest's website.

One of the questions addressed in the prior work of Sundaresan *et al.* was whether users achieve consistent performance. Their conclusion was that most of the ISPs provide consistent speeds, except for some ISP-based exceptions (Cablevision, and to a lesser extent, Cox), whose large fraction of users have inconsistent download speeds. We cannot directly compare our results with this prior work due to the inability to identify particular clients or users in our data. Instead, we indirectly evaluate consistent via scatterplot analysis in Figures 10 and 11. Figure 10 shows results for Cablevision, and Figure 11 shows results for Charter; we note that both of these ISPs are cable providers. Every point in the graph is one measurement from a user in the United States. In our measurements, we found that Cablevision exhibited the best upload speed consistencies (as defined by variability in the measurements), and we see that patterns in the download vs. upload scatter plots are very similar. These results suggest that users may indeed obtain consistent performance from these ISPs, although we cannot directly verify that. In terms of download speeds, both ISPs exhibit high variability: in both plots, download speeds are spread across the large interval, while upload speeds are largely localized in small intervals. Our results at least confirm the notion that upload speeds are more consistent than download speeds.

To compare cable operators with DSL operators, in Figures 12 and 13 we show the results of measurements for AT&T and Qwest operators, respectively. In general it seems that DSL operators show better clustering of points around their service plans. They also show higher variability in upload rates than cable operators.

In addition to download and upload throughput, our data also contain latency measurements between the user and Speedtest's server. Sundaresan *et al.* measure and make conclusions based on *last-mile latencies*, which is the latency from the gateway to the first hop in network. One of their results is that cable operators generally exhibit lower latencies than DSL operators. Although our dataset includes end-to-end latency measurements, we observe the same result. Figure 14 shows the latency distribution for cable and DSL operators. 60% of all the measurements for the cable operators are lower than 20 ms. The only exception is Cox, whose majority of users are in the 20–29 ms range. DSL users see higher latencies and more variance. Almost half of the measurements on Qwest reported latencies larger than 60 ms. Verizon's users with latency below 20 ms are their FiOS users.

Figure 15 shows average download throughputs for measurements with specific latencies. It is clear that the average download drops as latency increases. One explanation for this effect could be that measurements with bigger latencies were conducted under higher load. This explanation may correspond to findings of the study by Sundaresan *et al.*, which attribute the effect to large modem buffers. Another possible explanation is the well-known bias of TCP against longer round-trip times, which may result in lower throughputs achieved.

Sundaresan *et al.* also looked into how time of day affects user's performance. They observed the biggest difference between peak

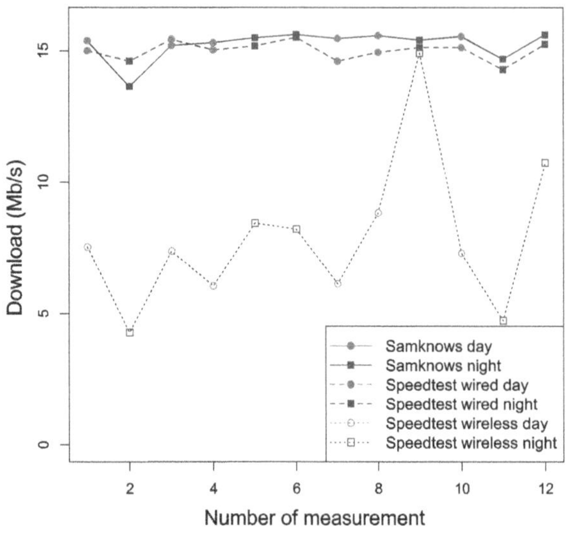

Figure 5: Download throughput as reported by Speedtest on wired and wireless network and SamKnows.

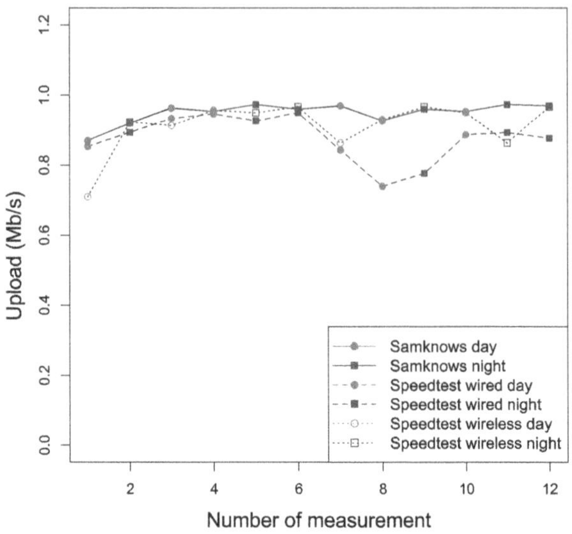

Figure 6: Upload throughput as reported by Speedtest on wired and wireless network and Samknows.

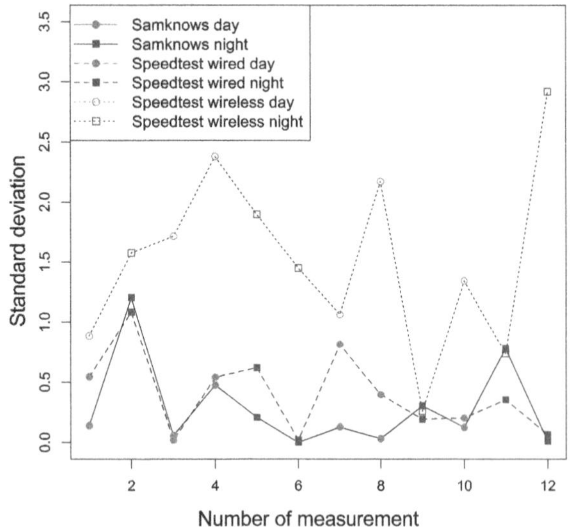

Figure 7: Standard deviation of download throughput of three consecutive runs of Speedtest on wired and wireless network and Samknows

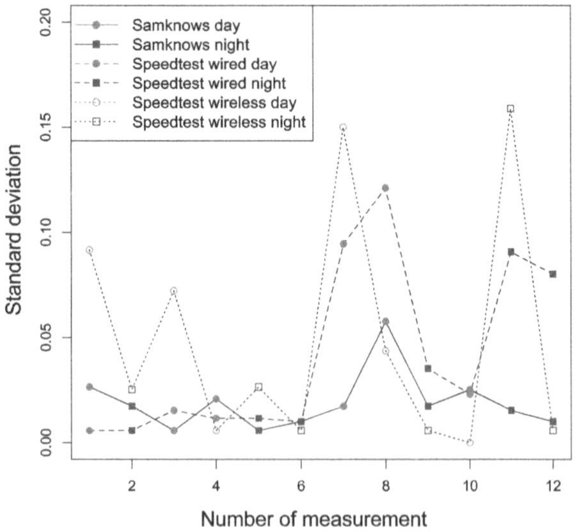

Figure 8: Standard deviation of upload throughput of three consecutive runs of Speedtest on wired and wireless network and Samknows

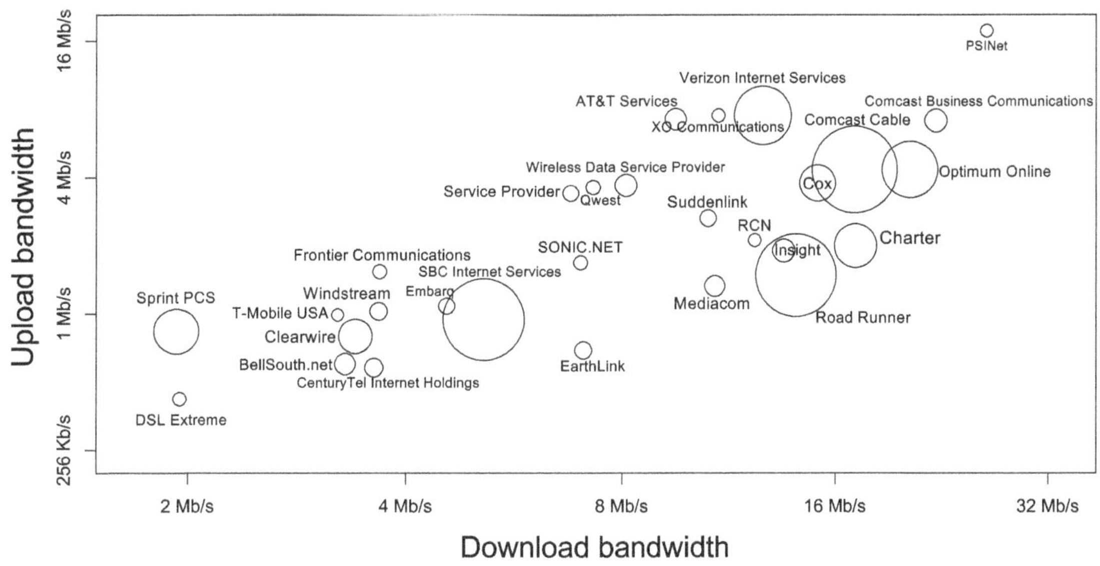

Figure 9: Average download/upload bandwidths for most frequent ISPs from US markets. Circle areas are proportional to number of measurements from that ISP.

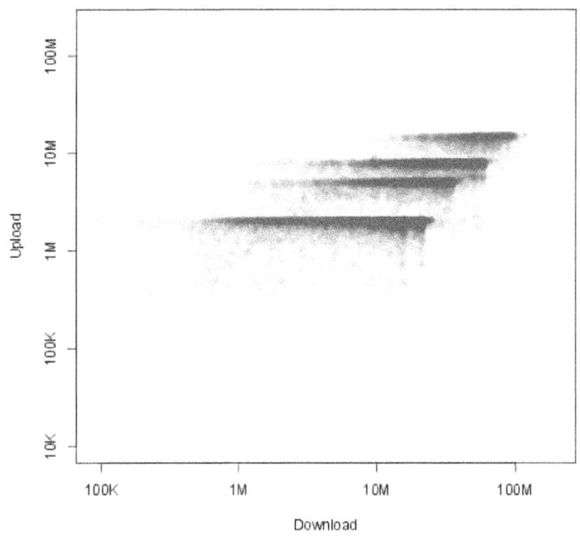

Figure 10: Scatter plot of download vs. upload throughput for Cablevision.

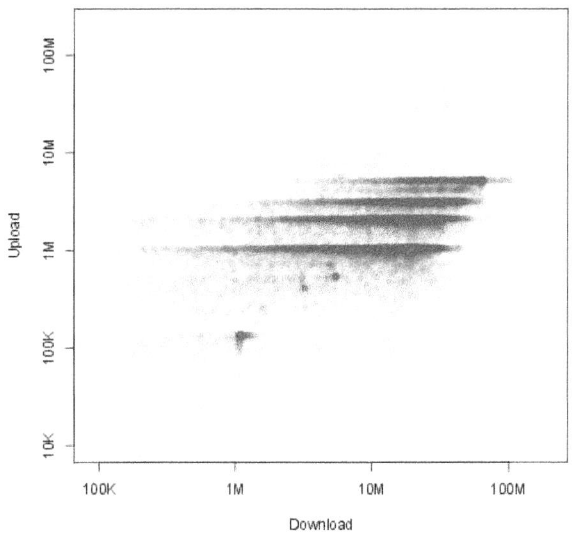

Figure 11: Scatter plot of download vs. upload throughput for Charter.

and worst performance of 40%. They also showed that some operators have consistent performance throughout, while the others exhibit degraded service during peak hours. To confirm their finding, we had to be careful due to potential time biases in our data. For example, during working hours most Speedtest experiments are likely conducted from businesses and universities, while during the evenings and nights, users run the experiments from their home networks. To overcome this limitation, we consider only experiments conducted on a Sunday. We limited our analysis to the Los Angeles metro area and we consider two operators, Cox and Time Warner. In prior work, Cox exhibited significant degradation during peak hours, while Time Warner showed consistent performance. Figure 16 shows the average download speed during specific hours of the day for Cox and Time Warner in the Los Angeles metro area. Our dataset confirms both findings by Sundaresan *et al.*. First, download speeds depend on time of day. Second, some operators have significant differences between peak and worst performance. Cox's peak average performance is two times better than the av-

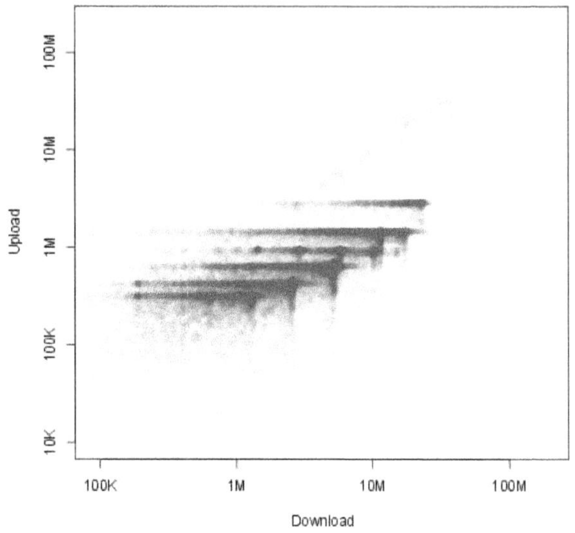

Figure 12: Scatter plot of download vs. upload throughput for AT&T.

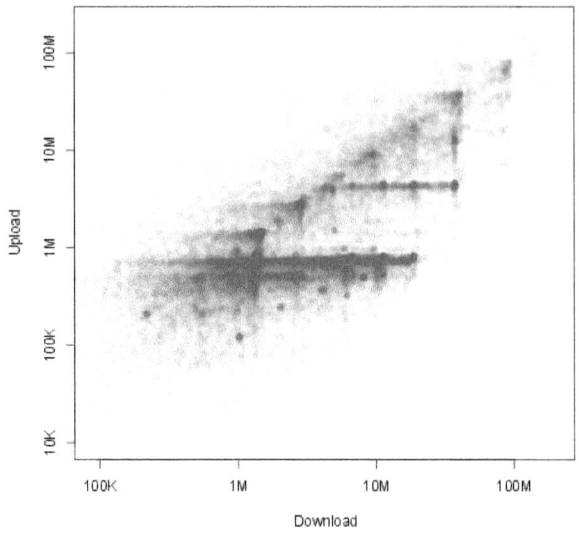

Figure 13: Scatter plot of download vs. upload throughput for Qwest.

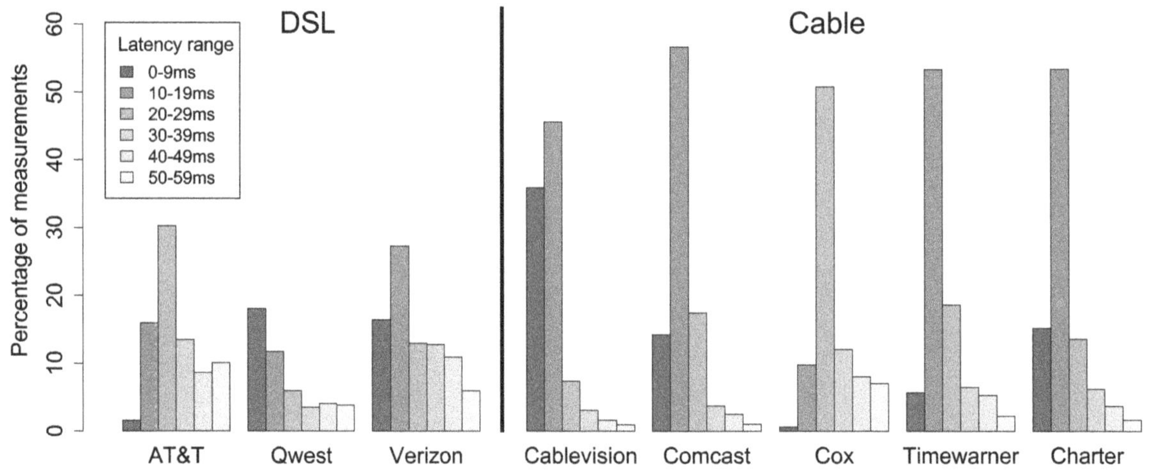

Figure 14: Latency distribution for operators from US markets.

erage download speed during busy times. Time Warner showed a slowdown of only 26%.

4.3 New Findings

In addition to analyzing prior results in light of our Speedtest data, we observed features not previously reported. Here we report on two of those: persistent low performance tests, and the impact of distance from the measurement server and network latency. Because of its wider perspective, these characteristics are more easily measured and observed with a dataset such as Speedtest, as compared with purpose-built and more narrowly deployed system like SamKnows.

4.3.1 Persistent low performance tests

During our analysis of download/upload scatter plots, we observed a number of high density dots in low performance areas, suggesting persistent low performance. For example, in Figure 11, we observed many measurements with a download speed a 1 Mb/s and upload speed of 120 kb/s. Comcast, Cox and Verizon also had similar artifacts with low performance, each with somewhat different specific upload / download measurements. We hypothesize that these artifacts represent "cheap and slow" service plan offerings. While operators may no longer offer these low performance plans, it is clear that some of the customers have not yet switched to new service plans. Because the rates are much slower, the tests easily saturate the rate limits, yielding little variability in the resulting measurements.

However, we also observed more interesting high density points, which we could not explain by cheap service offerings. Speedtest's servers in Australia (Sydney, Melbourne, Perth) reported many measurements of 1.3 Mb/s download speed and 210 kb/s upload speed for all of Australia's biggest Internet operators (iiNet, Internode, Optus, Telstra, TPG). As an example, Figure 17 shows the scat-

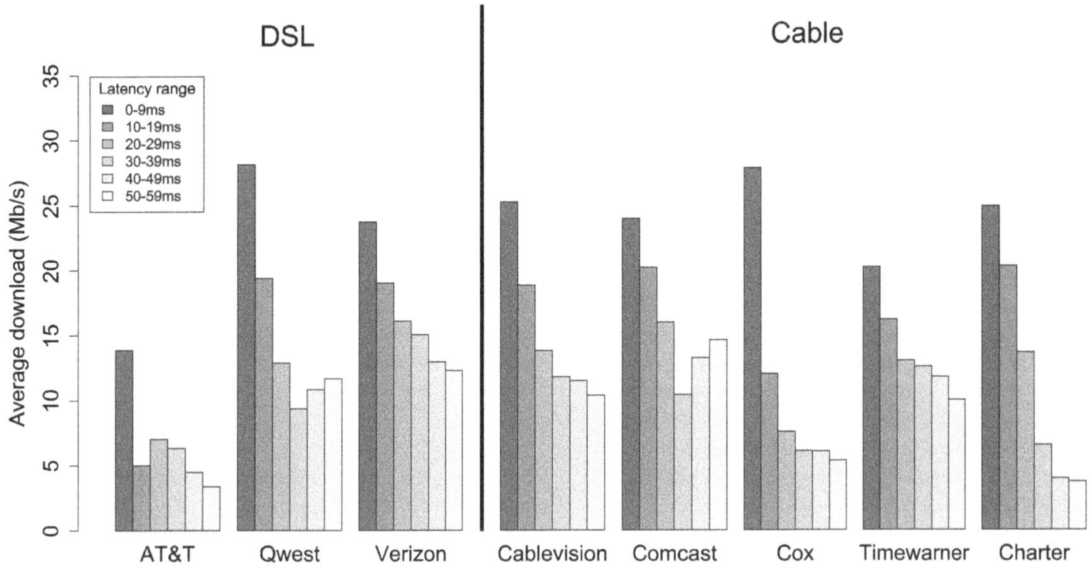

Figure 15: Average download speed with respect to latencies for operators from US markets.

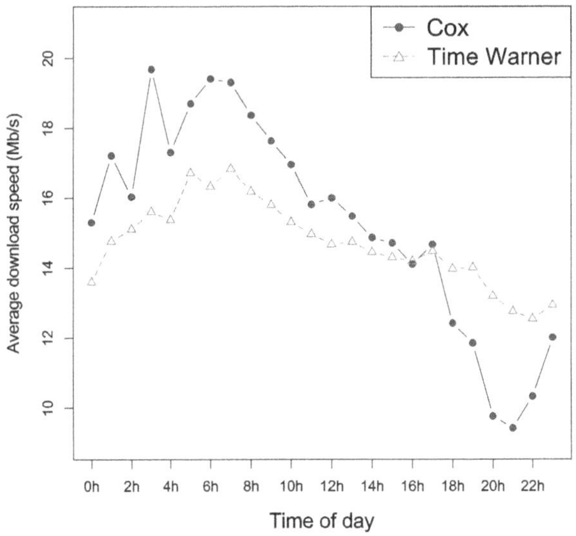

Figure 16: Average download performance for specific time of day. Analysis of Cox and Time Warner in Los Angeles, CA metro area.

ter plot of download and upload speeds for Optus Internet. The measurement that is consistent with other Australian operators is circled; other high-density points representing persistently low performance tests are not common to all the Australian operators.

One explanation for this phenomenon is that once a user exceeds the service plan's download quota, there is a resulting reduction in speed. However, websites for the above network operators state that speeds are usually reduced to 128, 256 or 512 kb/s, which we do not see in our results. The other possible explanation is that the patterns are related to old equipment or old configuration. Customers might not be achieving the internet speeds they are paying for because of old equipment that does not support faster speeds.

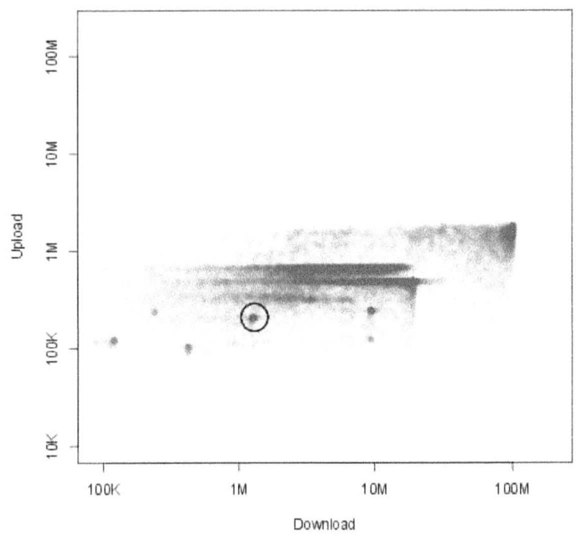

Figure 17: Scatter plot of download vs. upload throughput for Optus Internet in Australia

In almost all download/upload scatter plots, there are other high density points not connected to service plans offered by operators. Figure 11 shows two clusters below the common upload speed of 1 Mb/s and between 1 and 10 Mb/s download speeds. There are much more high density clusters in Figure 13, again mostly at low upload speeds. We intend to further investigate these data points in future work.

4.3.2 *Impact of distance on latency*

It is commonly assumed that as you increase geographic distance between end-points, network latency between them increases. With our dataset, we were able to provide empirical support for, and quantify that effect. We considered measurements in a radius of 600 miles from the server. Figure 18 plots the relation of latency and distance for AT&T, Charter and Comcast. We generally observe that as distance increases, so does network latency. This effect is especially true for Charter and Comcast on distances up to 150 miles. After 150 miles, both Charter's and Comcast's average latencies decrease, which is a surprising effect. There is a sudden increase in latency for measurements on AT&T's network around a distance of 100 miles. After that, the latency is almost constant up to 300 miles, where it starts increasing with distance again. An implication of these results is that although latency generally does correlate with geographic distance, network topology and connectivity of a provider clearly has an important impact on broadband performance for end-users.

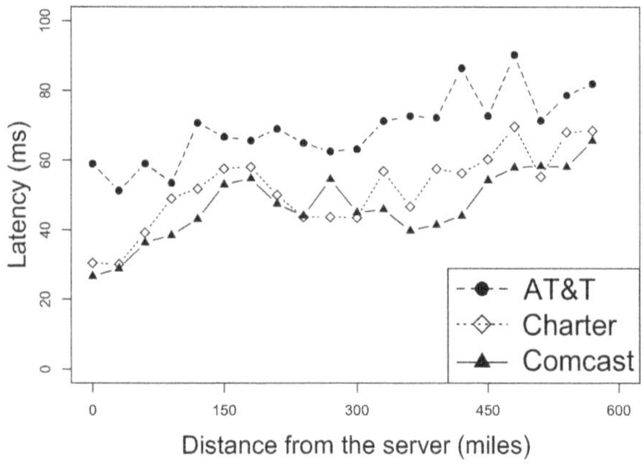

Figure 18: Impact of distance to latency for US operators.

4.4 Markets Beyond US

Figure 19 shows average download and upload speeds for all countries represented in our dataset. Note that the countries identified in the figure are from the perspective of the client host, not the Speedtest server. In cases where a Speedtest server is close to a country border, it is certainly possible for a client host to be within 200 mi and in a different country. Since we are interested in broadband access performance, we consider the country from which a test is initiated.

We observe that Hong Kong has the most developed Internet infrastructure by far with cheap and easily accessible fiber connections. Most European countries and the US have average download speeds larger than 5 Mb/s. Countries in the speed range from 2 Mb/s to 5 Mb/s are mostly South American or African. Both India and Indonesia have average download speeds lower than 2 Mb/s.

It is interesting to compare our findings with the findings of Kreibich *et al.* [15]. For most of the countries, the average speeds are twice as high in our dataset than what was reported in their study. There are also numerous relative performance differences. For example, Japan's average download speeds were reported to be almost two times faster than Hong Kong. In our measurements, we observe Hong Kong connections to be faster than those from Japan. We hypothesize that the number of users connecting over fiber in Hong Kong has increased, leading to average speeds that are now much faster than any other country.

Table 1: Number of measurements with download speed greater than 40 Mb/s and upload speed greater than 15 Mb/s broken down by servers.

Metro area	Fiber	Total
Hong Kong	428003	1476203
Budapest	110186	2197648
Tokyo	73388	641759
Los Angeles	62923	4448778
New York, NY	58075	2161745
San Francisco, CA	37944	1778681
Paris	30465	798004
Manchester	21396	2793875
Stockholm	21212	177703

On a global level, we examined fiber adoption rates in various countries and latencies of fiber connections. We also studied broadband connection infrastructural trends in developing countries.

4.4.1 *Fiber adoption*

For the purpose of the fiber connection analysis, we assume that every measurement with download speed greater than 40 Mb/s and upload speed greater than 15 Mb/s is over a fiber optic infrastructure.

Table 1 shows the number of high speed measurements broken down by individual metro area (which corresponds to a Speedtest server). We report only areas in which we observe at least 20,000 such measurements. In addition to Hong Kong, we also see high fiber adoption rates in Hungary, Japan, France, United Kingdom and Sweden. Note that in addition to home user fiber connections, these results also include measurements from universities and businesses.

4.4.2 *Fiber connection consistency and latency*

We compare operators offering fiber connections in different markets. In Hong Kong, the operator with the largest number of users is City Telekom. We compare it with DIGI, which offers fiber connection in Hungary, and Verizon FiOS, the most common high speed ISP in our US dataset.

Figures 20, 21 and 22 show scatter plots of measurements faster than 40 Mb/s download and 15 Mb/s upload for the above operators in their respective markets. Not only does Hong Kong have the largest fraction of high-speed internet users as shown above, but operators in Hong Kong market also offer higher speeds than operators from European and US markets, like DIGI and Verizon FiOS. Interestingly, City Telekom offers completely symmetric speeds for both upload and download. In prior work, Sundaresan *et al.* found that US operators provide better upload than download speed consistency. On Figure 20 for City Telekom in Hong Kong, we observe the opposite effect; there are more non-optimal measurements with upload rather than download degradation. DIGI, on the other hand, shows the same effect as US operators; very few measurements have below optimal upload, while there are lots of measurements with degraded download speeds.

We have shown in earlier sections that average download speed is lower on measurements with higher latencies for both cable and DSL operators. Is this also true for fiber connection? To study this question, we analyzed latency and download speeds from City Telekom and DIGI. We consider only measurements above 40 Mb/s download and 22 Mb/s upload speeds. We cut off measurements

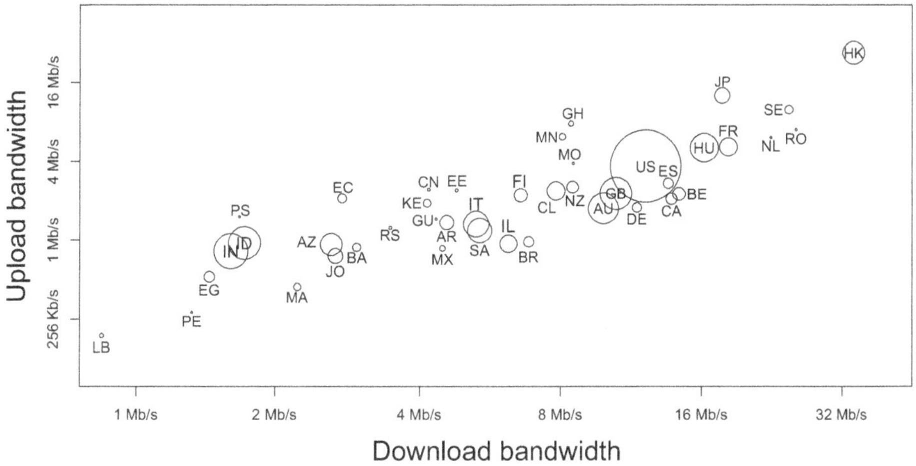

Figure 19: Average download/upload bandwidths for countries with most measurements. Countries identified are from the perspective of client hosts, not Speedtest servers. Circle areas are proportional to number of measurements initiated from that country.

with upload speeds between 15 and 22 Mb/s because we do not want to include data from the DIGI's suboptimal service plan we observed at bottom left part of the Figure 21.

Figure 23 shows both the latency distribution and the relation of average download speed to latency for DIGI and City Telekom. Users of Fiber connection see much lower latencies than users of cable and DSL operators. Most of the users have latencies in the range of 3 – 5 ms. The average download speed indeed decreases with latency. The effect is most noticeable in latency range from 1 – 5 ms, but is also true for latencies beyond 5 ms.

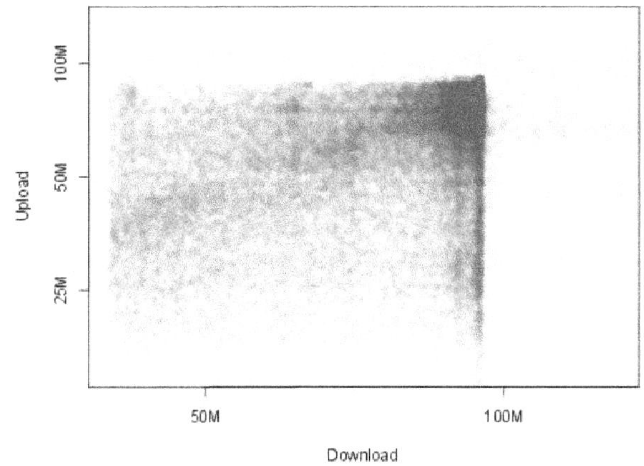

Figure 20: Scatter plot of download vs. upload throughput for City Telekom in Hong Kong.

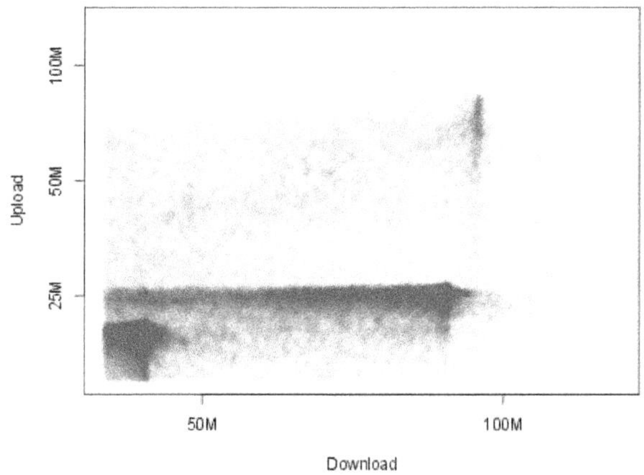

Figure 21: Scatter plot of download vs. upload throughput for DIGI in Hungary.

5. RELATED WORK

There is a growing body of studies that examine broadband access network performance. A number of earlier works focused on broadband access speeds in the context of peer-to-peer applications, *e.g.*, Lakshminarayanan *et al.* [16], and measurement methods for basic characterization of broadband access networks, such as the asymmetry in upload and download speeds, *e.g.*, Dischinger *et al.* [11] and Croce *et al.* [10]. For example, the authors of [11] found that download speeds exceed upload speeds by a factor of 10 in some cases, but that measured bandwidths matched speeds advertised by ISPs quite well at all times of day. They also found that DSL access links exhibit large latencies compared with cable modem access links. In contrast, as can be seen in the Appendix and in Figure 9, we find that instances in which there is an order of magnitude difference between download vs. upload to be the rare case and that in general, the gap has narrowed significantly.

While the aforementioned works employed active probe-based measurements, other studies have analyzed passive measurements collected from service provider networks. These measurements en-

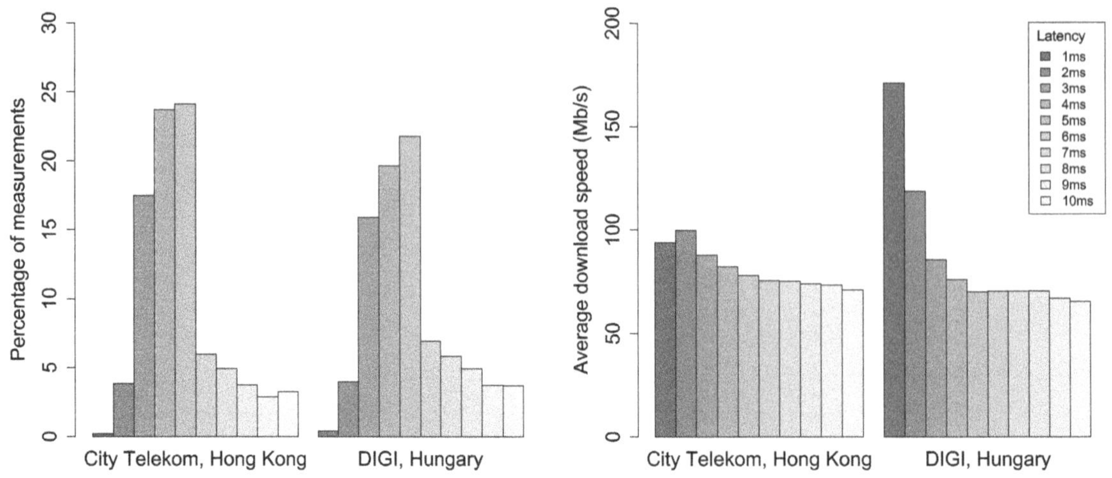

Figure 23: Latency distribution and relation of latency and average download speed for Fiber operators.

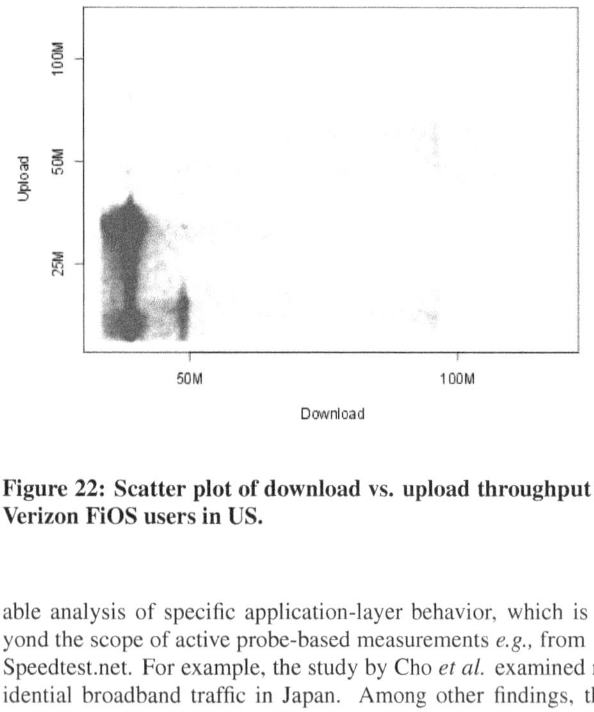

Figure 22: Scatter plot of download vs. upload throughput for Verizon FiOS users in US.

able analysis of specific application-layer behavior, which is beyond the scope of active probe-based measurements *e.g.,* from Speedtest.net. For example, the study by Cho *et al.* examined residential broadband traffic in Japan. Among other findings, their study showed that 63% of traffic was peer-to-peer, with many "heavy hitters", especially on fiber-connected access links. A more recent study by Maier *et al.* examined traffic from about 20,000 residential DSL customers from a large ISP in Europe [17]. In contrast to the earlier study in Japan, they found that HTTP traffic strongly dominates peer-to-peer traffic. They also found that delays from the home network to the ISP's gateway often exceed delays in the wide area, and that users rarely consume the full capacity of their access links (an observation also made in an earlier work by Siekkinen *et al.* [21]). Maier *et al.* suggested that users' achievable throughputs were often limited by suboptimal TCP settings.

More recent measurement studies to assess broadband access speeds and performance have been fueled, in part, by a sponsored project by the US Federal Communications Commission to assess broadband speeds and coverage, which is being managed by SamKnows [4, 9]. The recent study by Sundaresan *et al.* [22] used data collected by SamKnows for the FCC study, as well as measurement data produced by their own BISMark system, to evaluate a variety of characteristics of broadband access networks. For their study, both data sets are collected from processes running directly on the gateway router. In the BISMark system, upload and download throughputs are actively measured using a single-threaded HTTP connection, and other techniques are used to both actively and passively measure link characteristics (*e.g.,* the ShaperProbe tool is employed to measure capacity [14]). In contrast, the SamKnows throughput measurement method employs parallel TCP streams in order to be more likely to saturate the upload and download capacity. Among other issues, the authors examined ISP traffic shaping policies, differences among local access providers, and effects due to oversized buffers and effects of various modem models. As discussed in Section 4.1.1, differences between Speedtest vs. Samknows measurements are primarily due to SamKnows gateway-based deployment and cross-traffic avoidance. We make no argument that one is better than the other — simply that the provide different perspectives on broadband performance. However, Speedtest data clearly provides a broader perspective since it does not require whitebox deployment.

Similarly, work by Kreibich *et al.* on Netalyzr [15] has exposed effects of overbuffering on edge devices (*i.e.*, the "bufferbloat" problem [12]). Similar to Speedtest, Netalyzer is an applet that runs on client nodes and accesses dedicated servers to assess performance. Netalyzer differs from Speedtest by *(i)* providing measurements to users beyond latency and bandwidth, including *e.g.,* DNS response time, path MTU, and IPv6 support among others, *(ii)*, using EC2 for servers (instead of local servers), and *(iii)* using carefully constructed UDP streams instead of TCP transfers to measure bandwidth. Among other things, the study in [15] reports upload and download bandwidths in markets around the world. Their results show a more narrow range of bandwidths than observed in our data, most likely reflecting the nearly 3 year difference in data gathering.

This highlights the need for continuing analysis of broadband performance.

While devices deployed by SamKnows are available upon request by residential broadband users, many users rely on publicly available bandwidth testing services. Among these, Speedtest [3] is one of the most widely deployed. The Measurement Lab project also makes available the NPAD and NDT tools for network diagnostic and throughput testing [18]. These latter tools employ a single TCP connection for assessing throughput speeds. Bauer *et al.* examined the accuracy of various broadband access testing tools and found that while in-gateway measurement systems such as the one employed by SamKnows are the most accurate, the methods employed by the Speedtest application are also quite accurate [5]. Moreover, they found that tools that only use a single TCP connection for measuring throughputs tend not to be very accurate.

6. SUMMARY AND CONCLUSIONS

In this paper we revisit the issue of broadband performance using crowd-sourced data from `speedtest.net`. The objectives of our work are threefold: *(i)* to reconfirm prior results on broadband performance in the US, *(ii)* to expand on prior studies by investigating broadband performance details afforded by our data set, and *(iii)* to compare and contrast broadband performance in markets around the world. Our data set was collected over a 6 month period in 2011 from 59 metro markets around the world.

Our analysis of US markets focuses on reconfirmation of prior work by Sundaresan *et al.*. To begin, we report results of a case study that compares Speedtest measurements to SamKnows measurements. Our results show that there is high correlation between reported performance when Speedtest clients use wireline Ethernet, but Speedtest results are substantially lower when wireless Ethernet is used. The results of our evaluation of broadband performance in US markets are consistent with many of the prior performance studies. However, several of our results differ, for example in terms of service provider rankings. Our data reveal several additional features of broadband performance including tight clusters of lower performance (which we attribute to older service plans, older equipment or throttling), and the correlation between latency and distance to a server. Our analysis of non-US markets shows a broad spectrum of performance with Hong Kong at the high end, and India and Indonesia at the lower end.

In future work, we plan to use a broader set of Speedtest data to consider longitudinal characteristics of broadband deployments world wide. We also plan to investigate instances of anomalous conditions such as outages or step function jumps in performance that will provide a perspective on the robustness of broadband networks.

Acknowledgements

We thank our shepherd and the reviewers for their helpful suggestions and comments.

This work was supported in part by NSF grants CNS-0716460, CNS-0831427 and CNS-0905186, and CNS-1054985. Any opinions, findings, conclusions or other recommendations expressed in this material are those of the authors and do not necessarily reflect the view of the NSF.

We thank Ookla, Inc. and Andrew Bassett for generous access to the `Speedtest.net` performance data.

We thank Sam Crawford and SamKnows for the use of white-boxes in our experiments.

We also thank Anton Kapella for his fruitful suggestions and input on this work.

7. REFERENCES

[1] Ookla Documentation Wiki. http://wiki.ookla.com, 2011.
[2] Ookla, Inc. http://www.ookla.com, 2011.
[3] Speedtest.net. http://www.speedtest.net, 2011.
[4] SamKnows: Accurate broadband performance information for consumers, governments, and ISPs. `http://www.samknows.com/broadband/index.php`, 2012.
[5] S. Bauer, D. Clark, and W. Lehr. Understanding broadband speed measurements. In *38th Research Conference on Communication, Information and Internet Policy*, September 2010.
[6] S. Bauer, D. Clark, and W. Lehr. Powerboost. In *Proceedings of the ACM SIGCOMM workshop on Home networks*, 2011.
[7] R. Carlson. Network Diagnostic Tool. `http://www.internet2.edu/performance/ndt/`, February 2012.
[8] US Federal Communications Commission. National Broadband Plan. `http://www.broadband.gov/plan/`, 2011.
[9] US Federal Communications Commission. Measuring Broadband America. `http://www.fcc.gov/measuring-broadband-america`, 2012.
[10] D. Croce, T. En-Najjary, G. Urvoy-Keller, and E.W. Biersack. Capacity estimation of adsl links. In *Proceedings of ACM CoNEXT Conference*, 2008.
[11] M. Dischinger, A. Haeberlen, K.P. Gummadi, and S. Saroiu. Characterizing residential broadband networks. In *Proceedings of ACM Internet Measurement Conference*, 2007.
[12] J. Gettys and K. Nichols. Bufferbloat: Dark buffers in the internet. *Queue*, 9(11), November 2011.
[13] Google. Measurement Lab. `http://www.measurementlab.net`, 2012.
[14] P. Kanuparthy and C. Dovrolis. ShaperProbe: end-to-end detection of ISP traffic shaping using active methods. In *Proceedings of ACM Internet Measurement Conference*, 2011.
[15] C. Kreibich, N. Weaver, B. Nechaev, and V. Paxson. Netalyzr: Illuminating the edge network. In *Proceedings of ACM Internet Measurement Conference*, 2010.
[16] K. Lakshminarayanan and V.N. Padmanabhan. Some Findings on the Network Performance of Broadband Hosts. In *Proceedings of ACM Internet Measurement Conference*, 2003.
[17] G. Maier, A. Feldmann, V. Paxson, and M. Allman. On Dominant Characteristics of Residential Broadband internet Traffic. In *Proceedings of ACM Internet Measurement Conference*, 2009.
[18] M. Mathis, J. Heffner, P. O'Neil, and P. Siemsen. Pathdiag: Automated TCP Diagnosis. In *Proceedings of Passive and Active Measurement Conference*, 2008.
[19] MaxMind. The MaxMind IP Geolocation Servicel. `http://www.maxmind.com`, 2012.
[20] S. Perez. Nielsen: Cord Cutting and Internet TV Viewing on the Rise. `http://techcrunch.com`, February 2012.
[21] M. Siekkinen, D. Collange, G. Urvoy-Keller, and E. Biersack. Performance limitations of ADSL users: a case study. In *Proceedings of Passive and Active Measurement Conference*, 2007.
[22] S. Sundaresan, W. de Donato, N. Feamster, R. Teixeira, S. Crawford, and A. Pescapè. Broadband internet performance: A view from the gateway. In *Proceedings of ACM SIGCOMM '11*, Toronto, Canada, August 2011.

APPENDIX

The following table shows summary statistics and basic information on the Speedtest measurements included in our study.

Table 2: Number of measurements, average download and upload speeds and latency broken down by metro areas.

Region	Metro Area	Country Code	Tests	Download Mean (Stdev) Kb/s	Upload Mean (Stdev) Kb/s	Latency Mean (Stdev) millisec.
Europe	Barcelona	ES	323431	13384 (18471)	2704 (7264)	76 (161)
	Brussels	BE	495738	14380 (14404)	2374 (5701)	51 (164)
	Budapest	HU	2197648	16519 (27293)	5188 (12439)	50 (168)
	Frankfurt	DE	242569	12053 (16779)	1834 (3904)	118 (211)
	Manchester	UK	2793875	10718 (14322)	2328 (6176)	56 (119)
	Paris	FR	798004	19562 (49113)	5598 (24270)	59 (149)
	Rome	IT	1740709	5401 (9747)	1365 (6760)	74 (142)
	Sarajevo	BA	212119	2981 (5738)	893 (4145)	96 (267)
	Stockholm	SE	177703	26509 (40140)	10542 (23238)	50 (405)
	Turku	FI	515003	6484 (7953)	2273 (5183)	94 (155)
Asia	Hong Kong	HK	1476203	33955 (43730)	26988 (36826)	37 (137)
	Jakarta	ID	2852275	1743 (6250)	976 (4659)	133 (327)
	New Delhi	IN	3242544	1632 (3397)	844 (2045)	165 (278)
	Tokyo	JP	641759	18085 (29084)	13022 (18372)	70 (267)
	Ulaanbaatar	MN	109354	8261 (17064)	6326 (13437)	75 (200)
Africa	Accra	GH	68753	8561 (19282)	7900 (20609)	114 (291)
	Bamako	ML	19	244 (145)	143 (117)	489 (507)
	Cairo	EG	308805	1468 (3910)	539 (2771)	132 (347)
	Casablanca	MA	141558	2256 (3640)	451 (1933)	173 (240)
	Nairobi	KE	164759	4237 (11049)	1955 (6469)	164 (338)
Pacific	Auckland	NZ	381377	8689 (16535)	2605 (9791)	58 (167)
	Melbourne	AU	961180	12285 (18398)	1416 (4372)	56 (138)
	Perth	AU	353578	6254 (18409)	2028 (11248)	72 (168)
	Sydney	AU	1184639	9464 (17653)	2019 (9378)	50 (129)
	Tamuning	GU	12803	4137 (5869)	1384 (3899)	115 (198)
North America	Anchorage, AK	US	61144	4948 (7038)	1672 (6360)	144 (504)
	Bellingham, WA	US	433021	11978 (12793)	2436 (5181)	61 (153)
	Burlington, VT	US	101058	16554 (36229)	3963 (8671)	115 (249)
	Chicago, IL	US	1365027	13487 (22697)	4174 (12340)	53 (134)
	Dallas, TX	US	815938	10824 (17556)	3717 (9973)	76 (173)
	Flagstaff, AZ	US	55350	11822 (17760)	3260 (6548)	103 (197)
	Grand Forks, ND	US	84126	11774 (14269)	3192 (5425)	74 (161)
	Grand Rapids, MI	US	136568	7432 (10921)	2506 (5258)	95 (168)
	Honolulu, HI	US	127632	8536 (9948)	1834 (4526)	94 (130)
	Idaho Falls, ID	US	37079	6904 (12399)	2297 (4915)	131 (209)
	Lawrence, KS	US	170725	10525 (24911)	3553 (10067)	261 (432)
	Lexington, KY	US	368759	9800 (10433)	1887 (4865)	63 (140)
	Little Rock, AR	US	173791	7279 (9936)	1981 (4205)	90 (161)
	Los Angeles, CA	US	4448778	11377 (18100)	3215 (10473)	54 (139)
	Medford, OR	US	51780	13180 (15873)	3266 (10605)	74 (159)
	Miami, FL	US	740662	15977 (16262)	4114 (10271)	39 (112)
	New York, NY	US	2161745	16749 (20415)	4584 (8367)	50 (139)
	Pensacola, FL	US	143703	7916 (9085)	1961 (3617)	96 (145)
	Philadelphia, PA	US	489278	12736 (18220)	5474 (10544)	77 (189)
	Portland, ME	US	152908	9709 (11956)	2713 (6447)	91 (252)
	Provo, UT	US	31563	8648 (19535)	4427 (10258)	98 (189)
	San Francisco, CA	US	1778681	12384 (22480)	4764 (13072)	55 (147)
	Springfield, MO	US	458499	7561 (13952)	2047 (9096)	75 (143)
	Sumter, SC	US	78590	10560 (17325)	2460 (5852)	126 (234)
South America	Brasilia	BR	286197	6983 (8207)	995 (2751)	66 (180)
	Buenos Aires	AR	528919	4713 (9768)	1407 (5386)	72 (169)
	La Paz	BO	44925	752 (1428)	295 (1005)	315 (341)
	Quito	EC	213365	2800 (7660)	2123 (5885)	129 (294)
	Santiago	CL	935391	7928 (13115)	2415 (8278)	92 (359)
Middle East	Amman	JO	598767	2672 (4868)	759 (3263)	183 (292)
	Baku	AZ	1280475	2658 (4955)	948 (3383)	87 (196)
	Kabul	AF	1998	768 (1205)	585 (2025)	409 (689)
	Riyadh	SA	1595746	5487 (10381)	1212 (6274)	76 (175)
	Tel Aviv	IL	870621	6058 (6031)	943 (3133)	78 (197)

Obtaining In-Context Measurements of Cellular Network Performance

Aaron Gember, Aditya Akella
University of Wisconsin – Madison
{agember,akella}@cs.wisc.edu

Jeffrey Pang, Alexander Varshavsky, Ramon Caceres
AT&T Labs – Research
{jeffpang,varshavsky,ramon}@research.att.com

ABSTRACT

Network service providers, and other parties, require an accurate understanding of the performance cellular networks deliver to users. In particular, they often seek a measure of the *network performance users experience solely when they are interacting with their device*—a measure we call *in-context*. Acquiring such measures is challenging due to the many factors, including time and physical context, that influence cellular network performance. This paper makes two contributions. First, we conduct a large scale measurement study, based on data collected from a large cellular provider and from hundreds of controlled experiments, to shed light on the issues underlying in-context measurements. Our novel observations show that measurements must be conducted on devices which (*i*) recently used the network as a result of user interaction with the device, (*ii*) remain in the same macro-environment (e.g., indoors and stationary), and in some cases the same micro-environment (e.g., in the user's hand), during the period between normal usage and a subsequent measurement, and (*iii*) are currently sending/receiving little or no user-generated traffic. Second, we design and deploy a prototype active measurement service for Android phones based on these key insights. Our analysis of 1650 measurements gathered from 12 volunteer devices shows that the system is able to obtain average throughput measurements that accurately quantify the performance experienced during times of active device and network usage.

Categories and Subject Descriptors

C.4 [**Performance of Systems**]: Measurement techniques; C.2.3 [**Computer-Communication Networks**]: Network Operations—*Network monitoring*

Keywords

Active measurement, Cellular network performance, Device context

1. INTRODUCTION

Cellular data networks have become a main source of Internet access for hundreds of millions of users. Consequently, many parties require an accurate understanding of the performance that cellular networks deliver to users, e.g., the range of throughput, latency, and loss that users can experience in practice. Content providers need this to optimize application decisions; regulatory bodies need this to validate wireless broadband speeds; and network service providers need this for effective network management and efficient debugging.

Although many passive analysis techniques [17, 20] and mobile device tools for crowdsourcing active measurements [1, 2, 5, 6, 19, 33] have been developed, they mostly quantify the performance the cellular network can offer at random times, irrespective of whether users interact with their devices at these times and actually experience the consequences of the measured performance. For example, the speed of a background synchronization task conducted at night may not be relevant to most users, in contrast to the download speed of a movie a user is watching on-demand. We argue that in many important use-cases there is a need to obtain a measure of the *network performance users experience solely when they are interacting with their device.* Moreover, some parties may want to narrow their view of performance further, to focus on a specific scope of interest (e.g., morning commuters driving in Los Angeles). We refer to such measures of performance as *in-context measurements*, where *context* may refer to, e.g., whether or not a user is actively using their device, a device's position relative to the user (in pocket, in hand, etc.), or any of several other factors that may influence the cellular network performance a user experiences. §2 provides several example use-cases and discusses limitations of prior approaches in more detail.

Despite the need for in-context performance measures (as defined above), it has yet to be shown how one should go about capturing them, or even whether existing approaches are good enough. To this end, our paper makes two contributions: First, we use anonymized cellular network data from 20,000 subscribers of a large US-based cellular carrier and empirical results from 100s of controlled end-to-end experiments to examine the extent to which users' interactions with their devices quantitatively impact cellular network performance. Crucially, we find that measurements must be conducted in a manner that considers whether a user is actually using the device, what position a user puts the device in, and what activities a user is running on the device. Second, we leverage our empirical insights to de-

sign a crowdsourcing-based active measurement system for deriving in-context performance measures. We evaluate it using a real-world deployment spanning 12 volunteer users.
Empirical Study. (§3) Our empirical analysis addresses three questions that are central to obtaining in-context performance measurements: (i) How does performance differ when measured at the times users actually use their device as opposed to when devices are idle? (ii) What are the reasons for performance differences? In particular, to what extent do various contextual factors that manifest during active use, e.g., device position, motion, etc., impact measured performance? (iii) How should measurements be conducted to avoid conflating factors? In particular, what types of measurements and user traffic can overlap?

Active vs. Idle: Using network data from 20,000 subscribers, we find that, on average, latency is 16ms higher and loss rate is 6%-age points worse (~17% vs ~12%) near the times users actively use their device. This finding implies that a performance measurement scheme must take into account whether a user is actively using their device, otherwise measurements may overestimate network performance.

Impact of context: We conduct 100s of controlled end-to-end experiments in varying environments to identify the key contextual factors that affect measured performance. We observe that small changes in a device's position–e.g., moving a device from hand to pocket–can cause up to a 79% difference in measured throughput and, to a lesser extent, a difference in measured latency. We also confirm that changes in location by a few 100m and changes in whether a device is stationary or moving may cause >1Mbps difference in measured throughput and ~60ms difference in measured latency.

Measurement interference: Using our controlled end-to-end experiments, we quantify the impact of simultaneous device usage and measurement gathering—an important consideration for maximizing measurement opportunities. We observe that, despite the limited bandwidth and high latency of cellular links, web browsing or low-rate streaming can occur concurrently with measurements, while still obtaining accurate measurement results and suitable user experience.
Measurement System. (§4) A system for in-context measurement must decide *when* and on *which* devices to conduct measurements such that the results convey the cellular network performance users likely experience when they are interacting with their device. Our empirical study shows that measurements must be conducted only on devices which are active (for low-bandwidth measurements) or were recently-active (for measurements that may interfere with user actions). In the latter case, we must ensure that the device's context has not changed compared to its last active use.

To address these challenges, we design a measurement service for Android phones that leverages *crowdsourcing of active measurements.* We describe how to address key challenges, e.g., inferring user activity and monitoring the physical environment. We deployed the service across 12 volunteer cellular subscribers[1] over a three month period, gathering over 1650 measurements. Our analysis of these measurements shows that the system is able to obtain measures of mean throughput equivalent to the performance experienced during times of active device usage.

With a growing focus on the performance experienced by cellular subscribers from a variety of stakeholders, there is an urgent need for systems that provide the needed performance measures. Our work fills this gap both by showing what factors impact measurements to what degree, and by designing and evaluating an accurate measurement system.

[1]The volunteers include both customers and employees of a large US-based cellular carrier.

2. TOWARD CROWDSOURCED ACTIVE MEASUREMENTS

In this section, we present several use cases for cellular network performance measurements taken from the perspective of mobile devices, and then discuss the requirements measurements must meet to serve these use cases. We argue that existing approaches for measuring end-to-end performance meet the needs of some use cases, but they lack the ability to accurately measure specific metrics in situations where users actually use their device.

2.1 Use Cases and Requirements

Network service providers, content providers, regulatory agencies, and researchers all have a vested interest in measuring cellular network performance; we refer to these parties as *measurement admins.*
Network management. When customers complain, the failures they experienced may be a result of any combination of the mobile device, the network, user behavior (e.g., mobility), etc. Understanding the performance experienced by a certain device in similar contexts can help network providers eliminate confounding factors and narrow down the root cause.

A variety of issues may lead to network alarms being raised, e.g., RTT estimates or radio link control failures crossing key thresholds. It is often unclear if the events impact users, because they manifest as soft failures rather than loss of connectivity. Understanding the performance impact across a range of users is important for prioritizing alarm analysis.

Network providers continuously upgrade their networks but have difficulty understanding the impact on performance because of complex interactions between protocol layers [12, 29]. They benefit from conducting before-and-after user experience measurements in the areas where changes occurred.
Evaluating network providers. Some third parties collect measurements to compare different network providers (e.g., [5, 6]). In addition, regulatory bodies require accurate network speed measurements to evaluate the ubiquity of access to broadband capacities [3, 4]. In both these cases, measurements must accurately represent network performance in order to provide a fair and unbiased view for the public.
Application decision making. Time-sensitive applications (e.g., video streaming, multiplayer games, etc.) require accurate estimates of end-to-end performance to tune parameters such as buffer sizes and streaming rates. Since performance characteristics like delay change over time and space [25], estimating performance on demand is essential.
Measurement Requirements. Several common requirements emerge from these use cases.

1. Measurements should convey performance experienced in environments, and on devices, where users actually send/receive traffic, and more specifically, when users are *interacting with their device* (as opposed to performance at random times or when a device is unused).
2. Admins should be able to control the measurement and obtain specific metrics of interest. Only characteristics

of the cellular network which impact end-to-end performance should be depicted in measurement results.

3. Admins should be able to schedule measurements in a controlled scope of interest, e.g., devices used in an area where new infrastructure was deployed, or devices used indoors during peak times. Limiting measurements to controlled contexts helps admins identify the root cause of specific performance.

2.2 Need for a New Approach

Admins currently leverage a combination of passive analysis, field testing, and self-initiated reporting to understand cellular network performance. While these tools provide valuable views of performance, they do not entirely meet the requirements outlined above.

Network-based passive analysis. Network providers can instrument their infrastructure to passively estimate performance statistics based on user traffic [17, 20, 32]. However, it is difficult to determine or control what context mobile devices are in when they originate or receive the network traffic being measured, e.g., whether the device is indoors or outdoors. This limits the ability for administrators to focus their analysis on specific usage contexts. In addition, it can be difficult to eliminate the confounding factors of application variability [17]. Lastly, large scale passive analysis is only viable for admins with access to network infrastructure.

Field testing. Due to the manpower required and restrictions on access, it is impractical for field testing to cover the full range of physical contexts in which the network is used, e.g., to measure throughput in all buildings at many different times of day. Even if we crowdsource measurements from user devices for better coverage in time and space [33], we are unlikely to quantify the performance users experience when they are interacting with their device (§3.2, §3.3.1).

Self-initiated reporting. Admins also can rely on users to manually initiate active measurements and report performance anomalies [1, 2, 5, 6, 19]. However, these results will only capture a small subset of situations in which users interact with their device and the network: partially due to the need for manual initiation, and partially due to most users running these tools only when problems occur.

This paper advocates a new approach: *context-aware crowdsourcing of active measurements*. This measurement method enables a user's interactions with their device, along with the physical context of the device, to be considered when conducting measurements. This method also enables controlled metrics to be collected, without conflating factors external to the cellular network in our understanding of performance. In specific cases, passive analysis of application traffic may be an appropriate substitute for active measurements—e.g., it may be possible to use connections to Facebook to measure latency—but these measurements must be carefully filtered to only include passive observations from specific contexts.

To delineate the issues that determine the design of our approach, we first conduct a detailed measurement study of how users' interactions with their devices impact measured performance (§3). Then, we use the observations to design a measurement service prototype (§4).

3. EMPIRICAL STUDY

In this section, we examine the extent to which user's interactions with their device (or lack thereof), and other relevant factors (e.g., device position when not in use), impact in-context cellular network performance measurements. We analyze anonymized flow records and radio signaling data from 20,000 subscribers of a large US-based cellular carrier, and conduct 100s of end-to-end experiments from mobile devices under our control (§3.1). We start by looking at differences in performance between actual usage and idle periods (§3.2). We then investigate the impact of various contextual factors on the observed differences (§3.3). Finally, we examine the impact of overlap between measurement probes and user traffic (§3.4).

Identifier	*Release*	*Android Version*	*HSDPA/HSUPA 3G Speed (Mbps)*	*CPU (GHz)*	*RAM (MB)*
Phone A	May '11	2.3	Down 21, Up 3.6	1.2	512
Phone B	Jul '10	2.2	Down 7.2, Up 5.7	1.0	512
Phone C	Nov '10	2.1	Down 7.2, Up 2	0.8	512
Phone D	Jan '10	2.1	Down 7.2, Up 2	1.0	512

Table 1: Specifications for phones used in experiments

3.1 Datasets

Cellular Network Data. Our *network* dataset consists of anonymized flow records and radio resource control events from approximately 20,000 devices connected to a large US-based cellular provider. The devices are randomly sampled from a major metropolitan area, and only devices of a single device family are sampled (i.e., same OS and manufacturer). All device and user identifiers are anonymized to protect privacy without affecting the usefulness of our analysis.

Flow records for all traffic were collected on December 5–11, 2010 on the logical links between Serving GPRS Support Nodes (SGSNs) in the target metropolitan area and Gateway GPRS Support Nodes (GGSNs) in the UMTS core network. The data contains the following details, at one minute intervals, for each IP flow: initial cell sector, start and end timestamps, TCP header information, TCP handshake times [20], device identifiers, domain names, and application identifiers.[2]

Radio resource control (RRC) messages were collected on December 5–6, 2010 from the Radio Network Controllers (RNCs) in the target metropolitan area. RRC measurement and intra-frequency handover events were collected, with their relevant parameters. We post-process the data to extract: event timestamps, a list of cell sectors in the active set, and received signal code power (RSCP), i.e., signal strength.

Controlled Experiments. Our *context*[3] and *activity* datasets consist of latency and throughput measurements gathered using servers and devices under our control. Latency is measured using ping, with 1 KB (*context*) or 64 byte (*activity*) packets spaced 1 second apart. Downlink throughput is measured using iPerf, with observed bandwidth reported every 2 seconds (*context*) or 10 seconds (*activity*). All measurements are conducted on Android phones (Table 1) connected to the 3G UMTS network of the same carrier as above.

For the *context* dataset, latency and throughput measurements are conducted with the device in a variety of different positions and environments. The device positions in-

[2]Domain names are extracted from HTTP headers or DNS responses. Applications are identified using a combination of port information, HTTP headers, and other heuristics [15].
[3]The context dataset is available for download at: `http://cs.wisc.edu/~agember/go/imc2012dataset`

clude a user's hand, pocket, backpack, and desk/table. The environments vary in terms of geographic location, device movement speed (stationary, walking, city driving, highway driving), and place (indoors, outdoors, vehicle). For each environment, we conduct measurements on a single device model[4], and each measurement is run for either 1 or 5 minutes, depending on the environment. We conduct at least 5 measurements in each device position in each environment (in walking environments we only consider hand and pocket positions and in driving environments we do not consider desk/table), and we change device positions in a round-robin order to avoid bias due to temporal variation.

For the *activity* dataset, latency and throughput measurements are conducted on devices with and without user activities running simultaneously. The user activities include: web browsing, which loads 15 popular websites[5]; bulk downloads, which downloads a single large file 0.5-3MB in size; and streaming video, which models YouTube's streaming mechanism [9], sending a 4 minute video encoded at a specific bitrate. All measurements are conducted on devices in the same position and environment—stationary on a table indoors in a single geographic location. We conducted some measurements in a second location at different times, affirming that results from other environments are similar.

All figures in the paper identify the dataset used.

3.2 Active vs. Idle

The first step towards obtaining in-context cellular network performance measurements is to understand how performance differs between the times users actually use their devices versus the times the devices are unused. Specifically, we consider a device to be *active* when a user is interacting with the device (e.g., browsing the web, using a navigation application, playing music, etc.) and the activity requires sending/receiving data over the cellular network. A device is *idle* when the user is not interacting with the device (e.g., screen is off and no audio is playing), although background traffic (e.g., email sync) may still be present.

We compare the network performance of active devices to the performance of idle devices using the *network* dataset, accounting for the well-known effects of time [25], space [33], and resource allocation [28]. We find significant differences between the performance experienced by active and idle devices, implying that random measurements, conducted irrespective of whether a user is actually using their device, insufficiently capture an in-context view of performance.

3.2.1 Methodology

Estimating performance. To estimate network performance at different times and locations, we leverage the observation that each device in the *network* dataset has a TCP connection on which it sends and receives keep-alive messages approximately once every 30 minutes. This occurs whether the device is active or idle, and all devices connect to the same data center. We define each keep-alive event as a *measurement.*[6]

We estimate two performance metrics for each measurement: downlink loss rate and RTT. We estimate loss as the ratio of the number of bytes retransmitted over the number of bytes received: $(tcp\_datalen - seqno\_range)/seqno\_range$, where *tcp_datalen* is the total number of TCP payload bytes observed during the measurement and *seqno_range* is the difference between the minimum and maximum TCP sequence numbers observed. We estimate RTT using TCP handshake times when the measurement is preceded by a new TCP connection [20], as the connection is periodically reestablished by the device. There are approximately 2 million measurements in the network dataset.

Identifying active times. The network dataset does not give us direct indications of when a user is interacting with their device, so we infer a device is *active* based on the presence of network traffic that is likely to be triggered by user input. More specifically, we define an *active range* as the time range between the start and end times of flows that indicate user activity; active ranges are calculated on a per-user basis.

To differentiate flows that indicate user activity from background traffic flows (e.g., email polling and keep-alives), we analyze the periodicity of traffic for each <domain name, application> pair. Many applications send periodic traffic frequently while in active use (e.g., Facebook sends keep-alives every 1 minute), but the periodicity is much lower than background traffic (e.g., email polling every 10+ minutes). Based on manual inspection of the traffic patterns of the most used applications, we chose a periodicity threshold of 5 minutes to differentiate between the two categories of flows. If one of the top three periodicities for a <domain name, application> pair (excluding the keep-alive traffic described above) is longer than 5 minutes and appears as a spike in the frequency domain, we label the time ranges for flows belong to this pair as *unknown ranges*; this traffic is likely just background traffic but may indicate user activity. All other flows indicate active ranges.

We define any measurement that occurs within 10 minutes of an active range to be a *near active* measurement, and any measurement that occurs > 30 minutes from all active and unknown ranges to be an *idle* measurement. We ignore measurements that overlap or occur within 17 seconds of an active or unknown range to avoid measuring the effects of self-interference and to ensure near active and idle measurements both start in the same cellular radio state [28]. While our definitions of idle and near active times are inexact, we conjecture that the near active measurements are more likely to overlap actual active times than the idle measurements. Thus, these definitions are sufficient to demonstrate differences in active and idle measurements on average.

3.2.2 Results

Performance differences. We expect that performance will differ during different times of the day, as the traffic load on the network varies. So the first question we answer is: If we control for time of day, is the performance experienced by idle devices the same as active devices? Figures 1a and 1b show the mean latency and loss during each hour of the day for near active and idle devices; the error bars show 95% confidence intervals. We observe a clear difference in the

[4]We manually validated that multiple phones of the same model deliver similar performance under identical conditions.

[5]Based on Alexa, *http://www.alexa.com/topsites/countries/US.*

[6]While this connection is between the device and one of several different server IP addresses in the data center, the average performance of any subset of these connections should not be biased by the server selection algorithm. We statistically validated the server is chosen uniformly at random and all servers are co-located.

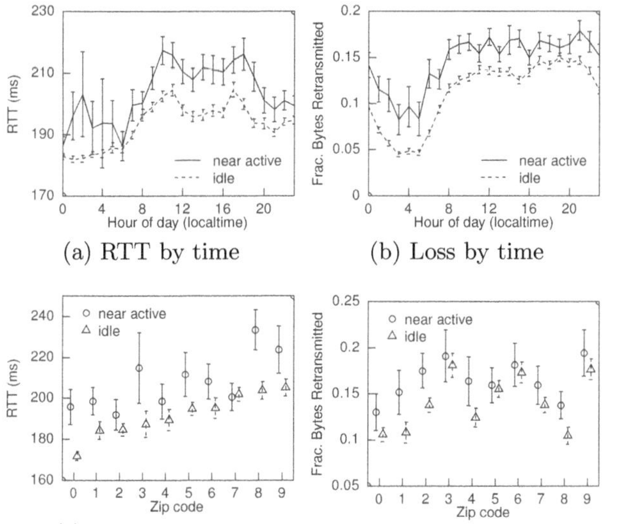

(a) RTT by time (b) Loss by time

(c) RTT by region (d) Loss by region

Figure 1: Distribution of latency and loss for active and idle devices in a large metropolitan area [*Network*]

near active and idle performance for most hours of the day. Measurements on idle devices have up to 16ms lower RTT; loss rates are lower by up to 6%-age points (or, 40% lower, relatively speaking) compared to near active measurements.

It has been shown that performance also differs between coarse-grain locations [33]. If we control for coarse-grain geographic location, is the performance experienced by idle devices the same as active devices? Figures 1c and 1d show the mean latency and loss for the 10 zipcodes with the most measurements for near active and idle devices. Again we see that measurements on idle devices have up to a 30ms lower RTT, and loss rates lower by up to 4%-age points (or, 26% on a relative scale) compared to near active measurements.

Thus, we conclude that the average performance of idle devices is *not* representative of the average performance of active devices, either at the same point in time, or within the same coarse geographic area. Including measurements from idle devices would overestimate performance, on average. Avoiding even such small overestimation is important, as minor differences in latency and loss can become magnified over the lifetime of a TCP connection. Moreover, studies have shown that even small increases in latency—as little as 100ms—can impact user retention [21].

Cause of differences. Two common causes of cellular performance variation—time of day and coarse geographic location—have already been accounted for in our examination of the performance differences between *active* and *idle* devices. We now consider three other possible causes.

First, we consider the duration of time a device has been idle. We calculate the Pearson's correlation coefficient between the idle duration and the RTT or loss. For both metrics, there is no correlation (0.0057 and -0.0045, respectively), indicating the duration of time since a device was last active does not impact its network performance.

Next, we consider signal strength. Figure 2a shows the mean signal strength across all near active and idle devices during each hour of the day; the error bars show 95% confidence intervals. We observe no significant difference in average signal strength for most hours of the day, indicating variations in signal strength are unlikely to cause the differences in latency and loss between active and idle devices. Our measurement system evaluation (§4.1) shows the effect of signal strength on measured throughput is also minimal.

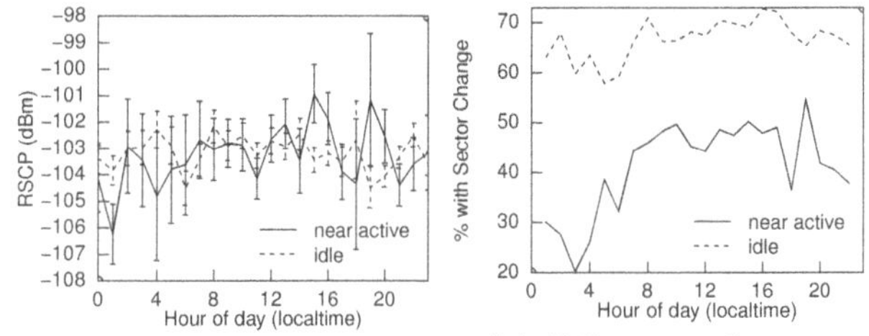

(a) Average signal strength (b) Cell sector changes

Figure 2: Possible causes of performance differences between active and idle devices [*Network*]

Finally, we consider differences between cell sectors as a possible cause of the performance differences. This consideration is prompted by Manweiler et al.'s observation that latency differs between cell sectors managed by different RNCs [25]. Figure 2b shows, for each hour of the day, the fraction of near active and idle devices which have changed cell sector since they were last active. We observe that a larger faction of idle devices are using different cell sectors, implying that differences between cell sectors—frequency, back-haul capacity, load, etc. [8]—are a possible cause of the performance differences between active and idle devices.

Summary. Our analysis indicates that the average network performance of active devices is worse than that of idle devices—the latency experienced by active devices is 16ms higher and the loss rate is 26% higher (~17% loss vs ~12% loss)—requiring measurements to be cognizant of whether devices are active to avoid overestimating network performance. Such differences in network performance cannot be attributed to idle duration or signal strength, but may be caused by differences between cell sectors. In the next section, we explore several other contextual factors, e.g., device position, that also likely cause the performance difference.

3.3 Impact of Physical Context

There are many factors that can contribute to differences in the end-to-end performance the network is capable of delivering to a device, including signal strength, signal fading and interference, handover rate, cell sector traffic load, and back-haul capacity. Several of these factors change over time as a result of what a user physically does with their mobile device—e.g., drives in a car with their device. In the previous section, we alluded to changes in these factors as possible explanations for the difference in achievable performance between active and idle devices. However, precisely accounting for changes in these low-level factors is extremely difficult, if not impossible.

We focus instead on the extent to which various aspects of a device's physical context—which influences these low-level factors—impacts measured performance. For example, changing a device's position from your hand to your pocket can change the signal characteristics, as can moving from indoors to outdoors. We use the *context* dataset (described in §3.1) to quantify the differences in performance between device positions—e.g., hand versus pocket—

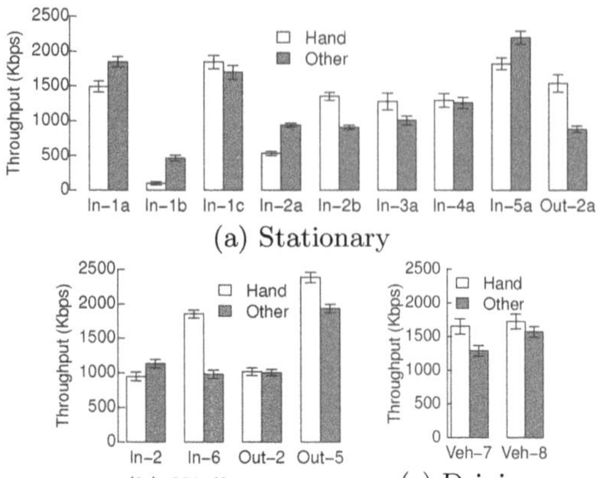

(a) Stationary

(b) Walking (c) Driving

Figure 3: Difference in mean throughput (with 95% confidence intervals) between hand and all other positions for various environments. Environments are named by place (*In*doors, *Out*doors, *Veh*icle), geographic location (1-8), and stationary spot (a-c). [*Context*]

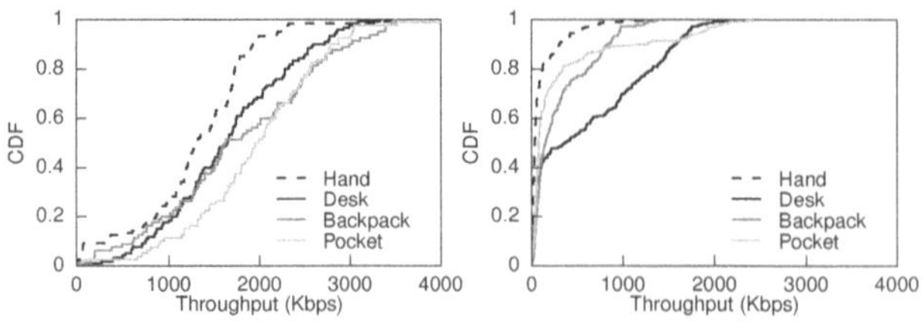

(a) In-1a (b) In-1b

Figure 4: Throughput in two offices in a building [*Context*]

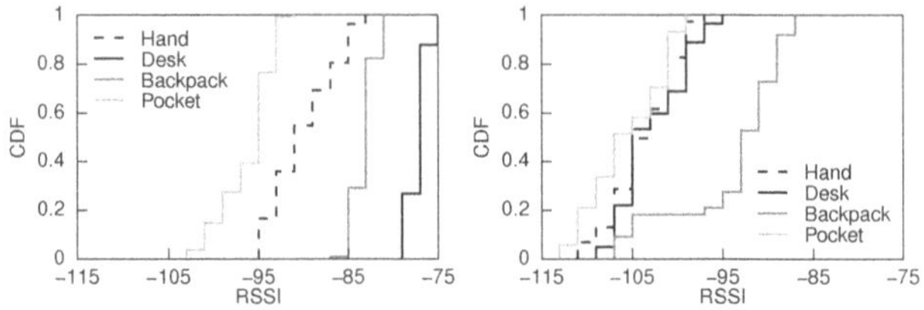

(a) In-1a (b) In-1b

Figure 5: RSSI during throughput measurements [*Context*]

and validate prior observations on performance differences associated with some changes in environment—e.g., moving from one room to another. We find that a device's position, location, and movement significantly and consistently influence measured performance.

3.3.1 Impact of Device Position

Users typically hold their mobile device in their hand when they are actively using the device, whereas they may place it on their desk or in their pocket or backpack when not in use. The device's signal characteristics will vary with each position, potentially resulting in different network performance. We quantify the differences in performance between several positions—a user's hand, pocket, backpack, and desk—to determine what effect, if any, minor position variation has on measurements. We observe different trends with different types of measurements, so we discuss throughput and latency measurements separately.

Throughput. In most environments, we observe a significant difference in throughput between device positions. Figure 3 shows the mean throughput measured with a device in a user's hand versus in other positions across various environments; the error bars show 95% confidence intervals. Mean throughput differs by up to 875Kbps between positions in some environments, but it may differ by less than 50Kbps.

Differences in measured throughput between device positions occur across all types of environments. Stationary devices may exhibit 35-660Kbps differences in throughput between positions, and moving devices may exhibit 20-875Kbps differences between positions. Similar variation in throughput differences exists for indoor and outdoor environments. Furthermore, there is no consistent trend as to whether performance in hand is always better or worse: mean throughput can be up to 47% better when the device is in the user's hand, or it can be up to 79% worse. Hence, throughput measurements must be cognizant of device position.

We look in detail at measured throughput across positions for a few of the environments to determine if we can attribute differences between positions to specific low-level factors. We consider two indoor stationary environments (*In-1a* and *In-1b*), which are different offices in the same building. However, similar trends in measurements and low-level factors hold for a user sitting at two different desks in a single office in a different building (indoor stationary environments *In-2a* and *In-2b*) and for users walking with their devices (environments *In-2*, *In-6*, *Out-2*, and *Out-5*).

Figure 4 shows CDFs of throughput across several measurements conducted in each device position in the two offices. In both offices, there are significant differences in the throughput distributions for each device position: the median throughput is 50% higher in pocket than in hand in In-1a and 917% higher on desk than in hand in In-1b. Furthermore, the ordering of throughput curves by device position is not consistent across the two offices.

We first consider signal strength as a possible explanation for the throughput differences between positions. Figure 5 shows the distribution of signal strength (RSSI) during our measurements in the two offices for each device position. There is a noticeable difference in median RSSI between positions: up to 18dB for In-1a and 12dB for In-1b. However, the ordering of the throughput curves does not match the ordering of the RSSI curves for either office. This suggests signal strength is not a primary factor.

We also consider cell sector, and its associated low-level factors, as a possible cause of throughput differences. However, we observe that all measurements conducted in In-1a occur over a single cell sector, and most measurements conducted in In-1b occur over that same cell sector, along with one other cell sector. This implies that cell sector is not a primary cause of the throughput differences between positions.

Our hypothesis is that small scale fading is the primary low-level factor causing differences in measured throughput across positions. Due to constructive and destructive interference of a signal's reflections off different objects in the environment, the signal power can be time and space varying even over small regions of space. This means that a device being in a user's hand versus their pocket, when the user is stationary, can result in significant differences in network performance. We would expect that the small scale fading would average out in moving environments, but since

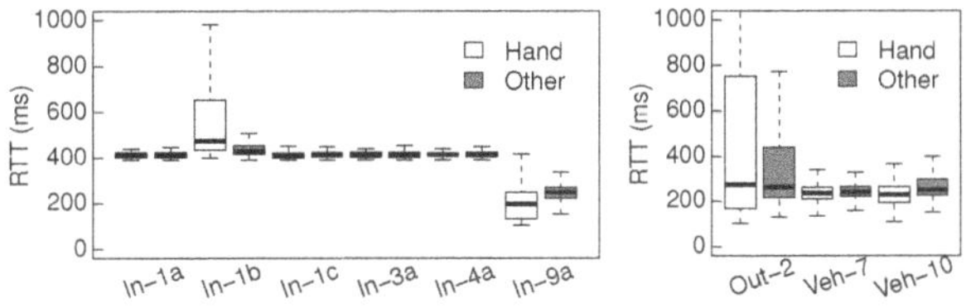

(a) Stationary (b) Moving

Figure 6: Difference in latency between hand and all other positions for various environments; boxes show 25th, 50th, and 75th %-tile, error bars show min and max [*Context*]

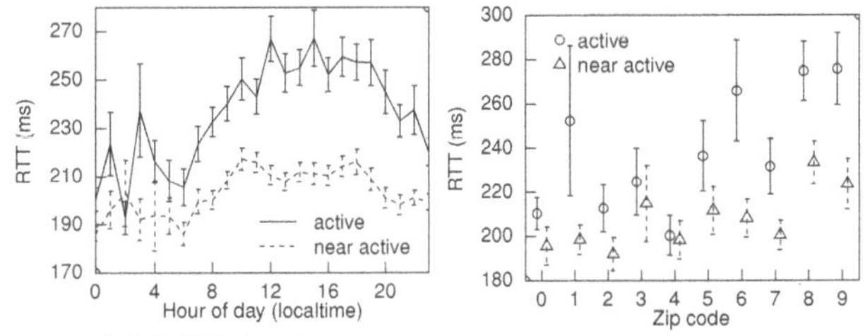

(a) RTT by time (b) RTT by region

Figure 7: RTTs with/without competing traffic [*Network*]

some objects do not move randomly—e.g., your pocket and a device within it moves in unison when you are walking—some regions of space may be consistently stuck in a null (destructive interference). Hence, we would still observe the effects of small scaling fading even when walking or driving.

Latency. In contrast to throughput measurements, latency measurements are less affected by device position. Figure 6 shows the median latency measured with a device in a user's hand versus in other positions across some of the same environments. We find that median latency tends to be equivalent across most environments, differing by more than 15ms in only one third of the environments. Furthermore, the worst-case (e.g., 75th percentile) measured latencies differ substantially between positions in only two environments.

Like throughput measurements, there is no consistent trend across environments as to when latency measurements will differ between device positions. However, our observation that median latency tends to be similar between device positions in the same environment agrees with previous findings [25] that latency is similar amongst mobile devices connected to the same cell sector. Overall, our findings suggest that median latency can be accurately measured irrespective of device position, but full distributions of latency require considering device positions.

3.3.2 *Impact of Environment*

In addition to changing the position of their mobile device, users may also change locations or transition between stationary and moving. These changes in environment have previously been shown to cause differences in end-to-end network performance [25, 33, 37]. We briefly discuss how our results compare with these findings.

Location. Measurements conducted using WiScape [33] showed that throughput differences of a few 100Kbps exist between locations as small as 250m apart. Similarly, Figure 3a shows a difference in measured throughput between three offices in the same building (environments *In-1a*, *In-1b*, and *In-1c*): the mean throughput of a device held in each of the three offices is 1491Kbps, 98Kbps, and 1842Kbps, respectively. All measurements are conducted in these offices within a timespan of about 2 hours and most measurements occur over the same cell sector, so these factors are unlikely to be major contributors to the measurement differences.

There also exists a difference, albeit less pronounced, in measured latency between locations (Figure 6a): median latency measured on a device held in each of the three offices is 416ms, 475ms, and 412ms, respectively. This discrepancy occurs despite most measurements occurring over the same cell sector, which others have shown to be the primary contributor of latency differences [25]. In summary, changes in location cause differences in measured performance.

Stationary versus moving. Tso et al. [37] showed that downlink throughput can decrease by over 1Mbps between a stationary environment and a public transportation environment (e.g., bus). Figure 3a shows a difference in measured throughput between stationary and moving devices in the same location (environment *2*): held devices moving at walking speeds indoors and outdoors have mean throughput of about 950Kbps, while stationary devices have mean throughput of 1540Kbps outdoors and a range of 533Kbps to 1351Kbps indoors. Thus, measurements conducted at even slow speeds can exhibit differences compared to measurements on stationary devices.

Summary. Our findings indicate that both device position and environment can impact measurement results. For example, an active device in a user's hand will experience different performance than an idle device in a user's pocket due to small scale fading. Additionally, differences in performance between environments can affect the accuracy of measurements if a device is typically active in some environments and idle in others. Therefore, *in-context measurements should not be conducted in positions or environments where devices are not active.*

3.4 Measurement Interference

The final factor we consider in conducting in-context performance measurements is the allowable overlap in measurements and user traffic. Many use-cases require specific metrics and results that depict only how characteristics of the cellular network impact end-to-end performance (§2.1). Hence, we want to avoid the concomitant effects of, and on, other traffic sent/received by devices under consideration. Additionally, we want to maximize the opportunities for conducting in-context measurements, since our earlier observations already require limiting measurements to devices which are active and in certain physical contexts.

We use the *network* and *activity* datasets to examine how user traffic—traffic resulting from user interactions with the device—impacts measurement results. We also study how active measurements may impact a user's experience.

3.4.1 *Impact on Measurement Results*

Latency measurements. We first examine the effect of self-interference caused by real flows, which encompass a wide range of traffic triggered by user interactions. We use the *network* dataset and the same methodology described in §3.2.1. Figure 7 shows the mean RTT over time and in different regions for measurements that overlap user-initiated flows (active) and nearby measurements that do not overlap user flows (near active); the error bars show 95% confidence

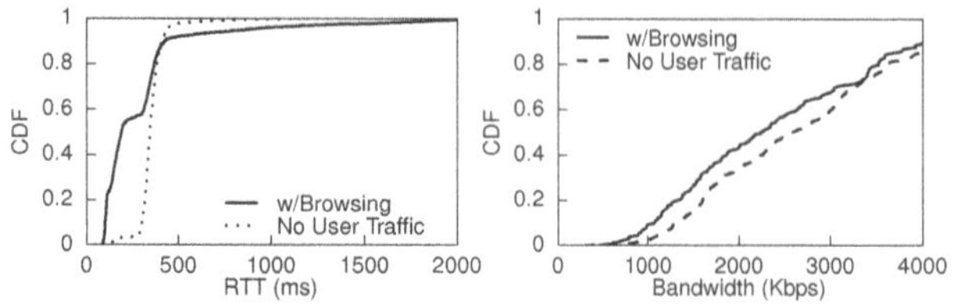

(a) Ping (b) iPerf

Figure 8: Measurements with web browsing [*Activity*]

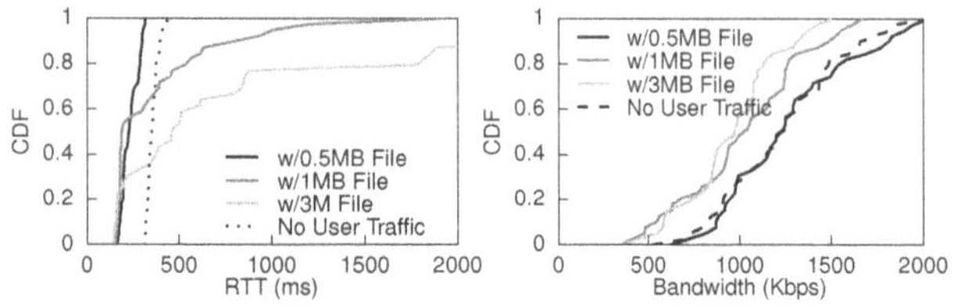

(a) Ping (b) iPerf

Figure 9: Measurements with bulk downloads [*Activity*]

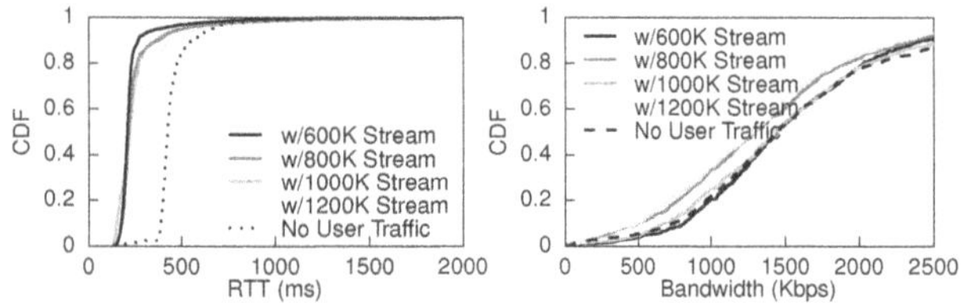

(a) Ping (b) iPerf

Figure 10: Measurements with video streaming [*Activity*]

intervals. We observe that mean RTT is about 20% (40ms) higher, during peak hours and in many regions, when measurements overlap with user traffic. This suggests that at least some types of concurrent user traffic will bias measurements.

We use the *activity* dataset to narrow the potential causes of this bias. We compare the RTTs reported by ping with and without three common types of user traffic: web browsing, bulk downloads, and video streaming (Figures 8a, 9a and 10a). We make three observations.

First, the lowest RTT measurements without user traffic are ≈150ms higher than the lowest RTTs reported during activities. This is due to effects from the radio resource control (RRC) state machine, which causes devices with low traffic volumes to stay in the *CELL_FACH* state, utilizing a low-bandwidth shared channel [29]. Operators need to adjust RTT measurements to account for this RRC effect.

Second, some user traffic significantly increases the tail of measured RTTs. In the presence of web browsing, 8% of measured RTTs are greater than 450ms, versus only 4% without web browsing (Figure 8a). The tail increase is even more pronounced for bulk downloads ≥ 1MB (Figure 9a).

Finally, the median RTT provides an accurate measure of latency only during short transfers and constant rate transfers. The median RTT with and without short web transfers is about 360ms (Figure 8a), as is the median RTT with and without video streaming (Figure 10a), due to the constant data transfer rate used after the initial video buffering period. In contrast, the median RTT measured during bulk downloads (Figure 9a) is only accurate for a small 0.5MB file, not the larger 1MB and 3MB downloads.

Throughput measurements. We also examine the bias

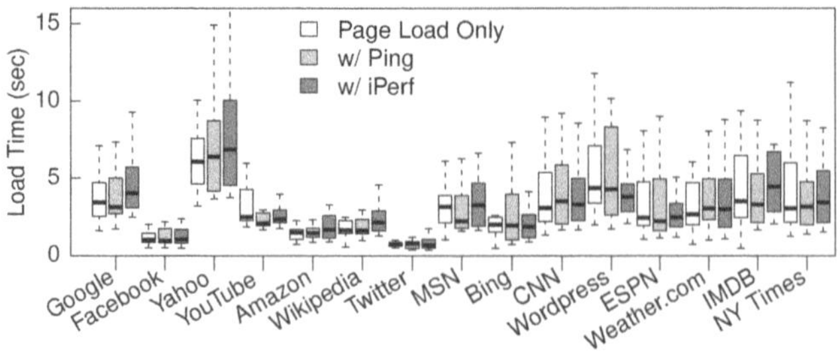

Figure 11: Page load times on *Phone A*; boxes show 25th, 50th, & 75th %-tile, error bars show min and max [*Activity*]

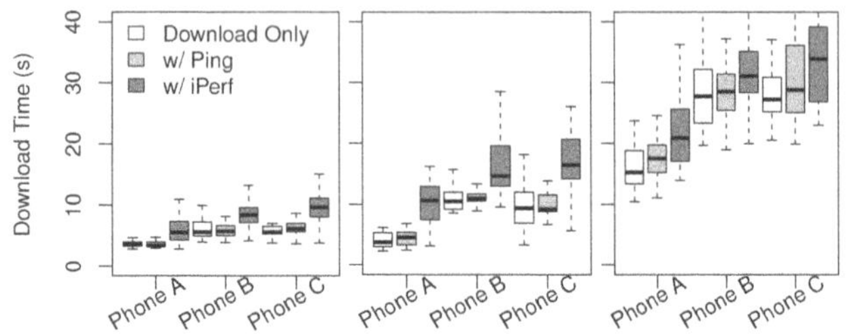

(a) 0.5MB (b) 1MB (c) 3MB

Figure 12: File download times; boxes show 25th, 50th, & 75th %-tile, error bars show min and max [*Activity*]

user traffic introduces in throughput measurements. Figures 8b, 9b and 10b show that measured throughput distributions are affected by all three categories of user traffic. As the peak bandwidth used by the user interaction increases, the impact on throughput measurements increases. For example, 1MB and 3MB bulk downloads are able to achieve higher peak bandwidths due to an increase in connection duration and a corresponding opportunity for TCP to probe for more bandwidth. A similar, though less pronounced effect, occurs as video streaming rates increase.

3.4.2 Impact on User Experience

We also consider the impact of active measurements on user experience, again using the *activity* dataset.

Web browsing. The median page load times—which includes both content retrieval and page rendering time—of 15 popular websites are unaffected by active latency or throughput measurements (Figure 11). We attribute the small variations (< 0.5s) for a few pages to transient network effects.

Bulk downloads. Applications relying on downloading data in bulk are affected by bandwidth-intensive throughput measurements. For files 0.5-3MB in size, throughput measurements cause download times to increase by 0.5s to 7s, with a 9% to 223% increase in variation (Figure 12). This time increase does not occur with web browsing because several small files (a few 100KB in total) are downloaded, keeping TCP congestion windows small and preventing the opportunity to achieve throughput levels that would be affected by co-occurring throughput measurements. Latency measurements have a much less pronounced impact on file download time: at most a 0.8s increase for a 1MB file.

Video streaming. Streaming is affected by both latency and throughput measurements. Table 2 shows the fraction of playback time spent buffering, which is a good indication of user experience [14]. Throughput measurements cause up to a 157% increase in the median buffering ratio, due to the high-bandwidth streaming requires. Latency measurements

	Median			Relative Increase	
Bit Rate	Only	w/Ping	w/iPerf	w/Ping	w/iPerf
600Kbps	0.00	0.00	0.00	0%	0%
800Kbps	0.00	0.01	0.09	11%	12%
1000Kbps	0.04	0.06	0.09	57%	114%
1200Kbps	0.07	0.09	0.19	24%	157%

Table 2: Streaming buffering ratios on *Phone B* [*Activity*]

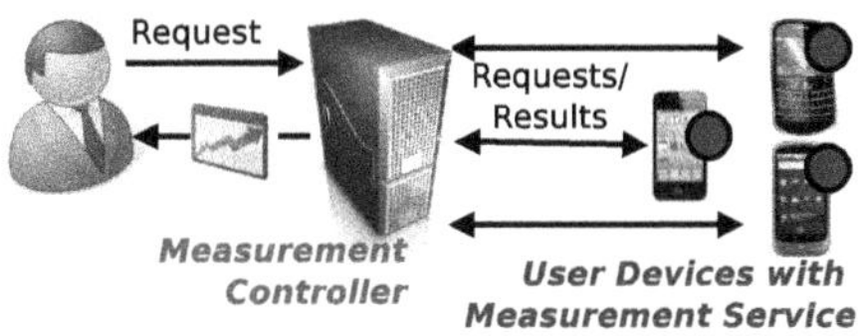

Figure 13: System architecture

cause up to a 57% increase in the median buffering ratio, as ping packets add jitter that impacts the ability to maintain a constant streaming ratio. Thus, any measurement activity could impact user experience for jitter-sensitive applications. **Summary.** Our findings indicate the measurements conducted in the presence of low-bandwidth user activities (e.g., web browsing or low-rate streaming) accurately portray median latency and throughput, while high-bandwidth user traffic causes overestimates of worst-case latency and underestimates of throughput. Measurement systems (passive or active) must consider these effects for in-context results to be accurate. Additionally, active measurement systems should avoid high-bandwidth measurements during user activities that heavily use the network, and no active measurements should be conducted during jitter-sensitive activities.

3.5 Summary of Observations

With a goal of obtaining a measure of the *performance users experience solely when they are interacting with their device*, we have analyzed cellular network performance across active and idle devices, various physical contexts, and several combinations of measurements and user traffic. Our findings indicate that measurements must be conducted:

- Only on active devices, otherwise measurements may overestimate network performance.
- On devices which are in the same positions and environments where the devices are actively used, otherwise mean throughput and worst-case latency measurements will be inaccurate.
- At times when only low-bandwidth, non-jitter-sensitive user traffic is present, otherwise measurement results will be skewed and user experience will be degraded.

These findings inform the design of our system for context-aware crowdsourcing of active measurements, discussed next. However, these observations can also be used to filter passive measurements to quantify the performance the network delivers solely when users are interacting with their device.

4. MEASUREMENT SYSTEM DESIGN

We now present the detailed design of a cellular network measurement system capable of crowdsourcing in-context active measurements from user devices. Our system consists of a logically centralized measurement controller and users' mobile devices running a local measurement service (Figure 13).

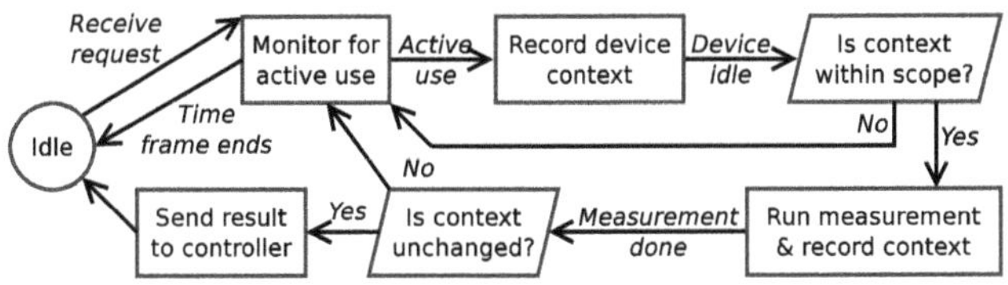

Figure 14: Measurement service decision process

Admins submit requests to the controller, specifying the metric of interest, the time frame and any constraints on which mobile devices to use. For instance, an administrator can request to measure latency on iPhones in Los Angeles during morning rush hour. The controller forwards the request to any viable participating mobile devices. After mobile devices conduct measurements, their results are received by the controller and aggregated for analysis by admins.

Users install our measurement service on their mobile device to conduct active measurements. The service (*i*) receives measurement requests, reports results, and sends coarse context updates to the controller, (*ii*) monitors network usage, screen state, and device sensors to identify opportunities to conduct an in-context measurement, and (*iii*) initiates the appropriate measurement when an opportunity arises. The service currently supports latency (ping), throughput (iPerf or bulk file download), streaming, and web page load time measurements, but it can be easily extended to gather other metrics. The local decision process used to initiate in-context measurements is shown in Figure 14.

Measurements are only conducted on devices which are *active* or were *recently-active*, to avoid overestimating network performance (§3.2). We consider a device to be active when a user is interacting with the device and the activity sends/receives data over the cellular network. Monitoring for active use is triggered by the receipt of a measurement request from the controller; we discuss the details below. When a device becomes idle, or if the device's usage of the network will not negatively impact the measurement (§3.4), we consider conducting a measurement.

A device's context is sensed and recorded while the device is active and while it is conducting a measurement. We check the context of an active device against the admin-specified scope of interest, conducting a measurement only if it matches. After the measurement finishes, we check if the position or environment changed in a way that impacts performance (§3.3), discarding the measurement if necessary; otherwise, the result is sent to the controller. When the specified measurement time frame ends, the service stops monitoring for measurement opportunities and returns to idle. We discuss the details of context monitoring below.

Our system conducts active measurements to avoid the confounding factors of application variability [17] and overlapping traffic (§3.4). However, our design could be easily modified to passively measure existing application traffic instead of conducting active measurements. The measurement decision process (Figure 14) would remain the same.

We now discuss how we address the challenges of active detection and context sensing in an energy-aware manner and describe their implementation on the Android platform.[7]

[7]Although our service is implemented for Android devices, we believe similar solutions could be ported to other mobile platforms.

Detecting Active. The Android platform generates an event when the screen turns on, which presumably means the user is interacting with their device. Subsequently, we can poll traffic counters for the cellular network interface to identify the presence of traffic from a user activity. However, some interactions may occur when the screen is off: listening to network-streamed audio or speaking into the microphone. Thus, we extend our monitoring to detect (using standard Android APIs) when the network is being used and either the screen is on, the microphone is on, or audio is playing.
Context Monitoring. Environment context can be obtained using existing solutions: cell sector identifier is often a sufficient indication of geo-location; mobility can be detected using cellular signals [34], GPS (used in our implementation), and accelerometers [31]; and indoors/outdoors detection can be based on the ability to obtain a GPS signal [30] or ambience fingerprinting [10].

Position changes are much more subtle. Existing accelerometer-based approaches for detecting a device's position on the human body are promising [11, 16], but no one has investigated the position changes we are interested in, e.g., moving a device from hand to backpack. We design a new approach that stems from a key observation: we do not need to identify the precise position of the device, only whether or not it has changed.

We detect changes in device position by monitoring for increases in the standard deviation of device acceleration. If the increase is significant enough, then significant device movement must have occurred—e.g., picking up the device from your desk—versus a slight device shift—e.g., tilting the device in your hand to see the screen better. Based on experimentation, we chose to sample the accelerometer at a rate of 4Hz, combine the acceleration along all three axis into a single acceleration vector, calculate the standard deviation over the last 15 samples, and signal changes in micro-environment when standard deviation exceeds $1m/s^2$.

To keep energy use low, we only sense the environment and position changes from the start of active use to the end of a corresponding measurement. If at any point we detect a change that affects whether a measurement is in-context (§3.3), we stop sensing until the next active use.

4.1 Evaluation

We evaluate our measurement system's accuracy in gathering in-context measurements, along with its position change detection accuracy and energy consumption. We show that measurements conducted under the constraints listed in §3.5 result in throughput metrics that closely match the performance users experience while interacting with their device. Furthermore, the mobile device service is able to detect position changes with a low false negative rate, and the energy burden imposed on devices is usually minimal.

4.1.1 In-context Measurement Accuracy

We deployed our measurement service prototype to the mobile devices of 12 volunteers over a three month period to evaluate how closely measurements gathered by our system match the cellular network performance these users experienced while interacting with their device. We focused on downlink TCP throughput, a common metric of interest which inherently captures other metrics (latency, loss, etc.).
Dataset. We measure downlink TCP throughput using a 20 second bulk file transfer from a server under our control. Throughput is calculated at one second intervals. Measurements were conducted (*i*) when the device's screen was on but no traffic was present, (*ii*) 20s after a device was active and the environment remained unchanged, and (*iii*) at random times regardless of current device usage or context. We refer to the three types of measurements as *ground truth*, *in-context*, and *random*, respectively.

We use measurements conducted under condition (*i*) as our *ground truth* for in-context performance, because times when the screen is on are times the user may engage in activities that use the network. We do not use passive measurements of actual application traffic because of the variability caused by application-specific factors (e.g., server location) [17] and the influence of cross-traffic from multiple applications (§3.4). Measurements conducted under condition (*ii*) are measurements we expect to be *in-context*, as the criteria for conducting these measurements satisfy the requirements outlined in §3.5. Hence, we compare these measurements against the ground-truth to verify our system can gather accurate in-context measurements of network performance.

We obtained 320 pairs of ground truth/in-context measurements and 607 random measurements. A few of these measurements (12 ground truth/in-context pairs, 14 random) were excluded because the measurement failed to start or complete. In 156 instances, the environment changed after a ground truth measurement was conducted; however, we still conducted a measurement in the idle period that followed (referred to as *environ-diff* measurements) to serve as a comparison to in-context measurements. Additionally, we obtained 284 ground truth measurements that did not have a corresponding in-context measurement, due to the lack of a sufficient idle period (<20s) between the device's screen turning off and then turning back on. These are likely caused by short power-saving screen timeouts. We use these *unpaired-active* measurements only for examining how various environment factors affect mean throughput.
Measurement Opportunities. Each of the volunteers contributed a different number of measurements to the dataset. Due to data plan constraints, the volunteers only ran our prototype for part of the three month period. The top of Figure 15 shows how many days each volunteer participated. Furthermore, the number of measurements contributed by a volunteer each day varies based on their device usage habits. The bars in Figure 15 show the average number of ground truth/in-context pairs, ground truth/environ-diff pairs, and random measurements conducted daily on each volunteer's device. The average number of measurement opportunities per day for each volunteer is the sum of the in-context and environ-diff counts, since these measurements are conducted when a user interacts with their device.

We make two important observations from Figure 15. First, the number of times per day volunteers interact with their device varies significantly. Some devices are used over 12 times per day, on average (e.g., volunteer 4), while other are used less than 3 times per day (e.g., volunteer 2).[8] Second, for most volunteers, 20% to 60% of measurements must be discarded due to changes in environment. This suggests

[8]This only includes instances when the device's screen is on for more than 10 seconds with no network traffic present; short device usage periods and background network usage also occur, but these are not adequate measurement opportunities.

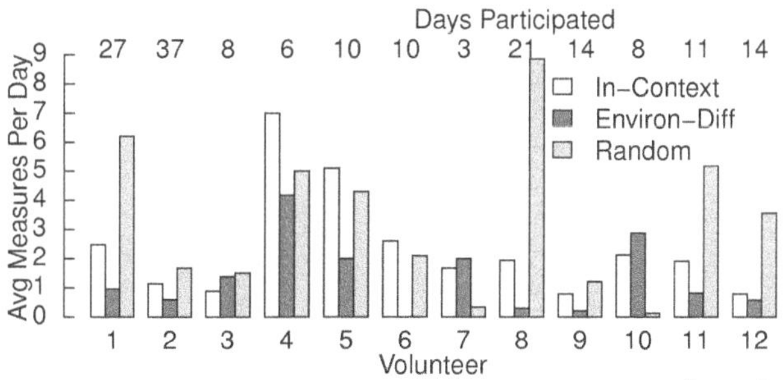

Figure 15: Measurement frequency by volunteer [*Eval*]

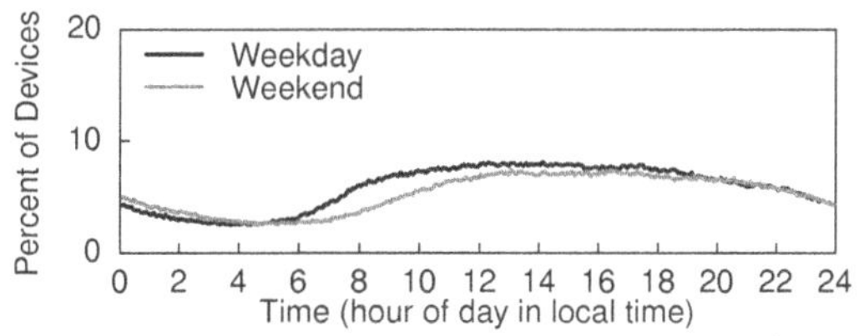

Figure 16: Measurement opportunities at scale [*Network*]

that analyses which do not account for context will include a significant number of results that are not in-context.

Since there are few measurement opportunities per-device per-day, we use the *network* dataset to examine whether there are sufficient opportunities across a large number of users. We consider a measurement opportunity to exist if a device has an active flow (according to our definition in §3.2.1) within a given 5-minute interval. As shown in Figure 16, measurement opportunities exist throughout the day on at least 2.5% of devices, with opportunities on as many as 8% of devices during peak hours on weekdays. Although these percentages are low, they translate to several tens of thousands of devices within a metro area.

Measurement Accuracy. We compare throughput performance across all volunteers for each hour of the day. Due to the sparsity of our collected dataset, we aggregate measurements from the entire three month evaluation period. Figure 17 shows the mean throughput, with 95% confidence intervals, for ground truth, in-context, and random measurements for each hour of the day. The mean throughput reported by ground truth and in-context measurements is approximately equivalent for 18 (75%) of the hours in a day. Two of the hours (4am, 5am) have zero or one measurement pairs, so a fair evaluation cannot be made. For three (11am, 1pm, 8pm) of the four hours when mean throughput differs between ground truth and in-context measurements, the difference can be attributed to a single measurement pair. The cause of these outlier pairs is unknown, but excluding them results in equivalent mean throughput between ground truth and in-context measurements.

Our data also confirms our earlier observation that random measurements provide inaccurate metric values (§3.2). The mean throughput reported by random measurements significantly differs from ground truth throughput for half of the hours. For several hours, the difference is more than 1 Mbps.

In practice, cellular networks offer a range of throughput performance, even within tightly controlled measurement conditions. We compare CDFs of throughput (graphs excluded for brevity) for the three types of measurements for each hour of the day to confirm that our system can accurately quantify this range of performance. We observe that, in addition to differences in mean throughput, the shape and range of the CDF curves for ground truth and in-context measurements are similar and the curves for in-context and random measurements are significantly different.

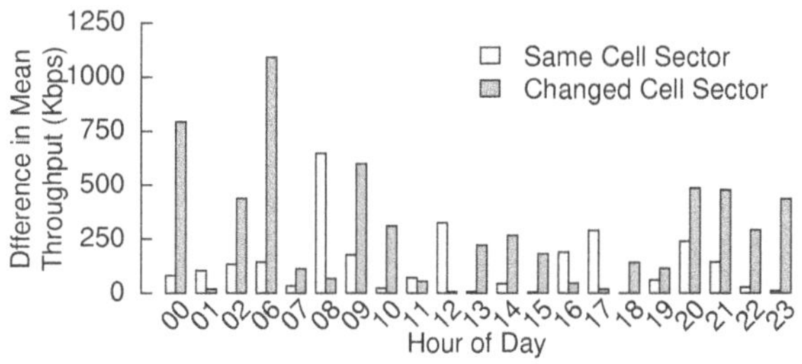

Figure 18: Effect of cell sector changes [*Eval*]

Environment Impact. We show the effect of changes in environment by comparing the mean throughput during ground truth measurements to both in-context and environ-diff measurements. Specifically, we use environ-diff measurements where the cell sector changes between the ground truth and environ-diff measurement. We aggregate the measurements by hour of day, and we exclude the three outlier ground truth/in-context measurement pairs discussed above. Figure 18 shows the absolute difference in average throughput between ground truth and in-context and between ground truth and environ-diff; the hours 3am-5am are excluded due to a lack of environ-diff measurements. We observe a significant inaccuracy in average throughput measurements for 15 of 21 hours (71%), confirming that changes in cell sector have an impact on measurement accuracy (§3.3). In several hours, the difference is over 0.5Mbps.

We further examine the impact of environment on measurement accuracy by examining which pieces of physical context are the most predictive of mean throughput. We consider nine factors: cell sector (LACID), location area (LAC), speed, indoors/outdoors, network connection type, signal strength, phone model, hour of day, and month. These factors are recorded for all measurements we obtained (including ground truth, in-context, environ-diff, and unpaired-active), along with the measured mean throughput.

We determine which factors are most influential by running the Reduced Error Pruning Tree (REPTree) algorithm in Weka [7]. REPTree builds a decision tree based on information gain, pruning the tree in a way that reduces decision errors. The accuracy of the tree is evaluated using 10-fold cross validation on our dataset. We limit the tree depth to 1, to determine the most predictive factor. Then, we exclude that factor from the dataset and re-run the REPTree algorithm to find the second most predictive factor; the process is repeated until all factors have been excluded.

We find that cell sector (LACID) is the most predictive of average throughput (with a raw absolute error of 619Kbps), indicating a change a cell sector has the biggest impact on measurement accuracy. The second most predictive factor is phone model, which we suspect is a result of differences in support for various 3G enhancements (e.g., HSDPA+) between devices. The ordering of the remaining seven factors from most predictive to least is: location area, hour of day, month, network connection type, indoors/outdoors, speed, and signal strength.

Summary. These findings indicate that our system is able

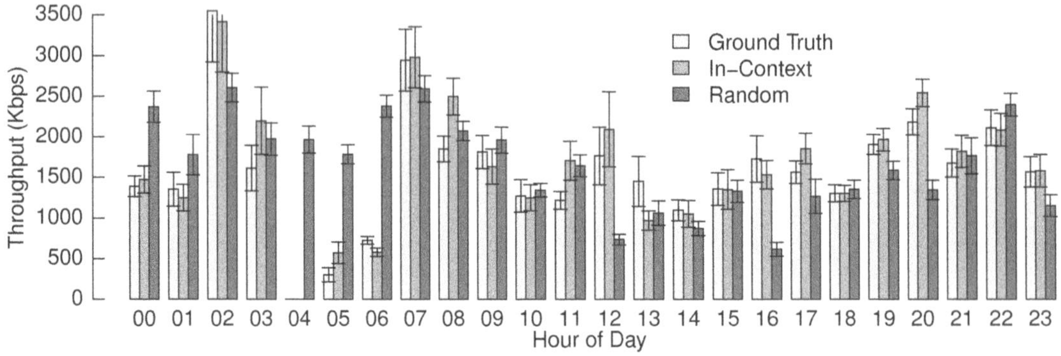

Figure 17: Mean throughput by hour of day; error bars show 95% confidence intervals [*Eval*]

Event	Correct	False Negatives	False Positives
Desk→Hand	7	0	-
Web browsing*	5	-	2
Hand→Pocket	7	0	-
In pocket*	7	-	0
Pocket→Hand	7	0	-
Hand→Desk	6	1	-

Table 3: Number of individuals for whom the service correctly/incorrectly detected position changes; *correct means not detecting any change in position

to accurately crowdsource in-context throughput measurements. Additionally, our findings on which environment factors are most predictive of throughput can be used to improve passive analysis techniques or other mobile applications seeking to approximate network performance, e.g., [25].

4.1.2 *Measurement Service Benchmarks*

Detecting Position Changes. To evaluate our accelerometer-based approach for detecting device position changes (§4), we asked 7 volunteers to perform a sequence of activities with their mobile devices. Users sitting at a desk were asked to pick up the device, browse to a website, then put the device in their pocket. After a minute, users were asked to remove the device from their pocket, make a phone call, and put the device back on the desk. Throughout the experiment, the service monitored for changes in position.

Table 3 shows the detection results from our user study. Our system correctly detected all but one position change, for a low false negative rate of 3%. However, some false positives occurred during the periods with no position change. No error in measurement accuracy occurs with false positives, but measurement opportunities are unnecessarily skipped.

Energy Usage. The exact energy used by the service depends on how frequently the device is active and how often measurements are requested. We broke down the service's process (Figure 14) into three pieces—idle, active monitoring, and context monitoring—and measured the energy consumed by each piece over a one minute interval. We ran the service on *Phone B* (Table 1 lists specifications), and read coarse-grained energy values from system counters every second. The device LCD was always off for consistency, and we subtracted the baseline energy the device consumes (20.5 Joules) when not running our service. We present results averaged over 30 one-minute runs for each function.

The energy consumed in one minute by each piece of the measurement service process is shown in Table 4. When the

Functionality	Energy Consumed in 1 Minute
Idle	0 Joules
Active Monitoring	0.44 Joules
Environment Monitoring (with GPS)	16.85 Joules
Environment Monitoring (no GPS)	0.15 Joules

Table 4: Energy consumed on *Phone B*

device is not active and no measurements are in progress, i.e., the service is idle, there is no noticeable energy consumption. The energy consumption slightly increases (to 0.44 Joules per minute) when the user interacts with the device and cellular interface traffic counters are monitored to detect network usage. Finally, energy consumption is the highest when using the GPS, accelerometer, and other events to detect environment changes. An optimized service could reduce this energy consumption significantly, by up to about 16 Joules, if movement speed and indoors/outdoors were detected without using the GPS.

4.2 Additional Issues

Scope of interest. As discussed in §2, admins often seek performance measurements for a narrower set of users corresponding to a specific usage environment, device specification etc. Our measurement service already tracks usage environment, and device specifications can be easily obtained, enabling the device itself to determine if it is currently in-scope. However, this suffers from scaling issues, as having each device make this decision means the measurement controller must broadcast measurement requests. To avoid this, we can conduct a preliminary filtering of devices at the measurement controller. Elements in the cellular network are already aware of some environment context and device details (e.g., cell location), enabling them to inform this preliminary filtering. The remaining context (e.g., precise geo-location) and specifications still require on-device filtering. Exactly which parameters to filter at the controller and which to filter on device requires trade-offs in scalability, device overhead, and potentially missed measurement opportunities, a subject we leave for future work.

Security. Mechanisms must be in place to prevent devices from reporting phony measurements and to protect the system from being compromised. Since the threat model is not fundamentally different from existing active measurement testbeds, ideas can be borrowed from prior techniques [27, 35] to help address these issues.

Scheduling. An admin may want to run multiple concurrent experiments, so scheduling them such that they do not

interfere is important. The bottleneck and complex protocol interactions in cellular networks is typically in the "last mile" [8], so limiting geographic overlap may be sufficient.
Incentives for deployment. To lure users to adopt measurement crowdsourcing, admins may use application features or monetary incentives. Existing measurement tools have successfully recruited thousands of volunteers with these approaches [1, 5, 18]. Monetary incentives is a feasible approach for network service providers since they control both billing and measurements.

5. RELATED WORK

Our analysis and measurement system is related to work in cellular performance studies and measurement testbeds.
Cellular performance studies. Numerous measurement studies of cellular network performance have been conducted, including studies on delay [23, 25], TCP performance [24, 26], fairness and performance under load [8, 36], and application specific performance [19]. While these studies shed light on performance trends, cellular network performance is constantly changing as network providers upgrade and reconfigure their networks. Instead, we designed a system for measuring performance on demand as network infrastructure and user devices continuously evolve. Moreover, our analysis offers previously unrecognized guidelines for performing in-context measurement of cellular networks.
Measurement testbeds. Automatically initiating active measurements from vantage points of interest has received prior attention in both the wired and wireless domains. NIMI [27] and Scriptroute [35] pioneered the idea of using voluntary hosts on the Internet to conduct active network measurements and addressed many important issues regarding security and sharing of resources. DipZoom [38], ATMEN [22], and CEM [13] extended these wired testbeds with matchmaking services, event-based measurement triggers, and endpoint crowdsourcing. WiScape [33] uses measurements conducted by mobile devices to evaluate the performance of wide area networks across time and space. It focuses on collecting a small number of measurement samples to adequately characterize performance in a given epoch and zone. Similar to our approach of opportunistic crowdsourcing, these systems conduct measurements from voluntary endpoints. However, our system is the first to address the question of where and when those measurements should be conducted to obtain results that quantify the network performance users experience solely when they are interacting with their device. Thus, the techniques we designed in this paper complement these previous systems, which mostly focused on policy and scheduling issues to avoid interference and limit network disruption.

6. CONCLUSION

We argue that there are several important scenarios where there is a need to obtain in-context performance measures, i.e., the performance the network can deliver when users are interacting with their mobile devices. We conducted a large-scale empirical study using data collected across cell subscribers and controlled experiments, and concluded that such measurements must be conducted on devices that are (*i*) actively used during the measurement time frame, (*ii*) currently exchanging limited user traffic, and (*iii*) in the same position and usage environment since the device was last used. Approaches that don't take these guidelines into account are very likely to give skewed results. Based on our findings, we designed a crowdsourcing-based active measurement system that allows various parties to obtain in-context measurements in a controlled fashion. We showed, using a three month study of our system deployed across 12 users, that our measurement results are very accurate.

7. ACKNOWLEDGEMENTS

We would like to thank our 12 volunteers for running our measurement system on their mobile devices. We would also like to thank our shepherd Dina Papagiannaki and the anonymous reviewers for their insightful feedback. This work is partially supported by the National Science Foundation under grants CNS-1050170, CNS-1017545 and CNS-0746531.

8. REFERENCES

[1] AT&T mark the spot. `research.att.com/articles/featured_stories/2010_09/201009_MTS.html`.

[2] MobiPerf. `http://mobiperf.com`.

[3] The national broadband plan. `http://broadband.gov`.

[4] Open internet. `http://openinternet.gov`.

[5] Root metrics. `http://rootmetrics.com`.

[6] Speedtest.net. `http://speedtest.net`.

[7] Weka. `http://www.cs.waikato.ac.nz/ml/weka`.

[8] V. Aggarwal, R. Jana, J. Pang, K. K. Ramakrishnan, and N. K. Shankaranarayanan. Characterizing fairness for 3g wireless networks. In *LANMAN*, 2011.

[9] S. Alcock and R. Nelson. Application flow control in YouTube video streams. *SIGCOMM CCR*, 41(2), 2011.

[10] M. Azizyan, I. Constandache, and R. Roy Choudhury. SurroundSense: mobile phone localization via ambience fingerprinting. In *MobiCom*, 2009.

[11] L. Bao and S. S. Intille. Activity recognition from user-annotated acceleration data. In *PERVASIVE*, 2004.

[12] M. C. Chan and R. Ramjee. TCP/IP performance over 3G wireless links with rate and delay variation. In *Mobicom*, 2002.

[13] D. R. Choffnes, F. E. Bustamante, and Z. Ge. Crowdsourcing service- level network event monitoring. *SIGCOMM CCR*, 40(4), 2010.

[14] F. Dobrian, A. Awan, D. Joseph, A. Ganjam, J. Zhan, V. Sekar, I. Stoica, and H. Zhang. Understanding the impact of video quality on user engagement. In *SIGCOMM*, 2011.

[15] J. Erman, A. Gerber, M. T. Hajiaghayi, D. Pei, and O. Spatscheck. Network-aware forward caching. In *WWW*, 2009.

[16] R. K. Ganti, P. Jayachandran, T. F. Abdelzaher, and J. A. Stankovic. Satire: a software architecture for smart attire. In *MobiSys*, 2006.

[17] A. Gerber, J. Pang, O. Spatscheck, and S. Venkataraman. Speed testing without speed tests: estimating achievable download speed from passive measurements. In *IMC*, 2010.

[18] D. Han and S. Seshan. A case for world-wide network measurements using smartphones and open marketplaces. Technical report, CMU, 2011.

[19] J. Huang, Q. Xu, B. Tiwana, Z. M. Mao, M. Zhang, and P. Bahl. Anatomizing application performance differences on smartphones. In *MobiSys*, 2010.

[20] H. Jiang and C. Dovrolis. Passive estimation of tcp round-trip times. *SIGCOMM CCR*, 32(3), 2002.

[21] R. Kohavi and R. Longbotham. Online experiments: Lessons learned. *Computer*, 40, 2007.

[22] B. Krishnamurthy, H. V. Madhyastha, and O. Spatscheck. Atmen: a triggered network measurement infrastructure. In *WWW*, 2005.

[23] M. Laner, P. Svoboda, E. Hasenleithner, and M. Rupp. Dissecting 3g uplink delay by measuring in an operational hspa network. In *PAM*, 2011.

[24] X. Liu, A. Sridharan, S. Machiraju, M. Seshadri, and H. Zang. Experiences in a 3g network: interplay between the wireless channel and applications. In *MobiCom*, 2008.

[25] J. Manweiler, S. Agarwal, M. Zhang, R. Roy Choudhury, and P. Bahl. Switchboard: a matchmaking system for multiplayer mobile games. In *MobiSys*, 2011.

[26] K. Mattar, A. Sridharan, H. Zang, I. Matta, and A. Bestavros. Tcp over cdma2000 networks: a cross-layer measurement study. In *PAM*, 2007.

[27] V. Paxson, J. Mahdavi, A. Adams, and M. Mathis. An architecture for large scale internet measurement. In *IEEE Comm. Magazine*, 1998.

[28] F. Qian, Z. Wang, A. Gerber, Z. M. Mao, S. Sen, and O. Spatscheck. Characterizing radio resource allocation for 3g networks. In *IMC*, 2010.

[29] F. Qian, Z. Wang, A. Gerber, Z. M. Mao, S. Sen, and O. Spatscheck. Profiling resource usage for mobile applications: A cross-layer approach. In *MobiSys*, 2011.

[30] L. Ravindranath, C. Newport, H. Balakrishnan, and S. Madden. Improving wireless network performance using sensor hints. In *NSDI*, 2011.

[31] S. Reddy, M. Mun, J. Burke, D. Estrin, M. Hansen, and M. Srivastava. Using mobile phones to determine transportation modes. *ACM Trans. Sensor Networks*, 6(2), 2010.

[32] F. Ricciato. Traffic monitoring and analysis for the optimization of a 3g network. *IEEE Wireless Communications*, 13(6), 2006.

[33] S. Sen, J. Yoon, J. Hare, J. Ormont, and S. Banerjee. Can they hear me now?: a case for a client-assisted approach to monitoring wide-area wireless networks. In *IMC*, 2011.

[34] T. Sohn, A. Varshavsky, A. Lamarca, M. Y. Chen, T. Choudhury, I. Smith, S. Consolvo, J. Hightower, W. G. Griswold, and E. D. Lara. Mobility detection using everyday gsm traces. In *Ubicomp*, 2006.

[35] N. Spring, D. Wetherall, and T. Anderson. Scriptroute: a public internet measurement facility. In *USITS*, 2003.

[36] W. L. Tan, F. Lam, and W. C. Lau. An empirical study on the capacity and performance of 3g networks. *IEEE Trans. on Mobile Computing*, 7(6), 2008.

[37] F. P. Tso, J. Teng, W. Jia, and D. Xuan. Mobility: a double-edged sword for hspa networks. In *MobiHoc*, 2010.

[38] Z. Wen, S. Triukose, and M. Rabinovich. Facilitating focused internet measurements. *SIGMETRICS Perform. Eval. Rev.*, 35(1), 2007.

Cell vs. WiFi: On the Performance of Metro Area Mobile Connections

Joel Sommers
Colgate University
jsommers@colgate.edu

Paul Barford
University of Wisconsin
pb@cs.wisc.edu

ABSTRACT

Cellular and 802.11 WiFi are compelling options for mobile Internet connectivity. The goal of our work is to understand the performance afforded by each of these technologies in diverse environments and use conditions. In this paper, we compare and contrast cellular and WiFi performance using crowd-sourced data from `Speedtest.net`. Our study considers spatio-temporal performance (upload/download throughput and latency) using over 3 million user-initiated tests from iOS and Android apps in 15 different metro areas collected over a 15 week period. Our basic performance comparisons show that *(i)* WiFi provides better absolute download/upload throughput, and a higher degree of consistency in performance; *(ii)* WiFi networks generally deliver lower absolute latency, but the *consistency* in latency is often better with cellular access; *(iii)* throughput and latency vary widely depending on the particular access type (*e.g.*, HSPA, EVDO, LTE, WiFi, *etc.*) and service provider. More broadly, our results show that performance consistency for cellular and WiFi is much lower than has been reported for *wired* broadband. Temporal analysis shows that average performance for cell and WiFi varies with time of day, with the best performance for large metro areas coming at non-peak hours. Spatial analysis shows that performance is highly variable across metro areas, but that there are subregions that offer consistently better performance for cell or WiFi. Comparisons between metro areas show that larger areas provide higher throughput and lower latency than smaller metro areas, suggesting where ISPs have focused their deployment efforts. Finally, our analysis reveals diverse performance characteristics resulting from the rollout of new cell access technologies and service differences among local providers.

Categories and Subject Descriptors

C.2.1 [**Network Architecture and Design**]: Wireless communication; C.4 [**Performance of Systems**]: Performance attributes; C.4 [**Performance of Systems**]: Measurement Techniques

General Terms

Design, Experimentation, Measurement, Performance

IMC'12, November 14–16, 2012, Boston, Massachusetts, USA.

Keywords

Cellular, WiFi

1. INTRODUCTION

Over the last five years there has been an explosion in the availability and use of mobile devices that are both cellular and 802.11 WiFi enabled. The combination of a short range, high-speed capability and a longer range, lower speed capability is compelling and enables a wide range of new mobile applications. Driven by the popularity of applications that run on hybrid cell phones such as the iPhone and Android-based devices, there is a large and growing demand for bandwidth by mobile users.

A vexing problem for WiFi enabled cell phone users, service providers and application designers is seeking out and supporting the connectivity option that provides the best and most reliable performance. Over shorter time scales issues that affect performance include local availability of services, load at a particular site, characteristics of the handset, and interference. Over longer time scales, performance is affected by issues such as the ongoing introduction of new technology and deployment of new service provider infrastructure.

To assist users in the effort of understanding their connectivity options, a number of commercial and open-source throughput testing applications are available. When invoked, these applications attempt to determine the maximum bandwidth for both uploads and downloads from the target device. At basis, these applications send streams of random bytes via HTTP (*e.g.*, data blobs through GET and POST methods) between the target device and a test server. The receiving application measures the bits/second received over small time periods (*e.g.*, one second) and reports the highest sustained rate that is achieved. Details of the specific mechanisms for selecting sending rates, measurements and reporting vary between applications. However, data gathered by these applications offer the possibility to provide unique insights into mobile device performance.

In this paper, we describe an investigation of mobile device performance using crowd-sourced data provided by one of the most popular and widely deployed mobile bandwidth testers, `Speedtest.net` [7]. This unique and rich data set includes information about the device operating system used for the test (iOS or Android), a unique handset identifier, GPS coordinates of the mobile device, time of test, upload and download speeds achieved, etc. Of equal importance is the fact that Speedtest servers are deployed in over 600 locations world wide and are used by tens of thousands of users on a daily basis.

The focus of our study is to understand the spatio-temporal characteristics of performance of WiFi-enabled cell phones in a selection of metro areas with different population densities and diverse geographic characteristics. We seek answers to basic questions such as: what is the relative performance of cellular vs. WiFi in a given geographic area? How does performance vary across local access providers, and how does cell and WiFi performance vary in sub-regions within the metro area? How does cellular and WiFi performance vary temporally in the metro area and in sub-regions within those areas? How consistent is performance for individual users over time? What specific features in the data differentiate observed performance? The long-term goal of our work is to formulate conclusions about the spatio-temporal aspects of WiFi enabled cell phone performance that will lead to improvements in the relevant protocols, configurations, and infrastructure.

Our evaluation indicates a rich yet complex set of characteristics of spatio-temporal performance of mobile devices in a metro area. As expected, we find absolute WiFi download and upload performance to be superior to cellular performance in most areas, and that WiFi exhibits a higher degree of performance consistency. We also find that WiFi latency measurements are at least a factor of two lower than cell latency in all areas, but that different providers can exhibit vastly different latency characteristics, and *consistency* in latency is often better with cellular access. Further, the absolute latency difference between cell and WiFi tends to be smaller in larger metro areas and the overall variability in latency is lower, suggesting that greater efforts have been made to optimize those cellular deployments. Although we find cell performance in large metro areas superior to performance in other areas, throughput and latency performance measures vary widely depending on the specific access type and service provider. Furthermore, we observe that while new cellular access technologies such as 4G LTE offer throughput speeds comparable to WiFi, the upload performance consistency is currently low, suggesting that these deployments are not yet fully optimized. More generally, our results show that performance consistency for cellular and WiFi is significantly lower than has been reported for *wired* broadband access. Our results also show that based on trends toward higher throughput cellular access technologies, connectivity decisions based solely on throughput may not be obvious in the future.

Recognizing the diversity of physical and IT infrastructures and time variations in usage patterns within a given metro area, our analysis includes evaluations of subareas over a variety of time windows. Our results show that download/upload performance in subareas follows a standard diurnal cycle but is highly variable. Specifically, we find that while WiFi performance tends to be more uniform across subareas, cell performance in subareas shows higher variability and there are fewer instances of subareas with consistently good performance. We find that subareas with consistently poor performance tend to be more localized in large metro areas for both cell and WiFi. These results have implications for both users and operators in terms of expectations for performance in both fixed and vehicular settings, for diagnosis of performance degradation and for future provisioning.

2. DATA

In this section we describe the unique data set that forms the basis of our study. We discuss Speedtest's deployment and performance measurement system. We also describe the Speedtest data that are the focus of our study and provide information about the metro areas in which the data were collected. Finally, we discuss how conclusions drawn from the data sets can be influenced by the areas and methods used for collection.

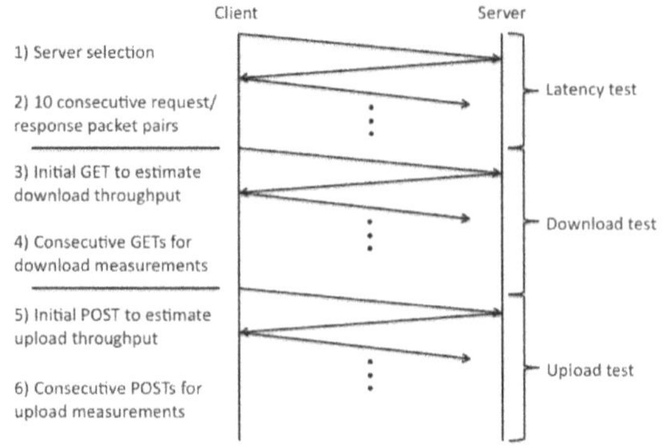

Figure 1: Packet exchange protocol initiated when the Speedtest application is started on a client system.

2.1 Speedtest Overview

`Speedtest.net` [7] is a bandwidth/performance evaluation platform that is managed and maintained by Ookla, Inc. [6]. The application can be run via a flash-based web site, and native apps are available for both Apple iOS-based devices (including iPod touches, iPhones, and iPads) and Android-based devices (including a variety of phones manufactured by HTC, Motorola, Samsung, and Sony Ericsson, among many others). Over 3B performance tests have been run since Speedtest began in 2006, with a significant increase in use over the past twelve months. Daily tests exceed 125K per day, globally.

Each Speedtest is initiated by the client (either a browser or mobile app) as shown in Figure 1. Upon invocation, a test request is directed to the Speedtest server that is deemed to be geographically nearest to the client. There are servers deployed in over 600 locations world wide. Per the Speedtest wiki [5], latency, download, and upload tests are conducted via HTTP (TCP port 80). Latency tests are based on request/response pairs with the average of 10 RTT ping-style tests reported for the latency measurement. Speedtest refers to the download and upload tests as "throughput tests", since their focus is on reporting download/upload speeds by transferring small files between client and server.

A download test begins with an initial transfer of a fixed-size file from server to client to establish an estimate for throughput. This initial test results in selection of another file that will be used for generating final test results. The size of the second file varies: smaller files are used when the initial estimate suggests lower bandwidth and larger files are used when the initial estimate suggests more bandwidth. The target test file is then transferred repeatedly (using naming tricks to prevent client caching) using up to 8 parallel HTTP threads (a configurable option). Throughput estimates based on these file transfers are provided at up to 30 times per second. The top 10% and bottom 30% of the throughput samples are discarded and the remaining samples are averaged to derive a throughput sample. The reason for this kind of sampling is to try to remove burst effects due to OS overhead and other effects and arrive at a maximum throughput estimate that corresponds to the expected case for the user. Test runs are tuned to be relatively short (maximum of tens of seconds) to enhance user experience. Upload tests are conducted in a similar fashion. We note that in prior work, Bauer *et al.* [12] found that the Speedtest method results in a fairly accurate characterization of last-mile performance.

In this work, we consider data collected from tests initiated from the iOS and Android apps. Each full test results in a rich log entry at

Table 1: **Summaries of census and Speedtest data from the 15 target metro areas that are the subject of our evaluation. Speedtest data are for the period from February 21, 2011 to June 5, 2011. US census data are from [14], European census data are from [28], Asian census data are from [1,3,4], and non-US per capita income (PCI) data are from [11].**

Location (market type)	Pop.	Metro Rank	Annual PCI	iOS Unique handsets	iOS # WiFi tests	iOS # cell tests	Android Unique handsets	Android # WiFi tests	Android # cell tests
New York, NY (large)	18.9M	1	$50.8K	89,356	246,222	78,729	97,994	100,794	353,784
Los Angeles, CA (large)	12.8M	2	$45.9K	150,804	425,197	105,901	174,221	181,928	606,564
Chicago, IL (large)	9.5M	3	$51.0K	27,018	62,997	12,084	41,482	34,437	104,667
Columbia, SC (medium)	768K	70	$41.7K	4,931	11,553	3,138	6,779	6,331	18,975
Syracuse, NY (medium)	663K	80	$39.8K	6,122	16,801	3,627	5,165	6,808	9,898
Madison, WI (medium)	569K	89	$49.2K	8,549	23,995	3,853	6,718	9,625	14,012
Jackson, TN (small)	115K	321	$36.6K	5,117	13,742	3,034	2,645	3,894	5,655
Lawrence, KS (small)	111K	329	$37.5K	3,231	8,164	1,893	3,917	4,058	11,498
Missoula, MT (small)	109K	331	$34.4K	860	2,479	604	526	872	806
Manchester, UK (europe)	2.2M	N/A	$41.4K	80,211	291,564	30,810	32,221	82,700	37,767
Brussels, BE (europe)	1.8M	N/A	$45.2K	22,624	48,085	11,033	4,311	7,192	3,964
Belgrade, SP (europe)	1.6M	N/A	$6.0K	3,849	11,606	1,477	9,599	18,865	13,101
Palembang, ID (asia)	1.5M	N/A	$2.0K	415	743	621	504	756	749
Almaty, KZ (asia)	1.4M	N/A	$6.9K	1,949	4,821	1,674	903	1,097	1,947
Ulaanbaatar, MN (asia)	1.1M	N/A	$1.6K	673	1,861	275	340	621	289

the local Ookla server that includes the client IP, device type and OS version, client geographic coordinates (longitude / latitude), server name and coordinates, great-circle distance from the client to the server (computed using the Haversine formula), timestamp, upload and download speeds (in kb/s), latency (in milliseconds), access type (cellular or WiFi), and the cellular carrier or WiFi network provider. In the Android data set, for some tests we have finer grained information about the specific cellular access type (*e.g.*, EDGE, HSPA, EVDO-A, or LTE). For the iOS data, no such fine-grained information exists; we only know whether the access is via cell or WiFi. For each of the apps, we also have a unique device fingerprint that allows us to identify measurements initiated by the same handset (user) even if the test is initiated using a different access technology or from a different service provider.

2.2 Data Sets Considered

The data we consider in our initial evaluation were collected from servers located in 15 metro areas over a period of 15 weeks from February 21, 2011 through June 5, 2011. In each case the metro areas are locations with Speedtest servers. Selection of the sites was based at a high level on attempting to amass a manageable data corpus, yet one that provides a broad perspective on cellular vs. WiFi performance in metro areas that are diverse in their geographic, socio-economic and behavioral characteristics. In particular, we focus on three different metro area types in the US, small (Lawrence, KS; Jackson, TN and Missoula MT), medium (Madison, WI; Syracuse, NY and Columbia SC) and large (New York, NY; Los Angeles, CA and Chicago, IL). We also include metro areas in Europe (Belgrade, Serbia; Brussels, Belgium and Manchester, United Kingdom), and in Asia/Pacific (Ulaanbaatar, Mongolia; Almaty, Kazakhstan and Palembang, Indonesia). The specific choices were made primarily based on market size with an attempt to select areas for each category that had roughly the same population. While the specific geographic boundaries of the US metro areas are defined by the US Census bureau, European and Asian markets do not define metro areas in the same way. Thus, for each server we only include tests that are conducted within a 100 km radius of a given server. Details of the individual metro areas and their associated Speedtest data sets can be found in Table 1. As shown in the table, the markets vary widely in terms of socio-economic characteristics and Speedtest use.

On average, we observe tests initiated by 7,551 handsets per day to the 15 servers for which we have data (3,863 by iOS users and 3,688 by Android users). From these handsets, an average of 14,961 individual tests are initiated per day from cellular access, and 15,521 per day using WiFi. Interestingly, for the Android app, there are 11,273 tests per day on average via cellular technology, and 4,380 via WiFi, while for the iOS app, there are only 2,464 tests via cellular technology per day on average, compared with 11,141 via WiFi. Also, in 9,230 cases, we observe the same handset in at least two different metro areas. Moreover, the distribution of the number of tests initiated per handset is skewed. On average, there are 6.0 tests per handset, with a (rather high) standard deviation of 17.4. Our data also include a great deal of diversity with respect to handset type and operating system version. Table 2 shows the unique number of devices and unique device/OS pairs (including different OS versions) per site, as well as the top three devices (and percentage share) for each site. Interestingly, while the number of tests per site is generally dominated by Android devices, the iPhone is the singularly most popular device, and other iOS-based devices are also very popular.

Data for each test include highly accurate GPS-derived geographic coordinates for the location of each test. The coordinates are only taken once during a test so we cannot tell from a single test whether or not a client was moving during a test. There are, however, instances in our data sets where multiple tests are run consecutively in relatively close geographic proximity and when plotted on a map, we can see that the positions follow roads perfectly. Thus, we can infer that a subset of our tests were run while users were traveling.

Figure 2 shows an example of the positions of all cellular clients that access the Los Angeles, CA, Manchester, UK and Lawrence, KS servers during the 15 week test period. Maps of WiFi client locations from these metro regions, and maps of client locations from other metro areas have similar profiles. In the large metro areas, cellular and WiFi tests are conducted with more uniformity over the highly populated metro area; in smaller metro areas, there are tight clusters of test locations in densely populated subregions with sparser use in less populated areas. In short, test locations correlate highly with population density. (In the Los Angeles, CA and Lawrence, KS plots shown in Figure 2, we show US zip code divisions, with more densely populated zip codes shaded darker than more sparsely populated zip codes.) This variable profile suggests

Table 2: Handset diversity: numbers of unique devices and device/OS pairs for each of the 15 servers, as well as the top three devices for each site (and percentage share of all devices for that site).

Location	Unique devices	Unique device+OS	Three most popular devices		
			1st (%)	2nd (%)	3rd (%)
New York, NY	473	1223	iPhone (26.0)	iPad (8.8)	HTC Supersonic (8.4)
Los Angeles, CA	558	1340	iPhone (24.9)	HTC Supersonic (10.7)	iPad (8.4)
Chicago, IL	320	925	iPhone (20.9)	HTC Mecha (13.3)	iPad (8.4)
Columbia, SC	125	265	iPhone (20.9)	HTC Mecha (14.7)	HTC Supersonic (9.8)
Syracuse, NY	124	253	iPhone (30.6)	iPad (12.0)	iPod touch (10.2)
Madison, WI	135	273	iPhone (29.9)	iPad (14.4)	iPod touch (12.3)
Jackson, TN	79	154	iPhone (46.1)	iPad (8.5)	Motorola Droid 2 (6.9)
Lawrence, KS	124	246	iPhone (26.4)	HTC Supersonic (20.4)	iPad (7.8)
Missoula, MT	51	99	iPhone (31.1)	iPad (17.7)	iPod touch (15.1)
Manchester, UK	412	899	iPhone (52.0)	iPad (11.7)	iPod touch (8.8)
Brussels, BE	178	354	iPhone (43.6)	iPad (11.4)	iPod touch (8.9)
Belgrade, SP	309	613	iPhone (18.2)	HTC Bravo (8.9)	HTC Buzz (8.2)
Palembang, ID	68	124	iPhone (29.4)	Samsung GT-P1000 (8.6)	iPad (8.2)
Almaty, KZ	124	239	iPhone (49.7)	iPad (11.2)	HTC Supersonic (4.6)
Ulaanbaatar, MN	94	158	iPhone (36.2)	iPad (15.6)	iPod touch (9.5)

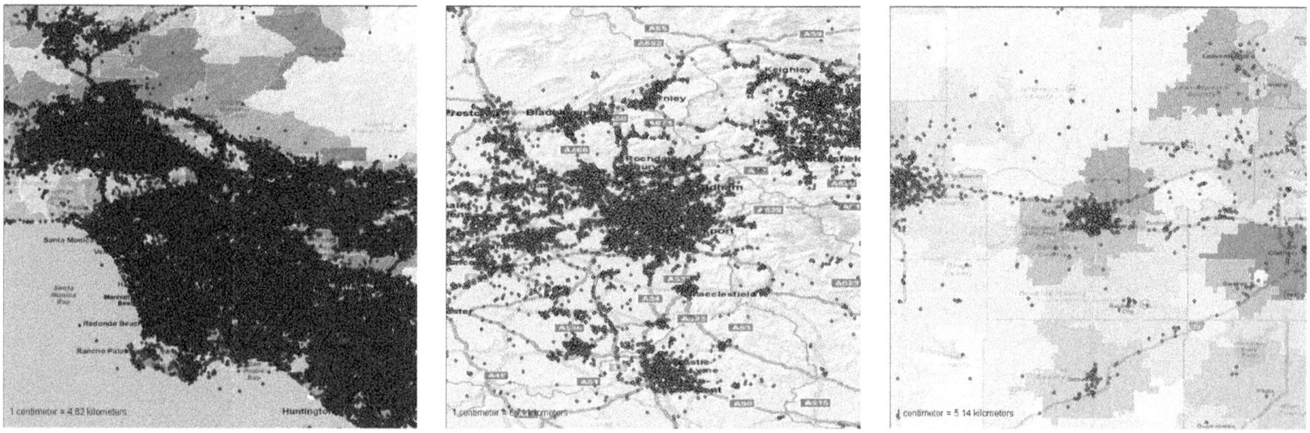

Figure 2: Locations of Speedtests by cellular users in the Los Angeles, CA (left), Manchester, UK (center) and Lawrence, KS (right) metro areas during the measurement period of February 21 to June 5, 2011. Area included in each plot is approximately 50km by 50km.

the need for a more detailed spatial analysis, which we describe in Section 3. In all cases, there is a high degree of overlap between cellular and WiFi test locations.

2.3 Discussion

We argue that the Speedtest data are compelling from the perspective of their richness, availability in a huge number of markets and broad adoption by users. However, there are several limitations that are important to acknowledge since they could influence the conclusions drawn from our study.

Speedtest data are crowd-sourced and rely on users invoking and running the throughput test application. While we have some ability to distinguish between handset types (for iOS devices, we do not know the hardware generation, but for Android devices, we have the specific model number), device configurations can vary, especially with jail-broken devices. Thus, there could be variations that could lead to biases in the test results. For example, we have no way of knowing whether a given test is run indoors or outdoors. Similarly, when and where the application is invoked depends entirely on how individuals derive value from the tests. We expect that the application will often be used when performance with the local default technology is perceived to be poor. Hence, the results of the performance tests might tend to be biased toward poor operating conditions for each technology. However, we have no way of establishing baselines for performance or assessing testing bias in each metro area that we consider other than appealing to statistical characterizations and the relatively large numbers of tests included in our data. Lastly, although we are able to identify individual users in our data via unique device identifiers, our comparisons between cellular and WiFi performance are at an aggregate level. In future work, we intend to carefully examine cellular versus WiFi performance on an individual user basis.

We are limited, to a certain extent, in our spatial analyses by the fact that we do not have up-to-date ground truth locations of all cell towers and WiFi access points that provided connectivity for handsets for all tests. In densely populated areas there are likely to be thousands of access points operated by many different providers. These would provide natural anchor points for spatial clustering of the performance data. The difficulty in assembling these data sets for diverse markets is substantial. While regulatory agencies such as the FCC keep databases of cell tower locations [16], they are often incomplete, and similar databases in non-US markets are sometimes difficult to obtain. However, we plan to consider cell tower locations as identified in sources such as [2] in future evaluations of our data. There are similar archives for WiFi access points *e.g.,* [8], but the completeness of these databases is unknown.

Economic considerations certainly come into play for all constituencies (users, service providers and application designers) mentioned or discussed in this paper. For users, connectivity may be subject to data transfer limits and traffic shaping. Although WiFi user plans are rarely data-quantity limited, they are partitioned among openly available for free, openly available for paying users, and private connectivity.

Service providers make decisions on infrastructure density based on many different issues including projected user growth, risks associated with losing customers due to under provisioning and geographic expansion of service. Finally, application designers must carefully consider how to manage data transfers so that user experience under expected conditions is acceptable. Otherwise, they risk losing customers. While these issues are fascinating and certainly play a role in the use of mobile devices, drawing explicit lines between the Speedtest measurements and economic issues is a subject of future study.

3. EVALUATION METHODOLOGY

Our evaluation takes a top-down approach to assessing the spatio-temporal performance characteristics of cellular and WiFi throughput and latency in the target metro areas. This section describes the methods that we use to evaluate Speedtest data toward the goal of being able to draw conclusions about the relative capabilities and robustness of each technology.

3.1 Basic Performance Characteristics

We begin by calculating the basic statistical characteristics of performance for each technology including maximum, average, minimum and standard deviation over the entire 15 week period in each of the 15 metro areas. This analysis does not distinguish between times of day or subregions within a given metro area. As such, it ignores the more complex and potentially interesting characteristics of performance. However, it does enables us to begin to understand the data from an aggregate perspective and establish simple rankings between area types (*i.e.,* large, medium, small, Europe, and Asia) and rankings of metro areas within each area type.

From this coarse view of the data, we drill down by analyzing per-handset performance measures. For the set of tests initiated by each handset in a metro region, we separate the series of tests by access technology (WiFi, cell, or some more detailed cell access type) and by service provider. To obtain the service provider, we use the IPv4 to autonomous system mapping data provided by `www.team-cymru.org`. From this grouping, we can compute summary statistics such as the median, mean, or 95th percentile for throughput and latency for a given handset (user) when using a given access provider and access technology in a given market. We then plot scatterplots of upload vs. download throughput to compare the throughput performance that different users obtain from different networks and access technologies. We also compute performance *consistency* measures using the same method of [33]. In particular, we plot CDFs of normalized per-handset throughput and latency performance. The normalization is performed by taking the average divided by the 95th percentile in the case of upload/download throughput, or taking the average divided by the 5th percentile in the case of latency.

3.2 Temporal Characteristics

The diurnal behavior of Internet traffic is one of its most well-known empirical characteristics. Prior studies of WiFi networks (*e.g.,* [22]) and cellular traffic (*e.g.,* [20]) have shown that diurnal usage patterns are also evident. The goal of our temporal analysis is to assess the extent to which client tests follow a diurnal pattern and how the expected diurnal use of cellular and WiFi has an impact on performance in our target metro areas. By drilling down on smaller time windows, we also expect to be able to observe and characterize anomalous events such as outages and periods of degraded service.

Our temporal analysis considers two characteristics: client use versus time, and performance versus time. In the case of the former, we plot the aggregate hourly invocations of the test application over the 15 week period. In the case of the latter, we plot the average hourly upload and download performance for cellular and WiFi over the 15 week period. We also compute the per-handset average normalized performance for each hour of the day, and the standard deviation of the normalized performance for each hour of the day, as in [33]. These measures allow us to determine whether certain hours in the day give consistently better or worse performance than others. Note that while we have a large number of total data points across all servers, the data are still quite temporally sparse. Thus, we do not examine time windows smaller than 1 hour. Nevertheless, these plots provide insights on how performance for each technology varies with time of day in each metro area.

3.3 Spatial Characteristics of Subregions

We believe that metro areas are a highly useful spatial aggregate for our study since they provide a sufficient corpus of daily data for temporal analysis and are commonly used in socio-economic analyses. Analyses at the metro area scale can enable the impact of large scale events such as storms or power outages to be evaluated. However, metro areas typically comprise hundreds of square miles, potentially thousands of cellular and WiFi access points and millions of users. As indicated above, this density can preclude identification of smaller scale unexpected or noteworthy events, which is a goal of our work. To that end, we also analyze performance in subregions for each metro area.

To analyze subregions, we generate a spatial interpolation of performance using a technique called inverse distance weighting (IDW) [32]. In IDW, the interpolated performance varies according to the distance away from measurement points. The method can produce a smooth contour of predicted performance based on measurement data, and we color each contour band depending on interpolated performance (*e.g.,* blue for good performance, yellow for intermediate performance, and red for poor performance).

With 15 weeks of data for each metro area, the question of the temporal selection of data for subregions is also important. Selections over longer time periods enable a first order perspective similar to what we conduct for entire metro areas, while selections over shorter time scales enable assessment of localized changes in performance, which is a goal of our work. Similar to our basic and temporal analyses, we consider subregion performance over the full 15 weeks as well as shorter intervals of days or hours.

Our spatial analysis is facilitated by the ArcGIS tool [19] —a widely used Geographic Information System that is easily adapted to processing the Speedtest data. With ArcGIS, we are able to perform IDW and kriging [29] analyses, among other types of spatial analyses. We are also able to overlay our plots on base maps that include roads and administrative or political boundaries, such as county, state and country borders, and postcode or zipcode divisions. ArcGIS exposes a Python-based API, which we heavily leveraged for our work. While this API does not expose all ArcGIS functionality, it enables repetitive tasks to be automated. In total, the scripts that were developed for Speedtest data analysis comprised several hundred lines of code, which we intend to make publicly available.

4. PERFORMANCE RESULTS

In this section we report the results of our spatio-temporal analyses of cellular and WiFi performance in the 15 target metro areas.

Table 3: Download throughput for cell and WiFi from the 15 target metro areas for full 15 week period. All values are in kb/s.

Location	Cell Mean (Stdev)	WiFi Mean (Stdev)	Cell 5th %	Cell Median	Cell 95th %	WiFi 5th %	WiFi Median	WiFi 95th %
New York, NY	3194.4 (4234.7)	7621.7 (5574.8)	108.0	1678.0	12922.0	404.0	7040.0	17617.0
Los Angeles, CA	2261.6 (2914.4)	6528.3 (5051.1)	62.0	1262.0	7607.0	352.0	5556.0	15376.0
Chicago, IL	3770.8 (4787.8)	8288.7 (6021.6)	125.0	2250.0	14014.0	396.0	7770.0	18598.0
Columbia, SC	4297.9 (6582.3)	4975.9 (4019.3)	113.0	1276.0	20681.0	254.0	4286.0	12222.0
Syracuse, NY	1634.4 (1916.7)	7866.5 (5288.0)	130.0	1143.0	4315.0	381.0	7914.0	16705.0
Madison, WI	1258.3 (1513.2)	6103.0 (4507.9)	99.0	895.0	3485.0	347.0	5742.0	14173.0
Jackson, TN	907.9 (728.4)	4251.9 (3767.2)	69.0	792.0	2138.0	223.0	3171.0	10926.0
Lawrence, KS	1878.8 (1919.5)	5771.0 (4969.5)	95.0	1182.0	5931.0	274.0	4623.5	15685.0
Missoula, MT	1014.4 (1013.0)	4672.8 (4203.0)	107.0	747.0	2607.0	283.0	3579.0	12952.0
Manchester, UK	1358.9 (1314.6)	5811.8 (4825.6)	28.0	1077.0	3842.0	267.0	4717.0	15635.0
Brussels, BE	1243.4 (1727.3)	8609.7 (5700.5)	61.0	902.0	4370.0	546.0	8171.0	18160.0
Belgrade, SP	1416.5 (1469.4)	3370.3 (2820.0)	35.0	884.0	4596.0	296.0	2952.0	8861.0
Palembang, ID	574.9 (819.8)	682.7 (866.6)	21.0	256.0	2312.0	43.0	457.0	1928.0
Almaty, KZ	1310.5 (1465.8)	3001.4 (3461.0)	26.0	783.0	4636.0	136.0	1855.0	9116.0
Ulaanbaatar, MN	1066.5 (999.4)	2263.3 (3346.0)	34.0	960.0	2595.0	90.0	975.0	10789.0

Table 4: Upload throughput for cell and WiFi from the 15 target metro areas for full 15 week period. All values are in kb/s.

Location	Cell Mean (Stdev)	WiFi Mean (Stdev)	Cell 5th %	Cell Median	Cell 95th %	WiFi 5th %	WiFi Median	WiFi 95th %
New York, NY	1804.6 (4577.9)	2873.2 (3314.6)	52.0	772.0	5428.0	177.0	2020.0	10094.0
Los Angeles, CA	1572.3 (4174.6)	2112.0 (3186.8)	62.0	715.0	4290.0	184.0	1022.0	9154.0
Chicago, IL	1587.0 (3412.5)	3025.4 (2325.9)	46.0	802.0	5289.0	265.0	3530.0	6539.0
Columbia, SC	1493.6 (2460.4)	1123.2 (2129.3)	47.0	708.0	5676.0	124.0	446.0	4422.0
Syracuse, NY	768.5 (1388.9)	2426.4 (3269.0)	74.0	683.0	1293.0	208.0	985.0	10919.0
Madison, WI	671.9 (1296.4)	1856.0 (2502.9)	55.0	478.0	1389.0	168.0	1064.0	5251.0
Jackson, TN	524.2 (745.7)	1771.1 (2579.0)	41.0	429.0	1258.0	101.0	930.0	6976.0
Lawrence, KS	634.6 (756.0)	2153.7 (2905.8)	45.0	554.0	1434.0	137.0	908.0	7773.0
Missoula, MT	719.2 (1834.6)	1188.4 (1907.9)	53.0	479.0	1890.0	124.0	731.0	4048.0
Manchester, UK	708.1 (755.3)	1384.6 (1950.7)	25.0	396.0	1659.0	180.0	745.0	5589.0
Brussels, BE	530.1 (657.7)	1699.3 (1622.1)	37.0	326.0	1773.0	233.0	1397.0	4185.0
Belgrade, SP	437.7 (709.8)	653.3 (1334.6)	32.0	351.0	1553.0	97.0	389.0	1618.0
Palembang, ID	156.8 (251.7)	514.2 (1269.1)	18.0	76.0	662.0	46.0	239.0	1596.0
Almaty, KZ	731.6 (830.0)	1455.5 (2736.0)	26.0	374.0	2497.0	58.0	829.0	6154.0
Ulaanbaatar, MN	277.6 (335.7)	2202.5 (3465.7)	29.0	154.0	926.0	55.0	846.5	10371.0

While we endeavor to be comprehensive in our reporting, the size of our data set and scope of our analyses precludes inclusion of all analyses due to space constraints. Thus, in a number of cases, we show figures and report findings that are exemplars of a broader set of results.

4.1 Basic Characteristics of Performance

4.1.1 *Aggregate Performance*

Our analysis begins by examining the general characteristics of cellular and WiFi performance in each of the target metro areas. These characteristics can be found in Tables 3, 4, and 5. The side-by-side comparison shows that WiFi provides better maximum and average performance for nearly all regions for upload and download performance and latency. One regional exception is Columbia, SC, which has a number of very high throughput cellular tests that cause the average and 95th percentile to be higher than WiFi. These tests are all from devices using the 4G LTE cell access technology, which has substantially higher throughput than some older access technologies. The tables also show that the difference in upload performance between WiFi and cell is much smaller than the difference in download performance.

In Figure 3 we show scatterplots of upload versus download performance for cell (left) and Wifi (right) for the Madison, WI metro area. Each data point is computed as the 95th percentile value for a given handset. These plots are representative of other metro areas. First, as with Tables 3 and 4, WiFi performance is generally higher than cell. We note that the highest cellular throughputs are for the LTE access technology. We also observe that for WiFi access, there are more obvious "tiered" performance bands evident, especially for AS7132 (AT&T) and AS20115 (Charter), than for the cellular access networks. Note that Figure 3 is annotated to point out some of these evident performance tiers in the upload direction. For WiFi networks, these bands likely represent different service plans available to customers. With cellular networks, there are not typically service plan limits on throughputs, but rather on total numbers of bytes transferred. Thus, the bands present in the cellular plot (around 600 kb/s upload, and just over 1 Mb/s upload, for UMTS and HSDPA) are more likely due to different modulation rates in the cellular access. We observe in the plot that the performance bands are most evident in the upload direction; especially for WiFi, there are no obvious download throughput tiers. We hypothesize that this difference is due to the typically asymmetric configuration of last-mile access technologies (*e.g.*, Cable and DSL), which makes it easier for the Speedtest application to saturate the available upload capacity. Lastly, we hypothesize that as higher speed cellular access technologies become more prevalent (e.g., LTE), providers may need to impose service plan rate limits similar to wired broadband access networks in order to better manage access network congestion.

In order to evaluate whether there are any significant performance differences between Android-based and iOS-based devices, we plot in the left plot of Figure 4 the median download for iOS devices versus the median download for Android devices computed for each local access carrier in each of the five metro area types. The right-hand plot shows median latency for iOS devices versus median latency for Android devices, again computed for each local access carrier. The plots are created from WiFi measurements only;

Table 5: **Latency for cell and WiFi from the 15 target metro areas for full 15 week period. All values are in milliseconds.**

Location	Cell Mean (Stdev)	WiFi Mean (Stdev)	Cell 5th %	Cell Median	Cell 95th %	WiFi 5th %	WiFi Median	WiFi 95th %
New York, NY	282.0 (575.9)	111.9 (261.8)	68.0	159.0	786.0	21.0	54.0	336.0
Los Angeles, CA	268.0 (354.2)	120.5 (314.4)	67.0	165.0	776.0	24.0	64.0	350.0
Chicago, IL	178.5 (318.9)	96.1 (227.1)	63.0	122.0	429.0	22.0	53.0	255.0
Columbia, SC	252.2 (316.8)	187.7 (313.6)	102.0	183.0	736.0	55.0	120.0	456.0
Syracuse, NY	238.9 (199.0)	131.2 (225.3)	115.0	171.0	558.0	29.0	73.0	358.0
Madison, WI	262.3 (267.8)	119.9 (258.1)	99.0	184.0	773.0	24.0	69.0	343.0
Jackson, TN	339.1 (363.9)	168.2 (309.4)	116.0	226.0	858.0	23.0	107.0	412.0
Lawrence, KS	323.5 (351.6)	177.3 (286.0)	95.0	250.0	778.0	30.0	113.0	470.0
Missoula, MT	360.3 (247.2)	190.3 (241.1)	165.0	314.0	687.0	47.0	115.0	412.0
Manchester, UK	335.2 (491.4)	129.7 (265.6)	98.0	221.0	912.0	34.0	92.0	313.0
Brussels, BE	281.6 (321.7)	103.8 (242.1)	84.0	203.0	755.0	28.0	67.0	238.0
Belgrade, SP	329.4 (475.7)	113.5 (379.0)	79.0	226.0	842.0	22.0	52.0	318.0
Palembang, ID	583.8 (1334.4)	371.7 (1144.5)	148.0	348.0	1095.0	62.0	179.0	917.0
Almaty, KZ	356.7 (663.3)	141.3 (405.0)	90.0	194.0	1114.0	27.0	77.0	364.0
Ulaanbaatar, MN	649.4 (1935.9)	239.3 (824.6)	76.0	216.0	1990.0	17.0	67.0	862.0

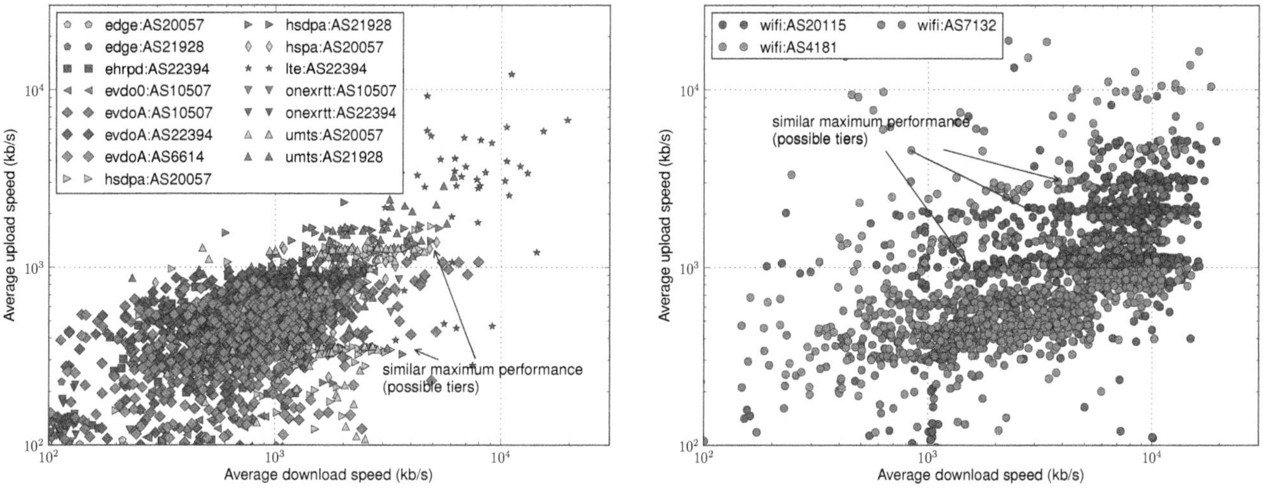

Figure 3: Scatterplots of upload versus download performance for cellular (left) and WiFi (right) for the Madison, Wisconsin metro area. Data points represent 95th percentile for a given handset. Points are colored based on service provider. and marker shapes are different for each access technology.

we do not show results for cellular tests due to the lack of detailed access technology information for iOS devices (we only know it is cellular, not what specific flavor). Interestingly, while throughput does not appear to be affected by OS version (the upload plot results are similar to the download plot shown), iOS appears to induce consistently higher latency measurements than Android. Since the same organization (Ookla) designed the app for each OS, we conclude that iOS either introduces significantly more buffering of network data, or its APIs are not optimized to deliver low packet-level latency.

Turning to a broader view of latency performance, we see in Table 5 a vast difference between cell and WiFi performance. Cell latencies are generally longer than WiFi, with mean cell latencies approaching or exceeding a third of a second in many cases, and very large 95th percentile latencies in all metro areas. Even the median cell latency is at least twice as large as WiFi latency for nearly all regions we consider (Columbia, SC is the only exception). Recall that for each server, we only consider tests carried out within a 100 km radius.

To examine the latency issue further, we plot in Figure 5 empirical cumulative distribution functions for WiFi connections and for specific cellular access technologies, for providers from which we see the most tests. The figure shows results for a large metro area (Chicago, IL) and a much smaller metro area (Lawrence, KS). First, we see that latencies for the larger Chicago market are generally smaller than for the Lawrence market. Indeed, for other metro areas, the trend is clearly toward shorter latencies for large cities and longer latencies for smaller cities. These results thus suggest that service providers expend more effort to engineer their networks for good performance in larger markets than smaller ones. We also see that specific latency distributions are highly provider dependent: for the Chicago plot, we see that the two curves showing WiFi latency distributions are highly dissimilar: one provider delivers quite low latencies, while another gives some of the worst latencies observed overall. We also observe that the latency profiles for all access types offered by a given provider often have similar characteristics. This is especially true for the Lawrence, KS plot, but also clearly evident in other metro areas (not shown). In other analyses (also not shown), we did not find any meaningful correlation between latency and distance to the server. This lack of correlation is likely due to packets traversing cellular backhaul networks that are possibly geographically far away from the local Speedtest server, an issue that has been identified in prior work [18,31].

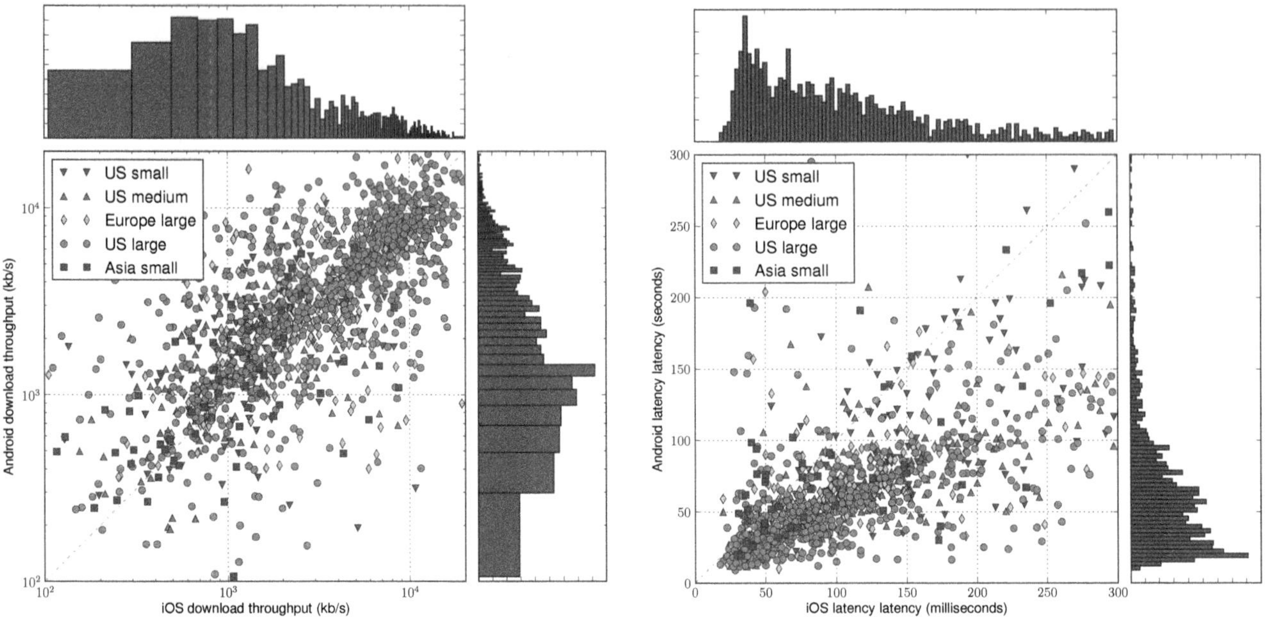

Figure 4: Scatterplots of iOS versus Android download and latency performance for WiFi. The left plot shows median download performance for iOS devices versus median download performance for Android devices, computed for each local access carrier in each of the five metro area types. The right plot shows similar results but for latency (i.e., median latency of iOS devices versus median latency of Android devices).

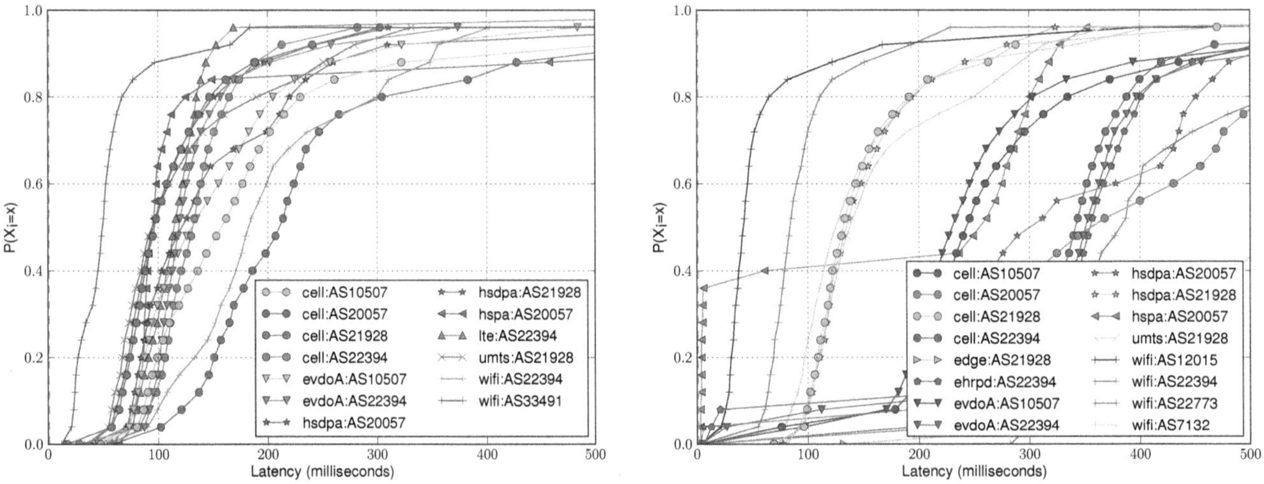

Figure 5: CDFs of latency for different access types; Chicago, IL (left) and Lawrence, KS (right).

4.1.2 Performance Consistency

We now examine *consistency* of performance results. We use the method of Sundaresan *et al.* [33]: for each handset (user), we construct cumulative distribution functions of normalized performance, where the normalization is computed as the mean divided by the 95th percentile. (For latency, instead of using the 95th percentile, we use the 5th percentile in the normalization computation.) The motivation behind each of these normalizations is to identify how far average measures deviate from *good* performance, where *good* is defined as the 95th percentile throughput and 5th percentile latency. We produce separate CDFs for each local access provider and for each access type. If throughputs are consistent, points along each CDF curve should be close to 1; any points less than 1 represent degraded performance. Likewise, if latency is consistent, we also expect to see points along each CDF curve to be close to 1. However, any deviations from *good* latency will result in normalized values higher than 1 (*i.e.*, inflated latencies). For each of the plots below, we only consider users for which we had at least 5 tests from which to compute a consistency measure; all other users' data are discarded. The authors of [33] found that download and upload performance for *wired* broadband access networks exhibited high consistency, except for a small number of service providers.

In Figure 6 we plot download (left), upload (center), and latency (right) performance consistency for Los Angeles (top) and Belgrade (bottom). Plots shown are representative of other metro areas. We observe in these plots a low degree of performance con-

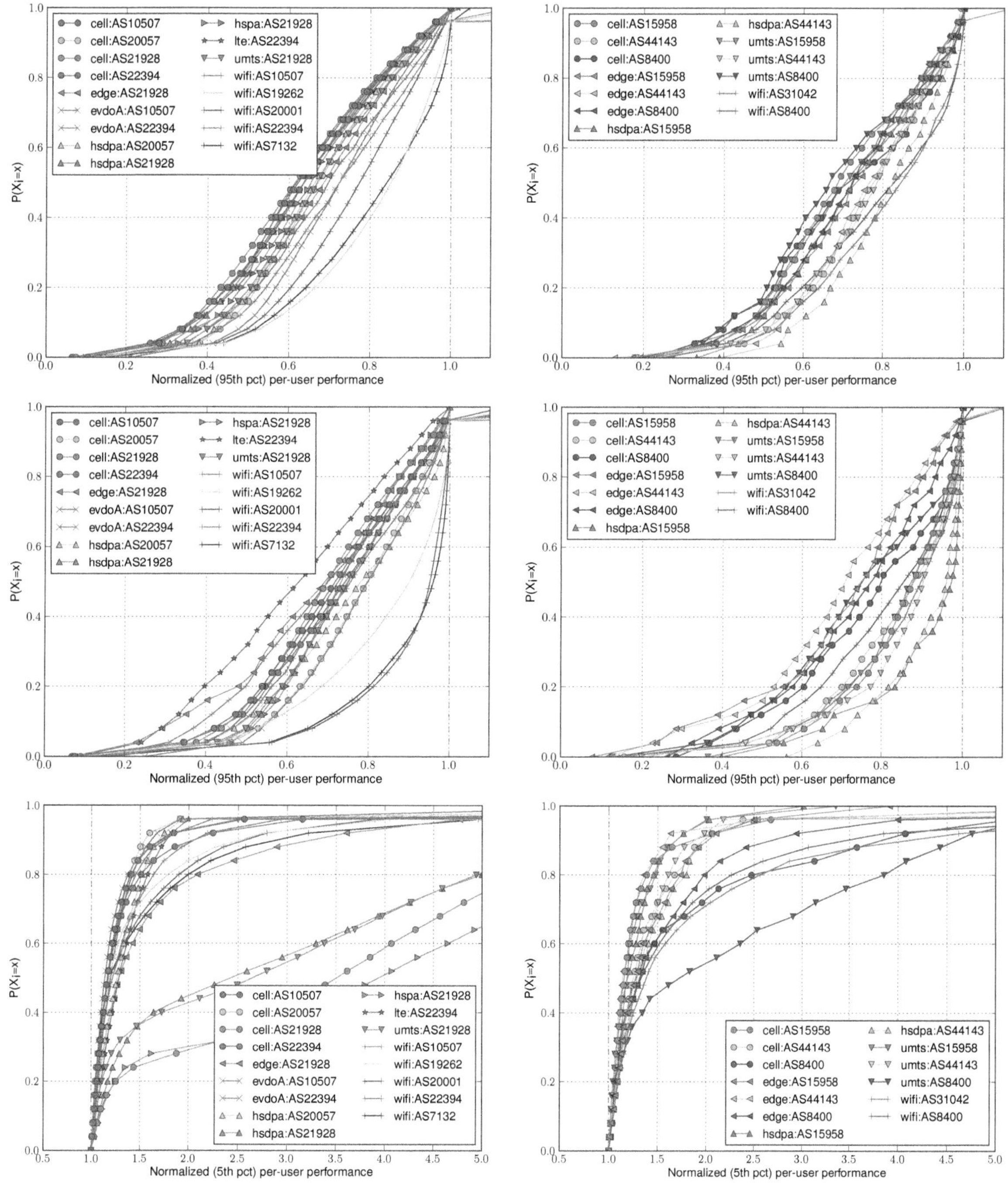

Figure 6: Performance consistency for Los Angeles (left) and Belgrade (right) for download (top), upload (middle), and latency (bottom). Plots shown are representative of other metro areas.

sistency, especially compared with the results of [33]. In their work, nearly all curves were very close to 1, representing highly consistent performance (the one exception was the Cable provider Charter). Our results are exclusively generated from wireless tests, and reveal that mobile users generally have to cope with much more variable performance than users on wired networks. In Figure 6, we also observe that WiFi upload/download performance is generally more consistent than cell upload/download, though it depends on the local access provider. Furthermore, in many cases, we see similar performance consistency characteristics for the various access technologies that a given service provider supports in a metro area (*c.f.* Figure 5). We hypothesize from these similarities that some providers use the same network "backhaul" infrastructure for both cellular and WiFi access in an effort to optimize their network infrastructures to minimize costs. Therefore, our hypothesis assumes that a shared bottleneck in the provider network is the cause of the observed similarity in performance consistency between cellular and WiFi. We intend to examine this hypothesis in detail in future work.

Interestingly, we observe that while LTE offers high absolute throughput performance, its upload performance consistency is poor. For example, in the Los Angeles upload consistency plot (top middle) in Figure 6, we see that LTE's performance consistency is lower than many other access types. Other metro areas show similar characteristics. We hypothesize that the cause for this behavior is simply that service providers have not yet optimized LTE installations, and have rather focused on getting services initially rolled out.

With respect to latency performance consistency, we see that while WiFi offers generally higher absolute throughputs and more consistent throughput, cellular latency is generally more consistent. In the case of Los Angeles (top right plot), except for one service provider that delivers poor performance consistency for most access types it offers (AS21928), WiFi latencies exhibit a lower degree of consistency than cellular access types. Similarly, for the Belgrade plot (lower right), 2 of the 4 least consistent access technologies are WiFi. We hypothesize that this lower degree of performance consistency is due to the effect of overbuffering at access routers. Many access routers are well known to exhibit latency pathologies due to overprovisioning of buffers [21, 33], and it is likely that user WiFi access is often through a home-grade router connected to a wired broadband connection. Another possibility for the lower degree of performance consistency in WiFi is higher contention for WiFi frequency bands, and differences between WiFi and cellular medium access control. However, since we observe the same pattern of lower consistency in WiFi across all metro areas—even the most sparsely populated ones where we would not expect the effect of contention to be significant—we believe that overbuffering is the more likely cause.

Lastly, we note that in different metro areas, there are clear instances of some service providers exhibiting generally poor performance consistency for all offered services. For example, AS21928 in Los Angeles, and to a lesser extent, AS8400 in Belgrade. This observation further supports the notion that performance for various access technologies offered by a given service provider exhibit similar qualities due to using the same backhaul infrastructure.

Main findings.

Absolute WiFi performance is better than cellular access, in general. Throughput performance does not appear to be correlated with operating system (iOS or Android), however latency measurements are generally higher with iOS devices, suggesting too much buffering or APIs that are suboptimally designed. Performance consistency of WiFi throughput is generally better than cellular, but cellular latency performance tends to be more consistent than WiFi. Lower consistency of WiFi latency is likely due to the impact of overbuffering at broadband access routers. Local providers exhibit similar performance consistency characteristics for all offered access types, suggesting that providers use the same backhaul infrastructure to support various last-mile access methods. Performance consistency for wireless access is markedly lower than has been reported for wired broadband access, with a great deal of variation depending on local service provider. The higher variability present with wireless access performance is likely due to variability in signal quality, deployment density of base stations and cell towers, and suboptimally designed service provider backhaul infrastructure, including distant placement of cellular gateway nodes [31].

4.2 Temporal Characteristics of Performance

Our temporal analysis begins by analyzing the frequency of use of the Speedtest application in the target regions. Figure 7 shows the number of hourly invocations of the application for cellular and WiFi over a two week period for six representative metro areas. The figures clearly show the characteristic diurnal pattern for each region and technology. We see that there are many hundreds of invocations of the Speedtest app per day in larger metro areas, but that the measurements are fairly sparse in smaller metro areas, with typically fewer than 10 invocations of the Speedtest applications per hour in Lawrence, KS. Lastly, we observe that in some markets there are similar numbers of invocations of the app over WiFi and cellular access (*e.g.*, New York, NY and Los Angeles, CA), but major differences in other markets (*e.g.*, Manchester, UK).

Next, we analyze the temporal characteristics of upload and download performance for cellular and WiFi. Figure 8 shows the hourly average upload and download performance for each technology over a 6 day period for one metro area from each of the five area types (notice the different y-axis scales for cellular (top) and WiFi (bottom)). We observe that for cellular access, the performance for all but the largest metro area is fairly similar over time; performance for the New York, NY region clearly stands above the others. This trend is similar for other metro areas in the five area types. The latency profiles in Table 5 and Figure 5 suggest that the better engineered cellular infrastructure for some providers in large metro areas has a clear impact on throughput performance. We observe that for WiFi connections, while the smallest metro areas have generally lower throughputs, the differences are not as great among the metro areas for WiFi as they are for cellular connections.

In other results (not shown due to space constraints), we observe that performance in the largest metro areas is better during non-peak hours (*i.e.*, early morning hours) than for other times of day. For other metro areas, there is no statistically significant difference in measured performance between peak and non-peak hours. We note that in Sundaresan *et al.* [33], the authors observed a distinct performance difference in peak versus off-peak hours, due to network load. We do not observe such a strong characteristic because of the significantly lower degree of performance consistency we see in our data.

Main findings.

We find higher throughput performance over time for larger metro areas, further supporting the notion that service providers expend more effort to engineer networks in more populous locations. We find some evidence for higher performance during off-peak hours and lower performance during peak hours, though to a lesser degree than has been reported for wired broadband access. The cause for this difference is likely due to the higher overall variability present

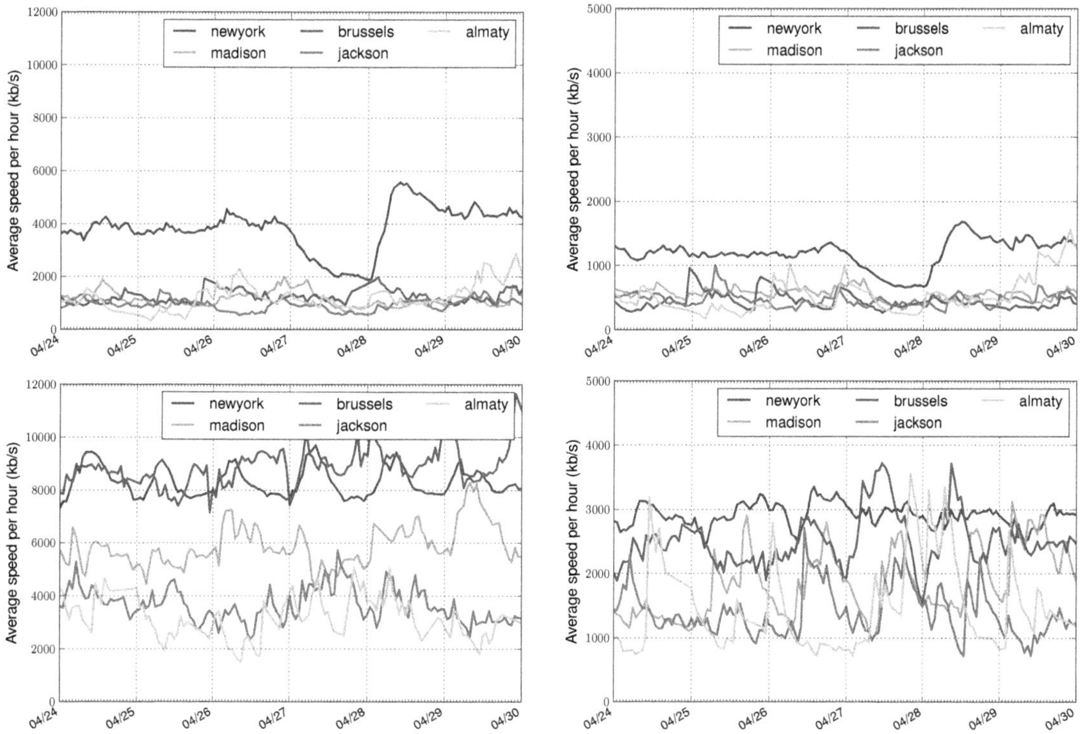

Figure 8: Average hourly performance for cellular downloads (top left), cellular uploads (top right), WiFi downloads (bottom left) and WiFi uploads (bottom right) for exemplars in each of the metro areas during April 24 to April 30, 2011.

in wireless access performance resulting from frequency band contention and overbuffering at edge routers.

4.3 Spatial Analysis of Subregion of Performance

Our spatial analysis of subregions within metro areas begins by considering spatial performance variations using the entire 15 week data set. To generate our plots below, we apply an inverse distance weighting interpolation [32] to the performance measurements over a region. Pixels are colored according to interpolated performance. In the plots below, we apply the following color symbology to upload/download performance: $<=$ 128 kb/s: red; between 128 kb/s and 256 kb/s: orange; between 256 kb/s and 512 kb/s: yellow; between 512 kb/s and 768 kb/s: green; between 768 kb/s and 1 Mb/s: cyan; between 1 Mb/s and 2 Mb/s: blue; $>$ 2 Mb/s: indigo. We apply this same symbology for both upload and download performance in order to make the plots visually comparable.

Figure 9 shows plots of interpolated upload performance for WiFi (top) and cell (bottom) for three different metro regions (Chicago, IL, Manchester, UK, and Lawrence, KS, left to right, respectively) over the 15 week data set. The plots show that upload performance is spatially variable. Since the plot is produced from the entire 15 week data collection period, regions in which the color is yellow or red suggest that there are subareas with consistently poor performance.

We also observe that although WiFi upload performance is broadly, on average, at least twice as fast as cellular performance (*c.f.* Table 4), the spatial performance characteristics reveal a much more complex picture. For the Chicago, IL metro area, we observe that WiFi upload performance is better across the entire region. However, when examining the Manchester, UK plots, we observe a clear separation in WiFi upload performance between areas closer to the city center and surrounding, more rural, areas. Although that pattern is somewhat less clear with cellular upload performance in Manchester, the areas of highest performance still generally lie closer to the Manchester city center, with larger and more prevalent areas of poor performance in surrounding, less urban, areas. A similar observation holds for the Lawrence, KS metro area and other areas (not shown). (Note that since the Chicago, IL metro area is extremely large, this pattern is not observable in the plots shown. Expanding the plotted region reveals poorer performance further away from the city center.)

We note that plots of download performance reveal similar variability in performance: there are subareas with consistently poor performance, and subareas that exhibit good performance. In future work, we intend to further examine spatial performance characteristics, and utilize available cell tower and WiFi maps, along with economic and population data, to drill down on the likely causes for the observed performance characteristics.

Main findings.

We see a high degree of spatial performance variability, with some metro areas exhibiting performance degradation as one moves further away from the metro area center. Observed performance differences are likely due to cellular tower and WiFi base station placement, and density of placements, as well as local contention due to load.

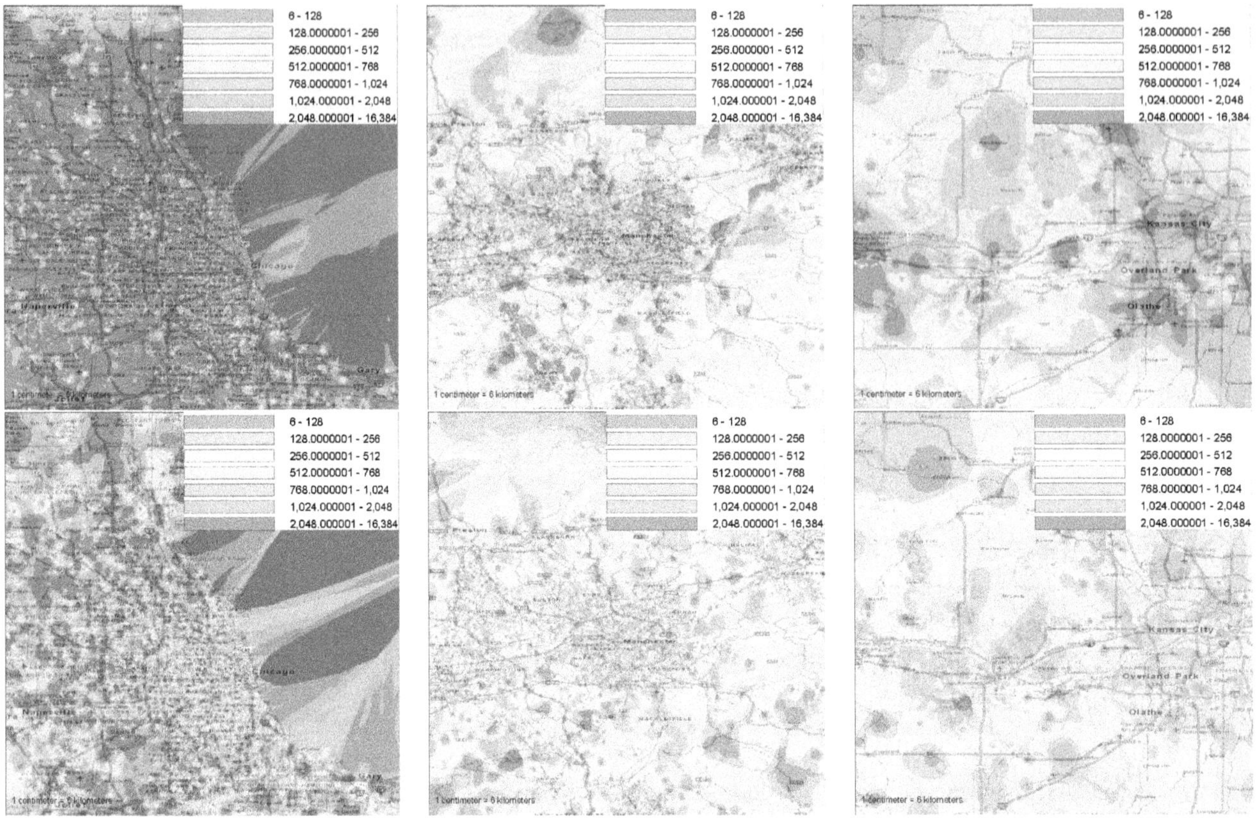

Figure 9: Inverse distance weighting interpolation plots for WiFi upload performance (top) and cellular (bottom) for Chicago, IL (left), Manchester, UK (center) and Lawrence, KS (right), for the entire 15 week data set.

5. RELATED WORK

There is a large and growing body of work that examines the behavior and characteristics of WiFi networks. Studies that are most closely related to ours have been focused on analyzing mobile use characteristics in live deployments. Birk *et al.* analyze the behavior and characteristics of a city-wide commercial WiFi mesh network in [13]. Their study is based on a diverse set of measurements of a 250 node mesh operated by a single provider. Their assessment of client performance was based on a set of targeted active measurements, and showed temporal variations with peak performance achieved during the day (since customers are primarily residential) in contrast to wireline networks. In a related study, Sen *et al.* propose a framework for client-assisted active measurement of wide-area wireless networks [30]. Similar empirical studies of WiFi behavior in localized settings include [9, 15, 22, 27]. More recently, LaCurts and Balakrishnan report results of an empirical study of 110 different WiFi mesh networks in diverse markets around the world [25]. While their study reveals a range of characteristics of these networks, it does not address client performance, which is our focus. While all of the aforementioned studies expand the body of knowledge on WiFi behavior, our work differs in objective, scope, measurement details and the fact that we include analysis of cellular performance.

There is also a growing literature on empirical studies of cellular networks. Tan *et al.* describe one of the first empirical studies of 3G cellular networks in [34]. Their work is focused in a single large metro area and includes an examination of client throughput and other performance characteristics using measurements of data transfers between a small set of smartphones and their servers. Their results show a wide range of variable behaviors (diurnal patterns, expanded RTT's during peak hours, etc.) that are consistent with a number of our observations. Other empirical studies of behavior in cellular networks include [24, 26, 31]. More recently, there have been several studies focused on smartphone performance. Falaki *et al.* use measurements from instrumented handsets to study diversity in smartphone traffic characteristics [20], while Huang *et al.* use a purpose-built application deployed on a large number of handsets to study smartphone application performance [23]. Shafiq *et al.* [31] and Elmokashfi *et al.* [18] recently examined cellular network performance characteristics. One particularly interesting finding from these studies is the impact that the topology of the cellular backhaul network plays in performance. Our work differs from these in its scope and focus on comparative analysis of cellular and WiFi.

There are several prior studies that investigate cellular and WiFi performance simultaneously. The notion of the combined use of cellular and WiFi in a vehicular setting is addressed in [10]. That study considers cellular and WiFi availability in three cities as the basis for their work. In [17], Deshpande *et al.* evaluate cellular and WiFi performance in the New York metro area, also in a vehicular setting. Measurements are taken with a laptop that is driven throughout the target area, which enables highly targeted spatio-temporal tests. Their results highlight the widely available, lower performance characteristics of cellular versus the lower availability, higher performance characteristics of WiFi. While there are similarities between these studies and our own, our results complement and expand the prior work by reporting client performance in diverse markets using a larger body of crowd-sourced data.

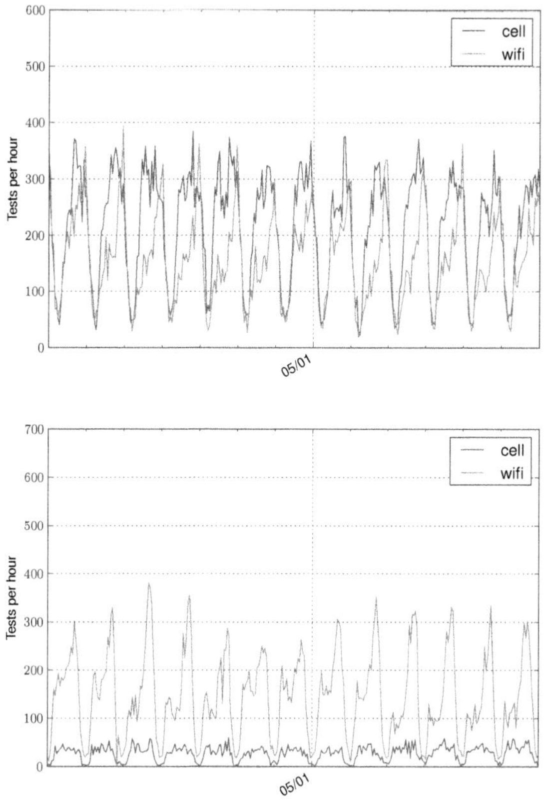

Figure 7: Cellular and WiFi tests conducted per hour in New York, NY (top) and Manchester, UK (bottom) metro areas for the two week period from 24 April, 2011 to 8 May, 2011.

6. SUMMARY AND CONCLUSIONS

Cellular and 802.11 WiFi are the *de facto* connectivity options for today's mobile users. The increasing availability of handsets and tablets that offer *both* connectivity options coupled with the the explosion of applications that demand high performance means that users are sensitive to throughput performance for each technology. In this paper, we present a measurement study of cellular and WiFi performance using crowd-sourced data from the widely used throughput testing application, Speedtest.net.

Our results reveal a wide range of characteristics of cellular and WiFi performance. The raw comparison between the two technologies shows that WiFi provides superior download performance, with maximum WiFi performance varying widely. The difference in upload performance is much smaller, yet is also highly variable. We also find that WiFi latency measurements are at least a factor of two lower than cell latency in all areas, but the *consistency* in latency is often better with cellular access. Overall, we find performance consistency for wireless access networks to be much lower than has been previously reported for wired networks. Temporal analysis reveals that performance is sensitive to time of day in the largest metro areas, with performance decreasing for both cellular and WiFi during the hours of peak use. Comparisons between metro areas shows that larger markets provide a consistently higher level of performance for both technologies, suggesting greater engineering effort and resources deployed in more populous regions. However, analysis within more localized regions shows high variability in performance for both technologies in all markets.

While the emphasis of our study is on a broad comparison of cellular and WiFi in metro areas, our current results suggest several conclusions about mobile performance. First, while WiFI offers superior download performance, the relatively predictable level of cellular performance for some network providers, coupled with its ubiquity make it a compelling option for all but the most bandwidth hungry apps. With the rollout of improve throughput access technologies like LTE, it may become the *preferred* option for wireless connectivity. Second, the stability and performance of both technologies in larger markets suggests that performance would be enhanced by further build out of both WiFi and cellular infrastructure in smaller markets.

In future work we plan to continue our investigation of Speedtest data. Specifically, we plan to expand the scope of study by considering additional markets. We also intend to drill down on the data in greater detail in order to better understand variations in performance, *e.g.*, by considering related datasets such as weather conditions during test periods and cell tower/WiFi access point locations. We also plan to investigate hypotheses posed in this paper concerning provider backhaul infrastructure and its impact on access performance, overbuffering in access routers, and wireless access contention. We are considering how to augment the Speedtest measurement protocol in order to better understand these and other performance observations. Finally, we plan to conduct targeted, hypothesis-driven experiments in different markets using the Speedtest application, again toward the goal of understanding the root causes of observed performance results.

Acknowledgements

This work was supported in part by NSF grants CNS-0716460, CNS-0831427 and CNS-0905186, and CNS-1054985. Any opinions, findings, conclusions or other recommendations expressed in this material are those of the authors and do not necessarily reflect the view of the NSF.

We thank Ookla, Inc. and Andrew Bassett for generous access to the `Speedtest.net` performance data.

We also thank Anton Kapella for his fruitful suggestions and input on this work.

7. REFERENCES

[1] Ulaanbaatar Statistics Bulletin. http://statis.ub.gov.mn, 2008.

[2] AntennaSearch.com. http://www.antennasearch.com, 2011.

[3] GeoNames Database. http://www.geonames.org, 2011.

[4] Kazakhstan Today. http://www.kt.kz, 2011.

[5] Ookla Documentation Wiki. http://wiki.ookla.com, 2011.

[6] Ookla, Inc. http://www.ookla.com, 2011.

[7] Speedtest.net. http://www.speedtest.net, 2011.

[8] Wireless Geographic Logging Engine. http://weigle.net, 2011.

[9] A. Balachandran, G. Voelker, P. Bahl, and P. Rangan. Characterizing User Behavior and Network Performance in a Public Wireless LAN. In *Proceedings of ACM SIGMETRICS*, Marina del Rey, CA, June 2002.

[10] A. Balasubramanian, R. Majahan, and A. Venkataramani. Augmenting Mobile 3G Using WiFi. In *Proceedings of ACM MobiSys '10*, San Francisco, CA, June 2010.

[11] World Bank. World Indicators Development Database. http://siteresources.worldbank.org/DATASTATISTICS/, 2011.

[12] S. Bauer, D. Clark, and W. Lehr. Understanding broadband speed measurements. In *38th Research Conference on Communication, Information and Internet Policy*, September 2010.

[13] V. Birk, S. Rayanchu, S. Saha, S. sen, V. Shrivastava, and S. Banerjee. A Measurement Study of a Commercial-grade Urban WiFi Mesh. In *Proceedings of ACM Internet Measurement Conference*, Vouliagmeni, Greece, October 2008.

[14] United States Census Bureau. Population and Housing Occupancy Status 2010. http://www.census.gov/popest/estimates.html, 2011.

[15] Y. Cheng, J. Bellardo, P. Benko, A. Snoeren, G. Voelker, and S. Savage. Solving the Puzzle of Enterprise 802.11 Analysis. In *Proceedings of ACM SIGCOMM '06*, Pisa, Italy, August 2006.

[16] US Federal Communications Commission. Geographic Information Systems. http://wireless.fcc.gov, 2011.

[17] P. Deshpande, X. Hou, and S. Das. Performance Comparison of 3G and Metro-Scale WiFi for Vehicular Network Access. In *Proceedings of ACM Internet Measurement Conference*, Melbourne, Australia, November 2010.

[18] A. Elmokashfi, A. Kvalbein, J. Xiang, and K. Evensen. Characterizing delays in Norwegian 3G networks. In *Passive and Active Measurement Conference*, March 2012.

[19] ESRI. ArcGIS Geographic Information Systems. http://www.esri.com, 2011.

[20] H. Falaki, R. Mahajan, S. Kandula, D. Lymberopoulos, R. Govindan, and D. Estrin. Diversity in Smartphone Usage. In *Proceedings of ACM MOBISYS '10*, San Francisco, CA, June 2010.

[21] J. Gettys and K. Nichols. Bufferbloat: Dark buffers in the internet. *Queue*, 9(11), November 2011.

[22] T. Henderson, D. Kotz, and I. Abyzov. The Changing Usage of a Mature Campus-wide Wireless Network. In *Proceedings of ACM MOBICOM '04*, Philadelphia, PA, October 2004.

[23] J. Huang, Q. Xu, B. Tiwana, Z. Mao, M. Zhang, and P. Bahl. Anatomizing Application Performance on Smartphones. In *Proceedings of ACM MobiSys '10*, San Francisco, CA, June 2010.

[24] K. Jang, M. Han, S. Cho, H. Ryu, J. Lee, and S. Moom. 3G and 3.5G Wireless Network Performance Measured from Moving Cars and High-speed Trains. In *Proceedings of ACM MICNET '09*, Beijing, China, September 2009.

[25] K. LaCurts and H. Balakrishnan. Measurement and Analysis of Real-World 802.11 Mesh Networks. In *Proceedings of ACM Internet Measurement Conference*, Melbourne, Australia, November 2010.

[26] X. Liu, A. Sridharan, S. Machiraju, M. Seshadri, and H. Zang. Anatomizing Application Performance on Smartphones. In *Proceedings of ACM MobiSys '10*, San Francisco, CA, June 2010.

[27] M. McNett and G. Voelker. Access and Mobility of Wireless PDA Users. *ACM Mobile Computing and Communications Review*, 9(2), April 2005.

[28] European Spatial Planning Observation Network. Study on Urban Functions. http://www.espon.eu/, 2007.

[29] M.A. Oliver and R. Webster. Kriging: A method of interpolation for geographical information systems. *Int. Journal of Geographic Information Systems*, 4(3), 1990.

[30] S. Sen, J. Yoon, J. Hare, J. Ormont, and S. Banerjee. Can they hear me how?: A case for a client-assisted approach to monitoring wide-area wireless networks. In *Proceedings of ACM Internet Measurement Conference*, Berlin, Germany, November 2011.

[31] M. Z. Shafiq, L. Ji, A. X. Liu, and J. Wang. Characterizing and modeling internet traffic dynamics of cellular devices. In *Proceedings of ACM SIGMETRICS '11*, San Jose, CA, June 2011.

[32] D. Shepard. A two-dimensional interpolation function for irregularly-spaced data. In *Proceedings of the 1968 23rd ACM national conference*, ACM '68, pages 517–524, 1968.

[33] S. Sundaresan, W. de Donato, N. Feamster, R. Teixeira, S. Crawford, and A. Pescapè. Broadband internet performance: A view from the gateway. In *Proceedings of ACM SIGCOMM '11*, Toronto, Canada, August 2011.

[34] F. Lam W. Tan and W Lau. An Empirical Study on 3G Network Capacity and Performance. In *Proceedings of IEEE INFOCOM*, Anchorage, AK, May 2007.

Network Performance of Smart Mobile Handhelds in a University Campus WiFi Network

Xian Chen, Ruofan Jin
University of Connecticut

Kyoungwon Suh
Illinois State University

Bing Wang, Wei Wei
University of Connecticut

ABSTRACT

Smart mobile handheld devices (MHDs) such as smartphones have been used for a wide range of applications. Despite the recent flurry of research on various aspects of smart MHDs, little is known about their network performance in WiFi networks. In this paper, we measure the network performance of smart MHDs inside a university campus WiFi network, and identify the dominant factors that affect the network performance. Specifically, we analyze 2.9TB of data collected over three days by a monitor that is located at a gateway router of the network, and make the following findings: (1) Compared to non-handheld devices (NHDs), MHDs use well provisioned Akamai and Google servers more heavily, which boosts the overall network performance of MHDs. Furthermore, MHD flows, particularly short flows, benefit from the large initial congestion window that has been adopted by Akamai and Google servers. (2) MHDs tend to have larger local delays inside the WiFi network and are more adversely affected by the number of concurrent flows. (3) Earlier versions of Android OS (before 4.X) cannot take advantage of the large initial congestion window adopted by many servers. On the other hand, the large receive window adopted by iOS is not fully utilized by most flows, potentially leading to waste of resources. (4) Some application-level protocols cause inefficient use of network and operating system resources of MHDs in WiFi networks. Our observations provide valuable insights on content distribution, server provisioning, MHD system design, and application-level protocol design.

Categories and Subject Descriptors

D.4.8 [**Performance**]: Measurements

General Terms

Performance, Measurement

IMC'12, November 14–16, 2012, Boston, Massachusetts, USA.

Keywords

Smart Mobile Handhelds, WiFi Networks, Performance Measurement

1. INTRODUCTION

Smart mobile handheld devices (MHDs) such as smartphones have been used for a wide range of applications including surfing web, checking email, watching video, accessing social networking services, and online games. Most MHDs are equipped with both cellular and WiFi interface cards. Whenever available, WiFi is still a preferred way for Internet connection due to its higher bandwidth, lower delay and lower energy consumption [9]. Although recently there is a flurry of studies on various aspects of smart MHDs (see Section 2), little is known about the network performance of smart MHDs in WiFi networks. Specifically, how is their network performance? What are the major factors that affect the network performance?

In this paper, we answer the above questions by measuring the performance of smart MHDs inside a university campus WiFi network. Specifically, our study is over a data set that is passively captured by a monitor placed at a gateway router in the University of Connecticut (UConn). The data set is collected over three days (2.9TB of data), containing traffic from various wireless devices, including MHDs such as iPhones, iPod touches, iPads, Android phones, Windows phones, and Blackberry phones, and wireless non-handheld devices (NHDs) such as Windows laptops and MacBooks. To understand the performance of MHDs, we first separate the traffic of MHDs from that of NHDs. Our focus is on MHDs; we describe the results on NHDs when necessary for comparison.

Analyzing the data set, we find HTTP is the dominant traffic type, accounting for over 92% of the TCP flows. We therefore focus on the performance of HTTP flows in this paper. The behavior of HTTP is complicated: we find many HTTP flows contain multiple HTTP requests, and a significant portion of an HTTP flow is idling (with no data packets). Hence, the traditional throughput metric (i.e., the amount of data downloaded in a flow divided by the total duration of the flow) may introduce bias in measuring the performance of HTTP flows. We therefore define a metric, *per-flow servicing rate*, i.e., the amount of data downloaded corresponding to HTTP requests in a flow divided by the downloading duration of the flow, to quantify the performance of an HTTP flow (see Section 4). This metric is interesting in its own right: it represents the network performance of an HTTP flow, while excluding the effect of various delays (e.g., client processing delays and user pause times) that are irrelevant to network performance. Our main findings are as follows.

- We observe that the best performance is achieved for the MHD flows served by an Akamai server cluster that is located close to UConn. Furthermore, 16% of the MHD flows are served by this server cluster, accounting for 35% of the bytes. Overall, a large percentage (38.4%) of MHD flows are served by well provisioned Akamai and Google servers, account for 62% of the bytes. Interestingly, these fractions are significantly larger than the corresponding values for NHDs, indicating that MHDs use Akamai and Google servers more heavily, which boosts their overall network performance. We also observe that Akamai and Google servers have adopted large initial congestion window, which contributes to the network performance of MHDs (particularly for short flows). On the other hand, we observe that most flows have low loss rates, indicating that loss rate is not a limiting factor in the campus WiFi network that we study.

- We find that MHDs tend to have longer local RTTs (i.e., delays within the university network) than NHDs. In addition, the number of concurrent flows has negative effect on performance, and the effect is more significant for MHDs than NHDs. These two differences between MHDs and NHDs might be caused by the inferior computation and I/O capabilities on MHDs. The effect of local RTT on network performance seems negligible due the fact that local RTT only takes a small portion of the RTT.

- We find that earlier versions of Android OS (before 4.X) cannot take advantage of the large initial congestion window adopted by many servers. While Android OS increases the receive window adaptively in every round trip time, it uses a very small initial receive window (much smaller than the initial congestion window adopted by Google and Akamai servers), which limits the performance of Andriod devices. In contrast, we observe that iOS uses a large static receive window, which fully exploits the benefit of large initial congestion window. On the other hand, most flows do not fully utilize the large receive window, potentially leading to unnecessary waste of resources on iOS devices.

- We find that some application-level protocols cause inefficient use of network and operating system resources of MHDs in WiFi networks. One example is the native YouTube application on iOS devices, which can use a large number of TCP flows to serve a single video. We suspect this is a design optimization for cellular networks, which is not suitable for WiFi networks.

Our findings highlight the impact of TCP parameters and application-level design choices on MHD network performance, providing valuable insights on content distribution, server provisioning, mobile system design, and application-level protocol design.

The rest of the paper is organized as follows. Section 2 describes related work. Section 3 describes data collection and classification. Section 4 introduces the performance metric. Section 5 describes our methodology. Section 6 presents network performance of MHDs, and explores the impact of network and application layer factors on the performance. Section 7 discusses what findings are specific to UConn WiFi network and what can be applied to other networks. Last, Section 8 concludes the paper and presents future research directions.

2. RELATED WORK

Several recent studies characterize the usage and traffics of MHDs in 3G cellular networks, public WiFi or residential WiFi networks. Trestian et al. analyze a trace collected from the content billing system of a large 3G mobile service provider to understand the relationship among people, locations and interests in 3G mobile networks [31]. Maier et al. study packet traces collected from more than 20,000 residential DSL customers to characterize the traffic from MHDs in home WiFi networks [21]. Falaki et al. employ passive sniffers on individual devices (Android and Windows Mobile smartphones) to record sent and received traffic, and provide a detailed look at smartphone traffic [11]. This study is limited to a small user population (43 users), and the traces were not separately analyzed for the different network interfaces (i.e., 3G and WiFi) being used, which have different properties. The study in [12] uses a larger population of 255 users, and characterizes intentional user activities and the impact of these activities on network and energy usage. Gember et al. compare the content and flow characteristics of MHDs and NHDs in campus WiFi networks [14]. We focus on network performance of MHDs in a campus WiFi network and the impact of various factors on the network performance of MHDs, which are not investigated in the above studies.

Huang et al. anatomize the performance of smartphone applications in 3G networks using their widely-deployed active measurement tool, 3GTest [16]. Tso et al. study the performance of mobile HSPA (a 3.5G cellular standard) networks in Hong Kong using extensive field tests [32]. Our study differs from them in that we study the network performance of MHDs in WiFi networks (instead of cellular networks). Furthermore, our study is based on large-scale traces collected passively from a university campus network, while the study in [16] adopts an active measurement tool and the study in [32] uses customized applications. The studies of [13, 26] report that iOS native YouTube player generates multiple TCP flows to stream a single video. We expand these studies by presenting the degree of inefficiencies caused by the large number of TCP flows and the main reason for the design choice in the player.

Several measurement studies are on university WiFi networks. However, MHDs have only been widely adopted recently, and none of those studies explores the network performance of MHDs as in our study. Our study builds upon the rich literature on understanding the behavior of TCPs and content distribution in operational environments (e.g., [19, 23, 20, 15, 30, 10, 4, 22]), and our observations confirm some of the findings in those studies.

Last, several other aspects of MHDs have been studied recently, including battery use and charging behaviors [6, 25], energy consumption [29, 5], and performance enhancement techniques (e.g., [24, 34]). Our study differs in scope from them.

3. DATA COLLECTION & CLASSIFICATION

We collect measurements at a monitoring point inside the University of Connecticut (UConn). The monitor is a commodity PC, equipped with a DAG card [2]. It is placed at a gateway router of UConn, capturing all incoming and outgoing packets through the router with accurate timestamps[1]. In particular, it captures up to 900 bytes of each packet, including application-level, TCP and IP headers. The campus network uses separate IP pools for Ethernet and Wireless LAN (WLAN). Since we are interested in the network performance of MHDs, which use the WLAN IP address pool, we use filters to capture only WLAN traffic.

We have collected two data sets. One data set is for three days, from 9am March 2 to 9am March 5, 2011. The other data set is for one day, from 9am April 23 to 9am April 24, 2012. Unless otherwise stated, we use the first data set (reasons for focusing on this data set and findings from the second data set are deferred to Section 6.9). In the following, we first provide a high-level view of the data, and then present methodology to separate MHD traffic from NHD traffic (the captured data set contains a mixture of traffic from both types of devices).

3.1 Data

Table 1 lists the number of packets captured during the three days. Overall, we collected over 5.8G packets (2.9 TB of data). Among them, 91.9% of the packets are carried by TCP. We only report the results obtained from the data collected on the first day; the statistical characteristics of the data on the other two days are similar[2].

Table 1: The number of packets captured during the three days.

	Day 1	Day 2	Day 3	Overall
incoming pkts	1.2G	1.4G	0.8G	3.5G
outgoing pkts	0.8G	1.0G	0.5G	2.3G
total pkts	2.0G	2.4G	1.4G	5.8G
% TCP pkts	91.8%	92.7%	90.8%	91.9%

We say a TCP flow is *valid* if it finishes three-way handshaking and does not contain a RESET packet[3]. Among the valid TCP flows, we identify the applications using destination port numbers (a recent study shows that this simple approach provides accurate results [20]). Table 2 lists the most commonly used applications, and the percentages of their traffic over all TCP traffic in terms of flows, packets and bytes, where the number of bytes in a packet is obtained from the IP header. We observe a predominant percentage (92.3%) of the TCP flows are HTTP flows. This is consistent with measurement results in other campus networks [14] and home environments [20]. In the rest of the paper, we focus on the network performance of HTTP flows; the performance of other protocols is left as future work.

[1]The campus network balances loads among two gateway routers. The load balancing strategy is set up so that data packets and ACKs in a TCP flow are through the same router.

[2]The amount of traffic on Day 3 is less than that of the other two days since Day 3 is a Friday.

[3]11.9% of the flows cotain a RESET packet.

Table 2: Percentage of the traffic from commonly used applications (in terms of flows, packets and bytes) over all the TCP traffic (Day 1).

Application	flows	packets	bytes
HTTP (80)	92.3%	82%	86.7%
HTTPS (443)	4.3%	8%	5.4%
IMAPS (993)	0.2%	0.28%	0.13%

3.2 Data classification

We refer to an HTTP flow that contains packets coming from and/or destinating to an MHD as an MHD flow (similar definition for an NHD flow). Since our captured data contains a mixture of MHD and NHD flows, we need to separate these two types of flows. The first approach we use to differentiate MHD and NHD flows is based on the keywords in the user-agent field in HTTP headers (MHDs and NHDs use different keywords) [21, 14]. Once the type of a flow is identified using the user-agent field, it provides us information on the type of the associated device (i.e., whether it is an MHD or NHD), which can be used to further identify the types of other flows. Specifically, if we know that a flow, f, from a device (the device is represented using an IP address) is an MHD flow, then we know all the flows that are concurrent with f and have the same source IP address as f are MHD flows[4]. If the type of an HTTP flow is not identified using the above two approaches, we use the knowledge that an IP address pool is dedicated to Apple mobile devices at UConn[5], and hence a flow using an IP address from this pool is an MHD flow. Using the above three approaches, we categorize 94.1% of the HTTP flows to be either MHD or NHD flows (91.9% of them are directly identified through the user-agent field, 6.7% are identified through the concurrent-flow approach, and the rest 1.4% are identified using the knowledge of the dedicated IP address pool). Specifically, we identify 0.7M MHD flows and 10.4M NHD flows, containing 38.8M and 821.1M packets, respectively. Further separation of the flows using other heuristics (e.g., TTL [21]) is left as future work.

We further identify the operating systems used by the MHDs and NHDs using the user-agent field. For MHDs, the dominant operating system is iOS, used in 96.2% of the MHD flows (iOS is used by iPhone, iPod touch, and iPad, with the percentages of flows as 65%, 26%, and 9%, respectively); and Android is the second most popular operating system, used in 3.2% of the MHD flows. For NHDs, the two dominant operating systems are OS X and Windows, taking 56.7% and 42.2% of the NHD flows, respectively; and Linux is at the third place, used by 1.1% of the NHD flows.

4. PERFORMANCE METRIC

As mentioned earlier, we mainly characterize the perfor-

[4]We can only classify the flows that are concurrent with f due to IP reassignment which can assign the same IP address to another device at another point of time.

[5]UConn network administrators set aside this dedicated pool to ease the management of IP addresses. Specifically, a device is assigned an IP address from this dedicated pool if its host name indicates that it is an Apple mobile device during the DHCP request phase.

mance of HTTP flows since HTTP is the predominant traffic type. The behavior of HTTP is complicated. For instance, modern browsers often open multiple TCP connections when browsing a web page [10]. Furthermore, an HTTP flow can send and receive multiple HTTP requests/responses. In our passive measurements, without any knowledge of the accessed content, it is difficult to correlate multiple TCP connections. We therefore focus on per-flow network performance, specifically, the performance that is the result of the complex interactions of myriad network and application related factors. In the following, we first describe our measurement results on HTTP flows, and then define a performance metric that we will use in the rest of the paper.

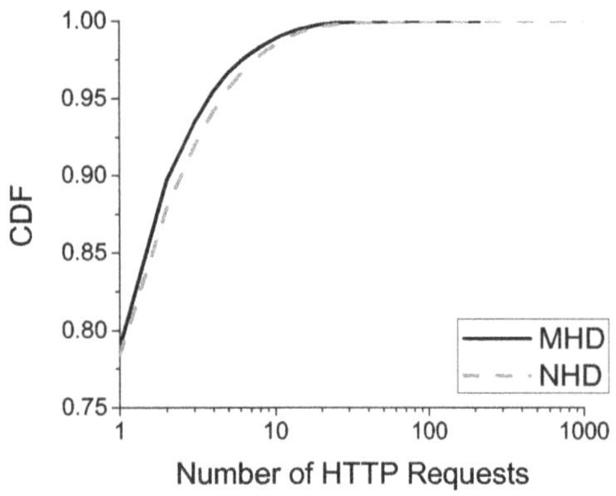

Figure 1: Distribution of the number of HTTP GET requests in an HTTP flow.

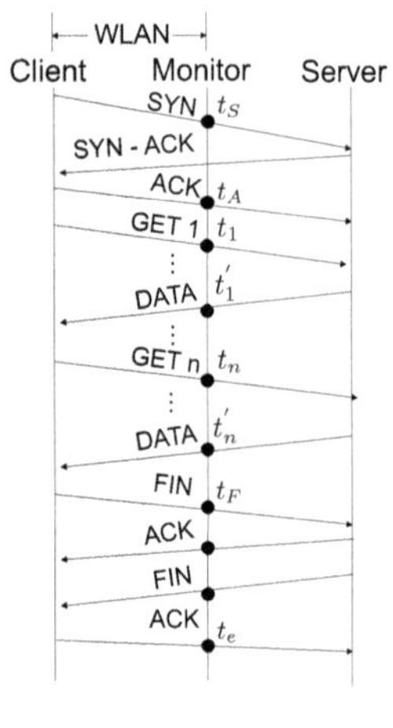

Figure 2: Illustration of a persistent HTTP flow.

We find that over 99% of the HTTP flows use HTTP 1.1, where TCP connections are persistent, i.e., each TCP connection allows multiple GET and POST commands. On the other hand, we observe only 6.5% of the HTTP flows contain POST commands. This is not surprising since most of the users in the campus network are content consumers. In the following, we ignore the HTTP flows with POST commands. Fig. 1 plots the distribution of the number of HTTP GET requests within an HTTP flow. Observe that over 20% of the HTTP flows contain at least two requests. The number

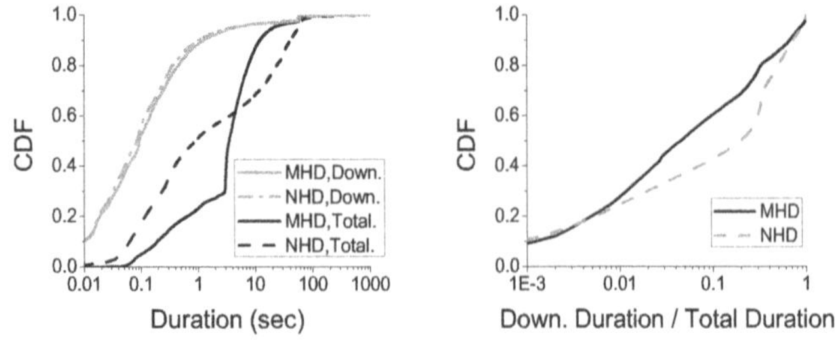

(a) (b)

Figure 3: (a) Total and downloading durations of MHD and NHD flows. (b) The ratio of downloading duration over total duration.

of requests in a flow can be as large as 100. In addition, NHD flows tend to contain a larger number of requests than MHD flows. This might be because regular web pages accessed by NHDs contain more objects than their mobile versions that are often accessed by MHDs [33].

Fig. 2 illustrates a persistent HTTP flow with n requests (the requests are sequential since we do not observe any pipelined requests in our trace where a request is sent out without waiting for the response of the previous request[6]). The measurement point sits between the client and server, capturing the packets with accurate timestamps. In particular, let t_S denote the timestamp of the SYN packet, t_A denote the timestamp of the ACK packet in the three-way handshaking, t_i denote the timestamp of the ith HTTP request, t_i' denote the timestamp of the last data packet corresponding to the ith HTTP request, t_F denote the timestamp of the first FIN packet, and t_e denote the timestamp indicating the end of a TCP flow. Then the measured duration of the HTTP flow at the measurement point is $t_e - t_S$, while the duration for data downloading is $\sum_{i=1}^{n}(t_i' - t_i)$. We refer to the former as *total duration* and the latter as *downloading duration*. Fig. 3(a) plots the distributions of the total and downloading durations for MHD and NHD flows. We observe that total durations can be significantly longer than downloading durations: the median downloading durations are 0.63s and 0.93s for MHD and NHD flows, respectively, while the median total durations are 5.06s and 15.45s for MHD and NHD flows, respectively. As shown in Fig. 3(b), the downloading duration is less than 10% of the total duration for respectively 60% and 42% of the MHD and NHD flows.

The difference between the downloading and total duration contains various delays inside an HTTP flow. Parts of the delays are for the three-way handshaking and TCP connection termination, and the rest of the delays are application idle/processing time. We divide the application idle/processing time into three parts. The first is the delay from finishing the three-way handshaking to the first GET request, defined as $T_S = t_1 - t_A$. The second is the sum of the delays from finishing one HTTP request to starting the next HTTP request, i.e., $T_G = \sum_{i=1}^{n-1}(t_{i+1} - t_i')$, and the last is the delay from finishing downloading the last object to start to close the TCP connection, i.e., $T_F = t_F - t_n'$. Fig. 4

[6]HTTP pipeline is not recommended and disabled in most browsers [3].

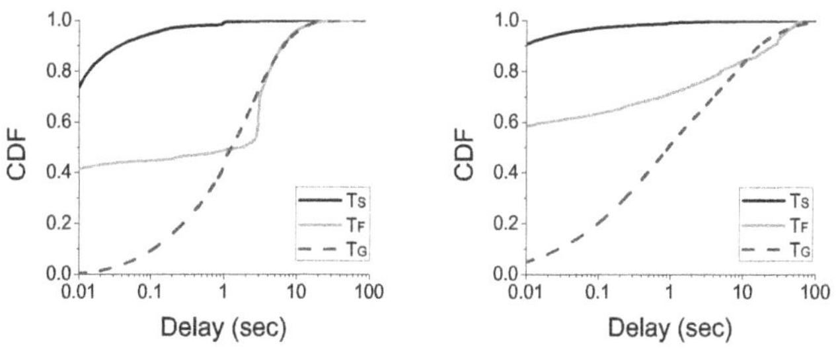

(a) MHD (b) NHD

Figure 4: Distribution of the various delays in an HTTP flow.

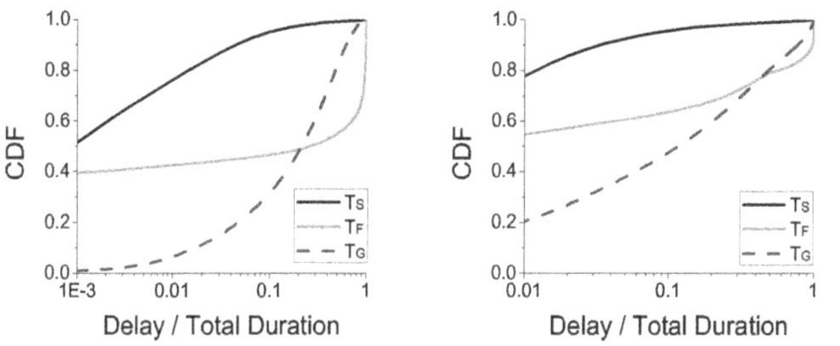

(a) MHD (b) NHD

Figure 5: Distribution of the ratios of the various delay over the total duration in an HTTP flow.

plots the distributions of the various delays. We observe that T_S is small for both MHD and NHD flows. Although a large fraction of the T_F values is small, it can be as large as several seconds for MHD flows and tens of seconds for NHD flows. The values of T_G are in a wide range from milliseconds to tens of seconds. Fig. 5 plots the CDF of the ratios of the various delay over the total duration.

In summary, the drastic difference between total duration and downloading duration highlights the importance of defining performance metric carefully: a traditional throughput metric, defined as the total amount of data downloaded divided by the total duration, can lead to biased results on the performance of HTTP flows. To exclude the effects of application-level delays on network performance, we define a performance metric, *per-flow servicing rate*, i.e., the total number of data bytes that are downloaded corresponding to HTTP requests divided by the downloading duration, to represent network performance. This metric represents the rate at which data are being fetched in an HTTP flow from a server to a client, while excluding the effect of various delays (e.g., client processing delays and user pause times) that are irrelevant to network performance.

5. METHODOLOGY

In the traces that we collected, MHDs are typically clients, requesting contents from servers outside UConn campus network. To understand the performance of MHD flows, we first group them according to their destinations. The rationale is that since the clients (i.e., MHDs) are at the same geographic location, the destinations (corresponding to the content servers) directly determine the network path. For the flows that are served by the same group of servers, we further divide the flows according to their lengths (in terms of number of packets inside the flow), since flow length affects the impact of the various TCP parameters and network path conditions on servicing rate. Specifically, short flows may terminate before finishing the slow-start phase in TCP, while long flows are more likely to reach congestion avoidance phase, and hence achieve more steady throughput.

In the following, we first describe server and flow classification, and then describe how we measure the various TCP and application-level characteristics.

5.1 Server Classification

We use two steps to study each flow destination IP address. First, we use reverse DNS lookup to find its domain name, and then query the IP registration information to determine the organization that registered the IP address. For the IP addresses that do not have a published domain name, we use the registration information only.

Table 3: Top five domain names for MHD and NHD flows (percentage is in terms of flows).

MHD	NHD
Akamai.com (26.1%)	Akamai.com (20.0%)
Google.com (12.3%)	Google.com (8.9%)
Facebook.com (10.0%)	Facebook.com (8.3%)
Amazon.com (6.8%)	Yahoo.com (5.9%)
Apple.com (5.0%)	Amazon.com (5.3%)

Table 3 presents the top five domain names of MHD flows that are obtained using reverse DNS lookup. We see that the largest percentage of MHD flows are served by Akamai CDN. Indeed, many widely used applications on MHDs are served by Akamai. For instance, when an iOS device downloads an application from Apple App Store, the data are actually downloaded from Akamai. In addition, some popular destinations, e.g., "fbcdn.net", are served by Akamai (we find 12% of MHD flows are destined to "fbcdn.net"). Following Akamai.com, Google.com is the second most frequently accessed domain name. This is not surprising: Google.com is one of the most frequently accessed web sites [1], and many MHDs have embedded Google applications (e.g., Google Map, Google Voice, Gmail). The third one is Facebook.com, which uses Akamai to serve many static contents, and use its own servers to serve many dynamic contents directly. The fourth one is Amazon.com, whose cloud services serve many popular applications running on iOS (e.g., Foursquare).

Since Akamai.com and Google.com are the top two domain names, we detail the network performance of the MHD flows that are served by Akamai and Google servers, as well as those served by the rest of the servers in Section 6. We also observe from Table 3 that 38.4% of MHD flows are served by Akamai CDN and Google servers. This percentage is significantly larger than the corresponding value for NHD flows (i.e., 28.9%). We believe the reason why MHD flows use Akamai and Google servers more heavily is that the destination hosts accessed by MHDs are less diverse than those accessed by NHDs [14]. Based on the host field in the HTTP request headers, we find around 6k distinct destination host domains from MHDs and 51k distinct destination host domains from NHDs. In addition, Table 4 lists the top 10 destination host domains accessed by MHD and NHD flows. We see for MHDs, accesses to the top ten host domains account for 39.2% of the MHD flows, while the percentage for NHDs (32%) is much lower. Last, we also observe from Table 4 that for MHDs, except for facebook.com and pandora.com, the other top eight host domains are all served by Akamai and Google, confirming the heavy usage of Akamai and Google servers by MHDs.

Table 4: Top ten destination host domains for MHD and NHD flows (percentage is in terms of flows).

MHD	NHD
fbcdn.net (12.0%)	fbcdn.net (12.9%)
facebook.com (10%)	facebook.com (6.5%)
apple.com (3.9%)	google.com (2.4%)
googlevideo.com (3.8%)	doubleclick.net (2.0%)
google.com (2.5%)	ytimg.com (1.7%)
admob.com (1.6%)	quantservec.om (1.6%)
doubleclick.net (1.5%)	yieldmanager.com (1.5%)
youtube.com (1.4%)	tumblr.com (1.2%)
google-analytics.com (1.3%)	twitter.com (1.1%)
pandora.com (1.2%)	yahoo.com (1.1%)

5.2 Flow Length Classification

For the flows that are served by the same server category, we divide the flows according to their lengths into three groups, denoted as G_1, G_2, and G_3. Specifically, G_1 contains short flows, with one to ten data packets, G_2 and G_3 contain longer flows, with at least 10 and 50 data packets, respectively. We make the above grouping since many web pages belong to G_1 [10], while long video streaming sessions may belong to G_3[7]. Table 5 lists the number of flows, packets and bytes (calculated from packet size in IP header) of the various groups. Observe that around 75% of the flows are short G_1 flows.

Table 5: Information of the various groups of MHD flows (for the data collected on Day 1).

	G_1	G_2	G_3
flows	0.5M	0.2M	0.03M
packets	2.9M	25.1M	19.0M
bytes	2.3GB	22.8GB	19.4GB

5.3 TCP flow characteristics

We now describe how we estimate the various TCP flow characteristics, including RTT, loss rate, local RTT and loss rate, server's initial congestion window, client's advertised receive window, and the maximum window size.

We use the techniques in [19] to obtain a sequence of RTT samples for a flow, and use the median to represent the flow's RTT. Packet losses are detected when observing triple duplicate ACKs, or a retransmission that is caused by timeout[8]. Local RTT represents the delay that a TCP flow experiences locally, inside a local-area network (i.e., the UConn campus network in our context). Similarly, local loss rate represents the loss rate that a TCP flow experiences inside a local-area network. In our study, both local RTT and local loss rate can be directly obtained from the measurements at the monitoring point since it is at the edge of the local-area network (see details in [7]).

The server's initial congestion window size (icwnd) has a significant impact on the flow downloading rate. It determines the amount of data that the server can send in the first window. If the icwnd is too small, the sender needs to pause and waits for ACKs before transmitting again; on the other hand, if it is too large, the sender pushes too much data into the network, and congestion could happen [10]. We infer the icwnd based on the packet arrival times at the monitoring point. Specifically, we obtain an estimate of the icwnd as n when observing the first window of n packets arriving close in time at the the monitoring point. The first window is dynamically estimated based on RTTs using the technique in [19]. This approach will underestimate the icwnd if the application does not have sufficient amount of data to send in the first window. To avoid potential underestimation, we only apply the approach to HTTP flows that contain at least one GET request and the data corresponding to the first GET request contain at least 20 packets. The constraint of at least 20 data packets (corresponding to at least 20KB when each packet is at least 1000 bytes) is based on the literature that servers can choose a large icwnd, e.g., between 10KB to 20KB [10, 23]. To obtain a server's icwnd, we infer a series of icwnd values from all of the flows that are served by this server and satisfy the requirements stated earlier, and then obtain the average, median, and maximum from these inferred values (our measurements indicate that a server's icwnd can vary among the flows). In Section 6.4, we only report the results from servers that have at least 10 estimates.

Client's advertised receive window, constantly reported from the client to the server, states the size of the available receive buffer, i.e., the maximum size of data that a sender transmits to the receiver before the data is acknowledged by the receiver. The receive window field in the TCP header is 16 bits, limiting the maximum size of receive window to 64KB. However, if both TCP server and client support window scaling option, they can agree upon a window scaling factor, which is the multiplier to the 16-bit receive window field. For example, if window scaling factor is 4, the maximum receive window that a client can specify is 256KB.

At each time point, the server's available window is the minimum of the client's advertised receive window and server congestion window. We also measure the maximum window of each flow during its lifetime. The maximum window has impact on the network performance as well: it determines the maximum amount of data that the sender can transmit in one RTT, which affects the maximum downloading rate.

5.4 Application layer characteristics

We consider the following three application-level characteristics. The first is the design of application-level proto-

[7]We also consider another group, G_4, which contains flows with at least 100 packets. The results of G_4 are similar to those of G_3, and hence are not reported in this paper.

[8]These are inferred losses at the TCP level. The loss rate thus estimated is an overestimate since the inferred losses may be due to long delays, not actual losses.

cols. In particular, we consider the protocol for YouTube videos. This is motivated by the popularity of this application and the large amount of video data in our trace (38% of the data are video contents). Secondly, we examine how servers respond to requests for different types of contents (e.g., video, image and texts). For this purpose, we define *application response time* as the delay from the first GET message to the first responding data packet for an HTTP request (the delay is measured at the monitoring point). Last, we quantify the relationship between the number of concurrent TCP flows and per-flow servicing rate. The rationale behind this is that the number of concurrent TCP flows might be an indicator of the amount of CPU and I/O activities on an MHD device. We calculate the amount of concurrent TCP flows for a flow as follows. Consider a flow f. Since the number of its concurrent flows can vary over time, we divide time into 0.3s bins, and count the number of concurrent flows in each bin, and then obtain the average number of concurrent flows during f's life-time as its number of concurrent flows. We only consider concurrent flows for long flows, specifically, the flows in G_3.

6. NETWORK PERFORMANCE OF MHDS AND RELATED FACTORS

In this section, we first present network performance of MHDs and then investigate how network and application layer factors affect the performance. Unless otherwise stated, we mainly report the results of iOS devices (i.e., iPhone, iPod touch, iPad) that account for 96.2% of the MHD flows.

As shown in Table 4, a large percentage (38.4%) of MHD flows are served by Akamai and Google servers. Using a commercial database [17], we identify that the Akamai servers are located in four main clusters, respectively 40km, 113km, 517km, and 966km away from UConn. Furthermore, consistent with the Akamai DNS design policy that gets servers close to end users [15], we find 90% of the MHD Akamai flows are served by the first two close-by server clusters. IP registration information reveals that all Akamai servers in the 40km range belong to the University of Hartford (only one hop away from UConn network), while it does not reveal any detailed information for the servers in the other distance ranges. We therefore refer to the first two server clusters as Akamai-Hartford and Akamai-113km, respectively. In the rest of the paper, we classify the servers into four clusters: Akamai-Hartford, Akamai-113km, Google[9], and other servers.

Figures 6(a), (b), and (c) plot per-flow servicing rate distributions of G_1, G_2 and G_3 flows, respectively. The results for all four server clusters are plotted in the figure. For the same server cluster, we observe larger per-flow servicing rate for longer flows because longer flows allow the congestion window to ramp up. Overall, Akamai-Hartford servers provide the best performance, with median servicing rates of 4.7Mbps, 5.9Mbps, and 6.5Mbps for G_1, G_2, and G_3 flows, respectively. For G_2 and G_3 flows, we observe a clear stochastic order: the performance achieved by Akamai-Hartford servers is the best, followed by Akamai-113km, Google, and the other servers. For G_1 flows, the performance achieved by Google servers is superior to that of Akamai-113km servers, and is superior to that of Akamai-Hartford servers at low percentiles, a point that we will return later.

Existing studies (e.g., [28, 26]) have shown that video servers may control the sending rate of video flows, which can affect per-flow servicing rate of those flows. In the traces that we collected, we confirm that YouTube flash videos to NHDs are indeed rate controlled. On the other hand, videos to NHDs are predominantly mp4 videos, which are not rate controlled. Therefore, per-flow servicing rates of MHD flows presented in Fig. 6 are not affected by rate control mechanisms. We next investigate the impact of various network and application-layer factors on MHD network performance.

6.1 RTT

We observe that RTTs to Akamai-Hartford servers tend to be the lowest, followed by Akamai-113km, Google, and the other servers. The main reason for the lowest RTTs to Akamai-Hartford servers is the close geographic distance and good network provisioning (both the University of Hartford where the servers are deployed and UConn belong to Connecticut education network). Fig. 7 plots the RTT distributions of G_2 MHD flows served by the four server clusters (results for G_1 and G_3 flows are similar). The median RTT of the flows served by Akamai-Hartford servers is 8.5ms, while for Akamai-113km, Google, and other servers, the median RTTs are respectively 2.3, 4.3, and 10.3 times larger. For the four server clusters, their relative order in terms of RTT is consistent with their relative performance as shown in Fig. 6. That is, a server cluster with lower RTTs tends to provide better performance. This is not surprising since RTT is a major factor that affects network performance.

What is more interesting is perhaps the large percentage of data that is served by the first three server clusters. Specifically, 58% of the MHD data bytes are served by the first three server clusters, much larger than the corresponding value (41%) for NHDs. Furthermore, 16% of the MHDs flows (accounting for 35% of the data) are served by Akamai-Hartford servers, the server cluster that provides the best performance. As described earlier, we believe that these large percentages originate from the fact that the most popular services accessed by MHDs are provided by major companies such as Facebook, Google, and Apple that use CDN services heavily. The large percentage of data served by Akamai and Google servers boost the overall network performance of MHDs.

6.2 Local RTT

We observe that long MHD flows tend to experience larger local RTTs than short MHD flows. As an example, Fig. 8(a) plots local RTT distributions of G_1, G_2, and G_3 MHD flows served by Akamai-Hartford server cluster (results for the other three server clusters are similar). We see that local RTT of G_1 flows is smaller than that of G_2 flows, which is in turn smaller than that of G_3 flows. In addition, we observe that local RTT of MHDs tends to be larger than that of NHDs. One example is shown in Fig. 8(b), which plots local RTT distributions of G_3 MHD and NHD flows served by Akamai-Hartford servers. Using *t-test* [18], we confirm that

[9]Google does not publish the location information of its data centers. Therefore we cannot simply use the database [17] to determine the geographic locations of Google servers. Hence we present the aggregate results of all Google servers. It is possible to determine the geographic location of the servers using RTT [30]. Dividing the servers into clusters according to their geographic locations and investigating their respective performance are left as future work.

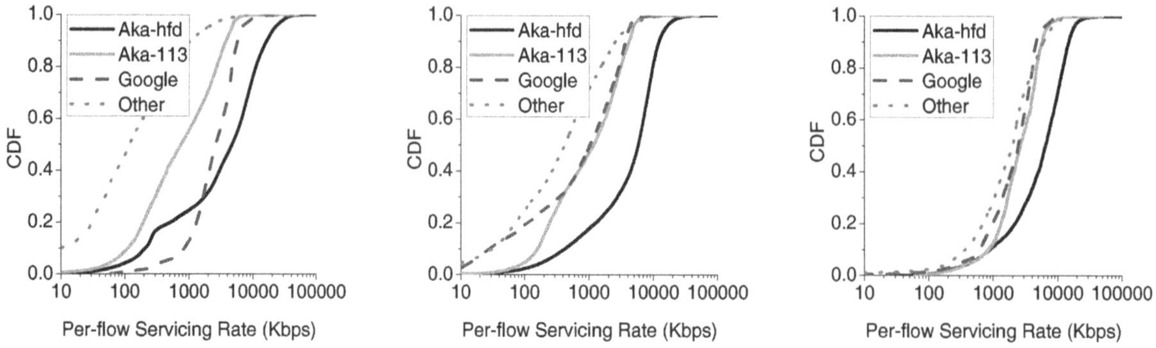

(a) G_1 (b) G_2 (c) G_3

Figure 6: Per-flow servicing rate of MHD flows served by the four server clusters.

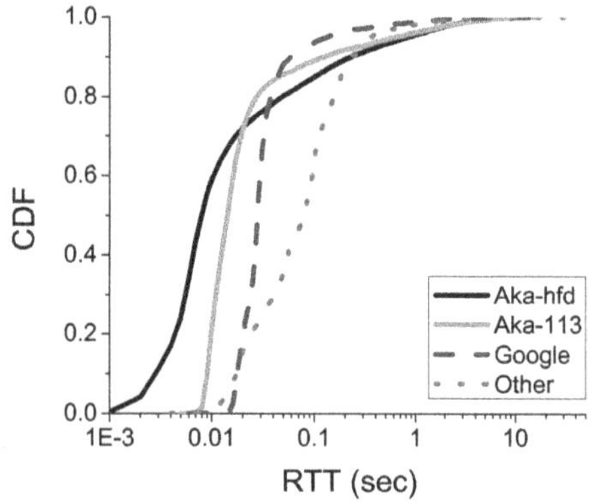

Figure 7: RTT distributions of G_2 flows served by the four server clusters.

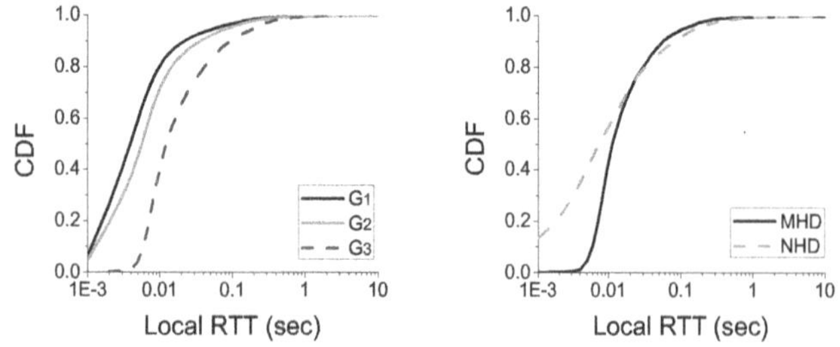

(a) (b)

Figure 8: (a) Local RTT for the MHD flows served by Akamai-Hartford servers. (b) Local RTT of G_3 MHD and NHD flows served by Akamai-Hartford servers.

the above two observations indeed hold statistically. Specifically, for the MHD flows served by the same server cluster, the average local RTT of G_i flows is statistically smaller than that of G_j flows, $i < j$; and for G_i flows, the average local RTT of MHD flows is statistically larger than that of NHD flows, $i = 1, 2, 3$. The reason might be limited computation and I/O capabilities on MHDs, which lead to longer processing time for longer flows, as well as longer processing time than that on NHDs (a more in-depth study using active measurements is left as future work). On the other hand, except for Akamai-Hartford servers, local RTT is only a small portion of RTT (the ratio of local RTT over RTT is below 0.2 for 10% to 56% of the flows). Therefore, the impact of local RTT on per-flow servicing rate is negligible. We also observe a small fraction of local RTTs that are longer than 100ms, a point we will return to in Section 6.3.

6.3 Loss Rate

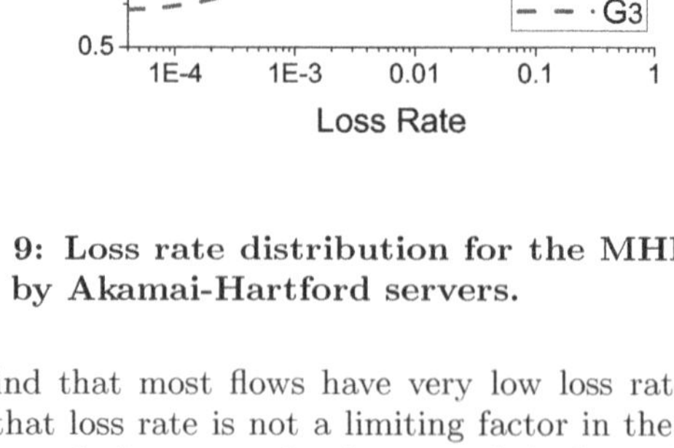

Figure 9: Loss rate distribution for the MHD flows served by Akamai-Hartford servers.

We find that most flows have very low loss rates, indicating that loss rate is not a limiting factor in the campus WiFi network that we study. An example is shown in Fig. 9, which plots loss rate distribution of the MHD flows served by Akamai-Hartford servers (results for the other three server clusters have similar trend). We observe that, for G_1, G_2 and G_3 flows, respectively 86%, 74% and 54% of the flows have zero loss. Furthermore, 90% of G_3 flows have loss rates below 0.02. The loss rate of a short flow can be large, which is however due to the artifact of small flow size (i.e., even a small number of losses can lead to high loss rate). We also find that all of the losses occur outside UConn (i.e., local loss rate is zero). This, however, does not mean that there is no loss at the MAC layer. We observe that a small percentage (around 3%) of local RTTs are longer than 100ms (see Fig. 8(a)). These long local RTTs might be caused by MAC-layer retransmissions and back-off times. Our measurements captured at the monitoring point does not contain MAC layer information; validating this conjecture through measurements captured at MAC layer is left as future work.

6.4 Initial Congestion Window

We find that Akamai and Google servers have adopted large initial congestion window. Specifically, the median initial congestion window of Akamai-Hartford servers is between 5 and 6KB, and the maximum initial congestion window is between 10 and 12KB. For Akamai-113km servers, 79% and 19% of the servers have median initial congestion window of 8KB and 5.5KB, respectively; the maximum initial congestion window is as large as 15KB. Google's adoption of large initial congestion window is even more aggressive: 98% of the Google servers use a median initial congestion window of 14KB (consistent with the advocated value of 15KB [10]), and the largest initial congestion window can be as large as 25KB. The rest of the servers (i.e., those other than Akamai and Google servers) have not adopted large initial congestion window as aggressively. Specifically, 61% of them use initial congestion window smaller than 4KB.

Large initial congestion window is particularly beneficial to short flows that can be completed in one RTT when initial congestion window is large. The more aggressive initial congestion window adopted by Google servers leads to its superior performance in serving G_1 flows: we observe from Fig. 6(a) better performance from Google servers than Akamai-113km servers at low percentiles despite that RTT to Google servers tends to be larger than that to Akamai-113km (RTT distributions for G_1 flows are similar to those for G_2 flows, which is plotted in Fig. 7). Furthermore, a smaller fraction of G_1 flows served by Google servers has very low servicing rate, as shown in Fig. 6(a). Even for G_2 flows, we observe similar servicing rates between flows served by Akamai-113km and Google servers (Fig. 6(b)) despite of the more dramatic differences in RTT (Fig. 7).

On the other hand, adopting larger initial congestion window can lead to congestion in the network. The study in [10] shows that this is only true for slow network connections. From our results, we do not observe significantly different loss rates from the server clusters that adopt different initial congestion windows.

6.5 Advertised Receive Window

We find that both iOS and Andriod operating systems support window scaling. When connecting to servers that support window scaling (e.g., we find all Akamai and Google servers support window scaling), the receive window advertised by iOS devices is 128KB[10], implying that the maximum window of a flow is 128KB. In contrast to the static

[10]The windows scaling factor is 4, leading to receive window of 256KB. However, we observe that the receive window is reduced to 128KB at the end of three-way handshake.

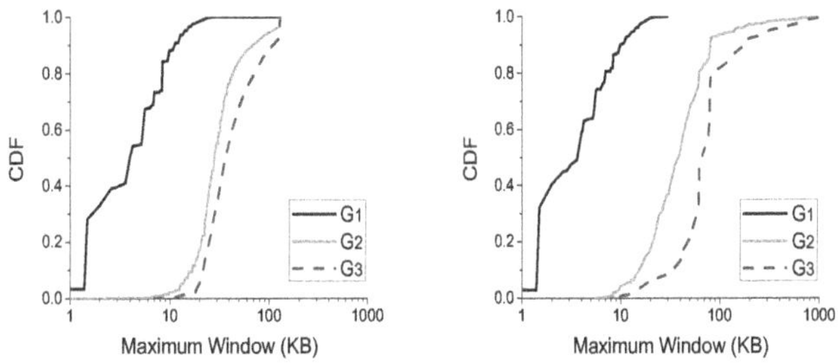

(a) iOS (b) Android

Figure 10: Distribution of maximum window size for iOS and Android flows served by Google servers.

large receive window advertised by iOS devices, Andriod devices dynamically adjust receive window every round trip time, starting from a fairly small size of 5KB. Furthermore, since the receive window can grow dynamically, the maximum window size can be larger than 128KB.

The different design choices adopted by iOS and Andriod devices have the following implications. First, we find the large receive window of iOS devices cannot be fully utilized by most flows. To illustrate this, we plot the distribution of maximum window size of iOS flows that are served by Google servers, as shown in Fig. 10(a). The reason for choosing Google server cluster is that it serves the highest percentage of video flows among all the four server clusters (the percentage is 30.5%), and video flows tend to be longer than other types of flows, and hence are more likely to reach large window size. From Fig. 10(a), we see that only 8% of G_3 flows reach the maximum window limit of 128KB, and the percentages for G_1 and G_2 flows are even lower, indicating that the large receive window of 128KB could potentially cause unnecessary waste of resources on iOS devices (whether it wastes resources or not depends on the kernel memory allocation mechanism: If the iOS kernel preallocates the memory for the socket, this causes waste of resources; otherwise, it does not waste resources).

Secondly, the very small receive window adopted by Andriod devices, while conserving resources, making Andriod devices unable to take advantage of large initial congestion window adopted by many servers (recall TCP congestion window is the minimum of the sender and receiver window), and hence can lead to inferior performance, particularly for short flows. As we shall see in Section 6.9, this is indeed the case (Section 6.9 reports findings from the data set collected in 2012, which contains more Andriod traffic and hence allows us to draw more convincing statistical conclusions regarding Andriod traffic). The adverse effect of small receive window may be even more dramatic in cellular networks where the round trip time can be significantly larger than that in WiFi networks.

Thirdly, since the receive window of Andriod devices is adjusted dynamically, it can grow to large values. Fig. 10(b) plots the distribution of maximum window size for Android flows that are served by Google servers. Indeed, we observe 9% of G_3 flows reach maximum window sizes larger than 128KB, while the maximum window size is bounded below 128KB for iOS flows. We suspect that since the receive window of Andriod devices can grow to large values, Android devices can achieve better performance for very long flows.

Our dataset, however, does not contain sufficient number of very long flows from Android devices (even in the data set that was collected in April 2012, which contains much more traffic from Android devices) to statistically verify the above conjecture.

Summarizing the above, we believe dynamic receive window adopted by Andriod devices is a suitable choice for resource limited MHDs. On the other hand, using very small initial receive window (e.g., 5KB) is too conservative, which can lead to inferior performance, particularly for short flows. How to choose receive window for MHDs to be both resource efficient and performance enhancing is beyond the scope of this paper, but is an interesting problem that we leave as future work.

6.6 Application-level Protocol

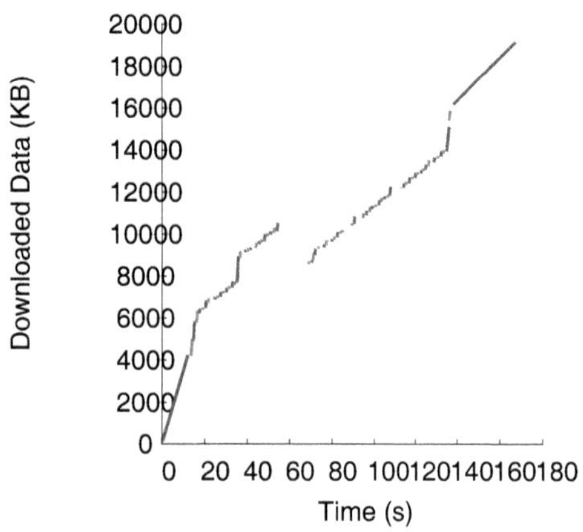

Figure 11: A series of 75 TCP flows is used to download one YouTube video when using the native YouTube application on an iOS device. The figure shows the starting and ending times of each TCP flow with the requested range. For better clarity, we use different colors (red and blue) to represent two adjacent TCP flows.

We find that some application-level protocols for MHDs are highly optimized for cellular networks, which may cause inefficient use of network and operating system resources of MHDs in WiFi networks. The native YouTube player in iOS is an example. When using this player, video contents are downloaded in segments; each segment is requested in a separate TCP connection, using the HTTP Range header field to specify the requested portion of the video [13]. While it has been reported in literature that multiple TCP connections are used to serve a single YouTube video [13, 26], we find, surprisingly, the number of TCP connections can be extremely large. Fig. 11 shows an example where a series of 75 TCP flows (most of them very short-lived) are used to download a single YouTube video. Considering the overhead of creating new TCP connections and the slow-start phase at the beginning of a TCP connection, using so many short-lived TCP flows to serve a single video does not seem to be sensible. We suspect this is a design choice that tries to cope with TCP timeouts (e.g., caused by long delays originated from handoffs, disconnections, and MAC-level retransmission) in cellular networks [8]. For example, the handoff in cellular network can take more than one second, which might cause TCP timeout and reduced congestion window (in the worst case, the congestion window might be reduced to one). Therefore, it might make sense to open a new TCP connection to take advantage of large initial congestion window to overcome the impact of the significantly degraded throughput.

We again find the design choices taken by iOS and Android devices are different: Android devices use only one TCP flow to download a single YouTube video. How to optimize application-level protocols for MHDs, considering the characteristics of both cellular and WiFi networks, is an interesting problem, but is beyond the scope of this paper.

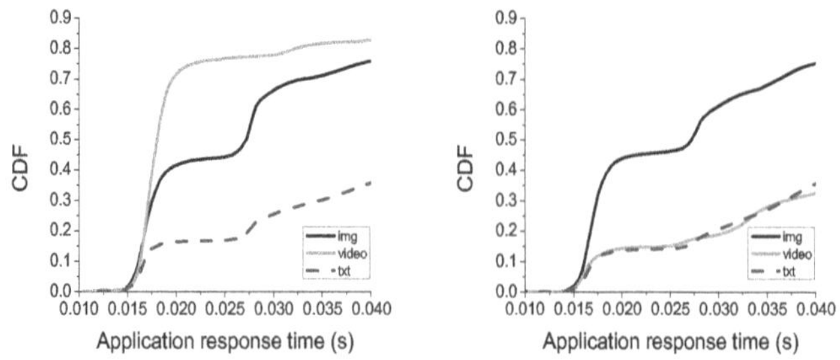

(a) MHD (b) NHD

Figure 12: Application response time for MHD and NHD flows that are served by Google servers.

6.7 Application Response Time

We investigate application response time for different types of content to understand whether servers use different mechanisms based on content type (recall application response time represents the delay from the first GET message to the first responding data packet for an HTTP request). Fig. 12(a) plots application response time distribution for three types of contents, video, image and text, that are served by Google servers. Most of the requested videos are YouTube videos, which are destined to Google servers because Google has migrated YouTube servers to its own network infrastructure after acquiring YouTube [30]. We observe from Fig. 12(a) that, perhaps surprisingly, videos have the lowest response time, followed by images and text. The reason why videos have the lowest response time might be that users tend to watch popular videos (note that YouTube iOS application has "Featured" and "Most Viewed" categories, convenient for users to select and watch those popular videos) and servers cache popular videos, leading to low response time. The slowest response time for texts might be because most of the requests for texts query search engines, which can take a longer time to respond.

Interestingly, the results for NHDs (see Fig. 12(b)) differ from those for MHDs: for NHDs, the response times for videos and texts are similar. We do not know the exact reasons that cause the difference between MHDs and NHDs. One observation is that the user interface for NHDs differ from that in MHDs: for NHDs, YouTube suggests related videos based on a user's preference (such as browsing history, local cache, etc.) while for MHDs, YouTube suggests featured and most viewed videos. Further investigation is left as future work.

In Fig. 12, we observe that the distribution of the response times for image flows that are served by Google contains

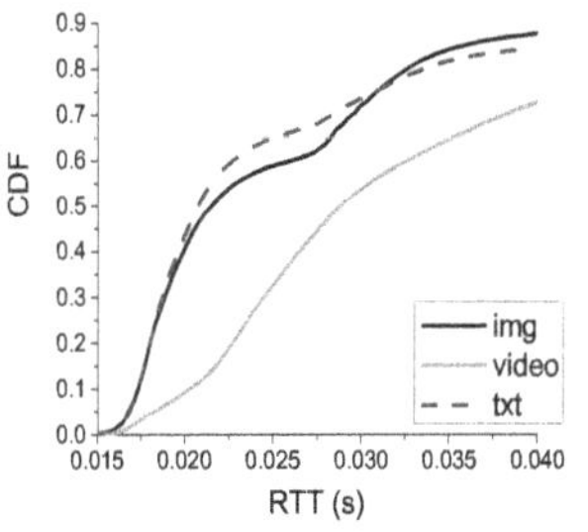

(a) MHD

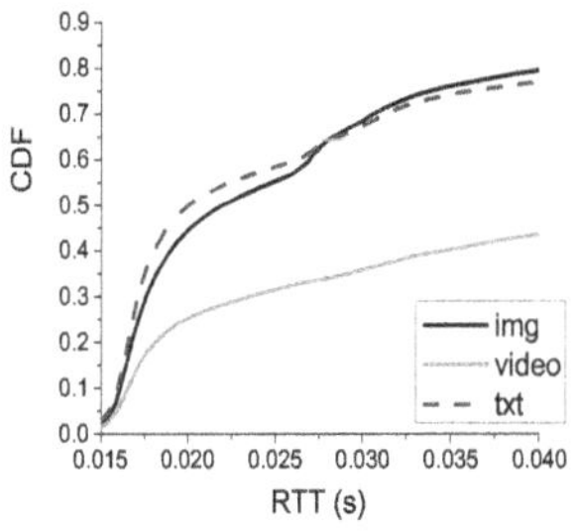

(b) NHD

Figure 13: RTT for MHD and NHD flows that are served by Google servers.

two modes. We conjecture that this is because the images are served by two clusters of servers, one closer to UConn than the other. Since Google data center information is not disclosed to the public, we try to infer the Google server locations through the RTT distribution [30]. Fig. 13 presents the RTT distributions for the flows with different content types. We indeed observe that the RTT distribution for image flows contains two modes, implying that they may be served by two clusters of servers at different geographic locations.

6.8 Number of Concurrent TCP Flows

As stated in Section 5.4, the number of concurrent TCP flows might be an indicator of the amount of CPU and I/O activities on an MHD device. We next present the relationship between the number of concurrent TCP flows and per-flow servicing rate.

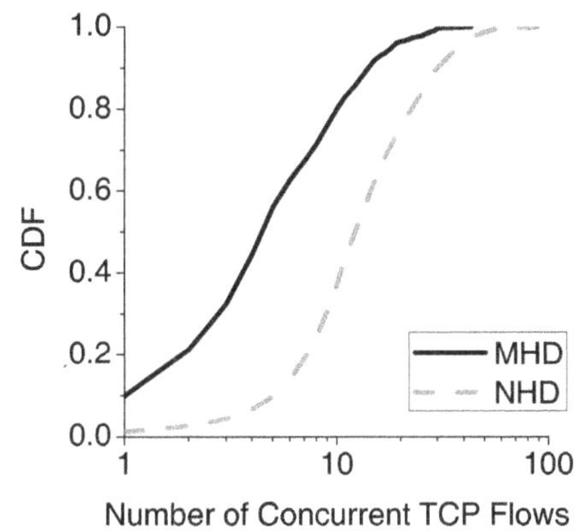

Figure 14: Average number of concurrent TCP flows for G_3 flows served by Akamai-113km servers.

We find that many G_3 flows have more than one concurrent TCP flow. Fig. 14 plots the distribution of the average number of concurrent TCP flows for G_3 flows served by Akamai-113km servers (for comparison, the results for both MHDs and NHDs are plotted in the figure). For MHDs, over 90% of the G_3 flows have more than one concurrent TCP flow, and there can be tens of concurrent flows. The results for the other three server clusters are similar (figure omitted). Intuitively, a larger number of concurrent flows on an MHD may lead to less resources to each flow, and hence lower per-flow servicing rate. To verify this conjecture, we obtain the correlation coefficient between the average number of TCP flows that are concurrent with a G_3 video flow and the per-flow servicing rate of the G_3 video flow. We find that the correlation coefficients are -0.03, -0.4 and -0.29 for G_3 video flows served by Akamai-Hartford, Akamai-113km and Google servers, respectively. The negative values indicate that indeed more concurrent flows can lead to lower per-flow servicing rates. The correlation is more significant for video flows served by Akamai-113km and Google. For the flows served by Akamai-Harford, the less significant correlation might be due to the superior performance achieved by this server cluster, which makes the effect of other factors less visible.

For comparison, let us look at the distribution of the average number of concurrent TCP flows for G_3 NHD flows in Fig. 14. Not surprisingly, the number of concurrent TCP flows on NHDs can be much larger than that on MHDs. On the other hand, we observe less significant correlation between the number of concurrent TCP flows and per-flow servicing rates on NHDs: in general, the negative correlation coefficient varies between -0.12 and -0.10 for the NHD flows served by the four server clusters. This less significant correlation may be due to superior computation and I/O capabilities on NHDs.

6.9 Findings from the 2012 Data Set

In the previous sections, we have presented the results from the data set collected in March 2011. We next report the results from the data set collected in April 2012.

In this data set, we find that only 64.7% of the TCP flows use HTTP, compared to 92.3% in the 2011 data set. On the other hand, the percentage of HTTPS flows has increased from 4.3% to 25.3%. This sharp increase is caused by the fact that many popular web sites such as Google, Facebook, and Hotmail, add the functionality to access their services using HTTPS, which protects users' privacy especially when they use public WiFi access points. For the rest of the TCP flows (11%), we do not observe any dominant application protocol.

Since the percentage of HTTP flows in the 2012 data set is much lower than that in the 2011 data set, and our approach to classifying MHD and NHD flows cannot be applied to the non-HTTP flows (since it uses User-Agent field in HTTP headers), leaving a large percentage (36.3%) of the TCP flows in the 2012 data set not analyzed, we have focused on the 2011 data set in this paper. We next describe the main results from analyzing the HTTP flows in the 2012 data set (developing new approaches to identify the device types for the non-HTTP flows in the 2012 data set, and analyzing their characteristics are left as future work). In the interests of space, we only present the main findings that differ from those from the 2011 data set.

- We observe that more MHD and NHD flows are served by Akamai and Google servers. Specifically, 43.5% of MHD flows and 38.4% of NHD flows are served by these two sets of servers, respectively. The number of distinct destination host domains accessed by MHDs has increased significantly to 9.3k (compared to 6k in the 2011 data set), while for NHDs, the increase is less dramatic (from 51k to 53k). The destination host domains accessed by MHDs are still less diverse than those accessed by NHDs. This is also evidenced by the observation that for MHDs, 38% of the flows are destined to the top ten host domains, while for NHDs, the percentage is 29%.

- We find that Google has deployed a set of servers (containing 12 IP addresses) very close to UConn, in the Connecticut Education Network at Hartford. Similar to the Akamai-Hartford server, this set of close-by Google servers provide high per-flow servicing rate due to small RTTs. We find 2.8% of MHD flows are served by these servers. In addition, analyzing the content type, we find that they mainly serve Youtube traffic (account for 45% of the MHD flows from these servers).

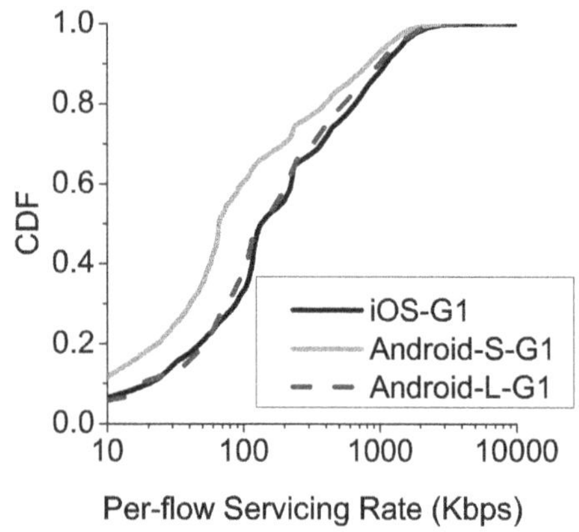

Figure 15: Distribution of per-flow servicing rate of G_1 iOS and Android flows that are served by Google servers from the 2012 data set, where Android-S-G1 corresponds to Andriod flows using small initial receive window (5KB) and Android-L-G1 corresponds to Andriod flows using large initial receive window (14KB).

- The amount of Android MHD flows has increased to 10% (compared to 3.2% in the 2011 data set), indicating the increasing popularity of Android devices. In addition, we observe 12% of the Android flows start with a significantly larger advertised receive window of 14KB, compared to the small initial receive window of 5KB that is observed predominantly in the 2011 data set. This larger initial receive window was adopted by newer versions of Android OS (starting from Android OS 4.X), and allows Android devices to better utilize the larger initial congestion window adopted by many servers. Fig. 15 plots the distribution of per-flow servicing rate of iOS and Andriod flows that are served by Google servers. We separate the Android flows into two groups, one using initial receive window of 5KB, and the other using initial receive window of 14KB. We only plot the results for G_1 flows; the results for G_2 and G_3 flows are consistent. Fig. 15 shows that iOS devices outperform Android devices that use small initial receive window, a point that we made in Section 6.5. On the other hand, the performance of Android devices that have adopted large initial receive window is comparable to that of iOS devices.

7. DISCUSSION

Our study has been conducted in a specific WiFi network, UConn campus WiFi network. A natural question is what findings from our study are specific to UConn network and what are applicable to other WiFi networks.

- Our findings related to hardware and software of MHDs and application-level protocols are not specific to UConn network, and hence we believe that they are equally applicable to other WiFi networks.

- The content delivery infrastructures in other networks may differ significantly from that perceived by UConn network. On the other hand, we believe MHDs in other networks also use Akamai and Google servers heavily because the most popular services accessed by MHDs are provided by major companies such as Facebook, Google, and Apple that use Akamai and Google servers heavily. The extent of usage and whether the usage by MHDs is heavier than that by NHDs in other networks, however, depend on the popularity of the applications in other networks.

- The use of Akamai and Google servers can also boost the network performance of MHDs in other networks in the US due to small RTTs provided by these servers. Specifically, the study of [15] reports that Akamai tends to deploy CDN sites close to the end users, and among all of the Akamai services, the 10th percentile and median of delays to Akamai are around 10ms and 20ms, respectively (these delays are comparable to the median delays of 8.5ms and 20ms from UConn campus to the two closest Akamai sites); Google is reported to provide similar RTT performance to most of the users in the US [27].

- The loss rates and RTTs in other networks may be significantly larger than those in UConn network. This implies that local losses and RTTs may play a significant role in network performance of MHDs in other networks. In addition, large initial congestion window adopted by many servers may not be strictly beneficial in other networks.

8. CONCLUSION AND FUTURE WORK

In this paper, we have studied the network performance of MHDs inside UConn campus network. We find that, compared to NHDs, MHDs use well provisioned Akamai and Google servers more heavily, which boosts the overall network performance of MHDs. Furthermore, MHD flows, particularly short flows, benefit from the large initial congestion window that has been adopted by Akamai and Google servers. Secondly, MHDs tend to have longer local delays inside the WiFi network and are more adversely affected by the number of concurrent flows. Thirdly, Android OS cannot take advantage of the large initial congestion window adopted by many servers, while the large receive window adopted by iOS is not fully utilized by most flows, leading to waste of resources. Last, some application-level protocols cause inefficient use of network and operating system resources of MHDs in WiFi networks. Our observations provide valuable insights on content distribution, server provisioning, MHD system design, and application-level protocol design.

As future work, we plan to use active controlled experiments to understand why local RTTs of MHDs tend to be larger than those on NHDs, and to understand the bottleneck(s) of MHD flows. We also plan to study network performance of MHDs in other public WiFi networks. For instance, we believe that WiFi hotspots (e.g., hotspots in Starbucks) and other campus WiFi networks might have different network characteristics (e.g., higher loss rates and higher RTTs) as well as different content popularity among users. Furthermore, the content delivery infrastructure may differ significantly from that perceived by UConn network. Quantifying the network performance of MHDs and identifying the performance limiting factors in a wide range of settings will provide us better insights on designing network services for MHDs. Last, we plan to study how the performance of 3G cellular network differs from that of WiFi in our campus network and when/why users on campus switch from one network interface to another network interface.

Acknowledgement

The work was supported in part by NSF CAREER Award 0746841. We thank J. Farese, R. Kocsondy, J. Pufahl, and S. Maresca (UConn) for their help with the monitoring equipment and their assistance in gathering the data. We thank Ilhwan Kim and Jaewan Jang (NHN) and D. Xuan (Ohio State University) for helpful discussions. We also thank the anonymous reviewers for their insightful comments, and our shepherd A. Balasubramanian for many helpful suggestions.

9. REFERENCES

[1] Alexa. http://www.alexa.com.

[2] DAG card. http://www.endace.com.

[3] HTTP Pipelining. http://en.wikipedia.org/wiki/HTTP_pipelining.

[4] M. Allman, S. Floyd, and C. Partridge. Increasing TCP's initial window, 2002. RFC 3390.

[5] N. Balasubramanian, A. Balasubramanian, and A. Venkataramani. Energy consumption in mobile phones: a measurement study and implications for network applications. In *Proc. of ACM IMC*, 2009.

[6] N. Banerjee, A. Rahmati, M. D. Corner, S. Rollins, and L. Zhong. Users and batteries: Interactions and adaptive energy management in mobile systems. In *Proc. of ACM Ubicomp*, 2007.

[7] X. Chen, B. Wang, K. Suh, and W. Wei. Passive online wireless LAN health monitoring from a single measurement point. *ACM Mobile Computer Comm. Review*, 14, November 2010.

[8] C. M. Choon and R. Ram. Improving TCP/IP performance over third-generation wireless networks. *IEEE Transactions on Mobile Computing*, 2008.

[9] P. Deshpande, X. Hou, and S. R. Das. Performance comparison of 3G and metro-scale WiFi for vehicular network access. In *Proc. of ACM IMC*, 2010.

[10] N. Dukkipati, T. Refice, Y. Cheng, J. Chu, T. Herbert, A. Agarwal, A. Jain, and N. Sutin. An argument for increasing TCP's initial congestion window. *ACM SIGCOMM CCR*, 40:26–33, June 2010.

[11] H. Falaki, D. Lymberopoulos, R. Mahajan, S. Kandula, and D. Estrin. A first look at traffic on smartphones. In *Proc. of ACM IMC*, 2010.

[12] H. Falaki, R. Mahajan, S. Kandula, D. Lymberopoulos, R. Govindan, and D. Estrin. Diversity in smartphone usage. In *Proc. of ACM MobiSys*, 2010.

[13] A. Finamore, M. Mellia, M. Munafo, and S. G. Rao. YouTube everywhere: Impact of device and infrastructure synergies on user experience. In *Proc. of ACM IMC*, 2011.

[14] A. Gember, A. Anand, and A. Akella. A comparative study of handheld and non-handheld traffic in campus WiFi networks. In *Proc. of PAM*, 2011.

[15] C. Huang, A. Wang, J. Li, and K. W. Ross. Measuring and evaluating large-scale CDNs. Technical Report MSR-TR-2008-106, Microsoft Research, 2008.

[16] J. Huang, Q. Xu, B. Tiwana, Z. M. Mao, M. Zhang, and P. Bahl. Anatomizing application performance differences on smartphones. In *Proc. of ACM Mobisys*, 2010.

[17] IP2Location. http://www.ip2location.com.

[18] R. Jain. *The art of computer systems performance analysis - techniques for experimental design, measurement, simulation, and modeling.* Wiley professional computing. Wiley, 1991.

[19] S. Jaiswal, G. Iannaccone, C. Diot, J. Kurose, and D. Towsley. Inferring TCP connection characteristics through passive measurements. In *Proc. of IEEE INFOCOM*, 2004.

[20] G. Maier, A. Feldmann, V. Paxson, and M. Allman. On dominant characteristics of residential broadband Internet traffic. In *Proc. of ACM IMC*, 2009.

[21] G. Maier, F. Schneider, and A. Feldmann. A first look at mobile hand-held device traffic. In *Proc. of PAM*, 2010.

[22] A.-F. Mohammad, E. Khaled, R. Benjamin, and G. Igor. Overclocking the Yahoo!: CDN for faster web page loads. In *Proc. of ACM IMC*, 2011.

[23] F. Qian, A. Gerber, Z. M. Mao, S. Sen, O. Spatscheck, and W. Willinger. TCP revisited: a fresh look at TCP in the wild. In *Proc. of ACM IMC*, 2009.

[24] M.-R. Ra, J. Paek, A. B. Sharma, R. Govindan, M. H. Krieger, and M. J. Neely. Energy-delay tradeoffs in smartphone applications. In *Proc. of ACM MobiSys*, 2010.

[25] A. Rahmati and L. Zhong. Human battery interaction on mobile phones. *Elsevier Pervasive and Mobile Computing Journal*, 5(5), 2009.

[26] A. Rao, Y.-S. Lim, C. Barakat, A. Legout, D. Towsley, and W. Dabbous. Network characteristics of video streaming traffic. In *Proc. of ACM CoNext*, 2011.

[27] K. Rupa, M. H. V., S. Sridhar, J. Sushant, K. Arvind, A. Thomas, and G. Jie. Moving beyond end-to-end path information to optimize CDN performance. In *Proc. of ACM IMC*, 2009.

[28] A. Shane and N. Richard. Application flow control in YouTube video streams. *SIGCOMM Computer Comm. Review*, 41, 2011.

[29] A. Shye, B. Sholbrock, and G. Memik. Into the wild: Studying real user activity patterns to guide power optimization for mobile architectures. In *Proc. of IEEE/ACM MICRO*, 2009.

[30] R. Torres, A. Finamore, J. Kim, M. Mellia,

M. Munafo, and S. Rao. Dissecting video server selection strategies in the YouTube CDN. In *Proc. IEEE ICDCS*, 2011.

[31] I. Trestian, S. Ranjan, A. Kuzmanovic, and A. Nucci. Measuring serendipity: connecting people, locations and interests in a mobile 3G network. In *Proc. of ACM IMC*, 2009.

[32] F. P. Tso, J. Teng, W. Jia, and D. Xuan. Mobility: a double-edged sword for HSPA networks: a large-scale test on Hong Kong mobile HSPA networks. In *Proc. of ACM MobiHoc*, 2010.

[33] D. Zhang. Web content adaptation for mobile handheld devices. *Communications of the ACM*, 50(2), February 2007.

[34] Z. Zhuang, K.-H. Kim, and J. P. Singh. Improving energy efficiency of location sensing on smartphones. In *Proc. of ACM MobiSys*, 2010.

Tackling Bufferbloat in 3G/4G Networks

Haiqing Jiang[1], Yaogong Wang[1], Kyunghan Lee[2], and Injong Rhee[1]
North Carolina State University, USA [1] Ulsan National Institute of Science and Technology, Korea [2]
{hjiang5, ywang15, rhee}@ncsu.edu khlee@unist.ac.kr

ABSTRACT

The problem of overbuffering in the current Internet (termed as bufferbloat) has drawn the attention of the research community in recent years. Cellular networks keep large buffers at base stations to smooth out the bursty data traffic over the time-varying channels and are hence apt to bufferbloat. However, despite their growing importance due to the boom of smart phones, we still lack a comprehensive study of bufferbloat in cellular networks and its impact on TCP performance. In this paper, we conducted extensive measurement of the 3G/4G networks of the four major U.S. carriers and the largest carrier in Korea. We revealed the severity of bufferbloat in current cellular networks and discovered some ad-hoc tricks adopted by smart phone vendors to mitigate its impact. Our experiments show that, due to their static nature, these ad-hoc solutions may result in performance degradation under various scenarios. Hence, a dynamic scheme which requires only receiver-side modification and can be easily deployed via over-the-air (OTA) updates is proposed. According to our extensive real-world tests, our proposal may reduce the latency experienced by TCP flows by 25% $\sim$ 49% and increase TCP throughput by up to 51% in certain scenarios.

Categories and Subject Descriptors

C.2.2 [**Computer-Communication Networks**]: Network Protocols

General Terms

Design, Measurement, Performance

Keywords

Bufferbloat, Cellular Networks, TCP, Receive Window

1. INTRODUCTION

Bufferbloat, as termed by Gettys [10], is a phenomenon where oversized buffers in the network result in extremely long delay and other performance degradation. It has been observed in different parts of the Internet, ranging from ADSL to cable modem users [5, 17, 26]. Cellular networks are another place where buffers are heavily provisioned to accommodate the dynamic cellular link (Figure 1). However, other than some ad-hoc observations [24], bufferbloat in cellular networks has not been studied systematically.

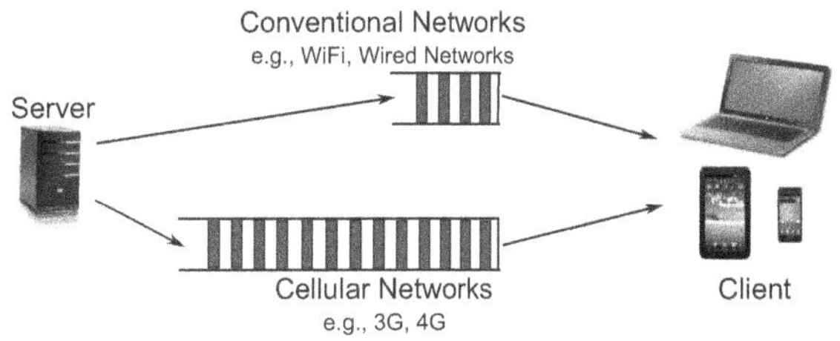

Figure 1: Bufferbloat has been widely observed in the current Internet but is especially severe in cellular networks, resulting in up to several seconds of round trip delay.

In this paper, we carried out extensive measurements over the 3G/4G networks of all four major U.S. carriers (AT&T, Sprint, T-Mobile, Verizon) as well as the largest cellular carrier in Korea (SK Telecom). Our experiments span more than two months and consume over 200GB of 3G/4G data. According to our measurements, TCP has a number of performance issues in bufferbloated cellular networks, including extremely long delays and sub-optimal throughput. The reasons behind such performance degradation are two-fold. First, most of the widely deployed TCP implementations use loss-based congestion control where the sender will not slow down its sending rate until it sees packet loss. Second, most cellular networks are overbuffered to accommodate traffic burstiness and channel variability [20]. The exceptionally large buffer along with link layer retransmission conceals packet losses from TCP senders. The combination of these two facts leads to the following phenomenon: the TCP sender continues to increase its sending rate even if it has already exceeded the bottleneck link capacity since all of the overshot packets are absorbed by the buffers. This results in up to several seconds of round trip delay. This extremely long delay did not cause critical user experience problems today simply because 1) base stations typically has separate buffer space for each user [20] and 2) users do not multitask on smart phones very often at this point. This means only a single TCP flow is using the buffer space. If it is a short-lived flow like Web browsing, queues will not build up since the traffic is small. If it is a long-lived

IMC'12, November 14–16, 2012, Boston, Massachusetts, USA.

flow like downloading a file, long queues will build up but users hardly notice them since it is the throughput that matters rather than the delay. However, as the smart phones become more and more powerful (e.g., several recently released smart phones are equipped with quad-core processors and 2GB of memory), users are expected to perform multi-tasking more often. If a user is playing an online game and at the same time downloading a song in the background, severe problem will appear since the time-sensitive gaming traffic will experience huge queuing delays caused by the background download. Hence, we believe that bufferbloat in 3G/4G networks is an important problem that must be addressed in the near future.

This problem is not completely unnoticed by today's smart phone vendors. Our investigation into the open source Android platform reveals that a small untold trick has been applied to mitigate the issue: the maximum TCP receive buffer size parameter (*tcp_rmem_max*) has been set to a relatively small value although the physical buffer size is much larger. Since the advertised receive window (*rwnd*) cannot exceed the receive buffer size and the sender cannot send more than what is allowed by the advertised receive window, the limit on *tcp_rmem_max* effectively prevents TCP congestion window (*cwnd*) from excessive growth and controls the RTT (round trip time) of the flow within a reasonable range. However, since the limit is statically configured, it is sub-optimal in many scenarios, especially considering the dynamic nature of the wireless mobile environment. In high speed long distance networks (e.g., downloading from an oversea server over 4G LTE (Long Term Evolution) network), the static value could be too small to saturate the link and results in throughput degradation. On the other hand, in small bandwidth-delay product (BDP) networks, the static value may be too large and the flow may experience excessively long RTT.

There are many possible ways to tackle this problem, ranging from modifying TCP congestion control algorithm at the sender to adopting Active Queue Management (AQM) at the base station. However, all of them incur considerable deployment cost. In this paper, we propose dynamic receive window adjustment (DRWA), a light-weight, receiver-based solution that is cheap to deploy. Since DRWA requires modifications only on the receiver side and is fully compatible with existing TCP protocol, carriers or device manufacturers can simply issue an over-the-air (OTA) update to smart phones so that they can immediately enjoy better performance even when interacting with existing servers.

DRWA is similar in spirit to delay-based congestion control algorithms but runs on the receiver side. It modifies the existing receive window adjustment algorithm of TCP to indirectly control the sending rate. Roughly speaking, DRWA increases the advertised window when the current RTT is close to the minimum RTT we have observed so far and decreases it when RTT becomes larger due to queuing delay. With proper parameter tuning, DRWA could keep the queue size at the bottleneck link small yet non-empty so that throughput and delay experienced by the TCP flow are both optimized. Our extensive experiments show that DRWA reduces the RTT by 25% $\sim$ 49% while achieving similar throughput in ordinary scenarios. In large BDP networks, DRWA can achieve up to 51% throughput improvement over existing implementations.

In summary, the contributions of this paper include:

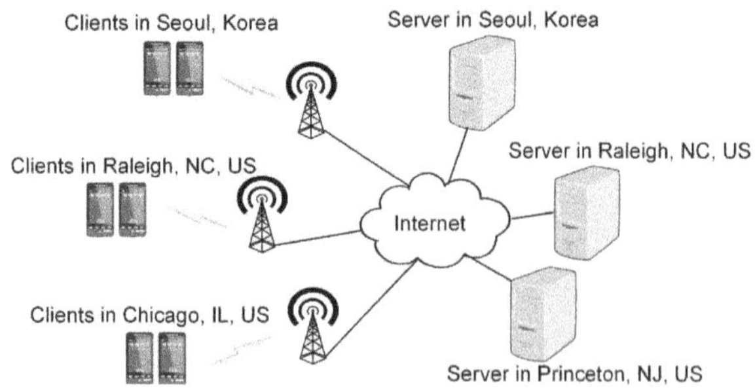

(a) Experiment testbed

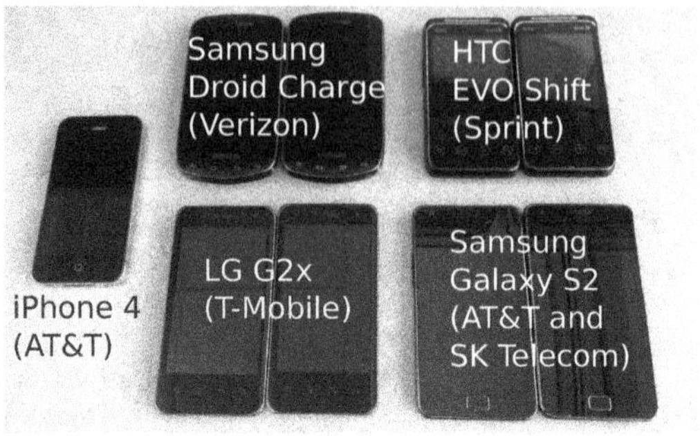

(b) Experiment phones

Figure 2: Our measurement framework spans across the globe with servers and clients deployed in various places in U.S. and Korea using the cellular networks of five different carriers.

- We conducted extensive measurements in a range of cellular networks (EVDO, HSPA+, LTE) across various carriers and characterized the bufferbloat problem in these networks.
- We anatomized the TCP implementation in state-of-the-art smart phones and revealed the limitation of their ad-hoc solution to the bufferbloat problem.
- We proposed a simple and immediately deployable solution that is experimentally proven to be safe and effective.

The rest of the paper is organized as follow. Section 2 introduces our measurement setup and highlights the severity of bufferbloat in today's 3G/4G networks. Section 3 then investigates the impact of bufferbloat on TCP performance and points out the pitfalls of high speed TCP variants in cellular networks. The abnormal behavior of TCP in smart phones is revealed in Section 4 and its root cause is located. We then propose our solution DRWA in Section 5 and evaluate its performance in Section 6. Finally, alternative solutions and related work are discussed in Section 7 and we conclude our work in Section 8.

2. OBSERVATION OF BUFFERBLOAT IN CELLULAR NETWORKS

Bufferbloat is a phenomenon prevalent in the current Internet where excessive buffers within the network lead to exceptionally large end-to-end latency and jitter as well as throughput degradation. With the recent boom of smart phones and tablets, cellular networks become a more and more important part of the Internet. However, despite the

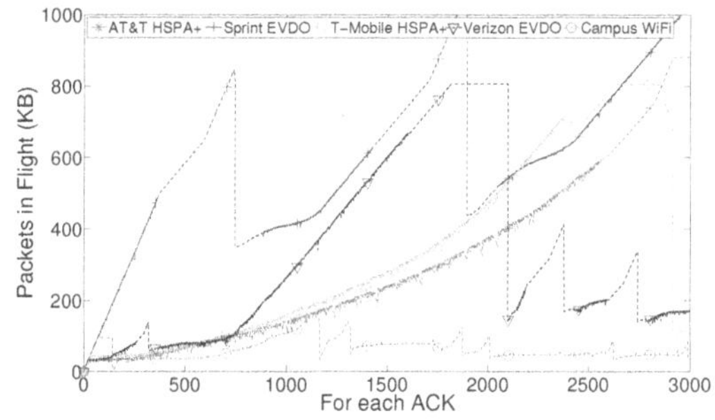

Figure 3: We observed exceptionally fat pipes across the cellular networks of five different carriers. We tried three different client/server locations under both good and weak signal case. This shows the prevalence of bufferbloat in cellular networks. The figure above is a representative example.

abundant measurement studies of the cellular Internet [4, 18, 20, 23, 14], the specific problem of bufferbloat in cellular networks has not been studied systematically. To obtain a comprehensive understanding of this problem and its impact on TCP performance, we have set up the following measurement framework which is used throughout the paper.

2.1 Measurement Setup

Figure 2(a) gives an overview of our testbed. We have servers and clients deployed in various places in U.S. and Korea so that a number of scenarios with different BDPs can be tested. All of our servers run Ubuntu 10.04 (with 2.6.35.13 kernel) and use its default TCP congestion control algorithm CUBIC [11] unless otherwise noted. We use several different phone models on the client side, each working with the 3G/4G network of s specific carrier (Figure 2(b)). The signal strength during our tests ranges from -75dBm to -105dBm so that it covers both good signal condition and weak signal condition. We develop some simple applications on the client side to download data from the server with different traffic patterns (short-lived, long-lived, etc.). The most commonly used traffic pattern is long-lived TCP flow where the client downloads a very large file from the server for 3 minutes (the file is large enough so that the download never finishes within 3 minutes). Most experiments have been repeated numerous times for a whole day with a one-minute interval between each run. That results in more than 300 samples for each experiment based on which we calculate the average and the confidence interval.

For the rest of the paper, we only consider the performance of the downlink (from base station to mobile station) since it is the most common case. We leave the measurement of uplink performance as our future work. Since we are going to present a large number of measurement results under various conditions in this paper, we provide a table that summaries the setup of each experiment for the reader's convenience. Please refer to Table 1 in Appendix A.

2.2 Bufferbloat in Cellular Networks

The potential problem of overbuffering in cellular networks was pointed out by Ludwig et al. [21] as early as 1999 when researchers were focusing on GPRS networks. However, overbuffering still prevails in today's 3G/4G networks. To estimate the buffer space in current cellular networks,

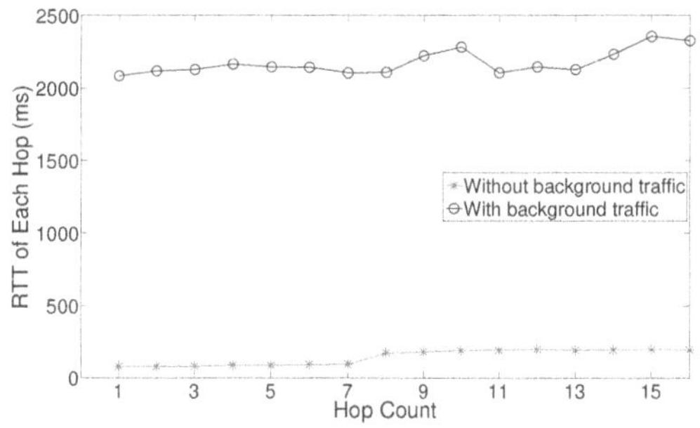

Figure 4: We verified that the queue is built up at the very first IP hop (from the mobile client).

we set up the following experiment: we launch a long-lived TCP flow from our server to a Linux laptop (Ubuntu 10.04 with 2.6.35.13 kernel) over the 3G networks of four major U.S. carriers. By default, Ubuntu sets both the maximum TCP receive buffer size and the maximum TCP send buffer size to a large value (greater than 3MB). Hence, the flow will never be limited by the buffer size of the end points. Due to the closed nature of cellular networks, we are unable to know the exact queue size within the network. Instead, we measure the size of packets in flight on the sender side to estimate the buffer space within the network. Figure 3 shows our measurement results. We observed exceptionally fat pipes in all four major U.S. cellular carriers. Take Sprint EVDO network for instance. The peak downlink rate for EVDO is 3.1 Mbps and the observed minimum RTT (which approximates the round-trip propagation delay) is around 150ms. Therefore, the BDP of the network is around 58KB. But as the figure shows, Sprint is able to bear more than 800KB of packets in flight!

As a comparison, we ran a similar experiment of a long-lived TCP flow between a client in Raleigh, U.S. and a server in Seoul, Korea over the campus WiFi network. Due to the long distance of the link and the ample bandwidth of WiFi, the corresponding pipe size is expected to be large. However, according to Figure 3, the size of in-flight packets even in such a large BDP network is still much smaller than the ones we observed in cellular networks.

We extend the measurement to other scenarios in the field to verify that the observation is universal in current cellular networks. For example, we have clients and servers in various locations over various cellular networks in various signal conditions (Table 1). All the scenarios prove the existence of extremely fat pipes similar to Figure 3.

To further confirm that the bufferbloat is within the cellular segment rather than the backbone Internet, we designed the following experiment to locate where the long queue is built up. We use *Traceroute* on the client side to measure the RTT of each hop along the path to the server and compare the results with or without a background long-lived TCP flow. If the queue is built up at hop x, the queuing delay should increase significantly at that hop when background traffic is in place. Hence, we should see that the RTTs before hop x do not differ much no matter the background traffic is present or not. But the RTTs after hop x should have a notable gap between the case with background traffic and the case without. The results shown in Figure 4 demonstrate that the queue is built up at the very first hop. Note that there could be a number of components between the mo-

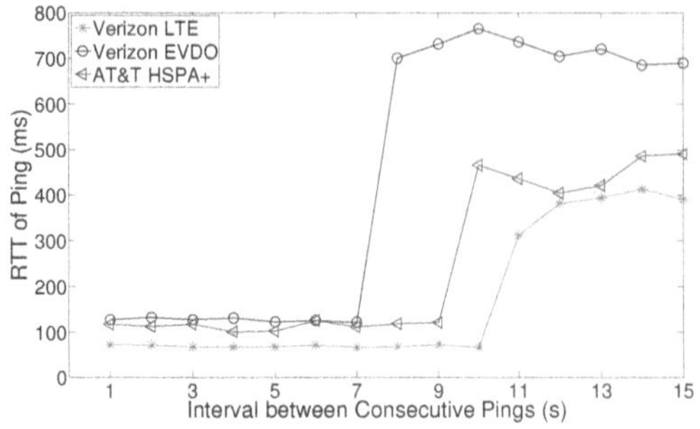

Figure 5: RRC state transition only affects short-lived TCP flows with considerable idle periods in between (> 7s) but does not affect long-lived flows.

bile client and the first IP hop (e.g., RNC, SGSN, GGSN, etc.). It may not be only the wireless link between the mobile station and the base station. Without administrative access, we are unable to diagnose the details within the carrier's network but according to [20] large per-user buffer are deployed at the base station to absorb channel fluctuation.

Another concern is that the extremely long delays we observed in cellular networks are due to Radio Resource Control (RRC) state transitions [1] rather than bufferbloat. We set up the following experiment to demonstrate that these two problems are orthogonal. We repeatedly *ping* our server from the mobile station with different intervals between consecutive *pings*. The experiment has been carried out for a whole day and the average RTT of the *ping* is calculated. According to the RRC state transition diagram, if the interval between consecutive *pings* is long enough, we should observe a substantially higher RTT due to the state promotion delay. By varying this interval in each run, we could obtain the threshold that would trigger RRC state transition. As shown in Figure 5, when the interval between consecutive *pings* is beyond 7 seconds (specific threshold depends on the network type and the carrier), there is a sudden increase in RTT which demonstrates the state promotion delay. However, when the interval is below 7 seconds, RRC state transition does not seem to affect the performance. Hence, we conclude that RRC state transition may only affect short-lived TCP flows with considerable idle periods in between (e.g., Web browsing), but does not affect long-lived TCP flows we were testing since their packet intervals are typically at millisecond scale. When the interval between packets is short, the cellular device should remain in CELL_DCH state and state promotion delays would not contribute to the extremely long delays we observed.

3. TCP PERFORMANCE OVER BUFFERBLOATED CELLULAR NETWORKS

Given the exceptionally large buffer size in cellular networks as observed in Section 2, in this section we investigate its impact on TCP's behavior and performance. We carried out similar experiments to Figure 3 but observed the congestion window size and RTT of the long-lived TCP flow instead of packets in flight. As Figure 6 shows, TCP congestion window keeps probing even if its size is far beyond the BDP of the underlying network. With so much overshooting, the extremely long RTT (up to 10 seconds!) as shown in Figure 6(b) is not surprising.

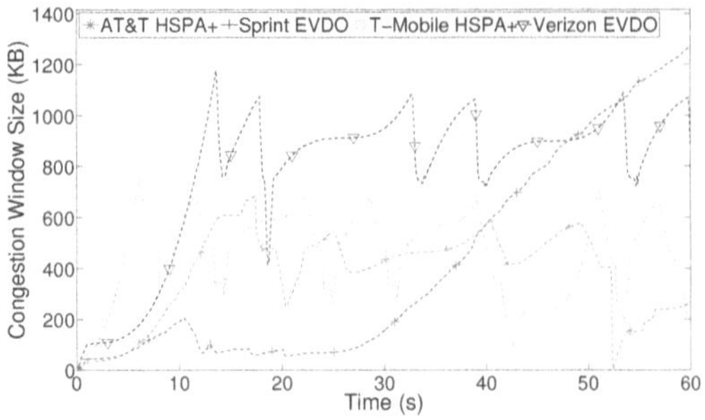

(a) Congestion Window Size

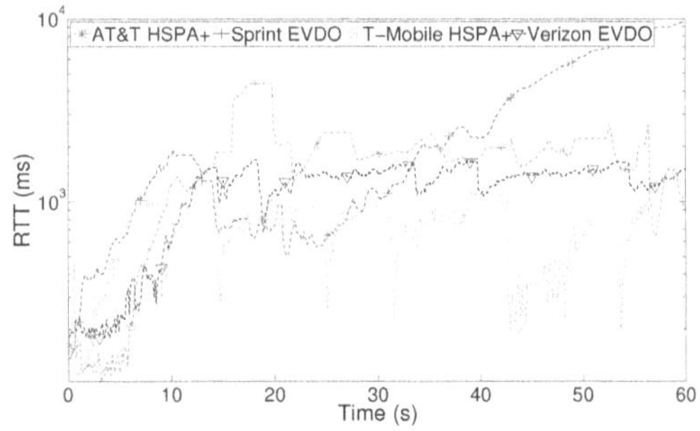

(b) Round Trip Time

Figure 6: TCP congestion window grows way beyond the BDP of the underlying network due to bufferbloat. Such excessive overshooting leads to extremely long RTT.

In the previous experiment, the server used CUBIC as its TCP congestion control algorithm. However, we are also interested in the behaviors of other TCP congestion control algorithms under bufferbloat. According to [32], a large portion of the Web servers in the current Internet use high speed TCP variants such as BIC [30], CUBIC [11], CTCP [27], HSTCP [7] and H-TCP [19]. How these high speed TCP variants would perform in bufferbloated cellular networks as compared to less aggressive TCP variants like TCP NewReno [8] and TCP Vegas [2] is of great interest.

Figure 7 shows the *cwnd* and RTT of TCP NewReno, Vegas, CUBIC, BIC, HTCP and HSTCP under AT&T HSPA+ network. We left CTCP out of the picture simply because we are unable to know its internal behavior due to the closed nature of Windows. As the figure shows, all the loss-based high speed TCP variants (CUBIC, BIC, HTCP, HSTCP) overshoot more often than NewReno. These high speed variants were originally designed for efficient probing of the available bandwidth in large BDP networks. But in bufferbloated cellular networks, they only make the problem worse by constant overshooting. Hence, the bufferbloat problem adds a new dimension in the design of an efficient TCP congestion control algorithm.

In contrast, TCP Vegas is resistive to bufferbloat as it uses a delay-based congestion control algorithm that backs off as soon as RTT starts to increase. This behavior prevents *cwnd* from excessive growth and keeps the RTT at a low level. However, delay-based TCP congestion control has its own problems and is far from a perfect solution to bufferbloat. We will further discuss this aspect in Section 7.

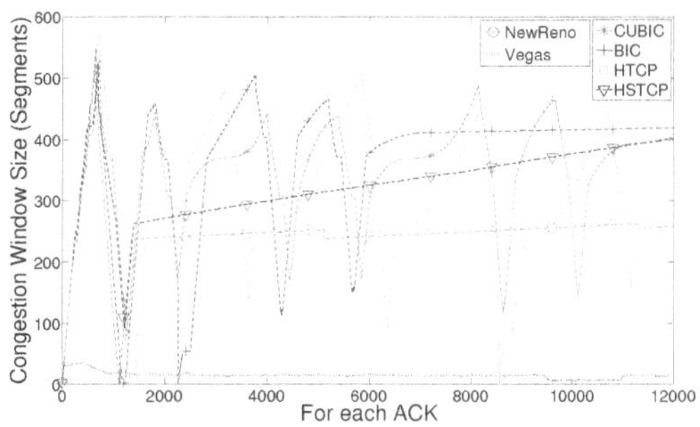

(a) Congestion Window Size

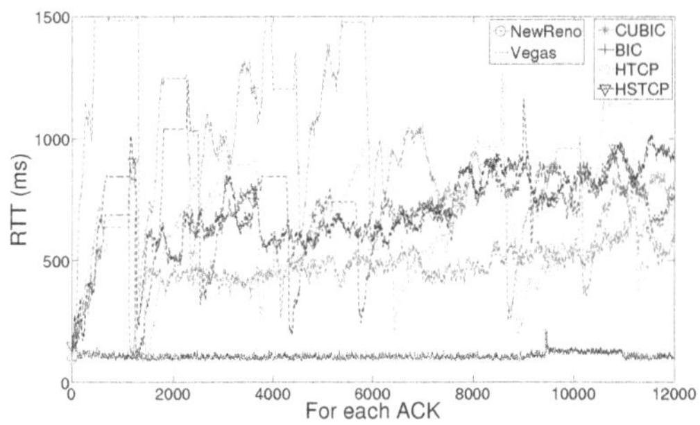

(b) Round Trip Time

Figure 7: All the loss-based high speed TCP variants (CUBIC, BIC, HTCP, HSTCP) suffer from the bufferbloat problem more severely than NewReno. But TCP Vegas, a delay-based TCP variant, is resistive to bufferbloat.

4. CURRENT TRICK BY SMART PHONE VENDORS AND ITS LIMITATION

The previous experiments used a Linux laptop with mobile broadband USB modem as the client. We have not looked at other platforms yet, especially the exponentially growing smart phones. In the following experiment, we explore the behavior of different TCP implementations in various desktop (Windows 7, Mac OS 10.7, Ubuntu 10.04) and mobile operating systems (iOS 5, Android 2.3, Windows Phone 7) over cellular networks.

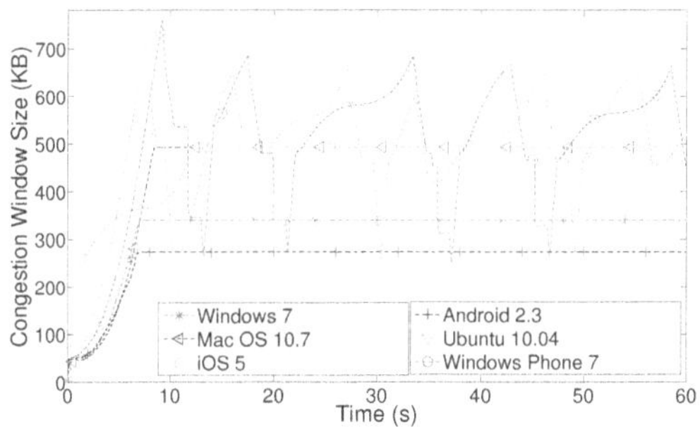

Figure 8: The behavior of TCP in various platforms over AT&T HSPA+ network exhibits two patterns: "flat TCP" and "fat TCP".

Figure 8 depicts the evolution of TCP congestion window when clients of various platforms launch a long-lived TCP flow over AT&T HSPA+ network. To our surprise, two types of *cwnd* patterns are observed: "flat TCP" and "fat TCP". Flat TCP, such as observed in Android phones, is the phenomenon where the TCP congestion window grows to a constant value and stays there until the session ends. On the other hand, fat TCP, such as observed in Windows Phone 7, is the phenomenon that packet loss events do not occur until the congestion window grows to a large value far beyond the BDP. Fat TCP can easily be explained by the bufferbloat in cellular networks and the loss-based congestion control algorithm. But the abnormal flat TCP behavior caught our attention and revealed an untold story of TCP over cellular networks.

4.1 Understanding the Abnormal Flat TCP

How could the TCP congestion window stay at a constant value? The static *cwnd* first indicates that no packet loss is observed by the TCP sender (otherwise the congestion window should have decreased multiplicatively at any loss event). This is due to the large buffers in cellular networks and its link layer retransmission mechanism as discussed earlier. Measurement results from [14] also confirm that cellular networks typically experience close-to-zero packet loss rate.

If packet losses are perfectly concealed, the congestion window may not drop but it will persistently grow as fat TCP does. However, it unexpectedly stops at a certain value and this value is different for each cellular network or client platform. Our inspection into the TCP implementation in Android phones (since it is open-source) reveals that the value is determined by the *tcp_rmem_max* parameter that specifies the maximum receive window advertised by the Android phone. This gives the answer to flat TCP behavior: the receive window advertised by the receiver crops the congestion windows in the sender. By inspecting various Android phone models, we found that *tcp_rmem_max* has diverse values for different types of networks (refer to Table 2 in Appendix B for some sample settings). Generally speaking, larger values are assigned to faster communication standards (e.g., LTE). But all the values are statically configured.

To understand the impact of such static settings, we compared the TCP performance under various *tcp_rmem_max* values in AT&T HSPA+ network and Verizon LTE network in Figure 9. Obviously, a larger *tcp_rmem_max* allows the congestion window to grow to a larger size and hence leads to higher throughput. But this throughput improvement will flatten out once the link is saturated. Further increase of *tcp_rmem_max* brings nothing but longer queuing delay and hence longer RTT. For instance, when downloading from a nearby server, the RTT is relatively small. In such small BDP networks, the default values for both HSPA+ and LTE are large enough to achieve full bandwidth utilization as shown in Figure 9(a). But they trigger excessive packets in flight and result in unnecessarily long RTT as shown in Figure 9(b). This demonstrates the limitation of static parameter setting: it mandates one specific trade-off point in the system which may be sub-optimal for other applications. Two realistic scenarios are discussed in the next subsection.

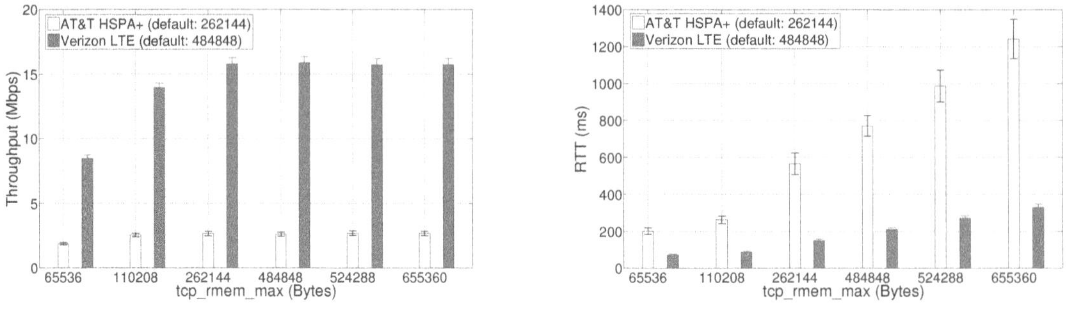

(a) Throughput (b) Round Trip Time

Figure 9: Throughput and RTT performance of a long-lived TCP flow in a *small* BDP network under different *tcp_rmem_max* settings. For this specific environment, 110208 may work better than the default 262144 in AT&T HSPA+ network. Similarly, 262144 may work better than the default 484848 in Verizon LTE network. However, the optimal value depends on the BDP of the underlying network and is hard to be configured statically in advance.

4.2 Impact on User Experience

Web Browsing with Background Downloading: The high-end smart phones released in 2012 typically have quad-core processors and more than 1GB of RAM. Due to their significantly improved capability, the phones are expected to multitask more often. For instance, people will enjoy Web browsing or online gaming while downloading files such as books, music, movies or applications in the background. In such cases, we found that the current TCP implementation incurs long delays for the interactive flow (Web browsing or online gaming) since the buffer is filled with packets belonging to the background long-lived TCP flow.

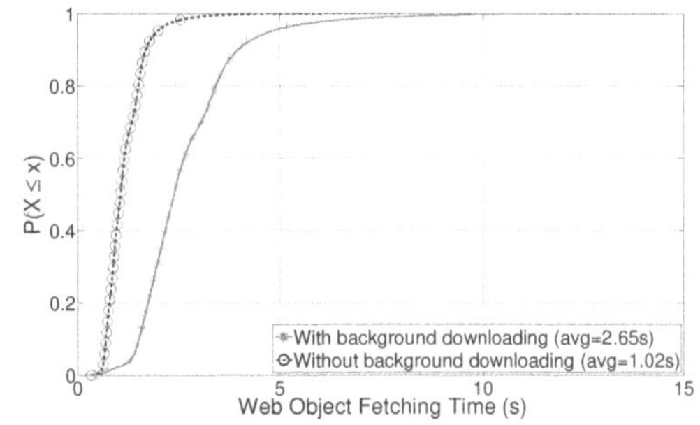

Figure 10: The average Web object fetching time is 2.6 times longer when background downloading is present.

Figure 10 demonstrates that the Web object fetching time is severely degraded when a background download is under way. In this experiment, we used a simplified method to emulate Web traffic. The mobile client generates Web requests according to a Poisson process. The size of the content brought by each request is randomly picked among 8KB, 16KB, 32KB and 64KB. Since these Web objects are small, their fetching time mainly depends on RTT rather than throughput. When a background long-lived flow causes long queues to be built up, the average Web object fetching time becomes 2.6 times longer.

Throughput in Large BDP Networks: The sites that smart phone users visit are diverse. Some contents are well maintained and CDNs (content delivery networks) are assisting them to get "closer" to their customers via replication. In such cases, the throughput performance can be satisfactory since the BDP of the network is small (Figure 9). However, there are still many sites with long latency due to their remote locations. In such cases, the static setting of *tcp_rmem_max* (which is tuned for moderate latency case) fails to fill the long fat pipe and results in sub-optimal throughput. Figure 11 shows that when a mobile client in Raleigh, U.S. downloads contents from a server in Seoul, Korea over AT&T HSPA+ network and Verizon LTE network, the default setting is far from optimal in terms of throughput performance. A larger *tcp_rmem_max* can achieve much higher throughput although setting it too large may cause packet loss and throughput degradation.

In summary, flat TCP has performance issues in both throughput and delay. In small BDP networks, the static setting of *tcp_rmem_max* may be too large and cause unnecessarily long end-to-end latency. On the other hand, it may be too small in large BDP networks and suffer from significant throughput degradation.

5. OUR SOLUTION

In light of the limitation of a static *tcp_rmem_max* setting, we propose a dynamic receive window adjustment algorithm to adapt to various scenarios automatically. But before discussing our proposal, let us first look at how TCP receive windows are controlled in the current implementations.

5.1 Receive Window Adjustment in Current TCP Implementations

As we know, the TCP receive window was originally designed to prevent a fast sender from overwhelming a slow receiver with limited buffer space. It reflects the available buffer size on the receiver side so that the sender will not send more packets than the receiver can accommodate. This is called TCP flow control, which is different from TCP congestion control whose goal is to prevent overload in the network rather than at the receiver. Flow control and congestion control together govern the transmission rate of a TCP sender and the sending window size is the minimum of the advertised receive window and the congestion window.

With the advancement in storage technology, memories are becoming increasingly cheaper. Currently, it is common

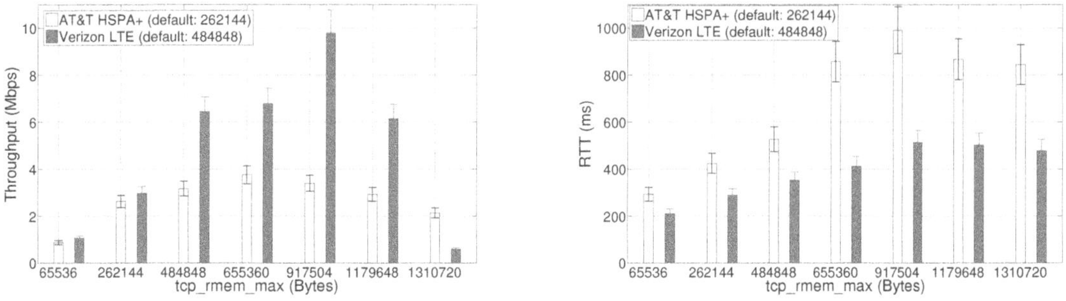

(a) Throughput (b) Round Trip Time

Figure 11: Throughput and RTT performance of a long-lived TCP flow in a *large* BDP network under different *tcp_rmem_max* settings. The default setting results in sub-optimal throughput performance since it fails to saturate the long fat pipe. 655360 for AT&T and 917504 for Verizon provide much higher throughput.

to find computers (or even smart phones) equipped with gigabytes of RAM. Hence, buffer space on the receiver side is hardly the bottleneck in the current Internet. To improve TCP throughput, a receive buffer auto-tuning technique called Dynamic Right-Sizing (DRS [6]) was proposed. In DRS, instead of determining the receive window based by the available buffer space, the receive buffer size is dynamically adjusted in order to suit the connection's demand. Specifically, in each RTT, the receiver estimates the sender's congestion window and then advertises a receive window which is *twice the size* of the estimated congestion window. The fundamental goal of DRS is to allocate enough buffer (as long as we can afford it) so that the throughput of the TCP connection is never limited by the receive window size but only constrained by network congestion. Meanwhile, DRS tries to avoid allocating more buffers than necessary.

Linux adopted a receive buffer auto-tuning scheme similar to DRS since kernel 2.4.27. Since Android is based on Linux, it inherits the same receive window adjustment algorithm. Other major operating systems also implemented customized TCP buffer auto-tuning (Windows since Vista, Mac OS since 10.5, FreeBSD since 7.0). This implies a significant role change for the TCP receive window. Although the functionality of flow control is still preserved, most of the time the receive window as well as the receive buffer size is undergoing dynamic adjustments. However, this dynamic adjustment is unidirectional: DRS increases the receive window size only when it might potentially limit the congestion window growth but never decreases it.

5.2 Dynamic Receive Window Adjustment

As discussed earlier, setting a static limit on the receive window size is inadequate to adapt to the diverse network scenarios in the mobile environment. We need to adjust the receive window dynamically. DRS is already doing this, but its adjustment is unidirectional. It does not solve the bufferbloat problem. In fact, it makes it worse by incessantly increasing the receive window size as the congestion window size grows. What we need is a bidirectional adjustment algorithm to rein TCP in the bufferbloated cellular networks. At the same time it needs to ensure full utilization of the available bandwidth. Hence, we build our DRWA proposal on top of DRS and Algorithm 1 gives the details.

DRWA uses the same technique as DRS to measure RTT on the receiver side when the TCP timestamp option [15] is

Algorithm 1 DRWA

1: Initialization:
2: $tcp\_rmem\_max \leftarrow a\ large\ value$;
3: $RTT_{min} \leftarrow \infty$;
4: $cwnd_{est} \leftarrow data\_rcvd$ in the first RTT_{est};
5: $rwnd \leftarrow 0$;
6:
7: RTT and minimum RTT estimation:
8: $RTT_{est} \leftarrow$ the time between when a byte is first acknowledged and the receipt of data that is at least one window beyond the sequence number that was acknowledged;
9:
10: **if** TCP timestamp option is available **then**
11: $RTT_{est} \leftarrow$ averaging the RTT samples obtained from the timestamps within the last RTT;
12: **end if**
13:
14: **if** $RTT_{est} < RTT_{min}$ **then**
15: $RTT_{min} \leftarrow RTT_{est}$;
16: **end if**
17:
18: DRWA:
19: **if** data is copied to user space **then**
20: **if** $elapsed\_time < RTT_{est}$ **then**
21: return;
22: **end if**
23:
24: $cwnd_{est} \leftarrow \alpha * cwnd_{est} + (1 - \alpha) * data\_rcvd$;
25: $rwnd \leftarrow \lambda * \frac{RTT_{min}}{RTT_{est}} * cwnd_{est}$;
26: Advertise $rwnd$ as the receive window size;
27: **end if**

not available (Line 8). However, if the timestamp option is available, DRWA uses it to obtain a more accurate estimation of the RTT (Line 10–12). TCP timestamp can provide multiple RTT samples within an RTT whereas the traditional DRS way provides only one sample per RTT. With the assistance of timestamps, DRWA is able to achieve robust RTT measurement on the receiver side. We also surveyed that both Windows Server and Linux support TCP timestamp option as long as the client requests it in the initial SYN segment. DRWA records the minimum RTT ever seen in this connection and uses it to approximate the

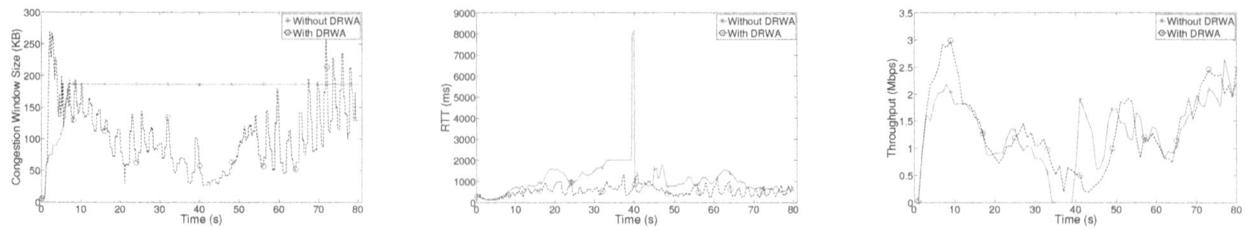

(a) Receive Window Size (b) Round Trip Time (c) Throughput

Figure 12: When the smart phone is moved from a good signal area to a weak signal area and then moved back, DRWA nicely tracks the variation of the channel conditions and dynamically adjusts the receive window size, leading to a constantly low RTT but no throughput loss.

round-trip propagation delay when no queue is built up in the intermediate routers (Line 14–16).

After knowing the RTT, DRWA counts the amount of data received within each RTT and smooths the estimated congestion window by a moving average with a low-pass filter (Line 24). α is set to 7/8 in our current implementation. This smoothed value is used to determine the receive window we advertise. In contrast to DRS who always sets $rwnd$ to $2 * cwnd_{est}$, DRWA sets it to $\lambda * \frac{RTT_{min}}{RTT_{est}} * cwnd_{est}$ where λ is a tunable parameter larger than 1 (Line 25). When RTT_{est} is close to RTT_{min}, implying the network is not congested, $rwnd$ will increase quickly to give the sender enough space to probe the available bandwidth. As RTT_{est} increases, we gradually slow down the increment rate of $rwnd$ to stop TCP from overshooting. Thus, DRWA makes bidirectional adjustment of the advertised window and controls the RTT_{est} to stay around $\lambda * RTT_{min}$. More detailed discussion on the impact of λ will be given in Section 5.4.

This algorithm is simple yet effective. Its ideas stem from delay-based congestion control algorithms but work better than they do for two reasons. First, since DRWA only *guides* the TCP congestion window by advertising an adaptive receive window, the bandwidth probing responsibility still lies with the TCP congestion control algorithm at the sender. Therefore, typical throughput degradation seen in delay-based TCP will not appear. Second, due to some unique characteristics of cellular networks, delay-based control can work more effectively: in wired networks, a router may handle hundreds of TCP flows at the same time and they may share the same output buffer. That makes RTT measurement noisy and delay-based congestion control unreliable. However, in cellular networks, a base station typically has separate buffer space for each user [20] and a mobile user is unlikely to have many simultaneous TCP connections. This makes RTT measurement a more reliable signal for network congestion.

However, DRWA may indeed suffer from one same problem as delay-based congestion control: inaccurate RTT_{min} estimation. For instance, when a user move from a location with small RTT_{min} to a location with large RTT_{min}, the flow may still memorize the previous smaller RTT_{min} and incorrectly adjust the receive window, leading to potential throughput loss. However, we believe that the session time is typically shorter than the time scale of movement. Hence, this problem will not occur often in practice. Further, we may supplement our algorithm with an accelerometer monitoring module so that we can reset RTT_{min} in case of fast movement. We leave this as our future work.

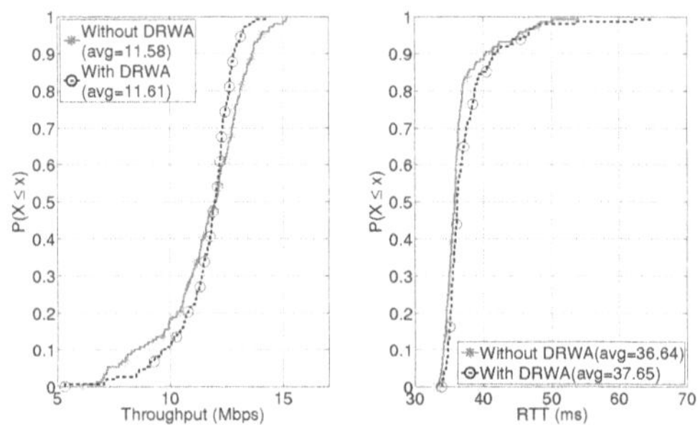

Figure 13: DRWA has negligible impact in networks that are not bufferbloated (e.g., WiFi).

5.3 The Adaptive Nature of DRWA

DRWA allows a TCP receiver to dynamically report a proper receive window size to its sender in every RTT rather than advertising a static limit. Due to its adaptive nature, DRWA is able to track the variation of the channel conditions. Figure 12 shows the evolution of the receive window and the corresponding RTT/throughput performance when we move an Android phone from a good signal area to a weak signal area (from 0 second to 40 second) and then return to the good signal area (from 40 second to 80 second). As shown in Figure 12(a), the receive window size dynamically adjusted by DRWA well tracks the signal strength change incurred by movement. This leads to a steadily low RTT while the default static setting results in an ever increasing RTT as the signal strength decreases and the RTT blows up in the area of the weakest signal strength (Figure 12(b)). With regard to throughput performance, DRWA does not cause any throughput loss and the curve naturally follows the change in signal strength.

In networks that are not bufferbloated, DRWA has negligible impact on TCP behavior. That is because, when the buffer size is set to the BDP of the network (the rule of thumb for router buffer sizing), packet loss will happen before DRWA starts to rein the receive window. Figure 13 verifies that TCP performs similarly with or without DRWA in WiFi networks. Hence, we can safely deploy DRWA in smart phones even if they may connect to non-bufferbloated networks.

5.4 The Impact of λ

λ is a key parameter in DRWA. It tunes the operation region of the algorithm and reflects the trade-off between

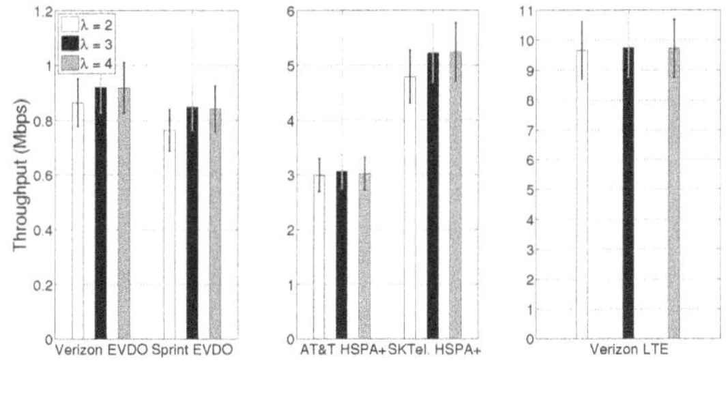

(a) Throughput

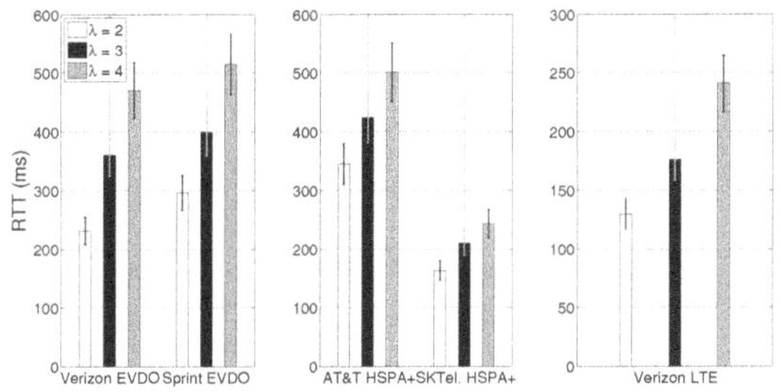

(b) Round Trip Time

Figure 14: The impact of λ on the performance of TCP: $\lambda = 3$ seems to give a good balance between throughput and RTT.

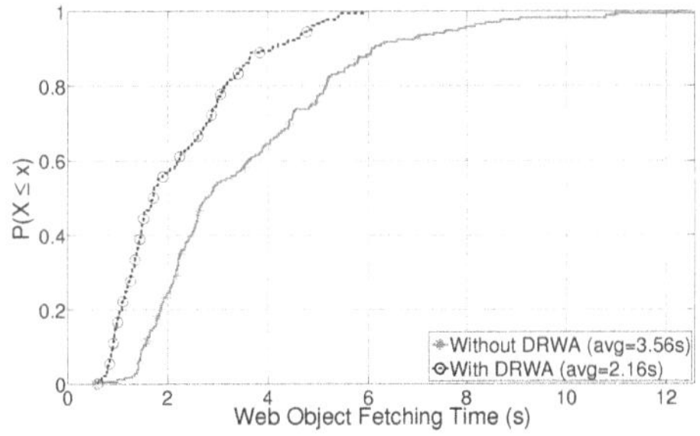

(a) Web Object Fetching Time

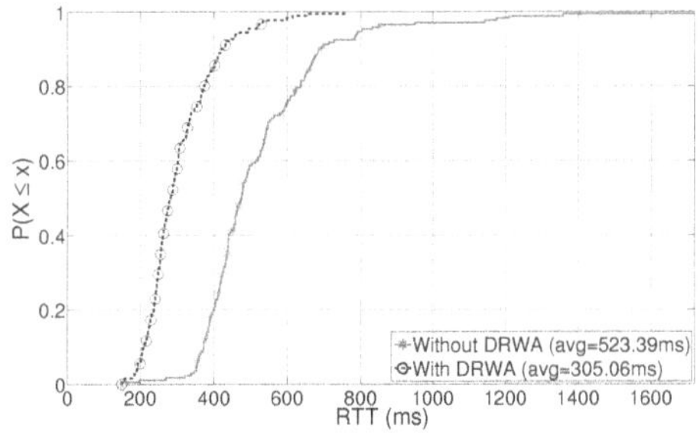

(b) Round Trip Time

Figure 15: DRWA improves the Web object fetching time with background downloading by 39%.

throughput and delay. Note that when RTT_{est}/RTT_{min} equals to λ, the advertised receive window will be equal to its previous value, leading to a steady state. Therefore, λ reflects the target RTT of DRWA. If we set λ to 1, that means we want RTT to be exactly RTT_{min} and no queue is allowed to be built up. This ideal case works only if 1) the traffic has constant bit rate, 2) the available bandwidth of the wireless channel is also constant and 3) the constant bit rate equals to the constant bandwidth. In practice, Internet traffic is bursty and the channel condition varies over time. Both necessitate the existence of some buffers to absorb the temporarily excessive traffic and drain the queue later on when the load becomes lighter or the channel condition becomes better. λ determines how aggressive we want to be in keeping the link busy and how much delay penalty we can tolerate. The larger λ is, the more aggressive the algorithm is. It will guarantee the throughput of TCP to be maximized but at the same time introduce extra delays. Figure 14 gives the performance comparison of different values of λ in terms of throughput and RTT[1]. This test combines multiple scenarios ranging from small to large BDP networks, good to weak signal, etc. Each has been repeated 400 times over the span of 24 hours in order to find the optimal parameter setting. As the figure shows, $\lambda = 3$ has some throughput advantage over $\lambda = 2$ under certain scenarios. Further increasing it to 4 does not seems to improve throughput but only incurs extra delay. Hence, we set λ to 3 in our current implementation. A potential future work is to make this parameter adaptive.

[1] We plot different types of cellular networks separately since they have drastically different peak rates. Putting LTE and EVDO together will make the throughput differences in EVDO networks indiscernible.

5.5 Improvement in User Experience

Section 4.2 lists two scenarios where the static setting of *tcp_rmem_max* may have a negative impact on user experience. In this subsection, we demonstrate that, by applying DRWA, we can dramatically improve user experience in such scenarios. More comprehensive experiment results are provided in Section 6.

Figure 15 shows Web object fetching performance with a long-lived TCP flow in the background. Since DRWA reduces the length of the queue built up in the cellular networks, it brings 42% reduction in RTT on average, which translates into 39% speed-up in Web object fetching. Note that the absolute numbers in this test are not directly comparable with those in Figure 10 since these two experiments were carried out at different time.

Figure 16 shows the scenario where a mobile client in Raleigh, U.S. launches a long-lived TCP download from a server in Seoul, Korea over both AT&T HSPA+ network and Verizon LTE network. Since the RTT is very long in this scenario, the BDP of the underlying network is fairly large (especially the LTE case since its peak rate is very high). The static setting of *tcp_rmem_max* is too small to fill the long fat pipe and results in throughput degradation. With DRWA, we are able to fully utilize the available bandwidth and achieve 23% ~ 30% improvement in throughput.

6. MORE EXPERIMENT RESULTS

We implemented DRWA in Android phones by patching their kernels. It turned out to be fairly simple to implement DRWA in the Linux/Android kernel. It only takes around 100 lines of code. We downloaded the original kernel source codes of different Android models from their manufacturers' website, patched the kernels with DRWA and recompiled

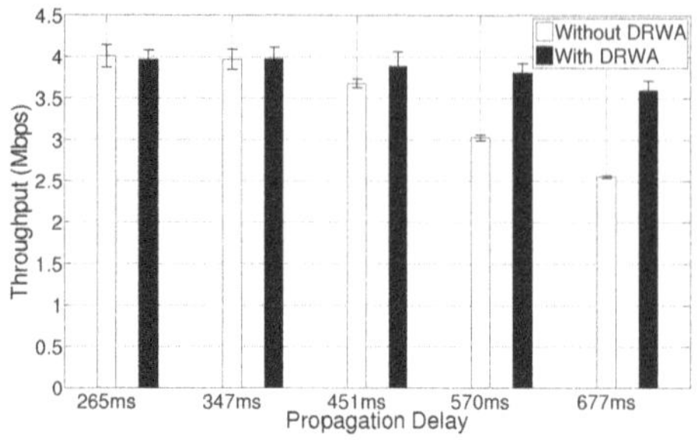

(a) Improvement in AT&T HSPA+: -1%, 0.1%, 6%, 26% and 41%

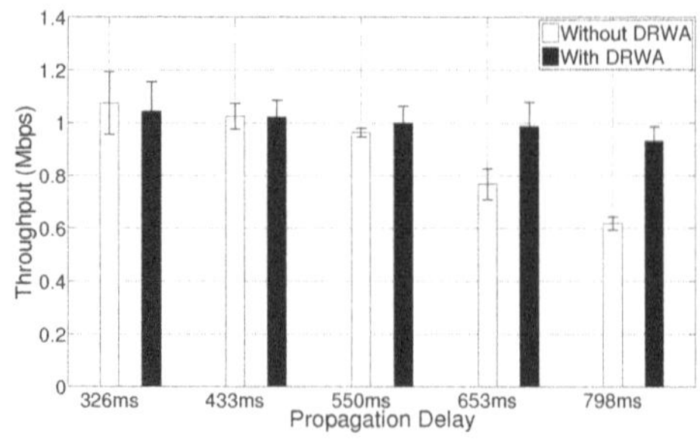

(b) Improvement in Verizon EVDO: -3%, -0.3%, 4%, 29% and 51%

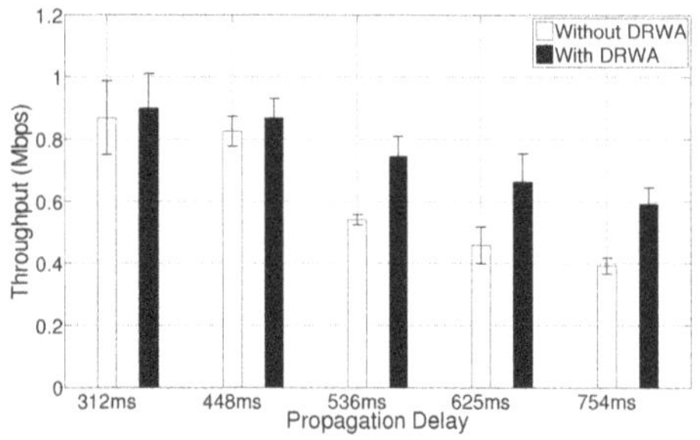

(c) Improvement in Sprint EVDO: 4%, 5%, 37%, 45% and 51%

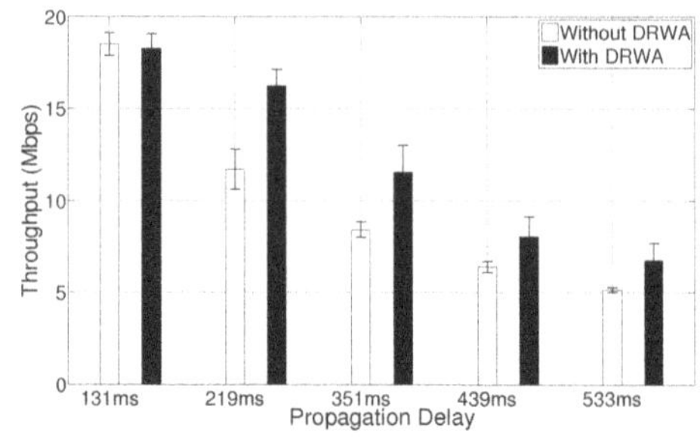

(d) Improvement in Verizon LTE: -1%, 39%, 37%, 26% and 31%

Figure 17: Throughput improvement brought by DRWA over various cellular networks: the larger the propagation delay is, the more throughput improvement DRWA brings. Such long propagation delays are common in cellular networks since all traffic must detour through the gateway [31].

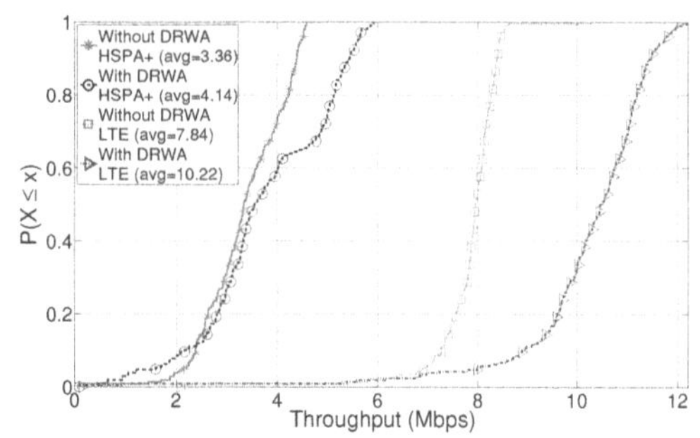

Figure 16: DRWA improves the throughput by 23% in AT&T HSPA+ network and 30% in Verizon LTE network when the BDP of the underlying network is large.

them. Finally, the phones were flashed with our customized kernel images.

6.1 Throughput Improvement

Figure 17 shows the throughput improvement brought by DRWA over networks of various BDPs. We emulate different BDPs by applying *netem* [12] on the server side to vary the end-to-end propagation delay. Note that the propagation delays we have emulated are relatively large (from 131ms to 798ms). That is because RTTs in cellular networks are indeed larger than conventional networks. Even if the client and server are close to each other geographically, the propagation delay between them could still be hundreds of milliseconds. The reason is that all the cellular data have to go through a few IP gateways [31] deployed across the country by the carriers. Due to this detour, the natural RTTs in cellular networks are relatively large.

According to the figure, DRWA significantly improves the TCP throughput in various cellular networks as the propagation delay increases. The scenario over the Sprint EVDO network with the propagation delay of 754ms shows the largest improvement (as high as 51%). In LTE networks, the phones with DRWA show throughput improvement up to 39% under the latency of 219ms. The reason behind the improvement is obvious. When the latency increases, the static setting of *tcp_rmem_max* fails to saturate the pipe, resulting in throughput degradation. In contrast, networks with small latencies do not show such degradation since the static value is large enough to fill the pipe. According to our experiences, RTTs between 400 ms and 700 ms are easily observable in cellular networks, especially when using services from oversea servers. In LTE networks, TCP throughput is even more sensitive to *tcp_rmem_max* setting. The BDP can be dramatically increased by a slight RTT increase. Therefore, the static configuration easily becomes sub-optimal. However, DRWA is able to keep pace with the varying BDP.

6.2 RTT Reduction

In networks with small BDP, the static *tcp_rmem_max* setting is sufficient to fully utilize the bandwidth of the network. However, it has a side effect of long RTT. DRWA manages to keep the RTT around λ times of RTT_{min}, which is substantially smaller than the current implementations in networks with small BDP. Figure 18 shows that the reduction in RTT brought by DRWA does not come at the cost of the throughput. We see a remarkable reduction of RTT

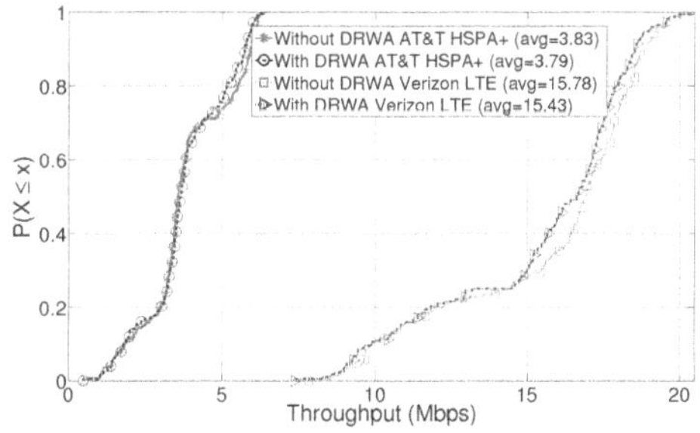

(a) Throughput in HSPA+ and LTE networks

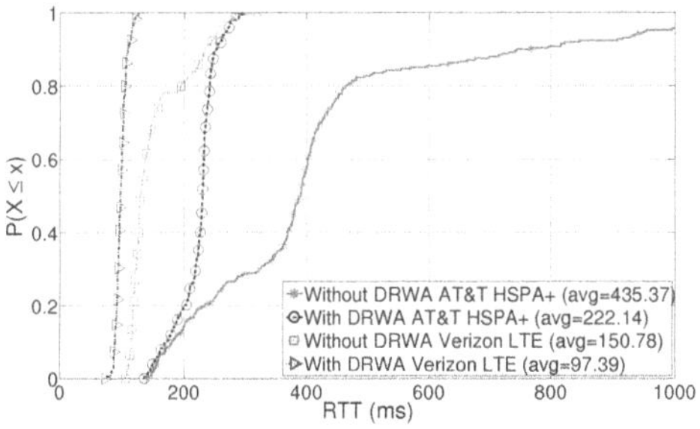

(b) RTT in HSPA+ and LTE networks

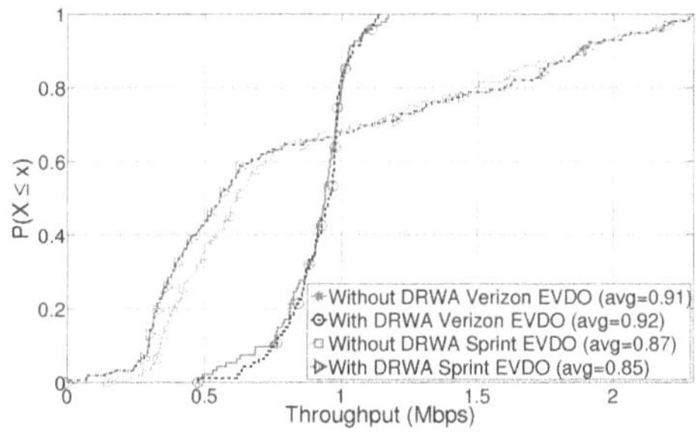

(c) Throughput in EVDO networks

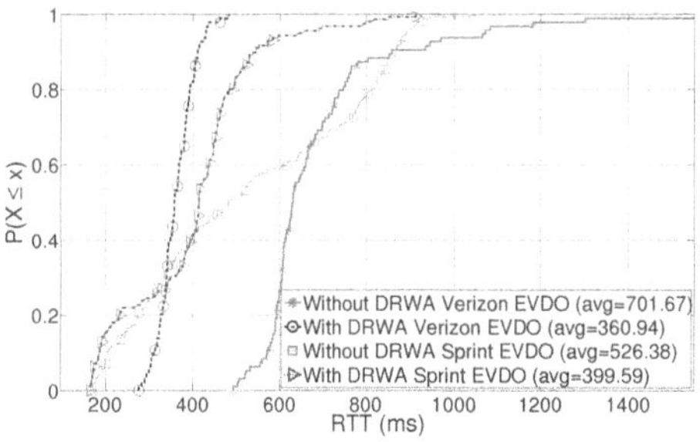

(d) RTT in EVDO networks

Figure 18: RTT reduction in small BDP networks: DRWA provides significant RTT reduction without throughput loss across various cellular networks. The RTT reduction ratios are 49%, 35%, 49% and 24% for AT&T HSPA+, Verizon LTE, Verizon EVDO and Sprint EVDO networks respectively.

up to 49% while the throughput is guaranteed at a similar level (4% difference at maximum).

Another important observation from this experiment is the much larger RTT variation under static *tcp_rmem_max* setting than that with DRWA. As Figures 18(b) and 18(d) show, the RTT values without DRWA are distributed over a much wider range than that with DRWA. The reason is that DRWA intentionally enforces the RTT to remain around the target value of $\lambda * RTT_{min}$. This property of DRWA will potentially benefit jitter-sensitive applications such as live video and/or voice communication.

7. DISCUSSION

7.1 Alternative Solutions

There are many other possible solutions to the bufferbloat problem. One obvious solution is to reduce the buffer size in cellular networks so that TCP can function the same way as it does in conventional networks. However, there are two potential problems with this simple approach. First, the large buffers in cellular networks are not introduced without a reason. As explained earlier, they help absorb the busty data traffic over the time-varying and lossy wireless link, achieving a very low packet loss rate (most lost packets are recovered at link layer). By removing these extra buffer space, TCP may experience a much higher packet loss rate and hence much lower throughput. Second, modification of the deployed network infrastructure (such as the buffer space on the base stations) implies considerable cost.

An alternative to this solution is to employ certain AQM schemes like RED [9]. By randomly dropping certain packets before the buffer is full, we can notify TCP senders in advance and avoid long RTT. However, despite being studied extensively in the literature, few AQM schemes are actually deployed over the Internet due to the complexity of their parameter tuning, the extra packet losses introduced by them and the limited performance gains provided by them. More recently, Nichols et al. proposed CoDel [22], a parameterless AQM that aims at handling bufferbloat. Although it exhibits several advantages over traditional AQM schemes, they suffers from the same problem in terms of deployment cost: you need to modify all the intermediate routers in the Internet which is much harder than updating the end points.

Another possible solution to this problem is to modify the TCP congestion control algorithm at the sender. As shown in Figure 7, delay-based congestion control algorithms (e.g., TCP Vegas, FAST TCP [28]) are resistive to the bufferbloat problem. Since they back off when RTT starts to increase rather than waiting until packet loss happens, they may serve the bufferbloated cellular networks better than loss-based congestion control algorithms. To verify this, we compared the performance of Vegas against CUBIC with and without DRWA in Figure 19. As the figure shows, although Vegas has a much lower RTT than CUBIC, it suffers from significant throughput degradation at the same time. In contrast, DRWA is able to maintain similar throughput while reducing the RTT by a considerable amount. Moreover, delay-based congestion control protocols have a number of other issues. For example, as a sender-based solution, it requires modifying all the servers in the world as compared to the cheap OTA updates of the mobile clients. Further, since not all receivers are on cellular networks, delay-based flows will compete with other loss-based flows in other parts of the network where bufferbloat is less severe. In such sit-

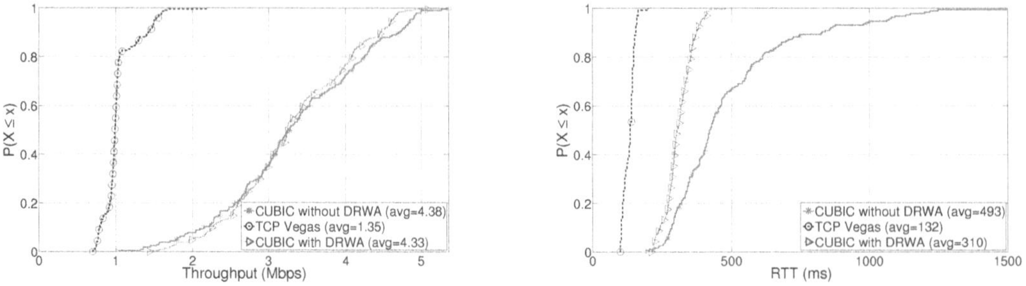

(a) Throughput (b) Round Trip Time

Figure 19: Comparison between DRWA and TCP Vegas as the solution to bufferbloat: although delay-based congestion control keeps RTT low, it suffers from throughput degradation. In contrast, DRWA maintains similar throughput to CUBIC while reducing the RTT by a considerable amount.

uations, it is well-known that loss-based flows unfairly grab more bandwidth from delay-based flows [3].

Traffic shaping is another technique proposed to address the bufferbloat problem [26]. By smoothing out the bulk data flow with a traffic shaper on the sender side, we would have a shorter queue at the router. However, the problem with this approach is how to determine the shaping parameters beforehand. With wired networks like ADSL or cable modem, it may be straightforward. But in highly variable cellular networks, it would be extremely difficult to find the right parameters. We tried out this method in AT&T HSPA+ network and the results are shown in Figure 20. In this experiment, we again use *netem* on the server to shape the sending rate to different values (via token bucket) and measure the resulting throughput and RTT. According to this figure, lower shaped sending rate leads to lower RTT but also sub-optimal throughput. In this specific test, 4Mbps seems to be a good balancing point. However, such static setting of the shaping parameters could suffer from the same problem as the static setting of *tcp_rmem_max*.

In light of the problems with the above-mentioned solutions, we handled the problem on the receiver side by changing the static setting of *tcp_rmem_max*. That is because receiver (mobile device) side modification has minimum deployment cost. Vendors may simply issue an OTA update to the protocol stack of the mobile devices so that they can enjoy a better TCP performance without affecting other wired users. Further, since the receiver has the most knowledge of the last-hop wireless link, it could make more informed decisions than the sender. For instance, the receiver may choose to turn off DRWA if it is connected to a network that is not severely bufferbloated (e.g., WiFi). Hence, a receiver-centric solution is the preferred approach to transport protocol design for mobile hosts [13].

7.2 Related Work

Adjusting the receive window to solve TCP performance issues is not uncommon in the literature. Spring et al. leveraged it to prioritize TCP flows of different types to improve response time while maintaining high throughput [25]. Key et al. used similar ideas to create a low priority background transfer service [16]. ICTCP [29] instead used receive window adjustment to solve the incast collapse problem for TCP in data center networks.

There are a number of measurement studies on TCP performance over cellular networks. Chan et al. [4] evaluated

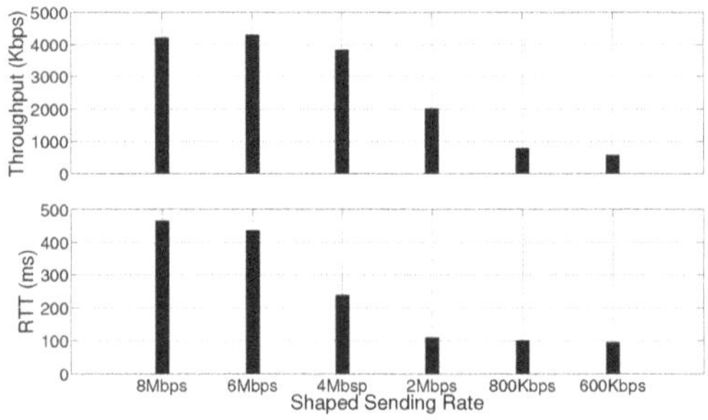

Figure 20: TCP performance in AT&T HSPA+ network when the sending rate is shaped to different values. In time-varying cellular networks, it is hard to determine the shaping parameters beforehand.

the impact of link layer retransmission and opportunistic schedulers on TCP performance and proposed a network-based solution called Ack Regulator to mitigate the effect of rate and delay variability. Lee [18] investigated long-lived TCP performance over CDMA 1x EVDO networks. The same type of network is also studied in [20] where the performance of four popular TCP variants were compared. Prokkola et al. [23] measured TCP and UDP performance in HSPA networks and compared it with WCDMA and HSDPA-only networks. Huang et al. [14] did a comprehensive performance evaluation of various smart phones over different types of cellular networks operated by different carriers. They also provide a set of recommendations that may improve smart phone users experiences.

8. CONCLUSION

In this paper, we thoroughly investigated TCP's behavior and performance over bufferbloated cellular networks. We revealed that the excessive buffers available in the existing cellular networks void the loss-based congestion control algorithms and the ad-hoc solution that sets a static *tcp_rmem_max* is sub-optimal. A dynamic receive window adjustment algorithm was proposed. This solution requires modifications only on the receiver side and is backward-compatible as well as incrementally deployable. Experiment results show that our scheme reduces RTT by 24% $\sim$ 49% while preserving similar throughput in general cases or improves the throughput by up to 51% in large BDP networks.

The bufferbloat problem is not specific to cellular networks although it might be most prominent in this environment. A more fundamental solution to this problem may be needed. Our work provides a good starting point and is an immediately deployable solution for smart phone users.

9. ACKNOWLEDGMENTS

Thanks to the anonymous reviewers and our shepherd Costin Raiciu for their comments. This research is supported in part by Samsung Electronics, Mobile Communication Division.

10. REFERENCES

[1] N. Balasubramanian, A. Balasubramanian, and A. Venkataramani. Energy Consumption in Mobile Phones: a Measurement Study and Implications for Network Applications. In *IMC'09*, 2009.

[2] L. S. Brakmo, S. W. O'Malley, and L. L. Peterson. TCP Vegas: New Techniques for Congestion Detection and Avoidance. In *ACM SIGCOMM*, 1994.

[3] L. Budzisz, R. Stanojevic, A. Schlote, R. Shorten, and F. Baker. On the Fair Coexistence of Loss- and Delay-based TCP. In *IWQoS*, 2009.

[4] M. C. Chan and R. Ramjee. TCP/IP Performance over 3G Wireless Links with Rate and Delay Variation. In *ACM MobiCom*, 2002.

[5] M. Dischinger, A. Haeberlen, K. P. Gummadi, and S. Saroiu. Characterizing Residential Broadband Networks. In *IMC'07*, 2007.

[6] W.-c. Feng, M. Fisk, M. K. Gardner, and E. Weigle. Dynamic Right-Sizing: An Automated, Lightweight, and Scalable Technique for Enhancing Grid Performance. In *PfHSN*, 2002.

[7] S. Floyd. HighSpeed TCP for Large Congestion Windows. IETF RFC 3649, December 2003.

[8] S. Floyd and T. Henderson. The NewReno Modification to TCP's Fast Recovery Algorithm. IETF RFC 2582, April 1999.

[9] S. Floyd and V. Jacobson. Random Early Detection Gateways for Congestion Avoidance. *IEEE/ACM Transactions on Networking*, 1:397–413, August 1993.

[10] J. Gettys. Bufferbloat: Dark Buffers in the Internet. *IEEE Internet Computing*, 15(3):96, May-June 2011.

[11] S. Ha, I. Rhee, and L. Xu. CUBIC: a New TCP-friendly High-speed TCP Variant. *ACM SIGOPS Operating Systems Review*, 42:64–74, July 2008.

[12] S. Hemminger. Netem - emulating real networks in the lab. In *Proceedings of the Linux Conference*, 2005.

[13] H.-Y. Hsieh, K.-H. Kim, Y. Zhu, and R. Sivakumar. A Receiver-centric Transport Protocol for Mobile Hosts with Heterogeneous Wireless Interfaces. In *ACM MobiCom*, 2003.

[14] J. Huang, Q. Xu, B. Tiwana, Z. M. Mao, M. Zhang, and P. Bahl. Anatomizing Application Performance Differences on Smartphones. In *ACM MobiSys*, 2010.

[15] V. Jacobson, R. Braden, and D. Borman. TCP Extensions for High Performance. IETF RFC 1323, May 1992.

[16] P. Key, L. Massoulié, and B. Wang. Emulating Low-priority Transport at the Application Layer: a Background Transfer Service. In *ACM SIGMETRICS*, 2004.

[17] C. Kreibich, N. Weaver, B. Nechaev, and V. Paxson. Netalyzr: Illuminating the Edge Network. In *IMC'10*, 2010.

[18] Y. Lee. Measured TCP Performance in CDMA 1x EV-DO Networks. In *PAM*, 2006.

[19] D. Leith and R. Shorten. H-TCP: TCP for High-speed and Long-distance Networks. In *PFLDnet*, 2004.

[20] X. Liu, A. Sridharan, S. Machiraju, M. Seshadri, and H. Zang. Experiences in a 3G Network: Interplay between the Wireless Channel and Applications. In *ACM MobiCom*, 2008.

[21] R. Ludwig, B. Rathonyi, A. Konrad, K. Oden, and A. Joseph. Multi-layer Tracing of TCP over a Reliable Wireless Link. In *ACM SIGMETRICS*, 1999.

[22] K. Nichols and V. Jacobson. Controlling Queue Delay. *ACM Queue*, 10(5):20:20–20:34, May 2012.

[23] J. Prokkola, P. H. J. Perälä, M. Hanski, and E. Piri. 3G/HSPA Performance in Live Networks from the End User Perspective. In *IEEE ICC*, 2009.

[24] D. P. Reed. What's Wrong with This Picture? The end2end-interest mailing list, September 2009.

[25] N. Spring, M. Chesire, M. Berryman, V. Sahasranaman, T. Anderson, and B. Bershad. Receiver Based Management of Low Bandwidth Access Links. In *IEEE INFOCOM*, 2000.

[26] S. Sundaresan, W. de Donato, N. Feamster, R. Teixeira, S. Crawford, and A. Pescapè. Broadband Internet Performance: a View from the Gateway. In *ACM SIGCOMM*, 2011.

[27] K. Tan, J. Song, Q. Zhang, and M. Sridharan. Compound TCP: A Scalable and TCP-Friendly Congestion Control for High-speed Networks. In *PFLDnet*, 2006.

[28] D. X. Wei, C. Jin, S. H. Low, and S. Hegde. FAST TCP: Motivation, Architecture, Algorithms, Performance. *IEEE/ACM Transactions on Networking*, 14:1246–1259, December 2006.

[29] H. Wu, Z. Feng, C. Guo, and Y. Zhang. ICTCP: Incast Congestion Control for TCP in Data Center Networks. In *ACM CoNEXT*, 2010.

[30] L. Xu, K. Harfoush, and I. Rhee. Binary Increase Congestion Control (BIC) for Fast Long-distance Networks. In *IEEE INFOCOM*, 2004.

[31] Q. Xu, J. Huang, Z. Wang, F. Qian, A. Gerber, and Z. M. Mao. Cellular Data Network Infrastructure Characterization and Implication on Mobile Content Placement. In *ACM SIGMETRICS*, 2011.

[32] P. Yang, W. Luo, L. Xu, J. Deogun, and Y. Lu. TCP Congestion Avoidance Algorithm Identification. In *IEEE ICDCS*, 2011.

APPENDIX

A. LIST OF EXPERIMENT SETUP

See Table 1.

B. SAMPLE *TCP_RMEM_MAX* SETTINGS

See Table 2.

Figure	Client				Server		Network	
	Location	Signal Strength	Model	Traffic Pattern	Location	Congestion Control	Carrier	Network Type
3	Raleigh Chicago Seoul	Good Weak	Linux Laptop	Long-lived TCP	Raleigh Princeton Seoul	CUBIC	AT&T Sprint T-Mobile Verizon SK Telecom	HSPA+ EVDO LTE WiFi
4	Raleigh	Good	Galaxy S2	Traceroute Long-lived TCP	Raleigh	CUBIC	AT&T	HSPA+
5	Raleigh	Good	Galaxy S2 Droid Charge	Ping	Raleigh	-	AT&T Verizon	HSPA+ EVDO LTE
6	Raleigh	Good	Linux Laptop	Long-lived TCP	Raleigh	CUBIC	AT&T Sprint T-Mobile Verizon	HSPA+ EVDO
7	Raleigh	Good	Linux Laptop	Long-lived TCP	Raleigh	NewReno Vegas CUBIC BIC HTCP HSTCP	AT&T	HSPA+
8	Raleigh	Good	Linux Laptop Mac OS 10.7 Laptop Windows 7 Laptop Galaxy S2 iPhone 4 Windows Phone 7	Long-lived TCP	Raleigh	CUBIC	AT&T	HSPA+
9	Raleigh	Good	Galaxy S2 Droid Charge	Long-lived TCP	Raleigh	CUBIC	AT&T Verizon	HSPA+ LTE
10	Raleigh	Good	Galaxy S2	Short-lived TCP Long-lived TCP	Raleigh	CUBIC	AT&T	HSPA+
11	Raleigh	Good	Galaxy S2 Droid Charge	Long-lived TCP	Seoul	CUBIC	AT&T Verizon	HSPA+ LTE
12	Raleigh	Good Weak	Galaxy S2	Long-lived TCP	Raleigh	CUBIC	AT&T	HSPA+
13	Raleigh	Good	Galaxy S2	Long-lived TCP	Princeton	CUBIC	-	WiFi
14	Raleigh Seoul	Good Weak	Galaxy S2 Droid Charge EVO Shift	Long-lived TCP	Raleigh	CUBIC	AT&T Verizon Sprint SK Telecom	HSPA+ LTE EVDO
15	Raleigh	Good	Galaxy S2	Short-lived TCP Long-lived TCP	Raleigh	CUBIC	AT&T	HSPA+
16	Raleigh	Good	Galaxy S2 Droid Charge	Long-lived TCP	Seoul	CUBIC	AT&T Verizon	HSPA+ LTE
17	Raleigh	Good	Galaxy S2 Droid Charge EVO Shift	Long-lived TCP	Raleigh	CUBIC	AT&T Verizon Sprint	HSPA+ LTE EVDO
18	Raleigh	Good	Galaxy S2 Droid Charge EVO Shift	Long-lived TCP	Raleigh	CUBIC	AT&T Verizon Sprint	HSPA+ LTE EVDO
19	Raleigh	Good	Galaxy S2	Long-lived TCP	Raleigh	CUBIC Vegas	AT&T	HSPA+
20	Raleigh	Good	Galaxy S2	Long-lived TCP	Raleigh	CUBIC	AT&T	HSPA+

Table 1: The setup of each experiment

	Samsung Galaxy S2 (AT&T)	HTC EVO Shift (Sprint)	Samsung Droid Charge (Verizon)	LG G2x (T-Mobile)
WiFi	110208	110208	393216	393216
UMTS	110208	393216	196608	110208
EDGE	35040	393216	35040	35040
GPRS	11680	393216	11680	11680
HSPA+	262144	-	-	262144
WiMAX	-	524288	-	-
LTE	-	-	484848	-
Default	110208	110208	484848	110208

Table 2: Maximum TCP receive buffer size (*tcp_rmem_max*) in bytes on some sample Android phones for various carriers. Note that these values may vary on customized ROMs and can be looked up by looking for "setprop net.tcp.buffersize.*" in the *init.rc* file of the Android phone. Also note that different values are set for different carriers even if the network types are the same. We guess that these values are experimentally determined based on each carrier's network conditions and configurations.

Breaking for Commercials: Characterizing Mobile Advertising

Narseo Vallina-Rodriguez†, Jay Shah†, Alessandro Finamore‡
Yan Grunenberger◇, Hamed Haddadi§, Konstantina Papagiannaki◇, Jon Crowcroft†
University of Cambridge†, Politecnico di Torino‡, Telefonica Research◇
Queen Mary University of London§
name.surname@cl.cam.ac.uk†, finamore@tlc.polito.it‡, {yan,dina}@tid.es◇
hamed@eecs.qmul.ac.uk§

ABSTRACT

Mobile phones and tablets can be considered as the first incarnation of the post-PC era. Their explosive adoption rate has been driven by a number of factors, with the most signifcant influence being applications (apps) and app markets. Individuals and organizations are able to develop and publish apps, and the most popular form of monetization is mobile advertising.

The mobile advertisement (ad) ecosystem has been the target of prior research, but these works typically focused on a small set of apps or are from a user privacy perspective. In this work we make use of a unique, anonymized data set corresponding to one day of traffic for a major European mobile carrier with more than 3 million subscribers. We further take a principled approach to characterize mobile ad traffic along a number of dimensions, such as overall traffic, frequency, as well as possible implications in terms of energy on a mobile device.

Our analysis demonstrates a number of inefficiencies in today's ad delivery. We discuss the benefits of well-known techniques, such as pre-fetching and caching, to limit the energy and network signalling overhead caused by current systems. A prototype implementation on Android devices demonstrates an improvement of 50% in terms of energy consumption for offline ad-sponsored apps while limiting the amount of ad related traffic.

Keywords

Energy, Advertisement, Smartphones, Traffic, Cellular, Caching

Categories and Subject Descriptors

D.4.8 [**Performance**]: Measurements

1. INTRODUCTION

Mobile application (app) markets have been a major success and adoption factor for smartphones, allowing individuals and organizations to develop and sell apps to interested users. The App Store from Apple and Google Play (previously named Android Market) from Google are the two major platforms where developers sell or freely share their apps. Both Apple and Google have played a major role in democratizing revenues related to mobile apps. In particular, considering that 73% of the apps in Google Play are free [1], it can be expected that free apps tend to obtain a larger number of downloads than paid apps[1]. The revenue model adopted by many free apps includes advertisements (ads) that are embedded in the app and displayed at various points during use. The adoption of the ad model in mobile apps has strong implications for both the users and the network. As an example, a recent study shows that 65-75% of the energy consumed in a gaming app (Angry Birds) on Android devices is spent by third party advertising modules [2].

Mobile advertising has been the focus of recent research, targeting the system design [3], energy [2, 4], and privacy aspects of ad services [5, 6]. However, there is still very little known about the ad delivery mechanisms adopted in current mobile networks. This happens primarily because existing work tends to focus on the inspection of traffic generated by a small number of popular apps. In this work, we aim to characterize and quantify ad traffic in real mobile networks. For that, we study a data trace covering one day of traffic for more than 3 million subscribers of a major European mobile carrier.

In such an attempt, we develop a methodology for the classification of ad traffic that incorporates the inspection of the SDKs provided by ad networks, traffic inspection of mobile apps, as well as rules extracted through a web log obtained from the aforementioned network. Using a rule set comprising 122 rules, we classify traffic into *i)* ad networks, *ii)* analytics, and *iii)* mediation services, and study its characteristics along a number of dimensions (traffic volume, frequency, type of content, etc.) for three major mobile platforms found in the trace. Our analysis reveals several properties of the mobile ad ecosystem:

- The mobile ad ecosystem is overcrowded and unmoderated, with AdMob and other Google services being the leaders.
- Ads are not just a strain on Android devices but are also prominent on Apple devices.
- Ads account for 1% of all mobile traffic in our data set, a significant component of the daily traffic of each device. Re-

[1]Although no ground truth data has been publicly available to confirm this conjecture.

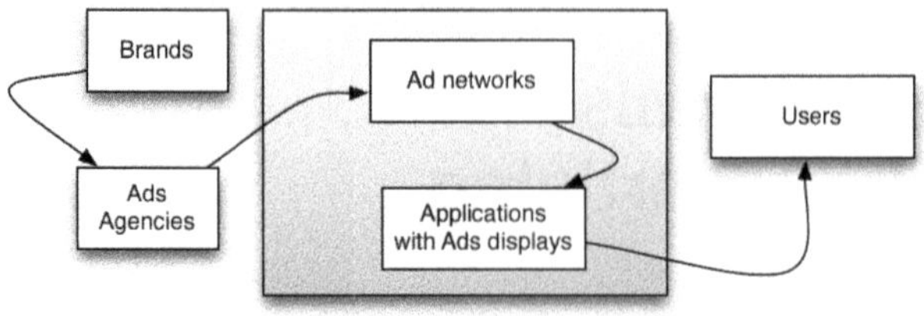

Figure 1: The mobile advertising ecosystem and the interaction of the players within it.

Provider	Retrieval Mechanism		Refresh Interval (s)	
	Push	Pull	Min	Max
AdMob	✓	✓	12	120
Millennial Media		✓	15	N/A
InMobi		✓	20	N/A

Table 1: Description of the refresh intervals and retrieval mechanisms supported by three popular ad networks.

sults show that for 3% of Android devices, ads account for more than 1 MB, while for Apple devices this is even higher and corresponds to more than 3 MB.

- Mobile ad traffic is mainly composed of *static* images and text files that are likely to be *re-downloaded*, with refresh intervals in the order of just a few seconds.
- Mobile ad traffic is the only type of network activity for some apps.

On a wired network, the transmissions of traffic can be assumed to be "free", however on a mobile network these are accompanied by control channel signalling overhead, use of scarce spectrum resources and battery implications. Low refresh intervals for downloading objects that have already been fetched previously further depletes the scarce resources of mobile networks. Moreover, solutions, such as pre-fetching and caching, are well understood in the system and networking community to readily provide solutions to a more spectrum-aware and energy-aware delivery of ads. Leveraging these techniques, we developed a system, called *AdCache*, that enables energy efficient and network friendly cache-based ad delivery, built on the intrinsic characteristics of ad traffic and mobile apps. AdCache enables the retrieval of ads under optimal network connectivity conditions for later display to the user, hence avoiding excessive energy wastage, signalling strains on the network and worsening the app responsiveness. We implement and test AdCache on Android devices and show that it is able to reduce the energy consumption of mobile advertising in offline apps by up to 50% even with a low ad refresh interval of 20 seconds.

2. EXTRACTING AD TRAFFIC

The mobile ad ecosystem, as detailed by Leontiadis et al [1], comprises multiple players: *brands* wanting to attract consumers, *ad agencies* designing ad campaigns for brands, *ad networks* used for distribution, *publishers* who create and publish mobile apps, and *users* to which ads are shown. *Mediation services* are an additional player that integrates several ad networks, allowing publishers to combine different ad networks and switch between them on the fly. Their main advantage is that they can potentially increase the publisher's revenues as if one ad network fails to return an ad at its slot, it can try another ad network to fill this gap.

Rank	Application Name	Category	Ad Provider
1	Facebook	Social Network	N/A
2	Talking Pierre	Entertainment	MobClix
3	Ceramic Destroyer	Arcade	AdMob
4	WhatsApp	Communication	N/A
5	Cartoon Camera	Photo	MobFox, MadVerti
6	Skype	Communication	N/A
7	Angry Birds	Arcade	Burstly
8	Onavo	Tools	N/A
9	Talking Tom Cat 2	Entertainment	MobClix
10	Viber	Communication	N/A

Table 2: Usage of ad networks on the top 10 most popular free mobile apps in the UK (As of 27th Feb. 2012).

URL domain	Object path	Type	Role
media.admob.com	adk-core-v40.js	Ad Net	Conf. Script
*.g.doubleclick.net	mads/gma	Ad Net	Get Ad
*.googlesyndication.com	pagead/simgad	Ad Net	Get Ad
*.googlesyndication.com	pagead/js	Ad Net	Static content
*.googlesyndication.com	pagead	Ad Net	Static content
*.g.doubleclick.net	aclk	Ad Net	Report Click

Table 3: Extract of the rule set for AdMob.

Ad networks and publishers are pursuing common objectives. Ad networks wish to maximize the number of clicks on ads through targeting the right users to satisfy the demands of the advertisers. Meanwhile, publishers are looking to maximize their revenue by increasing their click-through rate (the number of clicks on an ad divided by the number of times an ad is shown), using mediation services to fill up their advertising space, and obtain profiling information for targeting. Rather than inspecting all the relations between the players in this complex ecosystem, we focus our interest on the distribution mechanism used by ad networks and ad-sponsored apps running on the device, as depicted in Figure 1.

2.1 Understanding ad networks' SDKs

The ecosystem leverages the relative simplicity in incorporating ads in mobile app development. Ad networks provide a Software Development Kit (SDK) that enables integration of ads into mobile apps, hiding the protocol peculiarities. As shown in Table 1, popular ad networks such as AdMob, Millennial Media and InMobi allow developers to define which kind of ads are embedded, how they are delivered (push/pull techniques) and how often they are refreshed. The most common type of ad in mobile apps are banners (they are placed at the top or bottom of the screen and span its width) and interstitials (full-screen ads, covering a large part or all of the screen for a short period of time). Unlike banners, interstitials are typically shown as users transition between different activities in the app. Banners are usually composed by text, images, and Javascript code.

The protocols used by ad networks for fetching and reporting are generally based on plain HTTP requests using REST APIs, with most using HTTP GET methods. However, the ad networks studied differ slightly in the way they interact. As an example, AdMob acts as an internal mediation service to aggregate all Google's services (e.g. Doubleclick and AdSense) whereas InMobi only requires a single HTTP POST request per action. Millennial Media needs two HTTP connections with two different servers: one to get the ad, and the other one to get the associated static content.

Figure 2: Example of a real work flow for AdMob. The device incorporates the three power modes for mobile interfaces, and the transitions between them. Transport layer details are not included. The HTTP requests include the domain name and the strings used to identify the semantics in bold.

Figure 2 shows an example of a real work flow for an offline app requesting AdMob ads and the action triggered on a user click. The figure highlights the semantics of the HTTP requests (shown in Table 3) and some of the domains used by AdMob. Once a radio channel has been established, the client performs a DNS lookup and the necessary HTTP transactions. As we can see, AdMob comprises several services and the number of HTTP requests can be considerably high. A number of intermittent connections are going to be initiated depending on the refresh interval, causing costly transitions between the different radio power modes. To our benefit however, the resulting HTTP "conversations" tend to have a consistent structure, allowing one to derive a number of regular expressions that could be used in the classification of ad traffic.

2.2 Identification of ad traffic

Table 2 lists the top 10 most popular free apps on Google Play, as of 27th Feb. 2012, and the category that each app belongs to. Manually inspecting the traffic on a device, we also identified the ad networks used by each app. We can see how, only considering this small set, the ad ecosystem is highly diverse with a number of different players, potentially following different approaches in the delivery of ads.

To classify ad traffic accurately, we need to be able to incorporate such diversity. We perform such a task in two ways: *i)* by capturing traces from app execution to understand the cause-effect relationships (e.g. launching an ad-sponsored mobile app, requesting and clicking on the ad displayed), or *ii)* by inspecting traffic traces that are collected within a provider in order to identify peculiar characteristics of the traffic (e.g. hostnames or URL parameters). In the former case, we will be able to only inspect the ad delivery strategy chosen by the app publisher. In the latter case, we can further obtain information about the strategies followed by multiple publishers, as well as the diversity in ad delivery, as manifested through the use of different mediation services, and ad networks. In both cases, however, the fundamental challenge at hand is to be able to derive a comprehensive set of rules to classify the flows that are related to ad networks, mediation services, and any possible analytics traffic, that facilitates the targeting of users with relevant ads.

With that in mind, we have used four different techniques. First, we manually inspected the ad network SDKs and their documentation (if publicly available) to capture the way they use the network. Second, we installed a number of popular ad-based apps on an Android phone, and ran *tcpdump* to inspect what kind of services they use and the network traffic they generate, including the HTTP requests. Third, we created our own app that displayed an ad banner, and connected it with the most popular ad networks, to characterize the network behavior observed across a variety of ad networks. Lastly, we analyzed a trace containing all HTTP transactions car-

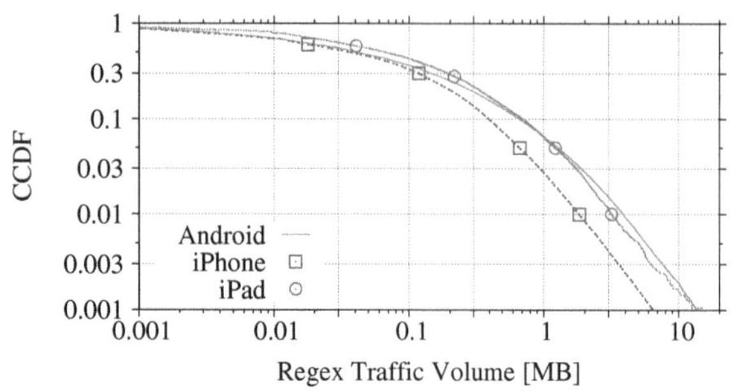

Figure 3: CCDF of the volume of ad traffic per user.

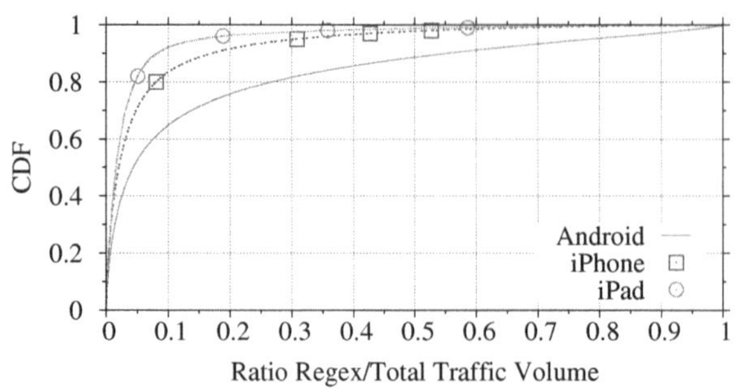

Figure 4: The fraction of mobile ad ecosystem traffic over the total traffic.

ried out by more than 3 million subscribers during a whole day on a mobile network covering an entire country in Europe. In this latter case, we made sure to filter out traffic resulting from non-mobile devices, given that the network in question allows tethering and offers 3G USB dongles that are used by non-mobile devices to connect to the mobile network.

The combination of the four processes, mentioned above, helped us obtain a set of 122 rules featuring regular expressions that are able to parse a URL and classify traffic as *i)* ad network, *ii)* analytics, *iii)* mediation service, or *iv)* other. The rule set also helps us to identify the type of action to be performed given a HTTP request. In Table 3, we show some examples of the rules obtained. Each rule, defined by a domain and URL object path, identifies the type of service, goal of the request (e.g. obtain configuration script, an ad or reporting a click), ad network and HTTP request method (e.g. POST vs. GET) used. The compiled dictionary is publicly available at [7].

3. AD TRAFFIC CHARACTERISATION

In this section we characterize ad traffic leveraging on a data set containing 1.7 billion traffic connections, which corresponds to 22TB of volume downloaded on 13th Aug. 2011 by more than 3 million subscribers of a major European mobile network. The data set comprises all TCP traffic, excluding HTTPS, seen by acceleration proxies installed on the network, that also cache and compress content for more efficient delivery. To the best of our knowledge, and according to the level of traffic at the peering point of this provider, we estimate the proportion of the secure traffic to be 11.5%.

The monitoring activity at each vantage point is reported in a set of text log files. Each entry in the logs contains a set of standard information, such as IP addresses, port numbers, number of bytes downloaded, and other HTTP specific information, such as content type, HTTP user agent, and HTTP response code. User information is anonymized but consistently hashed to a unique ID. Each line of the logs corresponds to a different TCP connection performed by a user.

The operator under study allows tethering and 3G connectivity through a USB dongle. In order to ensure that our analysis focuses on ad traffic generated truly by mobile devices and apps, we have filtered out this traffic. To achieve this we used a methodology based on the inspection of the HTTP user agent, normally including information about the Operating System (OS) of the device. All PC users, as well as those found to be using more than one OS during the day, have been filtered out from the original data set. This amount of traffic is not negligible, corresponding to 29.6% of the bytes downloaded by 7.2% of the users. This step further allows us to study ad delivery against the type of the platform used, e.g. Android, iPhone and iPad.

In what follows, we study the ad, mediation, and analytics traffic (called regex traffic for short) extracted from the sanitized mobile data set. We want to highlight that analytics services provide a standard framework to control the general activity of apps so they are not adopted in ad-sponsored apps only. However, we decided to include them in the analysis for completeness. We focus our characterization along five main axes: *i)* overall volume of ad services, *ii)* main actors, *iii)* type of ad content, *iv)* generating apps, and *v)* ad frequency.

3.1 Ad volume

Figure 3 shows the Complementary Cumulative Distribution Function (CCDF) of the regex traffic volume. While this traffic only corresponds to 31 kB per day for 50% of the devices, the distributions are characterized by their long tails. We can see how 10% and 1% of the iPhone devices download more than 400 kB and 2 MB of advertising related content respectively, while Android and iPad devices consume even more. Unexpectedly, the top 5 users together have consumed 1.35 GB, 701 MB and 124 MB just for regex traffic on Android, iPhone and iPad respectively. The single top users account for 458 MB, 167 MB and 31 MB for the three platforms.

These values might be the indication of outliers in the population. To better evaluate the weight of the regex traffic, Figure 4 reports the Cumulative Distribution Function (CDF) of the ratio between the volume of regex traffic and the total volume of traffic consumed by each user in the entire day. We can see that the traffic caused by the mobile ad ecosystem players is a strong component of the users' traffic. In particular, for 20% of iPad devices this traffic accounts for more than 4.7% of their traffic, while for iPhone devices it is 7.6%. This phenomenon is even more critical for Android users with 50% of them having more than 5% their total volume related to regex traffic.

3.2 Main actors

The regex data set contains three classes of ad traffic: ad networks, analytics services, and mediation services. These classes do not have the same weight on the aggregate volume. Table 4 reports the percentage of users, flows, and bytes for the three classes of traffic across the three most popular mobile platforms. We can see some differences across the device types. In particular, Android and iPhone present similar shares while for iPad both mediation and analytics services are less adopted. More than 90% of the volume is delivered by the ad networks, but we can also notice a sharp component of "control" traffic related to analytics and mediation services.

	%Users			%Flows			%Bytes		
Devtype	AN	AS	MS	AN	AS	MS	AN	AS	MS
Android	81.3	61.0	32.2	65.7	15.6	18.3	90.7	2.5	6.8
iPhone	77.3	60.0	23.6	65.5	22.2	12.3	89.4	5.7	4.9
iPad	88.4	35.8	13.7	87.2	6.9	5.9	96.9	1.5	1.6

AN = Ad Net., AS = Analytics Serv., MS = Mediation Serv.

Table 4: Breakdown of regex traffic with respect to class of traffic and device type.

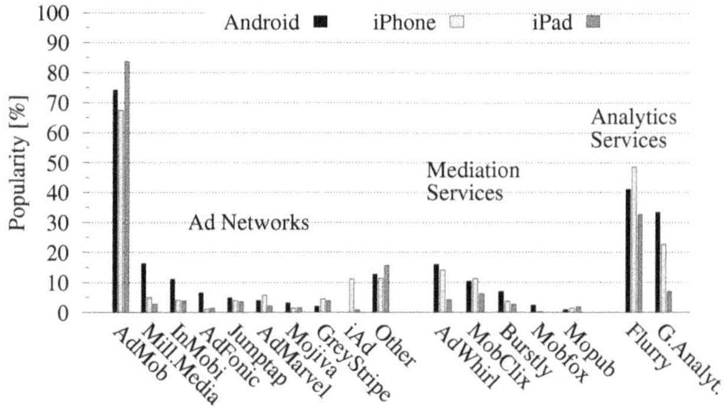

Figure 5: Ads and analytics services popularity.

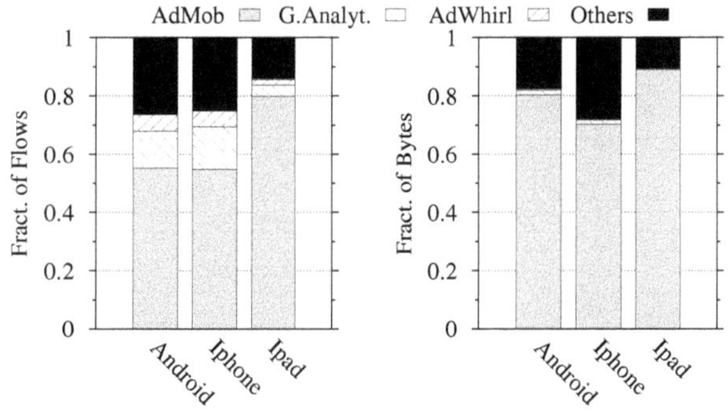

Figure 6: The fraction of flow and bytes of Google services.

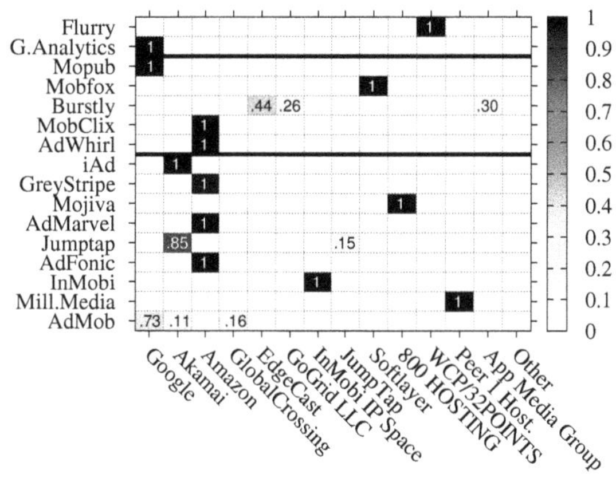

Figure 7: Distribution of the volume of each ad and analytics service among the organization contacted. The y-axis reports the ad service names sorted as in Figure 5 and the x-axis reports the set of organizations used by the ad services.

In Figure 5 we show the main ad networks, mediation and analytics services found in our data, along with their popularity (in terms of the percentage of users using them). The figure is partitioned into three areas, marking each type of service. The three different bars capture the statistics for each type of mobile platform. Services are sorted with respect to the popularity for Android devices with iAd (Apple's advertising service) added for completeness even though it is available only for Apple devices. AdMob is clearly the dominant service across all the ad networks serving 74.5%, 67.5% and 84.2% of all users. The remaining portion of the market is shared across many other ad networks with Millennial Media and InMobi leading only on Android devices. Furthermore, more than 10% of the users communicate with services outside the top 10, underlining the overcrowded nature of this ecosystem of services. Interestingly, the market share of iAd in iPad is modest, being overtaken even by smaller ad networks, such as GreyStripe and Jumptap. Mediation services are dominated by AdWhirl, MobClix, and Burstly, but in this case the differences are less significant than for ad networks.

Google's main source of income is advertising[2]. The prominent presence of Google in the mobile ad ecosystem is also clearly visible as AdMob, Google Analytics, and AdWhirl (open source but under Google's umbrella) are the dominating services. This dominance can be seen in terms of both popularity (Figure 5) and also in terms of volume and flows (Figure 6). In more detail, Google services on Android devices account for 73% and 80% of ad flows and bytes respectively whereas for iPhone devices the fraction of volume is lower due to the presence of iAd which accounts for 8% of the total bytes. AdMob's presence is even stronger on the iPad as it accounts for almost 90% of the total ad traffic on the platform.

Finally, Google Analytics and Flurry are the only two analytics services we could identify in the data set. The analysis reveals that these services are very popular across mobile apps, going beyond the values obtained by mediation services. The limited popularity of mediation services across mobile users indicates that mobile apps are more likely to interact directly with ad networks, namely AdMob, instead of relying on third party agencies. We hypothesize that this might be related to service quality, economical aspects, or implementation details, however we cannot demonstrate this with our data collection.

3.3 Type of ad content

As we schematically reported in Figure 2, ad traffic content is a combination of images, HTML and Javascript code. Inspecting the HTTP content type header field, we found that static content such as `'image/*'` accounts for 31.4%, 41.7%, and 49.1% of Android, iPhone, and iPad devices' ad volume respectively. The remaining portion is instead shared between `'text/javascript'` and `'text/html'` which are generally used to configure the client, dynamically load an ad and define its visual layout. Displaying such kind of content on a mobile app also affects performance as it requires a browser component to run completely embedded within a native app.

While images are static objects by definition, different scripts are also used to define the ad layout and behavior or client configurations, so they are more subject to change. To inspect the time variability of the content, we set up a simple experiment. We selected the top 1000 most popular objects for each device type, i.e., the content requested by the majority of the devices in the data set, with each set of objects requested once per hour from a PC over a day. Comparing the objects returned we found that for 95% of

[2] `http://investor.google.com/financial/tables.html`

Top AdMob Android Apps

Rank	App Name	Category	Users (%)
1	Angry Birds	Arcade	11.48
2	Advanced Task Killer	System Tools	9.77
3	Soccer Scores (FotMob)	Sports	3.53
4	Drag Racing	Arcade	2.69
5	Bubble Blast	Arcade	2.69

Top AdMob iPhone Apps

Rank	App Name	Category	Users (%)
1	TV Guide	Entertainment	5.96
2	Grindr	Dating	4.21
3	iFooty	Sports	4.01
4	Words with Friends	Arcade	3.51
5	Solitaire	Arcade	2.80

Table 5: Top apps requesting AdMob ads both in Android and iPhone. The right column indicates the percentage of users that had installed the app out of the total users with AdMob traffic for a given platform.

the cases there are no differences and many objects in the remaining 5% corresponds to scripts differing only because of timestamps embedded in the code, proving that ad content for mobile apps is static.

Inspecting the hostnames and server IPs we have noticed that the content is usually served through Content Delivery Networks (CDNs). For each ad service we identified the CDN/hosts they use, measuring the amount of bytes served by the CDN/host and normalizing the values with respect to the total volume of each ad service. To retrieve this information we relied on a commercial database provided by MaxMind[3] that maps an IP address to the name of the organization (AS, CDN, network operator, hosting company, etc.) that owns it. In Figure 7, we report a heat map to show the relationships between ad services and the CDN/hosts serving their content. The y-axis reports the ad service names sorted as in Figure 5. The services are grouped together according to the three classes of services previously introduced: analytics services, mediation services and ad networks. The x-axis reports the set of organizations used by the ad services. From the market point of view, the heat map is sparse, given that most ad services use a different organization for serving content. Most of the ad services are served by a single organization, except AdMob, Burstly and Jumptap, all of which balance the volume downloaded across 2 or 3 organizations. Beside Google, the only exception is Amazon which is preferred to Akamai by many ad services.

3.4 Greedy apps requesting ads

Traffic classification of mobile apps is not a trivial task. The methodologies available in the literature are usually based on the inspection of both the user agent and URL of HTTP requests [8]. However, we found these techniques inaccurate especially for Android where the user agent is usually not customized by app publishers. Considering the URLs of ad traffic, we noticed some parameters related to configuration (e.g., format and size of the ad), and tracking info (e.g., country code, GPS position) but we found also some identifiers related to the app name generating the traffic. In particular, some ad services identify apps using a hash code, the package name (e.g., *com.rovio.angrybirds*) or the real name (e.g., *Angry Birds*). While package names can be mapped to the real name using information available on the market, this is not true for hash codes which are created by the service when the publisher registers the app. Given these constraints, we decided to focus only on app using AdMob since *i*) is the most popular ad service (as seen in Figure 5) and *ii*) is the only service we found having the documentation describing the URLs parameters related to the app name[4].

[3]http://www.maxmind.com/app/organization

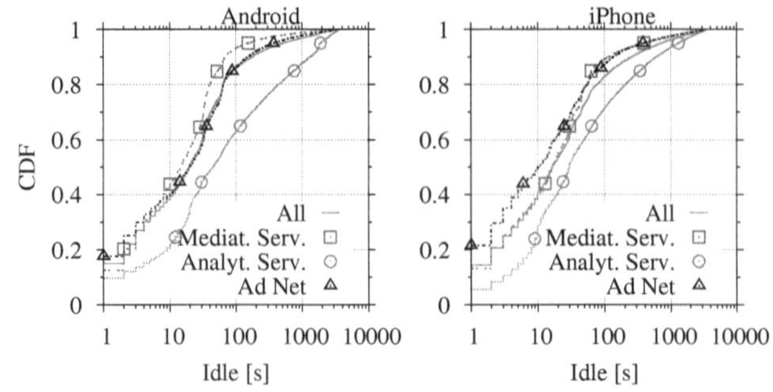

Figure 8: CDF of the interleave between consecutive activity periods.

In Table 5 we report the top 5 apps, on Android and iPhone, requesting ads from AdMob either directly using the SDK or via mediation services. For each app listed, we detail the category and the popularity, defined as the ratio between the number of devices using the app and the number of devices contacting AdMob. Most of the apps listed do not require the network access to use their intended functionality. This is the case with games such as *Angry Birds*, *Bubble Blast*, and system tools such as *Advanced Task Killer*. Other apps related to sport, TV/cinema or social networking, such as *Grindr*, instead require network access to perform properly. As we will see later in more detail, in the first case ads not only represent a "waste" in volume but they also increase the energy consumption since downloads are likely to be happening outside of other network activity.

Comparing the device types, we notice differences in the distribution of the popularity and app categories. For Android, the popularity is skewed with the first two apps accounting for 20% of all devices. For iPhone, instead the differences in the popularity are smoother. Interestingly, Angry Birds is top for Android but it is 20th for iPhone with a popularity of only 0.66%. We also noticed that AdMob served more ads to games on Android than to iPhone as eight out of the top 10 Android apps would operate offline if it did not display mobile ads.

3.5 Ad traffic frequency

Ad traffic is, by nature, periodic, and one of the important parameters controlling it is the refresh interval, i.e. how frequently the mobile app requests an ad. We have also seen that this traffic is mainly static and, given the finite catalog of ads available from a service, an object might be requested multiple times. In this section we investigate the frequency of ad traffic considering both these effects, starting from the characterization of traffic aggregates and then moving more to the details of the specific objects.

3.5.1 *Request interval*

As described in Section 2.1, different ad services adopt different protocols to deliver and manage ads. Reverse engineering is a difficult and time consuming task so we decided to opt for a more general approach to capture the frequency of the traffic grouping flows

[4]For iPhone devices the app name is usually carried in the `app_name` parameter. For Android devices it can be deduced from the app package name specified in the `msid` URL parameter.

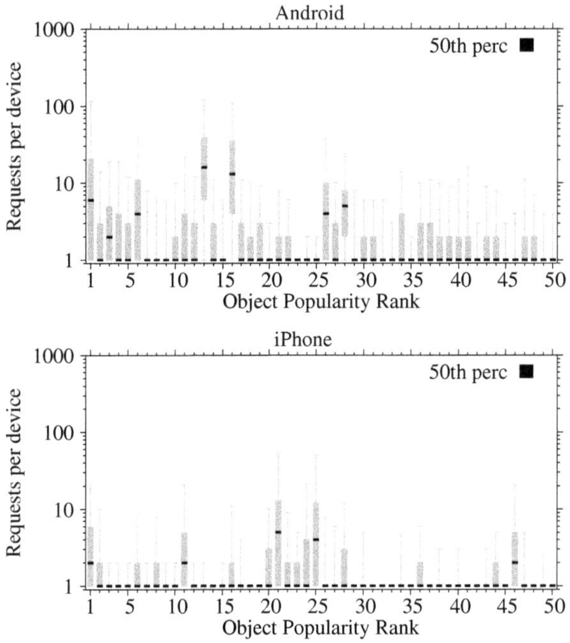

Figure 9: Box plots of the number of requests each device performs for the top 50 most popular objects on Android and iPhone devices.

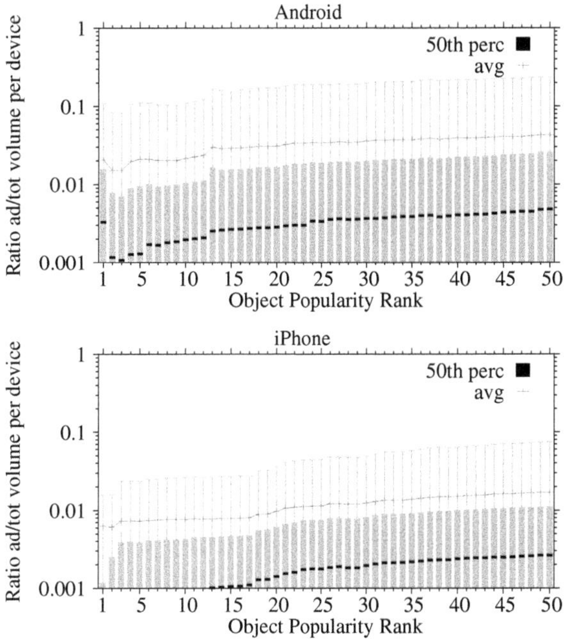

Figure 10: Box plots of the fraction of cumulated volume related to the 50 most popular objects on Android and iPhone devices.

in time: we define an *activity period* as a group of concurrent flows such that two consecutive flows *flow-A* and *flow-B* are part of the same group if $start(flow_A) < start(flow_B) < end(flow_A)$. In this way, we cluster the traffic in time and studying the interleave between activity periods gives us an indication of the traffic frequency.

In Figure 8 we report the CDF of the interleave between two consecutive activity periods. Each of the three classes of ad traffic is considered individually and we also report the aggregate for completeness. We can see that Android and iPhone handsets present similar distributions (this is true also for iPad but not reported due to its similarity) but differences emerge between the different classes of traffic. In fact, analytics services are less interactive than mediation services which typically generate multiple flows in a very short period of time as they need to communicate both with its servers and the ad network to report the action and obtain the ad respectively (as seen in Figure 2). Despite the static nature of ad traffic, 40% of the activity periods are interleaved by less than 10 seconds and more than 80% in less than 100 seconds.

3.5.2 Re-downloads

Given the static nature of ad traffic content, it is reasonable to expect that the SDKs provide some caching capabilities to limit the number of re-downloads of the objects, but instead they use standard HTTP libraries. Studying the HTTP response codes, we found that only 5% of the requests from Android devices receive a "`HTTP 304 Not Modified`" reply while this accounts for only 2% of requests from Apple devices. The limited adoption of conditional HTTP requests suggests that, in presence of multiple requests for the same object, it is very likely that it is re-downloaded.

In order to verify this assumption, for each object requested we computed its popularity as the ratio between the number of devices requesting such an object and the total number of devices that had ad traffic. For each object ranked in the top 50, we computed the distribution of the number of times such an object was requested by each device. The box plots shown in Figure 9 report the 5th, 25th, 75th and 95th percentile of each distribution. The median is equal to 1 for most of the objects but their distribution is heavy tailed. In particular, this is more notorious for Android devices, likely due to potential bugs in the HTTP libraries as reported by [9]. Nevertheless, different objects present different distributions. In particular, the objects presenting the highest number of requests (13/16th for Android and 20/25th for iPhone) correspond to requests generated by Angry Birds.

Figure 10 reports the distribution of the cumulated volume caused by all HTTP requests, to the top 50 objects, as a fraction of the total traffic generated by each device. Considering Android devices, we can see that the volume related to the top 10 objects is limited, as most of the devices have a median of 0.002%. However, the distributions are heavy tailed and for 25% of the devices the top 10 objects account for 1% of the total volume. Despite the fact that 1-2% of user volume may appear to be negligible, this fraction relates to very few objects. It is interesting that such a small set of content can have this impact of the overall traffic of a device. Moreover, this waste is not just related to volume as the unnecessary transmissions also have energy costs.

4. ADS AND MOBILE NETWORKS: ENERGY IMPLICATIONS

Most mobile devices boast a 3G network interface running on the UMTS standard, with an IP stack of upper layers protocols. In order to maximize the efficiency of spectrum allocated to these networks, each terminal (or *user equipment* in UMTS terminology) is associated with the *Radio Resource Control* (RRC) state machine that is responsible for the actual behavior in terms of bandwidth, power consumption and latency of the physical layer. While the specific parameters might have different values from one network provider to another [10], most networks define three power modes: IDLE which corresponds to no connection; CELL_DCH (dedicated

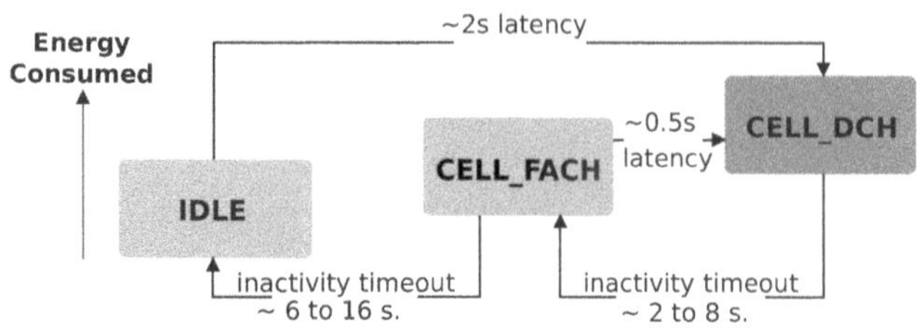

Figure 11: A common 3G wireless RRC state machine.

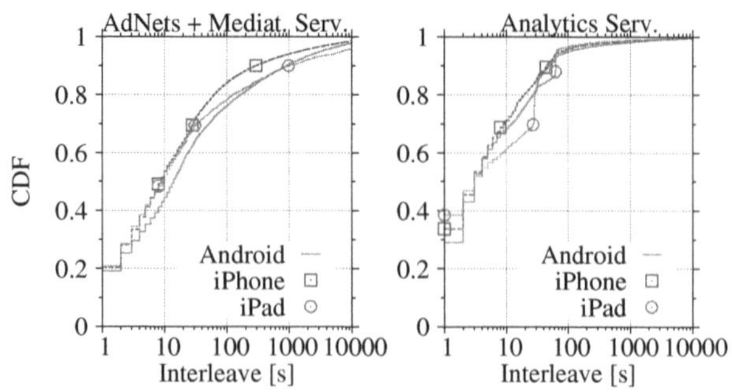

Figure 12: CDF of the interleave for each pure activity period.

channel), the highest power state with highest throughput and lowest latency; CELL_FACH (forward access channel) used to reduce the latency caused by going from IDLE to CELL_DCH in case another transmission occurs within a few seconds after the previous transmission[5]. All promotions are based on traffic volume whereas demotions are triggered by inactivity timers defined by the network operators, as shown in Figure 11.

In the previous sections we have seen how ad traffic has an intrinsic intensity due to the frequent communications between apps and ad networks, and we also observed that some requests lead to a waste of traffic as it may result in objects being re-downloaded. In this section, we will characterize and quantify the effect of ad traffic on power consumption. We start by investigating the isolation of ad traffic with respect to the RRC state machine, and then present the power consumption results obtained using an extensive set of active experiments in a controlled environment.

4.1 Ad traffic isolation

In Section 3.4 we have seen that some of the most popular ad-sponsored apps are likely to use the network only to download ads. Furthermore, a recent study revealed that 60% of the free apps in the Android market require network access against 30% of paid apps [1]. This suggests that ad traffic will likely be isolated, i.e., found when the device is not generating any other traffic. Using the concept of activity periods as previously introduced, we can define that ad traffic is isolated if the activity periods are *i) pure* - only contain ad traffic, and *ii) interleaved* - the device has been silent for some time before sending ad traffic. Due to the limitations of our dataset, the isolation factor can be only computed without including other non-TCP traffic such as DNS lookups so the results obtained represent the upper bound. Moreover, since analytics services are not strictly related to advertising, for this analysis we will consider them separately, while grouping ad networks and mediation service traffic into a single class.

We found that 81.1%, 68.2% and 69.7% of activity periods are pure for Android, iPhone and iPad devices respectively. While it is possible that some apps are actually using the network, the lower percentages obtained for Apple devices is likely due to *push notifications*, a background service characterized by persistent long lived connections used by the servers to send updates to the devices only when needed. When a device is using this service, it is common to have at least one push notification in each activity period, even if it might not generate any traffic during that period of time. This intuition is confirmed by the fact that filtering this traffic the percentages of pure activity periods increase to 78.5% and 74.3% for iPhone and iPad respectively. Interestingly, we found that 12-20.4% of the pure activity periods contains only analytics traffic, while only less than 1% has all three services. This shows that analytics traffic is not generated simultaneously with ad networks and mediation services traffic.

For each pure activity period identified, we measured the interleave, i.e. the amount of silence preceding the group of flows. In Figure 12 we report the CDF of the interleaves separating analytics services from the other types of traffic and detailing the results for different device types. Considering analytics services, we can observe that the distributions are very similar between the device types. Nearly 50% of the activity periods happen within the first 2-3 seconds from the last communication, and 94.8% within 1 minute. Instead, ad networks and mediation services present opposite characteristics. Moreover, interleaves are larger than for analytics services, with 20% of activity periods having more than 1 minute for iPhone devices, while 40% and 32% happen within 6 seconds.

We also note that for ad networks and mediation services the interleaves distribution is very similar to the results of Figure 8. Analytics services present clear differences as they are not strictly related to ad traffic. We noticed that 80% of the pure analytics activity periods are preceded by mixed activity periods, and that the opposite holds for ad networks and mediation services. Overall, we state that ad traffic is isolated and the high interleaves found indicate that the device radio is likely to be in the IDLE power mode when they request ad traffic.

4.2 Energy consumption of ad networks

The previous sections revealed several inefficiencies caused by mobile ad traffic with implications on mobile networks and the battery life of mobile devices. However, the mobile network data set does not capture the activity on the RNC or lower layer traces, so we were not able to estimate the real impact of ad traffic on the battery life from the network traces.

In this section we describe a set of active experiments run on a real device with a power meter to accurately estimate the power impact of mobile ad traffic. We take advantage of the fact that ad traffic is generally found in isolation, so there is generally no background traffic. While the traffic analysis has exhibited the presence of analytic services traffic, we have seen that the nature of this traffic is less interactive than traffic generated by mediation services and ad networks.

4.2.1 Methodology

We used a purpose-built app for evaluation, requesting ads from the three most popular ad networks (AdMob, Millennial Media and InMobi). The app only contains an ad slot at the bottom of the screen, to avoid incurring any extra CPU, I/O, and network costs. This allows us to focus the energy evaluation solely on the cost

[5]There is also an optional CELL_PCH (Cell paging channel) between IDLE and CELL_FACH.

Average current consumption (mA)

Power Mode	Mobile Network	Wi-Fi
Airplane Mode. Idle	2.1(0.1)	
Airplane Mode. Min Bright.	109.4 (0.1)	
Airplane Mode. Max Bright.	140 (1.4)	
Idle	3.3 (0.1)	5.4 (0.4)
Min brightness	110.6 (0.2)	118.6 (1.2)
Max brightness	141.3 (0.3)	149.4 (1.0)

Table 6: Average current consumption for a Samsung Galaxy Nexus S. In brackets, the standard deviation.

of fetching, displaying, and refreshing ads. The ad size used was 480×80 pixels across all networks tested (standard banners).

Measurements were taken with different refresh intervals (20, 40, 60 and 80 seconds), on 3G and Wi-Fi, each done ten times for three minutes under controlled conditions. Since we could not present detail on the amount of ad traffic potentially offloaded on Wi-Fi networks in our traffic analysis, we included the wireless interface on the energy evaluation, as many users use Wi-Fi when available. For 3G, the experiments were carried under good network conditions on a large European operator. The network type was 3G and the signal strength varied from 16 to 21 ASU (max is 31). The Wi-Fi experiments were done on a public Wi-Fi access point connected to a DSL line with background traffic. The intervals were chosen to give a good estimate of the real cost that publishers are adding to offline apps by including ads.

The popular Monsoon high-resolution Power Monitor was used to measure the current consumption by the device while running the app. To ensure that the conditions were kept constant, the brightness and volume were set to the minimum level, whereas notifications were disabled and all other apps were closed. The display is required to be active as otherwise the ads do not refresh.

4.2.2 *Baseline energy consumption*

Table 6 shows the energy costs in mA[6] for the basic power modes of a Samsung Galaxy Nexus S. These values are specific for the device used in the study, and will vary for other devices. These values aim to describe the standard configuration of a modern mobile device without any CPU and network-intense activity being executed (only basic OS activity was allowed). As can be seen, one of the most energy-intense resources is the display. The current values obtained are similar to previous experiments which tried to benchmark the energy consumption in modern mobile devices [11]. Being connected to a mobile network is more efficient than keeping the device connected to Wi-Fi APs. It should be noted that the higher variability in the results for Wi-Fi is caused by background broadcast traffic existing in the network. Wi-Fi results are highly dependent of the access point in use. The obtained results represent a worst case scenario as the energy consumption of Wi-Fi clients depends on the support of power saving mode on the access point and the characteristics of the mobile terminal itself [12].

4.2.3 *Energy cost: fetching ads under mobile networks and Wi-Fi*

The parameters that publishers can control such as the refresh interval and retrieval mechanism significantly impact the power costs. Figure 13 shows the current expenditure for different refresh intervals for the ad networks under study on both 3G and Wi-Fi. The

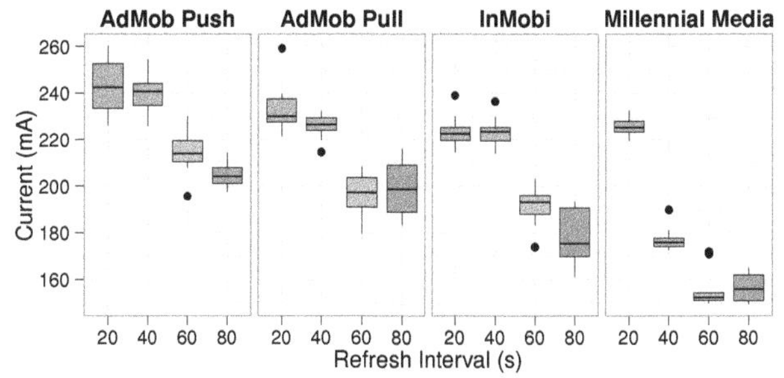

(a) Mobile Networks (3G)

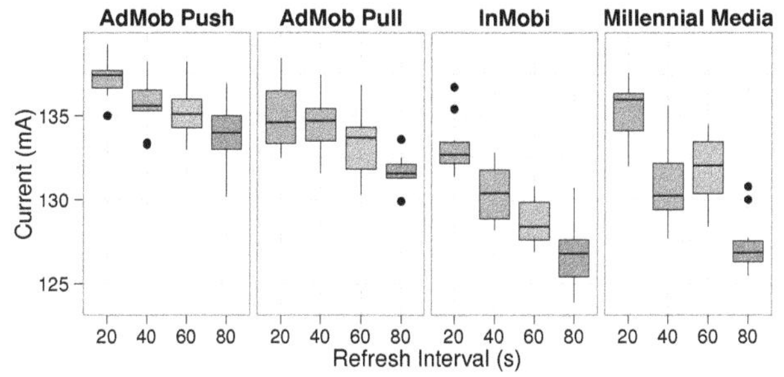

(b) Wi-Fi

Figure 13: Current drain of AdMob, Millennial Media and InMobi for banners at different refresh intervals and type of connectivity: Mobile Networks (3G) (a) and Wi-Fi (b).

results reveal that Google's Cloud-To-Device[7] push technologies can add some energy overhead due to their encryption mechanisms. Nevertheless, independently of the technology, a low refresh interval can more than double the current consumption (if there is no background traffic) in comparison to the baseline measurements described in Section 4.2.2. Importantly, the power overhead caused by the refresh interval is more notorious on 3G than in Wi-Fi due to their characteristic power models. Nevertheless, the results might vary in a real-world scenario as other apps might generate other flows that overlap, hence the power overhead is subsidized among different flows.

Using *tcpdump*, we identified that publishers' control on the retrieval mechanism and refresh interval used are not the only source of energy inefficiency on devices. Usually, the HTTP/1.1 request created by the SDK have the KeepAlive option enabled in order to fetch several objects in the same request. Even if each ad network relies on a single content provider as reported in Figure 7, different objects are usually downloaded from different servers and not transferred on a single TCP connection. In this case the KeepAlive feature is worthless and often forces the 3G radio interface to go from IDLE or CELL_FACH to CELL_DCH. This is the case of AdMob (also observed in other Google's services such as Gmail and Google Search), in which servers and clients have a connection timeout of 6 seconds, forcing the mobile interface to remain active (or even to go from IDLE to DCH) only to send TCP's FIN notification. Figure 14 shows the throughput for AdMob and Millennial Media for 3 minutes from an offline app requesting ads every 40 seconds. We can identify small throughput peaks caused by the FIN-ACK notifications in AdMob, whereas the active close used in Millennial Media presents a cleaner figure. These small

[6]To obtain power values in mW, values should be multiplied by the voltage (4V). To obtain the impact on the battery life (assuming that the app is running continuously), the battery capacity (in mAh) should be divided by the current consumption.

[7]`https://developers.google.com/android/c2dm/`

peaks can immediately cause RNC transitions and energy waste on the devices. This is the main reason behind AdMob having a higher power cost in comparison to Millennial Media and InMobi, both of which tend to close the connection immediately after the transaction is completed. Nevertheless, we have seen that when the server is the one performing the active close, as found in InMobi, it often experiences *Failure to send* `FIN` *notification promptly*. If this happens, the client will try to close the connection with the server after 1 minute (the default `fin_wait` timeout, specified in the proc filesystem) also forcing the 3G radio interface to go to a dedicated channel (CELL_DCH) in vain as the gateway/NAT in the mobile network might have closed the connection already. Millennial Media's client and server try to simultaneously perform the active close, reducing such inefficiencies. This guarantees that most of the network usage is compressed in the shortest time interval. Interestingly, AdMob and InMobi servers identify the type of network of the client to adapt the behavior of the system accordingly. The TCP connections remain open when the phone is connected with Wi-Fi despite the memory overhead for the servers required to keep an open TCP connection.

The results shown in this section are the worst case scenario for a pure offline app that does not require any network access but for displaying mobile ads. If the app is online by nature, the power overhead caused by ad traffic can be amortized whenever the app requires network access for its normal activity. However, a more detailed evaluation of the impact of background traffic requires a good characterisation of mobile traffic for different apps which is still an open and interesting research problem by itself. In the future, proposals, such as SPDY[8] from Googlem could offer better efficiency in downloading resources on the Internet by using parallelization and flow management to outperform HTTP. SPDY might present an elegant solution to the problem we have depicted here, but it will rely mostly on the global adoption of the solution in all web servers and web browsers, something proven to be difficult with previous proposals, such as WebM[9].

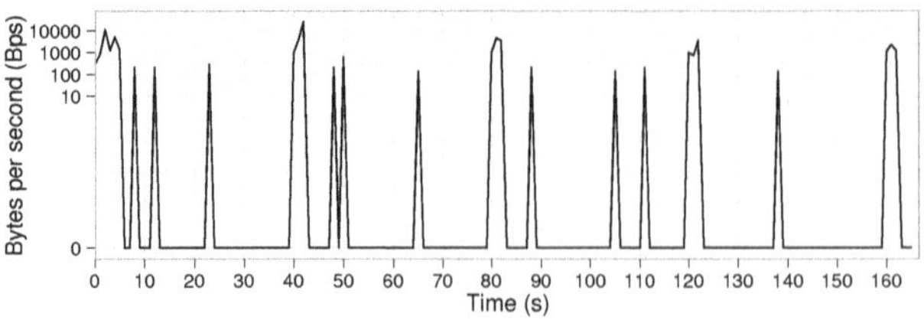

(a) AdMob

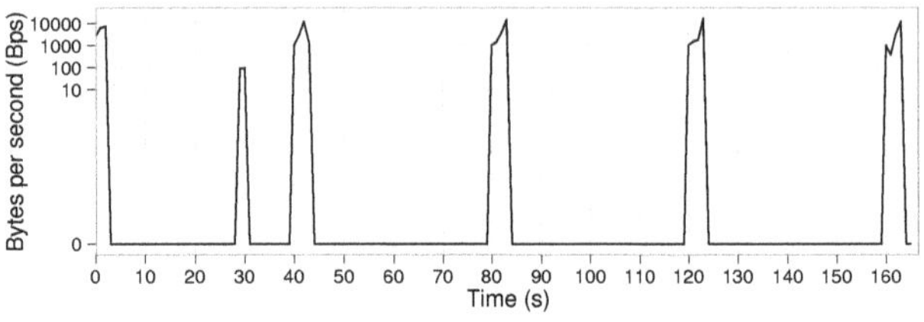

(b) Millennial Media

Figure 14: Throughput for AdMob (a) and Millennial Media (b) at a refresh interval of 40 seconds. We can clearly see the throughput peaks caused by the FIN notifications in AdMob, forcing the radio interface to change up to (or remain in) higher power states for longer periods of time.

5. EVALUATING IMPROVEMENT STRATEGIES THROUGH ADCACHE

The mobile ecosystem is maintained by a model that encourages publishers to (ab)use the features provided by ad networks to increase their revenues. Ad traffic is usually found in isolation so it forces offline apps to be online in order to obtain mobile ads. As a consequence, the volume of ad traffic per user is significant; 1% of mobile users have more than 2 MB of ad traffic per day, much of which is usually composed by objects such as images and Javascript that are constantly being re-downloaded. Such high download rates cause an important energy overhead, which is also aggravated by multi-party services and an inefficient protocol design. In Section 4.2, we observed that displaying ads on an app over a period of three minutes can more than double the power consumption at the lowest refresh interval.

Aggressive advertising strategies have pushed some users to adopt defensive strategies, for example, millions of users have installed the AdFree ad blocker app on Android. However these solutions are not ideal as they often involve changes to the `hosts` file to redirect traffic to localhost, generating firewall rules (by `iptables`) or turning off connectivity altogether. Furthermore, they are also a major disadvantage to publishers as it completely breaks their intended revenue model. The ideal solution is an ad delivery mechanism that is friendly to all the end-users, ad networks and publishers.

There are two feasible approaches to reduce the traffic volume and power overhead of ad networks: *i)* avoiding redundant transmissions and *ii)* reducing the number of transitions between the power modes in mobile networks. Conceptually, ad traffic contains static content by default, even for targeted ads. Mobile ads are not generated in real time, they are the result of planned campaigns by the advertisers mainly distributed over CDNs, as described in Section 3.3.

Based on these constraints, we designed *AdCache* for Android devices. The following sections will detail its architecture, describing the way it fulfils the requirements for state of the art commercial ad platforms and their features such as user profiling. AdCache is bandwidth and energy-aware by exploiting simple techniques such as connectivity awareness, batching and caching. Although privacy was not an initial objective, AdCache's design allows preserving users' privacy in a similar manner to MobiAd [5] and PrivAd [6].

5.1 Mobile agent

Figure 15 describes the AdCache architecture on a mobile device. As a proof of concept, the server functionality is provided by a mock ad network responsible for handling and serving the requests from the mobile clients. The mobile agent is a continuously running background service that prefetches ads into a data structure and serves them locally on requests by apps at the minimum power cost. The data structure is persistent (even when phone reboots), and is filled completely when the agent is initially started with a set of ads specified by the ad network and is then updated periodically. Ads are prefetched based on their Time To Live (TTL) value, defined by the ad network to remove outdated or invalid ads.

The mobile agent acts as the coordination point for delivering ads to apps installed on the device, making sure that no single app re-

[8] `http://dev.chromium.org/spdy`

[9] `http://www.appleinsider.com/articles/12/03/14/mozilla_considers_h264_video_support_after_googles_vp8_fails_to_gain_traction.html`

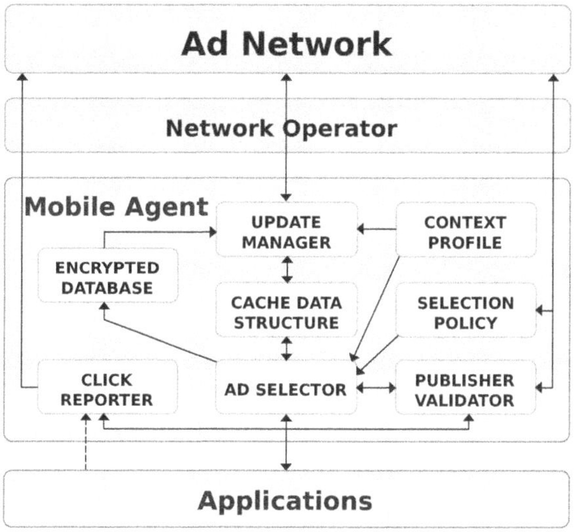

Figure 15: The AdCache architecture.

quests ads excessively and that radio access is given consciously. The ads are served according to a policy defined by the server, which is injected on the mobile agent whenever it has to be updated. Among other features, the policies assign priority to a given set of ads that takes into account the importance of some campaigns over others.

Cache updates and synchronisation tasks are event-based, triggered by satisfactory network conditions, timeouts (re-sync period set 2 hours by default but can be customized by the ad network), app requests, and expiration of all cached ads. These design decisions have three immediate effects: *i)* there are no cache misses *ii)* ads will not be pre-fetched if there are enough valid ads or there is no app demand hence reducing traffic volume and *iii)* allows AdCache to efficiently use network and energy-intense resources by exploiting batching techniques. The server also has the ability to push new ads to the client if needed.

Targeted ads

AdCache includes an opt-in profile in the mobile agent which the user is able to fully control. If they opt-in, this private information will be used by the ad network to deliver targeted ads, otherwise, standard ads will be delivered. Users' data is securely stored locally and apps do not have access to it.

For location awareness, location information is obtained using passive methods such as Android's Passive Location Provider[10] or mobile network information. In the latter case, AdCache delegates the task of performing the network positioning lookups on services such as Skyhook wireless to the server rather than adding an additional HTTP request on the device. Location is also used to update the cache. If the user is moving and there are apps requesting ads, the update interval is reduced dynamically to a value predefined by the network in order to provide more relevant ads quicker to the user if needed.

Reporting support

Statistics for the views are securely stored locally in an encrypted database. The reports are batched and uploaded to the server during cache updates rather than reporting them immediately. To avoid fraudulent actions, on receiving a message from a new publisher (based on their app package and publisher ID), the mobile agent validates the publisher's authenticity by contacting the ad network. The database is secured with tokens obtained from the ad network when starting the cache which are refreshed on each cache update. We use a dynamic token instead of a static token to avoid reverse engineering attacks. The downside of this is that if the client service is killed, the token, that had been stored in memory, is lost and the database has to be thrown away. This loss is not ideal, however it can be considered acceptable when compared to allowing an attacker (once the password is discovered) to delete and/or generate fake reports. As a consequence, user clicks are reported immediately to the server as the network interface will already be in a connected power mode when downloading the advertised content. This reduces the possibility of losing a click report if the service is stopped (unless network connectivity is not available at this time, in which case it will be cached), while also allowing AdCache to synchronize the reports and update the cache. This decision is based on the fact that click actions for AdMob (using the rule reported in Table 3) are not popular across many mobile users. Only 4.06%, 4.34% and 5.19% of the users for Android, iPhone and iPad respectively had performed at least one click on an AdMob ad. This metric should not be confused with the click-through rate, generally used to measure the success of an online advertising campaign for a particular website, and requires further investigation that we would like to explore in the future. The current consumption of performing such action on the device under study is 350 mA on 3G and 200 mA on Wi-Fi approximately.

Smart network usage

AdCache monitors the network conditions of the mobile interface (i.e., signal strength and type of network). This is done in order to temporarily defer the update if the network conditions are not ideal. In fact, the benefits of using AdCache on Wi-Fi are minor when compared to the 3G case.

When the mobile device is connected by Wi-Fi, AdCache operates like an ordinary ad network, by fetching one ad at a time as the power and network overhead is minimum. This is done so AdCache can deliver the most relevant ads to the user without any significant power cost. Nevertheless, under these network conditions, the cache attempts to prefetch fresher ads or update the metadata of existing ads which will be served once Wi-Fi connectivity is lost.

Privacy

The privacy and security issues highlighted in studies such as [1], [13] and [6] were considered. AdRisk [3] found that sensitive information accessed by some SDKs included call logs, user phone numbers and lists of all the apps a user has installed. A side effect of the AdCache design is that the permissions required for advertising are decoupled from the ones required for the intended purpose of the app. In fact, local user profiling helps to preserve user privacy as AdRisk [3] proposes.

5.2 AdCache evaluation

To evaluate the power cost of using AdCache, we used the same refresh intervals from Section 4.2.1 for three different type of ad: static banner, animated banner and text ads. A fourth case in which AdCache serves a randomly chosen type was also evaluated to emulate the behavior of existing ad networks. The animated ad type was purposely built to be particularly costly in terms of CPU usage, thus we could establish an upper bound on cost of supporting such a feature. We collected two sets of results, one where the mobile

[10]Android's PassiveLocationProvider reports location changes obtained from A-GPS or network positioning systems only if another app is actively doing so.

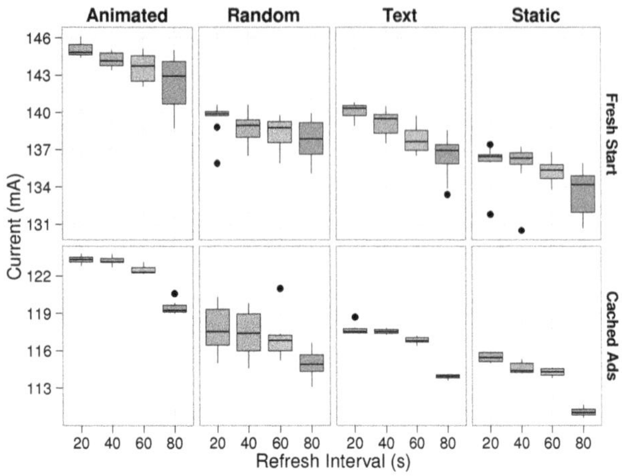

(a) Mobile Network (3G)

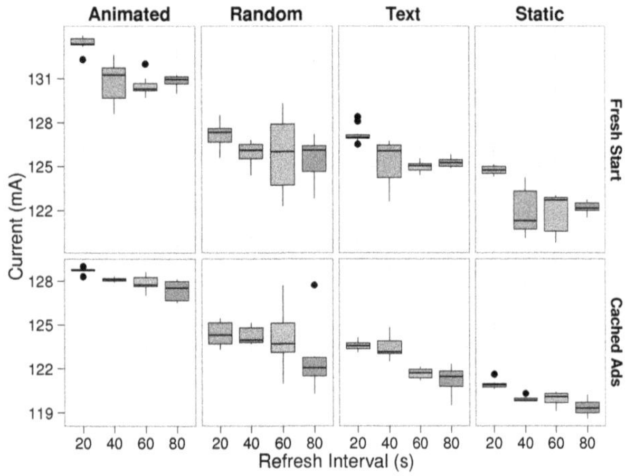

(b) Wi-Fi

Figure 16: Current drain of AdCache with different refresh intervals for animated and static banner ads, text ads and random ads under different connectivity conditions: Mobile Network (3G) (a) and Wi-Fi (b).

client has an empty cache (worst case), and the second with the cache already running and with valid ads already pre-fetched (best case). On a fresh start, 15 ads (10 image-based and 5 text-based ads) were downloaded to the device from a mock server hosted in the US. The time required to download all the ads on a fresh start varies from 10 to 12 seconds on 3G, this includes the channel allocation time.

As we show in Figure 16(a), AdCache has a significantly lower average current consumption when compared to existing ad networks (Figure 13). The power overhead compared to the baseline values for minimum brightness shown in Table 6 is small as a result of batching and pre-fetching. In Table 7, we compare the current drain of AdCache with the existing ad networks under study for the minimum and maximum refresh interval on 3G. For a 20 second refresh interval, *the power consumption is halved when compared to existing ad networks over a 3 minute period.* Interestingly, the effect of the refresh interval is not as notorious as in existing ad networks (Figure 13) where it reduces the number of network

Ad Network		Refresh Interval (s) 20	80
AdMob	Push	242.7 (12.2)	204.6 (5.5)
	Pull	233.4 (10.6)	198.8 (12.2)
InMobi		223.7 (6.8)	178.6 (12.0)
Millennial Media		225.5 (3.7)	156.4 (6.1)
AdCache *Fresh Start*	Animated	140.1 (0.6)	142.8 (2.1)
	Random	139.5 (1.4)	137.8 (1.7)
	Text	145.1 (0.6)	136.5 (1.7)
	Static	136.1 (1.6)	133.6 (1.8)

Table 7: Comparison of the average current consumption (standard deviation in brackets) for the different ad-networks with the maximum and minimum refresh intervals on 3G and AdCache if the cache is empty (worst case scenario).

transactions. For a 1,500 mAh battery, this implies that if the app was running continuously, the battery life could be extended from 6 hours to more than 12 hours. On the other hand, if the mobile agent has prefetched ads already, the ad is displayed almost instantly at a minimal power cost as I/O and CPU cost is negligible compared to wireless interfaces. Likewise, the cost over Wi-Fi (Figure 16(b)) is also slightly improved over existing ad networks. The small variability below 10 mA on the current cost for the Wi-Fi measurements is caused by background traffic. In a real deployment scenario, the current consumption can vary between the upper and the lower bounds depending on the advertising campaigns, user mobility and the expiration time of the ads.

Data plans can have relatively low data allowances, thus AdCache is also important in monetary terms for the end user. AdCache does not repeatedly download the same objects as was found with current ad networks, and also batches activity reports. In Section 3.5.2, we saw that 1% of the user's total daily traffic is wasted as a consequence of the repeated downloads of objects. Furthermore, mobile operators can also benefit from AdCache as the client communicates with the ad network less frequently, thus the amount of signalling traffic and the implications on the scarce radio spectrum in the mobile network are likely to be reduced significantly as a consequence of minimising unnecessary HTTP requests.

6. RELATED WORK

The ad ecosystem has been subject to several research studies focusing primarily on privacy issues. MobiAd [5] and PrivAd [6] suggest local profiling and ad serving in order to protect the user privacy, using a third party as an anonymization stage. In these solutions, a profiling agent receives a large selection of ads via a third party proxy, displaying those which match the user's interests. Clicks are also sent using third parties in order to keep the anonymity of the user intact. However these solutions perform a number of CPU-intensive cryptographic operations and are likely to increase communication overhead. In [1], the authors perform a large scale crawl of the Android app market based on the metadata about required permissions. They describe the mobile ecosystem based on free mobile apps and the imbalance of privacy in the ecosystem, as many apps are free and depend on targeted ads to generate revenue [14]. In AdRisk [3] the authors found that more than half the apps on the Android platform include aggressive ad libraries that download and run code from remote servers, while accessing personal information such as call logs and installed app lists.

While a lot of effort has been taken on privacy, only a small set of work focuses on performance issues and energy. In [4] the authors analyzed the mobile traffic patterns of 43 mobile users across two different mobile platforms using packet sniffers. They find daily traffic generation patterns of users and highlight the inefficiencies caused by the generally small transfer size of packets. Both [1] and [13] suggest the need to decouple the flow of information between publishers, users and ad networks to better optimize energy consumption. Eprof [2] is the first energy profiler for smartphone apps. It found that as much as 75% of the energy consumed by free apps is spent on mobile advertising.

The characteristics of the current mobile stacks and the tied relationship with energy management have been extensively studied in the recent literature. Studies cover topics ranging from the lowest level of the 3G network stack with the radio resource allocation management [10] to the highest level of the stack with the impact of Javascript and HTML code in web pages [15] on mobile devices. Other pieces of work tried to analyze the impact of middle boxes [16], along with other contributions such as [17] and [18].

Caching has been a popular solution for constrained systems and networks, specially those with poor connectivity conditions. Caching has been proposed already as an efficient way of saving energy on mobile networks [12]. In [19], the authors aim to reduce the bandwidth cost of mobile apps by proposing an HTTP proxy-based caching mechanism. They also highlight the potential inefficiencies that can be found in terms of energy. In our work, we prove the efficiency of an independent caching system using a variety of energy measurements on 3G and Wi-Fi. AdCache also provides the ability to separate permissions between advertising and app functionality, hence enabling AdCache to be a privacy-preserving profiler and advertising system.

The works described above are usually based on active experiments performed on a set of smartphones. To the best of our knowledge, this paper presents the first in-depth analysis of the ad network and mediation services ecosystem conducted on traffic from a real network. We did not limit our analysis to a single device type or ad agency, but instead we consistently compared Android, iPhone and iPad devices. We found several inefficiencies considering the wastage of both energy and bandwidth, and we designed AdCache to limit them.

7. CONCLUSION

In this paper, we undertook the first in-depth analysis of a large mobile ad traffic data set. Our findings confirm on a large scale that: *i)* ad networks impact a large proportion of users, especially on Android, but also on iPhone and iPad; *ii)* the ad ecosystem for mobile apps is mainly dominated by Google services (e.g. AdMob, AdWhirl and Google Analytics); *iii)* ad traffic can be a significant fraction of the total traffic of the users; *iv)* mobile ad traffic is responsible for important energy and network overhead by forcing offline apps to become online apps; and *v)* many of these requests are redundant due to the lack of caching capabilities in the SDKs. By taking a closer look at the popular AdMob service, we identify that the typical session of such traffic is quite short and very similar to the demotion timeouts used by the 3GPP network technology.

We identify a clear incompatibility of the current ad distribution mechanisms with the quasi-static nature of ad content. During the analysis of the data set, we have been surprised to see the impact of the user profiling traffic. We noticed a significant number of transmissions to analytic services with similar energy and bandwidth usage issues as seen in ad networks.

We demonstrate the advantages of a caching approach through the implementation and evaluation of AdCache, a first step into reducing the impact of ad traffic on battery life and controlling the traffic generated by ad networks. We demonstrate AdCache's viability in terms of energy savings to tackle the identified issues related to ads traffic. Our future objectives go along two points, first of which, we are planning to characterize the mobile ad ecosystem in greater detail, specially from an economics perspective, taking advantage of the potential of the rule set. Second, we would like to continue researching an energy and spectrum efficient ad delivery mechanism by introducing more embedded logic, enabling more offline capabilities such as user profiling, analytics support and greater fine-grained targeted advertising.

Acknowledgements

Narseo Vallina-Rodriguez is partially funded by a Qualcomm Innovation Fellowship and Alessandro Finamore by the EU-IP project mPlane funded by the European Commission under the grant n-318627. The authors would also like to thank the anonymous reviewers and our shepherd Chen-Nee Chuah (UC Davids) for constructive feedback on preparation of the final version of this paper. We also wish to thank Steve Uhlig (Queen Mary, University of London), Vijay Erramilli (Telefonica Research), Charalampos Rotsos, Steve Hand, Ilias Leontiadis, Christos Efstratiou, and Daniele Quercia (University of Cambridge) for insightful comments and feedback.

8. REFERENCES

[1] Ilias Leontiadis, Christos Efstratiou, Marco Picone, and Cecilia Mascolo. Don't kill my ads!: balancing privacy in an ad-supported mobile application market. In *Proceedings of the Twelfth Workshop on Mobile Computing Systems & Applications*, HotMobile '12, pages 2:1–2:6, New York, NY, USA, 2012. ACM.

[2] Abhinav Pathak, Y. Charlie Hu, Ming Zhang, Paramvir Bahl, and Yi-Min Wang. Fine-grained power modeling for smartphones using system call tracing. In *Proceedings of the sixth conference on Computer systems*, EuroSys '11, pages 153–168, New York, NY, USA, 2011. ACM.

[3] Michael C. Grace, Wu Zhou, Xuxian Jiang, and Ahmad-Reza Sadeghi. Unsafe exposure analysis of mobile in-app advertisements. In *Proceedings of the fifth ACM conference on Security and Privacy in Wireless and Mobile Networks*, WISEC '12, pages 101–112, New York, NY, USA, 2012. ACM.

[4] Hossein Falaki, Dimitrios Lymberopoulos, Ratul Mahajan, Srikanth Kandula, and Deborah Estrin. A first look at traffic on smartphones. In *Proceedings of the 10th annual conference on Internet measurement*, IMC '10, pages 281–287, New York, NY, USA, 2010. ACM.

[5] Hamed Haddadi, Pan Hui, and Ian Brown. Mobiad: private and scalable mobile advertising. In *Proceedings of the fifth ACM international workshop on Mobility in the evolving internet architecture*, MobiArch '10, pages 33–38, New York, NY, USA, 2010. ACM.

[6] Saikat Guha, Alexey Reznichenko, Kevin Tang, Hamed Haddadi, and Paul Francis. Serving ads from localhost for performance, privacy, and profit. In *In Proceedings of the 8th Workshop on Hot Topics in Networks*, 2009.

[7] Ad Regex Dictionary. `http://www.retitlc.polito.it/finamore/mobileAdRegexDictionary.xlsx`, 2012.

[8] Qiang Xu, Jeffrey Erman, Alexandre Gerber, Zhuoqing Mao, Jeffrey Pang, and Shobha Venkataraman. Identifying diverse usage behaviors of smartphone apps. In *Proceedings of the 2011 ACM SIGCOMM conference on Internet measurement*

conference, IMC '11, pages 329–344, New York, NY, USA, 2011. ACM.

[9] Feng Qian, Kee Shen Quah, Junxian Huang, Jeffrey Erman, Alexandre Gerber, Zhuoqing Mao, Subhabrata Sen, and Oliver Spatscheck. Web caching on smartphones: ideal vs. reality. In *Proceedings of the 10th international conference on Mobile systems, applications, and services*, MobiSys '12, pages 127–140, New York, NY, USA, 2012. ACM.

[10] Feng Qian, Zhaoguang Wang, Alexandre Gerber, Zhuoqing Morley Mao, Subhabrata Sen, and Oliver Spatscheck. Characterizing radio resource allocation for 3G networks. In *Proceedings of the 10th annual conference on Internet measurement*, IMC '10, pages 137–150, New York, NY, USA, 2010. ACM.

[11] Aaron Carroll and Gernot Heiser. An analysis of power consumption in a smartphone. In *Proceedings of the 2010 USENIX conference on USENIX annual technical conference*, USENIXATC'10, pages 21–21, Berkeley, CA, USA, 2010. USENIX Association.

[12] Niranjan Balasubramanian, Aruna Balasubramanian, and Arun Venkataramani. Energy consumption in mobile phones: a measurement study and implications for network applications. In *Proceedings of the 9th ACM SIGCOMM conference on Internet measurement conference*, IMC '09, pages 280–293, New York, NY, USA, 2009. ACM.

[13] Paul Pearce, Adrienne Porter Felt, Gabriel Nunez, and David Wagner. Addroid: Privilege separation for applications and advertisers in android. In *Proceedings of ACM Symposium on Information, Computer and Communications Security*, AsiaCCS'12. ACM, 2012.

[14] William Enck, Peter Gilbert, Byung-Gon Chun, Landon P. Cox, Jaeyeon Jung, Patrick McDaniel, and Anmol N. Sheth. Taintdroid: an information-flow tracking system for realtime privacy monitoring on smartphones. In *Proceedings of the 9th USENIX conference on Operating systems design and implementation*, OSDI'10, pages 1–6, Berkeley, CA, USA, 2010. USENIX Association.

[15] Narendran Thiagarajan, Gaurav Aggarwal, Angela Nicoara, Dan Boneh, and Jatinder P. Singh. Who killed my battery?: analyzing mobile browser energy consumption. In *Proceedings of the 21st international conference on World Wide Web*, WWW '12, pages 41–50, New York, NY, USA, April 2012. ACM.

[16] Zhaoguang Wang, Zhiyun Qian, Qiang Xu, Zhuoqing Mao, and Ming Zhang. An untold story of middleboxes in cellular networks. *SIGCOMM Comput. Commun. Rev.*, 41(4):374–385, August 2011.

[17] Narseo Vallina-Rodriguez and Jon Crowcroft. Energy management techniques in modern smartphones. *Communications Surveys Tutorials, IEEE*, PP, 2012.

[18] H. Haverinen, J. Siren, and P. Eronen. Energy consumption of always-on applications in wcdma networks. In *Vehicular Technology Conference, 2007. VTC2007-Spring. IEEE 65th*, pages 964 –968, april 2007.

[19] Azeem J. Khan, V. Subbaraju, Archan Misra, and Srinivasan Seshan. Mitigating the true cost of advertisement-supported "free" mobile applications. In *HotMobile'12*, 2012.

Screen-Off Traffic Characterization and Optimization in 3G/4G Networks

Junxian Huang
University of Michigan

Feng Qian
University of Michigan

Z. Morley Mao
University of Michigan

Subhabrata Sen
AT&T Labs - Research

Oliver Spatscheck
AT&T Labs - Research

ABSTRACT

Today's cellular systems operate under diverse resource constraints: limited frequency spectrum, network processing capability, and handset battery life. We consider a novel and important factor, handset *screen status*, *i.e.*, whether the screen is on or off, which was ignored by previous approaches for optimizing cellular resource utilization. Based on analyzing real smartphone traffic collected from 20 users over five months, we find that off-screen traffic accounts for 58.5% of the total radio energy consumption although their traffic volume contribution is much smaller. Such unexpected results are attributed to the unique cellular resource management policy that is not well understood by developers, leading to cellular-unfriendly mobile apps. We then make a further step by proposing *screen-aware* optimization, by leveraging the key observation that screen-off traffic is much more delay-tolerant than its screen-on counterpart due to a lack of user interaction. Our proposal can better balance the key tradeoffs in cellular networks. It saves up to 60.92% of the network energy and reduces signaling and delay overhead by 25.33% and 30.59%, respectively.

Categories and Subject Descriptors

C.2.1 [**Network Architecture and Design**]: wireless communication; C.4 [**Performance of Systems**]: design studies, performance attributes

Keywords

Screen-off traffic, cellular network, traffic optimization, fast dormancy, batching, LTE, radio resource optimization

1. INTRODUCTION

Smartphones with cellular data access have become increasingly popular across the globe, with the wide deployment of 3G and emerging LTE [1] networks, and a plethora of applications of all kinds. Cellular networks are typically characterized by limited radio resources and significant device power consumption for network communications. The battery capacity of smartphones cannot be easily improved due to physical constraints in size and weight. Hence, battery life remains a key determinant of end-user experience. Given the limited radio resources in these networks and device battery capacity constraints, optimizing the usage of these resources is critical for cellular carriers and application developers.

In 3G and 4G cellular networks, the user equipment (UE) must stay in a high-power state, occupying radio resources for some required time before the allocated resource is released by the network, and then the UE enters a low power state. This required time period, also known as the Radio Resource Control (RRC) tail [6], is necessary and important for cellular networks to prevent frequent state promotions (resource allocation), which can cause unacceptably long delays for the UE, as well as additional processing overheads for the radio access network [4, 12]. Today's cellular carriers use a static and conservative setting of the tail time in the order of many seconds, and previous studies have revealed this tail time to be the root cause of energy and radio resource inefficiencies in both 3G [15, 6, 11, 7] and 4G networks [9]. Various optimization solutions have been proposed to address this problem, *e.g.*, the use of fast dormancy [2, 3, 16] and client-side traffic shaping and scheduling [14, 18, 6]. In addition, specialized energy saving techniques for mobile applications have been proposed for specific applications [21, 10] and for specific protocols [5].

In this paper we consider a novel angle to the above problem and explore the impact of **screen status**, *i.e.*, whether the screen is on or off, on the device's network traffic patterns. The screen status is easy to monitor for most mobile OSes. We propose that the screen-off traffic should not be treated the same as the screen-on traffic for traffic optimization purposes, and the former can be optimized more aggressively. The main intuition is that the user (and possibly application) behavior have significant differences when the screen is on *v.s.* off, resulting in different traffic patterns and different performance requirements. When the screen is off, there is a much higher chance that the user is not actively interacting with the device and the network traffic is most likely to be more delay tolerant. Hence we can be more aggressive in optimizing this traffic using techniques such as batching and fast dormancy. In contrast, when the screen is on, it is harder to predict the delay sensitivity of the network traffic and aggressive optimizations may harm the user experience. To validate this intuition, we characterize the screen-off traffic for a real-world user data set and evaluate the benefits of us-

IMC'12, November 14–16, 2012, Boston, Massachusetts, USA.

ing "screen-aware" optimization for balancing UE energy savings and the resulting overheads in radio resource usage and response delay.

The proposed screen-aware optimization focuses on the overall device traffic, and is complementary to other efficiency improvement efforts, *e.g.*, better application design. While it is important for individual mobile applications to be better designed, the power state on a device is a function of the traffic pattern across all the running applications. Another advantage is that the approach works across both optimized and unoptimized (*e.g.*, legacy) applications.

The main contributions of this study are as follows:

- We perform the first characterization of screen-off traffic using 20 smartphone users' traffic over a 5 month interval. We compare the differences between screen-off and -on traffic patterns, both overall and for different individual applications.

- We find that although the number of packets and total payload for screen-off traffic are smaller than that of screen-on traffic, the former accounts for a disproportionate majority of the total network energy consumed by a device - 58.55% for all users, and up to 73.53% for some user.

- Evaluating various optimization techniques using an LTE RRC state machine energy model, we find that fast dormancy, for the same parameter settings, generates more energy savings and less signaling/delay overhead for screen-off traffic, compared with that for screen-on traffic. This can be attributed to the different traffic patterns for the two traffic classes. In total, the screen-aware optimization achieves 60.92% energy savings, 25.33% reduction in signaling overhead, and 30.59% reduction in channel scheduling delays, compared with the default smartphone settings.

2. METHODOLOGY

We next describe the data set used in this study, the burst analysis methodology, as well as the network and power simulation methodology.

2.1 UMICH data set

The UMICH data set [9] totals 118 GB and consists of five-month (05/12/2011 $\sim$ 10/12/2011) data (both cellular and WiFi) from 20 volunteers who used smartphones running Android 2.2. There are three types of data: *(i)* packet traces in **tcpdump** format including both headers and payload, *(ii)* the process name responsible for sending or receiving each packet, using the method described in [17] by correlating the socket, inode, and process ID in Android in realtime, and *(iii)* screen on/off status data with a sampling rate of $1Hz$. We strictly follow an anonymous analysis procedure to protect the users' privacy.

In order to associate individual packets with their screen status, we define a time window $[t_1, t_2]$ to be a screen-on (or screen-off, respectively) window if "all" the screen samples in this window have screen-on (or screen-off) status. Then we classify a packet as either screen-on or off if its timestamp falls respectively into any screen-on or screen-off window, and unknown otherwise. One reason for the occurrence of the unknown category is data collection errors.

2.2 Burst Analysis Methodology

In order to understand the screen-off traffic pattern and its impact on radio resource and device energy, we use the following traffic model for burst analysis. Intuitively, a burst is a continuous data transfer with preceding and succeeding idle times. For each user, the traffic trace is a sequence of network packets, $P_i (1 \leq i \leq n)$. Notice that P_i could be either downlink or uplink. If the timestamp of P_i is defined to be t_i, we have $t_i \leq t_j$ for any $i < j$. Using a burst threshold **BT**, the packets are divided into ***bursts***, *i.e.*, $\{P_p, P_{p+1}, \cdots, P_q\}$ belongs to a burst B, if and only if: *i)* $t_{k+1} - t_k \leq$ **BT** for any $k \in \{p, \cdots, q-1\}$, *ii)* $t_{q+1} - t_q >$ **BT** and *iii)* $t_p - t_{p-1} >$ **BT**. We define the inter-burst time **IBT** for burst B to be the time gap following this burst, *i.e.*, $t_{q+1} - t_q$. In this paper, we empirically choose to use **BT** = 2 seconds, which is validated to be larger than most packet gaps for 3G/4G networks within a continuous data transfer, such as downloading a web object.

2.3 LTE Network and Power Simulation Methodology

For evaluating optimization performance, we rely on network and power simulations. In this paper, we focus on the emerging LTE cellular technology to understand the energy and radio resource overhead of a particular packet trace. However, since there are important similarities in the network and power models for the LTE and 3G UMTS networks [8, 13, 19], *e.g.*, distinct energy states with very different power consumptions, long tail times *etc.*, the overall conclusions apply to 3G as well.

Specifically, we use the LTE 4G network and power simulation model, as well as three important performance metrics E, S and D, detailed in our earlier work [9]. E is the total UE network energy - the energy consumed by the device's cellular network interface. A previous study [20] indicates that this network energy typically accounts for a third of the energy drain on the phone. Given that E is larger when the allocated radio resource is occupied by the UE for a longer duration, reducing E is aligned with reducing the total radio resource occupation time. S is defined to be the signaling overhead, *i.e.*, the number of RRC promotions from **RRC_IDLE** (the idle state for LTE) to **RRC_CONNECTED** (the high-power state for LTE) triggered by the packets in a specific trace. Such state transitions cause significant signaling loads on the RAN and reducing this overhead is therefore important. D is the user-perceived channel scheduling delay, including promotion delay, caused by state promotions from **RRC_IDLE** to **RRC_CONNECTED**, and paging delay caused by UE's sleeping before checking the data channel (a mechanism in the cellular network to save energy). Reducing D is desirable as it improves user experience.

2.4 Traffic Optimization Methodology

In this paper, we mainly focus on two traffic optimization techniques:

(i) *Fast dormancy (FD)* [2, 3] is a mechanism in 3G networks for reducing the amount of tail time incurred by a device by quickly demoting it to a low energy RRC state without waiting for the tail timer to expire. In our simulations, we explore fast dormancy in an LTE setting, motivated by the fact that LTE, like 3G, also suffers from a serious tail problem [9]. Our fast dormancy-based optimization works as follows: when the UE has not observed any network activity for some idle time T_i, it sends a special RRC message to

	# of packets (million)	%
Total	131.49	100%
Screen on	72.50	55.13%
Screen off	47.14	35.84%
Unknown	11.85	9.02%

Table 1: Packet statistics of the UMICH data set.

the network to make the allocated radio resource be released earlier, instead of occupying it for the whole RRC tail. After the radio resource is released, the UE switches to the low power idle state (**RRC_IDLE** for LTE networks), saving energy. The setting of T_i is important for balancing the tradeoffs among UE energy saving (ΔE), signaling overhead (ΔS) and channel scheduling delay (ΔD), *i.e.*, a smaller T_i would results in a larger ΔE at the cost of larger ΔS and ΔD, and *vice versa*.

(ii) *Batching* is a widely used traffic shaping technique, which has been discussed in previous studies [6, 14]. In this study, batching uses two parameters, source window size α (seconds) and target window size β (seconds), and $\alpha > \beta$. For each α seconds long time window $[t, t+\alpha]$, packets within $[t, t+\alpha-\beta]$ are delayed and batched with those inside $[t+\alpha-\beta, t+\alpha]$. Notice that if α/β is too large, the limited bandwidth of the cellular network could become the bottleneck, making the batching impossible. So in this study, we make sure that our choice of α and β results in acceptable bandwidth usage for LTE networks.

3. CHARACTERISTICS OF SCREEN-OFF TRAFFIC

In this section, we present packet characteristics and burst analysis of screen-off traffic in the UMICH data set. Then we compare screen-on and screen-off traffic and scrutinize the top applications generating screen-off traffic.

3.1 Packet Characteristics of Screen-off Traffic

Using the methodology described in §2.1, we classify all packets to be screen-on, screen-off or unknown. Table 1 lists the number of packets in different categories. Among the total 131.49 million packets, 55.12% of them are screen-on packets and 35.85% are screen-off packets, with 9.02% unknown. The possible reasons for unknown packets are multifold, including that voluntary users may have accidentally killed the data collector. For the unknown category, we conservatively choose not optimize it for either screen-on or screen-off traffic optimization.

The top section of Table 2 lists the packet characteristics of both screen-on and screen-off traffic. Packet payload size refers to the size in bytes of an IP packet excluding the TCP/UDP and IP headers, and payload for a given process is the sum of the packet payload sizes of all packets corresponding to that process. We notice that screen-off traffic has far less packets (35.84% of total) than screen-on traffic (55.13% of total), much smaller total payload (27.26% for screen-off and 64.31% for screen-on traffic), and smaller average downlink packet payload size.

To understand individual process behavior within screen-off traffic, we scrutinize the top processes sorted by the number of screen-off packets, in the bottom section of Table 2. In the second column, titled "Off payload", we observe that some processes have most of their payload transferred during screen-off sessions, *e.g.*, Genie Widget, Epicurious Recipe, *etc.* Especially for Yahoo! Sportacular, 80.45% of all its payload is transferred when the screen is off. This is possibly due to the background behaviors of these processes, involving either periodically pulling updates from servers or traffic triggered by server-initiated push notifications. In terms of the % of downlink payload, compared to other processes, Skypekit, Gmail, Sportacular and Facebook have smaller proportions of their respective total downlink payloads associated with the screen-off states. These processes also have a smaller average downlink packet size (<500B). In contrast, a process like **android.process.media** has an average size of 1388B, indicating that most packets have a size of MTU (maximum transmission unit, ~1500B). This shows that for screen-off traffic, application behavioral diversity still exists similar to that of screen-on traffic.

A group of processes share quite similar behavior patterns, including Google Music, **/system/bin/mediaserver** and **android.process.media**, which have larger payload (>2GB), and >99% of the payload is downlink. Their average downlink packet sizes are close to the MTU and average uplink packet sizes are close to 0. Also, their ratio of downlink packets is close to 2/3. This is because TCP's delayed ACK would generate one uplink ACK packet for every two downlink data packets, resulting in a ratio of 2/3 of downlink packets. These observations suggest that Google Music is downloading large amount of data, as it can run in the background allowing users to listen to the music with the screen off. Similarly, although **/system/bin/mediaserver** and **android.process.media** are not actual applications, they are used by other applications, such as Pandora, to download contents for users while the screen is off. However, this group of processes does not necessarily have higher energy consumption compared with the remaining processes, and we explore this in more detail in latter sections.

3.2 Burst Analysis of Screen-off Traffic

Following the methodology in §2.2, Table 3 lists the results of the burst analysis for screen-off traffic, with that of screen-on traffic listed for comparison purposes.

We observe that screen-off traffic contains much more bursts than screen-on traffic, although the total number of packets for screen-off traffic is smaller. For screen-off traffic, bursts are smaller in terms of the number of downlink/uplink packets and payload. Especially, for average downlink payload per burst, screen-on traffic is 7 times that for screen-off traffic. In addition, the average burst length and the **IBT** following bursts for screen-off traffic are both shorter than those of screen-on traffic. The above observations indicate that screen-off bursts are smaller in size and duration and appear more often — such behavior is likely to cause longer channel occupation time in the high energy RRC state and therefore incur significant battery usage.

By studying the screen-off burst behavior of individual processes, we classify them into two separate groups. The first group, which we call *Gathered* group, includes Genie Widget, Google Music, **/system/bin/mediaserver** and **android.process.media**. These processes have a small number of larger bursts in terms of the number of uplink/downlink packets per burst and the average downlink payload. Notice that the uplink payload for these bursts is not necessarily large, since a small uplink payload of HTTP request can result in a large file download. The *Gathered* group also has longer bursts and longer trailing **IBT** in average, indicating a less frequent appearance.

Traffic type	Payload (GB) / %[a]	% of downlink payload	# of packets ($\times 10^6$) / %[b]	% of downlink packets	Avg downlink packet payload size (B)	Avg uplink packet payload size (B)
Screen-on	51.47 / 64.31%	96.31%	72.50 / 55.13%	60.71%	1126	67
Screen-off	21.82 / 27.26%	93.52%	47.14 / 35.84%	52.60%	823	63
Process name	**Off payload (GB) / %[c]**	**% of downlink off payload[d]**	**# of off packets ($\times 10^6$) / %[e]**	**% of downlink off packets[f]**	**Avg downlink off packet payload size (B)**	**Avg uplink off packet payload size (B)**
Genie Widget	1.76 / 72.21%	97.01%	3.80 / 73.16%	49.97%	901	28
Google Music	3.13 / 57.14%	99.91%	3.30 / 57.02%	68.60%	1384	3
Epicurious Recipe	1.65 / 70.05%	99.22%	2.69 / 69.29%	50.46%	1212	10
/system/bin/mediaserver	2.39 / 10.09%	99.77%	2.66 / 11.05%	66.95%	1342	6
android.process.media	2.35 / 28.42%	99.98%	2.37 / 29.06%	71.55%	1388	1
Skypekit[g]	0.04 / 25.54%	48.44%	2.07 / 46.73%	48.32%	22	22
Facebook	0.46 / 32.96%	86.13%	1.95 / 40.67%	42.55%	487	58
Yahoo! Sportacular	0.23 / 80.45%	83.53%	1.94 / 81.05%	41.98%	238	34
Gmail	0.39 / 46.00%	63.65%	1.33 / 54.46%	47.70%	400	208

[a] Payload refers to the total screen-on/off payload, and % is relative to the total payload of all traffic.
[b] % relative to the total number of packets of all traffic.
[c] Off payload refers to the screen-off payload of the specific application, and % is relative to the total payload of this application.
[d] % of downlink screen-off payload of the specific application relative to the total screen-off payload of that application.
[f] % of downlink screen-off packet count of the specific application relative to the total screen-off packet count of that application.
[g] Full process name: /data/data/com.skype.raider/files/skypekit, which is not the actual Skype application (com.skype.raider).

Table 2: Packet characteristics of screen-on/off traffic and top processes for screen-off traffic.

Traffic type	# of bursts	Avg[a] # of uplink packets	Avg[a] # of downlink packets	Avg[a] uplink payload (B)	Avg[a] downlink payload (KB)	Avg[a] burst length (sec)	Avg[a] `IBT` following (sec)
Screen-on	650,941	43.75	67.62	2910.44	76.17	2.92	335.13
Screen-off	1,910,939	11.69	12.98	739.78	10.68	1.37	113.60
Process name	**# of bursts**	**Avg[a] # of uplink packets**	**Avg[a] # of downlink packets**	**Avg[a] uplink payload (B)**	**Avg[a] downlink payload (KB)**	**Avg[a] burst length (sec)**	**Avg[a] `IBT` following (sec)**
Genie Widget	5,952	319.73	319.36	8852.48	287.88	17.87	3,892.87
Google Music	5,297	195.69	427.56	505.54	591.92	4.53	5,111.50
Epicurious Recipe	63,236	21.07	21.46	202.22	26.01	0.67	159.34
/system/bin/mediaserver	8,163	106.44	215.53	669.82	289.35	5.01	14,451.70
android.process.media	1,442	461.88	1,156.93	246.99	1,605.84	19.83	123,565.00
Skypekit	42,744	25.08	23.46	555.38	0.52	1.93	832.79
Facebook	203,535	5.49	4.07	318.83	1.98	0.86	547.23
Yahoo! Sportacular	133,785	8.39	6.07	285.44	1.45	1.52	261.78
Gmail	105,478	6.60	6.02	1375.30	2.41	1.17	2,002.60

[a] Each "avg" in this table stands for the average value per burst.

Table 3: Burst analysis of screen-on/off traffic and top processes for screen-off traffic.

The rest of the processes fall into the second group, called the *Scattered* group, which generate significantly more bursts and on average, these bursts contain less packets and smaller downlink payload. In addition, these bursts are shorter in duration and appear more frequently. A representative process from this group is Facebook, which includes over 200,000 bursts, and the major reason for this behavior of Facebook is the periodic keep-alive transfers [14].

Based on this comparison, we believe that it is both easy and important for mobile application developers to optimize their application behaviors during the screen-off stage, *e.g.*, for delay-insensitive traffic, they can batch the data into larger bursts, or even eliminate the screen-off data transfers if they are not necessary.

4. RADIO RESOURCE, ENERGY IMPACT AND OPTIMIZATION

Using the network and power model simulation (§2.3), we now evaluate the radio resource and energy impact of screen-off traffic and evaluate some optimization approaches.

4.1 Radio Resource and Energy Impact of Screen-off Traffic

Table 4 presents highlights of the simulation results using the LTE network and power model defined in our previous work [9]. ΔE, ΔS and ΔD represents the change of network energy, signaling overhead and channel scheduling delay after removing the traffic of an application or type, and a negative value indicates a reduction. The results indicate that, compared to screen-on traffic, screen-off traffic clearly has larger impact on the network energy E, as well as S and D. For example, removing all screen-off traffic reduces the total network energy by 58.55%, and for one user, this reduction is as high as 73.53%.

Comparing the *Gathered* group and *Scattered* group discussed in §3.2, the former has very small impact on E, S and D, while the later has a substantial impact. This is because, for the *Scattered* group, a large number of small bursts could result in a large number of RRC tails if the **`IBT`**s among these bursts are larger than the tail time and a long channel occupation time otherwise. For example,

Traffic type	ΔE %[a]	Min $\|\Delta E\|$ %[c]	Max $\|\Delta E\|$ %[c]	ΔS %[a]	ΔD %[a]
Screen-on	-22.18%	3.78%	38.11%	-14.87%	-17.57%
Screen-off	-58.55%	12.39%	73.53%	-58.03%	-54.46%

Process name	ΔE %[b]	Min $\|\Delta E\|$ %[c]	Max $\|\Delta E\|$ %[c]	ΔS %[b]	ΔD %[b]
Genie Widget	-0.34%	0%	2.46%	0.11%	-0.81%
Google Music	-0.12%	0%	1.68%	-0.02%	-0.08%
Epicurious Recipe	-1.63%	0%	26.06%	-1.78%	-0.94%
/system/bin/mediaserver	-0.13%	0%	1.08%	0.02%	-0.16%
android.process.media	-0.08%	0.01%	0.52%	0.02%	-0.05%
Skypekit	-0.96%	0%	7.32%	-0.24%	-0.51%
Facebook	-5.25%	0%	34.68%	-5.82%	-4.15%
Yahoo! Sportacular	-3.01%	0%	20.04%	-1.88%	-1.44%
Gmail	-1.18%	0.04%	4.59%	-0.69%	-1.47%

[a] ΔE, ΔS and ΔD are calculated by removing all screen-on/off traffic from the original traces
[b] ΔE, ΔS and ΔD are calculated by removing the screen-off traffic of one process from the original traces
[c] Min and max refer to the minimum and maximum energy saving $|\Delta E|$ across all users, respectively.

Table 4: Radio resource and energy impact of screen-on/off traffic and top processes for screen-off traffic.

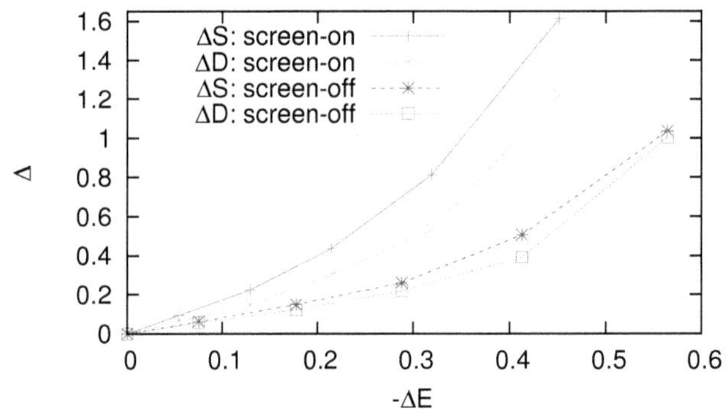

Figure 1: Effectiveness comparison of fast dormancy.

although the Facebook process does not generate the most screen-off traffic, it has the largest energy impact among all processes, *i.e.*, 5.25% of the total network energy can be saved by only removing Facebook's screen-off traffic, and for some users this number could be as high as 34.68%.

4.2 Traffic Optimization

Based on the above analysis, we find that screen-off traffic has a clearly different pattern compared to screen-on traffic, and accounts for a huge proportion of the UE network energy E, signaling overhead S and channel scheduling delay D. At the same time, because screen-off traffic is likely to be more delay-tolerant (see discussions in §1), it is more amenable to more aggressive optimization efforts. Intuitively a traffic optimization approach that is appropriately tuned to the two different traffic categories would yield significant efficiencies. To verify this intuition, we study two common optimization techniques, fast dormancy and batching.

We first compare applying fast dormancy to screen-on and screen-off traffic with a separate T_i settings. The default setting of the `RRC_CONNECTED` inactivity timer is 11.58 seconds for a major LTE ISP [9]. In Figure 1, we vary the setting of T_i from 10 seconds to 2 seconds with a step-size of 2 seconds (from left to right in Figure 1) and calculate the $\Delta(E, S, D)$ relative to when fast dormancy is not applied. We observe that for the same T_i setting, there is a higher energy saving ΔE and a lower ΔS and ΔD for screen-off traffic, compared with screen-on traffic, and these gaps are larger when T_i is smaller, *i.e.*, applying fast dormancy more aggressively. So in order to achieve the same energy saving for screen-off and screen-on traffic, the T_i should be set to a much smaller value for screen-on traffic, incurring much larger ΔS and ΔD. However, the responsiveness requirement when the screen is on is actually higher, hence a higher ΔD for screen-on traffic is not acceptable. A better strategy would be being more aggressive (a smaller T_i) for screen-off traffic, which produces significant energy savings, and more conservative (a relatively larger T_i) for screen-on traffic, which limits the negative impact on user experience, though with less energy savings. For example, when $T_i = 8s$, there is 42% energy savings with 52% ΔS and 40% ΔD for screen-off traffic, and when $T_i = 4s$, for screen-on traffic, though the energy saving is small (24%), ΔS (43%) and ΔD (30%) are also limited. With these two fast dormancy settings, for the whole traffic, we can achieve 34% energy saving, with 47.04% ΔS and 35.21% ΔD. This is a better tradeoff than one single T_i setting for both screen-on and screen-off traffic.

Besides fast dormancy, batching [14, 6] is also proposed for optimizing mobile traffic. In Table 5, we compare fast dormancy and batching under different settings for all applications together, and also individually for two applications, Facebook representing the *Scattered* group and Google Music representing the *Gathered* group. For fast dormancy, with reduced E, there is increased S, D, while for batching, all E, S, D are decreased. This is because for fast dormancy, since UE demotes to `RRC_IDLE` earlier, there would be more promotions resulting in increased S, D, while for batching, since the traffic pattern is altered, scattered packets are gathered into groups and hence there are less promotions. Notice that the metric D here does not include the delay of packets incurred by batching. In this work, we only focus on batching for screen-off traffic, since any delay for screen-on traffic is likely to be more perceptible to users.

In Table 5, when applying fast dormancy to all applications, we set a different T_i for screen-on/off traffic, *i.e.*, $T_{i,on}$ and $T_{i,off}$. For simplicity, let $<a, b>$ stands for the case when $T_{i,on} = a$ seconds and $T_{i,off} = b$ seconds. Based on Figure 1, we empirically select two values for $T_{i,on}$ and $T_{i,off}$, 4s as an aggressive setting and 8s as a conservative setting. Compared with $<8, 8>$, reducing $T_{i,on}$ to 4s, *i.e.*, $<4, 8>$, only saves 4.21% energy additionally.

Process name	Optimization	Settings	ΔE[a]	ΔS[a]	ΔD[a]
All applications	Fast dormancy	$T_{i,on}$[b] = 8s, $T_{i,off}$[b] = 8s	-16.39%	16.95%	13.14%
		$T_{i,on}$ = 4s, $T_{i,off}$ = 8s	-20.60%	28.29%	21.26%
		$T_{i,on}$ = 8s, $T_{i,off}$ = 4s	-34.44%	47.04%	35.21%
		$T_{i,on}$ = 4s, $T_{i,off}$ = 4s	-38.66%	58.38%	43.31%
	Batching	Only for screen-off, α = 50s, β = 10s	-22.33%	-6.24%	-11.27%
		Only for screen-off, α = 50s, β = 5s	-27.15%	-6.24%	-10.67%
		Only for screen-off, α = 100s, β = 10s	-36.72%	-30.00%	-33.43%
		Only for screen-off, α = 100s, β = 5s	-40.79%	-30.00%	-34.25%
	Fast dormancy + Batching	$T_{i,on}$ = 8s, $T_{i,off}$ = 4s, batching only for screen-off traffic, α = 100s, β = 5s	-60.92%	-25.33%	-30.59%
Facebook[c]	Fast dormancy + Batching	$T_{i,on}$ = 8s, $T_{i,off}$ = 4s, batching only for screen-off traffic, α = 100s, β = 5s	-60.19%	-36.27%	-34.93%
Google Music[c]	Fast dormancy + Batching	$T_{i,on}$ = 8s, $T_{i,off}$ = 4s, batching only for screen-off traffic, α = 100s, β = 5s	-57.30%	7.12%	-21.11%

[a] $\Delta E, S, D$ are relative to the E, S, D of all traffic for the specific application.
[b] $T_{i,on}$ is the inactivity threshold of fast dormancy for screen-on traffic, and $T_{i,off}$ is for screen-off traffic.
[c] For these two application rows, we consider the traffic of *only* one specific application, excluding that from other applications.

Table 5: Traffic optimization with fast dormancy and batching.

And $<8,4>$ has 11.34% reduction in S and 8.10% reduction in D, with only 4.22% less energy saving, compared with $<4,4>$. This verifies that a different setting for $T_{i,on}$ and $T_{i,off}$ balances the tradeoff of saving energy and reducing overhead, and we select $<8,4>$ as a reasonable setting. Notice that there are other possible parameter settings representing different aggressiveness with different energy saving and overhead, which may be more appropriate for different settings.

In Table 5, batching applied to the screen-off traffic is able to reduce all E, S, and D. Notice that we do not apply batching for screen-on traffic since it may affect the user experience, *e.g.,* when the user is waiting for a response at real time. We observe that most of the screen-off traffic (in terms of the energy impact) is less delay-sensitive, *e.g.,* push notification, since user interaction is not involved. However, there are also some exceptions for screen-off applications which requires real-time data transfer, *e.g.,* when the user is making a VoIP call with the screen off. Ideally, traffic from these delay-sensitive applications should not be batched even during screen-off stage. In this study, we do not attempt to completely solve this problem, instead, we show an upper bound of the benefit by batching all screen-off traffic. In reality, we need to prioritize delay-sensitive traffic during screen-off stage, and we leave it to future study. In §2.4, we discuss that the choice of α and β values is limited by the available bandwidth for 3G/4G networks. Comparing among the empirically selected candidate settings in Table 5, α = 100s and β = 5s is a better setting, which saves up to 40.79% energy, with a 30.00% reduction in S and 34.25% in D. Notice that the α and β settings studied are just example settings that work well in practice. The goal is to demonstrate the benefit of batching for screen-off traffic and the selection of optimal settings is left to future work.

Then we evaluate applying fast dormancy and batching jointly for all applications and for two sample applications, with the settings specified in Table 5. For all applications, there is a total network energy saving of 60.19%, with 25.33% reduction in S and 30.59% reduction in D. Facebook has similar energy saving, and due to its more "scattered" traffic pattern for screen-off traffic, the batching optimization results in even more reduction for S and D. However, for Google Music, whose traffic is already "gathered" as large bursts, the impact of fast dormancy is more obvious than batching, hence the reduction for D is smaller and there is even an increase in S, unlike the other two scenarios.

5. DISCUSSIONS AND CONCLUSION

In this study, we took a first step towards understanding the impact of screen status on cellular application traffic behavior. Our evaluations in the context of LTE cellular networks, show that although the number of packets and total payload for screen-off traffic are much smaller than that for screen-on traffic, the former accounts for a disproportionate majority (58.55%) of the total network energy consumed by a device. Exploration of resource optimization techniques like fast dormancy and batching indicate that the strategy of optimizing the screen-off traffic more aggressively than screen-on traffic can realize substantial resource savings, without adversely impacting user experience.

We are pursuing this research further, first to explore screen-off traffic in greater detail and explore optimization strategies tailored to the potentially different delay-requirements of subsets of that traffic. Second, in this paper, our optimization strategies imposed the strict constraint that screen-on traffic should not suffer any additional delays that come with traffic shaping approaches. In reality, some limited delay jitter would be tolerable depending on the application and traffic semantics - this is be an additional source of resource optimization beyond the savings we have shown in this paper. Finally, logistics permitting, it would be nice to extend the study to a larger user group.

6. ACKNOWLEDGEMENT

We thank Chen-nee Chuah for her many helpful comments and suggestions for improving the final version of this paper. We also thank the anonymous reviewers for their feed- back and helpful suggestions. This research was partially supported by the National Science Foundation under grants CNS-1111699, CNS-1059372, CNS-0939707, and CNS-1050157.

7. REFERENCES

[1] 3GPP LTE. `http://www.3gpp.org/LTE`.

[2] UE "Fast Dormancy" behavior. 3GPP discussion and decision notes R2-075251, 2007.

[3] Configuration of fast dormancy in release 8. 3GPP discussion and decision notes RP-090960, 2009.

[4] System impact of poor proprietary fast dormancy. 3GPP discussion and decision notes RP-090941, 2009.

[5] Y. Agarwal, R. Chandra, A. Wolman, P. Bahl, K. Chin, and R. Gupta. Wireless wakeups revisited: energy management for VoIP over WiFi smartphones. In *MobiSys*, 2007.

[6] N. Balasubramanian, A. Balasubramanian, and A. Venkataramani. Energy Consumption in Mobile Phones: A Measurement Study and Implications for Network Applications. In *IMC*, 2009.

[7] M. Chuah, W. Luo, and X. Zhang. Impacts of Inactivity Timer Values on UMTS System Capacity. In *Wireless Communications and Networking Conference*, 2002.

[8] H. Holma and A. Toskala. HSDPA/HSUPA for UMTS: High Speed Radio Access for Mobile Communications. John Wiley and Sons, Inc., 2006.

[9] J. Huang, F. Qian, A. Gerber, Z. M. Mao, S. Sen, and O. Spatscheck. A Close Examination of Performance and Power Characteristics of 4G LTE Networks. In *MobiSys*, 2012.

[10] S. Kang, J. Lee, H. Jang, H. Lee, Y. Lee, S. Park, T. Park, and J. Song. Seemon: scalable and energy-efficient context monitoring framework for sensor-rich mobile environments. In *MobiSys*, 2008.

[11] C.-C. Lee, J.-H. Yeh, and J.-C. Chen. Impact of inactivity timer on energy consumption in WCDMA and CDMA2000. In *the Third Annual Wireless Telecommunication Symposium (WTS)*, 2004.

[12] P. P. C. Lee, T. Bu, and T. Woo. On the Detection of Signaling DoS Attacks on 3G Wireless Networks. 2007.

[13] J. Perez-Romero, O. Sallent, R. Agusti, and M. Diaz-Guerra. Radio resource management strategies in UMTS. John Wiley and Sons, Inc., 2005.

[14] F. Qian, Z. Wang, Y. Gao, J. Huang, A. Gerber, Z. M. Mao, S. Sen, and O. Spatscheck. Periodic Transfers in Mobile Applications: Network-wide Origin, Impact, and Optimization. In *World Wide Web*, 2012.

[15] F. Qian, Z. Wang, A. Gerber, Z. M. Mao, S. Sen, and O. Spatscheck. Characterizing Radio Resource Allocation for 3G Networks. In *IMC*, 2010.

[16] F. Qian, Z. Wang, A. Gerber, Z. M. Mao, S. Sen, and O. Spatscheck. TOP: Tail Optimization Protocol for Cellular Radio Resource Allocation. In *Proc. ICNP*, 2010.

[17] F. Qian, Z. Wang, A. Gerber, Z. M. Mao, S. Sen, and O. Spatscheck. Profiling Resource Usage for Mobile Applications: a Cross-layer Approach. In *MobiSys*, 2011.

[18] M. Ra, J. Paek, A. Sharma, R. Govindan, M. Krieger, and M. Neel. Energy-delay tradeoffs in smartphone applications. In *MobiSys*, 2010.

[19] S. Sesia, I. Toufik, and M. Baker. LTE: The UMTS Long Term Evolution From Theory to Practice. John Wiley and Sons, Inc., 2009.

[20] A. Shye, B. Sholbrock, and M. G. Into the wild: Studying real user activity patterns to guide power optimization for mobile architectures. In *Micro*, 2009.

[21] Y. Wang, J. Lin, M. Annavaram, Q. Jacobson, J. Hong, B. Krishnamachari, and N. Sadeh. A framework of energy efficient mobile sensing for automatic user state recognition. In *MobiSys*, 2009.

Configuring DHCP Leases in the Smartphone Era

Ioannis Papapanagiotou
ECE, NC State University
Raleigh, NC
ipapapa@ncsu.edu

Erich Nahum
IBM Research
Hawthorne, NY
nahum@us.ibm.com

Vasileios Pappas
IBM Research
Hawthorne, NY
vpappas@us.ibm.com

ABSTRACT

The Dynamic Host Configuration Protocol (DHCP) was introduced nearly 20 years ago as a mechanism for hosts to automatically acquire IP addresses. While the protocol remains the same, its usage has evolved, especially in the last decade with the introduction of mobile devices and wireless local area networks. In this paper we investigate the impact that new types of wireless devices, such as smartphones, have on DHCP. We use two one-month long traces, collected at a corporate and an educational network, and we compare side-by-side DHCP usage patterns. We develop a novel passive fingerprinting technique based on DHCP messages to determine the device type and operating system. We show that DHCP implementations vary among device types and have an effect on DHCP lease durations. To improve network address utilization, without introducing any protocol changes, we propose a new leasing strategy which takes into account device types. This strategy, compared to current approaches, improves the address utilization without considerably increasing the DHCP overhead.

Keywords

Mobile, Smartphones, DHCP, OS Fingerprinting

Categories and Subject Descriptors

C.2.3 [**Computer-Communication Networks**]: Network Operations—*Network Management*

1. INTRODUCTION

The Dynamic Host Configuration Protocol (DHCP) [8] enables devices to attach to networks without manual configuration. It does, however, require manual configuration of access policies at the DHCP servers. One of the most critical parameter of the DHCP server configuration is the lease duration, indicating how long a device can use an IP address. Setting up proper DCHP lease values has been an art rather than a science. Long lease times can lead to exhaustion of the network address pool assigned for DHCP, while short ones can result in increased broadcast traffic and unnecessary activation of wireless interfaces by power limited devices.

There have been few studies on the DHCP lease times [7, 11], both of which were done before the onslaught of smartphones in local area networks. Smartphones present a challenge in correctly configuring DHCP leases. A single device may acquire multiple IP addresses during a day due to its continuous attachment, in either asleep or active mode, with the campus-wide wireless networks. For example, as a student moves from one side of the campus to another, her devices can re-associate with various campus subnets, acquiring a different address each time. In this scenario, setting DHCP lease times even as low as one hour may not necessarily be enough to reduce network address utilization.

To further understand the impact of smartphone devices on DHCP lease times, we analyze two one-month long packet traces, collected from a corporate and an educational network. We make the following contributions:

- We develop a novel device and operating system fingerprinting technique based on DHCP messages, which significantly improves the accuracy upon previous fingerprinting techniques that are based on HTTP user-agent information [12].
- We show that DHCP message exchanges vary both across device types (e.g., laptops, smartphones) and across operating systems (e.g., iOS, Android, Windows, Mac OS X, Linux), with each device type contributing a different amount of DHCP related traffic and having a varying effect on the network address utilization.
- We propose a new DHCP leasing strategy that does not require any protocol changes, and which takes advantage of the varying usage patterns per device type. Using simulation results, driven by our traces, we show that the new strategy, compared to current approaches, improves the network address utilization sixfold without considerably increasing DHCP overhead.

2. DHCP BACKGROUND

DHCP [8] enables automatic network configuration of hosts in TCP/IP networks, with a message exchange between hosts and DHCP servers. A *discover* message is broadcasted to locate available servers. The listening server replies with an *offer*, which contains the offered IP address. The client generates a *request* ("selecting" state) asking for offered param-

Trace Type	Corporate	Educational
Dates (2012)	Feb 29-Mar 25	Jan 15-Feb 15
Client MAC Addresses	2980	8726
Client IP Addresses	3435	1968
Wireless Subnets	8 * /23	/21
Leases	1h or 12h	15 min
DHCP Packets	2.16M	3.48M
TCP/UDP Bytes	2.5TB	4.9TB

Table 1: Dataset Properties

eters from one server and implicitly declining offers from all others. However, there are other occasions in which a client issues a *request* message, such as confirming correctness of previously allocated address after, e.g., system reboot ("init-reboot" state), or extending the lease on a particular network address ("renewing" or "rebinding" state[1]).

The server responds to a request with either an *acknowledgment*, if the request is granted, or a *negative acknowledgment*, in the case where the parameters are incorrect or the lease has expired. The *acknowledgment* contains the lease time for which the network address will be valid, either as a new lease, or as an update. The client may extend its lease with subsequent *request* messages sent periodically after half the lease period. For example, if the lease time is 14400 seconds, and the client is still active after 7200 seconds, it can generate a *request* message at that time to notify the server. If the lease time expires, the server assumes that the device has been disconnected from the network. The client can issue an explicit *release* message, but this is not mandated by the RFC.

Finally, an *inform* message is sent from the client to the server to ask for local configuration parameters. This only happens when the client already has an externally configured network address.

3. PACKET TRACE ANALYSIS

We capture packet traces from two large wireless local area networks, one from a corporate office network and one from an educational campus network. Table 1 summarizes the two traces, including their static lease policies.

Using the traces, we analyze the two types of data. First, we examine DHCP packets, in order to uniquely identify devices using MAC addresses, classify them based on the device type and the operating system, analyze network address utilization and emulate different lease policies. Second, we capture TCP and UDP packets using Bro 2.0 [1] to create summary log files for TCP and UDP flows, which enables us to determine the time periods in which devices are active.

3.1 Device Classification

We classify device types and operating systems by applying an *a-priori* learning algorithm [5] to generate association rules, using as input labels the following fields in the DHCP packets:

- *Host-Name*: Some devices set their host-name to a string that can identify the type of the device. For example, many iOS smartphones have names that follow the pattern of '*-iPhone', where * usually corresponds to a string related to the user.

[1]The RFC defines the "renewing" and "rebinding" as different states. Their only difference is the way they request a lease extension, i.e., broadcast or multicast.

		Corporate		Educational	
Device	**OS**	#	%	#	%
Laptop	All	2176	73.02	3970	45.50
	Windows	1787	59.97	2819	32.31
	Mac OS X	385	12.92	1131	12.96
	Linux	4	0.13	20	0.23
Smartphone	All	735	24.66	4489	51.44
	iOS	577	19.36	3069	35.17
	Android	126	4.24	1334	15.29
	BlackBerry	31	1.04	84	0.96
	Win Mobile	1	0.03	2	0.02
Other	All	69	2.32	267	3.06
	Cisco VoIP	9	0.32	-	-
	Unidentified	60	2.01	267	3.06
All		2980	100	8726	100

Table 2: Distribution of Devices in the Trace

- *Vendor-Name*: Some devices include in the vendor-name a string that can uniquely identify their operating system. For example, most versions of Microsoft Windows include the string 'MSFT'[3].
- *Parameter-Request*: Some devices generate a unique set and/or ordering of options that can be used for identification. For example, Android devices have the following options: '1 121 33 3 6 28 51 58 59'.
- *Organization Unique Identifier*: Using the IANA Ethernet assignments [2], we determine the vendor of the interface and then we identify if that vendor can be directly mapped to a specific type of device.

To quantify the confidence of the rules, we used standard data mining metrics: Support $supp(X)$ is defined as the portion of all devices that satisfy the rule x. Confidence $conf(X \Rightarrow Y)$ of an association rule $X \Rightarrow Y$ is defined as $supp(X \cap Y)/supp(X)$, where $supp(X \cap Y)$ is the support of rule $X \wedge Y$, namely, the portion of all devices that satisfy both rule X and Y. The rules that have high confidence in at least one direction ($conf(X \Rightarrow Y)$ and $conf(Y \Rightarrow X)$), and are not contradictory, are broken into their corresponding itemsets X and Y. Those rules are then used for potential classification. For example, [host-name contains 'Android'] $\Rightarrow$ [Parameter-Request-List contains '1 121 33 3 6 28 51 58 59'] happens with confidence 100%. The reverse direction [Parameter-Request-List contains '1 121 33 3 6 28 51 58 59'] $\Rightarrow$ [host-name contains 'Android'] happens with confidence 82.35%, and the remaining 17.63% are related to a device that neither has 'Android' in the host name (e.g., when the user has modified the default host-name) nor any other name from another device type. Now a host-name that contains 'Android' or a Parameter-Request-List that contains '1 121 33 3 6 28 51 58 59', can be used to classify Android devices. In other words, we assume no ground-truth but quantify every rule.

While we use an existing classification approach, we are unaware of any previous work that has used an unsupervised learning algorithm, fed with DHCP data, in order to classify devices and operating systems. Previous wireless device classification approaches were based on information in the HTTP user-agent header [12] and were able to classify up to 82% of devices. Table 2 shows the results of our approach on the two collected traces, indicating that more than 97% of the devices were classified.

Type	Corporate			Educational		
	(%)	Mean	Median	(%)	Mean	Median
iOS	51.6	251	140	35.74	158	38
Android	5.88	123	58	11.44	117	37
BlackBerry	2.68	200	48	0.88	135	42
Windows	31.16	51	24	39.6	190	45
Mac OS	7.08	52	48	12.38	148	38
Other	2.2	-	-	0.4	-	

Table 3: DHCP Requests

Corporate			
Type	Select	Init-Reboot	Renew
iOS	13.19	85.62	1.19
Android	72.40	17.52	10.09
BlackBerry	94.05	0.00	5.95
Windows	33.53	23.99	42.48
Mac OS X	20.33	56.18	22.49
Educational			
Type	Select	Init-Reboot	Renew
iOS	13.06	57.4	29.54
Android	28.46	10.78	60.76
BlackBerry	35.53	0	64.47
Windows	3.99	10.39	85.62
Mac OS X	4.91	8.79	86.3

Table 4: Relative (%) of DHCP Request Types

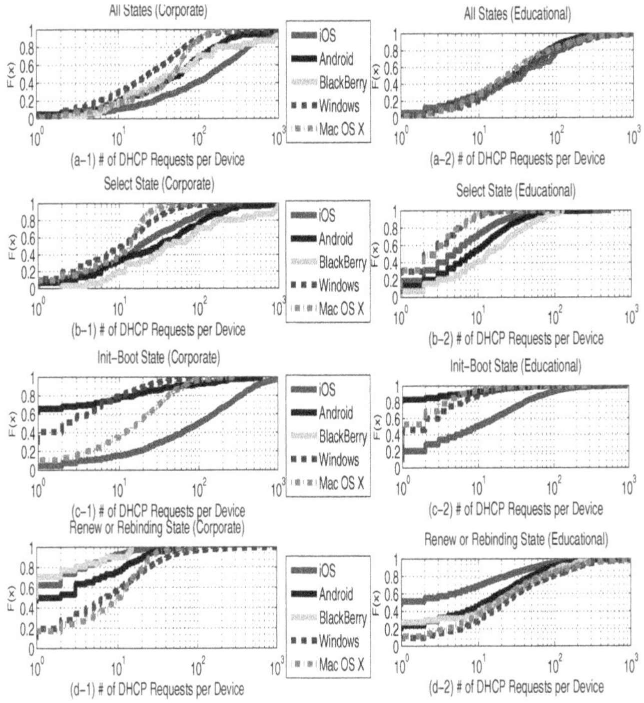

Figure 1: CDF of the number DHCP *Request* messages in the Corporate and Educational network

3.2 Lease Time Analysis

Using the DHCP-based device classification of the previous section, we analyse the DHCP request messages. Table 3 shows the acknowledged DHCP request messages[2] for each device type, as a percentage of the total requests, as well as the absolute mean and median values. We observe distinct behavioral differences between the corporate and educational network. In the corporate network, smartphones, especially iOS devices, generate considerably more DHCP requests on average as compared to laptops. In contrast, in the educational network all devices generate roughly the same number of requests. Figure 1(a), which shows the cumulative distribution of requests per device type, illustrates this more clearly. This difference between the corporate and educational network is due to the smaller lease time of the educational network, forcing all devices to generate frequent lease renewal requests, as shown by the larger number of requests per device in that network.

To better understand the differences, we present the distribution of DHCP request message types in Table 4. In the educational network, with the exception of the iOS devices, the majority of the DHCP requests are renewals. In contrast, in the corporate network a considerably smaller percentage of the requests are renewals. Given the small number of renewal requests in the corporate network, other types of requests become more prominent, revealing a number of distinctions between device types. For example, iOS devices, and to a lesser extent Mac OS X devices, generate a large proportion of init-reboot requests. In contrast, Android and BlackBerry devices generate mainly select requests, meaning once they acquire a new address, they rarely contact the DHCP server again.

This difference between Apple and other devices is attributed to the implementation of DNAv4 [4] in iOS and Mac OS X [6, 13]. DNAv4 optimizes the re-attachment to a previously connected network by attempting to reuse a previous but still valid configuration, by reducing the number of DHCP exchange messages and by using unicast ARP requests[3].

Finally, in Figure 2, we plot the interarrival time of the DHCP request messages. The first graph corresponds to the educational network, and the second two to the corporate network (with leases of one hour and twelve hours respectively). We also indicate with a dotted vertical line the time corresponding to half of the lease time. This is the time at which a DHCP client requests a lease extension. In the educational network, we observe that the majority of the request messages are generated at half of the lease time, indicating that they are renewal requests. In the corporate network, where the lease times are larger, the devices generate far fewer requests for renewing an IP address.

3.3 Network Access Patterns

Proper setting of DHCP lease times depends on the amount of time devices stay active in the network, i.e., the amount of time they send or receive data[4]. For a particular host, as identified by its MAC address, we define the following:

- *Active Time*: The time period, starting at the initial DHCP lease offer, up to the time a *Release* message has been issued[5] or the last time that any packet was generated, before the next lease offer.

[2] We use the acknowledged requests so that we do not account for messages generated by DHCP relays.

[3] In our trace we observed unicast ARP requests associated with DHCP init-reboot requests coming from Apple devices.

[4] Note that the active time does not depend on the configuration of lease times.

[5] In both traces a *release* message is issued in < 0.1% of the leases, with an exception in Windows laptops of the corporate environment which is issued in 6.8% of the leases.

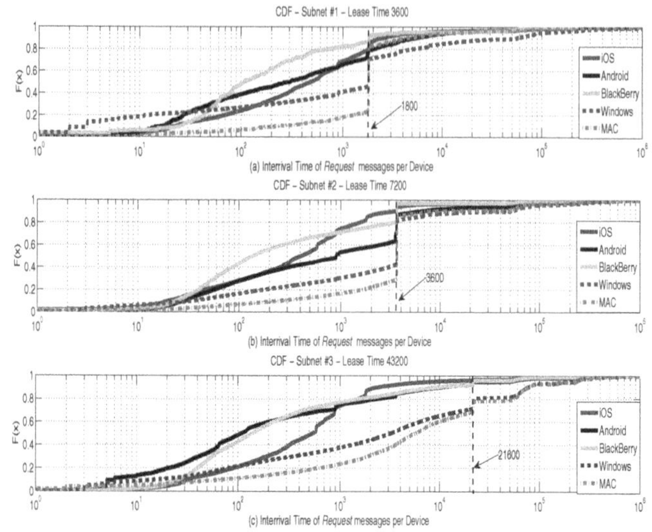

Figure 2: CDF of the interrival time of *Request* messages with different *Lease Time* setting

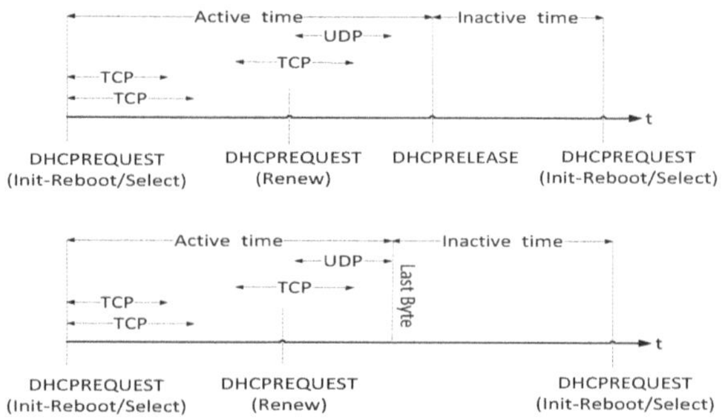

Figure 3: Calculating Active and Inactive times.

- *Inactive Time*: The time period between the end of an active period and the beginning of the next active period.

Active time starts when a device receives a DHCP acknowledgement message as a response to a DHCP request message. From the request messages, we exclude those generated when the client is either in the renewing or the rebinding state, as their purpose is to update the lease duration. However, we include the ones from the init-reboot state, where the objective is to reconfigure the leases. An illustration of active and inactive times is depicted in Figure 3.

Figure 4 shows active and inactive times for the different types of devices. We observe that smartphone active times are much smaller compared to laptop active times. We also see that active times for iOS devices are smaller than the active times of other smartphones. This happens due to a combination of reasons related to: *i)* the way users use laptops and smartphones, and *ii)* the different policies related to energy management between laptops and smartphones. User behaviour is difficult to analyze without having direct access on the devices, but we can clearly understand the effects of different energy management policies on the active

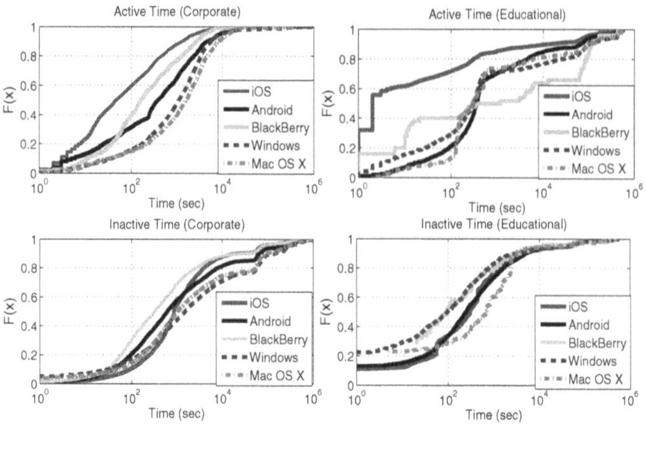

Figure 4: CDFs of Active and Inactive durations.

and inactive times. For laptops the policy has been to keep the wireless interfaces always active, while for cellphones the interface can switch off after some period of inactivity. In iOS devices, if the device is not plugged in to power and the device display is switched off, the Wi-Fi interface is also switched off and the cellular network becomes the primary interface. On the other hand, in Android devices the user is allowed to configure the WiFi sleep policy[6], although there is not a unique default policy.

Finally, it is interesting to point out that in the educational network there are a large number of smartphone devices, especially iOS devices, that have an active time of one minute or less. We attribute this to the fact that when users roam from one part of the campus to another, their devices associate with some subnets for only a brief period of time[7].

4. DHCP LEASE POLICIES

Ideally, a DHCP lease allocation policy should account for the differences in behavior of the various mobile devices. The goals of this policy should be to minimize the following, in decreasing priority:

- *Address space utilization*: The policy should use as little of the available address space as possible, in order to support the most concurrent users.
- *Broadcast traffic*: The policy should cause as few broadcasts as necessary, since broadcasts wake idle clients and consume power.
- *Server load*: The policy should minimize the load on the DHCP server, to reduce the related capex and opex expenses of running the server (including power).

We do this in two steps: first, we look at the behavior of the devices in isolation when varying the lease times over several orders of magnitude. Then, based on those behaviors, determine an approach that best meets the above goals. We wrote a simulator that, given a trace, reproduces the DHCP behavior and outputs the above metrics.

[6]There are various sleep policies: never sleep, never sleep when plugged in, sleep when screen turns off, sleep after 15 min, etc.

[7]We confirmed this with the educational network administrators, who also say that this was one of the reasons that they set the lease time to a relatively short 900 seconds.

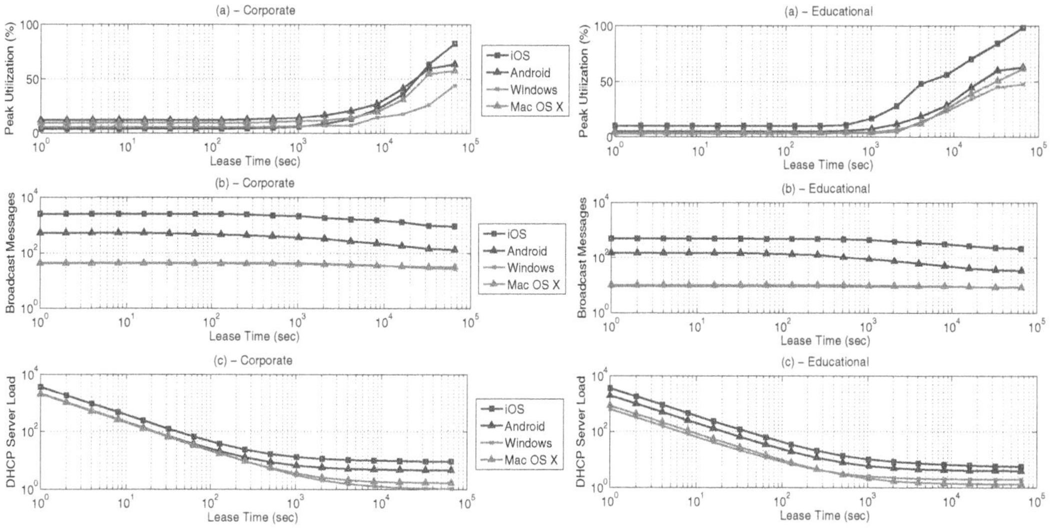

Figure 5: (a) Address space utilization (b) Broadcast messages (c) Server load, versus lease time, averaged per day and per device.

Figure 5 shows the results from our simulator. Broadly, one can see the tension between the goals in the three sets of graphs. Shorter lease times utilize the address space most efficiently, but cause large amounts of broadcast traffic and high server load. Large lease times minimize broadcasts and server load, but at the expense of poor address space utilization.

Looking more closely, in Figure 5a we see that address space utilization stays relatively flat versus lease times for each device type up until some threshold, after which utilization starts to grow logarithmically. In the corporate network and for iOS devices, the threshold is 10^3 seconds; for Androids, $2 * 10^3$ seconds, and for laptops, $4 * 10^3$ seconds. In the educational network, the same pattern holds, but with half the threshold. This is an artifact of the shorter active periods in the educational network as illustrated in Figure 4. As lease times go up, many leases are wasted on devices that have transitioned into the inactive period. This issue becomes more prevailent in smartphone devices since users have shorter access times and are more mobile compared to laptops.

In Figure 5b we observe that lease duration does not affect the number of broadcast messages generated by the laptops in both networks. Laptop users have long active times, therefore the majority of their DHCP messages are renews, which are unicast. In contrast, the number of broadcasts generated by smartphones is sensitive to the lease time. Shorter lease times incur larger numbers of broadcasts. This is because short lease time results in smartphones generating more request messages from the "selecting" state, as leases expire faster, and new leases require a full DCHP handshake, which incurs extra broadcast traffic.

In Figure 5c, we see that server load levels off at about 1,000 seconds for smartphones, but 10,000 seconds for laptops. This is due to the longer active times of the laptop users, as was shown in Figure 4.

Given these behaviors, we evaluated and compared the following DHCP lease policies:

- *Static policies*: Fixed lease times of 15 minutes, 30 minutes, and 12 hours, for all devices.
- *Exponential adaptation* [11], which allocates a short lease to a client once it arrives, and doubles the lease time every time the client renews its lease.
- *Differential lease*, which allocates different lease times based on the device type. We choose values based on our analysis of Figure 5. In the corporate network: iOS devices get 1000 seconds, Androids 2000 seconds, and Windows and Mac OS X 4000 seconds. In the educational network: iOS devices get 500 seconds, Androids 1000 seconds, and Windows and Mac OS X 2000 seconds.

Figure 6 shows the results of our simulations. We see that our differential lease policy provides a good tradeoff between our goals for both networks. It is very efficient in address utilization, almost as much as the 15 minute lease policies, yet creates less broadcast traffic and server load. Exponential adaptation, on the other hand, uses a large amount of address space, but produces low amounts of broadcast traffic and DHCP server load on a daily basis.

Different environments may have different priorities among the goals outlined above, depending on their address space size, distribution of clients (smartphones vs. laptops), etc. However, using static values requires a manual tuning process to determine the right tradeoff for the environment. Moreover, setting small static leases may have an adverse impact on the user experience. Devices have to reassociate in the wireless network when a lease expires, which in some cases can take several seconds. Our differential lease policy allows devices that tend to have longer active times to receive longer leases. Hence, it should work well across many environments, with less administrative intervention as the mixture of devices continues to change.

5. RELATED WORK

Although most wireless networks are configured to dynamically allocate IP addresses, relatively few studies exam-

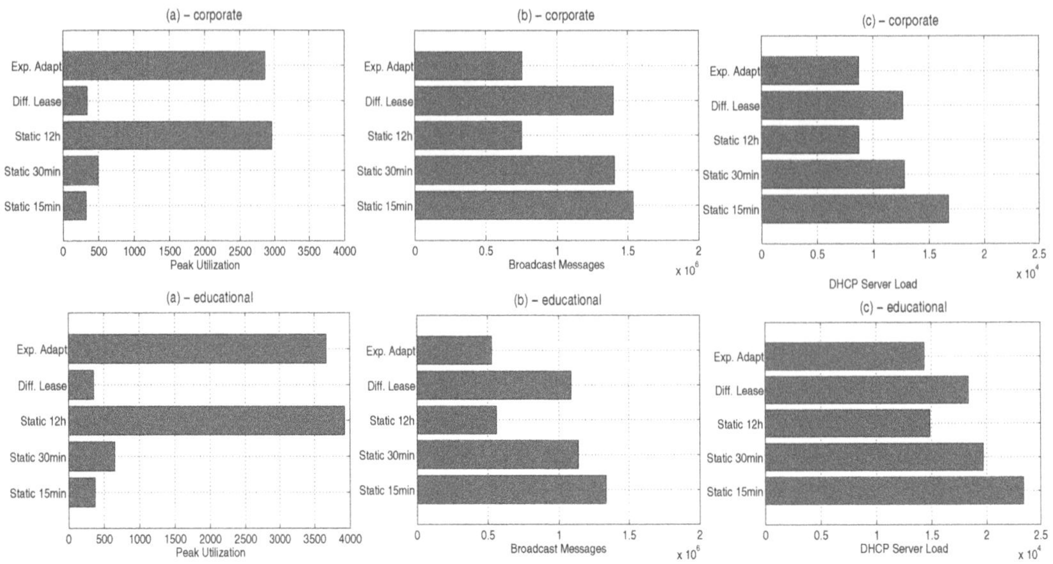

Figure 6: (a) Address space utilization (b) Broadcast messages (c) Server load, for various policies averaged per day

ine DHCP. Brick *et al.* [7] investigated the impact of lease times on DHCP performance. Khadikar *et al.* [11] studied the effects of longer DHCP lease times on address space utilization. Our work is the first to differentiate the device types and study the DHCP usage patterns of smartphones. Additionally, in contrast to previous studies, we combine DHCP and TCP/UDP behavior in order to better understand network usage patterns for each device type. Finally, our work is the first to propose DHCP leasing policies that account for the various device types and their behaviours.

With respect to device classification, Maier *et al.* [12] used a combination of IP TTL and HTTP *user-agent* information to classify device types among smartphones. Similarly, Erman *et al.* [9] identified devices based on the *user-agent* string only. Gember *et al.* [10] cross-validated the *user-agent* results with the organization unique identifier of the MAC address. In contrast, we use a different classification approach based solely on DHCP information. Our approach, in addition to being more accurate compared to the previous art, enables new DHCP leasing policies that account for different device types. Using our device classification technique, such policies can be implemented in current DHCP server software without requiring any protocol changes.

6. CONCLUSION

It has become of increasing importance for network administrators to properly allocate DHCP lease times, due to the variety of devices connected to wireless local area networks. In this paper, we show that smartphones are primary responsible for the increase in the network address utilization, and fixed lease time policies are far from optimal, even when DHCP lease times are as low as one hour. In contrast, fix leased times of 15 minutes, while they significantly decrease address utilization, produce unnecessary DHCP related overhead. To reduce this overhead, we propose a differential lease policy that assigns different lease values to each device type. The policy makes use of a novel device fingerprinting technique done at the DHCP server, without requiring any protocol changes. The main benefit of this new DHCP lease policy is that it is insensitive to the actual mixture between laptop and smartphone devices, thus removing the need to manually tune DHCP lease times as the mixture of devices continues to change.

7. REFERENCES

[1] The Bro network security monitor. `http://bro-ids.org/`.

[2] Ethernet number registration. `http://www.iana.org/assignments/ethernet-numbers`.

[3] Microsoft DHCP vendor and user classes. `http://support.microsoft.com/kb/266675`.

[4] B. Aboba, J. Carlson, and S. Cheshire. RFC 4436 - Detecting Network Attachment in IPv4 (DNAv4). IETF - `http://www.ietf.org/rfc/rfc4436.txt`, March 2006.

[5] R. Agrawal, R. Srikant, et al. Fast algorithms for mining association rules. In *VLDB*, 1994.

[6] Apple. DHCP client software. `http://www.opensource.apple.com/source/bootp/bootp-198.2/IPConfiguration.bproj/dhcp.c`.

[7] V. Brik, J. Stroik, and S. Banerjee. Debugging DHCP performance. In *Proceedings of the 7th ACM SIGCOMM Internet Measurement Conference*, pages 257–262. ACM, 2004.

[8] R. Droms. Dynamic host configuration protocol. IETF RFC, March 2007.

[9] J. Erman, A. Gerber, K. Ramakrishnan, S. Sen, and O. Spatscheck. Over the top video: The gorilla in cellular networks. In *IMC*. ACM, 2011.

[10] A. Gember, A. Anand, and A. Akella. A comparative study of handheld and non-handheld traffic in campus wi-fi networks. In *Passive and Active Measurement*, pages 173–183. Springer, 2011.

[11] M. Khadilkar, N. Feamster, M. Sanders, and R. Clark. Usage-based DHCP lease time optimization. In *Proceedings of the 7th ACM SIGCOMM Internet Measurement Conference*, pages 71–76. ACM, 2007.

[12] G. Maier, F. Schneider, and A. Feldmann. A first look at mobile hand-held device traffic. In *Passive and Active Measurement*. Springer, 2010.

[13] D. Simmons. Rapid DHCP redux. `http://cafbit.com/entry/rapid_dhcp_redux`.

Video Telephony for End-consumers: Measurement Study of Google+, iChat, and Skype

Yang Xu, Chenguang Yu, Jingjiang Li and Yong Liu
Department of Electrical and Computer Engineering
Polytechnic Institute of New York University
Brooklyn, NY, USA 11201
{yxu10, cyu03, jli12}@students.poly.edu, yongliu@poly.edu

ABSTRACT

Video telephony requires high-bandwidth and low-delay voice and video transmissions between geographically distributed users. It is challenging to deliver high-quality video telephony to end-consumers through the best-effort Internet. In this paper, we present our measurement study on three popular video telephony systems on the Internet: Google+, iChat, and Skype. Through a series of carefully designed active and passive measurements, we are able to unveil important information about their key design choices and performance, including application architecture, video generation and adaptation schemes, loss recovery strategies, end-to-end voice and video delays, resilience against random and bursty losses, etc. Obtained insights can be used to guide the design of applications that call for high-bandwidth and low-delay data transmissions under a wide range of "best-effort" network conditions.

Categories and Subject Descriptors

C.2 [**Computer-Communication Networks**]: Network Protocols

Keywords

Measurement, Video conferencing

1. INTRODUCTION

The Internet has fundamentally changed the way people communicate, ranging from emails, text-messages, blogs, tweets, to Voice-over-IP (VoIP) calls, etc. We are now experiencing the next big change: *Video Telephony*. Video telephony was originally conceived in 1920s. Due to its stringent bandwidth and delay requirements, for years, business customers have been paying high prices to utilize specialized hardware and software for video encoding, mixing and decoding, and dedicated network pipes for video distribution.Video telephony had little success in the end-consumer market, until very recently. The proliferation of video-capable consumer electronic devices and the penetration of increasingly faster residential network accesses paved the way for the wide adoption of video telephony. Two-party video chat and multi-party video conferencing services are now being offered for free or at low prices to end-consumers on various platforms. Notably, Apple iChat [15], Google+ Hangout [11], and Skype Video Calls [26] are among the most popular ones on the Internet.

Video conferencing requires high-bandwidth and low-delay voice and video transmission. While Skype encodes high-quality voice at data rate of $40kbps$, a Skype video call with good quality can easily use up bandwidth of $900kbps$ [34]. While seconds of buffering delay is often tolerable even in live video streaming, in video conferencing, user Quality-of-Experience (QoE) degrades significantly if the one-way end-to-end video delay goes over 350 milli-seconds [17]. To deliver good conferencing experience to end-consumers over the *best-effort* Internet, video conferencing solutions have to cope with user device and network access heterogeneities, dynamic bandwidth variations, and random network impairments, such as packet losses and delays. All these have to be done through video generation and distribution *in real-time*, which makes the design space extremely tight. This motivates us to conduct a measurement study of three existing solutions: iChat, Google+, and Skype, to investigate *how they address video conferencing challenges and how well they do it on the Internet.* Specifically, our study is focused on the following issues about their key design choices and their delivered user conferencing experiences.

- **System Architecture:** A natural conferencing architecture is Peer-to-Peer (P2P), where users send their voice and video to each other directly. Skype employs P2P for VoIP and two-party video chat. While P2P achieves low-delay, it comes short at achieving high-bandwidth: a residential user normally cannot upload multiple high-quality video streams simultaneously. While video conferencing servers can be employed to relay users' voice and video, data relay often incurs longer delay than direct transfer. Conferencing servers have to be strategically located and selected to balance the bandwidth and delay performance of voice and video relay between geographically distributed users.

- **Video Generation and Adaptation:** To cope with receiver heterogeneity, a source can generate single video version at a rate *downloadable* by the weakest receiver. One-version design unnecessarily limits the received

IMC'12, November 14–16, 2012, Boston, Massachusetts, USA.

video quality on other stronger receivers. Alternatively, multiple video versions can be generated, either directly by the source or by relay servers through transcoding. Different video versions will be sent to different receivers, matching their download capacities. In a simple multi-version design, each video version is encoded and transmitted separately. It incurs high encoding and bandwidth overhead. *Scalable Video Coding* (SVC) encodes video into multiple layers. It is appealing to adopt SVC in video conferencing to realize multi-version design with greatly reduced overhead.

- **Packet Loss Recovery:** To achieve reliability in realtime streaming, the conventional wisdom is to use Forward Error Correction (FEC) coding, instead of retransmission. However, in video conferencing, video has to be encoded and decoded in realtime. To avoid long FEC encoding and decoding delays, FEC blocks have to be short. This largely reduces FEC's coding efficiency and robustness against bursty losses. Meanwhile, retransmission is viable if the network delay between sender and receiver is small. Unlike FEC, retransmission adds redundancy only as needed, and hence is more bandwidth-efficient. Redundant retransmissions can also be used to protect important packets against bursty losses. The choice between FEC and retransmission is tightly coupled with system architecture and video generation.
- **User Quality-of-Experience:** Ultimately, the performance of a video conferencing system is evaluated by the delivered user conferencing experiences, which are highly sensitive to various voice and video quality metrics, such as end-to-end voice and video delay, synchronization between voice and video, video resolution, frame-rate and quantization, etc. To provide stable conferencing services to end consumers over the Internet, it is extremely important for a conferencing system to be adaptive to varying network conditions and robust against random network impairments. We systematically study the delivered user conferencing experiences of each system in a wide range of real and emulated network scenarios. We further investigate the implications of the design choices made by each system on their delivered user experiences.

It is admittedly challenging and ambitious to come up with conclusive answers for these questions. All three systems use proprietary protocols and encrypt data and signaling messages. There is very limited public information about their architectures and protocols. To address these challenges, we undertake an extensive measurement campaign and systematically measure the three systems as *black-boxes*. We observe and analyze their behaviors and performances through a set of carefully designed active and passive measurement experiments. Extrapolating from the measurement results, we are able to unveil important information about their system architecture, video encoding and adaptation, loss recovery and delivered user QoE. Our major findings are summarized as following.

1. While P2P is promising for voice conferencing and two-party video calls, P2P alone is not sufficient to sustain high-quality multi-party video conferencing. The design choices and performance of multi-party video conferencing systems are largely affected by the availability of bandwidth-rich server infrastructures.
2. Conferencing server locations not only impact the delivered user delay performance, but also affect the design of loss recovery mechanism and the achieved loss resilience. When servers are located close to end users, retransmission is more preferable than FEC to recover from random and bursty losses. Data relays through well-provisioned server networks can deliver low-delay and high-bandwidth voice and video transfers between geographically distributed users.
3. To deliver high-quality video telephony over the Internet, realtime voice and video generation, protection, adaptation, and distribution have to be *jointly* designed. Various voice and video processing delays, incurred in capturing, encoding, decoding and rendering, account for a significant portion of the end-to-end delays perceived by users.
4. Compared with multi-version video coding, layered video coding can efficiently address user access heterogeneity with low bandwidth overhead. With layered coding, content-aware prioritized selective retransmissions can further enhance the robustness of conferencing quality against random and bursty losses.

The rest of the paper is organized as follows. We briefly discuss the related work in Section 2. Our measurement platform is introduced in Section 3. Then we study the application architectures of the three systems in Section 4. Video generation and adaptation strategies are investigated in Section 5. Voice and video delay performances are measured in Section 6. In Section 7, we investigate their loss recovery strategies, and measure their resilience against bursty losses and long delays. The paper is concluded in Section 8.

2. RELATED WORK

Most of the previous measurement studies of realtime communications over the Internet were focused on Skype's VoIP service. Baset *et al* [1] first analyzed Skype's P2P topology, call establishment protocol, and NAT traversal mechanism. Since then, a lot of papers have been published on Skype's overlay architecture, P2P protocol, and VoIP traffic [2, 12]. Some other studies [3, 14, 33] focused on the quality of Skype's voice-over-IP (VoIP) calls. Huang *et al.* investigated Skype's FEC mechanism and its efficiency for voice streaming [14, 33]. In [3], the authors proposed a user satisfaction index model to quantify VoIP user satisfaction. Cicco *et al.* [4] proposed a congestion control model for Skype VoIP traffic.

More recently, there are some measurement work on video telephony. Cicco *et al.* [5] measured the responsiveness of Skype video calls to bandwidth variations. They conclude that Skype's response time to bandwidth increase is too long. In [34], we conducted an extensive measurement study of Skype two-party video calls under different network conditions. Based on the measurement results, we propose models for Skype video calls' rate control, FEC redundancy, and video quality. According to a year 2010 survey [18], most of the eighteen surveyed multi-party video conferencing systems before Skype and Google+ are sever-based. The maximum number of conferencing participants supported by each system ranges from 4 to 24.

3. MEASUREMENT PLATFORM

Our video telephony measurement effort was initiated in December 2010, right after Skype introduced its beta service of multi-party video conferencing. Since then, we have been continuously taking measurement of Skype. In June 2011, Google+ Hangout introduced its video conferencing service for users in *friend circles*. To obtain a broader view, we extended our study to Google+, as well as Apple's iChat.

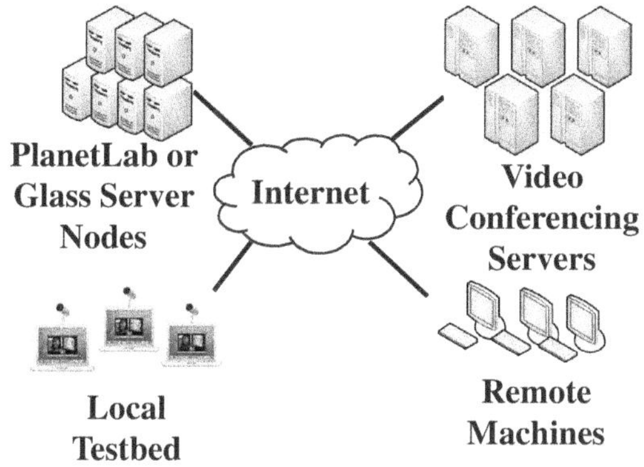

(a) Overall Testbed

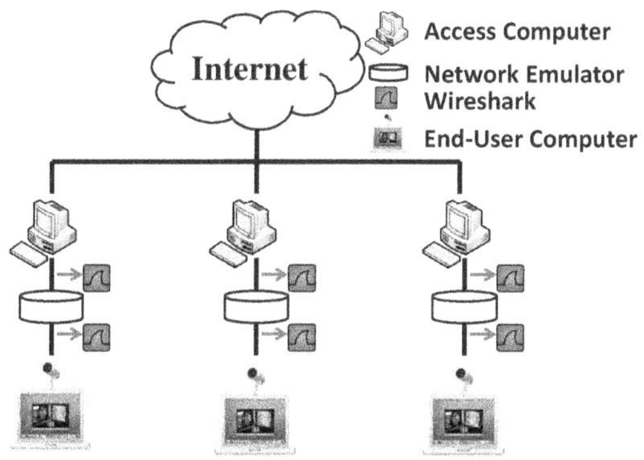

(b) Local Testbed

Figure 1: Testbed to Measure the Three Video Conferencing Systems

As illustrated in Fig 1(a), our measurement platform consists of three major components: local testbed within NYU-Poly campus network, remote machines of friends distributed all over the world, and Planetlab [22] and Glass Server [27] nodes at selected locations. Experimental video calls are established either only between our local machines, or between local machines and remote friends' machines. Planetlab and Glass Server nodes are employed for active probing to geolocate video conferencing servers. To emulate a video call, we choose a standard TV news video sequence "Akiyo" from JVT (Joint Video Team) test sequence pool. The sequence has mostly head and shoulder movements. It is very similar to a video-call scenario. We inject the video sequence into video conferencing systems using a virtual video camera tool [7]. This ensures the transmitted video contents are consistent and repeatable.

As illustrated in Fig 1(b), to emulate a wide range of network conditions, we install software-based network emulator, NEWT[20], on our local machines. It emulates a variety of network attributes, such as propagation delay, random or bursty packet loss, and available network bandwidth. We use Wireshark [31] to capture detailed packet-level information before and after the network emulators. iChat, Google+ and Skype all report technical information about video quality through application window, such as video rates, frame rates, RTT, etc. [21] We use a screen text capture tool [23] to capture these information periodically. The sampling interval is 1 second. Most of the measurement experiments are automated. All the reported statistics in the rest of the paper are drawn from a large number of samples.

4. SYSTEM ARCHITECTURE

There are three main architectures for networked applications: client-server, peer-to-peer, and hybrid of the two. Skype delivers a scalable VoIP service using P2P, where users connect to each other directly as much as possible. In a video conference, a source encodes his video at a rate much higher than that of voice, and might have to send the encoded video to multiple receivers. From the bandwidth point of view, a pure P2P design might not be sustainable. We now investigate the application architectures adopted by the three video telephony systems.

4.1 Methodology

For each system, we set up video calls and use Wireshark to capture packets sent out and received by each computer. Each user in the conference generates voice and video packets constantly at significant rates. In our Wireshark trace analysis, we capture those TCP and UDP sessions, whose durations are long enough (at least half of the conference session time) and data rates are significant (larger than 5*kbps*), as voice or video flows. To get the right topology and differentiate between signaling packets, voice packets and video packets, we conduct three stages of experiments. In the first stage, each user sets his voice and video on to form a video conference. In the second stage, users only set voice on to form a voice conference. In the third stage, all users shut down their videos and mute their voices. We compare the recorded flow sessions in the three stages. Consequently, we identify voice flows, video flows, and signaling flows.

4.2 iChat is P2P

iChat employs a P2P architecture and users in a conference form a star topology at the application layer as shown in Fig. 2(a). The central hub is the conference initiator, i.e., the user who initiated the conference. Only the conference initiator has the right to add people into the conference or close the entire conference. A normal user uploads his voice and video data to the initiator through one UDP flow, and also downloads other participants' voice and video data from the initiator through another UDP flow. Participants use UDP port 16402. Voice and video are transported using the RTP protocol [13]. Normal users only connect to the initiator. There is no direct connection between two normal users. iChat cannot work if UDP traffic is blocked.

4.3 Google+ is Server-centric

Google+ video calls, both two-party and multi-party, always use server-centric topology, as illustrated in Fig. 2(b).

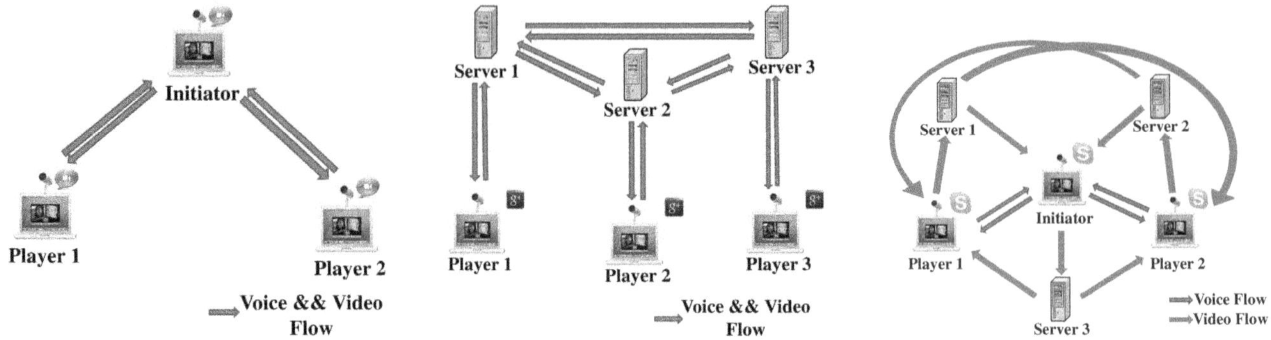

(a) iChat (b) Google+ Hangout (c) Skype multi-party

Figure 2: System Architectures of the iChat, Google+, and Skype

Each user sends his voice and video to a dedicated proxy server, and also receives other users' voice and video from that server. There is no direct transmissions between users. Generally, different users choose different proxy servers. Thus, the proxy servers need to communicate with each other to exchange users' voice and video. Each user opens four connections with his proxy server on the same server port (Port 19305). Most of the time, these four connections all use UDP. TCP is used only when we deliberately block UDP traffic. There is a trick [21] to access various statistics of Google+. The statistics show that two of the four flows carry voice and video respectively. Google+ also uses RTP protocol to transmit voice and video. The other two flows' payloads conform to the format of RTCP protocol. We infer that those two flows carry signaling information.

4.4 Skype is Hybrid

For two-party video calls, Skype uses direct P2P transmission for voice and video if the two users can establish a direct connection [34]. When three or more users are involved, the network topology is shown in Fig. 2(c). Voice is still transmitted using P2P. Similar to iChat, the conference initiator acts as the central hub. A normal user uploads his voice to the initiator and downloads other users' voice from the initiator. In a conference with three users, the upload flow rate from a normal user to the initiator is around $40kbps$. And the download rate from the initiator to that user is around $50kbps$, less than the total rate of two separate voice flows. This indicates that the initiator might use *sound mixing technique* to combine voices of multiple users into one voice stream. For video transmission, each user uploads his video to a Skype server, which relays the video flow directly to all other users in the conference, without going through another relay server. Different users normally choose different relay servers.

Similar to Google+, Skype mostly uses UDP to transmit voice and video, and only switches to TCP if UDP is blocked. Different from Google+ and iChat, Skype does not use RTP and RTCP. In addition to voice and video flows, we also observe some low-rate flows between servers and users. We conjecture that these small flows are for signaling.

4.5 Conferencing Server Placement

Google+ and Skype employ relay servers. If servers are not properly located and selected for users, voice and video relay will incur long delays that significantly degrade users' experience of realtime interaction in a conference. To determine the server locations of Skype and Google+, we set up video conferences with our friends all over the world. Table 1 shows the Google+ server IP addresses used by our friends from different locations. When using a popular geolocation tool Maxmind [19] to geo-locate those IP addresses, we were surprised that all Google+ server IP addresses are geo-located to Mountain View, CA, USA. However, this seems incorrect. In Table 1, we also report the measured RTT between our friends' machines and their corresponding proxy Google+ servers. The RTT results suggest that most of our friends are assigned to Google+ servers within short network distances, except for the two friends in Australia. Thus, we infer that Google+ hangout deploy conferencing servers all over the world.

Table 1: RTT to Google+ Hangout Servers

Friend Location	Server IP	RTT (ms)
Hong Kong, CHN	74.125.71.127	3.49
Armagh, UK	173.194.78.127	8.88
Rio de Janeiro, BRA	64.233.163.127	9.02
New York, USA	173.194.76.127	14.2
Aachen, DE	173.194.70.127	20.00
Toronto, CA	209.85.145.127	26.76
San Jose, USA	173.194.79.127	28.89
Brisbane, AU	72.14.203.127	147
Canberra, AU	74.125.31.127	147

We did similar experiments for Skype. We found that the server IP addresses for our friend machines are all located in the subnet of 208.88.186.00/24. Maxmind [19] reports that those servers are in Estonia. To verify this, we select Planetlab [22] and Glass Server [27] nodes to ping Skype servers randomly picked from the identified subnet and report the RTT results in Table 2. From nodes located in New York and Hong Kong, we also pinged all possible IP addresses in the subnet. The RTT results are consistent with the corresponding values from these two locations listed in Table 2. This suggests that those Skype servers are likely in the same physical location. Even if the bit propagation speed is exactly the speed of light ($3 \cdot 10^8$ meters/sec), the RTT between New York and Estonia is about 44.4ms (11,314km) [16], which is even larger than the measured RTT in Table 2. Thus, Skype servers can't be located in Estonia. To geolocate Skype servers, we did additional traceroute experiments from different locations. We found that the last-hop router IP addresses are all located near New Jersey area. This is consistent with Table 2, where the location with the smallest RTT is New Haven. Thus, we infer that Skype servers are located near the New Jersey/New York area. As will be shown in the following sections, server locations not only directly impact users' delay performance, but also have implications on the design and performance of loss recovery mechanisms of Google+ and Skype.

Table 2: RTT to Skype Video Relay Servers

PlanetLab/Glass Server Locations	RTT (ms)
New Haven, USA	17.4
New York, USA	25.9
Washington, USA	31.3
Vancouver, CA	61.41
San Jose, USA	67.5
London, UK	99.2
Guayaquil, EC	111
Saarbrucken, DE	138
Oulu, FIN	151
Rio de Janeiro, BRA	176
Tel Aviv, IL	207
Canberra, AU	222
Hong Kong, CHN	226
Brisbane, AU	266
West Bengal, IN	324

5. VIDEO GENERATION AND ADAPTATION

In a video conference, each source encodes and uploads his video in realtime. To cope with network bandwidth variations, the encoded video rate on a source first has to be adapted to his available uplink bandwidth. Additionally, in multi-party video conferencing, each source has multiple receivers, potentially with different download capacities. The source video encoding rate also has to be adapted to receivers' download capacities. In an *one-version* design, a source generates single video version that can be downloaded by the weakest receiver, and sends that version to all receivers. This unnecessarily limits the received video quality on stronger receivers. It is more desirable for a source to send different receivers different video qualities, maximally matching their download capacities. In a simple *multi-version* design, a source uses different video encoding parameters to generate multiple versions of the same video, and simultaneously uploads those versions to the server/receivers. One obvious drawback is that, as an end-host, a source might not have enough bandwidth to upload multiple versions. Alternatively, a source can send one copy of his video to a server, which then transcodes it into multiple versions at lower qualities. The third option is the *multi-layer* design, where a source encodes a video into multiple layers, using the recent scalable video coding techniques, such as SVC [25] or MDC [29]. A receiver can decode a basic quality video after receiving the base layer. Higher video quality can be obtained as more video layers are received. Recent advances in SVC coding has brought down the layered video encoding overhead to 10% [30]. With multi-layer coding, a source only needs to send out all layers using upload bandwidth slightly higher than the one-version design, and realizes the effect of multi-version design by allowing different receivers download different numbers of layers, matching their download capacities. It does not require server transcoding. It is robust against bandwidth variations and packet losses: a basic quality video can still be decoded as long as the base layer is received reliably.

5.1 Methodology

Since there is no public information about their video generation and adaptation strategies, we design experiments to trigger video adaptation by manipulating source upload bandwidth and receiver download bandwidth. In our local testbed, for all users involved in the conference, we set up one user as the sender, turn on his video and use the other users purely as receivers. We denote such a setting as a *sub-conference*, which is a basic component of the whole conference. As illustrated in Fig. 1, the bandwidth of the sender and receivers can all be set by the network emulator NEWT. We collect video information from the application window. We also record the packets using Wireshark [31] for offline video payload analysis.

5.2 Video Encoding Parameters

To cope with bandwidth variations, all three systems encode video using a wide range of parameters, as shown in Table 3. From the perspective of a viewer, the perceived video quality is mostly determined by three video encoding parameters: resolution, frame rate, and quantization. The frame rates can vary from 1 FPS (Frame-Per-Second) to 30 FPS for each system. In our experiments, the ranges of the observed resolution values are also listed in Table 3. Skype and Google+ adapt video resolution to network bandwidth. iChat's video resolution is determined by the number of users in the conference. For example, the resolution is always set to be 640×480 in the case of two-party call. When three or more users involved in the conference, the resolution becomes 320×240 or 160×120. And once the resolution is set at the beginning, it will not be changed afterward, no matter how we change the bandwidth setting. We cannot directly measure the quantization adaptation for any of the three systems.

Table 3: Video Rate and Resolution Ranges

System	Rate (kbps)	Resolutions
iChat	49 ~ 753	640*480,320*240,160*120
Google+	28 ~ 890	640*360,480*270,320*180 240*135,160*90,80*44
Skype	5 ~ 1200	640*480,320*240,160*120

5.3 Video Adaptation

When the upload link bandwidth of a sender varies, the video rate out of the sender changes correspondingly. Generally, for these three systems, the higher the upload link bandwidth, the larger the sending rate. When the upload bandwidth is too small, they will automatically shutdown the video. This shows that the three systems have their own available network bandwidth probing algorithms to determine the video quality to be encoded. To study video adaptation to receiver bandwidth heterogeneity, we set receivers' download capacities to different levels.

5.3.1 iChat uses One-version Encoding

We found that iChat uses *one-version encoding:* heterogenous receivers always receive the same video version, and the receiver with the lowest download capacity determines the video quality sent out by the sender. No video trans-coding, nor layered coding, is employed.

5.3.2 Skype uses Multi-version Encoding

When there is a large variability in receivers' download capacities, Skype employs *source-side multi-version encoding.* For example, in a video conference of one sender and three receivers, receiver 1, receiver 2 and receiver 3's download capacities are set to 150 kbps, 400 kbps and 2000 kbps respectively. The sender generates three video versions and uploads them to the relay server, which distributes one of the three video versions to the appropriate receiver. In this case, the received video rates on receiver 1, 2, and 3 are 70 kbps, 200 kbps, and 500 kbps, respectively. Server-side transcoding was not observed. In our experiments, the largest number of video versions that a sender can generate is three. When receiver capacity variability is small, or the sender upload capacity is low, Skype uses one-version encoding and sends to all receivers the same video quality.

5.3.3 Google+ uses Multi-layer Encoding

Google+ always give different video qualities to heterogenous receivers. For example, we only limit the download capacity of one receiver, say receiver 2, to 500 kbps. On the sender side, the encoded video rate is 835.7 kbps, with resolution of $640*360$ and frame rate of 30 FPS. On receiver 1, the received video rate is 386.9 kbps, with resolution of $640*360$, and frame rate of 14 FPS. On receiver 2, the received video rate is 168.6 kbps, with resolution of $320*180$, and frame rate of 14 FPS. The perceptual video quality on both receiver 1 and receiver 2 are consistent and acceptable. The experiment environment is not fully controlled. Video flows between our experiment machines and Google+ servers traverse the Internet, and have to compete with cross traffic. This explains that the received quality on receiver 1 is lower than the original video sent out by the sender, although we didn't add any bandwidth constraint on receiver 1.

To gain more insight about how the two video qualities are generated, we examine the packets captured on the sender and receivers. Both Google+ and iChat use RTP[13] protocol for voice and video transmission. Even though video payload cannot be directly decoded to reveal how video is generated, several fields in RTP headers enable us to infer the video coding strategy employed by Google+. According to RTP header format specification [24], "Sequence Number" field increments by one for each RTP data packet sent, and can be used by the receiver to detect packet loss and restore packet sequence. In Google+, video packets generated by one source form a unique sequence. "Timestamp" field records the sampling instant of the first octet in the RTP data packet. In Google+ RTP packet traces, we observe that a flight of packets with consecutive sequence numbers carry the same timestamp. We infer that those packets belong to the same video frame. The common timestamp is indeed the generation time of the frame. If a packet is the last one in a frame, then its "Marker" field is set to 1; otherwise the value is 0. Thus, we infer that the "Marker" field can be used to identify the boundary between two adjacent video frames. Since different machines use different initial sequence numbers, to match video frames between the sender and receivers, we instead use the "Timestamp", "Marker" and "Length" fields.

In Table 4, we match the RTP packets sent out by the sender and received by the two receivers based on their Timestamps, Marker (labeled 'M') and Length. (Packets in the same row have the same values in these three fields.) In the aligned table, the sender sent out five video frames, both receiver 1 and receiver 2 only received two frames. While receiver 1 received all packets of those two frames, receiver 2 only received the first two packets of those two frames. It should be noted that sequence numbers in receiver 1 and receiver 2 are consecutive. The lost packets/frames are not due to packet losses. Instead, it is the video relay server who decides not to send those frames/packets to receivers based on their bandwidth conditions.

Both receivers can decode the video with decent quality. This suggests that Google+ employs multi-layer coding. Since receiver 1 can decode the video even though some frames are missing, the layered coding used by Google+ achieves *temporal scalability*: video frames are temporally grouped into layers, such that a high frame-rate video generated by the sender can still be decoded at a lower frame-rate by a receiver even if a subset of frames/layers are dropped. Since receiver 2 can decode video even though it lost some packets within each frame, the layered coding used by Google+ also achieves *spatial scalability*: a video frame is encoded into spatial layers at the sender, such that even if some spatial layers are lost, the receiver can still decode the frame at lower resolution and larger quantization. In the experiment, we observe that no matter how low the download bandwidth of a receiver is, the received video resolution is at least one quarter of the resolution of the original video. This shows that the encoded video only has two spatial layers. This is reasonable, because spatial layers incur much higher encoding overhead than temporal layers. Thus, the number of spatial layers could not be too large.

We also developed a script and analyzed other RTP packet traces of Google+. It is verified that Google+ employs layered video coding with temporal and spatial scalability. Different layers have different importances for video decoding. Consequently, one should use different realtime transmission and protection strategies for different layers. As will be shown in the later sections, prioritized loss recovery scheme can be designed for layered video coding to achieve high robustness against packet losses.

6. VOICE AND VIDEO DELAY

To facilitates realtime interactions between users, video conferencing systems have to deliver voice and video with short delays. User conferencing experience degrades significantly if the one-way end-to-end video delay goes over 350 milli-seconds [17]. In this section, we study the delay performance of the three systems.

6.1 Methodology

The end-to-end voice/video delay perceived by a user is the sum of delays incurred by realtime voice/video capturing, encoding, transmission, decoding, and rendering. We can divide the end-to-end delay into four portions. Let T_e be the voice/video capturing and encoding delay at the sender, T_n be the one-way transmission and propagation delay on the network path between the sender and the receiver, T_s

Table 4: RTP Packet Headers in Google+

M	Timestamp	Length (bytes)	Sequence Number		
			Sender	Receiver1	Receiver2
0	2063696701	1269	61603	44445	52498
0	2063696701	1113	61604	44446	52499
0	2063696701	1278	61605	44447	
0	2063696701	1234	61606	44448	
0	2063696701	1283	61607	44449	
0	2063696701	1277	61608	44450	
0	2063696701	1077	61609	44451	
1	2063696701	989	61610	44452	
0	2063699269	621	61611		
1	2063699269	560	61612		
0	2063703362	1086	61613		
0	2063703362	485	61614		
0	2063703362	1167	61615		
1	2063703362	1048	61616		
0	2063706604	543	61617		
1	2063706604	914	61618		
0	2063709620	1276	61619	44453	52500
0	2063709620	1067	61620	44454	52501
0	2063709620	1272	61621	44455	
0	2063709620	1267	61622	44456	
0	2063709620	1279	61623	44457	
0	2063709620	1276	61624	44458	
1	2063709620	736	61625	44459	

be the server or super-node processing time ($T_s = 0$, if there is no server or super-node involved), and T_d be the video or voice decoding and playback delay at the receiver. Thus, the one-way voice (video) delay is:

$$T = T_e + T_n + T_s + T_d. \quad (1)$$

Obviously, it is not sufficient to just measure the network transmission delay T_n. We therefore measure end-to-end delay by emulating a real user's experience.

6.1.1 One-way Voice Delay

To record one-way voice delay, we employ a repeatable "Tick" sound as the voice source and inject it to the sender using a virtual microphone [28]. In our local testbed, we set up three computers side by side, as illustrated in Fig. 3(a). One computer is the voice sender, another one is the voice receiver. The sender repeatedly sends the "Tick" sound to the receiver. The third computer emulates a user and "hears" (records) the sound injected to the voice sender and the sound coming out of the receiver using a sound recording software [10]. [1] We can visually analyze the captured sound signal in that software. Fig. 3(b) shows a recorded sound wave sample. In the upper subfigure, we observe two sequences of impulses at different amplitudes. Since we set the volume of the sender's speaker significantly lower than the receiver's speaker, the impulses with smaller amplitudes correspond to the repeated "Ticks" sent by the sender, the impulses with larger amplitudes are the received "Ticks" on the receiver. On the sender, we set the time interval between two "Tick"s to be 1,000 ms, larger than the expected voice delay, so that we can match a large impulse with the preceding small impulse. The lower subfigure is the zoom-in view of the two adjacent sound impulses. Each impulse is indeed a waveform segment with rich frequency components.

[1]The sender uses a virtual microphone to inject the "Tick" sound to conferencing system. Consequently, the received sound on the receiver will NOT be looped back to system.

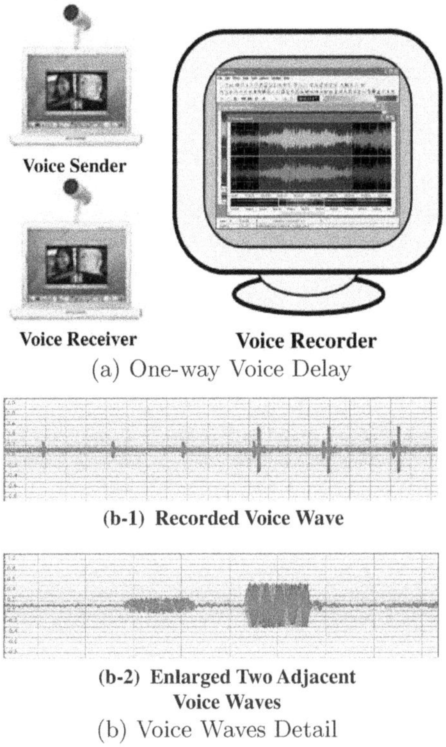

(a) One-way Voice Delay

(b) Voice Waves Detail

Figure 3: Testbed to Measure Vioce Delay

We use the time-lags between the first peaks of two adjacent segments as the one-way voice delays.

6.1.2 One-way Video Delay

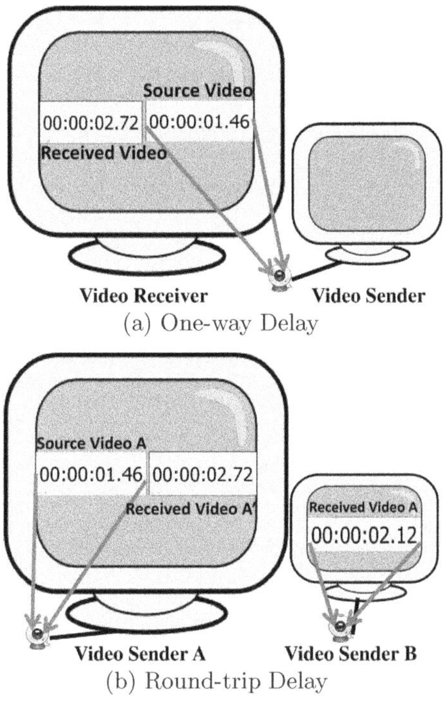

(a) One-way Delay

(b) Round-trip Delay

Figure 4: Testbed to Measure Video Delay

To measure video delay, we similarly emulate a user's video experience by simultaneously "viewing" (recoding) the original video on the sender and the received video on the receiver using a video capturing program. As illustrated in Fig. 4(a), we set up two computers side-by-side in our local testbed, one as the sender, the other as the receiver. We run a stopwatch program [8] on the *receiver* side, and focus the sender's video camera on the stopwatch window on the receiver's screen. The sender transmits the stopwatch video captured from the receiver screen back to the receiver using one of the three conferencing systems. There are two stopwatch videos on the receiver's screen: the original stopwatch video, and the copy captured by the sender then transmitted back through the video conferencing system. At any given time, the difference between the two stopwatches is the one-way end-to-end video delay perceived by the receiver. For the example in Fig. 4(a), the original stopwatch shows time "00:00:02.72" second and the received copy of the stopwatch shows time "00:00:01.46" second. Thus, the video delay in this case is $1,260$ ms. We use a software program running on the receiver to capture the snapshots of the receiver screen 10 times every second. We then use a software [6] to convert the captured pictures into mono-color, and extract stopwatch images from the mono-color pictures. Finally, the stopwatch readings will be decoded from stopwatch images using an Optical Character Recognition (OCR) software [9]. It should be noted that if the received video quality is bad, the OCR software cannot decode the stopwatch readings correctly. We skip those undecodable samples in our delay calculation. The undecodable picture ratio can also be used to infer the received video quality.

6.1.3 *Round-trip Video Delay*

The previous method does not work if the sender and the receiver are not in the same location. We develop another method to measure the *round-trip video delay* between two geographically distributed computers. As illustrated in Fig. 4(b), we run a stopwatch program on user A. A uses his camera to capture the stopwatch as its source video, and transmits it to user B using one of the three conferencing systems. The received stopwatch video is now displayed on B's screen. Then B focuses his camera on the received video from A, and sends the captured video back to A by using the same conferencing system. Then on A's screen, we can observe two stopwatch videos: the original one, and the one that is first sent to B, then recaptured and sent back to A by B. The clock difference between the two stopwatches on A reflects the summation of one-way video delay from A to B, and the one-way video delay from B back to A, in other words, the *round-trip video delay*. If we assume the two directions are symmetric, then the one-way video delay is roughly half of the round-trip delay. After the cameras on A and B are properly positioned, we only need to take screen shots on A. We can further use the same approach as in the one-way video delay case to process the data and get a large number of delay samples.

6.2 One-way Voice and Video Delay

We first test the one-way delay between users in our local testbed. All user computers are connected to the same router. The network delay along the direct connection between them is almost negligible.

Table 5: One-way Delay Performance (ms)

Systems		Video	Voice
Google+		180	100
Skype Two-Party		156	110
Skype Multi-party	initiator to normal	230	130
	normal to normal	230	190
iChat Two-Party		220	220
iChat Multi-party	initiator to normal	220	220
	non-initi. to non-initi.	270	270

The voice delay and video delay performances for three systems are listed in Table 5. For Google+, the average video delay is $180ms$, larger than the voice delay of $100ms$. As studied in Section 4.3, Google+ uses server-centric architecture. The round trip network delay between our local testbed and the allocated Google+ server is $14ms$. The addition delays are due to voice and video processing on both ends. It takes longer to process video than voice. Skype two-party calls use direct P2P transmissions for voice and video. Since network delays between machines in local testbed are almost zero, the measured one-way delays are mostly due to voice/video processing. *This suggests that voice and video processing can take a significant portion of the delay allowance of good-quality video conferencing.*

As studied in Section 4.4, Skype multi-party call employs different overlay topologies for voice and video transmissions. The voice flow from a non-initiator to another non-initiator has to be transmitted to the initiator first. The initiator will do some processing, like voice mixing and recoding. Thus, the voice delay between an initiator and a non-initiator is shorter than the voice delay between two non-initiators. Since video has to be first sent to Skype servers then relayed to receivers, Skype video delay is larger than voice delay. Video and voice are *unsynchronized*. The voice and video delay gap is as large as $100ms$ when we consider the case from an initiator to a normal user.

iChat transmits video and voice in one RTP flow. For two-party calls, video and voice are synchronized. For multi-party conferences, when voice and video flows are transmitted from the initiator to non-initiators, delay performance is the same as the two-party case. The voice and video delays between two non-initiators are longer than those between the initiator and non-initiators. Since the network delays are negligible, the additional delays are mostly for the initiator to combine packets generated by different sources into one RTP flow before sending it to a receiver.

6.3 Round-trip Video Delay

We also measure the round-trip video delays (video RTTs) between New York City and Hong Kong, New York City and Singapore when using Google+ Hangout and Skype Multi-party conferencing systems respectively. From Figure 5, in both cases, video RTTs of Google+ are much smaller than those of Skype. For the case between New York and Singapore, Google+'s mean video RTT is only about $579ms$, with standard deviation of $44ms$. We can approximate the one-way video delay by half of the video RTT. Google+'s one-way video delay is about $290ms$, within the $350ms$ delay allowance. To the contrary, Skype's mean video RTT is about $1,048ms$, with standard deviation of $239ms$. The corresponding one-way delay is over the delay allowance. Between New York City and Hong Kong, the average one-way video delay of Google+ is $374ms$, again much shorter than Skype's average delay of $788ms$.

From the topology study in Section 4, in Skype, video generated by a source is directly relayed by a server to all receivers. Video flows from a source to its assigned Skype relay server and from the relay server to the receivers all have to traverse the public Internet. They have to compete with background network traffic. To the contrary, Google+ deploy relay servers located all around the world, and a user is mostly connected to a close-by server. The transmission between Google+ relay servers likely traverse their own private backbone network with good QoS guarantee. This way Google+ voice and video relays incur much less random network losses and delays than Skype's voice and video relays over the public Internet. Additionally, as will be shown in the following section, Google+'s loss recovery scheme is more efficient than Skype, which also leads to shorter end-to-end video delay.

7. ROBUSTNESS AGAINST LOSSES

One main challenge of delivering video telephony over the best-effort Internet is to cope with unpredictable network impairments, such as congestion delays, random or bursty packet losses. To achieve reliability in realtime streaming, the conventional wisdom is to use packet-level forward error correction (FEC) coding, instead of retransmissions, which would incur too much delay. Unfortunately, in video conferencing, to avoid long FEC encoding and decoding delays, FEC blocks have to be short. This largely reduces the FEC coding efficiency and its robustness against bursty losses. If the network delay between the sender and the receiver is short, e.g. RTT of $20ms$ between our local testbed and Google+ servers, retransmissions might be affordable within an end-to-end delay allowance of $350ms$. Unlike FEC, retransmission adds in redundancy only as needed, and hence is more bandwidth-efficient. Redundant retransmissions can also be used to protect important packets against bursty losses. In this section, we investigate how the three systems recover from packet losses, and how robust they are against random and bursty losses.

7.1 Methodology

We set up multi-party conferences using machines in our local testbed. We conduct two sets of experiments by injecting packet losses using network emulators. In the first set of experiments, we add upload losses on the video sender side. In the second set, we add download losses on only one of the receivers. Because we capture packets before and after the loss module, we can figure out which packets are lost. Through packet trace analysis, we can also search for packets that have similar payloads as the lost ones to check whether retransmission is employed or not. At the same time, we monitor the application window to collect statistics on video rates and total data rates to calculate redundant transmission ratios.

7.2 Skype uses FEC

In our Skype experiments, we never found any retransmission of lost packets. From Skype's technical window, we can easily observe gaps between the total data rates and video rates. Previous studies [33, 34] suggest that Skype employs aggressive Forward Error Correction (FEC) coding for VoIP and two-party video calls. We infer that the observed rate gaps are also due to FEC. Let r_v be the actual video rate, r_s be the actual sending rate. FEC redundancy ratio ρ is calculated as the ratio between the redundant traffic rate and the total sending rate:

$$\rho = \frac{r_s - r_v}{r_s} \tag{2}$$

The experiment results of adding random upload losses are shown in Table 6. The reported video rates are the same on the sender and two receivers. Surprisingly, the sender always adds significant redundancy even if we don't introduce any additional packet losses. (Note that, since the upload flow traverses the Internet to reach Skype server, the sender might still incur some packet losses. Since we don't know the actual loss rate, we can't get a precise FEC model for Skype's multi-party calls similar to the model for the two-party calls in [34].) On the other hand, the redundancy ratios on the two receivers are pretty low, even though the download flows also have to traverse the Internet. One possible explanation is that Skype tries hard to protect video uploaded by a source, because any lost video during the upload has quality implications on all receivers. As we introduce additional losses, the video rate goes down significantly, and the FEC ratio increases. However, due to the initial high FEC ratio, the increase trend is not obvious when we further increase the loss rate. When the loss rate is really high, Skype significantly drops its video rate and the total sending rate. This is consistent with the observation for Skype two-party call in [34].

The results for download losses are shown in Table 7. Again, the reported video rates are the same on the sender and two receivers. We only add random download losses to receiver 1. The FEC ratio is much less aggressive than in the upload loss case. But there is still a trend that as the loss rate increases, more FEC packets are added into the video flow of receiver 1. In Table 6, we can also observe that quite often the download flow rates on the two receivers are lower than the upload rate of the sender. This suggests that the relay server first removes FEC packets from the received data, and then adds new FEC packets to each download flow. Results of Table 7 shows that the two receivers in different conditions receive the same video rate with different FEC ratios. Thus, we infer that relay server monitors network conditions of receivers and calculate different FEC ratios for different receivers.

7.3 Google+ uses Selective Persistent Retransmission

As shown in Section 4.3, a Google+ user only interacts with a Google+ server for video upload and download. In our experiments, we only focus on one video sender and one video receiver. We first set up a machine as a video sender and inject random packet losses to its uplink. Then we capture the packets before and after the network emulator so that we can identify the lost packets. In our packet trace analysis, if two packets have the same "Timestamp" and "Sequence Number", we treat them as redundant transmissions of the same packet. (Payload analysis shows that the bit information of those matched packets are almost the same except for several bits). Thus, we can identify retransmissions of lost packets. Detailed results are presented in Table 8. As more losses are injected, more retransmissions

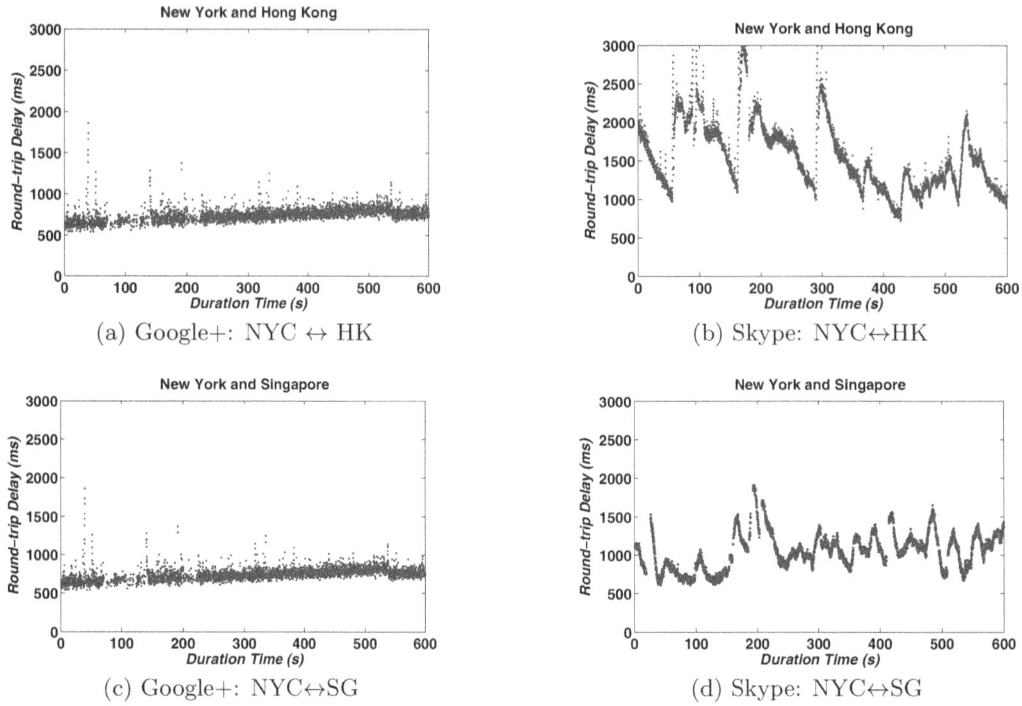

Figure 5: Round-trip Video Delays of Google+ and Skype

Table 6: FEC Adaptation at Skype Sender Side

Video Rate (kbps)	Video Sender Side			Video Receiver 1		Video Receiver 2	
	Upload Loss Ratio	Upload Rate (kbps)	FEC Ratio ρ_s	Received Rate (kbps)	FEC Ratio ρ_r	Received Rate (kbps)	FEC Ratio ρ_r
513.48	0	974.00	0.47	542.62	0.05	542.56	0.05
474.26	0.02	1108.00	0.57	519.61	0.09	522.05	0.09
460.37	0.05	1019.50	0.55	487.84	0.06	488.19	0.06
225.05	0.08	496.57	0.55	241.80	0.07	241.32	0.07

appear in the flow. However, the sender video FPS doesn't change too much when we increase upload loss from 0% to 20%. We calculate video rate as total rate minus retransmission rate. Google+ strives to maintain a high video upload rate even under high packet losses. This is similar to Skype's high FEC protection for video uploading. The *recovery ratio* is defined as the fraction of lost packets that are eventually received by the receiver. It shows that Google+ implements *selective retransmission*, only half of the lost packets are recovered. The *persistent ratio* defines the fraction of packets retransmitted at least once that are eventually received by the receiver. A persistent ratio of 1 means that if Google+ attempts to retransmit a packet, it will persistently retransmit the packet until it is received successfully. Since Google+ uses layered video coding, where packets from the lower video layers are more important for decoding. We conjecture Google+ applies *selective persistent retransmission* to packets of the lower video layers first. In all experiments, Google+ consistently offers good video quality, even under 20% uplink loss.

The results of adding download losses on the receiver is shown in Table 9. It shows a different trend. The received video frame rate, the total rate, and video rate inferred from retransmission rate all decrease as the download loss rate increases. This suggests that Google+ servers use packet loss as a signal to infer network congestion. As packet loss rate increases, it not only retransmits important lost packets, but also proactively reduces the number of video layers to be sent to a receiver. The recovery ratio and persistent ratio are more or less the same as the upload loss case. Because we cannot control packet loss outside of our local testbed, we still observe packet retransmissions even if the injected packet loss rate is zero. We also tried downlink loss rate of 40%. Surprisingly, Google+ still offers reasonably good perceptual video quality.

Table 8: Google+ Retransmission: Uplink

Loss Rate	Video FPS	Total Rate (kbps)	Retran. Rate (kbps)	Rcvry. Ratio	Persis. Ratio
0	29.97	826.0	0.9	-	-
0.05	29.98	836.9	24.2	0.46	1.00
0.10	29.97	885.7	52.1	0.46	1.00
0.20	29.98	857.2	101.4	0.45	1.00

To gain more insights about Google+'s loss recovery s-

Table 7: FEC Adaptation at Skype Relay Server Side

Video Rate (kbps)	Video Sender Side		Video Receiver 1			Video Receiver 2	
	Upload Rate (kbps)	FEC Ratio ρ_s	Download Loss Ratio	Relay Send Rate (kbps)	FEC Ratio ρ_r	Received Rate (kbps)	FEC Ratio ρ_r
513.48	974.00	0.47	0	542.62	0.05	542.56	0.05
478.52	1163.87	0.59	0.02	653.40	0.27	505.43	0.05
440.94	955.72	0.54	0.05	949.73	0.54	465.82	0.05
343.73	821.43	0.58	0.08	824.39	0.58	363.88	0.06

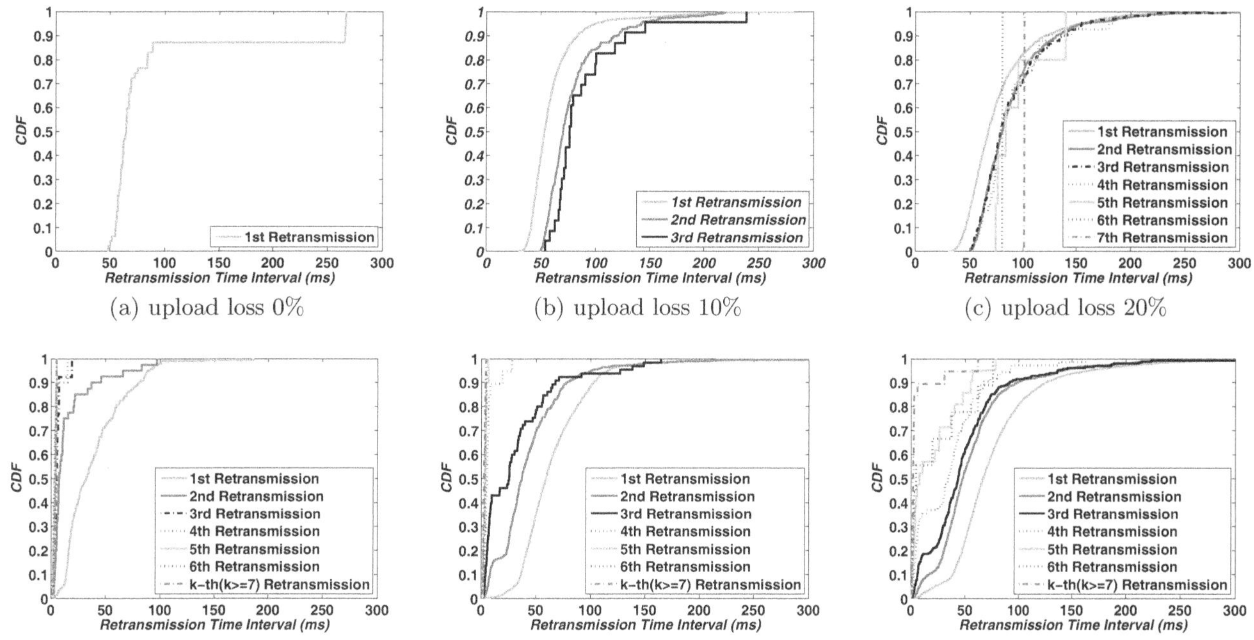

(a) upload loss 0% (b) upload loss 10% (c) upload loss 20%

(d) download loss 0% (e) download loss 10% (f) download loss 20%

Figure 6: CDF of Retransmission Time Intervals for Google+ Hangout

Table 9: Google+ Retransmission: Downlink

Loss Rate	Video FPS	Total Rate (kbps)	Retran. Rate (kbps)	Rcvry. Ratio	Persis. Ratio
0	27.91	810.8	4.4	-	-
0.05	27.07	827.3	35.2	0.51	1.00
0.10	20.158	744.3	67.4	0.60	1.00
0.20	19.231	677.7	116.4	0.64	1.00

trategy, we collect more statistics about its packet retransmissions. Table 10 lists how many retransmissions Google+ attempted to reliably transfer a packet at different packet loss rates. Most of the time, retransmission is done within one or two tries. Sometimes, a packet is retransmitted many times, with the highest up to 18 times. We define the *k-th retransmission interval* as the time lag between the kth retransmission and the $(k-1)th$ retransmission of the same packet (the original transmission is considered as the $0th$ retransmission). Table 11 presents the mean and standard deviation of retransmission intervals. For reference, the RTT between our machines and Google+ server is 14 ms. And the CDFs of retransmission intervals are plotted in Figure 6. In general, the retransmission intervals on the uplink are longer than the downlink. On the uplink side, 60% of the first retransmissions happen within $70ms$ after the first original packet transmission, which is about 3.75 times of the RTT. The retransmissions on the video uploader side all need to wait for such a long time. This is to avoid wasting valuable user upload bandwidth in retransmitting delayed, instead of lost, packets. On the downlink side, Google+ servers retransmit lost packets more aggressively with shorter intervals. Aggressive retransmissions might waste some server bandwidth, but recover faster from losses. Many of the N-th ($N \geq 5$) retransmissions are attempted within $5ms$ after the previous retransmission. This batch retransmission strategy is likely used to deal with severe and/or bursty packet losses.

7.4 iChat's Retransmission Strategy

iChat also uses retransmission to recover from packet losses. We did similar measurement for iChat as for Google+. The results for its retransmissions are shown in Table 12 and Table 13. Unlike Skype and Google+, video FPS decreases when upload losses are induced. However, that value doesn't change too much under download loss. Different from Google+, iChat does not do selective retransmission. It always retransmit lost packets. But, its retransmission is not

Table 10: Retransmission Probability in Google+

Loss Rate	1st	2nd	3rd	4th	5th	6th	k-th ($k \geq 7$)
Uplink: 0	1.00						
Uplink: 0.05	0.9492	0.0477	0.0023	0.0008			
Uplink: 0.10	0.8963	0.0947	0.0090				
Uplink: 0.20	0.7996	0.1620	0.0293	0.0080	0.0009	0	0.0002
Downlink: 0	0.8058	0.1311	0.0146	0.0097	0.0049	0.0146	0.0194
Downlink: 0.05	0.8845	0.0958	0.0101	0.0032	0.0032	0.0005	0.0027
Downlink: 0.10	0.8677	0.1125	0.0140	0.0027	0.0003	0.0003	0.0024
Downlink: 0.20	0.7691	0.1793	0.0376	0.0100	0.0023	0.0008	0.0010

Table 11: Mean and Standard Deviation(SD) for Retransmission Intervals in Google+

Loss Rate	1st		2nd		3rd		4th		5th		6th		k-th ($k \geq 7$)	
	Mean (ms)	SD (ms)	Mean (ms)	SD (ms)	Mean (ms)	SD (ms)	Mean (ms)	SD (ms)	Mean (ms)	SD (ms)	Mean (ms)	SD (ms)	Mean (ms)	SD (ms)
Uplink: 0	90.14	68.66												
Uplink: 0.05	64.69	31.12	70.47	14.90	61.56	9.13	56.88	0						
Uplink: 0.10	60.28	26.82	79.62	30.05	89.63	39.44								
Uplink: 0.20	77.49	38.00	89.63	36.00	90.15	36.32	90.89	34.34	93.72	27.15	79.83	0	101.08	0
Downlink: 0	39.35	27.52	15.97	21.55	5.54	4.47	4.86	3.87	3.41	1.11	3.40	1.08	3.91	0.85
Downlink: 0.05	80.35	122.62	40.72	36.66	16.33	34.32	4.56	2.70	4.76	6.00	2.69	1.18	2.17	0.90
Downlink: 0.10	66.03	34.10	45.14	42.45	32.36	36.21	6.70	6.37	3.41	1.39	3.44	0.89	2.64	0.83
Downlink: 0.20	77.84	57.05	58.59	57.97	53.16	64.31	35.14	31.59	20.86	22.85	23.06	28.58	6.87	14.83

persistent. Most of the time, it just tries to retransmit lost packet once as shown in Table 14. There is no guarantee that a lost packet will be successful recovered. Even though the recovery ratios reported in Table 12 and Table 13 are higher than those reported in Table 8 and Table 9, since iChat does not employ layered coding and prioritized retransmission, a lost video packet may prevent decoding of multiple video frames. Consequently, iChat's video quality under losses is much worse than Google+, even though they both use retransmissions to recover from packet losses. This suggests that layered video coding not only adapts to user heterogeneity well, but also enhances video quality resilience against losses. Due to the space limit, more results about iChat retransmission strategies can be found in our technical report [32].

Table 12: iChat Retransmission: Uplink

Upload Loss	Video FPS	Sending Rate	Retrans. Rate	Rcvry. Ratio
0	25.1	365.7	0	-
0.02	19.8	363.0	7.0	0.95
0.10	19.6	411.5	34.4	0.81

Table 13: iChat Retransmission: Downlink

Loss Rate	Video FPS	Total Rate	Retrans. Rate	Rcvry. Ratio
0	25.1	365.8	0	-
0.02	24.3	401.7	7.8	0.95
0.10	24.2	447.3	37.7	0.81

Table 14: Retransmission Probability in iChat

Case	1st	2nd
Downlink loss 0.02	1.00	
Downlink loss 0.10	1.00	
Uplink loss 0.02	0.9960	0.0040
Uplink loss 0.10	0.9975	0.0025

7.5 Robustness of Conferencing Quality

We use end-to-end video delay defined in Section 6 as a measure of the delivered conferencing quality. If the video can be continuously delivered to the receiver in realtime, the measured video delay from the stopwatch video should be consistently low. Since the original stopwatch continuously advances, losses of video frames on the receiver side will lead to large measured video delays. Additionally, if the received stopwatch video quality is bad, the text recognition tool, OCR, cannot decode the clock reading. The recognition ratio of OCR is an indirect measure of the received video quality. In this section, we compare the robustness of the three systems against bursty losses and long delays.

Packet losses can be bursty, especially on wireless links. We use the network emulator to generate bursty losses on the download link. For each loss burst, 4 $\sim$ 5 packets are dropped in batch. Table 15 compares the stopwatch recognition probabilities of the three systems under different bursty loss rates. The stopwatch video transmitted in iChat quickly become uncodable, this is consistent with our own video perception. The recognition probability remains high in Google+ and Skype, indicating that their delivered quality is stable up to 4% bursty losses.

Figure 7 compares the one-way video delay performances of Google+ and Skype. When we don't introduce any additional loss, both Google+ and Skype are able to maintain a low and stable video delay, with average about 200 ms. As we introduce additional bursty losses, Skype incurs large and highly-variable one-way video delays, as shown in Fig-

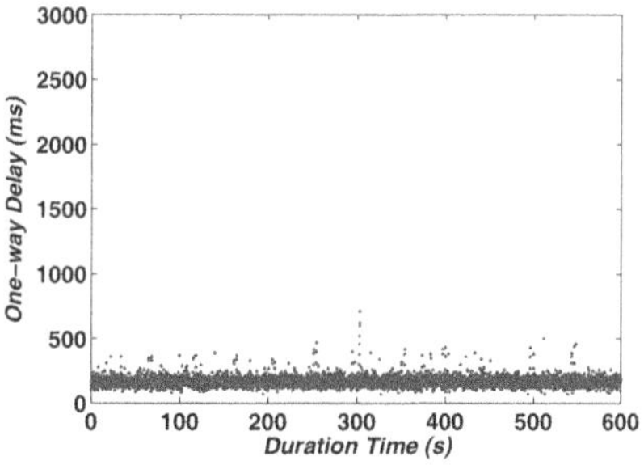

(a) Google+ Bursty Loss 0%

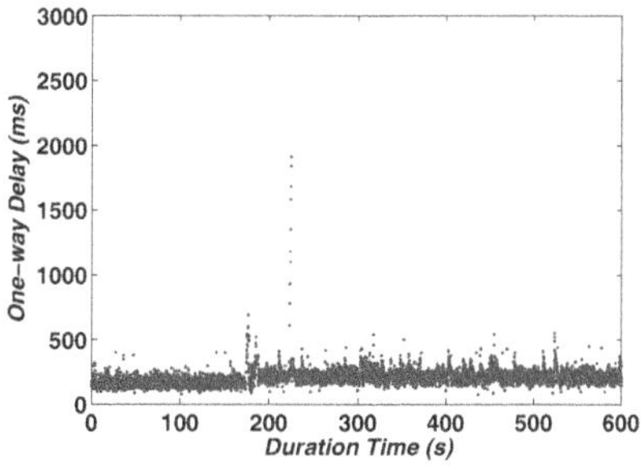

(b) Google+ Bursty Loss 2%

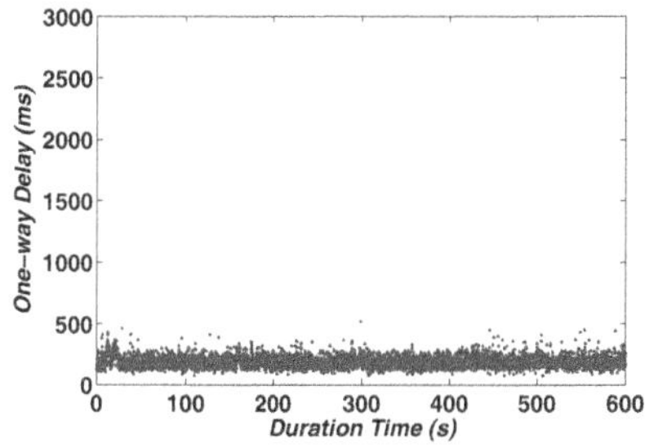

(c) Google+ Bursty Loss 4%

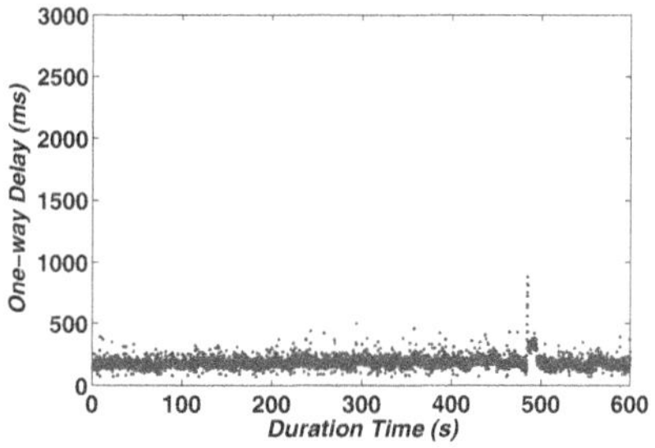

(d) Skype Bursty Loss 0%

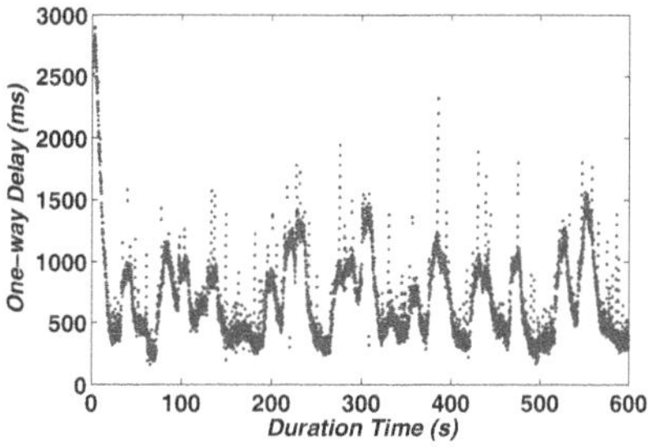

(e) Skype Bursty Loss 2%

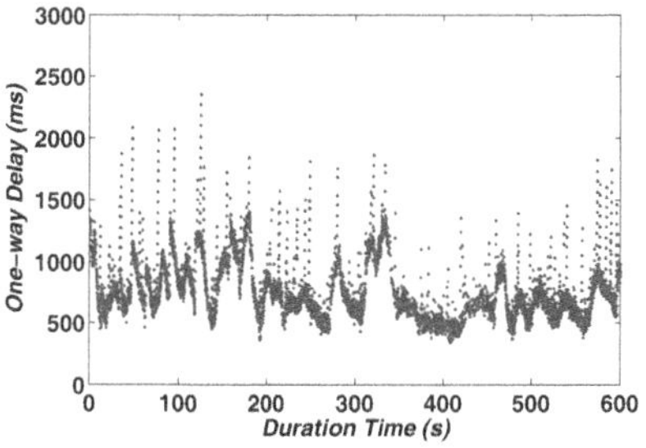

(f) Skype Bursty Loss 4%

Figure 7: One-way Video Delay For Google+ and Skype under Different Bursty Loss Probabilities

Table 15: Digital Clock Recognition Probability

Case	iChat	Google+	Skype
No Loss	0.90	0.86	0.88
2% Bursty loss	0.46	0.90	0.90
4% Bursty loss	0.10	0.76	0.92

ure 7(e) and Figure 7(f). This suggests that the FEC scheme adopted by Skype cannot efficiently recover from bursty losses. At frame rate of 30 frames/second, each lost frame leads to an additional video delay of $33ms$. Consecutive lost frames leads to delay pikes in the figures. Google+'s selective and persistent retransmissions can recover from bursty losses well. It can always do batch retransmissions for packets of the base layers upon bursty losses. The receiver can decode video as long as all packets of the base layer are received. As a result, Google+ is able to maintain low video delays up to 4% bursty losses in Figure 7(b) and Figure 7(c).

Compared with employing FEC, one main drawback of using retransmission is that it does not work well when the network delay between the sender and the receiver is large. To investigate the impact of network delay on the efficiency of retransmission, we set constant random loss to the download link of Skype and Google+, then we change RTT by introducing propagation delay on the access link of our local machines using the network emulator. Figure 8 compares the mean and variance of one-way video delay of both systems at different RTTs. Skype's one-way video delay curves are almost the same at no loss and 8% random losses. As RTT increases by Δ, the one-way video delay increases by roughly $\frac{\Delta}{2}$. This suggests that Skype's FEC efficiency is almost independent of RTT. To the contrary, when no loss is induced, Google+'s one-way video delay curve is almost the same as Skype's curve. Almost no retransmission is needed.

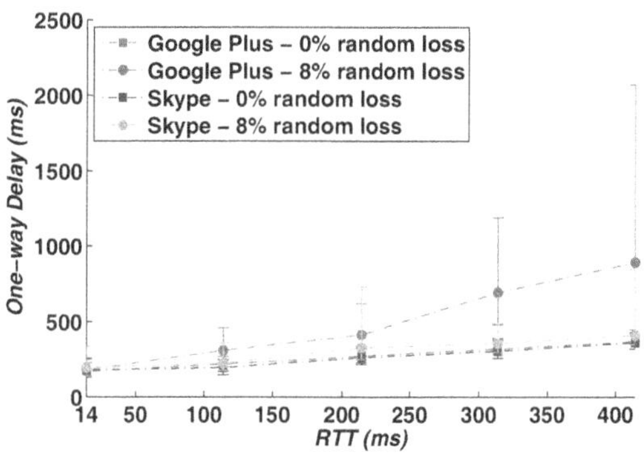

Figure 8: Google+ and Skype Delay Performances under Different Network Delays

When the random loss is set to be 8%, the video delay curve ramps up quickly, with increasingly higher variances. This suggests that FEC is preferable over retransmissions if RTT is large, loss is random, and loss rate is not too high.

8. CONCLUSION

In this paper, we present our measurement study of three popular video telephony systems for end-consumers. Through a series of carefully designed active and passive measurements, we were able to unveil important information about their design choices and performances. Our study demonstrated that pure P2P architecture cannot sustain high-quality multi-party video conferencing services on the Internet, and bandwidth-rich server infrastructure can be deployed to significantly improve user conferencing experiences. We also demonstrated that, in the extremely tight design space of video conferencing system, video generation, protection, adaptation and distribution have to be jointly considered. Various voice/video processing delays, incurred in capturing, encoding, decoding and rendering, account for a significant portion of the end-to-end delays perceived by users. Compared with multi-version video coding, layered video coding can more efficiently address user access heterogeneity. When relay servers are well-provisioned and selected, per-hop retransmission is more preferable than FEC to recover from random and bursty losses. With layered video coding, prioritized selective retransmissions can further enhance the robustness of conferencing quality against various network impairments. Our findings can be used to guide the design of new video conferencing solutions, as well as an increasing array of network applications that call for high-bandwidth and low-delay data transmissions under a wide range of "best-effort" network conditions.

9. ACKNOWLEDGMENT

The authors would like to thank Prof. Yao Wang, Dr. Hao Hu and Prof. Xinggong Zhang for discussions on video coding techniques. They also would like to thank the anonymous reviewers and the Shepherd Dr. Ming Zhang for their valuable feedbacks and suggestions to improve the paper quality. The work is partially supported by USA NSF under contracts CNS-0953682 and CNS-0916734.

10. REFERENCES

[1] S. A. Baset and H. G. Schulzrinne. An analysis of the skype peer-to-peer internet telephony protocol. In *Proceedings of IEEE INFOCOM*, pages 1–11, April 2006.

[2] D. Bonfiglio, M. Mellia, M. Meo, N. Ritacca, and D. Rossi. Tracking down skype traffic. In *Proceedings of IEEE INFOCOM*, pages 261–265, Apr 2008.

[3] K. Chen, T. Huang, P. Huang, and C. Lei. Quantifying skype user satisfaction. In *Proceedings of ACM SIGCOMM*, volume 36, Oct 2006.

[4] L. D. Cicco, S. Mascolo, and V. Palmisano. A mathematical model of the skype voip congestion control algorithm. In *Proceedings of IEEE Conference on Decision and Control*, Dec 2008.

[5] L. D. Cicco, S. Mascolo, and V. Palmisano. Skype video congestion control: an experimental investigation. *Computer Networks*, 55(3):558 – 571, Feb 2011.

[6] Comic Enhancer Pro. Homepage. http://www.comicer.com/stronghorse/.

[7] e2eSoft. Vcam: Webcam emulator. `http://www.e2esoft.cn/vcam/`.

[8] Free Stopwatch. Homepage. http://free-stopwatch.com/.

[9] FreeOCR. Homepage. http://www.freeocr.net/.

[10] GoldWave. Homepage. http://www.goldwave.com/.

[11] Google+. Homepage. `https://plus.google.com/`.

[12] S. Guha, N. Daswani, and R. Jain. An Experimental Study of the Skype Peer-to-Peer VoIP System. In *Proceedings of the 5th International Workshop on Peer-to-Peer Systems*, pages 1–6, Santa Barbara, CA, February 2006.

[13] H. Schulzrinne, S. Casner, R. Frederick and V. Jacobson. Rtp: A transport protocol for real-time applications. http://tools.ietf.org/html/rfc3550.

[14] T. Huang, K. Chen, and P. Huang. Tuning skype redundancy control algorithm for user satisfaction. In *Proceedings of IEEE INFOCOM*, pages 1179–1185, April 2009.

[15] iChat. Homepage. `http://www.apple.com/macosx/apps/all.html#ichat`.

[16] Infoplease. Homepage. http://www.infoplease.com/atlas/calculate-distance.html.

[17] J. Jansen, P. César, D. C. A. Bulterman, T. Stevens, I. Kegel, and J. Issing. Enabling composition-based video-conferencing for the home. *IEEE Transactions on Multimedia*, 13(5):869–881, 2011.

[18] Y. Lu, Y. Zhao, F. A. Kuipers, and P. V. Mieghem. Measurement study of multi-party video conferencing. In *Networking*, pages 96–108, 2010.

[19] MaxMind. Homepage. http://www.maxmind.com/.

[20] Microsoft Resarch Asia. Network Emulator for Windows Toolkit (NEWT). `http://blogs.msdn.com/b/lkruger`.

[21] Paul Spoerry. Hidden features in google+ hangouts. http://plusheadlines.com/hidden-features-googleplus-hangouts/1198/.

[22] PlanetLab. Homepage. http://www.planet-lab.org/.

[23] Renovation Software. Text grab for windows. `http://www.renovation-software.com/en/text-grab-sdk/textgrab-sdk.html`.

[24] RTP protocol Fields. Homepage. http://www.networksorcery.com/enp/protocol/rtp.htm.

[25] H. Schwarz, D. Marpe, and T. Wiegand. Overview of the Scalable Video Coding Extension of the H.264/AVC Standard. *IEEE Trans. Circuit and System for Video Technology*, 17:1103–1120, Sep. 2007.

[26] Skype. Homepage. `http://www.skype.com`.

[27] Traceroute.org. Homepage. http://www.traceroute.org/.

[28] Virtual Audio Cable. Homepage. http://software.muzychenko.net/eng/vac.htm/.

[29] Y. Wang, A. Reibman, and S. Lin. Multiple Description Coding for Video Delivery. *Proceedings of the IEEE*, 93, Jan. 2005.

[30] M. Wien, H. Schwarz, and T. Oelbaum. Performance Analysis of SVC. *IEEE Trans. Circuit and System for Video Technology*, 17:1194–1203, Sep. 2007.

[31] Wireshark. Homepage. http://www.wireshark.org/.

[32] Y. Xu, C. Yu, J. Li, and Y. Liu. Video telephony for end-consumers: Measurement study of google+, ichat, and skype. `http://eeweb.poly.edu/faculty/yongliu/docs/imc12tech.pdf`, 2012.

[33] T. yuan Huang, K. ta Chen, and P. Huang. Could skype be more satisfying? a QoE-Centric study of the fec mechanism in an internet-scale voip system. *IEEE Network*, 24(2):42, Mar 2010.

[34] X. Zhang, Y. Xu, H. Hu, Y. Liu, Z. Guo, and Y. Wang. Profiling Skype Video Calls: Rate Control and Video Quality. In *Proceedings of IEEE INFOCOM*, March 2012.

Range Tomography: Combining the Practicality of Boolean Tomography with the Resolution of Analog Tomography

Sajjad Zarifzadeh
szarifzadeh@gmail.com
Georgia Tech

Madhwaraj Gowdagere
madhwarajgk@gmail.com
Georgia Tech

Constantine Dovrolis
constantine@gatech.edu
Georgia Tech

ABSTRACT

The objective of early network tomography approaches was to produce a point estimate for the performance of each network link (Analog tomography). When it became clear that the previous approach is error-prone in practice, research shifted to Boolean tomography where each link is estimated as either "good" or "bad". The Boolean approach is more practical but its resolution is too coarse. We propose a new tomography framework that combines the best of both worlds: we still distinguish between good and bad links (for practicality reasons) but we also infer a range estimate for the performance of each bad link. We apply the *Range tomography* framework in two path performance metric functions (Min and Sum) and propose an efficient algorithm for each problem. Together with simulations, we have also applied Range tomography in three operational networks allowing us to identify the location of bad links and to estimate their performance during congestion episodes. We also compare the proposed method with existing Analog and Boolean tomography algorithms.

Categories and Subject Descriptors

C.2.3 [**Computer-communication Networks**]: Network Operations—*Network management, Network monitoring*; C.4 [**Performance of Systems**]: Measurement techniques

Keywords

Network tomography, localization, performance metric

1. INTRODUCTION

The objective of network tomography is to infer the internal characteristics of a network (e.g., link delay and loss rate, topology) from end-to-end path measurements. As a research area, network tomography is both interesting and significant. It is interesting because the underlying estimation problem is typically under-constrained (more unknowns than equations) and so its solution requires creative and domain-specific additional constraints and objectives. Further, network tomography combines the art of active probing with the science of statistical inference. Network tomography is also significant in practice because it allows users and network administrators to monitor and troubleshoot a set of network paths of interest without having direct access to every router and switch in those paths. This is particularly important in the context of interdomain paths, i.e., paths that traverse more than one network provider. Additionally, as IP-based networks move towards performance-based Service Level Agreements (SLAs) tomographic methods will become even more valuable. In fact, the motivation for this work resulted from an actual system that is used to monitor in real-time the performance of network paths that interconnect a large number of scientific research labs around the world using end-to-end measurements.

The first efforts in network tomography, about 15 years ago, focused on the most challenging instance of the problem: estimate the actual performance (e.g., loss rate or delay variation) of every link in the monitored network [1, 2]. We refer to those tomographic methods as *Analog* because they provide a real-valued performance estimate for each link. Analog tomography is a very challenging problem for several reasons, some of which are related to the underlying path measurements. For instance, those early methods assume that if two paths go through a single and shared lossy link, their measured path loss rates will be equal. This may be true if the measurements last for a very long period, assuming that the network load is stationary and the routes do not change. In practice, however, network conditions change significantly with time, and so the path measurements must be performed in short time intervals (e.g., one minute) before they become stale [3]. To make things worse, the probing frequency cannot be too high because the path measurements can then affect the underlying network performance [4]. So, Analog tomography methods need to work with noisy path estimates that result from short-term active measurements.

In 2003, Duffield proposed a paradigm shift in network tomography [5]. Instead of trying to estimate the actual performance of a link, it is more practical to only infer whether the link's performance is "good" versus "bad". This approach is referred to as *Boolean tomography* and it has also been followed by other researchers [6, 8]. Here, path measurements become much simpler (just detect congested paths) and so they can take place in shorter time periods and with fewer probes. The problem, of course, is that the result of the tomographic process has low resolution: just a single bit for

IMC'12, November 14–16, 2012, Boston, Massachusetts, USA.

each link. This may be sufficient if the objective is to simply identify severe congestion. In practice, however, the congestion level of network links varies widely and even though an application or operator may be satisfied with a loss rate of 0.1% or a queueing delay of 50msec, another may find these congestion levels unacceptable.

In this work, we propose a new approach in network tomography that attempts to combine the higher resolution of Analog tomography with the practicality of Boolean tomography. The path measurements are still classified as good or bad, to exploit the fact that most network paths typically operate without congestion [15]. This allows us to quickly remove a large number of links from the problem, as long as they only appear in good paths. For the remaining paths, we aim not only to identify bad links, but also to estimate a *range* (interval) for their actual performance. The width of the resulting range depends on the variability in the underlying path measurements: more accurate path measurements will result in narrower range estimates. We refer to the proposed framework as *Range Tomography*.

We apply the Range tomography framework in two path performance formulations: a *Min function* in which a path's performance is determined by the link with the minimum performance, and a *Sum function* in which a path's performance is determined by the sum of its links' performance values. Min is more appropriate for metrics such as available bandwidth, while Sum can be used for delay and (as an approximation) for loss rate. For each formulation we propose an efficient algorithm to identify bad links and estimate their performance range. The algorithms are first evaluated with simulations in three real topologies. Simulations are not ideal, but they allow us to examine the false positives, false negatives and accuracy of Range tomography under controllable and repeatable experiments. We performed these simulations under both random and bursty loss processes, showing the significant impact of the latter in network tomography methods. Further, we compare the proposed algorithms with "canonical" methods from Analog and Boolean tomography.

We have also applied the proposed methods in practice to detect and localize congestion events in three operational large networks, where the number of monitored paths varies between 70-3600. Even though we cannot use those real-world experiments for validation (we do not have access to routers and switches in those networks), they show some interesting points. First, in practice, there is rarely more than one bad link in the monitored paths and so the false positive/negative probability is close to zero. Second, the actual congestion level of those bad links can vary widely, and so it is important to also estimate a congestion range instead of a single bit.

The rest of the paper is structured as follows. In Section 2, we describe the Range Tomography problem. In Sections 3 and 4, we consider the Min and Sum formulations, respectively. In Section 5, we evaluate tomography methods using simulations. We present a short summary of the experimental results in Section 6. Section 7 discusses the related work and we conclude in Section 8.

2. RANGE TOMOGRAPHY

In this section, we motivate, state and explain the Range Tomography problem.

2.1 Problem statement

We are given a set of N measurement points or hosts, referred to as *sensors* $S = \{s_1, ..., s_N\}$. Each sensor measures the end-to-end path performance, with respect to a certain metric such as loss rate, one-way delay or available bandwidth, to all other sensors. We are interested to localize performance problems, with respect to the corresponding metric, in the set Π of $N \times (N-1)$ paths between sensors. The forwarding paths between sensors can be "mapped" at the IP-layer using traceroute-like tools (such as Paris traceroute [22]). Each path is represented by a sequence of links and each link is represented by the IP address of the corresponding router or host interface. Let $G = (V, E)$ be the directed graph constructed from the union of all paths between sensors.

Suppose that $p_{i,j}$ denotes the path from sensor s_i to sensor s_j, and $m_{i,j}$ is the *actual* performance of $p_{i,j}$ for a given performance metric in the time interval of interest. We assume that there is a function f that expresses the performance of a path based on the performance of its constituent links,

$$m_{i,j} = f(\{x_l | \forall l \in p_{i,j}\}) \tag{1}$$

where x_l is the *actual* performance of link l. We refer to f as the *path metric function*. For instance, in the case of available bandwidth, the performance of the end-to-end path is determined by the link with the minimum available bandwidth. Thus, the function f for available bandwidth is based on the *MIN* operator. In the case of delay, jitter and (as an approximation) loss rate, the path performance can be estimated by the sum of link performances. Hence, the function f would be the *SUM* operator for those metrics. In network tomography, we attempt to invert function f and estimate the performance of some links given the measured performance of a set of paths that traverse those links. As in other instances of tomography, this "inversion problem" is typically ill-defined and it can be solved only if we impose additional constraints, optimization objectives and assumptions [10].

In practice, the performance of a network path must be measured with low frequency probing (i.e., the probing traffic load should be low compared to the capacity of the path), and in short time intervals (due to dynamic network conditions). Hence, the measured path performance can be significantly different than the actual path performance. In other words, the measured performance of two paths sharing the same bottleneck link can be different even though their actual performance is the same. Let $\tilde{m}_{i,j}$ be the *measured* performance of path $p_{i,j}$ in the time interval of interest. Because of the previous limitations of the measurement process, we typically have that $m_{i,j} \neq \tilde{m}_{i,j}$, while the difference between the two metrics can vary significantly over different paths. To illustrate this issue, consider the following simple example. Assume that the packet drops at a link l follow a Bernoulli random process with probability $x_l = 0.01$, while the measurement process sends $n = 1000$ probing packets on that link. The variance of the measured packet losses is $n\,x_l\,(1 - x_l)$ and so the standard deviation ($\approx \sqrt{10}$) is significant compared to the expected number of packet losses at link l (10 packets).

In the following, we introduce the Range Tomography framework as a way to deal with the previous uncertainty in path measurements. First, we inherit from Boolean tomography the notion that paths and links can be distinguished

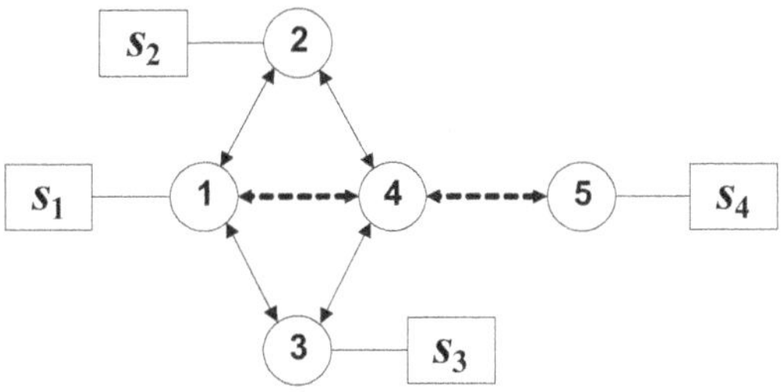

Figure 1: A simple network example with four sensors. The dashed lines indicate lossy links.

as "good" versus "bad". Formally, a path $p_{i,j}$ is called *bad* if its measured performance $\tilde{m}_{i,j}$ is worse than a threshold δ (δ may be zero, as in the case of loss rate for example). Similarly, a link is *bad* if its performance metric is worse than δ, otherwise it is *good*. After we infer the bad links from path measurements, we also estimate the performance of every bad link with a "range estimate" for its metric. In other words, we start with path point measurements and end up with link range estimates. To this end, we first identify and group paths that are likely affected by the same bad link and then use the measured performance of these paths to determine a narrow *performance range* for that link.

Definition 1. Two paths $p_{i,j}$ and $p_{k,l}$ are α-*similar* (represented by $p_{i,j} \parallel p_{k,l}$), if their relative performance difference is within a parameter α,

$$\frac{|\tilde{m}_{i,j} - \tilde{m}_{k,l}|}{min(\tilde{m}_{i,j}, \tilde{m}_{k,l})} \leq \alpha \quad (2)$$

where α is a positive parameter that quantifies the accuracy of the measurement process (we also say that the measurements $\tilde{m}_{i,j}$ and $\tilde{m}_{k,l}$ are α-*similar*). α is related to the measurement process (e.g., size of probing packets, probing frequency, probing method) and to the characteristics of the estimated path performance process. The parameter α can be estimated experimentally, measuring paths that are known to be limited by the same bottleneck link. The relative difference of the resulting path measurements should be less than the chosen value of α. In the rest of this section, we assume that α is given as an input to the network tomography process. In Section 5, we discuss how we estimated α in our experiments.

Let us consider the example of Figure 1. $p_{i,j}$ is the shortest path from s_i to s_j. End-to-end measurements indicate that the paths $p_{1,4}, p_{2,4}, p_{3,4}$ are lossy; their measured loss rates are 15%, 5% and 7%, respectively. All remaining paths are good. Boolean tomography would choose the link from node-4 to node-5, represented by (4,5), as the only bad link because it appears on all lossy paths. However, choosing a single lossy link cannot explain why these paths have so different loss rates. If $\alpha = 0.5$, paths $p_{2,4}$ and $p_{3,4}$ are α-similar. Then, one plausible solution is that link (4,5) (shared by the two α-similar paths) has a loss rate between 5% and 7% while link (1,4) on $p_{2,3}$ has a loss rate between 8% and 10%. In general, the notion of α-similar paths improves the network tomography process in two ways: 1) As opposed to Analog tomography, we can avoid the incorrect detection of multiple bad links in paths that show different performance even though they are affected by the same bad link. 2) Unlike Boolean tomography, when the paths sharing the same bad link are not α-similar, we can conclude that there are additional bad links (as in the previous example).

Let $\tilde{x}_l = [s_l..e_l]$ denote the performance range assigned to link l (i.e., the actual performance of l is estimated to be between s_l and e_l). $|\tilde{x}_l|$ denotes the width of range $\tilde{x}_l$. We define next how to examine whether the assigned link performance ranges are consistent with the path performance measurements.

Definition 2. The performance ranges assigned to bad links on a path $p_{i,j}$ are *consistent* with the measured performance of $p_{i,j}$ if there is at least one value in each of these ranges that would satisfy the path performance constraint in (1). We denote the consistency relation as:

$$\begin{aligned}&\tilde{m}_{i,j} \simeq f(\{\tilde{x}_l | \forall l \in p_{i,j}\}) \text{ if:}\\&\forall l \in p_{i,j}, \exists t_l \in \tilde{x}_l : \tilde{m}_{i,j} = f(\{t_l | \forall l \in p_{i,j}\})\end{aligned} \quad (3)$$

To illustrate the previous definition, consider the following example. Suppose that the measured loss rate of a path $p_{i,j}$ is 1% and there are two bad links l_1 and l_2 in that path. The performance range of both links is estimated as [1%-2%]. Obviously, these range estimates are not consistent with the path measurement. On the contrary, if the performance ranges are both [0.4%-0.6%], then they are consistent with the measured path loss rate. In this case, we also say that the performance ranges assigned to l_1 and l_2 *justify* the bad path $p_{i,j}$ ($p_{i,j}$ is then called *justified* path).

Before stating the Range Tomography problem more formally, we need to make the following assumptions:

(1) There are no spatial correlations between different bad links.[1]

(2) The routing paths between sensors remain constant during the measurement process.[2]

(3) A path is bad, if and only if, there is at least one bad link in that path.

Given the directed graph G and a measurement for each path in Π, the Range Tomography problem can be stated as follows:

Range Tomography (RT) problem: *Infer all bad links in G and assign a performance range to each bad link so that:*

1. *The number of bad links is minimized.*
2. *The assigned performance ranges to bad links are consistent with the path performance measurements, $\forall p_{i,j} \in \Pi : \tilde{m}_{i,j} \simeq f(\{\tilde{x}_l | \forall l \in p_{i,j}\})$.*

In practice, it is not common to have multiple bad links at the same time (this is also observed in our experimental results in Section 6). So, as it is common in Boolean tomography, we consider an optimization objective that aims to minimize the number of detected bad links. Without

[1] To the extent of our knowledge, there is no prior evidence that such correlations are common or significant in practice. We make this assumption so that we can calculate the performance of a path from the performance of its constituent links through a simple function.

[2] If the network deploys multipath routing, we need to make sure that both the Paris-traceroute packets and the probing packets sent from one sensor to another use the same port numbers so that they follow the same forwarding path.

this objective, the solution of the RT problem can result in several false positives. The complexity of the RT problem depends on the metric function f. In the following two sections, we consider two specific instances of the function f that can be used to capture different performance metrics.

3. MIN METRIC FUNCTION

We first consider a function that determines the performance of path $p_{i,j}$ as the minimum performance among all links in that path,

$$m_{i,j} = min_{\forall l \in p_{i,j}}\{x_l\} \qquad (4)$$

We refer to this instance of the RT problem as *RT-Min*. The previous function can be used for performance metrics such as capacity or available bandwidth, because these metrics are mostly determined by a single "bottleneck" link. In the rest of this section, we will refer to available bandwidth as the performance metric of interest (even though the proposed algorithm is applicable to any metric that satisfies the previous path performance constraint). We say a path (or a link) is *bad* if its available bandwidth is less than a threshold δ.

3.1 Solution and analysis for RT-Min

Definition 3. A bad link l is *detectable* if there is at least one path $p_{i,j}$ traversing l such that (I) there is no other bad link in $p_{i,j}$ **OR** (II) other bad links in $p_{i,j}$ have higher available bandwidth than link l.

The above condition implies that for every bad link l, there should be at least one path $p_{i,j}$ such that l is the bottleneck link of that path.

Definition 4. A good link l is *removable*, if there is at least one good path traversing l.

Lemma 1. Assume that there is no measurement error, i.e. $\tilde{m}_{i,j} = m_{i,j}, \forall p_{i,j} \in \Pi$. In that ideal case, the available bandwidth of every bad link can be determined if (I) all good links are removable, **AND** (II) all bad links are detectable.

The proof is straightforward and it is omitted. If both conditions of Lemma-1 hold, we can use the following method (referred to as *Min-Ideal*) to estimate the available bandwidth of the bottleneck link for every bad path. First, "mark" all links in good paths as good; the rest of the links are "unmarked". Then, select the bad path p_b with the highest available bandwidth among the remaining paths and assign the available bandwidth of p_b to all unmarked links on p_b (p_b is then labeled as *justified* and all links in p_b are marked). We repeat the previous step until there is no unjustified path in Π.

However, the two conditions of Lemma-1 (good links are removable and bad links are detectable) may not be true in practice. In addition, the measurement process is always error-prone. Therefore, we need to consider an algorithm that can *infer* bad links, even when the assumptions of Lemma-1 are not met.

Based on the complexity analysis of the Boolean tomography problem [8], it is easy to see that the RT-Min problem is also NP-hard[3]. So, we need to approximate solution of RT-Min with heuristics. Our solution to this problem, referred to as *Min-Tomo*, is based on the following two principles:
I) As in the case of *Min-Ideal*, the *Min-Tomo* algorithm runs iteratively, and in each iteration it considers the bad path p_b that has the highest available bandwidth among all remaining paths. Paths that are α-similar with p_b are then grouped into the set Ω.
II) Since good links are not necessarily removable, it is possible that we consider a link as bad even though it is good, and vice versa. To reduce this classification error, *Min-Tomo* greedily selects the link l that is traversed by the largest number of bad paths in Ω and marks it as bad. The intuition is that it is unlikely that a large number of bad paths traverse a good link, without *any* good path traversing that link.[4] Additionally, this greedy heuristic aims to minimize the number of links identified as bad.

The pseudo-code of *Min-Tomo* is presented in Algorithm 1. We first mark all links on every good path as good (line 3). Then, we consider the path with the highest available bandwidth among all bad paths. Let p_b be such a path. Instead of considering only path p_b, we consider the set of paths that are α-similar with p_b (this set is referred to by Ω in line 7). We then select link l_m as the link that is shared most between paths in Ω. In the case of a tie, we select the link which is traversed by most unjustified paths (lines 17 and 18). We also check in line 11 that there is at least one path that is α-similar with p_b and traverses l_m. Taking $\bar{r}$ as the average available bandwidth of paths going over l_m (line 19), the performance range of l_m is determined in line 20 so that every value in the range $\tilde{x}_{l_m}$ is α-similar with $\bar{r}$. We label all paths traversing l_m as *justified* (line 21), if their available bandwidth falls in the performance range $\tilde{x}_{l_m}$. We repeat this process until there is no unjustified path.

The estimated ranges produced by *Min-Tomo* satisfy the consistency requirement for the following reason. Let $h(l_m)$ be the highest available bandwidth path traversing l_m. Suppose there are several paths that are α-similar with $h(l_m)$ and traverse l_m. Let $\Phi(l_m)$ be the set of these paths. In the RT-Min problem, the range $\tilde{x}_{l_m}$ assigned to a link l_m is consistent with the measured performance of path $p_{i,j} \in \Phi(l_m)$ if the measurement $\tilde{m}_{i,j}$ belongs in the range $\tilde{x}_{l_m}$. It can be shown that this is true for every path in $\Phi(l_m)$ if we select the range $\tilde{x}_{l_m}$ as shown in line 20.

The run-time complexity of *Min-Tomo* is $O(|\Pi|^2 + |\Pi|\,|E|)$. The running time for a network with about 1000 bad paths and 4600 links is less than 5.5msec on a workstation with a 2.6GHz Intel i5 processor.

4. SUM METRIC FUNCTION

In this section we consider the following path metric function,

$$m_{i,j} = \sum_{\forall l \in p_{i,j}} x_l \qquad (5)$$

The corresponding range tomography problem is referred to as *RT-Sum*. The Sum metric function can capture performance metrics such as delay and jitter. Under the previous spatial independence assumption, the path loss rate is given by

$$m_{i,j} = 1 - \prod_{\forall l \in p_{i,j}} (1 - x_l) \qquad (6)$$

[3]To prove this we have to consider the simplified case where the available bandwidth of all bad links is the same. In that case, the RT-Min problem is the same with the Boolean tomography problem, which is NP-hard [8].

[4]The analysis of three real topologies, described in Section 5, confirms this intuition.

Algorithm 1 Min-Tomo

Require: Set of all links E
Require: Set of all paths Π
Require: The measured available bandwidth of every path in Π, $\tilde{m}_{i,j}, \forall p_{i,j} \in \Pi$

Initialize $R = \Pi$ {set of unjustified paths}
Initialize $U = E$ {set of unmarked links}
Remove from R and U all good paths and all links on good paths, respectively.
$h(l) = argmax_{\forall p_{i,j} \in R}\{\tilde{m}_{i,j}\}, \forall l \in U$ {path with highest available bandwidth going over l}
while $R \neq \varnothing$ **and** $U \neq \varnothing$ **do**
  $p_b = argmax_{\forall p_{i,j} \in R}\{\tilde{m}_{i,j}\}$ {path with highest available bandwidth in R}
  $\Omega = \{p_{i,j} | p_{i,j} \in R, p_{i,j} \parallel p_b\}$ {set of paths which are α-similar with p_b}
  $num(l) = |\{p_{i,j} | l \in p_{i,j}, p_{i,j} \in R\}|$ {number of unjustified paths going over l}
  for each link l in U **do**
    $C(l) =$ set of paths in Ω containing l
    if $h(l) \parallel p_b$ **then**
      $score(l) = |C(l)|$ {number of paths in $C(l)$}
    else
      $score(l) = 0$
    end if
  end for
  $L_m = argmax_{l \in U} score(l)$ {set of links with the maximum score}
  $l_m = argmax_{l \in L_m} num(l)$ {link with the maximum score and maximum number of unjustified paths going over it}
  $\bar{r} = avg\{\tilde{m}_{i,j} | p_{i,j} \in \Omega, l_m \in p_{i,j}\}$ {average available bandwidth of paths in Ω going over l_m }
  $\tilde{x}_{l_m} = [\bar{r}(\frac{1}{1+\alpha}), \bar{r}(1+\alpha)]$ {performance range of link l_m }
  $R = R - \{p_{i,j} | l_m \in p_{i,j}, p_{i,j} \in R, \tilde{m}_{i,j} \in x_{l_m}\}$ {Now, some paths going over l_m are justified}
  $U = U - \{l_m\}$
end while
return $\tilde{x}_l, \forall l \in E$

However, if the link loss rates are low and there are few lossy links in each path, the two formulas give similar results (e.g., in the case of three lossy links each with 1% loss rate, the actual loss rate is about 2.97% even though the Sum approximation gives 3%). In the rest of this section, we consider loss rate as the performance metric of interest, and we refer to bad links as "lossy" (i.e., δ=0).

4.1 Solution and analysis for RT-Sum

We first present a necessary condition for the identification of lossy links assuming error-free measurements.

Definition 5. A lossy link l is *detectable-1* if there is at least one path $p_{i,j}$ traversing l such that there is no other lossy link in $p_{i,j}$. A lossy link l is *detectable-n* ($n > 1$) if it is either *detectable-(n-1)* **OR** there is at least one path $p_{i,j}$ traversing l such that all other lossy links on $p_{i,j}$ are *detectable-(n-1)*.

Lemma 2. Assume there is no measurement error, i.e., $\tilde{m}_{i,j} = m_{i,j}, \forall p_{i,j} \in \Pi$. The loss rate of every lossy link can be determined if (I) all good links are removable **AND** (II) all lossy links are *detectable-n* ($n \geq 1$).

Proof: Under the previous conditions, we can use the following method (referred to as *Sum-Ideal*) to estimate the loss rate of lossy links. Let U be the set of links identified as lossy. Based on the recursive definition of *detectable-n* links, there should exist at least one path that traverses only one link in U. Suppose $p_{i,j}$ is such a path, traversing link $l \in U$. Hence, the loss rate of l is the same as the loss rate of $p_{i,j}$ ($x_l = m_{i,j}$). We remove l from U and then subtract the loss rate of l from the loss rate of every path traversing l. In the next iteration, there should again exist at least one path that traverses only one link of U; otherwise, the remaining links in U would not be *detectable-n* ($n \geq 1$). We repeat this process until the set U is empty. In each iteration, one link is removed from U, and so this algorithm is guaranteed to determine the loss rate of every bad link.

However, the two conditions of Lemma-2 may not be true in practice. We conducted a simple experiment to evaluate how often those two conditions are violated in three real topologies (described in Section 5). We randomly select a number of lossy links and assign a loss rate to them from a uniform distribution. The percentage of lossy links that are *not detectable-n* is quite low in all three topologies (less than 2% on average when up to 10% of links in the ESNet topology are lossy). But, the percentage of good links that are *not* removable is higher (around 7% when up to 10% of links in ESNet are lossy). In other words, it is possible that all paths traversing a good link are bad. Therefore, we need to consider an algorithm that can *infer* lossy links, even when the conditions of Lemma-2 are not met.

The RT-Sum problem is also NP-hard. To prove this, it is enough to consider the case where all lossy paths have the same loss rate. The solution in that case is the same with the solution of the Boolean tomography problem. We approximate the solution of the RT-Sum problem with a heuristic, referred to as *Sum-Tomo*, which is based on the following three principles:

I) In each iteration, we only consider the set of paths that are α-similar with the path that has the lowest loss rate. This set is referred to as Ω.
II) Similar to *Min-Tomo*, we greedily choose the link l that is traversed by the maximum number of lossy paths in Ω.
III) We subtract the assigned loss rate of a detected bad link from all paths traversing that link.

The pseudo-code of *Sum-Tomo* is presented in Algorithm 2. The input arguments are the same with *Min-Tomo* in Algorithm 1 and they are omitted. After removing good paths and their links (in line 3), we consider the path p_b with the lowest loss rate; let Ω be the set of paths that are α-similar with p_b (line 6 and 7). In line 14, we greedily choose link l_m as the link that is traversed by most paths in Ω (if there are multiple such links, the link that is traversed by most unjustified paths is chosen). We calculate $\bar{r}$ as the average loss rate of paths in Ω that traverse l_m (line 15), and so the performance range of l_m (line 16) is such that every point in $\tilde{x}_{l_m}$ is α-similar with $\bar{r}$. We then mark all paths (traversing l_m) as *justified* (line 17), if their loss rate is within the performance range of l_m. In that case, we also subtract the average loss rate $\bar{r}$ from the loss rate of all paths that traverse l_m (line 18).

The run-time complexity of *Sum-Tomo* is also $O(|\Pi|^2 + |\Pi||E|)$. The *Sum-Tomo* algorithm can only approximate

Algorithm 2 Sum-Tomo

Initialize $R = \Pi$ {set of unjustified paths}
Initialize $U = E$ {set of unmarked links}
Remove from R and U all good paths and all links on good paths, respectively.
Initialize $r_{i,j} = \tilde{m}_{i,j}, \forall p_{i,j} \in R$ {the loss rate of $p_{i,j}$ which has not been justified yet}
while $R \neq \varnothing$ **and** $U \neq \varnothing$ **do**
  $p_b = argmin_{\forall p_{i,j} \in R}\{r_{i,j}\}$ {path with lowest loss rate in R}
  $\Omega = \{p_{i,j} | p_{i,j} \in R, p_{i,j} \parallel p_b\}$ {set of paths which are α-similar with p_b, using $r_{i,j}$ instead of $m_{i,j}$}
  $num(l) = |\{p_{i,j} | l \in p_{i,j}, p_{i,j} \in R\}|$ {number of lossy paths going over l}
  for each link l in U **do**
    $C(l)$ = set of paths in Ω containing l
    $score(l) = |C(l)|$ {number of paths in $C(l)$}
  end for
  $L_m = argmax_{l \in U} score(l)$ {set of links with the maximum score}
  $l_m = argmax_{l \in L_m} num(l)$ {link with the maximum score and maximum number of lossy paths going over it}
  $\bar{r} = avg\{r_{i,j} | l_m \in p_{i,j}, p_{i,j} \in \Omega\}$ {average loss rate of paths in Ω going over l_m }
  $\tilde{x}_{l_m} = [\bar{r}(\frac{1}{1+\alpha}), \bar{r}(1+\alpha)]$ {performance range of link l_m }
  $R = R - \{p_{i,j} | p_{i,j} \in R, r_{i,j} \in \tilde{x}_{l_m}\}$ {Some paths going over l_m are now justified}
  $r_{i,j} = max\{0, r_{i,j} - \bar{r}\}, \forall p_{i,j} \in R, l_m \in p_{i,j}$ {Update loss rate of paths going over l_m}
  $U = U - \{l_m\}$
end while
return $\tilde{x}_l, \forall l \in E$

the optimal solution to the RT-Sum problem for two reasons. First, as in the case of *Min-Tomo*, it may not return the minimum number of bad links. Second, as opposed to *Min-Tomo*, *Sum-Tomo* may violate the consistency constraint. To understand how this can happen consider the following example. Assume we have three links l_1, l_2 and l_3, and three lossy paths $p_1 =< l_1 >$, $p_2 =< l_1, l_2 >$ and $p_3 =< l_2, l_3 >$. The measured path loss rates are 3%, 4% and 2%, respectively. Suppose that $\alpha = 0.1$. The *Sum-Tomo* algorithm would only detect l_1 and l_2 as lossy links, with the same loss rate range [1.8%-2.2%] for both links. Note that these ranges are *not* consistent with the measurement for path p_1. A consistent solution in this example would be that all three links are lossy and their loss rate ranges are $x_{l_1} = [2.7\% - 3.3\%]$, $x_{l_2} = [0.9\% - 1.1\%]$ and $x_{l_3} = [0.9\% - 1.1\%]$. Notice however that this solution results in more lossy links that the solution provided by *Sum-Tomo*. In other words, there can be a trade-off between minimizing the number of inferred lossy links and satisfying the consistency requirement. In fact, in the *RT-Sum* problem, we can show that finding a solution that satisfies the consistency requirement is NP-hard[5] (assuming that the performance ranges cannot contain zero loss rate).

[5]The proof uses a reduction to the *Exact-Set-Cover* problem [9].

5. EVALUATION

This section presents an evaluation study of different tomography algorithms using simulations on real topologies. For brevity, we only consider the *RT-Sum* problem and the loss rate metric.

5.1 Simulation model

We have developed a packet-level event-driven simulator to evaluate tomography algorithms under various network conditions. In each simulation run, we first set the number of lossy links to c. We vary c to examine how different tomography algorithms perform as the likelihood of lossy links increases. We then select the lossy links in the underlying network and assign an average loss rate to each of them. In the following results, the link loss rates are drawn from a Lognormal distribution with mean 0.04 and standard deviation 0.1[6] (these parameters were estimated from a large set of loss rate measurements in about 3600 Planetlab paths). The loss rate of the remaining links is set to zero.

We consider two loss processes:
(I) A Bernoulli random process where each arriving packet at a link is dropped with a given probability (equal to that link's loss rate).
(II) A Gilbert random process where the link's state varies between good and congested. In the good state, the link does not drop packets. In the congested state, the link drops arriving packets with a certain probability. The duration of the good and congested states follows an exponential distribution (with average duration T_{good} and T_{cong}, respectively). The loss probability in the congested state is calculated so that the long-term loss rate, across both good and congested time periods, is equal to the assigned average loss rate for that link.

The Gilbert process can better capture the bursty congestion events that are commonly observed in practice, especially when T_{cong} is much shorter than T_{good}. In our simulations, we have examined two cases for T_{good} and T_{cong}: 1) they are both set to 10sec and, 2) T_{good} is set to 100sec and $T_{cong} = 10sec$. The results with the first pair of values are similar to the Bernoulli case, and so we only report the results with the second pair of values.

To measure path loss rates, we simulate sending 4000 probing packets in each path at a rate of ten packets per second (i.e., the measurement duration is 400 seconds). If the measured path loss rate is less than 0.1%, the path is good (i.e. $\delta = 0.1\%$). The actual loss rate of a lossy link l is the ratio of probing packets (across all paths traversing l) that have been dropped at l.

We consider three IP-layer network topologies. Two of them (Internet2 and ESNet) have been provided to us by the corresponding operators. The third was obtained running Paris-traceroute [22] between 100 PlanetLab hosts. In more detail, the three topologies are:

1. The Internet2 topology, interconnecting 9 Internet2 sensors (located at the major PoPs of Internet2). It includes 44 links (all with known IP addresses) and 72 paths. The average path length is around 4 hops.

2. The ESNet topology, interconnecting 22 ESNet sensors (located at the major PoPs of ESNet). It includes 117

[6]But, we limit the maximum loss rate to 20%.

links (all with known IP addresses) and 382 paths. The average path length is around 6 hops.

3. The "PlanetLab topology", resulting from full-mesh Paris-traceroute measurements between 100 PlanetLab hosts at different sites. This topology includes 4672 links and 5917 paths. The average path length is about 15 hops.

In each of the previous topologies, there are some links that have the same *path cover set* (the path cover set of a link is the set of paths traversing that link). When two or more links have the same path cover set, it is impossible to distinguish those links and detect which of them (if any) is bad. Hence, as in previous work [15, 24], we group links with the same path cover set together[7] and localize *bad link groups* instead of bad links. The size of such groups is a topological property of the underlying network. The average group size is around 1.8 in the PlanetLab topology, while it is almost 1.0 in ESNet and Internet2.

In each simulation run, we select a topology and then select lossy links either randomly or based on a distribution that favors links close to the edge of the network (about 80% of the lossy links are at most three hops away from at least one sensor). This second approach allows us to simulate scenarios where congestion takes place mostly at the periphery of the network rather than the core.

We consider the following metrics. Let I be the set of lossy links and O be the set of lossy links inferred by a tomography algorithm. The *precision* is the ratio of links that are correctly identified as lossy to the total number of inferred lossy links, $precision = \frac{|I \bigcap O|}{|O|}$. The *recall* is the ratio of links that are detected correctly as lossy to the actual number of lossy links, $recall = \frac{|I \bigcap O|}{|I|}$. The precision and recall parameters capture the frequency of *false positives* and *false negatives*, respectively.[8] Let Q be the set of lossy links whose performance range is accurately estimated, i.e., the performance range assigned to a link in Q includes the actual loss rate of that link. The *accuracy* is defined as the ratio of inferred lossy links whose loss rate range is accurately estimated, $accuracy = \frac{|Q|}{|I \bigcap O|}$.

We consider two methods to set the α parameter. The first method (*Method-1*) relies on prior measurements in which the ground truth about the identity of bad links is known (e.g., using SNMP data from routers). The second method (*Method-2*) does not require any prior knowledge. Specifically, in Method-1 we calculate the variation of the measured end-to-end loss rates in all paths that traverse a single lossy link, and set α to the minimum value with which all these paths are α-similar. In the simulation experiments, Method-1 gives $\alpha \approx 0.3$ for Bernoulli losses, and about 0.5 for Gilbert losses. In Method-2, we first remove links that appear in good paths, as well as links that are traversed by only a small number of bad paths (say 3). For each remaining link, we compute the average loss rate $\bar{r}$ of all paths traversing that link, and determine the minimum value of α with which the loss rate of every such path is α-similar with $\bar{r}$. We finally use the median of the previous α values. The rationale in Method-2 is that if a link is traversed by multiple bad paths it is probably a bad link, and so we set α so that most such links are traversed by α-similar paths. There are two cases in which this assumption is incorrect: when a good link is identified as bad (false positive) and when a path traverses more than one bad link. However, as shown in the simulation results of this section and the experimental results of the next section, the likelihood of these two events is low in practice. In addition, by taking the median of α values across all links traversed by multiple bad paths, we reduce the impact of these events.

We compare *Sum-Tomo* with two other tomography algorithms: the Boolean *Tomo* method [8] and the Analog *Norm* method ("L1-norm minimization with non-negativity constraints") [23]. *Norm* starts with similar constraints as in (1) and solves them heuristically using a certain error minimization approach (the estimated link loss rates may not satisfy the path equations exactly, but they minimize the corresponding inference error favoring solutions that involve fewer lossy links). Some recent tomography algorithms, such as *Netscope* [15] and *LIA* [24], apply the previous norm minimization method but additionally they rely on the variance of link loss rates over multiple measurement snapshots. We do not consider such methods because they require multiple measurement snapshots (with 1,000-10,000 probing packets in each snapshot), and so they are less robust to load variations and routing changes. Our focus is on short-term measurements, and so we only compare our method with the original *Norm* algorithm. The precision and recall of *Norm* are computed by comparing the returned point estimates with the threshold δ (so that we can determine the set of bad links according to that method). To calculate the accuracy of *Norm*, we first convert the reported point estimates to range estimate using the relation shown in line-16 of Algorithm 2.

The results of each simulation are repeated 200 times. The standard error for all results in this section is negligible (mostly between 0.005 and 0.02) and so we simply show the average across all runs.

5.2 Results

We start with the ESNet topology. Figure 2 shows the results with three tomography algorithms in ESNet, when the number of lossy links varies from 1 to 20 (i.e., up to about 20% of the total links in that network). Lossy links are selected randomly and the loss process follows the Bernoulli model. The value of α is set based on Method-1; a comparison with Method-2 is given later in this section (Figure 5). Since *Tomo* is not able to determine the loss rate of links, Figure 2c only compares the results of *Sum-Tomo* and *Norm*. As the number of lossy links increases, we see a degradation in the performance of all tomography algorithms. This is because more lossy links create more lossy paths, and hence fewer links can be accounted as good at the initial step of the algorithms. Therefore, the tomography methods have to opt their candidate lossy links from a larger set, which increases the localization errors.

As illustrated in Figure 2a, the precision of *Tomo* and *Sum-Tomo* is very close. However, the recall of *Sum-Tomo* is higher than of *Tomo* by up to 13% (Figure 2b). The reason is that *Tomo* does not consider the loss rate of lossy paths and it simply aims to find the minimum set of links shared between such paths. This approach can be clearly wrong, however, because a link can justify different paths

[7] These groups of links over a path correspond to the Minimal Identifiable Link Sequence (MILS), defined in [25].

[8] In tomography, a false positive refers to detecting a link as bad while it is good.

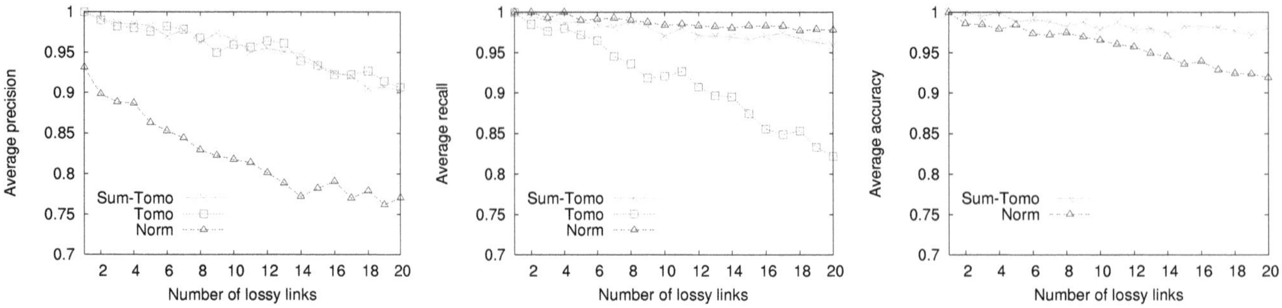

(a) Precision (b) Recall (c) Accuracy

Figure 2: Results of different algorithms obtained in ESNet when actual link loss rates follow Bernoulli process.

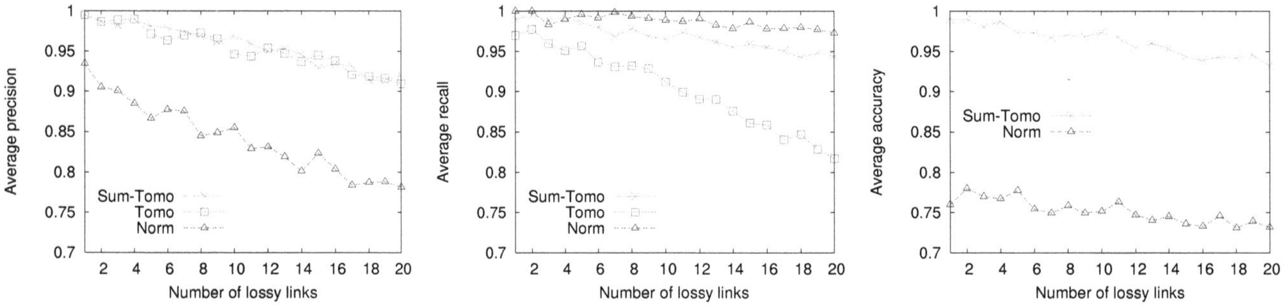

(a) Precision (b) Recall (c) Accuracy

Figure 3: Results of different algorithms obtained in ESNet when actual link loss rates follow Gilbert process.

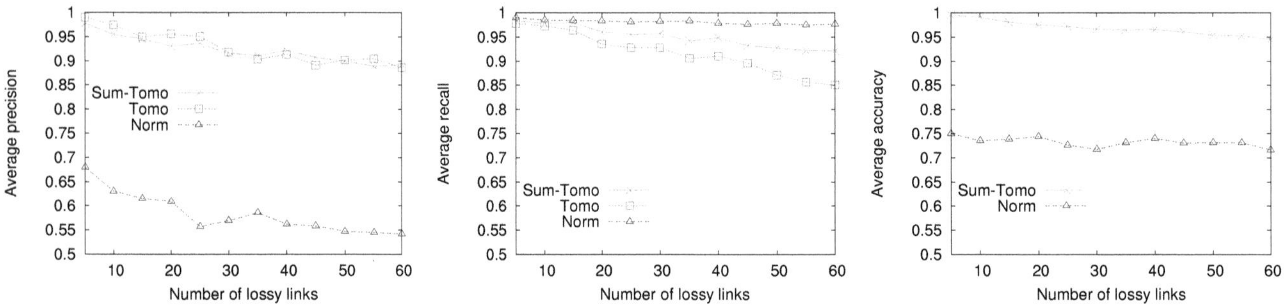

(a) Precision (b) Recall (c) Accuracy

Figure 4: Results of different algorithms obtained in PlanetLab when actual link loss rates follow Gilbert process.

even though their loss rates are very different. Hence, *Tomo* often identifies fewer lossy links. On the contrary, *Norm* usually selects more lossy links to justify the loss rate of every lossy path (the number of links reported by *Norm* as lossy is 30% more than *Sum-Tomo*). This is the reason that *Norm* gives low precision and high recall. Moreover, the accuracy results in Figure 2c show that *Sum-Tomo* can estimate a loss rate range for lossy links quite well. Specifically, if a link is correctly detected by *Sum-Tomo* as lossy, then with a high probability (above 95%) its loss rate range includes the actual loss rate of that link.

The results of the previous algorithms in the Internet2 topology are very similar with the results in the ESNet topology (when considering the same fraction of lossy links), and so they are omitted.

Figure 3 shows the results of the three tomography algorithms in ESNet, when lossy links are selected randomly and their loss process follows the Gilbert model. Comparing the results of Figures 2 and 3, note that the precision of all algorithms does not change much. In addition, the recall of *Tomo* remains the same because the binary state of a path remains the same under these two loss processes. However, we observe a small decrease (by about 2%) in the recall of *Sum-Tomo* and *Norm*, compared to Figure 2b. With the Gilbert process, the measured loss rate of a path can be significantly different from the actual loss rate of its constituent links, and so the value of α should be higher. This means that each link that is detected by *Sum-Tomo* as lossy can justify more lossy paths, and so *Sum-Tomo* may fail to identify some lossy links. Nonetheless, the recall of *Sum-*

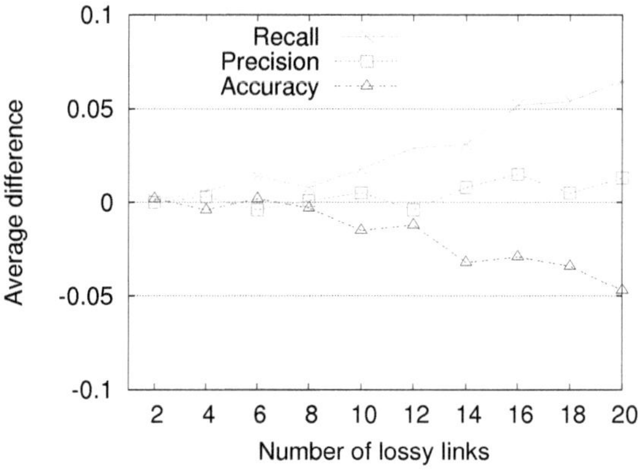

Figure 5: The difference in the results of *Sum-Tomo* with Method-1 versus Method-2 for the selection of α.

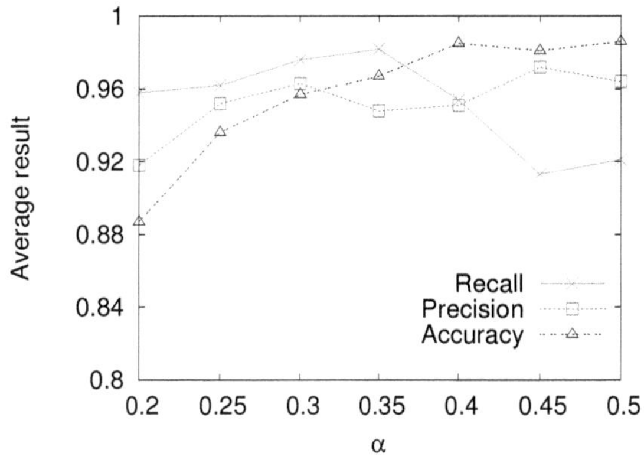

Figure 6: The sensitivity of various parameters to the value of α.

Tomo is still considerably higher than that of its Boolean counterpart (by up to 10%), while it remains close to the recall of *Norm*. Because the Gilbert process introduces more error in the path measurements, the accuracy of both *Sum-Tomo* and *Norm* algorithms declines (Figure 2c). However, because the Analog approach is more sensitive to measurement errors, we see a larger accuracy decrease in *Norm* (by about 25%).

Similarly, Figure 4 shows results obtained with the PlanetLab topology. Here, the loss process follows the Gilbert model while the selection of lossy links has the previously mentioned edge-network bias (α is the same as before). Because the PlanetLab topology is much larger, we consider up to 60 lossy links (about 5% of the total number of links in that network). Figure 4a shows that the precision of *Tomo* and *Sum-Tomo* are close. However, as shown in Figure 4b, the recall of *Sum-Tomo* is higher than that of *Tomo*. This is again because *Tomo* selects fewer links to justify lossy paths (e.g. about 10% fewer links than *Sum-Tomo*). On the other hand, the precision of *Norm* is quite low, as it does not capture that paths sharing the same lossy link may measure different loss rates. So, it reports about 40% more lossy links than *Sum-Tomo*. The accuracy of the loss rate ranges assigned to lossy links by *Sum-Tomo* is always higher than 94%.

The width of the loss rate ranges assigned to bad links depends on the parameter α. When we use the Bernoulli loss model (i.e. $\alpha \approx 0.3$), the width of the resulting loss rate range is about 50% of the center value. For example, when the center of the loss rate range is 0.04, the reported range is from 0.03 to 0.05. With the Gilbert loss model (i.e. $\alpha \approx 0.5$), the width of the loss rate range is about 80% of the center value.

In comparison to a random selection of lossy links, the edge-network bias results in a small decrease (between 2-3%) in precision and recall for *Tomo* and *Sum-Tomo*. This is because fewer paths traverse edge links than core links, and so in some cases these two greedy tomography algorithms fail to select the right lossy link because they prefer to select the most shared link (which is often in the network core).

We now focus on the selection of α, comparing Method-1 with Method-2. Here, we use the ESNet topology, while lossy links are selected randomly and the link loss rates follow the Gilbert process. Figure 5 shows the differences in precision, recall and accuracy between Method-1 and Method-2. Method-1 provides better estimates for α, as it relies on prior measurements in which the ground truth is known. The difference between the two methods is negligible when the number of lossy links is not high (e.g., less than 10% of all network links). With more lossy links, the recall obtained with Method-2 is worse (by up to 6%), while the accuracy improves (by at most 5%). The precision remains roughly the same. The reason is that, when there are many lossy links, Method-2 over-estimates the value of α since each bad path is more likely to traverse more than one lossy link. Then, *Sum-Tomo* becomes more similar to the Boolean *Tomo* algorithm, which yields lower recall, as noted earlier. On the other hand, Method-2 gives higher accuracy because the performance ranges become wider as a result of a larger α.

Finally, we investigate the sensitivity of the precision, recall and accuracy metrics to the value of α. Here, we use the ESNet topology, while losses follow the Bernoulli process. We fix the number of lossy links to 10 (i.e. about 10% of the network's links are lossy). The value of α resulting from Method-1 and Method-2 is around 0.3 and 0.4, respectively. We vary α around these two values, from 0.2 to 0.5. As Figure 6 shows, the accuracy is always improved with increasing α because the estimated loss rate range becomes wider. The precision has an increasing trend with α because each link that is detected as lossy can potentially justify more bad paths, and so *Sum-Tomo* detects fewer links as lossy. For the same reason, the recall drops significantly as we increase α above the value recommended by Method-1 or Method-2. In fact, when α is sufficiently high the *Sum-Tomo* algorithm behaves similar with the Boolean tomography algorithm *Tomo*.

In summary, the errors with *Sum-Tomo* increase as the number of lossy links increases, their locations are moved closer to the edge of the network, and their loss rate varies rapidly over time.

6. EXPERIMENTAL RESULTS

We have conducted extensive experiments on real networks to understand the practical issues involved in network tomography and to examine the behavior of Range Tomography algorithms in practice. In fact, the main purpose of this section is to show the characteristics of actual congestion events in Internet paths and to illustrate how the *Sum-Tomo* algorithm localizes such events. We first present our method to detect congestion events, and analyze the results of that detection phase. We then use the *Sum-Tomo* algorithm to localize those congestion events.

6.1 Detection of congestion events

We performed our experiments over three real networks: Internet2, ESNet, and PlanetLab (the same topologies that were described in Section 5, except that the PlanetLab topology here consists of 60 sensors). The measurement data for Internet2 and ESNet have been provided to us by the corresponding network operators, while the measurement data for PlanetLab were obtained by us running the same measurement tools that are used in Internet2 and ESNet.

The forwarding paths between sensors were measured using Paris-traceroute [22] every 30 minutes. Because multipath forwarding is common in practice (as reported by [26]), it is necessary to use tools such as Paris-traceroute to avoid false inference of paths that do not actually exist in the network. We measured the one-way delay variations and the loss rate in each path with active measurements (using OWAMP), sending ten UDP 60-byte packets per second. In the following results, we analyze a 3-day PlanetLab data set, a 35-day Internet2 data set, and a 14-day ESNet data set.

Generally speaking, we define a *congestion event* as a significant increase in the path one-way delays and/or as the appearance of packet losses. Specifically, if we observe a significant increase in the path one-way delay for at least k consecutive packets, relative to the path's base delay, we detect a congestion event in that path. This approach falsely detects congestion events in two cases: I) when the forwarding path between the two sensors changes (e.g. due to a routing change or because of an NTP clock adjustment), or II) when there is a CPU context-switch event in either sensor, causing a short-term disruption in the measurement process. In the former, we observe a level-shift (rising or falling) in the one-way packet delays. In the latter, we observe a sudden substantial increase in the one-way packet delays, followed by a linear decrease towards the base delay. Specifically, if we observe an increase of at least 80ms in the one-way delay of two consecutive packets, we detect the start of a context-switch event; the event lasts until the delay returns back to its base level[9]. We preprocess the data set to remove all detected context-switches and level-shifts before applying the tomography algorithm.

6.2 Detection results

Table 1 shows the congestion event detection results for the three data sets. The frequency of level-shifts is quite low in all three networks (especially, in ESNet), suggesting that the paths in these networks are stable over several hours. On the other hand, the frequency of context-switches is relatively high in ESNet and PlanetLab paths, indicating that sensors are often highly-loaded (Internet2 sensors are much better in this aspect). The frequency of congestion events is much higher in Internet paths between PlanetLab hosts, while this frequency is quite small in ESNet.

[9]The base delay of a path at time t is set to the median of the one-way delays among the last 100 packets received in that path before t.

Table 1: The results of the detection process on three networks. The value in each cell represents the average occurrence frequency per day and per path.

	Level-shift	Context-switch	Congestion
Internet2	0.01	0.011	0.002
ESNet	0.0002	0.48	0.0002
PlanetLab	0.007	0.61	0.005

Figure 7a shows the distribution of congestion event duration in the PlanetLab network. About 95% of the congestion events last less than 30 seconds. These durations become even shorter in Internet2 and ESNet (the maximum duration is 27sec and only 5% of congestion events last more than 20 seconds in those two networks). This result clearly contradicts the assumption made by several tomography methods that the network conditions (e.g., congestion level at different links) remain constant for long periods of time. It becomes clear that *tomography methods should be able to produce results based on short-term measurements.*

Table 2 summarizes statistics about lossy congestion events (congestion events with at least one lost packet)[10]. The frequency of lossy congestion events is negligible in Internet2 and ESNet, but it is large in PlanetLab paths. More than 50% of the lossy congestion events include just one lost packet, while there are at most 4 packet losses in about 80% of such events (the loss rate is below 1% in about 80% of lossy congestion events).

It is important to note that several tomography methods rely on loss rate to infer and localize congestion events. The previous results imply that most congestion events do not introduce any packet losses, and if there are losses the loss rate is often very low (making it difficult to estimate the loss rate in practice with a limited frequency of probing packets). For these reasons, we define congestion events based on one-way delay variations in the rest of this section.

Table 2: The number and frequency of lossy congestion events (over all congestion events) in the three data sets.

	# lossy events	Frequency of lossy events	# lost packets
Internet2	6	0.2%	1
ESNet	0	0%	0
PlanetLab	535	16.5%	[1-320]

Assume we have detected a congestion event in a path between the kth and l^{th} probing packets. We use the average one-way delay increase during that period to quantify the *congestion magnitude* M,

$$M = \frac{\sum_{i=k}^{l} (d_i - d_{base})}{l - k} \tag{7}$$

where d_{base} is the base one-way delay (estimated as the median one-way delay of the last 1000 probing packets before the kth packet). A higher value of M indicates heavier congestion in that path. Figure 7b shows the congestion magnitude distribution in the PlanetLab network. The average delay increase during half of the congestion events is less

[10]Note that we have ignored cases where all packets sent (or received) over every path to (or from) a specific host are dropped because the problem then can be easily associated with the corresponding sensor and its local-area network.

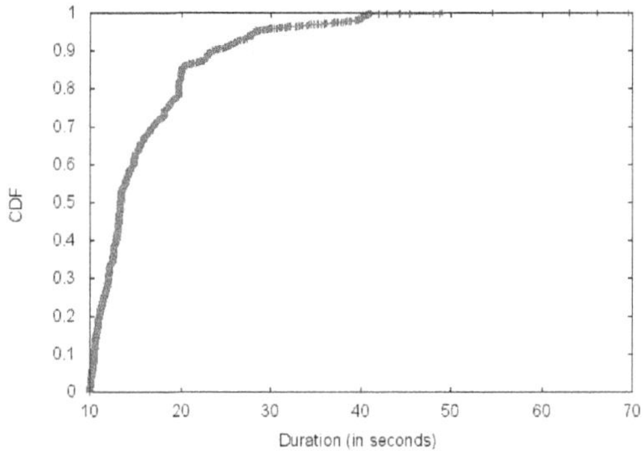

(a) CDF of congestion duration

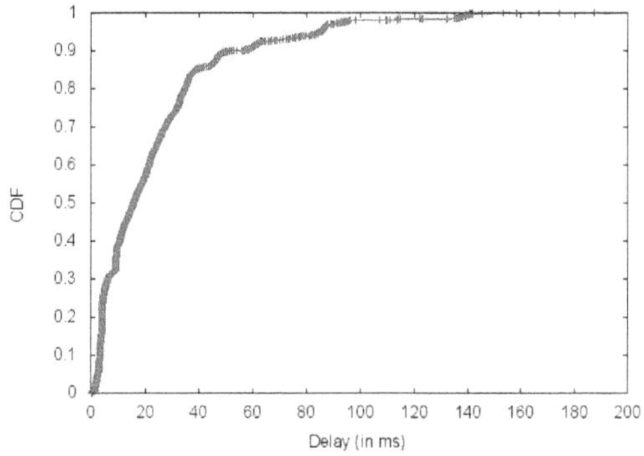

(b) CDF of congestion magnitude

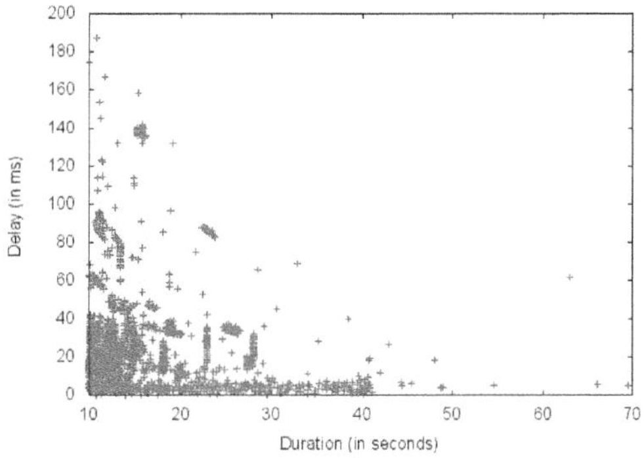

(c) Congestion magnitude vs. congestion duration

Figure 7: Results of the detection process in PlanetLab.

than $20ms$, and it does not exceed $50ms$ in 90% of those events. The distribution of M in the other two networks has the same trend, but the maximum value of M is at most $60ms$ there. Finally, Figure 7c shows the magnitude of congestion events versus their duration. It is interesting to see that heavier congestion events usually last for shorter durations, emphasizing again that a practical tomography method should be able to work with short-term measurements. It should be noted here that network tomography methods cannot localize congestion events that are very short in duration because it is hard to reliably detect such events, and further to estimate their magnitude, with active measurements. For instance, even if the probing frequency is 10 packets per second, a congestion event that lasts for three seconds introducing a loss rate of 1% would probably not be observed by the probing stream. However, because the Range Tomography methods do not require a long measurement history or precise estimates of path performance, they are able to localize congestion events that last for at least few tens of seconds, as shown in the following results.

6.3 Localization results

We run the *Sum-Tomo* algorithm on the detected congestion events to localize congested links. Ideally, we expect that a congested link causes the same congestion event (in terms of duration and congestion magnitude) to paths that traverse that link. However, these congestion periods do not exactly overlap in practice due to lack of perfect clock synchronization in the measurement hosts. Therefore, we consider the time interval that covers all overlapping congestion periods as the designated congestion period that the tomography method analyzes.

We then compute the congestion magnitude M in every path during that designated period. To distinguish good paths from bad paths, we set the threshold δ as the minimum congestion magnitude over all detected congestion events in that network (the value of δ is around $2ms$ in practice). The α parameter is determined based on Method-2, introduced in Section 5.1. This process results in α=2 in Internet2 and ESNet, and α=1.2 in PlanetLab. In our experiments, we ignore paths containing links with unknown IP addresses (only happens in the PlanetLab data set).

It is not possible to directly validate the results of the *Sum-Tomo* algorithm because we do not have access to the routers and switches along each path. Instead, we use the indirect validation method introduced in [19]. In this method, the measured paths in each period are divided in two groups, *inference paths* and *validation paths*. Each link should be included in both sets. The inference paths are then used to identify congested links and to estimate their congestion magnitude range using the *Sum-Tomo* algorithm. Then, we use the validation paths to examine if the ranges that were computed based on the inference paths are consistent with the measured congestion magnitude of the validation paths. Finally, we measure the *validation error* as the fraction of bad links in which the estimated congestion magnitude range

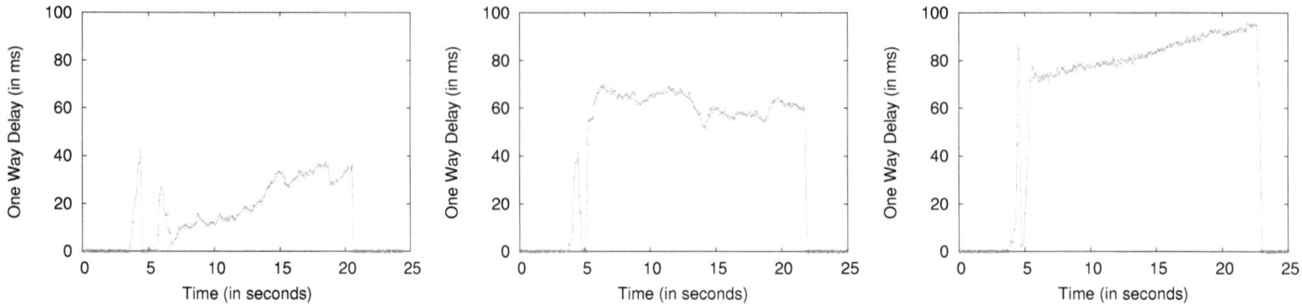

(a) Delay timeseries of a path traversing a congested link l_1. (b) Delay timeseries of a path traversing a congested link l_2. (c) Delay timeseries of a path traversing both congested links l_1 and l_2.

Figure 8: The timeseries of one-way packet delays measured in three paths during a congestion event in Internet2. The delays are relative to the base delay in that path (i.e., they represent one-way delay increase due to queueing). There are two congested links during this episode. Paths in (a) and (b) traverse two different congested links, but the path in (c) traverses both links. Note that the sum of the delay increase in (a) and (b) results to roughly the same delay increase we observe in (c).

for a link is *not* consistent with the measured congestion magnitude in the corresponding validation path.

Overall, we analyzed 254 congestion events in Internet2, 336 events in ESNet, and 159 events in PlanetLab. In almost all events, *only one congested link* was identified as the root cause of the congestion event. Specifically, more than 97% of congested paths in all three networks include just one congested link, and only 0.5% of paths contain more than two congested links (we did not find any path with four congested links in our data sets).

The validation error in all three data sets was zero. In addition, the time-series of one-way delay variations in the inference and validation paths are highly correlated in the time domain when the corresponding congested paths traverse the same congested link. For instance, the time-series in Figure 8 show an interesting example of a congestion event in Internet2 that involves two congested links. The congestion magnitude range assigned to links is mostly below 70ms in PlanetLab, and mostly less than 40ms in Internet2 and ESNet.

7. RELATED WORK

We refer the reader to a thorough review [10] for a coverage of the prior work until 2004.

In Analog tomography, a typically under-constrained linear system of equations models the relation between path and link parameters (assuming that the topology is known). Techniques from parametric or non-parametric statistical inference, jointly with additional constraints, assumptions and optimization objectives, are then used to infer the most likely values of the link parameters from the measured path parameters [10, 11]. For instance, Shavitt et al. [12] estimate link delays using a least-squares method, Bu et al. [13] use expectation-maximization to infer link loss rates, while Chen et al. [14] use Fourier domain analysis to infer link delays. NetScope [15] is a recent method that estimates link loss rates also considering the observed loss rate variances. Ghita et al. study the case that different links can be correlated (all other related work assumes independent links) [16]. The application of Analog tomography in practice has been rather limited for several reasons. First, they require accurate end-to-end path measurements, which are hard to get in short timescales and without intrusive probing. Second, some link-level parameters may not be statistically identifiable, meaning that different assignments of link-level metrics produce the same statistical distribution of path measurements [5, 6, 7]. Third, Analog methods can be computationally intensive [7].

Duffield introduced the Boolean tomography framework in 2003 [5, 7], while Nguyen and Thiran compared Analog with Boolean tomography [17]. NetDiagnoser [8] extends Boolean tomography to multiple sources and destinations. Kompella et al. [18] consider a similar approach to detect "silent failures" in MPLS/IP networks using active measurements between edge routers. Nguyen and Thiran introduce a Boolean method to infer link state probabilities from multiple measurements over time, and then using those probabilities to identify congested links [6]. Bayesian approaches to infer lossy links have also been proposed [19]. The authors in [20] use prior link state probabilities to diagnose the underlying cause behind the faulty state of links. Barford et al. have proposed a framework to detect and localize performance anomalies using active probe-based measurements [21]. To reduce probing overhead, they give an algorithm to select the paths that should be probed at any point in time.

8. CONCLUSIONS

We proposed a new tomography framework that combines the best features of Analog and Boolean tomography. Range tomography estimates a range estimate for each bad link, instead of aiming to infer a point estimate or a binary estimate for every link. We applied the range tomography framework in two path performance metric functions (Min and Sum) and presented an efficient heuristic for each function. The *Min-Tomo* algorithm considers only the lowest-performance link over a path, while the *Sum-Tomo* algorithm considers the sum of the performance metrics for all bad links in that path.

Simulation results show that the proposed tomography method performs much better than earlier Boolean and Analog techniques in terms of precision, recall and accuracy. For instance, *Sum-Tomo* generates up to 35% less false positives than the Analog Norm-minimization method, while its false negative error is less than the Boolean Tomo method by up to 15%. Moreover, the accuracy of the resulting range estimates is always high (more than 93%).

We have also applied the *Sum-Tomo* method in three operational networks to detect and localize congested links and to estimate their congestion magnitude. According to an indirect validation method, the resulting link range estimate is consistent with the measured path congestion magnitude in every congestion event we have analyzed. The experimental results also emphasize that congestion events in Internet paths are often short-lived, and so any practical tomography methods should be accurate even if the path measurements result from few probes and they are error-prone. Finally, at least for the networks we measured in this study, we often see only one bad link during any congestion event, and rarely more than 2-3 bad links.

Acknowledgements

We are grateful to Partha Kanuparthy for his help with the detection logic and data management. We also thank Jason Zurawski from Internet2, and Joe Metzger, Brian Tierney and Andrew Lake from ESnet for providing us with the OWAMP data sets. We are also grateful to the anonymous reviewers and our "shepherd", Matthias Grossglauser, for their constructive comments.

This research was supported by the U.S. Department of Energy under grant number DE-FG02-10ER26021.

9. REFERENCES

[1] R. Caceres, N.G. Duffield, J. Horowitz, D. Towsley. Multicast-Based Inference of Network Internal Loss Characteristics. *IEEE Trans. on Information Theory*, 45(7), 2462-2480, 1999.

[2] M. Coates, R. Nowak. Network loss inference using unicast end-to-end measurement, In *Proc. ITC Conf. IP Traffic, Modeling and Management*, 2000.

[3] Y. Zhang, N. Duffield, V. Paxson, S. Shenker. On the Constancy of Internet Path Properties. In *ACM SIGCOMM Workshop on Internet Measurement*, 2001.

[4] M. Roughan. Fundamental Bounds on the Accuracy of Network Performance Measurements. In *ACM SIGMETRICS*, 2005.

[5] N. Duffield. Simple network performance tomography. In *Proc. ACM IMC*, 2003.

[6] H. Nguyen, and P. Thiran. The Boolean Solution to the Congested IP Link Location Problem: Theory and Practice. In *Proc. IEEE INFOCOM*, 2007.

[7] N. Duffield. Network Tomography of Binary Network Performance Characteristics. In *IEEE Trans. Information Theory*, 52, 2006.

[8] A. Dhamdhere, R. Teixeira, C. Dovrolis, C. Diot. NetDiagnoser: Troubleshooting network unreachabilities using end-to-end probes and routing data. In *Proc. ACM CoNEXT*, 2007.

[9] M. R. Garey, and D. S. Johnson. *Computers and Intractability: A Guide to the Theory of NP-Completeness*. W. H. Freeman and Co., 1979.

[10] R. Castro, M. Coates, G. Liang, R. Nowak, B. Yu. Network Tomography: Recent Developments. *Statistical Science*, 19(3):499-517, 2004.

[11] R. Caceres, N. Duffield, S. Moon, D. Towsley. Inference of Internal Loss Rates in the MBone. In *Proc. IEEE Global Internet*, 1999.

[12] Y. Shavitt, X. Sun, A. Wool, B. Yener. Computing the unmeasured: An algebraic approach to internet mapping. In *Proc. IEEE INFOCOM*, 2001.

[13] T. Bu, N. Duffield, F. L. Presti, D. Towsley. Network tomography on general topologies. In *Proc. ACM SIGMETRICS*, 2002.

[14] A. Chen, J. Cao, T. Bu. Network tomography: Identifiability and fourier domain estimation. In *Proc. IEEE INFOCOM*, 2007.

[15] D. Ghita, H. Nguyen, M. Kurant, K. Argyraki, P. Thiran. Netscope: Practical Network Loss Tomography. In *Proc. IEEE INFOCOM*, 2010.

[16] D. Ghita, K. Argyraki, P Thiran. Network Tomography on Correlated Links. In *Proc. ACM IMC*, 2010.

[17] H. X. Nguyen, and P. Thiran. Binary versus analogue path monitoring in IP networks. In *LNCS*, Vol. 3431, Jan. 2005, p. 97.

[18] R. R. Kompella, J. Yates, A. Greenberg, A. C. Snoeren. Detection and Localization of Network Blackholes. In *Proc. IEEE INFOCOM*, 2007.

[19] V. Padmanabhan, L. Qiu, H. Wang. Server-based Inference of Internet Link lossiness. In *Proc. IEEE INFOCOM*, 2003.

[20] S. Kandula, D. Katabi, J.-P. Vasseur. Shrink: A Tool for Failure Diagnosis in IP Networks. In *Proc. ACM SIGCOMM MineNet Workshop*, 2005.

[21] P. Barford, N. Duffield, A. Ron, and J. Sommers. Network Performance Anomaly Detection and Localization. In *Proc. IEEE INFOCOM*, 2009.

[22] B. Augustin et al. Avoiding traceroute anomalies with Paris traceroute, In *Proc. ACM IMC*, 2006.

[23] H. H. Song, L. Qiu, Y. Zhang. NetQuest: A Flexible Framework for Large-Scale Network Measurement. In *Proc. ACM SIGMETRICS*, 2006.

[24] H. X. Nguyen, and P. Thiran. Network Loss Inference with Second Order Statistics of End-to-End Flows. In *Proc. ACM IMC*, 2007.

[25] Y. Zhao, Y. Chen, D. Bindel, Towards Unbiased End-to-End Network Diagnosis, In *Proc. ACM SIGCOMM*, 2006.

[26] M. Luckie, A. Dhamdhere, K. Claffy, D. Murrell. Measured impact of crooked traceroute. In *ACM SIGCOMM CCR*, Vol. 41, Issue 1, 2011.

On Traffic Matrix Completion in the Internet

Gonca Gürsun
Department of Computer Science
Boston University
goncag@cs.bu.edu

Mark Crovella
Department of Computer Science
Boston University
crovella@cs.bu.edu

ABSTRACT

The ability of an ISP to infer traffic volumes that are not directly measurable can be useful for research, engineering, and business intelligence. Previous work has shown that *traffic matrix completion* is possible, but there is as yet no clear understanding of which ASes are likely to be able to perform TM completion, and which traffic flows can be inferred.

In this paper we investigate the relationship between the AS-level topology of the Internet and the ability of an individual AS to perform traffic matrix completion. We take a three-stage approach, starting from abstract analysis on idealized topologies, and then adding realistic routing and topologies, and finally incorporating realistic traffic on which we perform actual TM completion.

Our first set of results identifies which ASes are best-positioned to perform TM completion. We show, surprisingly, that for TM completion it does not help for an AS to have many peering links. Rather, the most important factor enabling an AS to perform TM completion is the number of direct customers it has. Our second set of results focuses on which flows can be inferred. We show that topologically close flows are easier to infer, and that flows passing through customers are particularly well suited for inference.

Categories and Subject Descriptors

C.2.3 [**Network Operations**]: Network monitoring; C.2.5 [**Local and Wide-Area Networks**]: Internet — BGP

Keywords

Interdomain Routing, Matrix Completion

1. INTRODUCTION

Interdomain traffic – the traffic flowing between autonomous systems – is the fundamental workload of the Internet. It reflects global economic activity and information flow. Knowledge of interdomain traffic volumes is therefore of immense engineering, scientific and societal interest.

On a more local scale, knowledge of interdomain traffic volumes has great value for business intelligence. Consider an ISP that is pondering a bid for a competitor's customer. That ISP has a significant advantage if it knows how much business the competitor currently does with the customer (i.e., how much traffic they exchange), and how the customer's traffic would impact the ISP's network should the customer change providers.

Unfortunately, broad knowledge of interdomain traffic volumes on the Internet is hard to come by. The inherently distributed architecture of the AS-level Internet means that there is no single place where all Internet-wide traffic can be measured, and the competitive relationship of the commercial Internet means that sharing such information across organizational boundaries is unlikely. The authors in [10] review the situation and note that an inter-AS traffic matrix is an "elusive object."

Hence we are prompted to turn to statistical inference where direct measurement is impossible. The problem can be cast in terms of a *traffic matrix* – measurements of traffic volume from sources (rows) to destinations (columns). Any given AS can observe some of the elements of this matrix – namely, exactly the traffic that flows through the AS. Can an AS ever 'fill in' the missing entries (corresponding to traffic *not* flowing through the AS) thereby 'completing' the matrix? Doing so would give the AS a view of a much larger set of traffic volumes, or even of traffic volumes across the entire Internet.

Surprisingly, recent work has suggested that in some cases, a single AS *can* complete at least some of the missing portions of its traffic matrix [2, 27]. The general idea (described in detail in Section 2) is as follows. The first step is to note that traffic matrix elements show strong statistical regularities. There are predictable relationships between elements, such that missing elements can often be cast in terms of linear functions of observable elements. One way of describing this phenomenon is to note that traffic matrices often have *low effective rank* (which we define in Section 2). The second step is to apply methods of statistical inference that are recently emerging in the signal processing community, termed *matrix completion*. These methods are specifically designed to perform missing-element inference on matrices that have low effective rank. A wide variety of such methods have now been developed [3, 4, 5, 17, 25].

The key to matrix completion is the ability to observe a sufficiently useful subset of the matrix entries. If enough en-

IMC'12, November 14–16, 2012, Boston, Massachusetts, USA.

tries, in the right positions, can be observed, the rest of the entries can be 'filled in.' In the context of interdomain traffic matrices, this question relates to the network's AS-level connectivity and routing patterns. Some ASes, by virtue of their topological position and commercial roles, may observe enough traffic passing through their networks to allow them to infer traffic volumes *not* passing through their networks. Initial studies have shown existence proofs that such inference is possible [2, 27]. The question is – for whom? For which ASes is traffic matrix completion most likely to be successful? And, for those ASes that can infer some TM elements, which elements can they infer?

Those questions are the focus of this paper. We seek to understand *which* ASes are likely to be able to perform TM completion, *which* elements they can infer, and *why*. We seek to answer these questions from two standpoints: from an analytical standpoint, we look for graph-theoretic properties of the AS topology that lead to increased traffic inference ability for an AS. And from a practical standpoint, we look to answer to these questions in terms of metrics that relate to an ISP's business and engineering relationships – e.g., how many customers and peering links it has.

To do so, we provide a framework for analyzing the inference capability of a given AS based on its position in the AS graph and the set of paths that pass through it. This is the first contribution of our paper, and is independently useful, for example, when an individual AS seeks to evaluate its own inference capability. However, once having developed this framework, our second contribution is to apply the framework to a large AS graph to investigate actual ASes and their TMs.

The first stage of our work explores the relationship between TM completion ability and certain idealized graph models. We develop an algorithm that allows us to prove a lower bound on TM completion ability, and using it we gain insight into how TM completion ability relates to local graph topology.

The second stage of our work brings realistic routing into the picture. For this we rely on an extensive survey of the AS-level Internet, comprising over 100 million AS paths, captured at a single time. This rich dataset allows us to explore how TM completion ability varies over the set of all ASes in the Internet.

Finally, the third stage of our work applies actual matrix completion to realistic TMs across ASes in the Internet. For each AS we evaluate its accuracy when completing a TM comprising about 30 million elements, of which between 0.001% and 0.3% are actually visible to the AS, depending on the set of AS paths that flow through it.

The three stages of our effort mutually support our primary conclusions. We find that the key to TM inference ability lies in the *set of customers* of an AS. Our analysis and measurements show that an AS's customers provide the AS with crucial knowledge of interdomain traffic flows needed for TM completion. When asking which flows are most readily estimated, we find that the closer a flow passes to an AS in the BGP graph, the more readily it may be estimated; and when an AS seeks to specifically recover the entries of flows that pass through another AS, it is most successful when the other AS is a neighbor – especially, when the other AS is a customer.

2. BACKGROUND & RELATED WORK

2.1 Definitions

A *traffic matrix* (TM) is an $m \times n$ matrix T in which T_{ij} is a measure of the traffic flowing from a set of IP addresses $\mathscr{S}_i$ to a set of IP addresses $\mathscr{D}_j$ during a specific time interval. At any moment, the *view* of a network P consists of all the source-destination pairs (s,d) such that any traffic flowing from s to d will at some point pass through P. A network's view can be captured in the form of an $m \times n$ *visibility matrix* M, where $M_{ij} = 1$ if traffic from $\mathscr{S}_i$ to $\mathscr{D}_j$ passes through P, and zero otherwise.

A key property for traffic matrices in our work is *low effective rank*. If an $m \times n$ matrix T can be factored into an $m \times d$ matrix X and a $d \times n$ matrix Y, such that $XY = T$, then T has rank (no greater than) d. If $d \ll \min(m,n)$ then we say T has *low rank*. When working with measurement data, a matrix T may be strictly speaking full rank, but nonetheless well-approximated by a low-rank matrix. That is, if there exists a rank d matrix T' such that $T \approx T'$, we say that T has low effective rank. For example, we may use a least-squares criterion: $T \approx T'$ if $\sum_{i,j}(T_{ij} - T'_{ij})^2 / \sum_{i,j} T_{ij}^2$ is small enough. Low rank is important because it means that elements of T are related; only a small amount of information (X and Y) is needed to construct T, so some elements of T can be computed as linear functions of other elements. Likewise, if a matrix has low effective rank, then some elements can be approximated as linear functions of other elements.

In this work, TMs will be organized as either node-to-node TMs (in our idealized examples in Section 3) or AS-to-prefix TMs (when using real topologies in Sections 4 and 5).

2.2 Properties of Traffic Matrices

Our work deals with large-scale inference of traffic matrices that span ASes. While an interdomain TM remains an "elusive object" [10], a few previous studies have built models of interdomain traffic. The work described in [13] estimates Web-related interdomain traffic, using server logs from a large CDN provider. The work described in [8] brings more AS-specific information to the table, including business relationship, population size, and AS role, and fuses this information to form estimates of interdomain traffic volume. These models and methods inform our work, but the focus of our work is not explicitly on modeling TMs. Rather, we only assume that TMs show low effective rank.

Indeed, there is considerable evidence that traffic matrices often show low effective rank. In [19], the authors document low effective rank in measurements of temporal traffic matrices, in which each column is a time-series of the traffic volume between a source-destination pair. In [2], the authors present a similar result for measurements of spatial traffic matrices, in which the rows represent the sources and the columns represent the destinations (as do the matrices in this paper). More generally, traffic matrix modeling often assumes that TMs have low effective rank. The often-used *gravity* models are rank-1 models; such models have been used, for example, in [9, 20, 22, 23, 26]. Likewise, the authors in [12] show that a rank-2 model is a good fit to measured TMs. Finally, a number of papers have explicitly relied on the property of low effective rank in TMs as the basis for their results [2, 18, 27].

In this paper we start from the assumption that TMs show

low effective rank. However, we do not assume that TMs have any *particular* effective rank; our analyses and experiments treat matrix rank k as a parameter.

2.3 Traffic Matrix Completion

Our paper applies ideas from matrix completion to traffic at the AS level. Matrix completion is a relatively new area in statistical inference with a number of recent results [5, 17]. The matrix completion problem consists of recovering a low-rank matrix from a subset of its entries. Let the $m \times n$ matrix T having rank $k \ll min(m,n)$ be unknown, except for a subset of its entries Ω which are known. If the set Ω contains enough information, and T meets a condition called *incoherence,* then there is a unique rank-k matrix that is consistent with the observed entries.

Recently, a variety of algorithms have been proposed that solve the matrix completion problem under various assumptions [3, 4, 5, 17, 25]. These algorithms are typically analyzed under the assumption that the locations of the known entries of T are distributed uniformly at random across the matrix. However, matrix completion can be possible when the location of entries are not uniformly spread across the matrix. In particular, the algorithm in [21] does not assume uniformly spread entries, and furthermore has a more general capability. Rather than focusing exclusively on matrix completion, it can also be used to identify *which* elements of a matrix can be recovered, even when full completion is not possible. It is this property of the algorithm that we make use of in our work. We review this algorithm and our use of it in the next subsection.

Given the tendency for traffic matrices to show low effective rank, a number of authors have applied matrix completion to different types of TMs. In particular, the authors in [27] develop algorithms for accurately recovering missing values (due to measurement failures) in intra domain TMs in which the sources and destinations are in the observer's network. And in the study mentioned previously, the authors in [2] develop methods for inferring traffic volumes for traffic that does not pass through the observer's network, and hence cannot be measured. In [2], the authors show that a network P can infer the traffic that does not flow through P but flows through its direct customer network T. However [2] only demonstrates this for one particular pair of networks and does not give insight into when TM completion is possible in general. In contrast, our paper asks the broader question - what relationship should P and T have in order for TM completion to be successful.

2.4 ICMC and AICMC

To analyze the ability of an AS to perform matrix completion, we adopt a particular algorithm from the matrix completion literature called *Information Cascading Matrix Completion (ICMC)* [21]. ICMC can be applied to matrices that are exactly low-rank, or approximately low-rank; for simplicity in the description below we describe it as applied to an exactly low-rank matrix. However extensions to deal with approximately low-rank matrices are not difficult, as described in [21].

We use ICMC as a tool for exploring the TM completion ability of ASes. The advantage of using ICMC as compared to other matrix completion algorithms is that it identifies which matrix elements can definitely be recovered in a given setting. That is how we use it in this Section and Sections 4 and 5. However, not all matrix completion algorithms work in this elementwise, all-or-nothing fashion; other algorithms try to form estimates of all missing elements. Hence we confirm our results by using a different matrix completion algorithm in Section 6.

ICMC assumes that the $m \times n$ matrix T having rank k is *non-degenerate*, meaning that T can be factored into the matrices $X \in \mathbb{R}^{m \times k}$ and $Y \in \mathbb{R}^{k \times n}$ such that any k rows of X are linearly independent, any k columns of Y are linearly independent, and $XY = T$. The basic idea of ICMC is to progressively compute rows of X and columns of Y so that $(XY)_{ij} = T_{ij}$, $\forall (i, j) \in \Omega$.

In fact, our goal in this paper is not performing matrix completion per se, but rather identifying *whether* and *when* matrix completion is possible. Hence we employ ICMC in a manner we refer to as *abstract* ICMC, or *AICMC*.

AICMC may be expressed in terms of operations on a bipartite graph, as shown in Figure 1. The graph consists of two sets of vertices, $U = \{u_i, i = 1, \ldots, m\}$ and $V = \{v_j, j = 1, \ldots n\}$. An edge exists between u_i and v_j if $(i, j) \in \Omega$; otherwise no edge exists. Thus there is a correspondence between vertex u_i and row i of X; and there is a correspondence between vertex v_j and column j of Y.

AICMC progresses by successively marking vertices as 'infected,' which means that the corresponding row of X or column of Y can be recovered. The set L consists of infected u vertices, and R consists of infected v vertices. Infection propagates through the graph: v_j can be infected if there are at least k edges from v_j to vertices in L. Analogously, infecting u_i requires at least k edges from u_i to vertices in R. When no more nodes can be infected, the set L identifies the rows of X that can be recovered, and R identifies the recoverable columns of Y. The authors in [21] prove the correctness of this process for recovering X and Y.

Figure 1 shows an example visibility matrix and corresponding bipartite graph. This process is shown in the figure for $k = 1$. Starting with infected vertex u_1, each step progressively infects nodes on alternating sides of the bipartite graph. While in this case the final set of infected nodes corresponds to the largest connected component, note that for $k > 1$ the final set of infected nodes is not necessarily the largest connected component.

To start the algorithm, one notes that the solution X, Y is not unique, and hence without loss of generality the algorithm can be initiated by setting any k rows of X to the $k \times k$ identity matrix, and marking the corresponding k vertices as infected (forming the initial population of the set L). Beginning from this initial set of infected nodes, the algorithm proceeds by alternately adding to the sets R and L. When these sets contain all vertices in the graph, the entire matrix is recovered at rank k.

That said, one can set aside the graph interpretation and express AICMC simply in terms of an observer's visibility matrix M. Note that $M_{ij} = 1$ iff $(i, j) \in \Omega$. AICMC proceeds as follows

1. Choose k rows of M and set L to those rows.

2. If L contains all rows of M and R contains all columns of M, stop - the matrix T can be fully recovered. Otherwise:

    (a) For every column of M such that there are at least k 1s in rows from set L, add the column to R. If there are no such columns, stop.

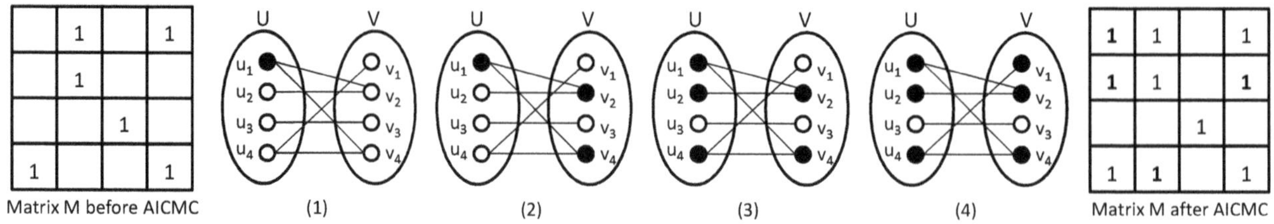

Figure 1: AICMC Example: T is a 4×4 data matrix (not shown) of rank $k = 1$. T's known elements correspond to the positions of the 1s in its visibility matrix M (left side of the figure). The steps of AICMC are: (1) $L = \{u_1\}$, (2) $R = \{v_2, v_4\}$, (3) $L = \{u_1, u_2, u_4\}$, (4) $R = \{v_1, v_2, v_4\}$. The algorithm stops at the end of (4). The completed elements are $(1,1), (2,1), (2,4)$, and $(4,2)$ - 1s shown in bold in M (right side of the figure).

(b) For every row of M such that there are at least k 1s in columns from set R, add the row to L. If there are no such rows, stop.

3. Go to 2.

At completion, an element (i, j) can be recovered if row i is in L and column j is in R. Thus AICMC allows us to examine an AS's visibility matrix, and identify, for each invisible element, whether it can be recovered at a given rank (or approximate rank) k. In Figure 1 the recoverable elements are shown on the right side of the figure. Note that if an AS can complete its TM at rank k, it can complete it at any rank $r \leq k$.

2.5 Interdomain Topology

A central aspect of our work is establishing a connection between the AS-level topology of the Internet, and the ability of individual ASes to do traffic matrix completion. Hence we rely on the considerable body of work that has characterized the AS level topology, of which we can only review a portion here.

At the highest level, the AS graph is usually characterized as having roughly three distinguishable parts [6, 15, 16, 24]. Forming the center of the graph is a mesh-like core that is a clique or 'almost' a clique. This core is fed by a collection of ASes in provider-customer relationships that are 'tree-like' but not strictly trees. Finally the vast majority of ASes are *stubs,* ASes at the edge of the network having no customers themselves. A number of methods have been proposed for organizing ASes into a small number of *tiers* [15, 24].

In our work we seek a finer-grained and less arbitrary measure of centrality in the AS graph than tiers, and so we turn to a tool for graph analysis called *k-core decomposition* [1] [1]. K-core decomposition separates the vertices of a graph into successive sets called "shells". These are operationally defined: the 1-shell consists of all nodes of degree 1, plus all nodes that become degree-1 when degree-1 nodes are removed. Removing all such nodes leaves only nodes of degree-2 and higher, and the process repeats. As described in [6], this is a parameter-free way of characterizing the AS graph, and it naturally identifies a 'nucleus' (innermost shell) of the graph which is observed to consist of major provider ISPs, major IXPs, CDNs and content providers. In our data the nucleus is shell 58, containing 120 ASes. Each node in the nucleus is connected to about 70% of the other nodes.

[1]Note that parameter k used in k-core decomposition represents degree order It is unrelated to rank parameter k we use throughout the paper.

Our knowledge of the AS level graph is derived from measurements, and is generally understood to be imperfect. A good review of the issues is presented in [10], but a persistent concern is that maps of the AS graph miss links, in particular peering links [7]. Missing links may result in some inaccuracy in certain graph metrics we use: k-core decomposition, degree, number of peers and number of customers. For that reason we do not base results on precise values of these metrics, but rather focus on the trends seen as these metrics vary. However missing links do *not* cause inaccuracies for our key metrics: completion ability and expected rank (defined below). This is because (as explained in Section 4.1) we select a subset of all AS paths in such a way that these metrics are known with high confidence.

Finally, a portion of our results relies on the classification of AS-AS links as customer-provider or peer-peer (we do not consider sibling-sibling links). For this we rely on the body of knowledge that has been built up on how to do this classification since [14], and in particular rely on the comprehensive approach used in [11].

3. ANALYSIS

Our first step is to develop high-level insight about the relationship between graph topologies and the opportunity for traffic inference. We do that by establishing provable lower bounds on traffic matrix completion in various idealized networks. These models necessarily ignore important aspects of the AS level Internet (e.g., they assume shortest-path, symmetric routing) but our goal here is to build intuition. Later, in Sections 4 and 5, we will examine real AS level graphs.

Each of our idealized models starts with a particular graph $G = (V, E)$, with $|V| = n$. Each node $v_i \in V$ sends one traffic flow to every node $v_j \in V$ (including v_i itself). All flows travel over shortest paths, assuming edges have unit weight. In each graph we designate an *observer node*, denoted v_o; we will analyze the observer's ability to do traffic inference.

The information available to the observer node is summarized in a *visibility matrix* M of size $n \times n$. We set $M_{ij} = 1$ if the flow from v_i to v_j passes through v_o and so is measurable by v_o; otherwise we set $M_{ij} = 0$. By convention we assign v_o to matrix index 1. Thus the first row and the first column of M are always fully populated with 1s, since all traffic that originates or terminates at v_o is visible to v_o. Furthermore, because of our assumptions about flow routing, M is symmetric.

To find a lower bound on the traffic inference capabilities of v_o, we apply Abstract ICMC (AICMC) to M as described in

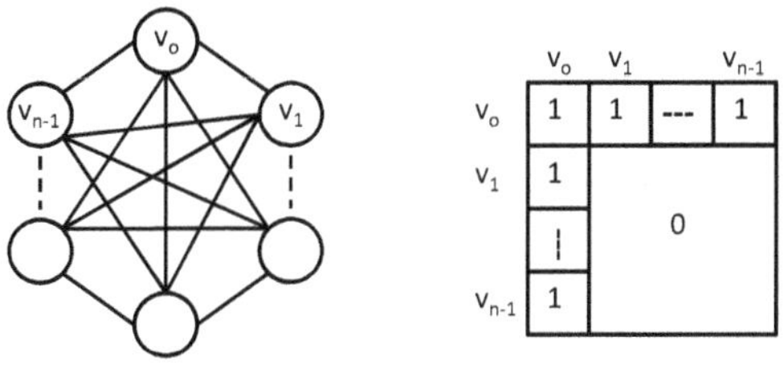

Figure 2: Full mesh network.

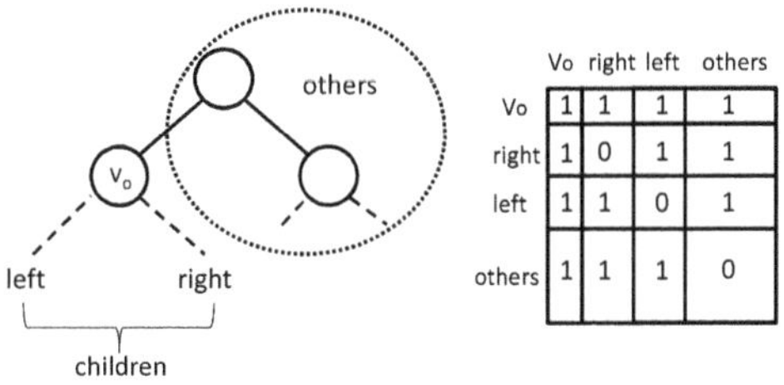

Figure 3: Example tree.

Section 2.4. Using AICMC we can identify invisible elements of the network-wide traffic matrix that can be recovered by v_o, assuming the traffic matrix is rank k. For simplicity, we ask the following question in each case: For what values of k can v_o recover the entire TM? Larger values of k imply a greater ability to do TM completion.

We study a progression of idealized networks, starting with highly decentralized networks, then moving to trees and tree-like networks, and finally considering some more specialized topologies that are inspired by the connection pattern of ASes in the Internet.

3.1 Idealized Networks

We study three idealized networks: a clique, and two trees that differ in terms of size and degree.

Clique: In a clique (a full mesh), there is a direct link between every pair of nodes (Figure 2). As a result, the observer node v_o can only measure flows having itself as either source or destination, resulting in the visibility matrix shown in the Figure.

PROPOSITION 3.1. *Given a full mesh with n nodes, (a) the observer can complete its TM for $k = 1$; and (b) the observer cannot complete its TM at any rank $k > 1$.*

PROOF. For (a): in the initial step we choose the first row of M and set L to that row, i.e. $L = \{1\}$. Next, all columns are added to R, i.e. $R = \{1, \ldots, n\}$, since they all have 1s in the first row of M. Finally, all the rest of the rows are added to L, i.e. $L = \{1, \ldots, n\}$, since they all have 1s in the first column of M.

For (b): when $k > 1$, the initial step chooses k rows of M and sets L to those rows. However, no choice of k rows yields more than one column with k 1s, so completion is impossible at rank $k > 1$. □

Trees: Figure 3 shows an example tree and the visibility matrix of an arbitrary observer node, v_o. Node v_o has two children, which form the roots of its *left* and *right* subtrees (extension to the case where v_o has more than two children is straightforward). Nodes besides v_o and its children are referred to as *others*. The visibility matrix reflects the fact that the observer can measure traffic between nodes in its subtrees and others, and traffic between nodes in its right and left subtrees. The observer cannot measure traffic flowing only within the right subtree, or within the left subtree, or among others.

PROPOSITION 3.2. *Given a tree containing an observer node v_o with (at least) two children, as in Figure 3, let n_r be the number of nodes in the right subtree, n_l be the number of nodes in the left subtree, and n_o be the number of other nodes. If $n_r \geq k-1$, $n_l \geq k-1$, and $n_o \geq k-1$, the observer can complete its TM at rank k.*

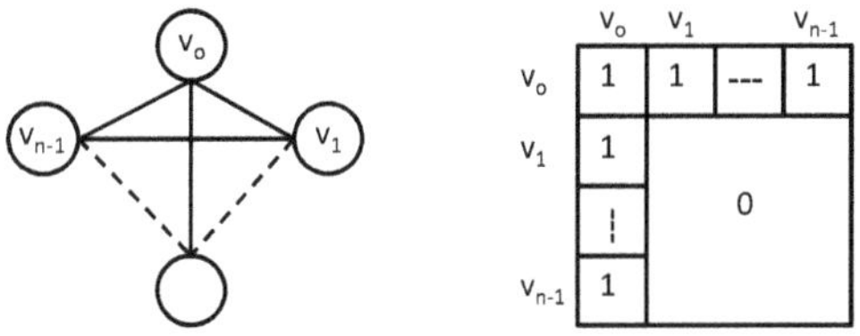

Figure 4: Mesh-of-Trees

PROOF. Let $\mathcal{N}_l$ be the indices of the left children, $\mathcal{N}_r$ be the indices of the right children, and $\mathcal{N}_o$ be the indices of the other nodes. The initial step chooses the first k rows of M and sets L to those rows, i.e. $L = \{1, \ldots, k\}$. Next, the columns that correspond to the indices of the observer, left children, and the others are added to R, i.e. $R = \{1, \mathcal{N}_l, \mathcal{N}_o\}$, since they have at least k 1s in the rows of L due to the assumption $n_r \geq k-1$. Next, all the remaining rows are added to L, i.e. $L = \{1, \ldots, n\}$, due to the assumptions $n_l \geq k-1$ and $n_o \geq k-1$. Finally, the columns that correspond to right children are are added to R, i.e. $R = \{1, \ldots, n\}$ since they have at least $3k-2$ 1s in the rows of L. □

Note that the proposition does *not* hold if the observer has only one child; observation of traffic *between* children is important for overall traffic matrix completion.

The previous proposition showed that the number of customers in each subtree matters. Next, we show that local connectivity (node degree) matters as well.

PROPOSITION 3.3. *Given a tree (a star) consisting of an observer node v_o connected to d other individual nodes, the observer can complete its TM at rank k, where $2k \leq d+1$.*

PROOF. In this topology, the observer v_o sees the traffic between any pair of nodes. This results in a visibility matrix M in which all elements are 1s except the last $n-1$ elements in the diagonal. In the initial step we choose the first k rows of M and set L to those rows, i.e. $L = \{1, \ldots, k\}$. Next, the columns that correspond to the indices greater than k are added to R, i.e. $R = \{1, k+1, \ldots, n\}$ since they have k 1s in each of the rows of L. Next, all the remaining rows are added to L, i.e. $L = \{1, \ldots, n\}$, since they have at least k 1s due to the assumption $2k \leq d+1$. Finally, all the remaining columns are added to R, i.e. $R = \{1, \ldots, n\}$ since they have at least $2k-1$ 1s in the rows of L. □

Thus there are two node characteristics that influence the ability to complete the TM in a tree: the observer can complete

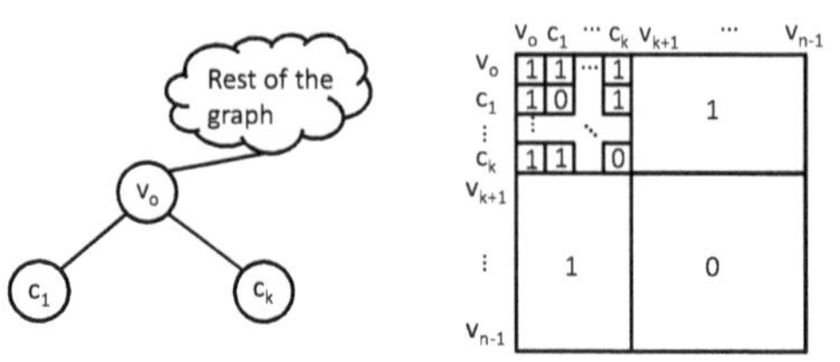

Figure 5: A node with k single-parent customers

its TM if the number of nodes in each of its subtrees is high enough, or if its degree is high enough.

3.2 Internet-Like Graphs

Now we turn to graph models that are intended to capture aspects of the Internet topology at the AS level. We apply the idealized graph models studied above to various Internet-inspired topologies. Again, these models ignore important aspects of the AS level Internet, but we build some intuition about the AS level Internet by studying them.

Our first model is a full mesh of nodes, each of which is the root of a subtree, as illustrated in Figure 4. This model is intended to capture some aspects of the relationship between top-tier ASes, as described in Section 2.5.

PROPOSITION 3.4. *Given a mesh of trees in which each mesh node v_i is the root of a tree, the observer mesh node v_o has at least two child trees each of size at least $n_c \geq k-1$, and the sum of the sizes of all other trees (including the roots) is $\geq k-1$, the observer node v_o can fully complete its visibility matrix at rank k.*

PROOF. Straightforward adaptation of Proposition 3.2. □

This example shows that even though a node participates in a decentralized mesh (as for example happens at the top of the AS hierarchy), if it has enough nodes in its subtrees it can complete its traffic matrix.

Single-Parent Stub Customers: Next we turn to analyze models of AS topologies that are more typical further down in the AS hierarchy. We define *single-parent customers* as nodes that use only one provider to connect to the rest of the network during the time interval in which measurements are taken. Note that single-parent customers are not necessarily single-homed customers — they may have multiple providers, but they only route traffic through one provider at any given time.

A node with single-parent customers can see the traffic between these customers and the rest of the network. Figure 5 (left) shows an observer v_o that has k single-parent customers, $c_1, \ldots, c_k$, which are stub networks. Figure 5 (right) shows the visibility matrix of v_o.

PROPOSITION 3.5. *Given a network of size n, an observer v_o that has k single-parent stub customers can complete its visibility matrix M at rank k, where $n \geq 2k+1$.*

PROOF. In the initial step we choose the first k rows of M and set L to those rows, i.e. $L = \{1, \ldots, k\}$. Next, the columns that correspond to the indices $v_o, c_k, v_{k+1}, \ldots, v_n$, are added to R, i.e. $R = \{1, k+1, \ldots, n\}$. Next, the row that corresponds to c_k is added to L, i.e. $L = \{1, \ldots, k+1\}$. Next, the columns that correspond to $c_1, \ldots, c_{k-1}$ are added to R, i.e. $R = \{1, \ldots, n\}$. Finally, the rows that correspond to $v_{k+1}, \ldots, v_n$ are are added to L, so that $L = \{1, \ldots, n\}$. Note that this is a simple extension of Proposition 3.3. □

An important loss of visibility occurs when some customers have peering relationships. If two customers c_i and c_j have a peering relationship, v_o can not see the traffic between them. This yields a visibility matrix like Figure 5, but with two more 0 entries on the upper left submatrix. In general, this type of peering relationship can happen between more than one pair of customers. In the worst case, all customers have peering relationships and this makes the upper left part of M all 0s except for its first row and column.

PROPOSITION 3.6. *Given a network of size n, for an observer v_o that has k single-parent stub customers, if at least $k-p-1$ of its customers have no more than p peering links with other customers, where $p \geq 0$ and $n \geq 2k+1$, then v_o can complete its TM at rank $r = k-p$.*

PROOF. Assume that the customers are indexed (starting from 2) in order of increasing number of peering links. In the initial step we choose the first r rows of M and set L to those rows, i.e. $L = \{1, \ldots, r\}$. Next, the columns that correspond to v_o, v_{k+1}, ..., v_n have r 1s in the rows of L. The columns that correspond to customers are not guaranteed to have r 1s; it depends on the number of peering links they have. Therefore, $R = \{1, k+1, \ldots, n\}$. Next, the rest of the rows that correspond to the customers are added to L, i.e. $L = \{1, \ldots, k+1\}$ due to the assumption that $n > 2k+1$. After this point, the columns that are not added to R yet are $\{2, \ldots, k+1\}$. These correspond to the customers c_1, ..., c_k. Likewise, the rows that are not added to L are v_{k+1}, ..., v_k. For these rows to be added, at least $r-1$ columns that correspond to the customers should have at least r 1s. Rewriting this statement for $r = k-p$, to complete the matrix at rank $k-p$, at least $k-p-1$ columns that correspond to the customers should have at least $k-p$ 1s. If an AS has p peering links, then it has $k-p$ 1s in its corresponding column. This shows that in order to complete the matrix at rank $k-p$, at least $k-p-1$ customers should have no more than p peering links with other customers. □

This shows that the presence of a limited amount of peering links diminishes, but does not necessarily destroy, the observer's ability to complete its TM.

Single-Parent Customer Trees: Next, we consider non-stub single-parent customers. We refer to the set of all single-parent descendants of the observer as its *Single-Parent Customer (SPC) Tree*. Figure 6 shows a SPC tree example. In this example, v_o cannot observe traffic between c_1 - c_2, c_1 - c_3, c_2 - c_3, or c_4 - c_5. Note that this creates the same visibility matrix as the case where all nodes $c_1, \ldots, c_5$ are stubs, but with peering relationships between the pairs (c_1, c_2), (c_2, c_3), (c_1, c_3), and (c_4, c_5).

PROPOSITION 3.7. *Given a node v_o and its SPC tree, any subtree of v_o which consists of d nodes creates the same visibility matrix as the case where the nodes are stubs, and there are peering links between each pair of nodes of the subtree.*

PROOF. Clear by construction. □

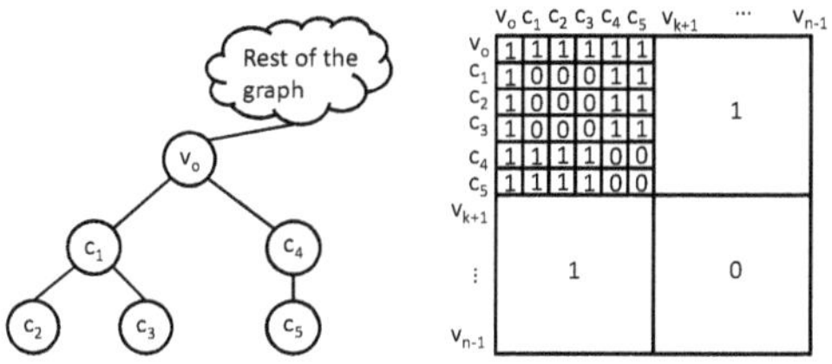

Figure 6: Single-Parent customer tree example.

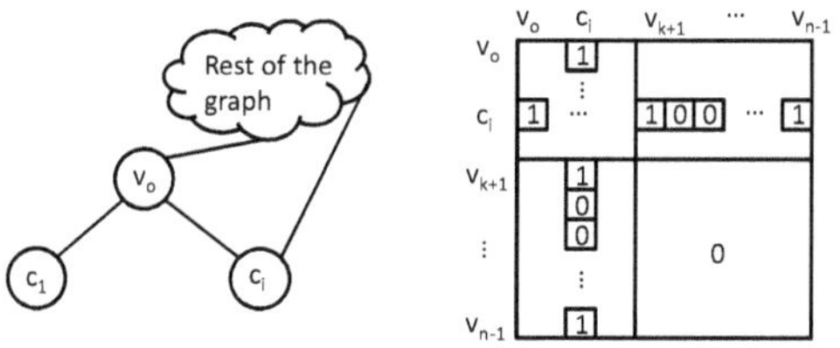

Figure 7: Multi-Parent customers.

Thus a subtree of size d has the same completion effect as d stubs, each having $d-1$ peering links. Thus, given an observer v_o and its SPC tree, proposition 3.7 and 3.6 can be used together to determine matrix completion ability at any rank. For example, the network in Figure 6 is equivalent to one having five stub customers, each having no more than 2 peering links, and so v_o can complete its matrix at rank 3.

PROPOSITION 3.8. *Consider a network of size n, and a node v_o which has a SPC tree that consists of m subtrees of sizes $d_1, \ldots, d_m$. Let k be the total number of customers in this SPC tree s.t. $d_1 + \cdots + d_m = k$ and $2k+1 \leq n$. Let the size of some subtrees be smaller than $p+1$, i.e., $d_1, \ldots, d_i \leq p+1$, where $p \geq 0$. For v_o to complete its visibility matrix M of rank $r = k-p$, it must be true that $d_1 + \cdots + d_i \geq k-p-1$.*

PROOF. Follows from Propositions 3.6 and 3.7. □

Multi-Parent Customers: Finally, we consider the influence of multi-parenting on the ability of a node to do TM completion. We define *multi-parent customers* as nodes that use multiple providers to connect to the rest of the network during the time interval in which measurements are taken. Note that all multi-parent customers are multi-homed customers.

Assume that the observer v_o has a multi-parent customer c_i. Customer c_i exchanges traffic with some nodes in the rest of the graph, as well as the other customers of v_o, through v_o. However, c_i also exchanges traffic with some other nodes in the rest of the graph through other providers. The example graph in Figure 7 yields the visibility matrix shown in the Figure.

PROPOSITION 3.9. *Given a network of size n, an AS v_o, which has $c+1$ multi-parent customers out of k customers, is guaranteed to fully complete its visibility matrix M at rank $k-c$, where $c \geq 0$ and $n > 2k+1$.*

PROOF. Assume that the customers are indexed (starting from 2) in the order of decreasing number of 1s in their rows. In the initial step we choose the first $k-c$ rows of M and set L to those rows. Due to the assumption that $n > 2k+1$, the densest rows correspond to $v_o, c_1, \ldots, c_{r-1}$, i.e. $L = \{1, \ldots, r\}$. Next, if none of the customers were multi-homed, the columns that correspond to $v_o, v_{k+1}, \ldots, v_n$ since they would have r 1s. However, if some of the customers are multi-homed, then the columns that correspond to the ASes which they send/receive traffic to/from through other providers may have less than r 1s. For instance, consider an AS v_j which all $c+1$ multi-homed customers send/receive traffic to/from through other providers, then its corresponding column has $k-c$ 1s. This implies that completion at ranks higher than $k-c$ is not guaranteed for v_o. □

Thus, Proposition 3.9 can not provide a guarantee that a multi-parent customer can improve an node's TM completion ability. However, in practice there are a number of ways in which the flows sent by the multi-parent node through the observer may contribute to TM completion ability. First, they may nonetheless provide sufficient visibility to improve TM completion, since the Proposition only establishes a lower bound on ICMC's performance; and second, the additional visibility may be useful when using inference methods other than ICMC.

In summary, the examples in this section have provided a number of insights into the relationship between graph topology and TM completion ability. First, we find that the decentralized nature of meshes is a strong impediment to TM completion. On the other hand, tree structures can be suitable for TM completion, and two aspects of a tree are important: increasing the degree of the observer node and increasing the number of nodes in each subtree both tend to improve TM completion.

Applying these models to Internet-like topologies, Proposition 3.4 suggests that despite its mesh-like nature, the topological relationship of top-tier ASes is amenable to TM completion. For ASes further down in the AS hierarchy, Proposition 3.5 shows the value of having single-parent customers, while Proposition 3.6 shows that peering relationships between one's customers are detrimental, but only in a limited way, to TM completion. Propositions 3.7 and 3.8 show that when one's customers themselves are providers, nodes deeper in the tree contribute more limited information for TM completion.

Taken together, Propositions 3.5 and 3.8 show that it is good to have a large single-parent customer tree, and it is better for those nodes to be arranged in a wide tree rather than a deep tree. For example, we can compare two organizations of a SPC tree, as shown in Figure 8. Consider the case when an AS v_o has k ASes in its SPC tree (and assume the network as a whole is large enough). When all of v_o's descendants are its direct customers (a), it can complete its TM at rank k. In comparison, when only two of v_o's descendants are direct customers (b), that is, its customers are grouped in two subtrees each of size $k/2$, it can only complete at rank at most $k/2$.

4. WHICH ASES CAN DO TM COMPLETION?

The analyses in the previous section provide some insight regarding the best conditions for TM completion, but they have a number of drawbacks. First, although the previous analyses give some indication of what conditions are best to allow an AS to perform TM completion, it is not clear *where* in the Internet those conditions are most prevalent. Second, the analyses assume highly idealized network models, which differ sig-

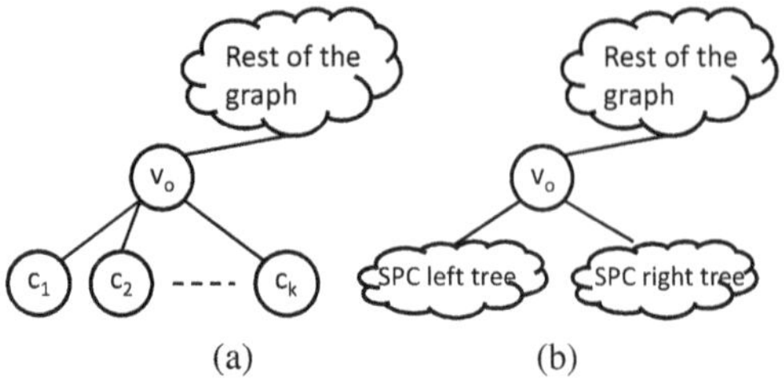

Figure 8: Comparison of two SPC trees.

nificantly from the actual AS topology. For example, the analyses assume there is a single source and destination in each node, and that routing is shortest-path and symmetric. These assumptions are all invalid in the AS-level Internet.

In this section we evaluate the ability of real ASes to do TM completion. Our goal in doing so is twofold: first, we seek to verify that the positive results from Section 3 hold in practice – namely, that TM completion is possible, at least for certain rank matrices, in the real Internet. Second, we seek to answer a set of natural follow-on questions. In particular, we would like to know: (1) Given that the analyses in the previous section suggested that TM completion may be possible at different 'locations' in the Internet (ie, among top-tier ISPs as well as ISPs lower in the AS hierarchy), where in fact is the opportunity for TM completion greatest? And: (2) Given that the analyses in the previous section pointed to various factors that can influence TM completion ability, what factors are actually most significant in the Internet?

4.1 Data

To answer these questions we analyze a large survey of AS paths in use in the Internet. Our data consists of a snapshot of all active BGP paths in use by 376 ASes *(monitors)*, taken at midnight UTC on August 6th, 2010. The dataset consists of over 100 million AS paths, and contains 524,761 unique prefixes. (Note that not all BGP tables show paths to all prefixes.) Because these paths are the *active* paths at the time of collection, each path represents the sequence of ASes that traffic will flow through when going from the particular monitor to the path's destination prefix.[2]

Next we select a subset of monitors and a subset of prefixes such that, for every monitor and every prefix, our dataset has the AS path from the monitor to the prefix. This results in 133 monitors and 225,041 prefixes.

Because we have the path from every monitor to every destination, we can construct visibility matrices for every AS appearing in the dataset – 28,763 ASes. These visibility matrices have size $133 \times 225{,}041$; for each entry in each visibility matrix, we can determine whether its value is 0 or 1. This is because we have the AS path corresponding to each element of the matrix, and to determine the 0-1 status of that element for a particular observer AS, we simply need to check whether the observer AS appears on that AS path. So our input to the analyses below consists of over 28,000 visibility matrices, each of which consists of about 30 million elements, known with high confidence.

Of course, these visibility matrices are only a portion of the complete visibility matrix of each AS, so our analyses in this section concern each AS's attempt to apply matrix completion to a portion of its TM.

In some our results, we make use of AS relationships (customer/provider and peer/peer); for that purpose we use the AS relationship labeling performed and published by CAIDA [11], which is based on the most comprehensive methodology available at present.

4.2 Metrics

We characterize an observer AS in two ways: via standard metrics used in the study of complex networks, and using metrics that capture networking-specific properties. First, to measure "centrality" of an observer AS, we use its *k-core decomposition shell* (or just "k-shell") [1]. As described in Section 2.5, the k-core decomposition identifies shells (vertex sets) of a graph that are nested, and successively more densely interconnected. Since we have seen in Section 3 that node degree is significant, we also measure each observer's *degree* (the number of ASs that are adjacent along a BGP path with the observer). Finally, we also consider networking-specific metrics: the number of customers of the observer, and the number of peers of the observer.

Each observer's TM completion ability depends on the rank k at which TM completion is attempted, with higher rank indicative of more accurate completion ability. In most cases in our data, observers cannot complete their entire TMs. However, AICMC identifies the subset of elements that can be recovered for any given rank. Thus rather than asking "at what rank k can the entire TM be recovered?" as we did in Section 3, here we use a different metric, which we call *expected rank*. Expected rank is defined as the expected value of the maximum rank at which a randomly chosen entry can be recovered. To compute the metric, we take the average over all non-visible entries of the maximum rank at which the element can be recovered (using zero when the element cannot be recovered at any rank).

Note that the matrices we use in this section are not structured the same way as those in Section 3. For example, matrices in this section are not symmetric, and are indexed differently. Because of this, rank values cannot be compared directly. Hence our focus is on how effective rank varies, rather than its specific value.

4.3 Results

We first consider whether centrality in the Internet as measured by k-shell is a good predictor of TM completion ability. For this, we look at the top 500 ASes in terms of k-shell number. Figure 9(a) shows a scatterplot of k-shell versus expected rank, and Figure 9(b) shows expected rank for ASes in order of decreasing k-shell number. In the this figure, values have been smoothed to reduce the effects of noise.

The figures show that centrality as measured by k-shell has some relationship to completion ability, but the relationship is not strong. Among ASes in the innermost shell (the nucleus), many have low completion ability. In fact, on average ASes in the core have lower completion ability than those 'just outside' the nucleus.

[2]We are ignoring possible configuration errors, false BGP advertisements, or path changes that have not yet reached the monitors – each of which we expect to have negligible effects on our results.

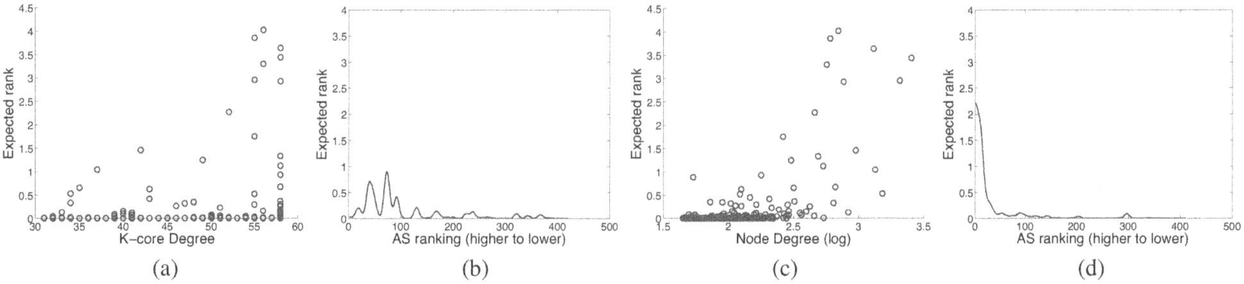

Figure 9: Expected rank as a function of (a),(b) k-shell and (c),(d) degree.

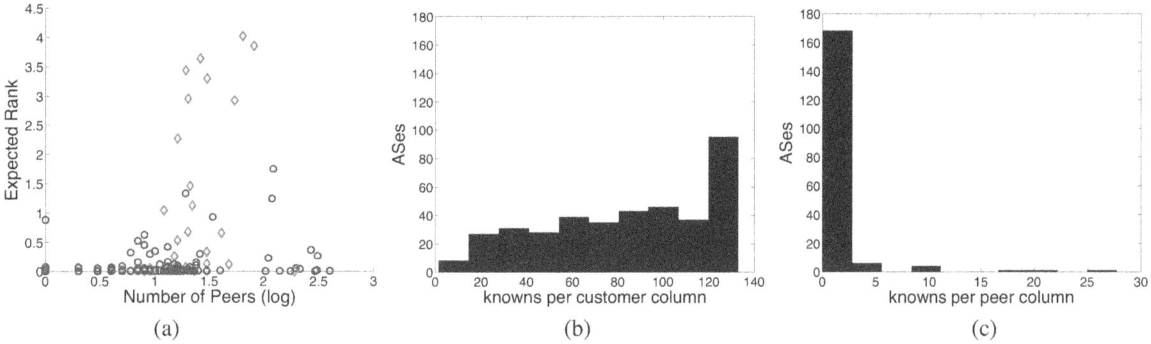

Figure 11: Effect of peers vs. customers completion ability.

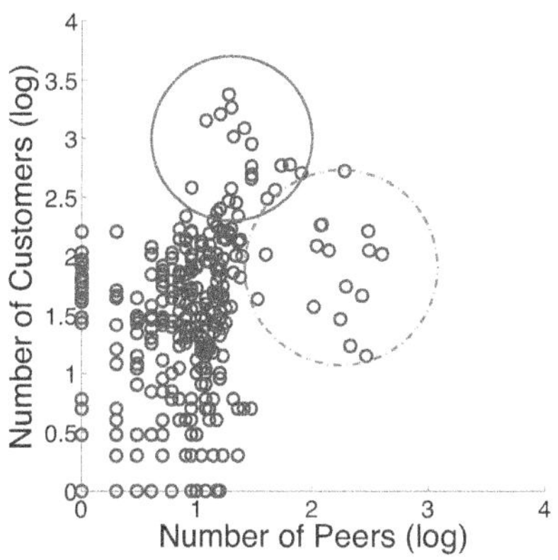

Figure 10: Peer degree vs. customer degree.

Since centrality *per se* is not a strong indicator of completion ability, we turn to the analyses in Section 3 to guide our intuition. Proposition 3.3 showed that increasing the degree of a node can increase its TM completion ability. The relationship between degree and TM completion ability is shown in Figures 9(c) and 9(d). The figures show that degree is a much better predictor of completion ability than centrality.

However, close examination of Figures 9(c) shows that some of the very highest-degree ASes have poor completion ability. Further consideration of the implications of Proposition 3.3 suggest an explanation that sharpens our understanding. The proposition was based on the assumption of shortest-path routing, and so does not directly apply to the AS graph. In particular, in the AS graph, a link may be between customer and provider, or it may be between two peers. The topology considered in Proposition 3.3 resulted in traffic between nodes flowing through the observer, and so links in that case were analogous to customer-provider links. In contrast, in the AS graph, traffic between two peers of the observer does *not* flow through the observer, because peers do not transit traffic for other peers.

This suggests that we should separate a node's degree into two components: the number of customer links, and the number of peer links.[3] This separation is shown in Figure 10, which plots customer degree against peer degree across the highest-degree ASes. The figure shows that high-degree ASes tend to fall into two different groups (shown in circles): some have more customer links than peer links, while others have more peer links than customer links.

Thus, it makes sense to analyze these two groups separately. If our analysis based on Proposition 3.3 is correct, ASes with high customer degree should show increased TM completion ability, while those with high peer degree should not necessarily show high completion ability.

This is in fact confirmed by our results, which are shown in Figure 11. Figure 11(a) shows TM completion ability versus the number of peers of the observer AS. There is no strong relationship between number of peers and completion ability; in fact the ASes with the greatest number of peers (more than 100) all have quite poor completion ability. In the figure, the red diamonds correspond to those ASes with the highest number of customers; it can be seen that these are the ASes with the greatest completion ability, but which typically have intermediate peer degree.

We can understand this difference by examing the influence of customers and peers on the visibility matrix of the

[3]The number of provider links per AS in our data is usually quite small and we ignore them in this analysis.

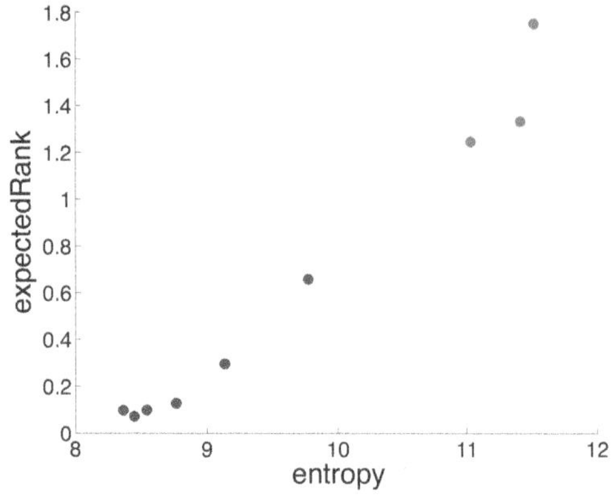

Figure 12: Expected rank vs. entropy for ASes having comparable densities.

observer AS. We do this by examining how many knowns (visible flows) are contributed to an observer AS on average by a customer and by a peer, for the set of ASes in Figure 11(a). Figure 11(b) shows a histogram of this quantity for customers, and Figure 11(c) shows the result for peers. The histograms show that often, a customer provides a highly dense column of the visibility matrix, while a peer typically provides very few entries in the visibility matrix. In particular, a single-parent stub customer provides a complete column.

In this regard, it is also important to note that improving completion ability is not simply a matter of maximizing the number of visible elements in the AS's traffic matrix. It is important *where* in the matrix the visible elements appear. In general, it is better for visible elements to be broadly distributed across columns and rows of the matrix. To demonstrate this fact, we select a set of 9 ASes with comparable density of visible elements — all ASes for which the number of visible elements lies in the range $(4\times10^5, 6\times10^5)$. To characterize the dispersion of visible elements we measure their entropy across columns. That is, for a matrix M of size $m\times n$, we compute $E = -\sum_{j=1}^{n}\frac{C_j}{N}log(\frac{C_j}{N})$ where C_j is the total number of knowns in column j and N is the total number of knowns in the entire matrix.

The relationship between entropy and expected rank for the 9 ASes is shown in Figure 12. When this entropy measure is large, visible elements are dispersed throughout the columns, while when it is small, visible elements are concentrated in few columns. The figure shows that ASes with very similar numbers of visible flows can vary considerably in their completion ability, and that completion ability is much better when visible elements are spread widely across the columns of the matrix.

In summary, our results in this section confirm key elements of our analysis from the previous section. In particular, our results point to the importance of having customers as a resource for TM completion. Further, we find that ASes best at TM completion are not generally those with a large number of peers, nor do they tend to be in the innermost, densest-connected k-shell.

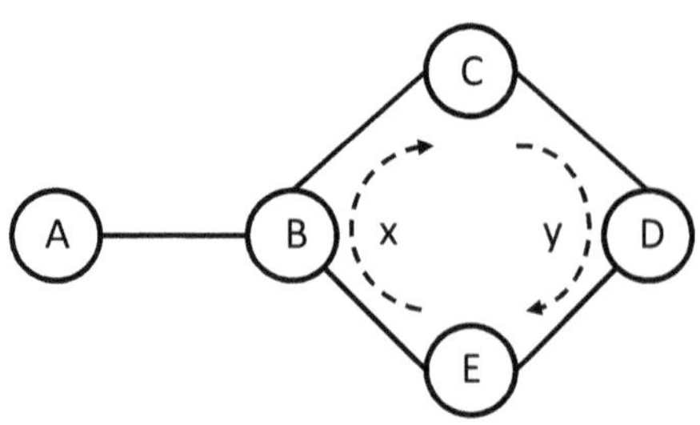

Figure 13: Computing distance to a flow. Flows x and y take AS paths of $E-B-C$ and $C-D-E$, respectively. The distance between A and flow x is 1 while the distance between A and flow y is 2.

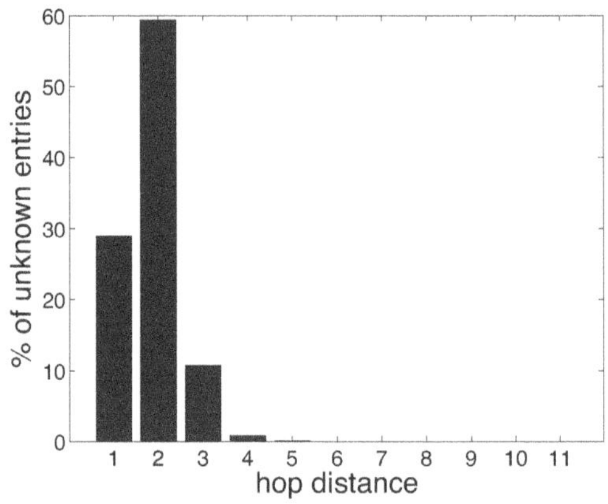

Figure 14: Distance to all flows.

5. WHICH ELEMENTS CAN BE RECOVERED?

While the results in the last section focused on comparing ASes globally across the Internet, we now turn to questions that are specific to individual ASes. Since a given AS may only be able to recover some of its invisible elements, it is important to develop an understanding of *which* elements are most readily estimated.

To capture the relationship between an AS and a flow that is invisible to that AS, we define a metric for distance between an AS and a flow. Figure 13 illustrates how flow distances are computed. For any given AS and flow, we find the shortest-path distance in the AS graph between the observer AS and each AS that the flow passes through. The distance between the AS and flow is the minimum of these shortest path distances. Of course, the distance to a known flow is zero.

To get a sense of typical distance values, we measure the distribution of distances across all (AS,flow) pairs. The result is shown in Figure 14. The figure shows that around 60% of unknown flows are distance 2 away from the observer ASes. Distances 1 and 3 follow by 30% and 10%, respectively; the percentage of unknowns that are further away is negligible. Thus, most unknown flows are at least two hops away from the observer AS.

Our first set of results characterizes the distance to flows that can be recovered, aggregating across all ASes. Figure 15 shows the fraction of unknown flows that can be recovered at

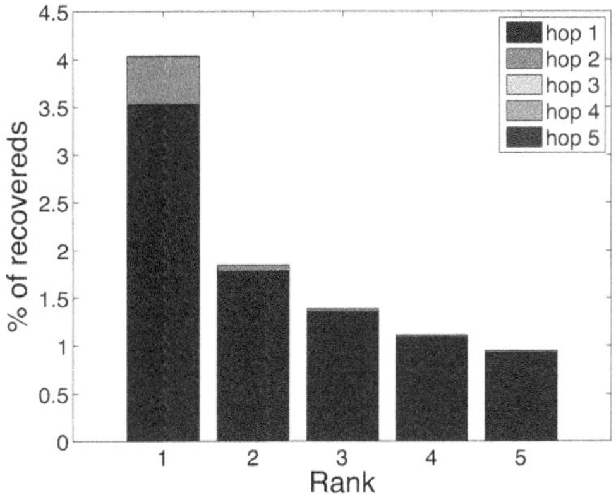

Figure 15: Distance to recovered flows.

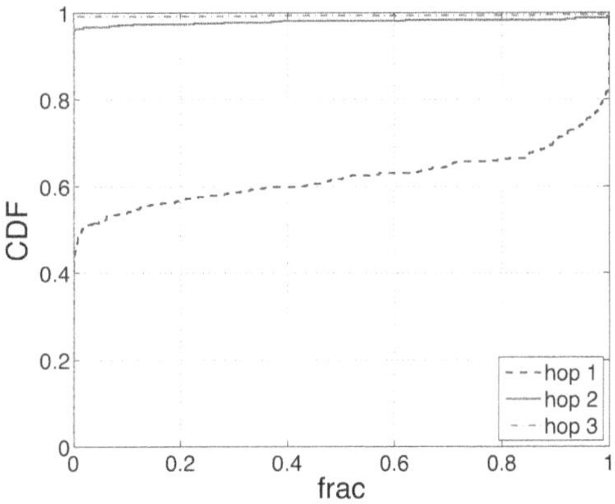

Figure 16: Success rate of targeted completion: fraction of target-visible unknowns that can be recovered in the predictor.

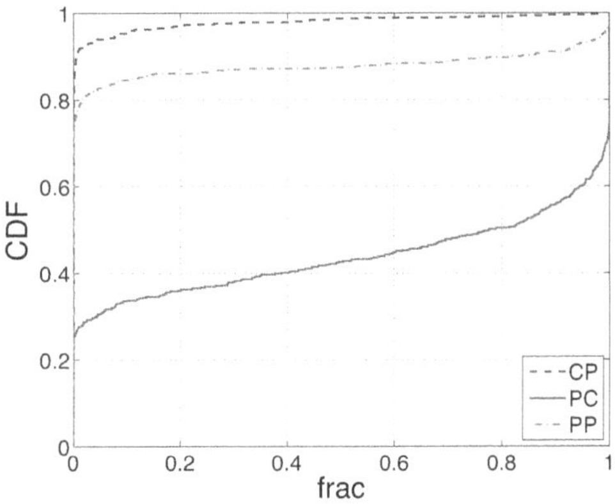

Figure 17: Success rate of targeted completion by predictor-target relationship.

each hop distance for varying rank values. At all rank values, the flows that ASes recover are primarily at distance 1. Only at rank 1 is there a non-negligible amount of flows recovered at distance 2 (despite the fact that distance 2 flows are much more numerous, as shown in Figure 14). The percentage of recovered unknowns at hop distance 3 and greater is negligible at any rank. These results show that there is a strong relationship between the distances to a particular flow and the potential to recover the flow. In particular, the unknown flows that an observer AS is most likely to recover are those that pass through its direct neighbors.

An important set of questions from a business intelligence standpoint concerns the ability of one AS (a *predictor*) to infer the set of flows that pass through some other particular AS (a *target*). We call this *targeted TM completion*. For example, consider the case described in the Introduction: an ISP may wish to know how much business a competitor is doing with a prospective customer. In this case the first ISP is the predictor and its competitor is the target.

To understand the ability of an AS to do targeted TM completion, we consider pairs of *(predictor, target)* ASes. Each pair has an associated hop distance in the AS graph. After constructing all such pairs and measuring their distance, we randomly sample 500 pairs at each distance. We then measure the fraction of the flows visible in the target that were filled-in during TM completion in the predictor. That is, let V be the set of elements visible in the target, U the set of unknown (invisible) flows in the predictor, and R the set of recovered flows in the predictor. Then for every pair we compute the fraction $frac = |V \cap R|/|V \cap U|$.

The results are shown in Figure 16 as a CDF across all 500 pairs at each hop distance. The figure shows that for pairs at hop distance 2 or 3, very little targeted completion is possible – in more than 95% of such cases, no targeted completion can be performed. However the situation is quite different for hop distance 1, which corresponds to ASes that are adjacent in the AS graph. In that case, only 45% of predictors cannot do any targeted completion. Most predictors can do some targeted completion, and for 19% of the predictors, *all* of their target's flows can be recovered. Thus, if an AS wishes to do targeted completion, its best targets are its neighbors.

While an AS's neighbors make the best targets, it is important to note that an AS can have a variety of different kinds of neighbors. We focus on three business/routing relationships that may exist between predictor and target: they may be *customer-provider* (CP), *provider-customer* (PC), or *peer-peer* (PP). Starting with our previous set of 1-hop AS pairs, we divide pairs into these three groups and examine the same metric as before (fraction of target unknowns completed). In the CP group, the predictor seeks to estimate flows passing through its provider; in the PC group, the predictor seeks to estimate flows passing through its customer; and in the PP group, the predictor is estimating flows passing through a peer.

The results are shown in Figure 17. The differences between the three cases is sharp. The least opportunity for targeted completion occurs when estimating a provider's flows; only about 10% can estimate any provider traffic. The situation is slightly better for peers: about 20% can estimate some peer flows, and a small percentage can estimate all of a peer's flows. However, the situation is very different for customer flows. Most providers can estimate a significant fraction of their customer's flows; and 30% can recover all of the flows passing through their customers.

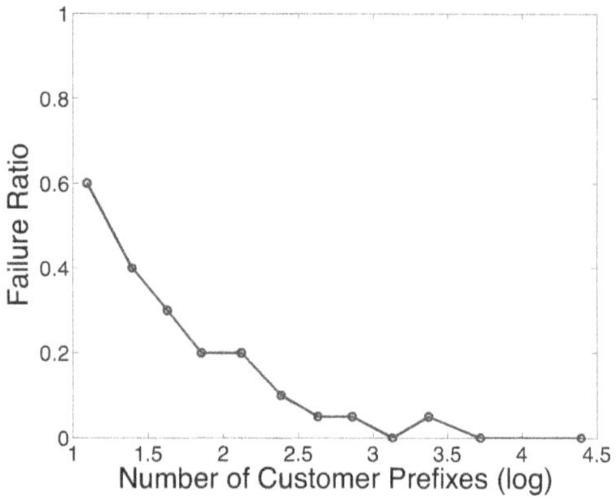

Figure 18: Estimation failure rate vs. number of customer prefixes.

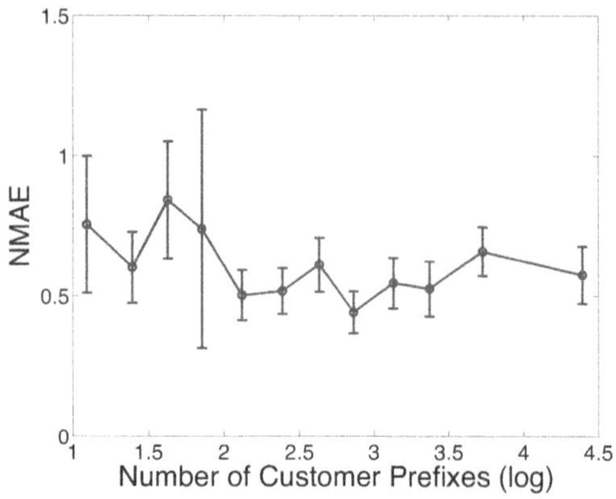

Figure 19: NMAE vs. number of customer prefixes.

6. ESTIMATION ACCURACY

Our results so far are in fact somewhat conservative: AICMC identifies when an element is surely estimable, but this does not mean that estimation of other elements is necessarily inaccurate in practice, particularly when using estimation algorithms other than ICMC. In general, it is important to confirm that the trends observed when using AICMC to analyze visibility matrices in fact agree with the results obtained when actually performing TM completion.

6.1 Approach

In order to confirm that our results are valid in practice, we perform actual matrix completion as it would be done by each AS. We provide each AS with only the knowledge of the TM entries as determined by its visibility matrix. We then perform matrix completion to estimate the entries that are invisible to that AS. Note that the fraction of the 30 million matrix elements visible to any AS varies from 0.3% (for the small number of ASes with highest density) down to 0.001% and lower for the vast majority of ASes.

Our focus is on evaluating how AS's visibility affects its TM completion ability, so it is important that we use similar traffic for studying each AS. We do not want our results to be affected by the differing nature of traffic in each AS (and obtaining actual traffic measures for each of the ASes in our dataset is out of the question in any case). Hence we take a single traffic matrix R (of real traffic, measured in the Géant network) and use it to populate each AS's TM. The traffic matrix R is a 54×54 submatrix of the entire Geant TM, and we have chosen rows and columns for R such that all 2,916 elements are visible to Geant (and therefore represent valid measurements). The elements of R consist of traffic flowing from ASes to prefixes, which matches the organization of our visibility matrices. We then populate an experimental TM D of size $133 \times 225{,}041$ by tiling D with copies of R. Although R is a rank of 54 matrix, our analysis of R (not shown) estimates its effective rank as 2 (95% of the variation in R can be captured in a rank-2 matrix), and so the rank of D is 54 and effective rank of D is 2 as well.

Since one of our goals in this section is to validate previous results that relied on ICMC, it is important that we use a different matrix completion algorithm for these experiments. For that reason we turn to an algorithm that works very differently from ICMC, namely *LMaFit* [25]. While ICMC works by incrementally constructing the matrix factors X and Y at full accuracy, LMaFit works by computing progressively more accurate versions of X and Y (in their entirety) via successive over-relaxation. LMaFit terminates when it (1) converges to a solution, meaning that visible elements are accurately represented in the solution or (2) detects an inability to converge, in which case LMaFit reports failure.

For each AS, we proceed as follows: First, we identify the visible elements of D (using the same visibility matrices as in Section 4). We next set the invisible elements in D to be zero. We then apply LMaFit to estimate the missing elements of D (using D's effective rank of 2 as the input value of k for LMaFit) yielding either failure, or a completed matrix $\hat{D}$.

We evaluate the results using two metrics: first, we want to know *whether* matrix completion can succeed: for this we note whether LMaFit succeeds in each case. Second, we want to know the *accuracy* of estimation that is possible in each case, which we measure using Normalized Mean Absolute Error (NMAE):

$$NMAE = \frac{\sum_{(i,j)\notin\Omega} |D_{ij} - \hat{D}_{ij}|}{\sum_{(i,j)\notin\Omega} D_{ij}}.$$

Note that the accuracy metric only applies to those cases where TM completion is successful.

6.2 Results

Our results compare number of prefixes announced by an AS's customers with its estimation failure rate and estimation accuracy. We sample 20 ASes in logarithmically spaced bins across the entire range of number of prefixes. In Figures 18 and 19, each point is the bin average, and 95% confidence intervals are shown in Figure 19.

Figure 18 shows that there is a strong relationship between number of customer prefixes and success rate of LMaFit. This is entirely consistent with the results in Section 4 and confirms that the ASes with large customer set can successfully perform TM completion. Figure 19 shows that the accuracy of TM completion can be quite good — generally between 0.5 and 1. Thus, as long as TM completion is possible, it can be done with high accuracy.

In fact, we find this last point to be true across all the experiments, i.e. regardless of the metric used to characterize ASes, average NMAE is consistently in the range of 0.5 to 1, and there is no significant change in NMAE across metric values. This applies not just to number of customer prefixes, but to k-shell number and degree. In all cases, as long as TM completion is possible, it can be done with relatively high accuracy.

Thus, the metric that gives the most insight into TM completion ability is failure rate. We find that k-shell number is not a good indicator of low failure rate, whereas node-degree is (results not shown). This confirms our results from Section 4, and underscores that ASes with good ability to complete their TMs are generally those whose customers advertise large numbers of prefixes.

7. DISCUSSION

While the results in this study are suggestive, they do not precisely identify the TM completion ability of ASes. One reason is that in Sections 4 and 5 we are only working with a portion of each AS's visibility matrix. Although the visibility matrices we use have over 30 million elements, this is only about 0.5% of the full visibility matrix of an AS. That said, we have no reason to believe that the matrix portions we study are unusual.

Additionally, our results start from the assumption that TMs have low effective rank. While this fact has been empirically observed in numerous studies (as described in Section 2.2), all such observations to date have been at limited scale (hundreds or thousands of rows or columns). When considering TMs of the size in this paper (hundreds of thousands of columns) it is an open question whether and to what degree the property of low effective rank holds. However, this is a concern only if the AS seeks to complete its *entire* TM. For the results in Section 5 (including the business case described in Section 1) an AS is only concerned with completing a relatively small portion of its TM.

Broadly, the analytic and empirical sides of our study combine to yield a number of insights. In particular, our results suggest that:

- *ASes in the innermost k-shell of Internet are not necessarily effective at TM completion.* Proposition 3.4 showed that densely-meshed nodes can do TM completion, but only to a rank limited by the number of their customers. Empirically we find that densely-meshed ASes are not uniformly strong at TM completion (Figure 9(a)). In particular, the ASes that have the most peers are not especially well suited to complete their TMs (Figure 11(a)).

- *ASes with many single-homed customers are best suited to perform TM completion.* Propositions 3.5 and 3.8 show that it is good to have a large single-parent customer tree, and it is better for those nodes to be arranged in a wide tree rather than a deep tree. Empirically we find ASes with many customers are most effective at TM completion (Figure 11(a),(b)) and that an AS's customers contribute a large number of visible elements useful for TM completion (Figure 11(b)).

- *ASes are most effective at completing matrix entries that correspond to 'nearby' flows.* Flows that pass through neighboring ASes are more easily estimated than flows that do not pass through neighboring ASes (Figure 15). It seems that typical routing structures imply that flows that pass through neighbor ASes are more likely to have sources or destinations in common with visible flows, thus making recovery more likely.

- *When targeting specific ASes for completion, customer traffic is most readily estimated.* Among (predictor, target) AS pairs, the greatest completion ability exists when the predictor and target are neighbors (Figure 16) and in particular when the target is the customer of the predictor (Figure 17). Thus, not only do customers provide important information for completing TMs, but they are particularly good targets for TM completion.

The picture that emerges is that ASes with many direct single-homed customers have a particularly advantageous platform for performing TM completion. This suggests that ASes with many customers have a perhaps-underappreciated resource: not only do customers provide revenue, but the patterns of traffic that they send contain considerable information about traffic in other, more distant parts of the Internet.

8. CONCLUSION

In this paper we have investigated the application of the emerging concept of matrix completion to the specific case of Internet traffic matrices. The ability to perform matrix completion on TMs would provide considerable benefit spanning scientific, engineering, and commercial domains. Our goal is to understand how the structure of Internet routing and topology affects the ability of a given AS to estimate traffic flows that it cannot measure. We start by building intuition through analysis and we then deepen and extend our understanding using measurements of actual Internet routing.

We find that many ASes have the ability to perform at least partial TM completion. However which ASes are best at completion, and which elements they can recover, depends strongly on the local topology of the network. In particular, our study focuses attention on an AS's customers as its most important resource for TM completion. Customers provide rich information about traffic patterns; for example, a large array of single-homed stub customers provides an AS with the ability to infer invisible traffic even when the missing traffic is relatively complex (high rank). This suggests that many ASes scattered throughout the Internet have visibility into local traffic patterns that is well suited to inferring the nature of more distant, unmeasurable traffic.

9. ACKNOWLEDGEMENTS

This work was supported by NSF grants CNS-0905565, CNS-1018266, CNS- 1012910, and CNS-1117039. The authors thank the IMC referees and shepherd for their help in improving the paper. The authors also thank Renesys, Inc. for providing the data used in this paper.

10. REFERENCES

[1] J. I. Alvarez-Hamelin, L. Dall'Asta, A. Barrat, and A. Vespignani. k-core decomposition: a tool for the visualization of large scale networks. Technical report, Arxiv, 2005.

[2] V. Bharti, P. Kankar, L. Setia, G. Gürsun, A. Lakhina, and M. Crovella. Inferring invisible traffic. In *Proceedings of CoNEXT*, Philadelphia, PA, 2010.

[3] J.-F. Cai, E. J. Candès, and Z. Shen. A singular value thresholding algorithm for matrix completion. *SIAM J. on Optimization*, 20, March 2010.

[4] E. J. Candès and Y. Plan. Matrix completion with noise. *CoRR*, abs/0903.3131, 2009.

[5] E. J. Candès and B. Recht. Exact matrix completion via convex optimization. *Found. Comput. Math.*, 9(6):717–772, 2009.

[6] S. Carmi, S. Havlin, S. Kirkpatrick, Y. Shavitt, and E. Shir. A model of internet topology using k-shell decomposition. In *PNAS*, volume 104, pages 11150–11154, July 2007.

[7] H. Chang, R. Govindan, S. Jamin, S. J. Shenker, and W. Willinger. Towards capturing representative AS level Internet topologies. *Computer Networks*, 44(6):737–755, 2004.

[8] H. Chang, S. Jamin, Z. Mao, and W. Willinger. An empirical approach to modeling inter-AS traffic matrices. In *Proceedings of IMC*, 2005.

[9] H. Chang, S. Jamin, and W. Willinger. To peer or not to peer: Modeling the evolution of the Internet's AS-level topology. In *Proceedings of Infocom*, 2006.

[10] H. Chang, M. Roughan, S. Uhlig, D. Alderson, and W. Willinger. The many facets of Internet topology and traffic. *Networks and Heterogeneous Media*, 1(4):569–600, 2006.

[11] X. Dimitropoulos, D. Krioukov, M. Fomenkov, B. Huffaker, Y. Hyun, kc claffy, and G. Riley. AS relationships: Inference and validation. *ACM SIGCOMM CCR*, 37(1):29–40, 2007.

[12] V. Erramilli, M. Crovella, and N. Taft. An independent-connection model for traffic matrices. In *Proceedings of IMC*, pages 251–256, 2006.

[13] A. Feldmann, N. Kammenhuber, O. Maennel, B. Maggs, R. De Prisco, and R. Sundaram. A methodology for estimating interdomain web traffic demand. In *Proceedings of IMC*, 2004.

[14] L. Gao. On inferring autonomous system relationships in the internet. *IEEE/ACM Trans. Netw.*, 9:733–745, December 2001.

[15] Z. Ge, D. R. Figueiredo, S. Jaiswal, and L. Gao. On the hierarchical structure of the logical Internet graph. In *In Proceedings of SPIE ITCOM*, pages 208–222, 2001.

[16] G.Siganos, S.L.Tauro, and M.Faloutsos. Jellyfish: A conceptual model for the AS Internet topology. *Journal of Communications and Networks*, 2006.

[17] R. H. Keshavan, S. Oh, and A. Montanari. Matrix completion from a few entries. `http://arxiv.org/abs/0901.3150`, 2009.

[18] A. Lakhina, M. Crovella, and C. Diot. Diagnosing network-wide traffic anomalies. In *Proceedings of ACM SIGCOMM 2004*, pages 219–230, August 2004.

[19] A. Lakhina, K. Papagiannaki, M. Crovella, C. Diot, E. D. Kolaczyk, and N. Taft. Structural analysis of network traffic flows. In *Proceedings of SIGMETRICS '04/Performance '04*, New York, NY, USA, 2004. ACM.

[20] A. Medina, N. Taft, K. Salamatian, S. Bhattacharyya, and C. Diot. Traffic matrix estimation: Existing techniques and new directions. In *Proceedings of ACM SIGCOMM*, 2002.

[21] R. Meka, P. Jain, and I. S. Dhillon. Matrix completion from power-law distributed samples. In *Proceedings of NIPS*, December 2009.

[22] M. Roughan. First order characterization of Internet traffic matrices. Invited paper at the 55th Session of the International Statistics Institute, April 2005.

[23] M. Roughan. Simplifying the synthesis of internet traffic matrices. *SIGCOMM Comput. Commun. Rev.*, 35:93–96, October 2005.

[24] L. Subramanian, S. Agarwal, J. Rexford, and R. Katz. Characterizing the Internet hierarchy from multiple vantage points. In *In Proc. IEEE INFOCOM*, 2002.

[25] Z. Wen, W. Yin, and Y. Zhang. Solving a low-rank factorization model for matrix completion by a nonlinear successive over-relaxation algorithm. Technical report, Rice University, 2010.

[26] Y. Zhang, M. Roughan, C. Lund, and D. Donoho. Estimating point-to-point and point-to-multipoint traffic matrices: An information-theoretic approach. *IEEE/ACM Transactions on Networking*, 13(5):947–960, 2005.

[27] Y. Zhang, M. Roughan, W. Willinger, and L. Qiu. Spatio-temporal compressive sensing and internet traffic matrices. *SIGCOMM Comput. Commun. Rev.*, 39(4):267–278, 2009.

DNS to the Rescue: Discerning Content and Services in a Tangled Web

Ignacio N. Bermudez
Politecnico di Torino,
Torino, Italy
ignacio.bermudez@polito.it

Marco Mellia
Politecnico di Torino,
Torino, Italy
marco.mellia@polito.it

Maurizio M. Munafò
Politecnico di Torino,
Torino, Italy
maurizio.munafo@polito.it

Ram Keralapura
Narus Inc.,
Sunnyvale, CA
rkeralapura@narus.com

Antonio Nucci
Narus Inc.,
Sunnyvale, CA
anucci@narus.com

ABSTRACT

A careful perusal of the Internet evolution reveals two major trends - explosion of cloud-based services and video streaming applications. In both of the above cases, the owner (e.g., CNN, YouTube, or Zynga) of the content and the organization serving it (e.g., Akamai, Limelight, or Amazon EC2) are decoupled, thus making it harder to understand the association between the content, owner, and the host where the content resides. This has created a tangled world wide web that is very hard to unwind, impairing ISPs' and network administrators' capabilities to control the traffic flowing in their networks.

In this paper, we present DN-Hunter, a system that leverages the information provided by DNS traffic to discern the tangle. Parsing through DNS queries, DN-Hunter tags traffic flows with the associated domain name. This association has several applications and reveals a large amount of useful information: (*i*) Provides a fine-grained traffic visibility even when the traffic is encrypted (i.e., TLS/SSL flows), thus enabling more effective policy controls, (*ii*) Identifies flows even before the flows begin, thus providing superior network management capabilities to administrators, (*iii*) Understand and track (over time) different CDNs and cloud providers that host content for a particular resource, (*iv*) Discern all the services/content hosted by a given CDN or cloud provider in a particular geography and time interval, and (*v*) Provides insights into all applications/services running on any given layer-4 port number.

We conduct extensive experimental analysis and show results from real traffic traces (including FTTH and 4G ISPs) that support our hypothesis. Simply put, the information provided by DNS traffic is one of the key components required for understanding the tangled web, and bringing the ability to effectively manage network traffic back to the operators.

IMC'12, November 14–16, 2012, Boston, Massachusetts, USA.

Categories and Subject Descriptors

C.2 [**Computer-Communication Networks**]: Miscellaneous; C.4 [**Performance of Systems**]: Measurement Techniques

General Terms

Measurement, Performance

Keywords

DNS, Service Identification.

1. INTRODUCTION

In the past few years, the Internet has witnessed an explosion of cloud-based services and video streaming applications. In both cases, content delivery networks (CDN) and/or cloud computing services are used to meet both scalability and availability requirements. An undesirable side-effect of this is that it decouples the owner of the content and the organization serving it. For example, CNN or YouTube videos can be served by Akamai or Google CDN, and Farmville game can be accessed from Facebook while running on Amazon EC2 cloud computing platform, with static content being retrieved from a CDN. This may be even more complicated since various CDNs and content owners implement their own optimization mechanisms to ensure "spatial" and "temporal" diversity for load distribution. In addition, several popular sites like Twitter, Facebook, and Google have started adopting encryption (TLS/SSL) to deliver content to their users [1]. This trend is expected to gain more momentum in the next few years. While this helps to protect end-users' privacy, it can be a big impediment for effective security operations since network/security administrators now lack the required traffic visibility. The above factors have resulted in "tangled" world wide web which is hard to understand, discern, and control.

In the face of this tangled web, network/security administrators seek answers for several questions in order to manage their networks: (*i*) What are the various services/applications that contribute to the traffic mix on the network? (*ii*) How to block or provide certain Quality of Service (QoS) guarantees to select services?

While the above questions seem simple, the answers to these questions are non-trivial. There are no existing mechanisms that can provide comprehensive solutions to address the above issues. Consider the first question above. A typical approach currently used by network administrators is to rely on DPI (deep packet inspection) technology to identify traffic based on packet-content signatures. Although this approach is very effective in identifying unencrypted traffic, it severely falls short when the traffic is encrypted. Given the popularity of TLS in major application/content providers, this problem will amplify over time, thus rendering typical DPI technology for traffic visibility ineffective. A simple approach that can augment a DPI device to identify encrypted traffic is to inspect the certificate during the initial handshake[1]. Although this approach gives some visibility into the applications/services, it still cannot help in identifying specific services. For instance, inspecting a certificate from Google will only reveal that it is Google service, but cannot differentiate between Google Mail, Google Docs, Blogger, and Youtube. Thus administrators need a solution that will provide fine-grained traffic visibility even when the traffic is encrypted.

Let us now focus on the second question which is even more complex. Consider the scenario where the network administrator wants to block all traffic to Zynga games, but prioritize traffic for the DropBox service. Notice that both of these services are encrypted, thus severely impairing a DPI-based solution. Furthermore, both of these services use the Amazon EC2 cloud. In other words, the server IP-address for both of these services can be the same. Thus using IP-address filtering does not accomplish the task either. In addition the IP-address can change over time according to CDN optimization policies. Another approach that can be used in this context is to introduce certain policies directly into the local name servers. For example, the name server does not resolve the DNS query for zynga.com in the above example, thus blocking all traffic to Zynga. Although this approach can work effectively for blocking certain services, it does not help when administrators are interested in prioritizing traffic to certain services. Administrators face the same situation when they want to prioritize traffic to *mail.google.com* and *docs.google.com*, while de-prioritizing traffic *blogspot.com* and *youtube.com* since all of these services can run over HTTPS on the same Google platform.

In this work, we propose DN-Hunter, a novel traffic monitoring system that addresses all of the above issues in a completely automated way. The main intuition behind DN-Hunter is to correlate the DNS queries and responses with the actual data flows in order to effectively *identify* and *label* the data flows, thus providing a very fine grained visibility of traffic on a network. It helps network administrators to keep track of the mapping between users, content owners, and the hosts serving the content even when this mapping is changing over time, thus enabling them to enforce policies on the traffic at any time with no manual intervention. In addition, network administrators could use DN-Hunter to dynamically reroute traffic in order to use more cost-effective links (or high bandwidth links as the policies might dictate) even as the content providers change the hosts serving the content over time for load balancing or other economic reasons.

At a high level, the methodology used in DN-Hunter seems to be achievable by performing a simple reverse DNS lookup using the server IP-addresses seen in traffic flows. However, using reverse DNS lookup does not help since it does not return accurate domain (or the sub-domain) names used in traffic flows.

The main contributions of this work are:

- We propose a novel tool, DN-Hunter, that can provide *fine-grained traffic visibility* to network administrators for effective policy controls and network management. Unlike DPI technology, using experiments on real traces, we show that DN-Hunter is very effective even when the traffic is encrypted clearly highlighting its advantages when compared to the current approaches. DN-Hunter can be used either for active or passive monitoring, and can run either as a stand-alone tool or can easily be integrated into existing monitoring systems, depending on the final intent.
- A key property of DN-Hunter is its ability to identify traffic *even before the data flow starts*. In other words, the information extracted from the DNS responses can help a network management tool to *foresee* what kind of flows will traverse the network. This unique ability can empower proactive traffic management policies, e.g., prioritizing all TCP packets in a flow (including the critical three-way-handshake), not just those packets that follow a positive DPI match.
- We use DN-Hunter to not only provide real-time traffic visibility and policy controls, but also to help gain better understanding of how the dynamic web is organized and evolving today. In other words, we show many other applications of DN-Hunter including: (*i*) *Spatial Discovery:* Mapping a particular content to the servers that actually deliver them at any point in time. (*ii*) *Content Discovery:* Mapping all the content delivered by different CDNs and cloud providers by aggregating the information based on server IP-addresses. (*iii*) *Service Tag Extraction:* Associating a layer-4 port number to the most popular service seen on the port with no a-priori information.
- We conduct extensive experiments using five traffic traces collected from large ISPs in Europe and North America. The traces contain full packets including the application payload, and range from 3h to 24h. These ISPs use several different access technologies (ADSL, FTTH, and 3G/4G) to provide service to their customers, thus showing that DN-Hunter is effective in several different contexts. Furthermore, DN-Hunter has been implemented and currently deployed in three operative vantage points since March 2012.

Although DN-Hunter is a very effective tool in any network administrator's arsenal to address issues that do not have a standard solution today, there are some limitations as well. First, the effectiveness of DN-Hunter depends on the visibility into the DNS traffic of the ISP/enterprise. In other words, DN-Hunter will be rendered useless if it does not have visibility into the DNS queries and responses along with the data flows from the end-users. Second, DN-Hunter does not help in providing visibility into applications/services that do not depend on DNS. For instance, some peer-to-peer applications are designed to work with just IP-addresses and DN-Hunter will be unable to label these flows. Third, automatic

[1]During TLS negotiation, the server certificate contains a plain text string with the name being signed.

Table 1: Dataset description.

Trace	Start [GMT]	Duration	Peak DNS Responses Rate	#Flows TCP
US-3G	15:30	3h	7.5k/min	4M
EU2-ADSL	14:50	6h	22k/min	16M
EU1-ADSL1	8:00	24h	35k/min	38M
EU1-ADSL2	8:40	5h	12k/min	5M
EU1-FTTH	17:00	3h	3k/min	1M

and smart algorithms must be devised to dig into the information exposed by DN-Hunter. In this paper, we provide some examples of how the information extracted from the DNS traffic can be used. We believe that the applications of DN-Hunter are not limited to the ones presented in this work, and novel applications can leverage the information exposed by DN-Hunter.

The rest of the paper is organized as follows: Sec. 2 introduces the datasets we use in this paper. In Sec. 3 we describe the architecture and design details of DN-Hunter. Sec. 4 presents some of our advanced analytics modules while Sec. 5 provides extensive experimental results. We discuss correct dimensioning and deployment issues in Sec. 6. We highlight the major differences between DN-Hunter and some existing approaches in Sec. 7 and conclude the paper in Sec. 8.

2. DATASETS AND TERMINOLOGY

In this section, we provide insight into the datasets used for experimental evaluation along with some basic DNS terminology used henceforth in this paper.

2.1 Experimental datasets

All our datasets are collected at the Points-of-Presence (PoP) of large ISPs where the end customers are connected to the Internet. The five datasets we use in this paper are reported in Tab. 1. In all of these traces activities from several thousands of customers are monitored. In all the 5 datasets, we capture full packets including the application payload without any packet losses. For the sake of brevity, Tab. 1 only reports the start time and trace duration, the peak time DNS response rate, and the number of TCP flows that were tracked. Each trace corresponds to a different period in 2011. The first dataset is a trace collected from a large North American 3G/4G mobile operator GGSN aggregating traffic from a citywide area. The second dataset originates from a European ISP (EU2) which has about 10K customers connected via ADSL technology. The last three datasets correspond to traffic collected from different vantage points in the same European ISP (EU1). The vantage points are located in three different cities - two ADSL PoPs and one Fiber-To-The-Home (FTTH) access PoP.

Currently, DN-Hunter has been implemented in a commercial tool as well as *Tstat* [2]. The latter has been deployed in all the three vantage points in EU1 and has been successfully labeling flows since March 2012. Some of the results in this paper are derived from this deployment.

2.2 DNS Terminology

DNS is a hierarchical distributed naming system for computers connected to the Internet. It translates "domain names" that are meaningful to humans into IP-addresses required for routing. A DNS name server stores the DNS records for different domain names.

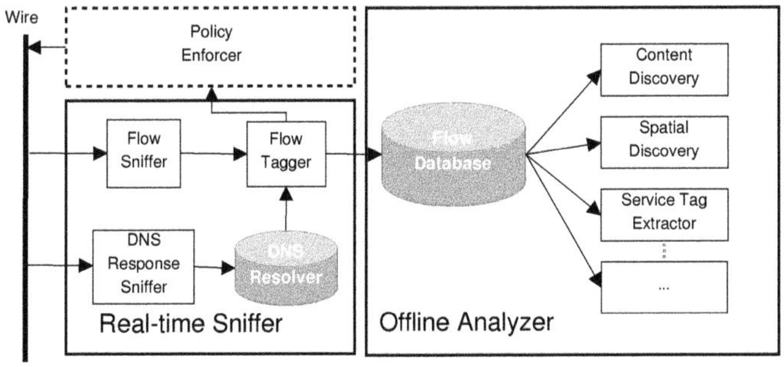

Figure 1: DN-Hunter architecture overview

A domain name consists of two or more "labels" that are conventionally concatenated, and delimited by dots, e.g., *www.example.com*. These names provide meaningful information to the end user. Therefore labels naturally convey information about the service, content, and information offered by a given domain name. The labels in the domain name are organized in a hierarchical fashion. The Top-Level Domain (TLD) is the last part of the domain name - *.com* in the above example; and sub-domains are then pre-pended to the TLD. Thus, *example.com* is a subdomain of *.com*, and *www.example.com* is a subdomain of *example.com*. In this paper, we refer to the first sub-domain after the TLD as "second level domain"; it generally refers to the organization that owns the domain name (e.g., *example.com*). Finally *Fully Qualified Domain Name* (FQDN) is the domain name complete with all the labels that unambiguously identifies a resource, e.g., *www.example.com*.

When an application needs to access a resource, a query is sent to the local DNS server. This server responds back with the resolution if it already has one, else it invokes an iterative address resolution mechanism until it can resolve the domain name (or determine that it cannot be resolved). The responses from the DNS server carry a *list of answers*, i.e., a list of $serverIP$ addresses that can serve the content for the requested resource.

Local caching of DNS responses at the end-hosts is commonly used to avoid initiating new requests to the DNS server for every resolution. The time for which a local cache stores a DNS record is determined by the Time-To-Live (TTL) value associated with every record. It is set by the authoritative DNS name server, and varies from few seconds (e.g., for CDNs and highly dynamic services) to days. Also, memory limits and timeout deletion policies can affect local caching at the client OS. However, as we will see later, in practice, clients cache DNS responses for typically less than 1 hour.

3. DN-Hunter ARCHITECTURE

A high level overview of DN-Hunter architecture is shown in Fig. 1. It consists of two main components: *real-time sniffer* and *off-line analyzer*. As the name indicates, the sniffer labels/tags all the incoming data flows in *real time*. The output from the sniffer can be used for online policy enforcement (using any available policy enforcing tool) and/or can be stored in a database for off-line analysis by the analyzer component. Note that the sniffer can be a passive

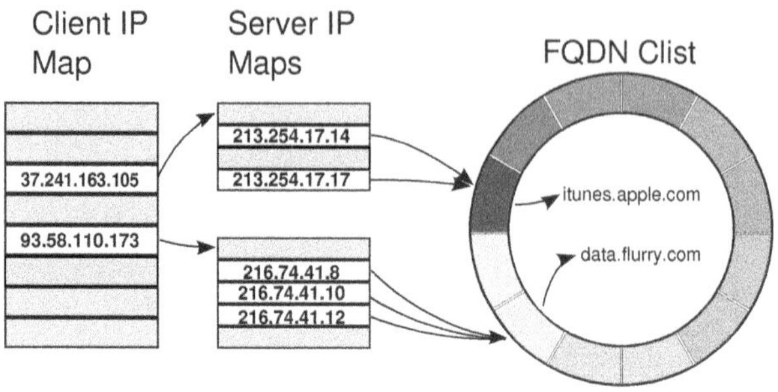

Figure 2: DNS Resolver data structures

component instead of being active if the policy enforcer is not implemented. For the ease of exposition, in this work, we assume that the real-time sniffer component is a passive monitoring component.

3.1 Real-Time Sniffer Component

The sniffer has two low-level sniffing blocks: (*i*) *Flow sniffer* which reconstructs layer-4 flows by aggregating packets based on the 5-tuple *Fid* = (*clientIP*, *serverIP*, *sPort*, *dPort*, *protocol*), and (*ii*) *DNS response sniffer* which decodes the DNS responses, and maintains a local data structure called the *DNS Resolver*. The DNS resolver maintains a mapping between client IP, domain names queried, and the server IP(s) included in the DNS response. In particular, for each response, it stores the set of *serverIP* addresses returned for the fully qualified domain name (FQDN) queried, associating them to the *clientIP* that generated the query.

All data flows reconstructed by the flow sniffer is passed on to the *Flow Tagger* module. The flow tagger module queries the DNS resolver to tag the incoming *clientIP*, *serverIP* pair. The flow tagger will tag the incoming flow with the "label" (i.e., the FQDN) and sends the flow to the policy enforcer (to enforce any policy on the flow including blocking, redirection, rate limiting, etc.) and/or the database for off-line analysis.

3.1.1 DNS Resolver Design

The key block in the real-time sniffer component is the DNS Resolver. Its engineering is not trivial since it has to meet real-time constraints. The goal of the DNS Resolver is to build a replica of the client DNS cache by sniffing DNS responses from the DNS server. Each entry in the cache stores the *FQDN* and uses the *serverIP* and *clientIP* as look-up keys. To avoid garbage collection, *FQDN*s are stored in a first-in-first-out FIFO circular list, *Clist*, of size L; a pointer identifies the next available location where an entry can be inserted. L limits the cache entry lifetime and has to properly match the local resolver cache in the monitored hosts.

Lookup is performed using two sets of tables. The first table uses the *clientIP* as key to find a second table, from where the *serverIP* key points to the most recent *FQDN* entries in the *Clist* that was queried by *clientIP*. Tables are implemented using C++ maps[2], in which the elements are sorted from lower to higher key value following a specific strict weak ordering criterion based on IP addresses. Let N_C and $N_S(c)$ represent the number of monitored clients and the number of servers that client c contacts, respectively. Assuming L is well-dimensioned, the look-up complexity is $O(\log(N_C) + \log(N_S(c)))$. N_C depends on the number of hosts in the monitored network. $N_S(c)$ depends on the traffic generated by clients. In general, $N_S(c)$ is in the order of a few hundreds. Note that when the number of monitored clients increase, several load balancing strategies can be used. For example, two resolvers can be maintained for odd and even fourth octet value in the client IP-address.

```
1:  INSERT(DNSresponse)
2:  Input: DNSresponse
3:  (FQDN, ClientIP, answerList) ← decode(DNSresponse
4:  DNEntry ← newDNEntry(FQDN)
5:  mapServer ← mapClient.get(clientIP)
6:  if mapServer = null then
7:     mapServer ← new MapServer()
8:     mapClient.put(clientIP, mapServer)
9:  end if
10: for all serverIP in answerList do
11:    /* replace old references */
12:    if exists mapSever.get(serverIP) then
13:       OLDEntry ← mapSever.get(serverIP)
14:       OLDEntry.removeOldReferences()
15:    end if
16:    /* Link back and forth
17:    references to the new DNSEntry */
18:    mapServer.put(serverIP, DNEntry)
19:    MSEntry ← mapServer.get(serverIP)
20:    DNEntry.insert(MSEntry)
21: end for
22: /* insert next entry in circular array */
23: OldDNEntry ← Clist.nextEntry()
24: OldDNEntry.deleteBackreferences()
25: Clist.nextEntry ← DNEntry
26:
27: LOOKUP(ClientIP, ServerIP)
28: Input: ClientIP and ServerIP of a flow
29: Output: FQDN of ServerIP as requested by ClientIP
30: mapServer ← mapClient.get(clientIP)
31: if mapServer contains serverIP then
32:    DNEntry ← mapServer.get(serverIP)
33:    return DNEntry.FQDN
34: end if
```

Algorithm 1: DNS Resolver pseudo-code

Fig. 2 depicts the internal data structures in the DNS resolver. Algorithm 1 provides the pseudo code of the "insert()" and "lookup()" functions that access the data structures in Fig. 2. Since DNS responses carry a list of possible *serverIP* addresses, more than one *serverIP* can point to the same *FQDN* entry (line 11-22). When a new DNS response is observed, the information is inserted in the *Clist*, eventually removing old entries (line 12-15)[3]. When an entry in the DNS circular array is overwritten, the old *clientIP* and *serverIP* keys are removed from the maps before inserting the new one (line 25).

3.1.2 DNS traffic characteristics

Using the above algorithm for tagging (or labeling) incoming data flows, we conducted several experiments to accomplish the following goals: (*i*) Understand how much information DNS traffic can expose in enabling traffic visibility, and (*ii*) Understand how to correctly dimension the DNS resolver data structures.

[2]Unordered maps, i.e., hash tables, can be used as well to further reduce the computational costs

[3]In this case the information about the old FQDN is lost and may create some ambiguity. See Sec. 6 for more details.

Protocol	EU1-ADSL1	EU1-ADSL2	EU1-FTTH
HTTP	92% (4.4M)	90% (2.7M)	91% (683k)
TLS	92% (0.4M)	86% (196k)	84% (50k)
P2P	1% (6k)	1% (1.3k)	0% (48)
	EU2-ADSL	**US-3G**	
HTTP	97% (5.8M)	75% (445k)	
TLS	96% (279k)	74% (83k)	
P2P	1% (4.2k)	8% (8k)	

Table 2: DNS Resolver hit ratio

To address the first goal, we compute the DNS hit ratio. In other words, DNS hit ratio represents the fraction of data flows that can be successfully associated with a FQDN. The higher is the hit ratio, the more successful is DN-Hunter in enabling traffic visibility. Intuition suggests that all client-server services/applications rely on the DNS infrastructure and hence DN-Hunter will be able to accurately identify them. However, certain peer-to-peer services/applications do not use the DNS infrastructure and thus evade detection in DN-Hunter. Tab. 2 confirms this intuition. It details, for each trace, the number of DNS hits and the corresponding percentage of flows that were resolved, considering the subset of HTTP, TLS, and P2P flows. In this experiment, we consider a warm-up time of 5 minutes (i.e., we track all flows, but ignore the statistics contributed by the flows in the first 5 mins of the trace).

As expected, HTTP and TLS flows show a very high hit ratio, with the majority of cache-miss occurring in the initial part of the trace when the end host operating system local resolver cache resolves the query locally and limits the queries to the DNS server. P2P data flows are hardly preceded by DNS resolutions, and hence it results in a very low hit ratio[4].

When considering only HTTP and TLS data flows, we see that the hit ratio mostly exceeds 90% for all traces except US-3G. When considering only the last hour of each trace, the DNS hit ratio increases further close to 100% in all traces but US-3G. In the case of US-3G, we hypothesize that the adoption of tunneling mechanisms over HTTP/HTTPS for which no DNS information is exposed may be the cause of lower DNS Resolver efficiency. Furthermore, device mobility may also affect our results: our tool may observe flows from devices entering the coverage area after performing a DNS resolution outside the visibility of our monitoring point. Thus our tool might miss the DNS response resulting in a cache-miss. More details about the DNS traffic characteristics that affects DN-Hunter dimensioning is provided in Sec. 6.

3.1.3 DN-Hunter vs. DNS reverse lookup

The information that the sniffer component extracts is much more valuable than the one that can be obtained by performing active DNS reverse lookup of $serverIP$ addresses. Recall that the reverse lookup returns only the designated domain name record. Consider Tab. 3 where we randomly selected 1,000 $serverIP$ for which the Sniffer was able to associate a FQDN. We have considered the EU1-ADSL2 dataset for this experiment. We then performed active DNS reverse lookup queries of the $serverIP$ addresses and compared the returned FQDN with the one recovered by the sniffer. In 29% of cases, no answer was returned by the reverse lookup while in 26% of the lookups the two answers were totally different from each other. All the other queries had at least had a partial match. In fact, only 9% of the reverse lookups completely matched the results from the sniffer while the rest of the 36% only matched the second-level domain name. These results are not surprising since single servers are typically serving several FQDNs (see Sec. 5). In addition to this, reverse lookup poses scalability issues as well.

[4]P2P hits are related to BitTorrent tracker traffic mainly.

Same FQDN	9%
Same 2nd-level domain	36%
Totally different	26%
No-answer	29%

Table 3: DN-Hunter vs. reverse lookup

3.2 Off-Line Analyzer Component

Although the sniffer module provides deep visibility into the services/applications on the wire in real-time, some analytics cannot be performed in real-time. In other words, dissecting and analyzing the data in different ways can expose very interesting insights about the traffic. The off-line analyzer component does exactly this. It contains several intelligent analytics that can extract information from the flows database by mining its content. In the next section, we will present a few sample analytics. However, several other analytics can be added into the system easily.

4. ADVANCED ANALYTICS

In this section we describe some advanced analytics using the data stored in the labeled flows database to automatically discover information and discern the tangled web.

4.1 Spatial Discovery of Servers

Today, CDNs and distributed cloud-based infrastructures are used to meet both scalability and reliability requirements, decoupling the owner of the content and the organization serving it. In this context some interesting questions arise: (*i*) Given a particular resource (i.e., a FQDN) what are all the servers or hosts that deliver the required content?, (*ii*) Do these servers belong to the same or different CDNs?, and (*iii*) Do CDNs catering to the resource change over time and geography? (*iv*) Are other resources belonging to the same organization served by the same or different set of CDNs?

DN-Hunter can easily answer all of the above questions. Algorithm 2 shows the pseudo-code for the Spatial Discovery functionality in DN-Hunter. The spatial discovery module first extracts the second-level domain name from the FQDN (line 4), and then queries the labeled flows database (line 5) to retrieve all $serverIP$ addresses in flows directed towards the second-level domain (i.e., the organization). Then, for every FQDN that belongs to the organization, the spatial discovery module will extract the $serverIP$ addresses that can serve the request (line 6-9) based on the DNS responses. This enables the module to: (*i*) Discover the information about the structure of servers (single server, or one/many CDNs) that handle all queries for the organization, (*ii*) Discover which servers handle a more specific resource. For example, different data centres/hosts may be serving the content for *mail.google.com* and *scholar.google.com*, and (*iii*)

```
SPATIAL DISCOVERY(FQDN)
Input: The targeted FQDN
Output: ranked list of serverIP addresses
2ndDomain ← FQDN.split()
ServerSet ←
    FlowDB.queryByDomainName(2ndDomain)
FQDNset ← 2ndDomain.query()
for all FQDN in FQDNSet do
    FQDN.ServerSet ←
        FlowDB.queryByDomainName(FQDN)
end for
Return(FQDN.ServerSet.sort(), ServerSet.sort())
```

Algorithm 2: Spatial Discovery Analytics Algorithm

Automatically keep track of any changes in *serverIP* addresses that satisfy a given FQDN over time. Note that the ability of DN-Hunter to easily track temporal and spatial changes in the FQDN-*serverIP* address mapping also enables some basic anomaly detection. While out of scope of this paper, consider the case of DNS cache poisoning where a response for certain FQDN suddenly changes and is different from what was seen by DN-Hunter in the the past. We can easily flag this scenario as an anomaly, enabling the security operator to take some action if required.

4.2 Content Discovery

As we saw in the previous subsection, a particular resource can be served by one or more CDNs or cloud infrastructures, and the spatial discovery analytics module provides deep insights into this. However, it is also important to understand tangle from another perspective. In other words, we need to answer the following questions: (*i*) Given a particular CDN what are the different resources that they host/serve? (*ii*) What is the popularity of particular CDNs in different geographies? (*iii*) Given two CDNs, what are the common resources that they both host?, and (*iv*) Does a given CDN focus on hosting content for certain types of services (like real-time multimedia streaming, mail, etc.)?

Once again DN-Hunter can answer the above questions easily based on the mapping stored in the flows database and using the whois database to associate IP addresses to CDNs. The complete algorithm for the content discovery module is shown in Algorithm 3. The algorithm takes a *ServerIPSet*, i.e., the set of *serverIP* addresses belonging to one or more CDNs, and extracts all the FQDNs associated with them (line 4-7). Depending on the desired granularity level, either the complete FQDN or only part of the FQDN (say, the second-level domain) can be considered. If only the second-level domains are considered, then the algorithm will return all the organizations served by the set of *serverIP* addresses provided as input. However, if only service tokens are used (we will discuss this in the next sub-section), then the algorithm will return which popular services are hosted by the input *serverIP* addresses.

4.3 Automatic Service Tag Extraction

Identifying all the services/applications running on a particular layer-4 port number is a legacy problem that network administrators encounter. Even today there are no existing solutions that can identify all applications on any given layer-4 port number. In fact, the network administrators depend on DPI solutions to address this problem. DPI technology can only provide a partial solution to this problem due to two reasons: (1) Several services/applications use encryption and hence bypass DPIs, and (2) DPI devices can only identify those services/applications for which they already have a signature, thus severely limiting the coverage.

```
 1: CONTENT DISCOVERY(ServerIPSet)
 2: Input: The list of targeted serverIP
 3: Output: The list of handled FQDNs
 4: DomainNameSet ← FlowDB.query(ServerIPSet)
 5: for all FQDN in DomainNameSet do
 6:     TokenSet ← DomainName.split(FQDN)
 7: end for
 8: for all Token in TokenSet do
 9:     Token.score.update()
10: end for
11: Return(Tokens.sort())
```

Algorithm 3: Content Discovery Analytics Algorithm

```
 1: TAG EXTRACTION(dPort, k)
 2: Input: targeted dPort, k of tags to return
 3: Output: The ranked list of tags
 4: DomainNameSet ← FlowDB.query(dPort)
 5: for all FQDN in DomainNameSet do
 6:     TokenSet ← DomainName.split(NoTLD|NoSLD)
 7: end for
 8: for all Token in TokenSet do
 9:     Token.score.update()
10: end for
11: Return(Tokens.sort(k))
```

Algorithm 4: Service Tag Extraction Analytics Algorithm

DN-Hunter provides a simple and automated way to address the above issue. The algorithm for extracting service tags on any layer-4 port number is shown in Algorithm 4. The input to the algorithm are the target port number and the k value for the top-k services to be identified. The algorithm first retrieves all FQDNs associated to flows that are directed to *dPort* (line 4). Each FQDN is then tokenized to extract all the sub-domains except for the TLD and second-level domain. The tokens are further split by considering non-alphanumeric characters as separators. Numbers are replaced by a generic N character (lines 5-7). For instance, *smtp2.mail.google.com* generates the list of tokens {smtpN, mail}.

We use the frequency of tokens as measure of "relevance" of the token for the targeted port (lines 8-10). To mitigate the bias due to some clients generating a lot of connections to a FQDN having the same token X, we use a logarithmic score. Mathematically, let $N_X(c)$ be the number of flows originated by *clientIP* c having the token X. Then the score of X is:

$$score(X) = \sum_{c} \log(N_X(c) + 1) \quad (1)$$

Tokens are then ranked by score and the top-k tokens are returned to the users (line 11). Depending on the final goal, different criteria can be applied to limit the list of returned tokens. For instance, the list can simply be limited to the top 5%, or to the subset that sums to the n-th percentile. Typically, the score distribution is very skewed, as we will show in Sec. 5.

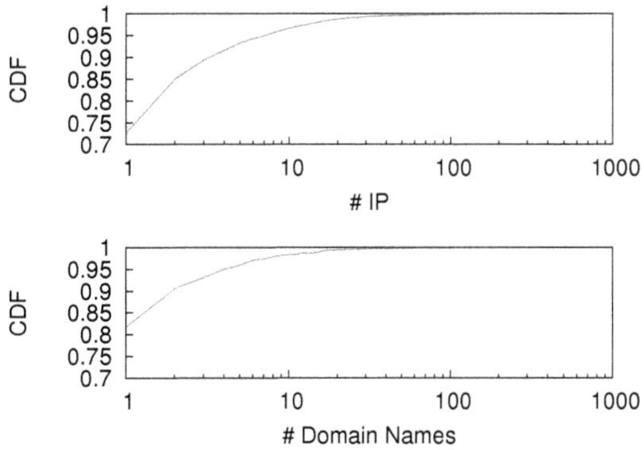

Figure 3: Number of *serverIP* addresses associated to a FQDN (top) and number of FQDN associated to a *ServerIP* (bottom). EU2-ADSL.

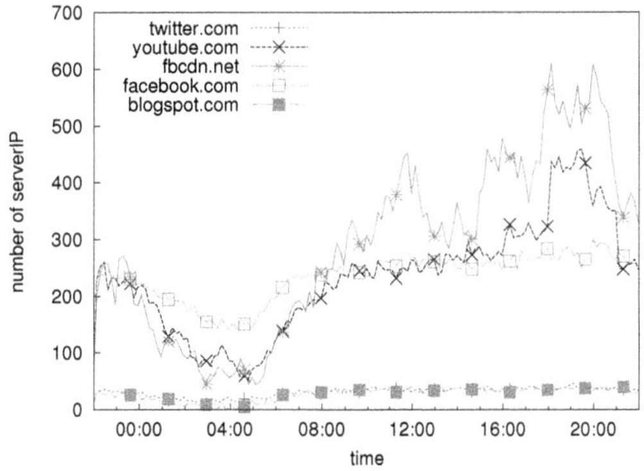

Figure 4: Number of IP addresses serving some particular 2nd-level domain name. EU1-ADSL2.

5. EXPERIMENTAL RESULTS

In this section, we present the results from using DN-Hunter on the traces mentioned in Sec. 2. We begin the discussion here by showing evidence of how tangled is the web today in terms of content, content providers, and hosts serving the content. We then present the results that clearly highlight the advantages of using DN-Hunter in an operational network compared to the existing solutions for traffic visibility and policy enforcement. In fact, DN-Hunter is now implemented as part of two different DPI tools and is deployed to provide traffic visibility to network operators. In the second half of this section we will present results from our advanced analytics modules to demonstrate the wide applicability and usefulness of DN-Hunter.

5.1 The Tangled Web

The basic hypothesis of this paper is that the web today is intertwined with content, content providers, and hosts serving the content that are continually changing over time and space. Hence we need a methodology that can assist in restoring clarity to operators regarding their network traffic. The top plot of Fig. 3 reports, for each FQDN, the overall number of *serverIP* addresses that serve it. In the bottom plot of Fig. 3 we show the opposite - the number of different FQDNs a single *serverIP* address serves. Fig. 3 was generated using the EU2-ADSL dataset, however, all the other datasets produced very similar result. We can clearly see that one single *serverIP* is associated to a single FQDN for 73% of *serverIPs*, and 82% of FQDNs map to just one *serverIP*. But more important to note is that there are FQDNs that are served by hundreds of different *serverIP* addresses. Similarly a large number of FQDNs are served by one *serverIP*. Notice the x-axis in this figure is presented in log scale.

Just looking at the one-to-many mapping between FQDN and *serverIP* addresses reveals only a small part of the complexity. Now let us add time into the mix. Fig. 4 shows the number of *serverIP* addresses that have been observed responding to some selected well-known second-level domains. We consider time bins of 10min, covering a 24h period from EU1-ADSL2 dataset. For some of the domains (like fbcdn.net and youtube.com) we can clearly see a diurnal pattern with more *serverIPs* being used during late evening when compared to early morning. In fact, for *youtube.com* we can see that there is a big and sudden jump in the number of *serverIPs* between 17:00 and 20:30. This reflects a change in the YouTube policies, triggered by the peak-time load. The domain *fbcdn.net* (owned by Akamai and serving Facebook static content) shows similar characteristics with more than 600 different *serverIP* addresses serving content in every 10min interval between 18:00 and 20:00. Finally, some of the other domains like *blogspot.com* (aggregating more than 4,500 total FQDN) are served by less than 20 *serverIPs* even during peak traffic hours.

Fig. 5 reports the number of different FQDNs that were served every 10min by different CDNs and cloud providers over a period of 24h. The MaxMind organization database was used to associate *serverIP* addresses to organization. We can clearly see that Amazon serves more than 600 distinct FQDN in every 10 min interval during peak hours (11:00 to 21:00). In total, Amazon served 7995 FQDNs in a day. While Akamai and Microsoft also serve significant number of FQDNs during peak hours, other CDNs like EdgeCast serve less than 20 FQDNs.

Another aspect worth noting here is that association between FQDNs and CDNs change over time and space (i.e., geography). Due to space constraints we do not present these results here. However, all of the above results clearly show why it is very hard to discern and control the traffic in today's networks! In fact, there is clear need for a solution like DN-Hunter that can track these changes seamlessly to ensure traffic visibility at any point in time. Surprisingly, the results presented in this section for motivating the need for a solution like DN-Hunter could not have been produced if we did not have DN-Hunter!

5.2 Traffic Visibility and Policy Enforcement

The key feature of DN-Hunter is to provide a "label" (i.e., the FQDN that the client was contacting) to every flow in the network automatically. To show how this labeling evolves over time, we show the results from our live deployment in EU1-ADSL2 for a period of 18 days in April, 2012. In Fig. 6 we report the total number of unique FQDNs over time. The plot shows the growth of unique entities - FQDNs, second-level domains, and *serverIP* - over time. Once again we can clearly see the diurnal pattern where the increase in unique entities is much higher during the day than the night. After a steep growth during the first few days, the

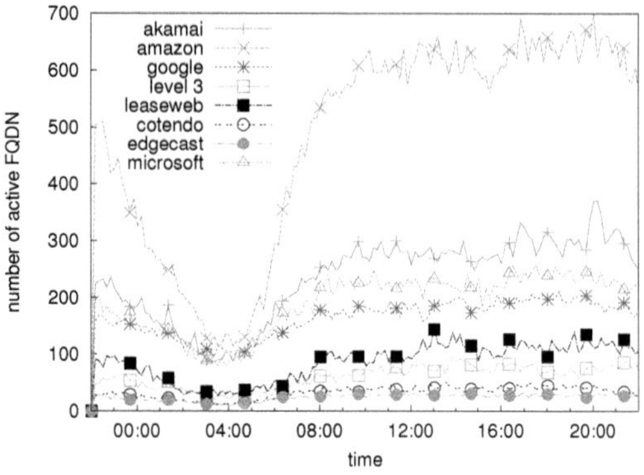

Figure 5: Number of FQDN served by CDNs through a day. EU1-ADSL2.

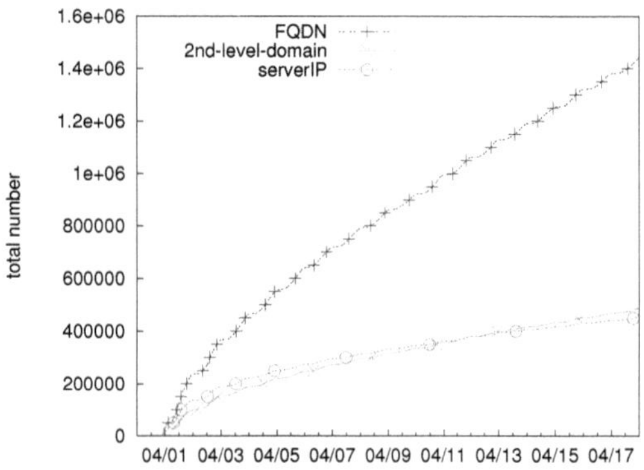

Figure 6: Unique FQDN, 2nd level domain names and IP birth processes. EU1-ADSL2 live.

number of unique *serverIP* addresses and second-level domains reach a saturation point and do not grow much. This result basically indicates that the same *serverIP* addresses are used to serve the contents for the same organizations (i.e., second-level domains). However, a surprising result is regarding the unique FQDNs. As we can see, the number of unique FQDNs keeps increasing even after 18 days of observation. In 18 days we saw more than 1.5M unique FQDNs and it was still growing at the rate of about 100K per day. This reflects the fact that the content being accessed on the Internet keeps growing, with new services popping up regularly. The main take away point is that in order to get fine-grained traffic visibility (and thus be applied for policy enforcement), it is critical to use a tool like DN-Hunter that can dynamically keep track of the content and their association with content providers and the hosts serving the content.

5.2.1 *The Case of Encrypted Traffic*

As we mentioned earlier, one of the main advantages of DN-Hunter when compared to traditional DPI solutions is its ability to label encrypted (TLS/SSL) flows. Traditional DPI solutions cannot identify encrypted traffic by inspecting the packet content and matching it against a signature. However, the DPI solution can be modified to inspect the certificates exchanged during the TLS/SSL handshake to figure out the server name of the organization that will provide the content.

Certificate equal FQDN	18%
Generic certificate	19%
Totally different certificate	40%
No certificate	23%

Table 4: Comparison between the server name extracted from TLS certificate-inspection and the FQDN using DN-Hunter. EU1-ADSL2.

In order to compare the certificate inspection approach with DN-Hunter, we implemented the certificate inspection functionality in Tstat. Tab. 4 compares certificate inspection approach with DN-Hunter for all TLS flows in the EU1-ADSL2 dataset. Results show that DN-Hunter clearly outperforms the certificate inspection approach. For 23% of the flows in the trace there was no certificate, while for 40% of the flows the server name in the certificate was totally different from the FQDN. For the other 37% of the flows that matched the second-level domain name in the FQDN, only 18% matched the complete FQDN. The main problems with the certificate inspection approach are three-fold: (*i*) The server name can be "generic", e.g., **.google.com*, thus not giving the fine-grained visibility into the actual services. (*ii*) The server name may indicate the server used by the hosting CDN and may not reflect anything about the service, e.g., *a248.akamai.net* in the certificate for providing Zynga content, and (*iii*) Certificate exchange might happen only the first time a TLS/SSL server is contacted and all other flows following that will share the trust. Thus using such an approach is almost infeasible.

5.3 Spatial Discovery of Servers

The main goal of the spatial discovery module is to track a particular resource (FQDN or second-level domain) to understand which *serverIPs* and CDNs serve the requested content. For the ease of exposition, in this section, we will focus on two specific second-level domains - LinkedIn and Zynga. Fig. 7 shows the mapping between the various FQDNs of LinkedIn and the CDNs serving the content in US-3G dataset. The oval nodes represent DNS tokens extracted from the FQDNs, while arcs connect the tokens to reconstruct the FQDN. The numbers in these tokens are represented as a generic letter, N. The rectangular nodes group tokens by the CDN hosting them based on the information from the MaxMind database. To illustrate the concept better let us consider the leftmost branch in Fig. 7. The complete FQDN is the concatenation of all the tokens, i.e., *mediaN.linkedin.com*. These FQDNs are served by Akamai CDN using 2 servers and accounts for 17% of the total flows destined to *linkedin.com*. In order to limit the size of the figure, we have hidden 7 different tokens in the rightmost branch of the tree.

From the figure, it is easy to see that LinkedIn relies on the service offered by several CDN providers. Only the *www.linkedin.com* FQDN along with 7 other FQDNs are served by Linkedin managed servers. Most of the static content is served by hosts in three different CDNs - Akamai, CDNetwork, and Edgecast. In fact, EdgeCast serves 59% of all flows with a single *serverIP* address. On the

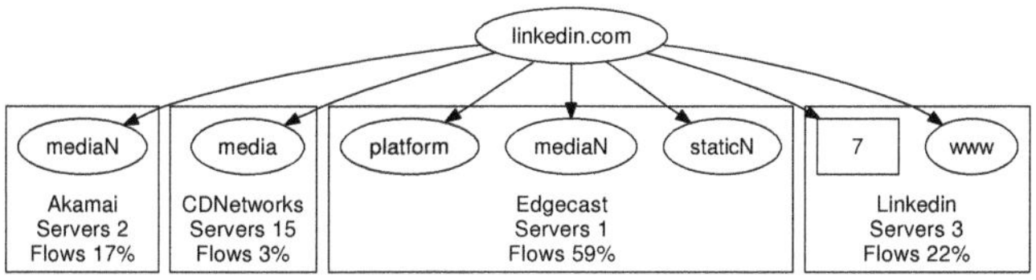

Figure 7: Linkedin.com domain structure served by two CDNs. US-3G.

contrary, CDNetworks, serves only 3% of flows with 15 different *serverIP* addresses.

Let us now consider the second sample domain - Zynga (see Fig. 8). We can see that Amazon EC2 cloud service provides computational resources required for the games while Akamai CDN hosts most of the static content. Some services/games like MafiaWars are served directly by Zynga owned servers. Interestingly, about 500 Amazon *serverIP* addresses are contacted and they handle 86% of all Zynga flows. Akamai serves fewer requests (7%); yet, 30 different *serverIP* are observed.

Given that the off-line analyzer relies on actual measurement of network traffic, it is able to capture both the service popularity among the monitored customers, and the bias induced by the server selection and load balancing mechanisms. To elaborate this further, let us consider Fig. 9. Each of the three sub-figures corresponds to a different content provider (i.e., the second-level domain name). For each of these content providers we plot the access patterns in three of our traces (EU1-ADSL1, US-3G, and EU2-ADSL). In other words, the x-axis in each of these graphs are the CDNs hosting the content and the y-axis represents different traces. Notice that for every CDN, the figure shows all the accessed *serverIP* addresses that belong to the CDN. Hence the width of the column representing each CDN is different. Also, the gray scale of each block in the graph represents the frequency of access; the darker is a cell, the larger is the fraction of flows that a particular *serverIP* was responsible for. The "SELF" column reports cases in which the content providers and content hosts are the same organization.

The top graph in Fig. 9 shows the access pattern for Facebook. We can see that in all the datasets, most of the Facebook content is hosted on Facebook servers. The only other CDN used by Facebook is Akamai, which uses different *serverIP* in different geographical regions. In the middle graph, we can see that Twitter access patterns are a little different. Although, Twitter relies heavily on its own servers to host content, they also rely heavily on Akamai to serve content to users in Europe. However, the dependence on Akamai is significantly less the US. The bottom graph shows the access patterns for Dailymotion, a video streaming site. Dailymotion heavily relies on Dedibox to host content both in Europe and US. While they do not host any content in their own servers in Europe, they do serve some content in the US. Also, in the US they rely on other CDNs like Meta and NTT to serve content while they rely a little bit on Edgecast in Europe.

5.4 Content Discovery

Although the spatial discovery module provides invaluable insight into how a particular resource is hosted on various

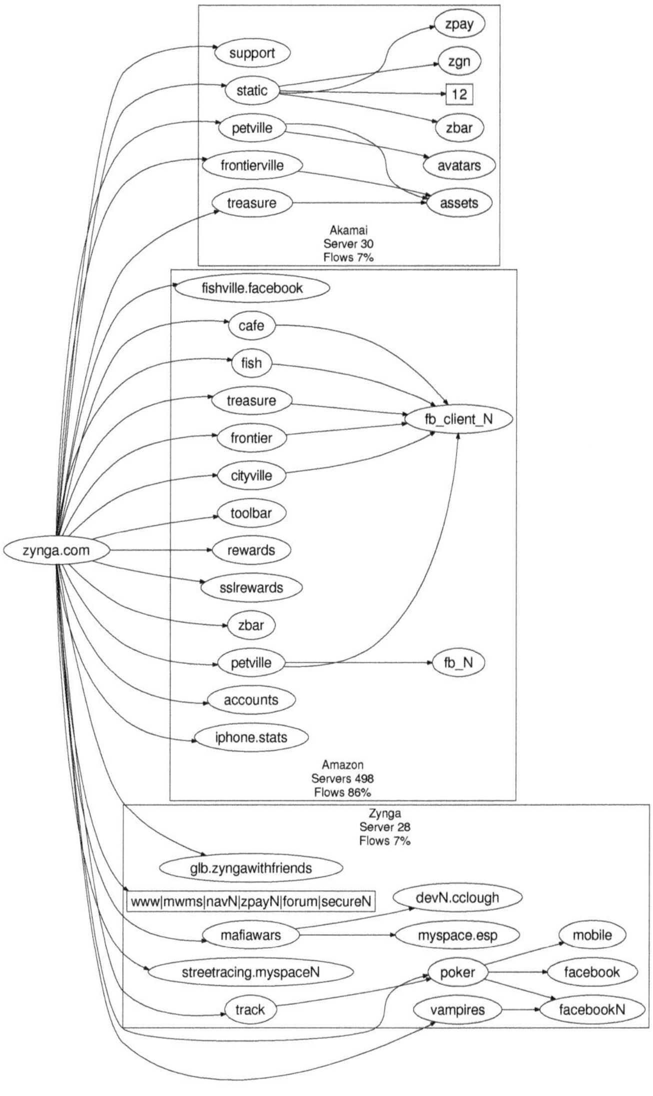

Figure 8: Zynga.com domain structure served by two CDNs. US-3G.

CDNs, it does not help in understanding the complete behavior of CDNs. In the content discovery module our goal is to understand the content distribution from the perspective of CDNs and cloud service providers. Tab. 5 shows the top-10 second-level domains served by the Amazon EC2 cloud in EU1-ADSL1and US-3G. Notice that one dataset is from Europe and the other from US. We can clearly see that the top-10 in the two datasets do not match. In fact, some of the popular domains hosted on Amazon for US users like admarvel, mobclix, and andomedia are not accessed on Amazon by European users, while other domains like cloutfront, invitemedia, and rubiconproject are popular in both the datasets. This clearly shows that the popularity and access patterns of CDNs hosting content for different domains depend on geography; extrapolating results from one geography to another might result in incorrect conclusions.

5.5 Automatic Service Tag Extraction

Another interesting application of DN-Hunter is in iden-

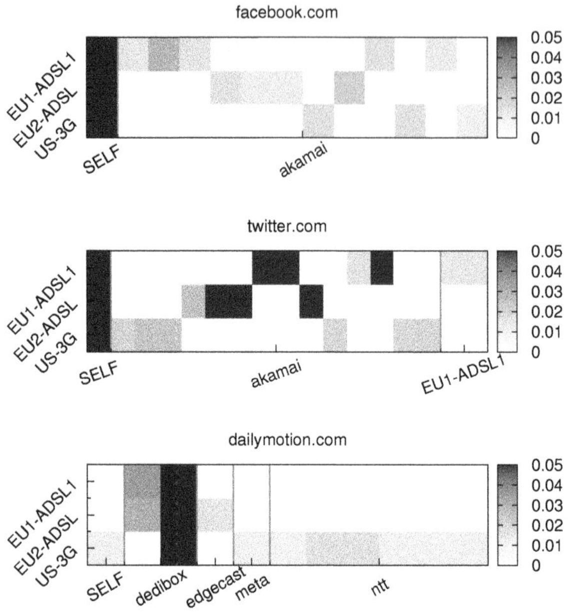

Figure 9: Organizations served by several CDN according to viewpoint.

Rank	US-3G	%	EU1-ADSL1	%
1	cloudfront.net	10	cloudfront.net	20
2	invitemedia.com	10	playfish.com	16
3	amazon.com	7	sharethis.com	5
4	rubiconproject.com	7	twimg.com	4
5	andomedia.com	5	amazonaws.com	4
6	sharethis.com	5	zynga.com	4
7	mobclix.com	4	invitemedia.com	2
8	zynga.com	3	rubiconproject.com	2
9	admarvel.com	3	amazon.com	2
10	amazonaws.com	3	imdb.com	1

Table 5: Top-10 domains hosted on the Amazon EC2 cloud.

tifying all the services/applications running on a particular layer-4 port number. This application is only feasible due to the fined grained traffic visibility provided by DN-Hunter. To keep the tables small, we only show the results extracted on a few selected layer-4 ports for two data sets - EU1-FTTH (Tab. 6) and US-3G(Tab. 7). In these tables we show the list of terms along with the weights returned by the Service Tag Extraction Analytics algorithm (Algorithm 4). The last column in each of these tables is the ground truth obtained using Tstat DPI and augmented by Google searches and our domain knowledge.

We can clearly see that the most popular terms extracted in both the datasets in fact represents the application/service on the port. Some of them like pop3, imap, and smtp are very obvious by looking at the top keyword. However, some of the other are not very obvious, but can be derived very easily. For example, consider the port 1337. TCP port 1337 is not a standard port for any service and even a google search for TCP port 1337 does not yield straight forward results. However by adding "exodus" and "genesis", the main keywords extracted in DN-Hunter, to the google search along

Port	Keywords	GT
25	(91)smtp, (37)mail, (22)mxN, (19)mailN, (18)com, (17)altn, (14)mailin, (13)aspmx, (13)gmail	SMTP
110	(240)pop, (151)mail, (68)popM, (33)mailbus	POP3
143	(25)imap, (22)mail, (12)pop, (3)apple	IMAP
554	(1)streaming	RTSP
587	(10)smtp, (3)pop, (1)imap	SMTP
995	(101)pop, (37)popN, (31)mail, (20)glbdns (20)hot, (17)pec	POP3S
1863	(21)messenger, (5)relay, (5)edge, (5)voice, (2)msn, (2)com, (2)emea	MSN

Table 6: Keyword extraction example considering well-known ports. EU1-FTTH.

Port	Keywords	GT
1080	(51)opera, (51)miniN	Opera Browser
1337	(83)exodus, (41)genesis	BT Tracker
2710	(62)tracker, (9)www	BT Tracker
5050	(137)msg, (137)webcs, (58)sip, (43)voipa	Yahoo Messager
5190	(27)americaonline	AOL ICQ
5222	(1170)chat	Gtalk
5223	(191)courier, (191)push	Apple push services
5228	(15022)mtalk	Android Market
6969	(88)tracker, (19)trackerN, (11)torrent, (10)exodus	BT Tracker
12043	(32)simN, (32)agni	Second Life
12046	(20)simN, (20)agni	Second Life
18182	(92)useful, (88)broker	BT Tracker

Table 7: Keyword Extraction for frequently used ports; Well-known ports are omitted. US-3G.

with TCP port 1337 immediately shows that this port in US-3G dataset is related to www.1337x.org BitTorrent tracker.

5.6 Case Study - appspot.com Tracking

In this section, we want to present a surprising phenomenon that we discovered using DN-Hunter's ability to track domains. Let us consider the domain *appspot.com*. *Appspot* is a free web-apps hosting service provided by Google. The number of applications, CPU time and server bandwidth that can be used for free are limited. Using the labels for various flows in the labeled flows database, we extract all traffic associated with services. This allows to understand the kind of applications and services that are hosted in the Appspot cloud.

Fig. 10 shows the most relevant applications hosted on *appspot* as a word cloud where the larger/darker fonts represent more popular applications. Although *appspot* is intended to host legacy applications, it is easy to see that users host applications like "open-tracker", "rlskingbt", and the like. A little more investigation reveals that these applications actually host *BitTorrent* trackers for free. With the help of the information from DN-Hunter and also the Tstat DPI deployed at the European ISP, we find that there are several trackers and other legacy applications running in the *appspot.com* site. We present the findings in Tab. 8. As we can see, BitTorrent trackers only represent 7% of the applications but constitute for more flows than the other applications. Also, when considering the total bytes exchanged for each of these services, the traffic from client-to-server gen-

Figure 10: Cloud tag of services offered by Google Appspot. EU1-ADSL2 during live deployment.

Service Type	Services	Flows	C2S	S2C
Bittorrent Trackers	56	186K	202MB	370MB
General Services	824	77K	320MB	5GB

Table 8: Appspot services. EU1-ADSL2 live.

erated by the trackers is a significantly large percentage of the overall traffic.

In Fig. 11 we plot the timeline (in 4hr intervals) of when the trackers were active over a period of 18 days. A dot represents that the tracker was active at that time interval. We assign each tracker an id, starting at 1 and incrementally increasing based on the time when the tracker was first observed. Of all the 45 trackers seen in the 18 day period, about 33% (colored in red, ids 1-15) of them remained active for all the 18 days. Trackers with ids 26-31 (colored in blue) exhibit a unique pattern of on-off periods. In other words, all of these trackers were accessed during the same time intervals. Such a synchronized behavior indicates, with high probability, that one BitTorrent client was part of a swarm, so that when the client was active, the tracker was accessed. Similar considerations hold for the trackers with ids 33-34 (colored in green), which was seen accessed on May 5th for the first time.

Finally, trackers with ids larger than 33 highlight a birth process according to which a new tracker is born and accessed by only a few BitTorrent clients. This is due to the particular environment the trackers live: since Appspot limits the amount of resource an application can use for free, new trackers are born once they run out to resources. Indeed, checking the status of the trackers during May 15th 2012, we verified that most of them, while still existing as FQDN, run out of resources and made unavailable by Google. They live as *zombies*, and some BitTorrent clients are still trying to access them.

6. DIMENSIONING THE FQDN CLIST

In Sec. 3, we presented the design of the DNS resolver. One of the key data structures of the DNS resolver is the FQDN Clist. Choosing the correct size for the Clist is critical to the success of DN-Hunter. In this section we will present a methodology to choose the correct value of L (size of the Clist) and the real-time constraint implication.

Fig. 12 shows the Cumulative Distribution Function (CDF) of the "first flow delay", i.e., the time elapsed between the observation of the DNS response directed to *clientIP* and the first packet of the *first* flow directed to one of the *serverIP* addresses in the answer list. Semilog scale is used for the sake of clarity. In all datasets, the first TCP flow is observed

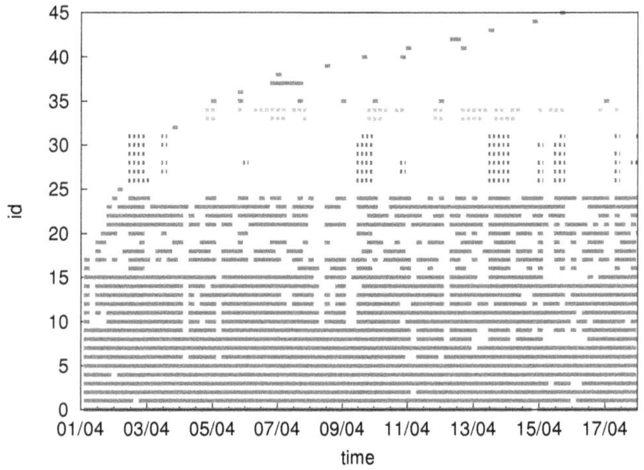

Figure 11: Temporal evolution of the BitTorrent trackers running on Appspot.com. EU1-ADSL2 during live deployment.

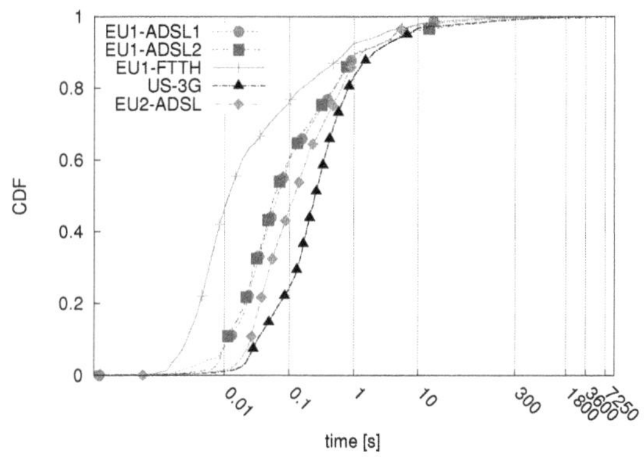

Figure 12: Time elapsed between DNS response and the *first* TCP flow associated to it.

after less than 1s in about 90% of cases. Access technology and sniffer placement impact this measurement; for instance, FTTH exhibits smaller delays, while the 3G technology suffers the largest values.

Interestingly, in all traces, for about 5% of cases the first flow delay is higher than 10s, with some cases larger than 300s. This is usually a result of aggressive pre-fetching performed by applications (e.g., web browsers) that resolve all FQDNs found in the HTML content before a new resource is actually accessed. Tab. 9 quantifies the fraction of "useless" DNS responses, i.e., DNS queries that were not followed by any TCP flow. Surprisingly, about half of DNS resolutions are useless. Mobile terminals are less aggressive thus resulting in lower percentage of useless responses.

Trace	Useless DNS
EU1-ADSL1	46%
EU1-ADSL2	47%
EU1-FTTH	50%
EU2-ADSL	47%
US-3G	30%

Table 9: Fraction of useless DNS resolution.

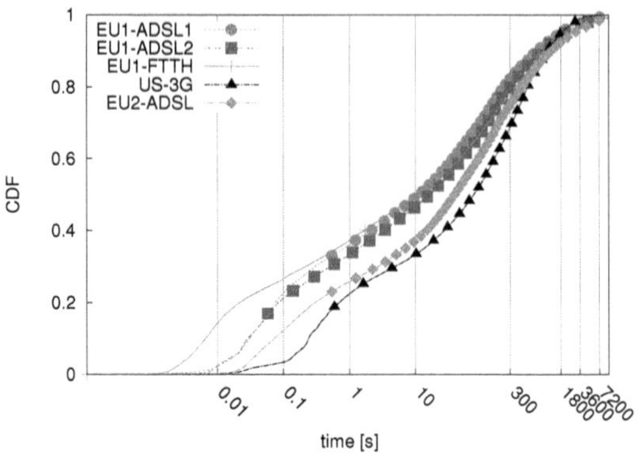

Figure 13: Time elapsed between a DNS response and *any* TCP flow associated to it.

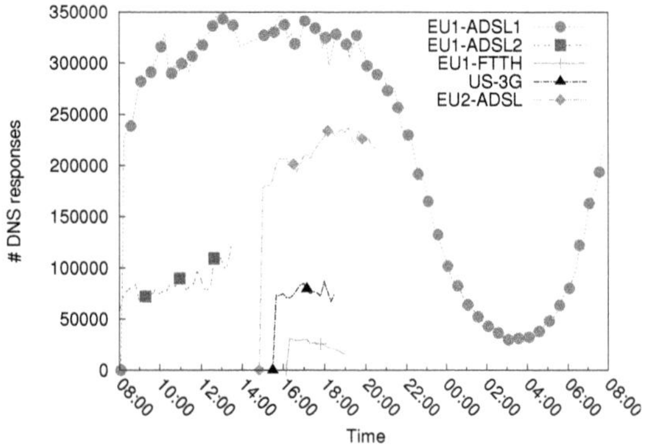

Figure 14: DNS responses observed during a day by intervals of 10 minutes in EU1-ADSL1.

Fig. 13 shows the CDF of the time elapsed between the DNS response and *any* subsequent TCP flow the client establishes to any of the *serverIP* addresses that appeared in the answer list. It reflects the impact of caching lifetime at the local DNS resolver at clients. The initial part of the CDF is strictly related to the first flow delay (Fig. 12); subsequent flows directed to the same FQDN exhibit larger time gaps. Results show that the local resolver caching lifetime can be up to few hours. For instance, to resolve about 98% of flows for which a DNS request is seen, *Clist* must handle an equivalent caching time of about 1 hour.

Fig. 14 shows the total number of DNS responses observed in 10m time bins. As we can see, at the peak time about 350,000 requests in EU1-ADSL1 dataset. In this scenario, considering a desired caching time of 1h, L should be about 2.1M entries to guarantee that the DNS resolver has an efficiency of 98%.

We have also checked the number of *serverIP* addresses returned in each DNS response. Since the *clientIP* can choose any one of the *serverIP* addresses to open the data connection, all of the *serverIP* addresses must be stored in the DNS resolver. The results from all the datasets are very similar with about 40% of responses returning more than one *serverIP* address. About 20-25% of responses include 2-10 different ip-addresses. Most of these are related to servers managed by large CDNs and organizations. For example, up to 16 *serverIPs* are returned when querying any Google FQDN. The maximum number exceeds 30 in very few cases.

Trace	Total Test	Generic coll.	Severe Coll
US-3G	1.3M	0.7%	0.6%
EU2-ADSL	11.9M	0.7%	0.3%
EU1-ADSL1	4.9M	0.01%	0.004%
EU1-ADSL2	2.6M	0.1%	0.05%
EU1-FTTH	680k	1.6%	0.9%

Table 10: DN-Hunter Collision Ratio

6.1 Collision probability in practice

Now we consider the possibility of collisions when the same *clientIP* is accessing two or more FQDNs hosted at the same *serverIP*. DN-Hunter would return the last observed FQDN, thus possibly returning incorrect labels. We call this event a "collision". We examined the traces to see how frequently such situation occurs. We observed was that the most common reason for this is due to HTTP redirection, e.g., *google.com* being redirected to *www.google.com* and then to *www.google.it*, all FQDNs being served by the same *serverIP*. Hence, two types of collisions are possible: (*i*) generic collision, and (*ii*) severe collision. The latter accounts for the cases in which the two conflicting FQDNs have different second level domain names, e.g., *google.com* and *youtube.com*.

Collisions can occur in DN-Hunter when the same *clientIP* address contacts the same *serverIP* address several times during the period of our traces. In the second column of Tab. 10 we report the total number of flows that are potential candidates for collision in DN-Hunter. If the domain name that DN-Hunter return for the two successive flow from the same <*clientIP*, *serverIP*> pair is the same, then we declare that there is no collision. If the returned domain name is different, then we declare that a collision has occurred. If a collision occurs, then we examine the domain names to determine if the collision is a generic one or a severe one. The second column of Tab. 10 reports the total number of potential candidate flows for collision. The third and the fourth columns report the percentage of the potential collision candidates that translate into generic and severe collisions respectively. As we can clearly see, the collision rate is extremely low in all the traces used for evaluation. In fact, we observe that more than 70% of collisions occur within a 1 second interval, suggesting that these collisions could be a result of HTTP redirection. Although, these are collisions might not impact the accuracy of DN-Hunter, in Tab. 10 we still consider them to be collisions and give a conservative estimate. In summary, the problem of collisions has minimal impact on the operational value of DN-Hunter.

Finally, note that it is possible to extend DN-Hunter to return all possible labels associated to a flow instead of only the latest one, thus giving the network administrator the ability to resolve the collisions using more advanced policies than by strictly using the latest FQDN.

6.2 Deployment issue

DN-Hunter is a passive sniffer which assumes to observe DNS and data traffic generated by the end-users. The natural placement of the sniffer is at the network boundaries, where end-users' traffic can be observed. The Flow Sniffer and the DNS Response Sniffer may also be placed at different vantage points, e.g., the latter may be located in front of (or integrated into) the internal DNS server to intercept all DNS queries. Considering DNS traffic sniffing, DNSSEC [3] poses no challenge since it does not provide confidentiality to DNS traffic. DNSCrypt [4], a recent proposal to encrypt DNS traffic, on the contrary, would make the DNS Response Sniffer ineffective. DNSCrypt is not yet widely deployed and it requires significant DNS infrastructure [4] changes to be pragmatic in the near future [5].

DN-Hunter labels TCP flows using $(clientIP, serverIP)$ pair as the key. In scenarios where the same $clientIP$ is shared by multiple end-hosts via NAT/connection sharing tools, DN-Hunter may associate the wrong FQDN to the flow,causing a possible collision. Notice that this can happen only if the end-hosts are initiating connection at almost the same time to the same $serverIP$ (which has been returned when requesting two different FQDN). This can also happen when a end-user is using multiple applications (e.g., multiple browsers windows/tabs opened at the same time) to access different services running on the same $serverIP$ at the same time. We cannot quantify how probable these events are in practice in our traces, and given the very low collision probability (see Sec. 6.1), we expect this to be a marginal problem in the considered scenarios. We argue that in access scenarios where single households are allowed to share the internet connection among few terminals, the collision probability is still marginal. However, in the scenario where there are several hundreds (or thousands) of users behind NAT and the monitoring point for DN-Hunter is after the NAT, DN-Hunter will be severely impaired. Deploying DN-Hunter before the NAT will result in accurate results.

7. RELATED WORK

DNS has been a popular area of research over the past few years. I this section we will highlight the main differences between DN-Hunter and some of the other related works.

The first set of related work focusses on exploring the relationship between CDNs and DNS mainly to study the performance and load balancing strategies in CDNs [6–8]. Ager et al. [9] complement this by proposing an automatic classifier for different types of content hosting and delivery infrastructures. DNS traces actively collected and provided by volunteers are analyzed, in an effort to provide a comprehensive map of the whole Internet. DN-Hunter is similar in spirit, but leverages DNS information in a completely passive manner and focuses on a broader set of analytics.

Similar to our work, [10, 11] focus on the relationship between FQDNs and the applications generating them mainly in the context of botnet detection. However, in DN-Hunter, we mainly focus on identifying and labeling various applications in the Internet. Furthermore, we focus on some advanced analytics to shed light on problems that are critical for untangling the web.

[12] analyze the DNS structure using available DNS information on the wire. The authors define 3 classes of DNS traffic (canonical, overloaded and unwanted), and use the "TreeTop" algorithm to analyze and visualize them in realtime, resulting in a hierarchical representation of IP traffic fractions at different levels of domain names. DN-Hunter goes beyond the visualization of DNS traffic as the set of domain names being used by users in a network, and provides a much richer information to understand today's Internet.

The same authors above extend their analysis on DNS traffic in [13]. Their proposal is similar to the DN-Hunter Sniffer goal, even if not designed to work in real time: flows are labeled with the original resource name derived from the DNS (as in the Flow Database). Then, flows are classified in categories based on the labels of the DNS associated entries. This allows to recover the "volume" of traffic, e.g., going to .com domain, or to apple.com, etc. Authors then focus on the study of breakdown of traffic volumes based on DNS label categories. As presented in the paper, DN-Hunter Analyzer performs much more advanced information recovery out of DNS traffic.

In [14], the authors focus on security issues related to DNS prefetching performed by modern Internet browsers, specifically the fact that someone inspecting DNS traffic can eventually reconstruct the search phrases users input in the search boxes of the browser. Their methodology is somewhat similar to the one DN-Hunter uses to associate tags to network ports, but the objective is completely different.

Note CDN content discovery and mapping the geographical locations of servers is a topic that could have been addressed without the introduced approach. Yet, the major plus of DN-Hunter is that it is completely passive, and very simple. It provides information to the ISP that naturally reflects its end-users habits along with the configuration CDNs adopt for serving traffic generated by ISP's end-users. In other words, it reflects the "current" usage of the network with respect to the traffic and external events (like CDN policy changes).

8. CONCLUSIONS

In this work we have introduced DN-Hunter, a novel tool that links the information found in DNS responses to traffic flows generated during normal Internet usage. Explicitly aimed at discerning the tangle between the content, content providers, and content hosts (CDNs and cloud providers), DN-Hunter unveils how the DNS information can be used to paint a very clear picture, providing invaluable information to network/security operators. In this work, we presented several applications of DN-Hunter, ranging from automated network service classification to dissecting content delivery infrastructures.

As notable examples, we have shown how DN-Hunter is helpful (i) in providing a fine-grained traffic visibility even when the traffic is encrypted (i.e., TLS/SSL flows), (ii) in identifying flows even before the flows begin, thus providing superior network management capabilities to administrators, (iii) in observing and tracking how CDNs and cloud providers host content for a particular resource over time, and (iv) in discerning the services/contents hosted by a CDN or cloud provider. We believe that the applications of DN-Hunter the Analyzer in particular, are not limited to the ones presented in this work, and novel applications can leverage the information exposed by the labeled flows database.

DN-Hunter has been deployed in actual ISP networks, providing network administrators enhanced traffic visibility and the ability to perform detailed forensics if required. A key challenge for the future is to devise automatic algorithms to mine the amount of data exposed by DN-Hunter and by network monitoring tools in general. We believe that this challenge is common to the network monitoring and measurement community, and modern tools have to be devised to dig into this enormous volume of data.

Acknowledgments

The research leading to these results has received funding from Narus Inc. and from the European Commission under the Seventh Framework Programme (FP7 2007-2013) with the Grant Agreement n. 318627 - Integrated Project "mPlane - an Intelligent Measurement Plane for Future Network and Application Management".

9. REFERENCES

[1] V. Gehlen, A. Finamore, M. Mellia, and M. Munafò. Uncovering the big players of the web. In *TMA Workshop*, pages 15–28, Vienna, AT, 2012.

[2] A. Finamore, M. Mellia, M. Meo, M.M. Munafo, and D. Rossi. Experiences of internet traffic monitoring with tstat. *Network, IEEE*, Vol.25, N.3, pages 8–14, May 2011.

[3] R. Arends et. Al. RFC 4033 - DNS Security Introduction and Requirements, March 2005.

[4] Introducing DNSCrypt (Preview Release), February 2011. `http://www.opendns.com/technology/dnscrypt/`

[5] B. Ager, H. Dreger, and A. Feldmann. Predicting the DNSSEC Overhead using DNS Traces. In *40th Annual Conference on Information Sciences and Systems*, pages 1484–1489. IEEE, 2006.

[6] S. Triukose, Z. Wen, and M. Rabinovich. Measuring a Commercial Content Delivery Network. In *ACM WWW*, pages 467–476., Hyderabad, IN, 2011.

[7] A.J. Su, D.R. Choffnes, A. Kuzmanovic, and F.E. Bustamante. Drafting Behind Akamai: Inferring Network Conditions Based on CDN Redirections. *IEEE/ACM Transactions on Networking*, Vol.17, N. 6, pages 1752–1765, 2009.

[8] C. Huang, A. Wang, J. Li, and K.W. Ross. Measuring and Evaluating Large-scale CDNs. In *ACM IMC*, pages 15–29, Vouliagmeni, GR, 2008.

[9] B. Ager, W. Mühlbauer, G. Smaragdakis, and S. Uhlig. Web Content Cartography. *ACM IMC*, pages 585–600, Berlin, DE, 2011.

[10] H. Choi, H. Lee, H. Lee, and H. Kim. Botnet Detection by Monitoring Group Activities in DNS Traffic. In *IEEE CIT* , pages 715–720., Fukushima, JP, 2007.

[11] S. Yadav, A.K.K. Reddy, AL Reddy, and S. Ranjan. Detecting Algorithmically Generated Malicious Domain Names. In *ACM IMC*, pages 48–61., Melbourne, AU, 2010.

[12] D. Plonka and P. Barford. Context-aware Clustering of DNS Query Traffic. In *ACM IMC*, pages 217–230., Vouliagmeni, GR, 2008.

[13] D. Plonka and P. Barford. Flexible Traffic and Host Profiling via DNS Rendezvous. In *Workshop SATIN*, 2011.

[14] S. Krishnan and F. Monrose. An Empirical Study of the Performance, Security and Privacy Implications of Domain Name Prefetching. In *IEEE/IFIP DSN*, Boston, MA, 2011.

Taster's Choice: A Comparative Analysis of Spam Feeds

Andreas Pitsillidis* apitsill@cs.ucsd.edu
Chris Kanich† ckanich@cs.uic.edu
Geoffrey M. Voelker* voelker@cs.ucsd.edu
Kirill Levchenko* klevchen@cs.ucsd.edu
Stefan Savage* savage@cs.ucsd.edu

*Department of Computer Science and Engineering
University of California, San Diego

†Department of Computer Science
University of Illinois at Chicago

ABSTRACT

E-mail spam has been the focus of a wide variety of measurement studies, at least in part due to the plethora of spam data sources available to the research community. However, there has been little attention paid to the suitability of such data sources for the kinds of analyses they are used for. In spite of the broad range of data available, most studies use a single "spam feed" and there has been little examination of how such feeds may differ in content. In this paper we provide this characterization by comparing the contents of ten distinct contemporaneous feeds of spam-advertised domain names. We document significant variations based on how such feeds are collected and show how these variations can produce differences in findings as a result.

Categories and Subject Descriptors

E.m [**Data**]: Miscellaneous; H.3.5 [**Information Storage and Retrieval**]: On-line Information Services

General Terms

Measurement, Security

Keywords

Spam e-mail, Measurement, Domain blacklists

1. INTRODUCTION

It is rare in the measurement of Internet-scale phenomena that one is able to make comprehensive observations. Indeed, much of our community is by nature opportunistic: we try to extract the most value from the data that is available. However, implicit in such research is the assumption that the available data is *sufficient* to reach conclusions about the phenomena at scale. Unfortunately, this is not always the case and some datasets are too small or too biased to be used for all purposes. In this paper, we explore this issue in the context of a common security measurement domain: e-mail spam.

On the one hand e-mail spam is plentiful—everyone gets it—and thus is deceptively easy to gather. At the same time, the scale of the e-mail spam problem is enormous. Industry estimates (admittedly based on unknown methodology) suggest that spammers sent well over 100 billion e-mails each day in 2010 [16]. If true, then even a spam corpus consisting of 100,000 messages per day would constitute only *one ten thousandth of one percent* of what occurred globally. Thus, except for researchers at the very largest e-mail providers, we are all forced to make extrapolations by many orders of magnitude when generalizing from available spam data sources. Further, in making these extrapolations, we must assume both that our limited samples are sufficiently unbiased to capture the general behavior faithfully and that the behavior is large enough to be resolved via our measurements (concretely, that spam is dominated by small collections of large players and not vice versa). However, we are unaware of any systematic attempt to date to examine these assumptions and how they relate to commonly used data sources.

To explore these questions, we compare contemporaneous spam data from ten different data feeds, both academic and commercial, gathered using a broad range of different collection methodologies. To address differences in content, we focus on the Internet domain names advertised by spam messages in such feeds, using them as a *key* to identify like messages. Using this corpus, corresponding to over a billion messages distributed over three months, we characterize the relationships between its constituent data sources. In particular, we explore four questions about "feed quality": purity (how much of a given feed is actually spam?), coverage (what fraction of spam is captured in any particular feed?), timing (can a feed can be used to determine the start and end of a spam campaign?) and proportionality (can one use a single feed to accurately estimate the relative volume of different campaigns?).

Overall, we find that there are significant differences across distinct spam feeds and that these differences can frequently defy intuition. For example, our lowest-volume data source (comprising just over 10 million samples) captures more spam-advertised domain names than all other feeds combined (even though these other feeds contain two orders of magnitude more samples). Moreover, we find that these differences in turn translate into analysis limitations; not all feeds are good for answering all questions. In the remainder of this paper, we place this problem in context, describe our data sources

IMC'12, November 14–16, 2012, Boston, Massachusetts, USA.

and analysis, and summarize some best practices for future spam measurement studies.

2. BACKGROUND

E-mail spam is perhaps the only Internet security phenomenon that leaves no one untouched. Everybody gets spam. Both this visibility and the plentiful nature of spam have naturally conspired to support a vast range of empirical measurement studies. Some of these have focused on how to best filter spam [3, 5, 7], others on the botnets used to deliver spam [11, 30, 42], and others on the goals of spam, whether used as a vector for phishing [25], malware [12, 22] or, most commonly, advertising [17, 18].

These few examples only scratch the surface, but importantly this work is collectively not only diverse in its analyses aims, but also in the range of data sources used to drive those same conclusions. Among the spam sources included in such studies are the authors' own spam e-mail [3, 44], static spam corpora of varied provenance (e.g., Enron, TREC2005, CEAS2008) [10, 26, 34, 41, 44], open mail proxies or relays [9, 28, 29], botnet output [11, 30], abandoned e-mail domains [2, 13], collections of abandoned e-mail accounts [39], spam automatically filtered at a university mail server [4, 31, 35, 40], spam-fed URL blacklists [24], spam identified by humans in a large Web-mail system [42, 43], spam e-mail filtered by a small mail service provider [32], spam e-mail filtered by a modest ISP [6] and distributed collections of honeypot e-mail accounts [36].

These data sources can vary considerably in volume — some may collect millions of spam messages per day, while others may gather several orders of magnitude fewer. Intuitively, it seems as though a larger data feed is likely to provide better coverage of the spam ecosystem (although, as we will show, this intuition is misleading). However, an equally important concern is how differences in the *manner* by which spam is collected and reported may impact the *kind* of spam that is found.

To understand how this may be, it is worth first reflecting on the operational differences in spamming strategies. A spammer must both obtain an address list of targets and arrange for e-mail delivery. Each of these functions can be pursued in different ways, optimized for different strategies. For example, some spammers compile or obtain enormous "low-quality" address lists [15] (e.g., based on brute force address generation, harvesting of Web sites, etc.), many of which may not even be valid, while others purchase higher quality address lists that target a more precise market (e.g., customers who have purchased from an online pharmacy before). Similarly, some spam campaigns are "loud" and use large botnets to distribute billions of messages (with an understanding that the vast majority will be filtered [12]) while other campaigns are smaller and quieter, focusing on "deliverability" by evading spam filters.

These differences in spammer operations in turn can interact with differences in collection methodology. For example, spam collected via MX honeypots (accepting all SMTP connections to a quiescent domain) will likely contain broadly targeted spam campaigns and few false positives, while e-mail manually tagged by human recipients (e.g., by clicking on a "this is spam" button in the mail client) may self-select for "high quality" spam that evades existing automated filters, but also may include legal, non-bulk commercial mail that is simply unwanted by the recipient.

In addition to properties of how spam data is *collected*, how the data is *reported* can also introduce additional limitations. For example, some data feeds may include the full contents of e-mail messages, but many providers are unwilling to do so due to privacy concerns. Instead, some may redact some of the address information, while, even more commonly, others will only provide information about the spam-advertised URLs contained with a message. Even within URL-only feeds there can be considerable differences. Some data providers may include full spam-advertised URLs, while others scrub the data to only provide the fully-qualified domain name (particularly for non-honeypot data, due to concern about side-effects from crawling such data). Sometimes data is reported in raw form, with a data record for each and every spam message, but in other cases providers aggregate and summarize. For example, some providers will de-duplicate identically advertised domains within a given time window, and domain-based blacklists may only provide a single record for each such advertised domain.

Taken together, all of these differences suggest that different kinds of data feeds may be more or less useful for answering particular kinds of questions. It is the purpose of this paper to put this hypothesis on an empirical footing.

3. DATA AND METHODOLOGY

In this work we compare ten distinct sources of spam data (which we call *feeds*), ranging in their level of detail from full e-mail content to only domain names of URLs in messages. Comparisons between feeds are by necessity limited to the lowest common denominator, namely domain names. In the remainder of this paper we treat each feed as a source of spam-advertised domains, regardless of any additional information available.

By comparing feeds at the granularity of domain names, we are implicitly restricting ourselves to spam containing URLs, that is, spam that is a Web-oriented advertisement in nature, at the exclusion of some less common classes of spam (e.g., malware distribution or advance fee fraud). Fortunately, such advertising spam is the dominant class of spam today.[1]

3.1 Domains

Up to this point, we have been using the term "domain" very informally. Before going further, however, let us say more precisely what we mean: a *registered domain*—in this paper, simply a *domain*—is the part of a fully-qualified domain name that its owner registered with the registrar. For the most common top-level domains, such as COM, BIZ, and EDU, this is simply the second-level domain (e.g., "ucsd.edu"). All domain names at or below the level of registered domain (e.g., "cs.ucsd.edu") are administered by the registrant, while all domain names above (e.g., "edu") are administered by the registry. Blacklisting generally operates at the level of registered domains, because a spammer can create an arbitrary number of names under the registered domain name to frustrate fine-grained blacklisting below the level of registered domains.

[1]One recent industry report [37] places Web-oriented advertising spam for pharmaceuticals at over 93% of all total spam volume.

3.2 Types of Spam Domain Sources

The spam domain sources used in this study fall into five categories: botnet-collected, MX honeypots, seeded honey accounts, human identified, and blacklists. Each category comes with its own unique characteristics, limitations and tradeoffs that we discuss briefly here.

Botnet. Botnet datasets result from capturing instances of bot software and executing them in a monitored, controlled environment such that the e-mail they attempt to send is collected instead. Since the e-mail collected is only that sent by the botnet, such datasets are highly "pure": they have no false positives under normal circumstances.[2] Moreover, if we assume that all members of a botnet are used in a homogeneous fashion, then monitoring a single bot is sufficient for identifying the spamming behavior of the entire botnet. Botnet data is also highly accessible since a researcher can run an instance of the malware and obtain large amounts of botnet spam without requiring a relationship with any third-party security, mail or network provider [11]. Moreover, since many studies have documented that a small number of botnets are the primary source of spam e-mail messages, in principle such datasets should be ideally suited for spam studies [11, 21, 30]. Finally, these datasets have the advantage of often being high volume, since botnets are usually very aggressive in their output rate.

MX honeypot. MX honeypot spam is the result of configuring the MX record for a domain to point to an SMTP server that accepts all inbound messages. Depending on how these domains are obtained and advertised, they may select for different kinds of spam. For example, a newly registered domain will only capture spam using address lists created via brute force (i.e., sending mail to popular user names at every domain with a valid MX). By contrast, MX honeypots built using abandoned domains or domains that have become quiescent over time may attract a broader set of e-mail, but also may inadvertently collect legitimate correspondence arising from the domain's prior use. In general MX honeypots have low levels of false positives, but since their accounts are not in active use they will only tend to capture spam campaigns that are very broadly targeted and hence have high volume. Since high-volume campaigns are easier to detect, these same campaigns are more likely to be rejected by anti-spam filters. Thus, some of the most prevalent spam in MX-based feeds may not appear frequently in Web mail or enterprise e-mail inboxes.

Seeded honey accounts. Like MX honeypots, seeded honey accounts capture unsolicited e-mail to accounts whose sole purpose is to receive spam (hence minimizing false positives). However, unlike MX honeypots, honey accounts are created across a range of e-mail providers, and are not limited to addresses affiliated with a small number of domains. However, since these e-mail addresses must also be seeded—distributed across a range of vectors that spammers may use to harvest e-mail address lists (e.g., such as forums, Web sites and mailing lists)—the "quality" of a honey account feed is related both to the number of accounts and how well the accounts are seeded. The greater operational cost of creating and seeding these accounts means that researchers generally obtain honey account spam feeds from third parties (frequently commercial anti-spam providers).

Honey accounts also have many of the same limitations as MX-based feeds. Since the accounts are not active, such feeds are unlikely to capture spam campaigns targeted using social network information (i.e., by friends lists of real e-mail users) or by mailing lists obtained from compromised machines [14]. Thus, such feeds mainly include low-quality campaigns that focus on volume and consequently are more likely to be captured by anti-spam filters.

Human identified. These feed are those in which humans actively nominate e-mail messages as being examples of spam, typically through a built-in mail client interface (i.e., a "this is spam" button). Moreover, since it is primarily large Web mail services that provide such user interfaces, these datasets also typically represent the application of human-based classification at very large scale (in our case hundreds of millions of e-mail accounts). For the same reason, human identified spam feeds are not broadly available and their use is frequently limited to large Web mail providers or their close external collaborators.

Human identified spam feeds are able to capture "high quality" spam since, by definition, messages that users were able to manually classify must also have evaded any automated spam filters. As mentioned before, however, such feeds may underrepresent the high-volume campaigns since they will be pre-filtered before any human encounters them. Another limitation is that individuals do not have a uniform definition of what "spam" means and thus human identified spam can include legitimate commercial e-mail as well (i.e., relating to an existing commercial relationship with the recipient). Finally, temporal signals in human-identified spamfeeds are distorted because identification occurs at human time scales.

Domain blacklists. Domain blacklists are the last category of spam-derived data we consider and are the most opaque since the method by which they are gathered is generally not documented publicly.[3] In a sense, blacklists are meta-feeds that can be driven by different combinations of spam source data based on the organization that maintains them. Among the advantages of such feeds, they tend to be broadly available (generally for a nominal fee) and, because they are used for operational purposes, they are professionally maintained. Unlike the other feeds we have considered, blacklists represent domains in a binary fashion—either a domain is on the blacklist at time t or it is not. Consequently, while they are useful for identifying a range of spam-advertised domains, they are a poor source for investigating questions such as spam volume.

While these are not the only kinds of spam feeds in use by researchers (notably omitting automatically filtered spam taken from mail servers, which we did not pursue in our work due to privacy concerns), they capture some of the most popular spam sources as well as a range of collection mechanisms.

3.3 False Positives

No spam source is pure and all feeds contain false positives. In addition to feed-specific biases (discussed above), there is a range of other reasons why a domain name appearing in a spam feed may have little to do with spam.

[2]However, see Section 4.1 for an example of domain poisoning carried out by the Rustock botnet.

[3]However, they are necessarily based on some kind of real-time spam data since their purpose is to identify spam-advertised domains that can then be used as a dynamic feature in e-mail filtering algorithms.

Feed	Type	Domains	Unique
Hu	Human identified	10,733,231	1,051,211
URIBL	Blacklist	n/a	144,758
DBL	Blacklist	n/a	413,392
MX_1	MX honeypot	32,548,304	100,631
MX_2	MX honeypot	198,871,030	2,127,164
MX_3	MX honeypot	12,517,244	67,856
Ac_1	Seeded honey accounts	30,991,248	79,040
Ac_2	Seeded honey accounts	73,614,895	35,506
Bot	Botnet	158,038,776	13,588,727
Hyb	Hybrid	451,603,575	1,315,292

Table 1: Summary of spam domain sources (feeds) used in this paper. The first column gives the feed mnemonic used throughout.

First, false positives occur when legitimate messages are inadvertently mixed into the data stream. This mixing can happen for a variety of reasons. For example, MX domains that are lexically similar to other domains may inadvertently receive mail due to sender typos (see Gee and Kim for one analysis of this behavior [8]). The same thing can occur with honeypot accounts (but this time due to username typos). We have also experienced MX honeypots receiving legitimate messages due to a user specifying the domain in a dummy e-mail address created to satisfy a sign-up requirement for an online service (we have found this to be particularly an issue with simple domain names such as "test.com").

The other major source of feed pollution is chaff domains: legitimate domains that are not themselves being advertised but co-occur in spam messages. In some cases these are purposely inserted to undermine spam filters (a practice well documented by Xie *et al.* [42]), in other cases they are simply used to support the message itself (e.g., image hosting) or are non-referenced organic parts of the message formatting (e.g., DTD reference domains such as w3.org or microsoft.com). Finally, to bypass domain-based blacklists some spam messages will advertise "landing" domains that in turn redirect to the Web site truly being promoted. These landing domains are typically either compromised legitimate Web sites, free hosting Web services (e.g., Google's Blogspot, Windows Live domains or Yahoo's groups) or Web services that provide some intrinsic redirection capability (e.g., bit.ly) [18]. We discuss in more detail how these issues impact our feeds in Section 4.1.

3.4 Meet the Feeds

Table 1 lists the feeds used in this study. We assign each feed a concise label (e.g., Ac_2) identifying its type, as described earlier. Of these ten feeds, we collected MX_1 and Bot directly. We receive both blacklist feeds (DBL and URIBL) by subscription. Provider agreements preclude us from naming the remaining feeds (Ac_1, MX_2, Ac_2, MX_3, Hyb, Hu). One feed, Hyb, we identify as a "hybrid." We do not know the exact collection methodology it uses, but we believe it is a hybrid of multiple methods and we label it as such.

Referring to Table 1, the *Domains* column shows the total number of samples we received from the feed during the three-month period under consideration. Thus, the Hu feed included only a bit over ten million samples, while the Bot feed produced over ten times that number. The *Unique* column gives the number of unique registered domain names in the feed.

With the exception of the two blacklists, we collected the feeds used in this paper in the context of the Click Trajectories project [18] between August 1st, 2010 and October 31st, 2010. The Click Trajectories project measured the full set of resources involved in monetizing spam—what we call the spam value chain. One of the resources in the value chain is Web hosting. To identify the Web hosting infrastructure, we visited the spam-advertised sites using a full-fidelity Web crawler (a specially instrumented version of Firefox), following all redirections to the final storefront page. We then identified each storefront using a set of hand-generated content signatures, thus allowing us to link each spam URL to the goods it was advertising.

We use the results of this Web crawl to determine whether a spam domain, at the time it is advertised, led to a live Web site.[4] Furthermore, we determined if this site was the storefront of either a known online pharmacy selling generic versions of popular medications, a known replica luxury goods store, or a known "OEM" software store selling unlicensed versions of popular software. These three categories — pharmaceuticals, replica goods, software — are among the most popular classes of goods advertised via spam [18, 20]. Based on this information, we refer to domains as *live* if at least one URL containing the domain led to a live Web site, and *tagged* if the site was a known storefront.

Finally, because we obtained the blacklist feeds after the completion of the Click Trajectories work, we could not systematically crawl all of their domains. Thus the entries listed in the table only include the subset that *also* occurred in one of the eight base feeds. While this bias leads us to undercount the domains in each feed (thus underrepresenting their diversity), this effect is likely to be small. The DBL feed contained 13,175 additional domains that did not occur in any of our other base feeds (roughly 3% of its feed volume) while the URIBL feed contained only 3,752 such domains (2.5% of its feed volume).

4. ANALYSIS

We set out to better understand the differences among sources of spam domains available to the researcher or practitioner. The value of a spam domain feed, whether used in a production system for filtering mail or in a measurement study, ultimately lies in how well it captures the characteristics of spam. In this paper we consider four qualities: *purity*, *coverage*, *proportionality*, and *timing*.

Purity is a measure of how much of a feed is actually spam domains, rather than benign or non-existent domains.

Coverage measures how much spam is captured by a feed. That is, if one were to use the feed as an oracle for classifying spam, coverage would measure how much spam is correctly classified by the oracle.

Proportionality is how accurately a feed captures not only the domains appearing in spam, but also their relative frequency. If one were tasked with identifying the top 10 most spammed domains, for example, proportionality would be the metric of interest.

Timing is a measure of how accurately the feed represents the period during which a domain appears in spam.

[4]With feeds containing URLs, we visited the received URL. Otherwise, for feeds containing domains only, we prepended `http://` to the domain to form a URL.

Feed	DNS	HTTP	Tagged	ODP	Alexa
Hu	88%	55%	6%	1%	1%
DBL	100%	72%	11%	<1%	<1%
URIBL	100%	85%	22%	2%	2%
MX_1	96%	83%	20%	9%	8%
MX_2	6%	5%	<1%	<1%	<1%
MX_3	97%	83%	16%	9%	7%
Ac_1	95%	82%	20%	8%	5%
Ac_2	96%	88%	33%	10%	11%
Bot	<1%	<1%	<1%	<1%	<1%
Hyb	64%	51%	2%	12%	10%

Table 2: Positive and negative indicators of feed purity. See Section 4.1 for discussion.

Most often with timing we care about how quickly a domain appears in the feed after it appears in spam in the wild.

Unfortunately, all of the measures above presuppose the existence of an ultimate "ground truth," a platonic absolute against which all feeds can be compared. Sadly, we have no such feed: barring the challenges of even defining what such a feed would contain, the practical difficulty of capturing all spam (however defined) is immense. We can still gain useful insight, however, by comparing feeds to each other. In particular, for coverage and timing, we combine all of our feeds into one aggregate super-feed, taking it as our ideal. For proportionality, we measure the relative frequency of spam domains in incoming mail seen by a large Web mail provider, allowing us to compare the relative frequencies of domains in a spam feed to their frequencies in a representative e-mail feed.

In the remainder of this section, we evaluate the spam domain feeds available to us (summarized in Table 1) with respect to the qualities described above.

4.1 Purity

The purity of a feed is a measure of how much of the feed is actually spam, rather than benign or non-existent domains. Very simply, purity is the fraction of the feed that are spam domains. We refer to these spam domains appearing in the feed as *true positives*, and non-spam domains appearing in the feed as *false positives*. Purity is thus akin to *precision* in Information Retrieval or *positive predictive value* in Statistics.

The importance of purity varies from application to application. If the feed is used to directly filter spam (by marking any message containing a domain appearing in the feed as spam), then purity is of paramount importance. On the other hand, for a measurement study, where spam domains are visited and further analyzed, low purity may tax the measurement system, but generally has little impact on the results once filtered.

Operationally, the nature of the false positives matters as well. While non-existent domains appearing in the feed are merely a nuisance, benign domains can lead to highly undesirable false positives in the filtering context.

Table 2 shows several purity indicators for each feed. The first three (*DNS*, *HTTP*, and *Tagged*) are positive indicators—larger numbers mean higher purity. The last two (Alexa and ODP) are negative indicators, with larger numbers meaning lower purity.

4.1.1 Non-existent Domains

The DNS column shows the proportion of domains in the feed that were registered, based on several major TLDs. Specifically, we checked the DNS zone files for the COM, NET, ORG, BIZ, US, AERO, and INFO top-level domains between April 2009 and March 2012, which bracket the measurement period by 16 months before and 16 months after. Together these TLDs covered between 63% and 100% of each feed. We report the number of domains in these TLDs that appeared in the zone file.

Blacklists, seeded honey accounts, and two of the three MX honeypot feeds consisted largely of real domains (over 95%). Human-identified spam and the hybrid feed were lower, at 88% and 64%, levels at which non-registered domains pose little harm operationally or experimentally.

Two feeds—Bot and MX_2—exhibit unusually low registration levels, however. Most of these relate to a single phenomenon, a period of several weeks during which the Rustock botnet was sending randomly-generated domains [19, 38]. Such bogus domains cost spammers nearly nothing to generate, while costing spam filter maintainers and spam researchers considerably more in dealing with them.

The HTTP column shows the fraction of domains in the feed that responded to an HTTP request (with a code 200 reply) made to any of the URLs received from the feed during the measurement period. Like the DNS registration measure, HTTP responses indicate that a feed contains live URLs (whether spam or not). Some amount of HTTP failures are inevitable, and we see success rates in the 51% to 88% range for most feeds, with the exception of the same two feeds—Bot and MX_2—discussed above.

4.1.2 Known Spam

An HTTP response still does not mean that a domain is not a benign domain accidentally included in the list. To get at the true spam domains, we turn to the Web content tagging carried out in the context of the Click Trajectories project [18]. Recall from Section 3.4 that these are domains that lead to storefronts associated with known online pharmacies, replica stores, or software stores.

Such domains constituted 11–33% of domains in high-purity feeds. Note that while these domains are less than a third of all domains in a feed, they cover the bulk of the spam by volume [18].

4.1.3 Benign Domains

Finally, the ODP and Alexa columns indicate the number of domains in the feed that appeared in Open Directory Project [27] listings and the Alexa top 1 million Web sites [1] list. We expect that nearly all of these domains are benign, and their appearance in a feed is erroneous.[5]

There are at least three reasons why a benign domain might appear in spam. Benign domains may be included in a message by the spammer. A phishing e-mail, for example, may contain some legitimate links to the service being phished. In some cases, a legitimate e-mail may be inadvertently sent to a honeypot or honey account. For example, if an MX honey-

[5]While nothing prohibits a spam domain from appearing on the Alexa list or in the Open Directory listings, these domains are usually short-lived because their utility, and therefore use, is reduced with domain blacklisting. We expect both lists to be overwhelmingly composed of domains incompatible with spam advertising.

pot uses an abandoned, previously-used domain, it may still receive legitimate traffic from its former life. A third cause of benign domains appearing in spam are legitimate services being used by the spammer as a redirection mechanism. By using a URL shortening service, for example, the spammer can evade domain blacklists by hiding behind an established domain.

Using spam domain feeds to drive a production spam filtering system thus runs the risk of false positives. Because blacklists are intended specifically for this task, they have the fewest false positives: only 2% of domains in the URIBL feed, and less than 1% of DBL domains, intersected the ODP and Alexa lists.

4.1.4 Removing Impurities

In the analysis ahead of us, these impurities skew the results and thus obscure the picture. To better understand the useful contributions of each feed, we remove all non-responsive domains and all domains we believe are likely benign. Specifically, for each feed, we take only the set of domains for which we receive at least one successful HTTP response and from this set remove all domains appearing on the Open Directory and Alexa list. (These are the domains listed in the *HTTP* column of Table 2 less those counted in the *ODP* and *Alexa* columns.) We call these ***live*** domains.

In several instances, data collected by the Click Trajectories project [18] allows us to see deeper into the nature of domain, namely into the affiliate programs and affiliates behind each domain. For this analysis, however, we are limited to the set of ***tagged*** domains. We remove Alexa and ODP domains from this set as well. Table 3 shows the number of distinct domains of each type in the feed. In the remainder of the paper, we state explicitly whether a measurement uses live or tagged domains.

We have chosen to explicitly remove Alexa-listed and ODP-listed domains from the set of live and tagged domains used in the remainder of the paper. As discussed in Section 4.1.3, live and even tagged domains may contain domains in the Alexa and ODP listings. An otherwise benign domain may be tagged if it is abused by a spammer as a redirection mechanism, as noted above. Unfortunately, the stakes are high when it comes to such false positives. These same Alexa and ODP domains—comprising less than 2% of the domains in a blacklist—are disproportionately more popular than spam domains. Figure 3 shows the fraction of spam messages containing such domains. In many feeds, these handful of benign domains comprise as much as 90% of live domain volume. Working at the granularity of registered domains, even a single URL redirecting to a spam site can affect the standing of an entire domain.

Practitioners must take great care in choosing which domains to blacklist and whether to blacklist each instance at the registered name or finer granularity. It is not the purpose of this paper, however, to design the perfect blacklist or blacklisting mechanism, and so we leave the question of how best to deal with potential false positives without a full and satisfactory resolution. For our analysis, we take the conservative approach and remove such suspect domains.

4.2 Coverage

Roughly speaking, coverage is a measure of how many spam domains a feed contains. In an operational context, greater coverage—more spam domains—means more spam filtered. For a measurement study or system evaluation, more spam domains means more comprehensive results. In this section, we consider how coverage varies across our ten spam domain feeds. But domains do not exist in a vacuum: they are a projection of external entities into the domain name system, and it is often these entities that are the object of our interest. In the world of spam, these take the form of affiliate programs and affiliates. In Section 4.2.3 we compare feeds on the visibility they provide into that world.

4.2.1 Domains

Table 3 shows the number of live and tagged domains in each feed in the *Total* column. Recall that *live* domains are those that resulted in at least one successful Web visit to a URL containing the domain, while *tagged* domains are those for which the final Web site is a known storefront (Section 3.4).

In absolute terms, whether one considers live domains or tagged domains, the largest contributor of unique instances is the human-identified spam domain feed Hu, despite also being the smallest feed in terms of absolute volume (see Table 1). The reason for this coverage is undoubtedly that this particular provider has hundreds of millions of accounts and thus their customers are likely to be targets of virtually any spam campaign. In turn, we believe that the reason this feed has low volume is that as users identify e-mails as "spammy" the included domains are used to filter subsequent inbound messages. Thus, high-volume campaigns are unlikely to have high representation in such a feed.

Clearly, if one had to choose only one feed to provide maximum coverage, it would be that feed. Unfortunately, outside large mail providers, such data is not widely available to the research community. Instead, the readily-available blacklists—DBL and URIBL—are an excellent alternative, providing more tagged domains than any other feed besides Hu.

Exclusive domains. So far, we have been comparing feeds in terms of their absolute coverage: the total number of spam domains contributed. Given a choice of one feed, one may well pick the largest one by this measure. A feed's value, however, may be in its differential contribution, that is, in the domains it provides that are in no other feed. We term domains that occur in exactly one feed *exclusive* domains. Across our feeds, 60% of all live domains and 19% of all tagged domains were exclusive to a single feed.

Table 3 shows number of exclusive domains provided by each feed in the *Excl.* column. The relationship between the numbers of distinct domains in a feed and the number of exclusive domains is also shown graphically in Figure 1; the left plot shows this relationship for live domains, and the right plot shows it for tagged domains. In both plots, the x axis denotes to the number of distinct domains on a logarithmic scale, while the y axis denotes number of exclusive domains in each feed on a logarithmic scale. Dotted lines denote fixed exclusive domain proportions. For example, the Hyb feed lies just under the 100% line, indicating that most of its live domains—just over 65%—are exclusive.

Figure 1 makes apparent that the Hu and Hyb feeds make the greatest contribution in terms of the distinct number of domains they contribute as well as the number of domains exclusive to each feed. The number of tagged domains is about an order of magnitude less in each feed than the number of live domains, suggesting that spam belonging to

	All Domains		Live Domains		Tagged Domains	
Feed	Total	Excl.	Total	Excl.	Total	Excl.
Hu	1,051,211	534,060	564,946	191,997	64,116	11,356
DBL	413,355	0	298,685	0	46,058	0
URIBL	144,721	0	119,417	0	30,891	0
MX_1	100,631	4,523	72,634	1,434	19,482	29
MX_2	2,127,164	1,975,081	93,638	6,511	18,055	4
MX_3	67,856	6,870	49,659	2,747	10,349	2
Ac_1	79,040	3,106	58,002	798	15,242	2
Ac_2	35,506	3,049	26,567	972	11,244	31
Bot	13,588,727	13,540,855	21,265	3,728	2,448	0
Hyb	1,315,292	1,069,074	496,893	322,215	25,993	1,285

Table 3: Feed domain coverage showing total number of distinct domains (*Total* column) and number of domains exclusive to a feed (*Excl.* column).

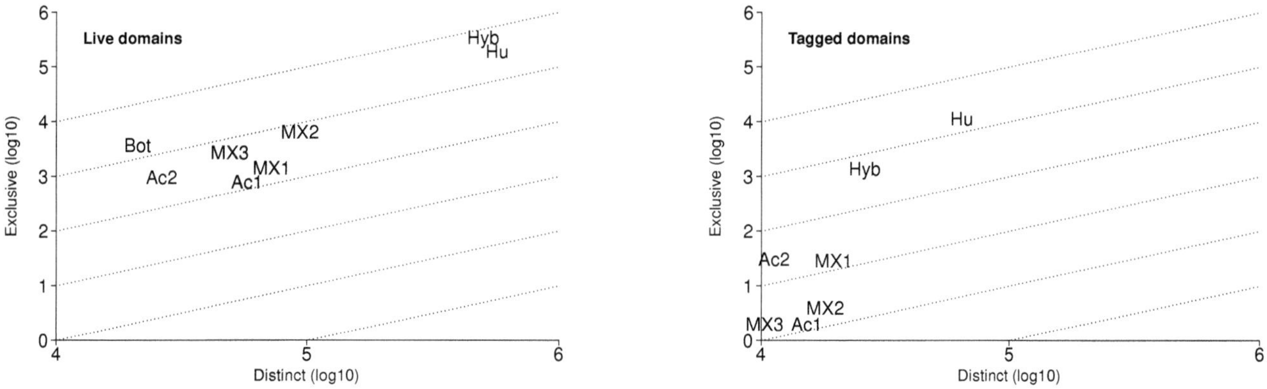

Figure 1: Relationship between the total number of domains contributed by each feed and the number of domains exclusive to each.

the categories represented by the tagged domains—online pharmacies, replica shops, and counterfeit software stores—is a small fraction of all spam. This is not so, however. As we will see in Section 4.3, these domains dominate the feeds in volume.

Figure 1 and Table 3 put the Bot feed in perspective. Although extremely valuable in identifying which domains are being spammed by which botnet, its contribution to the big picture is more limited. None of its tagged domains were exclusive, not a surprising fact given that bots are renowned for indiscriminate high-volume spamming. The roughly 3,700 exclusive live domains in the Bot feed are likely the result of the domain poisoning described earlier (Section 4.1), as fewer than 1% of all domains were legitimate (Table 2).

Pairwise comparison. In the preceding discussion of exclusive contribution, we were implicitly asking which feed, if it were excluded, would be missed the most. Next we consider the question of each feed's differential contribution with respect to another feed. Equivalently, we are asking how many domains from one feed are also in another. (Removing non-responsive and benign domains is particularly important for a meaningful comparison here.)

Figure 2 shows pairwise domain overlap as a matrix, with live domains plotted on the left and tagged domains on the right. For two feeds A and B, the cell in row A column B shows how many domains (percent) from feed B are in feed A, as well as the absolute number of such domains. Formally, the top and bottom numbers show

$$|A \cap B|/|B| \quad \text{and} \quad |A \cap B|.$$

For example, in the left-hand matrix, the cell in row Ac_1 column MX_1 indicates that Ac_1 and MX_1 have approximately 47,000 live domains in common, and that this number is 65% of the MX_1 feed. Note that these same 47,000 live domains constitute 81% of the Ac_1 feed (row MX_1 column Ac_1). In addition, the right-most column, labeled *All* contains the union of all domains across all feeds. The numbers in the *All* column thus indicate what proportion of all spam domains (the union of all feeds) is covered by a given feed.

Figure 2 once again highlights the coverage of the Hu and Hyb feeds. The Hyb feed covers 51% of all live domains (the union of all non-blacklist feeds), while the Hu feed covers 58%; the two feeds together covering 98% (not shown in matrix) of all live domains. When restricted to tagged domains only (Figure 2 right), the coverage of the Hu feed is an astounding 96%, while the contribution of Hyb drops to 39%. In fact, restricting the domains to tagged only (right-hand matrix) excludes many of the benign domains appearing in Hyb from the *All* column, *improving* the coverage of most feeds with respect to *All*.

Figure 2 also reveals that most feeds—especially Ac_1, MX_1, MX_2, and MX_3—are quite effective at capturing bot-generated spam domains. These feeds range from 12% to 21% bot-generated (tagged domains), although the true number is

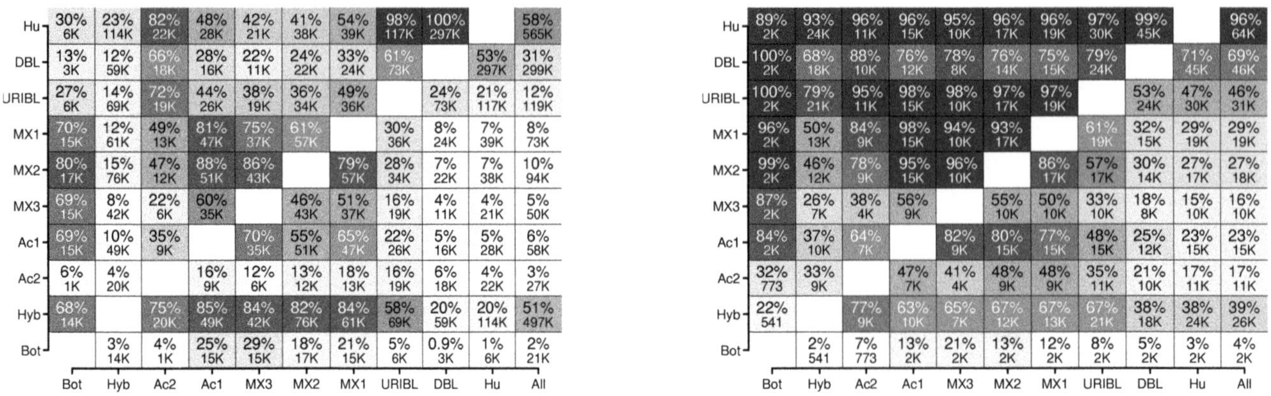

Figure 2: Pairwise feed domain intersection, shown for live (left) and tagged domains (right).

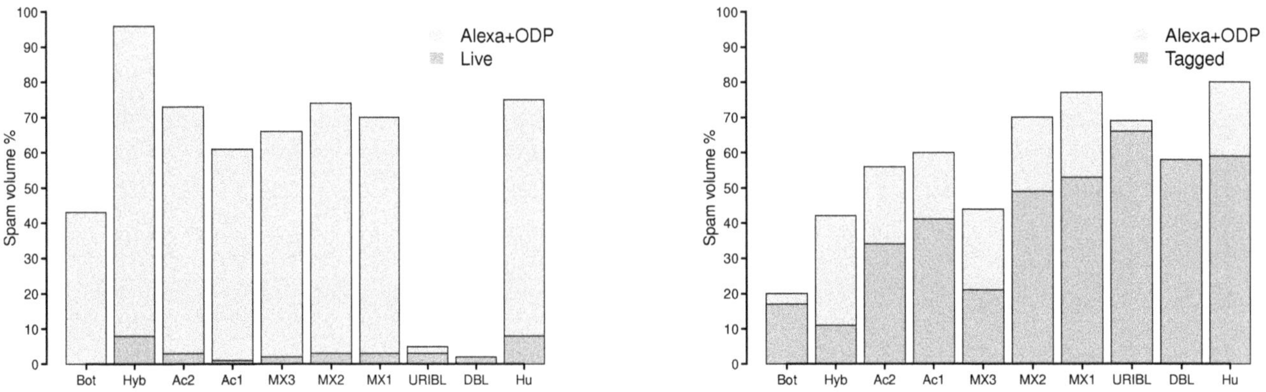

Figure 3: Feed volume coverage shown for live (left) and tagged domains (right).

likely higher given the limited set of bots included in the Bot feed. In turn, URIBL is quite effective at capturing these honeypot feeds (MX_1, MX_2, MX_3, Ac_1, and Ac_2), and both blacklists considerably overlap each other. Moreover, blacklists have a non-trivial overlap with the Hu feed. Despite these higher numbers, though, a gap still exists, as blacklists cannot replace the human identified dataset. Overall, this is a strong indicator of the strength of human-identified feeds, while also stressing the significance of blacklists.

4.2.2 *Volume*

While there are millions of URLs and thousands of domains spammed daily, the number of messages in which each appears can vary dramatically. We call the number of messages advertising a domain the *volume* of that domain. Here we consider the coverage of each feed with respect to the relative volume of spam it covers. To estimate this quantity, we solicited the help of a large Web mail provider to measure the volume of spam domains at their incoming mail servers.

The incoming mail oracle. We refer to this data source as our *incoming mail oracle*. For this measurement, we collected all live domains seen across all feeds, and submitted them to the cooperating mail provider. The provider reported back to us the number of messages (normalized) containing each spam domain, as seen by their incoming mail servers over five days during the measurement period. This provider handles mail for hundreds of millions of users. Although the measurement collected is not a perfectly uniform sample of all spam globally, we believe it to be a reasonable representative. Given the limited duration of the measurement—five days versus three months of feed data—these results should be interpreted with caution.

Figure 3 shows the volume of spam covered by the live and tagged domains in each feed. Recall that both live and tagged domains specifically exclude domains listed in the Alexa 1 million and domains appearing in the Open Directory Project listings (Section 4.1.4). In the figure, we've included the volume due to these Alexa and ODP domains occurring in each feed, shown stacked on top of the live and tagged volume bars. Before removing Alexa and ODP domains, the volume of live domains is dominated by these potential false positives. Among tagged domains, the volume attributed to Alexa and ODP domains (before exclusion) is much lower. These are domains which may have been used by the spammer as a redirection mechanism, either by abusing a legitimate service or via compromise. Of the feeds, the blacklists show the highest purity, as noted in Section 4.1.

With the Alexa and ODP domains excluded from the set of tagged domains, the URIBL blacklist provides the greatest coverage, followed by the Hu feed and DBL blacklist. At the opposite end, the Hyb feed provides only about a sixth of the coverage (by tagged domain volume) compared to URIBL, DBL, and Hu. Although it has nearly an order of magnitude more domains, its spam volume coverage is less than the Bot feed. One possibility is that this feed contains spam domains not derived from e-mail spam.

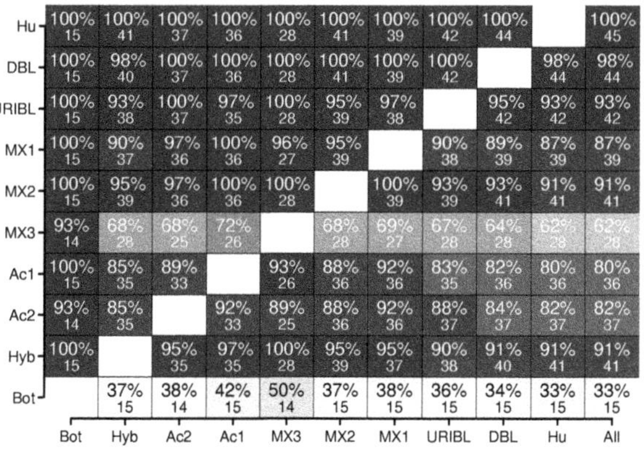

Figure 4: Pairwise feed similarity with respect to covered affiliate programs.

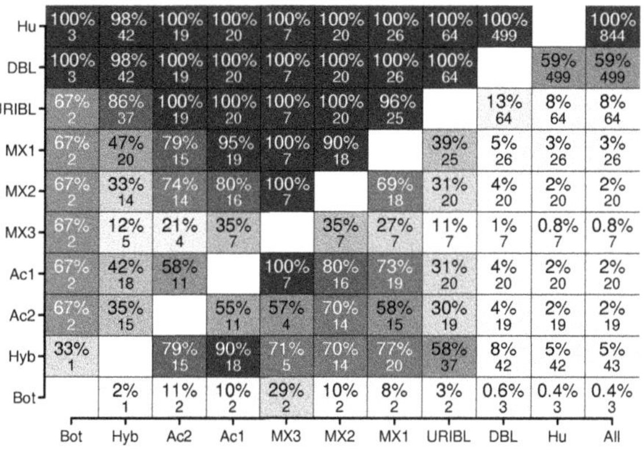

Figure 5: Pairwise feed similarity with respect to covered RX-Promotion affiliate identifiers.

4.2.3 *Affiliate Programs*

Up to this point, our focus has been the domains occurring in feeds, with the implicit understanding that domains represent a spam campaign. The relationship between a campaign and the domains it uses can be complex: a domain may be used in multiple campaigns, and a campaign may continuously cycle through several domains.

In fact, there is another level of structure beyond domains and campaigns: affiliate programs. Today, spammers operate primarily as advertisers, working with an affiliate program and earning a commission (typically 30–50%). The affiliate program handles Web site design, payment processing, customer service and fulfillment [33].

The prior Click Trajectories measurement effort [18] identified 45 leading affiliate programs specializing in pharmaceutical sales, replica luxury goods, and "OEM" software (this classification includes all the major players in each category that advertise via spam). We use the classification results of this project to define the tagged domains (Section 4.1). Here, we explore the tags themselves, that is, the affiliate programs associated with domains. Specifically, we consider the coverage of each feed with respect to *affiliate programs*.

Figure 4 shows the proportion of programs covered by each feed, relative to other feeds and all feeds combined. The representation is the same as Figure 2: each cell indicates the number of programs represented by the two feeds given by the row and column labels, and the top number of each cell expresses this intersection relative to the second program (identified by the column). For example, the cell in row MX_1 column Hyb indicates that 37 affiliate programs are seen in both feeds, and that these 37 programs represent approximately 90% of the 41 programs appearing in the Hyb feed.

Generally, most feeds do a good job covering all programs. The MX_3 feed has the second worst coverage, covering only 62% of all programs. Not surprisingly, the Bot feed has the worst coverage: only 15 programs. This poor coverage is partly because botnet operators frequently act as affiliates themselves and thus only advertise for a modest number of programs where they have spent the time to establish themselves. Even a botnet for rent will have a modest number of users and thus any given botnet will typically spam for a small number of programs in a given time.

4.2.4 *RX-Promotion*

In the affiliate marketing model for spam-advertised goods, the store site is usually hosted by the affiliate program itself, and not the spammer. For the affiliate program to determine which affiliate should receive credit for a sale, the URL itself must uniquely identify the affiliate. The most common mechanism is to assign each (major) affiliate a handful of dedicated domains.[6] Any sales generated via those domains are automatically credited to the appropriate affiliate.

One program, RX-Promotion, embeds an affiliate identifier in the page source of the storefront itself. This embedding allowed us to extract affiliate identifiers and map them to domains. In total, we were able to identify 846 distinct affiliate identifiers.

Affiliate coverage. Figure 5 shows the pairwise feed comparison matrix for RX-Promotion affiliate identifier coverage. Similar to affiliate program coverage, the human-identified feed Hu contributes the largest number of distinct affiliates. In this case, however, the difference between Hu and other feeds is more pronounced, with more than 40% of the affiliates found exclusively in Hu. The remaining feeds follow the same pattern as before. The MX honeypots (especially MX_1 and MX_2) continue to offer slightly greater coverage than seeded honey accounts (Ac_1 and Ac_2). Most striking is the paucity of affiliate IDs in the botnet feeds, confirming our earlier suspicion that botnet-originated affiliate program spam is associated with a single individual (the botnet operator).

Revenue coverage. The ultimate measure of an affiliate's success is the revenue he generates for the program. By this measure, a feed's value lies not in how many affiliates it covers, but in how much revenue it covers.

In a recent dispute between rival pharmacy affiliate programs, a number of RX-Promotion documents were leaked to the public [23]. One such document available to us, lists annual revenue generated by each RX-Promotion affiliate in 2010. Using these revenue statistics, we calculate affiliate coverage *weighted by affiliate revenue*. Figure 6 shows the revenue-weighted affiliate coverage of each feed.

The domains advertised in the smaller campaigns only found in Hu and DBL generate an order of magnitude more revenue than the sites advertised by bots and typically five times more than those sites seen in MX and honey account feeds. Overall, the results generally follow the affiliate cover-

[6]New domains must be constantly registered and assigned, as domains quickly become ineffective because of blacklisting.

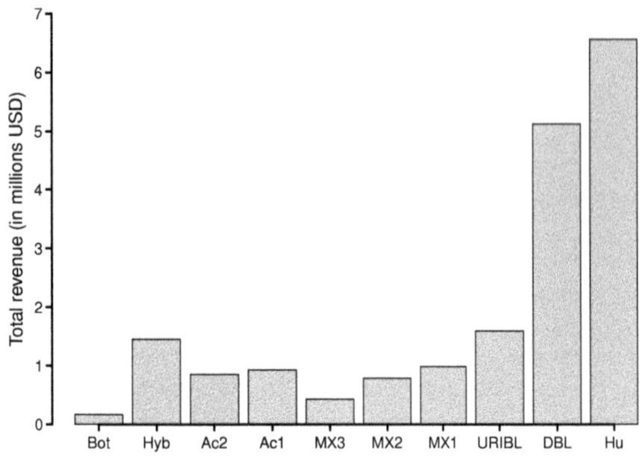

Figure 6: RX-Promotion affiliate coverage of each feed weighted by each affiliate's 2010 revenue.

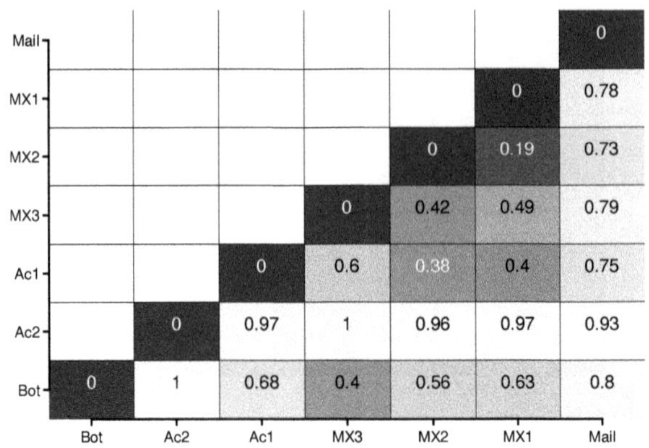

Figure 7: Pairwise variational distance of tagged domains frequency across all feeds. Shading is inverted (larger values are darker).

age shown in Figure 5, although the revenue-weighted results indicate a bias toward higher-revenue affiliates. While DBL covers only 59% of Hu affiliates, these affiliates represent over 78% of revenue covered by Hu.

4.3 Proportionality

An anti-spam system seeks to identify as many spam messages as possible, and in this context volume is a natural measure of a domain's importance. A blacklist that identifies the top 100 spammed domains by volume will identify more spam than a list of the same size consisting of infrequent domains. Similarly, domain take-downs are best prioritized to target high-volume domains first. To make these judgments, a spam domain feed must contain not only the domains themselves, but also their observed volume.

It happens that some of our feeds do provide volume information: each domain is listed with the number of times a domain was seen in spam, allowing relative domain volume and rank to be estimated. This section considers only feeds with volume information; the Hyb feed, Hu feed and both blacklist feeds (DBL and URIBL) have no associated volume information and are thus excluded from this analysis.

Empirical domain distribution and rank. The volumes associated with each domain define an empirical distribution on domains. That is, if a domain i has reported volume c_i in a feed, then the empirical domain probability distribution is c_i/m, where m is the total volume of the feed (i.e., $m = \sum_i c_i$).

Variation distance. Variation distance (also called "statistical difference" in some areas of Computer Science) is a straightforward metric frequently used to compare distributions. Formally, given two probability distributions (feeds) P and Q, let p_i be the empirical probability of domain i in P, and q_i the probability of the same domain in Q. (If a domain does not occur in a feed, its empirical probability is 0.) The variation distance is given by:

$$\delta = \frac{1}{2}\sum_i |p_i - q_i|.$$

Variation distance takes on values between 0 and 1, where $\delta = 0$ if and only if $P = Q$ (domains have the same probability in both), and $\delta = 1$ if P and Q are disjoint (no domains in common). Figure 7 shows pairwise measures of variation distance of tagged domains. (Because we round values to two decimal places, a variational distance of 1 in the figure may still allow for some domain overlap.)

Kendall rank correlation coefficient. Variation distance places more weight on more frequently occurring domains. In some cases, only the relative ranks of domains are of interest, and not the magnitudes of the empirical probabilities. The Kendall rank correlation coefficient (also called Kendall's tau-b) allows us to compare the relative ranking of domains between two distributions. In the case where all probabilities are distinct,

$$\tau = \frac{1}{n(n-1)}\sum_{i \neq j} \operatorname{sgn}\left[(p_i - p_j)(q_i - q_j)\right].$$

where $\operatorname{sgn}(x)$ is the familiar signum function. The sum is over all domains common to both feeds being compared, and n is the number of such domains. The Kendall rank correlation coefficient takes on values between -1 and 1, with 0 indicating no correlation, 1 indicating perfect positive correlation, and -1 indicating perfect negative correlation. If there are ties, i.e., $p_i = p_j$ or $q_i = q_j$ for some $i \neq j$, the denominator $n(n-1)$ must be adjusted to keep the full range between -1 to 1; we refer the reader to an appropriate Statistics textbook for details.

Figure 8 shows the pairwise tagged domain Kendall rank correlation coefficient between all feed pairs.

Pairwise comparison. Figures 7 and 8 show how well each pair of feeds agree in domain volume and rank. (The *Mail* column will be described shortly.) Qualitatively, both variation distance and Kendall rank correlation coefficient show similar results. The MX honeypot feeds and the Ac_1 honey account feeds exhibit similar domain distributions; these four also have many domains in common as seen in Figure 2.

The Bot feed brings a small number of domains, many of which also occur in the MX honeypot feeds and the Ac_1 feed (Figure 2). The volume of these domains, however, is significant; so much so, that in terms of domain proportions, the MX_3 feed is more like the Bot feed than any other feed, including the remaining MX honeypots.

The similarity in coverage and empirical domain probability distributions indicates that, roughly speaking, one MX honeypot feed is as good as another. By their nature, MX honeypots are targets of high-volume spammers who spam

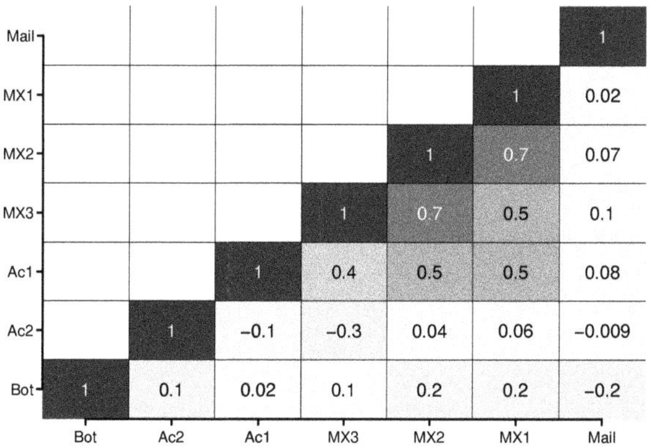

Figure 8: Pairwise Kendall rank correlation coefficient of tagged domain frequency across all feed pairs.

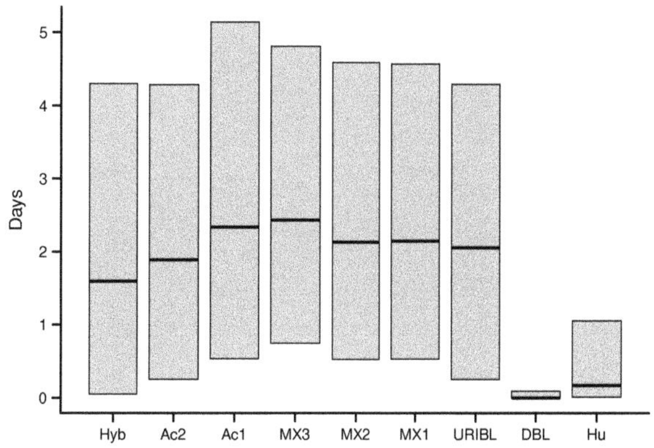

Figure 9: Relative first appearance time of domains in each feed. Campaign start time calculated from all feeds except Bot. Solid lines are medians; boxes range from the 25th to the 75th percentile.

randomly-generated names at all registered domains. By this process, it is just as easy to stumble upon one MX honeypot as another.

Comparison to real mail. In Section 4.2.2 we reported on the fraction of incoming spam—as seen by a major Web mail provider—covered by each feed. Here we use the same incoming mail oracle to determine the real-world relative volumes of spam domains, and compare those numbers to the relative domain volumes reported by each feed. We use only tagged domains appearing in at least one spam feed in the comparison: in the calculation of δ and τ, we set $p_i = 0$ for any domain i not appearing in the union of all spam feeds.

The *Mail* column in Figures 7 and 8 shows these results. The MX_2 feed comes closest to approximating the domain volume distribution of live mail, with Ac_1 coming close behind. As with coverage, the Ac_2 feed stands out as being most unlike the rest.

4.4 Timing

For both sides of the spam conflict, time is of the essence. For a spammer, the clock starts ticking as soon as a domain is advertised. It is only a matter of time before the domain is blacklisted, drastically reducing the deliverability of spam. While a domain is still clean, the spammer must maximize the number of messages delivered to potential customers. On the other side, blacklist maintainers strive to identify and blacklist spam domains as quickly as possible to maximize the volume of spam captured.

In this section we consider how well each spam feed captures the timing of spam campaigns. Specifically, we identify how quickly each feed lists spam domains, and, for feeds driven by live mail, how accurately they identify the end of a spam campaign. Unless noted otherwise, we restrict our analysis to tagged domains because we have the most confidence in their provenance.

Ideally, we would like to compare the time a domain first appears in spam with the time it first appears in a spam feed. Lacking such perfect knowledge about the start of each spam campaign, we instead take the *earliest* appearance time of a domain across all feeds as the *campaign start time*, and the *last* appearance time of a domain in live mail-based feeds as the *campaign end time*. For this analysis, we exclude the Bot feed because its domains have little overlap with the other feeds. As a result, including them greatly diminishes the number of domains that appear in the intersection of the feeds, and hence the number of domains that we can consider.

Taking the campaign start time and end time as described above, we define the *relative first appearance time* for a domain in a particular feed to the time between campaign start and its first appearance in the feed. In other words, we take campaign start time as "time zero" and calculate the relative first appearance time relative to this time. Put another way, the relative first appearance time is thus the *latency* of a feed with respect to a domain.

4.4.1 First Appearance Time

Figure 9 shows the distribution of relative first appearance times of domains in each feed. The bottom of the box corresponds to the 25th percentile, the top denotes the 75th percentile, and the solid bar inside the box denotes the median.

Both Hu and DBL are excellent early warnings of spam campaigns since they see most domains soon after they are used. The Hu feed sees over 75% of the domains within a day after they appear in any feed, and 95% within three days; DBL is delayed even less, with over 95% appearing on the blacklist within a day. Once again, the nature of these feeds lends themselves to observing wide-spread spam activity quickly: Hu has an enormous net for capturing spam, while DBL combines domain information from many sources. In contrast, the other feeds have much later first appearance times: they do not see roughly half of the domains until two days have passed, 75% until after four days, and 95% after ten. Operationally, by the time many of the domains appear in these feeds, spammers have already had multiple days to monetize their campaigns.

Of course, these results depend on both the set of domains that we consider and the sets of feeds we use to define campaign start times. When performing the same analysis on the larger set of live domains that appear in the same set of feeds, the first appearance times remain very similar to Figure 9: even for the broader set of domains, Hu and DBL see the domains multiple days earlier than the other feeds.

However, changing the set of *feeds* we consider does change relative first appearance times. Figure 10 shows similar

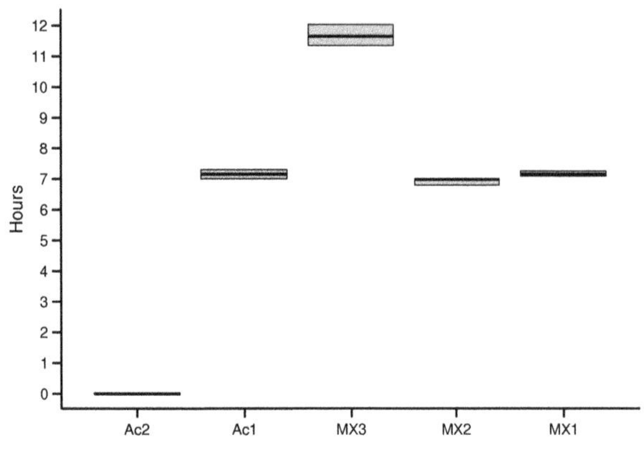

Figure 10: Relative first appearance time of domains in each feed. Campaign start time calculated from MX honeypot and honey account feeds only. Solid lines are medians; boxes range from the 25th to the 75th percentile.

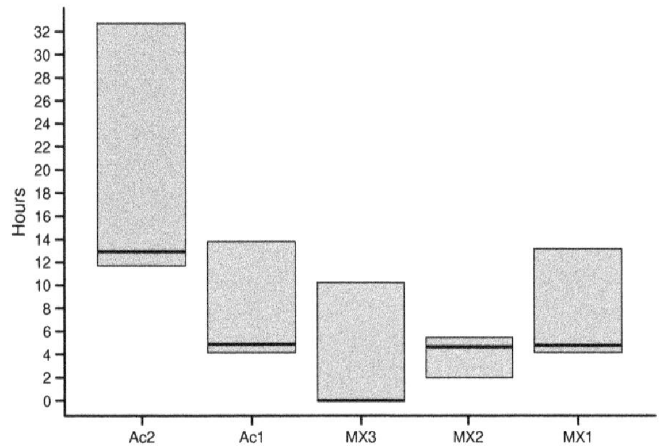

Figure 11: Distribution of differences between the last appearance of a domain in a particular and the domain campaign end calculated from an aggregate of the same five feeds. Solid lines are medians; boxes range from the 25th to the 75th percentile.

results as Figure 9, but with the Hu, Hyb, and blacklist feeds removed. (We chose these feeds because, as discussed further below, they all contain domains reported by users, which affects the last appearance times of domains.) Restricting the feeds we use to determine campaign start times reduces the total set of domains, but also increases the likelihood that a domain appears in all traces. When we focus on just the MX honeypot and account traces in this way, we see that relative to just each other they continue to have consistent first appearance times with each other, but the relative first appearance times are now very short (roughly less than a day). As with other metrics, these results show that timing estimates are quite relative and fundamentally depend on the feeds being considered.

4.4.2 Last Appearance Time

Last appearance times are often used to estimate when spam campaigns end. Figure 11 shows the time between the last appearance of a domain in a feed and the domain's campaign end time. As with Figure 10 we focus on only a subset of the feeds where the last appearance of a domain

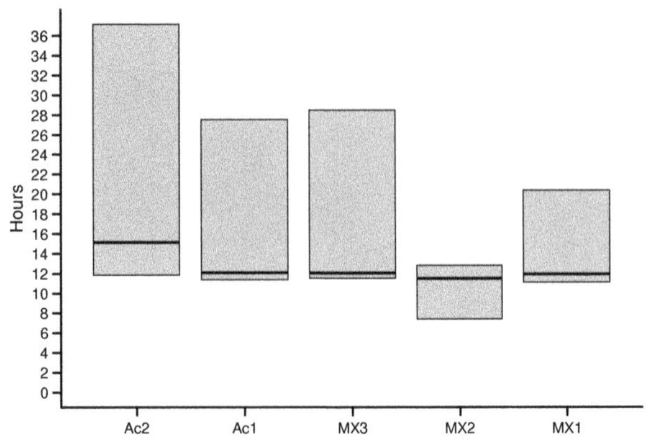

Figure 12: Distribution of differences between domain lifetime estimated using each feed and the domain campaign duration computed from an aggregate of those same five feeds. Solid lines are medians; boxes range from the 25th to the 75th percentile.

likely corresponds to when a spammer stopped sending messages using the domain: the MX honeypots and honeypot account feeds. Feeds like Hu, Hyb, and the blacklists all have domains reported by users. Since user reports fundamentally depend on when users read their mail and report spam, they may report spam long after a spammer has sent it.

Consistent with the first appearance times for the honeypot feeds, the feeds are similar to each other for last appearance times as well. The difference with the baseline are relatively short (a day or less), but have longer tails (the 95th percentiles for most are over a week).

4.4.3 Duration

Another common metric for spam campaigns is their duration: how long spammers advertise domains to attract customers. Figure 12 shows the differences in time durations of domains advertised in spam as observed by each feed relative to estimated campaign duration (campaign end time minus campaign start time). For each feed we calculate the *lifetime* of a domain in the feed using the first and last appearance of a domain just in that feed. Then we compute the difference between the domain lifetime in a feed and the estimated campaign duration. (Campaign duration is computed from the same five feeds and is always at least as long as the domain lifetime in any feed.) The box plots in the graph summarize the distributions of these differences across all domains in each feed.

The differences in duration estimates for the honeypot feeds are also consistent with their first and last appearance time estimates. The duration estimates across feeds are similar to each other, the duration estimates differ from the baseline by less than a day for half of the domains and roughly a day for 75% of the domains. The distribution tails are longer, though, with outliers underestimating durations by multiple weeks.

5. CONCLUSION

Most measurement studies focus on using data to infer new facts about the world. This goal is why we measure things—to put truth on an empirical footing. However, occasionally it is necessary to perform introspective studies such as this one to understand the limits of what we can conclude from available data.

While our analysis is not comprehensive, we have found significant variation among the ten feeds we did study. Based on these findings we recommend that researchers consider four different challenges whenever using spam data:

- Limited purity. Even the best spam feeds include benign domains and these domains should be anticipated in analyses. We should identify the "kinds" of benign domains that appear in a dataset and determine if their existence will bias results—in particular when spam feed data will be correlated with other data sources.

- Coverage limitations. MX and honey account spam sources are inherently biased towards loud broad campaigns. If we desire a broader view of what is advertised via spam and are unable to strike an arrangement with a large e-mail provider, operational domain blacklists are the next best source of such information.

- Temporal uncertainty. Studies of spam campaign timing should recognize how timing error can be introduced via different feeds. Botnet-based feeds are among the best for timing information, but naturally coverage is limited. Other feeds provide highly accurate "onset" information (e.g., blacklists and human-identified feeds) but may not provide a correspondingly accurate ending timestamp. This area is one where combining the features of different feeds may be appropriate.

- Lack of proportionality. It is tempting to measure the prevalence of one kind of spam in a feed and extrapolate to the entire world—"25% of all spam advertises eBooks!" or "My spam filter can block 99.99% of all spam". However, the significant differences in the makeup of the feeds we have studied suggests that any such conclusion is risky. For example, spam filter results trained on botnet output may have little relevance to a large Web mail provider. In general, we advise making such claims based on knowledge of the source data set. For example, MX-based honeypots may be appropriate for characterizing relative prevalence among distinct high volume spam campaigns.

While it is important to be aware of the limitations and challenges of spam feeds, an even more interesting question is what feeds one should use for related studies. The clear answer, as shown by our results, is that there is no perfect feed. Instead, the choice should be closely related to the questions we are trying to answer. It is still possible, though, to provide some general guidelines that would apply for most cases:

- Human identified feeds, which are provided by large mail providers, will usually be the best choice for most studies. They provide a clear advantage when it comes to coverage, due to their wide exposure, and allow for visibility inside low-volume campaigns. They do so with reasonable purity, but due to the presence of the human factor, filtering is required. On the other hand, we should avoid human identified feeds when we are interested in timing, and especially last appearance information.

- If it is not possible to get access to human identified feeds, due to their limited availability, high-quality blacklist feeds offer very good coverage and first appearance information. They also offer the best purity since they are usually commercially maintained, and have low false positives as their primary goal. Similar to human identified feeds, they are less useful for studies that rely on last appearance or duration information.

- When working with multiple feeds, the priority should be to obtain a set that is as diverse as possible. Additional feeds of the same type offer reduced added value, and this situation is especially true in the case of MX honeypot feeds.

- It is very challenging to obtain accurate information regarding volume and provide conclusions that apply to the entirety of the spam problem. Given our limited view into the global spam output, all results are inherently tied to their respective input datasets.

In a sense, the spam research community is blessed by having so many different kinds of data sources available to it. In many other measurement regimes the problem of bias is just as great, but the number of data sources on hand is far fewer. However, with great data diversity comes great responsibility. It is no longer reasonable to take a single spam feed and extrapolate blindly without validation. Our paper provides a basic understanding of the limitations of existing feeds and provides a blueprint for refining this understanding further.

Acknowledgments

We would like to thank the named and anonymous providers of our feeds, whose willingness to share data with us made a paper such as this possible. We are also grateful to Brian Kantor and Cindy Moore who have managed our systems and storage needs.

This work was supported by National Science Foundation grants NSF-0433668, NSF-0433702, NSF-0831138, by Office of Naval Research MURI grant N000140911081, and by generous research, operational and in-kind support from the UCSD Center for Networked Systems (CNS).

6. REFERENCES

[1] Alexa. Alexa top 500 global sites. `http://www.alexa.com/topsites`, June 2011.

[2] D. S. Anderson, C. Fleizach, S. Savage, and G. M. Voelker. Spamscatter: Characterizing Internet Scam Hosting Infrastructure. In *Proc. of 16th USENIX Security*, 2007.

[3] I. Androutsopoulos, J. Koutsias, K. Chandrinos, G. Paliouras, and C. D. Spyropoulos. An Evaluation of Naive Bayesian Anti-Spam Filtering. In *Proc. of 1st MLNIA*, 2000.

[4] R. Beverly and K. Sollins. Exploiting Transport-Level Characteristics of Spam. In *Proc. of 5th CEAS*, 2008.

[5] X. Carreras and L. Màrquez. Boosting Trees for Anti-Spam Email Filtering. In *Proceedings of RANLP-2001*, 2001.

[6] R. Clayton. How much did shutting down McColo help? In *Proc. of 6th CEAS*, 2009.

[7] H. Drucker, D. Wu, and V. N. Vapnik. Support vector machines for spam categorization. In *Proc. of IEEE Transactions on Neural Networks*, 1999.

[8] G. Gee and P. Kim. Doppleganger Domains. `http://www.wired.com/images_blogs/threatlevel/2011/09/Doppelganger.Domains.pdf`, 2011.

[9] P. H. C. Guerra, D. Guedes, W. M. Jr., C. Hoepers, M. H. P. C. Chaves, and K. Steding-Jessen. Spamming Chains: A New Way of Understanding Spammer Behavior. In *Proc. of 6th CEAS*, 2009.

[10] P. H. C. Guerra, D. Guedes, W. M. Jr., C. Hoepers, M. H. P. C. Chaves, and K. Steding-Jessen. Exploring the Spam Arms Race to Characterize Spam Evolution. In *Proc. of 7th CEAS*, 2010.

[11] J. P. John, A. Moshchuk, S. D. Gribble, and A. Krishnamurthy. Studying Spamming Botnets Using Botlab. In *Proc. of 6th NSDI*, 2009.

[12] C. Kanich, C. Kreibich, K. Levchenko, B. Enright, G. M. Voelker, V. Paxson, and S. Savage. Spamalytics: An Empirical Analysis of Spam Marketing Conversion. In *Proc. of 15th ACM CCS*, 2008.

[13] M. Konte, N. Feamster, and J. Jung. Dynamics of Online Scam Hosting Infrastructure. In *PAM*, 2009.

[14] C. Kreibich, C. Kanich, K. Levchenko, B. Enright, G. M. Voelker, V. Paxson, and S. Savage. On the Spam Campaign Trail. In *Proc. 1st USENIX LEET*, 2008.

[15] C. Kreibich, C. Kanich, K. Levchenko, B. Enright, G. M. Voelker, V. Paxson, and S. Savage. Spamcraft: An Inside Look at Spam Campaign Orchestration. In *Proc. of 2nd USENIX LEET*, 2009.

[16] M. Lee. Why My Email Went. `http://www.symantec.com/connect/blogs/why-my-email-went`, 2011.

[17] N. Leontiadis, T. Moore, and N. Christin. Measuring and Analyzing Search-Redirection Attacks in the Illicit Online Prescription Drug Trade. In *Proc. of USENIX Security*, 2011.

[18] K. Levchenko, A. Pitsillidis, N. Chachra, B. Enright, M. Félegyházi, C. Grier, T. Halvorson, C. Kanich, C. Kreibich, H. Liu, D. McCoy, N. Weaver, V. Paxson, G. M. Voelker, and S. Savage. Click Trajectories: End-to-End Analysis of the Spam Value Chain. In *Proc. of IEEE Symposium on Security and Privacy*, 2011.

[19] H. Liu, K. Levchenko, M. Félegyházi, C. Kreibich, G. Maier, G. M. Voelker, and S. Savage. On the Effects of Registrar-level Intervention. In *Proc. of 4th USENIX LEET*, 2011.

[20] M86 Security Labs. Top Spam Affiliate Programs. `http://www.m86security.com/labs/traceitem.asp?article=1070`, 2009.

[21] Marshal8e6 TRACELabs. Marshal8e6 Security Threats: Email and Web Threats. `http://www.marshal.com/newsimages/trace/Marshal8e6_TRACE_Report_Jan2009.pdf`, 2009.

[22] M. M. Masud, L. Khan, and B. Thuraisingham. Feature Based Techniques for Auto-Detection of Novel Email Worms. In *Proc. of 11th PACKDDD*, 2007.

[23] D. McCoy, A. Pitsillidis, G. Jordan, N. Weaver, C. Kreibich, B. Krebs, G. M. Voelker, S. Savage, and K. Levchenko. PharmaLeaks: Understanding the Business of Online Pharmaceutical Affiliate Programs. In *Proc. of the USENIX Security Symposium*, 2012.

[24] D. K. McGrath and M. Gupta. Behind Phishing: An Examination of Phisher Modi Operandi. In *Proc. of 1st USENIX LEET*, 2008.

[25] T. Moore and R. Clayton. Examining the Impact of Website Take-down on Phishing. In *Proceedings of the Anti-Phishing Working Group's 2nd annual eCrime Researchers Summit*. ACM, 2007.

[26] B. Nelson, M. Barreno, F. J. Chi, A. D. Joseph, B. I. P. Rubinstein, U. Saini, C. Sutton, J. D. Tygar, and K. Xia. Exploiting Machine Learning to Subvert Your Spam Filter. In *Proc. of 1st USENIX LEET*, 2008.

[27] ODP – Open Directory Project. `http://www.dmoz.org`, September 2011.

[28] A. Pathak, Y. C. Hu, , and Z. M. Mao. Peeking into Spammer Behavior from a Unique Vantage Point. In *Proc. of 1st USENIX LEET*, 2008.

[29] A. Pathak, F. Qian, Y. C. Hu, Z. M. Mao, and S. Ranjan. Botnet Spam Campaigns Can Be Long Lasting: Evidence, Implications, and Analysis. In *Proc. of 9th ACM SIGMETRICS*, 2009.

[30] A. Pitsillidis, K. Levchenko, C. Kreibich, C. Kanich, G. Voelkera, V. Paxson, N. Weaver, and S. Savage. Botnet Judo: Fighting Spam with Itself. In *Proc. of 17th NDSS*, 2010.

[31] Z. Qian, Z. Mao, Y. Xie, and F. Yu. On network-level clusters for spam detection. In *Proc. of 17th NDSS*, 2010.

[32] A. Ramachandran, N. Feamster, and S. Vempala. Filtering Spam with Behavioral Blacklisting. In *Proc. of 14th ACM CCS*, 2007.

[33] D. Samosseiko. The Partnerka — What is it, and why should you care? In *Proc. of Virus Bulletin Conference*, 2009.

[34] F. Sanchez, Z. Duan, and Y. Dong. Understanding Forgery Properties of Spam Delivery Paths. In *Proc. of 7th CEAS*, 2010.

[35] S. Sinha, M. Bailey, and F. Jahanian. Shades of Grey: On the effectiveness of reputation-based blacklists. In *Proc. of 3rd MALWARE*, 2008.

[36] O. Thonnard and M. Dacier. A Strategic Analysis of Spam Botnets Operations. In *Proc. of 8th CEAS*, 2011.

[37] Trustwave. Spam Statistics – Week ending Sep 2, 2012. `https://www.trustwave.com/support/labs/spam_statistics.asp`, September 2012.

[38] G. Warner. Random Pseudo-URLs Try to Confuse Anti-Spam Solutions. `http://garwarner.blogspot.com/2010/09/random-pseudo-urls-try-to-confuse-anti.html`, Sept. 2010.

[39] C. Wei, A. Sprague, G. Warner, and A. Skjellum. Identifying New Spam Domains by Hosting IPs: Improving Domain Blacklisting. In *Proc. of 7th CEAS*, 2010.

[40] A. G. West, A. J. Aviv, J. Chang, and I. Lee. Spam Mitigation Using Spatio-temporal Reputations From Blacklist History. In *Proc of 26th. ACSAC*, 2010.

[41] J. Whissell and C. Clarke. Clustering for Semi-Supervised Spam Filtering. In *Proc. of 8th CEAS*, 2011.

[42] Y. Xie, F. Yu, K. Achan, R. Panigrahy, G. Hulten, and I. Osipkov. Spamming Botnets: Signatures and Characteristics. In *Proceedings of ACM SIGCOMM*, 2008.

[43] L. Zhuang, J. Dunagan, D. R. Simon, H. J. Wang, I. Osipkov, G. Hulten, and J. Tygar. Characterizing Botnets from Email Spam Records. In *Proc. of 1st USENIX LEET*, 2008.

[44] J. Zittrain and L. Frieder. Spam Works: Evidence from Stock Touts and Corresponding Market Activity. Social Science Research Network, March 2007.

Crime Scene Investigation: SMS Spam Data Analysis

Ilona Murynets
AT&T Security Research Center
New York, NY
ilona@att.com

Roger Piqueras Jover
AT&T Security Research Center
New York, NY
roger.jover@att.com

ABSTRACT

The Short Messaging Service (SMS), one of the most successful cellular services, generates millions of dollars in revenue for mobile operators. Estimates indicate that billions of text messages are traveling the airwaves daily. Nevertheless, text messaging is becoming a source of customer dissatisfaction due to the rapid surge of messaging abuse activities. Although spam is a well tackled problem in the email world, SMS spam experiences a yearly growth larger than 500%. In this paper we present, to the best of our knowledge, the first analysis of SMS spam traffic from a tier-1 cellular operator. Communication patterns of spammers are compared to those of legitimate cell-phone users and Machine to Machine (M2M) connected appliances. The results indicate that M2M systems exhibit communication profiles similar to spammers, which could mislead spam filters. Beyond the expected results, such as a large load of text messages sent out to a wide target list, other interesting findings are made. For example, the results indicate that the great majority of the spammers connect to the network with just a handful of different hardware models. We find the main geographical sources of messaging abuse in the US. We also find evidence of spammer mobility, voice and data traffic resembling the behavior of legitimate customers.

Categories and Subject Descriptors

K.6.5 [**Security and Protection**]; K.4.1 [**Computers and Society**]: Public Policy Issues—*Abuse and crime involving computers*; C.2.3 [**Computer Communications Networks**]: Network Operations—*Network Monitoring*

General Terms

Experimentation, Measurement

Keywords

SMS, abuse, spam, traffic analysis, cellular networks

IMC'12, November 14–16, 2012, Boston, Massachusetts, USA.

1. INTRODUCTION

For the past three decades, the Short Messaging Service (SMS) has gained tremendous popularity throughout the world. Reports estimate billions of text messages handled daily by cellular providers' messaging infrastructures [19], generating millions of dollars of yearly revenue [7].

Being unquestionably successful, text messaging is steadily becoming an annoyance due to the surge of SMS fraudulent activities [16]. Spam is the commonly adopted name to refer to unwanted messages that are massively sent to a large number of recipients.

Spam is a well known and tackled problem in the context of e-mail. Multiple solutions detect and block spam e-mails daily resulting in a small amount of spam reaching customer's inboxes. This is considered a great achievement given the estimates indicating that 90% of the daily electronic mail traversing the Internet is spam [3].

In the case of text messaging abuse, the trend has been rapidly increasing with the introduction of unlimited messaging plans. Current studies estimate mobile SMS spam to be experiencing a steady yearly growth larger than 500% [8]. Effective anti-abuse messaging filters are deployed, sparing networks from spam text messages injected into cellular networks from the Internet. However, content-based algorithms used to detect e-mail spam, are less efficient in the case of SMS spam [11]. The length of an SMS is limited to only 160 characters [23] and customers often use acronyms, pruned spellings and emoticons which mislead detection algorithms. Thus, mobile originated SMS spam still remains a problem for cellular networks.

The criminals - spammers - connect aircards and cellphones to personal computers (PCs). These are used to send thousands of daily spam text messages, mostly using pre-paid SIM (Subscriber Identity Module) cards with unlimited messaging plans. The defense against such illegitimate activities often involves SIM shutdowns and account cancelations. This does not stop most spammers, though, who purchase multiple cards and swap them to limit the daily per-SIM volume [8].

Millions of illegitimate text messages are transmitted via cellular networks daily [16]. These messages consume network resources that could be allocated to legitimate services otherwise. SMS spam results also in a major inconvenience for cellular customers because, without an unlimited plan, the end user is paying at a per received message basis. Therefore, SMS spam potentially generates unwanted bill charges for some users leading to negative messaging experience and customer dissatisfaction. Spam also exposes smart-

Field	Data Type	Description
Time	SMS/Voice/Data	Transmission/Reception date and time
Originating number	SMS/Voice	Originating number
Terminating number	SMS/ Voice	Terminating number
Call type	SMS/Voice	Mobile originated/terminated SMS/call
Duration	Voice	Phone call time duration
Load	Data	IP traffic byte cound
IMEI	SMS/Voice/Data	International Mobile Equipment Identity
LAC-CID	SMS/Voice	Location Area Code and Cell ID
Lat-Long	SMS/Voice	Base Station Coordinates
Account age	SMS/Voice/Data	Time since contract activation
Customer segment	SMS/Voice/Data	Prepaid/Postpaid

Table 1: SMS/Voice/Data Call Detail Record fields

phone users to viruses. Often multiple fraudulent messaging activities such as phishing, identity theft and fraud [25] are related to SMS spam. SMS is also known as an entry vector for malware propagation [15].

In this paper we analyze the characteristics and communication patterns of SMS spammers. The analysis is based on mining SMS, Voice and IP network traffic from a tier-1 network operator in the United States. The behavior of over 9000 positively identified and known spammers is analyzed and compared to legitimate cell-phone users and embedded Machine to Machine (M2M) appliances. As will be shown throughout the paper, some M2M communication systems exhibit a behavior that resembles in some aspects that of an SMS spammer. The results of this investigation are being used to develop an advanced SMS spam detection engine, the details of which are out of the scope of this paper.

Beyond the expected results, such as the large load of messages sent by spammers to a widely geographically distributed target list, very interesting discoveries are presented in this paper. For example, the vast majority of spammers utilize just five different models of hardware to send the messages. Some of these devices are very popular feature phones that are reflashed to be used as cellular modem. In terms of traffic, spammers make a large number of phone calls, of very short duration, perhaps to mislead detection schemes that might discard accounts with a near-human voice communication profile. We also find the main geographical hot-spots (sources) of messaging abuse activities in the US and that some spammers launch very geographically targeted campaigns.

To the best of our knowledge, this paper is the first to

(a) analyze characteristics of fraudulent SMS spam traffic over a major cellular network

(b) analyze voice and IP communication patterns and device and location characteristics of accounts cancelled due to fraudulent SMS activities

(c) compare communication patterns of spammers, legitimate cell-phone users and M2M systems.

The rest of the paper is organized as follows. Section 2 describes the three data sets under analysis (SMS spammers, legitimate users and M2M systems) and how they are labeled. Section 3 presents the data analysis. In Section 4 we give some introductory comments on an SMS spam detection engine that has been designed based on the data analysis in this paper. Section 5 discusses the related work. Finally, the study is concluded with the closing remarks in Section 6.

2. EVIDENCE OF THE CRIME: DATA SET

The analysis presented in this paper is based on traffic data provided by a tier-1 cellular operator in the United States. The data sample contains Call Detail Records (CDR) of 9000 spammer accounts and almost 17000 legitimate accounts. This last set includes about 7000 Machine to Machine devices and 10000 post-paid family plans, from the one year period between March 2011 and February 2012.

CDRs are records logging each phone call, text message and data exchange in the network. If two communicating ends belong to the same provider, a duple of records is stored. The Mobile Originated (MO) record logs data of the transmitting party, while the Mobile Terminated (MT) one stores information of the receiver. Note that the MO and the MT records for the same transaction contain duplicated data, such as the originating number and the terminating number. IP (Internet Protocol) data traffic generates only MO logs.

Table 1 summarizes the CDR fields used in our analysis. The originating and terminating phone numbers are fully anonymized and only the first 8 digits of the International Mobile Equipment Identity (IMEI) are parsed, discarding individual serial numbers. This first portion of the device identifier, known as the Type Allocation Code (TAC), determines the manufacturer and model of the wireless device. In the case of a phone, the TAC indicates the manufacturer and model of the phone itself (e.g. Nokia Lumia 900) and, in the case of an M2M connected device, the TAC identifies the embedded cellular modem (e.g. Sierra Wireless Q2687).

The spammer data set is obtained as follows. A list of positively identified spamming accounts and their cancelation dates were provided by the Fraud Department of the cellular operator. The Fraud Department maintains a constantly updated white-list of known legitimate sources of large loads of text messages (i.e. Twitter, American Idol alerts, etc) so they are never confused with spam. Therefore, this data set contains exclusively spammer accounts that were identified and disconnected from the network.

The legitimate account data set is obtained in two steps. First legitimate user accounts are selected and then legitimate M2M appliances are catalogued and included to the set. Our analysis of spammer accounts revealed that 99 64%

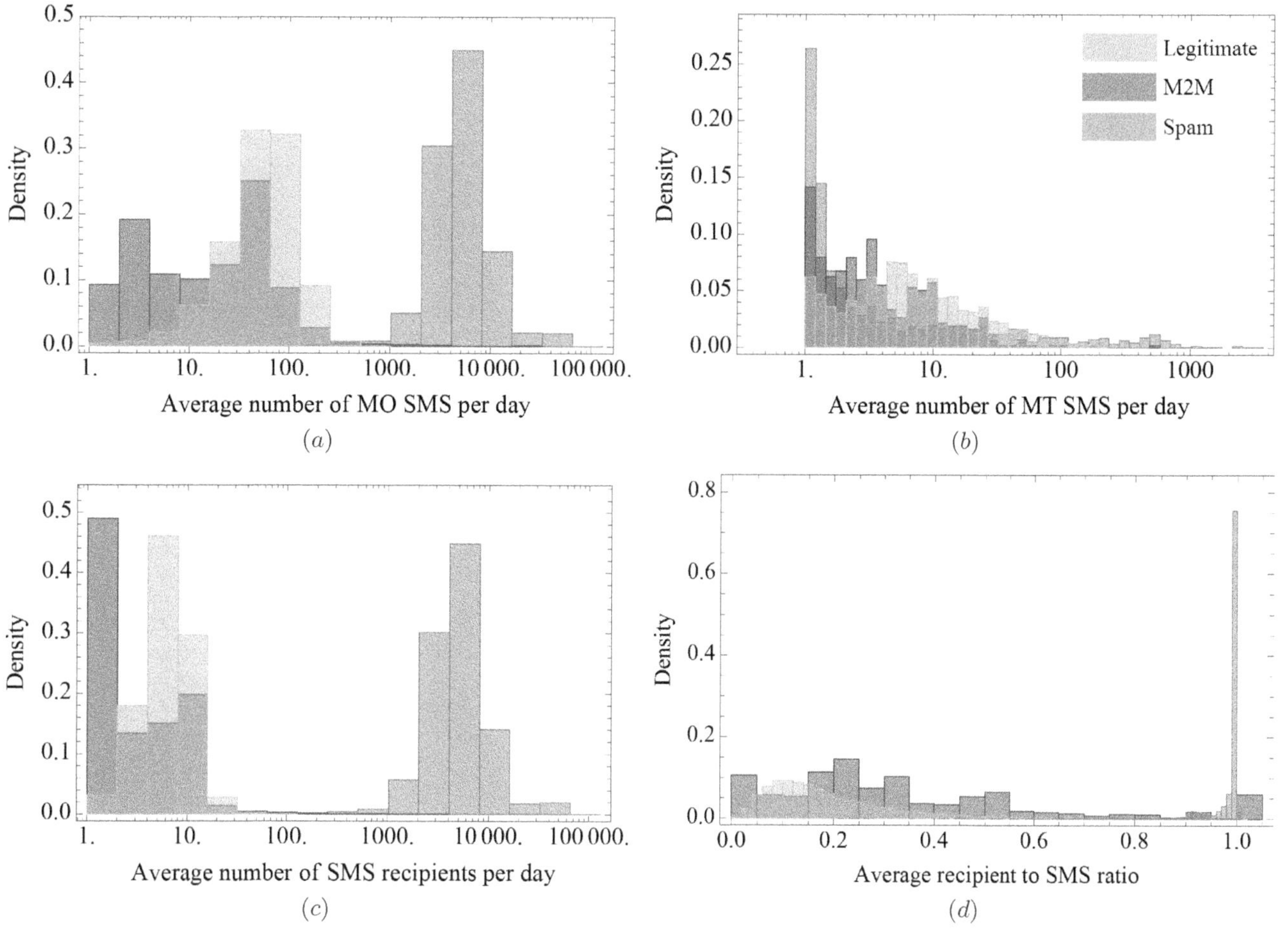

Figure 1: Messaging pattern of spammers (red), legitimate customers (green) and M2M (blue)

of spammers have prepaid plans. Therefore, the set of legitimate customers is drawn from a random and geographically uniform sample of post-paid family plan accounts, which are highly unlikely to be used by a spammer. This way we minimize the probability of having an unknown spammer mislabeled as legitimate. In parallel, M2M connected appliances are identified by the TAC and extracted from the operator's list of M2M approved devices. This is a database of the M2M devices that have been selected, tested and approved to operate on the provider's cellular network. These devices include connected appliances running all kinds of services. Some applications found in our data set are asset tracking, remote medical monitoring, security monitoring, Automatic Teller Machines and smart grid power meters. We discard, though, approved M2M systems with a Universal Serial Bus (USB) port because these could be used to send illegitimate messages if plugged to a spammer's computer.

Message abusing accounts stay alive for a short period of time (see Section 3.1), therefore we collected CDR records for spammer accounts for one week prior to cancelation. For each legitimate account we collected data for a random week between March 2011 and February 2012.

From the CDR data fields we extract multiple features that characterize customer communication patterns. For example, based on the time stamp of each MO SMS (and MO call) we calculate the intervals between two consecutive outgoing messages (and phone calls) and the number of outgoing messages (calls) per day. Based on the time stamps of MT SMSs (MT calls) we calculate the average number of MT messages (calls) per day. The response ratio is computed combining the average number of MO and MT messages (calls) per day. The terminating number field for SMS and voice traffic, also anonymized, is used to calculate the number of individual recipients and the number of different terminating area codes per day. From uplink and downlink byte counts we compute aggregated data usage per week.

Finally, geo-location data is extracted from the CDR records. The coordinates of the serving base station are recorded each time an SMS is transmitted. MO records contain the coordinates of the tower receiving the message in the uplink, whereas the MT record lists the base station delivering the SMS in the downlink. Based on this data fields, the location of a device can be estimated with an accuracy equivalent to the size of a cell or sector. If two communicating devices are connected to the same operator, we know approximate locations of both the sender and the receiver.

3. INVESTIGATION

This section describes the analysis of confirmed SMS spammer accounts that were canceled due to messaging abuse activities. The study compares communication pat-

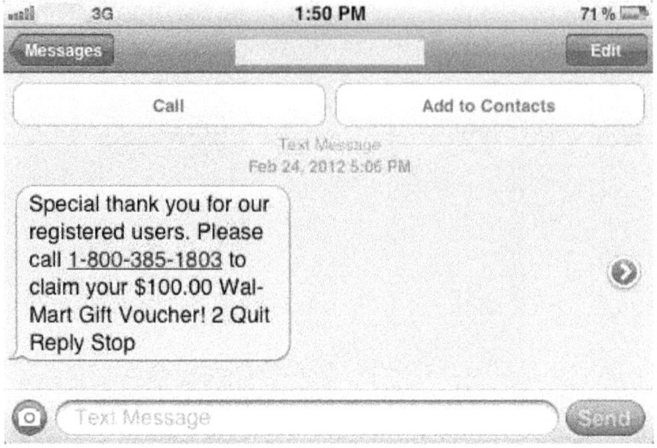

Figure 2: SMS spam message requesting a reply

terns of spammers to those of legitimate customers, both cell-phone users and M2M devices.

In all the figures throughout the paper, legitimate cell-phone users, M2M systems and spammers are represented in green, blue and red, respectively.

This section is organized in five subsections. We start with Subsection 3.1, which briefly describes the characteristics of the accounts of message abusers. Subsection 3.2 investigates the SMS spam traffic in general and Subsection 3.3 studies the location information of both spammers and their targets. Finally, Subsection 3.4 discusses tools used in messaging abuse and voice and data traffic are described in Subsection 3.5.

3.1 Spammer sketch: Account information

Detailed analysis of Call Detail Records indicates that the great majority of spammers (99.64%) are using pre-paid accounts. As the GSMA Messaging Anti-Abuse Working Group investigated [8], spammers purchase bulk SIM cards with unlimited messaging plans. These SIM cards are constantly switched to circumvent detection schemes and reduce the number of messages sent per day. Also they discard them once an account is canceled and continue spamming with a new one.

The average age of an illegitimate account is 7 to 11 days. This indicates that message abuse accounts are canceled rapidly on average. The account age of a legitimate user is often several months to a couple years.

3.2 The Crime: Messaging Abuse

Figures 1a and 1b compare the empirical histograms for the number of text messages sent and received by legitimate accounts, M2M and spammers. Intuitively, spammers generate a large load of messages. The number of spam SMSs is two orders of magnitude higher than that of legitimate user text messages and one order of magnitude above the number of messages from networked appliances.

Spammers not only send but also receive two orders of magnitude more messages than legitimate customers do. Although this behavior is, at first, unexpected, it can be explained by the nature of SMS spam messages. Upon reception of an unrequested text message, users sometimes attempt to reply to opt-out from the advertised service. Furthermore, actual spam messages often attempt to trick the recipient into replying to the message (Figure 2). Despite a small percentage of users will reply, the large amount of accounts targeted in a spam campaign results in many responses.

Figure 1c, which plots the distribution of the number of destinations, shows that legitimate accounts have a small set of recipients. Cell-phone users text on average to 7 contacts per day, while spammers hit a couple of thousand victims each day.

The ratio of the number of recipients to the number of messages, shown in Figure 1d, provides an additional insight. On average, spammers send one message to each victim. Legitimate users send multiple messages to a small set of destinations. For this specific feature, M2M appliances display a mixed distribution. Some devices send many messages to a small set of destinations while others transmit one single message to each destination. It is important to note that such M2M systems could be miss-labeled as message abusers by simple spam filters.

3.2.1 Response ratio

In subsection we investigate the ratio between the number of received and transmitted messages (response ratio). Although spammers receive a lot of messages, the response ratio is very different to that of a legitimate user. Figure 3 plots an example for a randomly selected spammer and legitimate user (with a post-paid family plan). The number of messages is equally normalized in both cases.

In the case of legitimate users, generally messages are sent in response to a previous message in a sequential way. Therefore, the response ratio close to 1. For spammers the amount of MT SMSs is proportionally very small to the number of transmitted messages. Therefore, the response ratio is close to 0.

3.2.2 Message timing and time series

This sub-section investigates timing characteristics of spam text messages. Due to the large load of SMSs spammers send, the intervals between two consecutive messages are short. On the other hand, both legitimate customers and M2M systems send messages less frequently. This can be observed in Figure 4a, which shows the distribution of the intervals between two sequential messages.

Figure 4b plots the distribution of the inter-message time entropy. Usually, spammers send messages at a constant rate using a computer. Legitimate users are less predictable. One cannot accurately estimate when the next text message will be sent given the time of the previous one. Inter-SMS intervals for spammers are less random resulting in low entropy values. On the other hand, intervals between two legitimate messages are random, with higher entropy.

Messaging activities of certain M2M devices are prescheduled. For example, smart grid meters report measurements periodically. Other applications, such as parking meters and ATMs, have communications initiated by humans. A message is sent each time a parking receipt is issued. Therefore, we observe a large number of M2M connected devices with a low value of the entropy, overlapping with spammers, and some with a higher value of the entropy, overlapping with legitimate users.

Beyond the large messaging load at a high frequency, we investigate what strategy spammers follow to transmit text messages over time. Figure 5 plots a typical example of the

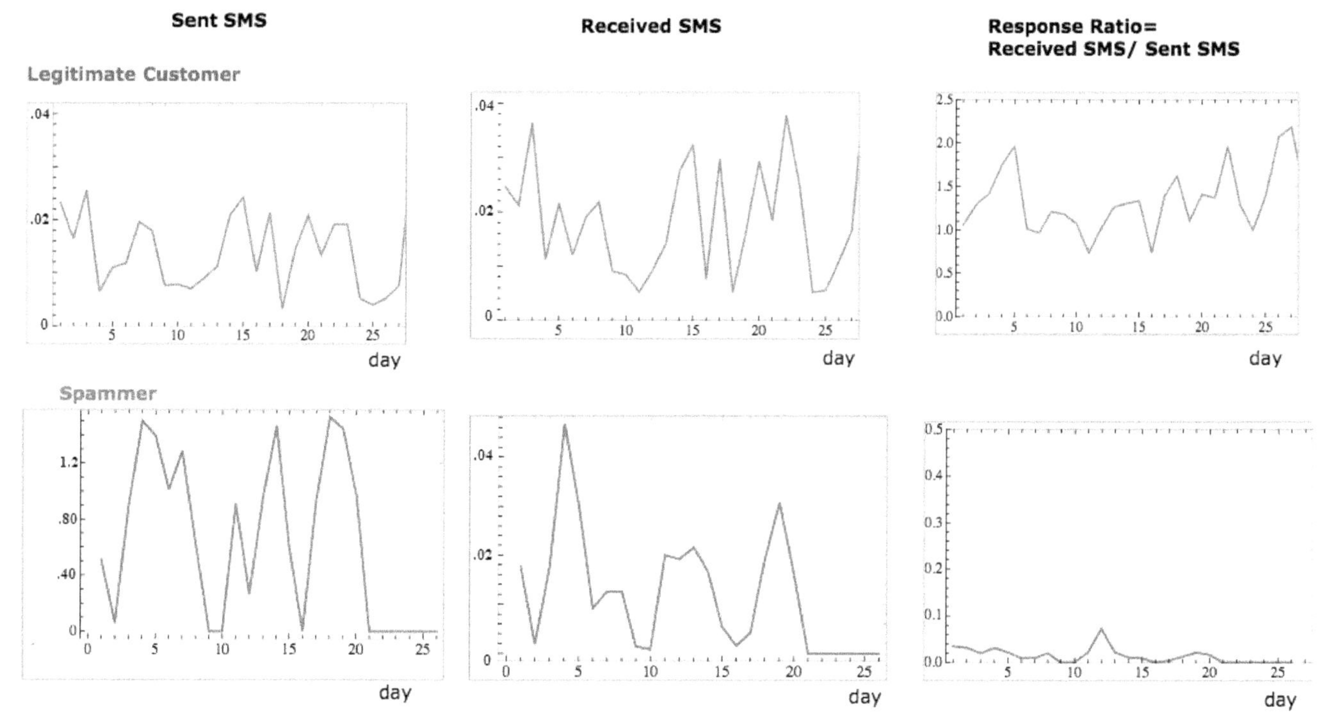

Figure 3: Example of normalized response ratio for a legitimate cell-phone user (green) and a spammer (red)

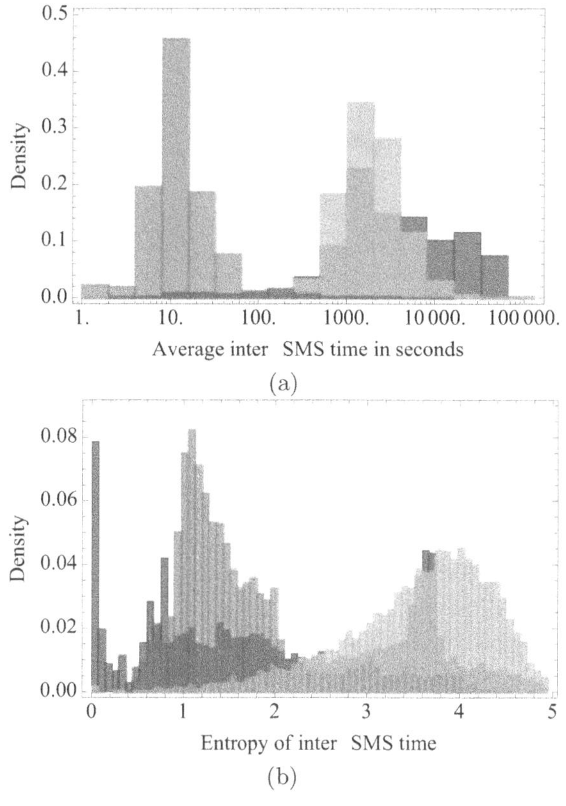

Figure 4: Distributions of the average inter-SMS time and its entropy for spammers (red), legitimate customers (green) and M2M (blue)

number of messages per minute sent over the span of one day. The results indicate that spammers focus the illegitimate activity during the day time. This might be to minimize the annoyance caused to recipients and lower the chances to be reported to spam detections services such as the 7726 service [1].

3.2.3 Message content

The analysis of the content of spam messages is out of the scope of this paper. However, we offer a brief glimpse of some of our findings. Querying the Cloudmark 7726 data-base of user reported spam messages [1], we access the content of the messages sent by positively identified spammers. Based on this data we determine that spammers based in far apart locations sometimes flood messages with exactly the same content. This could be an indication of either collaboration or a set of common sources both for revenue and content.

3.3 The Scene of the Crime

The next step of our analysis is to determine the geographical distribution of messaging abuse. We aim to find out where spammers base their activities and where the targets of such SMS traffic are located. Finally, we attempt to determine whether spammers are mobile or not.

3.3.1 Location of spammers and their targets

Figure 6 shows the locations of accounts identified for messaging abuse activities during the one year period under analysis. Data indicates that spammers are mainly located in California, specifically in the counties of Sacramento and Orange and in the surroundings of Los Angeles. Other notable sources of spam are observed in the New York/New Jersey/Long Island areas and in Miami Beach. Smaller sources of messaging abuse are found in Illinois, Michigan, North Carolina and Texas. Note that this does not im-

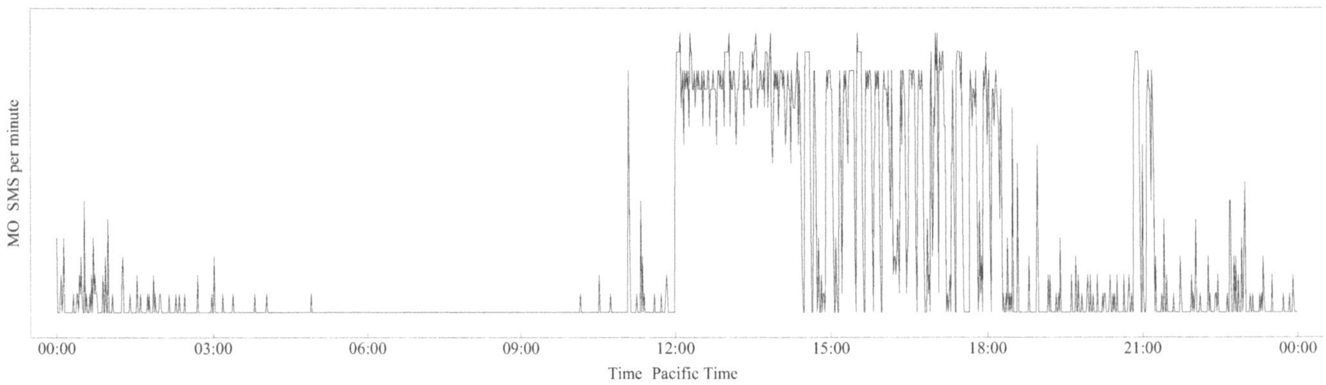

Figure 5: The number of messages sent per minute by a typical randomly selected spammer

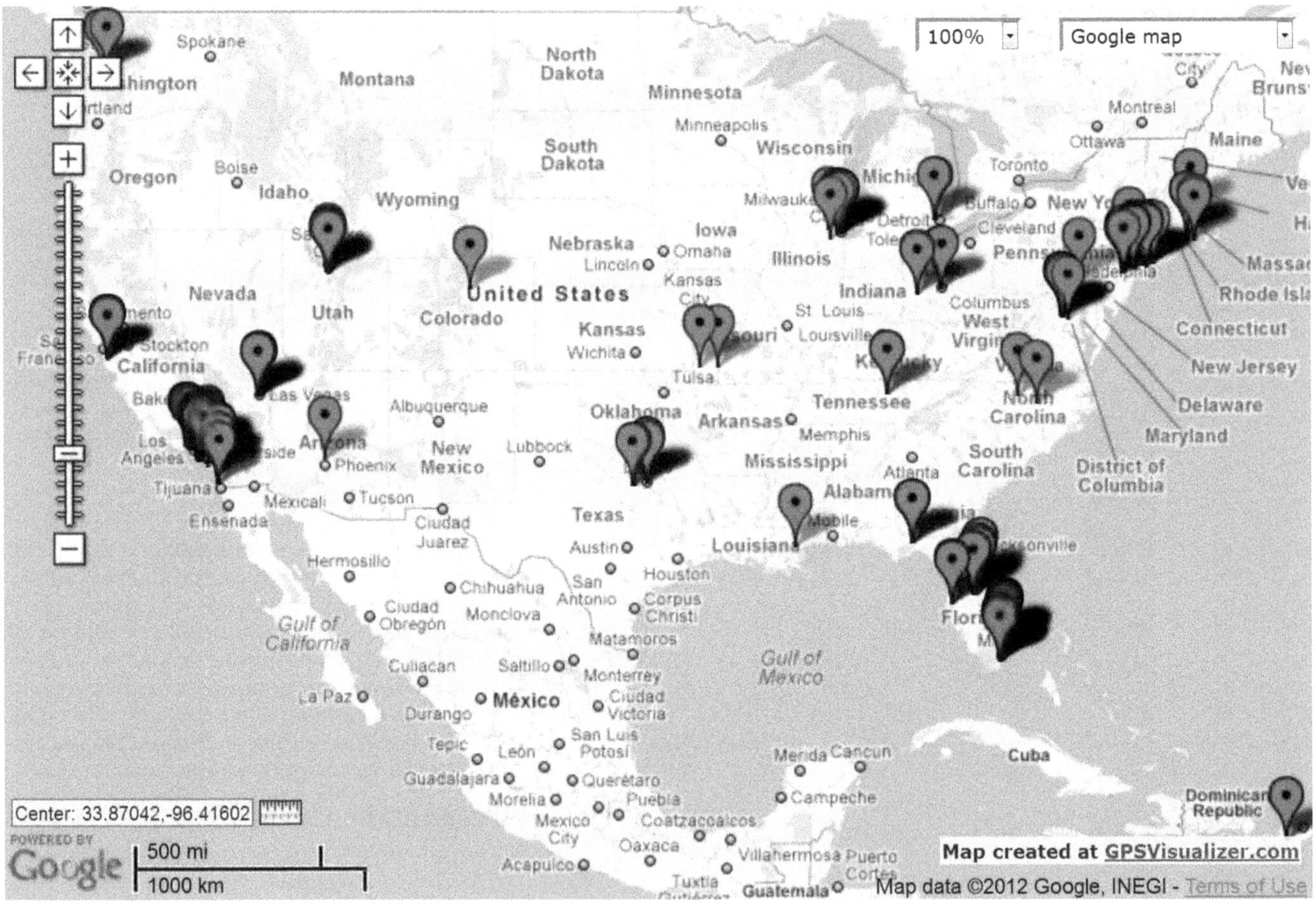

Figure 6: Location of SMS spammers.

ply that spam will always come from only these areas, but gives an indication of the non-uniform origin of SMS spam messages. Messaging abuse in the SMS world appears to originate from a few locations over the US.

Figures 7a and 7b show the recipients of SMS messages sent out in one day by a randomly selected spammer and legitimate customer respectively. Each map plots the source (spammer or legitimate user) with a pin and individual recipients with a diamond. Note that we only have location information for customers (recipients) subscribed to the cellular operator under analysis. The legitimate customer communicates only with a small number of contacts. Most of the recipients for the given user belong to the local area (i.e. the area around the subscriber's home) as well as several other locations (e.g. areas where the subscriber works, used to live or where friends and relatives reside). In contrast, the recipients of spam text messages appear to be distributed

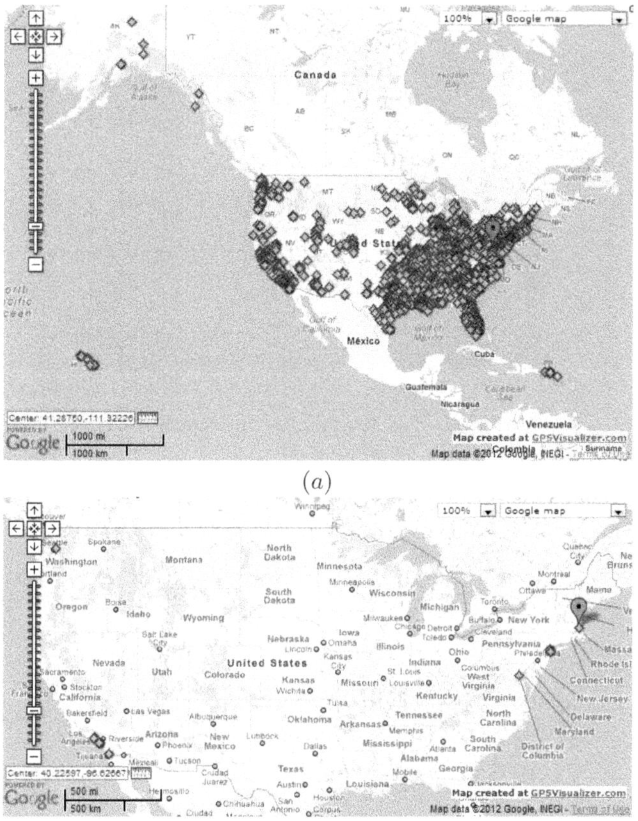

(a)

(b)

Figure 7: Example area code messaging pattern for a spammer (a) and a legitimate customers (b)

uniformly over the US population (the spammer sends messages to most area codes).

Figure 8a plots the distribution of the number of unique area codes contacted in one day by spammers, legitimate customers and M2M systems. Spammers are characterized by messaging a large number of area codes, always greater than those of cell-phone users and M2M. We observe, though, a small amount of spammers contacting a reduced number of area codes. Most M2M devices contact numbers just within one area code.

Independent of the number of unique area codes, it is interesting to know how often these area codes are contacted. Figure 8b plots the entropy of these area codes. In this context, entropy stands for the randomness of the connections in one day. A low value of the entropy implies that this specific user contacts repeatedly the same area codes. On the other hand, a high value of the entropy indicates a user that sends messages to a more random set of area codes.

Network enabled appliances report to specific servers and data collectors or, in the case of user applications (i.e. home monitoring), to a predefined set of cell-phones. Therefore, the entropy is the lowest. Spammers show a much more random set of SMS abuse targets with a high entropy. Further analysis of the spam data identifies a messaging strategy that consists of messaging numbers in ascendent order. Thus, sending bulk SMSs to each area code sequentially.

The aforementioned results are summarized in Figure 8c, which plots the correlation between the number of sent messages and the number of recipients. The linear relation in the case of SMS spammers is obvious. Both M2M systems and cell-phone users cluster around the bottom-left area of the graph. One can notice in the figure some M2M appliances sending up to 20000 messages to 1 single destination. This is a common situation in, for example, security or monitoring M2M applications in which reports are timely sent to a controlling server.

The relation between the ratio (number of message recipients)/(number of messages sent) and the average number of area codes reached by day is plotted in Figure 8d. Cell-phone users congregate at the bottom left of the Figure, with low destinations-to-messages ratio and a small set of contacted area codes. A great majority of spammers exhibit the opposite behavior, clustering on the top-right corner of the figure. Nevertheless, a substantial number of spammers with a different behavior is identified.

The spammers aggregated on the bottom-right corner of Figure 8d are message abusers that target very specific geographical regions. These accounts still send thousands of messages per day with a ratio close to one destination per message. However, the number of targeted area codes is in the range of the number of recipients from legitimate cell-phone users.

3.3.2 Do spammers move? Yes, they do!

In terms of mobility, one expects spammers to not move. Therefore, all messages should be handled by one single base station. Figure 9 plots the distribution of the number of base stations (Location Area Code - Cell ID, LACCI) a device is connected to in one day. Legitimate customers display a highly mobile behavior, with most of the users visiting at most 30 cells sectors. This number depends on many factors, such as the length of the daily commute. The distribution exhibits a long tail with a minority of highly mobile cell-phone users.

Spammers, as expected, are much less mobile. They still appear to traverse an average of about 4 cells or sectors. This might be due to the following reasons. On one hand, spammers might mount their equipment on a vehicle and drive around the area in an attempt to misguide detection schemes looking at device mobility. On the other hand, especially in the case of aircards, the hardware often connects to the network by means of a Third Generation (3G) technology. 3G wireless networks in the operator under study are based on Wideband Code Multiple Division Access (WCDMA). In such technology, the receiver can be physically connected to up to 6 sectors at the same time, combining the signal at the RAKE receiver [22]. Depending on the channel conditions and fading, the serving base station might fluctuate throughout this list of 6 LACCIs. This would result in CDR records from the same static device appearing to come from up to 6 different sectors.

Note that, though, based on the IMEI, we are able to determine the actual hardware used by the spammer to send messages. In the case of GSM devices, a cell-phone or cellular modem is at all time connected to, at most, one cell tower [6]. Camping on base stations miles away from each other definitively indicates movement.

The distribution of recipients' area codes for M2M is mixed. The majority of appliances are quasi-static, with most of their messaging load being handled by a couple of sectors. This corresponds to non-mobility M2M applications

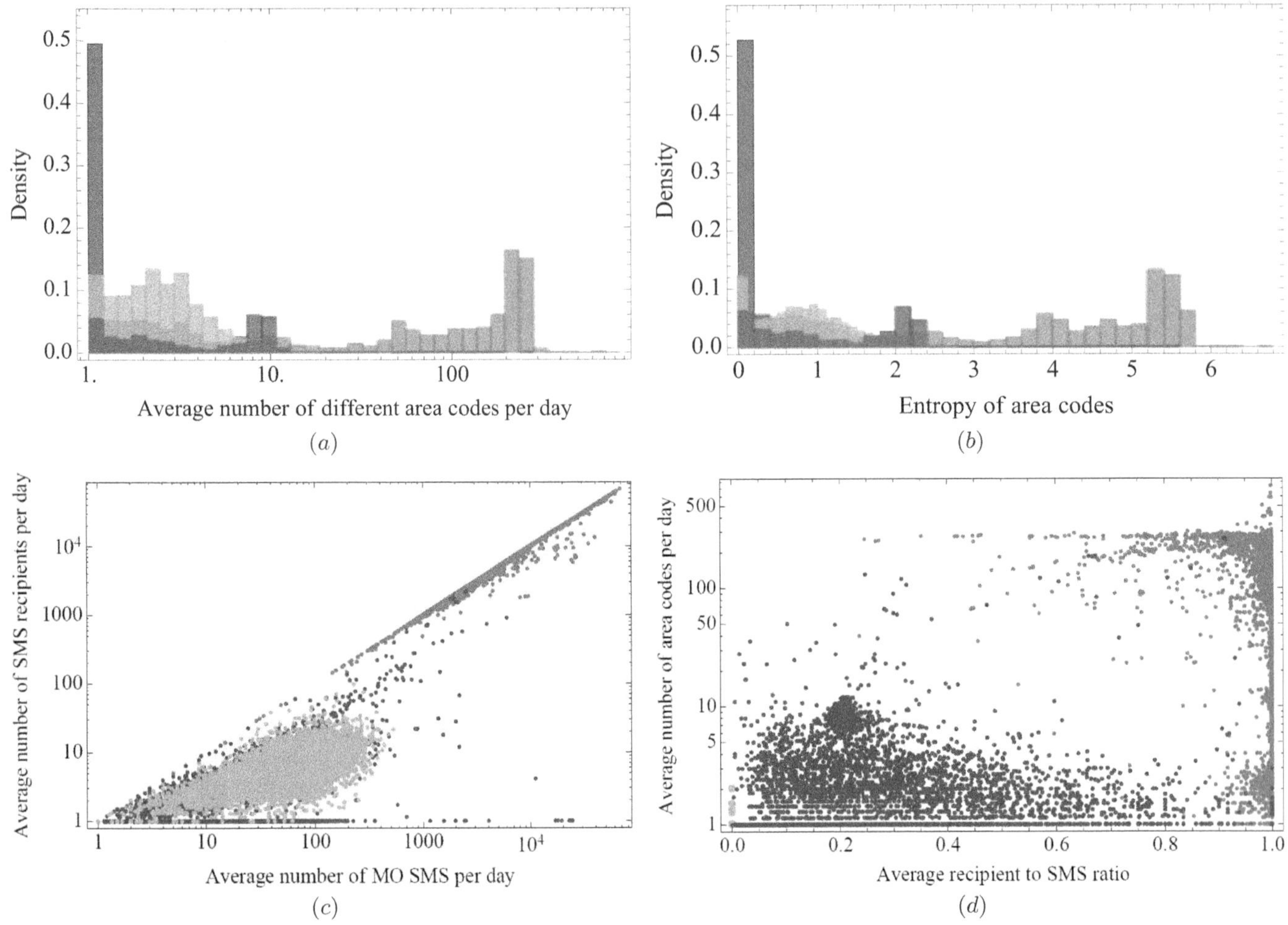

Figure 8: Distributions of the average number of destination area codes, their entropy and related scatter-plots for spammers (red), legitimate customers (green) and M2M (blue)

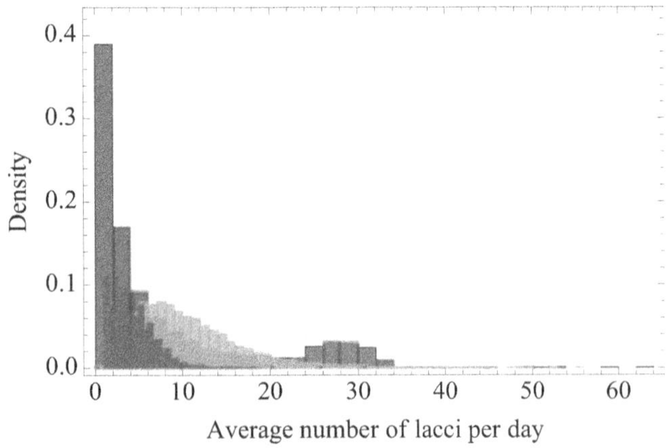

Figure 9: Distribution of the average daily number of base stations (LACCI) visited by spammers (red), legitimate customers (green) and M2M (blue)

such as alarms and smart grid readers. Another large set of devices are highly mobile, with an average of 28 sectors visited per day. In this case, these are mobile applications such as fleet control/monitoring and asset tracking.

The final answer to the question is found in Figure 10, which plots the observed locations of a randomly chosen spammer on the map of an undisclosed area. The legend indicates the length on the map that corresponds to 1 mile and 2km. Based on this information, it seems that certain spammers move while sending illegitimate SMSs. In the case of the example, this spammer is observed in the vicinity of cell sites as far as 4 miles apart. Computing the longest distance between the cell sites every spammer camps on indicates a maximum displacement of 15 miles.

3.4 The weapons of choice

Observations of the IMEI from CDR gives us an insight on the kind of device used to connect to the cellular network. Analyzing the TAC data from known and already canceled spamming accounts, we observe that an impressive 83% of the spammers identified in one year is sent from one of the top five identified devices. About 65% of the spammers in the US send messages with the top device.

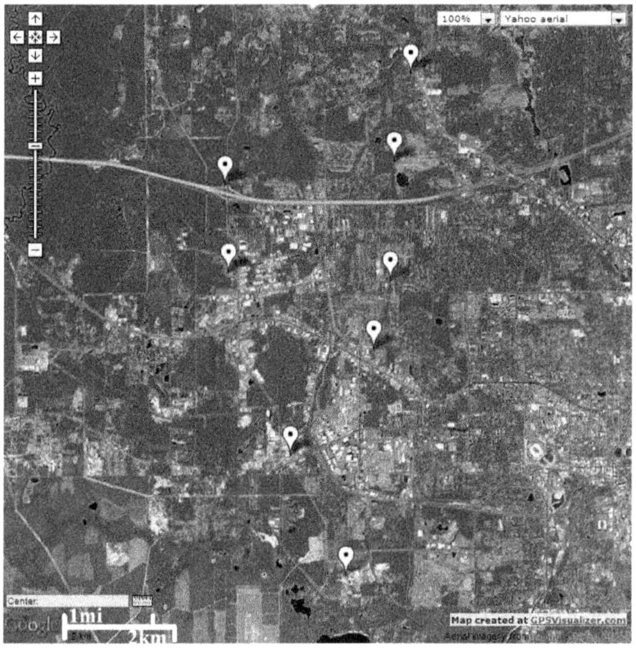

Figure 10: Example of observed locations for one spammer

Devices used by spammers are anonymized and ranked. The top 5 most frequently used devices are listed below.

1. USB Modem/Aircard A1
2. Feature mobile-phone M1
3. Feature mobile-phone M2
4. USB Modem/Aircard A2
5. USB Modem/Aircard A3

Thus spammers often rely on modems and aircards connected to a PC via USB interface. A1, A2 and A3 belong to this category. In parallel, spammers also use common feature phones as cellular modem. This might be done in order to mislead detection schemes by making messages appear to be originated at a legitimate cell-phone. Several resources can be found online with detailed instructions on how to re-flash typical feature phones from most manufacturers with custom firmware [2] [5] [4].

Note that these devices are legitimate hardware that spammers use for SMS abuse. All of them are used in legitimate applications, which provides cover for the spam. This is why we anonymize the make and model of these devices.

It is interesting to note that this specific traffic analysis indicates that at least 16% of the SMS traffic originated by all the A1 modems in the network is spam. This shows a clear preference of spammers for this particular cellular modem.

3.5 The Alibi: Voice and IP traffic

As observed in the previous sections, SMS spammers attempt to reach as many targets as possible by flooding large amounts of messages. This paper focuses on SMS spam analysis. Nevertheless, we include voice and IP traffic data in our study and the results are rather interesting. Spammers do generate both data and voice traffic, perhaps to increase the chances to go undetected through spam filters that search for non human-like communication traffic or perhaps other forms of fraud.

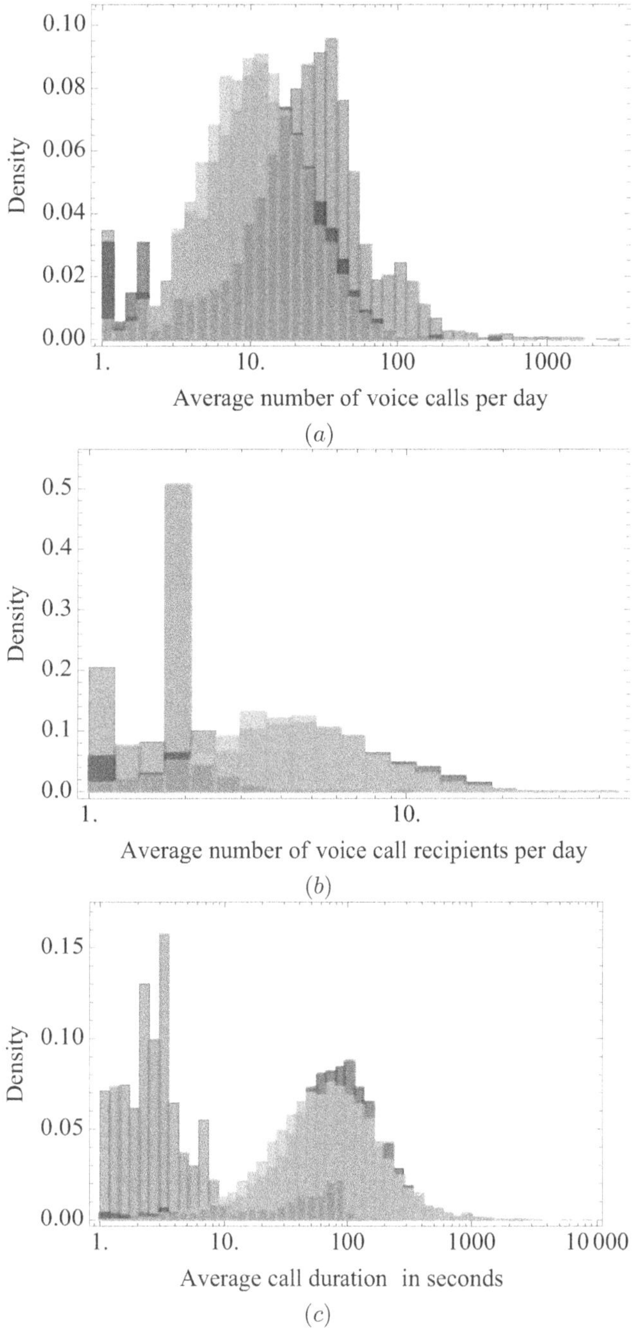

Figure 11: Distributions of the average number of (a) phone calls, (b) call destinations and (c) call durations for spammers (red), legitimate customers (green) and M2M (blue)

3.5.1 Voice calls

Figures 11a and 11b plot the empirical histograms of the number of phone calls and their recipients. Figure 11c corresponds to the empirical histogram of the duration of voice calls. On average, spammers make many more phone calls than legitimate users, however the average number of phone call destinations is much lower (Figures 11a and 11b). This number of phone calls could perhaps indicate that they are trying to mimic legitimate users. In terms of voice traffic duration, phone calls placed by spammers are much shorter than those of legitimate users, as it can be observed on Figure 11c. This is because, despite they seem to attempt to match the calling profile of a legitimate user, these calls cannot be sustained for a long time since the recipient will hang up. The short call duration could also indicate that these calls might be spam as well. Most of the times, the recipient of a spam call will hang up immediately.

Unlike in SMS traffic, spammers do not flood with calls a large number of recipients. They might be communicating with a small set of numbers that they know will pick up the call even though they might hang up quickly.

The results are further detailed in Figure 12. Figure 12a plots the average number of call destinations per day (y-axis) versus the average number of calls (x-axis), in log-log scale. One can see that spammers cluster around a large number of calls to a small set of destinations. In parallel, both cell-phone users and M2M devices make phone calls to a proportional set of destinations.

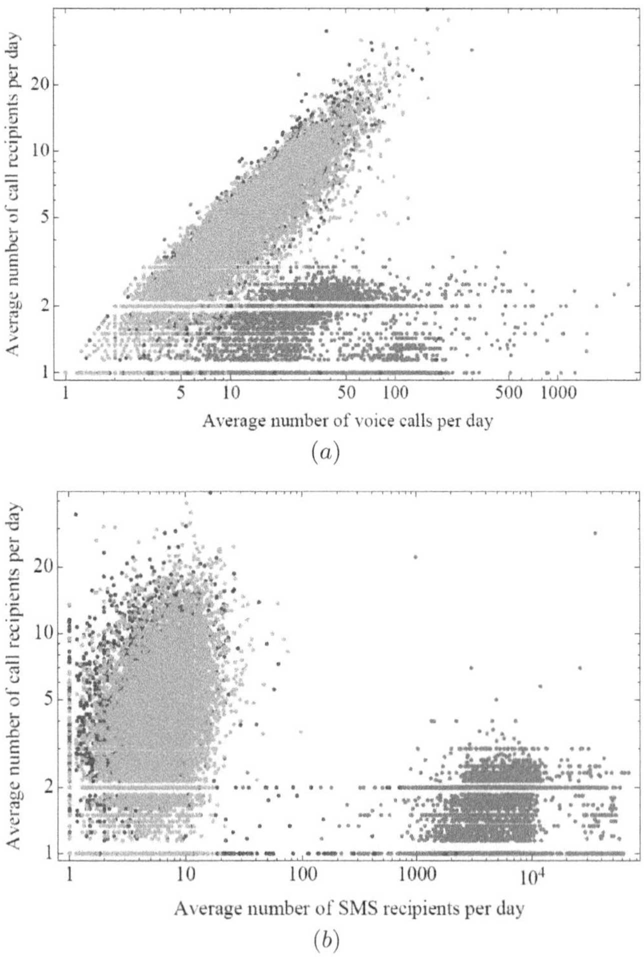

Figure 12: Correlation between number of calls and their recipients for spammers (red), legitimate customers (green) and M2M (blue)

The difference in behavior of spammers is highly accentuated in Figure 12b, which plots the average number of SMS destinations (x-axis) against the number of voice call destinations (y-axis). Spammers appear to be placing phone calls to a set of recipients that is much smaller than the set of targets for the text message abuse. This figure also hints that legitimate users, on average, tend to communicate to a larger set of contacts by phone than by text message. This could be explained based on the fact that cell-phone users rely on the extremely popular SMS service to communicate with friends and relatives. However, phone calls are made to this same set of users plus other contacts such as restaurants to make a reservation, the doctor's office to make an appointment, etc. Therefore, the set of call recipients will be larger than for SMSs.

3.5.2 IP traffic

Finally, we examine IP traffic. Figure 13 plots the distribution of the up-link and down-link byte counts related to the three account categories under analysis. Spammers generate a small amount of data, consisting on several small transactions.

Cell-phone users and M2M systems generate asymmetric IP data traffic. Regular users often consume more bandwidth in the downlink, by browsing videos, media and other kinds of content. Their uplink traffic is generally lower. M2M appliances have the opposite behavior. Used mostly as reporting tools for applications such as remote alarm and fleet control, they often generate a larger load in the uplink.

4. STOPPING THE CRIME

The results presented in this paper have been used to develop an accurate SMS spam detection engine. The description, details and results obtained are out of the scope of this paper, but will be submitted in the near future. In this section, though, we offer a brief overall glimpse.

An advanced SMS spam detection algorithm is proposed based on an ensemble of decision trees. Over 40 specific features are extracted from messaging patterns and processed through a combination of decision trees. Moreover, in order to speed up the spam detection process, the system focuses on features that only require one to a few messages to obtain. This algorithm also leverages the insights on M2M SMS messaging patterns described in this paper.

5. RELATED WORK

SMS spam has not been widely discussed in literture. Nevertheless, there is some work introducing different detection schemes. For example, the authors of [24] propose a detection engine based on analyzing the social network of connections of spammers. Other approaches are based on investigating the content of SMS spam messages [12].

There is plenty of literature on spam messaging analysis on other communication systems. The most widespread type of spam is electronic mail (email) spam. In this context, [17] presents interesting findings on how message abusers harvest large lists of email addresses to use as targets for their spam campaigns. The authors of [18] study the network-level behavior of spammers in the email world. Email messaging abuse is found to originate from a very few regions of the IP address space. This messages are generated from an immense swarm of bots, each one of them sending only a few

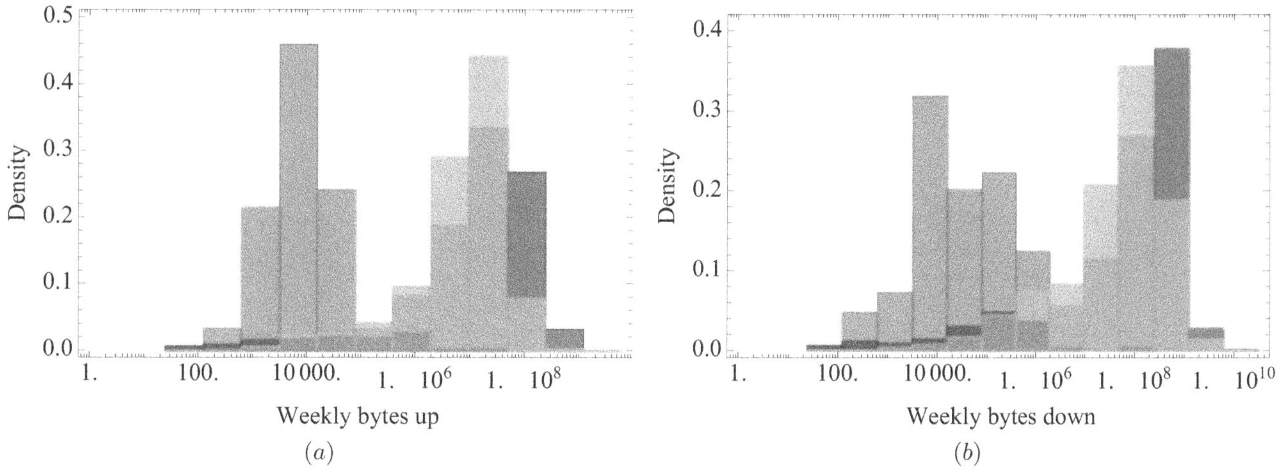

Figure 13: Data traffic pattern of spammers (red), legitimate customers (green) and M2M (blue)

pieces of mail over very short periods of time. It is interesting to note that this somehow correlates with the SMS spam world where, based on our data analysis in Section 3, messages are originated from a few geographic hot-spots and by accounts with a very short tenure. Based on the findings in [18], the authors of [26] proposed an algorithm to detect and track bot-nets based on email spam records.

Email spam has been a known problem for many years and there is already plenty of work proposing advanced detection schemes. For example, the authors of [13] study the effectiveness of DNS blacklisting and [10] presents a survey of known spam filtering techniques with particular emphasis on how well they work.

There is also some work analyzing other kinds of spam and messaging abuse. For example, [14] studies the traffic characteristics of tweet spam and propaganda. Message (tweet) abuse is generated by a small amount of playes that generate large amounts of messages, most of which appear to be retweets, in short periods of time. Other interesting works analyze messaging abuse and spam in the context of YouTube comments [20] and the blogosphere [21]. Finally, the authors of [9] study the risk of sophisticated context-aware spam that could result from information sharing on social networks.

6. CONCLUSIONS

In this paper we study characteristics and traffic patterns of SMS spam accounts based on real cellular network from a tier-1 provider in the United States. The results are compared against a sample of real traffic from legitimate cell-phone users and M2M devices.

Confirming the common presumption, we identify that 99.64% of the spammers connect using pre-paid accounts. The simple availability of such SIM cards make them the perfect tool for SMS abuse. Observations indicate an average age for the pre-paid accounts between 7 and 11 days. We also find indications of the preference spammers have for a very small set of hardware devices. Spam traffic analysis reveals that 84% of the spammers use one of the top 5 spamming tools in the US. In particular, 65% of the spammers choose to connect to the network with the top device.

We confirm common intuitions about spammers, such as the large number of text messages sent per day to a wide target list. Spammers generate two orders of magnitude more messages than cell-phone users and one order of magnitude greater than most M2M systems. These messages are sent mostly to different recipients, with a ratio of recipients to messages sent very close to one. Further investigation of the messaging flow indicates that spammers also receive a large number of messages. Nevertheless, the number of incoming SMS is relatively very low with respect to the number of transmitted spam texts.

The study of geo-location data identifies the areas of Sacramento, Los Angeles-Orange County and Miami Beach as the major spamming hot-spots in the US. From these locations, spammers launch very geographically distributed campaigns targeting all area codes uniformly. Nevertheless, some spammers are engaged in very geographically focused spamming campaigns. In terms of mobility, we conclude that spammers are often mobile around their local area.

Finally, spammers are found to generate a large number of very short phone calls and data transactions with a very small number of end points. This could be perhaps a strategy to mislead spam detection filters by replicating human-like network traffic behavior.

Our traffic analysis indicates that certain networked appliances have messaging behavior close to that of a spammer. A small number of M2M systems transmit a large number of SMSs per day. These are often devices that communicate with a large number of destinations as well. Despite not being very abundant, we identify a substantial number of M2M enabled objects with a ratio destination to number of messages very close to 1. These appliances communicate with a large set of area codes as well. However, these area codes have low entropy in the sense that the recipients of the messages are always the same. Based on the investigation in this paper, we identify Machine to Machine communications as an important player in SMS networks. Such systems should be taken into consideration when designing SMS spam detection and filtering schemes. Systems designed otherwise could incur the risk of blocking or erroneously labeling legitimate text messages as message abuse.

The results presented in this paper are being used to design an advanced SMS spam detection system.

ACKNOWLEDGEMENTS

The authors would like to thank Cheri Kerstetter, Rick Becker, Joel Casey, Jeff Bickford and Alex Bobotek for their help, comments and valuable suggestions.

7. REFERENCES

[1] GSMA Spam Reporting Service Overview. GSMA and Cloudmark. `http://www.gsma.com/spam-reporting-services-overview/`.

[2] Motorola RAZR V3 Reflash Files by MotoX. Cell Corner, February 2006. `http://www.cellcorner.com/unlock/phpBB2/post-19.html`.

[3] 2009 Annual Security Report. Symantec MessageLabs Intelligence, 2009. `http://www.symanteccloud.com/mlireport/2009MLIAnnualReport_Final_PrintResolution.pdf`.

[4] Samsung-Eternity Firmware Editor project. Google Code, July 2010. `http://code.google.com/p/samsung-firmware-tools/wiki/Summary`.

[5] Flashing Original or custom firmware on Nokia mobiles using Phoenix Service software. Digi-Passion, September 2011. `http://preview.tinyurl.com/7e38byq`.

[6] 3GPP: Global System for Mobile Communications. Digital cellular telecommunications system (phase 2+): Physical layer on the radio path: general description. Technical report 3GPP gsm 05.01. v5.0.0, 1996. `http://preview.tinyurl.com/8kgxzyq`.

[7] M. Ablot. SMS on the decline as third–party messaging gains traction. Wireless Inteligence, November 2011. `http://informationweek.com/news/healthcare/mobile-wireless/232301072`.

[8] A. Bobotek. Threat of Mobile Malware and Abuse. Messaging Anti-Abuse Working Group (MAAWG), October 2010. `http://wnss.sv.cmu.edu/wms/2010/wms_talk01.pdf`.

[9] G. Brown, T. Howe, M. Ihbe, A. Prakash, and K. Borders. Social networks and context-aware spam. In *Proceedings of the 2008 ACM conference on Computer supported cooperative work*, CSCW '08, pages 403–412, San Diego, CA, USA, 2008. ACM.

[10] G. Cormack. Email spam filtering: A systematic review. *Foundations and Trends in Information Retrieval*, 1(4):335–455, 2007.

[11] G. V. Cormack, J. M. G. Hidalgo, and E. P. Sánz. Feature engineering for mobile (SMS) spam filtering. In *Proceedings of the 30th annual international ACM SIGIR conference on Research and development in information retrieval*, SIGIR '07, pages 871–872, Amsterdam, The Netherlands, 2007. ACM.

[12] J. M. Gómez Hidalgo, G. C. Bringas, E. P. Sánz, and F. C. García. Content based sms spam filtering. In *Proceedings of the 2006 ACM symposium on Document engineering*, DocEng '06, pages 107–114, Amsterdam, The Netherlands, 2006. ACM.

[13] J. Jung and E. Sit. An empirical study of spam traffic and the use of dns black lists. In *Proceedings of the 4th ACM SIGCOMM conference on Internet measurement*, IMC '04, pages 370–375, Taormina, Sicily, Italy, 2004. ACM.

[14] C. Lumezanu, N. Feamster, and H. Klein. # bias: Measuring the tweeting behavior of propagandists. In *Sixth International AAAI Conference on Weblogs and Social Media*, Dublin, Ireland, 2012.

[15] I. Murynets and R. Piqueras Jover. How an SMS-Based malware infection will get throttled by the wireless link. In *Proceedings of IEEE ICC 2012 - Communication and Information Systems Security Symposium (ICC'12 CISS)*, Ottawa, Ontario, Canada, June 2012.

[16] N. Perlroth. Spam Invades a Last Refuge, the Cellphone. The New York Times, April 2012. `http://preview.tinyurl.com/7nwvm3g`.

[17] M. Prince, B. Dahl, L. Holloway, A. Keller, and E. Langheinrich. Understanding how spammers steal your e-mail address: An analysis of the first six months of data from project honey pot. In *Second Conference on Email and Anti-Spam*, CEAS '05, Stanford, CA, USA, 2005.

[18] A. Ramachandran and N. Feamster. Understanding the network-level behavior of spammers. In *ACM SIGCOMM Computer Communication Review*, volume 36, pages 291–302. ACM, 2006.

[19] V. Shannon. 15 years of text messages, a 'cultural phenomenon', December 2007. `http://www.nytimes.com/2007/12/05/technology/05iht-sms.4.8603150.html?pagewanted=all`.

[20] A. Sureka. Mining user comment activity for detecting forum spammers in youtube. *CoRR*, Vol. abs/1103.5044, 2011.

[21] A. Thomason. Blog spam: A review. In *Conference on Email and Anti-Spam*, CEAS '07, Mountain View, CA, USA, 2007.

[22] Universal Mobile Telecommunications System (UMTS). Physical layer procedures (FDD). 3GPP TS 25.214 Release 1999. v8.9.0, 1999. `http://preview.tinyurl.com/98ex9hw`.

[23] Universal Mobile Telecommunications System (UMTS). Digital cellular telecommunications system (phase 2+): Universal mobile telecommunications system (UMTS), technical realization of the short message service (SMS). Technical report 3GPP TS 23.040. v10.0.0, 2011. `http://preview.tinyurl.com/9cs3wdo`.

[24] C. Wang, Y. Zhang, X. Chen, Z. Liu, L. Shi, G. Chen, F. Qiu, C. Ying, and W. Lu. A behavior-based sms antispam system. *IBM Journal of Research and Development*, 54(6):3–1, 2010.

[25] N. Zablotskaya. Fraudulent spam. Securelist, July 2008. `http://www.securelist.com/en/analysis/204792012/Fraudulent_spam`.

[26] L. Zhuang, J. Dunagan, D. Simon, H. Wang, I. Osipkov, G. Hulten, and J. Tygar. Characterizing botnets from email spam records. In *Proceedings of the 1st Usenix Workshop on Large-Scale Exploits and Emergent Threats*, number 2 in LEET '08, pages 1–9, San Francisco, CA, USA, 2008. USENIX Association.

Longtime Behavior of Harvesting Spam Bots

Oliver Hohlfeld
TU Berlin / Telekom Innovation Laboratories
oliver@net.t-labs.tu-berlin.de

Thomas Graf
Modas GmbH
post@thomas-graf.de

Florin Ciucu
TU Berlin / Telekom Innovation Laboratories
florin@net.t-labs.tu-berlin.de

ABSTRACT

This paper investigates the origins of the spamming process, specifically concerning address harvesting on the web, by relying on an extensive measurement data set spanning over three years. Concretely, we embedded more than 23 million unique spamtrap addresses in web pages. 0.5% of the embedded trap addresses received a total of 620,000 spam messages. Besides the scale of the experiment, the critical aspect of our methodology is the uniqueness of the issued spamtrap addresses, which enables the mapping of crawling activities to the actual spamming process.

Our observations suggest that simple obfuscation methods are still efficient for protecting addresses from being harvested. A key finding is that search engines are used as proxies, either to hide the identity of the harvester or to optimize the harvesting process.

Categories and Subject Descriptors

C.2.3 [**Computer-communication networks**]: Network operations—*Network monitoring*; H.4.3 [**Information Systems Applications**]: Communications Applications—*Electronic mail*

General Terms

Measurement, Security

Keywords

Spam, E-Mail, Address Harvesting

1. INTRODUCTION

The presence of unsolicited bulk e-mail (spam), which has exceeded the volume of legitimate e-mail, remains a costly economic problem. Notwithstanding existing counteracting measures, spamming campaigns advertising products are profitable even when the amount of purchases being made is small relative to the amount of spam [12]. The apparent success of spamming campaigns motivates the understanding of spamming trends and their economics, which may provide insights into more efficient counteracting measures.

Many studies address the properties of spam e-mails, traffic, and campaigns [5, 31, 19, 22], infrastructures for spam dissemination (e.g., botnets) [6, 27, 11, 19, 31, 22, 30, 10], and detection and classification methods [29, 2, 6, 7, 9, 11, 30, 14, 13]. For instance, it has been shown that spam and non-spam traffic have significantly different properties which can be used for spam classification [5]. Much fewer studies address the origins of the spamming process, e.g., concerning *address harvesting*, which remains the primary means for spammers to obtain new target addresses. Addresses can be harvested in multiple ways, e.g., from public web pages by using crawlers [20] or by malicious software locally running on compromised machines [16]. Investigating the harvesting processes is particularly relevant as it leads to new insights about spammers, according to studies revealing the social network of spammers [28] or a rather superficial effort to conceal identity [20].

To explore the origins of the spamming process, this paper conducts a large scale study involving addresses harvested from public web pages. Concretely, to identify address harvesting crawlers, we have embedded more than 23 million unique spamtrap addresses in more than 3 million visits to web pages over the course of more than three years, starting in May of 2009. 0.5% of the embedded addresses received a total of 620,000 spam e-mails. The uniqueness property of the embedded spamtrap addresses enables the mapping between the crawling activity to the actual spamming process.

Our main findings can be summarized as follows: *i)* search engines are used as proxies, either for hiding the identity of the harvester or for optimizing the harvesting process and *ii)* simple obfuscation methods are still efficient for protecting addresses from being harvested.

In addition, we find that harvesting on our web sites is on the decline. Harvested addresses are mainly spammed in batches and are only used for a short time period. We show that harvester bots are still mainly run in access networks. One interpretation of our results is that only a few parties are involved in address harvesting, each causing different spam volumes. Our findings also suggest that the usage of some harvesting software is stable. Also, harvesters make little use of Tor as anonymity service to hide their identity. Our overall study provides thus an up-to-date view on spam origins which further reveals guidelines for webmasters to protect e-mail addresses.

Our data set can be obtained from [8].

IMC'12, November 14–16, 2012, Boston, Massachusetts, USA.

2. RELATED WORK

The method of identifying harvesting bots by issuing dynamically created addresses that are unique to each page request has been used for spam prevention and the identification of harvesters [24, 20, 25]. The first attempts in understanding the behavior of harvesters have been undertaken by Prince et al. [20] and Schryen [24] in 2005. Based on 2500 spam e-mails, Schryen [24] investigates whether the top level domain of an e-mail address is relevant for spammers and finds that .com addresses attract more spam. A more systematic study of address harvesting was done by Prince et al. [20] by using a distributed platform using 5000 participants to advertise spamtrap addresses and receive spam (Project Honey Pot). The authors present preliminary results on the average turnaround time of e-mails, User Agent strings used by harvester bots, and their geolocation. The data has been obtained over a period of six months and is based on an unstated number of spam e-mails. In particular, the paper classifies harvesters into two distinct categories by the message turnaround time: hucksters and fraudsters.

Aspects of address harvesting were revisited by Shue et al. [25] in 2009. Their study is based on 96 spam e-mails and studies the geolocation of harvesters, strength of presentation methods, turnaround times, and the aggressiveness of harvester bots expressed by the frequency of page visits.

Several spam prevention studies [3, 23] propose to pollute spammers' databases and thus to inflate the number of available recipients in order to reduce spam on legitimate accounts. In contrast, our study is concerned with dynamically generating spamtrap addresses for identifying the properties of address harvesting.

As trends in the world of spam and malware are changing fast, this paper presents an up-to-date view on address harvesting and content spamming. To the best of our knowledge, we are the first to present a large-scale data set spanning over more than three years that combines aspects of harvesting and comment spamming. In contrast to [24] and [25], our spam body consists of 620,000 spam e-mails and is larger by magnitudes. While we confirm previous findings, we also study new aspects such as *i)* the connection between harvesting and comment spamming activities, *ii)* the efficiency of blacklisting, *iii)* the usage of the Tor anonymity service, *iv)* host-level properties of bots, and *v)* the usage of search engines as proxies to hide the identity of harvesters.

3. METHODOLOGY & DATASETS

To study the properties of the address harvesting process of harvesters using web crawlers, we use a methodology relying on issuing unique spamtrap e-mail addresses via the web. As the addresses are uniquely generated for each page request, their usage can be directly mapped to a specific page request. The generated addresses are embedded into nine low-profile web pages of various types (gaming, private web pages, research group, etc., see Table 1) and popularities. This methodology is implemented in web sites by including a dynamic script that generates unique e-mail addresses for each page request and logs information about the visitors. The resulting distributed platform to advertise our spamtrap addresses and to receive spam is illustrated in Figure 1.

Webmasters are typically confronted with the dilemma of choosing a method for displaying e-mail addresses on the web: Should addresses be presented in a user-friendly or obfuscated way to prevent spam? Which presentation method is the most robust against address harvesters? To shed light on this dilemma, the information included in the web pages of our study consists of six different spamtrap addresses, each being displayed with one of the following presentation and obfuscation techniques: *i)* a *mailto:* link (**MTO**), *ii)* non-linked, plain-text address (**TXT**), *iii)* e-mail obfuscated in the form of *user [at] domain [dot] tld* (**OBF**), *iv)* obfuscated using Javascript code (**JS**), *v)* included in a hidden data field of a web form (**FRM**), and *vi)* plain-text address inside an HTML comment (**CMT**). All of the above described addresses consist of random strings of 10 characters each (*RND IDs*, e.g., "jdi4gj8bzx"). We use random strings as they are sufficiently hard to guess. Table 1 shows the total number of embedded random IDs per web page, as well as the respective measurement periods. Note that the number of random IDs correlates with the number of monitored page requests for each web site.

In addition to random strings, we issue realistic looking addresses containing random combinations of first and last names generated from phone book records (*Name IDs*, e.g., "john.doe"). These addresses were introduced in January 2010, six months after the random IDs. The number of embedded addresses per web page is shown in Table 1. Compared to random strings, the assumption is that realistic looking addresses are harder to identify as spamtrap addresses, but are also easier to guess. As the total number of possible firstname × lastname combinations is much smaller than the total number of possible random IDs, we only issue name IDs using the *MTO* embedding method, to avoid running out of addresses. Webmasters often append strings to displayed addresses that are to be removed by users, causing bots to extract non-existent addresses. Therefore, by using the MTO method, we embed name addresses twice in each web page: once by using the regular address and once by appending a "_remove_" tag.

E-mail addresses are advertised by appending different domains and TLDs. Our e-mail domains are handled by several mail exchange servers located in different networks. Servers which are under our control run a qsmtpd SMTP server that captures the complete SMTP transactions and accepts any incoming mail. Other servers provide us the unfiltered e-mail feed via IMAP. We consider any e-mail sent to trap addresses as spam.

As harvesters can only be identified once the first spam is received, we log basic information such as the requesting IP for all page visits. In addition, web site operators provided us with complete access logs since January 2010. This extended information allows us to analyze further properties such as user agent strings submitted by visitors.

As our web pages cover a variety of different genres and popularities, this selection is arguably representative. By monitoring a relatively small number of web pages concentrated in Germany, the conclusions of this study are conceivably biased. However, this bias creates the opportunity to look at a focussed set of web pages and study locality in the harvesting process.

4. HARVEST AND SPAM ACTIVITIES

This section presents the main properties of address harvesting bots. We present statistics on page requests made by bots, geolocation of bots, the usage of our spamtrap addresses, fingerprints of bots, the robustness of methods

Site	Type	Country	Start of Rnd IDs	Issued Rnd IDs (% spammed)	Issued MTO Rnd IDs (% spammed)	Issued Name IDs (% spammed)	End
A	Private blog	DE	2009-05-16	791,890 (0.23%)	144,769 (0.45%)	211,851 (0.12%)	2010-11-29
B	Gaming web site	DE	2009-05-16	2,807,925 (0.06%)	469,804 (0.19%)	929,147 (0.03%)	2012-08-24
C	Private web site	DE	2009-05-16	21,558 (0.53%)	3,890 (1.54%)	5,938 (0.12%)	2011-03-28
D	Mail archive	DE	2009-05-16	5,191,288 (1.75%)	917,836 (3.20%)	1,518,105 (0.68%)	2012-08-24
E	Private web page	DE	2009-05-17	1,097 (0.00%)	197 (0.00%)	320 (0.00%)	2012-08-17
F	Private web page	DE	2009-05-16	400,490 (0.54%)	70,424 (1.47%)	118,481 (0.09%)	2011-10-30
G	Spamtap page	DE	2010-01-14	998132 (0.29%)	166,408 (0.54%)	332,694 (1.07%)	2012-08-24
H	Research group	DE	2010-01-24	7,582,332 (0.07%)	1,372,051 (0.17%)	2,094,329 (0.04%)	2012-08-24
I	Fake email provider	US	2010-07-09	34,500 (0.19%)	5,750 (0.26%)	11,500 (0.03%)	2011-05-16

Table 1: Data Set Overview

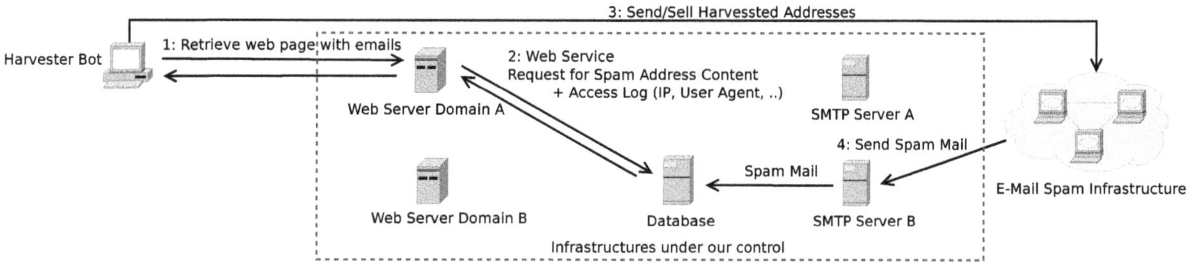

Figure 1: Measurement Methodology: Multiple web servers offer unique spamtrap addresses. Spam e-mails are received by multiple SMTP servers in multiple locations. Note that infrastructures used for harvesting and for sending spam might be run by different entities.

used to display e-mail addresses on the web, the efficiency of blacklisting, the usage of anonymity services, the relationship to comment spam, and the role of search engines.

4.1 Network Level Properties

We start by analysing the requests made by harvesting bots to the monitored web sites. By request we denote a page retrieval which resulted in spam to at least one of the retrieved e-mail addresses. Figure 2(a) shows *i)* the total number of page requests per month and *ii)* the page requests by harvesters. The figure shows a decline in harvesting activity at the monitored sites, especially compared to comment spam as malicious activity (cf. § 4.6). Conceivable reasons for this decline are: *i)* our sites get blacklisted over time, *ii)* increasing e-mail turnaround time or, *iii)* less usage of web crawlers for address harvesting.

In total, we classified 1251 hosts as harvesters and obtained DNS records for 90% of the hosts. For the remaining 10%, no DNS record could be obtained from the authoritative DNS servers, but *whois* information. Inspecting a random subset of hosts led to mostly access networks. To our surprise, we classified 20% of the hosts as search engines whose requests originated from legitimate address spaces associated to Google, Microsoft, and Yahoo. We discuss this issue further in § 4.7. Requests by a search engine crawler that resulted in spam are shown in Figure 2(a).

To study how requests by harvesting bots are spread over time, address space, and volume, Figure 2(b) shows a volume classification for the requests per day and IP. For most of the bots, only a small number of page requests resulting in spam can be observed (maximum 9871 requests per IP and day). A few regions in the IP address space show activity over multiple months, visible as horizontal bars. We found DSL customers by a German ISP to be the most dominant ones in March and July to August of 2010. However, the Google bot showed the longest time stability.

The figure also shows several heavy-hitters; six hosts retrieved around 10,000 pages—corresponding to 80,000 e-mail IDs—each on a single day. Manually inspecting these hosts revealed that most of the IP addresses belong to a single provider in Romania. We found 24 distinct IPs originating from this network, none of them having a DNS record. Page requests by these IPs span over almost the entire monitoring period and are responsible for a major fraction of the received spam (see Figure 3(b)). We observed requests to five of our web sites, of which 99% belong to web site D (mail archive).

To connect access statistics with the actual spam volume, we show the number of received spam e-mails vs. the page requests per IP in Figure 2(c). In many cases, only one or two page requests per IP are observed. However, the spam volume sent to addresses advertised in those requests was substantial.

We were further interested in whether harvesting machines are primarily hosted by infected machines located in residential or business access lines, or by operating dedicated servers. For this classification, we *i)* firstly apply a reverse DNS lookup to obtain host names and *ii)* secondly look for specific text patterns in the obtained host names. We classify hosts as DSL or Cable hosts if their host name contains key words such as "dsl", "customer", "dialin", etc. According to our classification heuristic, 73% of the IPs belong to ADSL or Cable access providers. This shows that harvester bots are still primarily run in residential access networks.

To study further properties of the hosts running bot software, we collected statistics about open TCP/UDP ports by port scans since mid 2011. To reduce the traffic caused by port scans and to focus our scans on harvesters, we limited our port scans to hosts blacklisted by Project Honeypot (note that we can only mark harvesters in retrospect after the first spam arrival). Only 13 hosts that we scanned harvested e-mail addresses from our web sites. Six of the scanned hosts had port 3389 open (typically used for remote

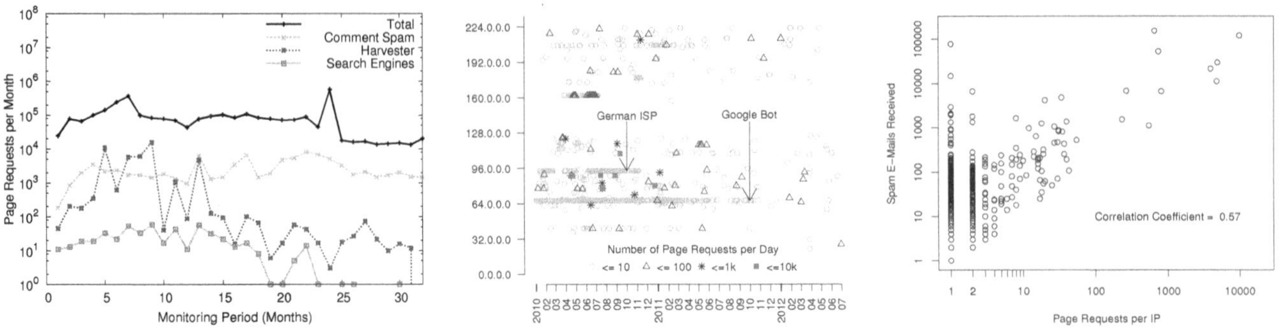

(a) Total Page Requests (b) Page Requests per Day and IP (c) Page Requests vs. Received Spams

Figure 2: Bot Visits to our web sites that lead to spam

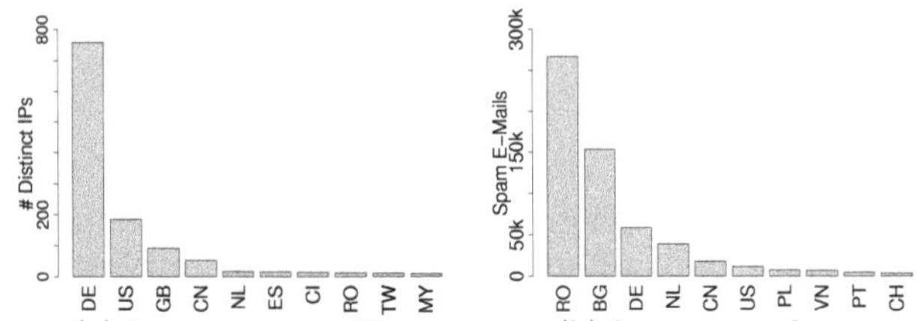

(a) by requesting IPs (b) by spam volume

Figure 3: Top 10 Harvesting Countries

control of Windows systems), four port 22 (remote control of Unix systems), and five port 80 (HTTP).

Lastly, we study the geolocation of the observed IP addresses. By solely looking at the number of distinct IPs per country (see Figure 3(a)), the bias in our data set towards web sites in Germany is reflected in the geolocation of harvesting machines: 60.6% of all bot IPs are located in Germany. Looking at AS information, we find that the majority of harvesting requests originate from AS3320 (Deutsche Telekom residential access lines) in Germany.

However, are the German harvester bots also responsible for most of the spam volume? By looking at the total spam volume caused per harvesting location leads to a different distribution (see Figure 3(b)); harvester bots in Romania and Bulgaria caused 72% of the received spam. All the 675 Bulgarian page requests were made by a single IP located in a Bulgarian ISP in November 2010 (we observed 24 distinct IPs from Romania, as mentioned earlier). The German bots that made up for 60% of all the distinct IPs were only responsible for 10% of the spam.

4.2 E-Mail Address Usage

What happens to e-mail addresses after they were harvested? We investigated this aspect by focusing on the usage of harvested addresses. Concretely, we denote the time between the address being harvested and their first usage as the *turnaround time* and show its distribution in Figure 4. 50% of the addresses received the first spam e-mail within four days after being harvested. The slowest observed turnaround was 1068 days, whereas the fastest was 64 seconds. Focusing the analysis only on addresses advertised to search engines led to slower turnaround times (not shown in the figure); 50% of the addresses were spammed within 11 days after a visit by a search engine bot. We found the fastest turnaround to be one day, while the slowest was 611 days.

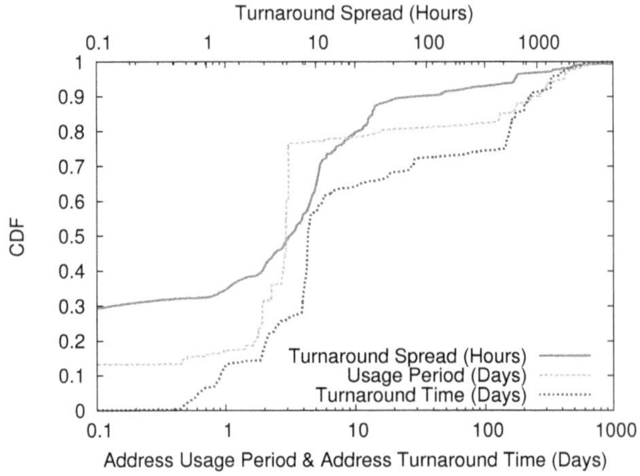

Figure 4: E-Mail Address Usage

As we embedded multiple addresses in one page, we were interested whether they were also simultaneously used for the first time. Therefore, we selected all RND addresses which received more than one spam e-mail (78%) and grouped them by page requests. We denote the *spread* in turnaround times as the range (max-min) of turnaround times for the addresses embedded in one request. A low spread indicates that all addresses in one request were firstly spammed within the same period. The distribution of the spread in hours is shown in Figure 4 (note the upper axis). 80% of the pages show a spread of less than a day (99% for search engines), and 27% of 0 seconds (94% for search engines) meaning that all extracted addresses simultaneously received their first spam. This finding suggests that spam to our spamtrap addresses was mainly sent in batches.

We also computed the amount of time that our addresses receive spam, denoted here as the *usage period.* 11% (16% for the search engines) of all addresses which received at least two spam e-mails were used for less than a second, 17% (40%) for less than a day, and 78% (51%) for less than a week. The longest observed usage of an e-mail address was 1068 days (749 days). We mention that our monitoring period spanned over 1202 days.

Comparing addresses advertised to search engine bots reveals various usage patterns; these addresses tend to be sent more often in batches to addresses embedded within a page. They also tend to have a slower turnaround time and a longer usage period. We further mention that only 558 addresses advertised to search engines were spammed, making this subset less representative than the whole data set.

4.3 Fingerprinting: User Agent Strings

In Figure 5 we show the usage of user agent strings submitted by harvesters bots in the HTTP header of the page request to our web sites. Figure 5(a) shows the use of user agents on a per-request basis. Note that the variability is modulated by heavy-hitters as shown in Figure 2(b); thus a per-IP classification shifts the popularity of user agents.

Note the variation over time visible in Figure 5(a) and 5(b) (also in Figure 6). One inference from this observation is the existence of only a few parties that harvest addresses from our sites. Depending on their activity, they can strongly skew a given quarter's statistics. Also, differences in Figure 5(a) and 5(b) suggest that the addresses harvested by different parties are not homogeneously used and caused different spam volumes.

We observed that 19% of the classified hosts as harvesters submitted a user agent string mimicking those of major search engines. By resolving IP addresses to AS numbers, we find that only 5% of the hosts using the Google bot user agent do not originate from the Google AS and are thus mimicking the Google bot. These 5% of the hosts are located in various ISPs and hosting sites (including Amazon EC2) located in seven different countries. Checking the *whois* records for each IP revealed various providers that cannot be associated directly to Google. 95% are indeed legitimate requests from the true Google AS. We did not observe a case of faked user agents for Yahoo's Slurp and Microsoft's Bing bots.

Seven years after the study of Prince [20], we find the Java user agent (e.g. "Java/1.6.0_17"), classified in our figures as "Script" and reported by [20], still to be present. Visits by this user agent span over the entire data set. We find this user agent to be used by 3% of the hosts classified as harvester. However, these hosts account for 88% of the page requests leading to spam, whereas spamtrap addresses harvested by these hosts account for 55% of the total spam, indicating that our data is skewed by one type of harvesting. In particular, the majority of the hosts located in Romania (cf. § 4.1) supplied the Java user agent string. These visits caused 99.9% of the spam volume that can be traced back to harvester bots in Romania. We found only a single host submitting six requests using "Mozilla/2.0 (compatible; NEWT ActiveX; Win32)" as user agent. This finding indicates that the usage of some harvesting software is fairly stable.

Out of curiosity, we personally replied to incoming spam in a few cases. In one case, a personalised response was received 10 minutes after our inquiry, originating from a residential access line located in the Netherlands. To our surprise, the IP from which the e-mail was sent matched the IP to which the address was issued a few days before (the harvester bot did use the "Java" user agent). It is often speculated that harvesting and mass e-mailing are two different processes, which might be conducted by different entities. However, this example shows the contrary, as the spammer did run the harvesting bot on his/her computer or used the same bot as proxy. This observation calls for further investigation.

4.4 Address Presentation Method Robustness

One aspect concerning webmasters is how to display e-mail addresses on the web to prevent spam: in a user-friendly or an obfuscated way? To address this issue, we study the robustness of presentation techniques by displaying our spamtrap addresses using a set of different presentation and obfuscation methods. For each spamtrap address which received spam, we show the relative share of spammed addresses for the used presentation methods in Figure 6.

As expected, a significant portion of spam was received by addresses presented in easy to parse plain text or as *mailto:* link. While some of the plain text obfuscated addresses (OBF) were harvested, none of the addresses presented using Javascript code received any spam. Concerning addresses advertised to search engine bots, the majority of the spammed addresses were presented using MTO (60.7%) and TXT (38.4%). Bots using the Java user agent only parsed addresses presented using MTO and TXT. These findings suggest that simple obfuscation methods, in particular Javascript, are still quite efficient to protecting addresses from being harvested.

4.5 Efficiency of Blacklisting & Usage of Anonymity Services

We query the IP based spam blacklist provided by Project Honeypot for each page request to our monitored sites at the time of the visit. Blacklist data has been collected over a period of 13 months since July 2011 and aims to evaluate the efficiency of blacklisting for blocking harvester bots. During this period, we received visits by 318 hosts that were classified as harvesting spam bots. 26% of the visiting hosts were marked by Project Honeypot as harvester.

In addition, we were interested if harvesters use anonymity services—such as Tor—to hide their identity. While the default configuration of Tor exit nodes blocks traffic to port 25—used to send spam—access to port 80—used to retrieve e-mail addresses from the web—is not prohibited by default. This could make Tor more attractive to harvesters than to spammers. To check if requests originated from the Tor network, we queried the list of Tor exit nodes when a page was requested. Tor usage statistics were collected over a period of five months starting in 2012. In this period, only 0.03% of the total requests to our web sites originated from the Tor network. However, we did not receive any request using Tor that was classified as harvesting activity.

We note that the short evaluation time conceivably biases these observations, but suggests that harvesters do not make an effort to conceal their identity.

4.6 Are Comment Spammers Harvesters?

Comment spam [1, 17, 26, 21, 15] exploits the existence of web forms that are designed to let users upload content. Examples of legitimate use are: i) commenting to blogs, discussion boards, or Youtube videos, ii) messaging to webmasters, and iii) uploading files such as videos or images. Crawlers that traverse the web, download and parse web pages are needed for both activities, i.e., comment spamming and address harvesting. Given the required effort, it would be efficient to simultaneously run both activities, i.e., harvesting addresses while sending comment spam. But do spammers make a business out of both harvesting addresses *and* delivering comment spam?

To test this hypothesis, we include trap web forms in addi-

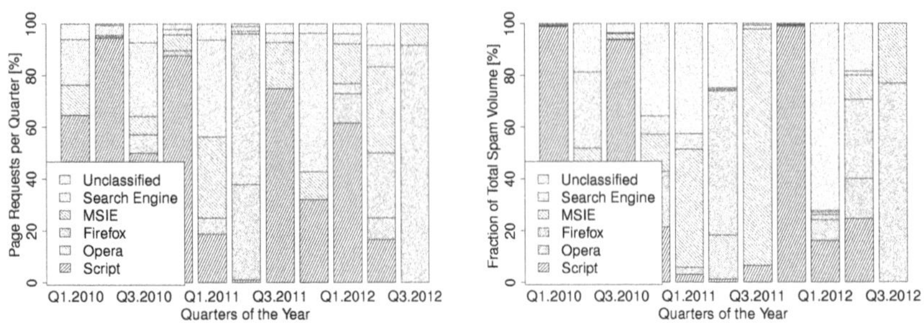

(a) by page requests (b) by spam volume

Figure 5: User Agents Strings of Harvesting Bots

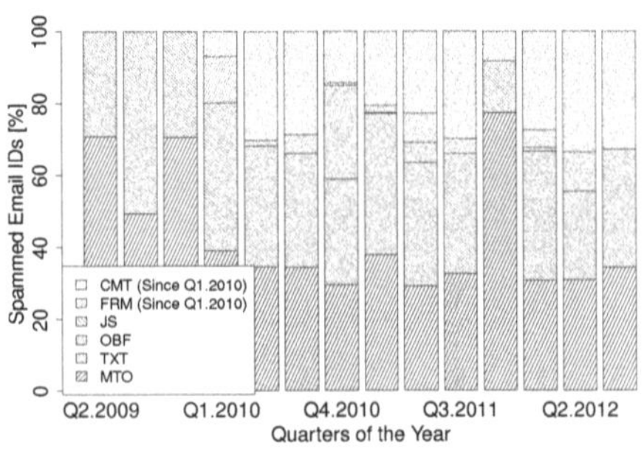

Figure 6: Spammed Email IDs by Presentation Method

tion to spamtrap addresses in web pages. Like the spamtrap addresses, our trap forms are not rendered by the browser and are thus invisible to normal users. We therefore assume any data sent over trap forms to be sent by bots. As these forms can have any structure, we replicated forms used for placing comments by the Wordpress software, frequently used to run blogs and web sites. Over a period of more than two years, we received 89,158 comment spams from 9312 distinct IP addresses. In the period of July 2010 to May 2011, five harvester hosts originating from four different countries submitted empty forms in which they could have technically sent comment spam. These hosts submitted five different user agents strings, including the Java user agent we discussed earlier. However, none of the e-mail addresses issued to comment spam bots was spammed. This suggests that comment spam bots do not harvest e-mail addresses.

To further study the differences between comment spam bots and harvesting bots, we repeated the analysis presented in § 4.1 - § 4.5 for the comment spam data set (not shown here). Our findings suggest that harvesting and comment spamming are uncorrelated activities, run using different software, and are most likely run by different entities. In this way, comment spammers do not (yet?) exploit the feasibility of simultaneously extracting and selling e-mail addresses on the market.

4.7 Harvesting: Role of Search Engines

We now address the role of search engines in the context of address harvesting. To our surprise, we received spam to spamtrap addresses advertised only to major search engine bots, i.e., Google, Microsoft, and Yahoo. In particular, 0.5% of the spamtrap addresses delivered *only* to search engines received 0.2% of the total spam. We define visits by search engines as requests made by crawlers that originate from the Google, Microsoft, and Yahoo ASes. All of the visits originating from those ASes used the proper user agent of the respective search engine bot. Concretely, 13% of the hosts classified as harvester originated from the Google AS, 3.7% from the Microsoft AS, and 1.2% from the Yahoo AS. We observe this behavior on all sites over the entire measurement period (cf. Figure 2(b) for the Google bot).

While the impact of the harvesting techniques to the overall spam volume and the number of harvested addresses is rather small, that very existence is a surprising result that has not been previously reported. It suggests that harvesters use search engines as a proxy to either *i)* hide their own identity or *ii)* optimize the harvesting process itself. As harvesters did not try to hide their identities by either using anonymity services or by masquerading as legitimate browsers by sending common user agent strings, option *ii)* seems more likely. In fact, we were able to find harvesting software that offers the functionality of querying search engines. Concretely, the advertisement for ECrawl v2.63 [18] states: "Access to the Google cache (VERY fast harvesting)". The Fast Email Harvester 1.2 "collector supports all major search engines, such as Google, Yahoo, MSN" [4]. This finding suggests that web site operators should not advertise e-mail addresses to search engine bots. It also calls for a further systematic investigation.

5. CONCLUSIONS

We have presented a longitudinal study of address harvesting that is based on a large-scale data set and that gives an up-to-date view on spam origins. We show that some aspects of harvesting are fairly stable over time, e.g., the existence of a certain user agent that has been observed for years, and the poor performance of harvesting software in breaking obfuscation methods. One interpretation of our results suggest that only a few harvesting parties are active, each causing different spam volumes. We also find that new aspects arise in the harvesting process, such as the emerging trend in the usage of legitimate search engines as proxies for address harvesting. Other observations point to the decline of harvesting activity on our sites and the existence of only a small set of hosts being responsible for a major fraction of the received spam.

Our findings reveal several guidelines for webmasters, e.g., *i)* to continue using obfuscation methods for displaying e-mail addresses on the web, e.g., by using Javascript code, *ii)* to restrict embedding e-mail addresses in web sites sent to legitimate browsers, and in particular not to search engine bots, *iii)* to rely on blacklists, e.g., provided by Project Honey Pot, to limit the likelihood of address harvesting.

6. ACKNOWLEDGEMENTS

We thank Bernhard Ager, Gregor Maier, Enric Pujol, and Nadi Sarrar for their insightful comments. Further, we thank the webmasters for including our scripts. We also thank the anonymous IMC reviewers and our shepherd Vern Paxson for their valuable comments and suggestions to improve this manuscript. Last but not least, we thank all the anonymous spammers and harvesters for making this study possible.

7. REFERENCES

[1] S. Abu-Nimeh and T. Chen. Proliferation and detection of blog spam. *IEEE Security and Privacy*, 8(5):42–47, Sept. 2010.

[2] I. Androutsopoulos, J. Koutsias, K. V. Chandrinos, G. Paliouras, and C. D. Spyropoulos. An evaluation of Naive Bayesian anti-spam filtering. In *Workshop on Machine Learning in the New Information Age*, pages 9–17, 2000.

[3] A. Antonopoulos, K. Stefanidis, and A. Voyiatzis. Fighting spammers with spam. In *International Symposium on Autonomous Decentralized Systems*, 2009.

[4] eMarkSofts. Fast email harvester 1.2. `http://fast-email-harvester.smartcode.com/info.html`, 2009.

[5] L. H. Gomes, C. Cazita, J. M. Almeida, V. Almeida, and W. Meira, Jr. Characterizing a spam traffic. In *ACM IMC*, pages 356–369, 2004.

[6] G. Gu, J. Zhang, and W. Lee. BotSniffer: Detecting botnet command and control channels in network traffic. In *Network and Distributed System Security Symposium*, 2008.

[7] S. Hao, N. A. Syed, N. Feamster, A. G. Gray, and S. Krasser. Detecting spammers with snare: spatio-temporal network-level automatic reputation engine. In *USENIX security symposium*, pages 101–118, 2009.

[8] O. Hohlfeld. IMC 2012 address harvesting data set. `http://www.net.t-labs.tu-berlin.de/~oliver/harvesting/`, 2012.

[9] T. Holz, C. Gorecki, K. Rieck, and F. C. Freiling. Measuring and detecting fast-flux service networks. In *Network and Distributed System Security Symposium*, 2008.

[10] X. Hu, M. Knysz, and K. G. Shin. Measurement and analysis of global IP-usage patterns of fast-flux botnets. In *IEEE INFOCOM*, pages 2633–2641, 2011.

[11] J. P. John, A. Moshchuk, S. D. Gribble, and A. Krishnamurthy. Studying spamming botnets using botlab. In *USENIX NSDI*, pages 291–306, 2009.

[12] C. Kanich, C. Kreibich, K. Levchenko, B. Enright, G. M. Voelker, V. Paxson, and S. Savage. Spamalytics: An empirical analysis of spam marketing conversion. In *ACM Conference on Computer and Communications Security*, pages 3–14, 2008.

[13] J. Kim, K. Chung, and K. Choi. Spam filtering with dynamically updated URL statistics. *IEEE Security and Privacy*, 5(4):33–39, July 2007.

[14] M. Knysz, X. Hu, and K. G. Shin. Good guys vs. bot guise: Mimicry attacks against fast-flux detection systems. In *IEEE INFOCOM*, pages 1844–1852, 2011.

[15] P. Kolari, A. Java, and A. Joshi. Spam in Blogs and Social Media, Tutorial . In *International Conference on Weblogs and Social Media*, 2007.

[16] C. Kreibich, C. Kanich, K. Levchenko, B. Enright, G. M. Voelker, V. Paxson, and S. Savage. Spamcraft: an inside look at spam campaign orchestration. In *USENIX LEET*, 2009.

[17] Y. Niu, H. Chen, F. Hsu, Y.-M. Wang, and M. Ma. A quantitative study of forum spamming using context-based analysis. In *Network and Distributed System Security Symposium*, 2007.

[18] Northworks Solutions Ltd. Ecrawl v2.63. `http://www.northworks.biz/software.html`, 2012.

[19] A. Pathak, F. Qian, Y. C. Hu, Z. M. Mao, and S. Ranjan. Botnet spam campaigns can be long lasting: evidence, implications, and analysis. In *ACM SIGMETRICS*, pages 13–24, 2009.

[20] M. B. Prince, B. M. Dahl, L. Holloway, A. M. Keller, and E. Langheinrich. Understanding how spammers steal your e-mail address: An analysis of the first six months of data from project honey pot. In *Collaboration, Electronic messaging, Anti-Abuse and Spam Conference*, 2005.

[21] A. Rajadesingan and A. Mahendran. Comment spam classification in blogs through comment analysis and comment-blog post relationships. In *Computational Linguistics and Intelligent Text Processing*, pages 490–501, 2012.

[22] A. Ramachandran and N. Feamster. Understanding the network-level behavior of spammers. In *ACM SIGCOMM*, pages 291–302, 2006.

[23] S. Roy, A. Pathak, and Y. C. Hu. Mitigating the impact of spams by internet content pollution. In *ACM SIGCOMM Poster*, 2007.

[24] G. Schryen. An e-mail honeypot addressing spammers' behavior in collecting and applying addresses. In *IEEE Information Assurance Workshop*, 2005.

[25] C. A. Shue, M. Gupta, J. J. Lubia, C. H. Kong, and A. Yuksel. Spamology: A study of spam origins. In *Collaboration, Electronic messaging, Anti-Abuse and Spam Conference*, 2009.

[26] A. Thomason. Blog spam: A review. In *Collaboration, Electronic messaging, Anti-Abuse and Spam Conference*, 2007.

[27] Y. Xie, F. Yu, K. Achan, R. Panigrahy, G. Hulten, and I. Osipkov. Spamming botnets: signatures and characteristics. *ACM CCR*, 38(4):171–182, Oct. 2008.

[28] K. S. Xu, M. Kliger, Y. Chen, P. J. Woolf, and A. O. Hero. Revealing social networks of spammers through spectral clustering. In *IEEE ICC*, 2009.

[29] L. Zhang, J. Zhu, and T. Yao. An evaluation of statistical spam filtering techniques. *ACM Transactions on Asian Language Information Processing*, 3(4):243–269, Dec. 2004.

[30] Y. Zhao, Y. Xie, F. Yu, Q. Ke, Y. Yu, Y. Chen, and E. Gillum. Botgraph: large scale spamming botnet detection. In *USENIX NSDI*, pages 321–334, 2009.

[31] L. Zhuang, J. Dunagan, D. R. Simon, H. J. Wang, and J. D. Tygar. Characterizing botnets from email spam records. In *USENIX LEET*, 2008.

Observing Common Spam in Tweets and Email

Cristian Lumezanu
NEC Laboratories America
Princeton, NJ
lume@nec-labs.com

Nick Feamster
University of Maryland
College Park, MD
feamster@cs.umd.edu

ABSTRACT

Spam is pervasive across many types of electronic communication, including email, instant messaging, and social networks. To reach more users and increase financial gain, many spammers now use multiple content-sharing platforms—including online social networks—to disseminate spam. In this paper, we perform a joint analysis of spam in email and social networks. We use spam data from Yahoo's web-based email service and from Twitter to characterize the publishing behavior and effectiveness of spam advertised across both platforms. We show that email spammers that also advertise on Twitter tend to send more email spam than those advertising exclusively through email. Further, we use DNS lookup information to show that sending spam on both email and Twitter correlates with a significant increase in coverage: spam domains appearing on both platforms are looked up by an order of magnitude more networks than domains using just one of the two platforms.

Categories and Subject Descriptors

C.2.3 [**Computer-communication networks**]: Network Operations; K.4.2 [**Computers and society**]: Social issues; H.0 [**Information systems**]: General

General Terms

Measurement, Security

Keywords

Twitter, email, spam, DNS, multiple platform spam

1. INTRODUCTION

Spam is an unwanted yet continual scourge in electronic communication; it infiltrates basic conversation tools, such as email and instant messaging, as well social-based content sharing platforms, such as OSNs and forums. A recent study shows that 89% of the 107 trillion emails sent in 2010 were spam [15]. Further, emerging social-based applications such as social networks, blogs, or video sharing websites, are also subject to abuse: 8% of the URLs shared on Twitter lead to malicious websites that host malware or scams [6].

To reach more users and maximize their financial gains, spammers are increasingly using multiple content-sharing platforms to disseminate the same malicious content. For example, several malware and phishing campaigns are carried over email, to target as many users as possible, but also over social networking platforms, where the trust-based social graph enables spammers to target those users who are more likely to click on their links [8,9]. In our analysis (§ 4), we discover over 700 scam, malware, and phishing domains that are advertised using both email and tweets over the course of a month.

In this paper, we take an initial step towards understanding the properties of spam across multiple platforms. We present a joint measurement study of spam across two popular content sharing platforms: email and social networking. We consider spam to be any message containing an URL that leads to a website that hosts malicious content such as malware, phishing, or scams. Using two message data sets, of emails to Yahoo accounts and tweets from Twitter, gathered for one month in March 2011, we provide a parallel view of the properties of spam and behavior of spammers. An important characteristic of our study is that it focuses on *both emails and tweets sent during the same time period.*

We characterize email and tweet spam from two different perspectives. First, we investigate the presence of spam on the two dissemination platforms (Section 4). We discover that 55% of all spam emails advertise scam domains that also appear on Twitter. Email spammers that advertise at least one domain on Twitter are likely to send more email spam overall during our measurement than those that send only email-exclusive spam.

Second, we seek to understand the effect of advertising spam on multiple platforms (Section 5). To the best of our knowledge, our study offers the first large-scale analysis on the behavior and effectiveness of spam sent during the same time period on both email and Twitter. Using DNS lookup data to estimate the number of clicks for each domain, we find that domains common to both emails and tweets receive an order of magnitude more clicks than domains exclusive to one platform.

Because the email data set is unfiltered while the tweets have already passed through Twitter's spam filters, our study has a few limitations. We cannot offer a complete comparison between email and tweet spam or establish a causal

IMC'12, November 14–16, 2012, Boston, Massachusetts, USA.

relationship between the presence of spam in tweets and in emails and its effectiveness. Notwithstanding, our results show that there is a positive correlation between publishing spam on multiple platforms and both the volume of email spam send by these publishers and the effectiveness of the spam being sent. This leads to a most important finding of our study: *incorporating information about Twitter spam publishing behavior into email spam filters (or vice versa) could increase their effectiveness in quickly identifying virulent spammers.*

Although we do not pursue the positive implications of our findings in this paper, we believe that the overlap between spam that appears in both email messages and tweets ultimately presents new opportunities for improving both the accuracy and speed of spam detection. Spam filters could leverage information about publishing behavior of spam across platforms to build better defenses. For example, discovering that spam URLs are consistently published on Twitter before email could help develop more accurate email blacklists. Further, understanding how and when spammers send common spam could reveal their strategies and how to counter them. Finally, understanding the presence and behavior of common spam would help existing spam fighting solutions developed for individual platforms [1, 2, 5–7, 10, 12, 16, 19] interact better with each other.

2. RELATED WORK

Most analyses of spam have focused exclusively on email [1, 11, 12, 19]. They characterize spam from various aspects such as the behavior of spammers [11, 12], the email contents [14], or the properties of spam hosting infrastructures [1]. More recently, several studies characterize spam in forums [10, 13], or in social networking applications such as Facebook and Twitter [2, 5–7]. Unlike previous work, we focus on spam that is sent on *multiple platforms (e.g., both email and Twitter) at the same time.* Such a joint analysis provides a new perspective on spam and allows us to better understand how spammers work and coordinate to increase their impact.

To fight spam sent across web services such as social networking or video sharing sites, Thomas *et al.* proposed Monarch, a spam URL filtering service [16]. Monarch compared email and tweet spam and found few features in common across the two platforms. This means that one would need to learn specific sets of rules to detect spam on each platform. We share a similar philosophy to Monarch, that generalizing spam fighting across multiple platforms can lead to faster and more efficient detection. However, unlike Thomas *et al.*, we focus on the spam that *is common across platforms* and characterize its prevalence, publishing behavior, and effectiveness.

3. DATA AND METHODS

In this section, we present the data sets used in our analysis and discuss how we identify spam messages. We use Twitter and Yahoo! Mail as representative applications for online social networks (OSNs) and email, respectively.

3.1 Data sets

To compare spam in tweets and email, we start with two sets of public messages, *Twitter* and *Yahoo*, both collected in March 2011. The *Twitter* data set contains public tweets gathered using the public Twitter streaming API. For each tweet we retrieve the publishing time, details on its author (*e.g.*, id, screen name, numbers of followers, friends, and statuses posted), as well as the text of the tweet. The *Yahoo* data set represents a snapshot of all incoming emails to Yahoo! Mail accounts as received by Yahoo's mail servers and it was privately shared by Yahoo!. The information available is the connecting IP, the time of the message, and the URLs contained in the message. Both data sets capture around 1%, extracted uniformly at random, of all messages sent on each platform in March 2011.

3.2 Spam identification

Because URLs are the primary method that spammers use to attract users to websites that host malicious content, we restrict our analysis on the tweets and emails that contain URLs. To identify spam messages, we take the following three steps. (1) We parse the text of each tweet and extract all URLs. (2) We find the final landing page for all links from tweets and emails that are hidden with URL shortening services or behind chains or redirections. (3) We use two sources to determine whether a URL leads to malicious content by comparing the URL of the final landing page with public URL blacklists and spamtrap emails. We describe below this final step in more detail.

URL blacklists contain domains and websites that are known to host malicious content such as scams and malware or participate in phishing campaigns. We check the domains in our data sets against several public URL blacklists in the first week of May 2011. URIBL and SURBL are DNS-based blacklists with domain names found in the body of spam emails, but generally not in legitimate emails. PhishTank lists phishing URLs voted by users. To detect malware, we use the list published by `malwaredomains.com`. Finally, for both malware and phishing domains, we use the Google Safebrowsing API to check against Google's constantly updated blacklists.

Blacklists are not always effective in detecting recently advertised spam domains or domains that are not frequently reused. Previous studies show that information about many spam domains and spammers fails to show up in blacklists even more than a month after the domain was first advertised [6, 12]. To improve the completeness of our study and detect even recently published spam domains, we use data from the spamtrap set up by Ramachandran and Feamster [11]. Because the spamtrap is associated with a DNS Mail Exchange (MX) record with no legitimate email addresses, all email that it receives is spam. For our measurement, we collect all URLs found in over 11 million emails received by the spamtrap between January and March 2011.

Although all emails received at the spamtrap are from spammers, the spam emails might still contain legitimate URLs to subvert anti-spam filters. We use the following simple heuristic to select the spamtrap URLs (and domains) that are more likely to be malicious. First, we whitelist all URLs with domains present in the Alexa top 10,000 most popular domains, under the assumption that popular domains rarely host spam. Second, we consider only domains that appear in more than 1,000 spamtrap emails. This is based on the assumption that, for spam to be effective, it must be distributed at scale [20].

Data set	Messages with URLs			
	All	Spam		
		blacklist	spamtrap	total
Yahoo	290,355,683	39,440,693	13,134,298	49,142,499
- Yahoo only	135,740,285 (47%)	29,755,924 (75%)	8,012,716 (61%)	34,159,814 (69%)
- Yahoo, common	186,552,390 (64%)	18,712,383 (47%)	8,881,790 (68%)	27,009,682 (55%)
Twitter	5,569,940	197,932	18,404	198,887
- Twitter only	496,303 (1%)	29 (<1%)	0 (0%)	29 (<1%)
- Twitter, common	5,159,890 (99%)	197,903 (>99%)	18,404 (100%)	198,858 (>99%)

Data set	Domains			
	All	Spam		
		blacklist	spamtrap	total
Yahoo	14,860,901	81,567	3,681	82,233
- Yahoo only	14,699,376 (>99%)	80,897 (99%)	3,601 (89%)	81,493 (99%)
- Yahoo, common	161,535 (< 0%)	670 (<1%)	80(2%)	740 (1%)
Twitter	283,936	676	80	746
- Twitter only	127,315 (45%)	6 (<1%)	0 (0%)	6 (<1%)
- Twitter, common	156,621 (55%)	670 (>99%)	80 (100%)	740 (>99%)

Table 1: Data sets used in our study. We collect the main data sets, *Yahoo* and *Twitter* in March 2011. The secondary data sets contain the messages with domains that appear only on Yahoo, only on Twitter, and on both. Percentages are computed of the values for the main data sets. Not all percentages add to 100% because there are messages with more than one URL where some URLs are unique to one platform and others are common to both. We also separate the messages and domains according to whether they are spam or not and to the method used to identify them as spam (blacklists or spamtrap).

3.3 Spam characterization

We use the methods described above to identify spam messages in the *Twitter* and *Yahoo* data sets. Table 1 shows the statistics with respect to spam domains and messages (tweets or emails) that contain spam URLs (focus on the data sets labeled "Yahoo" and "Twitter"). There are around two orders of magnitude more spam emails than tweets. This could be explained by the relative difference between the number of messages in the two data sets but it could also be due to the Twitter data being collected after filtering, as we explain below. The gap becomes smaller when we consider the amount of spam relative to the total number of messages on each platform: 17% of all emails are spam while, even after filtering, 4% of all tweets are spam. These numbers suggest that although Yahoo! Mail has many more users and daily messages than Twitter [4,18], Twitter is becoming a significant infrastructure for disseminating spam.

3.4 Limitations

Data sampling. Due to the large volume of tweets and emails, we analyze only 1% of the emails received by Yahoo servers and of the tweets sent in March 2011. Sampling can misrepresent the properties of the original message population, but we are confident that it has not distorted general trends: for example, the statistics about the prevalence of spam that we report are comparable to what previous studies have shown [6,17,20].

Spam filtering. The *Yahoo* data set contains information about emails captured *before* any spam filtering was performed, while the tweets in our data set have already passed through Twitter's spam filters. This can affect our results as follows:

1. It can underestimate the amount of Twitter spam, which in turn underestimates the common spam sent on both Twitter and email. However, even after filtering, we find a significant amount of tweets that are spam.
2. Twitter's filtering may skew the ratio between the amount of "common with Yahoo" and "exclusive to Twitter" spam (if exclusive domains are filtered more or less than common domains). We believe that, because Twitter uses email blacklists to fight spam [6], it is more likely that common domains are filtered more than exclusive domains, making our results in Section 4 an underestimation of reality.
3. Finally, while distorting the absolute view on common spam, the filtered tweets in our data sets can offer a more realistic perspective on the amount of common spam that *an email spam filter would see* if it had access to the publicly available Twitter stream. Our results in Section 4 suggest that email filters could be more effective if they incorporated Twitter spam publishing behavior in their analysis.

Spam identification. We use both blacklists and spamtrap emails to ensure that our knowledge about which domains host malicious content is as complete as possible. However, even then, we may still miss many spam domains. For example, neither blacklists nor spamtrap emails help us identify several Twitter-specific spam campaigns (*e.g.*, phishing for followers, buying retweets [6]). Because the focus of our paper is on common spam in email and Twitter, missing the Twitter-specific spam does not affect our results.

4. PRESENCE OF COMMON SPAM

We now study the presence of spam and the behavior of spammers across Twitter and email from two perspectives: How is common spam published across platforms?, and How do we identify it? Unsurprisingly, we find that the networks

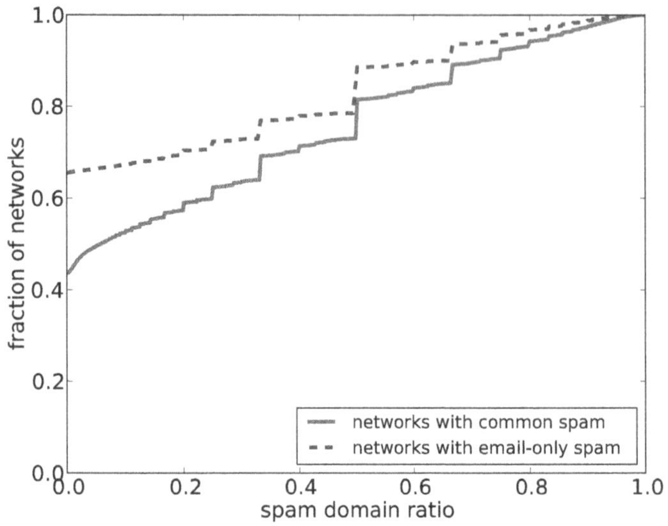

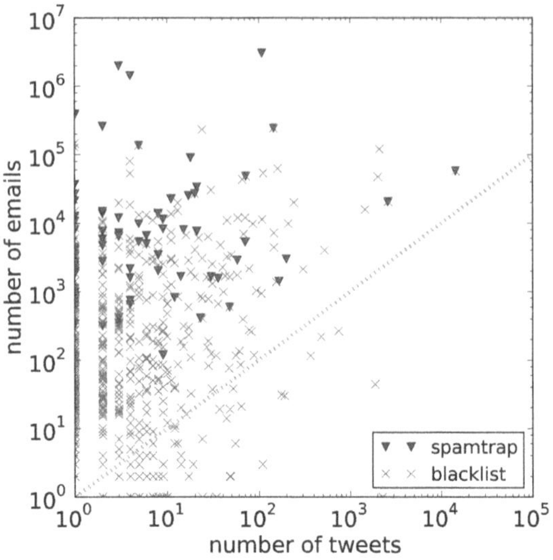

Figure 1: (left) Cumulative distribution for the spam domain ratio for /24 networks that send spam; the spam domain ratio for a network is the fraction of the number of spam domains to the total number of domains sent from them network; (right) Number of emails/tweets for each common spam domain; each point is associated to a common spam domain and has a different symbol according to how the domain was detected.

that advertise spam on both email and Twitter tend to send more spam overall than the networks that advertise spam exclusively through email. We also study the sources that allow us to identify spam and show that URL blacklists help identify the most spam, although spamtraps are also effective to discover high-volume spam domains.

We divide each data set into two secondary data sets, according to whether a message contains URLs that are published on both platforms or are exclusive to one platform. Table 1 presents details on the secondary data sets. There are 740 spam domains common to both Yahoo and Twitter which appear in 27M emails and 198K tweets. More than half (55%) of the spam emails contain domains that appear on Twitter. Because the tweets in our data set have already passed through Twitter's spam filters (as explained in Section 3.4), we cannot make a definitive assessment on the amount of common spam. However, because Twitter uses email blacklists to filter spam [6], if tweets were not filtered, we would likely have even more spam domains in common with email. Thus, the numbers in Table 1 could be interpreted as lower bounds for the amount of common spam.

4.1 Publishing behavior

We focus on the common spam domains that we do identify. We compare how much each domain is advertised across the two platforms. Only 10% of the common domains appear in more tweets than emails and 60% of the common domains appear in at least ten times as many emails as tweets. We also find that 99% of all domains that appear in tweets also appear in emails. These results could be an artifact of the pre-filtering of tweets (*e.g.*, if Twitter had already filtered the common spam that is more prevalent in tweets) or of using email-based blacklists to detect Twitter spam. However, if we take into account the total number of messages sent on the two platforms, the result could also mean that email is still a more pervasive platform for sending spam and that Twitter may be used simply as a backup for email. To better understand the implications of our observation, we are currently implementing Twitter-specific spam detection techniques [3] that are trained independently from email spam.

Next, we compare the spamming behavior of users that send spam on both platforms to that of users that send spam on only one platform. In doing so, we hope to understand whether common spam domains are associated with heavier spammers. We restrict our analysis to Yahoo users because we find little Twitter-only spam for a meaningful comparison. We extract the /24 networks from which every email was sent and group them into two categories: those from which at least one common spam domain was advertised and those from which no common spam, but at least one email-only spam domain, was sent. For each network, we compute the spam domain ratio as the fraction of spam domains to the total number of domains sent from the network.

The left graph in Figure 1 shows the distributions of the spam domain ratio for networks that originate common spam and networks that are never source for common spam. The networks that advertise at least one common spam domain have a higher ratio than those that do not. Although this observation does not necessarily imply a causal relationship between sending spam on multiple platforms and the volume of email spam, it does indicate a correlation that could be exploited by spam filters to improve their efficiency: networks that send spam domains that also appear on Twitter are likely to send more spam overall than those networks advertising domains that are exclusive to email.

4.2 Identification

Given that detecting common spam domains can help identify networks that are likely to send more spam, we ask what is the better source for detecting these domains.

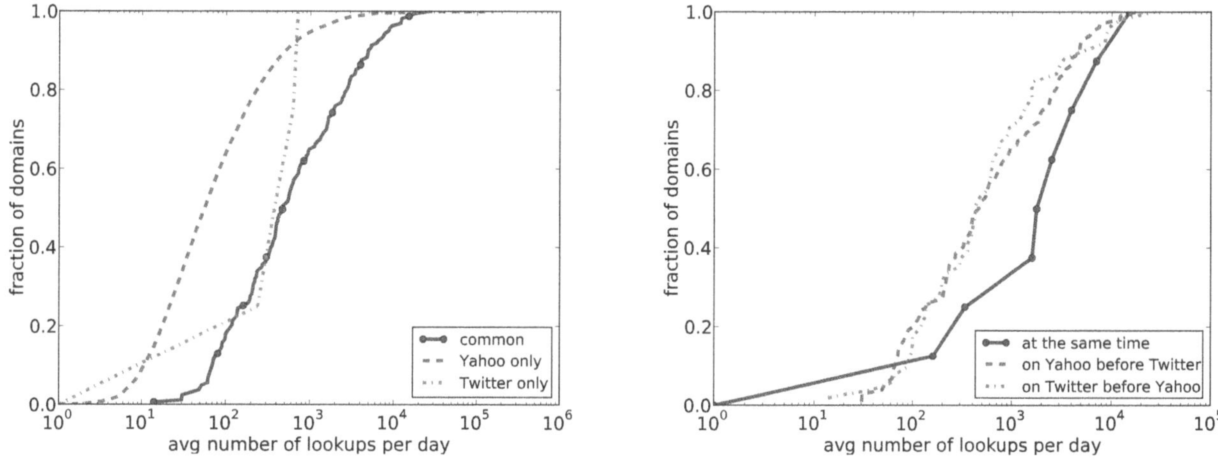

Figure 2: Cumulative distribution of the average number of unique networks querying for spam domains per day: (left) all spam domains, and (right) common spam domains.

We separate the spam messages according to the information source (blacklists or spamtrap) used to classify them as spam. Table 1 shows statistics about the results. Only 7% of all spam emails and 9% of all spam tweets could be identified using *both* sources, which is evidence for the lack of overlap between our spamtrap data and URL blacklists. Although spamtraps constitute an important source of information for building blacklists, oftentimes blacklists are not updated quickly enough to keep up with the "fresh" spam [12].

Although spamtraps appear to detect fewer spam domains than blacklists (4% of all email spam domains are identified using the spamtrap data), these domains are significant on email: they contribute to 27% of all email spam and to 33% of all common spam sent through emails. For Twitter, spamtrap data is less decisive, identifying only 9% of all tweets. For further evidence, the right graph of Figure 1 shows the number of tweets vs. the number of emails each common domain appears in. Each point is associated with a domain and has a different symbol according to whether the domain was identified as spam using blacklists or spamtrap data. In conclusion, *blacklists can identify most common spam, although spamtrap data is also effective in detecting the common domains that appear in many emails.*

5. EFFECTIVENESS OF COMMON SPAM

We presented evidence that there is a significant amount of common spam across tweets and emails: 55% of all spam emails and 99% of all spam tweets advertise content also published on the other platform. We seek now to better understand the role of each platform in the spammers' strategies. Is Twitter a backup for cases when email spam is not effective? Or do the platforms combine to capture a more diverse set of users, unattainable from a single medium?

To understand the effectiveness of spam on each platform, we use DNS lookup information collected by Verisign. Verisign manages the TLD nameservers responsible for the `.com` and `.net` domains. We obtained a data set with information about when each domain (ending in `.com` or `.net`) in our data set was looked up. We consider only those lookups performed during the time when our tweets and emails were sent (March 2011). The data set contains information about the /24 networks of recursive resolvers that looked up 66% of the common spam domains, 57% of the Yahoo exclusive domains, and 66% of the Twitter exclusive domains. To estimate the number of clicks on each domain, and implicitly its popularity, we use the number of unique /24 networks from which a DNS query is performed.

Figure 2(left) presents the distribution of the number of unique networks that lookup each spam domain in March 2011. There are around ten times more networks that lookup common spam domains than spam domains that are exclusive to email. We cannot make a definitive assessment for the Twitter exclusive domains due to their low number. We further separate the common domains according to when they were first advertised: on both platforms on the same day, on Twitter before email, and on email before Twitter. We plot the distributions for each category in Figure 2(right). The domains that are published for the first time on both platforms on the same day tend to receive more clicks than those that are published on different days.

We find that there is a positive correlation between publishing spam on multiple platforms and its effectiveness, measured as the number of unique networks that lookup the spam domains. Our data is insufficient to determine whether the number of dissemination platforms or some other unobserved property of the spammer (*e.g.*, some spammers may be sophisticated enough that they send high yield spam *and* use multiple dissemination platforms) is responsible for the increased effectiveness of spam. Notwithstanding, the association that we observe strengthens or finding from Section 4.1, that sharing spam information across platforms (*e.g.*, whether a spam domain appears on both Twitter and email) could help email spam filters detect the heavy and virulent spammers quicker.

Equating the number of clicks that a domain receives with the number of unique /24 networks from which DNS queries are performed for it can introduce bias in our results. Most importantly, due to caching of DNS information along the DNS hierarchy, not all clicks on an URL lead to queries to the TLD nameservers. However, we believe that the number of unique networks still reflects the *relative* popularity between domains. If anything, it may under-represent the more popular domains, for which it is more likely that a query is cached at a lower level resolver.

6. CONCLUSIONS

We presented a measurement study on the properties of common spam across multiple content sharing platforms. We focused on two popular web applications, Twitter and Yahoo! Mail. We make two main observations: (1) spam sent on both Twitter and email at the same time has a better exposure and a higher lookup rate than spam sent exclusively with email; and (2) spammers that advertise on both on email and Twitter send more email spam overall than spammers that advertise only on email.

The limitations of the data sets do not allow us to draw definitive conclusions about how spammers use Twitter and email. For example, we cannot determine whether there is causation or simply correlation between sending spam concurrently using multiple mechanisms and its virulence and volume. Notwithstanding, our results suggest that general solutions for detecting message abuse that incorporate information and features from multiple platforms at the same time may ultimately improve the accuracy and responsiveness of existing filters.

7. ACKNOWLEDGEMENTS

We thank our shepherd Christian Kreibich and the IMC reviewers for their valuable feedback. This project was supported by NSF grants CNS-0643974 and CNS-1111723, and by NSF grant 0937060 to the Computing Research Association for the CIFellows Project.

8. REFERENCES

[1] D. S. Anderson, C. Fleizach, S. Savage, and G. M. Voelker. Spamscatter: Characterizing internet scam hosting infrastructure. In *Usenix Security*, 2007.

[2] F. Benevenuto, G. Magno, T. Rodrigues, and V. Almeida. Detecting spammers on Twitter. In *CEAS*, 2010.

[3] F. Benevenuto, G. Magno, T. Rodrigues, and V. Almeida. Detecting spammers on twitter. In *CEAS*, 2010.

[4] Full metal email: Confessions of an 'anti-spam zealot'. `http://goo.gl/WL8IG`.

[5] H. Gao, J. Hu, C. Wilson, Z. Li, Y. Chen, and B. Y. Zhao. Detecting and characterizing social spam campaign. In *ACM IMC*, 2010.

[6] C. Grier, K. Thomas, V. Paxson, and M. Zhang. @spam: The underground on 140 characters or less. In *ACM CCS*, 2010.

[7] K. Lee, J. Caverlee, and S. Webb. Uncovering social spammers: social honeypots + machine learning. In *SIGIR*, 2010.

[8] Newest messaging malware targets Facebook and Twitter. `http://goo.gl/TrGkq`.

[9] Unstoppable new phishing attacks blanket Facebook, Twitter, Hotmail. `http://goo.gl/X0tdr`.

[10] Y. Niu, Y. min Wang, H. Chen, M. Ma, and F. Hsu. A quantitative study of forum spamming using contextbased analysis. In *NDSS*, 2007.

[11] A. Ramachandran and N. Feamster. Understanding the network-level behavior of spammers. In *ACM Sigcomm*, 2006.

[12] A. Ramachandran, N. Feamster, and S. Vempala. Filtering spam with behavioral blacklisting. In *ACM CCS*, 2007.

[13] Y. Shin, M. Gupta, and S. Myers. Prevalence and mitigation of forum spamming. In *IEEE Infocom*, 2011.

[14] Spam forensics: Reverse-engineering spammer tactics. `http://goo.gl/Y9wmk`.

[15] Symantec messagelabs intelligence: 2010 annual security report. `http://www.messagelabs.com/mlireport/MessageLabsIntelligence_2010_Annual_Report_FINAL.pdf`.

[16] K. Thomas, C. Grier, J. Ma, V. Paxson, and D. Song. Design and evaluation of a real-time URL spam filtering service. In *IEEE Security & Privacy*, 2011.

[17] State of twitter spam. `http://goo.gl/M4X5M`.

[18] Twitter finally reveals all its secret stats. `http://goo.gl/07kzP`.

[19] Y. Xie, F. Yu, K. Achan, E. Gillum, M. Goldszmidt, and T. Wobber. How dynamic are ip addresses? In *ACM Sigcomm*, 2007.

[20] Y. Xie, F. Yu, K. Achan, R. Panigrahy, G. Hulten, and I. Osipkov. Spamming botnets: signatures and characteristics. In *ACM Sigcomm*, 2008.

Beyond Friendship: Modeling User Activity Graphs on Social Network-Based Gifting Applications

Atif Nazir
Dept. of Computer Science
University of California–Davis
anazir@ucdavis.edu

Alex Waagen
Dept. of Applied Math
University of California–Davis
awaagen@math.ucdavis.edu

Vikram S. Vijayaraghavan
Dept. of Physics
University of California–Davis
vikram@ms.physics.ucdavis.edu

Chen-Nee Chuah
Dept. of Elecrical Engineering
University of California–Davis
chuah@ucdavis.edu

Raissa M. D'Souza
Dept. of Computer Science
University of California–Davis
raissa@cse.ucdavis.edu

Balachander Krishnamurthy
AT&T Labs–Research
bala@research.att.com

ABSTRACT

We employ user activity data from three highly popular gifting applications on Facebook to study the evolution of user activity on applications through the most commonly-used growth mechanism, namely Application Requests. We find user activity graphs differ from friendship graphs in large part due to the inherent directionality of user activity, and node transience. Our results show that, unlike degree distributions in friendship graphs, activity graphs exhibit strong asymmetry in in- and out-degree distributions, and that out-degrees are not accurately described by currently known parametric distributions. As such, user activity graphs cannot be simulated through existing intent- and feature-driven algorithms that can model friendship graphs.

We present a novel probabilistic growth model for user activity on the gifting genre of social applications. Our model decouples in- and out-degrees based on their distinct nature exhibited by our empirical data. We use the insight that regardless of increasing, declining or stable user activity, gifting application user activity exhibits the same graph structure. Our model produces synthetic graphs that consist of disconnected components with low clustering of nodes, and exhibit degree structures very similar to our real activity data. We discuss the benefits and shortfalls of our model and its applicability to other types of OSN-based applications, such as social games. To the best of our knowledge this study is the first to explore and model user activity growth processes on OSN-based applications.

Categories and Subject Descriptors: C.2.0 [Computer - Communication Networks]: General; H.4.3 [Information Systems Applications]: Communications Applications

General Terms: Measurement, Algorithms

Author Keywords: Online Social Networks, Social Games, Social Gifting, Facebook, Applications, Algorithms

1. INTRODUCTION

Over the last five years, Facebook has become the most widely used Online Social Network (OSN) with a user base of over 950 million, and through its Developer Platform, Facebook supports a rich social application eco-system that has become a $6+ billion industry as of 2012. This growing importance of OSNs has spurred massive academic interest in OSNs, resulting in research that has focused on studying friendship graphs [15, 2, 23, 1]. Meanwhile, considerably less is known about *user activity* on social networks, even though researchers have argued the greater importance of studying user activity over simple friendship formation [22, 7, 29, 24, 25, 21]. This lack of research on user activity is due to privacy issues related to sharing of user activity data [12], which have resulted in lack of availability of such data for research purposes.

OSN friendship graphs differ significantly from user activity graphs (UAGs). We know that while friendship graphs consist of static friendship relations that rarely change between user pairs, UAGs are dynamic in nature due to the constant activity. Also, user activity on OSNs may or may not be reciprocal, whereas OSN friendships always are.[1] This means OSN friendship graphs are undirected, whereas UAGs are directed in nature. Furthermore, user activity on OSNs is not always based on the underlying friendship graph,[2] and UAGs exhibit temporal variance in graph properties that do not exist for OSN friendship graphs [16]. Due to these differences, existing work on friendship graphs is inapplicable to UAGs.

A number of questions regarding UAGs from social applications remain unanswered, including whether or not it is possible to model UAGs from social applications, just as researchers have modeled OSN friendship graphs. Our intent is to explore the possibility of modeling UAGs from all social applications on the largest OSN, Facebook. These

[1]Relationships on Twitter do not qualify as friendships, but rather as user-follower relations.

[2]For example, adaptations of board games such as Scrabble to Facebook applications have mostly been played with random application users rather than one's OSN friends.

applications utilize one or all four growth mechanisms available on Facebook to achieve growth in user base. These growth mechanisms are Application Requests (ARs), Newsfeed Stories, Emails, and Paid Advertising (see Section 3.1). Among these, only ARs are used by *all* Facebook applications. Based on this last observation, this paper focuses on understanding the growth of UAGs through ARs by studying, and modeling, UAGs from one genre of Facebook applications, namely, gifting applications. We say a social application is in the gifting genre if it consists of only one feature, and that this feature enables inter-user sharing of virtual gifts through ARs.

Our survey of the top 250 Facebook applications shows that gifting is the second-most popular genre of Facebook applications behind gaming, and that *all* Facebook gaming applications use gifting as a feature to increase growth. Furthermore, since gifting applications use only the AR mechanism, their UAGs are simpler to model than applications that use more than just the AR growth mechanism. *As a starting point to model UAGs from social applications, we investigate modeling UAGs from only gifting applications in this paper.* We use static snapshots of empirical UAGs from *three popular gifting applications* on Facebook to study the growth of UAGs. This approach of studying evolution of a graph by studying its static snapshots has been advocated previously ([10]), and it enables us to address the following questions regarding UAGs:

(1) How do UAGs from social applications differ from friendship graphs obtained from OSNs?

Unlike creation and deletion of friendships on OSNs, we have previously observed year-round dynamic patterns in the UAGs obtained from one gaming and three gifting applications [16]. In addition to daily and weekly variations in user activity, reliably high user activity is observed during special occasions and holidays (Valentine's Day, New Year, Christmas, etc.). Also unlike friendship graphs where friendships are almost always mutual, user activity is not always reciprocal. The lack of reciprocity in user activity gives rise to distinct in- and out-degree distributions. Furthermore, in our gifting UAGs, there is an explicit cost associated with initiation of activities (outgoing edges); i.e., the total number of activities that can be initiated by a user is capped at a limit. This is due to a throttling mechanism used by Facebook to limit spam in the network, which amplifies the distinction between in- and out-degree distributions.

(2) Existing graph models generate 'acceptable' synthetic friendship graphs [19, 13]. Do these models suffice when modeling user activity from social gifting applications?

We evaluate intent- and feature-driven algorithms (such as Nearest Neighbor and Forest Fire) reported to generate graphs that are statistically similar to OSN friendship graphs. We find the procedures employed in the original as well as existing hybrid versions of these algorithms are too simplistic to generate gifting UAGs. For instance, our results show that our gifting UAGs exhibit degree structures that are more complex than for friendship graphs. In particular, out-degree distributions in our UAGs cannot be explained simply by power-laws, and are not summarized by any known parameterized distribution. In contrast, OSN friendship graphs exhibit degree structures that are often explained by single power-laws [3].

(3) What key features should be considered to model UAGs from gifting applications? How do these features change with time?

Research on friendship graph modeling suggests a small number of metrics that are sufficient to summarize friendship graphs, i.e., clustering coefficients, degree distributions, and number/size of connected components [19]. We explore these metrics in conjunction with more focused user behavior metrics from our applications i.e., likelihoods of interacting with inactive users and targeting new users, and distributions of user lifetimes and number of daily interactions.

Our analysis of gifting UAGs shows that degree distributions as well as connected component size distributions tend to stabilize over approximately one week of user activity. Clustering coefficients are too small to reliably stabilize for our gifting applications, while the number of connected components do not stabilize, but instead may increase or decrease given the phase of the application's lifetime. We also observe that all metrics vary from week to week, depending on overall trends in application usage.

(4) Finally, is it possible to model user activity on a class of social applications that utilize the same underlying growth mechanism?

We use our understanding of the social application growth process to provide an algorithm tailored to a class of applications, namely *gifting*, that uses one particular growth mechanism, namely *ARs*. Unlike existing friendship models, our algorithm decouples in- and out-degrees to provide synthetic graph structures similar to our gifting UAGs. Our algorithm uses application-specific metrics such as active user duration, distribution of daily number of activities, etc. as inputs to facilitate accuracy of the synthetic graph produced. By varying inputs to this algorithm, we show its efficacy in generating *weekly* synthetic graphs for *all* of the gifting applications we study. We also perform rigorous analysis of the degree distributions produced by our algorithm. This analysis provides a mathematical formula that describes the expected distribution in activity level among users.

To the best of our knowledge, this is the first attempt to model UAGs from OSN-based applications. Due to similarity of structure and the pervasive use of ARs, we believe our model is applicable to other Facebook gifting applications as well. Our findings can be leveraged to forecast a gifting application's usage. The synthetic UAGs generated by our model provide an alternative to sharing large data sets that may violate user privacy.

We begin this paper with a discussion of related work in Section 2, followed by a discussion of our methodology, including the graph metrics we use to model gifting UAGs, in Section 3. We analyze measurements for our selected graph metrics in Section 4, and present our UAG growth model in Section 5 with a discussion of its potential uses. We discuss future work and conclude the paper in Section 6.

2. RELATED WORK

Spurred by the increasing relevance of OSNs to online user activity, there has been an increase in analyses of OSNs over the last few years [11]. While some researchers have analyzed usage patterns of popular OSNs, others have focused on graph theoretic properties of OSNs such as YouTube [15].

Research into OSN network growth has resulted in multiple algorithms that produce synthetic graphs to mimic OSN friendship graph properties. These algorithms derive concepts from earlier graph theory [18], including algorithms for offline social network growth, such as Nearest Neighbor, Random Walk, Barabasi-Albert, and so on [19]. Moreover, some research marries preferential attachment with latent node characteristics to study OSN network growth [9].

Researchers have also studied time-varying OSN graphs [20, 8]. Gummadi *et al.* report on the strength of user interactions on Facebook using indigenous OSN applications in [25]. They find that communication decreases among users from the point of friendship formation due to relationship fatigue. Leskovec *et al.* propose that graphs over time do not follow the same patterns or exhibit the same attributes as they did when they were initially formed, and presents the Forest Fire algorithm to model OSN network growth [13]. Other research has focused on information dissemination patterns on OSNs [21, 2]. Li *et al.* have suggested that in complex networks, relying on statistical methods cannot provide an idea of which features are essential to the topology's formation [14]. Instead, they propose that knowledge of the building blocks of network activity is essential to understand growth of networks. Furthermore, Holme *et al.* propose studying static snapshots of graphs to study evolution of temporal networks [10].

The lack of availability of real data sets from OSNs has slowed research into growth patterns on OSNs. This is especially true for social applications on OSNs, for which high-level statistical analyses exist ([5, 16, 17, 6]), yet whose growth processes have not been studied.

Our social applications provide us a unique opportunity to study the growth of OSN-based applications [16, 17]. We believe the observation of Gummadi *et al.* on user fatigue holds true for social applications as well, since application novelty can explain early application growth and user fatigue could account for its decline. We find that growing and aged graphs exhibit different patterns ([13]) for UAGs as well. To the best of our knowledge, this paper is the first to study and model growth of user activity on social applications.

3. METHODOLOGY AND RATIONALE

Our end-goal is to study growth processes of all OSN-based applications. However, due to limited access to OSN application data, we use only applications on the largest OSN, Facebook, as a case study.

3.1 Growth Mechanisms of OSN Applications

Facebook applications allow subscribed users to interact with non-subscribing users to encourage application growth on the OSN. We define a *subscribing* user on a Facebook application as someone who has 'logged in' to the application through an installation screen presented by Facebook for that application. Moreover, online social applications belong to different genres. While some of the more complex applications (games) target audience that seek high engagement in OSN applications,[3] other simpler applications (gifting) target casual users i.e., users that spend only a short time on social applications.

Application statistics websites ([27], [26]) rank Facebook applications according to Monthly Active Users (MAU) [16]. Our review of these rankings indicates that gaming and gifting applications are the two largest sets of Facebook applications. In particular, our review (using Developer Analytics [27]) in January 2012 showed that 74.4% of the top 250 Facebook applications by MAU were Flash or text-based gaming applications, while 9.43% were gifting applications, followed by other smaller genres of applications.[4]

We study growth processes for social applications using the OSN-based application architecture (Figure 1(a)), discussed in [16]. These growth processes depend on the growth mechanisms employed by social applications. Facebook provides the following growth mechanisms:

- **Application Requests (ARs)**: Facebook users are able to send ARs to their friends, allowing them to recruit friends to applications free of cost. The AR growth mechanism is illustrated by steps 1 and 5 in Figure 1(a). If User A sends an AR to User B, the sending user performs step 1 and the OSN (asynchronously) performs step 5 for User B. When a user receives an AR, she can either *accept* it or *ignore* it. Accepting an AR presents non-subscribing users with an installation page, and subscribed users are shown the reason(s) they were sent an AR. An AR is sent by a subscribing user to any friend on Facebook, whether subscribed to the application or not. Facebook limits the number of these outgoing requests on a given application through an internal spam-control algorithm. For our applications, the daily per-user AR limit for an application was typically 20, but could be as high as 60. There are, however, no limits on ARs a user may receive.
- **Newsfeed Stories**: Newsfeed stories are personalized posts on a user's profile made through applications by subscribed users. Facebook controls the visibility of Newsfeed stories to users' friends through an internal algorithm that prioritizes a story's importance to the viewing user. A Newsfeed story can be posted by a subscriber to any friend, whether subscribed to the application or not. Our review shows 88% of the top 250 applications prompt users to share a Newsfeed story in at least one sequence of actions. Note that due to the algorithm Facebook uses to display Newsfeed stories to users, as well as the passive nature of Newsfeed stories compared to ARs, the latter have been more reliable for application growth in our experience.
- **Emails**: Pending a subscribed user's approval, Facebook allows applications to send e-mail notifications to their personal e-mail addresses when an event occurs. Since users often perceive allowing e-mail access to social applications as a security risk, developers do not use this communication channel often. We found only 36% of the top 250 applications at least ask users for their email addresses, but it is not practical to measure how often this mechanism is utilized due to the complex nature of user flows in most gaming applications.
- **Paid Advertising**: Application developers on Facebook may purchase advertisements to boost subscription growth. However, we are unable to discern how widely this mechanism is used by analyzing the applications alone. Anecdotally, most social games tend to use advertisements to increase subscription growth.

Our review of the top 250 Facebook applications suggests applications may use one or all growth mechanisms.

[3]Higher user engagement translates into higher average revenue generated per subscriber.

[4]Since the genre listings of applications can be inaccurate, we categorized the top 250 applications manually.

However, *all* applications use ARs. *Our data allows us to study specifically the growth process arising from use of ARs through UAGs from Facebook-based gifting applications.* We define a *gifting application* as an application that 1) uses only ARs for growth and inter-user communication, and 2) only allows users to share themed images (gifts) through ARs with their Facebook friends.

3.2 Measuring Gifting Application UAGs

We employ UAGs from three Facebook gifting applications to study application growth through the AR growth mechanism. The architecture of the Platform used is shown in Figure 1(a). We say a single user *activity* occurs on a gifting application when steps 1 and 5 are performed by the sending user A, and the OSN, respectively. The third-party application servers record the sending and receiving users' Facebook UIDs with the time at which the activity was generated. We only studied anonymized data for our research.

Each node in the UAG represents a Facebook user, and each directed edge from User A to User B represents an AR sent from User A to User B. Note that our UAGs are multigraphs, i.e., User A may have multiple directed edges to User B. Our UAGs were obtained through server-side measurements of the following Facebook-based gifting applications, which were owned and operated by Manakki, LLC:

- **iHeart**: Launched in June 2009, iHeart grew to 30 million monthly active users by December 2009, and was installed by 76 million users on Facebook by August 2010. Our user activity traces capture 2.2 billion activities. Users share decorative heart-shaped graphics with their Facebook friends.
- **iSmile**: Launched in August 2008, iSmile was installed by 43 million users on Facebook by August 2010. Our user activity traces for iSmile capture 1.5 billion user activities. Users share graphics of smiling characters with their Facebook friends.
- **Hugged**: Launched in February 2008, Hugged was installed by 28 million users on Facebook by August 2010. Our user activity traces for Hugged capture 1.6 billion user activities. Users share graphics of hugging characters with their Facebook friends.

iHeart was a very popular application that ranked in the top three applications on Facebook by MAU in December 2009. We use iHeart to drive and evaluate the development of our UAG growth model, and employ UAGs from Hugged and iSmile to test this model's applicability to other gifting applications. Figure 1(b) shows user activity on iHeart for 13 months after its launch, and indicates three distinct periods of activity on iHeart: the ramp-up user activity period (until week 49, 2009), the short-lived peak user activity period (weeks 50-51, 2009), and the declining user activity period. The sharp fluctuations in user activity in all three phases indicate real-world events/holidays, where user activity usually spikes before the occasion and then falls during the event, with exceptions such as Mother's Day (week 19, 2010). This three-phase lifetime user activity is evident on all of our social applications, is attributed to application novelty and eventual user fatigue, and is less prominent on longer-lasting applications such as Farmville [28].

In order to perform analysis that is representative of all three phases of our applications' user activity and lower processing times for our analysis, we use the periods of activity for iHeart shown in Table 1. This sample of user activity periods captures all variations in application lifetime phases, stable/increasing/declining user activity and special real-world events. We use the same 10 weeks' data from Hugged and iSmile to test our UAG growth model, but only list week 34-2009 in Table 1 for brevity.

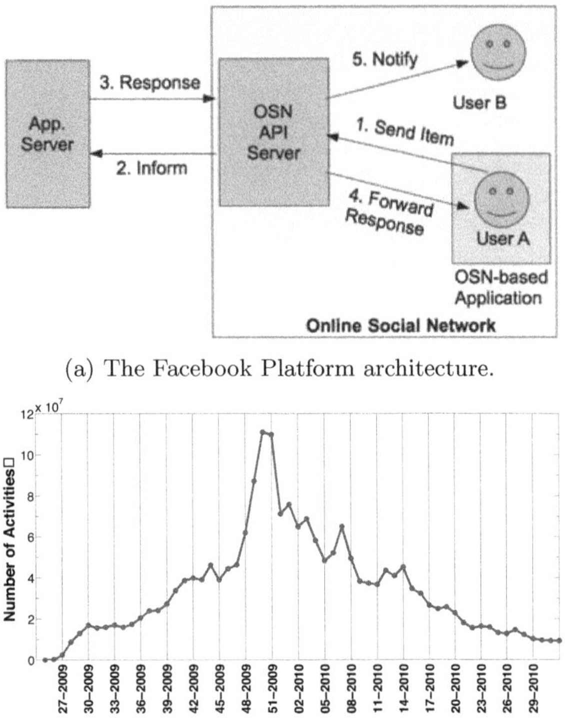

(a) The Facebook Platform architecture.

(b) The total number of hearts sent per week on iHeart across 13 months. We see three user activity periods for iHeart: increasing activity (upto 50-2009), peak activity (50-2009) and declining activity (01-2010 onwards). Sharp dips/spikes in user activity are due to holidays and special real-world events. From left to right, these dips are due to: Halloween, Thanksgiving, Christmas/New Year, and Valentine's Day.

Figure 1: The Platform architecture used by our applications, and user activity for iHeart.

In our traces, a week's user activity starts at 12:00:01AM Pacific Time on Sunday, and ends on the following Sunday at 12:00:00AM. We discuss the reason for selecting weekly user activity periods over shorter and longer choices in Section 4. We performed analysis and simulations for all listed weekly activity periods. However, due to the similarity in results from a given phase's weekly periods, we only present results for one week from each phase: we use week 34-2009 as a representative week for the pre-peak phase, week 50-2009 for the peak phase, and week 26-2010 for the post-peak phase.

We discuss the metrics we use to model our UAGs next.

3.3 Understanding Social Application Growth

Existing friendship models generate synthetic graphs that reproduce the following key graph properties:

- *Clustering Coefficient (CC)*: The CC of a node $v \in V$ is the ratio of number of edges between neighbors x of v (such that $\exists(x, v) \in E$) and the total number of

Table 1: **Relevant measurements for weekly UAGs from iHeart, Hugged and iSmile. Our weekly activity periods belong to all three phases of an application's lifetime: pre-peak (P-), peak (P) and post-peak (P+). Section 3.3 defines α, β, γ^d, γ_m, M and N_0.**

App.	Week	Phase	Users	Activities	α	β	γ_d	γ_m	M	N_0
iHeart	34-2009	P-, Stable	9.85M	11.8M	0.541	0.875	1.75	0.77	20	0.52M
	38-2009	P-, Increasing	14.7M	18.4M	1.82	0.74	0.512	0.867	20	0.80M
	45-2009	P-, Spiky	22.3M	29.6M	0.477	0.863	1.71	0.80	20	1.17M
	50-2009	P, Stable	44.7M	110M	0.414	0.899	1.75	1.09	60	1.37M
	01-2010	P+, Declining	31.4M	43.8M	0.459	0.879	1.72	0.87	24	1.57M
	06-2010	P+, Spiky	30.95M	47.59M	0.452	0.869	1.57	0.85	24	1.61M
	14-2010	P+, Declining	19.0M	23.7M	0.516	0.878	1.80	1.09	20, 24	1.12M
	19-2010	P+, Spiky	11.59M	13.0M	0.592	0.889	2.14	0.99	26	0.83M
	26-2010	P+, Stable	9.89M	11.1M	0.629	0.904	1.95	0.93	26	0.62M
	30-2010	P+, Declining	6.51M	6.86M	0.644	0.899	2.05	1.07	20, 26	0.52M
iSmile	34-2009	P-, Stable	5.28M	7.17M	0.697	0.901	2.67	0.69	20	0.28M
Hugged	34-2009	P-, Stable	2.72M	3.55M	0.727	0.899	2.79	1.06	20	0.14M

edges possible between those neighbors. The CC of a graph is the average of individual nodes' CCs.

- *Degree Distribution*: The degree distribution $\forall k : P(k)$ of a graph is the fraction of nodes with degree k. If there are N nodes where n_k have degree k, $P(k) = n_k/N$. We distinguish between in- and out-degrees.
- *Connected Components*: Two nodes x and y belong to one connected component if an undirected path between x and y exists. A component's nodes are only connected with other nodes in the same component. We look at *number* of components, as well as *percentage of users in the largest* components.

Existing research uses these properties to summarize the static structure of OSN graphs [19]. We want a growth model that reproduces the above properties, including distinct in- and out-degree distributions, for our UAGs. Our findings show these graph metrics stabilize around a week's aggregate user activity for our applications (Section 4). We use this finding to simulate only weekly user activity to simplify our growth model. Our model differentiates between active, and inactive users. *Active* users send at least one AR in a week's UAG, and *inactive* users only receive, and do not send, ARs in a week's UAG.

The social application growth processes are dependent on use of different growth mechanisms. We believe the following list of application-specific parameters must be used in a growth model for gifting applications.

- *Probability of Sending to New Targets (α)*: This is the probability a user will target a previously unseen user through ARs in our UAGs.
- *Probability a User Remains Inactive (β)*: Inactive users may or may not be subscribed to our applications. The subscribed inactive users, even though they may visit the application, do not send ARs. The parameter β represents the probability a user will remain inactive in a weekly UAG.
- *Active User Duration (d_x)*: Nodes in UAGs are more transient in nature as compared to friendship graphs. In order to capture this transience in our model, we use the distribution of the number of days an active user appears in a given week's UAG as a parameter. Our measurements suggest d_x is power-law distributed, with exponent γ_d.
- *Daily ARs Sent (m_x)*: Even though our UAGs show limits on ARs per day, users may not exhaust these limits. Furthermore, some users may visit an application but not send any ARs at all. This parameter captures the distribution of number of ARs users send on a given day, which is important for generating accurate degree distributions. Our measurements suggest m_x is power-law distributed, with exponent γ_m.

Note that user activity on social applications is continuous, i.e., users in one time period are responsible for incoming users in the consecutive time period. We have previously reported that almost 80% of all AR acceptees visit the application within 48 hours of receiving the AR [16]. If we consider weekly snapshots of user activity, a proportion of users never receive ARs in the current week, yet appear in the UAG regardless. These are the *seeding users* responsible for continued activity on the application in the given week. Along with the daily AR limit (M), we use the number of seeding users (N_0) as an *external constraint* in our model.

4. CASE STUDY: UAGS FROM IHEART

This section presents the defining features of UAGs observed in our most popular application, iHeart. As mentioned in Section 3.1, iHeart shares structure and design with other gifting applications on Facebook. We build our algorithm to simulate iHeart's UAGs first, and then test it on our other gifting applications. We use the activity periods listed in Table 1 for this analysis.

Our findings suggest graph metrics do not stabilize in hourly or daily activity traces. We measure convergence times for the key graph metrics to gauge the minimum period required for metric stability in our UAGs.

4.1 Convergence of Key Graph Metrics

We define the *convergence* time Z as the amount of time it takes for metric values to stabilize for our UAGs. More specifically, $Z = \min z$ such that $f(z+1) - f(z) \approx 0$, where $f(z)$ represents metric values measured from a UAG of the first z days in a given time period.

Degree Distributions: We measured Z for in- and out-degree distributions on iHeart by comparing aggregated user activity (starting at Sunday) for the 10 time periods listed in Table 1. The function $f(z)$ represents the CDF of user activity over z days for the in- or out-degree distribution.

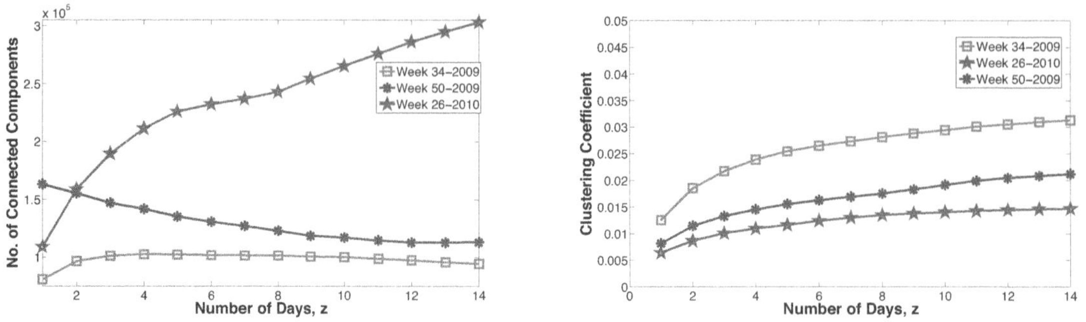

(a) Number of connected components.

(b) Clustering coefficient.

Figure 2: The number of connected components and clustering coefficients over 14 days of aggregated user activity for iHeart, starting at Sunday for weeks 34-2009 (pre-peak), 50-2009 (peak) and 26-2010 (post-peak).

The resulting $f(z+1) - f(z)$ values, or Euclidean Distances (EDs) indicate a small distance between $f(2)$ and $f(1)$ (i.e., one and two days' aggregate user activity) for both in- and out-degrees, and that this difference decreases monotonically as z increases. The in- and out-degree distributions stabilize roughly at $z = 7$ days, with ED $\leq$ 2.5% for all 10 weekly activity periods. An exception occurs when new content is introduced during week days, where out-degree distribution EDs spike to up to 34%. However, we observe ED $\leq$ 2.5% as we approach the end of the week.

Connected Components: We look at two metrics with regards to connected components in our UAGs: the *number* of connected components and the *percentage of users in the largest* connected component.

In general, we find that as more users interact through ARs, the *number* of distinct connected components grows. However, unlike degree distributions, in our applications the number of connected components behaves differently for pre-peak, peak and post-peak activity periods. In the peak activity period the number stabilizes over the course of a week, but it does not converge in either pre-peak or post-peak activity periods. Figure 2(a) shows this behavior for the representative periods on iHeart. More specifically, the number of connected components declines when z increases for pre-peak activity periods, indicating that increasing AR activity between users merges the largest component with smaller, fragmented components. In post-peak activity periods, in contrast, the number of connected components increases as z increases. User fatigue is a possible explanation for this phenomenon, i.e., users take longer to return to the application leading to formation of small (up to 110 node) components that do not connect with the largest component as quickly as in the pre-peak periods.

The percentage of users in the largest component, however, does stabilize for our UAGs. If $f(z)$ represents the percentage of users in the largest connected component, we find that $f(z+1) - f(z) \leq 0.5\%$ where $z \geq 6$ for all time periods considered (Table 1). For different time periods, however, $f(7)$ varies between 90.17% and 94.89%. Note that the second largest components for our weekly UAGs are of negligible size (less than 20 nodes).

Clustering Coefficients (CC): Figure 2(b) shows the CC for undirected iHeart UAGs for three representative periods 14 days of activity. We have previously discussed the effect of user engagement on CCs in UAGs from social applications in [16], where we showed a highly engaging gaming application exhibited high node clustering (CC = 0.8). In contrast, Figure 2(b) shows the CC is very small for iHeart, but that increasing z results in slightly higher CC. Note that the aim of this study is to provide a growth model that approximates gifting UAGs as a first step. Therefore, we seek to generate synthetic graphs with low or no clustering of nodes rather than graphs with precisely the same number of clusters as in our empirical UAGs.

A weekly snapshot of user activity captures a full cycle of low and high user activity for OSN-based applications [16]. Moreover, since gifting applications are non-recurrent (compared to social gaming applications), less than 10% of users return in a consecutive week. This high churn of users means every week's user activity can almost be treated independently. Our results show both degree distributions and percentage of users in the largest connected components stabilize within 7 days of user activity. Therefore, we focus only on weekly time periods for our first UAG growth model.

4.2 Approximating Degree Distributions

Existing research indicates power laws may partially explain degree distributions in OSN graphs [15, 19]. However, our measurements indicate that known parametrized distributions do not accurately fit the full range of the degree distributions for gifting UAGs. Unfortunately, this means that the simple growth mechanisms known to give rise to the parameterized distributions (such as preferential attachment which leads to power laws, or multiplication of independent random variables with leads to log-normal distributions) do not suffice to explain growth of our UAGs. To demonstrate the lack of fit, we attempt to fit the candidate distributions shown in Table 2 to our real user activity data.

We perform Goodness of Fit (GoF) tests for potential candidate distributions (Table 2) for iHeart UAGs. We use the Kolmogorov-Smirnov (KS) statistic between the data and parametric fits to measure applicability of the distributions to our UAGs. The KS statistic is suggested as a reliable GoF measure for heavy-tailed distribution approximation [4]. We do an exhaustive search of the parameter space to find the best fit that minimizes the error for a given distribution.

First, consider *in-degree distributions*. The KS statistic indicates that both PL and PLED provide fits with good statistical accuracy, while LN, SE and EXP are orders of magnitude higher for all weekly UAGs (see Table 3). Be-

Distribution	P(x)	Valid Range of Parameters
Power law (PL) or Algebraic Decay	$ax^{-\gamma}$	$0 < a, \gamma < \infty$
Power law w/ Exp. Decay (PLED)	$ax^{-\gamma}\exp(-x/\tau)$	$0 < a, \gamma, \tau < \infty$
Exponential (EXP)	$a\exp(-x/\tau)$	$0 < a, \tau < \infty$
Stretched Exp. (SE)	$\frac{a}{b}(x/b)^{a-1}\exp(-(x/b)^a)$	$0 < a, \tau < \infty$
Log-normal (LN)	$\frac{1}{x\sqrt{2\pi\sigma^2}}\exp(-(\log x - \mu)^2/2\sigma^2)$	$0 < \mu, \sigma < \infty$

Table 2: Candidate distributions to approximate our UAGs' degree structures.

Week	GoF	In-degree				
		PL	PL-EXP	SE	LN	EXP
34-2009	KS	1.16E-04	3.21E-05	0.1412	0.0806	0.0694
50-2009	KS	7.87E-04	2.85E-04	0.0695	0.1361	0.0548
26-2010	KS	3.49E-04	1.28E-04	0.1052	0.0623	0.0536

Table 3: GoF measures for in-degree distributions for weekly iHeart user activity.

Week	GoF	Out-degree, Bulk				
		PL	SE	LN	EXP	PLED
34-2009	KS	3.99E-03	0.0914	0.0744	0.1857	9.69E-03
50-2009	KS	0.0163	0.3687	0.2886	0.4533	0.0571
26-2010	KS	5.04E-03	0.2375	0.1654	0.2886	0.0834

Table 4: GoF measures for out-degree (bulk) distributions for weekly iHeart user activity.

Week	GoF	Out-degree, Tail				
		LN	PL	EXP	SE	PLED
34-2009	KS	5.39E-03	6.58E-03	5.77E-03	5.41E-03	5.49E-03
50-2009	KS	3.82E-04	3.34E-04	4.49E-04	4.38E-04	6.289E-03
26-2010	KS	7.32E-03	7.11E-03	7.75E-03	7.74E-03	0.0195

Table 5: GoF measures for out-degree (tail) distributions for weekly iHeart user activity.

Week	In-degree Fit	Out-degree Fit		
	γ_i	γ_o	μ	σ
34-2009	3.394	0.7443	1.661	1.135
50-2009	3.628	0.7436	2.145	1.296
26-2010	3.457	0.9202	1.9414	0.9143

Table 6: Parameters of the distributions that best fit the data. In-degrees were fit using PL with exponent γ_i, while out-degrees' *bulk* were fit using algebraic decay with exponent γ_o and *tail* with LN with mean μ and standard deviation σ.

tween PL and PLED, the latter is more accurate for the early portion of the distribution, yet PL captures tail events better, is a simpler distribution, and achieves overall accuracy very close to the PLED fit. Figure 3 shows an example PL fit (starting at $k = 12$) to the week 34-2009 UAG from iHeart, and Table 6 shows the best-fit distribution parameter values for the three representative weeks.

Now consider *out-degree distributions.* Figure 3 shows an example out-degree distribution for week 34-2009. The algebraic 'steps' in weekly out-degree distributions occur at multiples of daily AR limits (shown as M in Table 1). Note that more than 88% of AR senders in any week have out-degrees less than the daily AR limit, i.e., only a small fraction of users send 20 or more ARs in a given week.

We find that the out-degree distributions are best fit by splitting the data into two parts at the daily AR limit: we call the data up to the daily AR limit the *bulk* of the distribution, while degrees above the daily AR limit are the *tail* of the distribution. This is because the behavior exhibited by the *bulk* differs significantly from the *tail*, highlighting the fact that 1) most users do not exhaust the daily AR limit, and 2) most users visit gifting applications once a week due to low engagement [16]. The KS statistic indicates the out-degree distributions for the *bulk* are explained best by an algebraic decay (PL), followed by PLED, SE, EXP and LN, in that order, whereas the *tail* can be reasonably fit using either an LN or PL distribution, as shown in Tables 4 and 5. The KS statistic is not extremely sensitive to tail events, and visual inspection confirms that LN provides a better fit to the tail for all weeks studied. Figure 3 shows an example best fit for out-degrees, and Table 6 shows the best-fit distribution parameter values for the three representative weeks. We performed these fits by removing all multiples of daily AR limits to reduce distortion in KS values.

Thus a power law can reasonably fit the in-degree distribution, but no simple parametric distribution describes the full out-degree distribution. Even when fitting the out-degree with two different distributions, the values of the parameters for these distributions vary considerably as seen in Table 6. As such, we cannot explain UAG growth via a simple mechanism like preferential attachment or multiplicative growth. Our findings are valid for all other weekly periods (Table 1) as well.

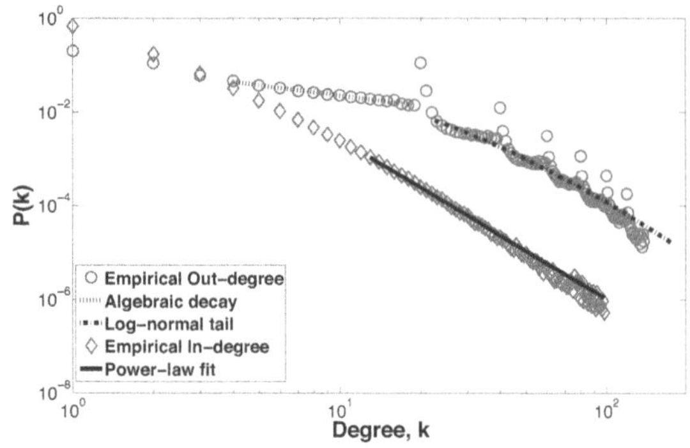

Figure 3: In- and out-degrees for weeks 34-2009 along with parametric distributions that fit. In-degrees were fit using PL (exponent 2.90), while out-degrees' *bulk* were fit using algebraic decay (exponent 0.744) and *tail* with LN (mean $\mu = 1.66$ and standard deviation $\sigma = 1.135$).

4.3 Relevant Metrics for Modeling Growth

As discussed in Section 3.3, certain key metrics are needed to model gifting UAGs. These metrics will serve as input parameters for our modeling algorithm.

Probability of Sending to New Targets (α): Table 1 shows the probability of sending hearts to a new user ranges from 0.41 to 0.73 in weekly UAGs. Also, users are more likely to target new users in lower activity periods.

Probability a User Remains Inactive (β): Our measurements show (Table 1) the probability a randomly selected user is inactive throughout a week is in a very narrow range between 0.85 and 0.91 for iHeart, i.e., it is more or less stable throughout iHeart's lifetime.

Active User Duration (d_x): Our measurements show between 70% to 75% of active users in a given week are only active for a day, and this percentage decays approximately as a power law with number of days active (e.g., only between 1.5% and 2% users are active for all seven days). Table 1 shows the weekly PL exponent of this distribution (γ_d).

Daily ARs Sent (m_x): Our measurements show that the distribution of ARs generated per day follows a power law for iHeart. Our algorithm uses the exponent, γ_m, of this PL distribution, and its values are shown in Table 1.

Additionally, Table 1 shows measurements for our *external constraint* on the seeding users (N_0) for a given week. We observe the lowest proportion of seeding users at peak activity, and highest proportion during lowest user activity. Week 45-2009 (Thanksgiving) is an exception since only four days of the week see high user activity, followed by three days of very low user activity (Figure 1(b)) as the Thanksgiving weekend kicked in.

4.4 Fitting Graph Models to iHeart UAGs

Existing research on growth processes on OSNs has yielded viable candidate models for friendship graphs [19]. We tested some of the more promising algorithms for our applications, in particular the original versions of the Nearest Neighbor, Watts-Strogatz, Barabasi-Albert and Forest Fire algorithms. All of these algorithms rely mainly on preferential attachment, and do not distinguish between behaviors of different types of nodes resulting in out-degree structures that are not representative of our UAGs. However, these algorithms do provide decent approximations of in-degrees for our UAGs. This is evident from the KS statistic values measured using synthetic graphs from these models against all weekly degree distributions from iHeart. Example KS statistic values for the Nearest Neighbor and Forest Fire algorithms against the week 34-2009 UAG from iHeart are shown in Table 7.[5] Figure 4 shows the degree structures that resulted in the lowest average KS values from these models against those from the week 34-2009 UAG for iHeart.

Period	Model	KS_{in}	L_{in}	KS_{out}	L_{out}
34-2009	FF	0.2117	7.81	0.6671	70.3
34-2009	NN	0.1768	7.65	0.7839	183.01

Table 7: Error measurements for in- and out-degrees for the weekly iHeart data using directed Forest Fire (FF) and Nearest Neighbor (NN) models.

5. MODELING GIFTING APPLICATIONS

The algorithm described in this section produces synthetic graphs with degree structures similar to UAGs for our gifting applications while preserving low clustering of nodes. We will show how our algorithm succeeds in capturing the difference in in- and out-degree distributions, which were not reproduced by previous models. We also provide steady-state equations (Section 5.4) for the synthetic distributions as a means to gauge user activity levels on gifting applications without running possibly time-consuming simulations.

5.1 Our UAG Growth Model

We have shown our UAGs exhibit similar structure across different weekly periods in terms of low clustering of nodes, and class of distribution functions that approximate the real degree distributions. However, the parameter values for these distributions that best fit the data differ significantly from week to week. This variability in UAGs must be captured by our algorithmic model. The basics of our growth model are as follows:

Our UAG growth model operates at discrete *timesteps* t, where each timestep represents a day of user activity. Let G_t denote the graph at the beginning of timestep t. The graph G_0 is a set of N_0 isolated nodes, which correspond to initial seeding users. Seeding users send ARs in each turn they are active. They send ARs to new users (i.e., 'recruit' them) with probability α, and to existing users chosen preferentially by in-degrees otherwise. When a user is recruited, with probability β she will choose to remain inactive throughout the process, and otherwise will be active at the beginning of the next timestep. Each user is assigned a fixed duration and daily output of ARs. The duration d_x of user x corresponds to the number of timesteps x is active, and the per-timestep output m_x of x corresponds to the number of ARs sent by x daily. After 7 timesteps, the resulting synthetic graph G_7 is produced. The structure of G_7 should be comparable to our UAGs.

Algorithm 1 shows the pseudocode for our UAG growth model. This algorithm uses *four* input parameters (α, β, γ_d and γ_m as described in Section 3.3), as well as two external constraints M and N_0. In the pseudocode, IPL(γ,t) and

[5]The L metric is defined in Section 5.2.

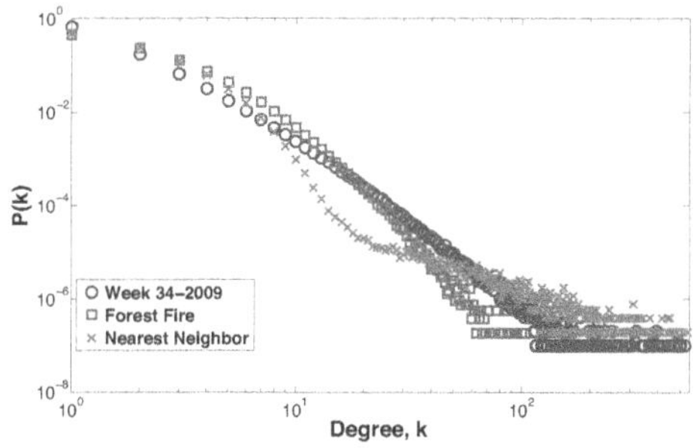

(a) In-degree distribution comparison.

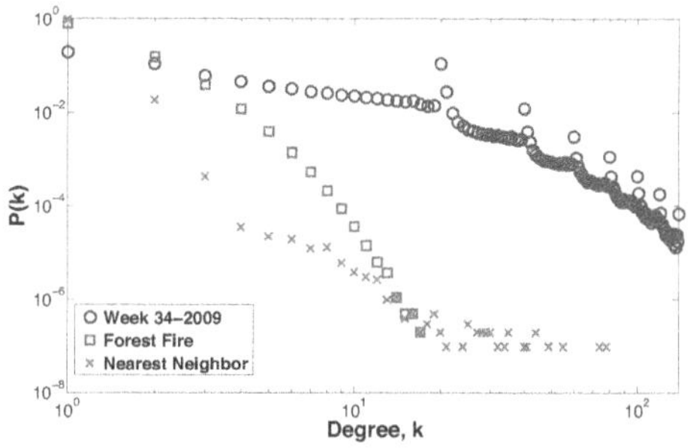

(b) Out-degree distribution comparison.

Figure 4: Visual comparison of degree structures for Nearest Neighbor, Forest Fire algorithms with the week 34-2009 UAG from iHeart.

RPL(γ,t) are integer- and real-valued PL distributed random variables (respectively) of exponent γ with a cut-offat t. Moreover, the variable act_x is the number of timesteps a user has previously been active, and $diff_x$ is the difference between $\lfloor m_x \rfloor d_x$ and the ultimate out-degree $\lfloor m_y d_y \rfloor$ of x.

5.2 Synthetic vs. Empirical UAGs

We implemented Algorithm 1 in Python and tested it on all 10 weeks of iHeart, iSmile and Hugged user activity. However, for brevity's sake, we only present results of simulations using UAGs from weeks 34-2009, 50-2009, 26-2010 for iHeart, and week 34-2009 for iSmile and Hugged.

We evaluate our simulated graphs' degree structures using two goodness of fit measures. In Section 4.2 we used the KS statistic to evaluate our degree distribution fits. However, the KS metric does not capture variance in tails as accurately as, say, the chi-squared metric. Therefore, we use an additional quantity we call L, which is analogous to chi-square on a log scale. Given two positive, integer-valued random variables X and Y, we define:

$$L(X,Y) = \sum_{k=1}^{\infty} [\log \Pr(X=k) - \log \Pr(Y=k)]^2 \log(\frac{k+1}{k})$$

Note that $\log(\frac{k+1}{k}) = \log(k+1) - \log(k)$. Hence L can be viewed as a discrete equivalent of the L_2 measure $d(f,g) = \int((f(x) - g(x))^2 dx)$ on a log-log scale.

Table 8 shows the KS and L values for our simulations using the 4-parameter model that is Algorithm 1, and Figure 5 shows the plots for the same. The KS and L values suggest the empirical degree structure is reasonably well-modeled in the 'typical' week represented by week 34-2009. For comparison, note the significantly larger L_{out} values in Table 7 for out-degree distributions generated by the Forest Fire and Nearest Neighbor models for week 34-2009 on iHeart. The larger L_{out} values demonstrate that Algorithm 1 performs significantly better than either Forest Fire or Nearest Neighbor in modeling out-degree distributions for our applications. Furthermore, L_{in} values in Tables 8 and 7 show that Algorithm 1 significantly outperforms both Forest Fire and Nearest Neighbor algorithms for in-degrees as well. Given the simplicity of the attachment rule used in our model, the fact that the in-degree distributions are captured so well is surprising. This is evidence that the dynamics of the real system may be similar to the 'Preferential Attachment with recruitment' dynamics in our model.

Our simulations using the 4-parameter model, however, result in synthetic graphs with comparatively large L values for the peak (week 50-2009) and post-peak (week 26-2010) periods for iHeart. This is a result of our inability to measure the degree of preference a user employs when sending ARs. Occurrences such as this are due to the inability of simple metrics to capture behavior of users in social graphs [19]. To remedy this, we introduce two additional parameters and refer to this as the *6-parameter version* of the model shown by Algorithm 1. The 6-parameter model is identical to the 4-parameter version in all aspects except the choice of the Active User Duration d_x and Daily ARs Sent m_x. In the 6-parameter model, these are approximated by LN distributions rather than PL distributions. LN distributions require *two* parameters whereas PL distributions only required one, so that the total number of parameters becomes 6.

Table 8 shows the L and KS values for our UAGs using the 6-parameter model. Our 6-parameter model simulations show that in some cases the error measurements actually grow larger compared to our 4-parameter model, but only slightly so. On the other hand, some of the error in the measurements can be dramatically reduced (out-degrees for iHeart). In week 50-2009, L_{out} drops from 18.08 to 0.62 when the 6-parameter model is used, and in week 26-2010 it drops from 7.75 to 1.44. An example resulting distribution using the 6-parameter model is shown in Figure 6.

Furthermore, as mentioned in Section 4.1, our UAGs exhibit very low clustering of nodes. Our UAG growth model's synthetic graphs similarly exhibit little or no clustering of nodes with CCs less than 0.0005. Our synthetic graphs also consist of connected components of size distributions similar to our UAGs. That is, more than 90% of users belong to one connected component, and the second largest component is of negligible size. We provide proof of the disconnectedness of our model's synthetic UAGs in Section 5.4.

5.3 Observations for our Growth Model

By demonstrating our algorithm works well on three gifting applications, we have shown it is possible to model UAGs for a class of social applications. *By decoupling in- and out-degrees and recognizing different types of users, our model provides a very close approximation of degree structures that result from use of the AR growth mechanism.* As in our empirical UAGs our model produces disconnected graphs such that most nodes belong to one connected component. Our synthetic graphs also exhibit little to no clustering of nodes.

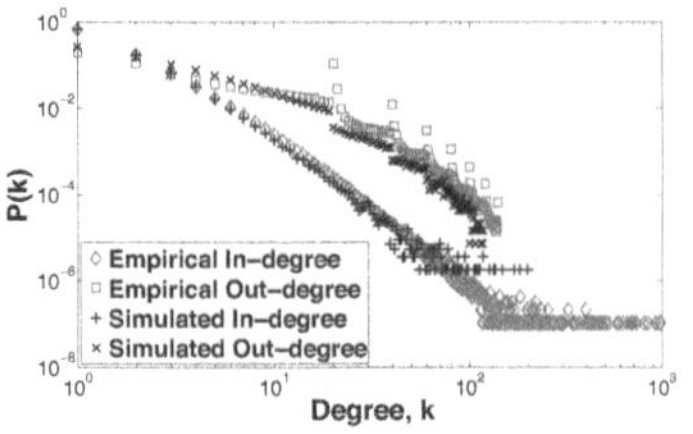

(a) Week 34-2009 for iHeart.

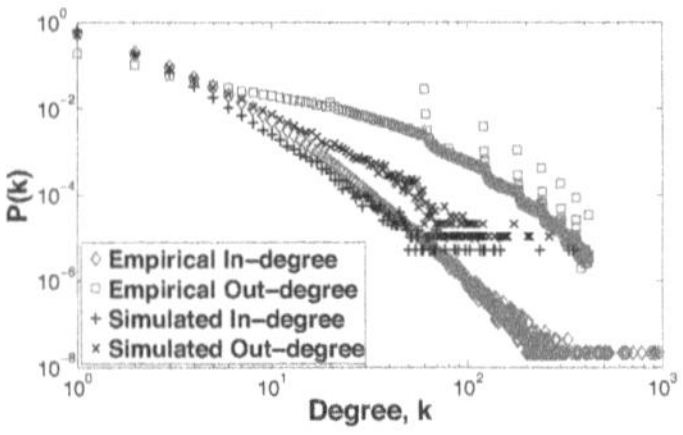

(b) Week 50-2009 for iHeart.

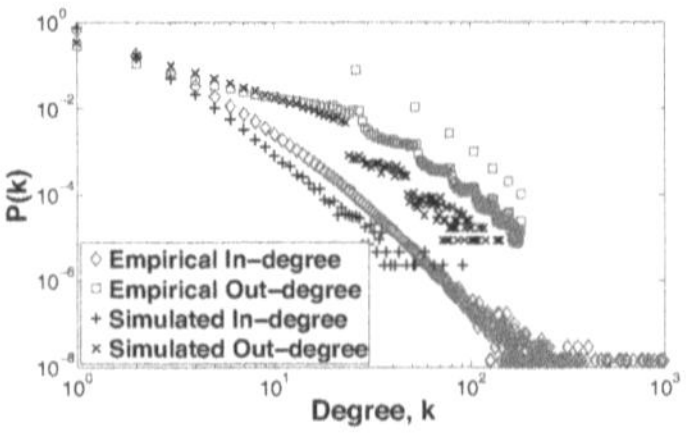

(c) Week 26-2010 for iHeart.

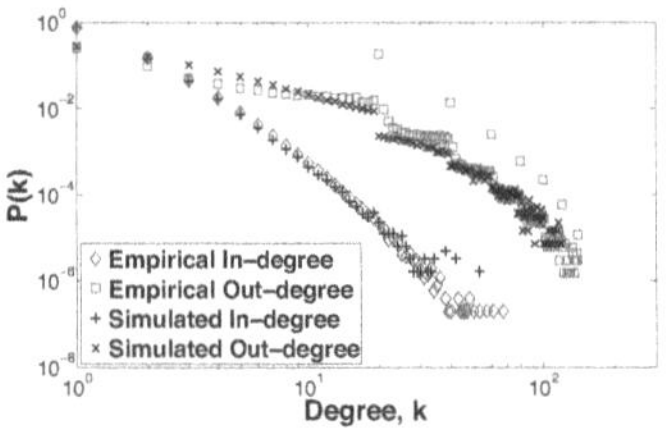

(d) Week 34-2009 for iSmile.

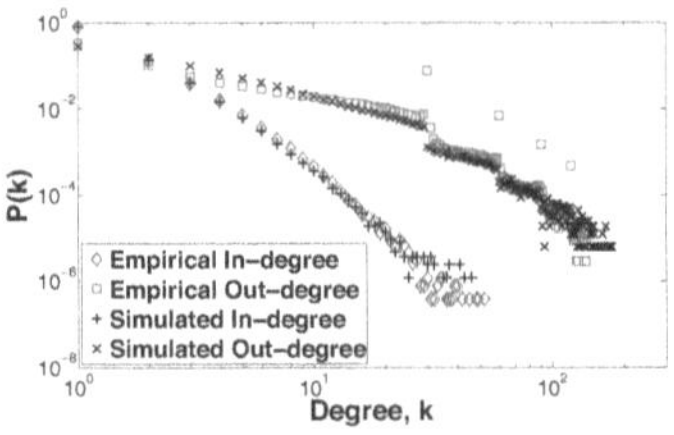

(e) Week 34-2009 for Hugged.

Figure 5: Simulated degree structures with 4 parameters.

		4 Parameter Model				6 Parameter Model			
App.	**Period**	KS_{in}	L_{in}	KS_{out}	L_{out}	KS_{in}	L_{in}	KS_{out}	L_{out}
iHeart	34-2009	0.002	0.77	0.002	2.07	0.004	1.5	0.004	0.69
	50-2009	0.01	2.07	0.01	18.08	0.002	4.23	0.002	0.62
	26-2010	0.0067	3.68	0.0067	7.75	0.0069	3.12	0.007	1.44
Hugged	34-2009	0.0001	0.27	0.0001	1.1	0.0003	0.56	0.0005	2.03
iSmile	34-2009	9.6e-005	0.38	9.6e-005	1.17	0.0002	0.63	0.0003	1.78

Table 8: Error measurements for in-degree and out-degree for the weekly UAGs.

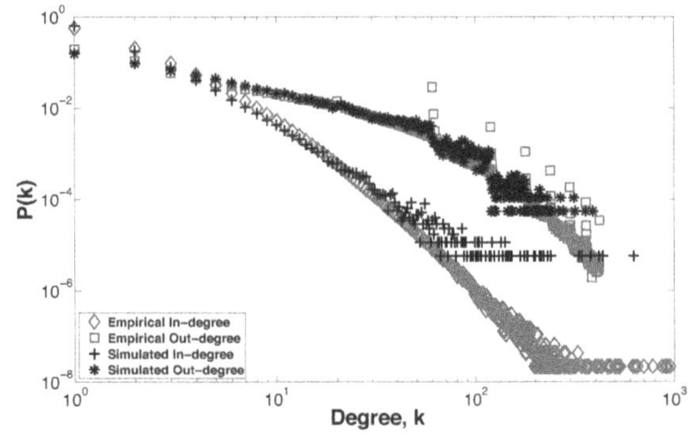

Figure 6: Simulated degree structures with 6 parameters for week 50-2009, iHeart.

Our 4-parameter model already works significantly better than existing algorithms, and the 6-parameter model works exceptionally well. We therefore do not require extensive information to model UAGs for gifting applications.

Our model potentially provides an alternative to sharing large data sets of application user activity, and since these graphs are synthetic, it also alleviates the violation of user privacy when sharing such data. Furthermore, given social applications exhibit weekly and yearly temporal patterns in user activity [16], our model is a step towards predicting user activity on other classes of social applications as well. Such a model is useful to application developers that wish to forecast an application's usage, and seek a reliable tool to help optimize growth strategies and advertising budgets. For instance, a developer might wish to buy N_0 application users from an advertising company to jumpstart (seed) their new application. Our model can provide them an approximation of user activity up to a week after application launch, which also helps them predict resource usage to minimize problems such as application downtime in the future.

5.4 Deriving Steady-State Results

Our UAG growth model allows us to run simulations given some knowledge of target graphs. However, simulating activity graphs for millions of users can be time consuming, for e.g., some of our simulations with 10 million nodes required over 5 hours to complete. We can lower our reliance on simulations through steady-state equations for degree distributions generated by our growth model. Using these equations, we can gauge statistics that convey user activity levels (such as the ratio of power to casual users) without running simulations. In this section, we probabilistically derive these distributions. We also provide a theoretical proof that our UAG growth model creates synthetic graphs with more than a single connected component.

Asymptotic Degree Distributions

Mathematical analysis allows us to obtain steady-state properties which assume the graph is infinite. However, our interest here is in producing a finite graph that captures 7 days of user activity. We find that the simulated degree distributions converge to the steady-state mathematical re-

Algorithm 1 Produces a model for weekly UAGs.

Require: N_0, M, α, β, γ_d, γ_m.
Initialize the network G_0 as a set of N_0 isolated nodes.
for all $x \in G_0$ **do**
  Activate x.
  $d_x \leftarrow IPL(\gamma_d, 7)$
  $m_x \leftarrow RPL(\gamma_m, M)$
  $diff_x \leftarrow \lfloor m_x d_x \rfloor - \lfloor m_x \rfloor d_x$
  $act_x \leftarrow 0$
end for
for $i = 0 \rightarrow 6$ **do**
  for all Active nodes x **do**
    if $diff_x \geq act_x$ **then**
      $dailyOutput \leftarrow \lfloor m_x \rfloor$
    else
      $dailyOutput \leftarrow \lfloor m_x \rfloor + 1$
    end if
    for $j = 1 \rightarrow dailyOutput$ **do**
      $coinflip \leftarrow uniform(0, 1)$
      if i = 1 and j = 1 **then**
        Add a self loop (x, x) to G_1
      else if $coinflip \leq \alpha$ **then**
        Add isolated node y to G_{i+1}
        Add the edge (x, y) to G_{i+1}
        $coinflip \leftarrow uniform(0, 1)$
        if $coinflip \geq \beta$ **then**
          Mark y for activation.
          $d_y \leftarrow IPL(\gamma_d, 7)$
          $m_y \leftarrow RPL(\gamma_m, M)$
          $diff_y \leftarrow \lfloor m_y d_y \rfloor - \lfloor m_y \rfloor d_y$
          $act_y \leftarrow 0$
        end if
      else
        Choose a random edge (y, z)
        Add the edge (x, z) to G_{i+1}.
      end if
    end for
    $d_x \leftarrow d_x - 1$
    $act_x \leftarrow act_x + 1$
    if $d_x = 0$ **then**
      Deactivate x.
    end if
  end for
  for all Marked nodes m **do**
    Activate m.
  end for
end for
  return G_7.

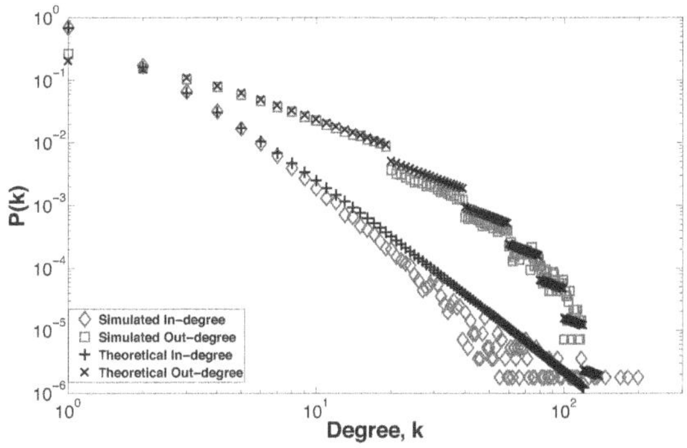

Figure 7: Simulated versus theoretical degree distributions for week 34-2009 from iHeart.

sults quickly as the number of seeding nodes (N_0) increases. Figure 7 shows example theoretical steady-state, as well as simulated, degree distributions for the week 34-2009 UAG on iHeart. Figure 7 shows that this theoretical formulation is indeed in agreement with our simulation results. The formulation is as follows:

First, consider out-degrees. Define N_t as the number of newly activated nodes at the tth timestep and N as the total number of nodes. If we assume that $x \in N_t$, where x is chosen uniformly at random, then the out-degree of x is a random variable $\lfloor m_x d_{x,t} \rfloor$ where $d_{x,t} = d_x 1_{d_x \leq 7-t} + (7-t) 1_{d_x > 7-t}$. The indicator random variable 1_A outputs 1 if the event A has occurred, and 0 otherwise. The general formula for out-degree is as follows:

$$\Pr(deg_{out}(x) = j) = \sum_{k=0}^{7} \frac{N_k}{N} \Pr(m_x d_{x,k} \in (j, j+1))$$

To calculate the in-degree, first define $N_{k,t}$ as the number of nodes of in-degree k after t edges have been added. If $p_{k,t}$ is the probability of observing a node of in-degree k after t edges have been added, then $p_{k,t} = \frac{t}{n} a_{k,t}$, where n is the number of nodes in the graph after t edges have been added. Dropping the t subscript in any of these variables denotes the asymptotic limit as $t \rightarrow \infty$.

$$\begin{aligned} N_{1,t} &= N_{1,t-1} - N_{1,t-1}(1-\alpha)t - 1 + \alpha \\ N_{2,t} &= N_{2,t-1}[1 - \frac{2(1-\alpha)}{t-1} - \frac{(1-\alpha)}{n}] + \\ &\quad + N_{1,t-1}[\frac{(1-\alpha)}{t-1}] \\ &\vdots \\ N_{k,t} &= N_{k,t-1}[1 - \frac{k(1-\alpha)}{t-1} - \frac{(1-\alpha)}{n}] + \\ &\quad + N_{k-1,t-1}[\frac{(k-1)(1-\alpha)}{t-1}] \end{aligned}$$

Using these master equations, we derive a recursive formula for p_k shown as Equation (1), which can be used to calculate p_k in time linear in k, and can also be approximated in closed form. This approximation is found by taking logs of both sides of Equation (1) and by replacing the resultant sum with an integral. This also shows that for large k, p_k decays as a PL with exponent $1 + \frac{1}{1-\alpha}$. Note that Equation (1) allows exponents strictly larger than 2.

$$\begin{aligned}
p_1 &= \frac{t}{n}\frac{\alpha}{1+(1-\alpha)} = \\
&= \frac{t}{N_0 + (1-\alpha)*t}\frac{\alpha}{1+(1-\alpha)} = \\
p_k &= \frac{t}{n}(p_{k-1})\frac{k-1}{\frac{1}{(1-\alpha)}+k} = \\
&= \frac{t}{N_0 + (1-\alpha)*t}(p_{k-1})\frac{k-1}{\frac{1}{(1-\alpha)}+k}
\end{aligned} \tag{1}$$

Connectivity

Although our model relies on a modified form of Preferential Attachment, unlike graphs with pure Preferential Attachment, our synthetic graphs are disconnected with some very small components, as in our empirical UAGs. The theorem below shows that with high probability, the synthetic graph produced is not entirely connected, and in fact for sufficiently large N_0 has a component of any fixed size.

PROPOSITION 1. *Given any fixed integer t^*, the graph G_{t^*} has multiple weakly connected components.*

PROOF. First note that $N_k \leq (M+1)N_{k-1}$, so that $N_{t^*} \leq (M+1)^{t^*} N_0$. It follows that $\frac{N_0}{N_{t^*}} \geq \frac{1}{(M+1)^{t^*}} > 0$ and thus N_0 is proportional to N_{t^*} for any choice of parameters. Let x be a node in G_t, and suppose y is a node that is sending out a heart. Since all nodes in G_t have in-degree at least 1, the probability that y sends the heart to x is at most $\frac{1}{N_t}$. Since $0 < \frac{N_0}{N_{t^*}} \leq \frac{N_t}{N_{t^*}}$ it follows that the probability that a node x of in-degree 1 receives a heart is $O(\frac{1}{N_{t^*}})$ at any given time step. The out-degree of any node is bounded by the constant Mt^*, and so the probability that x receives no hearts at all throughout the process is $(1 - O(\frac{1}{N_{t^*}}))^{Mt^* N_{t^*}} = \Omega(e^{-Mt^*})$. It follows that some non-vanishing portion of nodes in N_t receive no hearts after time $t-1$, and some non-vanishing portion of nodes in N_0 receive no hearts from other users.

Moreover, there is some non-vanishing portion of nodes in N_0 which have out-degree 1 and are connected to a node with out-degree 0. If both nodes receive no other hearts throughout the process, which will occur with probability $\Omega(e^{-2Mt^*})$, they form a component of size 2. Therefore, with high probability a portion of the nodes in N_0 will be contained in a component of size 2. Similarly it can be shown with high probability that for any $k = o(\log N_{t^*})$ there is at least on component of size k for sufficiently large n. □

6. CONCLUSION AND FUTURE WORK

We have provided insight into user activity on Facebook-based gifting applications, and have presented our methodology to create the first UAG growth model for a class of social applications that use only ARs for growth. Our algorithm requires little information to produce synthetic graphs for gifting applications, and provides a feasible alternative to sharing large data sets that may violate user privacy. Together with our steady-state equations for the synthetic degree structure, our algorithm may serve as an efficient user activity prediction tool to application developers.

Our work is a first step towards modeling user activity from social applications, and as such it does suffer from some shortcomings. Specifically, our growth model does not currently differentiate between male and female users, even though we speculate there are differences in gender-wise user behavior, and it only simulates weekly UAGs without tying multiple weeks' graphs into, say, a monthly or yearly UAG. A further (albeit minor) issue is that the very low clustering of nodes in our empirical UAGs is not accurately represented in our synthetic graphs, where the clustering is in fact even lower. It is important for future work to resolve these issues to create a more flexible UAG growth model.

We wish to create an algorithm that simulates UAGs from non-gifting social applications as well. While the gifting genre of applications is the second largest on at least Facebook, gaming applications are the largest and most lucrative. This is due to the fact that social gaming itself is now a 5+ billion dollar industry, and shows no signs of declining with the advent of mobile platforms such as iPhone and Android. Modeling UAGs from *gaming* applications is, however, a highly challenging task due to use of growth mechanisms in addition to ARs (Section 3.1), and the wide variety of possible in-game activities that affect their growth.

A cursory glance at the top ten Facebook gaming applications reveals most, if not all, games incorporate a select few mechanisms to drive growth and increase user engagement. Social games differ from their counterparts in the same genre due to the extent of importance a given mechanism is afforded. Mechanics such as leader boards, periodic item give-aways, holiday-themed in-game items and non-friend interactions drive user engagement and subscribership growth, while pure growth mechanisms include gifting in-game items to OSN-resident friends. The common use of engagement and growth mechanisms in social games hints at a possible general growth model for social games.

A successful model for gaming applications must incorporate characteristics of social gaming user activity such as high clustering coefficients, presence of strong community structures, high average time spent per user, and lower organic subscriber growth compared to gifting applications [16]. For now, quantitative measurements from non-gifting applications are lacking, and this prevents research into creating a more elaborate model.

Our work is the first step towards modeling social applications that use a combination of growth mechanisms, and it begins to alleviate the lack of availability of social application data to the research community. We hope this work will encourage research into activity models for non-gifting social applications as well.

Acknowledgements

We thank Manakki, LLC for the donation of anonymized activity data. This work is supported in part by AT&T Labs–Research, Google Research Award, Defense Threat Reduction Agency, Basic Research Award No. HDTRA1-10-1-0088, and the Army Research Laboratory under Cooperative Agreement Number W911NF-09-2-0053.

7. REFERENCES

[1] Backstrom, L., et al. Four degrees of separation. In *ArXiv, Social and Information Networks* (2011).

[2] Cha, M., et al. Characterizing social cascades in flickr. In *ACM SIGCOMM Workshop on Online Social Networks (WoSN)* (2008).

[3] Chierchetti, F., et al. Models for the compressible web. In *Proc. of the Symposium on Foundations of Computer Science* (2009).

[4] Clauset, A., et al. Power-law distributions in empirical data. In *SIAM Review* (2009).

[5] Gjoka, M., et al. Poking facebook: Characterization of osn applications. In *ACM SIGCOMM Workshop on Online Social Networks (WoSN)* (2008).

[6] Gjoka, M., et al. Walking in facebook: A case study of unbiased sampling of osns. In *Proc. IEEE INFOCOM* (2010).

[7] Golder, S., et al. Rhythms of Social Interaction: Messaging within a Massive Online Network. In *International Conference on Communities and Technologies* (2007).

[8] Guo, F., et al. Recovering temporally rewiring networks: model-based approach. In *Proc. of International Conference on Machine Learning* (2007).

[9] Handcock, M. S., et al. Model-based clustering for social networks. In *Journal of the Royal Statistical Society, Series A* (2007).

[10] Holme, P., and Saramäki, J. Epidemic spreading in scale-free networks. In *Physical Review* (2011).

[11] Krishnamurthy, B. A measure of online social networks. In *Proc. International Conference on Communication Systems and Networks* (2009).

[12] Krishnamurthy, B., et al. On the leakage of personally identifiable information via online social networks. In *ACM SIGCOMM Workshop on Online Social Networks (WoSN)* (2009).

[13] Leskovec, J., et al. Graphs over time: Densification laws, shrinking diameters and possible explanations. In *International Conference on Knowledge Discovery and Data Mining* (2005).

[14] Li, L., et al. A first principles approach to understanding the internet's router-level topology. In *Proc. ACM SIGCOMM* (2004).

[15] Mislove, A. and M. Marcon and K. Gummadi and P. Druschel and B. Bhattacharjee Measurement and Analysis of Online Social Networks. In *Proc. ACM IMC* (2007).

[16] Nazir, A., Raza, S., and Chuah, C.-N. Unveiling facebook: A measurement study of social network based applications. In *Proc. ACM IMC* (2008).

[17] Nazir, A., Raza, S., Gupta, D., Chuah, C.-N., and Krishnamurthy, B. Network level footprints of facebook applications. In *Proc. ACM IMC* (2009).

[18] Newman, M. E. J. The structure and function of complex networks. In *SIAM Review* (2003).

[19] Sala, A., et al. Measurement-calibrated graph models for social network experiments. In *Proc. of World Wide Web Conference* (2010).

[20] Sharan, U., and Neville, J. Temporal-relational classifiers for prediction in evolving domains. In *Proc. of International Conference on Data Mining* (2008).

[21] Tang, J., et al. Temporal distance metrics for social network analysis. In *ACM SIGCOMM Workshop on Online Social Networks (WoSN)* (2009).

[22] Torkjazi, M., Rejaie, R., and Willinger, W. Hot today, gone tomorrow: On the migration of myspace users. In *ACM SIGCOMM Workshop on Online Social Networks (WoSN)* (2009).

[23] Ugander, J., Karrer, B., et al. The anatomy of the facebook social graph. In *ArXiv, Social and Information Networks* (2011).

[24] Valafar, M., et al. Beyond friendship graphs: a study of user interactions in flickr. In *ACM SIGCOMM Workshop on Online Social Networks (WoSN)* (2009).

[25] Viswanath, B., Mislove, A., Cha, M., and Gummadi, K. P. On the evolution of user interaction in facebook. In *ACM SIGCOMM Workshop on Online Social Networks (WoSN)* (2009).

[26] App data. http://appdata.com/.

[27] Developer analytics. http://developeranalytics.com/.

[28] Farmville. https://apps.facebook.com/onthefarm/.

[29] Wilson, C., Boe, B., et al. User interactions in social networks and their implications. In *ACM EuroSys* (2009).

Inside Dropbox: Understanding Personal Cloud Storage Services

Idilio Drago
University of Twente
i.drago@utwente.nl

Marco Mellia
Politecnico di Torino
mellia@tlc.polito.it

Maurizio M. Munafò
Politecnico di Torino
munafo@tlc.polito.it

Anna Sperotto
University of Twente
a.sperotto@utwente.nl

Ramin Sadre
University of Twente
r.sadre@utwente.nl

Aiko Pras
University of Twente
a.pras@utwente.nl

ABSTRACT

Personal cloud storage services are gaining popularity. With a rush of providers to enter the market and an increasing offer of cheap storage space, it is to be expected that cloud storage will soon generate a high amount of Internet traffic. Very little is known about the architecture and the performance of such systems, and the workload they have to face. This understanding is essential for designing efficient cloud storage systems and predicting their impact on the network.

This paper presents a characterization of Dropbox, the leading solution in personal cloud storage in our datasets. By means of passive measurements, we analyze data from four vantage points in Europe, collected during 42 consecutive days. Our contributions are threefold: Firstly, we are the first to study Dropbox, which we show to be the most widely-used cloud storage system, already accounting for a volume equivalent to around one third of the YouTube traffic at campus networks on some days. Secondly, we characterize the workload users in different environments generate to the system, highlighting how this reflects on network traffic. Lastly, our results show possible performance bottlenecks caused by both the current system architecture and the storage protocol. This is exacerbated for users connected far from storage data-centers.

All measurements used in our analyses are publicly available in anonymized form at the SimpleWeb trace repository: `http://traces.simpleweb.org/dropbox/`

Categories and Subject Descriptors

C.2 [**Computer-Communication Networks**]: Miscellaneous; C.4 [**Performance of Systems**]: Measurement Techniques

General Terms

Measurement, Performance

Keywords

Dropbox, Cloud Storage, Internet Measurement.

1. INTRODUCTION

Recent years have seen the introduction of cloud-based services [18], offering people and enterprises computing and storage capacity on remote data-centers and abstracting away the complexity of hardware management. We witness a gold rush to offer on-line storage capabilities, with players like Microsoft, Google and Amazon entering the market at the end of April 2012. They face a crowded scenario against popular solutions like Box.com, UbuntuOne, and Dropbox. The latter, active since 2007, currently counts over 50 million users, uploading more than 500 million files daily.[1]

It is thus not surprising that cloud storage has gained increasing momentum within research community. Some works explicitly consider system architecture design [12], while others focus on security and privacy issues concerning the storage of user data [19]. Considering commercial offers, little is known, with most players providing proprietary solutions and not willing to share information. Some studies present a comparison among different storage providers [13, 17]: by running benchmarks, they focus on the user achieved performance, but miss the characterization of the typical usage of a cloud service, and the impact of user and system behavior on personal storage applications.

In this paper, we provide a characterization of cloud-based storage systems. We analyze traffic collected from two university campuses and two Points of Presence (POP) in a large Internet Service Provider (ISP) for 42 consecutive days. We first devise a methodology for monitoring cloud storage traffic, which, being based on TLS encryption, is not straightforward to be understood. We then focus on Dropbox, which we show to be the most widely-used cloud storage system in our datasets. Dropbox already accounts for about 100GB of daily traffic in one of the monitored networks – i.e., 4% of the total traffic or around one third of the YouTube traffic at the same network. We focus first on the service performance characterization, highlighting possible bottlenecks and suggesting countermeasures. Then, we detail user habits, thus providing an extensive characterization of the workload the system has to face.

To be best of our knowledge, we are the first to provide an analysis of Dropbox usage on the Internet. The authors

[1] `http://www.dropbox.com/news`

of [11] compare Dropbox, Mozy, Carbonite and CrashPlan, but only a simplistic active experiment is provided to assess them. In [16], the possibility of unauthorized data access and the security implications of storing data in Dropbox are analyzed. We follow a similar methodology to dissect the Dropbox protocol, but focus on a completely different topic. Considering storage systems in general, [8, 9] study security and privacy implications of the deployment of data deduplication – the mechanism in place in Dropbox for avoiding the storage of duplicate data. Similarly, [1] presents a performance analysis of the Amazon Web Services (AWS) in general, but does not provide insights into personal storage. Finally, several works characterize popular services, such as social networks [7, 15] or YouTube [3, 6]. Our work goes in a similar direction, shedding light on Dropbox and possibly other related systems. Our main findings are:

• We already see a significant amount of traffic related to personal cloud storage, especially on campus networks, where people with more technical knowledge are found. We expect these systems to become popular also at home, where penetration is already above 6%.

• We highlight that Dropbox performance is mainly driven by the distance between clients and storage data-centers. In addition, short data transfer sizes coupled with a per-chunk acknowledgment mechanism impair transfer throughput, which is as little as 530kbits/s on average. A bundling scheme, delayed acknowledgments, or a finer placement of storage servers could be adopted to improve performance.

• Considering home users' behavior, four groups are clear: 7% of people only upload data; around 26% only download, and up to 37% of people do both. The remaining 30% abandon their clients running, seldom exchanging files.

• Interestingly, one of the most appreciated features of Dropbox is the simplified ability to share content: 30% of home users have more than one linked device, and 70% share at least one folder. At campuses, the number of shared folders increases, with 40% of users sharing more than 5 folders.

Our findings show that personal cloud storage applications are data hungry, and user behavior deeply affects their network requirements. We believe that our results are useful for both the research community and ISPs to understand and to anticipate the impact of massive adoption of such solutions. Similarly, our analysis of the Dropbox performance is a reference for those designing protocols and provisioning data-centers for similar services, with valuable lessons about possible bottlenecks introduced by some design decisions.

The remainder of this paper is organized as follows: Sec. 2 provides insight into the Dropbox architecture. Sec. 3 describes our data collection and compares the popularity of well-known cloud-based storage systems. Sec. 4 presents a characterization of Dropbox performance. User habits and the generated workload are presented in Sec. 5. While those sections mostly focus on the usage of the Dropbox client software, Sec. 6 discusses the less popular Web interface. Finally, Sec. 7 concludes this paper, and Appendix A provides some additional characteristics of Dropbox storage traffic.

2. DROPBOX OVERVIEW

2.1 The Dropbox Client

The Dropbox native client is implemented mostly in Python, using third-party libraries such as *librsync*. The application is available for Microsoft Windows, Apple OS X and Linux.[2] The basic object in the system is a *chunk* of data with size of up to 4MB. Files larger than that are split into several chunks, each treated as an independent object. Each chunk is identified by a SHA256 hash value, which is part of meta-data descriptions of files. Dropbox reduces the amount of exchanged data by using delta encoding when transmitting chunks. It also keeps locally in each device a database of meta-data information (updated via incremental updates) and compresses chunks before submitting them. In addition, the client offers the user the ability to control the maximum download and upload speed.

Table 1: Domain names used by different Dropbox services. Numeric suffixes are replaced by a `X` letter.

sub-domain	Data-center	Description
`client-lb/clientX`	Dropbox	Meta-data
`notifyX`	Dropbox	Notifications
`api`	Dropbox	API control
`www`	Dropbox	Web servers
`d`	Dropbox	Event logs
`dl`	Amazon	Direct links
`dl-clientX`	Amazon	Client storage
`dl-debugX`	Amazon	Back-traces
`dl-web`	Amazon	Web storage
`api-content`	Amazon	API Storage

Two major components can be identified in the Dropbox architecture: the *control* and the *data storage* servers. The former are under direct control of Dropbox Inc., while Amazon Elastic Compute Cloud (EC2) and Simple Storage Service (S3) are used as storage servers. In both cases, sub-domains of `dropbox.com` are used for identifying the different parts of the service offering a specific functionality, as detailed in Tab. 1. HTTPS is used to access all services, except the *notification* service which runs over HTTP.

2.2 Understanding Dropbox Internals

To characterize the usage of the service from passive measurements, we first gained an understanding of the Dropbox client protocol. We performed several active experiments to observe what information is exchanged after a particular operation. For instance, among others, we documented the traffic generated when adding or removing files on local folders, when downloading new files and when creating new folders. During our data collection, Dropbox client version 1.2.52 was being distributed as the stable version.[3]

Since most client communications are encrypted with TLS, and no description about the protocol is provided by Dropbox, we set up a local testbed, in which a Linux PC running the Dropbox client was instructed to use a *Squid* proxy server under our control. On the latter, the module *SSL-bump*[4] was used to terminate SSL connections and save decrypted traffic flows. The memory area where the Dropbox application stores trusted certificate authorities was modified at run-time to replace the original Dropbox Inc. certificate by the self-signed one signing the proxy server. By means of this setup, we were able to observe and to understand the Dropbox client communication.

[2] Mobile device applications access Dropbox on demand using APIs; those are not considered in this work.

[3] `http://www.dropbox.com/release_notes`

[4] `http://wiki.squid-cache.org/Features/SslBump`

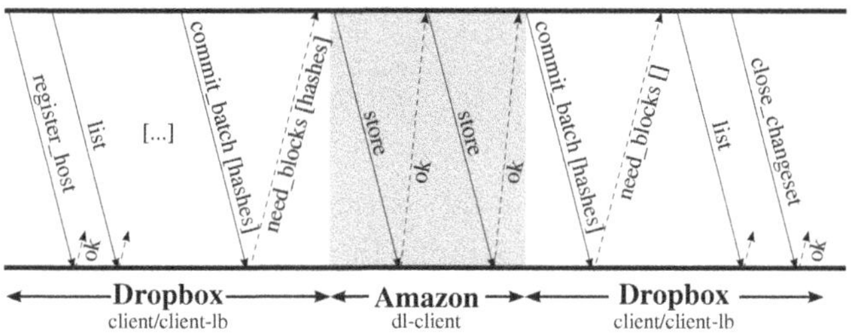

Figure 1: An example of the Dropbox protocol.

For instance, Fig. 1 illustrates the messages we observed while committing a batch of chunks. After registering with the Dropbox control center via a `clientX.dropbox.com` server, the *list* command retrieves meta-data updates. As soon as new files are locally added, a *commit_batch* command (on `client-lb.dropbox.com`) submits meta-data information. This can trigger *store* operations, performed directly with Amazon servers (on `dl-clientX.dropbox.com`). Each chunk *store* operation is acknowledged by one *OK* message. As we will see in Sec. 4, this acknowledgment mechanism might originate performance bottlenecks. Finally, as chunks are successfully submitted, the client exchanges messages with the central Dropbox servers (again on `client-lb.dropbox.com`) to conclude the transactions. Note that these messages committing transactions might occur in parallel with newer *store* operations.

A complete description of the Dropbox protocols is outside the scope of this paper. We, however, exploit this knowledge to tag the passively observed TCP flows with the likely commands executed by the client, even if we have no access to the content of the (encrypted) connections. In the following, we describe the protocols used to exchange data with the Dropbox control servers and with the storage servers at Amazon.

2.3 Client Control Flows

The Dropbox client exchanges control information mostly with servers managed directly by Dropbox Inc. We identified three sub-groups of control servers: (i) Notification, (ii) meta-data administration, and (iii) system-log servers. System-log servers collect run-time information about the clients, including exception back-traces (via Amazon, on `dl-debug.dropbox.com`), and other event logs possibly useful for system optimization (on `d.dropbox.com`). Since flows to those servers are not directly related to the usage of the system and do not carry much data, they have not been considered further. In the following we describe the key TCP flows to the meta-data and notification servers.

2.3.1 Notification Protocol

The Dropbox client keeps continuously opened a TCP connection to a notification server (`notifyX.dropbox.com`), used for receiving information about changes performed elsewhere. In contrast to other traffic, notification connections are *not encrypted*. Delayed HTTP responses are used to implement a push mechanism: a notification request is sent by the local client asking for eventual changes; the server response is received periodically about 60 seconds later in case of no change; after receiving it, the client immediately sends a new request. Changes on the central storage are instead advertised as soon as they are performed.

Each device linked to Dropbox has a unique identifier (*host_int*). Unique identifiers (called *namespaces*) are also used for each shared folder. The client identifier is sent in notification requests, together with the current list of namespaces. Devices and number of shared folders can, therefore, be identified in network traces by passively watching notification flows. Finally, different devices belonging to a single user can be inferred as well, by comparing namespace lists.

2.3.2 Meta-data Information Protocol

Authentication and file meta-data administration messages are exchanged with a separate set of servers, (`client-lb.dropbox.com` and/or `clientX.dropbox.com`). Typically, synchronization transactions start with messages to meta-data servers, followed by a batch of either *store* or *retrieve* operations through Amazon servers. As data chunks are successfully exchanged, the client sends messages to meta-data servers to conclude the transactions (see Fig. 1). Due to an aggressive TCP connection timeout handling, several short TLS connections to meta-data servers can be observed during this procedure.

Server responses to client messages can include general control parameters. For instance, our experiments in the testbed reveal that the current version of the protocol limits the number of chunks to be transferred to at most 100 per transaction. That is, if more than 100 chunks need to be exchanged, the operation is split into several batches, each of at most 100 chunks. Such parameters shape the traffic produced by the client, as analysed in Sec. 4.

2.4 Data Storage Flows

As illustrated in Fig. 1, all *store* and *retrieve* operations are handled by virtual machines in Amazon EC2. More than 500 distinct domain names (`dl-clientX.dropbox.com`) point to Amazon servers. A subset of those aliases are sent to clients regularly. Clients rotate in the received lists when executing storage operations, distributing the workload.

Typically, storage flows carry either *store* commands or *retrieve* commands. This permits storage flows to be divided into two groups by checking the amount of data downloaded and uploaded in each flow. By means of the data collected in our test environment, we documented the overhead of *store* and *retrieve* commands and derived a method for labeling the flows. Furthermore, we identified a direct relationship between the number of TCP segments with the `PSH` flag set in storage flows and the number of transported chunks. Appendix A presents more details about our methodology as well as some results validating that the models built in our test environment represent the traffic generated by real users satisfactorily. We use this knowledge in the next sections for characterizing the system performance and the workload.

2.5 Web Interface and Other Protocols

Content stored in Dropbox can also be accessed through Web interfaces. A separate set of domain names are used to identify the different services and can thus be exploited to distinguish the performed operations. For example, URLs containing `dl-web.dropbox.com` are used when downloading private content from user accounts. The domain `dl.dropbox.com` provides public direct links to shared files. As shown in Sec. 6, the latter is the preferred Dropbox Web interface.

Table 2: Datasets overview.

Name	Type	IP Addrs.	Vol. (GB)
Campus 1	Wired	400	5,320
Campus 2	Wired/Wireless	2,528	55,054
Home 1	FTTH/ADSL	18,785	509,909
Home 2	ADSL	13,723	301,448

In addition, other protocols are available, like the LAN Synchronization Protocol and the public APIs. However, these protocols do not provide useful information for the aim of this paper. They are therefore mostly ignored in the remainder of this paper.

3. DATASETS AND POPULARITY

3.1 Methodology

We rely on passive measurements to analyze the Dropbox traffic in operational networks. We use Tstat [5], an open source monitoring tool developed at Politecnico di Torino, to collect data. Tstat monitors each TCP connection, exposing information about more than 100 metrics[5], including client and server IP addresses, amount of exchanged data, eventual retransmitted segments, Round Trip Time (RTT) and the number of TCP segments that had the `PSH` flag set [14].

Specifically targeting the analysis of Dropbox traffic, we implemented several additional features. First, given that Dropbox relies on HTTPS, we extracted the TLS/SSL certificates offered by the server using a classic DPI approach. Our analysis shows that the string `*.dropbox.com` is used to sign all communications with the servers. This is instrumental for traffic classification of the services. Second, we augmented the exposed information by labeling server IP addresses with the original Fully Qualified Domain Name (FQDN) the client requested to the DNS server [2]. This is a key feature to reveal information on the server that is being contacted (see Tab. 1) and allows to identify each specific Dropbox related service. Third, Tstat was instructed to expose the list of device identifiers and folder namespaces exchanged with the notification servers.

3.2 Datasets

We installed Tstat at 4 vantage points in 2 European countries and collected data from March 24, 2012 to May 5, 2012. This setup provided a pool of unique datasets, allowing us to analyze the use of cloud storage in different environments, which vary in both the access technology and the typical user habits. Tab. 2 summarizes our datasets, showing, for each vantage point, the access technologies present in the monitored network, the number of unique client IP addresses, and the total amount of data observed during the whole period.

The datasets labeled *Home 1* and *Home 2* consist of ADSL and Fiber to the Home (FTTH) customers of a nation-wide ISP. Customers are provided with static IP addresses, but they might use WiFi routers at home to share the connection. *Campus 1* and *Campus 2* were instead collected in academic environments: *Campus 1* mostly monitors wired workstations in research and administrative offices of the Computer Science Department in a European university. *Campus 2* accounts for all traffic at the border

[5]See `http://tstat.tlc.polito.it` for details.

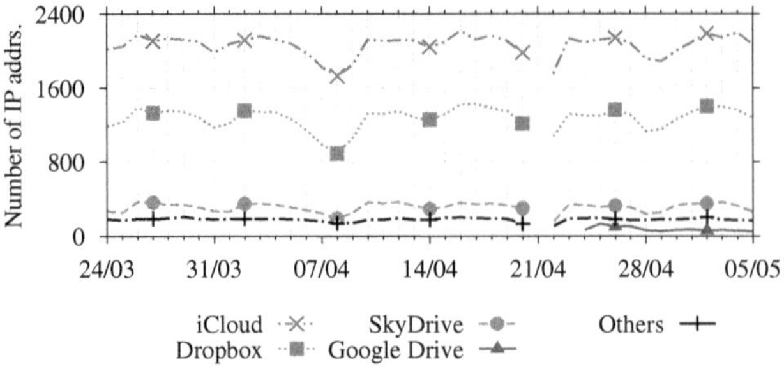

(a) IP addresses

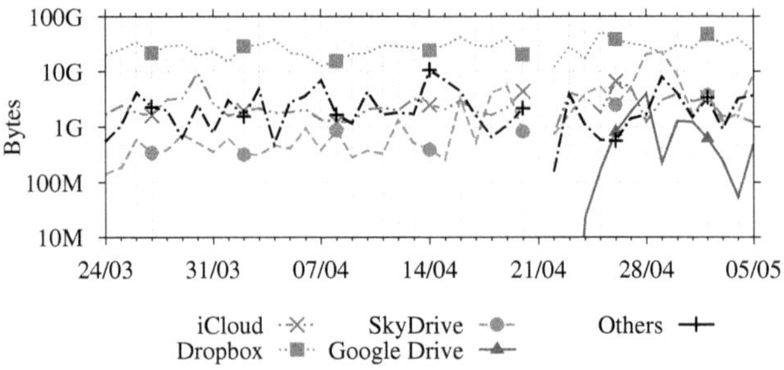

(b) Data volume

Figure 2: Popularity of cloud storage in *Home 1*.

routers of a second university, including campus-wide wireless access points and student houses. In this latter scenario, NAT and HTTP proxy-ing are very common, and DNS traffic was not exposed to the probe. For privacy reasons, our probes export only flows and the extra information described in the previous section. All payload data are discarded directly in the probe. To complete our analysis, a second dataset was collected in *Campus 1* in June/July 2012.

3.3 Popularity of Different Storage Providers

We present a comparison of the popularity of cloud-based storage systems. We explicitly consider the following services: *Dropbox*, *Google Drive*, *Apple iCloud* and *Microsoft SkyDrive*. Other less known services (e.g., *SugarSync*, *Box.com* and *UbuntuOne*) were aggregated into the *Others* group. We rely on both the extracted TLS server name and DNS FQDN to classify flows as belonging to each service.

We first study the popularity of the different services in terms of unique clients. We use the *Home 1* dataset because IP addresses are statically assigned to households and, therefore, are a reliable estimation of the number of installations. Fig. 2(a) reports[6] the number of distinct IP addresses that contacted at least once a storage service in a given day. iCloud is the most accessed service, with about 2,100 households (11.1%), showing the high popularity of Apple devices. Dropbox comes second, with about 1,300 households (6.9%). Other services are much less popular (e.g., 1.7% for SkyDrive). Interestingly, Google Drive appears immediately on the day of its launch (April 24th, 2012).

Fig. 2(b) reports the total data volume for each service in *Home 1*. Dropbox tops all other services by one order of magnitude (note the logarithmic y-scale), with more than 20GB of data exchanged every day. iCloud volume is limited

[6]A probe outage is visible on April 21, 2012.

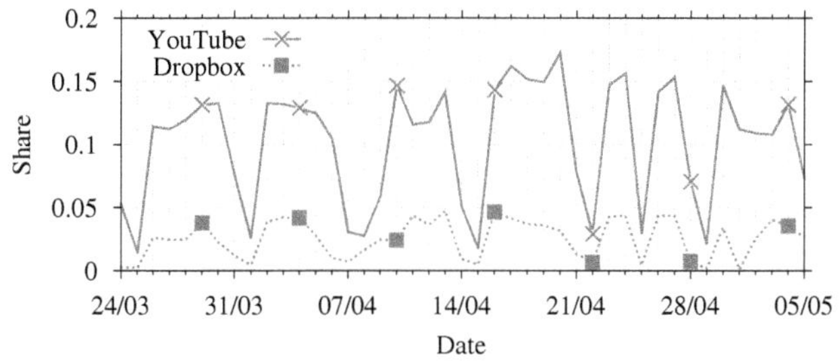

Figure 3: YouTube and Dropbox in *Campus 2*.

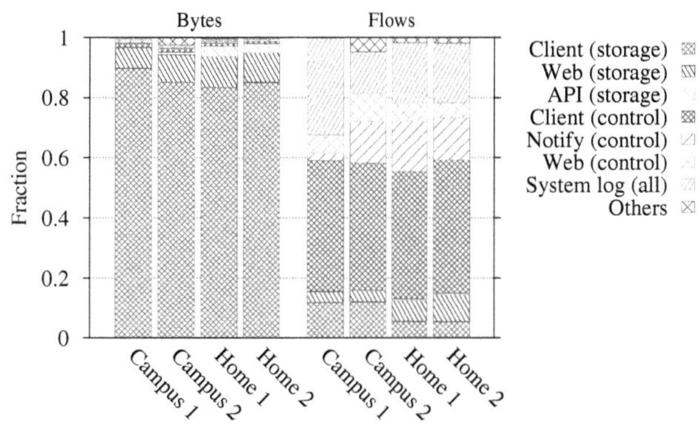

Figure 4: Traffic share of Dropbox servers.

Table 3: Total Dropbox traffic in the datasets.

Name	Flows	Vol. (GB)	Devices
Campus 1	167,189	146	283
Campus 2	1,902,824	1,814	6,609
Home 1	1,438,369	1,153	3,350
Home 2	693,086	506	1,313
Total	4,204,666	3,624	11,561

despite the higher number of devices, because the service does not allow users to synchronize arbitrary files. SkyDrive and Google Drive show a sudden increase in volume after their public launch in April.

Fig. 3 compares Dropbox and YouTube share of the total traffic volume in *Campus 2*. Apart from the variation reflecting the weekly and holiday pattern, a high fraction is seen for Dropbox daily. Note that in this network the traffic exchanged with Dropbox is close to 100GB per working day: that is already 4% of all traffic, or a volume equivalent to about one third of YouTube traffic in the same day!

These findings highlight an increasing interest for cloud-based storage systems, showing that people are eager to make use of remote storage space. Cloud-based storage is already popular, with 6-12% of home users regularly accessing one or more of the services. Although the popularity of the recently launched systems may increase in the future, in the following we restrict our attention to Dropbox only, since it is by far the most used system in terms of traffic volume at the moment. Dropbox overall traffic is summarized in Tab. 3, where we can see the number of flows, data volume, and devices linked to Dropbox in the monitored networks. Our datasets account for more than 11,000 Dropbox devices, uniquely identified by their *host_int* (see Sec. 2.3.1). The traffic generated by the Web interface and by public APIs is also included. In total, more than 3.5TB were exchanged with Dropbox servers during our capture.

4. DROPBOX PERFORMANCE

4.1 Traffic Breakdown: Storage and Control

To understand the performance of the Dropbox service and its architecture, we first study the amount of traffic handled by the different sets of servers. Fig. 4 shows the resulting traffic breakdown in terms of traffic volume and number of flows. From the figure, it emerges that the Dropbox client application is responsible for more than 80% of the traffic volume in all vantage points, which shows that this application is highly preferred over the Web interfaces for exchanging data. A significant portion of the volume (from 7% to 10%) is generated by direct link downloads and the main Web interface (both represented as *Web* in Fig. 4). In home networks, a small but non-negligible volume is seen to the Dropbox API (up to 4%). Finally, the data volume caused by control messages is negligible in all datasets.

When considering the number of flows, the control servers are the major contributors (more than 80% of the flows, depending on the dataset). The difference on the percentage of notification flows – around 15% in *Campus 2*, *Home 1* and *Home 2*, and less than 3% in *Campus 1* – is caused by the difference in the typical duration of Dropbox sessions in those networks, which will be further studied in Sec. 5.5.

4.2 Server Locations and RTT

We showed in previous sections that the Dropbox client protocol relies on different servers to accomplish typical tasks such as file synchronization. Dropbox distributes the load among its servers both by rotating IP addresses in DNS responses and by providing different lists of DNS names to each client. In the following, we want to understand the geographical deployment of this architecture and its consequences on the perceived RTT.

4.2.1 Server Locations

Names in Tab. 1 terminated by a numerical suffix are normally resolved to a single server IP address[7] and clients are in charge of selecting which server will be used in a request. For instance, meta-data servers are currently addressed by a fixed pool of 10 IP addresses and notification servers by a pool of 20 IP addresses. Storage servers are addressed by more than 600 IP addresses from Amazon data-centers. Fig. 5 shows the number of contacted storage servers per day in our vantage points. The figure points out that clients in *Campus 1* and *Home 2* do not reach all storage servers daily. In both *Campus 2* and *Home 1*, more servers are instead contacted because of the higher number of devices on those vantage points. Routing information suggests that control servers are located in the U.S. West Coast (likely in California), while storage servers are in the U.S. East Coast (apparently in Amazon's Northern Virginia data-centers).

In order to verify the current Dropbox setup worldwide, we performed active measurements using the PlanetLab. By selecting nodes from 13 countries in 6 continents, we checked which IP addresses are obtained when resolving the Dropbox DNS names seen in our passive measurements, as well as the

[7]Meta-data servers are addressed in both ways, depending on the executed command, via `client-lb` or `clientX`.

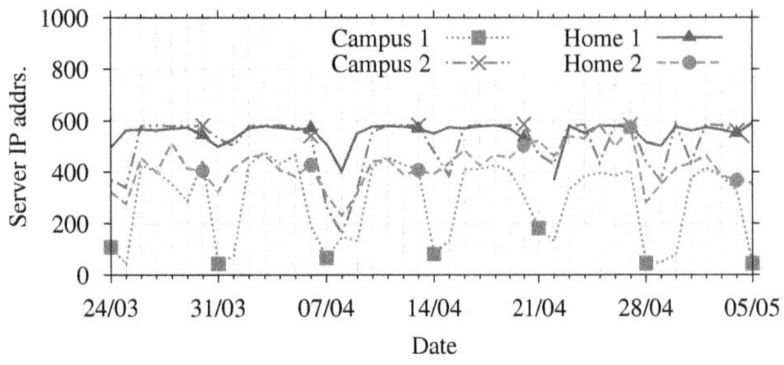

Figure 5: Number of contacted storage servers.

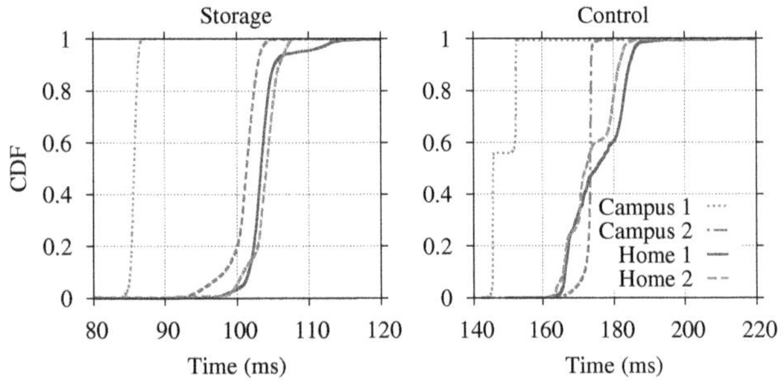

Figure 6: Distribution of minimum RTT of storage and control flows. Note the different x-axes.

routes and RTT when contacting the servers. The experiment shows that the same set of IP addresses is always sent to clients regardless of their geographical locations. This is valid for both control and storage domain names. Route information and RTT suggest that the same U.S. data-centers observed in our passive measurements are the only ones used worldwide. That is, Dropbox is, as for now, a service centralized in the U.S. Considering that more than half of the Dropbox clients are outside the U.S.[8], and the high amount of traffic observed in our vantage points, the traffic exchanged between the clients and the data-centers is likely to be already very relevant in the core network.

4.2.2 *Storage and Control RTT*

A deeper analysis of the RTT at our four vantage points reveals more details of the physical implementation of the Dropbox architecture. Sec. 4.4 will show that the RTT has a major impact on the service performance. Fig. 6 shows, separately for storage (left) and control flows (right), the CDF of the minimum RTT in flows where at least 10 RTT samples could be obtained (see [14]). The figure accounts only for the RTT between our probes and the servers, to filter out the impact of the access technologies (e.g., ADSL).

The RTTs to storage servers at Amazon remained stable during our measurements, meaning that no significant changes in the network topology happened. The differences in RTTs among the vantage points are related to the countries where the probes are located. This constant RTT during our 42 days of measurements is another strong indication that a single data-center was used by all users in our vantage points. The RTTs to the control servers are less constant. In both *Campus 1* and *Home 2*, the curve presents small

[8]`http://www.dropbox.com/news`

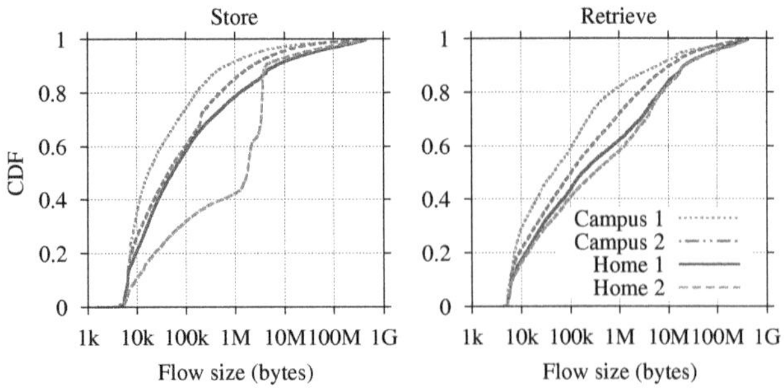

Figure 7: Distribution of TCP flow sizes of file storage for the Dropbox client.

steps (less than 10ms). We assume that they are caused by changes in the IP route, since the same behavior is not noticeable in all probes. Also in this case, the measurements hint to a central control server farm. Finally, it is interesting to note the high difference in the RTT between control and storage data-centers. This is probably caused by the physical distance between them inside the U.S.

4.3 *Retrieve* and *Store* Flows

4.3.1 *Flow Size*

As shown in Fig. 4, most traffic is generated by storage operations. Fig. 7 depicts the CDF of the flow size for storage operations. Since SSL is used, we observe a minimum flow size of approximately 4kB. The flows have a maximum size of approximately 400MB because of current run-time parameters of Dropbox: batches are limited to a maximum of 100 chunks, each smaller than 4MB, as described in Sec. 2.

From Fig. 7 it emerges that a significant percentage of flows (up to 40% in some cases) exchange less than 10kB, meaning that they are composed mostly by SSL handshake messages and a small amount of user data. A very high percentage of flows (varying from 40% to 80%) consist of less than 100kB. We conjecture that two factors are causing this behavior: (i) the synchronization protocol sending and receiving file *deltas* as soon as they are detected; (ii) the primary use of Dropbox for synchronization of small files constantly changed, instead of periodic (large) backups.

Comparing the CDFs for the *retrieve* and *storage* operations, we can see that *retrieve* flows are normally larger than the *store* ones. This is particularly visible in *Campus 1*, *Campus 2* and *Home 1* datasets. For instance, while 60% of *store* flows in *Home 1* have no more than 100kB, the percentage is about 40% for *retrieve* flows in the same network. This can be partially explained by the first batch synchronization happening when sessions are started. Besides that, we observed a high number of devices using Dropbox only for downloading content. This usage will be analyzed further in the coming sections.

We also highlight a remarkably discrepancy in the CDF for *store* flows in *Home 2*. A single device was submitting single chunks in consecutive TCP connections during several days in our capture. This caused the CDF to be strongly biased toward the maximum chunk size used by Dropbox (4MB). We could not determine whether this behavior is due to problems in the Dropbox client manifested in this single device, or another legitimate use of the service.

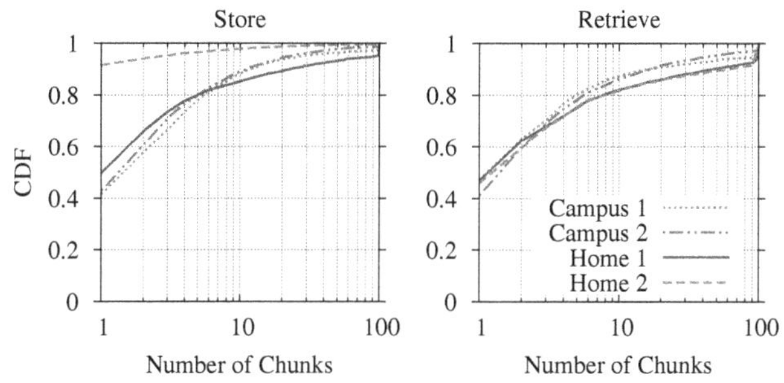

Figure 8: Distribution of the estimated number of file chunks per TCP flow.

4.3.2 *Chunks per Batch*

Fig. 8 depicts the CDF of the estimated number of chunks per flow. The curves show that most batches are composed by a small number of chunks. Storage flows have no more than 10 chunks in more than 80% of the cases in all datasets. *Home 2* distribution diverges because of the single client behaving abnormally described in the previous section. These distributions reinforce our conjecture about the dominance of deltas and small files in Dropbox usage habits: most flows are very small and composed by few chunks. Most of the remaining flows have the maximum allowed number of chunks per batch and, therefore, are strongly shaped by the protocol design of Dropbox.

4.4 Storage Throughput

Our measurements in Sec. 4.2 indicate that Dropbox relies on centralized data-centers for control and storage. This raises the question on the service performance for users not located near those data-centers.

The throughput of the storage operations is certainly one of the key performance metrics. Fig. 9 depicts the throughput achieved by each storage flow in *Campus 2*. The figure shows separate plots for the *retrieve* and *store* operations. Similar plots would be obtained using *Campus 1* dataset. *Home 1* and *Home 2* are left out of this analysis since the access technology (ADSL, in particular) might be a bottleneck for the system in those networks. The x-axis represents the number of bytes transferred in the flow, already subtracting the typical SSL overheads (see Appendix A for details), while the y-axis shows the throughput calculated as the ratio between transferred bytes and duration of each flow (note the logarithmic scales). The duration was accounted as the time between the first TCP SYN packet and the last packet with payload in the flow, ignoring connection termination delays. Flows are represented by different marks according to their number of chunks.

Overall, the throughput is remarkably low. The average throughput (marked with dashed horizontal lines in the figure) is not higher than 462kbits/s for *store* flows and 797kbits/s for *retrieve* flows in *Campus 2* (359kbits/s and 783kbits/s in *Campus 1*, respectively). In general, the highest observed throughput (close to 10Mbits/s in both datasets) is only achieved by flows carrying more than 1MB. Moreover, flows achieve lower throughput as the number of chunks increases. This can be seen by the concentration of flows with high number of chunks in the bottom part of the plots for any given size.

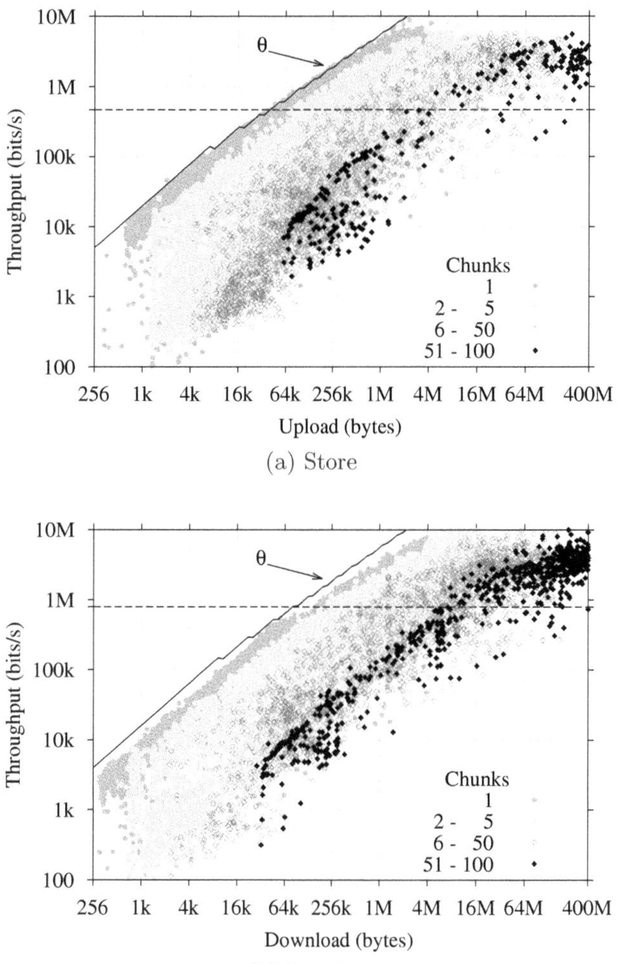

(a) Store

(b) Retrieve

Figure 9: Throughput of storage flows in *Campus 2*.

TCP start-up times and application-layer sequential acknowledgments are two major factors limiting the throughput, affecting flows with a small amount of data and flows with a large number of chunks, respectively. In both cases, the high RTT between clients and data-centers amplifies the effects. In the following, those problems are detailed.

4.4.1 *TCP Start-up Effects*

Flows carrying a small amount of data are limited by TCP slow start-up times. This is particularly relevant in the analyzed campus networks, since both data link capacity and RTT to storage data-centers are high in these networks. Fig. 9 shows the maximum throughput θ for completing the transfer of a specific amount of data, assuming that flows stayed in the TCP slow start phase. We computed the latency as in [4], with initial congestion window of 3 segments and adjusting the formula to include overheads (e.g., the 3 RTTs of SSL handshakes in the current Dropbox setup).

Fig. 9 shows that θ approximates the maximum throughput satisfactorily. This is clear for flows with a single chunk, which suffer less from application-layer impediments. The bound is not tight for *retrieve* flows, because their latency includes at least 1 server reaction time. Note that the through-

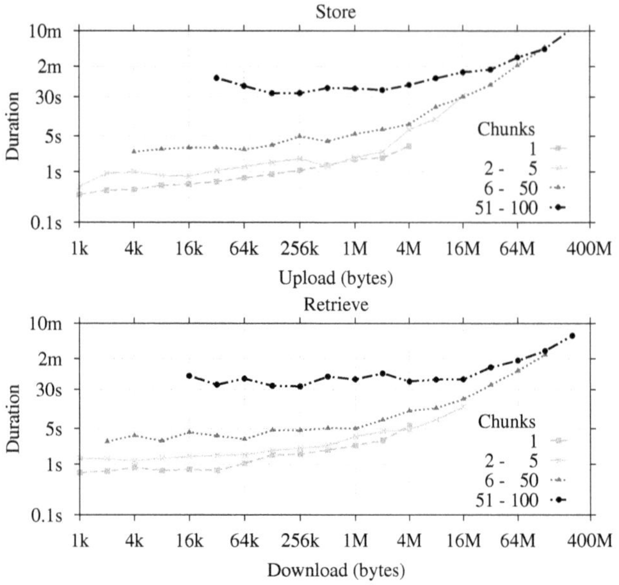

Figure 10: Minimum duration of flows with diverse number of chunks in *Campus 2*.

put can still be limited by other factors, such as the explicit user selection of transfer limits, or possible network congestion. However, when considering only flows with a single chunk, more than 99% of the *store* flows and around 95% of the *retrieve* flows in *Campus 1* have no TCP retransmissions. These percentages are lower in *Campus 2* (88% and 75%) because of the wireless access points. Single-chunk flows with no retransmissions experience throughput close to the limit (e.g., -17% on average for *store* flows in *Campus 1*), confirming that the TCP start-up is their main bottleneck.

4.4.2 Sequential Acknowledgments

Flows with more than 1 chunk have the sequential acknowledgment scheme (Fig. 1) as a bottleneck, because the mechanism forces clients to wait one RTT (plus the server reaction time) between two storage operations. Naturally, flows carrying a large number of small chunks suffer relatively more from this impediment than flows with large chunks. Fig. 8 shows that more than 40% of the flows have at least 2 chunks and are potentially affected by that.

Flows with several chunks are also affected by the previously described factors. Besides that, the Dropbox client keeps storage connections opened for a short interval after transferring a chunk, waiting for new chunks. Therefore, some flows in Fig. 9 might have a longer duration because they were reused during this idle interval. To remove these effects and highlight the impact of sequential acknowledgments, we divide the x-axis of Fig. 9 in slots of equal sizes (in logarithmic scale) and, for each slot, select the flow with maximum throughput in each of the four groups shown in the figure. Fig. 10 depicts the duration of these representative flows. Flows with more than 50 chunks, for instance, always last for more than 30s, regardless of their sizes. Considering the RTT in *Campus 2*, up to one third of that (5-10s) is wasted while application-layer acknowledgments are transiting the network. The remaining duration is mainly due to the server and the client reaction times between chunks.

Table 4: Performance in *Campus 1* before and after the deployment of a bundling mechanism.

	Mar/Apr		Jun/Jul	
	Median	Average	Median	Average
	Flow size			
Store	16.28kB	3.91MB	42.36kB	4.35MB
Retrieve	42.20kB	8.57MB	70.69kB	9.36MB
	Throughput (kbits/s)			
Store	31.59	358.17	81.82	552.92
Retrieve	57.72	782.99	109.92	1293.72

4.5 Implications and Recommendations

Our measurements clearly indicate that the application-layer protocol in combination with large RTT penalizes the system performance. We identify three possible solutions to remove the identified bottlenecks:

1. Bundling smaller chunks, increasing the amount of data sent per storage operation. Dropbox 1.4.0, announced in April 2012, implements a bundling mechanism, which is analyzed in the following;

2. Using a delayed acknowledgment scheme in storage operations, pipelining chunks to remove the effects of sequential acknowledgments;

3. Bringing storage servers closer to customers, thus improving the overall throughput.

Note that the first two countermeasures target only the application-layer bottleneck. The third one, while valid for any on-line service, would have the extra positive impact of removing heavy storage traffic from the core of the Internet.

4.5.1 Improvements in Dropbox 1.4.0

The latest version of Dropbox adds two commands (*store_batch* and *retrieve_batch*), allowing several chunks to be submitted in a single operation.[9] Single-chunk commands are still in use: the system decides at run-time whether chunks will be grouped or not. We use extra data captured in *Campus 1* during June and July 2012 to quantify the effects of this mechanism on the system performance.

Tab. 4 compares the flow size and the throughput distributions before and after the deployment of Dropbox 1.4.0. The increase in the median flow size shows that flows become bigger, likely because more small chunks can be accommodated in a single TCP connection in this version. The averages are less affected, since only smaller flows profit from the mechanism. Both the median and the average throughput, on the other hand, are dramatically improved. The average throughput of *retrieve* flows, for instance, is around 65% higher in the newest dataset.

Since both the new batch commands and the old single-chunk commands are still executed sequentially, there seems to exist room for improvements in the protocol. A complete characterization of that is, however, out of scope of this paper. Such an analysis will be performed in future work, along with an study of the effectiveness and possible drawbacks of each of our recommendations.

[9]Number of chunks and TCP segments with the `PSH` flag set do not have a direct relation in this version anymore.

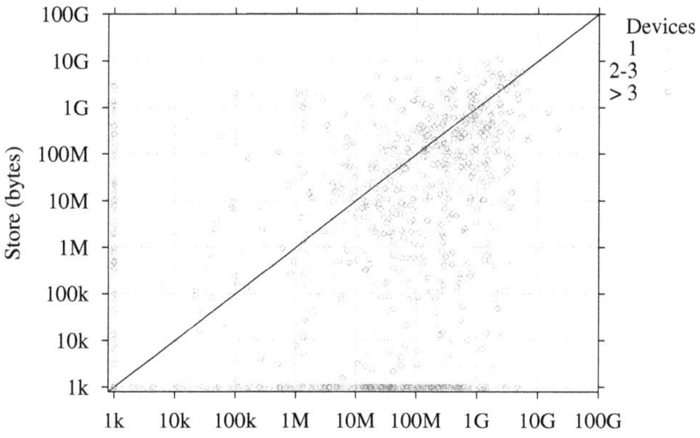

(a) Home 1

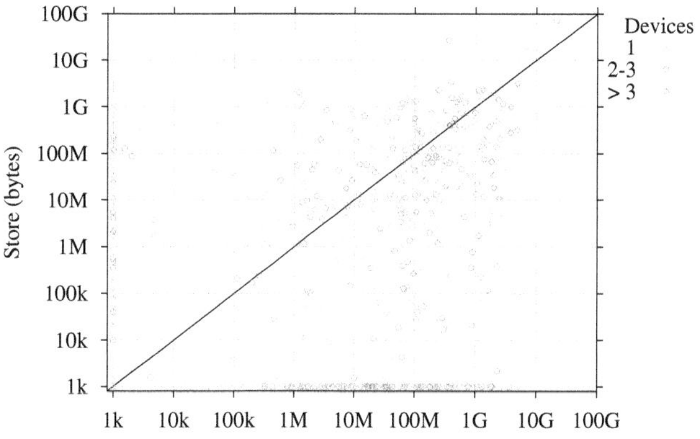

(b) Home 2

Figure 11: Data volume stored and retrieved from Dropbox in each household.

5. SERVICE WORKLOAD

5.1 Storage Volume

In this section we correlate ISP customers (IP addresses) in home networks and the total storage volume in *retrieve* and *store* operations. The amount of retrieved and stored data per household is depicted in Fig. 11. Each IP address is represented by a point and different symbols are used to illustrate the number of devices behind the IP address. Note that we placed all cases with less than 1kB on the axes because of the logarithmic scales. The figure accounts only for transfers made from the Dropbox client. Similarly to Sec. 4.4, the typical overhead of SSL negotiations were subtracted from the transferred amount.

Fig. 11 shows that Dropbox users tend to download more than upload. This is visible in the density of points below the diagonals. Overall, the total downloaded data in *Campus 2* is 2.4 times higher than the total uploaded data. This ratio is equal to 1.6 and 1.4 in *Campus 1* and *Home 1*, respectively. *Home 2* is an exception: The ratio is around 0.9 in this network. Some customers massively uploading content created this divergence. These customers appear on the top right corner of Fig. 11(b). Note that one of these customers is also responsible for the bias in the CDF depicted in Fig. 7.

In both datasets, four usage scenarios can be identified: (i) *Occasional* users, which abandon their Dropbox clients, hardly synchronizing any content (points close to the origins); (ii) *upload-only* users that mainly submit files (points close to the y-axes); (iii) *download-only* users, executing predominantly *retrieve* operations (points close to the x-axes); (iv) *heavy* users that both store and retrieve large amounts of data (points along the diagonals). The proportion of users in each group explains the overall relation between downloads and uploads seen in Fig. 11.

Tab. 5 quantifies the groups. The IP addresses are divided according to the following heuristics: IP addresses that have less than 10kB in both *retrieve* and *store* operations are included in the *occasional* group; IP addresses that have more than three orders of magnitude of difference between upload and download (e.g., 1GB versus 1MB) are included in either *download-only* or *upload-only*; all others are in the *heavy* group. For each group, the table shows the group percentage of IP addresses and sessions, the total transferred data, the average number of days in which the devices were seen on-line, and the average number of devices per household.

The *occasional* group represents around 30% of the total IP addresses in both vantage points. As expected, customers in this group exchange a negligible amount of data and stay on-line in Dropbox less time when compared to others. They also have the lowest average number of devices. This group, therefore, marginally generates any load to the system.

The *upload-only* group accounts for around 7% of the IP addresses, and is responsible for a significant amount of uploads (21% in *Home 1* and 11% in *Home 2*). Considering their low number of devices, users in this group seem to be interested in Dropbox for backups and for the submission of content to third-parties or to geographically dispersed devices. The opposite behavior can be concluded for the *download-only* group. This group is, however, very significant in both number of IP addresses (26% in *Home 1* and 28% in *Home 2*) and transferred volume (25% and 28%, respectively). Similarly to the *upload-only* group, a moderate number of devices per IP address is seen in this group.

Finally, accounting for 37% of IP addresses in *Home 1* and 33% in *Home 2*, the *heavy* group is responsible for most of the volume transferred by Dropbox clients. Customers in this group have a high number of devices (above 2 on average), appeared on-line more than 60% of the days in our capture and are responsible for more than 50% of the Dropbox sessions. The usage of Dropbox for synchronization of devices in a household seems to be the typical scenario in this group. Those are, therefore, the users causing the biggest impact on both system workload and network utilization.

5.2 Devices

In this section we describe the distribution of the number of devices residing in the same LAN. Devices connected to the same LAN can make use of the LAN Sync Protocol for synchronizing files without retrieving duplicated content from the cloud. Fig. 12 depicts the distribution of the number of devices per IP address in *Home 1* and *Home 2*.

In around 60% of the households using the Dropbox client, there is only a single device linked to the service. Most of the remaining households have up to 4 devices and, not surprisingly, are part of the *heavy* group identified in the previous section. By inspecting a subset of notification connections in *Home 1*, we observed that in around 60% of households

Table 5: **Fraction of IP addresses and sessions, retrieved and stored data volume, average number of days on-line, and average number of devices of the different user groups in *Home 1* and *Home 2*.**

Group	*Home 1*						*Home 2*					
	Addr.	Sess.	Retr.	Store	Days	Dev.	Addr.	Sess.	Retr.	Store	Days	Dev.
Occasional	0.31	0.15	-	-	16.37	1.22	0.32	0.18	-	-	15.52	1.13
Upload-only	0.06	0.06	-	84GB	19.74	1.36	0.07	0.04	-	26GB	20.42	1.37
Download-only	0.26	0.24	135GB	-	21.53	1.69	0.28	0.23	57GB	-	17.37	1.34
Heavy	0.37	0.54	417GB	321GB	27.54	2.65	0.33	0.55	147GB	193GB	27.10	2.16

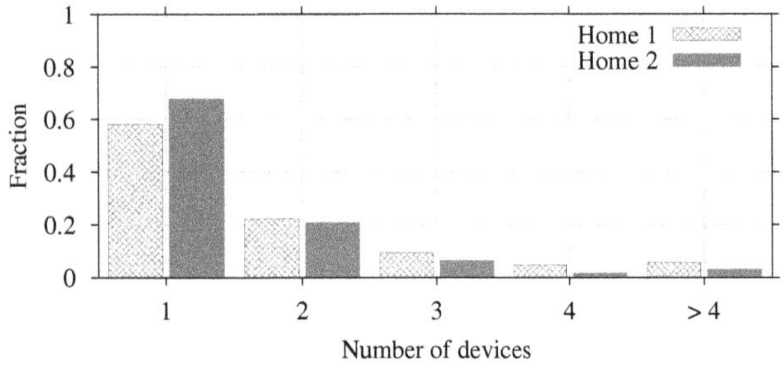

Figure 12: Distribution of the number of devices per household using the Dropbox client.

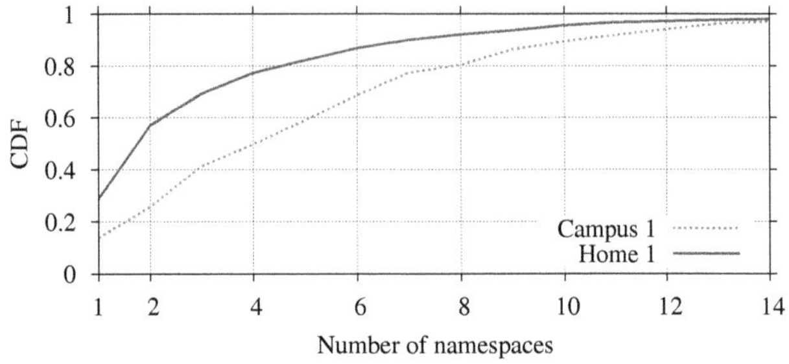

Figure 13: Number of namespaces per device.

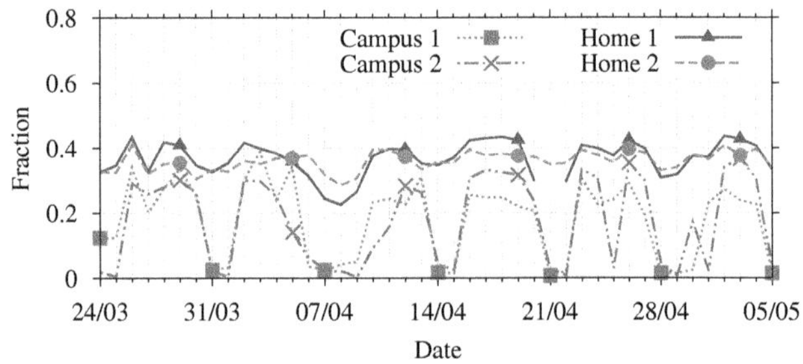

Figure 14: Distinct device start-ups per day – fraction of the number of devices in each probe.

with more than 1 device (around 25% of the total), at least 1 folder is shared among the devices. This further confirms our findings about the typical use of Dropbox among *heavy* users for the synchronization of devices. Since the LAN Sync Protocol traffic does not reach our probes, we cannot quantify the amount of bandwidth saved in these households by the use of the protocol. We can conclude, however, that no more than 25% of the households are profiting from that. The remaining users always rely on central storage data-centers for their data transfers.

5.3 Shared Folders

In order to measure to what extent Dropbox is being used for content sharing or collaborative work, we analyze namespace identifications in *Home 1* and *Campus 1* traffic (in *Home 2* and *Campus 2* this information was not exposed). Fig. 13 shows the distribution of the number of namespaces per device. By analyzing *Campus 1* data in different dates, it is possible to conclude that the number of namespaces per device is not stationary and has a slightly increasing trend. Fig. 13 was built considering the last observed number of namespaces on each device in our datasets.

In both networks the number of users with only 1 namespace (the users' root folder) is small: 13% in *Campus 1* and 28% in *Home 1*. In general, users in *Campus 1* have more namespaces than in *Home 1*. The percentage of users having 5 or more namespaces is equal to 50% in the former, and 23% in the latter. When considering only IP addresses assigned to workstations in *Campus 1*, each device has on average 3.86 namespaces.

5.4 Daily Usage

We characterize whether the use of the Dropbox client has any typical seasonality. Fig. 14 shows the time series of the number of distinct devices starting up a Dropbox session in each vantage point per day. The time series are normalized by the total number of devices in each dataset. Around 40% of all devices start at least one session every day in home networks, including weekends.[10] In campus networks, on the other hand, there is a strong weekly seasonality.

At a finer time scale (1 hour bins), we observe that the service usage follows a clear day-night pattern. Fig. 15 depicts the daily usage of the Dropbox client. All plots were produced by averaging the quantities per interval across all working days in our datasets.

Fig. 15(a) shows the fraction of distinct devices that start a session in each interval, while Fig. 15(b) depicts the fraction of devices that are active (i.e., are connected to Dropbox) per time interval. From these figures we can see that Dropbox usage varies strongly in different locations, following the presence of users in the environment. For instance, in *Campus 1*, session start-ups have a clear relation with employees' office hours. Session start-ups are better distributed during the day in *Campus 2* as a consequence of the transit of students at wireless access points. In home networks, peaks of start-ups are seen early in the morning and during the evenings. Overall, all time series of active devices (Fig. 15(b)) are smooth, showing that the number of active users at any time of the day is easily predictable.

[10]Note the exceptions around holidays in April and May.

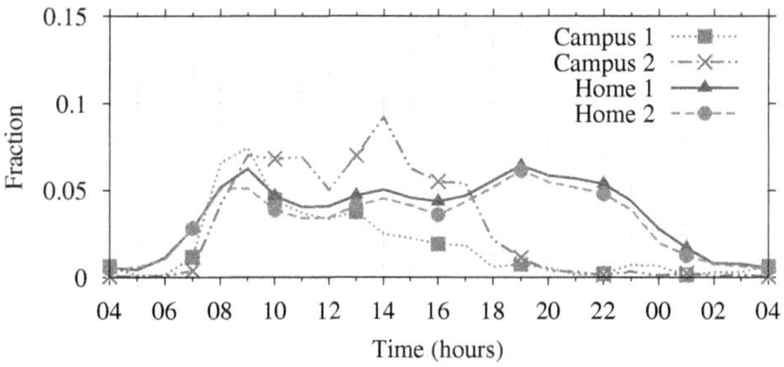

(a) Session start-ups

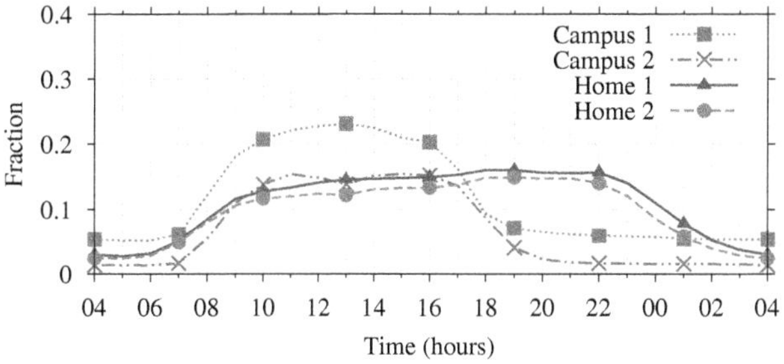

(b) Active devices

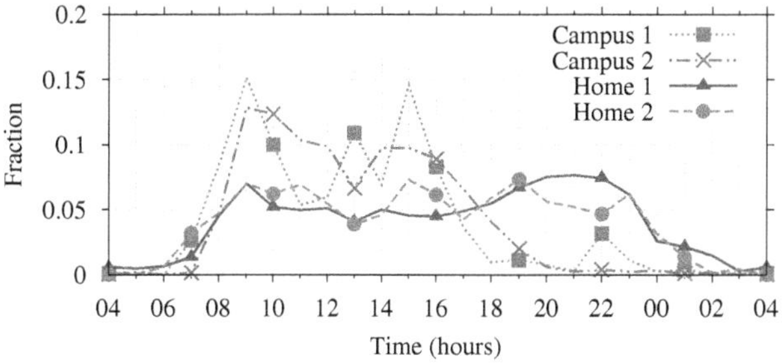

(c) Retrieve

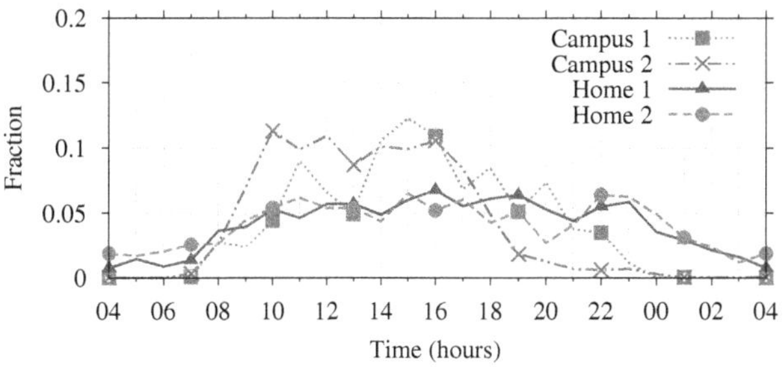

(d) Store

Figure 15: Daily usage of Dropbox on weekdays.

Fig. 15(c) and 15(d) depict the fraction of the total number of bytes exchanged in each time interval in *retrieve* and *store* functions, respectively. Fig. 15(c) shows that the number of bytes received in *retrieve* operations has a correlation with client start-ups. This suggests that the first synchronization after starting a device is dominated by the download of content produced elsewhere, instead of the upload of content produced while off-line. Although other patterns are visible in the figures, such as the concentration of downloads in the morning in *Campus 1* and in the evening in *Home 1*, both series are still very noisy at this level of aggregation.

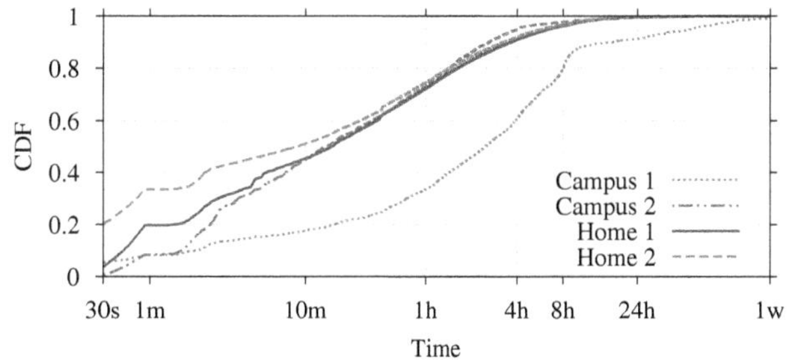

Figure 16: Distribution of session durations.

5.5 Session Duration

We analyze the session duration based on the TCP flows to notification servers. *Home 1*, *Home 2*, and *Campus 2* have a similar behavior in general, as shown in Fig. 16, with an exception for the number of short-lived sessions. In both home networks, a significant number of notification flows are terminated in less than 1 minute. A closer inspection reveals that most of those flows are from few devices. Their divergent TCP behavior suggests that network equipment (*e.g.* NAT or firewalls – see [10]) might be terminating notification connections abruptly. Considering the normal operation of the Dropbox protocol, notification connections are re-established immediately after that.

Most devices in *Home 1*, *Home 2* and *Campus 2* stay connected up to 4 hours in a single session. In *Campus 1*, a significantly higher percentage of long-lasting sessions is seen. This can be explained by the prevalence of workstations in a typical 8-hours work routine. Inflections at the tail of the distributions are seen in all curves, as a consequence of the devices kept always on-line.

5.6 Implications

The results in this section help to understand the current usage of the Dropbox client. This is needed, for instance, for provisioning data-centers and networks to handle cloud storage traffic. Our analysis of typical user behaviors reveals that users have different interests on the application. For instance, although Dropbox is already installed in more than 6% of the households (see Sec. 3.3), less than 40% of these households are fully using its functionalities, i.e., synchronizing devices, sharing folders etc. Interestingly, the results are very similar in both home networks, reinforcing our conclusions. The very high amount of traffic created by this limited percentage of users motivates our expectations that cloud storage systems will be among the top applications producing Internet traffic soon. Geographically dispersed sources as well as longitudinal data are, however, necessary to check whether the conclusions of this section can be generalized, as more people adopt such solutions.

6. WEB STORAGE

In addition to the client application, Dropbox allows users to access shared folders and files using both its main Web interface and a direct link download mechanism. In the following, we analyze the usage of these interfaces. Fig. 17 presents the CDFs of the number of bytes in the storage flows of the Dropbox main Web interface. Separate CDFs for uploads and downloads are presented.

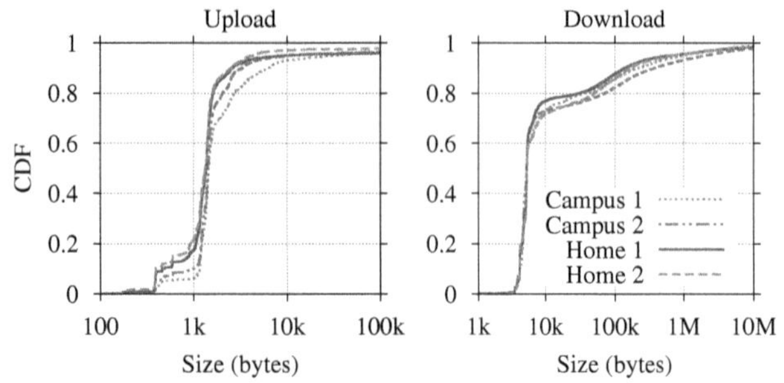

Figure 17: Storage via the main Web interface.

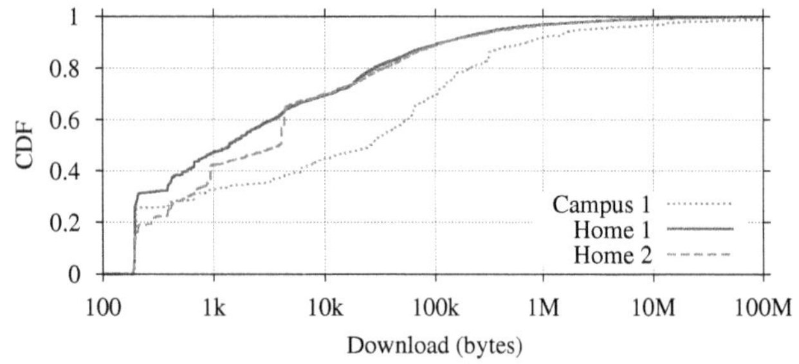

Figure 18: Size of direct link downloads.

Considering the number of uploaded bytes, it becomes clear that the main Web interface is hardly used for uploading content. More than 95% of the flows submitted less than 10kB. When considering downloaded bytes, up to 80% of flows exchanged less 10kB. These distributions are, however, strongly biased toward the SSL handshake sizes for two reasons: (i) the Dropbox interface retrieves thumbnails from storage servers using SSL; (ii) Web browsers open several parallel connections when retrieving those HTTP objects. The remaining flows have less than 10MB in more than 95% of the cases, showing that only small files are normally retrieved from this Web interface.

Additionally, we analyze flows related to direct link downloads. Note that these flows correspond to 92% of the Dropbox Web storage flows in *Home 1*, confirming that this mechanism is highly preferred over the main Dropbox Web interface. Fig. 18 shows the CDF of the size of direct link downloads.[11] Since these downloads are not always encrypted, the CDF does not have the SSL lower-bound. Interestingly, only a small percentage of direct link downloads is bigger than 10MB, suggesting that their usage is not related to the sharing of movies or archives.

7. CONCLUSIONS

To the best of our knowledge, we are the first to analyze the usage of Dropbox on the Internet. Our analysis assessed the increasing interest on cloud-based storage systems. Major players like Google, Apple and Microsoft are offering the service. We showed that, in this landscape, Dropbox is currently the most popular provider of such a system.

By analyzing flows captured at 4 vantage points in Europe over a period of 42 consecutive days, we showed that Dropbox is by now responsible for a considerable traffic volume. In one of our datasets, for instance, Dropbox is already equivalent to one third of the YouTube traffic.

We presented an extensive characterization of Dropbox, both in terms of the system workload as well as the typical usage. Our main findings show that the Dropbox service performance is highly impacted by the distance between the clients and the data-centers, which are currently located in the U.S. The usage of per-chunk acknowledgments in the client protocol combined with the typically small chunk sizes deeply limits the effective throughput of the service. In this paper, we identified two possible improvements to the protocol: (i) the usage of a chunk bundling scheme; (ii) the introduction of delayed acknowledgments. We showed that the recent deployment of a bundling mechanism improved the system performance dramatically. In addition, we expect that the overall performance will be improved by the deployment of other data-centers in different locations.

Regarding the typical workload of the Dropbox system, our analysis showed a variety of user behaviors. For instance, a considerable number of users take full advantage of the Dropbox functionalities, actively storing and retrieving files and sharing several folders. However, we also noted around one third of users completely abandoning their clients, seldom exchanging any data during the 42 days of observations.

[11] Uploads are not shown since a single HTTP request is sent. *Campus 2* is not depicted due to the lack of FQDN.

8. ACKNOWLEDGMENTS

This work has been carried out in the context of the TMA COST Action IC0703, the EU-IP project *mPlane* and the IOP GenCom project *SeQual*. *mPlane* is funded by the European Commission under the grant n-318627. *SeQual* is funded by the Dutch Ministry of Economic Affairs, Agriculture and Innovation via its agency Agentschap NL.

9. REFERENCES

[1] A. Bergen, Y. Coady, and R. McGeer. Client Bandwidth: The Forgotten Metric of Online Storage Providers. In *Proceedings of the 2011 IEEE Pacific Rim Conference on Communications, Computers and Signal Processing*, PacRim'2011, pages 543–548, 2011.

[2] I. Bermudez, M. Mellia, M. M. Munafò, R. Keralapura, and A. Nucci. DNS to the Rescue: Discerning Content and Services in a Tangled Web. In *Proceedings of the 12th ACM SIGCOMM Conference on Internet Measurement*, IMC'12, 2012.

[3] M. Cha, H. Kwak, P. Rodriguez, Y.-Y. Ahn, and S. Moon. I Tube, You Tube, Everybody Tubes: Analyzing the World's Largest User Generated Content Video System. In *Proceedings of the 7th ACM SIGCOMM Conference on Internet Measurement*, IMC'07, pages 1–14, 2007.

[4] N. Dukkipati, T. Refice, Y. Cheng, J. Chu, T. Herbert, A. Agarwal, A. Jain, and N. Sutin. An Argument for Increasing TCP's Initial Congestion Window. *SIGCOMM Comput. Commun. Rev.*, 40(3):26–33, 2010.

[5] A. Finamore, M. Mellia, M. Meo, M. M. Munafò, and D. Rossi. Experiences of Internet Traffic Monitoring with Tstat. *IEEE Network*, 25(3):8–14, 2011.

[6] A. Finamore, M. Mellia, M. M. Munafò, R. Torres, and S. G. Rao. YouTube Everywhere: Impact of Device and Infrastructure Synergies on User

Experience. In *Proceedings of the 11th ACM SIGCOMM Conference on Internet Measurement*, IMC'11, pages 345–360, 2011.
[7] M. Gjoka, M. Sirivianos, A. Markopoulou, and X. Yang. Poking Facebook: Characterization of OSN Applications. In *Proceedings of the First Workshop on Online Social Networks*, WOSN'08, pages 31–36, 2008.
[8] S. Halevi, D. Harnik, B. Pinkas, and A. Shulman-Peleg. Proofs of Ownership in Remote Storage Systems. In *Proceedings of the 18th ACM Conference on Computer and Communications Security*, CCS'11, pages 491–500, 2011.
[9] D. Harnik, B. Pinkas, and A. Shulman-Peleg. Side Channels in Cloud Services: Deduplication in Cloud Storage. *IEEE Security and Privacy*, 8(6):40–47, 2010.
[10] S. Hätönen, A. Nyrhinen, L. Eggert, S. Strowes, P. Sarolahti, and M. Kojo. An Experimental Study of Home Gateway Characteristics. In *Proceedings of the 10th ACM SIGCOMM Conference on Internet Measurement*, IMC'10, pages 260–266, 2010.
[11] W. Hu, T. Yang, and J. N. Matthews. The Good, the Bad and the Ugly of Consumer Cloud Storage. *ACM SIGOPS Operating Systems Review*, 44(3):110–115, 2010.
[12] A. Lenk, M. Klems, J. Nimis, S. Tai, and T. Sandholm. What's Inside the Cloud? An Architectural Map of the Cloud Landscape. In *Proceedings of the 2009 ICSE Workshop on Software Engineering Challenges of Cloud Computing*, CLOUD'09, pages 23–31, 2009.
[13] A. Li, X. Yang, S. Kandula, and M. Zhang. CloudCmp: Comparing Public Cloud Providers. In *Proceedings of the 10th ACM SIGCOMM Conference on Internet Measurement*, IMC'10, pages 1–14, 2010.
[14] M. Mellia, M. Meo, L. Muscariello, and D. Rossi. Passive Analysis of TCP Anomalies. *Computer Networks*, 52(14):2663–2676, 2008.
[15] A. Mislove, M. Marcon, K. P. Gummadi, P. Druschel, and B. Bhattacharjee. Measurement and Analysis of Online Social Networks. In *Proceedings of the 7th ACM SIGCOMM Conference on Internet Measurement*, IMC'07, pages 29–42, 2007.
[16] M. Mulazzani, S. Schrittwieser, M. Leithner, M. Huber, and E. Weippl. Dark Clouds on the Horizon: Using Cloud Storage as Attack Vector and Online Slack Space. In *Proceedings of the 20th USENIX Conference on Security*, SEC'11, 2011.
[17] G. Wang and T. E. Ng. The Impact of Virtualization on Network Performance of Amazon EC2 Data Center. In *Proceedings of the 29th IEEE INFOCOM*, pages 1–9, 2010.
[18] Q. Zhang, L. Cheng, and R. Boutaba. Cloud Computing: State-of-the-Art and Research Challenges. *Journal of Internet Services and Applications*, 1:7–18, 2010.
[19] M. Zhou, R. Zhang, W. Xie, W. Qian, and A. Zhou. Security and Privacy in Cloud Computing: A Survey. In *Sixth International Conference on Semantics Knowledge and Grid*, SKG'10, pages 105–112, 2010.

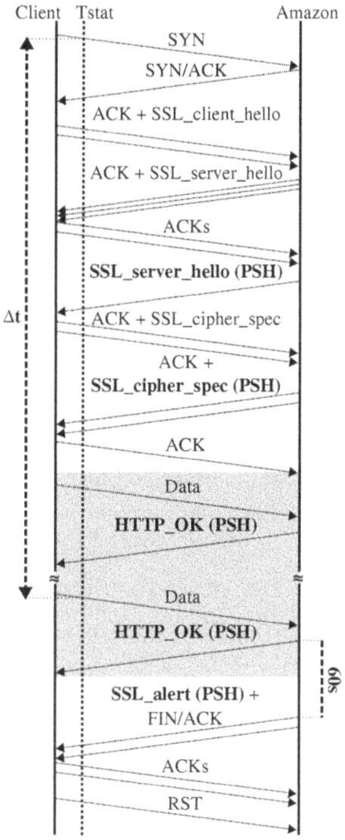

(a) Store

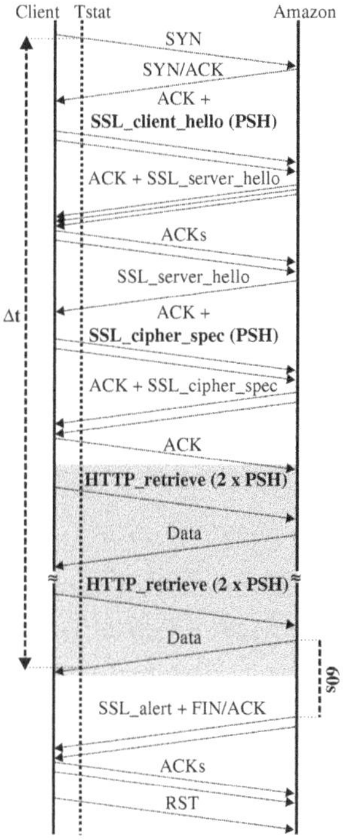

(b) Retrieve

Figure 19: Typical flows in storage operations.

APPENDIX

A. STORAGE TRAFFIC IN DETAILS

A.1 Typical Flows

Fig. 19 shows typical storage flows observed in our testbed. All packets exchanged during initial and final handshakes are depicted. The data transfer phases (in gray) are shortened for the sake of space. Key elements for our methodology, such as TCP segments with `PSH` flag set and flow durations, are highlighted. To confirm that these models are valid in real clients, Tstat in *Campus 1* was set to record statistics about the first 10 messages delimited by TCP segments with `PSH` flag set. In the following, more details of our methodology and the results of this validation are presented.

A.2 Tagging Storage Flows

Storage flows are first identified using FQDNs and SSL certificate names, as explained in Sec. 3.1. After that, they are classified based on the number of bytes sent by each endpoint of the TCP connection. The method was built based on the assumption that a storage flow is used either for storing chunks or for retrieving chunks, but never for both. This assumption is supported by two factors: (i) when both operations happen in parallel, Dropbox uses separate connections to speed up synchronization; (ii) idle storage connections are kept open waiting for new commands only for a short time interval (60s).

Our assumption could be possibly violated during this idle interval. In practice, however, this seems to be hardly the case. Fig. 20 illustrates that by plotting the number of bytes in storage flows in *Campus 1*. Flows are concentrated near the axes, as expected under our assumption.

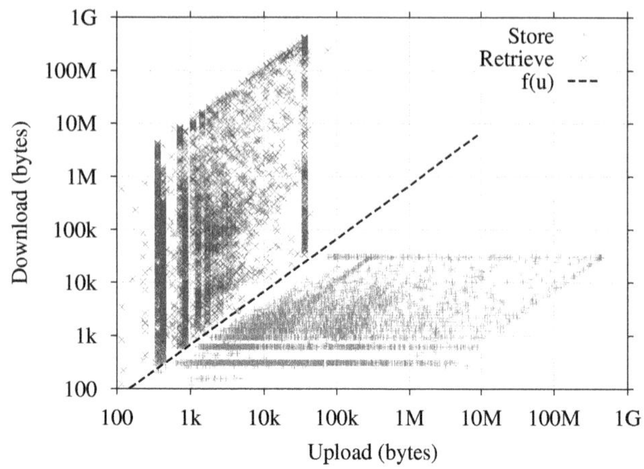

Figure 20: Bytes exchanged in storage flows in *Campus 1*. Note the logarithm scales.

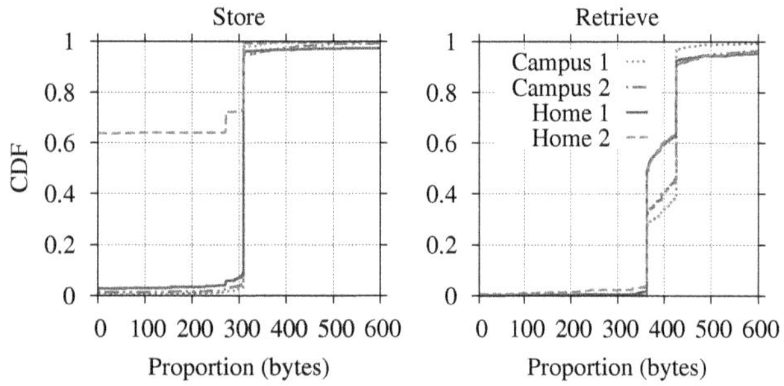

Figure 21: Payload in the reverse direction of storage operations per estimated number of chunks.

Flows in Fig. 20 are already divided into groups. The limit between *store* and *retrieve* regions is determined by the function $f(u) = 0.67(u - 294) + 4103$, where u is the number of uploaded bytes. This function was empirically defined using the extra information collected in *Campus 1*, where the following was observed:

- Both *store* and *retrieve* operations require at least 309 bytes of overhead from servers;
- *Store* and *retrieve* operations require at least 634 and 362 bytes of overhead from clients, respectively;
- Typically, SSL handshakes require 294 bytes from clients and 4103 bytes from servers.

$f(u)$ is centralized between the regions determined according these constants. For improving visualization, SSL overheads are subtracted from each point in the figure.

Since client machines in *Campus 1* are relatively homogenous, the gap between the two groups is very clear in this dataset. More variation in message sizes is observed at other vantage points. SSL handshakes, in particular, are affected by different software configurations. However, this does not change considerably the regions of each storage operation when compared to *Campus 1*.

Finally, we quantify the possible error caused by violations of our assumption. In all vantage points, flows tagged as *store* download less 1% of the total storage volume. Since this includes protocol overheads (e.g., HTTP_OK messages in Fig. 19), mixed flows marked as *store* might have only a negligible impact in our results. Similar reasoning is valid for *retrieve* flows.

A.3 Number of Chunks

The number of chunks transported in a storage flow (c) is estimated by counting TCP segments with `PSH` flag set (s) in the reverse direction of the transfer, as indicated in Fig. 19. For *retrieve* flows, $c = \frac{s-2}{2}$. For *store* flows $c = s - 3$ or $c = s - 2$, depending on whether the connection is passively closed by the server or not. This can be inferred by the time difference between the last packet with payload from the client and the last one from the server: when the server closes an idle connection, the difference is expected to be around 1 minute (otherwise, only a few seconds). Tstat already records the timestamps of such packets by default.

We validate this relation by dividing the amount of payload (without typical SSL handshakes) in the reverse direction of a transfer by c. This proportion has to be equal to the overhead needed per storage operation. Fig. 21 shows that for the vast majority of *store* flows the proportion is about 309 bytes per chunk, as expected. In *Home 2*, the apparently misbehaving client described in Sec. 4.3 biases the distribution: most flows from this client lack acknowledgment messages. Most *retrieve* flows have a proportion between 362 and 426 bytes per chunk, which are typical sizes of the HTTP request in this command. The exceptions (3% – 8%) might be caused by packet loss in our probes as well as by the flows that both stored and retrieved chunks. Our method underestimates the number of chunks in those cases.

A.4 Duration

Fig. 19 shows the duration used when computing the throughput of a storage flow (Δt). Since initial TCP/SSL handshakes affect users' perception of throughput, the first SYN packet is taken as the begin of the transfer. Termination handshakes, on the other hand, are ignored. In *store* flows, the last packet with payload sent by the client is considered the end of the transfer. In *retrieve* flows, the last packet with payload is normally a server alert about the SSL termination. We compensate for that by subtracting 60s from the duration of *retrieve* flows whenever the difference between the last packet with payload from the server and the one from the client is above 60s.

Because of our monitoring topology, Δt does not include the trip time between clients and our probes. Δt is, therefore, slightly underestimated. Fig. 19 also shows that 4 or 5 RTTs are needed before the client starts to send or to receive data. In some cases, this already accounts for about 500ms in the flow duration. Note that the initial TCP congestion window in place at servers was forcing a pause of 1 RTT during the SSL handshake. This parameter has been tuned after the release of Dropbox 1.4.0, reducing the overhead.

Reducing Allocation Errors in Network Testbeds

Jelena Mirkovic
USC/ISI
4676 Admiralty Way, Ste 1001
Marina Del Rey, USA
sunshine@isi.edu

Hao Shi
USC/ISI
4676 Admiralty Way, Ste 1001
Marina Del Rey, USA
shihao@isi.edu

Alefiya Hussain
USC/ISI
4676 Admiralty Way, Ste 1001
Marina Del Rey, USA
alefiya@isi.edu

ABSTRACT

Network testbeds have become widely used in computer science, both for evaluation of research technologies and for hands-on teaching. This can naturally lead to oversubscription and resource allocation failures, as limited testbed resources cannot meet the increasing demand.

This paper examines the causes of resource allocation failures on DeterLab testbed and finds three main culprits that create perceived resource oversubscription, even when available nodes exist: (1) overuse of mapping constraints by users, (2) testbed software errors and (3) suboptimal resource allocation. We propose solutions that could resolve these issues and reduce allocation failures to 57.3% of the baseline. In the remaining cases, real resource oversubscription occurs. We examine testbed usage patterns and show that a small fraction of unfair projects starve others for resources under the current first-come-first-served allocation policy. Due to interactive use of testbeds traditional fair-sharing techniques are not suitable solutions. We then propose two novel approaches – Take-a-Break and Borrow-and-Return – that temporarily pause long-running experiments. These approaches can reduce resource allocation failures to 25% of the baseline case by gently prolonging 1–2.5% of instances. While our investigation is done on DeterLab testbed's data, it should apply to all testbeds that run Emulab software.

Categories and Subject Descriptors

C.2.1 [**Computer Communication Networks**]: Network Architecture and Design; C.2.3 [**Computer Communication Networks**]: Network Operations

Keywords

network testbeds, Emulab, resource allocation

1. INTRODUCTION

The last decade brought a major change in experimentation practices in several areas of computer science, as researchers migrated from using simulation and theory to using network testbeds. Teachers are also shifting from traditional lecture-oriented courses to more dynamic and realistic teaching styles that incorporate testbed use for class demonstrations or student assignments. These diverse groups of users each have important deadlines that they hope to meet with help of testbeds, such as conference and research demonstration deadlines, class projects, class demonstrations, etc.

Current testbed resource allocation practices are not well aligned with these user needs. Most testbeds deploy no automated prioritization of allocation requests, serving them on first-come-first-served basis [24, 3, 2, 7, 10], which makes it impossible to guarantee availability during deadlines. In this paper we focus on testbeds that allow users to obtain exclusive access to some portion of their resources. As user demand grows, these testbeds experience overload that leads to allocation failures. Most testbeds further let users keep allocated resources for as long as needed [24, 3, 2]. While there are idle detection mechanisms that attempt to reclaim unused resources, users can and do opt out of them. Based on our experience from managing DeterLab most experiments are interactive, which means that resource allocations should last at most a day. Thus long-running experiments reflect a user's unwillingness to release resources at the end of their work day. We believe this occurs primarily because: (1) testbeds lack mechanisms to easily save disk state on multiple machines and recreate it the next day, and (2) users have no guarantee that resources will be available the next day. Some users request help of testbed staff to reserve resources for major deadlines. Since many testbeds lack reservation mechanisms [24, 3, 2], these are done manually by staff pulling requested machines out from the available pool. This often occurs early, so staff could guarantee availability, but it wastes resources and increases testbed overload.

Testbeds need better and more predictable allocation strategies as they evolve from a novel to a mainstream experimentation platform. Our main goal in this paper is to understand the reasons for resource allocation failures and to propose changes in testbed operation that would reduce these. We survey related work in Section 2. We then introduce our terminology and data in Sections 3 and 4. We explain the resource allocation problem in network testbeds in Section 5. We then examine reasons for resource allocation failures in the DeterLab testbed's [3, 5] operation during 8 years of its existence in Section 6. DeterLab is a public testbed for security experimentation, hosted by USC/ISI and UC Berkeley. In early 2012 it had around 350 general PCs and several tens of special-purpose nodes. While it is build on Emulab technology, its focus is on cyber security research, test and evaluation. It provides resources, tools, and infrastructure for researchers to conduct rigorous, repeatable experiments with new security technologies, and test their effectiveness in a realistic environment. DeterLab is used extensively both by security researchers and educators. It also experiences intensive internal use for development of new testbed technologies.

IMC'12, November 14–16, 2012, Boston, Massachusetts, USA.

We find that 81.5% of failures occur due to a *perceived* resource shortage, i.e., not because the testbed lacks enough nodes, but because it lacks enough of the *right* nodes that the user desires. As user desires and testbed allocation strategies act together to create the shortage of the nodes that are in current demand, we next investigate how much relaxing user constraints (Section 7) or improving resource allocation strategy (Section 8) help reduce allocation failures. Finally, we investigate if changes in testbed resource allocation policy would further improve resource allocation both in cases of perceived and in cases of true resource shortage in Section 9. We conclude in Section 10.

While we only had access to DeterLab's dataset, this testbed's resource allocation algorithms and practices derive from the use of Emulab software [24], which is used extensively by 40+ testbeds around the world [1]. Our findings should apply to these testbeds.

Main contributions of our paper are:

- This is the first analysis of causes for resource allocation failures in testbeds. We find that 81.5% of failures occur due to a perceived resource shortage, when in fact there are sufficient nodes to host a user's request. Around half of these cases occur because of inefficient testbed software, while the rest occur because of over-specification in user's resource requests.
- We closely examine the resource allocation algorithm used in Emulab testbeds – `assign` [20] – and show that it often performs suboptimally. We propose an improved algorithm – `assign+` – that reduces allocation failures to 77% of those generated by `assign`, while running 10 times faster and preserving more of the limited resources, such as interswitch bandwidth.
- We propose improvements to testbed resource allocation strategy by gently relaxing user constraints, to reduce resource allocation failures to 68.1% of those generated by `assign`.
- We propose modifications to testbed resource allocation policy that reshuffle allocated experiments to make space for new ones. This further reduces allocation failures to 57.3% of those generated by `assign`.
- We identify and demonstrate the need for some fair sharing and prioritization of user allocation requests at times of true overload. We propose two ways to modify testbed resource allocation policy to achieve these effects: Take-a-Break and Borrow-and-Return. In both, resources from long-running experiments are reclaimed and offered to incoming ones, but in Take-a-Break they are held as long as needed, while in Borrow-and-Return they are returned back to the original experiment after 4 hours. We show that both these approaches improve fairness of resource allocation, while reducing allocation failures to 25.3 – 25.6% of those generated by `assign`.
- During the course of our study we have also identified tools that testbeds need to develop either to better serve their users or to become more stable. We suggest five such improvements throughout the paper.

All the data used in our study is anonymized and publicly released at `http://nsl.isi.edu/TestbedUsageData`.

2. RELATED WORK

The wide adoption of emulation testbeds in the networking research community has spurred studies on different approaches for designing and managing them. For example, the resource management mechanisms for Globus and PlanetLab are contrasted and compared extensively by Ripeanu [21]. Additionally, Banik et. al [4] conduct empirical evaluations for different protocols that can provide exclusive access to shared resources on PlanetLab. The StarBED project has several unique solutions for emulation that include configuring the testbed and providing mechanisms for experiment management [18, 19]. These works either evaluate pros and cons of specific testbed management mechanisms or propose how to build testbeds, but do not investigate resource allocation algorithms, which is our focus.

Testbed usage and design practices have also attracted research attention. Hermenier and Ricci examine the topological requirements of the experiments on the Emulab testbed [24] over the last decade [9]. They propose a way to build better testbeds by: (1) increasing the heterogeneity of node connectivity, (2) connecting nodes to different switches to accommodate heterogeneous topologies without use of interswitch bandwidth, and (3) purchasing smaller and cheaper switches to save costs. Our work is orthogonal to theirs and focuses on optimizing allocation software and policies, regardless of testbed architecture. Kim et. al characterize the PlanetLab testbed's [7] usage over the last decade [13]. Their results indicate that bartering and central banking schemes for resource allocation can handle only a small percentage of total scheduling requirements. They do not propose better resource allocation algorithms, even though they identify the factors that account for high resource contention or poor utilization.

Yu et al. in [25] propose collecting allocation requests during a time window and then allocating testbed resources to satisfy the constraints of this request group. They employ a greedy algorithm to map nodes and path splitting to map links. Besides, they perform online migration to change the route or splitting ratio of a virtual link, which re-balances the mapping of virtual topologies to maximize the chance of accepting future requests. Their methods consider the general mapping problem at a high-level way, but do not take into account heterogeneity of testbed nodes. Besides, queuing allocation requests in network testbeds would introduce potentially large delays that users would not tolerate. Chowdhury et al. in [6] utilize mixed integer programming to solve the resource allocation problem, but their constraints are limited to CPU capacity and distance between the locations of two testbed nodes. J. Lu et. al [15] develop a method for mapping virtual topologies onto a testbed in a cost-efficient way. They consider traffic-based constraints but do not consider node heterogeneity or node features.

In a broader setting, ISPs tend to address resource allocation problems by over provisioning their resources (bandwidth). This solution does not readily apply to network testbeds. First, testbeds have limits on how many machines they can host that stem from the space, weight, cooling and power capacity of the rooms that host them. Second, testbeds are hosted by academic institutions and funded through grants – this limits both human and financial resources for purchase and maintenance of hardware. Finally, testbed use exhibits heavy tails along many dimensions (see Section 9.2), which prevents prediction of future resource needs.

Clusters and data centers face similar resource allocation issues as testbeds [8, 11, 23]. In [8], Ghodsi et al. propose dominant resource fairness (DRF) for resource allocation in data centers. This approach achieves fair allocation of heterogeneous resources between users who prioritize them differently. Unfortunately, like other fair-sharing approaches, DRF is not readily applicable to testbeds (see Section 9.2 for more details) due to interactive nature of experimentation and due to different value of long vs short experiments. In [11], Hindman et al. describe a platform called Mesos for sharing clusters, by allowing multiple resource allocation frameworks to run simultaneously. Mesos offers resource shares to the frameworks, based on some institutional policy, e.g., fair share, and they decide which offers to accept and which tasks to allocate on them. Some principles from [11], such as resource offers, may apply to testbeds, but they assume users that are way more sophisticated and informed about resource allocation than testbeds currently have. Condor [23] is a workload management system for compute-intensive jobs that aims to harness unused resources on heterogeneous and distributed hardware and can migrate data and jobs as nodes become available. While some Condor ideas may apply to network testbeds to achieve instance migration (see Section 9) testbed nodes are usually heavily customized by users, which prevents fine-grain migration that Condor excels at.

3. TERMINOLOGY

We now introduce several terms that relate to network testbed use and illustrate them in Figure 1.

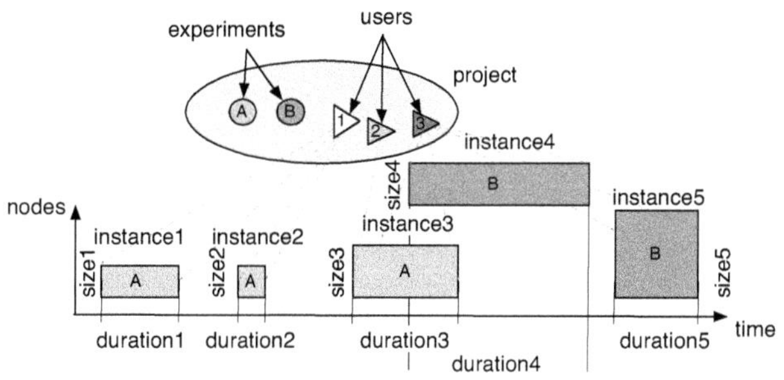

Figure 1: Terminology

An *experiment* is a collection of inputs submitted by a user to the testbed (one or more times) under the same identifier. These inputs describe experimenter's needs such as experiment topology, software to be installed on nodes, etc. We will say that each input represents a *virtual topology*. Experiments can be modified, e.g. by changing number of requested nodes or their connectivity. In Figure 1 there are two experiments A and B.

An *instance* is an instantiation of the experiment at the physical resources of the testbed. We say that an instance has *duration* (how long were resources allocated to it), *size* (how many nodes were allocated) and *virtual topology* (how were nodes connected to each other, what types of nodes were requested, what OS, etc.). The same experiment can result in multiple non-overlapping instances, one for each resource allocation. In Figure 1 there are five instances, three linked to the experiment A, and two linked to B. Release of the resources back to the testbed or instance modification denotes the end of a particular instance.

A testbed *project* is a collection of experiment definitions and authorized users, working on the same common project under a single *head-PI*. In Figure 1 there is one project with two experiments and three users.

An experiment can experience the following events: `preload`, `start`, `swapin`, `swapout`, `swapmod` and `destroy`. Events `preload`, `start` and `destroy` can occur only once during experiment's lifetime, while others can occur multiple times. Each event is processed by one or more testbed scripts and can result in a success or a failure. Figure 2 shows the state diagram of an experiment, where state transitions occur on successful events. A `preload` event leads to experiment's virtual topology being stored on the testbed, but no resources are yet allocated to the experiment – experiment exists in the *defined* state. A `swapin` event leads to resource allocation, changing the experiment's state to *allocated*. A `start` event is equivalent to a `preload` followed by a `swapin`. A `swapout` event releases resources from the experiment, changing its state to *defined*. A `swapmod` event can occur either in *defined* or in *allocated* state. It changes the experiment's definition but does not lead to state change. If a `swapmod` fails while the experiment is in *allocated* state, the testbed software automatically generates a `swapout` event and reverts experiment state to *defined*. A `destroy` event removes an experiment's virtual topology and state from the testbed but history of its events still remains. Table 1 shows the frequency of all experimental events in our dataset, which is described in the following Section.

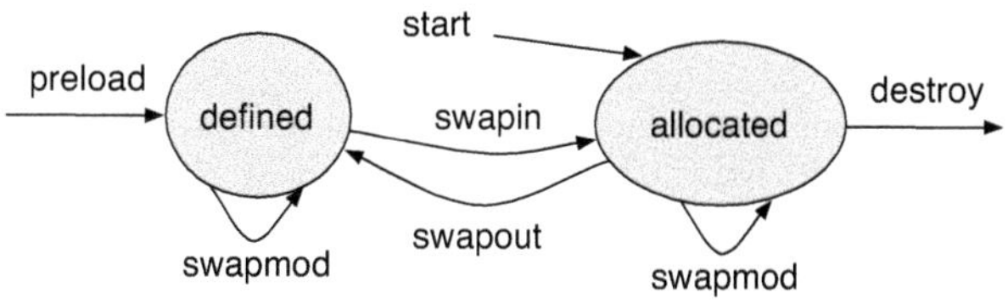

Figure 2: Experiment state diagram

4. DATA

We analyze eight years of data about DeterLab's operation collected from its inception in February 2004 until February 2012. As of February 2012, DeterLab had 154 active research projects (556 research users), 38 active class projects (1,336 users) and 11 active internal projects (95 users). The testbed consisted of 346 general PCs, and some special-purpose hardware. Half of the nodes are located at UCS/ISI, and other half at UC Berkeley. Table 2 shows the features of DeterLab's PCs.

DeterLab runs Emulab's software for experiment control [24], which means that all testbed management events such as node al-

Event	Count	Frequency
preload	10,472	4%
start	16,043	6.1%
swapin	101,275	38.6%
swapmod	36,819	14%
swapout	75,156	28.7%
destroy	22,575	8.6%
total	262,340	100%

Table 1: Frequency of experimental events in the dataset

Type	Disk (GB)	CPU (GHz)	Mem (GB)	Interf.	Count
1	250	2.133	4	4	63
2	250	2.133	4	4	63
3	72	3	2	4	32
4	72	3	2	5	32
5	36	3	2	4	61
6	36	3	2	5	60
7	36	3	2	9	4
8	238	1.8	4	5	31

Table 2: DeterLab's node types as of Jan 2011

Source	Data	Meaning
DB	`events`	Time, experiment, project, size, exit code for each event.
DB	`errors`	Time, experiment, cause and error message for each error.
FS	`/usr/testbed/expinfo`	Virtual topology, testbed resource snapshot, and resource allocation log for all successful and for some unsuccessful resource allocation requests.

Table 3: Types of data analyzed to recreate the experimental events and state of the testbed

location, release, user account creation, etc. are issued from one control node called `boss` and recorded in a database there. Additionally, some events create files in the file system on the `boss` node. We analyze a portion of database and file system state on this node that relates to resource allocations. We have database records about testbed events and any errors that occurred during processing of these events. We further have files describing virtual topologies and testbed state snapshots that were given to the allocation software – `assign` – and the allocation logs showing which physical nodes were assigned to each experiment instance. The virtual topology encodes user desires about the nodes they want, their configuration and connectivity. The testbed state snapshot gives a list of currently available nodes on the testbed, along with their switch connectivity, supported operating system images, features and feature weights (see Section 5 for explanation of these terms). Such snapshots are created on each attempted `start`, `swapin` or `swapmod`. The complete list of our data is shown in Table 3.

In our investigation we found that both database and file system data can be inconsistent or missing. This can occur for several reasons:

1. Different scripts may handle the same event and may generate database entries. It is possible for a script to behave in an unexpected manner or overlook a corner case, leading to inconsistent information. For example, for a small number of experiments we found that database entries show consecutive successful `swapin` events, which is an impossible state transition. We believe that this occurs because one script processes the event and records a success before the event fully completes. In a small number of cases another script detects a problem near the end of resource allocation and reverts the experiment's state to *defined* but does not update the database.

2. State transitions can be invoked manually by testbed operations staff, without generating recorded testbed events. For example, we found a small number of experiments in *allocated* state according to the database, while file system state indicated that they returned the resources to the testbed. This can occur when testbed operations staff manually evicts several or all experiments to troubleshoot a testbed problem.

3. Testbed policies and software evolve, which may lead to different recording of an event over time. For example in 2004–2006, when a user's request for experiment modification had a syntax error this was recoded in the database. This practice was abandoned in later Emulab software releases. Similarly, when a user's request for experiment modification failed due to temporary lack of testbed resources, this request and testbed's state snapshot were recorded in the file system on the `boss` node. This practice was abandoned in early 2007 making it difficult to understand and troubleshoot resource allocation errors.

4. In a small number of cases software generating unique identifiers for file names storing virtual topology and testbed state snapshot had low randomness leading to newer files overwriting older ones within the same experiment. This means that file system state for some instances is missing.

During our analysis, we detect and either correct or discard entries with inconsistencies. We also attempt to infer missing data wherever possible, by combining the database and the file system information.

Suggestion 1: *Testbeds need better software development practices that start from a system model and verify that developed code matches the model, e.g., through model checking and unit testing.* While it is impossible to eliminate all bugs in a large codebase, a systematic tying of code to requirements and models would help eliminate inconsistencies in record-keeping and even facilitate automated detection and forensics of testbed problems.

5. TESTBED MAPPING PROBLEM

We now explain some specifics of testbed operation that relate to resource allocation, using Figure 3 to illustrate them. Many of the concepts in this Section were first introduced in [20].

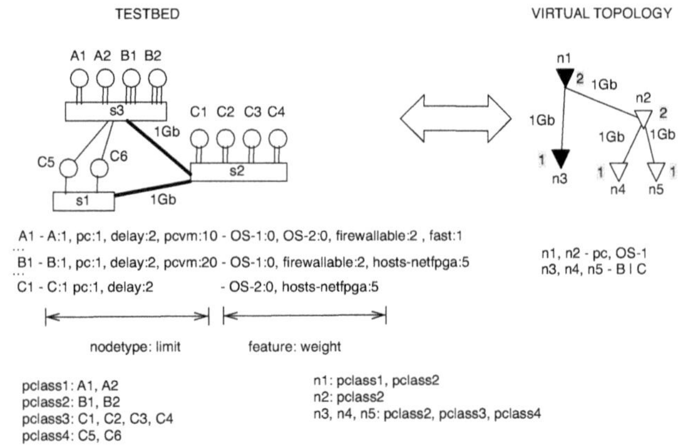

Figure 3: Illustration of the network testbed mapping problem

Over time network testbeds acquire nodes of different hardware types leading to heterogeneity. Types can differ in number of network interfaces, processor speed, memory size, disk space, etc. In Figure 3 the drawing on the left shows a sample testbed architecture. There are three hardware types: *A*, *B* and *C*, with 2, 2 and 6 nodes respectively. Each physical node is connected to a switch. Because a single switch has a limited number of ports a testbed may have multiple switches connected by limited-bandwidth links, each hosting a subset of nodes. In Figure 3 there are three switches – *s1*, *s2* and *s3* – with interswitch links shown as thick lines between them. Often nodes of the same type are connected to the same switch. Sometimes it is beneficial to connect different node types to the same switch (e.g., nodes of type *A* and *B* are connected to *s1*) or to connect some nodes to two different switches (e.g., nodes *C5* and *C6* connect to *s1* and *s3*). DeterLab has instances of all three node-to-switch connection types in its current architecture.

Users submit their experiment configuration requests to the testbed as a *virtual topology*. One such topology is shown in the right drawing in Figure 3. A resource allocation algorithm attempts to solve the *testbed mapping problem* [20]. It starts from the virtual topology and a snapshot of the testbed state and attempts to find the best selection of hardware that satisfies experimenter-imposed and testbed-imposed constraints.

Testbed-imposed constraints consist of limitations on available nodes of any given type, limitations on number of node interfaces, and limited interswitch link bandwidth. Experimenter-imposed constraints are encoded in the virtual topology as *desires* and consist of: (1) **Node type constraints** – a virtual node must be mapped to specific hardware type, (2) **OS constraints** – a virtual node must run specific OS, (3) **Connectivity constraints** – a virtual node should have specific number of network interfaces and must be connected to another node by a link of specific bandwidth. Node type and OS constraints are encoded explicitly by annotating nodes in the virtual topology, and the connectivity constraints are implied in the topology's architecture. For example, in Figure 3, explicit constraints request nodes *n1* and *n2* to be of type *pc* and run OS 1, while nodes *n3*, *n4* and *n5* should be of type *B* or *C*. Implicit connectivity constraints require that *n2* be mapped to a node with at least 3 network interfaces, *n1* to a node with at least 2 interfaces, and the rest to nodes with at least 1 interface. Each link is required to have 1 Gbit bandwidth. This limits the number of virtual links that can be allocated to an interswitch link and in turn invalidates some mapping of virtual to physical nodes that would oversubscribe interswitch bandwidth. Emulab software further lets users specify **fixed mappings**: virtual nodes that map to specific physical nodes (e.g. a user may request *n1* to be mapped to *A1*). This sometimes helps `assign` algorithm to find a solution, where it would otherwise miss it. We elaborate on reasons for fixed mappings in the next Section.

The notion of the *node type* [20] extends beyond simple hardware types in two ways. First, a physical node can "satisfy" multiple node types and may host multiple instances of the same type. For example, node *A1* (see annotations at the bottom left in Figure 3) can host one virtual node of type *A*, one virtual node of type *pc*, two virtual nodes of type *delay*, or ten virtual nodes of type *pcvm* (virtual machine installed on a physical node). Second, a user can specify a *vclass* – a set of node types instead of the single type for any virtual node, e.g. in Figure 3 a user has asked for nodes *n3*, *n4* and *n5* to be either of type *B* or of type *C*. *vclasses* can be hard – requiring that all nodes be assigned to the same node type from *vclass* (e.g., all are *B* or all are *C*) – and soft – allowing mixed type allocations, from the same *vclass* (e.g., each could be *B* or *C*). In DeterLab's operation we have only encountered use of soft *vclasses*. Corresponding to experimenter's desires, physical nodes have *features*. For example, in Figure 3 there are the following features: (1) OS 1 runs on types *A* and *B*, (2) OS 2 runs on types *A* and *C*, (3) firewallable feature is supported by types *A* and *B*, (4) hosts-netfpga feature is supported by types *B* and *C*. Each feature is accompanied by a *weight* that is used during resource allocation process to score and compare different solutions.

Testbeds create *base* OS images for all their users, for popular OS types like Linux, Windows and Free BSD. Over time testbed staff creates newer versions of base images but the old ones still remain on the testbed and are used, we believe due to inertia. Testbeds further allow users to create custom disk images as a way of saving experimental state between allocations. These images are rarely upgraded to new OS versions. As testbeds grow, old custom and base images cannot be supported by new hardware. Thus virtual topologies with such images can be allocated only to a portion of the testbed and OS desires turn into mapping constraints.

Suggestion 2: *Testbeds need mechanisms that either provide state saving without disk imaging, or help users to upgrade their custom images automatically to new OS versions. Experiment specifications (virtual topologies) should also be upgraded automatically to use newer base OS images. This would eliminate OS-based constraints and improve allocation success.*

An *acceptable* solution to the testbed mapping problem meets all experimenter-imposed and testbed-imposed constraints. We note that honoring an interswitch bandwidth constraint is a choice and not a must. Testbed software can allocate any number of virtual links onto the interswitch substrate, but if it oversubscribes this substrate and if experimenters generate full-bandwidth load on the virtual links they may experience lower than expected performance. In our example in Figure 3 it is possible to allocate links *n2-n4* and *n2-n5* on the same 1 Gbit interswitch link, but if the experimenter sends 1 Gbit of traffic on each of them at the same time half of the traffic will be dropped. There are two choices when evaluating if interswitch bandwidth constraint is met: (1) evaluation can be done only within the same experiment assuming no other experiment uses the same interswitch link, and (2) evaluation can be done taking into account all experiments that use the same interswitch link. In practice, solution (1) is chosen because it improves the resource allocation success rate. Risk of violating experimenter's desires is minimal because the incidence of multiple experiments using the same interswitch link and generating high traffic at the same time is low.

The *best* solution to the testbed mapping problem is such that minimizes interswitch bandwidth consumption and minimizes unwanted features on selected physical nodes – these are the features that are present on the nodes but were not desired by the experimenter. Doing so improves the chance of success for future allocations. In face of these allocation goals the testbed mapping problem becomes NP-hard, because the number of possible solutions is too large to be exhaustively searched for the best one.

6. WHY ALLOCATIONS FAIL

A resource allocation may fail for a number of reasons such as a syntax error in the user's request, a testbed software failure, a policy violation by a user's request, etc. In this paper we only investigate resource allocation failures that occur due to temporary shortage of testbed resources. This means that the same virtual topology would successfully allocate on an empty testbed. We will call these TEMP failures and classify them into the following categories:

1. **FIXED:** Virtual topology specified a fixed mapping of some virtual nodes to specific physical nodes but testbed could not obtain access to these nodes.

2. **TYPE:** Virtual topology had node type constraint that could not be met by the testbed.

3. **OS:** Virtual topology had OS constraint that could not be met by the testbed.

4. **CONNECT:** The testbed could not find a node with sufficient interfaces.

5. **INTERSWITCH:** The allocation algorithm found a solution but the projected interswitch bandwidth usage exceeded link capacity.

6. **TESTBED:** There is a problem in the testbed's software that only becomes evident during resource allocation. One such problem occurs when `assign` [20] – the current allocation algorithm – fails to find a solution even though one exists.

Categories FIXED, TYPE, OS, CONNECT and INTERSWITCH stem directly from the way testbeds address the testbed mapping problem (see the previous Section) – a failure to satisfy user or testbed constraints will fall into one of these five categories. In our analysis of TEMP failures on DeterLab we further find that bugs in testbed configuration and software occasionally lead to TEMP failures, *when in reality there are available resources to satisfy user and testbed constraints*. This leads us to create the TESTBED category. One could view TEMP failures that fall into TESTBED category as false TEMP failures, since they do not occur due to a temporary resource shortage.

We first investigate why TEMP failures occurred historically on the DeterLab's testbed. We start with the records from the DeterLab's database that contain experiment identifier, time and alleged cause of each failure, as well as the error message generated by the testbed software. The database only has records for failures that occurred after April 13, 2006. There are 24,206 records, out of which 11,176 have their cause classified as TEMP in the database. We use the error messages to classify these TEMP failures into the categories above. We find that 47.5% are TYPE failures, 18.5% are FIXED failures, 15.7% are OS failures, 3.8% are CONNECT failures and only 0.5% are INTERSWITCH failures. In 13.5% of cases the error message indicates that mapping failed, but does not give the specific reason. Finally there are 0.2% of failures that occur due to a policy violation or a semantic problem in the experimenter's request but are misclassified as TEMP failures.

While the above analysis offers a glimpse into why specific allocations failed, we would like to know how many failures occur due to *true overload* – there are not enough nodes on the testbed – and how many occur due to *perceived overload* – there are enough nodes on the testbed but experimenter or testbed constraints are violated. Cases of *perceived overload* could be eliminated either by relaxing experimenter's constraints or by improving testbed software. To answer these questions we need to match each TEMP failure to the virtual topology and the testbed state snapshot that were given to `assign` so we could mine the desired and the available number of resources. We perform this matching in the following way:

1. We link each TEMP failure to a resource allocation log file showing details of the allocation process, by matching the time of the TEMP failure with the timestamp of the file.

2. From the log file we mine the file names of the virtual topology and the testbed state snapshots that were used by the resource allocation software, i.e. the `assign` algorithm.

3. In 2007, DeterLab testbed stopped saving the virtual topology and the testbed state files for failed allocations so we must infer them from other data. To infer the virtual topology we identify the testbed event (`swapmod` or `swapin`) that led to that specific TEMP failure. For failures that occurred on a `swapin` event, we attempt to find a previous successful `swapmod` or `swapin` of the same experiment and link it to a virtual topology using the same process from steps 1 and 2. We associate this topology with the TEMP failure. To infer the testbed state at the time of TEMP failure, we process the testbed state snapshots chronologically up to the time of the failure and infer from those the physical node features and testbed architecture (connections and bandwidth between nodes and switches). We also take the last testbed snapshot created before the TEMP failure and extract the list of available nodes at the time. We then process any `swapout` events between the time of the last snapshot and the TEMP failure, and add the released nodes to the available pool. This gives us the testbed state at the time of TEMP failure. Then we combine all this information and generate the testbed snapshot in the format required by the `assign` algorithm. This inference process may result in an incorrect testbed state only if some of the available nodes become unavailable in the time between the last testbed snapshot and the TEMP failure. This can happen due to a hardware error, a manual reservation by the testbed staff, or because some of the nodes released by the `swapout` events in that short time interval failed to reload the default OS and required manual intervention by testbed staff. While hardware errors and manual reservations are rare on DeterLab, reload failures occur daily but usually affect a handful of nodes. We thus believe that most of our inferred testbed snapshots are correct.

We were able to match 9,066 out of 11,176 TEMP failures in this manner – they form the *matched-failure* set that we analyze further. We focus only on demand and availability of general PC nodes, since only a small fraction of instances request special hardware. Only 1,679 of TEMP errors or 18.5% occur because of a true overload, meaning that there are less PCs than desired. This means that 81.5% of TEMP errors could potentially be reduced or eliminated by improving testbed software or by educating users how to minimize their use of constraints. To identify TESTBED errors we run both the `assign` and our `assign+` allocation algorithm (described in the Section 8.2) on the remaining 7,387 pairs in the *matched-failure* set.

We next modify virtual topologies in the *matched-failure* set to remove fixed mappings, because they seem to often harm allocations, as evidenced by a high number of FIXED failures. In many cases fixed mappings are inserted not by a user but by the testbed software when a running instance is being modified, e.g. by adding or removing nodes. This enables the testbed to keep the currently allocated nodes associated with the instance and just drop some (in case of removing nodes) or add a few more. However, if some of the allocated nodes become unresponsive the entire resource allocation fails. We believe that this is an incorrect model, and the testbed should fall back to the strategy of releasing all nodes and allocating from the entire available node pool. Another reason for fixed mappings occurs in a case when nodes of a given type may differ based on their location, and a user prefers some locations over others. We argue that these cases would be better handled through node features or through creation of location-specific node types, since fixed mappings allow users to select only one out of several possible node choices.

We find that `assign+` can successfully allocate resources in 1,392 cases, or 15.3% of our *matched-failures* set. We further find that both `assign` and `assign+` succeed in 2,251 or 24.8% of cases. It is possible that the original failure, recorded in the database, was a "bad run of the luck" event for `assign`, due to its randomized search strategy (see Section 8.1 for more details). It is further possible that the original failure occurred due to a failure of some other testbed software and was recorded as a TEMP failure. Either way, we classify these failures as TESTBED failures. Finally, we find that in 456 cases or 5% allocation failed due to a spelling error in the database in some switch names. These entries are used when testbed snapshots are created, and a spelling error leads to a disconnected testbed. We thus conclude that 3,288 or 36.3% of TEMP errors occur due to experimenter's constraints, 4,099 or 45.2% occur due to testbed software and 1,679 or 19.5% occur due to true overload. There are thus three ways of addressing the allocation problem: (1) helping users understand and reduce the constraints on their topologies, (2) designing better resource allocation algorithms and (3) enforcing some fair sharing of resources. We explore each of these strategies in the following sections.

Suggestion 3: *Testbeds should develop automated self-checking software that detects events such as spelling errors in the database records, real switch and node disconnections, etc., well before they lead to resource allocation failures.*

7. RELAXING USER CONSTRAINTS

We now explore how much user constraints influence allocability of instances on DeterLab. We first match all the successfully allocated instances in our dataset with their virtual topology and the state of the empty testbed that existed at the time of their allocation. For each topology, we simulate the checks in the testbed mapping software for node type, OS and connectivity constraints on this empty testbed. We limit our checks only to those nodes in the virtual topology that can be allocated on general PCs, and the testbed state only includes these PCs. For each node we record the *nodescore*, showing the percentage of testbed that can satisfy this node's constraints. For example, if a user asked for a node of type A or B with OS 1 and if there are 30 nodes of type A, 30 of type B and 20 of type C in the testbed, with OS 1 supported on A and C, the *nodescore* for this node would be $30/80 = 0.375$ because it can only be allocated to nodes of type A. We then calculate the *topscore*, averaging all the *nodescore*'s in the virtual topology.

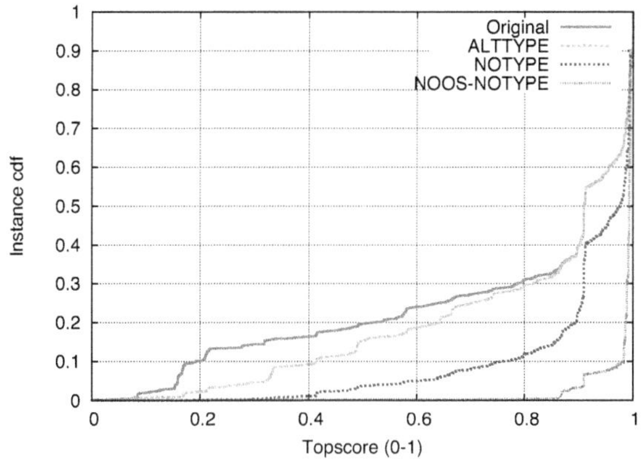

Figure 4: *Topscore* values when we vary type restrictions

The red line in the Figure 4 shows the cumulative distribution function (cdf) of all the *topscores* in the original topologies. There are 30% of topologies that can allocate on less than 80% of the testbed, 20% can allocate on less than half of the testbed and 10% can allocate on less than 20% of the testbed. To identify the effect of the node type, OS and connectivity constraints on the allocability we modify virtual topologies in the following ways: (1) **ALTTYPE:** We allow use of alternative node types that have similar or better hardware features than the user-specified node type; these are described in more detail in Section 8.4, (2) **NOTYPE:** We completely remove the node type constraint, (3) **NOOS-NOTYPE:** We remove both the node type and the OS constraints; the OS constraint can be removed by users upgrading their experiments to use newer OS versions that are supported by all testbed hardware. Effect of these strategies on the allocability is also shown in Figure 4. Use of alternative types improves the allocability, especially of

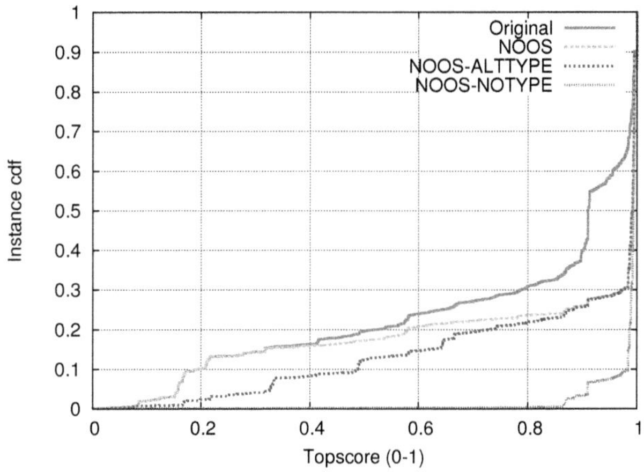

Figure 5: *Topscore* values when we vary OS restrictions

those topologies that were previously severely restricted. There are now 15% of topologies now allocate on less than half of the testbed and only 2% allocate on less than 20% of the testbed. Removal of node type constraints has a profound effect. Only 11% of topologies now allocate on less than 80% of the testbed, only 3% on less than half of the testbed and only 0.1% on less than 20% of the testbed. Finally, removing all node type and OS constraints leads to only 0.3% of topologies to allocate on less than 80% of the testbed.

We next explore the effect of (1) **NOOS:** Removing OS restrictions, (2) **NOOS-ALTTYPE:** Removing OS restrictions and using alternative node types. The effect of these strategies is shown in Figure 5. Removal of OS constraints leads to 23% of topologies that can allocate on less than 80% of the testbed, 17% can allocate on less than half of the testbed and 10% can allocate on less than 20% of the testbed. If we add to this use of alternative types, 21% of topologies that can allocate on less than 80% of the testbed, 12% can allocate on less than half of the testbed and only 2% can allocate on less than 20% of the testbed.

We do not explore how changing connectivity would influence allocability, because connectivity constraints only affect a small number of topologies, and lower the allocability by a small value. This is reflected in **NOOS-NOTYPE** line in Figure 5 where it departs from 1 to values 0.9–1 for about 15% of topologies.

This section has laid out strategies that users can deploy themselves to improve allocability of their topologies. But, how likely is this to happen, i.e. are users flexible about their constraints? To answer this, we try to characterize evolution of virtual topologies in our dataset by first pairing failed allocations with the first following successful allocation in the same experiment and then comparing their topologies. We manage to pair 2,124 out of our 9,066 virtual topologies from the *matched-failures* set. In 956 of those pairs the topologies differ: in 639 cases a user has modified node type or OS constraint, and in 322 cases a user has reduced the topology's size. We conclude that users naturally relax their constraints when faced with an allocation failure about half of the time. When we examine how long it takes a user to converge to a "good" set of constraints we find that half of the users discover the constraint set that leads to successful allocation within one hour, 66% within 4 hours, and 78% within a day. But this distribution is heavy-tailed with the tail going into year-long values, possibly due to the user abandoning the experiment and returning to it much later.

Having automated tools that identify and propose alternative constraints to users would improve this convergence time, and would improve user experience. We believe that such an interactive dialogue with the user would work better then letting users specify how important certain constraints are to them, since this more actively engages the user and informs them about possible trade-offs.

Suggestion 4: *Testbeds need tools that help users evaluate trade-offs between different constraint sets and automatically suggest modifications that improve allocability. This could be done prior to the actual attempt to allocate resources.*

8. IMPROVING RESOURCE ALLOCATION

We now explain how `assign` algorithm works and how we improve it in `assign+`.

8.1 `assign`

In [20] Ricci et al. propose and evaluate the `assign` algorithm as a solver for the testbed mapping problem. Because this problem is NP-hard, Ricci et al. propose to solve it using simulated annealing [14] – a heuristic that performs a cost-function-guided exploration of a solution space. Simulated annealing starts from a random solution and scores it using a custom *cost function* that evaluates its quality. It then perturbs the solution using a *generation function* to create the next one. If this solution is better than the previous one it is always accepted; otherwise it is accepted with some small probability, controlled by *temperature*. This helps the simulated annealing to get out of the locally optimal solutions and find the global optimum. At the beginning of the search, the temperature is set to a high value, leading to most solutions being accepted. Over time the temperature is lowered, following a custom *cooling schedule*, making the algorithm converge to a single "best" solution. There is no guarantee that the algorithm will find the best solution but it should find one that is much better than a random assignment, and fairly close to the best one. Obviously, as algorithm runs longer its chance of finding the global optimum increases but so does the runtime. To guarantee time-bounded operation, `assign`'s runtime is limited, which may sometimes make it miss a possible solution.

To condense the search space, Ricci et al. introduce the concept of *pclasses* – sets of nodes that have the same node types, features, network interfaces and switch connections. In Figure 3 we identify four *pclasses*. Virtual nodes are then mapped to *pclasses*. The `assign` algorithm starts from the set of all *pclasses* and precomputes for each virtual node a list of *pclasses* that are acceptable candidates. It then moves all the virtual nodes into *unassigned* list and, at each step, tries to map one node from this list to a *pclass*. When all the nodes have been assigned, the algorithm tries in each step to remap one randomly selected virtual node to another *pclass*. Each solution is scored by calculating a penalty for used interswitch bandwidth and for unwanted features. The actual scoring function is quite complex but it approximately adds up unwanted feature weights and fixed link penalties. A lower score denotes a better solution. In the end `assign` selects the solution with the lowest score as the best one. Algorithm 1 gives a high-level overview of `assign`'s operation.

Algorithm 1 `assign` pseudocode.

```
generate pclasses; put all virtual nodes into unassigned set
map each virtual node to candidate pclasses
repeat
    assign one node from unassigned to a pclass
until unassigned = ∅
repeat
    solution = remap one virtual node to a different pclass
    score solution; solutions+ = solution
until sufficient iterations or average score low
select the lowest scored solution as best
```

8.2 `assign+`

In designing `assign+` our main insight was to use expert knowledge of network testbed architecture to identify allocation strategies that lead to minimizing interswitch bandwidth. These strategies are deployed deterministically to generate candidate solutions, instead of exploring the entire space of possible allocations via simulated annealing, which significantly shortens the run time. We also recognized that allocating strongly connected node clusters in experiment topologies together leads to preservation of interswitch bandwidth and shortens the run time. In the long run these strategies also lead to better distribution of instances over heterogeneous testbed resources.

Like `assign`, `assign+` generates *pclasses* and precomputes for each virtual node a list of *pclasses* that are acceptable candidates. It then generates *candidate lists*, aggregating virtual nodes that can be satisfied by the same candidate *pclasses*. For example, in Figure 3 *n1* can be satisfied by *pclass1* or *pclass2*, *n2* can be satisfied only by *pclass2* because it requires three network interfaces, and *n3*, *n4* and *n5* can be satisfied by *pclass2*, *pclass3* or *pclass4*. Each *pclass* has a size which equals the number of currently available testbed nodes that belong to it. Next, the program calls its `allocate` function five times, each time exploring a separate allocation strategy.

The main idea of the `allocate` function is to divide the virtual topology into several connected subgraphs and attempt to map each subgraph or its portion in one step, if possible. Only if this fails, the function attempts to map individual virtual nodes. This reduces the number of allocation steps, while minimizing the interswitch bandwidth, because connected nodes are mapped in one step whenever possible.

The `allocate` function first breaks the virtual topology into several connected partitions attempting to minimize the number of cut edges. Our partitioning goal is to create a large number of possible partitions, where smaller partitions can be subsets of larger ones. This allows us flexibility to map these partitions to different-sized *pclasses*. We achieve this goal by traversing the topology from edges to the center and forming parent-child relationships, so that nodes closer to the center become parents of the farther nodes.

Graph partitioning problem has many well-known solutions (e.g. [12]), but these either require the number of partitions to be known in advance – whereas we want to keep this number flexible – or they are too complex for our needs. We employ the following heuristic to generate the partitions we need. We start from virtual nodes with the smallest degree and score them with number 1, also initializing round counter to 1. In each consecutive round, links that are directly connected to the scored nodes are marked, if the peer on the other side of the link is either not scored yet or is scored with the higher number. The peer becomes a "parent" of the scored node if it does not already have one. The process stops when all nodes in the virtual topology have been scored. We illustrate the scores for nodes in the virtual topology in Figure 3. Black nodes belong to one partition and white ones to the second one. Node *n2* is the parent of nodes *n4* and *n5* and node *n1* is the parent of the node *n3*.

Next, the `allocate` function traverses the candidate list from the most to the least restricted, attempting to map each virtual node and, if possible, its children. Let us call the virtual node that is currently being allocated the *allocating* node. The most restricted candidate list has the smallest number of *pclasses*. In our example this is the list for node *n2*. The function calculates the number of virtual nodes that must be allocated to this list and the number of physical nodes available in the list. If the first is larger than the second the entire mapping fails. Otherwise, we calculate for each parent node in the candidate list two types of children pools: *minimum pool* and *maximum pool*. Both calculations only include those children that have not yet been allocated. The minimum pool relates to the candidate list and contains all the children of the node that must be allocated to this list. The maximum pool relates to each *pclass* in the candidate list and contains all the children of the given parent node that can be allocated to this *pclass*. In our example, when we allocate *n1* its minimum pool would be empty because neither *n4* nor *n5* must be allocated to *pclass2*, while the maximum pool would contain *n4* and *n5* for *pclass2*. The `allocate` function traverses each *pclass* in the current candidate list in an order particular to each allocation strategy we explore. This order is always from the most to the least desirable candidate. It first tries to allocate the allocating node and its maximum pool. If there are no resources in any of the *pclasses* of the candidate list it tries to allocate the allocating node and its minimum pool. If this also fails, it tries only to allocate the allocating node. If this fails the entire mapping fails.

Algorithm 2 `assign+` pseudocode.

```
generate pclasses
map each virtual node to candidate pclasses
generate candidate lists
for strategy = (PART, SCORE, ISW, PREF, FRAG) do
    solution = allocate(strategy)
    score solution; solutions+ = solution
end for
select the solution with the lowest interswitch bw as best
break ties by selecting solution with the lowest score
```

There are five allocation strategies we pursue in the calls to the `allocate` function: PART, SCORE, ISW, PREF and FRAG. Each strategy uses expert knowledge of possible network testbed architectures to generate candidate solutions that are supposed to minimize interswitch bandwidth use. The success of each strategy depends on the available resources and the size and user-specified constraints in a given virtual topology. The first strategy – PART – minimizes partitions in the virtual topology by allocating *pclasses* from largest to smallest size. This improves packing of future instances and also reduces number of interswitch links. The second – SCORE – minimizes the score of the allocation by allocating *pclasses* from those with the smallest to those with the largest score. We explore different ways to score a *pclass*, e.g., based on how many features it supports, based on how often it is requested, or a combination of both. When we score by features we do not use feature weights, but instead just add up counts of supported features. The next three allocation strategies prefer those *pclasses* that already host parents or children of the allocating node, thus minimizing interswitch bandwidth demand. In addition to parent/child host preference, the ISW strategy also prefers those *pclasses* that have high-bandwidth interswitch links to *pclasses*, which host neighbors of the allocating node. This only makes a difference when interswitch links have different capacities, in which case ISW will minimize the risk of mapping failure due to interswitch bandwidth oversubscription. In addition to parent/child host preference, the PREF strategy also prefers those *pclasses* that share a switch with *pclasses*, which host neighbors of the allocating node. This minimizes use of interswitch bandwidth because communication is contained within one switch, even though it occurs among different *pclasses*. The PREF strategy tries to both minimize the interswitch bandwidth and to minimize partitions in the virtual topology by allocating from *pclasses* with the largest to those with the smallest product of their preference and size. The FRAG strategy only deploys parent/child preference and tries to use the smallest number of *pclasses* by allocating from *pclasses* with the largest to those with the smallest product of their preference and size.

At the end, the `allocate` function records the candidate solution and then tries to further reduce interswitch bandwidth cost by running Kernighan-Lin graph partitioning algorithm [12] to exchange some nodes between *pclasses* if possible. Each exchange generates a new candidate solution. The algorithm stops when no further reduction is possible in the interswitch bandwidth. Each solution's score is the sum of scores of all the physical nodes in it.

After all calls to the `allocate` function return, `assign+` chooses the best solution. This solution has the smallest interswitch bandwidth. If multiple such solutions exist, the one with the smallest score is selected. Algorithm 2 gives a high-level overview of `assign+`'s operation.

8.3 Evaluation

Algorithm	Failed allocations (out of 19,258)	% Baseline
`assign`	1,176 (mean)	100%
`assign+.1`	905	77%
`assign+.1m`	983	83.6%
`assign+.2m`	917	78%
`assign+.at`	801	68.1%
`assign+.mig`	701	59.6%
`assign+.atmig`	674	57.3%
`assign+.tb`	298	25.3%
`assign+.borrow`	301	25.6%

Table 4: Evaluation summary for allocation failure rates

To compare the quality of found solutions and the runtime of `assign` and `assign+`, we needed a testbed state (hardware types and count, node types, features, weights and operating systems supported by each hardware type, node and switch connectivity), and a set of resource allocation requests. We reconstruct the state of the DeterLab testbed on January 1, 2011 using virtual topology and testbed state snapshot data from the filesystem. To make the allocation challenging, we permanently remove 91 PC nodes from the available pool, leaving 255. While this may seem extreme, our analysis of testbed state over time indicates that often this many or more PCs are unavailable due to either reserved but not yet used nodes or to internal testbed development. We seed the set of resource allocation requests with all successful and failed allocations on DeterLab in 2011. Each request contains the start and end time of the instance and its virtual topology file. For failed allocations, we generate their desired duration according to the duration distribution of successful allocations. Finally, we check that there are no overlapping instances belonging to the same experiment. If found, we keep the first instance and remove the following overlapping instances from the workload. We test this workload both with `assign` and `assign+` on empty testbed and remove 1.3% of instances that fail with both algorithms, because the reduced-size testbed does not meet experimenter's constraints. We will label this final simulation setup "2011 synthetic setup". We then attempt to allocate all workload's instances, and release them in order dictated by their creation and end times, evolving the testbed state for each allocation and each release. Evaluation results are summarized in Table 4.

Figure 6 shows the allocation failure rate over time on this setup for both algorithms. Since `assign` deploys randomized search,

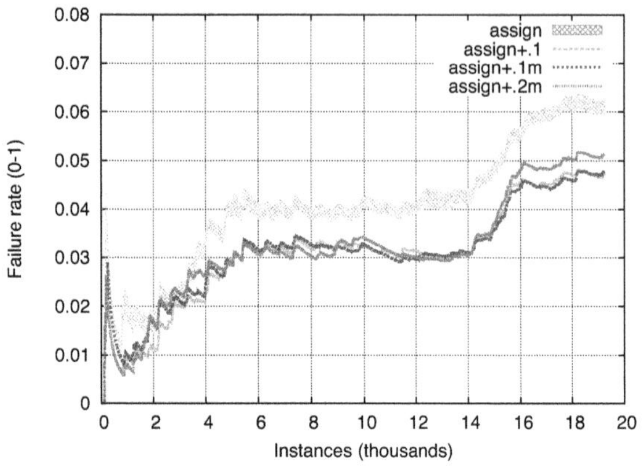

Figure 6: Allocation failure rates

we show the mean and the standard deviation of its 10 runs. We test several approaches to score calculation: `assign+.1` deploys `assign`-like approach, where node types with more unwanted features are penalized higher, (2) `assign+.1m`, same as `assign+.1` but with memory, so node types that are requested more often receive a higher penalty when allocated, and (3) `assign+.2m` scores nodes only by how often they are requested. In case of `assign`, the failure rate starts small and increases to almost 6% by the end of the simulation. Curves for different flavors of `assign+` have the similar shape but the failure rate is always below that for `assign`, reaching 4.7% at the end. Overall, `assign+` creates only 77% of allocation failures generated by `assign`. `assign`-like score calculation outperforms the one that depends only on user request frequency. In the rest of the paper we use `assign+.1` under `assign+` label.

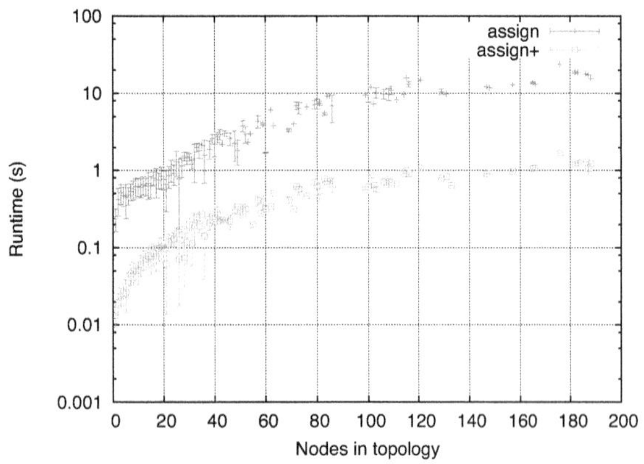

Figure 7: Runtime versus topology size

Figure 7 shows the runtime of `assign` and `assign+` versus topology size, with y-axis being in the log scale. For both algorithms the runtime depends on the size and complexity of the virtual topology, and the number and diversity of available nodes on the testbed. We show the average of runtimes for each topology size and the error bars show one standard deviation around the mean. `assign+` is consistently around 10 times faster than `assign`, thanks to its deterministic exploration of the search space.

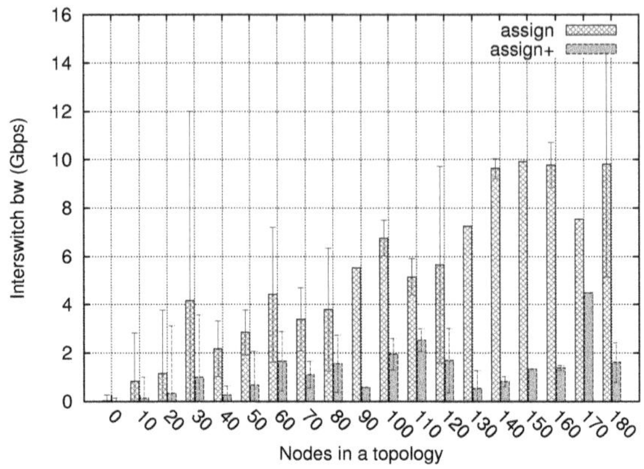

Figure 8: Interswitch bandwidth versus topology size

Figure 8 shows the interswitch bandwidth allocated by `assign` and `assign+` versus topology size. We group allocations into bins based on the virtual topology size, with step 10, and show the mean, with error bars showing one standard deviation. Here too, `assign+` significantly outperforms `assign` on each topology size. On the average, `assign+` allocates only 23% of the interswitch bandwidth allocated by `assign` .

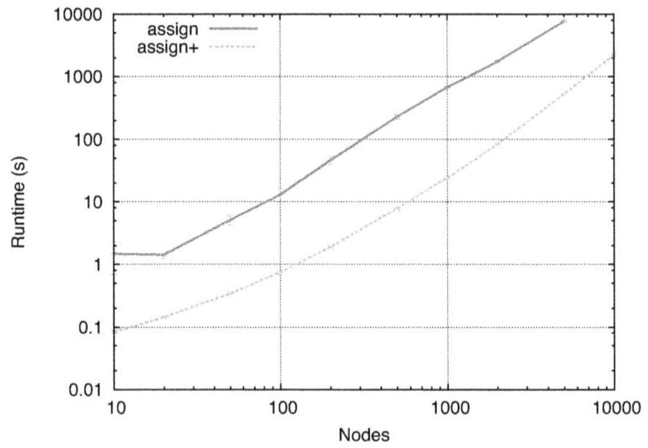

Figure 9: Scalability

We further test the scalability of both algorithms by using Brite [16] to generate realistic, Internet-like topologies of larger sizes. These topologies are more complex and more connected than those found in most testbed experiments [9] and thus challenge allocation algorithms. We generate 10 topologies each of the size 10, 20, 50, 100, 200, 500, 1,000, 2,000, 5,000 and 10,000 nodes. For each node we request `pcvm` type (virtual machines), making it possible to allocate large topologies on our limited testbed architecture. Each allocation request runs on an empty testbed. Figure 9 shows means and standard deviations for runtime of `assign` and `assign+` versus the topology size, both on log scale. `assign+` again outperforms `assign` having about 10 times shorter runtime. `assign` further fails to find a solution for 10,000-node topologies, while assign+ finds it. assign+ only allocates interswitch bandwidth in 5,000 and 10,000 node cases, while assign allocates it for much smaller topologies. We believe that mechanisms that limit assign's runtime for large topologies interfere with its ability to find a good solution that minimizes the interswitch bandwidth.

8.4 Alternative Types

We now assume that users request specific node types because they need some well-provisioned resource such as a large disk or a fast CPU. We explore if we can further improve resource allocation success by expanding experimenter's node type constraint to equivalent or better hardware. In real deployment this would have to be done only with user's consent. We only consider disk, CPU and memory specifications. We start from DeterLab's node types in January 2011, as shown in Table 2, and identify for each type *alternative types* that have same or better features in these three dimensions.

Figure 10 shows the effect of using alternative types on allocation success of assign+, under the label assign+.at. It creates 68.1% of failed allocations generated by assign.

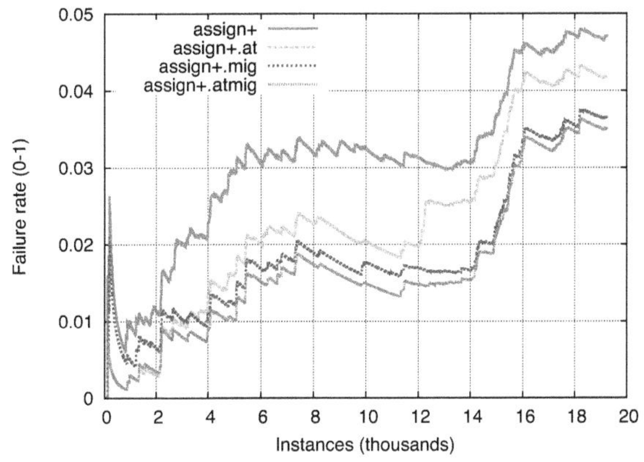

Figure 10: Allocation failure rates for assign+, when using alternative types and migration

9. CHANGING ALLOCATION POLICY

The approaches in the previous section change the resource allocation strategy, but do not change the allocation policy on testbeds that allows users to hold resources for arbitrarily long times without interruption. In this section we investigate if changes in resource allocation policy would further improve allocation success. We examine two such changes:

1. *Experiment migration* – where running instances can be migrated to other resources in the testbed (that still satisfy user-specified constraints) to make space for the allocating instance.

2. *Fair sharing* – where running instances can be paused if they have been running for a long time and are currently idle, so their resources can be borrowed by an allocating instance.

We acknowledge that either of these changes would represent a major shift in today's network testbeds' philosophy and use policy. Yet such shift may be necessary as testbeds become more popular and the demand on their resources exceeds capacity. Our work helps evaluate potential benefits of such policy changes.

Further, the above changes are potentially disruptive for some instances that rely on the constancy of hardware allocated to them for the duration of their lifetime. We assume that users would have mechanisms to opt out of these features, i.e. they could mark their experiment as "do not migrate" or "do not pause". We further assume that, if the benefits of these policy changes seem significant, testbeds would develop mechanisms to seamlessly migrate or pause and restart instances that would be minimally disruptive to users. Finally, we emphasize that instances could be migrated and/or paused only during idle times, when allocated machines exhibit no significant terminal, CPU, disk or network activity. Emulab software looks for such idle machines each 10 minutes, and records each machine's state (idle/non-idle) in the database, overwriting the previous state. We have collected these reports for one year to investigate the extent of idle time in instances. Figure 11 shows the distribution of the total idle time in four classes of instances: those that last < 12, 12-24 h, 1-7 days and > 7 days. All instances have significant idle time and long-lived instances are often idle for more than a week! This leads us to believe that our proposed policy modifications would apply to many instances and would not disrupt their existing dynamics.

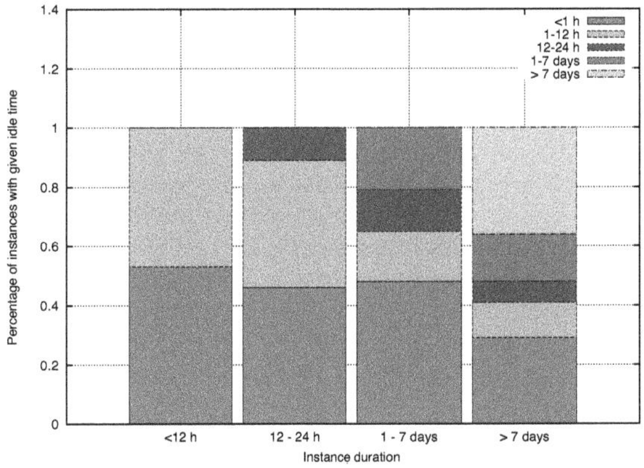

Figure 11: Idle times for instances of different duration

9.1 Migration

We now explore how much we can improve resource allocation by performing experiment migration. This would include stopping some allocated instances and moving their configuration and data to other testbed machines to "make space" for the allocating instance. While there exist techniques in distributed systems that can migrate running processes to another physical node [17], we propose a much lighter-weight migration that would only move instances that are idle at the time. The simplest implementation of such migration would be to image all disks of the experimental machines, and load those images to new machines, but that would require a lot of time and disk space.

We test the migration on our "2011 synthetic setup". If a regular resource allocation fails, we identify any instance that holds node types requested by the allocating instance and is idle as the *migration candidate*. We then order candidates from the smallest to the largest and attempt to migrate them one at a time. To do so we reclaim resources from the migration candidate, try to allocate the allocating instance, and then try to reallocate the migration candidate. Allocation succeeds only if both of these actions succeed. Otherwise we restore the old state and try the next candidate. We only record a failure for the allocating instance if all migrations fail. In real deployment this can be easily simulated, without disturbing any instances, until the successful combination is found.

Figure 10 shows the allocation failure rate when using migration during `assign+` under `assign+.mig` label, and when combining migration and alternative types, under `assign+.atmig` label. We assume that a migration candidate is always idle in our simulation. Migration lowers the allocation failure rate to 59.6% of that generated by `assign`. Adding the alternative types to migration has a minor effect, lowering the allocation failure rate to 57.3% of that generated by `assign`.

Suggestion 5: *Testbeds need better state-saving mechanisms that go beyond manual disk imaging, to support migration.*

9.2 Fair-Sharing

When demand for a shared resource exceeds supply, a usual approach is to enforce fair sharing and penalize big users. Traditional fair sharing where every user (or in testbed case every project) receives a fair share of resources works well when: (1) users have roughly similar needs for the resource, or (2) the demand does not heavily depend on the resource allocation success and jobs are scheduled in fixed time slots. In the first case, one can implement quotas on use, giving each user the same amount of credit and replenishing it on periodic basis. In the second case, one can implement fair queuing (e.g., [22]), allocating jobs from big users whenever there is leftover resource from the small ones. Unfortunately, neither of these approaches works well for testbeds.

Many measures of testbed usage exhibit heavy-tail properties that violate the first assumption about users having similar needs. For example, the distributions of instance size and duration is heavy-tailed (Figure 12(a) and 12(b)): most instances are short and small, but there are a few very large or very long instances that dominate the distribution. If we assume that fairness should be measured at the project level, heavy tail property manifests again. The distribution of node-hours per project (Figure 12(c)), obtained by summing the products of size and duration in hours for all its instances, is also heavy tailed. The second assumption is violated because most fair-sharing algorithms are designed for fixed-size jobs while testbed instances have a wide range of durations that are not known in advance.

We now quantify the extent of unfairness on DeterLab testbed. We define a project as "unfair" if it uses more than its fair share of PCs in a week. While we focus on PC use, similar definitions can be devised for specific node types. We choose a week-long interval to unify the occurrence of heavy use due to any combination of large instances, long instances or many parallel instances in a project. A fair share of resources is defined as total number of possible node-hours in a week, taking into account available and allocated PCs, divided by the total number of active projects in that week. A project can be classified as unfair one week and fair the other week.

Figure 13 shows the percentage of total possible node-hours used by unfair and by fair projects each week during 2011. There are 114 projects active during this time, each of which has been fair at some point during the year; 27 projects have also been unfair. There were total of 3,126 TEMP failures in 2011, averaging 58.7 failures per project when it is unfair, and 26.1 failures per project, when it is fair. While an unfair project has more than double the errors of a fair project, this is expected, because unfair projects request more

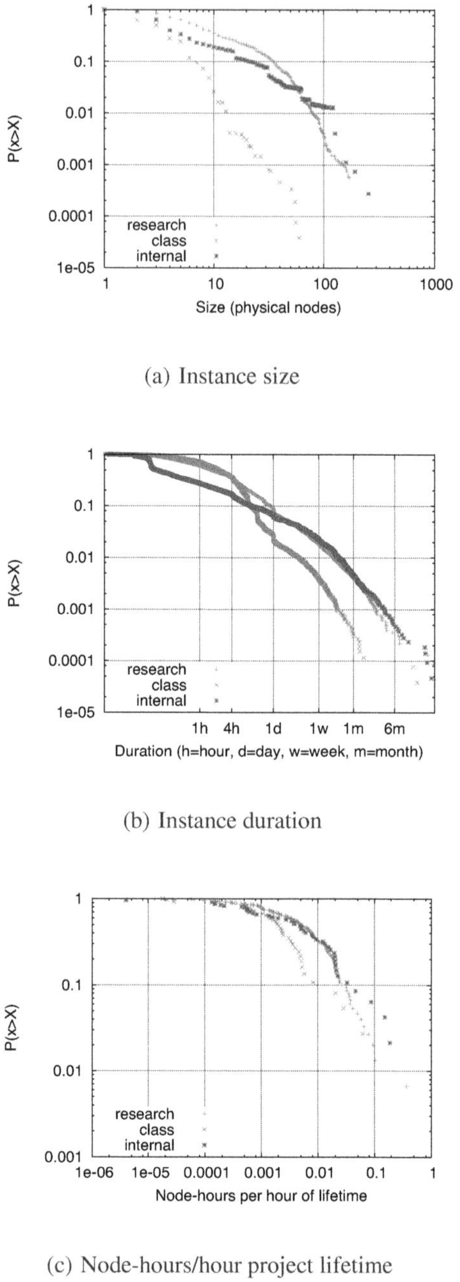

Figure 12: Heavy tails in testbed use measures

allocations per second, their allocations are larger and have longer duration.

Penalizing big testbed users is difficult because large use in research projects seems to be correlated with publications. We manually classify research projects on DeterLab as "outcome projects" if they have published one or more peer-reviewed publication, or MS and PhD thesis, in which they acknowledge use of DeterLab. We find 48 outcome projects and 104 no-outcome projects. We then define an instance as big if it uses 20 nodes or more, and as long if it lasts one day or longer. Only 9% of instances are big and 5% are long. Outcome projects have on the average 99 big and 33 long instances, while no-outcome projects have 10 big and 8 long instances. Thus big instances and long instances that lead to unfair testbed use seem to be correlated with research publications, and good publicity for the testbed, and are thus very valuable to testbed owners. It would be unwise to alienate these users or discourage heavy testbed use. Instead, we want to gently tip the scale in favor of small users when possible.

We identify three design goals for fairness policy on testbeds:

1. **Predictability.** Any fairness approach must allow users to accurately anticipate when they may be penalized.
2. **User control.** Actions taken to penalize a user must depend solely on their actions, and testbeds should offer opt-out mechanisms.
3. **On-demand.** Resources should be reclaimed only when there is an instance whose allocation fails, and whose needs can be satisfied by these resources.

One approach to tipping the scale would be to reclaim some resources from unfair projects until their use is reduced to a fair share. This would violate all three design goals, because unfair status changes depending on how many other projects are active, and freed resources could sit unused on the testbed. Another approach would be to reclaim resources on demand from an instance that has used the most node-hours. Again this leads to unpredictable behavior from the user's point of view, and it may interrupt short-running but large instances that are difficult to allocate again. We opt for the strategy that reclaims resources on demand from the longest-running instance, as long as it has been running for more than one day and is currently idle. This lets users identify which of their instances may be reclaimed in advance. We propose two possible approaches to fair allocations: Take-a-Break and Borrow-and-Return.

9.3 Take-a-Break

In Take-a-Break approach, when a resource allocation fails, we identify any instance that holds node types that are requested by the allocating instance and is currently idle, as the *break candidate*. We then select the candidate that has been running the longest and, if its age is greater than one day, we release its resources to the allocating instance. The break candidate is queued for allocation immediately, and an attempt is made to allocate it after any resource release.

Figure 14 shows the rate of allocation failures for Take-a-Break approach under the `assign.tbreak` label. We also deploy migration and alternative node types. We assume that a break candidate is always idle in our simulation. Failure rate is strikingly

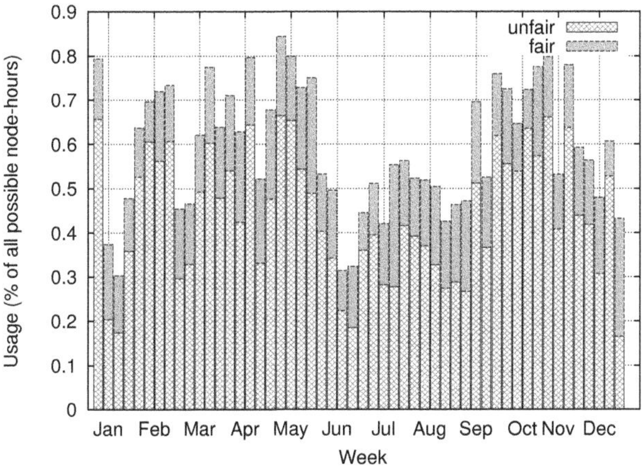

Figure 13: Usage of fair and unfair projects in 2011.

low, reaching 1.5% by the end of our simulation even though the density of allocated instances is increased. Overall, `assign+` with Take-a-Break creates only 25.3% of failed allocations generated by `assign`. This comes at the price – duration of 177 instances is prolonged. Half of these instances experience delays of up to 1 hour, 79% up to 4 hours, and 97% up to 1 day. Only six instances are delayed more than one day, the longest delay being 1.67 days. Looking at relative delay, 72% of instances are only delayed up to 1% compared to their original duration, 94% of instances are delayed by at most 10% and the worst delay doubles the instance's duration.

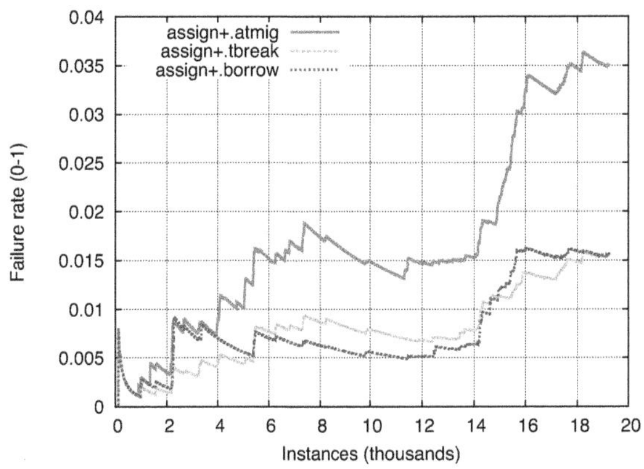

Figure 14: Error rates for `assign+` when using Take-a-Break and Borrow-and-Return approaches.

We now verify if we have tipped the scale in favor of fair projects. We first apply the fairness calculation to the allocations resulting from running `assign+` on our "2011 synthetic setup" and obtain similar usage patterns, to those seen in the real dataset, except that the allocation failures are reduced because we were removing overlapping instances during workload creation and we started with an empty testbed. There were 14.5 failures per project when it is unfair, and 3.98 failures per project, when it is fair. We then apply the same calculation to the allocations resulting from running `assign+` with Take-a-Break on our "2011 synthetic setup" and we count both allocation failures and forcing an instance to take a break as "failures". We find that there are 18.6 failures per project when it is unfair, and 1.62 failures per project, when it is fair. Thus unfair projects are slightly penalized and the failure rate of fair projects is more than halved.

9.4 Borrow-and-Return

While Take-a-Break approach helps fair projects obtain more resources, it forces instances whose resources have been reclaimed to wait for unpredictable duration. Borrow-and-Return approach amends this. Its design is the same as Take-a-Break approach, but resources are only "borrowed" from long-running instances for 4 hours, after which they are returned to their original owner. Users receiving these borrowed nodes would be alerted to the fact that the nodes will be reclaimed at a certain time. Instances interrupted this way are queued and allocated as soon as possible.

Figure 14 shows the rate of allocation failures for Borrow-and-Return approach, under the `assign.borrow` label. We also deploy migration and alternative node types. Allocation failure rate is similar to that of Take-a-Break approach – 25.6% of that of the `assign` . Duration of 583 instances is prolonged. 80% of these instances experience delays of up to 1 hour, 96% up to 4 hours, and 99% up to 1 day. Only five instances are delayed more than one day, the longest delay being 1.9 days. Looking at relative delay, 25% of instances are delayed up to 1% compared to their original duration, 76.1% of instances are delayed by at most 10%, 97% are delayed by at most 100% and the worst delay extends the instance's duration 4.5 times. This approach seems to find a good middle ground between heavily penalizing long instances, like Take-a-Break does, and doing nothing. Fairness of Borrow-and-Return approach is slightly worse than that of Take-a-Break, leading to the average of 18.9 failures for unfair projects, and 2.3 for fair projects.

10. CONCLUSIONS

Network testbeds are extensively used today, both for research and for teaching, but their resource allocation algorithms and policies have not evolved much since their creation. This paper examines the causes for resource allocation failures in Emulab testbeds and finds that 31.9% of failures could be avoided through: (1) providing better information to users about the cost of and the alternatives to their topology constraints, and (2) better resource allocation strategies. The remaining failures can be reduced to 25.3% of the original by applying a gentle fair-sharing strategy such as Take-a-Break or Borrow-and-Return. The main challenge in designing fair testbed allocation policies lies in achieving fairness, while being sensitive to human user needs for predictability and while nurturing heavy users that bring most value to the testbed. Our investigation is just the first of many that need to be undertaken to reconcile these conflicting, but important goals.

11. ACKNOWLEDGMENTS

This material is based upon work supported by the National Science Foundation under Grant No. 1049758. Any opinions, findings, and conclusions or recommendations expressed in this material are those of the authors and do not necessarily reflect the views of the National Science Foundation.

12. REFERENCES

[1] Other Emulab Testbeds. `https://users.emulab.net/trac/emulab/wiki/OtherEmulabs`.

[2] Schooner WAIL (Wisconsin Advanced Internet Laboratory). `http://www.schooner.wail.wisc.edu`.

[3] R. Bajcsy, T. Benzel, M. Bishop, et al. Cyber Defense Technology Networking and Evaluation. *Communications of the ACM*, 2004.

[4] S. M. Banik, L. P. Daigle, and T. H. Chang. Implementation and Empirical Evaluations of Floor Control Protocols on Planetlab Network. In *Proceedings of the 47th Annual Southeast Regional Conference, ACM-SE 47*, 2009.

[5] T. Benzel. The Science of Cyber Security Experimentation: The DETER Project. In *Proc. of 2011 Annual Computer Security Applications Conference (ACSAC)*, December 2012.

[6] N. M. M. K. Chowdhury, M.R. Rahman, and R. Boutaba. Virtual network embedding with coordinated node and link mapping. In *Proc. of INFOCOM 2009*, pages 783–791, 2009.

[7] B. Chun, D. Culler, et al. Planetlab: an Overlay Testbed for Broad-coverage Services. *ACM SIGCOMM Computer Communication Review*, 33(3):3–12, 2003.

[8] Ali Ghodsi, Matei Zaharia, Benjamin Hindman, Andy Konwinski, Scott Shenker, and Ion Stoica. Dominant resource fairness: Fair allocation of multiple resource types. In *Proceedings of the 8th USENIX Conference on Networked Systems Design and Implementation*, 2011.

[9] F. Hermenier and R. Ricci. How to Build a Better Testbed: Lessons From a Decade of Network Experiments on Emulab. In *TridentCom*, 2012.

[10] J.P. Herron, L. Fowler, and C. Small. The GENI Meta-Operations Center. In *Proc. of IEEE Conf. on eScience*, pages 384–385. IEEE Computer Society, 2008.

[11] Benjamin Hindman, Andy Konwinski, Matei Zaharia, Ali Ghodsi, Anthony D. Joseph, Randy Katz, Scott Shenker, and Ion Stoica. Mesos: a platform for fine-grained resource sharing in the data center. In *Proceedings of the 8th USENIX conference on Networked Systems Design and Implementation*, 2011.

[12] B. W. Kernighan and S. Lin. An Efficient Heuristic Procedure for Partitioning Graphs. *The Bell system technical journal*, 49(1):291–307, 1970.

[13] W. Kim, A. Roopakalu, K.Y. Li, and V.S. Pai. Understanding and Characterizing PlanetLab Resource Usage for Federated Network Testbeds. In *Proc. of the ACM SIGCOMM*, pages 515–532. ACM, 2011.

[14] S. Kirkpatrick, C. D. Gelatt, and M. P. Vecchi. Optimization by Simulated Annealing. *Science*, 220(4598):671–680, 1983.

[15] J. Lu and J. Turner. Efficient mapping of virtual networks onto a shared substrate. *Washington University in St. Louis, Tech. Rep*, 2006.

[16] A. Medina, A. Lakhina, I. Matta, et al. BRITE: An Approach to Universal Topology Generation. In *Proc. of MASCOTS*, pages 346–. IEEE Computer Society, 2001.

[17] Dejan S. Milojicic, Fred Douglis, Yves Paindaveine, Richard Wheeler, and Songnian Zhou. Process migration. *ACM Comput. Surv.*, 32(3):241–299, September 2000.

[18] T. Miyachi, K. Chinen, and Y. Shinoda. Automatic Configuration and Execution of Internet Experiments on an Actual Node-based Testbed. In *Proc. of Tridentcom*, 2005.

[19] J. Nakata, S. Uda, T. Miyaclii, et al. Starbed2: Large-scale, Realistic and Real-time Testbed for Ubiquitous Networks. In *Proc. of TridentCom*, 2007.

[20] R. Ricci, C. Alfeld, and J. Lepreau. A Solver for the Network Testbed Mapping Problem. *SIGCOMM Comput. Commun. Rev.*, 33(2):65–81, 2003.

[21] M. Ripeanu, M. Bowman, S. Chase, et al. Globus and Planetlab Resource Management Solutions Compared. In *Proc. of International Symposium on High Performance Distributed Computing*, pages 246 – 255, 2004.

[22] I. Stoica, S. Shenker, and H. Zhang. Core-stateless Fair Queueing: a Scalable Architecture to Approximate Fair Bandwidth Allocations in High-speed Networks. *IEEE/ACM Trans. Netw.*, 11(1):33–46, 2003.

[23] Douglas Thain, Todd Tannenbaum, and Miron Livny. Distributed Computing in Practice: the Condor Experience. *Concurrency - Practice and Experience*, 17(2-4):323–356, 2005.

[24] B. White, J. Lepreau, L. Stoller, et al. An Integrated Experimental Environment for Distributed Systems and Networks. In *Proc. of OSDI*, pages 255–270, December 2002.

[25] M. Yu, Y. Yi, J. Rexford, and M. Chiang. Rethinking Virtual Network Embedding: Substrate Support for Path Splitting and Migration. *ACM SIGCOMM Comp. Comm. Rev.*, 38(2):17–29, 2008.

Sharing the Cost of Backbone Networks
Cui Bono?

Laszlo Gyarmati*, Rade Stanojevic*, Michael Sirivianos†, Nikolaos Laoutaris*
*Telefonica Research, †Cyprus University of Technology
{laszlo,rade,nikos}@tid.es, michael.sirivianos@cut.ac.cy

ABSTRACT

We study the problem of how to share the cost of a backbone network among its customers. A variety of empirical cost-sharing policies are used in practice by backbone network operators but very little ever reaches the research literature about their properties. Motivated by this, we present a systematic study of such policies focusing on the discrepancies between their cost allocations. We aim at quantifying how the selection of a particular policy biases an operator's understanding of cost generation.

We identify F-discrepancies due to the specific *function* used to map traffic into cost (*e.g.*, volume vs. peak rate vs. 95-percentile) and M-discrepancies, which have to do with where traffic is *metered* (per device vs. ingress metering). We also identify L-discrepancies relating to the *liability* of individual customers for triggered upgrades and consequent costs (full vs. proportional), and finally, TCO-discrepancies emanating from the fact that the *cost of carrying a bit* is not uniform across the network (old vs. new equipment, high vs. low energy or real estate costs, *etc.*).

Using extensive traffic, routing, and cost data from a tier-1 network we show that F-discrepancies are large when looking at individual links but cancel out when considering network-wide cost-sharing. Metering at ingress points is convenient but leads to large M-discrepancies, while TCO-discrepancies are huge. Finally, L-discrepancies are intriguing and esoteric but understanding them is central to determining the cost a customer inflicts on the network.

Categories and Subject Descriptors

C.2.3 [**Computer-Communication Networks**]: Network Operations; J.4 [**Social and Behavioral Sciences**]: Economics

Keywords

cost sharing, backbone network, network economics, fairness

IMC'12, November 14–16, 2012, Boston, Massachusetts, USA.

1. INTRODUCTION

After several years of growth during which Internet Service Providers (ISPs) have enjoyed healthy profit margins, we are entering a new era in which margins are progressively declining. This is due to intense competition that pushes prices down, while at the same time traffic increases faster than the ability of technology to reduce capital (CAPEX) and operational (OPEX) expenses. The viability of an ISP in such a competitive ecosystem will largely depend on its ability to understand and manage its costs.

Understanding and optimizing the total cost of ownership (TCO) of a network, *i.e.* both CAPEX and OPEX, is an important aspect of network operations and therefore it has received substantial attention from procurement, network development, and network planning departments of large telcos [23]. However, the impact of individual customers on the cost of the network, which in the case of backbone networks are other (smaller) networks and big enterprises, is much less understood. There are multiple reasons for this, including the difficulties of monitoring usage statistics for each customer at each device, variable per device TCO, and non-linearities of cost-capacity functions. There is also the issue of which customer's additional traffic demand forces the operator to upgrade his network in order to maintain the Service Level Agreement (SLA) for all customers, that is, which customer is liable for a *triggered upgrade* and to what extent.

Overcoming such challenges and quantifying in detail how individual customers affect the TCO of a network is crucial and can be used for provisioning and operations purposes, including routing and peering. It can also be used for creating better tariff schemes, *e.g.*, to give discounts to customers inflicting low costs or justify premiums in the opposite case. Tariffs are also influenced by additional factors including regulation, competition, and demand, and thus their relationship to cost is not necessarily directly proportional. In this paper we analyze a wide range of cost-sharing policies used in practice by backbone operators and contrast their outcome using extensive input data from a tier-1 backbone network, including 590 ingress interfaces to large customers, 691 main backbone links, and 71 core routers spread over 3 continents. Our main objective is to see *how the selection of a certain cost-sharing policy impacts the picture that an operator has about which customers generate high costs.*

Our main contributions are:

- The development of a methodology for studying multiple facets of cost-sharing in multi-resource environments such as a backbone network. [1]

- We analyze multiple cost-sharing policies of varying complexity and accuracy under various settings. Our analysis reveals large discrepancies among different policies when splitting the cost of an individual network element among the customers that use it: in 20% of cases the ratio of costs associated by two different policies is under 0.5 or over 2. This in turn implies that operators must be careful in selecting among different policies since their cost-allocation outcomes may vary widely for individual devices or small networks.
- The above is a negative result but luckily it becomes less severe when one considers cost-sharing among all the devices that constitute a large network. In this case, individual discrepancies at the device level cancel out as one sums them up across a network. This in turn points to an opportunity for selecting cost-sharing policies from the least complicated side of the spectrum without risking much sacrifice in terms of accuracy.
- Metering only at ingress links (which is the de-facto norm in monitoring the customer's usage) may greatly under- or over-estimate the actual costs, depending on the locality of the traffic and temporal characteristics of the customer.
- We study additional aspects of cost-sharing related to the issues of liability for triggered upgrades, and discrepancies due to non-uniform TCO costs of different network elements.

The structure of the paper is as follows. In Section 2 we give an overview on what determines the cost of a backbone network and present why the sharing of these costs is a challenging task. We present our methodology in Section 3, where we introduce four different aspects that affect the quantified costs of the customers. We describe our datasets in Section 4. We investigate the costs of customers and the severity of the different types of discrepancies in Section 5. Afterwards, we review the related work in Section 6 while we draw the conclusions of our work in Section 7.

2. BACKGROUND

What contributes to the cost of a backbone? The cost of a network consists of CAPEX and OPEX for all devices and Points-of-Presence (PoPs). The CAPEX is the one-time cost paid whenever equipment is bought and installed [23]. It depends on the amount of traffic the device must carry at a specific level of Quality-of-Service (QoS). A key observation is that *the capacity needed to guarantee a certain QoS depends on the peak traffic that needs to be carried.* This is because for a given capacity, QoS is minimized when the traffic peaks.

The OPEX corresponds to operational costs such as real estate, energy, and personnel. It also depends on the amount of traffic and the QoS; however, that dependence is more elastic. The cost sharing policies we discuss are generic enough to capture both CAPEX and OPEX with appropriate parameterization.

[1]Our methodology is sufficiently general to be applied in settings beyond backbone networks, such as 3G networks, datacenters, *etc.*, but we do not examine such cases here.

Why is it difficult to split cost among customers? From the above discussion, one may conclude that splitting the cost among customers is straightforward: for each device of the network each customer should pay in proportion to his contribution to the peak traffic carried by the device and then sum up over all devices. Things, however, are not that simple:

- **Accounting complications.** It is difficult to know for each network device the contribution of each customer to its peak. This is because backbone operators need to measure and keep state at many points in the network, which requires costly monitoring equipments. In addition, computing traffic rates introduces the problem of identifying the appropriate time-scale for the computation owing to the limited resources of the monitoring tools.
- **Liability complications.** If we were to build from scratch a new network for a fixed set of customers of known demand, then the cost attributed to each customer should be proportional to the sum of its contributions to the peaks of individual devices. Splitting costs based on the contribution to the peak is indeed exact, but only for this "offline problem". However, in reality, networks are not deployed as a single event but grow organically with the addition of new customers and the ramping up of their traffic. Under this more realistic case, peak-based cost-sharing is not guaranteed to be fair. Consider for example the case in which a network is already operating at the maximum utilization allowed by QoS constraints and a small new customer triggers an expensive upgrade that leads to a new network with plentiful unallocated capacity (upgrades typically involve large jumps, *e.g.*, 1Gbps to 2.5Gbps, to 10Gbps, *etc.*). Peak-based cost sharing would attribute to the new customer only a small fraction of the overall cost. Is that fair? The answer depends on what happens with the unallocated capacity. If the network can easily sell it to new or existing customers then indeed it is fair. If, however, selling this leftover capacity is not guaranteed, then the new customer may have a larger liability for the upgrade costs.

For the above reasons, we will present a methodology in which we first compare among policies of varying complexity, and then switch to comparing among policies that assign different liability levels.

3. METHODOLOGY

In this section, we present a thorough classification of the discrepancies between methods when a backbone operator quantifies the costs that its customers inflict on the network. By *discrepancy* we mean the difference in a customer's costs according to two cost sharing policies. Each type of discrepancy reveals a separate facet of the challenge of customer cost quantification. These facets relate to the following questions:

- How does the backbone operator compute the cost of the customers?

- What kind of traffic metering does the backbone operator apply in the network?
- Which customers are liable for the incurred costs?
- How diverse are the costs of the components of the network?

Before presenting the taxonomy of discrepancies, we first introduce the metric we use to quantify the discrepancies of a pair of cost sharing procedures. Let N denote the set of customers who utilize resources in the network. Let A and B denote the sets of costs allocated to each customer using two different cost sharing policies. It holds that $|A| = |B| = |N|$. Accordingly, $a_i \in A$ denotes the cost of customer $i \in N$ quantified based on the first cost sharing policy while $b_i \in B$ represents customer i's cost based on the second policy. We define the discrepancy of the costs of customer i as

$$d(a_i, b_i) = \max\left\{\frac{a_i}{b_i}, \frac{b_i}{a_i}\right\} \quad (1)$$

We use this measure of discrepancy because it describes the relation of the costs with a simple, comprehensible value. We use several statistics of the customers' individual discrepancies to quantify the discrepancy of two cost sharing policies including the 95th percentile and the median.

We now describe how we determine the aggregate cost that the sharing policies distribute. A network consists of various network devices, such as routers and links. Let L denote the set of devices of the network. Let $x_i^l(t)$ denote the traffic volume of customer $i \in N$ on network device $l \in L$ during the time interval $t \in [1, T]$. Furthermore, let c^l denote the cost of network device $l \in L$.

The cost of a specific device depends on the maximum amount of traffic that it has to carry during a certain time interval. Thus, we obtain c^l by examining the available capacity rates of the device (*e.g.*, 1 *Gbps*, 10 *Gbps*, *etc.*) and then using the cost of the smallest device whose capacity satisfies the requested Service Level Agreement (SLA) for the given traffic demand. We assume that the backbone operator fulfills its SLA by upgrading its devices when utilization hits the 50% threshold. To this end, we assume that the costs follow a step function $C : \mathbb{R} \to \mathbb{R}$. Thus, the cost of device l is

$$c^l = C\left(\max_{t\in T} \sum_{i\in N} x_i^l(t)\right) \quad (2)$$

3.1 F-discrepancies

The first source of discrepancies between cost allocation methods is the *function* that the backbone operator uses to compute the contribution of the customers to the aggregate cost. We next present four policies that strike different balances between precision and resource needs, which we discuss in more details at the end of this section. We consider these methods because backbone operators apply some of these policies (*e.g.*, the 95Percentile-Customer and the Aggregate-Peak-Device) in practice to determine the costs a customer inflicts and consequently the price the customers pays. For example, one can easily map some of the tariffs (*e.g.*, based on the purchased raw capacity or on the 95th percentile of the traffic) used in practice to the introduced policies (*e.g.*, Volume-Customer and 95Percentile-Customer).

- **Volume-Customer.** We measure the amount of data that a single customer sends on a specific network device (e.g., on a single link) for the whole analyzed time period. Afterwards, we share the cost of the device proportionally to the traffic volumes of the customers using it. Hence, the cost of customer i for device l is:

$$c_i^l = c^l \cdot \frac{\sum_{t\in T} x_i^l(t)}{\sum_{j\in N}\sum_{t\in T} x_j^l(t)} \quad (3)$$

- **95Percentile-Customer.** We distribute the cost of the device proportional to the 95th percentile [12] of the customers' traffic that traverses the particular device:

$$c_i^l = c^l \cdot \frac{P_{95}\left(\ldots, x_i^l(t), \ldots\right)}{\sum_{j\in N} P_{95}\left(\ldots, x_j^l(t), \ldots\right)} \quad (4)$$

where $P_{95}()$ denotes the 95th percentile of the arguments.

- **Peak-Customer.** Under this policy, we share the expenditure of the network device proportional to the customers' maximum usage volumes for the given time interval:

$$c_i^l = c^l \cdot \frac{\max_{t\in T} x_i^l(t)}{\sum_{j\in N} \max_{t\in T} x_j^l(t)} \quad (5)$$

- **Aggregate-Peak-Device.** Backbone operators plan the capacity of the network based on the maximum utilization, *e.g.*, the 50% of the capacity of a device is larger than the expected maximum of the traffic that traverses it. Accordingly, we distribute the cost of the devices based on the contribution of individual customers to the peak utilization. Assuming that the peak utilization of device l happens at time step $t_m = \arg\max_t \sum_{j\in N} x_j^l(t)$, we allocate the following cost to customer i as:

$$c_i^l = c^l \cdot \frac{x_i^l(t_m)}{\sum_{j\in N} x_j^l(t_m)} \quad (6)$$

We evaluate F-discrepancies by comparing a policy with Aggregate-Peak-Device, which shares the costs in a fair way when it is guaranteed that new unallocated capacity from an upgrade will soon find a customer to amortize it. The F-discrepancies of the policies arise from the misalignment of traffic peaks: the peak of a customer's traffic may not coincide with the peak of the aggregate traffic the device carries.

Illustrative example: Let us assume that two customers utilize device l_1 with the time-series depicted in Fig. 1. Based on the time-series we compute the costs of the customers. The percentages of the cost that customer 1 covers are 69.9%, 56.2%, 60%, and 53.3% of the total cost of the device for the Volume-Customer, Peak-Customer, 95Percentile-Customer, and Aggregate-Peak-Device policies, respectively. For example, in case of the 95Percentile-Customer policy, customer 1 has a traffic of 0.9 Gbps while the cumulative traffic is 1.5 Gbps resulting in 60% cost share. The main cause behind the discrepancies of the costs are the misalignment of the customers' peak, and that the different policies consider diverse parts of the time-series to compute a value that describes the traffic of the customer.

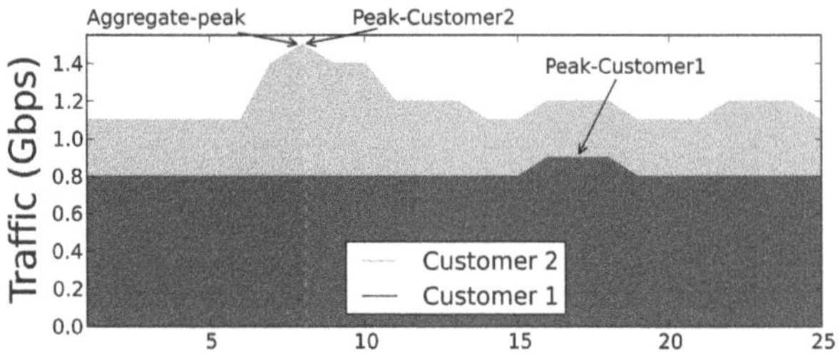

Figure 1: Illustrative example for F-discrepancies. The misalignment of the customers' peak causes cost differences across policies.

The introduced policies quantify the cost of the customers using different functions on a per device basis. The F-discrepancies of the customers emerge at two different levels:

- **Device-level discrepancies.** We compute separately for each network device the discrepancy among different policies based on the customers' costs. In this case, the set of costs is

$$\left\{c_i^l \mid \forall i \in N\right\}, l \in L \tag{7}$$

and has cardinality $|N||L|$. For example, the F-discrepancy of customer i in case of policies a and b is $d(a_i^l, b_i^l)$.

- **Network-level discrepancies.** We first summarize the costs of a customer over all the devices of the network, *i.e.*, we compute the total cost of each customer. Afterwards, we compute the discrepancies of the policies. In this case, the set of the costs over which we compute the discrepancies is

$$\left\{\sum_{l\in L} c_i^l \mid \forall i \in N\right\} \tag{8}$$

and has cardinality $|N|$. For example, for policies a and b the F-discrepancy of customer i is $d(\sum_{l\in L} a_i^l, \sum_{l\in L} b_i^l)$.

3.2 M-discrepancies

The traffic *metering* method is the second source of discrepancies. The resource requirements of the traffic monitoring tools depend on the resolution of metering. The main cause behind the M-discrepancies is the trade-off that backbone operators face: increasing the precision of the metering improves the validity of the quantified cost, however, this comes with an elevated cost for traffic monitoring. We study the two corner cases of traffic metering:

- **Customer-Ingress.** Each customer has several ingress devices through which it injects its traffic to the network. The backbone operator keeps track of the customers' usage solely on the ingress devices. This is the least expensive metering method. The operator uses the ingress traffic time-series to share the network-wide expenditures among the customers.

- **Customer-per-Device.** If the backbone operator deploys more advanced network monitoring tools, it can capture the time-series of the customers not only on the ingress devices but on all the devices located in the network. This is the most expensive metering method and is typically done using NetFlow technology, which comes at a high procurement and administration cost. Metering the actual traffic on each network device allows the backbone operator to compute the costs of the customers based on the device specific time-series. Therefore, the backbone operator faces a trade-off: more accurate expenditure sharing vs. more cost efficient operation.

We define the M-discrepancies as follows. First, we compute the cost of customer i on each device l using a given cost allocation function (*e.g.*, based on the Volume-Customer policy of Section 3.1), and we compute the network-level cost of customer i as $\sum_{l\in L} c_i^l$. Second, we compute using the given cost allocation function the customer's share (c_i^*) of the network's total cost ($c = \sum_{l\in L} c^l$) using the ingress traffic time-series of the customers. The total ingress traffic of customer i is $x_i^*(t) = \sum_{l\in I_i} x_i^l(t)$ where I_i denotes the set of ingress devices that customer i has. Accordingly, the M-discrepancy of customer i is

$$d_i\left(\sum_{l\in L} c_i^l, c_i^*\right) \tag{9}$$

where d_i is our metric of discrepancy (Eq. 1).

Illustrative example: Let us now assume that the ingress traffic of the customers is as we show in Fig. 2. The backbone network consists of two devices: L_1 on which the traffic of the customers is as depicted in Fig. 1 and L_2 which is solely utilized by customer 1 with a constant traffic of 1 *Gbps*. For illustration purposes, we separate the two flows of customer 1, one on L_1 and the other on L_2, with a dashed line in the Fig. 2. Because the traffic on device L_2 is modest it can be transmitted on a 2.5 *Gbps* device while the capacity of L_1 should be 10 *Gbps*. The diverse device capacities imply diverse costs as well. In the case of ingress metering, *i.e.*, sharing the cost of the network just based on the aggregate traffic shown in Fig. 2, the cost of customer 1 is 83.9%, 73.1%, 76%, and 72% of the cost of the whole network for the Volume-Customer, Peak-Customer, 95Percentile-Customer, and Aggregate-Peak-Device policies, respectively. However, if we measure the traffic of the customers on all the devices then customer 1's shares of costs are 75.9%, 65%, 68%, and 62.7%. If we compare these cost fractions we encounter large discrepancies caused by the level of the metering.

3.3 L-discrepancies

The third type of discrepancies is caused by the different types of customer *liability* as discussed in Section 2. We will examine the following policies:

- **Aggregate-Peak-Device.** This is the already introduced policy that is the measure of fairness when the customer liability is proportional to the aggregate peak of devices.

- **Trigger.** With this policy, the backbone operator allocates the cost of the device exclusively to the customer

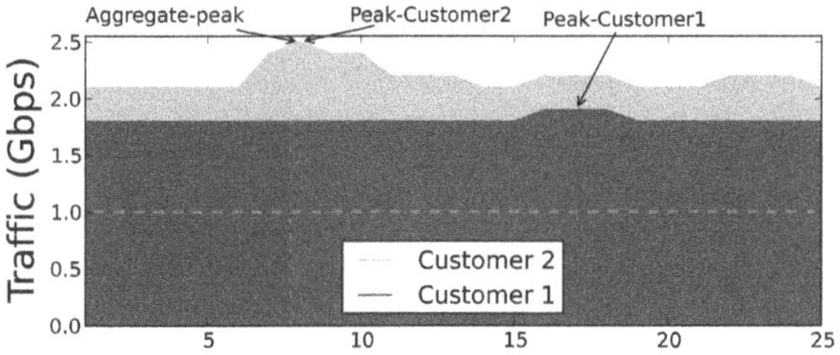

Figure 2: Illustrative example for M-discrepancies: metering traffic only at the ingress link causes customer 1 to have a larger share of the cost than if we meter at all devices.

that triggered the capacity upgrade. This policy is applied when the backbone operator is not confident that it can sell the newly obtained but unallocated capacity.[2]

To this end, the backbone operator utilizes the historical traffic patterns of the customers and their arriving order. For example, the cost of the first customer is equal to the cost of the device that is capable to transmit his traffic demand. We assume that the customers are numbered based on their arriving order while t_i denotes the time when the customer started to use the network. Accordingly, the cost of customer i in case of the Trigger policy is

$$c_i^l = C(\max_{t \le t_i} \sum_{j \in \{N|j \le i\}} x_j^l(t)) - C(\max_{t \le t_i} \sum_{j \in \{N|j < i\}} x_j^l(t_i)) \tag{10}$$

The main drawbacks of Trigger are: a) it assigns cost only to the customer whose traffic trigger upgrades and 0 to everyone else, therefore order of arrival can have a huge impact on the costs attributed to a customer; and b) it is difficult to compute Trigger since it requires extensive historical data on the order of customer arrival and traffic build up.

- **Shapley.** The Shapley cost sharing policy lies between the two above presented extremes; the Aggregate-Peak-Device and Trigger policies. It assigns to customers partial liability for upgrades, thereby avoiding the all-or-nothing assignments of Triggers. Therefore it is less strict than Trigger but more strict than Aggregate-Peak-Device since it assigns "averaged" liabilities rather than proportional liabilities based on a single time interval when a device peaks.

  The main advantage of the Shapley over the Aggregate-Peak-Device policy is that its allocations are more stable than that of the Aggregate-Peak-Device policy in view of customer churn. For example, let us imagine that the aggregate peak traffic of a device is P and appears at t_1. We also assume that the device at time t_2 has load $P - \epsilon$. Now let us suppose that customer X is responsible for 90% of P at t_1 and 1% of $P - \epsilon$ at t_2. Then if a small 2ϵ customer leaves from P at t_1 then the peak will move to t_2 and X will go from paying 90% to paying only 1% after a tiny 2ϵ perturbation of the aggregate traffic. On the contrary, the Shapley policy is aware of such situations as it takes into account all the local maxima of the aggregate traffic in quantifying the costs of the customers.

  Under the Shapley policy, the cost of each customer is proportional to its average marginal contribution to the device's total cost. Particularly, let us consider all the possible $S \subset N$ subsets (coalitions) of the customers who utilize resources of the network device l. The cost of coalition S depends on the aggregate traffic volume of the participants, *i.e.*, it is equal to the cost of a network device that has sufficient capacity:

$$v^l(S) = C\left(\max_{t \in T} \sum_{j \in S} x_j^l(t)\right) \tag{11}$$

  Based on the v cost function of the coalitions, we compute the Shapley value of customer i as

$$\phi_i(v^l) = \frac{1}{N!} \sum_{\Pi \in S_N} \left(v^l(S(\Pi, i)) - v^l(S(\Pi, i) \setminus i)\right) \tag{12}$$

  where Π is a permutation of arrival order of the set N and $S(\Pi, i)$ denotes the set of players who arrived no later than i. The $(\phi_1(v), \ldots, \phi_N(v))$ Shapley values describe the fair distribution of costs in the case of the $S = N$ grand coalition. Fair in a way that it satisfies four intuitive fairness criteria [1, 13, 22]. We quantify the cost of customer i based on its Shapley value for the device l as

$$c_i^l = c^l \cdot \frac{\phi_i(v^l)}{\sum_{j \in N} \phi_j(v^l)} \tag{13}$$

  While computing the aggregate traffic volumes of the coalitions, we assume that the routing inside the network is static, *i.e.*, removing some traffic from the network device does not affect the traffic volumes of other customers (*e.g.*, the backbone operator does not apply load balancing mechanisms).

Illustrative example: We present the traffic patterns of two customers and the thresholds where the capacity of the device needs to be upgraded in Fig. 3. Customer 1 is liable for 53.3% and 87.5% of the cost of the device in case of the Aggregate-Peak-Device and Shapley policies. The peak of the aggregate traffic happens in a time step where the customers' traffic volumes are balanced. Although there are local maxima where the traffic of customer 2 is small, it is not considered by the Aggregate-Peak-Device policy. From a Shapley policy viewpoint, the traffic peak of customer 1 is too large to be transmitted with a lower-capacity device, *i.e.*, its traffic is mainly responsible for the total cost of the device. If we assume that customer 1 arrived first it causes 100% of the costs according to the Trigger policy because its peak needs a larger-capacity device whose leftover capacity can be used by customer 2 afterwards.

Customers can have both *device-* or *network-level* L-discrepancies, depending on whether we consider the costs

[2]Recall that upgrades generally involve large jumps that can leave substantial unallocated capacity.

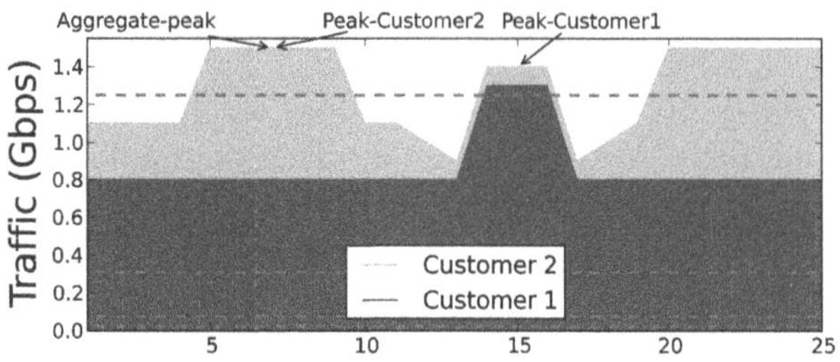

Figure 3: Illustrative example for L-discrepancies

of the customers on particular devices (*e.g.*, c_i^l) or on the aggregate (*e.g.*, $\sum_{l \in L} c_i^l$).

3.4 TCO-discrepancies

The final class of discrepancies is related to the *Total Cost of Ownership (TCO)* of different devices of the network. Due to the heterogeneous nature of the network—caused by the geographic and technological differences of its parts—the same traffic patterns imply diverse expenditures for the backbone operator on different devices. Therefore, additional discrepancies occur when we consider the TCO of the network in more detail. The following levels of TCO impact the costs and the discrepancies of the customers:

- **Pieces of costs.** Even if the capacity of two particular equipment are equal, their costs can vary significantly due to technology differences (newer vs. older generation), location (cost of shipping), differences in purchase price, *etc.*.
- **Point-of-Presence (PoP) costs.** The backbone network operator deals with diverse costs at each geographic location where it has a presence. The causes behind the varying costs include but are not limited to the following factors: energy (*e.g.*, the energy price in Germany can be twice as much as in the UK), facility costs (*e.g.*, the rental cost of office space in Hong Kong can be four times higher than in Germany [9]), taxation, and personnel costs.

Contrary to the former types of discrepancies, in the case of the TCO only network-level discrepancies exist. At the network level, where we summarize the costs of the customers across all the devices, additional discrepancies appear due to the diverse costs of the equipments.

Formally, we define the network-level TCO-discrepancy of customer i as

$$d\left(\sum_{l \in L} c_i^l, \sum_{l \in L} c^l \cdot \frac{\sum_{l \in L} e_i^l}{\sum_{l \in L} \sum_{i \in N} e_i^l}\right) \quad (14)$$

where the first term considers the diverse costs of the devices contrary to the second. e_i^l denotes the cost of customer i in case of device l assuming uniform cost across all the devices ($e^l = e^*, \forall l \in L$).

Illustrative example: If we consider the traffic pattern of the customers in Fig. 1 but we assume that the cost of the investigated device is five times more than before, *e.g.* it is located in a developing country, the costs of the customers also increase by a factor of 5. Accordingly, the TCO-discrepancy is 5 in the case of all the customers.

3.5 Discussion

The cost sharing methods introduced strike various trade-offs in terms of computational complexity, amount of required information, and accuracy. The Volume-Customer, Peak-Customer, Aggregate-Peak-Device, and 95Percentile-Customer policies require the least *computational resources* due to their sum, maximum, and percentile computations. The Trigger method determines when the device upgrade thresholds are surpassed. Finally, the Shapley policy has the largest complexity as it computes the costs based on the sub-coalitions of the customers. For computational reasons, we consider the 15 largest customers per network device in our evaluations to quantify the Shapley costs. On average, these customers cover 96% of the traffic of the devices.

In terms of the amount of *information*, all the policies except the Shapley and Trigger are similarly modest. They utilize single values for the historical usage (sum and maximum, respectively) and the current traffic volumes. However, the Shapley policy uses the whole time-series of traffic volumes to compute the costs. The information need of the Trigger policy is even larger as it needs both the historical traffic volumes of the customers and their arriving orders.

From a *fairness* point of view, the Aggregate-Peak-device policy is the absolute measure of fairness when the customer liability is proportional to the aggregate peak of devices (Section 3.3). Otherwise, the liability of the triggered network upgrade should be considered. The Shapley policy lies in between the two extreme policies because: a) unlike Trigger, it does not allocate the cost only to the late-comers but to the previous customers as well by considering all possible orders of arrivals; and b) unlike Aggregate-Peak-Device, it does not consider only the time instance of the peak utilization.

We postpone the analysis of the cost sharing policies' *accuracy* to Section 5 where we present a thorough investigation of the policies based on dataset-driven evaluations. Our comparative study has the following structure. We first compare the Aggregate-Peak-Device policy with other more practical, albeit less accurate policies. Then, we compare the Aggregate-Peak-Device policy with the Shapley policy and comment on how much error is introduced ignoring the local peaks.

4. DATASETS

We use several datasets from a tier-1 backbone network, which interconnects with other ISPs that it serves. In our dataset, the network consists of 26 Points of Presence (PoPs) and each customer connects to the network at one or more PoPs through one or more interfaces. Overall there are 590 ingress links, and each ingress link is used by exactly one customer. Internally, the backbone has 71 routers and 691 links, which are typically used by more than one customer. We collected detailed NetFlow-based statistics for each of the internal and ingress links including the traffic volumes to and from each customer on every link in the network. Such information allows us to assess which customer uses which component in the shared infrastructure and how it affects the load on each component.

The per-link and per-customer traffic statistics cover the period from 18 March 2012 to 10 April 2012, with a 2-hour granularity (*i.e.*, reporting volumes sent and received within 2 hours). We have two additional datasets containing time-series with a 5-min and 30-min granularity for one day and one week, respectively. The traffic aggregated over all ingress links peaks at around 1.35 *Tbps* in both inbound and outbound directions. Thus, without loss of generality, we utilize the time-series of the customers' incoming traffic.

The cost of a network link depends on the one hand on the capacity of the interface, *i.e.*, how much traffic it is capable of forwarding. On the other hand, the geographic location and the applied technology have an impact as well. Hardware costs, energy prices, deployment costs, and taxation, among others, contribute to the cost of a network device. Thereby, it is challenging to accurately quantify the cost of every single device.

To estimate the cost of the network links, we use the wholesale point-to-point transport price database of TeleGeography [29]. We stress that these are the prices of wholesale physical layer circuits, however, do not differ substantially from the actual cost of ownership. In our empirical analysis, we apply the prices of network links with different bandwidth, ranging from E-1 (2 *Mbps*) throughout STM-4 (622 *Mbps*) and 2.5G waves to 40G waves (40000 *Mbps*). The costs of these links define a step function for the network expenditures. Exact values can be provided to interested parties if confidentiality requirements are met. As future work, we intend to extend our analysis using more detailed expenditure datasets that contains information on the OPEX costs related to for example power supply, hosting centers, *etc.*.

5. DATA-DRIVEN EVALUATION

In this section we use the datasets introduced in Section 4 to evaluate the various discrepancies discussed in Section 3. In case of the F-, M-, and L-discrepancies, we use a uniform cost function for the network devices to focus on the specific properties of cost-sharing.

5.1 F-discrepancies

We start by looking at the effect of the function applied to the traffic of a customer.

5.1.1 Device-level F-discrepancies

To showcase the intricacies of F-discrepancies we start with an example based on a backbone link between two major PoPs in Europe. The monthly cost of this link is $2163. In Fig. 4 we plot the amount of this cost attributed to each one of the 10 largest customers according to the four different policies detailed in Section 3.1. The F-discrepancy, *i.e.*, the ratio of the cost computed by the Aggregate-Peak-Device policy and the cost computed by the simpler policy X∈ [Volume-Customer, 95Percentile-Customer, Peak-Customer] is as high as 2.36 for customer 4 in this example. This particular customer impacts the aggregate peak of the device disproportionally more than the other customers when we focus on the traffic volumes of the customers. For several other customers the F-discrepancies are much milder, *i.e.*, the different cost-sharing policies are more or less in agreement.

We now look at F-discrepancies across all customers and all links in our dataset. In Fig. 5, we plot the the F-discrepancies for the three simpler policies and we summarize the main statistics in Table 1. The results show generally high F-discrepancies. For example, 60% of the customers are assigned 25% higher or lower cost than the

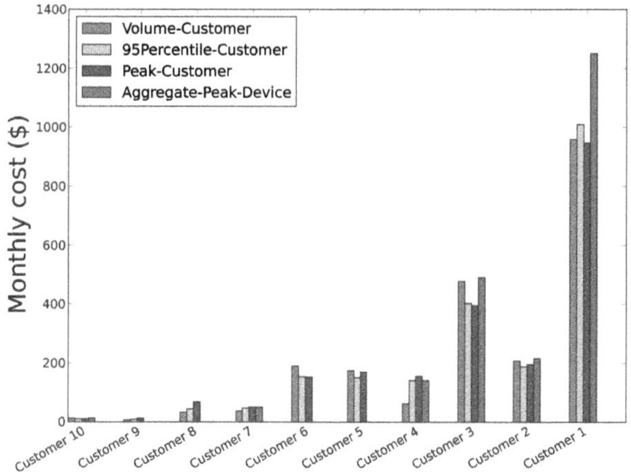

Figure 4: Device-level cost of customers for varying cost-sharing policies. Link between two European PoPs.

Method	>25%	95th percentile	median
Volume-Customer	0.592	63.07	1.372
Peak-Customer	0.520	89.55	1.263
95Percentile-Customer	0.508	80.79	1.259

Table 1: Device-level F-discrepancies compared to the Aggregate-Peak-Device policy.

real one they inflict according to Aggregate-Peak-Device. F-discrepancies are particularly high for Volume-Customer and smaller for Peak-Customer and 95Percentile-Customer. The last two policies are sensitive to peaks, albeit those of particular customers instead of peaks of the aggregate traffic on the device. Volume-Customer is even less accurate since it is not looking at any peaks, but only at aggregate volume over a longer time scale.

One may expect that there is a strong correlation between the traffic volumes and the discrepancies of the policies. For example, the other policies may always overestimate the cost of customers, compared to the Aggregate-Peak-Device, if the customers inject a large amount of traffic. However, our results refute this as we illustrate in Fig. 6, where we present the F-discrepancies as a function of the traffic volumes.

To illustrate the differences between the policies, Fig. 7 depicts a portion of the time-series of a link where a large F-discrepancy (3.07) exists between the Volume-Customer and the Aggregate-Peak-Device policies. The figure shows the traffic pattern of the customer with the large F-discrepancy and the aggregate traffic pattern of the other customers. The traffic of the customer is marginal compared to the traffic of the others, yielding a very low Volume-Customer cost. However during the peak, the customer with the large discrepancy contributes a significant portion to the aggregate traffic, thereby inducing a 3.07 times higher Aggregate-Peak-Device than Volume-Customer cost.

Summary and implications: In the case of device-level discrepancies, numerous and substantial F-discrepancies exist. This implies that backbone operators should apply the Aggregate-Peak-Device policy for computing the costs in case of a single device instead of the simpler policies.

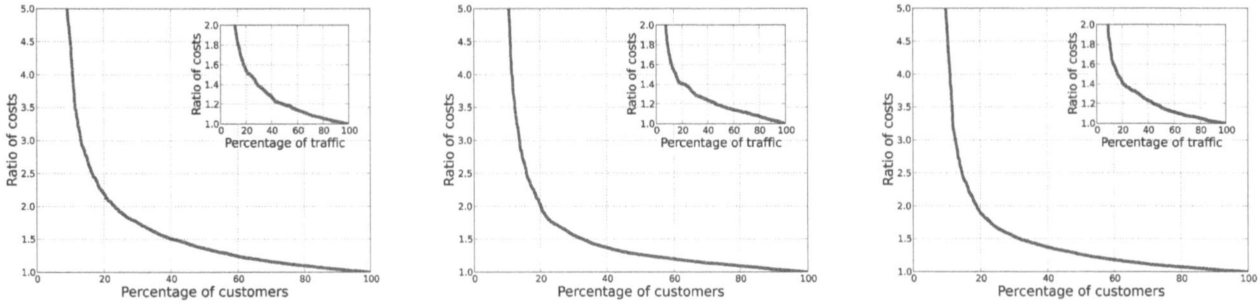

(a) Volume-Customer (b) Peak-Customer (c) 95Percentile-Customer

Figure 5: Distribution of the device-level F-discrepancies between the simpler cost-sharing policies and the Aggregate-Peak-Device policy. Distributions are based on the percentage of the customers and the traffic (insets). All the policies have high F-discrepancies, especially the F-discrepancies of the Volume-Customer policy are large.

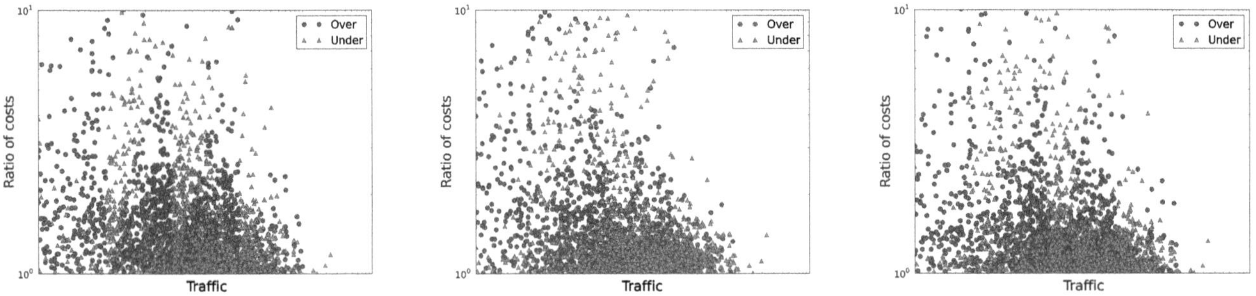

(a) Volume-Customer (b) Peak-Customer (c) 95Percentile-Customer

Figure 6: There does not exist a strong correlation between the traffic volumes and the discrepancies of the policies. Moreover, there is no significant difference between the over- and under-estimation of the costs. The axes are logarithmically scaled.

5.1.2 Network-level F-discrepancies

We now examine F-discrepancies in the context of the entire network. We do this by summing the costs of a customer over all the network's devices. We present the relative aggregate costs of the 10 largest customers in Fig. 8; we consider the largest cost as the baseline. We present the F-discrepancies of the policies in Table 2. The results reveal that F-discrepancies at the network-level are much smaller than at the device-level. For example, the network-level median F-discrepancies are ~40% less than the device-level ones. This is because in large networks positive and negative cost differences at each device cancel each other out, thus the cost predictions of the simpler policies become more aligned.

Summary and implications: F-discrepancies although important for individual links or small networks tend to become less significant for larger networks. Thus, backbone operators can use simpler policies than the Aggregate-Peak-Device without running a high risk of miscalculating the costs of the customers if they are just interested in the aggregate costs of the customers.

Method	>25%	95th percentile	median
Volume-Customer	0.5	3.141	1.251
Peak-Customer	0.35	12.71	1.151
95Percentile-Customer	0.37	5.046	1.181

Table 2: Network-level F-discrepancies compared to the Aggregate-Peak-Device policy.

5.2 M-discrepancies

Next we compute the discrepancy between the customer's network-level cost derived by (1) metering its traffic at its ingress links (Customer-Ingress or CI) and (2) metering its traffic on each device that the customer uses (Customer-per-Device or CD). All of the policies result in high M-discrepancies (ratios as high as 34) as summarized in Table 3.

Up to this point, we analyzed the impact of different discrepancies separately. Next, we quantify the joint effect of F-discrepancies and M-discrepancies, *i.e.*, how large can the difference be between the most and the least accurate combination of function and metering schemes. We do this by comparing the network-level costs of customers under the Volume-Customer+CI, Volume-Customer+CD, and

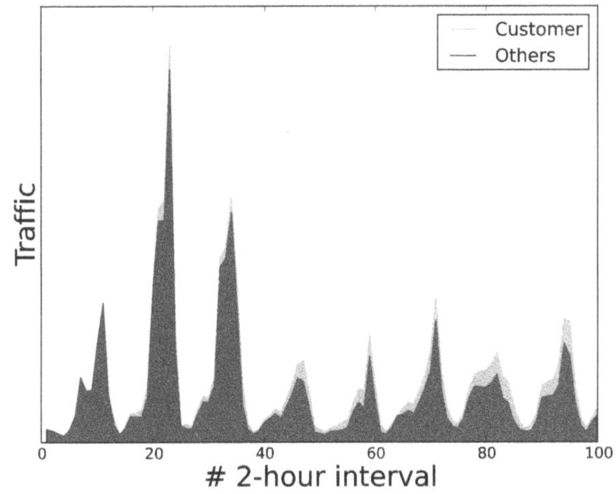

Figure 7: Time-series of the traffic of a customer with a large (3.07) F-discrepancy on a single link. Volume-Customer vs. Aggregate-Peak-Device policy.

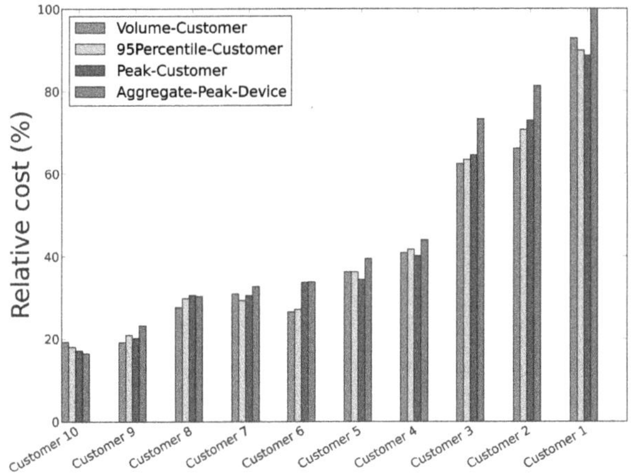

Figure 8: Aggregate relative costs of the 10 largest customers; comparison normalized by the largest cost.

Aggregate-Peak-Device+CI policies with the nominally accurate one, namely, the Aggregate-Peak-Device+CD policy. The results are summarized in Table 4. The Volume-Customer policy has the smallest M-discrepancy, that is, the median ratio of the Customer-Ingress and the Customer-per-Device costs is 1.5. On the contrary, the Aggregate-Peak-Device policy yields the largest M-discrepancies. The reason behind this is twofold. First, when metering traffic at the ingress links, traffic that results in peaks at individual links does not result in peaks of the aggregate ingress traffic. Second, under Customer-Ingress, the Aggregate-Peak-Device policy takes into account only the time interval with the largest aggregate traffic while the peaks of the internal devices may happen in other time intervals neglected by the Aggregate-Peak-Device+CI policy. We observe that under the Aggregate-Peak-Device+CI combination, the costs diverge by at least 25% for 76% of the customers. In addition we note that under the Volume-Customer+CI policy and metering, the discrepancy can be as high as 32.

Method	>25%	95th pct	median
Volume-Customer	0.695	34.53	1.543
Peak-Customer	0.752	32.34	1.738
95Percentile-Customer	0.750	19.10	1.630
Aggregate-Peak-Device	0.763	28.52	1.801

Table 3: Network-level M-discrepancies of the cost-sharing policies. Comparison of the Customer-Ingress and the Customer-per-Device costs of the customers.

Method	>25%	95th pct	median
Volume-Customer+CI	0.760	32.69	1.816
Aggregate-Peak-Device+CI	0.763	28.52	1.801
Volume-Customer+CD	0.500	3.141	1.251
Aggregate-Peak-Device+CD	0.0	1.0	1.0

Table 4: Discrepancies with the Aggregate-Peak-Device policy using Customer-per-Device (real traffic) metering (CI – Customer-Ingress, CD – Customer-per-Device).

Summary and implications: The level at which the backbone operator meters the traffic of the customers has a large impact on the quantified costs. Based on the medians, the most and the least accurate policies diverge by 80%. Therefore, the backbone operators should apply sophisticated metering strategies (*e.g.*, network-wide deployment of NetFlow-capable traffic monitoring devices) in order to accurately quantify the costs of the customers. Moreover, the simple methods are no longer aligned with the real cost of the customers (*i.e.*, with the Aggregate-Peak-Customer policy) if the traffic is metered on the ingress links. From an accuracy point of view, this implies that backbone operators should reconsider the pricing of IP transit services, which they currently price based on simpler policies such as the 95Percentile one.

5.3 L-discrepancies

Next, we focus on the L-discrepancies. Out of the three policies described in Section 3.3, one, the Trigger policy, requires historic information on customer arrival events as well as customer traffic information on long time scales that relate to network upgrade events. Since we do not have full historic information on all the links, we approximate the Trigger policy as follows. We assume for each customer he was the last one arriving to the network. Then we compute the marginal cost contribution of the customer as the actual cost of the device minus the cost of the device without the traffic of the customer. Formally, we quantify the marginal contribution of customer i as:

$$m_i^l = C\left(\max_{t\in T}\sum_{j\in N} x_j^l(t)\right) - C\left(\max_{t\in T}\sum_{j\in N\setminus\{i\}} x_j^l(t)\right) \quad (15)$$

Finally, we allocate the cost of the device to the customers in proportion to their marginal contributions:

$$c_i^l = c^l \cdot \frac{m_i^l}{\sum_{j\in N} m_j^l} \quad (16)$$

In the following, we refer to this method as Trigger*.

Method	>25%	95th percentile	median
Shapley	0.674	472.4	1.497
Trigger*	0.861	1188	2.475

Table 5: Device-level L-discrepancies compared to the Aggregate-Peak-Device policy.

5.3.1 Device-level L-discrepancies

We present the L-discrepancies in Table 5 by computing the ratio between X∈ [Trigger*,Shapley] and the Aggregate-Peak-Device policy. L-discrepancies are quite high (ratios up to 1180) pointing to the fact that liability can bias significantly the cost-sharing picture that a telco has. For example, if we compute costs based on the Trigger* and based on the Aggregate-Peak-Device policy, the gap between the two is very large: in more than 85% of the cases the L-discrepancy is larger than 25%. The Trigger* policy allocates the cost in a full-liability fashion, while the Aggregate-Peak-Device policy applies a proportional liability scheme. Our empirical results confirm that the Shapley policy, which estimates the customers' average contribution to the capacity upgrade considering every possible arriving order, lies in between these two extremes. Again, the difference between the costs of the Shapley and the Aggregate-Peak-Device policy is substantial: the median ratio of the costs is 1.5; however, in some cases the ratio can be larger than 400.

We further examine the L-discrepancy between the Aggregate-Peak-Device and the Shapley policies. In Fig. 9 we plot the L-discrepancies for all customers and all links as a function of the traffic volumes, which the customers had on the particular device in the analyzed time period. The magnitude of the L-discrepancy is inversely proportional to the traffic volumes. Thus, smaller customers tend to have larger L-discrepancies. Small customers usually do not significantly influence the peak utilization of the devices, *i.e.*, they have some marginal share of the costs. However, they may trigger a capacity upgrade of the link and therefore have a larger share of the costs because of the link's step-based cost function. The figure also reveals that whether the Shapley policy over- or under-estimates the Aggregate-Peak-Device policy' costs is not significantly influenced by the customers' traffic volume or by the magnitude of their L-discrepancies.

We present in Fig. 10 a part of the time-series of a customer with a large L-discrepancy (3.25) along with the aggregate time-series of the other customers who utilize the same link. The dashed horizontal lines denote the traffic volumes where the capacity of the link needs to be upgraded. The traffic of the customer is small enough to be transmitted over a link with lower capacity. However, the traffic of the other customers pushes the link to have larger capacity and thus larger cost. The Shapley policy considers this fact when it computes the average marginal contribution of the customer. As a result, the cost of the customer is less than if we compute it based solely on time of the largest utilization of the device. On the contrary, the Aggregate-Peak-Customer focuses only on the time-interval when the link has its aggregate peak. The particular customer has significant share of the aggregate peak and thus of the cost of the link according to the Aggregate-Peak-Customer. This however masks who is responsible for the link's larger capacity. However, this single time-interval masks the fact that the specific customer is not responsible for the link's needing a larger capacity.

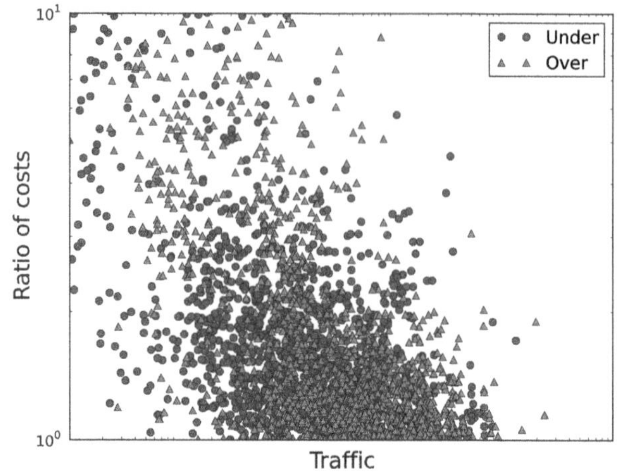

Figure 9: Device-level L-discrepancies as a function of the traffic volumes. The Shapley policy both over- or underestimates the Aggregate-Peak-Device policy.

Method	>25%	95th percentile	median
Shapley	0.54	179.3	1.316
Trigger*	0.771	231.2	1.767

Table 6: Network-level L-discrepancies compared to the Aggregate-Peak-Device policy.

5.3.2 Network-level L-discrepancies

We show the network-level L-discrepancies in Table 6. At the network level, the number and the magnitude of the L-discrepancies is smaller than at the device level. Nevertheless, for more than 50% of the customers the costs are off by at least 25%. The median L-discrepancies of the policies are notable too, *e.g.*, 1.3 under the Shapley policy.

Summary and implications: The liability of network upgrades plays an important role in the quantification of the costs of customers in backbone networks. The median value of L-discrepancies is at least 1.3 while the L-discrepancies impact more than half of the customers with at least 25%. The implication of the results is that if the backbone network is not built in one-shot but is rather organically grown and upgraded then the Aggregate-Peak-Customer policy may induce cross-subsidization problems: customers may be accounted for costs of upgrades for which they are not liable (or not in that degree). From a customer point of view, this cross-subsidization may not be tolerated in a long-run given the competitive environment of the backbone networks. That is the customers may select other backbone network operator where they are not liable for the costs of others. From the operator point of view, the large L-discrepancies dictate that he needs to take them under serious consideration. If it is anticipated that the market for backbone services will be healthy, the operator should choose the Aggregate-Peak-Device policy. If however, he expects difficulties in selling its capacity, our results indicate that Shapley should be the policy of choice.

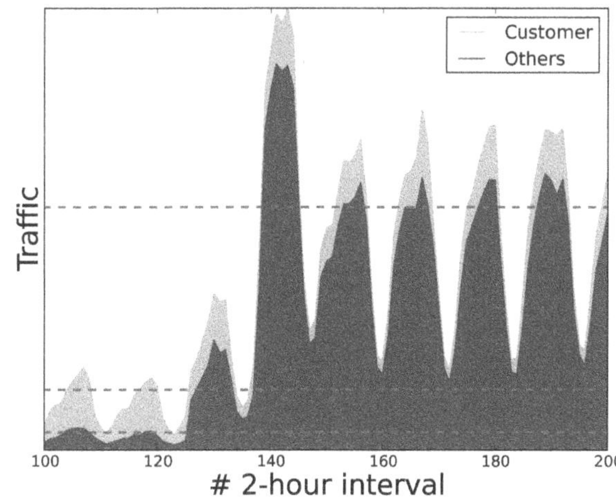

Figure 10: Time-series of a customer with large (3.25) L-discrepancy (Shapley vs. Aggregate-Peak-Device policy). The dashed lines represent the traffic volumes where the capacity of the link needs to be upgraded.

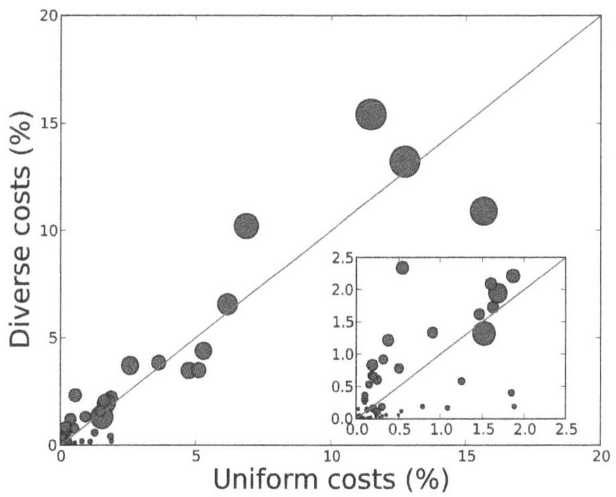

Figure 11: The customers' total costs for the uniform and diverse link costs using the Aggregate-Peak-Device cost-sharing policy; the size of the circles is proportional to the aggregate traffic volume of the customers.

Method	>25%	95th percentile	median
Volume-Customer	0.830	961.1	4.305
Peak-Customer	0.802	933.1	4.187
95Percentile-Customer	0.817	922.4	4.079
Aggregate-Peak-Device	0.840	862.1	4.019
Shapley	0.830	761.1	3.460

Table 7: Network-level TCO-discrepancies, *i.e.*, the costs of the customers based on uniform vs. diverse link costs

5.4 TCO-discrepancies

In this section we take into account that our dataset contains a geographically distributed set of links with diverse costs as we introduced in Section 4. We compute the TCO-discrepancies by computing the ratio between the customers' costs given links with uniform and diverse costs. In Fig. 11 we illustrate the TCO-discrepancies under the Aggregate-Peak-Device policy. Each customer is affected by the TCO-discrepancies. The difference between the two costs can be as high as 5% of the cost of the entire network.

We report the quantified TCO-discrepancies of five policies in Table 7. The results show generally extreme TCO-discrepancies; some customers have TCO-discrepancies as high as 900. In addition, 80% of the customers are assigned 25% higher or lower cost when the diverse costs of the links is considered. The Shapley value is affected the least based on the medians of the TCO-discrepancies.

Summary and implications: TCO-discrepancies have a very large impact on the costs of the customers. The median ratio of the customers' costs is as high as a factor of four. Similar to the L-discrepancies, cross-subsidization problems arise if the impact of TCO differences is neglected. Backbone operators are aware of the fact that different parts of their network have different TCOs. The implication of our results is that this diversity should also be reflected in the quantification of the customers' costs— and eventually in the tariffs too, based on which customers are charged.

Method	>25%	Median
Peak-Customer (5-min)	0.3	1.157
Peak-Customer (30-min)	0.3	1.157
Peak-Customer (2-hour)	0.35	1.151
Volume-Customer (5-min)	0.49	1.261
Volume-Customer (30-min)	0.51	1.261
Volume-Customer (2-hour)	0.50	1.251
95Percentile-Customer (5-min)	0.27	1.186
95Percentile-Customer (30-min)	0.4	1.186
95Percentile-Customer (2-hour)	0.37	1.181
Shapley (5-min)	0.56	1.359
Shapley (30-min)	0.54	1.359
Shapley (2-hour)	0.54	1.316

Table 8: The impact of time intervals on the network-level discrepancies. The policies are compared to the Aggregate-Peak-Device policy for the same time interval.

5.5 Sensitivity analysis

We investigate the robustness of the cost-sharing policies from two additional angles. First, we quantify the costs of the customers for time-series with 5-minute, 30-minute, and 2-hour intervals. We compare the network-level costs of the methods to the Aggregate-Peak-Device policy in Table 8, where the two policies are compared based on the same time interval. The results reveal that all the policies are affected equally, *i.e.*, the duration of the time-interval does not introduce additional discrepancies among the schemes. For example, the median ratios of the costs based on the Volume-Customer and the Aggregate-Peak-Device policies are 1.261, 1.261, and 1.251 in the case of the datasets with 5-minute, 30-minute, and 2-hour intervals, respectively.

Second, backbone operators apply different utilization thresholds at which they upgrade the capacity of their devices. We compute the costs of the customers in the case

Upgrade policy	>25%	95th percentile	Median
40%	0.642	512.5	1.453
50%	0.673	472.4	1.497
60%	0.689	451.3	1.542

Table 9: Network-level discrepancy for varying network upgrade thresholds (Aggregate-Peak-Device vs. Shapley policy).

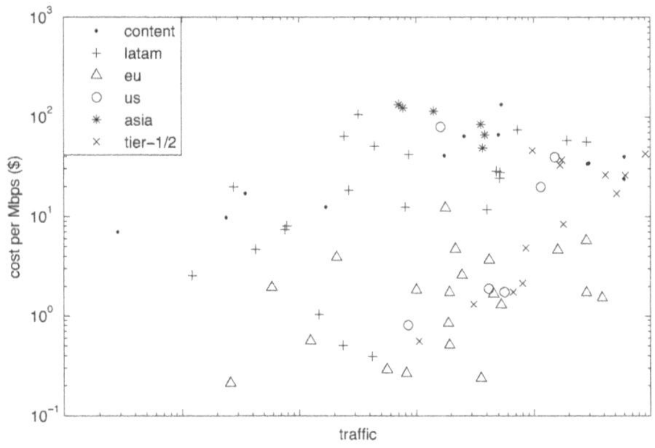

Figure 12: Cost per $Mbps$ for different types of customers.

of 40%, 50%, and 60% threshold values and quantify the ratio between the customers' costs based on the Aggregate-Peak-Device and the Shapley policies (Table 9). Similar to the time intervals, the impact of the network upgrade policy is modest. The median ratio of the costs increases only by 0.1 if the upgrade threshold is increased from 40% to 60%.

Summary and implications: Neither the time-intervals, over which we aggregate the traffic of the customers, nor the upgrade policy, which is determined by the utilization level when the capacity of a device is upgraded, have a significant impact on the discrepancies between the different cost-sharing policies.

5.6 Costs in different type of customers

We next dive deeper into the costs and focus on the different types of the customers present in our datasets. In Fig. 12 we depict the cost per $Mbps$ and the peak data rate for all customers classified into six different types: content ISPs, tier 1/2 ISPs, and EU, Latin American, US and Asian access providers. We consider the network-level costs quantified based on the Aggregate-Peak-Device policy. The figure reveals the following three main properties of the costs. First, the cost per $Mbps$ of individual customers covers a wide range of several orders of magnitude. Second, even within a single type of customer, one can expect large variability of cost per $Mbps$ though there is a tendency for lower costs for the EU/US ISPs, compared to the LatAM and Asian ones. This is a consequence of the fact that the EU/US ISPs send most of their traffic to EU/US and thus utilize lower-cost infrastructure. Finally, content providers fall consistently in the range of 'expensive' customers (over 10$ per $Mbps$) in terms of the cost per $Mbps$ served. This indicates that a large fraction of their traffic crosses expensive intercontinental links. We were able to justify this assumption based raw data in our datasets.

6. RELATED WORK

We refer to the textbook of Courcoubetis and Weber [8] for a thorough treatment of pricing in communication networks. A workshop version preceded this work [14] where we focused on the different cost-sharing policies that can be applied in backbone networks. Our current work extends that preliminary work with the following: a) we propose a methodology for cost-sharing in backbone networks and introduce the different types of discrepancies; b) we evaluate the liability facet of the cost-sharing domain; and c) we utilize a much richer dataset that describes the traffic patterns of a backbone network with three-times more links.

Several studies investigated how to reduce the transit costs including ISP peering [2, 11, 10], CDNs [24], P2P localization [6], and traffic smoothing [20]. Dimitropoulos et al. [12] presented a comprehensive analysis of the 95th percentile pricing. A proposal by Laoutaris et al. [16, 15] showed how traffic can be transferred in the network without increasing the 95th percentile of the customers. A recent proposal by Stanojevic et al. [27] proposes to the customers of transit providers to form a coalition to reduce their transit costs. Valancius et al. [30] show that a small number of pricing tiers are enough to extract close-to-optimal efficiency in the transit provider. In our work we augment the price efficiency analysis of [30] with a methodology that quantifies how individual customers affect the cost of running the network that demonstrate the complex nature of the customers' costs in the real-world networks.

Motiwala [21] et al. developed a cost model that operators can use to evaluate the costs of their routing and peering decisions. Their study is complementary to ours, as we can use their model to assess the CAPEX and OPEX cost of the network instead of using our step function (Section 3). A difference is that we primarily focus on how the cost can be more fairly and accurately distributed among the customers of an operator.

The net neutrality debate is in many ways related to the question of who is responsible for the costs in the network [7], and our work contributes towards better understanding of such costs.

Due to the desirable fairness properties [1, 13, 22] of the Shapley value [25], recent studies proposed pricing and cost sharing mechanisms using Shapley values. Briscoe [3, 4] motivates the usage of mechanisms that share the costs of the users fairly as a way to reduce widely known cross-subsidization[3] of the common infrastructure that often happens in the communication networks [5]. Cooperative approaches for cost sharing are investigated in case of interdomain routing [19, 26] and IP multicast [1, 13]. Ma et al. [17, 18] presented a fair revenue sharing method for ISPs that quantifies the importance of each ISP in the Internet ecosystem. The work of Stanojevic et al. [28] is the closest to ours. The authors empirically investigated the temporal usage effects using the Shapley and the 95Percentile-Customer method. This work is different in several ways: a) we focus on the costs of the large customers of a backbone network with geographically diverse links; b) we study additional cost

[3]The phenomenon in which a small set of customers is subsidized by a large fraction of other customers of the service.

sharing policies and aspects such as liability and TCO; and c) we study a more detailed cost and traffic dataset.

7. CONCLUSIONS

With the increasing traffic volumes, intense market competition, and technological barriers, most commercial backbone operators are faced with the challenge of maintaining healthy profit margins. Providing services to their customers, which are often ISPs themselves, carries significant maintenance and upgrade costs. Attributing these costs to individual customers is critical for ensuring smooth operations of the backbone network as well as offering fair tariffs to customers. However, the process of quantifying the cost contribution of customers in a distributed backbone network is far from simple involving the complex interaction of many factors ranging from temporal/spatial characteristics of the customers and non-linear cost-capacity relationships to measurement infrastructure issues and high variability of the component costs.

In this paper, we make a step towards understanding the relationship between several cost-sharing policies and how they affect the individual customers. While our analysis reveals several important properties of the backbone network cost-sharing, there are many questions that remain open. For example, how can one utilize the global view of cost allocation per customer to create simple yet profitable tariffs? Based on our findings, such tariffs should include device-level expenditures and measurements to assure its accuracy. Another open research question is how tariffs inspired by the presented cost sharing policies would alter the behavior of the customers, *i.e.*, their traffic patterns to minimize their expenditures. Additionally, it would be interesting to study if our observed properties of the cost-sharing could be mapped to other types of networks that are spatially less diverse but serve a more populous customer base, such as the residential broadband or 3G access networks.

Acknowledgement

We would like to thank Juan Manuel Ortigosa, Emilio Sepulveda, and Gabriel Bonilha from Telefonica for their valuable insights. This work and its dissemination efforts have been supported in part by the ENVISION FP7 project of the European Union.

8. REFERENCES

[1] Aaron Archer, Joan Feigenbaum, Arvind Krishnamurthy, Rahul Sami, and Scott Shenker. Approximation and collusion in multicast cost sharing. *Games and Economic Behavior*, 47(1):36 – 71, 2004.

[2] Brice Augustin, Balachander Krishnamurthy, and Walter Willinger. Ixps: mapped? In *Proceedings of the 9th ACM SIGCOMM conference on Internet measurement conference*, IMC '09, pages 336–349, New York, NY, USA, 2009. ACM.

[3] Bob Briscoe. Flow rate fairness: dismantling a religion. *SIGCOMM Comput. Commun. Rev.*, 37(2):63–74, 2007.

[4] Bob Briscoe. A Fairer, Faster Internet. *IEEE Spectrum*, 45(12):42–47, 2008.

[5] Kenjiro Cho, Kensuke Fukuda, Hiroshi Esaki, and Akira Kato. The impact and implications of the growth in residential user-to-user traffic. SIGCOMM '06, pages 207–218, New York, NY, USA, 2006. ACM.

[6] David R. Choffnes and Fabián E. Bustamante. Taming the torrent: a practical approach to reducing cross-isp traffic in peer-to-peer systems. In *Proceedings of the ACM SIGCOMM 2008 conference on Data communication*, SIGCOMM '08, pages 363–374, New York, NY, USA, 2008. ACM.

[7] kc claffy. "network neutrality": the meme, its cost, its future. *SIGCOMM Comput. Commun. Rev.*, 41(5):44–45.

[8] C. Courcoubetis and R. Weber. *Pricing and Communications Networks*. John Wiley & Sons, Ltd, 2003.

[9] Cushman & Wakefield. Office Space Across the World, 2012.

[10] A. Dhamdhere, C. Dovrolis, and P. Francois. A Value-based Framework for Internet Peering Agreements. In *Teletraffic Congress (ITC), 2010 22nd International*, 2010.

[11] Amogh Dhamdhere and Constantine Dovrolis. The internet is flat: modeling the transition from a transit hierarchy to a peering mesh. In *Proceedings of the 6th International COnference*, Co-NEXT '10, pages 21:1–21:12, New York, NY, USA, 2010. ACM.

[12] Xenofontas Dimitropoulos, Paul Hurley, Andreas Kind, and Marc Stoecklin. On the 95-percentile billing method. In Sue Moon, Renata Teixeira, and Steve Uhlig, editors, *Passive and Active Network Measurement*, volume 5448 of *Lecture Notes in Computer Science*, pages 207–216. Springer Berlin, Heidelberg, 2009.

[13] Joan Feigenbaum, Christos H. Papadimitriou, and Scott Shenker. Sharing the cost of multicast transmissions. *Journal of Computer and System Sciences*, 63(1):21 – 41, 2001.

[14] L. Gyarmati, M. Sirivianos, and N. Laoutaris. Simplicity vs Precision: Sharing the Cost of Backbone Networks. In *NetEcon 2012 - Seventh Workshop on the Economics of Networks, Systems, and Computation*, 2012.

[15] Nikolaos Laoutaris, Michael Sirivianos, Xiaoyuan Yang, and Pablo Rodriguez. Inter-datacenter bulk transfers with netstitcher. In *Proceedings of the ACM SIGCOMM 2011 conference*, SIGCOMM '11, pages 74–85, New York, NY, USA, 2011. ACM.

[16] Nikolaos Laoutaris, Georgios Smaragdakis, Pablo Rodriguez, and Ravi Sundaram. Delay tolerant bulk data transfers on the internet. In *Proceedings of the eleventh international joint conference on Measurement and modeling of computer systems*, SIGMETRICS '09, pages 229–238, New York, NY, USA, 2009. ACM.

[17] Richard T. B. Ma, Dah ming Chiu, John C. S. Lui, Vishal Misra, and Dan Rubenstein. Internet economics: the use of shapley value for isp settlement. In *Proceedings of the 2007 ACM CoNEXT conference*, CoNEXT '07, pages 6:1–6:12, New York, NY, USA, 2007. ACM.

[18] Richard T. B. Ma, Dah-ming Chiu, John C. S. Lui, Vishal Misra, and Dan Rubenstein. On cooperative settlement between content, transit and eyeball

internet service providers. In *Proceedings of the 2008 ACM CoNEXT Conference*, CoNEXT '08, pages 7:1–7:12, New York, NY, USA, 2008. ACM.

[19] Ratul Mahajan, David Wetherall, and Thomas Anderson. Negotiation-based routing between neighboring isps. In *Proceedings of the 2nd conference on Symposium on Networked Systems Design & Implementation - Volume 2*, NSDI'05, pages 29–42, Berkeley, CA, USA, 2005. USENIX Association.

[20] M. Marcon, M. Dischinger, K.P. Gummadi, and A. Vahdat. The Local and Global effects of Traffic Shaping in the Internet. In *Third International Conference on Communication Systems and Networks (COMSNETS)*, 2011.

[21] Murtaza Motiwala, Amogh Dhamdhere, Nick Feamster, and Anukool Lakhina. Towards a cost model for network traffic. *SIGCOMM Comput. Commun. Rev.*, 42(1):54–60.

[22] HervĂŠ Moulin and Scott Shenker. Strategyproof sharing of submodular costs:budget balance versus efficiency. *Economic Theory*, 18:511–533, 2001. 10.1007/PL00004200.

[23] W. B. Norton. *The Internet Peering Playbook: Connecting to the Core of the Internet.* DrPeering Press, 2012.

[24] L. Qiu, V.N. Padmanabhan, and G.M. Voelker. On the Placement of Web Server Replicas. In *IEEE INFOCOM*, pages 1587–1596, 2001.

[25] L. S. Shapley. A value for n-person games. *Annals of Mathematical Studies*, 1953.

[26] Gireesh Shrimali, Aditya Akella, and Almir Mutapcic. Cooperative interdomain traffic engineering using nash bargaining and decomposition. *IEEE/ACM Trans. Netw.*, 18(2):341–352, April 2010.

[27] Rade Stanojevic, Ignacio Castro, and Sergey Gorinsky. Cipt: using tuangou to reduce ip transit costs. In *Proceedings of the Seventh COnference on emerging Networking EXperiments and Technologies*, CoNEXT '11, pages 17:1–17:12, New York, NY, USA, 2011. ACM.

[28] Rade Stanojevic, Nikolaos Laoutaris, and Pablo Rodriguez. On economic heavy hitters: shapley value analysis of 95th-percentile pricing. In *Proceedings of the 10th ACM SIGCOMM conference on Internet measurement*, IMC '10, pages 75–80, New York, NY, USA, 2010. ACM.

[29] TeleGeography. Wholesale IP transit price database, `http://www.telegeography.com/`.

[30] Vytautas Valancius, Cristian Lumezanu, Nick Feamster, Ramesh Johari, and Vijay V. Vazirani. How many tiers?: pricing in the internet transit market. In *Proceedings of the ACM SIGCOMM 2011 conference*, SIGCOMM '11, pages 194–205, New York, NY, USA, 2011. ACM.

Content Delivery and the Natural Evolution of DNS

Remote DNS Trends, Performance Issues and Alternative Solutions

John S. Otto Mario A. Sánchez John P. Rula Fabián E. Bustamante
Northwestern University
{jotto,msanchez,john.rula,fabianb}@eecs.northwestern.edu

ABSTRACT

Content Delivery Networks (CDNs) rely on the Domain Name System (DNS) for replica server selection. DNS-based server selection builds on the assumption that, in the absence of information about the client's actual network location, the location of a client's DNS resolver provides a good approximation. The recent growth of remote DNS services breaks this assumption and can negatively impact client's web performance.

In this paper, we assess the end-to-end impact of using remote DNS services on CDN performance and present the first evaluation of an industry-proposed solution to the problem. We find that remote DNS usage can indeed significantly impact client's web performance and that the proposed solution, if available, can effectively address the problem for most clients. Considering the performance cost of remote DNS usage and the limited adoption base of the industry-proposed solution, we present and evaluate an alternative approach, *Direct Resolution*, to readily obtain comparable performance improvements without requiring CDN or DNS participation.

Categories and Subject Descriptors

C.2.4 [**Communication Networks**]: Distributed Systems—*Distributed applications*; C.2.5 [**Communication Networks**]: Local and Wide-Area Networks—*Internet*; C.4 [**Performance of Systems**]: Measurement techniques

General Terms

Experimentation, Measurement, Performance

Keywords

CDN, Content distribution, DNS, DNS extension, Internet, measurement

IMC'12, November 14–16, 2012, Boston, Massachusetts, USA.

1. INTRODUCTION

Content Delivery Networks (CDNs) replicate content across geographically distributed sets of servers and redirect clients to nearby replicas to reduce web access time. Since first emerging in the mid 1990s, CDNs have become the primary vehicle for distributing content over the Internet. Today, 74% of the top 1,000 sites and 89% of their pageviews[1] use CDNs to deliver content to clients (Fig. 2). Over the last decade the CDN industry has grown to include a large and diverse set of over 49 companies including regional focused ones (e.g. Accelia) and global services such as Akamai and Level3.[2]

CDNs rely on the Domain Name System (DNS) for both dynamic request routing and replica server selection. For server selection, CDNs base their decision on the IP address of a client's local DNS resolver. This approach builds on the assumption that, in the absence of information about the client's actual network location, the location of its resolver provides a good approximation. The recent growth in remote DNS usage challenges this assumption.

This paper investigates the impact of recent DNS evolution on the web experience of end users. Over the past few years there has been a significant increase in the use of remote DNS services, including public DNS. Remote DNS offers a number of potential advantages to both service providers and end users. For service providers, strategically placed, remote DNS server clusters offer economies of scale and simplified management, among other benefits. For users, such services can yield better DNS performance, availability and security. The relative importance of such benefits to end users partially explains the observed growth in public DNS usage. OpenDNS has recently reported a 2× increase in users of their service over 2010-2012 [20, 21]. In our own survey (Fig. 3) based on data from the EdgeScope project [5], we found that the public DNS user base has grown by 27% annually over the last 21 months. As of December 2011, 8.6% of users in this dataset relied on a public DNS service.

While remote DNS services could indeed result in better DNS performance for end users, by breaking the assumption made by CDN mapping approaches they may yield worse end-to-end web performance. To illustrate the scope and extent of this effect, we compare the *minimum* time to fetch content from Akamai's CDN when using local and remote DNS servers from different locations in North America. Fig-

[1] As ranked by Alexa.com, accounting for 48% of all Internet pageviews.
[2] `http://cdnlist.com`; July 2011

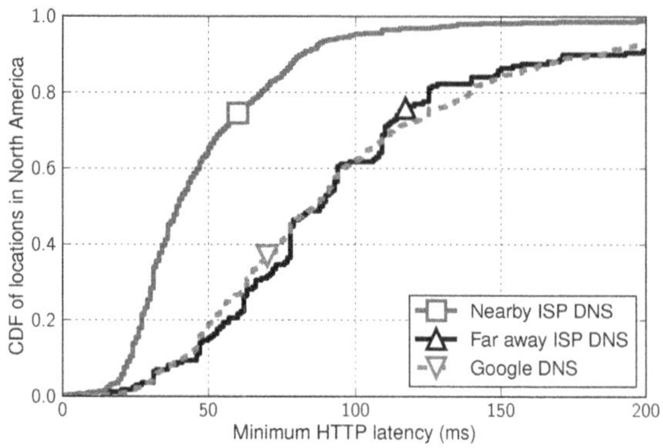

Figure 1: For North America, minimum HTTP latency to get Akamai content using near or far ISP DNS, and Google DNS. 27% of locations have "far away" ISP DNS (latency >50 ms). Median case's access latency is *doubled* for far-away and Google vs. nearby ISP DNS.

ure 1 plots the minimum latency for the different locations using *nearby* (latency <50 ms) and *faraway* ISP DNS and Google DNS.[3] Web access latency is a significant factor in user satisfaction [7,26]. As the figure shows, remote DNS—both public DNS and far-away ISP DNS—has a major impact on CDN access latency. Latency doubles in the median case and *triples* for the worst 10% of locations. These results extend and are consistent with those in Ager et al. [1]; we find that a large fraction of ISPs' DNS services, as much as 27%, are distant from their users and therefore result in significant reductions in CDN performance.

In this paper, we present results from a large-scale study of the end-to-end impact of remote DNS usage on CDN performance (§ 4). Based on experiments conducted from 10,923 end-hosts across 99 countries, we show that for 90% of the sampled locations, the set of CDN replicas selected based on public DNS services has *no overlap* with those selected based on the client location. This error results in a 60% increase in end-to-end latency in the median case and up to 3× increase for 20% of the sampled location.

The potential negative impact of remote DNS usage on web performance motivates the recently proposed edns-client-subnet EDNS0 extension [3]. This extension, put forward by a collaboration of several CDNs and DNS service providers [28], allows DNS recursive resolvers to pass along clients' subnet information that could be used by CDNs to improve replica server selection. A key challenge to this approach is adoption, as it requires the commitment of both CDN and DNS services to be effective. We report on the first study of the adoption of the proposed edns-client-subnet extension and its potential benefits for public DNS service users (§4.3). We find that the proposed extension could be effective at reducing the impact of public DNS usage on CDN performance. Our results show that, assuming wide adoption, the proposed extension can reduce the impact of public DNS usage to less than 80% for 80% of locations (30% for the median case). However, in a survey of the top 1,000 most popular sites, we find that only 9% of sites use CDNs that support the extension.

We introduce *Direct Resolution* (*DR*) an alternative solution (§5) that obtains comparable performance improvements to the DNS extension. Our end-host solution enables incremental adoption by affected users, and does not rely on support from either DNS services or CDNs. The approach leverages the cache of an end host's recursive resolver to efficiently map a Canonical Name (CNAME) to an authoritative name server, but directly contacts the authoritative server to obtain a precise redirection for the client. We have implemented *DR* as part of *namehelp*, a tool based on a popular DNS benchmark utility [18] to both provide a comparative evaluation of DNS service and web performance and act as a DNS proxy that implements *DR* to improve CDN mappings. Naïvely using *DR* for all CDN queries improves end-to-end performance for 49% of locations. *namehelp* avoids this penalty and achieves strictly better performance than recursive DNS alone by only using *DR* when it has previously improved end-to-end performance.

[3]To put this in context, the average network latency between U. Washington in Seattle, WA and Georgetown U. in Washington, D.C. is ≈ 83 ms.

Contributions

Recent studies [1, 9, 12] have shown that the use of public DNS services can complicate the mapping of clients to replica servers or data centers done by CDNs and cloud service providers, while Huang et al. [8] and Khosla et al. [12] discuss possible approaches to mitigate the performance penalty. Our work extends significantly these previous efforts, contributing:

- The first study of the end-to-end web performance impact of remote DNS on CDNs from users' perspectives in access networks.
- The first evaluation of the proposed edns-client-subnet extension, its potential performance and level of adoption.
- The design and experimental evaluation of a novel end-system solution that provides comparable benefits to the extension and is readily available for users to install.

After providing some background, we expand on each of these contributions. We close the paper with a discussion of closely related work in §6 and our concluding thoughts in §7.

2. BACKGROUND

Since their emergence in the mid 1990s, CDNs have become the primary vehicle for delivering content over the Internet. To estimate the reliance of popular sites on CDNs, we conducted a survey of the top 1,000 most popular sites, as ranked by Alexa.com. For each site, we download its index page and linked web objects. We used several techniques to determine if a site uses CDNs, including detection of HTTP redirection to CDN domains or use of CNAME entries in DNS resolutions. Since there are other methods of redirecting to a CDN (e.g. domain delegation) that we do not capture, these results are a lower bound on the use of CDNs in popular sites.

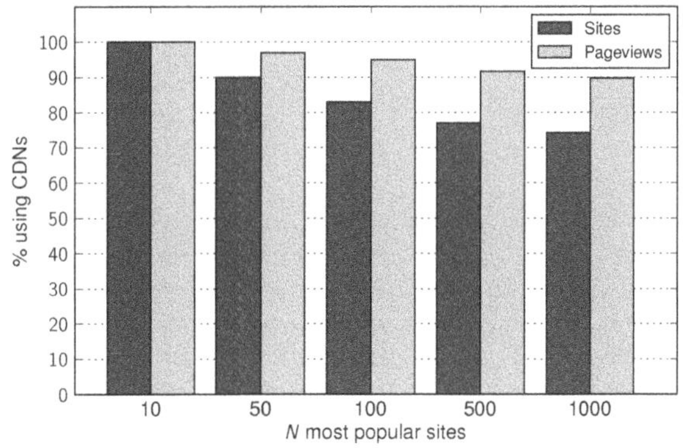

Figure 2: Fraction of the top N most popular sites and their pageviews that use CDNs. Over 70% of the top 1,000 sites and 89% of their pageviews utilize CDNs.

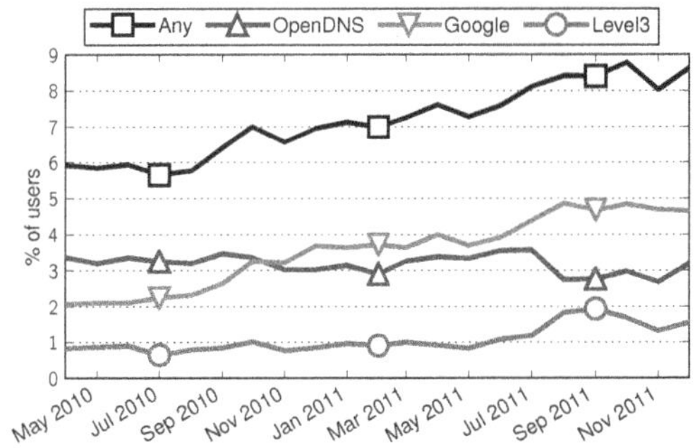

Figure 3: % of users with public DNS configured on their computer over the last 21 months. "Any" shows the combined adoption percentage of these services. Public DNS usage is growing by 27% annually.

Figure 2 summarizes our findings. The figure plots both the fraction of "Sites" (blue/dark) and "Pageviews" (green/light) using CDNs in the top N most popular sites. As the figure shows, all sites in the top 10 and over 70% of those in the top 1,000 rely on CDNs. Weighting CDN use by pageviews results in an even larger fraction of top sites using CDNs. Across all views to the top 1,000 sites—accounting for 48% of all pageviews—9 out of 10 require loading objects from a CDN.

In general, for a web client to retrieve content for a web page, the first step is to use DNS to resolve the server-name portion of the content's URL into the address of a machine hosting it. If the web site uses a CDN, the content will be replicated at several hosts across the Internet. A popular way to direct clients to those replicas dynamically is DNS redirection. With DNS redirection, a client's DNS request is redirected to an authoritative DNS name server that is controlled by the CDN, which then resolves the CDN server name to the IP address of one or more replica servers [13]. DNS redirection can be used to deliver full or partial site content. With the former, all DNS requests for the origin server are redirected to the CDN. With partial site content delivery, the origin site modifies certain embedded URLs so that requests for only those URLs are redirected to the CDN. CDNs typically select a (set of) replica to serve the request from based on the network and geographic region of the local DNS server. While a reasonable approximation when clients and their local DNS resolvers are topologically close, the use of remote DNS services can yield less than optimal redirections.

Over the past few years there has been a significant increase in the use of remote DNS services,[4] including public DNS. To analyze longitudinal trends in remote DNS usage, we use 21 months of user DNS configuration data from the EdgeScope project (April 2010 through December 2011). EdgeScope [5] collects data from BitTorrent [32] users, including host configuration and host and network measurement statistics. The dataset includes information reported by 47,119 users located in 197 countries and 4,613 ASes, giving us a diverse and global perspective on DNS usage by BitTorrent users.

We quantify public DNS adoption by counting the users having configured well-known IP addresses for these services at different points over the observed period. Figure 3 shows the observed trends in combined (labeled *Any*) and individual public DNS service adoption for the three most popular: Google, OpenDNS and Level3. Overall, we found a 27% annual growth rate in public DNS adoption, reaching 8.6% of sampled users in December 2011. Google's DNS service showed the most significant growth—a 74% annual increase—which resulted in it becoming the most-used public DNS service (overtaking OpenDNS) in November 2010. For 70% of these public DNS users, the public service is configured as their primary (22%) or only option (48%).

While subject to a potential "geek bias", our results are indicative of an overall increasing trend of public DNS use.[5] Indeed, our observed growth trends are consistent with those reported by OpenDNS showing a 2× increase in users of their service over 2010-2012 [20, 21].

2.1 Industry response

The increased use of remote DNS services, with its potential impact on web performance, has motivated a recent response from industry. Several companies, including Google, OpenDNS and EdgeCast, have proposed the "edns-client-subnet" DNS extension ("`ECS`") to the IETF [3] as part of the "Global Internet Speedup" initiative [28].

The proposed extension provides a mechanism for recursive DNS resolvers to pass client location information to CDN authoritative DNS servers. This enables CDNs to factor in the client's actual location in redirection decisions. The extension is specified as a EDNS0 [30] option that is appended to the DNS query and contains the client's network prefix. The length of the prefix is a parameter determined by the recursive resolver.

Assuming that *both the DNS service and the CDN* support the extension, the approach enables CDNs to transparently improve the quality of redirections. It is straightforward to determine whether a DNS service or CDN supports the

[4]While anecdotal, evidence of this trend can be seen in reports of DNS service outages in national ISPs, typically affecting large geographic regions [34, 35].

[5]`http://voices.washingtonpost.com/fasterforward/2010/11/comcast\_internet\_or\_any\_other.html`

extension by sending a request to recursive or authoritative DNS servers. If the ECS option is present in the response, the extension is supported.

3. METHODOLOGY

In this section, we describe our methodology to experimentally evaluate the interactions between remote DNS and CDNs.

We base our analyses on data contributed by 10,923 end hosts distributed across 99 countries and 752 ASes, providing a diverse set of vantage points. In terms of geography, 59% of the hosts are spread across 35 European countries, 21.9% are from the United States, 5.5% are located in Asia, and 3.9% are in Oceania. Our dataset was collected over a 127 day period between September 12th, 2011 and January 16th, 2012.

Each end host runs an instance of an ISP characterization plugin for the Vuze BitTorrent client [32]; users download our software and allow us to collect measurement results. Each host reports: local configuration information, the results of DNS resolutions, HTTP request timing statistics, and results of traceroutes and pings to CDN and DNS servers.

For our study, we chose different public DNS services and CDNs based on popularity and deployment architectures. The set of public DNS services we measured includes two of the most popular: Google Public DNS and OpenDNS. Our set of CDNs, which includes Akamai, EdgeCast, Google and Limelight, covers a variety of deployment models, ranging from servers sparsely deployed at points of presence to servers located inside the networks of end users. For each CDN, we manually selected a small (<10 KB) web object hosted by that CDN. This enabled us to evaluate the end-to-end performance using 2 steps: (1) clients query DNS for the object's hostname to obtain a CDN redirection, and then (2) request the object via HTTP from the CDN's edge server.

We define each /24 IP prefix from which we have measurements to be a vantage point "location" and aggregate measurements taken by nodes in the prefix. In the remainder of the paper, we analyze the distributions across these "locations". To ensure the significance of our results, we require at least 3 measurements from each location. For each combination of vantage point location, DNS service and CDN, we select the *best case results* (i.e. minimum latencies) for comparison.

Our experiments are designed to minimize their impact on the monitored services. We use caching at each node to avoid multiple probes to the same server, and randomly schedule experiments to reduce the likelihood of concurrent measurements launched from different hosts.

3.1 Obtaining CDN redirections

We use iterative DNS resolution to obtain CDN redirections that are not affected by the location of the ISP or public DNS servers.

End hosts typically resolve DNS names by querying a recursive DNS resolver operated by an ISP or public service. The recursive resolver makes several queries on behalf of the end host, caches the responses, and returns the answer to the end host.

Using iterative resolution, an end host can act as its own recursive resolver. Since the host directly contacts the authoritative DNS servers, CDNs can base their replica server selections on the client's *actual network location*.

To obtain CDN redirections that are effectively informed by client location, we follow two approaches to cover the cases where the edns-client-subnet DNS extension is *and* is not supported.

DNS extension supported. To query combinations of DNS services and CDNs where the extension *is supported*, we implement a stub resolver that adds the ECS option with a specified IP prefix to a query and forwards the request to a recursive resolver. This method of querying with the ECS option is possible due to a provision in the specification to support hierarchies of DNS resolvers; if the ECS option is already present in a query, it should not be modified by a recursive resolver. Since our stub resolver generates the option, we can evaluate the impact of providing different amounts of client information (i.e. prefix length) on CDN redirections.

DNS extension not supported. To evaluate the DNS extension's approach for DNS services or CDNs that *do not* support the extension, we emulate its characteristics: the latency to receive the answer, and the CDN's answer based on the client's location. We determine the latency to receive an answer by simply querying the DNS service for a name that is cached on the server. To obtain a CDN answer based on the client's location, we use iterative resolution to directly query the CDN's authoritative DNS server. As we show in §4.2, redirections via iterative lookup generally provide best-case HTTP performance. As a result, our emulated ECS query gives redirections equivalent to using the extension and providing the client's full IP address.

3.2 Measuring DNS services

Public DNS services are typically offered on BGP anycast-enabled IP addresses, allowing all users to configure the same server IP address. Probing public DNS services can present a challenge for network-level measurements, as some anycast-enabled addresses do not respond to ICMP pings.

To determine the recursive DNS resolver's globally routable *unicast IP address* so that we can probe it directly, we use a technique similar to that used by Huang et al. [9]. We operate an authoritative DNS server that answers queries with the IP address of the recursive DNS resolver sending the query. This approach works because resolvers that answer queries on an anycast IP interface use a *separate unicast interface* to communicate with other authoritative DNS servers; our service returns this unicast IP address for the recursive resolver. Clients send a DNS query to the public DNS service's anycast IP address and receive its globally routable unicast IP address in the DNS response; this gives the client a mapping between the public DNS service and the unicast IP address for the recursive resolver. Clients report these mappings, which enables us to identify public resolvers in our dataset.

Filtering configured public DNS services. To obtain ISPs' DNS servers in a scalable manner, we start out with users' DNS configurations and exclude known public DNS services. Since users may have public DNS services configured on either their computer or a DNS-proxying middlebox, we must filter out both cases. First, we conservatively filter well-known public DNS anycast IP addresses (e.g. 8.8.8.8 for Google DNS) configured on the user's computer. Then, using the result of our previously

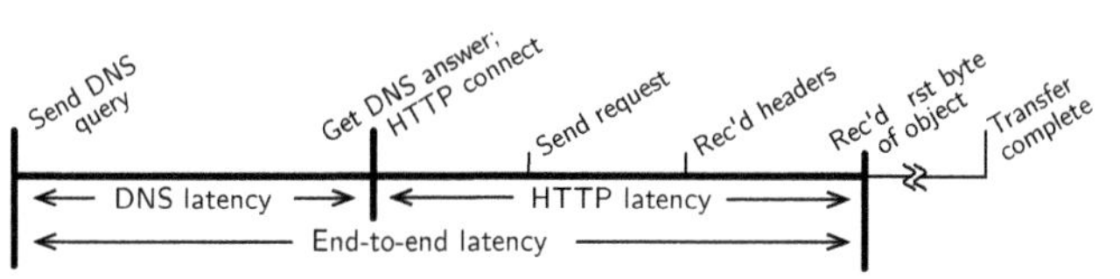

Figure 4: Timeline of DNS and CDN interactions, and the components we consider when measuring latency in this work.

described approach to determine a DNS server's *unicast IP address*, we can see through any proxies (e.g. middlebox) and determine the underlying DNS server. We exclude data when the underlying DNS server is in a /24 prefix where we have previously located public DNS servers via directly probing the public DNS services' well-known addresses.

We use ping latency to measure network distance. To reduce the impact of transient spikes in latency, we probe each DNS service's anycast and unicast addresses with three ICMP pings and select the minimum latency.

3.3 Measuring CDNs

We measure end-to-end latency for each pair of DNS and CDN services using the combined latency of DNS lookup and HTTP request (Fig. 4).

- DNS lookup: Time to obtain a CDN redirection, from querying a recursive DNS resolver until receiving an answer
- HTTP request: Time from initiating a connection to a replica server, to receiving the first byte of an object from an CDN edge server via HTTP

For each CDN studied, we select one of their customer's small web objects to request. To factor out any differences due to varying object size across CDNs, we compute access latency based on the time needed to receive *the first byte* of the object. We conduct each DNS and HTTP `GET` request twice in close succession so that the requested object will be served from the server's cache on the second request; we use the smaller latency.

3.4 Baseline for performance comparison

One issue we faced in our analyses was determining how to compare the performance of different approaches for obtaining CDN redirections. We initially considered using the performance when using ISP DNS as our baseline. However, several issues with ISP DNS mean that it is not always an appropriate choice as a baseline. For instance, the use of remote DNS architectures may break the assumption of proximity between client and resolver. Also, some ISP DNS services exhibit high latencies and poor cache performance due to load balancing [1]. Another alternative we considered is using the performance of redirections seen via iterative DNS resolution; however, factors such as CDN load balancing between replica server clusters may affect the redirections resulting in suboptimal performance.

We determine baseline performance by selecting each location's *best* performance from any CDN redirection mechanism, including using ISP DNS, public DNS services and iterative resolution. We compare the performance of CDN redirection approaches' aggregate distributions of performance relative to this baseline.

To compare the end-to-end performance of different approaches to obtaining CDN redirections, we compute *for each location* the baseline DNS latency to obtain a CDN redirection, and the baseline HTTP latency to download an object from the CDN. We define our baseline DNS performance as the minimum latency to obtain a DNS response from *any* ISP or public DNS service. This represents the latency to obtain a cached answer from the nearest recursive DNS resolver. For our baseline HTTP performance, we use the minimum observed HTTP latency for that CDN in that location. This value represents the best-possible CDN performance we observed from the location—typically, the latency to obtain a cached object from the nearest CDN server. Our end-to-end performance baseline is defined as the sum of the DNS and HTTP baseline latencies. This represents an idealized best-case scenario in which the nearest DNS returns a cached CDN redirection, the redirection yields the nearest CDN replica server, and the requested object is cached on the replica server.

4. DNS–CDN INTERACTION

To examine the impact that different DNS services have on several aspects of CDN performance, we first look at differences in the replica servers seen when obtaining CDN redirections using ISP DNS, public DNS services and iterative resolution. Next, we compare the impact of these approaches on the resulting HTTP performance. Finally, we evaluate the end-to-end performance benefit of using the edns-client-subnet extension and the degree of its adoption.

4.1 Redirection similarity

When a client requests a redirection, a CDN may consider factors beyond proximity, including server or network load. As a result of these transient effects, a client may see not one but rather a collection of replica servers. Over time, this collection reveals patterns in which some replica servers are seen more frequently than others. We aggregate redirections based on replica servers' /24 IP prefix since these servers are often deployed in clusters. We build a "ratio map" to represent these aggregated redirections, which maps each replica server cluster to the fraction of redirections specifying that cluster [2,27].

We analyze these ratio maps of CDN redirections obtained via different DNS services, estimating the degree of similarity between them. Previous work has shown that this similarity can be used to estimate the proximity between nodes [2,27].

We use *cosine similarity* to quantify the similarity between ratio maps on the assumption that clients with equivalent sets of redirections, i.e. client sees the same replica servers, should yield comparable HTTP performance. Given two ratio maps, we extract two equal-length vectors—one for each ratio map. Cosine similarity between the two vectors A and B quantifies the degree of overlap between the vectors computed as their dot product divided by the product of their lengths. Cosine similarity yields a value in the range $[0, 1]$:

$$cos\_sim = \frac{A \cdot B}{\|A\|\|B\|}$$

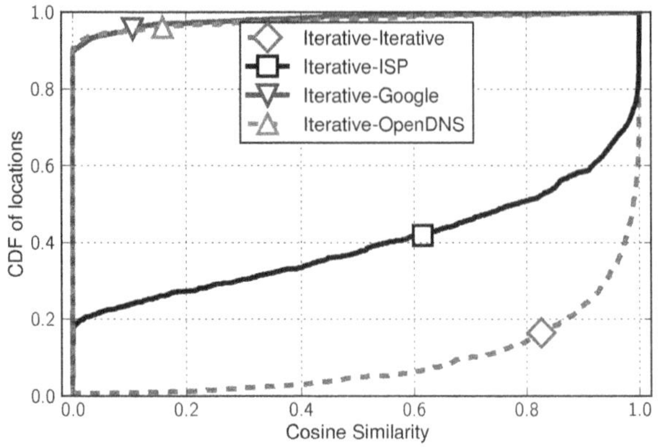

(a) Akamai

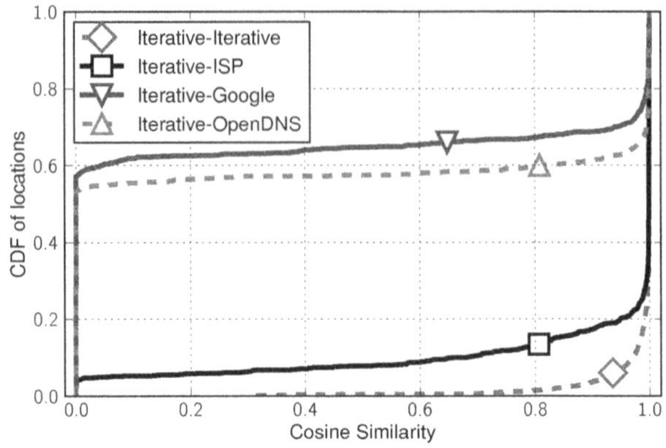

(b) Limelight

Figure 5: CDFs of cosine similarity for Akamai and Limelight CDN redirections by DNS lookup. Compared to Iterative, ISP DNS has some similarity in at least 80% of locations. However, for 90% of locations there is no similarity in Akamai redirections via public DNS.

When $cos\_sim = 0$, the sets of redirections have no clusters in common. Values greater than 0 indicate that some clusters are seen in both sets; $cos\_sim = 1$ means that the sets of clusters seen are equivalent. We ensure the significance of this analysis by requiring that each location's ratio map comprises *at least* 3 redirections (see §3). This enables us to capture load balancing behavior when computing the similarity of CDN redirections.

We use cosine similarity to estimate differences in redirections resulting from ISP and public DNS, to those resulting from iterative resolution. Redirections seen via ISP or public DNS are based on the location of the DNS resolver—not the client. Since iterative resolution yields CDN redirections based on client location, any differences indicate potential for redirections to suboptimal replica server clusters. Figure 5 plots the cosine similarities seen in Akamai and Limelight CDN redirections between iterative and ISP or public DNS services.

The "Iterative-Iterative" curves show similarity between random subsets of iterative redirections, and are the upper bound on similarity for a CDN's redirections. If CDN redirections were static, we would expect this value to always equal 1; however, they are dynamic and responsive to several factors including system load and network conditions. Cosine similarity values <1 reflect these variations in redirections. We find that, for the "upper bound" of similarity, we see higher similarity for CDNs with fewer data centers (e.g. Limelight) as there will likely be fewer variations in redirections.

Iterative and ISP redirections have the highest similarity, with 80% of locations having some Akamai replica server clusters in common. In contrast, the "Iterative-Google" and "Iterative-OpenDNS" curves reveal very low similarity—in 90% of locations, there is no similarity in the set of Akamai redirections.

These trends are the same for Limelight redirections, except that public DNS is able to match iterative's redirections in a larger fraction (43%) of locations. While ISP and public DNS resolvers both result in different redirections compared to iterative lookups, the effect is significantly larger for public DNS services.

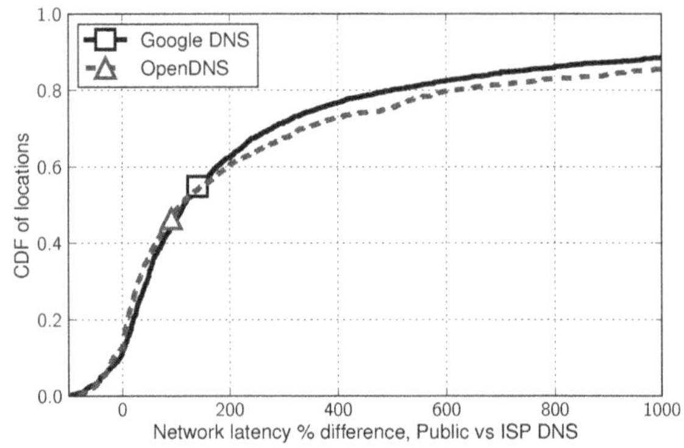

Figure 6: CDF of % difference in network latency to public vs. ISP DNS resolvers. Public DNS servers are farther away in 90% of locations and more than twice as far in 50%.

One possible explanation for the differences in cosine similarity seen with public DNS vs ISP DNS is their distance from the client. Since CDNs' replica server mappings are indicative of the location of the recursive DNS resolver, increased distance to a resolver is expected to correlate with lower similarity in redirections. To test this hypothesis, Fig. 6 plots the percent difference in latency to public DNS resolvers relative to ISP DNS latency. For half of our locations, public DNS servers are at least *twice as far away* as ISP DNS servers. This explains the lower similarity we find in redirections via public DNS.

Our cosine similarity analysis serves as a useful indicator for the *potential* impact of using a given DNS service. Having a cosine similarity value <1 is a *necessary but not sufficient* condition for a DNS service to affect performance. For instance, ISP DNS may provide different redirections compared to Iterative, but both of the CDN mappings could provide equivalent performance. In the next section, we directly compare the quality of HTTP performance using CDN redirections obtained via different DNS services.

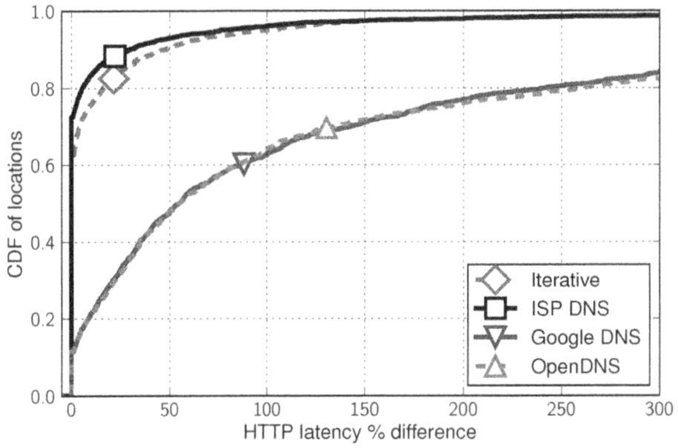

(a) Akamai

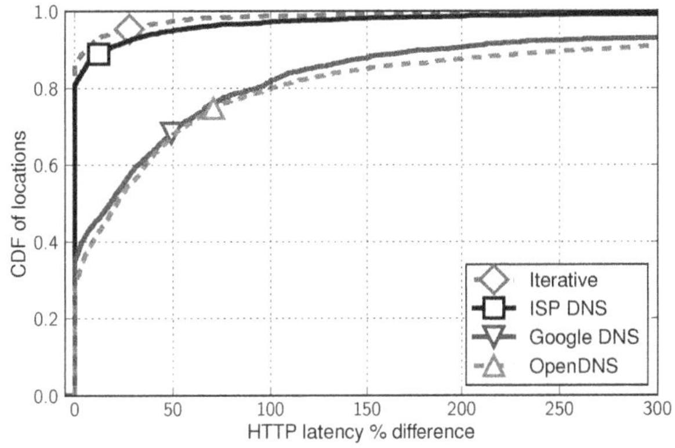

(b) Limelight

Figure 7: CDF of % difference in HTTP latency using iterative, ISP or public DNS relative to our ideal baseline, for Akamai and Limelight. Replica servers seen via ISP DNS and iterative lookups generally provide the best-case HTTP latency. Public DNS services often yield redirections with higher latencies, with a 2× increase for 35% (Akamai) and 18% (Limelight) of locations.

4.2 HTTP performance

To understand the impact of the differences in CDN redirections between DNS approaches, we analyze the resulting HTTP performance obtained through each. As our metric, we use the latency to establish a connection to a CDN replica server and start downloading an object. This latency is an important measure of CDN performance. When loading web pages, low latencies are essential to attaining low page load times. In the case of high-bandwidth streaming (e.g. HD video), lower latency connections allow for higher transfer rates.

We evaluate the quality of CDN redirections via iterative, ISP and public DNS resolutions relative to our ideal baseline HTTP latency. Figure 7 plots the percent difference in HTTP latency—the time to receive the first byte of an object—of these DNS resolution approaches. Both iterative and ISP DNS redirections match the best-case HTTP performance in 70% (Akamai) and 80% (Limelight) of locations. In contrast, public DNS's redirections only achieve this for 15% (Akamai) and 40% (Limelight) of locations. Since Limelight's CDN architecture has relatively fewer data centers, the increased distance to the public DNS server is less likely to affect the client's replica server mapping. Still, public DNS results in at least double the HTTP latency for 35% (Akamai) and 18% (Limelight) of locations.

For some sampled locations, we find that iterative resolution does not always result in optimal performance. In these cases, several factors beyond client location may affect the redirections obtained from the CDN, including load balancing between server clusters [29]. In practice, this source of noise in CDN redirections is negligible in comparison to the overall results that we report.

4.2.1 *Cause of performance differences*

To better understand the components of HTTP latency, we examine two possible explanations: load and proximity of edge servers. These analyses will determine the reason for the differences in HTTP performance we observe between DNS services.

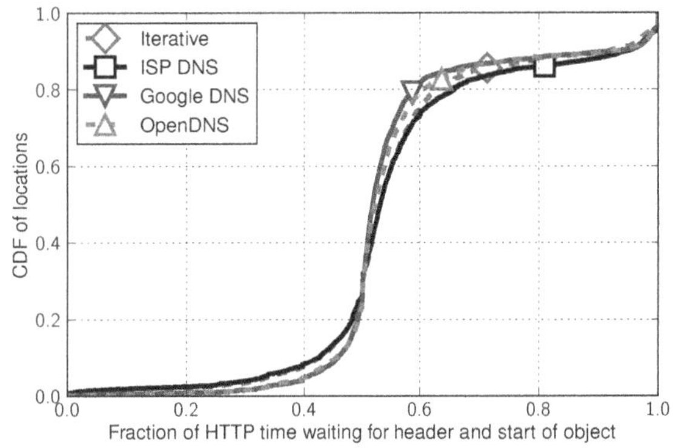

Figure 8: CDF of the fraction of the HTTP interaction spent waiting for a response, comparing redirections via several DNS services. Under load, servers queue requests, increasing this parameter from the expected value of 0.5. The distributions are nearly identical; there are no systematic differences in server load.

We test whether server load (and therefore response time) differ significantly between the edge servers seen via each DNS service. Since keeping edge server load low is one of the main goals of CDNs in general, we expect that our requests for cached objects should be served with minimal delay. We validate this hypothesis in Fig. 8, which plots CDFs of the fraction of the HTTP latency spent waiting to receive the response header and first byte of the requested object, for both lookups via public and ISP DNS. The intuition is that an HTTP request requires 2 round-trips to the server: the first to establish a connection, and the second to request the content. If the server is not heavily loaded, then the request will not be queued, and a request for a cached object can be returned immediately—in this case, the fraction of time

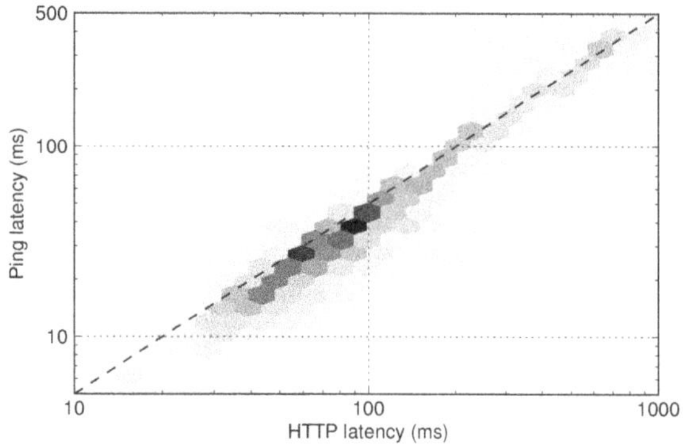

Figure 9: Heat map of HTTP and ping latency to replica servers aggregated across our experiments; darker bins indicate higher density of samples. The dashed black line shows the expected value, where HTTP latency is 2× ping latency. The variables are strongly correlated ($r = 0.88$). Network latency is the dominant factor in HTTP performance.

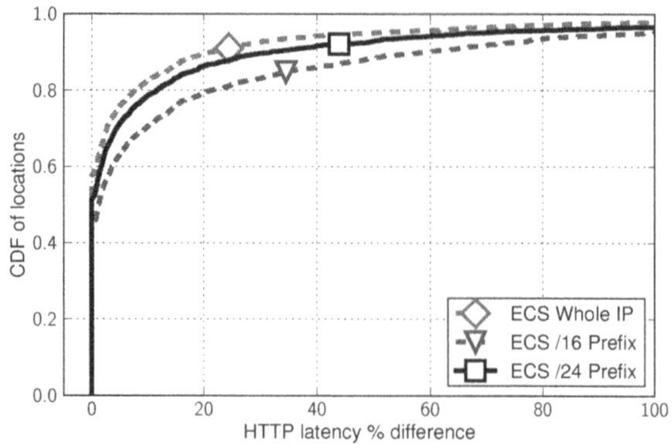

Figure 10: CDFs of HTTP latency relative to our ideal baseline, for varying amounts of client information included in an ECS-enabled lookup. Providing a client's /24 prefix provides nearly the same performance as giving the whole IP address for Google CDN. When only providing the /16 prefix of the client's address, HTTP latency is higher than when giving the /24 prefix for about 30% of locations.

spent on the second round-trip should be the same as the first, or 50% of the total request time. We find that in 70% of cases, this metric is within 10% of the expected value, and find no significant differences between these distributions. This indicates that server load is not systematically different for CDN replica servers seen via any DNS service.

Next, we evaluate network latency's relationship to overall HTTP latency. In an HTTP interaction, requesting and receiving an object requires 2 round trips: the first to establish the connection, and the second to request and receive the object. In Fig. 9 we plot a heat map showing the relationship between HTTP and network latency, with the black line showing the expected relationship in which HTTP latency is twice the network latency. We find a strong correlation between these two variables ($r = 0.88$, $n = 629252$), indicating that network latency has a significant impact on overall HTTP latency.

4.3 Better performance using client location

The previous analysis shows that using remote DNS services results in significantly different CDN redirections, often leading to reduced HTTP performance. The "edns-client-subnet" DNS extension [3] provides a way to expose client location information, part of the client's IP address, to CDNs as an approach to address this.

In the following paragraphs we present the first study on the efficacy of the proposed extension. For our evaluation, we follow the methodology for obtaining CDN redirections using the extension in §3.1. We close the section with a survey of the current extent of its adoption.

4.3.1 Performance improvement with client location

The `ECS` extension functions by passing part of the client's network address to the CDN's authoritative DNS server to aid in selecting an appropriate replica server. Choosing the amount of client information to provide requires several considerations. Exposing fine-grained client location information could enable the CDN to provide more accurate redirections, but might also result in the recursive resolver having to cache additional `ECS`-specific mappings—one for each client prefix—for every CDN domain name.

We evaluate the impact of providing different amounts of client location information via the extension on HTTP performance. For this experiment, we query Google DNS servers for a Google CDN name. Figure 10 plots the % difference in HTTP latency of redirections of `ECS` queries with either the client's /16 prefix, /24 prefix, or the client's whole IP address. For 60% of locations, giving the /16 and /24 prefixes are sufficient to obtain equivalent performance to giving the whole IP address. In the remaining locations, the /24 prefix provides slightly better mappings than the /16 prefix. For instance, giving the /16 prefix, 9% of locations have at least 50% increase in HTTP latency compared to the whole IP address—giving the /24 prefix, only 3% have a 50% increase. We also conducted this analysis for lookups to an EdgeCast CDN name, and found no difference between providing the /16 prefix, /24 prefix or the whole IP address. *For these CDNs*, we find that a /16 prefix is typically sufficient to provide equivalent mappings to the whole IP address. For a subset of locations, using /24 prefixes can result in marginal performance improvements compared to /16 prefixes.

We stress that these results are not generally applicable to CDNs due to variations in their deployments of edge servers. We would expect to see similar results for CDNs with *like deployments*, since users would be mapped to edge server locations with equivalent granularity in terms of their network location. For CDN architectures with edge servers in *more* locations (e.g. in end-users' networks), we expect that providing more prefix information would result in a greater performance improvement than we observed. However, lacking a CDN with such a deployment that also supports the extension, we cannot experiment directly with the impact of varying amounts of client location information on the performance of this CDN deployment model.

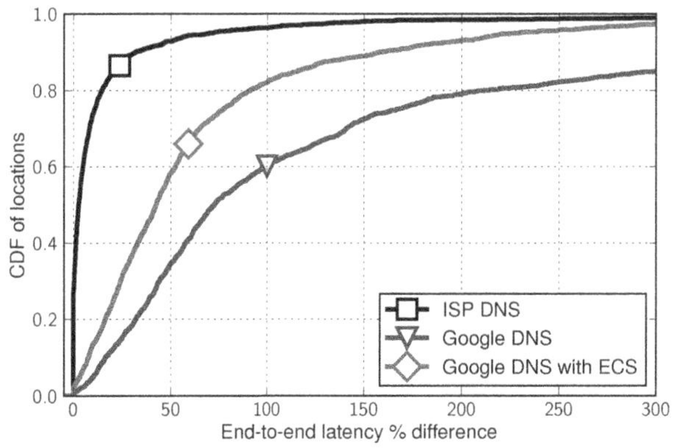

(a) Akamai

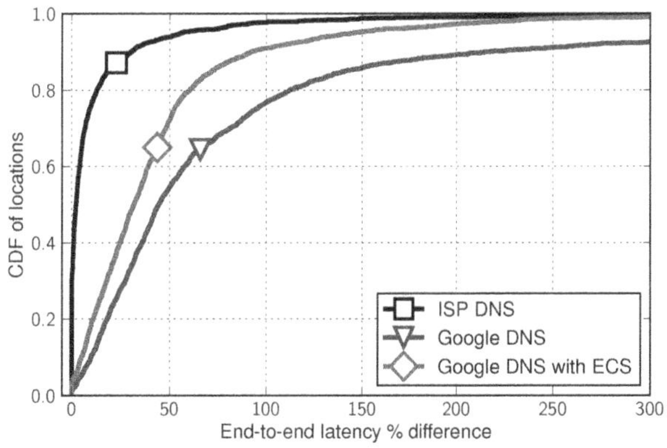

(b) Limelight

Figure 11: CDFs of end-to-end latency % difference, comparing ISP DNS and public DNS with and without the extension, for requests to Akamai and Limelight CDNs. Values are relative to the ideal end-to-end latency baseline. Using the extension significantly improves end-to-end performance. For Akamai, the extension improves median performance by 40%; for the top 20% of locations, it reduces latency by 60%.

To understand the impact of the extension in the context of end-to-end performance, we compare the performance of public DNS with and without ECS to ISP DNS. Figure 11 plots relative end-to-end latency for accessing objects on the Akamai and Limelight CDNs. Since neither of these CDNs currently support the ECS extension, we simulate it by using answers provided by iterative DNS lookups.

Using ECS provides a significant performance improvement over public DNS resolution without ECS. For instance, the median latency difference for Akamai lookups without ECS was 61%; with ECS, this was only 33%. The benefits of using the extension are most apparent in the upper tail of the distribution. Without the extension, 15% of locations had a 4× penalty from using public DNS; with the extension, this fraction of locations is less than 5%. Overall, the ECS approach provides a significant end-to-end performance advantage when using remote DNS services.

4.3.2 *Extension challenges*

Our analysis has demonstrated the potential benefits of the edns-client-subnet DNS extension for reducing the CDN performance impact of using remote DNS. To realize its performance benefits, however, both the DNS service and CDN must support the extension. In the following paragraphs, we evaluate and discuss the current level of support for the extension.

As part of our measurement experiments, we probed users' ISP DNS servers as well as several public DNS services to check if they supported the extension. Google DNS was the *only public service* that supported the extension. We also found *no ISP DNS services* that supported the extension, this despite the growing use of "remote DNS" architecture by ISPs and its potential performance cost.

To determine the impact of the extension on aggregate web performance, we test popular web sites to see if any of the CDNs they use support the extension. We determine the fraction of web sites and pageviews that utilize the extension to improve client performance. This analysis follows the model we used in §2 for evaluating the fraction of sites using CDNs; here, we also test whether each CDN supports the extension.

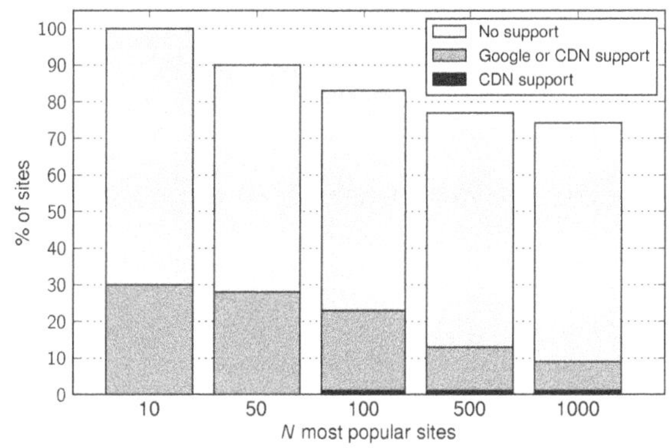

Figure 12: Breakdown of popular sites using CDNs, based on whether the CDNs used support the edns-client-subnet DNS extension. Each bar's overall height shows the % of sites using at least one CDN. The height of the middle region shows the % of sites using a CDN that supports the extension, while the bottom region shows the % of sites when excluding Google sites and services. Only 9% of sites in the top 1,000 use CDNs that support the extension.

Figure 12 plots the fraction of sites using CDNs in the N most popular sites. Each site is categorized by whether the CDNs used support the ECS extension. Adoption to date is quite limited: out of the top 1,000 sites, only 9% employ a CDN supporting the extension. Most sites are in this category because they either are a Google site (e.g. www.google.co.uk) or they use a Google service such as advertising, site analytics or hosted libraries (e.g. jQuery). Setting aside these Google-related sites, we find that only 1% of sites use a non-Google CDN that supports the extension. For the remaining 65% of sites using CDNs without ECS support, their clients are potentially receiving suboptimal CDN redirections and increased page load times.

There is a technical explanation for why CDNs may not have yet adopted the extension. Some large CDNs make their redirection decisions by mapping DNS servers onto a set of "core points" in the network, which are in turn mapped to the CDN's infrastructure [4]; this initial mapping step is non-trivial. Under this approach, the problem is that the CDN cannot directly utilize the information provided by the extension. Neither of the possible solutions—generating a much more extensive set of mappings or changing the overall approach for redirecting clients—are attractive to the CDN. This issue presents a significant barrier to adoption of the extension.

In summary, our analyses have shown that the edns-client-subnet DNS extension has significant potential to improve performance by conveying a client's location to CDNs' authoritative DNS servers to inform their redirection decisions. However, current adoption of the extension is limited to a few CDNs; only 9% of the top 1,000 most popular sites benefit from the potential performance improvements of the extension.

5. AN END HOST SOLUTION

In this section, we present *Direct Resolution* (*DR*), a readily available, end host solution that improves CDN performance when using remote DNS. Our approach is motivated by the potential performance benefits of the proposed DNS extension and its low adoption levels. *DR* does not require the participation of either DNS services or CDNs. We first describe *DR* and explain the intuition and process behind it. We evaluate the impact *DR* has on improving end-to-end CDN performance. Finally, we describe "*namehelp*", an implementation of *DR* that attain performance comparable to the edns-client-subnet DNS extension.

5.1 Approach

In our previous analysis we rely on iterative DNS resolution to attain the best possible redirections and, thus, the highest HTTP performance. The iterative resolution approach, however, is not a suitable solution by itself given its high resolution latency. With iterative resolution, a client must conduct several queries that traverse the DNS hierarchy and translate Canonical Names (CNAME) entries from customer domain names to CDN domains (e.g. `wwwimages.adobe.com` to `a1953.x.akamai.net`) before obtaining an answer. Recursive DNS servers can often answer a client's query faster than if the client used iterative resolution itself. This is because recursive servers answer queries for many clients, enabling them to answer many queries from cache or with few additional queries.

The *Direct Resolution* approach composes the best aspects of recursive DNS servers and iterative resolution to obtain improved CDN redirections. Figure 13 diagrams the high-level *DR* process. *DR* leverages the cache of a recursive DNS server to quickly translate customer domain names to CDN names and determine the CDN's authoritative CDN server to contact (Query #1). However, instead of using the CDN redirection obtained via the recursive server, the client *directly contacts the CDN's authoritative server* (Query #3) as in iterative resolution. The resulting CDN redirection is the same as that which iterative resolution would return but without the iterative latency penalty.

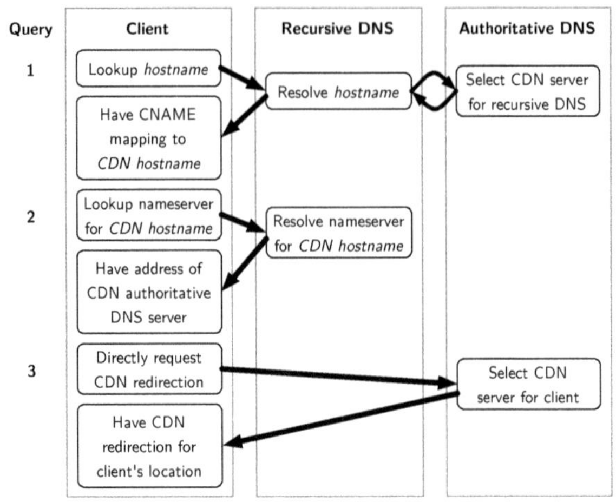

Figure 13: Sequence diagram for *Direct Resolution*.

5.2 CDN redirections using Direct Resolution

In Fig. 13, we outline the 3 steps to obtain a CDN redirection using *DR*. As an example to illustrate how *DR* works, we walk through the steps to obtain a CDN redirection for an object linked on a website (`website.com`) that is served by a CDN (`somecdn.com`).

Query #1 of this process is identical to the query a client makes when using an ISP or public DNS service: the client requests the IP address for `website.com`. The answer includes the requested IP address, as well as any Canonical Name (CNAME) entries to show how the queried domain name was resolved. CNAME entries tell us which CDN hosting the requested object (e.g. `somecdn.com`).

After the first query, the client has obtained a CDN redirection to the client; however, the redirection is based on the *location of the recursive DNS server*. The subsequent queries provide the client with a CDN redirection based on its own location.

To directly query the CDN for a redirection requires that client know the IP address of `somecdn.com`'s authoritative DNS server. Sometimes this information is provided as part of the information in the first query. Most times, however, the authoritative server is not typically included in the DNS response but we may have the answer in a local cache. Alternatively, If the client does not know the authoritative DNS server, then it issues Query #2 asking the recursive DNS server for the authoritative DNS server for `somecdn.com`.

At this point, the client knows the address of the authoritative server and can directly obtain a CDN redirection (Query #3). The CDN's response contains a redirection based on the client's location. The client can then use the CDN redirection from Query #3 to address the server and download the objects for `website.com` from the CDN.

5.3 Performance evaluation

Since our *DR* approach for obtaining CDN redirections is functionally equivalent to iterative DNS resolution, we will

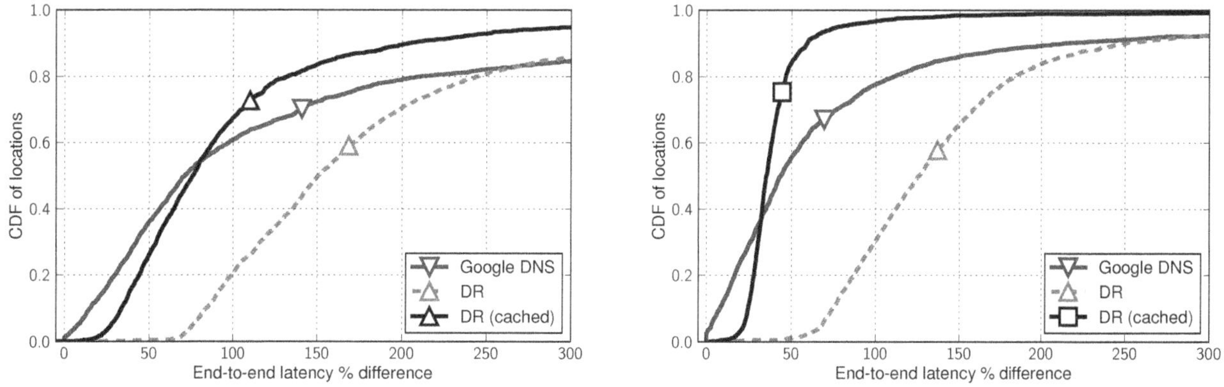

(a) Akamai (b) Limelight

Figure 14: CDFs of end-to-end latency difference relative to the best-case latency, comparing "Google DNS" with *DR* when the CDN server is not known ("DR") or is cached ("DR (cached)"). "DR (cached)" can provide significantly improved performance compared to "Google DNS".

receive mappings to the same set of edge servers. Since HTTP requests to edge servers are agnostic to *how* the edge server mappings were obtained, we expect that the HTTP performance under *DR* will match that of iterative resolution. As we reported in §4.2, this yields best-case HTTP performance.

To evaluate the *DR* approach in terms of end-to-end performance, however, we must also account for the latency to obtain the CDN redirection. Depending on whether the client has the CDN's authoritative DNS server address in its cache, this entails either two or three queries. When the authoritative server's address is not known, the client must make two queries to the recursive server and one query to the CDN's authoritative server. If the authoritative server is cached, then the client contacts the recursive server and then the authoritative server.

We compare the end-to-end performance of our *DR* approach—with and without knowing the authoritative server—with the performance of simply using a remote DNS service. Figure 14 plots the distribution of % difference in end-to-end latency compared to our ideal baseline, across our measurement locations, for both Akamai and Limelight CDNs. For example, using Akamai, the median location's end-to-end latency when using Google DNS is 60% higher than the ideal baseline. When using *DR*, having the CDN's authoritative DNS server cached ("DR (cached)") provides significantly better performance than when it is not cached ("DR"). Compared to Google DNS, "DR (cached)" provides significant performance improvement, especially in the upper tail of the distribution. Comparing directly Google DNS and "DR (cached)", our solution provides lower end-to-end performance in 49% of locations.

This comparison between our approach and remote DNS shows that the HTTP performance benefits from better CDN redirection do not always outweigh the latency of *DR*'s additional DNS query. We address this by proposing that a client determines whether it should conduct *DR*'s additional queries to obtain a better redirection. For the purpose of our evaluation, we assume the existence of an oracle that determines whether it makes sense to use *DR* or simply the CDN redirection from remote DNS. One way to implement

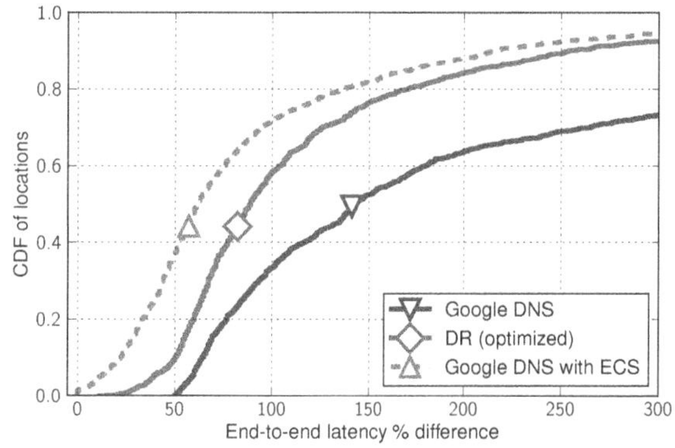

Figure 15: CDFs of end-to-end latency difference vs. best-case latency, for locations with > 50% remote DNS penalty. "DR (optimized)" shows performance for using an oracle to decide whether to use *DR*. This significantly improves on remote DNS performance, and is within a constant factor of the performance of "Google DNS with ECS".

this would be to use the results of previous redirections; when a prior *DR* redirection resulted in the same answer as that seen via remote DNS, *DR* would not be used and the client would return the redirection seen via remote DNS in Query #1.

To evaluate *DR*, we focus on the set of locations where remote DNS usage has the most impact. We select those locations in which the penalty from using remote DNS is at least 50%. This subset comprises 65% of the total set of locations. For these locations, Fig. 15 plots the distributions of % difference in end-to-end latency for Akamai CDN relative to our ideal baseline for *optimized DR* and remote DNS with and without the edns-client-subnet DNS extension.

Generally, *optimized DR* provides significantly improved performance compared to remote DNS. In the median case, *optimized DR* provides 1.6× better performance than remote

DNS (88% vs. 142%) and is even better at the 90th percentile (2.5× better). One reason is that in the extreme cases of poor performance using remote DNS, the HTTP latency to distance CDN edge servers dominates; *optimized DR* can provide significant improvements via nearer edge servers.

We also examine the relative performance of *optimized DR* and remote DNS with the edns-client-subnet DNS extension, finding that the distributions of performance match closely. *Optimized DR* is within 42% of the edns-client-subnet extension's performance in the median case (88% vs 62%) and within 18% at the 90th percentile. The difference in performance between these two approaches is generally consistent across the distribution, and is primarily due to the additional DNS request that the *DR* approach must make to obtain an edge server mapping.

Overall, these results show that the *optimized DR* approach not only attains performance within a constant factor of remote DNS with the edns-client-subnet DNS extension, but that it also significantly improves performance relative to just using remote DNS.

5.4 Implementation

We have implemented our optimized *DR* approach in *namehelp*, a DNS proxy that runs on the user's computer as a daemon and requires no modifications to the operating system. Our implementation is available for download.[6] *namehelp* compares the performance of alternative DNS services with respect to CDN performance, and presents the results to the user. We consider additional implementations, such as integration into operating systems or middleboxes, as future work.

5.4.1 DNS proxy daemon

To provide the benefits of our optimized *DR* approach, *namehelp* functions as a DNS proxy running on the user's computer. Configuring the DNS proxy simply requires the user to specify her DNS server as "localhost", so that all DNS requests will be directed to *namehelp*.

namehelp listens on the default port (53) for DNS queries, and forwards them to a configured recursive DNS service. Simple domain name responses are returned immediately by the *namehelp* proxy with no latency penalty. If the response from the recursive DNS contains a CDN redirection (e.g. a CNAME record), we invoke our *DR* approach to improve the CDN redirection before returning an answer.[7]

5.4.2 Performance comparison utility

namehelp also includes a DNS benchmarking tool based on *namebench* [18]. To compare DNS services, we adopt *namebench*'s approach, which makes queries to both public and ISP DNS servers for a set of domain names. By default, a list of popular sites from Alexa.com is used, but users can use their web browser history to personalize the results. Using the results of these tests, it ranks DNS servers by mean response time and shows potential server-specific issues to the user (e.g. NXDOMAIN hijacking [31]).

namehelp benchmarking service extends the functionality of *namebench* to evaluate CDN performance via different DNS services. Tests can be run against a list of popular websites, or tailored with a user's browsing history. In addition, the tool also probes DNS services to test for edns-client-subnet support, given its potential performance benefits when available (§4.3).

To evaluate end-to-end CDN performance provided by a DNS service, *namehelp* benchmarking downloads the selected web pages and their linked objects (i.e. images, scripts and stylesheets) using the given DNS service to resolve domain names. We determine end-to-end latency using the methodology from §3.3. We adopt a single-threaded architecture for downloading web objects for simplicity. Although optimizations for downloading web objects (e.g. parallel connections and HTTP pipelining) could change the *overall time* necessary to download a web page, our approach yields *comparable* results of end-to-end performance between public DNS services. Caching of DNS lookups and HTTP objects when possible minimizes the test's run time and the bandwidth consumed.

The results of these tests are presented to the user, enabling her to make an informed decision regarding which DNS service to use based not only on DNS performance (as *namebench*) but also including the resulting CDN performance.

6. RELATED WORK

Our work builds upon and significantly extends a number of past studies on DNS, CDNs and their interaction.

CDNs. In an early study by Krishnamurthy et al. [13], the authors evaluate characterize the benefits of CDNs from the client perspective. Johnson et al. [10] studied the redirection performance of CDNs and conclude that they succeed not by selecting optimal servers, but rather by avoiding making bad decisions. Wang et al. [33] analyze methods of maximizing CDN's objectives of improving response time and system throughput under a wide range of loads. Nygren et al. [19] describe several aspects of the Akamai's network, and Triukose et al. [29] studies Akamai's performance. WhyHigh [14] is a tool used by Google to identify and diagnose client performance issues from the CDN's perspective. Although a detailed view of a CDN's network is a valuable perspective for evaluating a CDN, a persistent challenge is accurately capturing the end-user's perceived performance under the range of alternative settings. In this work, we capture this end user's perspective to accurately characterize the end-to-end performance impact of remote DNS usage.

DNS and CDNs. DNS is a critical component of the Internet infrastructure and, since Mockapetris and Dunlap's [17] retrospective study, has been the subject of several measurement analysis (e.g. [1, 11, 15, 16, 22, 25]) and proposed design alternatives (including [23, 24]). A number of studies [1, 9, 12, 16, 25] have evaluated different aspects of DNS-based redirections and CDNs. Mao et al. [16] determine that this is sufficient for coarse-grained (e.g. AS-level) server selection, but not as precise at the granularity of BGP prefixes. Shaikh et al. [25] find the ping time to a client's DNS server is a poor predictor of ping time to the actual client. The recent growth in usage of remote DNS services, such as OpenDNS [20, 21] and Google DNS [6], has motivated studies on the implications of remote DNS and its interactions with CDN redirections. In a preliminary study of DNS resolvers by Ager et al. [1], the authors report

[6] http://aqualab.cs.northwestern.edu/projects/namehelp

[7] *namehelp* can be extended to detect CDNs configured via domain delegation by using a whitelist containing CDNs' authoritative DNS servers.

that typically-employed load balancing techniques have a detrimental effect on the efficacy of DNS caching and that public DNS-based redirection is less likely to point users to an available copy of content within their own network. Huang et al. [9] documented that a user's nearest public DNS server is considerably farther away than that user's ISP-provided DNS server, and that using a more-distant public DNS server resulted in redirections to edge servers that were farther away. Our work builds on and extends these studies by evaluating the end-to-end performance impact of remote DNS on CDNs and conducting an extensive diagnosis of the results.

Solutions. Several approaches have been proposed to address the poor interaction between remote DNS and CDN redirections. Khosla et al. [12] studied the interaction between "cloud-based" remote DNS and Akamai redirections and discussed several possible approaches to mitigate the performance penalty. Huang et al. proposed an application-level solution to address the mismatch between client and local DNS resolvers [8]. Several industry players have formed the "Global Internet Speedup" [28] collaboration. This group advocates for the adoption of the proposed edns-client-subnet DNS extension [3], which passes along part of a client's IP address to CDNs to improve DNS-based server selection decisions. Our work presents the first evaluation of the performance benefits and adoption of this DNS extension. In addition, we are the first to propose and evaluate a general client-based solution that allows *unmodified applications* to enjoy the benefits of improved redirections. We present *Direct Resolution*, an alternative end-host approach to the industry proposed DNS extension, describe *namehelp*, an implementation of the *DR* approach and evaluate its performance benefits.

7. CONCLUSION

We explored the end-to-end impact of using remote DNS services on CDN performance and presented the first evaluation of an industry-proposed solution to the problem. We showed that remote DNS usage can indeed significantly impact client's web performance and that the proposed solution, if available, can effectively address the problem for most clients. Considering the performance cost of remote DNS usage and the limited adoption base of the industry-proposed solution, we present and evaluate *Direct Resolution*, an alternative approach to readily obtain comparable performance improvements without requiring CDN or DNS participation. We have implemented our approach as part of *namehelp*, a DNS proxy running on the client local host. *namehelp* also provides a benchmark service, comparing the impact of alternative DNS services on CDN performance. We have made *namehelp* publicly available. We continue to monitor the adoption of the edns-client-subnet DNS extension by DNS services and CDNs. We are also studying approaches for evaluating the potential performance benefits of this extension when providing partial client location information, while investigating alternative heuristics to improve *namehelp*'s performance.

Acknowledgements

We would like to thank our shepherd, Alan Mislove, and the anonymous reviewers for their valuable feedback and assistance. We are always grateful to Paul Gardner for his assistance with Vuze and the users of our software for their invaluable data. This work was supported in part by the National Science Foundation through Awards CNS 0644062, CNS 0917233 and CNS 0855253 and by a generous Google Faculty Research Award.

8. REFERENCES

[1] B. Ager, W. Mühlbauer, G. Smaragdakis, and S. Uhlig. Comparing DNS resolvers in the wild. In *Proc. of IMC*, 2010.

[2] D. R. Choffnes and F. E. Bustamante. Taming the torrent: A practical approach to reducing cross-ISP traffic in peer-to-peer systems. In *Proc. of ACM SIGCOMM*, 2008.

[3] C. Contavalli, W. van der Gaast, S. Leach, and D. Rodden. Internet-draft: Client subnet in DNS requests, 2011. `http://tools.ietf.org/html/draft-vandergaast-edns-client-subnet-00`.

[4] G. Economou. How Akamai maps the net: an industry perspective, 2010. `http://www.akamai.com/dl/akamai/economu_mapping_the_internet.pdf`.

[5] EdgeScope – sharing the view from a distributed Internet telescope. `http://aqualab.cs.northwestern.edu/projects/EdgeScope`.

[6] Google Public DNS. `http://code.google.com/speed/public-dns/`.

[7] J. Hamilton. The cost of latency, October 2009. `http://perspectives.mvdirona.com/-2009/10/31/TheCostOfLatency.aspx`.

[8] C. Huang, I. Batanov, and J. Li. A practical solution to the Client-LDNS mismatch problem. *ACM CCR*, 42, 2012.

[9] C. Huang, D. A. Maltz, A. Greenberg, and J. Li. Public DNS System and Global Traffic Management. In *Proc. of IEEE INFOCOM*, 2011.

[10] K. L. Johnson, J. F. Carr, M. S. Day, and M. F. Kaashoek. The measured performance of content distribution networks. *Computer Communications*, 24, 2001.

[11] J. Jung, E. Sit, H. Balakrishnan, and R. Morris. DNS Performance and the Effectiveness of Caching. *IEEE/ACM Transactions on Networking*, October 2002.

[12] R. Khosla, S. Fahmy, and Y. C. Hu. Content retrieval using cloud-based DNS. In *Proc. of IEEE Global Internet Symposium*, 2012.

[13] B. Krishnamurthy, C. Wills, and Y. Zhang. On the use and performance of content distribution networks. In *Proc. of ACM IMW*, 2001.

[14] R. Krishnan, H. V. Madhyastha, S. Srinivasan, S. Jain, A. Krishnamurthy, T. Anderson, and J. Gao. Moving beyond end-to-end path information to optimize CDN performance. In *Proc. of IMC*, 2009.

[15] R. Liston, S. Srinivasan, and E. Zegura. Diversity in DNS performance measures. In *Proc. of ACM IMW*, 2002.

[16] Z. M. Mao, C. D. Cranor, F. Douglis, M. Rabinovich, O. Spatscheck, and J. Wang. A precise and efficient evaluation of the proximity between web clients and their local DNS servers. In *Proc. of USENIX ATC*, 2002.

[17] P. V. Mockapetris and K. J. Dunlap. Development of the Domain Name System. In *Proc. of ACM SIGCOMM*, Oct. 1998.

[18] *namebench*. http://code.google.com/p/namebench/.

[19] E. Nygren, R. K. Sitaraman, and J. Sun. The Akamai network: a platform for high-performance Internet applications. *ACM SIGOPS Operating Systems Review*, 44, August 2010.

[20] OpenDNS. More than 1 percent of the world's Internet users now using OpenDNS for a safer, faster, smarter and more reliable connection, March 2010. http://www.opendns.com/about/announcements/160.

[21] OpenDNS. Security industry leader dan hubbard joins opendns as chief technology officer, March 2012. http://www.opendns.com/about/announcements/303.

[22] V. Pappas, D. Wessels, D. Massey, S. Lu, A. Terzis, and L. Zhang. Impact of configuration errors on DNS robustness. *IEEE J.Sel. A. Commun.*, April 2009.

[23] K. Park, V. S. Pai, L. Peterson, and Z. Wang. CoDNS: improving DNS performance and reliability via cooperative lookups. In *Proc. of USENIX OSDI*, 2004.

[24] V. Ramasubramanian and E. G. Sirer. The design and implementation of a next generation name service for the Internet. In *Proc. of ACM SIGCOMM*, 2004.

[25] A. Shaikh, R. Tewari, and M. Agrawal. On the effectiveness of DNS-based server selection. In *Proc. of IEEE INFOCOM*, 2001.

[26] S. Souders. High performance web sites: 14 rules for faster loading pages, June 2009. http://stevesouders.com/docs/velocity-20090622.ppt – Statistic attributed to Greg Linden.

[27] A.-J. Su, D. R. Choffnes, F. E. Bustamante, and A. Kuzmanovic. Relative network positioning via CDN redirections. In *Proc. of ICDCS*, 2008.

[28] The Global Internet Speedup. A Faster Internet. http://www.afasterinternet.com.

[29] S. Triukose, Z. Web, and M. Rabinovich. Measuring a commercial content delivery network. In *Proc. of WWW*, 2011.

[30] P. Vixie. Extension mechanisms for DNS (EDNS0), 1999. http://www.ietf.org/rfc/rfc2671.txt.

[31] P. Vixie. What DNS is Not. ACM Queue, November 2009. http://queue.acm.org/detail.cfm?id=1647302.

[32] Vuze, Inc. Vuze. http://www.vuze.com.

[33] L. Wang, V. Pai, and L. Peterson. The effectiveness of request redirection on CDN robustness. In *Proc. of USENIX OSDI*, 2002.

[34] L. Whitney. Comcast customers hit by another major outage. *CNET News*, December 6 2010. http://news.cnet.com/8301-1023_3-20024692-93.html.

[35] L. Whitney. Major outage hits Comcast customers. *CNET News*, November 29 2010. http://news.cnet.com/8301-1023_3-20023949-93.html.

Measuring the Deployment of IPv6: Topology, Routing and Performance

Amogh Dhamdhere
CAIDA
Univ. of California, San Diego
amogh@caida.org

Matthew Luckie
CAIDA
Univ. of California, San Diego
mjl@caida.org

Bradley Huffaker
CAIDA
Univ. of California, San Diego
bhuffake@caida.org

Kc Claffy
CAIDA
Univ. of California, San Diego
kc@caida.org

Ahmed Elmokashfi
Simula Research
Oslo, Norway
ahmed@simula.no

Emile Aben
RIPE NCC
Amsterdam, NL
emile.aben@ripe.net

ABSTRACT

We use historical BGP data and recent active measurements to analyze trends in the growth, structure, dynamics and performance of the evolving IPv6 Internet, and compare them to the evolution of IPv4. We find that the IPv6 network is maturing, albeit slowly. While most core Internet transit providers have deployed IPv6, edge networks are lagging. Early IPv6 network deployment was stronger in Europe and the Asia-Pacific region, than in North America. Current IPv6 network deployment still shows the same pattern. The IPv6 topology is characterized by a single dominant player – Hurricane Electric – which appears in a large fraction of IPv6 AS paths, and is more dominant in IPv6 than the most dominant player in IPv4. Routing dynamics in the IPv6 topology are largely similar to those in IPv4, and churn in both networks grows at the same rate as the underlying topologies. Our measurements suggest that performance over IPv6 paths is comparable to that over IPv4 paths if the AS-level paths are the same, but can be much worse than IPv4 if the AS-level paths differ.

Categories and Subject Descriptors

C.2.2 [**COMPUTER-COMMUNICATION NETWORKS**]: Network Protocols—*Routing Protocols*

Keywords

IPv6, BGP, Internet topology, routing, performance

General Terms

Experimentation, Measurement

1. INTRODUCTION

The Internet operations, engineering and research communities are putting significant attention into a relatively new version (actually 15 years old) of the Internet Protocol – IP version 6 (IPv6) [1] – designed to solve several architectural limitations of the existing IPv4 protocol. The most essential characteristic of IPv6 is that it has provides orders of magnitude more address space than the world's foreseeable IP connectivity needs. IPv6 has become especially pertinent in the last two years because the global Internet address allocation architecture relies on the presence of a free pool of IP addresses to allocate to sites operating Internet infrastructure. The Internet Assigned Numbers Authority (IANA) exhausted its unallocated address pool in February 2011, and the Asia-Pacific region (represented by the APNIC RIR) followed suit in April 2011. The remaining RIRs too are expected to run out of unallocated addresses in the next few years [2]. This exogenous pressure from IPv4 address scarcity has driven widespread adoption of IPv6 into modern operating systems and network equipment. Major network operators and content providers are deploying IPv6 on both a trial and production basis [3], and some governments are mandating IPv6 support [4, 5]. But there is little hard data about how mature the IPv6 network is in terms of composition, topology, routing, and performance.

While IPv6 penetration remains small compared to IPv4, the IPv6 network topology has shown two distinct growth phases – for both ASes and AS links, an initial linear growth ($y{=}ax{+}b$) followed by exponential ($y{=}ae^{bx}$) gives the best fit with the data, with the change in trajectory occurring around 2008. The exponents for ASes and AS links are 0.13 and 0.16, respectively (Figure 1). It is interesting that the IPv4 network topology growth shifted from exponential to linear a decade ago [6]. While the current exponential growth of IPv6 hints that it may finally have shifted from an experimental or "toy" network to production, the nature of its growth is still largely undocumented. Which network types and geographic regions contribute the most? Does the growing IPv6 network appear to converge toward the existing IPv4 network? How do routing dynamics in IPv6 compare to IPv4? Does performance over IPv6 paths approach that over IPv4 paths?

In this study we use historical BGP archives and recent active measurements of the public IPv4 and IPv6 network infrastructures to analyze the state of maturity of IPv6 de-

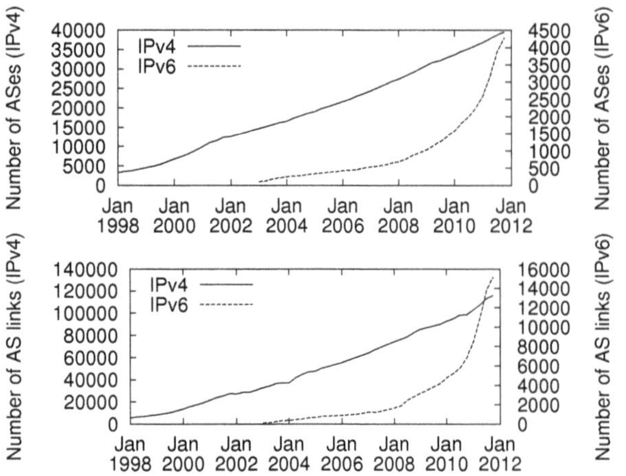

Figure 1: Both AS nodes and links grow linearly in IPv4 but exponentially (as of 2007) in IPv6.

ployment along three dimensions: topology, routing, and performance. Section 2 describes the data sources and supporting analysis techniques we use throughout the paper. We find that the IPv6 network is maturing, as indicated by its increasing similarity in size and composition (Section 3), AS path congruity (Section 4), topological structure (Section 5), and dynamics (Section 6), to the public IPv4 Internet. While core Internet transit providers have mostly deployed IPv6, edge networks are lagging behind. While all geographic regions show exponential growth in IPv6 adoption, early IPv6 deployment was stronger in Europe and the Asia-Pacific region than in North America. The IPv6 network is characterized by the presence of a single prominent player, Hurricane Electric (HE). Hurricane Electric currently appears in between 20% and 95% of IPv6 AS paths seen from different vantage points, and is more prominent in IPv6 than the most prominent player in IPv4. Further, when IPv4 and IPv6 AS paths differ, HE is the network most often added to the IPv6 path. Routing dynamics in the IPv6 topology are largely similar to those in IPv4. While routing churn grows linearly in IPv4 and super-linearly in IPv6, it is important to note that these trends match those of the underlying IPv4 and IPv6 AS topology growth. In terms of performance (Section 7), our measurements show that IPv6 data-plane performance closely matches IPv4 performance when the AS-level paths are the same, while it can be significantly worse when AS-level paths differ.

2. DATASETS AND METHODS

We use a variety of data sources and analysis methods, which we summarize here, providing more detail in sections that use specific data. Our analysis of the IPv6 Internet's size, routing behavior, and structure (Sections 3-5) relies on publicly available historical BGP tables. Section 6 uses BGP updates from the same public repositories to analyze routing dynamics of the IPv4 and IPv6 networks over time. We gather our own data using active measurements from five vantage points around the world, to compare and correlate IPv4 and IPv6 performance with other growth parameters. To compare the composition of the IPv4 and IPv6 graphs according to type of networks, we classify the business types of ASes using the algorithm presented in our previous work [6] and the business relationships of the links between them (*e.g.*, customer, provider, peer) using Gao's algorithm [7].

BGP topology data

We collected historical BGP data from the two major public repositories at RouteViews [8] and RIPE [9]. We rely only on these two data sources because no other source of topological/routing data (routing registries, traceroutes, looking glass servers, etc.) provides historical information. Routeviews and RIPE started collecting IPv4 BGP data as early as 1998; the first IPv6 collector, however, became active in 2003. Consequently, our IPv4 data spans 14 years from 1998 to 2011, while the IPv6 data is from 2003 to 2011. The use of Routeviews/RIPE repositories of BGP data has been shown to inadequately expose the *complete Internet topology* [10, 11, 12] – although this data captures most ASes, it misses a significant fraction of peering and backup links at the edges of the Internet [13, 12, 14]. However, we are mainly interested in customer-provider links used most of the time. AS links revealed by short term failures and transient routing events can "confuse" an evolutionary study, misinterpreting link disappearances and appearances due to transient failures as link deaths and births respectively. For example, the primary link l_p between ASes X and Y fails at time t_1, causing the activation of a backup link l_b between ASes X and Z. l_p is repaired at t_2 and the connectivity returns to its original state. Since we focus on primary links, our goal is to ignore the transient event during (t_1, t_2) and not detect l_b. On the other hand, a change of routing policy that makes l_b the primary link should be detected as the death of l_p and the birth of l_b. To remove backup and transient links, we apply the method of "majority filtering" described in our previous work [6] on the set of BGP AS paths obtained from BGP table dumps at Routeviews and RIPE collectors. We do not use BGP updates to construct our topology snapshots, as these reveal backup and transient links which we want to filter. The majority filtering method works as follows. For both IPv4 and IPv6, we construct a topology snapshot by collecting 5 sets of AS paths over a duration of 3 weeks, only using AS paths that were seen in a majority of those five samples. We collect such a topology snapshot every 3 months, resulting in 56 snapshots of the IPv4 topology and 36 snapshots of the IPv6 topology. We refer the reader to our previous work [6] for a detailed description of the data collection and pre-processing.

BGP routing dynamics data

Our comparative analysis of routing dynamics of the IPv4 and IPv6 infrastructures is based on BGP updates collected by the Routeviews project. Routeviews collectors run BGP sessions with routers (or *monitors*) in many networks. Each monitor sends a BGP update to the collector every time there is a change in the preferred path from the monitor to a destination prefix. We use update traces from two Routeviews collectors: Routeviews6 for IPv6 data and Oregon-IX for IPv4 data. The IPv4 updates span the period from 1 Jan 2003 to 16 Feb 2012, while the IPv6 updates span 7 May 2003 through 16 Feb 2012. We use monitors from five networks that contributed both IPv4 and IPv6 routing data throughout the study period: AT&T, Hurricane Electric (HE), NTT-America, and Tinet, and IIJ. AT&T's IPv4 monitor was unavailable for three months in 2003, and its IPv6 monitor was unavailable between May 2005 and May

2007. Tinet's IPv6 monitor was unavailable between June 2008 and June 2010. If the multi-hop BGP session between a monitor and the collector is broken and re-established (session reset), the monitor re-announces all its known paths, producing large bursts of updates. This is a local artifact of the Routeviews measurement infrastructure, and does not represent genuine routing dynamics. We use the method developed by Zhang *et al.* [15] to identify and remove updates caused by session resets.

AS relationships

We use Gao's AS relationship classification algorithm [7] to infer the business relationship associated with each inter-AS link.[1] For each snapshot, we apply this algorithm to the set of IPv4 AS paths. Gao's algorithm classifies AS links into the following types: sibling, customer-provider, settlement-free peer, and unknown. Our focus is on customer-provider and settlement-free peering links, so we exclude the sibling and unknown classes, which account for fewer than 1% of the AS links in any snapshot.

AS classification

In our previous work [6], we developed a method to classify ASes according to their expected business type. The method relies on a machine learning decision tree classifier which uses as input two properties inferred for each AS – the average number of customers and average number of peers over the lifespan of that AS. By peers we mean settlement-free peers in a routing sense; we cannot know for sure if there is a settlement between them. In that study we used this method to classify each AS into four classes – Enterprise Customer (EC), Small Transit Provider (STP), Large Transit Provider (LTP), and Content/Access/Hosting Provider (CAHP) – with an accuracy of 85%. Note that the AS types we consider are quite distinct from each other in terms of their function and business goals. It is thus reasonable to expect that ASes do not change from one AS type to another during their lifetime. We validated this assumption in our previous work by running the classification algorithm using only a two-year dataset; we found that only 3% of AS classifications changed as compared to the entire dataset [6]. For this study we repeated the classification algorithm using the 14-year dataset described above to obtain a new classification. Of the ASes present in both datasets, only 2.4% had a different classification. We assume that an AS has the same business type in IPv6 as in IPv4. We further classify ASes according to their primary geographical region of operation, as reflected in the RIR database (WHOIS) where the AS is registered: ARIN (North America), RIPE (Europe, Middle East, and the former USSR), APNIC (Asia/Pacific), AfriNIC (Africa), and LACNIC (Latin America).

Performance data

Similar to the method employed by Nikkhah *et al.* [16], we measure the average time to fetch a page from webservers registered in the DNS with IPv4 and IPv6 addresses that have the same origin AS number in the longest matching BGP route. We use the Alexa list of the one-million most popular websites in the Internet, testing up to three webservers for each origin AS. We try to avoid a common problem with throughput measurements, namely never getting out of TCP's slow start phase, by seeking to download a page that is at least 10,000 bytes. If the web site's root page is smaller than that, we fetch the smallest object embedded in that page that is at least 10,000 bytes[2]. While a threshold of 10,000 bytes is not always sufficient to get out of slow start, it seeks to balance the tradeoff between finding a large number of web objects to download, and ensuring that those objects are sufficiently large. We fetch each page three times from each webserver, alternating IPv4 and IPv6 transport sequentially. Each measurement begins approximately five seconds after the previous one completes to avoid competing measurements but also to minimize the chance of network topology changes mid-measurement. We also measure the forward AS-level IPv4 and IPv6 paths using traceroute with TCP probes immediately after the sequence of performance measurements completes. We collected this data from five vantage points: a state network in New York; a research network in Japan; a commercial ISP in Japan; a commercial network in the Netherlands; and an enterprise customer in the Netherlands. We sanitized our measurements as in [16]: We excluded from performance evaluation those measurements where the standard error of the mean download time (for either IPv4 or IPv6) was greater than 10% (at the 95% significance level), or the object sizes in IPv4 and IPv6 were not within 1% of each other. This filtering left us with 544 dual-stack ASes represented in our dataset, consisting of 233 ECs, 106 STPs, 10 LTPs, and 195 CAHPs according to the previously described classification. We used scamper's tbit and traceroute implementations [17]; the former includes a test that fetches a page, negotiating TCP SACK and TCP timestamps, and records all packets sent and received during the test, which allows us to further examine the packet traces to infer why performance may differ.

3. GROWTH TRENDS BY BUSINESS TYPE AND GEOGRAPHIC REGION

While overall growth rates indicate that IPv6 deployment is accelerating, these growth rates differ by (business) type of network and geographic region. Since IPv6 provides essentially the same functionality as IPv4, we hypothesize that as IPv6 matures, the distribution of business types in IPv6 should resemble that in IPv4. Geographic coverage of IPv6 may not exhibit the same convergence with IPv4 given the pre-existing allocation of IPv4 address space around the world and various levels of pressure by different national governments to promote IPv6.

3.1 Growth trends by business type

Figure 2 shows the fraction of networks over time from each of the four business types mentioned in Section 2, for the IPv4 (top panel) and IPv6 (bottom panel) topologies. Above each panel, we show the total number of ASes in the IPv4 and IPv6 graphs over which the fractions are computed. At least since 1998 (when historical BGP data became available), the IPv4 topology has always consisted of a large fraction of EC networks; currently 90% of ASes are EC, while STPs and CAHPs comprise most of the remaining 10%. In 2003 only 35% of IPv6 networks were of type EC, but this fraction has increased steadily, currently at 60%. The relatively large fractions of STPs and CAHPs in the

[1]We are in the process of developing and validating a new AS relationship classification algorithm, but for this study we use Gao [7].

[2]Nikkhah *et al.* [16] fetched the root page regardless of size.

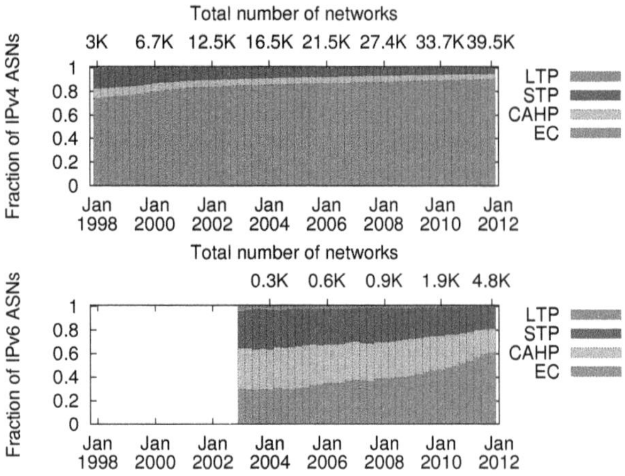

Figure 2: As IPv6 matures the fraction of EC ASes has grown from 35% to over 60% of the IPv6 graph, while IPv4 has seen little change, with ECs currently at 90%.

IPv6 topology suggests that IPv6 deployment has primarily occurred at the core of the network, driven by transit and content providers.

To further explore the evolution of business types in IPv6, we measure growth trends for each AS type in the IPv4 and IPv6 graphs. We find that ECs, STPs and CAHPs all grow linearly in IPv4 after 2001. The IPv6 graph has evolved differently. For ECs, STPs, and CAHPs, we find that an initial linear growth phase from 2003 (when data archiving began) until 2007-2008, followed by exponential growth until the present time gives the best fit with the data. The exponents for ECs, STPs, and CAHPs in the exponential growth phase are 0.16, 0.09, and 0.08, respectively.[3]

We also measure the growth rate (in ASes/month) of each business type in the IPv4 and IPv6 graphs (graph omitted due to space constraints). In both the IPv4 and IPv6 graphs, ECs show the highest growth rate, although the growth rate of ECs in the IPv4 graph (between 50 and 350 ASes/month over the last 14 years) has always been larger than in the IPv6 graph. Only since 2011 has the EC growth rate in IPv6 been comparable to that in the IPv4 graph. In fact, the growth rate of ECs in the IPv6 graph reached a peak of 182 ASes/month in mid-2011 and then declined, coincident with *World IPv6 Day* [18] in June 2011, and consistent with Aben's observation that the overall growth rate of IPv6 ASes peaked around the World IPv6 day [19]. The growth rate of STP and CAHP ASes in IPv4 has been almost constant over the last 14 years (between -2 and 20 ASes/month); interestingly, the growth rates for these types in the IPv6 graph are similar (between -2 and 40 ASes/month), and since 2010, the growth rates in IPv6 are larger than those in IPv4 (in fact, STPs and CAHPs show recent negative growth in the IPv4 graph). The recent spurt in the growth rate of IPv6 ECs to a level that is comparable with the growth rate of IPv4 ECs is encouraging: it implies that IPv6 deployment at the edges, which has historically lagged behind deployment at the core, is now catching up.

[3]We omit the graph due to space constraints

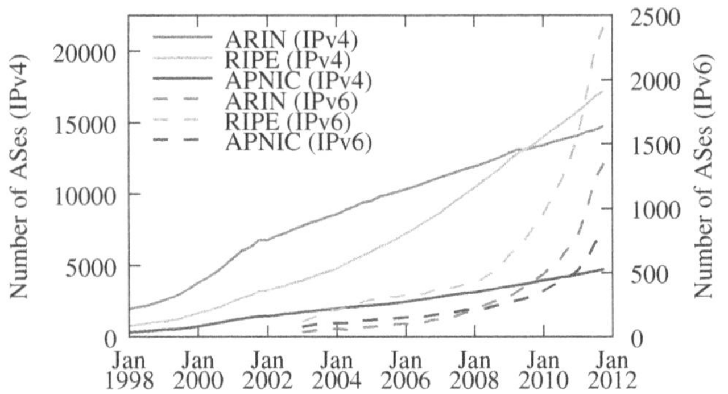

Figure 3: Regional growth in IPv4 and IPv6 ASes. RIPE overtook ARIN in the IPv4 graph in 2009; RIPE has always been ahead in IPv6.

3.2 Growth trends by geographical region

Figure 3 shows the number of ASes in different geographical regions over time, according to the RIR WHOIS mappings described in Section 2. We omit the two smallest registries (LACNIC and AfriNIC), which have so few ASes compared to the three large registries (ARIN, RIPE and APNIC) that they are barely visible in the graph. The graph shows that for IPv4, the growth rate of RIPE-registered ASes has exceeded that of ARIN-registered ASes for the last decade (though both ARIN and RIPE showed linear growth in this period), and as of 2009 the RIPE region has more ASes than the ARIN region, a big difference from the early days of IPv4. For the IPv6 graph, on the other hand, the growth trend for each of the ARIN, RIPE and APNIC registries shows two distinct periods since 2003 – an initial linear phase followed by an exponential phase (with exponents 0.13, 0.13 and 0.11, respectively) until the present time. For ARIN and RIPE, the change from linear to exponential happened around 2007-2008, while for APNIC it was at the start of 2009. Unlike IPv4, however, the RIPE region has always had more ASes in IPv6 than ARIN. APNIC had more ASes than ARIN until 2008, when the IPv6 AS growth rate in the ARIN region changed to exponential. *While the RIPE and APNIC regions led early adoption of IPv6, adoption in the ARIN region is accelerating, and the number of ARIN-registered and RIPE-registered ASes in IPv6 currently grow at the same rates.*

The business type classification of the previous section reveals more insight into growth across different geographic regions. Although growth in ECs in different regions mostly follows the same trends as for all ASes (shown in Figure 3), STPs and CAHPs behave differently. In the IPv4 graph, the growth rate of ARIN-registered STPs was almost identical to that of RIPE-registered STPs (around 5 ASes/month) until 2002. Since 2002, however, the growth rate of ARIN-registered STPs has slowed to 1.5 ASes/month, while that of RIPE-registered STPs is around 3 ASes/month. Consequently, the number of RIPE-registered STPs soon surpassed ARIN-registered STPs. This difference may derive from contrasting regulatory environments which led to more competition in the transit market in Europe than in North America. Another possible explanation is the tendency of small Eastern European networks to use Provider-Independent (PI) address space [20] which is typically advertised in BGP with its own ASN, rather than Provider-Aggregatable

Peer	ASN	Name	Type	BGP source	When
ACOnet	1853	Austrian Academic Computer Network	CAHP	RIS RRC 05	Oct 2003
IIJ	2497	Internet Initiative Japan	STP	Routeviews 2/6	Jul 2003
NTT	2914	NTT Global IP Network	LTP	Routeviews 2/6	Jul 2003
Tinet	3257	Tiscali International Network	LTP	Routeviews 2/6	Oct 2003
HE	6939	Hurricane Electric	LTP	Routeviews 2/6	Jul 2003
AT&T	7018	AT&T Services	LTP	Routeviews 2/6	Apr 2004
BIT	12859	BIT BV	STP	RIS RRC 03	Jan 2003

Table 1: BGP vantage points (VPs) providing both IPv4 and IPv6 routing data since 2003. Six of the seven networks are transit providers, which may bias our view of the topology because we miss peering links below.

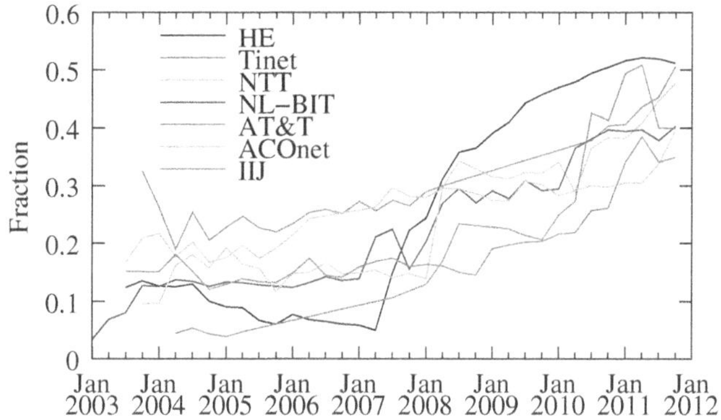

Figure 4: Fraction of dual-stacked origin ASes reachable over an identical AS-level path in both IPv4 and IPv6. Currently, more than 40% of the AS-level paths used to reach an origin are the same in both protocols.

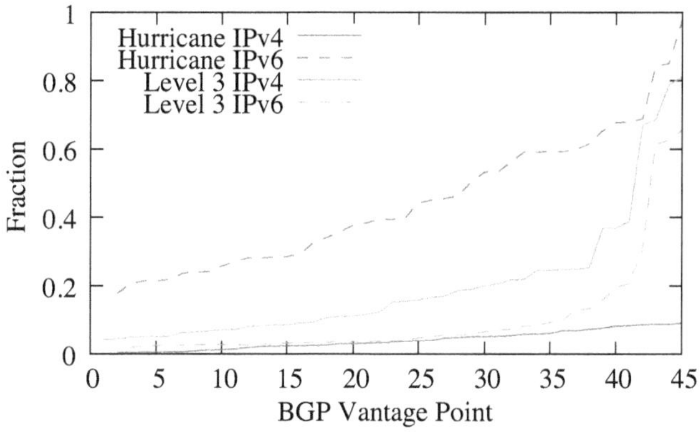

Figure 5: Fraction of origin ASes reached via an AS for each BGP vantage point in October 2011. Hurricane is relatively more prominent in the IPv6 topology than Level3 is in the IPv4 topology.

(PA) address space which is typically advertised in BGP by a provider network. In the IPv6 graph the number of STPs and CAHPs in the RIPE region has exceeded that of the ARIN region since 2003 (the start of IPv6 data collection), consistent with the stronger community pressure in Europe for operators to support IPv6, including European Commission funding for IPv6 deployment from its early stages.

4. EVOLVING STRUCTURE OF IPV4 AND IPV6 TOPOLOGIES: AS PATHS

Similar to our belief that the composition of a maturing IPv6 topology should look more like the IPv4 topology, we also expect a convergence to occur between the best AS path between a given pair of ASes in IPv4 and IPv6. Another reason to compare IPv4 and IPv6 AS path congruity is its correlation with performance. In Section 7 we show that *IPv6 data plane performance is worse than IPv4 when the AS paths differ, but when the AS paths are the same, IPv6 performance is comparable to that of IPv4.* Improved congruity between IPv4 and IPv6 paths seem to improve IPv6 performance, which is likely to further promote IPv6 deployment. To explore trends in congruity between IPv4 and IPv6 paths, we first calculate the fraction of AS paths from a given vantage point (VP) toward dual-stacked origin ASes (*i.e.*, ASes that advertise both IPv4 and IPv6 prefixes) that are identical in IPv4 and IPv6. If there are multiple IPv4 or IPv6 AS paths available between a given VP and an origin AS, we report it having an identical AS path if any of the paths are the same. If they differ, we dissect the differences, in terms of which ASes are added and removed from those paths. This analysis also reveals the presence of dominant players in the IPv6 topology.

We first measure the evolution of IPv6 from seven vantage points listed in Table 1 (four LTPs, two STPs, and one CAHP) which have provided BGP data to Routeviews and RIS since 2003. For each topology snapshot, we use the set of majority-filtered (as described in Section 2) AS paths exported by these six monitors. We remove all prepending from AS paths, and discard paths with AS sets or loops. This filtering process rejects 0.1% of AS paths due to AS sets or loops.

Identical AS paths in IPv4 and IPv6

Figure 4 plots the fraction of dual-stack paths that are identical in IPv4 and IPv6 from each vantage point over time. According to this metric, IPv6 paths are maturing slowly. In January 2004, 10-20% of paths were the same for IPv4 and IPv6; eight years later, 40-50% of paths are the same for six of the seven vantage points. The most significant trend in this data is the rise in prominence of Hurricane Electric. In April 2007 only 5% of its dual-stacked paths were identical, but in 2012 just over 50% of dual-stacked paths are the same from Hurricane's perspective.

Different ASes in IPv4 and IPv6 AS paths

Since only between 40% and 50% of the AS paths from different vantage points to dual-stacked origin ASes are the same, the next question is: how do the paths differ? We compute the AS edits required to make the IPv4 paths identical to the

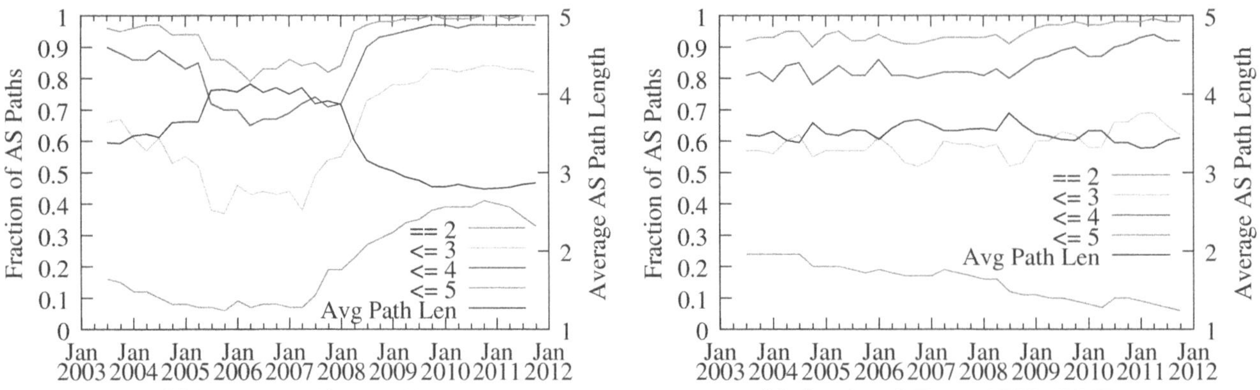

(a) Hurricane Electric, IPv6.

(b) Combined Tinet, NTT, IIJ IPv6.

Figure 6: Average AS path lengths to dual-stacked origin networks over time from different vantage points, and the fraction of paths of length 2 (directly connected), length ≤ 3, and so on. In January 2011, HE was directly connected to 40% of dual-stacked origin ASes in IPv6. Since 2003, other transit providers have observed the fraction of directly connected dual-stack ASes decrease.

IPv6 paths – specifically, which ASes are most often added and removed from AS paths that differ. Between 2011 and 2012 Hurricane Electric was added to between 20% and 50% of IPv6 paths that were different to a corresponding IPv4 path, depending on the vantage point. There were no other ASes added to IPv6 paths as frequently and consistently across vantage points as Hurricane. No AS is consistently missing from IPv4 paths.

ASes most frequently seen in AS paths

Next, we examine the AS paths from all BGP vantage points (VPs) that provide a full table[4] to Routeviews and RIPE collectors in October 2011 to determine the relative *prominence* of ASes in the IPv4 and IPv6 topologies. We define the *prominence* of an AS X to a VP as the fraction of origin ASes that are reached through it.[5] While the AS that appears most often depends on the VP in question, we find that for all IPv6 VPs, Hurricane Electric appears in the largest fraction of AS paths (between 20% and 95%, see Figure 5). Contrast this with the importance of Hurricane Electric in the IPv4 topology, where it appears in fewer than 10% of AS paths from any given vantage point. Level3 (AS3356), the largest player in the IPv4 space in terms of this metric, appears in between 5% and 80% of IPv4 AS paths, depending on the vantage point. This data suggests that *Hurricane Electric is more prominent in the IPv6 graph than the most prominent player in the IPv4 graph.*

AS path lengths in IPv4 and IPv6

Even though the IPv4 AS graph continues to grow in the number of ASes (linearly, after initial exponential growth until 2002), the average AS path length as measured from Routeviews/RIPE vantage points is *almost constant around 4 AS hops* since January 1998 [6]. We emphasize that this result is based on ASes that provide data to Routeviews and RIPE collectors, and does not necessarily reflect the average AS path length that an arbitrary AS sees. Figure 7 shows the average path length (in AS hops after removing AS prepending) in the IPv4 and IPv6 topologies over time, as measured from all Routeviews and RIPE vantage points. The average AS path length for IPv6 shows a *decreasing trend*, and showed a sharp decrease since 2008. This result is counter-intuitive, given the relative sparseness of the IPv6 topology as compared to the IPv4 topology. We dig deeper into the possible reasons for the decreasing IPv6 AS path length, by measuring the average AS path length from different IPv6 capable monitors over time.

Figure 6 shows the average AS path length seen from the perspective of Hurricane Electric (6(a)), and from the other vantage points (6(b)). The average path lengths from vantage points other than HE are similar, hence we group them together. The plot also shows the number of AS paths of length 2 (origin AS is directly connected to the VP), of length ≤ 3, and so on. Our main observation is that the average IPv6 AS path length seen by Hurricane Electric decreases, while for other transit providers it is almost constant. The fraction of ASes directly connected to Hurricane in IPv6 increased from 10% in Jan 2007 to 40% in Jan 2010, perhaps as a result of Hurricane's open peering policy in IPv6 [21]. Other transit providers saw the fraction of dual-stacked networks that are directly connected decline (indicated by the curve labeled "==2" in Figure 6(b)), further confirming the rising dominance of HE in the IPv6 topology. We conclude that the overall decreasing trend seen in the average IPv6 AS path length is due to this increasing dominance of HE in the IPv6 topology. We recommend caution in analyzing graph properties of the IPv6 AS topology; due to its relatively small size, the presence of even a few important ASes such as Hurricane Electric can significantly affect overall graph properties.

5. EVOLVING STRUCTURE OF IPV4 AND IPV6 TOPOLOGIES: AS GRAPHS

We next directly compare the IPv4 and IPv6 topologies over time. Again we hypothesize that as the IPv6 network matures, its topological structure should grow more congruent with IPv4's structure, *i.e.*, an increasing fraction of ASes and AS links will be common to both topologies, the most

[4]We define a VP as having a full table if it has BGP paths to at least 35,000 IPv4 ASes and 3,900 IPv6 ASes.

[5]This metric is related to *betweenness centrality*, but only uses paths observed from a single VP.

highly connected ASes should grow to be more similar in both topologies, and upstream IPv4 and IPv6 providers for the same edge AS should eventually converge.

5.1 Common ASes and AS links in the IPv4 and IPv6 graphs

For each topology snapshot, we find the set of ASes that are present in either the IPv4 or the IPv6 AS topology, which we call the combined topology. In each snapshot, more than 99% of ASes and more than 96% of AS links in the combined topology were present in the IPv4 topology, *i.e.*, *the number of ASes that are unique to the IPv6 topology is negligibly small.* Consequently, we focus most of our analysis on the set of ASes from the combined topology that were present in the IPv6 topology.

Common ASes present in IPv6 topology

Figure 8 shows the fraction of ASes from the combined topology that are present in the IPv6 topology. We measure these fractions for all ASes, and further classify ASes according to business type. We find that the fraction of ASes from the combined topology that are seen in the IPv6 topology varies widely depending on business type. Almost all LTPs are now seen in the IPv6 topology; The 3 exceptions are AS1 (owned by Level 3 Communications, but no longer the primary ASN), AS7132 (owned by AT&T. AS7018, also owned by AT&T is in the IPv6 topology), and AS3786 (owned by LG DACOM. AS9316 owned by the same organization is in the IPv6 topology). Significantly, *around 50% of STPs and CAHPs from the combined topology are also present in IPv6, while fewer than 10% of ECs are seen in the IPv6 topology.* Since the combined AS topology is dominated by ECs, the overall fraction of ASes seen in IPv6 is similarly low, which further confirms our earlier observation that IPv6 adoption is faster in the core of the network while the edge (ECs) has been slow to deploy IPv6.

We also measured the fraction of ASes from the combined topology that are present in IPv6, separately for each geographic region (figure omitted due to space constraints). *We find that this fraction is less than 20% for each geographic region.* As of late 2011, the APNIC region (for which 16% of ASes from the combined topology are present in IPv6) is slightly ahead of RIPE (14%), which is well ahead of ARIN (9%). Interestingly, this ordering is the same order in which the registries either ran out (APNIC in April 2011 [2]) or are projected to run out of IPv4 addresses (RIPE in August 2012, and ARIN in June 2013). As early as 2003, news

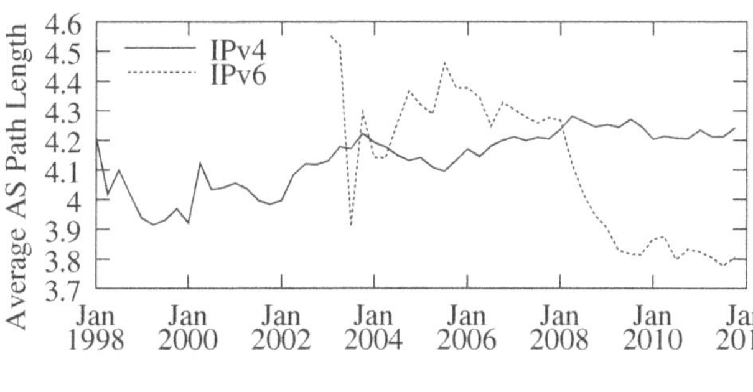

Figure 7: Average IPv4 AS path length is almost constant, while in IPv6 it decreases.

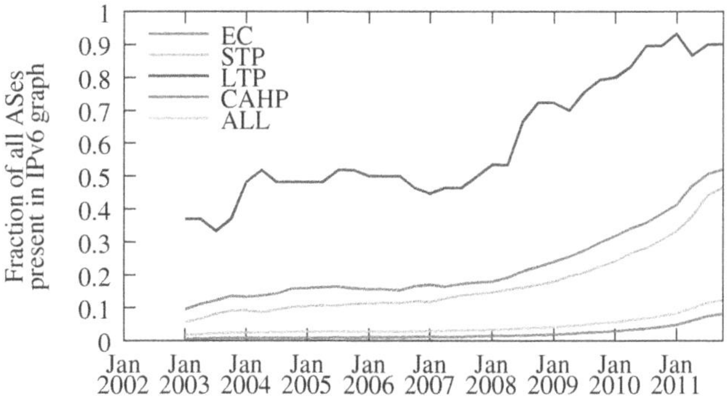

Figure 8: Fraction of ASes from the combined (IPv4+IPv6) graph that are present in the IPv6 graph, classified according to business type and geographical region. Less than 10% of ECs, while 90% of LTPs are present in the IPv6 graph.

reports claimed APNIC to run out of allocatable IPv4 addresses first, with RIPE and ARIN soon to follow [22].

ASes unique to the IPv6 topology

We briefly comment on the small set of ASes that were present only in the IPv6 topology. In our latest topology snapshot from October 2011, 109 ASes were only in the IPv6 topology. Of these, 42 ASes (34 ECs, 5 STP, and 3 CAHPs) were in the IPv4 topology in some previous snapshot (and hence we were able to assign business types to these ASes). Inspection of the as-names and descriptions of the other 67 ASes (as they appear in the RIR whois databases) reveals that 27 can be trivially matched with ASes in the IPv4 topology that have similar names and descriptions. This overlap hints at organizations using separate ASes to provide IPv4 and IPv6 connectivity. Furthermore, we found that 2 ASes unique to the IPv6 topology were administered by universities that used IPv4 address space announced from the respective national research and education networks ASes. This shows that organizational boundaries of the entities that manage ASes in the IPv4 and IPv6 topology do not always align.

Common top ASes

We measure the fraction of the top-K ASes (in terms of AS degree) from the IPv4 topology that are also top among the top-K ASes in the IPv6 topology. As the IPv6 network matures, we expect that the top ASes from the IPv4 topology will also appear as the top ASes in the IPv6 topology. Figure 9 shows the fraction of the top-K ASes from the IPv4 topology that are also among the top-K ASes in the IPv6 topology, for K=10, 50 and 100. This fraction has increased from around 20% in 2003 to more than 60% currently. Until 2008, however, the top-K fraction for K=10 was significantly smaller than that for K=50 and K=100, indicating that the largest ASes in the IPv4 topology were either not present in IPv6, or were not among the largest ASes in the IPv6 topology. This difference has decreased sharply in the last 3-4 years – currently 60% of the top-10 ASes from IPv4 are also in the top-10 for the IPv6 topology.

Common AS links

Finally, we are interested in the common set of AS links between the IPv4 and IPv6 topologies. As mentioned in

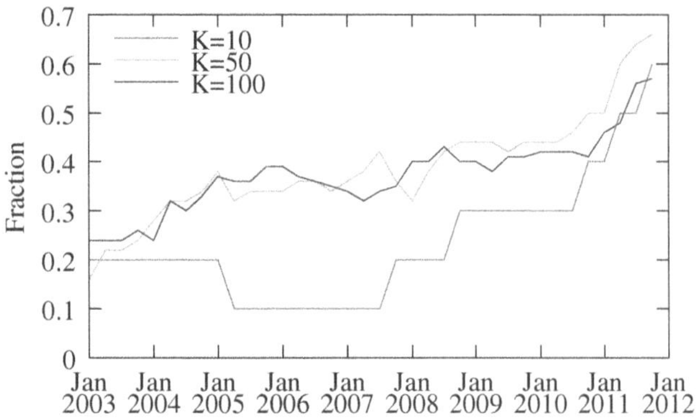

Figure 9: Fraction of ASes from the top-K ASes in the IPv4 graph that are also in the top-K ASes in the IPv6 graph. The fractions increase for different K values.

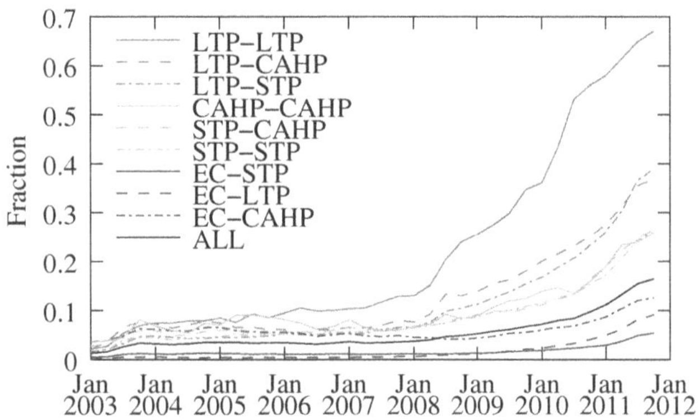

Figure 10: Fraction of AS links from combined (IPv4+IPv6) graph that are present in the IPv6 graph, classified according to business type of link endpoints.

Section 2, our BGP vantage points are likely to miss some AS links, particularly peering links lower in the hierarchy than the Routeviews/RIPE BGP monitors. We are, however, interested in the fraction of links from the IPv4 topology which were also seen in the IPv6 topology. The aforementioned visibility issues should affect both the IPv4 and IPv6 graphs similarly, and hence our analysis should not be impacted by missing peering links in the measured IPv4 and IPv6 topologies. Figure 10 shows the fraction of AS links from the combined topology that also appear in the IPv6 topology over time. We compute this fraction for all AS links and also classify them based on the business types of the endpoints. As with ASes, the fraction of AS links seen in the IPv6 topology is less than 20% for the overall graph. This fraction varies widely, however with the business type of the AS on each end of the link. Links involving ECs are the least represented in the IPv6 graph, while larger fractions of links involving STPs, LTPs, and CAHPs are seen in the IPv6 graph. This is again consistent with our previous finding that the pace of IPv6 adoption is higher in the core of the network but lags at the edge (represented by ECs).

6. EVOLVING DYNAMICS OF IPV4 AND IPV6 INFRASTRUCTURE

Continuing to explore our hypothesis that a maturing IPv6 network should look more like the IPv4 network, we compare the evolution of routing dynamics in IPv4 and IPv6. In particular, we focus on the evolution of update churn, correlation between the update churn seen from different vantage points, path exploration, and convergence times in IPv4 and IPv6. We focus on these metrics for the following reasons. First, we hypothesize that both IPv4 and IPv6 should show a similar relation between update churn and the size of the underlying topology. Second, due to business relationships and dense interconnection among ASes, churn becomes localized, and each vantage point does not see the same set of routing events. Consequently, correlation between update churn seen at different vantage points can serve as a measure of the maturity of the underlying network and business relationships. Finally, previous work has shown that end-to-end delays and loss rates are significantly higher during routing events [23]. It is thus useful to compare the extent of path exploration and routing convergence times during routing events. If these metrics are significantly worse in IPv6 as compared to IPv4, then it could deter the adoption of IPv6.

6.1 Churn as a function of topology size and vantage point

Interdomain routing scalability has been a topic of major concern in recent times [24, 25] for two reasons – increasing routing table size, and increasing rate of BGP updates (churn). The latter can be a more serious concern, because failing to process updates in a timely manner can trigger a wide-scale instability and result in traffic blackholing. Some of these concerns were put to rest by observations that churn in the IPv4 topology grows slowly [26, 27], and at the same rate as the underlying topology. More recently, however, Huston [28] compared IPv4 and IPv6 BGP update time series and concluded that while IPv4 churn has grown slowly (linear), IPv6 churn has been increasing exponentially. This qualitative difference between the evolution of update churn in IPv4 and IPv6 raised speculation on whether routing dynamics in IPv6 are fundamentally different from those in IPv4. In order to investigate these differences, we next compare the evolution of BGP churn in IPv4 and IPv6. We define churn as the rate of BGP updates received from a vantage point (*e.g.*, updates per day). This definition of churn is consistent with previous related work in the area.

Churn as a function of topology size

To understand how churn has evolved with respect to network size, we track the growth in the number of updates, normalized by the size of the underlying AS topology. To calculate this metric, we bin the total number of updates per day into three-month windows, find the median daily churn (using the average daily churn gives similar results) for each window, and divide it by the average number of ASes in the topology during that time window. Figure 11 plots this metric for IPv4 (top) and IPv6 (bottom).

In IPv6 this number has remained mostly stable since Jan 2004 at $\approx$ 3 updates per origin AS, except at the AT&T monitor which sees half that many. In IPv4, except for the AT&T and NTT monitors, this metric stabilized in 2006 at $\approx$ 5 updates per origin AS. Other monitors that peer

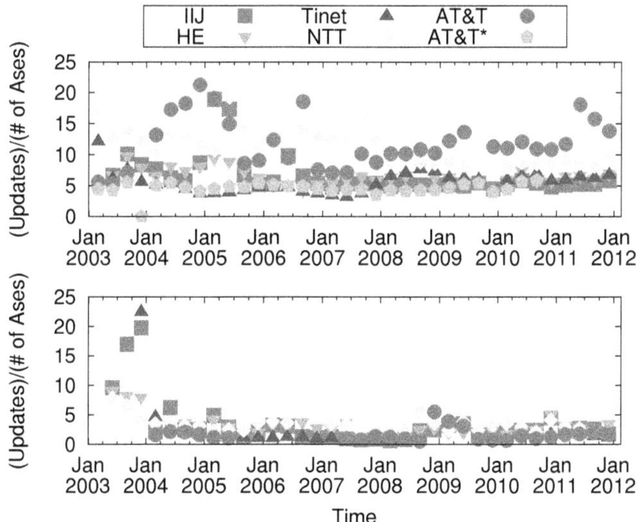

Figure 11: Churn growth in relation to topology size in IPv4 (top) and IPv6 (bottom). BGP churn, in both IPv4 and IPv6, grows linearly with the number of ASes.

with the Oregon-IX collector show similar behavior. We hypothesize that the anomalies exhibited by the AT&T and NTT monitors are caused by non-stationary periods, which we confirm by filtering out noise from the AT&T time series as described in [26] and plotted in Figure 11 (top panel) as AT&T*. Similar to the other monitors, this filtered AT&T* time series exhibits a stable ratio of 5 updates per origin AS.

To summarize, while previous work has pointed to the qualitatively different growth trajectories of IPv4 and Ipv6 churn, we showed that churn in both protocols grows at the same rate as the underlying topology. We emphasize that understanding the evolution of update dynamics requires examining more than temporal evolution; we must also consider the evolution of the underlying topology. Measuring churn normalized by the size of the underlying topologies reveals a richer picture, namely that *BGP update dynamics in IPv4 and IPv6 are qualitatively similar and their growth is a function of the growth in the number of ASes.* Explaining why the average number of updates per AS is 5 in IPv4 and 3 in IPv6 is an interesting open question. We believe that this has to do with the nature of the underlying topologies and prevalent operational practices such as business relationships and traffic engineering.

Churn seen from different vantage points

The churn seen from different vantage points can shed some light on the maturity of the underlying topology, because as ASes establish denser interconnections and enforce business relationships, *churn becomes more localized*, i.e., some routing events only affect a limited part of the Internet.

We calculate the cross-correlation between all pairs of daily churn time series in IPv6 and IPv4 respectively, for the monitors in Figure 11. We use the non-parametric Kendall's τ rank correlation coefficient [29], a measure of association between random variables based on the ranking of their sample data. Kendall's τ takes value in the range [-1,1]; a value of 1 denotes a perfect correlation and a value of -1 denotes anti-correlation. Figure 12 shows the calculated correlation

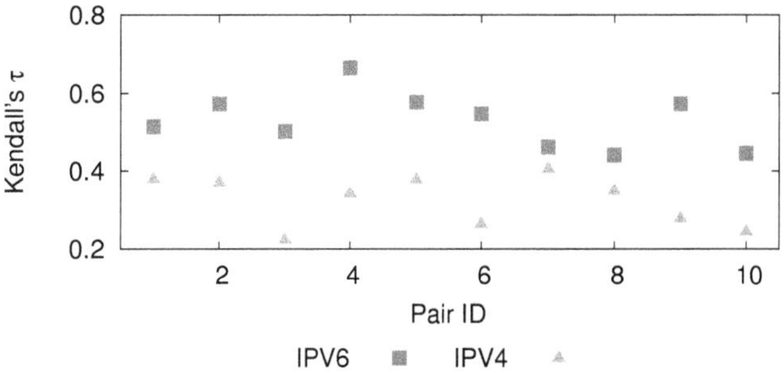

Figure 12: Correlation of the BGP churn time series across monitors. IPv6 monitors exhibit stronger correlation than IPv4 monitors.

coefficients between all pairs of IPv6 time series, as well as between all IPv4 pairs. IPv4 pairs show little correlation, with τ values mostly below 0.4, but IPv6 pairs show strong positive correlation, with τ values mostly above 0.5. The lack of correlation between IPv4 monitors indicates that churn is highly dependent on the location and configuration of the corresponding router. As stated earlier, this is likely due to denser interconnection and enforcement of business relationships in the IPv4 topology. We have studied this effect in our previous work, where we showed that correlation between IPv4 churn time series doubles after filtering out updates triggered by routing events that affect only a limited part of the Internet [26].

To summarize, we find that the churn seen by different BGP vantage points shows stronger correlation in IPv6 as compared to that in IPv4. Two factors might contribute to the stronger correlation between IPv6 time series than in IPv4. *First, the IPv6 AS graph is much smaller and thus provides less isolation (i.e., routing changes will have a larger scope of impact). A second possibility is that since IPv6 deployment is still at an early stage, business policies may be less enforced and monitored, which would also result in less isolation of BGP messages.* As IPv6 deployment proceeds, we expect both of these factors to change; the IPv6 topology is growing exponentially, interconnection is becoming denser, and business relationships in IPv6 will start to be enforced. Thus, we expect the correlation of IPv6 churn seen from different BGP monitors to decrease over time and become similar to that in IPv4.

6.2 Path exploration and convergence times

Routing changes have different outcomes. Some changes result in the withdrawal (addition) of a prefix from (to) the routing table. Other changes alter the reachability information to a prefix (e.g. rerouting). In addition, routing changes can be transient or long-lasting. The effects of routing instability on data plane characteristics such as loss rate have been well studied [23]. It is thus important to compare routing changes in IPv6 and IPv4. But, first we must identify and group prefix updates that constitute a routing change. When an underlying incident triggers a routing change, it often results in several updates for each affected prefix (i.e., convergence sequence). The duration of this convergence sequence is referred to as *convergence time*. A *prefix event* is a sequence of updates for a given prefix that are likely triggered by the same underlying cause. We use the definition

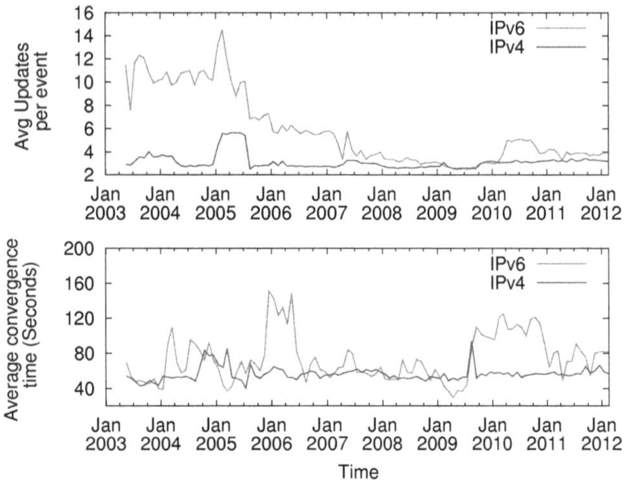

Figure 13: Comparing path exploration and convergence times (IIJ). The average number of updates per routing change event gradually converges between IPv4 and IPv6. The average convergence time in IPv6 is burstier, with a lower bound at a similar level as in IPv4.

by Wu *et al.* [30] to identify prefix events: *Two consecutive updates for the same prefix belong to the same prefix event if they are no more than 70 seconds apart. The maximum duration for a prefix event is set to 10 minutes. Events with duration longer than 10 minutes are considered to be flapping.* These prefix events can be classified based on the best known path to the affected prefix before and after the event [31, 32]. After identifying all prefix events in our time series, we compute two metrics reflecting their impact: path exploration (average number of updates observed per event) and convergence time. When a route to a prefix fails, BGP may explore several routes before converging to a new route or withdrawing the prefix altogether. A longer path exploration extends BGP convergence time which will likely impede data plane performance.

Path exploration

Path exploration is often more pronounced in events that lead to a complete withdrawal of a prefix (AW events) [32]. The top panel in Figure 13 compares the average number of updates per an AW event in IPv6 and IPv4 as seen from the perspective of IIJ[6]. In IPv4, this number has mostly remained stable below 4. We also observe a slight increase in post-withdrawal path exploration after 2009. In IPv6, on the other hand, this number was around 10 updates until early 2005, it then decreased gradually and stabilized around 4. When investigating AW events that took place in the first two years of the study period, we find that our monitors explored monotonically longer paths before sending the final withdrawal. In IIJ for example, the median length of the longest explored path was 18 hops in January 2004 and gradually dropped to stabilize around 7 hops in 2008. We can imagine two possible causes for this gradual reduction in path exploration. First, ten years ago only a few hundred ASes had deployed IPv6, and routing policies may have been less enforced, allowing exploration of many more alternative paths. Second, the early IPv6 graph was sparser, so paths were naturally longer (see Figure 7), leading to proportionally longer convergence times (i.e., more path exploration) [33]. The trends identified above are consistent across monitors.

[6]Due to space limitations, we only present results for the IIJ monitor. Other monitors show qualitatively similar results.

Convergence times

The bottom panel in Figure 13 shows the evolution of BGP convergence time from the perspective of IIJ, measured as the monthly average of all prefix event durations (i.e., the time difference between the first update and the last update in an event). The average convergence time in IPv4 is stable around 50 seconds, but is higher and less stable in IPv6. During 2004, IPv6 convergence time was slightly higher, similar to the path exploration metric. We also recorded two periods with sustained higher convergence times, in 2006 and 2010. A closer look at the data showed that the increase in 2006 was caused by one prefix that flapped between two paths that only differed in the ATOMIC_AGGREGATE attribute (i.e., one path is announced as aggregated while the other as not). The fact that a single prefix has a large impact on the measured convergence time is surprising. However, our data shows that the small size of the IPv6 routing system makes it vulnerable to such effects. The number of prefix events per day rose sharply from ≈ 200 before this instability to ≈ 350 due to the unstable prefix; this single flapping prefix experienced 150 instabilities per day. On the other hand, the number of prefix events per day is two orders of magnitude larger in IPv4 than in IPv6. When we exclude events related to this prefix, the convergence time drops to the same level as prior to the instability. A similar flapping that involved five prefixes caused the peak in 2010. We believe that this activity was triggered by an IGP misconfiguration in the origin AS. These peaks were evident in all monitors, consistent with the earlier observed strong correlation between IPv6 monitors. Apart from these anomalous periods, IPv6 generally matched IPv4 in terms of convergence time.

To summarize, *the evolution of path exploration and convergence time shows that the characteristics of routing changes in IPv6 are gradually becoming similar to those in in IPv4. This is an encouraging trend, as it suggests an increasing maturity in IPv6 deployment. Furthermore, any performance degradations resulting from routing changes in IPv6 should be no worse than we see in IPv4.*

7. IPV4 VS. IPV6 PERFORMANCE

Figure 14 plots the the relative performance as measured by relative download times for all five vantage points we use (method described at the end of Section 2). Confirming the results of Nikkhah *et al.* [16], 79% of paths we observed had IPv6 performance within 10% of IPv4 (or IPv6 had better performance) if the forward AS-level path was the same in both protocols, while only 63% of paths had similar performance if the forward AS-level path was different. However, our measurements (and theirs) are dominated by the path RTT because the transfers are typically small (although we only analyze measurements of transfers over 10K bytes). The dashed lines in Figure 14 plot the relative

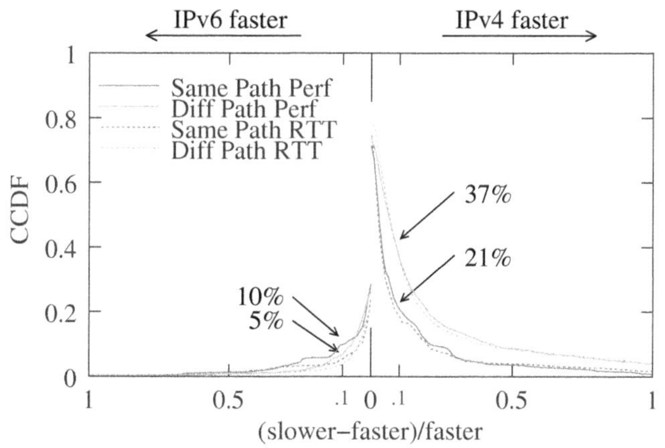

Figure 14: Relative performance between IPv4 and IPv6 measured by the relative mean fetch times (solid lines) and minimum SYN/ACK RTT (dashed lines). Because small pages (although over 10K bytes) are fetched, performance is dominated by relative RTT. The annotations at x=0.1 represent the points where performance is at least 10% worse in IPv4 or IPv6. IPv4 and IPv6 performance is more likely to be similar if the same AS-level paths are used for both IP protocols.

RTTs measured to the same (IPv4 and IPv6) webservers; the solid lines (relative fetch time) and the dashed lines (relative RTTs) are barely distinguishable. When IPv6 performance is better, it is more likely correlated with a different forward AS-level path. However, the correlation between RTT and fetch time is weaker when IPv6 performance is better, for reasons we do not yet understand.

Implications of correlation between performance and topological congruence

The significant correlation between data plane performance between two endpoints and the congruity of the AS path between them inspires us to ask: how far are we from topological parity between IPv4 and IPv6?

Recall from Section 4 that only 40-50% of AS paths are actually identical. There are several reasons why the AS paths in IPv4 and IPv6 could be different – the ASes or AS links seen on the IPv4 path may not be present in the IPv6 topology, or networks may simply choose different routes for IPv4 and IPv6. With the data available to us, we cannot confirm why the AS paths differ; we can, however, measure how much congruence between IPv4 and IPv6 AS paths is possible today. For each link in an IPv4 AS path toward a dual-stacked origin AS, we examine whether that link is present in the IPv6 topology, regardless of the AS path on which it appears. Figure 15 shows that currently, 60-70% of AS paths *could* be identical in IPv4 and IPv6 without configuring a new BGP peering session, because for these paths each IPv4 link is already present in the IPv6 topology, just not yet part of an observable BGP-policy-compliant path between the edges. We take a step further and examine what would happen if each IPv6-capable AS were to establish equivalent peerings in IPv6 and IPv4. Figure 16 shows the fraction of IPv4 AS paths where each AS on the path appears in the IPv6 topology. If current IPv6-capable ASes

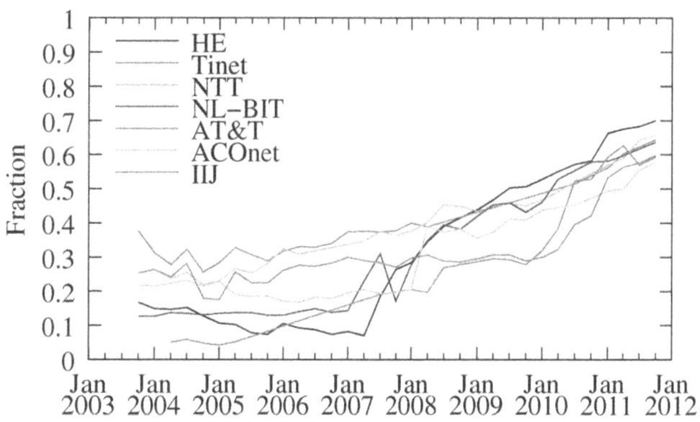

Figure 15: Fraction of dual-stack ASes reachable using an IPv4 AS path where all AS links in that path are in the IPv6 AS-level graph. If IPv6 BGP paths chosen were consistent with IPv4 paths, then 60% to 70% of ASes could be reached over a path congruent in IPv4 and IPv6.

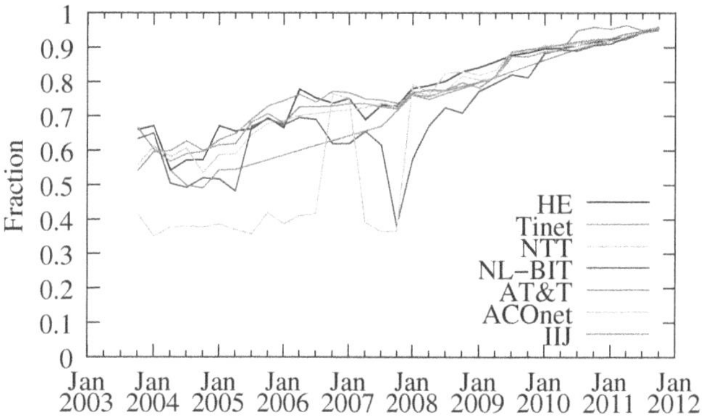

Figure 16: Fraction of dual-stack ASes reachable using an IPv4 AS path where all ASes in that path are in the IPv6 AS graph. If current IPv6 capable ASes established peerings equivalent in IPv4 and IPv6, then 95% of paths would be identical.

established equivalent peerings in IPv4 and IPv6, 95% of AS paths could be identical in IPv4 and IPv6, *i.e.*, for an AS link on such a path, both ASes are present in the IPv6 topology, and both ASes already peer in IPv4. If these ASes also started IPv6 peering, we could see the AS paths converge. These results are encouraging, but they are even more motivating when juxtaposed with performance measurements which show IPv4 and IPv6 data plane performance is comparable when the AS paths are the same. Together, these results demonstrate the undeniable benefit of BGP peering parity between IPv4 and IPv6 AS-level topologies.

8. RELATED WORK

Many attempts have been made to evaluate the status of IPv6 adoption and penetration [34, 35, 36, 37, 38, 39, 40, 41, 42, 43]. None have found significant activity, even though IPv6 has been implemented on all major network and host operating systems. Current levels of observable IPv6 activity fall well below 1% [40, 42, 43]. Google plots a time-series of the percentage of Google users that would access www.google.com over IPv6 if it had an IPv6 address, which moved from 0.1% in September 2008 to 0.6% in May 2012 [3]. By some accounts, IPv6 development is progressing faster in Asian countries, *e.g.*, China [44]. Notably, the 2008 Summer Olympics in Beijing was the first major world event with a presence on the IPv6 Internet [45]. These measurement studies were either focused on IPv6 *capability*, *i.e.*, how many websites and clients were IPv6 capable, or on the actual levels of IPv6 traffic on the network. In our work, we have focused on IPv6 deployment at the level of organizations, represented in BGP as Autonomous Systems. Huston and Michaelson [46] of APNIC examined a range of types of data collected over four years (January 2004 to April 2008) in search of IPv6 deployment activity. They analyzed interdomain routing announcements, APNIC's web access logs, and queries of reverse DNS zones that map IPv4 and IPv6 addresses back to domain names. All of their metrics showed some increase in IPv6 deployment activity starting in the second half of 2006, but they emphasized the data's limitations, since it mostly reflected some interest in IPv6 rather than usable IPv6 support. More recently, Michaelson [47] measured the disparity between IPv6 capability at the network level, and IPv6 capability of end-users. Karpilovski *et al.* [48] measured IPv6 deployment using data on address allocation, BGP routing, and traffic. They concluded that even though IPv6 address allocations were increasing, actual traffic levels remained negligible. Huston [49] continuously tracks the evolution of the IPv6 topology and routing, with some high-level comparisons with the current state of IPv4. Aben [50] provides an interactive look into the deployment of IPv6 at the AS-level, further divided by country. To the best of our knowledge, ours is the first work to compare and contrast IPv6 evolution with that of the IPv4 ecosystem.

BGP update dynamics and scalability have been active topics of research during the last decade or so, mostly for the IPv4 topology, *e.g.* [33, 32]. Lately, however, there has been some concern about the *scalability of BGP interdomain routing* [25]. Huston [28] compared update churn in IPv4 and IPv6, and found that while churn in IPv4 does indeed appear "flat", that in IPv6 increases exponentially. In this paper, we compared IPv4 and IPv6 update dynamics, and showed that they are qualitatively similar. The apparent difference between the absolute volume of IPv4 and IPv6 updates over time is simply a function of the different growth rates of the underlying topologies – the IPv4 topology grows linearly, while the IPv6 topology grows exponentially.

A recent measurement study by Nikkah *et al.* [16] compared performance (measured in terms of web page download times) over IPv4 and IPv6, with the goal of determining whether the control plane or the data plane was responsible for worse performance over IPv6. They found that while the data plane performs comparably in IPv4 and IPv6, differences in the control plane (routing) are responsible for performance differences seen between IPv4 and IPv6. We show web page download time is dominated by RTT because the pages fetched are typically small, so these performance measurements are dominated by delay rather than available bandwidth. We also demonstrate there is significantly more gain that could be made with the existing ASes that have deployed IPv6; if equivalent links are established in IPv6 as in IPv4 then 95% of existing paths could be identical.

9. CONCLUSIONS AND FUTURE WORK

With the Internet Assigned Numbers Authority (IANA) now having exhausted its pool of available IPv4 addresses, and the Regional Internet Registries (RIRs) scheduled to run out in the near future, there has been growing interest in how IPv6 is being deployed and used. In this paper, we undertook the first study of the evolution of IPv6 deployment, comparing and contrasting it with how IPv4 has evolved over the last decade and a half. Our findings hint that the IPv6 network is indeed maturing, and while the increasing pace of IPv6 uptake over the last two years is an encouraging sign, IPv6 adoption is distinctly non-uniform, both topologically and geographically. From the topological perspective, IPv6 deployment is ahead in the core of the network, driven by transit and content providers, while it lags at the edges, which mostly consist of enterprise customers. While the data at our disposal does not allow us to study *why* deployment is lagging at the edge, we conjecture that this is due to a lack of incentives for edge networks to deploy IPv6, given available alternative strategies, e.g., NAT. For many edge networks, deploying IPv6 represents a cost (transitioning infrastructure, training staff, increased management/troubleshooting overhead) without a tangible benefit. A single player, Hurricane Electric, predominates the IPv6 topology significantly more than the most predominant AS in the IPv4 topology. This suggests that several graph-theoretic metrics (e.g., average AS-path length) could be significantly skewed by the single large player in IPv6. In terms of geographical trends, IPv6 adoption is higher in Europe and the Asia Pacific region. We conjecture that adoption in the Asia-Pacific region was spurred by IPv4 address exhaustion, which happened first in that region. A big push toward IPv6 by network operators in the RIPE region could explain why Europe is ahead of North America. From the point of view of routing dynamics, we find that IPv6 behaves mostly like IPv4. The differences in the growth of the absolute volume of updates in IPv4 and IPv6 stem from the different growth rates of the two topologies – IPv4 now grows linearly in terms of ASes and prefixes, while IPv6 grows exponentially. Finally, we find that performance over IPv6 paths is comparable to that over IPv4 if the AS-level paths are the same, while it can be significantly worse when AS-level paths are different. Interestingly, we found that while only 40-50% of AS paths are currently identical in IPv4 and IPv6, up to 95% of AS paths could be identical, if current IPv6-capable ASes established equivalent peerings in IPv4 and IPv6.

There are several avenues for future work. First, we plan to keep collecting and processing topology and routing data for both IPv4 and IPv6. We plan to release to the research and operational communities periodic data tracking the evolution of IPv6 topology and routing, to enable comparison with IPv4 evolution over the last 15 years. We expect that such monitoring will become more useful as networks move toward deploying IPv6 in production. In particular, it will be interesting to measure if IPv6 deployment accelerated following the World IPv6 Launch [51] event, scheduled for June 6, 2012. Complementary to our efforts in measuring IPv6 deployment, we are developing a quantitative model of IPv6 adoption at the organization level, which we will parameterize and validate using our our ongoing measurements. A crucial factor in determining whether IPv6 is widely adopted is the end-to-end performance achievable over IPv6, and whether that performance is comparable to that achievable over IPv4. We plan to continue and extend our current IPv6 performance measurements to identify or rule out other causes of performance disparity beyond RTT, such as loss, fragmentation, segmentation, and packet reordering, and make results available to the community.

10. ACKNOWLEDGEMENTS

We would like to thank the anonymous reviewers and our shepherd, Sharon Goldberg, for their invaluable feedback which helped substantially in improving the quality of the paper. Amogh Dhamdhere, Matthew Luckie, Bradley Huffaker and Kc Claffy are supported by NSF grant CNS-1111449. Ahmed Elmokashfi is supported by the Norwegian Research Council, grant number 209954/S10. Emile Aben was supported by RIPE NCC, although the majority of his contribution was on his own time so as to not interfere with his RIPE-NCC responsibilites.

11. REFERENCES

[1] S. Deering and R. Hinden, "RFC 2460. Internet Protocol, Version 6 (IPv6) Specification," 1998.

[2] G. Huston, "IPv4 Address Report," 2009, `http://www.potaroo.net/tools/ipv4/index.html`.

[3] Google, "Google ipv6 implementors conference," 2010, `https://sites.google.com/site/ipv6implementors/2010/agenda`.

[4] Ram Mohan, "Will U.S. Government Directives Spur IPv6 Adoption?," September 2010, `http://www.circleid.com/posts/20100929_will_us_government_directives_spur_ipv6_adoption/`.

[5] Wikipedia, "IPv6 deployment," 2012, `http://en.wikipedia.org/wiki/IPv6_deployment#Deployment_by_country`.

[6] Amogh Dhamdhere and Constantine Dovrolis, "Twelve Years in the Evolution of the Internet Ecosystem," *IEEE/ACM Transactions on Networking*, vol. 19, no. 5, 2011.

[7] Lixin Gao, "On Inferring Autonomous System Relationships in the Internet," *IEEE/ACM Transactions on Networking*, vol. 9, no. 6, 2001.

[8] David Meyer, "University of Oregon Route Views Project," http://www.routeviews.org/.

[9] RIPE, "Routing Information Service (RIS)," 2008, `http://www.ripe.net/ris/`.

[10] Q. Chen, H. Chang, R. Govindan, S. Jamin, S. Shenker, and W. Willinger, "The Origin of Power-Laws in Internet Topologies Revisited," in *Proc. IEEE Infocom*, 2002.

[11] R. Cohen and D. Raz, "The Internet Dark Matter - On the Missing Links in the AS Connectivity Map," in *Proc. IEEE Infocom*, 2006.

[12] Y. He, G. Siganos, M. Faloutsos, and S. V. Krishnamurthy, "A Systematic Framework for Unearthing the Missing Links: Measurements and Impact," in *Proc. USENIX/SIGCOMM NSDI*, 2007.

[13] H. Chang and W. Willinger, "Difficulties Measuring the Internet's AS-Level Ecosystem," in *Proc. Annual Conference on Information Sciences and Systems*, 2006.

[14] Beichuan Zhang, Raymond Liu, Daniel Massey, and Lixia Zhang, "Collecting the Internet AS-level Topology," *ACM SIGCOMM CCR*, 2005.

[15] B. Zhang, V. Kambhampati, M. Lad, D. Massey, and L. Zhang, "Identifying BGP routing table transfers," in *MineNet '05: Proceedings of the 2005 ACM SIGCOMM workshop on Mining network data*, New York, NY, USA, 2005, pp. 213–218, ACM.

[16] Mehdi Nikkhah, Roch Guérin, Yiu Lee, and Richard Woundy, "Assessing IPv6 through web access a measurement study and its findings," in *Proc. ACM CoNEXT*, 2011, pp. 26:1–26:12.

[17] Matthew Luckie, "Scamper: a scalable and extensible packet prober for active measurement of the Internet," in *Proc. ACM SIGCOMM/USENIX IMC*, Nov. 2010.

[18] Internet Society, "World ipv6 day," 2011, `http://www.worldipv6day.org/`.

[19] Emile Aben, "World ipv6 day - what did we learn?," Presentation at APNIC32 meeting, 2011.

[20] Rene Wilhelm, "Members and Number Resources, One Year Later," Feb. 2011, `https://labs.ripe.net/Members/wilhelm/members-and-number-resources-1-year-later`.

[21] Hurricane Electric, "Hurricane electric peering policy," `http://www.he.net/peering.html`.

[22] RIPE NCC, "IPv4 - Running Out of Time?," 2003, `http://www.ripe.net/internet-coordination/ipv4-exhaustion/archive/ipv4-running-out-of-time`.

[23] Feng Wang, Zhuoqing Morley Mao, Jia Wang, Lixin Gao, and Randy Bush, "A measurement study on the impact of routing events on end-to-end internet path performance," in *Proc. ACM SIGCOMM*, 2006, pp. 375–386.

[24] Geoff Huston and Grenville Armitage, "Projecting future IPv4 router requirements from trends in dynamic BGP behaviour," in *Proc. ATNAC*, Dec 2006.

[25] David Meyer, Lixia Zhang, and Kevin Fall, "Report from the IAB workshop on routing and addressing," RFC 4984, 2007.

[26] Ahmed Elmokashfi, Amund Kvalbein, and Constantine Dovrolis, "BGP churn evolution: A perspective from the core," *IEEE/ACM Transactions on Networking*, vol. 20, no. 99, 2011.

[27] Geoff Huston, "BGP in 2009 (and a bit of 2010)," Presentation at ARIN XXV meeting, 2010.

[28] Geoff Huston, "The BGP World is Flat," Nov. 2011, `http://www.potaroo.net/ispcol/2011-12/flat.html`.

[29] Myles Hollander and Douglas A. Wolfe, *Nonparametric statistical methods*, Wiley, second edition, 1999.

[30] Jian Wu, Zhuoqing Morley Mao, Jennifer Rexford, and Jia Wang, "Finding a needle in a haystack: pinpointing significant BGP routing changes in an IP network," in *Proc. USENIX/SIGCOMM NSDI*, 2005.

[31] Craig Labovitz, G. Robert Malan, and Farnam Jahanian, "Origins of Internet routing instability," in *Proc. IEEE INFOCOM*, 1999.

[32] Ricardo Oliveira, Beichuan Zhang, Dan Pei, Rafit Izhak-Ratzin, and Lixia Zhang, "Quantifying path exploration in the Internet," in *Proc. ACM SIGCOMM/USENIX IMC*, 2006.

[33] Craig Labovitz, Abha Ahuja, Abhijit Bose, and Farnam Jahanian, "Delayed internet routing convergence," in *Proc. ACM SIGCOMM*, 2000, pp. 175–187.

[34] H. Ringberg, C. Labovitz, D. McPherson and S. Iekel-Johnson, "A One Year Study of Internet IPv6 Traffic," 2008, http://www.nanog.org/meetings/nanog44/presentations/Tuesday/Ringberg_measurement_N44.pdf.

[35] Lorenzo Colitti, Steinar H. Gunderson, Erik Kline, and Tiziana Refice, "Evaluating IPv6 adoption in the Internet," in *PAM 2010*, 2010, http://research.google.com/pubs/archive/36240.pdf.

[36] Mike Leber, "Global IPv6 Deployment Progress Report," 2006, http://bgp.he.net/ipv6-progress-report.cgi.

[37] M. Kuehne, "Examining Actual State of IPv6 Deployment," 2008, http://www.circleid.com/posts/81166_actual_state_ipv6_deployment/.

[38] Mark Prior, "IPv6 survey," 2009, http://www.mrp.net/IPv6_Survey.html.

[39] M. Abrahamsson, "some real life data," 2008, http://article.gmane.org/gmane.ietf.v6ops/9116.

[40] Emile Aben, "IPv4/IPv6 measurements for: RIPE NCC," November 2010, http://albatross.ripe.net/v6-clientresolver.

[41] Emile Aben, "Measuring IPv6 at Web Clients and Caching Resolvers," Mar. 2010, https://labs.ripe.net/Members/emileaben/.

[42] Craig Labovitz, "IPv6 Momentum?," http://asert.arbornetworks.com/2010/10/ipv6-momentum/.

[43] Roch Guerin, "IPv6 Adoption Monitor," http://mnlab-ipv6.seas.upenn.edu:8080/monitor/index.html.

[44] Ma Yan, "Construction of CNGI-CERNET IPv6 CPN," 2009, http://www.apan.net/meetings/kaohsiung2009/presentations/ipv6/cernet.pdf.

[45] "Olympic Games 2008," 2008, http://ipv6.beijing2008.cn/en.

[46] G. Huston and G. Michaelson, "Measuring IPv6 Deployment," 2008, http://www.nro.net/news/cisp-ipv6.pdf.

[47] G. Michaelson, "Measuring ipv6 at the network and the customer level," May 2012, http://www.potaroo.net/iepg/july2002/.

[48] Elliott Karpilovsky, Alexandre Gerber, Dan Pei, Jennifer Rexford, and Aman Shaikh, "Quantifying the Extent of IPv6 Deployment," in *Proc. PAM*, Apr 2009.

[49] G. Huston, "IPv6 Reports," http://bgp.potaroo.net/index-v6.html.

[50] Emile Aben, "IPv6 Enabled Networks," http://v6asns.ripe.net/v/6.

[51] Internet Society, "World ipv6 launch," June 2012, http://www.worldipv6launch.org/.

Measuring the Impact of the Copyright Amendment Act on New Zealand Residential DSL Users

Shane Alcock
University of Waikato
Hamilton, New Zealand
salcock@cs.waikato.ac.nz

Richard Nelson
University of Waikato
Hamilton, New Zealand
richardn@cs.waikato.ac.nz

ABSTRACT

The Copyright (Infringing File Sharing) Amendment Act 2011 (CAA) is a New Zealand law that aims to provide copyright holders with legal recourse when content is illegally shared over the Internet. This paper presents a study of residential DSL user behaviour using packet traces captured at a New Zealand ISP before, shortly after and several months after the CAA coming into effect. We use libprotoident to classify the observed traffic based on the application protocol being used to identify and examine any changes in traffic patterns that may be a result of the new law. We find that the use of peer-to-peer applications declined significantly once the CAA was in effect, suggesting a strong correlation. We also found that there were increases in tunneling, secure file transfer and remote access traffic amongst a small segment of the user population, which may indicate an increased uptake in the use of foreign seedboxes to bypass the jurisdiction of the CAA.

Categories and Subject Descriptors

C.2.3 [**Computer-Communication Networks**]: Network Operations

Keywords

P2P, seedbox, traffic classification, residential DSL, Internet law

1. INTRODUCTION

The use of Internet file sharing technologies for copyright infringement has received significant attention from lawmakers in many countries. France, South Korea and the United Kingdom were among the first to enact legislation allowing for a graduated response to copyright infringement on the Internet. These countries employ a "three-strikes" approach where the offender receives warnings for the first and second infringements but may have their Internet connection terminated if infringing continues.

IMC'12, November 14–16, 2012, Boston, Massachusetts, USA.

On the first of September 2011, New Zealand joined these countries with the Copyright (Infringing File Sharing) Amendment Act [15] (which we shall henceforth refer to as the CAA). The CAA implements a graduated response system whereby copyright owners can advise the user's ISP when they believe a subscriber has breached copyright. The copyright holder must pay a NZ $25 processing fee (approximately $20 US) to the ISP and the ISP in turn must then issue an infringement notice to the suspected party. After three infringements, the subscriber can be taken to the New Zealand Copyright Tribunal by the copyright holder where the subscriber can be fined up to NZ$15,000. The law also has a (currently inactive) provision for the termination of an offending subscriber's Internet connection.

The CAA received widespread media coverage both inside and outside of New Zealand and the vast majority of New Zealand Internet users will have been aware of the new law by the time it came into effect. However, media reports differed as to whether the law was having any impact on user behaviour, i.e. whether users had ceased file sharing. One major New Zealand ISP reported a 10% decrease in peer-to-peer (P2P) traffic, another stated that international traffic had declined but was unable to determine whether this was related to file sharing while a third claimed there had been no discernible impact on traffic volumes [18]. None of the three ISPs provided any detail as to the measurement approach used to reach the publicised conclusions.

Therefore, we have conducted an investigation into the application protocols used by residential DSL users in New Zealand, both prior and subsequent to the CAA coming into force, to analyse the effect of the CAA on the behaviour of Internet users. We have analysed packet traces captured from a single New Zealand ISP using libprotoident [19], a traffic classification library and compared the popularity of different applications (e.g., P2P, web, mail) both before and after the CAA came into effect.

Unlike earlier studies that have looked at the impact of similar laws in other countries, such as [9] and [10], our study is based on measurements of the traffic sent and received by a cross-section of Internet users. Using this approach, we can easily and effectively analyse the behaviour of a large group of Internet users in an objective fashion.

Our results show that P2P traffic had more than halved by the time the CAA became an active law, suggesting that there may be a strong correlation between anti-file-sharing legislation and the use of P2P applications. Traffic volumes also declined notably for newsgroups and encrypted transfers. By contrast, we observed that protocols which can be used as secure or private mechanisms for direct file transfers had become much more popular than they were prior to September 2011. These results suggest that, while the CAA may have had the intended effect of discouraging New Zealanders from partaking in P2P file sharing, some users have simply changed their approach to acquiring copyrighted material to avoid detection by rights-holders.

It should be noted that, due to the difficulties in obtaining suitable packet traces, this study has examined only a small portion of New Zealand Internet traffic and therefore we cannot irrefutably prove that the decline in P2P traffic has been caused by the new law. There are other possible reasons for the changes that we observed that cannot be ruled out with the data that we have: for example, a global trend in declining P2P traffic [12]. Therefore, the results of this study should be seen as an observation of a strong correlation that we believe is both interesting to the Internet research community and deserving of more detailed analysis in the future.

2. RELATED WORK

Other studies have examined the impact of laws similar to the CAA enacted in other countries. Dejean [10] surveyed a group of Internet users in Brittany following the enactment of the HADOPI law in France. They found that 25% of users had altered their downloading habits but less than 15% had ceased using peer-to-peer file sharing entirely. Many of those that had stopped using peer-to-peer had moved to alternative forms of file sharing, such as illegal streaming. Danaher [9] attempted to correlate the introduction of HADOPI with changes in online sales statistics for music. This study also suggested that HADOPI had a measurable impact, as song and album sales had increased significantly compared with other countries without similar legal ramifications for downloading copyrighted material.

Unlike the aforementioned research, we use Internet traffic classification techniques to conduct our study. Traffic classification has been a popular area of research over the past decade, especially with regard to identifying and analysing peer-to-peer traffic. The current state of the field has been well documented by several summary papers [7] [8] [16]. We used the libprotoident library [19] to classify the measured traffic for our study. Libprotoident is a lightweight payload inspection tool which uses only a small amount of application payload to identify the application protocol. This approach is similar to that used by Aceto et al. [3] with the PortLoad software but, unlike libprotoident, PortLoad is not publicly available nor has it been used to conduct any studies similar to this one.

With regard to identifying and measuring peer-to-peer traffic, Perényi [17] proposed a set of heuristics for identifying P2P traffic from NetFlow records. This technique was used to analyse the characteristics of P2P traffic observed at a Hungarian ISP, although they were only able to identify individual applications in cases where the default port was used. Another example is Hu [11] which developed behavioural profiles which could identify BitTorrent and PPLive traffic with high accuracy. There have also been studies using statistical and machine learning techniques to identify Internet applications [6] [13] [14]. These offer promising results but do not offer enough confirmed reliability for the analysis we intended to conduct, particularly with regard to identifying P2P traffic.

	Jan 2011	Sept 2011	Jan 2012
Start Date	06 Jan	12 Sept	16 Jan
Duration	7 days	8 days	8 days
Incoming Bytes	5,159 GB	5,079 GB	5,459 GB
Outgoing Bytes	919 GB	790 GB	896 GB
Active Subscribers	4928	4333	4135

Table 1: The trace sets used in this study. Incoming and outgoing bytes refer to the DSL network only. Active subscribers refers to unique IP addresses owned by the ISP that transmitted at least one packet.

3. METHODOLOGY

3.1 Data Sources

Packet traces that were captured using a passive monitor placed within the core network of a New Zealand ISP were used for this study. Although not large by New Zealand standards, the ISP offers DSL plans that are comparable in price, speed and data allowance with most competing ISPs in the New Zealand broadband market. The ISP operates on a nationwide basis and attracts customers from throughout the country, so we believe that the data set should be sufficiently representative for the purposes of our study.

The monitor was able to capture all bidirectional traffic for a subset of the ISP customer base. Each trace set was captured using an Endace DAG 4.3GE hardware capture card [2] and was entirely contiguous; all packets passing through the passive monitor between the start and end of the capture were written to disk. The trace sets are described in more detail in Table 1.

The timing of the captures was important for this study. The traces cover three distinct time periods: one week in January 2011, eight days in September 2011 and eight days in January 2012. The CAA came into effect on September 1, 2011. The January 2011 capture will therefore provide a suitable indication of user behaviour before the subscribers became conscious of the CAA. The September 2011 capture will demonstrate what, if any, immediate impact the new law may have had on user behaviour. Finally, the January 2012 capture will enable us to look at the possible effects of the CAA in the medium term and compare the traffic pattern with a similar time period from the previous year [1].

During the capture process, each packet was truncated to only contain the headers up to and including the transport header, i.e. the TCP or UDP header, plus an additional four bytes of application payload. The extra payload (captured with the permission of the ISP) allowed us to use libprotoident to classify the traffic, while minimising the potential impact on the privacy of the network users.

When performing the analysis, we used IP ranges provided by the technicians at the ISP to filter the captured traffic to only include traffic involving residential DSL subscribers. We chose to focus on residential DSL only as this user type was the principal intended target of the CAA. However, we will consider examining the effect of the CAA on other user classes, e.g. corporate Ethernet, in future work.

[1]Being different months, January and September may have had different traffic patterns for non-legislative reasons.

Category	Example Protocols
Chat	IRC, MSN, XMPP, Yahoo
Encryption	Unclassified SSL/TLS
Files	FTP, Rsync, SMB, Orbit
Gaming	Steam, Gamespy, XboxLive, WoW
Mail	SMTP, POP3, IMAP, IMAPS
NAT Traversal	STUN
News	NNTP
P2P	BitTorrent, Gnutella, EMule Pando, Manolito
P2P Structure	BitTorrent UDP, Gnutella UDP Emule UDP, Pando UDP
P2P TV	PPStream, PPLive
Remote	SSH, RDP, Teamviewer
Services	DNS, NTP
Streaming	RTMP, RTSP, Flash, Realplayer
Tunneling	TOR, OpenVPN, Teredo, ESP
VOIP	Skype, SIP, RTP, Teamspeak
Web	HTTP (incl. YouTube), HTTPS

Table 2: Categories supported by Libprotoident.

3.2 Analysis

We developed a program to read and analyse the packet traces using libtrace [4] and libprotoident [19]. Libtrace is a trace processing library that supports multiple capture formats and is required by libprotoident. Libprotoident is a traffic classification library that attempts to identify the application protocol being used by each flow observed in a packet trace using a technique known as lightweight packet inspection. Unlike deep packet inspection software, libprotoident only requires four bytes of application payload to be present in each captured packet. The version of libprotoident that we used, 2.0.5, supported over 200 unique application protocols including twelve P2P protocols and has been shown to achieve better accuracy than existing open-source deep packet inspection software [5].

The analysis program examined each flow that started and ended within the period covered by each trace set and reported the number of bytes downloaded, byte uploaded and active subscribers observed for each application protocol. Because the three data sets have different durations, the analysis and comparison of traffic volumes has been based on the mean amount of traffic observed per day rather than the total amount of traffic observed.

Each application protocol supported by libprotoident was also assigned to a category which described the purpose of the protocol, such as Web, P2P or Mail. The categories that were most prominent in our data sets are described in Table 2. In this paper, we present some results at the category level, as this can provide a clearer view of general user behaviour than examining popular individual applications.

One useful feature of our data set is that, unlike some DSL providers, the ISP that we have monitored assigned static IP addresses to DSL subscribers. We use the term subscriber to refer to a single premise that is being provided with broadband by the ISP. There may be multiple users associated with a single subscription; for example, residents of the same house who are sharing a broadband connection. We have assumed that a local IP address in a given trace set always corresponded to the same subscriber for the duration of the capture. This allowed us to investigate the number of

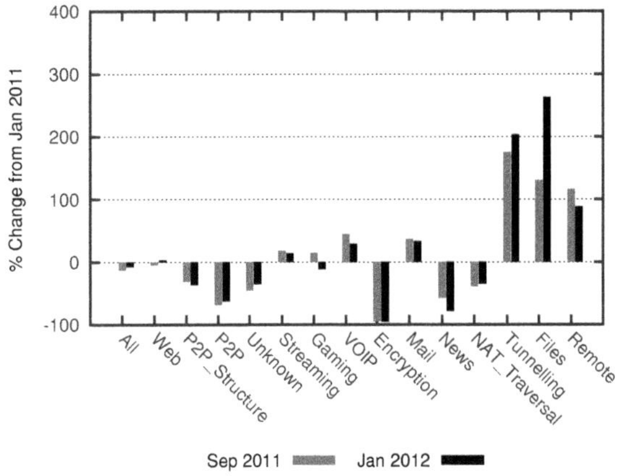

Figure 1: Bytes downloaded by residential DSL subscribers relative to the value observed in January 2011, broken down by application category.

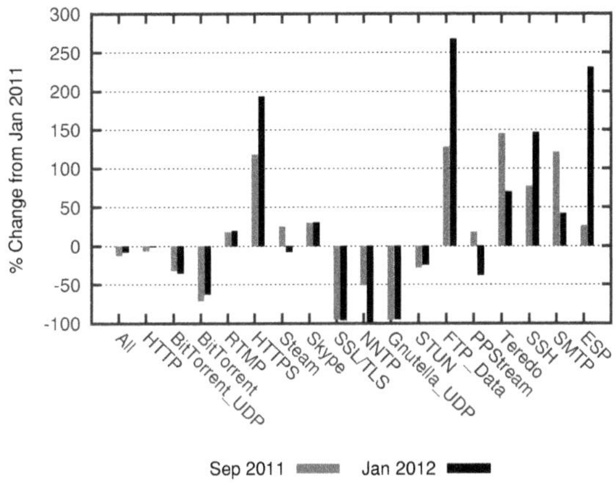

Figure 2: Bytes downloaded by residential DSL subscribers relative to the value observed in January 2011, broken down by application protocol.

subscribers using each application protocol or category over the course of each trace set. However, given the likelihood of customer churn over the course of several months, we did not extend this assumption across trace sets.

4. RESULTS

4.1 Bytes Transferred

Figures 1 and Figure 2 show the quantity of bytes downloaded by residential DSL subscribers relative to the value observed in January 2011, i.e. prior to the CAA coming into effect. Figure 1 shows the analysis on the category level whereas Figure 2 shows the results for a selection of individual application protocols. A category or protocol must have contributed at least one gigabyte per day in order to be included in either graph.

Overall, traffic across all categories decreased 7.5% in January 2012 compared with the volume observed in the previous year. Unencrypted web traffic was mostly static across all three trace sets but HTTPS traffic tripled between January 2011 and January 2012.

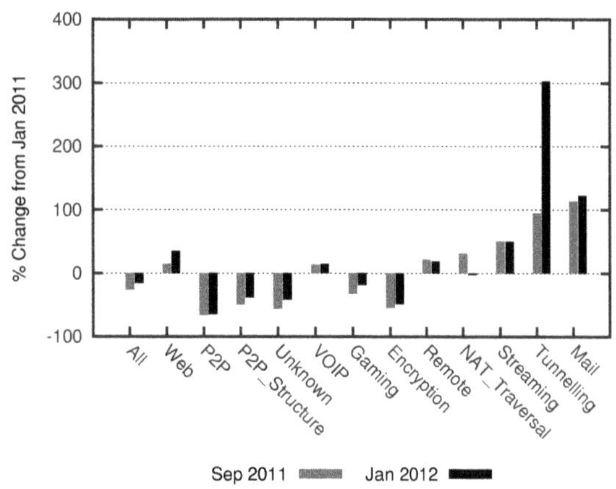

Figure 3: Bytes transmitted by residential DSL subscribers relative to the value observed in January 2011, broken down by application category.

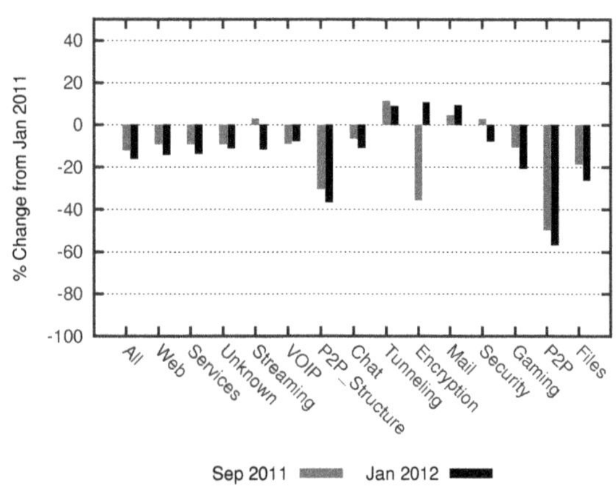

Figure 4: Active residential DSL subscribers using an application from each category, relative to the subscriber count in January 2011.

There were significant decreases in both the P2P and P2P structure categories. Downloaded traffic that was recognisable as P2P fell by 69% between January 2011 and September 2011 and recovered only slightly in January 2012. P2P structure traffic, i.e. P2P network maintenance traffic, was less affected but still decreased by 32% in September 2011. The primary cause for the decrease in both categories appeared to be a decline in BitTorrent usage. Also, Gnutella UDP traffic disappeared almost entirely from the ISP network, accounting for only 5% of the volume that it had in January 2011.

The Newsgroups and Encrypted categories also experienced sharp declines in traffic volumes in September 2011. Binary newsgroups are commonly used for sharing files (including copyrighted material) while many P2P file sharing applications use SSL to encrypt traffic. The decrease in encrypted traffic is likely because encryption does not protect against detection by copyright holders, as they detect infringements by finding New Zealand IP addresses participating in P2P networks that are sharing the copyrighted content. Some major newsgroup providers have been shut down in recent times, e.g. News-Service.com was closed in November 2011 [1], which may have caused the decline in NNTP traffic in the January 2012 dataset.

Unknown traffic also decreased in September 2011, which shows that the file sharing traffic did not move to new undetectable protocols. Rather, the decline in Unknown traffic leads us to believe that the converse may have been true: much of the Unknown traffic in January 2011 may have been encrypted P2P traffic that we were unable to detect using libprotoident.

By contrast, there were large increases in downloaded traffic matching the Files, Remote and Tunneling categories. Figure 2 shows that this was due to the growing use of protocols such as FTP, SSH, ESP (Encapsulating Security Protocol) and Teredo. Another protocol worth mentioning that is not present in Figure 2 is OpenVPN, which was seldom observed in January 2011 but was much more prominent in the later trace sets.

Our belief is that much of the growth in these categories can be attributed to users changing their file sharing approach. Rather than participating in P2P exchanges from home where they can be detected by copyright holders and issued an infringement notice under the CAA, the user downloads files using a seedbox located in a foreign country. The files are then copied directly back to their personal computer using either a secure tunnel, such as a VPN, or downloaded from a secure HTTP or FTP service running on the seedbox. This could also explain the large growth in HTTPS traffic.

While Files, Remote and Tunneling traffic has grown significantly, the total volume of traffic matching those categories was still relatively small compared with P2P traffic, as shown in Table 3. BitTorrent alone was still responsible for more downloaded traffic than any tunneling or remote access protocols. Furthermore, daily BitTorrent traffic decreased by 39 GB between January and September 2011 whereas growth in the daily traffic matching the Files, Remote and Tunneling categories was less than 5 GB for the same time period. Daily HTTPS traffic grew by 13 GB in the same time period, but it is unlikely that the entire increase can be attributed to seedboxes, e.g. online shopping, Internet banking and secure login to social media sites such as Facebook are also likely contributing factors.

Following the enactment of HADOPI in France, many users switched to using illegal streaming to access copyrighted content [10]. We also observed an increase in Streaming traffic in the September 2011 data set but the growth was not enough to suggest an uptake similar to that observed in France. This may be partly due to New Zealand's geographic isolation – the streaming sites hosted are not within New Zealand and the latency to foreign sites would likely result in a poor user experience. Rather, we suspect this increase is the result of increased uptake of legal radio, music and television streaming services which have developed an increased presence in New Zealand recently.

The CAA was also intended to target uploaders of copyrighted material. Figure 3 shows the traffic transmitted by residential DSL users, again broken down by category. Many of the trends observed in downloaded traffic were also present in uploaded traffic, such as the decrease in P2P file sharing and an increase in the Tunneling and Streaming categories. Outgoing Mail traffic had also increased significantly, although it is unlikely that this is related to the CAA.

	Jan 2011		Sep 2011		Jan 2012	
	GBs / day	Percentage	GBs / day	Percentage	GBs / day	Percentage
HTTP	469.3	68.7	441.3	72.3	465.4	70.9
BitTorrent UDP	55.8	8.2	38.0	6.2	36.1	5.5
BitTorrent	54.3	8.0	15.8	2.6	20.5	3.1
RTMP	20.8	3.0	24.6	4.0	24.9	3.8
HTTPS	11.2	1.6	24.3	4.0	32.7	5.0
Steam	10.2	1.5	12.7	2.1	9.4	1.4
Skype	9.1	1.3	11.9	1.9	11.9	1.8
SSL / TLS	7.3	1.0	0.4	0.1	0.4	0.1
NNTP	2.9	0.4	1.4	0.2	< 0.1	< 0.1
Gnutella UDP	2.0	0.3	0.1	< 0.1	0.1	< 0.1
FTP Data	1.1	0.2	2.4	0.4	3.9	0.6
Teredo	0.9	0.1	2.1	0.3	1.5	0.2
SSH	0.4	0.1	0.7	0.1	1.0	0.2
ESP	0.4	0.1	0.5	0.2	1.3	0.2
OpenVPN	< 0.01	< 0.1	1.4	0.2	1.6	0.2

Table 3: Bytes downloaded by DSL subscribers that matched each application protocol. "Percentage" refers to the proportion of traffic in the trace set that matched the protocol.

4.2 Active Users

We also examined the number of subscribers that were actively using each application protocol to assess whether the CAA had caused some subscribers to cease using P2P applications altogether. We defined a subscriber as actively using a protocol if a flow was observed where the subscriber had either transmitted a packet containing application payload or received at least one megabyte of application payload from the external host. The second condition ensured that we did not exclude one-way passive FTP transactions as these do not require the recipient to transmit any data.

Figure 4 shows the relative change in the number of subscribers actively using an application from each of the most prominent categories. Overall, the number of residential DSL subscribers decreased by 16% between January 2011 and January 2012. There is no obvious reason for this decline. The number of subscribers using Web, Services and Gaming traffic, i.e. categories that are largely unaffected by the CAA, fell by a similar amount. By contrast, the number of subscribers using P2P protocols shrank by a much greater amount, halving between January 2011 and January 2012.

Table 4 and Figure 5 show the percentage of subscribers that used certain application protocols and the average volume of traffic downloaded per day by a subscriber when using those protocols, respectively. BitTorrent was not widely used even before the CAA came into effect. Only 8.5% of subscribers actively used BitTorrent in January 2011. Following the enactment of the CAA, this value fell to 5.5% in September 2011 and declined further to 5.2% in January 2012. Also, the amount of traffic downloaded per BitTorrent user also decreased from 126 MB per day per user in January 2011 to 81 MB in January 2012. This matches the behaviour described in [10], where some French Internet users ceased using P2P altogether in response to the HADOPI law while others reduced their downloading activities.

Remarkably, OpenVPN traffic per user went from 600 KB per day in January 2011 to 116 MB per day in January 2012. It is possible that this is due to subscribers using OpenVPN to access seedboxes, although it is difficult to conclusively prove this with the data that we have. OpenVPN was only used by 0.3% of subscribers in January 2012 which suggests

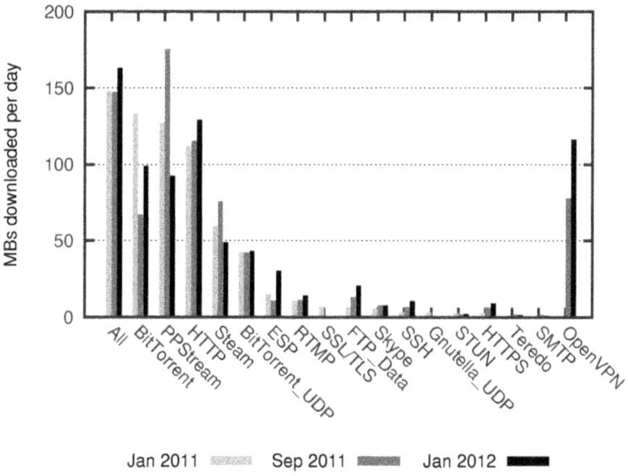

Figure 5: Mean bytes downloaded per day per active user, broken down by application protocol.

that the new usage of VPNs is restricted to a very small group of users. Other tunneling and file transfer protocols that were more popular, such as FTP, ESP and SSH, also exhibited an upward trend in the mean bytes downloaded per user, but the mean values were not as high as those observed for OpenVPN.

Teredo was another major contributor towards the growth in Tunneling usage. However, this is more likely due to the increased presence of IPv6 hosts providing content than P2P being tunneled over Teredo. The amount of Teredo traffic per active Teredo user was much less than what was observed for other Tunneling protocols and did not demonstrate the same upward trend.

5. CONCLUSIONS

In this paper, we presented the results of a study investigating changes in traffic patterns and Internet user behaviour following the Copyright (Infringing File Sharing) Amendment Act (CAA) 2011 which came into effect in New Zealand on 1 September 2011. We used libprotoident, an application protocol classification library, to analyse packet

	Jan 2011		Sep 2011		Jan 2012	
	Subscribers	Percentage	Subscribers	Percentage	Subscribers	Percentage
HTTP	4303	87.3	3919	90.4	3697	89.4
HTTPS	4297	87.2	3905	90.1	3697	89.4
RTMP	1978	40.1	2233	51.5	1802	43.6
Skype	1726	35.0	1580	36.5	1609	38.9
BitTorrent UDP	1348	27.4	926	21.4	858	20.8
SSL / TLS	1067	21.7	689	15.9	1181	28.6
Teredo	939	19.1	1070	24.7	1088	26.3
Gnutella UDP	588	11.9	233	5.4	233	5.6
BitTorrent	418	8.5	240	5.5	213	5.2
Steam	175	3.6	141	4.0	166	4.8
FTP Data	169	3.4	190	4.4	196	4.7
SSH	126	2.6	113	2.6	100	2.4
ESP	27	0.6	47	1.1	44	1.1
OpenVPN	7	0.1	18	0.4	14	0.3
NNTP	5	0.1	2	< 0.1	3	0.1

Table 4: The number of residential DSL subscribers that were using each application protocol in the data sets. "Percentage" refers to the proportion of all active subscribers that used the protocol.

traces captured at a single New Zealand ISP both before and after the law came into effect. In particular, the number of residential DSL subscribers that were using each application protocol as well as the volumes of traffic downloaded and uploaded by those users were examined.

Our main findings are summarised as follows:

- Traffic downloaded using P2P applications decreased to less than half the volume it had been prior to the CAA coming into effect. The decline persisted for several months afterward and many subscribers appeared to have ceased using P2P applications entirely.
- P2P uploads also decreased significantly following the introduction of the CAA. P2P traffic transmitted by DSL subscribers in January 2012 was a quarter of the amount transmitted in January 2011.
- FTP, tunneling and remote access protocols increased in popularity following the introduction of the CAA. The relative growth in these protocols compared with January 2011 was very large, e.g. 300% more tunneling traffic was received by residential DSL subscribers in January 2012 compared to the previous year.
- The number of active subscribers and traffic generated by tunneling, remote access and FTP remained much smaller than the corresponding values for P2P, suggesting that the observed growth in those protocols was not indicative of a widespread change in file sharing behaviour.
- Newsgroup traffic almost completely disappeared after the CAA came into effect, possibly suggesting that NNTP was being used almost exclusively for file sharing.

These results suggest that there is a strong correlation between the CAA coming into effect and the behaviour of New Zealand residential DSL users, at least in the short term. Many subscribers appear to have abandoned P2P file sharing entirely while the remaining P2P users downloaded less content on a per-user basis than they had previously. Other application protocol categories that were related to file sharing, including newsgroups, encrypted traffic and unclassified traffic, also experienced large declines in traffic volume.

Conversely, there was a distinct increase in the use of tunneling, secure file transfer and remote access applications amongst a small group of subscribers. We believe that this may be due to users responding to the CAA by changing their approach to file sharing to limit the likelihood of being detected by copyright holders. Rather than running P2P applications at home, people can use seedboxes located outside of New Zealand to download copyrighted material and transfer the files back to their home computer using HTTPS or a secure tunnel. However, we note that the decrease of P2P traffic observed in our study was much greater than the amount of new traffic that could be associated with tunneling and file transfers.

The results presented in this paper describe the behaviour of subscribers from one New Zealand ISP only. Other ISPs may offer subscription plans and data caps which may appeal more to the people who download copyrighted material. For example, one ISP may be more popular with "heavy" P2P users because they sell a subscription plan with a high off-peak data cap, whereas another ISP may only sell plans that target subscribers with small to medium data or bandwidth requirements. Although we believe that the subscriber base that we have measured is suitably representative, we also acknowledge that this study merely represents a single data point when it comes to evaluating the impact of the CAA overall. A comparative analysis with other New Zealand and international ISPs would ascertain whether the behaviour that we have highlighted is caused by the CAA rather than just strongly correlated.

Another avenue of future work will involve continuing this study over a longer period of time. At the time of writing, only three people have received a third strike under the CAA and the copyright holders elected not to take any of the cases to the Copyright Tribunal. Many copyright holders (in particular, movie and television studios) are not willing to pay the processing fee for issuing notices and the lack of enforcement of the CAA has been widely reported. As a result, it may prove that the decrease in P2P traffic that we have observed will only be temporary.

6. REFERENCES

[1] Curtain falls on News-Service.com (Press Release). http://www.news-service.com/cms/pressrelease20111108en.html (Accessed on 2012/08/16).

[2] Endace Technologies Ltd. http://www.endace.com.

[3] G. Aceto, A. Dainotti, W. de Donato, and A. Pescapè. PortLoad: Taking the Best of Two Worlds in Traffic Classification. In *INFOCOM IEEE Conference on Computer Communications Workshops , 2010*, pages 1 –5, March 2010.

[4] S. Alcock, P. Lorier, and R. Nelson. Libtrace: A Packet Capture and Analysis Library. *SIGCOMM Comput. Commun. Rev.*, 42(2):42–48. April 2012.

[5] S. Alcock and R. Nelson. Libprotoident: Traffic Classification Using Lightweight Packet Inspection. Technical report, University of Waikato. http://www.wand.net.nz/publications/lpireport.

[6] L. Bernaille, R. Teixeira, and K. Salamatian. Early Application Identification. In *Proceedings of the 2006 ACM CoNEXT Conference*, pages 6:1–6:12, 2006.

[7] A. Callado, C. Kamienski, G. Szabo, B. Gero, J. Kelner, S. Fernandes, and D. Sadok. A Survey on Internet Traffic Identification. *Communications Surveys and Tutorials*, 11(3):37 – 52, 2009.

[8] A. Dainotti, A. Pescapè, and K. Claffy. Issues and Future Directions in Traffic Classification. *IEEE Network*, 1(1):35–40, Jan 2012.

[9] B. Danaher, M. D. Smith, R. Telang, and S. Chen. The Effect of Graduated Response Anti-Piracy Laws on Music Sales: Evidence from an Event Study in France. http://ssrn.com/abstract=1989240, 2012.

[10] S. Dejean, T. Pénard, and R. Suire. Une première évaluation des effets de la loi Hadopi sur les pratiques des Internautes français. Technical report, University of Rennes, France, 2010. http://recherche.telecom-bretagne.eu/marsouin/IMG/pdf/NoteHadopix.pdf.

[11] Y. Hu, D.-M. Chiu, and J. C. Lui. Profiling and Identification of P2P Traffic. *Computer Networks*, 53(6):849 – 863, 2009.

[12] Internet Initiative Japan Inc. Traffic Shifting away from P2P File Sharing to Web Services. *Internet Infrastructure Review*, 8:25–30. August 2010.

[13] M. Crotti and M. Dusi and F. Gringoli and L. Salgarelli. Traffic Classification through Simple Statistical Fingerprinting. *ACM SIGCOMM Computer Communication Review*, 37(1):5–16, 2007.

[14] M. Pietrzyk and J-L. Costeux and G. Urvoy-Keller and T. En-Najjary. Challenging Statistical Classification for Operational Usage: the ADSL Case. In *Proceedings of the 9th ACM SIGCOMM conference on Internet measurement conference*, pages 122–135, 2009.

[15] New Zealand Public Act 11 of 2011. Copyright (Infringing File Sharing) Amendment Act 2011. http://www.legislation.govt.nz/act/public/2011/0011/latest/whole.html.

[16] T. T. T. Nguyen and G. J. Armitage. A Survey of Techniques for Internet Traffic Classification using Machine Learning. *IEEE Communications Surveys and Tutorials*, 10(1-4):56–76, 2008.

[17] M. Perényi, T. D. Dang, A. Gefferth, and S. Molnár. Identification and Analysis of Peer-to-Peer Traffic. *Journal of Communications*, 1(7):36–46, 2006.

[18] T. Pullar-Strecker. P2P downloads fall as 'Skynet' introduced. http://www.stuff.co.nz/technology/digital-living/5578590.

[19] WAND Network Research Group. libprotoident. http://research.wand.net.nz/software/libprotoident.php.

Author Index

www.ingramcontent.com/pod-product-compliance
Ingram Content Group UK Ltd.
Pitfield, Milton Keynes, MK11 3LW, UK
UKHW051416290926
15471UKWH00009B/1637

9 781450 31933